Best Books
for Children

Recent Titles in the
Children's and Young Adult Literature Reference Series
Catherine Barr, Series Editor

Green Reads: Best Environmental Resources for Youth, K–12
Lindsey Patrick Wesson

Best Books for Children: Preschool Through Grade 6. 9th Edition
Catherine Barr and John T. Gillespie

Literature Links to World History, K–12: Resources to Enhance and Entice
Lynda G. Adamson

A to Zoo: Subject Access to Children's Picture Books. 8th Edition
Carolyn W. Lima and Rebecca L. Thomas

Literature Links to American History, 7–12: Resources to Enhance and Entice
Lynda G. Adamson

Literature Links to American History, K–6: Resources to Enhance and Entice
Lynda G. Adamson

Celebrating Cuentos: Promoting Latino Children's Literature and Literacy in Classrooms
and Libraries
Jamie Campbell Naidoo

The Family in Literature for Young Readers: A Resource Guide for Use with Grades 4 to 9
John T. Gillespie

Best Books for High School Readers, Grades 9–12.
Supplement to the Second Edition
Catherine Barr

Best Books for Middle School and Junior High Readers, Grades 6–9.
Supplement to the Second Edition
Catherine Barr

Rainbow Family Collections: Selecting and Using Children's Books with Lesbian, Gay,
Bisexual, Transgender, and Queer Content
Jamie Campbell Naidoo

A to Zoo: Subject Access to Children's Picture Books. Supplement to the 8th Edition
Rebecca L. Thomas

Best Books for Children

PRESCHOOL THROUGH GRADE 6
Supplement to the 9th Edition

Catherine Barr

Children's and Young Adult Literature Reference

LIBRARIES UNLIMITED

AN IMPRINT OF ABC-CLIO, LLC
Santa Barbara, California • Denver, Colorado • Oxford, England

Library of Congress Cataloging-in-Publication Data
Barr, Catherine, 1951–
  Best books for children. Supplement to the 9th edition / Catherine
Barr.
     pages cm. — (Children's and young adult literature reference)
  "Preschool through grade 6."
  Includes bibliographical references and index.
  ISBN 978-1-59884-780-2 (hardback) — ISBN 978-1-61069-265-6 (ebook)
  1. Children—Books and reading—United States. 2. Children's
literature—Bibliography. 3. Best books—United States. I. Title.
  Z1037.G48 2010 Suppl.
  011.62—dc23   2012012003

ISBN: 978-1-59884-780-2
EISBN: 978-1-61069-265-6

17 16 15 14 13   1 2 3 4 5

This book is also available on the World Wide Web as an eBook.
Visit www.abc-clio.com for details.

Libraries Unlimited
An Imprint of ABC-CLIO, LLC

ABC-CLIO, LLC
130 Cremona Drive, P.O. Box 1911
Santa Barbara, California 93116-1911

This book is printed on acid-free paper ∞
Manufactured in the United States of America

Contents

Biography

The Arts and Language

History and Geography

Social Institutions and Issues

Personal Development

Physical and Applied Sciences

CONTENTS

Major Subjects Arranged Alphabetically

Preface

This is the supplement to the ninth edition of *Best Books for Children*. The primary aim of this work, as with the earlier editions, is to provide a list of books recommended to satisfy both a child's recreational reading needs and the demands of a typical school curriculum. These recommendations are gathered from a number of sources, which are discussed on the following pages. For greatest depth, coverage has been limited to the age group from preschool children through readers in grade 6.

Books that could be used with advanced sixth graders but are best suited to readers in grades 6 through 9 are listed in the companion volume *Best Books for Middle School and Junior High Readers* (2nd ed., Libraries Unlimited, 2009, and its supplement, published in 2011). It is suggested that this title be used to enrich collections for gifted fifth- and sixth-grade readers. A third volume, *Best Books for Senior High Readers* (2nd ed., Libraries Unlimited, 2009, with a supplement published in 2011), covers grades 9 through 12.

Of the 4,367 titles in this supplement, 4,074 are individually numbered main entries. The remaining 293 titles — those cited within the annotations — are additional recommended titles by the main entry author.

In most cases, at least two recommendations were required from the sources consulted for a title to be considered for listing. However, a single recommendation could also make a title a candidate for inclusion. This was particularly true of nonfiction books in a series. The reviewing policies of many journals do not allow for the inclusion of all titles in a series. Some give little or no coverage to series books, while others review only representative titles or list titles without reviews. Where only a single recommendation was available, the reviewing history of the series was taken into consideration and books in the series were often examined and evaluated by the editor from copies supplied by the publisher. In these cases, such criteria as availability, currency, accuracy, usefulness, and relevance were applied.

Several sources were used to compile this annotated bibliography. The major tools were current reviewing periodicals, principally *Booklist, Horn Book, Library Media Connection,* and *School Library Journal.*

It is hoped that this bibliography will be used in four ways: (1) as a tool to evaluate the adequacy of existing collections; (2) as a book selection instrument for beginning and expanding collections; (3) as an aid for giving reading guidance to children; and (4) as a base for the preparation of bibliographies and reading lists. To increase the book's usefulness, particularly in the two latter areas, the chosen titles are arranged under broad interest areas or, as in the case of nonfiction works, by curriculum-oriented subjects rather than by the Dewey Decimal Classification System. For example, a book on religious practices in colonial America might be cataloged under religion, but in this book it would be included with other books on "United States — Colonial Period." In this way, analogous titles that otherwise would be in separate sections are brought together and can be seen in relation to other books on the same broad topic.

In general, the titles that appear in the section Books for Younger Readers are those usually read to children or used in assisted-reading situations. The one exception in this section is the listing of "Books for Beginning Readers." This area contains books of fiction easy enough to be read by beginning readers; nonfiction beginning readers are integrated into the appropriate subject areas with mention in the annotation that the work is suitable for beginning readers. Interactive books, such as books containing tabs, pop-ups, or flaps, are integrated into appropriate sections but their annotations mention the nature of their format.

The "Imaginative Stories" section in the Picture Books area is divided into two categories: Fantasies and Imaginary Animals. The first contains both books that depict humans, usually children, in fanciful, unrealistic situations (many bordering on the supernatural) and books that include (as characters) such mythological beasts as dragons and unicorns. The Imaginary Animals category includes stories about anthropomorphized animals that engage in human activities (such as pigs going to school) and display human motivations and behavior.

Simple chapter books and similar nonfiction titles that bridge the reading abilities and interests of children in the upper primary grades and early middle grades are integrated into the appropriate sections for older readers and their annotations indicate that they are easily read.

In the Fiction for Older Readers areas, only general anthologies of short stories are included under "Short Stories and Anthologies." Collections of short stories on a single topic, such as sports stories, are found under that specific topic. In the fiction section labeled "Ethnic Groups," only those novels in which ethnicity is the central theme are included. Other novels that simply include members of minority groups are integrated into other more appropriate topical areas. Similarly, in the nonfiction Biography section under "African Americans," "Hispanic Americans," and "Native Americans," only those individuals who have been associated primarily with race-related activities are included. For example, a biography of Martin Luther King, Jr., would be found under "African Americans" but a life story of golfer Tiger Woods would be under sports biographies. Also in the nonfiction area, general books of science projects and experiments are found under "General Science — Experiments and Projects," but books of activities relating to a specific area of science are included in that area. Some types of books have been omitted from this bibliography. These include reference books such as dictionaries and encyclopedias, professional books (for example, other bibliographies), and such mass-market series as the Nancy Drew and Hardy Boys books.

A listing of "Major Subjects Arranged Alphabetically" provides both the range of entry numbers and page numbers for the largest subject areas covered in the volume. Other features also continued are the International Standard Book Number (ISBN) for both hardcover and paperback editions, series titles, and Dewey Decimal numbers for nonfiction titles. Review citations provide sources from which to obtain more detailed information about each of the books listed:

Booklist (BL)
Horn Book (HB)
Library Media Connection (LMC)
School Library Journal (SLJ)
Voice of Youth Advocates (VOYA)

The citing of only one review does not necessarily mean that the book received only a single recommendation; it might also have been listed in one or more of the other sources consulted. An asterisk following a review citation denotes an outstanding recommendation from that source.

Entry Information

Titles in the main section of the book are assigned an entry number. Entries contain the following information where applicable: (1) author or editor; (2) title; (3) suitable grade levels; (4) adapter or translator; (5) indication of illustrations or illustrator's name (usually only for picture books); (6) series title; (7) date of publication; (8) publisher and price of hardbound edition (LB=library binding); (9) ISBN of hardbound edition; (10) paperback (paper) publisher (if no publisher is listed, it is the same as the hardbound edition) and price; (11) ISBN of paperback edition; (12) number of pages; (13) annotation; (14) awards; (15) indication that an audiobook version is available; (16) indication that an ebook version is available; (17) Lexile measure; (18) review citations; (19) Dewey Decimal number.

Lexile measures may be preceded by a code, as in AD310. The codes are defined below; more information is available at lexile.com.

AD Adult Directed
NC Non-Conforming
HL High-Low
IG Illustrated Guide
GN Graphic Novel
BR Beginning Reading
NP Non-Prose

Indexes

Best Books for Children includes three indexes: author/illustrator, book title, and subject/grade level. Authors and illustrators are listed alphabetically by last name, followed by book titles and entry numbers; fiction titles are indicated by (F). The Title Index includes both main entry titles and internal titles cited within annotations, all with entry numbers and (F) notations.

The Subject/Grade Level Index includes thousands of subject headings. Within each subject, entries are listed according to grade-level suitabilities. For example, under the subject Humorous Stories there may be numerous entry numbers given first for Primary (P) readers; then for the Primary-Intermediate (PI) group; for the Intermediate (I) group; and for the Intermediate-Junior High (IJ) readers. This will enable the professional to select the most appropriate titles for use. Biographical entries are listed in this index by the last name of the subject of the biography. The following codes are used to give approximate grade level:

P   (Primary) preschool through grade 3
PI   (Primary-Intermediate) grades 2 through 4
I   (Intermediate) grades 4 through 6
IJ   (Intermediate-Junior High) grades 5 through 8 (or in a few cases some higher grades)

Specific, more exact grade-level suitabilities are given (parenthetically) for each book in its main text entry. To facilitate quick reference, all listings in all indexes refer the user to entry number, not page number.

Many people were involved in the preparation of this bibliography. I am especially grateful to Barbara Ittner of Libraries Unlimited for her encouragement and support, to Christine McNaull, who makes it all possible, and to Kristina Strain, who helps with many aspects of production.

Catherine Barr

Literature

Books for Younger Readers

Alphabet, Concept, and Counting Books

Alphabet Books

1 Baker, Keith. *LMNO Peas* (PS–1). Illus. by author. 2010, Simon & Schuster $16.99 (978-1-4169-9141-0). 40pp. An entertaining pea-oriented alphabetical introduction to occupations. (Rev: BL 2/1/10; SLJ 3/1/10*)

2 Basher, Simon. *ABC Kids* (PS–2). Illus. by author. 2011, Kingfisher $17.99 (978-0-7534-6495-3). 64pp. Beautifully designed illustrations accompany alliterative introductions to the letters of the alphabet. (Rev: BL 5/1/11; SLJ 3/1/11)

3 Bottner, Barbara. *An Annoying ABC* (PS–1). Illus. by Michael Emberley. 2011, Knopf $17.99 (978-0-375-86708-8); LB $20.99 (978-037596708-5). 32pp. Adelaide annoys Bailey first, then Bailey blames Clyde, and so forth to Zelda, when a chain of apologies starts. (Rev: BL 11/15/11; HB 11–12/11; SLJ 10/1/11*)

4 Brown, Margaret Wise. *Goodnight Moon ABC: An Alphabet Book* (PS–K). Illus. by Clement Hurd. 2010, HarperCollins $16.99 (978-0-06-189484-8). Unpaged. Well-known images and items from the beloved bedtime book are featured in this attractive alphabet book. (Rev: SLJ 7/1/10) [421]

5 Bruel, Nick. *A Bad Kitty Christmas* (K–3). Illus. by author. 2011, Roaring Brook $15.99 (978-159643668-8). 40pp. A rowdy alphabetical take on "The Night Before Christmas" in which Bad Kitty goes on a rampage after but eventually learns the true meaning of Christmas. (Rev: BLO 11/15/11; HB 11–12/11; SLJ 10/1/11)

6 Czekaj, Jef. *A Call for a New Alphabet* (K–2). Illus. by author. 2011, Charlesbridge $12.95 (978-1-58089-228-5); paper $5.95 (978-1-58089-229-2). 44pp. A disgruntled letter X complains about his place in the world — always stuck in the middle, hardly ever fronting words — until he realizes how much more responsibility the other letters have, and decides to stay just where he is. Lexile GN520L (Rev: BL 2/1/11; HB 5–6/11; SLJ 3/1/11)

7 deRubertis, Barbara. *Alexander Anteater's Amazing Act* (PS–1). Illus. by R. W. Alley. Series: Animal Antics A to Z. 2010, Kane LB $22.60 (978-1-57565-304-4); paper $7.95 (978-1-57565-300-6). 32pp. With a little help and encouragement from his friends, Alexander the Anteater practices and perfects a balancing routine for the school talent show in this vocabulary-building alphabet book, the first in a series of 26. (Rev: BL 3/15/10; LMC 5–6/10; SLJ 5/1/10)

8 Fuge, Charles. *Astonishing Animal ABC* (K–2). Illus. by author. 2011, Sterling $14.95 (978-1-4027-8645-7). 32pp. Full of alliteration, this entertaining alphabet book introduces animals from aardvark to an imaginary zak. (Rev: BLO 6/21/11; SLJ 7/11) [590]

9 Geisert, Arthur. *Country Road ABC: An Illustrated Journey Through America's Farmland* (PS–3). Illus. by author. 2010, Houghton Mifflin $17 (978-0-547-19469-1). 64pp. This alphabet book for older readers reveals much about rural life in the United States. (Rev: BL 4/15/10; SLJ 4/1/10) [630.973]

10 Herzog, Brad. *G Is for Gold Medal: An Olympics Alphabet* (2–4). Illus. by Doug Bowles. 2011, Sleeping Bear $15.95 (978-158536462-6). 32pp. This alphabet book with alliterative verses includes lots of information on the games, the athletes, and related traditions. (Rev: BL 12/1/11) [796.48]

11 Hudes, Quiara Alegría. *Welcome to My Neighborhood! A Barrio ABC* (PS–K). Illus. by Shino Arihara. 2010, Scholastic $16.99 (978-0-545-09424-5). 32pp. From "abuela" to "Z street," this alphabet book gives a gritty but warm image of an urban neighborhood. (Rev: BL 7/10; LMC 1–2/11; SLJ 10/1/10)

12 Lichtenheld, Tom, and Ezra Fields Meyer. *E-mergency!* (1–3). Illus. by Tom Lichtenheld. 2011, Chronicle $16.99 (978-0-8118-7898-2). 40pp. Rushing downstairs for breakfast the letter E falls and injures herself, leaving O to take her place and causing worldwide chaos. (Rev: BL 12/1/11*; SLJ 12/1/11)

13 Maass, Robert. *A Is for Autumn* (PS–2). Illus. 2011, Henry Holt $16.99 (978-0-8050-9093-2). 32pp. An alphabetical introduction to fall and its features — fallen leaves, back-to-school, Halloween, and so forth. (Rev: BL 9/1/11; SLJ 10/1/11)

14 McGuirk, Leslie. *If Rocks Could Sing: A Discovered Alphabet* (PS–3). Illus. by author. 2011, Tricycle $17.99 (978-1-58246-370-4); LB $20.99 (978-1-58246-395-7). 32pp. This unique alphabet book uses rocks that the author found on the beach to illustrate the letters. (Rev: BL 5/1/11; SLJ 5/1/11)

15 Murray, Alison. *Apple Pie ABC* (PS–1). Illus. by author. 2011, Hyperion/Disney $16.99 (978-1-4231-3694-1). 32pp. A simple story about a dog and an apple pie is told in one-line phrases beginning with sequential letters of the alphabet. (Rev: BLO 6/21/11; HB 7–8/11; SLJ 7/11)

16 O'Connell, Rebecca. *Danny Is Done with Diapers: A Potty ABC* (PS). Illus. by Amanda Gulliver. 2010, Whitman $16.99 (978-0-8075-1466-5). 32pp. From Adam to Zach, children learn the ABCs of using a toilet, washing hands, getting dressed, and so forth. (Rev: BL 3/15/10; SLJ 3/1/10)

17 Osornio, Catherine L. *The Declaration of Independence from A to Z* (1–4). Illus. by Layne Johnson. 2010, Pelican $16.99 (978-1-58980-676-4). Unpaged. This simple, alphabetical introduction will be a useful supplement for those studying the document. (Rev: LMC 8–9/10; SLJ 4/1/10)

18 Rosenthal, Amy Krouse. *Al Pha's Bet* (PS–1). Illus. by Delphine Durand. 2011, Putnam $16.99 (978-0-399-24601-2). 32pp. Faced with a disorganized mess of recently invented letters, Al Pha takes responsibility for arranging them just so in this fun, quirky story. (Rev: BL 8/11; LMC 11–12/11; SLJ 6/11)

19 Siddals, Mary McKenna. *Compost Stew: An A to Z Recipe for the Earth* (PS–2). Illus. by Ashley Wolff. 2010, Tricycle $15.99 (978-1-58246-316-2). 32pp. A rhyming, alphabetical recipe — with an engaging chorus — for making compost. (Rev: BL 2/15/10; SLJ 4/1/10)

20 Watterson, Carol. *An Edible Alphabet: 26 Reasons to Love the Farm* (PS–2). Illus. by Michela Sorrentino. 2011, Tricycle $16.99 (978-1-58246-421-3); LB $19.99 (978-1-58246-422-0). 48pp. From "Ants on Asparagus" to "Zoom Zoom Zucchini," rich collage illustrations and clever wordplay add appeal to this informative, farm-centric alphabet book. (Rev: BL 6/1/11; SLJ 7/11) [530]

21 Werner, Sharon. *Alphabeasties and Other Amazing Types* (K–4). Illus. by Sarah Forss. 2009, Blue Apple $19.99 (978-1-934706-78-7). Unpaged. Multiple typefaces grace this joyful alphabetical exploration of animals and vocabulary. (Rev: LMC 11–12/09; SLJ 10/1/09)

Concept Books

GENERAL

22 Aliki. *Push Button* (PS). Illus. by author. 2010, Greenwillow $16.99 (978-0-06-167308-5). 40pp. Only when his finger hurts too much does this toddler stop pushing any available buttons and consider other forms of entertainment. (Rev: BL 2/15/10*; HB 7–8/10; SLJ 4/1/10)

23 *American Babies* (PS). Illus. 2010, Charlesbridge $6.95 (978-158089280-3). 16pp. A companion volume to *Global Babies,* this board book offers close-up photographs of diverse babies accompanied by brief text. (Rev: BL 5/1/10*)

24 Bauer, Marion Dane. *Thank You for Me!* (PS–1). Illus. by Kristina Stephenson. 2010, Simon & Schuster $14.99 (978-0-689-85788-1). 32pp. Vibrantly illustrated, this book features rhymed text celebrating all the wondrous things a body is capable of. (Rev: BL 1/1/10; SLJ 2/1/10)

25 Bond, Felicia. *Big Hugs, Little Hugs* (PS). Illus. by author. 2012, Philomel $16.99 (978-0-399-25614-1). 32pp. Illustrations of all kinds of loving animals, both wild and domestic, show that there are many different ways to hug. (Rev: BL 1/12; SLJ 12/1/11)

26 Brocket, Jane. *Spiky, Slimy, Smooth: What Is Texture?* (PS–2). Illus. by author. Series: Clever Concepts. 2011, Millbrook LB $25.26 (978-0-7613-4614-2). 32pp. Brocket introduces the concept of texture using evocative words and bright, eye-catching photographs of various objects and foods. (Rev: BL 4/15/11; SLJ 5/1/11) [612.8]

27 Cocca-Leffler, Maryann. *Rain Brings Frogs: A Little Book of Hope* (PS–2). Illus. by author. 2011, HarperCollins $9.99 (978-0-06-196106-9). 32pp. Nate, a little boy who sees everything on the bright side, helps show readers see the good things in life. (Rev: BL 2/15/11; SLJ 2/1/11)

28 Costello, David Hyde. *I Can Help* (PS–K). Illus. by author. 2010, Farrar $12.99 (978-0-374-33526-7). 32pp. In this simple, charming story, the pattern of being the rescuer and rescued is repeated as one animal after another calls on his friends for help. (Rev: BL 1/1/10; LMC 1–2/10; SLJ 1/1/10)

29 Cousins, Lucy. *Maisy's Amazing Big Book of Learning* (PS–K). Illus. by author. 2011, Candlewick $14.99 (978-076365481-8). 48pp. Maisy the mouse's life is full of concepts as she counts, makes noises, jumps, watches the weather, and so forth; this oversize book has lots of lift-the-flap features. (Rev: BL 9/1/11)

30 Emberley, Ed. *Where's My Sweetie Pie?* (PS–1). Illus. by author. 2010, Little, Brown $7.99 (978-031601891-3). 14pp. Readers raise die-cut flaps as they hunt through the pages for the missing sweetie pie. (Rev: BL 2/1/10)

31 Fisher, Valorie. *Everything I Need to Know Before I'm Five* (PS–K). Illus. by author. 2011, Random House $17.99 (978-0-375-86865-8). 40pp. An appealing concept book covering numbers, opposites, shapes, colors, seasons, weather, and the alphabet. (Rev: BL 7/11; HB 7–8/11; SLJ 7/11)

32 Fleming, Denise. *Shout! Shout It Out!* (PS–1). 2011, Henry Holt $16.99 (978-0-8050-9237-0). 40pp. Readers are encouraged to vocalize with enthusiasm their knowledge of numbers, the alphabet, colors, animal names, and so forth. **e** (Rev: BL 3/1/11; HB 3–4/11; SLJ 2/1/11)

33 Gurth, Per-Henrik. *Hockey Opposites* (PS). Illus. by author. 2010, Kids Can $15.95 (978-155453241-4). 24pp. A simple introduction to opposites using ice hockey examples — out/in, win/lose, big/small, and so forth. (Rev: BL 9/1/10)

34 Hall, Michael. *My Heart Is Like a Zoo* (PS). Illus. by author. 2010, Greenwillow $16.99 (978-0-06-191510-9); LB $17.89 (978-0-06-191511-6). 32pp. Readers consider various emotions as they explore bright collages of zoo animals showing expressions such as "eager as a beaver," "angry as a bear," "brave as a lion." (Rev: BL 11/15/09; SLJ 2/1/10)

35 Henry, Jed. *I Speak Dinosaur* (PS–K). Illus. by author. 2012, Abrams $14.95 (978-141970233-4). 32pp. A young boy who has adopted the manners and roars of a dinosaur learns there might be better ways to behave in public. (Rev: BLO 3/1/12; LMC 8–9/12; SLJ 4/12)

36 Isadora, Rachel. *Say Hello!* (PS–1). Illus. by author. 2010, Putnam $16.99 (978-0-399-25230-3). 32pp. Carmelita and her mother greet their multicultural neighbors in a variety of languages, while their dog Manny sticks to "woof." (Rev: BL 2/15/10; LMC 5–6/10; SLJ 3/1/10)

37 Jocelyn, Marthe, and Nell Jocelyn. *Ones and Twos* (PS–1). Illus. by Marthe Jocelyn. 2011, Tundra $15.95 (978-1-77049-220-2). 24pp. Rhyming couplets follow a bird and a girl as they go about their everyday activities, highlighting instances of ones and twos. (Rev: BL 4/15/11; HB 9–10/11; SLJ 5/1/11*) [513.2]

38 Lobel, Anita. *Ten Hungry Rabbits: Counting and Color Concepts* (PS). Illus. by author. 2012, Knopf $9.99 (978-037586864-1); LB $12.99 (978-037596864-8). 24pp. A herd of 10 young bunnies are sent into the garden to gather a variety of different-colored fruits and vegetables for dinner in this numbers and colors concept story. (Rev: BL 1/1/12; HB 1–2/12; SLJ 1/12)

39 Mora, Pat. *Gracias / Thanks* (PS–2). Trans. by Adriana Dominguez. Illus. by John Parra. 2009, Lee & Low $17.95 (978-160060258-0). 32pp. In this bilingual picture book, a young boy gives thanks for all the simple and often taken-for-granted things in his life, like his pajamas and the crickets that sing at night. (Rev: BL 11/1/09*; HB 1–2/10; LMC 3–4/10)

40 Newman, Jeff. *Hand Book* (PS–K). Illus. by author. 2011, Simon & Schuster $15.99 (978-1-4169-5013-4). 40pp. A tale of the role of hands in our lives, from very basic toddler functions to adult uses. (Rev: BL 7/11; SLJ 7/11)

41 Olson-Brown, Ellen. *Ooh La La Polka-Dot Boots* (PS–K). Illus. by Christiane Engel. 2010, Ten Speed/Tricycle $14.99 (978-1-58246-287-5). 36pp. A game of dress-up in book form, this book features a multicultural array of characters showing off their favorite outfits in bright illustrations including polka-dot boots. (Rev: BL 1/1/10; SLJ 4/1/10)

42 Patricelli, Leslie. *Faster! Faster!* (PS–2). Illus. by author. 2012, Candlewick $15.99 (978-076365473-3). 32pp. The little girl we met in *Higher! Higher!* (2009) now urges her father to carry her faster and faster as she imagines he is a dog, a cheetah, an ostrich, and so forth. (Rev: BLO 10/15/11; SLJ 3/1/12)

43 Rotner, Shelley. *Shades of People* (PS–3). Illus. by Sheila M. Kelly. 2009, Holiday House $16.95 (978-0-8234-2191-6). 32pp. Celebrates the many different skin tones found around the world. ALSC Notable Children's Book, 2010. (Rev: BL 8/09; SLJ 9/1/09)

44 Seeger, Laura Vaccaro. *What If?* (PS–K). Illus. by author. 2010, Roaring Brook $15.99 (978-1-59643-398-4). 32pp. In this simple yet thought-provoking, almost wordless story about friendship and sharing, Seeger explores the different outcomes possible when three seals play with a beach ball. (Rev: BL 2/1/10; LMC 5–6/10; SLJ 4/1/10*)

45 Selig, Josh. *Red and Yellow's Noisy Night* (PS–2). Illus. by Little Airplane Productions. 2012, Sterling $14.95 (978-140279070-6). 28pp. Characters Red and Yellow learn about simple conflict resolution when Red decides to play a quiet song instead of loud music to help his friend to sleep. (Rev: BL 4/1/12; SLJ 5/1/12)

46 Siminovich, Lorena. *I Like Vegetables* (PS). Illus. by author. 2011, Candlewick $6.99 (978-0-7636-5283-8). 10pp. With tactile fabric sections in collages, this square board book introduces a variety of vegetables. (Rev: BL 7/11; SLJ 9/1/11)

47 Snicket, Lemony. *Thirteen Words* (K–2). Illus. by Maira Kalman. 2010, HarperCollins $16.99 (978-0-06-166465-6). 40pp. A quirky, playful book involving 13 words, a despondent bird, a dog, and a mezzo-soprano. (Rev: BL 9/1/10; SLJ 12/1/10)

48 Soltis, Sue. *Nothing Like a Puffin* (PS–2). Illus. by Bob Kolar. 2011, Candlewick $15.99 (978-0-7636-3617-3).

40pp. This exercise in similarities and differences compares a puffin to everything from a newspaper and a pair of blue jeans. (Rev: BL 12/1/11; SLJ 9/1/11)

49 Tafuri, Nancy. *All Kinds of Kisses* (PS–K). Illus. by author. 2012, Little, Brown $16.99 (978-0-316-12235-1). 32pp. This large-format picture book celebrates different kinds of kisses that animals — and people — share around the world. (Rev: BL 1/1/12; HB 1–2/12; SLJ 12/1/11)

50 Tillman, Nancy. *The Crown on Your Head* (PS). Illus. by author. 2011, Feiwel & Friends $16.99 (978-0-312-64521-2). 32pp. Celebrates the unique qualities endowed on every child, using a crown as an illustration. (Rev: BL 9/15/11; SLJ 9/1/11)

51 Tullet, Hervé. *The Book with a Hole* (PS–2). 2011, Abrams paper $14.50 (978-1-85437-946-7). Unpaged. This board book features a large hole in the middle of each illustration, which gives readers opportunities for interaction; simple text provides encouragement. Other books in this attractive, inventive series include *The Game of Finger Worms, The Game of Let's Go!, The Game of Light, The Game of Mix and Match, The Game of Mix-Up Art,* and *The Game of Patterns* (all 2011). (Rev: SLJ 9/1/11)

52 Tullet, Hervé. *Press Here* (PS–2). Illus. by author. 2011, Chronicle $14.99 (978-0-8118-7954-5). 56pp. This sturdy book encourages readers to tilt, twist, press, and blow on the pages to see colored dots move. (Rev: BL 4/1/11; HB 7–8/11; SLJ 4/11*)

53 Underwood, Deborah. *The Loud Book!* (PS). Illus. by Renata Liwska. 2011, Houghton Mifflin $12.99 (978-0-547-39008-6). 32pp. Noises from burping to whistling are celebrated in this book featuring the lively stuffed animals first seen in *The Quiet Book* (2010). (Rev: BL 1/1–15/11; SLJ 5/1/11*)

54 Underwood, Deborah. *The Quiet Book* (PS–K). Illus. by Renata Liwska. 2010, Houghton Mifflin $12.95 (978-0-547-21567-9). 32pp. Using young animals as characters, this picture book explores different kinds of quiet. (Rev: BL 2/15/10; SLJ 3/1/10*)

55 Van Fleet, Matthew. *Moo* (PS). Illus. by Brian Stanton. 2011, Simon & Schuster $16.99 (978-1-4424-3503-2). 18pp. This interactive board book looks at barnyard animals using simple text, tabs, flaps, and touch-and-feel elements. (Rev: BLO 11/15/11; SLJ 10/1/11) [636]

56 Verdick, Elizabeth. *Calm-Down Time* (PS). Illus. by Marieka Heinlen. Series: Toddler Tools. 2010, Free Spirit paper $7.95 (978-1-57542-316-6). Unpaged. This board book introduces the importance of calming down when overexcited and various strategies to use. (Rev: SLJ 6/1/10) [152.4]

57 Walsh, Joanna. *The Biggest Kiss* (PS–1). Illus. by Judi Abbot. 2011, Simon & Schuster $12.99 (978-1-4424-2769-3). 32pp. This tribute to kisses celebrates all different kinds, from fish kisses to penguin kisses

to the sweetest kisses of all. (Rev: BL 12/15/11; SLJ 11/1/11)

58 Wild, Margaret. *Itsy-Bitsy Babies* (PS). Illus. by Jan Ormerod. 2010, IPG/Little Hare $15.99 (978-1-921541-36-0). 24pp. A simple and charming rhyming celebration of the things that babies and toddlers do. (Rev: BL 11/10/10; SLJ 12/1/10)

COLORS

59 Basher, Simon. *Colors* (PS). Illus. by author. Series: Go! Go! BoBo. 2011, Kingfisher $6.99 (978-0-7534-6493-9). Unpaged. BoBo, a childlike character, plunges into six basic colors in this appealing board book. (Rev: BL 7/11; SLJ 8/1/11) [535.6]

60 Brocket, Jane. *Ruby, Violet, Lime: Looking for Color* (PS–2). Photos by author. Series: Jane Brocket's Clever Concepts. 2011, Millbrook LB $25.26 (978-0-7613-4612-8). 32pp. Bright photographs and vivid text illustrate the primary colors plus a few extras. **e** (Rev: SLJ 9/1/11)

61 Gibbs, Edward. *I Spy with My Little Eye* (PS–1). Illus. by author. 2011, Candlewick $14.99 (978-0-7636-5284-5). Unpaged. Part seek-and-find, part practice with colors, this engaging book features brightly colored illustrations and die-cut holes. (Rev: SLJ 6/11*)

62 Houblon, Marie. *A World of Colors: Seeing Colors in a New Way* (PS–2). Illus. 2009, National Geographic $16.95 (978-1-4263-0556-6); LB $25.90 (978-1-4263-0559-7). 48pp. In this sophisticated color book, each color is presented in a variety of different shades and tints while questions encourage readers to expand their perceptions. (Rev: BL 11/15/09; SLJ 10/1/09) [535.6]

63 Jay, Alison. *Red, Green, Blue: A First Book of Colors* (PS–3). Illus. by author. 2010, Dutton $16.99 (978-0-525-42303-4). 40pp. Children are introduced to colors through familiar nursery rhyme characters, from the three little (pink) pigs to Little Bo Peep's white sheep and Miss Muffet's scary black spider. (Rev: BL 5/15/10; SLJ 6/1/10)

64 Nunn, Daniel. *Yellow* (PS–K). Illus. Series: Colors All Around Us. 2012, Raintree LB $25.32 (978-143295748-3); paper $8.95 (978-143295757-5). 24pp. Yellow objects of all kinds — yolks, trucks, sunflowers, ducklings — are on display here. (Rev: BLO 3/1/12) [535.6]

65 Salzano, Tammi. *One Rainy Day* (PS). Illus. by Hannah Wood. 2011, ME Media/Tiger Tales $8.95 (978-158925860-0). 24pp. A duckling goes out for a walk in the rain in this padded board book designed to reinforce the names of colors. (Rev: BL 7/11)

66 Sterling, Kristin. *Blue Everywhere* (K–2). Series: Lightning Bolt Books — Colors Everywhere. 2010, Lerner LB $25.26 (978-0-7613-4588-6). 32pp. Highlights the presence of blue in the everyday world and its connection to emotional expression. Also use *Red Everywhere* and *Silver and Gold Everywhere* (both 2010). (Rev: LMC 3–4/10; SLJ 2/1/10) [535.6]

67 Stockland, Patricia M. *Pink* (PS–K). Illus. by Julia Woolf. 2011, ABDO LB $18.95 (978-161641138-1). 24pp. A simple approach to the color pink and the places it is often found. Also use *Orange, Gray,* and *Brown* (all 2011). (Rev: BL 5/1/11) [535.6]

68 Wolff, Ashley. *Baby Bear Sees Blue* (PS–K). Illus. by author. 2012, Simon & Schuster $16.99 (978-144241306-1). 40pp. Baby Bear sees colors all around him — yellow light, blue birds, red strawberries, orange butterflies, and more. e (Rev: BL 2/1/12; HB 3–4/12; SLJ 1/12)

PERCEPTION

69 Averbeck, Jim. *Except If* (PS–1). Illus. by author. 2011, Atheneum $12.99 (978-1-4169-9544-9). 40pp. An egg will become a baby bird, except if . . . . This intriguing book presents many alternative scenarios. (Rev: BL 12/1/10; HB 1–2/11; SLJ 2/1/11)

70 *Peek-a-Boo What?* (PS). Illus. by Elliot Kreloff. Series: Begin Smart. 2009, Sterling $10.95 (978-193461850-9). 18pp. Simple collage illustrations and die-cut holes enhance this repetitive rhymed board-book game of peek-a-boo. (Rev: BLO 11/15/09)

SIZE AND SHAPE

71 Basher, Simon. *Shapes* (PS). Illus. by author. Series: Go! Go! BoBo. 2011, Kingfisher $6.99 (978-0-7534-6494-6). Unpaged. BoBo, the bouncy baby with a Band-Aid on his head, explores various shapes. (Rev: BLO 11/28/11; SLJ 8/1/11) [516]

72 Dodd, Emma. *I Am Small* (PS). Illus. by author. 2011, Scholastic $8.99 (978-0-545-35370-0). 24pp. A baby penguin finds the size of the world quite scary, but recognizes that he feels quite safe in his mother's arms. (Rev: BL 12/15/11; SLJ 10/1/11)

73 Frazier, Craig. *Lots of Dots* (PS–K). Illus. by author. 2010, Chronicle $15.99 (978-0-8118-7715-2). Unpaged. Colorful, punchy illustrations show how dots and circles — scoops of ice cream, traffic signals, spotted animals, and more — can be seen everywhere. (Rev: SLJ 12/1/10)

74 Hall, Michael. *Perfect Square* (PS–3). Illus. by author. 2011, Greenwillow $16.99 (978-0-06-191513-0). 40pp. A perfect red square is transmogrified into a variety of new shapes in this satisfyingly simple square picture book. (Rev: BL 4/15/11; HB 3–4/11; SLJ 4/11*)

75 Intriago, Patricia. *Dot* (PS–K). Illus. by author. 2011, Farrar $14.99 (978-0-374-31835-2). 40pp. This inventive book explores the versatile possibilities of a simple dot; fresh, direct language and comic illustrations add humor. (Rev: BLO 8/11; HB 9–10/11; SLJ 8/11*)

76 Long, Ethan. *Up! Tall! and High!* (PS–1). Illus. by author. 2012, Putnam $15.99 (978-039925611-0). 40pp. A group of different birds try to outdo each other by being the tallest and flying the highest in this nicely illustrated story with lift-the-flap surprises. (Rev: BL 3/15/12; SLJ 2/1/12)

77 Nagel, Karen. *Shapes That Roll* (PS–2). Illus. by Steven Wilson. 2009, Blue Apple $14.99 (978-1-934706-81-7). Unpaged. A triangle, circle, and square have fun exploring and talking about other different kinds of shapes, from diamonds and stars to bananas and catchers' mitts in this bright, introduction to shapes. Lexile AD310 (Rev: SLJ 1/1/10)

78 Ray, Mary Lyn. *Stars* (PS–2). Illus. by Marla Frazee. 2011, Simon & Schuster $16.99 (978-1-4424-2249-1). 40pp. A celebration of the wonder of stars and the many places we find their shapes in our lives. (Rev: BL 10/15/11*; SLJ 10/1/11*)

79 Rayner, Catherine. *Ernest, the Moose Who Doesn't Fit* (PS–1). Illus. by author. 2010, Farrar $15.99 (978-0-374-32217-5). 32pp. An enormous moose struggles to solve his problem of being too big — too big, even, for a picture book spread — by enlisting the help of a chipmunk friend in this funny book with a gatefold. (Rev: BL 12/1/10; SLJ 10/1/10*)

80 Rissman, Rebecca. *Shapes in Sports* (PS–1). Illus. Series: Spot the Shape. 2009, Heinemann LB $14.50 (978-143292170-5). 24pp. Using crisp photographs, Rissman identifies a lot of interesting shapes found in sporting equipment and venues. (Rev: BL 9/1/09*) [516]

81 Schoonmaker, Elizabeth. *Square Cat* (PS–1). Illus. by author. 2011, Simon & Schuster $14.99 (978-1-4424-0619-3). 32pp. A square cat named Eula has a difficult life and longs to be like the other cats, and they — after first trying to minimize her squareness — work to convince her that her shape has its advantages. (Rev: BL 2/1/11; SLJ 1/1/11)

82 Shea, Susan A. *Do You Know Which Ones Will Grow?* (PS–2). Illus. by Tom Slaughter. 2011, Blue Apple $16.99 (978-1-60905-062-7). 38pp. This flap book posits a variety of playful questions about size, shape, and growth. (Rev: BL 5/1/11; SLJ 6/11*)

Counting and Number Books

83 Beaty, Andrea. *Hide and Sheep* (PS–2). Illus. by Bill Mayer. 2011, Simon & Schuster $15.99 (978-1-4169-2544-6). 32pp. A sleepy farmer's sheep escape to various locations in order to avoid shearing in this rhymed book that counts down from 10. (Rev: BL 4/1/11; SLJ 4/11)

84 Berkes, Marianne. *Over in Australia: Amazing Animals Down Under* (PS–2). Illus. by Jill Dubin. 2011, Dawn $16.95 (978-1-58469-135-8); paper $8.95 (978-

1-58469-136-5). 32pp. A wombat and a crocodile are among the animals presented in this rhyming counting book based on "Over in the Meadow"; includes facts and activities. (Rev: BL 3/15/11; LMC 10/11; SLJ 6/11)

85 Berkes, Marianne. *Over in the Forest: Come and Take a Peek* (PS–2). Illus. by Jill Dubin. 2012, Dawn $16.95 (978-158469162-4); paper $8.95 (978-158469163-1). 32pp. Introduces woodland animals using a refrain based on "Over in the Meadow" and offering many opportunities for counting. (Rev: BLO 4/15/12; SLJ 7/12)

86 Chall, Marsha Wilson. *One Pup's Up* (PS–K). Illus. by Henry Cole. 2010, Simon & Schuster $16.99 (978-1-4169-7960-9). 32pp. Readers can count up to 10 and back again as a litter of puppies tumble and play. (Rev: BL 4/15/10; SLJ 6/1/10)

87 Cuyler, Margery. *Guinea Pigs Add Up* (PS–2). Illus. by Tracey Campbell Pearson. 2010, Walker $16.99 (978-0-8027-9795-7). 32pp. Class pet guinea pigs offer a lesson in counting as they multiply. (Rev: BL 5/1/10; LMC 8–9/10; SLJ 7/1/10)

88 Degman, Lori. *One Zany Zoo* (K–1). Illus. by Colin Jack. 2010, Simon & Schuster $15.99 (978-1-4169-8990-5). Unpaged. A rollicking counting book in which the zoo animals are freed from their cages. (Rev: LMC 8–9/10; SLJ 7/1/10)

89 Dickinson, Rebecca. *Over in the Hollow* (PS–K). Illus. by Stephan Britt. 2009, Chronicle $15.99 (978-0-8118-5035-3). Unpaged. Count from 1 spider to 13 ghosts in this spooky and comic Halloween tale. (Rev: LMC 1–2/10; SLJ 10/1/09)

90 Durango, Julia. *Go-Go Gorillas* (PS–K). Illus. by Eleanor Taylor. 2010, Simon & Schuster $15.99 (978-1-4169-3779-1). 32pp. King Big Daddy's relatives are summoned to the Great Gorilla Villa in this lively, bouncy counting book that shows gorillas arriving in buses, hot-air balloons, and planes. Lexile AD530L (Rev: BL 5/1/10; SLJ 3/1/10)

91 Emberley, Rebecca, and Ed Emberley. *Ten Little Beasties* (PS–1). Illus. by authors. 2011, Roaring Brook $12.99 (978-1-59643-627-5). Unpaged. Count little beasties up to 10 and back again to the tune of "Ten Little Indians" or to the original melody offered on a related Web site. (Rev: SLJ 10/1/11)

92 Fox, Mem. *Let's Count Goats!* (PS–K). Illus. by Jan Thomas. 2010, Simon & Schuster $16.99 (978-1-4424-0598-1). 40pp. Goats in different shapes, sizes, colors, and numbers populate brightly colored, comic spreads, while simple text encourages readers to search, find, and count. (Rev: BL 10/1/10; SLJ 11/1/10)

93 Franco, Betsy. *Double Play* (PS–1). Illus. by Doug Cushman. 2011, Tricycle $15.99 (978-158246384-1); LB $18.99 (978-158246396-4). 32pp. At recess, Jill and Jake's activities offer the chance to count, add, and double numbers from 1 to 10. (Rev: BL 7/11; SLJ 6/11)

94 Franco, Betsy. *Zero Is the Leaves on the Tree* (PS–2). Illus. by Shino Arihara. 2009, Tricycle $15.99 (978-1-58246-249-3). 32pp. The concept of zero is introduced in a variety of creative ways. (Rev: BL 9/15/09; LMC 3–4/10; SLJ 9/1/09) [513]

95 Goldstone, Bruce. *100 Ways to Celebrate 100 Days* (PS–2). Illus. by author. 2010, Henry Holt $16.99 (978-0-8050-8997-4). 48pp. Bolstering reading and counting skills, this volume presents a wide variety of simple ways to celebrate the first 100 days of school. (Rev: BL 9/1/10; LMC 10/10; SLJ 7/1/10) [513]

96 Gravett, Emily. *The Rabbit Problem* (1–4). Illus. by author. 2010, Simon & Schuster $17.99 (978-1-4424-1255-2). Unpaged. If a pair of baby rabbits are put into a field, how many pairs will there be: a) At the end of each month? b) After one year? This book takes a clever and humorous approach to the Fibonacci problem. (Rev: HB 1–2/11; SLJ 12/1/10)

97 Himmelman, John. *Ten Little Hot Dogs* (PS–1). Illus. by author. 2010, Marshall Cavendish $12.99 (978-0-7614-5797-8). 32pp. Lively little dachshunds leap, play, pile, and snooze in this counting book. (Rev: BL 12/1/10; SLJ 9/1/10)

98 Long, Ethan. *One Drowsy Dragon* (PS–2). Illus. by author. 2010, Scholastic $16.99 (978-0-545-16557-0). Unpaged. An adult dragon is kept awake by 10 rambunctious youngsters in this bright counting book full of onomatopoeia. (Rev: LMC 10/10; SLJ 7/1/10)

99 MacDonald, Margaret Read, and Nadia Jameel Taibah. *How Many Donkeys? An Arabic Counting Tale* (K–2). Illus. by Carol Liddiment. 2009, Whitman $16.99 (978-0-8075-3424-3). 32pp. Jouha is having trouble counting his 10 donkeys in this eye-catching tale set in the Middle East and featuring both English and Arabic. (Rev: BL 9/15/09; LMC 11–12/09; SLJ 10/1/09) [398.2]

100 McGrath, Barbara Barbieri. *Teddy Bear Counting* (PS). Illus. by Tim Nihoff. 2010, Charlesbridge $16.95 (978-1-58089-215-5); paper $7.95 (978-1-58089-216-2). Unpaged. This colorful book uses appealing bear illustrations to present basic counting (1 to 12) as well as colors, shapes, addition and subtraction, and grouping numbers in sets. (Rev: SLJ 2/1/10)

101 Maloney, Peter, and Felicia Zekauskas. *One Foot Two Feet: An EXCEPTIONal Counting Book* (PS–K). 2011, Putnam $12.99 (978-0-399-25446-8). 48pp. Counting and vocabulary are combined in this interactive book that emphasizes how plural nouns differ from singular ones. (Rev: BL 6/1/11; SLJ 7/11*) [372.72]

102 Marino, Gianna. *One Too Many: A Seek and Find Counting Book* (PS–2). Illus. by author. 2010, Chronicle

$16.99 (978-0-8118-6908-9). 40pp. A wordless, cumulative — and beautifully illustrated — counting book in which groups of animals from 1 to 12 congregate on the pages until a final addition (a skunk) is just one too many. (Rev: BL 4/15/10; LMC 10/10; SLJ 5/1/10)

103 Marzollo, Jean. *Help Me Learn Numbers 0–20* (PS–1). Illus. 2011, Holiday House $15.95 (978-0-8234-2334-7). 32pp. Photographs and interactive rhymes that become more difficult as they progress teach children to count to 20. (Rev: BL 11/1/11; SLJ 9/1/11) [513.2]

104 Matzke, Ann H. *Make It 100!* (PS–K). Illus. Series: Little World Math Concepts. 2011, Rourke $22.79 (978-161741765-8); paper $7.96 (978-161741967-6). 24pp. Bright illustrations show a variety of ways to count to hundred. Also use *Plus 0, Minus 0* and *Plus 2, Minus 2* (both 2011). (Rev: BL 11/1/11)

105 Norman, Kim. *Ten on the Sled* (PS–2). Illus. by Liza Woodruff. 2010, Sterling $14.95 (978-1-4027-7076-0). 24pp. A sled careening down a frozen hill with 10 animals aboard gradually becomes a vehicle for 1 lonely caribou as the other passengers tumble out. (Rev: BLO 10/15/10; SLJ 12/1/10)

106 Otoshi, Kathryn. *Zero* (PS–3). Illus. by author. 2010, KO Kids $17.95 (978-0-9723946-3-5). 32pp. Zero has difficulty accepting her role, envying numbers that have value, but eventually realizes her real importance in this story with a message about being true to oneself. (Rev: BL 9/15/10*; LMC 3–4/11; SLJ 11/1/10)

107 Schulman, Janet. *Ten Easter Egg Hunters: A Holiday Counting Book* (PS). Illus. by Linda Davick. 2011, Knopf $8.99 (978-0-375-86787-3); LB $11.99 (978-0-375-96787-0). 32pp. An Easter bunny hides a basket full of eggs, and watches from a distance as a group of children hunts and finds them in this colorful counting book. **e** (Rev: BL 2/1/11; SLJ 2/1/11)

108 Sebe, Masayuki. *Let's Count to 100!* (PS–2). Illus. by author. 2011, Kids Can $16.95 (978-1-55453-661-0). 24pp. Attractive spreads show 100 animals, people, or objects organized in groups of 10, making the task of counting to 100 less daunting. (Rev: BLO 9/1/11; SLJ 9/1/11) [513.2]

109 Stutson, Caroline. *Cats' Night Out* (PS–K). Illus. by Jon Klassen. 2010, Simon & Schuster $15.99 (978-1-4169-4005-0). 32pp. Captivating, retro illustrations enhance this hip counting book in which cats dance the night away, doing the tango, rumba, boogie . . . (Rev: BL 2/15/10; SLJ 2/1/10)

110 Waber, Bernard. *Lyle Walks the Dogs: A Counting Book* (PS–K). Illus. by Paulis Waber. 2010, Houghton Mifflin $12.99 (978-0-547-22323-0). 24pp. Well-intentioned crocodile Lyle struggles to keep his 10 canine charges in line in his new job as dog-walker. (Rev: BLO 4/15/10; SLJ 5/1/10)

111 Wallace, Nancy Elizabeth. *Planting Seeds* (PS). Illus. 2010, Marshall Cavendish $7.99 (978-0-7614-5643-8). 24pp. A rabbit family plants, grows, and harvests carrots — and generously shares the feast — in this warm, clearly illustrated book that counts from 1 to 10. (Rev: BLO 4/1/10; SLJ 4/1/10)

112 Young, Cybele. *Ten Birds* (1–3). Illus. by author. 2011, Kids Can $16.95 (978-1-55453-568-2). 32pp. Counts down from 10 as small black birds use different contraptions to cross a river, collecting the hardware from a heap that subsides with the countdown. (Rev: BL 5/1/11; SLJ 4/11)

Bedtime Books and Nursery Rhymes

Bedtime Books

113 Bardhan-Quallen, Sudipta. *Chicks Run Wild* (PS–1). Illus. by Ward Jenkins. 2011, Simon & Schuster $15.99 (978-1-4424-0673-5). 32pp. A mama hen finally manages to exhaust her energetic brood of chicks in this funny bedtime story. (Rev: BL 1/1–15/11; SLJ 1/1/11)

114 Beaumont, Karen. *No Sleep for the Sheep!* (PS–2). Illus. by Jackie Urbanovic. 2011, Harcourt $16.99 (978-0-15-204969-0). 32pp. A sleepy sheep must deal with one interruption after another as his barnyard friends decide to join him, one at a time; excellent for read-alouds, with humorous and expressive artwork. Lexile AD650L (Rev: BL 4/15/11; HB 3–4/11; SLJ 4/11*)

115 Becker, Bonny. *A Bedtime for Bear* (PS–3). Illus. by Kady MacDonald Denton. 2010, Candlewick $16.99 (978-0-7636-4101-6). 48pp. A sleepover with Mouse proves challenging to Bear's usual bedtime routine, but in the end he's glad to have his friend. (Rev: BL 10/15/10; SLJ 8/1/10*)

116 Boelts, Maribeth. *Sweet Dreams, Little Bunny!* (PS). Illus. by Kathy Parkinson. 2010, Whitman $7.99 (978-080754589-8). 14pp. A mama bunny gently guides her little one off to bed in this board book. (Rev: BL 1/1–15/11)

117 Braun, Sebastien. *Back to Bed, Ed!* (PS–1). Illus. by author. 2010, Peachtree $15.95 (978-1-56145-518-8). Unpaged. A little mouse learns the secret to staying safe and comfortable in his own bed: a bevy of stuffed animal friends alongside. (Rev: SLJ 3/1/10*)

118 Butler, John. *Bedtime in the Jungle* (PS). Illus. by author. 2009, Peachtree $16.95 (978-1-56145-486-0). 32pp. As dusk arrives, the animals of the jungle settle down for the night; with verses inspired by "Over in the Meadow" and stunning illustrations. (Rev: BL 9/15/09; SLJ 9/1/09)

119 Christelow, Eileen. *Five Little Monkeys Reading in Bed* (PS–2). Illus. by author. 2011, Clarion $16.99

(978-0-547-38610-2). 40pp. Reading is so much fun that the five little monkeys just don't feel sleepy. (Rev: BL 10/15/11; SLJ 9/1/11)

120 Dahl, Michael. *Nap Time for Kitty* (PS). Illus. by Oriol Vidal. 2011, Capstone $7.99 (978-140485216-7). 20pp. A young kitten with no interest in nap time is finally persuaded to go to sleep. (Rev: BL 7/11)

121 Durand, Hallie. *Mitchell's License* (PS). Illus. by Tony Fucile. 2011, Candlewick $15.99 (978-0-7636-4496-3). 40pp. Three-year-old Mitchell gets to drive his father to bed, riding on his shoulders; a funny, active but satisfying bedtime book. (Rev: BL 3/1/11; SLJ 4/11)

122 Durango, Julia, and Katie Belle Trupiano. *Dream Away* (PS–2). Illus. by Robert Goldstrom. 2011, Simon & Schuster $16.99 (978-1-4169-8702-4). 32pp. A young boy is lulled to sleep as he and his father read a bedtime story about sailing through the stars. (Rev: BLO 7/11; SLJ 7/11)

123 Egielski, Richard. *The Sleepless Little Vampire* (PS–2). Illus. 2011, Scholastic $16.99 (978-0-545-14597-8). 32pp. A little vampire who can't sleep wonders which creature is keeping him up. Is it the werewolf? The spider? The skeletons? (Rev: BL 9/1/11; SLJ 7/11)

124 Feiffer, Kate. *No Go Sleep!* (K–3). Illus. by Jules Feiffer. 2012, Simon & Schuster $16.99 (978-144241683-3). 32pp. A stubborn baby is finally charmed into sleep by a pastel cast of forest animals, celestial bodies, and more in this sweet bedtime story. ℮ (Rev: BL 2/15/12; HB 3–4/12; SLJ 5/1/12*)

125 Fleming, Denise. *Sleepy, Oh So Sleepy* (PS). Illus. by author. 2010, Henry Holt $16.99 (978-0-8050-8126-8). 32pp. Baby animals go to sleep in this effective bedtime book. (Rev: BL 6/10*; HB 7–8/10; SLJ 7/1/10)

126 Fraser, Mary Ann. *Pet Shop Lullaby* (PS–2). Illus. by author. 2009, Boyds Mills $16.95 (978-1-59078-618-5). 32pp. A hamster spinning his exercise wheel disturbs his fellow pet shop inhabitants in this please-go-to-bed story. (Rev: BL 11/1/09; HB 1–2/10; SLJ 11/1/09)

127 Frederick, Heather Vogel. *Hide and Squeak* (PS). Illus. by C. F. Payne. 2011, Simon & Schuster $16.99 (978-0-689-85570-2). Unpaged. A father mouse patiently follows his young one's pre-bedtime capers before finally persuading him to sleep. (Rev: BL 1/1–15/11; SLJ 2/1/11)

128 Gal, Susan. *Night Lights* (PS–1). Illus. by author. 2009, Knopf LB $14.99 (978-0-375-95862-5). 32pp. A little girl, her mother, and dog share a variety of quiet evening activities on a summer night in this book that is wordless apart from the names of the various lights they see (street, fire, candle, star). (Rev: BL 12/1/09; SLJ 11/1/09*)

129 Gershator, Phillis. *Moo, Moo, Brown Cow! Have You Any Milk?* (PS–2). Illus. by Giselle Potter. 2011, Random House $16.99 (978-0-375-86744-6); LB $19.99

(978-0-375-96744-3). 40pp. A sheep contributes wool for a blanket, a cow milk for a bedtime snack, and so forth in this soothing barnyard bedtime story. (Rev: BL 6/1/11; HB 9–10/11; SLJ 6/11)

130 Gershator, Phillis, and Mim Green. *Who's Awake in Springtime?* (PS–2). Illus. by Emilie Chollat. 2010, Henry Holt $16.99 (978-0-8050-6390-5). 32pp. In this cumulative bedtime story with a find-and-seek twist, a host of animals playfully evades bedtime until it proves irresistible. (Rev: BL 12/15/09; LMC 1–2/10; SLJ 2/1/10)

131 Gorbachev, Valeri. *Shhh!* (PS–1). Illus. by author. 2011, Philomel $16.99 (978-0-399-25429-1). 32pp. A little boy tiptoes around the house while his brother naps, asking all his toys (clown, knights, tiger) to keep quiet. (Rev: BLO 10/15/11; SLJ 9/1/11)

132 Guthrie, James. *Last Song* (PS–K). Illus. by Eric Rohmann. 2010, Roaring Brook $10.99 (978-1-59643-508-7). 28pp. A squirrel family settles in for the night after a busy day in this nicely illustrated story based on a Scottish verse. (Rev: BL 10/15/10; SLJ 10/1/10)

133 Hayes, Geoffrey. *The Bunny's Night-Light: A Glow-in-the-Dark Search* (PS–K). Illus. by author. 2012, Random House $11.99 (978-0-375-86926-6); LB $14.99 (978-0-375-96926-3). 32pp. Bunny and his dad search the woods for the perfect night-light, dismissing the moon and fireflies before his mom figures out the perfect solution to the problem. (Rev: BL 1/1/12; SLJ 12/1/11)

134 Hill, Susanna Leonard. *Can't Sleep Without Sheep* (PS–1). Illus. by Mike Wohnoutka. 2010, Walker $16.99 (978-0-8027-2066-5). Unpaged. Ava just can't sleep, but the disgruntled sheep are exhausted and try to find suitable replacements, without success. (Rev: SLJ 9/1/10)

135 Howland, Naomi. *Princess Says Goodnight* (PS–K). Illus. by David Small. 2010, HarperCollins $16.99 (978-0-06-145525-4). 32pp. A little girl imagines herself a princess as she gets ready for bed, eating chocolate éclairs and practicing her curtsies. (Rev: BL 4/1/10; SLJ 4/1/10)

136 Hurd, Thacher. *The Weaver* (PS–2). Illus. by Elisa Kleven. 2010, Farrar $16.99 (978-0-374-38254-4). 32pp. High above the Earth, a young girl in a red dress sits on a cloud and weaves her observations of life below during the day and evening before going home to her own family. (Rev: BL 4/15/10; LMC 8–9/10; SLJ 6/1/10)

137 Iwamura, Kazuo. *Bedtime in the Forest* (PS–1). Illus. by author. 2010, NorthSouth $16.95 (978-0-7358-2310-5). 32pp. A trio of young squirrels want to stay up past their bedtimes to play with their owl friends, but eventually figure out an even better way to interact. (Rev: BL 8/10; SLJ 1/1/11)

138 Jadoul, Emile. *Good Night, Chickie* (PS). Illus. by author. 2011, Eerdmans $13.99 (978-0-8028-5378-3). 26pp. Finally reassured by Mother Hen that all is well, little Chickie tells his toy bunny that it's time to go to sleep. (Rev: BL 5/1/11; SLJ 2/1/11)

139 Kempter, Christa. *When Mama Can't Sleep* (PS). Illus. by Natascha Rosenberg. Series: Tuff Books. 2011, NorthSouth $6.95 (978-0-7358-4015-7). Unpaged. Mama can't sleep; nor can Papa, or Max, or teddy, or the dog. The only thing to do is all crawl into bed together. (Rev: SLJ 8/1/11)

140 Ketteman, Helen. *Goodnight, Little Monster* (PS–2). Illus. by Bonnie Leick. 2010, Marshall Cavendish $16.99 (978-0-7614-5683-4). Unpaged. Howling at the moon, worm juice and beetle bread, and picking bugs off ears are all part of the bedtime ritual for this young monster. (Rev: SLJ 9/1/10)

141 Kramer, Andrew. *Pajama Pirates* (PS–K). Illus. by Leslie Lammle. 2010, HarperCollins $16.99 (978-0-06-125194-8). 40pp. Dreamy illustrations enhance this story of three youngsters playing pirates before drifting off to sleep. (Rev: BLO 8/10; SLJ 9/1/10)

142 Lamb, Albert. *Tell Me the Day Backwards* (PS–1). Illus. by David McPhail. 2011, Candlewick $15.99 (978-0-7636-5055-1). 40pp. Before bed, a little bear and his mother lovingly rehash their eventful day. (Rev: BL 3/1/11; SLJ 3/1/11)

143 LaRochelle, David. *The Haunted Hamburger and Other Ghostly Stories* (PS–2). Illus. by Paul Meisel. 2011, Dutton $16.99 (978-0-525-42272-3). 40pp. A daddy ghost tells his offspring three short scary bedtime stories; fortunately, what's scary to ghosts is funny to readers. (Rev: BLO 8/11; HB 9–10/11; LMC 11–12/11; SLJ 8/1/11)

144 MacLachlan, Patricia. *Lala Salama: A Tanzanian Lullaby* (PS–K). Illus. by Elizabeth Zunon. 2011, Candlewick $16.99 (978-0-7636-4747-6). 32pp. As evening falls, a mother recalls the events of the day for her baby as they sit on the banks of Lake Tanganyika. (Rev: BL 12/1/11; SLJ 11/1/11)

145 McQuinn, Anna. *The Sleep Sheep* (PS–2). Illus. by Hannah Shaw. 2010, Scholastic $17.99 (978-0-545-23145-9). Unpaged. Sylvie turns to counting sheep in order to get to sleep, but the sheep are uncooperative. (Rev: SLJ 7/1/10)

146 Martin, Bill, and Michael Sampson. *Kitty Cat, Kitty Cat, Are You Going to Sleep?* (PS–K). Illus. by Laura J. Bryant. 2011, Marshall Cavendish $15.99 (978-0-7614-5946-0). 24pp. A young kitten reluctantly follows her mother's patient prompts about the process of getting ready for bed. (Rev: BL 3/15/11; SLJ 5/1/11)

147 Martin, Ruth. *Moon Dreams* (PS–K). Illus. by Olivier Latyk. 2010, Candlewick $16.99 (978-0-7636-5012-4). 32pp. Luna wonders where the moon goes during the day and dreams up fanciful, beautifully illustrated, scenarios. (Rev: BL 7/10; SLJ 4/11)

148 Perlman, Willa. *Good Night, World* (PS). Illus. by Carolyn Fisher. 2011, Simon & Schuster $16.99 (978-1-4424-0197-4). 40pp. A small child wishes good night to everything from the sun and the stars to his neighborhood and family. (Rev: BL 7/11; HB 9–10/11; SLJ 6/11)

149 Reidy, Jean. *Light Up the Night* (K–2). Illus. by Margaret Chodos-Irvine. 2011, Hyperion/Disney $16.99 (978-1-4231-2024-7). 40pp. A little boy takes a magic blanket tour of the universe before returning to his comfortable bed. (Rev: BL 11/15/11; HB 9–10/11; SLJ 9/1/11)

150 Rinker, Sherri Duskey. *Goodnight, Goodnight, Construction Site* (PS–K). Illus. by Tom Lichtenheld. 2011, Chronicle $16.99 (978-0-8118-7782-4). 32pp. As the sun sets, five construction site vehicles end their working day and bed down for the night. (Rev: BL 9/1/11*; SLJ 7/11*)

151 Rosenthal, Amy Krouse. *Bedtime for Mommy* (PS–K). Illus. by LeUyen Pham. 2010, Bloomsbury $16.99 (978-1-59990-341-5). 32pp. A determined child oversees her mother's progress to bed in this humorous role-reversal story. (Rev: BL 2/15/10; LMC 1–2/10; SLJ 3/1/10)

152 Ross, Tony. *I Want My Light On! A Little Princess Story* (PS–1). Illus. by author. 2010, Andersen $16.95 (978-0-7613-6443-6). Unpaged. Little Princess is petrified of ghosts until she meets one and discovers that it's as afraid of her as she is of it. (Rev: BL 7/10; SLJ 8/1/10)

153 Ruddell, Deborah. *Who Said Coo?* (PS). Illus. by Robin Luebs. 2010, Simon & Schuster $16.99 (978-1-4169-8510-5). 40pp. Various animal sounds interrupt Lulu the Pig as she's trying to sleep in this comic lullaby with a sweet ending. (Rev: BL 6/10; LMC 8–9/10; SLJ 8/1/10) [811.6]

154 Sartell, Debra. *Time for Bed, Baby Ted* (PS–K). Illus. by Kay Chorao. 2010, Holiday House $16.95 (978-0-8234-1968-5). 32pp. Toddler Ted is an expert at prolonging his bedtime routine, impersonating different animals and enticing his patient, good-natured dad to guess the correct animal before tucking him in. (Rev: BL 1/1/10; SLJ 3/1/10)

155 Saunders, Karen. *Baby Badger's Wonderful Night* (PS–2). Illus. by Dubravka Kolanovic. 2011, Egmont $16.99 (978-1-60684-172-3). Unpaged. Baby badger's dad takes him on a beautiful nighttime walk through the forest and shows him that the dark is not frightening after all. (Rev: SLJ 4/11)

156 Schaefer, Carole Lexa. *Who's There?* (PS–1). Illus. by Pierr Morgan. 2011, Viking $15.99 (978-0-670-01241-1). 32pp. Alone in the dark with his teddy bear, a little rabbit imagines all kinds of sources for the noises he hears; the illustrations are of completely unscary monsters. (Rev: BL 5/1/11; SLJ 7/11)

157 Shea, Bob. *Race You to Bed* (PS–1). Illus. by author. 2010, HarperCollins $16.99 (978-0-06-170417-8). 32pp. A hyperactive rabbit leads readers on a frenetic race — over hills, through a swamp, on a train — to bed in this rather energetic bedtime story. (Rev: BL 4/1/10; SLJ 2/1/10)

158 Smith, Danna. *Pirate Nap: A Book of Colors* (PS–K). Illus. by Valeria Petrone. 2011, Clarion $14.99 (978-0-574-57531-5). 40pp. Two brothers intent on seeing pirate possibilities all around the house strongly resist the idea that they should take a nap. (Rev: SLJ 8/1/11)

159 Srinivasan, Divya. *Little Owl's Night* (PS–K). Illus. by author. 2011, Viking $16.99 (978-0-670-01295-4). 32pp. Little Owl is having such a good time foraging through the night that he's sad to see the sun come up and realize that it's time for bed. (Rev: BL 10/15/11*; SLJ 11/1/11)

160 Steigemeyer, Julie. *Seven Little Bunnies* (PS). Illus. by Laura J. Bryant. 2010, Marshall Cavendish $15.99 (978-0-7614-5600-1). 24pp. Seven little bunnies resist bedtime with frenzied activities that eventually tire them out. (Rev: BL 2/15/10; SLJ 4/1/10)

161 Stills, Caroline, and Sarcia Stills Blott. *The House of 12 Bunnies* (PS–1). Illus. by Judith Rossell. 2012, Holiday House $16.95 (978-082342422-1). 24pp. Sophia the bunny searches the whole house for her book before finding it under her pillow in this book that offers counting and seek-and-find opportunities. (Rev: BL 3/1/12; SLJ 4/1/12)

162 Symes, Sally. *Yawn* (PS). Illus. by Nick Sharratt. 2011, Candlewick $7.99 (978-076365725-3). 24pp. Sean gives a yawn that passes to a cat, leading to a domino effect and general sleepiness. (Rev: BLO 11/15/11; HB 1–2/12; SLJ 1/12)

163 van Genechten, Guido. *No Ghost Under My Bed* (PS). Illus. by author. 2010, Clavis $16.95 (978-1-60537-069-9). 30pp. A little penguin named Jake asks his father to check around his room repeatedly before finally feeling safe enough to sleep. (Rev: BL 11/1/10; SLJ 10/1/10)

164 Verdick, Elizabeth. *Bedtime* (PS). Illus. by Marieka Heinlen. Series: Toddler Tools. 2010, Free Spirit paper $7.95 (978-1-57542-315-9). Unpaged. This board book introduces the importance of bedtime and various actions that can make children sleepy. (Rev: SLJ 6/1/10)

165 Watson, Wendy. *Bedtime Bunnies* (PS). Illus. by author. 2010, Clarion $15.99 (978-0-547-22312-4). 32pp. Five little bunnies get ready for bed in this lively book with minimal, onomatopoeic text. ℮ (Rev: BL 12/1/10; HB 11–12/10; SLJ 12/1/10*)

166 Wells, Rosemary. *Max and Ruby's Bedtime Book* (PS–1). Illus. by author. 2010, Viking $17.99 (978-0-670-01141-4). 48pp. At their bedtime, Grandma tells three stories about young rabbits Max and Ruby. (Rev: BL 7/10; HB 9–10/10; SLJ 6/11)

167 Willems, Mo. *Time to Sleep, Sheep the Sheep!* (PS–K). Illus. by author. 2010, HarperCollins $10.99 (978-0-06-172847-1). 32pp. Cat the Cat has a slumber party at which most of her friends (Sheep, Pig, Giraffe, and others) are all happy to get to bed — except Owl. (Rev: BL 5/1/10; HB 7–8/10; SLJ 7/1/10)

168 Yolen, Jane. *Creepy Monsters, Sleepy Monsters: A Lullaby* (PS–1). Illus. by Kelly Murphy. 2011, Candlewick $14.99 (978-0-7636-4201-3). 32pp. Diverse young monsters complete their daily dinner-bath-bedtime routine in this story with detailed illustrations. (Rev: BL 5/1/11; SLJ 6/11)

Nursery Rhymes

169 Ashburn, Boni. *Builder Goose: It's Construction Rhyme Time!* (1–3). Illus. by Sergio De Giorgi. 2012, Sterling $14.95 (978-140277118-7). 32pp. For the mechanically minded, this is a collection of nursery rhymes recast to include heavy equipment. (Rev: BL 3/1/12; SLJ 5/12) [398.8]

170 Duffy, Chris, ed. *Nursery Rhyme Comics: 50 Timeless Rhymes from 50 Celebrated Cartoonists* (PS–3). Illus. 2011, First Second $18.99 (978-159643600-8). 128pp. Talented cartoonists draw richly imagined versions of familiar nursery rhymes in this inspired collection. (Rev: BL 11/15/11*; SLJ 9/1/11) [741.5]

171 Hale, Sarah Josepha. *Mary Had a Little Lamb* (PS–1). Illus. by Laura Huliska-Beith. 2011, Marshall Cavendish $12.99 (978-0-7614-5824-1). 24pp. A timeless, lively new version of the nursery classic. (Rev: BL 3/15/11; SLJ 3/1/11) [811]

172 Hillenbrand, Will. *Mother Goose Picture Puzzles* (PS–1). Illus. by author. 2011, Marshall Cavendish $17.99 (978-0-7614-5808-1). 40pp. Twenty nursery rhymes, some familiar and some more obscure, are presented in rebus format. ℮ (Rev: BL 3/1/11; SLJ 4/11*) [398.2]

173 Mavor, Salley. *Pocketful of Posies: A Treasury of Nursery Rhymes* (PS–K). Illus. by author. 2010, Houghton Mifflin $21.99 (978-0-618-73740-6). 72pp. Familiar and not-so-familiar nursery rhymes and verses are presented with boldly textured illustrations that may incorporate shells, seeds, beads, and driftwood. ALSC Notable Children's Book, 2011; Boston Globe–Horn Book Award. ℮ (Rev: BLO 8/10; HB 11–12/10; SLJ 9/1/10) [398.8]

174 Moses, Will. *Mary and Her Little Lamb: The True Story of the Famous Nursery Rhyme* (1–3). Illus. by author. 2011, Philomel $17.99 (978-0-399-25154-2). 40pp. The true story behind the nursery rhyme — involving a sickly lamb, a kind young girl, and an 1800s

Massachusetts schoolhouse — is presented with folk-art illustrations. (Rev: SLJ 9/1/11)

175 Pinkney, Jerry. *Three Little Kittens* (PS–1). Illus. by author. 2010, Dial $16.99 (978-0-8037-3533-0). 32pp. The classic nursery rhyme of three kittens and their mittens is reinterpreted here with chant-along refrains and evocative pencil-and-watercolor art. (Rev: BL 9/1/10; SLJ 9/1/10) [398.8]

176 Taylor, Jane. *Twinkle, Twinkle, Little Star* (PS–1). Illus. by Jerry Pinkney. 2011, Little, Brown $16.99 (978-0-316-05696-0). Unpaged. A little chipmunk gazes into the sky and wonders at the sights he sees in this imaginative and beautifully illustrated picture book. (Rev: SLJ 11/1/11*) [821]

177 Tildes, Phyllis Limbacher. *Will You Be Mine? A Nursery Rhyme Romance* (PS–K). Illus. by author. 2011, Charlesbridge $17.95 (978-1-58089-244-5); paper $7.95 (978-1-58089-245-2). 32pp. Eighteen Mother Goose rhymes are arranged so they tell a larger story about a cat and poodle's nuptials in this attractively illustrated book. **e** (Rev: BL 1/1–15/11; SLJ 2/1/11) [398.8]

Stories Without Words

178 Baker, Jeannie. *Mirror* (PS–3). Illus. by author. 2010, Candlewick $18.99 (978-0-7636-4848-0). 40pp. Boys on opposite sides of the world — in Sydney, Australia, and in rural Morocco — are shown spending the day with their families in parallel wordless stories. (Rev: BL 2/15/11; SLJ 1/1/11*)

179 Cooper, Elisha. *Beaver Is Lost* (PS–2). Illus. by author. 2010, Random House $17.99 (978-0-375-85765-2). 40pp. A beaver hitches a ride on a logging truck and ends up having a big and sometimes frightening adventure in the big city, eventually finding his way home across a big lake. (Rev: BL 6/10; LMC 11–12/10; SLJ 6/1/10)

180 Day, Alexandra. *Carl's Snowy Afternoon* (PS). Illus. by author. 2009, Farrar $12.99 (978-0-374-31086-8). 32pp. With the babysitter preoccupied, Carl the Rottweiler and his young charge sneak off to attend a pond party on a snowy afternoon. (Rev: BL 11/15/09; SLJ 12/1/09)

181 Faller, Regis. *Polo and the Dragon* (PS–K). Illus. by author. 2009, Roaring Brook $9.99 (978-1-59643-498-1). 32pp. A young dog named Polo becomes trapped in ice when out sailing but a friendly dragon helps him get home safely; a wordless picture book. (Rev: BLO 11/1/09; SLJ 11/1/09)

182 Frazier, Craig. *Bee and Bird* (PS–1). Illus. by author. 2011, Roaring Brook $16.99 (978-1-59643-660-2). 40pp. A wordless tale about a bird and a bee sharing a journey using various forms of transportation. (Rev: BL 5/1/11; SLJ 7/11)

183 Hogrogian, Nonny. *Cool Cat* (PS–1). Illus. by author. 2009, Roaring Brook $17.99 (978-1-59643-429-5). Unpaged. Cool Cat is tired of his dreary neighborhood and transforms it with some paint and a lot of help from friends who appreciate the new, beautiful world. (Rev: HB 1–2/10; LMC 11–12/09; SLJ 10/1/09)

184 Lee, Suzy. *Shadow* (PS–1). Illus. by author. 2010, Chronicle $15.99 (978-0-8118-7280-5). Unpaged. This nearly wordless story that is read horizontally features a girl playing with shadows in a dark attic. (Rev: SLJ 11/1/10*)

185 Lehman, Barbara. *The Secret Box* (PS–2). Illus. by author. 2011, Houghton Mifflin $15.99 (978-0-547-23868-5). 48pp. In a school dormitory in the early 20th century, a young boy hides a mysterious box under the floorboards; as the generations roll by, the scenery around the dormitory changes, until the box is rediscovered by a modern-day boy; this wordless story is told in detailed watercolors. (Rev: BL 2/1/11; HB 7–8/11; SLJ 5/1/11)

186 Mayer, Mercer. *Octopus Soup* (K–2). Illus. by author. 2011, Marshall Cavendish $16.99 (978-0-7614-5812-8). Unpaged. An octopus has a series of misadventures in this wordless picture book. (Rev: SLJ 4/11)

187 Nolan, Dennis. *Sea of Dreams* (PS–4). Illus. by author. 2011, Roaring Brook $16.99 (978-1-59643-470-7). Unpaged. In this magical realism story, the inhabitants of a young girl's sandcastle escape at night, as the tide comes in and their home is washed away. (Rev: LMC 1–2/12; SLJ 11/1/11)

188 Raschka, Chris. *A Ball for Daisy* (PS–K). Illus. by author. 2011, Random House $16.99 (978-0-375-85861-1); LB $19.99 (978-0-375-95861-8). 32pp. A playful little dog gets depressed when another dog punctures her favorite ball in this effective wordless story. Caldecott Medal. (Rev: BL 6/1/11; HB 9–10/11; SLJ 8/1/11*)

189 Rodriguez, Beatrice. *The Chicken Thief* (PS–2). Illus. by author. 2010, Enchanted Lion $14.95 (978-1-59270-092-9). 32pp. A chicken's friends — a bear, a rabbit, and a rooster — set off in hot pursuit when she is captured by a fox in this wordless story. (Rev: BL 6/10; SLJ 8/1/10*)

190 Rodriguez, Béatrice. *Fox and Hen Together* (PS–1). Illus. by author. 2011, Enchanted Lion $14.95 (978-1-59270-109-4). Unpaged. Hen leaves Fox in charge of their egg and heads off on an ill-fated fishing trip with Crab; the entertaining, wordless sequel to *The Chicken Thief* (2010). The final volume in the trilogy is *Rooster's Revenge* (2011). (Rev: SLJ 7/11*)

191 Schories, Pat. *When Jack Goes Out* (PS–K). Illus. by author. 2010, Boyds Mills $13.95 (978-1-59078-652-9). 32pp. Jack the dog enjoys a night cavorting with fun-loving aliens, but does he want to go home with them? A wordless book. (Rev: BL 2/15/10; LMC 5–6/10; SLJ 2/1/10*)

192 Schubert, Ingrid, and Dieter Schubert. *The Umbrella* (PS–2). Illus. by authors. 2011, Lemniscaat $16.95 (978-1-9359-5400-2). Unpaged. A small black dog with a red umbrella takes readers on a trip through all Earth's climate zones, from arctic tundra to tropical rain forest in this wordless picture book. (Rev: SLJ 11/1/11)

193 Thomson, Bill. *Chalk* (K–3). Illus. by author. 2010, Marshall Cavendish $15.99 (978-0-7614-5526-4). 40pp. A wordless picture book in which three children find some chalk and draw pictures on a playground that come to life. ℮ (Rev: BLO 3/1/10; SLJ 4/1/10*)

194 Tolman, Marije, and Ronald Tolman. *The Tree House* (PS–1). Illus. by authors. 2010, Boyds Mills $17.95 (978-1-59078-806-6). Unpaged. A variety of different animals have carefree and kindhearted adventures in a magnificent treehouse in this wordless story. (Rev: SLJ 4/1/10)

Picture Books

Imaginative Stories

FANTASIES

195 Anderson, Derek. *Story County: Here We Come!* (PS–1). Illus. by author. 2011, Scholastic $16.99 (978-0-545-16844-1). 40pp. A farmer, a dog, a cow, a pig, and a chicken team up to create a colorful farm with crops such as jelly beans and pizza, all in a bouncy day. Lexile AD190L (Rev: BLO 1/1–15/11; SLJ 2/1/11)

196 Ashburn, Boni. *Over at the Castle* (PS–1). Illus. by Kelly Murphy. 2010, Abrams $15.95 (978-0-8109-8414-1). 32pp. The song "Over in the Meadow" is re-cast in a medieval setting in which the occupants of a castle go about their daily activities until dragons offer a fire display; a counting component adds an extra dimension. (Rev: BL 3/1/10; SLJ 5/1/10)

197 Baeten, Lieve. *The Clever Little Witch* (PS–2). Illus. by Wietse Fossey. 2012, NorthSouth $16.95 (978-073584079-9). 32pp. Lizzy's efforts to open a mysterious suitcase by using spells do not work, so she consults older witches and, with their advice, succeeds — to find a letter inviting her to attend Witch School. (Rev: BLO 4/15/12; SLJ 4/1/12)

198 Baeten, Lieve. *The Curious Little Witch* (PS–2). Illus. by author. 2010, NorthSouth $16.95 (978-0-7358-2305-1). 32pp. An over-curious young witch named Lizzy finds herself in the home of benevolent older witches, who enhance her broken broomstick and send her on her way. Also use *Happy Birthday, Little Witch*

(2011) in which Lizzy searches for her missing black cat. (Rev: BL 9/15/10; LMC 1–2/11; SLJ 11/1/10)

199 Banks, Kate. *The Eraserheads* (PS–2). Illus. by Boris Kulikov. 2010, Farrar $16.99 (978-0-374-39920-7). 40pp. Three animal-shaped erasers find themselves on a fantastic and dangerous trip as they try to help a young boy with his homework. (Rev: BL 1/1/10; SLJ 5/1/10)

200 Barnett, Mac. *Extra Yarn* (K–2). Illus. by Jon Klassen. 2012, HarperCollins $16.99 (978-0-06-195338-5). 40pp. Annabelle has a seemingly unending supply of yarn and knits sweaters for all the people, animals, and buildings of the town . . . and then an evil archduke arrives. Boston Globe–Horn Book Award. (Rev: BL 12/15/11*; HB 1–2/12; SLJ 12/1/11)

201 Bartoletti, Susan Campbell. *Naamah and the Ark at Night* (PS–1). Illus. by Holly Meade. 2011, Candlewick $16.99 (978-0-7636-4242-6). 32pp. In this reimagined story with rhyming text, Bartoletti pictures Noah's wife as a soothing singer who helps calm the animals and people aboard the Ark. (Rev: BL 11/1/11*; SLJ 7/11)

202 Bently, Peter. *King Jack and the Dragon* (PS–K). Illus. by Helen Oxenbury. 2011, Dial $17.99 (978-0-8037-3698-6). 32pp. Three diapered boys build a cardboard castle and fight dragons in this imaginative adventure with spare, rhyming text. (Rev: BL 9/1/11; SLJ 9/1/11*)

203 Biedrzycki, David. *Me and My Dragon* (K–2). Illus. by author. 2011, Charlesbridge $16.95 (978-1-58089-278-0); paper $7.95 (978-1-58089-279-7). Unpaged. A young boy imagines all the fun he could have with a pet dragon. ℮ (Rev: SLJ 7/11)

204 Bunting, Eve. *Pirate Boy* (PS–1). Illus. by Julie Fortenberry. 2011, Holiday House $16.95 (978-0-8234-2321-7). 32pp. Danny wonders about becoming a pirate but has his doubts about the wisdom of this plan; his mother reassures him that she will always come and get him. (Rev: BL 10/15/11; SLJ 9/1/11)

205 Burell, Sarah. *Diamond Jim Dandy and the Sheriff* (K–1). Illus. by Bryan Langdo. 2010, Sterling $14.95 (978-1-4027-5737-2). 32pp. Dustpan, Texas, finds itself in a tizzy when a friendly and talented rattlesnake comes to town. (Rev: BL 2/15/10; LMC 5–6/10; SLJ 3/1/10)

206 Calvert, Pam. *Princess Peepers Picks a Pet* (K–2). Illus. by Tuesday Mourning. 2011, Marshall Cavendish $16.99 (978-0-7614-5815-9). Unpaged. Princess Peepers loses her glasses on a trip to the forest to select a nice animal for the pet show at the Royal Academy for Perfect Princesses and mistakes a dragon for a unicorn. (Rev: SLJ 4/11)

207 Chabon, Michael. *The Astonishing Secret of Awesome Man* (PS–2). Illus. by Jake Parker. 2011, HarperCollins $17.99 (978-0-06-191462-1). 40pp. A young superhero describes and then demonstrates his amazing powers, admitting at the same time that Mom is always waiting at the Fortress of Awesome with cheese and crackers and chocolate milk. (Rev: BL 9/15/11; SLJ 8/1/11*)

208 Christelow, Eileen. *The Desperate Dog Writes Again* (PS–2). Illus. by author. 2010, Clarion $16.99 (978-0-547-24205-7). 40pp. Worried about her human's relationship with another human, Emma the dog consults Queenie, the canine advice columnist. (Rev: BL 10/15/10; SLJ 1/1/11)

209 Cleminson, Katie. *Cuddle Up, Goodnight* (PS–K). Illus. by author. 2011, Hyperion/Disney $15.99 (978-1-4231-3844-0). 32pp. A young boy and his animal friends — an elephant, a raccoon, a hippo, a polar bear — have a variety of daytime adventures, including mealtime, naptime, play time, and bath time, ending up with bedtime. (Rev: BL 1/1–15/11; HB 1–2/11; LMC 3/1/11; SLJ 2/1/11)

210 Cohen, Caron Lee. *Broom, Zoom!* (PS–K). Illus. by Sergio Ruzzier. 2010, Simon & Schuster $12.99 (978-1-4169-9113-7). 32pp. After an initial disagreement about who needs the broom most, Little Witch and Little Monster agree to share and cooperate. (Rev: BL 9/1/10; HB 9–10/10; SLJ 9/1/10)

211 Collins, Ross. *Doodleday* (PS–K). Illus. by author. 2011, Whitman $16.99 (978-0-8075-1683-6). 32pp. Henry is warned not to draw on Doodleday but he goes ahead and draws a fly, then a spider, and more; each successive animal comes to life and risks creating havoc until his mother rushes home to save the day. (Rev: BL 3/1/11; SLJ 5/1/11)

212 Cottringer, Anne. *Eliot Jones, Midnight Superhero* (PS–2). Illus. by Alex T. Smith. 2009, Tiger Tales $15.95 (978-1-58925-083-3); paper $7.95 (978-1-58925-416-9). Unpaged. Eliot becomes a superhero each night at midnight and embarks on a mission to save Earth from a giant meteor. (Rev: LMC 11–12/09; SLJ 9/1/09)

213 dePaola, Tomie. *Strega Nona's Harvest* (PS–3). Illus. by author. 2009, Putnam $16.99 (978-0-399-25291-4). 32pp. When Big Anthony grows more vegetables than he can handle, he leaves them for Strega Nona, who turns them into a grand feast. Lexile AD690L (Rev: BL 11/1/09; SLJ 10/1/09)

214 Duddle, Jonny. *The Pirate Cruncher* (PS–2). Illus. by author. 2010, Candlewick $15.99 (978-0-7636-4876-3). 38pp. Greedy pirates follow a mysterious fiddler who promises rich treasures, but a monster awaits instead. (Rev: BL 4/15/10; SLJ 5/1/10)

215 Dyer, Sarah. *Monster Day at Work* (PS–1). Illus. by author. 2010, Frances Lincoln $16.95 (978-1-84780-069-5). 28pp. It's Bring Your Child to Work Day and Monster Dad takes Monster Son (and the dog) along with him in this humorous story seen from the child's perspective. (Rev: BL 10/15/10; SLJ 1/1/11)

216 Egielski, Richard. *Captain Sky Blue* (PS–1). Illus. by author. 2010, Scholastic $17.95 (978-054521342-4).

32pp. In this action-packed, imaginative story, a young boy's favorite toy pilot becomes lost at sea but eventually makes it back home thanks to his bravery and some help from Santa. Lexile AD580L (Rev: BL 9/15/10; HB 11–12/10)

217 Ellis, Andy. *When Lulu Went to the Zoo* (PS–1). Illus. by author. 2010, Andersen $16.95 (978-0-7613-5499-4). 32pp. Empathetic 4-year-old Lulu invites the zoo's animals home with her in this zany, whimsical tale with eye-catching illustrations. (Rev: BL 1/1/10; SLJ 3/1/10)

218 Enderle, Dotti. *The Library Gingerbread Man* (PS–2). Illus. by Colleen M. Madden. 2010, Upstart $17.95 (978-1-60213-048-7). 32pp. A gingerbread man escapes from his story on the shelf at the library, and manages to elude a host of other literary characters in his pursuit for a grand adventure. (Rev: BLO 4/15/10; LMC 10/10; SLJ 6/1/10)

219 Fenton, Joe. *Boo!* (PS–1). Illus. by author. 2010, Simon & Schuster $12.99 (978-1-4169-7936-4). Unpaged. A little ghost does his best to scare his family but fails until he wanders into a white sheet. (Rev: SLJ 7/1/10)

220 Foley, Greg. *Willoughby and the Moon* (K–2). Illus. by author. 2010, HarperCollins $18.99 (978-0-06-154753-9). 40pp. Willoughby can't sleep when the moon disappears and discovers the moon in his closet with a giant snail that is look for his lost silver ball; shining illustrations enhance this quirky tale about fears and imagination. (Rev: BL 2/15/10; SLJ 5/1/10)

221 Fore, S. J. *Read to Tiger* (PS–1). Illus. by R. W. Alley. 2010, Viking $15.99 (978-0-670-01140-7). Unpaged. A little boy absorbed in his book is constantly disturbed by an annoying tiger, but finally convinces him that the story is worth listening to. (Rev: LMC 11–12/10; SLJ 8/1/10)

222 Foreman, Michael. *Fortunately, Unfortunately* (PS–2). Illus. by author. 2011, Andersen $16.95 (978-0-7613-7460-2). 32pp. On the way to return his grandmother's umbrella, young Milo has a number of lucky and unlucky encounters (with a whale, a pirate, dinosaurs, friendly aliens, and so forth). ℮ Lexile AD530L (Rev: BL 3/1/11; SLJ 2/1/11)

223 Gammell, Stephen. *Mudkin* (PS–1). Illus. by author. 2011, Carolrhoda $16.95 (978-0-7613-5790-2). 32pp. A strange, muddy little creature invites a young girl to join him in a glorious day of mud-filled activities in this almost wordless story. (Rev: BL 1/1–15/11*; SLJ 3/1/11)

224 Gleeson, Libby. *The Great Bear* (2–4). Illus. by Armin Greder. 2011, Candlewick $16.99 (978-0-7636-5136-7). Unpaged. A captive dancing bear in a medieval circus endures neglect and abuse until it finally rebels and escapes up into the sky. (Rev: SLJ 9/1/11)

15

225 Gore, Leonid. *The Wonderful Book* (PS–1). Illus. by author. 2010, Scholastic $16.99 (978-0-545-08598-4). 32pp. A red object is used for various purposes by the animals in the forest (a hat, a picnic table) before a little boy turns up and reads a story from it. (Rev: BL 10/15/10; LMC 1–2/11; SLJ 11/1/10)

226 Graham, Bob. *April and Esme, Tooth Fairies* (PS–2). Illus. by author. 2010, Candlewick $16.99 (978-0-7636-4683-7). Unpaged. Two young fairies are asked to make their first expedition, to collect Daniel Dangerfield's tooth. (Rev: BL 10/1/10*; HB 9–10/10*; LMC 1–2/11; SLJ 9/1/10)

227 Gravel, Elise. *Adopt a Glurb!* (1–3). Illus. by author. Series: Balloon Toons. 2010, Blue Apple $10.99 (978-160905037-5). 40pp. Gravel describes the benefits and drawbacks of adopting a glurb — a smelly little monster — in this funny book with cartoon illustrations. (Rev: BL 11/15/10)

228 Grey, Mini. *Traction Man and the Beach Odyssey* (PS–2). Illus. by author. 2012, Knopf $16.99 (978-037586952-5); LB $19.99 (978-037596952-2). 32pp. Action toy Traction Man and his sidekick Scrubbing Brush have an exciting adventure at the beach and meet Beach Time Brenda. (Rev: BL 4/15/12*; HB 7–8/12; SLJ 4/1/12*)

229 Harper, Charise Mericle. *Cupcake: A Journey to Special* (PS–1). Illus. by author. 2010, Hyperion/Disney $14.99 (978-1-4231-1897-8). 32pp. A plain vanilla cupcake receives advice from a friendly candle on how to decorate himself. (Rev: BL 3/1/10; HB 3–4/10; SLJ 6/1/10)

230 Henkes, Kevin. *My Garden* (PS–1). Illus. by author. 2010, Greenwillow $17.99 (978-0-06-171517-4); LB $18.89 (978-0-06-171518-1). 40pp. A young girl imagines her ideal garden, complete with never-dying flowers and chocolate rabbits. (Rev: BL 1/1/10; HB 3–4/10; SLJ 3/1/10*)

231 Hines, Anna Grossnickle. *I Am a Tyrannosaurus* (PS). Illus. by author. 2011, Tricycle $14.99 (978-1-58246-413-8); LB $15.99 (978-1-58246-414-5). 40pp. A little boy has a day of imaginative play acting out the behaviors of various dinosaurs. (Rev: BLO 3/14/11; SLJ 8/1/11)

232 Howe, James. *Brontorina* (PS–2). Illus. by Randy Cecil. 2010, Candlewick $15.99 (978-0-7636-4437-6). 32pp. An enormous dinosaur named Brontorina is determined to become a ballerina despite her many drawbacks. (Rev: BL 5/15/10*; LMC 10/10; SLJ 7/1/10)

233 Hughes, Shirley. *Jonadab and Rita* (PS–2). Illus. by author. 2011, IPG/Red Fox paper $11.99 (978-1-86-230313-3). 32pp. Minnie neglects her toy donkey Jonadab and he flies off for an exciting adventure. (Rev: BLO 8/11; SLJ 6/11)

234 Ichikawa, Satomi. *My Little Train* (PS–1). Illus. by author. 2010, Philomel $15.99 (978-0-399-25453-6). 40pp. A toy train travels across the broad expanse of living room carpet, depositing its animal passengers at different locales: a potted plant, the fishbowl, the couch. (Rev: BL 10/1/10; SLJ 11/1/10)

235 Jackson, Ellen. *The Seven Seas* (PS–2). Illus. by Bill Slavin and Esperança Melo. 2011, Eerdmans $15.99 (978-0-8028-5341-7). 36pp. As his teacher talks about geography, a young rabbit daydreams about exploring fantasy seas — a Pink Sea with flamingos and cotton candy clouds, and so forth. (Rev: BL 2/15/11; SLJ 2/1/11)

236 Jeffers, Oliver. *The Hueys in the New Sweater* (PS–1). Illus. by author. 2012, Philomel $10.99 (978-039925767-4). 32pp. A population of identical, humdrum creatures called Hueys finds a new perspective on life when a Huey named Rupert knits himself an orange sweater in this paean to individuality. (Rev: BL 5/15/12*)

237 Jeffers, Oliver. *Up and Down* (K–2). Illus. by author. 2010, Philomel $16.99 (978-0-399-25545-8). 40pp. A boy and his penguin friend share board games and make music together until the penguin decides he must learn to fly, and must do so alone. (Rev: SLJ 12/1/10*)

238 Jenkins, Emily. *Toys Come Home: Being the Early Experiences of an Intelligent Stingray, a Brave Buffalo, and a Brand-New Someone Called Plastic* (K–2). Illus. by Paul O. Zelinsky. 2011, Random House $16.99 (978-0-375-86200-7); LB $19.99 (978-0-375-96200-4). 144pp. A prequel to *Toys Go Out* (2006) and *Toy Dance Party* (2008), this book explores the history of the toys that came to be cherished by the Girl. (Rev: BL 9/15/11*; SLJ 10/1/11)

239 Johnson, Angela. *The Day Ray Got Away* (PS–2). Illus. by Luke LaMarca. 2010, Simon & Schuster $16.99 (978-0-689-87375-1). 40pp. A strong-willed parade balloon shaped like the sun makes a break for freedom — inspiring the other parade balloons to attempt an "uprising." Lexile AD610L (Rev: BL 8/10; HB 9–10/10; SLJ 9/1/10)

240 Johnson, D. B. *Palazzo Inverso* (K–3). Illus. by author. 2010, Houghton Mifflin $16 (978-0-15-23999-6.). 32pp. Channeling Escher, this picture book full of shifting perspectives features young Mauk, whose contributions to the design of a grand Palazzo are dizzy-making. (Rev: BL 2/15/10; SLJ 5/1/10)

241 Joosse, Barbara. *Old Robert and the Sea-Silly Cats* (PS–2). Illus. by Jan Jutte. 2012, Philomel $16.99 (978-039925430-7). 40pp. A lonely old sailor's life is changed when a group of cats — three performing, and one an endearing little soul with no apparent talents — moves in. (Rev: BL 4/1/12; LMC 10/12; SLJ 4/1/12)

242 Joyce, William. *The Man in the Moon* (PS–3). Illus. by author. Series: Guardians of Childhood. 2011, Atheneum $17.99 (978-1-4424-3041-9). 56pp. When he was a child in the Golden Age, the Man in the Moon (MiM) was attacked by Pitch, the King of Nightmares, and escaped to a faraway galaxy where he made friends with guardians including the Tooth Fairy and the Sandman to look after the children of Earth. (Rev: BL 10/1/11; SLJ 10/1/11)

243 Judge, Lita. *Red Sled* (PS–2). Illus. by author. 2011, Simon & Schuster $16.99 (978-1-4424-2007-6). Unpaged. A diverse group of animals enjoy a little girl's red sled during the night in this almost-wordless book. (Rev: LMC 1–2/12*; SLJ 10/1/11*)

244 Juster, Norton. *The Odious Ogre* (PS–1). Illus. by Jules Feiffer. 2010, Scholastic $17.95 (978-0-545-16202-9). 32pp. An ogre used to terrorizing villages is undone by a beautiful young girl who refuses to fear him; the illustrations add to the humor. **e** Lexile AD880L (Rev: BL 9/15/10; HB 11–12/10; LMC 1–2/11; SLJ 10/1/10*)

245 Kasbarian, Lucine, reteller. *The Greedy Sparrow: An Armenian Tale* (PS–2). Illus. by Maria Zaikina. 2011, Marshall Cavendish $17.99 (978-0-7614-5821-2). 32pp. A greedy sparrow keeps trading up the goods he's able to con his neighbors out of, eventually receiving well-deserved comeuppance in the end. **e** Lexile AD640L (Rev: BLO 2/14/11; SLJ 3/1/11)

246 Kent, Allegra. *Ballerina Swan* (PS–3). Illus. by Emily Arnold McCully. 2012, Holiday House $16.95 (978-082342373-6). 32pp. A young swan named Sophie who is eager to be a ballerina works hard and is eventually awarded a part in *Swan Lake*. (Rev: BL 3/15/12; SLJ 4/1/12*)

247 Kirk, Daniel. *Honk Honk! Beep Beep!* (PS–K). Illus. by author. 2010, Hyperion $15.99 (978-1-4231-2486-3). 32pp. A young boy's toys — father and son — enjoy a secret adventure before he awakens. (Rev: BL 6/10; SLJ 11/1/10)

248 Knudsen, Michelle. *Argus* (PS–3). Illus. by Andrea Wesson. 2011, Candlewick $15.99 (978-0-7636-3790-3). 32pp. Sally is presented with an odd egg in her class's egg-hatching project; it turns out to be a dragon, presenting a wealth of funny situations and challenging problems. Lexile AD420L (Rev: BL 1/1–15/11; LMC 5–6/11; SLJ 2/1/11)

249 Krause, Ute. *Oscar and the Very Hungry Dragon* (1–3). Illus. by author. 2010, NorthSouth $16.95 (978-0-7358-2306-8). Unpaged. Unlucky Oscar is sent from his village as a peace offering to a hungry dragon; fortunately his cunning and his cooking abilities trick the beast into eating haute cuisine rather than human flesh. (Rev: LMC 11–12/10; SLJ 10/1/10)

250 Krensky, Stephen. *Noah's Bark* (K–2). Illus. by Roge. 2010, Carolrhoda $16.95 (978-082257645-7). 32pp. Noah's animals make too many confusing sounds and Noah induces order by making them each choose their own sound. Lexile AD470L (Rev: BL 3/1/10; LMC 8–9/10)

251 Kroll, Steven. *Super-Dragon* (PS–2). Illus. by Douglas Holgate. 2011, Marshall Cavendish $16.99 (978-0-7614-5819-7). 32pp. Little Drago gets a bird to teach him to fly so he can enter a contest, at which he surprises and impresses his whole family. (Rev: BLO 3/25/11; LMC 8–9/11; SLJ 5/1/11)

252 Kroll, Steven. *The Tyrannosaurus Game* (K–2). Illus. by S. D. Schindler. 2010, Marshall Cavendish $17.99 (978-0-7614-5603-2). 32pp. Stuck inside on a rainy day, 12 students craft a progressive story about an imaginary dinosaur to pass the time. (Rev: BLO 3/1/10; LMC 8–9/10; SLJ 4/1/10)

253 Krosoczka, Jarrett J. *Ollie the Purple Elephant* (1–2). Illus. by author. 2011, Knopf $16.99 (978-0-375-86654-8); LB $19.99 (978-0-375-96654-5). Unpaged. A cat and an unhappy neighbor scheme to get rid of the purple elephant living in the McLaughlins' New York City apartment. **e** (Rev: SLJ 12/1/11)

254 Lacamara, Laura. *Floating on Mama's Song / Flotando en la cancion de mama* (K–3). Illus. by Yuyi Morales. 2010, HarperCollins $16.99 (978-006084368-7). 32pp. Mama sings, and miraculously begins to rise into the air in this bilingual picture book. (Rev: BL 8/10; SLJ 9/10)

255 Langdo, Bryan. *Tornado Slim and the Magic Cowboy Hat* (K–2). Illus. by author. 2011, Marshall Cavendish $17.99 (978-0-7614-5962-0). 32pp. A hat presented to Tornado Slim by a coyote brings nothing but trouble on a journey to Fire Gulch City. **e** (Rev: BLO 11/15/11; LMC 1–2/12; SLJ 9/1/11)

256 LaReau, Kara. *Otto: The Boy Who Loved Cars* (K–3). Illus. by Scott Magoon. 2011, Roaring Brook $15.99 (978-1-59643-484-4). 32pp. A little boy obsessed with race cars turns into one in this quirky fantasy that encourages readers to try new things. (Rev: BL 7/11; SLJ 8/1/11)

257 Lee, YJ. *The Little Moon Princess* (PS–3). Illus. by author. 2010, HarperCollins $16.99 (978-0-06-154736-2). 32pp. A sparrow and a princess work together to spread bright stars throughout the night sky in this beautifully illustrated story. (Rev: BL 5/1/10; SLJ 4/1/10)

258 Levine, Gail Carson. *Betsy Red Hoodie* (K–3). Illus. by Scott Nash. 2010, HarperCollins $16.99 (978-0-06-146870-4). 40pp. Shepherd Betsy (of 2002's *Betsy Who Cried Wolf!*) is off to grandma's house along with the sheep and her colleague Zimmo the wolf in this funny fractured tale. Lexile AD210L (Rev: BL 9/15/10; HB 9–10/10; SLJ 9/1/10)

259 Lichtenheld, Tom. *Cloudette* (PS–2). Illus. by author. 2011, Henry Holt $16.99 (978-0-8050-8776-5). 40pp. A kindhearted cloud too little to quench a whole field of crops finds a perfect application for her altruistic spirit: a tiny pond with a lone parched frog. **e** Lexile AD660L (Rev: BL 2/1/11; SLJ 2/1/11)

260 Long, Loren. *Otis and the Tornado* (PS–2). Illus. by author. 2011, Philomel $17.99 (978-0-399-25477-2). 40pp. When a tornado looms over the farm, Otis the tractor comes to the aid of the recalcitrant and ornery bull. (Rev: BL 9/1/11; SLJ 10/1/11)

261 McAllister, Angela. *Yuck! That's Not a Monster* (PS–2). Illus. by Alison Edgson. 2010, Good Books $16.99 (978-156148683-0). 32pp. Two warty and frightful monsters are miffed when their third egg hatches into something adorable. (Rev: BLO 5/15/10; SLJ 8/10)

262 McCarty, Peter. *The Monster Returns* (PS–K). Illus. by author. 2012, Henry Holt $16.99 (978-080509030-7). 40pp. In this sequel to *Jeremy Draws a Monster* (2009), the monster created in a drawing threatens to return and Jeremy asks his friends to help create new monsters — and a hospitable atmosphere. (Rev: BLO 12/15/11; SLJ 1/12)

263 McElligott, Matthew. *Even Monsters Need Haircuts* (PS–2). Illus. by author. 2010, Walker $14.99 (978-0-8027-8819-1). 40pp. Monsters do need haircuts, and once a month a normally obedient boy provides this service in his father's barbershop. (Rev: BL 8/10; SLJ 9/1/10)

264 McKinlay, Meg. *No Bears* (K–2). Illus. by Leila Rudge. 2012, Candlewick $15.99 (978-076365890-8). 32pp. Ella is determined to write a story without bears, but one keeps cropping up despite her best intentions and even plays a key role in this book with fairy-tale themes. (Rev: BL 4/1/12; HB 5–6/12; LMC 10/12; SLJ 5/1/12)

265 Maclear, Kyo. *Spork* (PS–2). Illus. by Isabelle Arsenault. 2010, Kids Can $7.95 (978-1-55337-736-8). 32pp. Frustrated with never fitting in, young Spork (who is part spoon and part fork) vies for acceptance until a new development makes the misfit utensil just what everyone needs. Lexile 740L (Rev: BL 9/15/10; SLJ 2/1/11)

266 McNamara, Margaret. *The Three Little Aliens and the Big Bad Robot* (PS–2). Illus. by Mark Fearing. 2011, Random House $16.99 (978-0-375-86689-0); LB $19.99 (978-0-375-96689-7). 40pp. In this story reminiscent of the Three Little Pigs, three lovable aliens — Bork, Gork, and Nklxwcyz — set off into space to build their own homes, taking care to watch out for the big, bad robot. (Rev: BL 10/15/11; SLJ 9/1/11)

267 Marciano, John Bemelmans. *Madeline at the White House* (PS–1). Illus. by author. 2011, Viking $17.99 (978-0-670-01228-2). 48pp. Madeline and her orphan friends arrive from Paris to cheer up neglected First Daughter Candle in this magical Capitol Hill romp. Lexile AD540L (Rev: BL 1/1–15/11; SLJ 3/1/11)

268 Mayer, Mercer. *Too Many Dinosaurs* (K–2). Illus. by author. 2011, Holiday House $16.95 (978-0-8234-2316-3). 32pp. A little boy who desperately wants a puppy ends up with a dinosaur egg instead, with interesting consequences. (Rev: BL 9/15/11; SLJ 9/1/11)

269 Mayhew, James. *Ella Bella Ballerina and Swan Lake* (PS–3). Illus. by author. 2011, Barron's $14.99 (978-0-7641-6407-1). 32pp. A music box transports young Ella Bella into Tchaikovsky's ballet, where she sees the story unfold. Lexile AD670L (Rev: BLO 7/11; SLJ 8/1/11)

270 Meadows, Michelle. *Traffic Pups* (PS–K). Illus. by Dan Andreasen. 2011, Simon & Schuster $15.99 (978-1-4169-2485-2). 32pp. Canine motorcyclists police their toy community's roads, helping where needed, and disciplining the occasional offender in this sequel to *Pilot Pups* (2008). (Rev: BLO 8/11; SLJ 6/11)

271 Metzger, Steve. *Detective Blue* (PS–2). Illus. by Tedd Arnold. 2011, Scholastic $16.99 (978-0-545-17286-8). 32pp. Detective (Little Boy) Blue searches for the missing Miss Muffet and encounters a variety of familiar nursery rhyme characters along the way. (Rev: BL 8/11; HB 9–10/11; LMC 11–12/11; SLJ 7/11*)

272 Metzger, Steve. *The Ice Cream King* (PS–1). Illus. by Julie Downing. 2011, Tiger Tales $15.95 (978-1-58925-096-3); paper $7.95 (978-1-58925-427-5). Unpaged. A new ice cream shop beckons young Teddy into a world of wonderful fantasy. (Rev: SLJ 4/11)

273 Moore, Jodi. *When a Dragon Moves In* (PS–2). Illus. by Howard McWilliam. 2011, Flashlight $16.95 (978-0-979974-67-0). Unpaged. A dragon moves into a boy's sandcastle and the two have great fun together but nobody will believe that he's there. (Rev: LMC 10/11*; SLJ 9/1/11)

274 Morrissey, Dean. *The Wizard Mouse* (K–2). Illus. by author. 2011, HarperCollins $16.99 (978-0-06-008066-2). Unpaged. A young field mouse named Rollie agrees to assist an aging wizard in keeping his kingdom of Muddmoor safe from attack. (Rev: SLJ 12/1/11)

275 Mortimer, Rachael. *Song for a Princess* (PS–1). Illus. by Maddy McClellan. 2010, Scholastic $17.99 (978-0-545-24835-8). Unpaged. A little brown bird manages to cheer up a sad princess by using the happy words he has collected from her stories. Lexile AD650L (Rev: LMC 1–2/11; SLJ 11/1/10)

276 Mull, Brandon. *Pingo* (K–2). Illus. by Brandon Dorman. 2009, Shadow Mountain $17.95 (978-1-60641-109-4). Unpaged. A young boy's imaginary friend becomes resentful when he's put aside for more mature interests, mischievously sabotaging Chad's life until, many years later, Chad returns to his old friend for company. (Rev: SLJ 1/1/10)

277 Murray, Laura. *The Gingerbread Man Loose in the School* (K–2). Illus. by Mike Lowery. 2011, Putnam $16.99 (978-0-399-25052-1). 32pp. The Gingerbread Man is upset when the class that created him takes off for recess, leaving him on his own. (Rev: BL 8/11*; SLJ 8/1/11)

278 Murray, Martine. *Henrietta Gets a Letter* (1–3). Illus. by author. 2010, IPG/Allen & Unwin paper $8.99 (978-174175451-3). 92pp. Henrietta recovers from a tantrum when she discovers a small fairy under her bed in this third installment in the series. (Rev: BL 1/1–15/11)

279 Muth, Jon J. *Zen Ghosts* (K–3). Illus. by author. 2010, Scholastic $17.99 (978-0-439-63430-4). 40pp. On Halloween, Stillwater the Zen Buddhist panda tells his three sibling friends a thought-provoking and spooky story. ⌒ Lexile AD530L (Rev: BL 9/15/10; SLJ 11/1/10)

280 Oldland, Nicholas. *Big Bear Hug* (K–2). Illus. by author. 2009, Kids Can $16.95 (978-1-55453-464-7); paper $4.99 (978-1-55453-482-1). Unpaged. An environmentally minded tree-hugging bear must make a decision when he comes across a man with an axe — and decides on the usual hug. (Rev: LMC 11–12/09; SLJ 10/1/09)

281 Ormerod, Jan. *Maudie and Bear* (PS–1). Illus. by Freya Blackwood. 2012, Putnam $16.99 (978-039925709-4). 48pp. A charmingly self-centered little girl leans on her accommodating, loyal friend Bear in this series of five short stories. (Rev: BL 1/1/12*; SLJ 1/12)

282 Owen, Karen. *I Could Be, You Could Be* (PS–1). Illus. by Barroux. 2011, Barefoot $16.99 (978-1-84686-405-6). 32pp. A young boy and girl have an adventure in imagination, mulling over the various things they could be — astronauts, dragons, chimps, and so forth. (Rev: BL 4/15/11; SLJ 5/1/11)

283 Palatini, Margie. *Goldie and the Three Hares* (PS–2). Illus. by Jack E. Davis. 2011, HarperCollins $16.99 (978-0-06-125314-0). 32pp. A family of hares finds itself with a bossy housemate — Goldilocks — and calls the Bears' house in desperation for advice on how to get her to leave. ℮ Lexile AD610L (Rev: BL 1/1–15/11; SLJ 3/1/11)

284 Pearce, Clemency. *Frangoline and the Midnight Dream* (K–2). Illus. by Rebecca Elliott. 2011, Scholastic $16.99 (978-0-545-31426-8). Unpaged. Frangoline is good by day but gets wild by night until she scares herself to the point where she wants to go home. (Rev: LMC 11–12/11; SLJ 7/11)

285 Perl, Erica S. *Dotty* (K–2). Illus. by Julia Denos. 2010, Abrams $16.95 (978-0-8109-8962-7). 32pp. Ida is a little embarrassed by her imaginary friend Dotty until she learns that her teacher also has a special friend. (Rev: BL 7/10; LMC 11–12/10; SLJ 8/1/10)

286 Pinder, Eric. *If All the Animals Came Inside* (PS–K). Illus. by Marc Brown. 2012, Little, Brown $16.99 (978-031609883-0). 40pp. A little boy imagines inviting a noisy and boisterous group of zoo animals into his house, and eventually decides the mess and chaos is too much for him and a dog and cat are quite enough. (Rev: BL 4/15/12; SLJ 4/1/12*)

287 Pinkwater, Daniel. *I Am the Dog* (PS–1). Illus. by Jack E. Davis. 2010, HarperCollins $16.99 (978-0-06-055505-4). 32pp. Young Jacob trades places with his dog in this zany romp. Lexile AD220L (Rev: BL 10/15/10; SLJ 10/1/10)

288 Plecas, Jennifer. *Pretend* (PS–1). Illus. by author. 2011, Philomel $15.99 (978-0-399-23430-9). 32pp. A boy and his father enjoy a fantasy that begins with the living room sofa being a boat at sea. (Rev: BL 5/1/11; SLJ 7/11)

289 Pulver, Robin. *Happy Endings: A Story About Suffixes* (K–3). Illus. by Lynn Rowe Reed. 2011, Holiday House $16.95 (978-0-8234-2296-8). 32pp. Hearing that Mr. Wright's class is to "tackle" suffixes, the suffixes take fright and disappear, leading the students on an interesting chase. Lexile AD430L (Rev: BL 4/15/11; LMC 11–12/11; SLJ 3/1/11)

290 Pym, Tasha. *Have You Ever Seen a Sneep?* (PS–K). Illus. by Joel Stewart. 2009, Farrar $16.95 (978-0-374-32868-9). 32pp. Have you ever seen a Sneep? A Snook? A Grullock or a Floon? Apparently if you have you will remember the encounter. (Rev: BL 9/15/09; LMC 11–12/09; SLJ 11/1/09)

291 Quattlebaum, Mary. *The Hungry Ghost of Rue Orleans* (K–2). Illus. by Patricia Castelao. 2011, Random House $15.99 (978-0-375-86207-6); LB $18.99 (978-0-375-96207-3). 32pp. Fred is a very happy ghost in his New Orleans home until it is turned into a restaurant, and his efforts to scare the customers away seem counterproductive. (Rev: BL 9/15/11; SLJ 9/1/11)

292 Ray, Jane. *The Dollhouse Fairy* (PS–3). Illus. by author. 2010, Candlewick $16.99 (978-0-7636-4411-6). 32pp. When Rosy's beloved father goes to the hospital, she misses the time they used to spend on her dollhouse and, playing there by herself, she discovers that a fairy with a broken wing has moved in. (Rev: BL 6/10*; SLJ 8/1/10)

293 Reynolds, Aaron. *Snowbots* (PS–1). Illus. by David Barneda. 2010, Knopf $16.99 (978-0-375-85873-4); LB $19.99 (978-0-375-95873-1). Unpaged. A gaggle of robot children enjoy a frosty day of outdoor play in this lively, rhyming story. (Rev: SLJ 11/1/10)

294 Reynolds, Aaron. *Superhero School* (K–3). Illus. by Andy Rash. 2009, Bloomsbury $16.99 (978-1-59990-166-4). 32pp. When the teachers at Leonard's superhero school are kidnapped by ice zombies, the young students rise to the occasion and defeat the foe using their math skills. (Rev: SLJ 9/1/09)

295 Rosen, Michael. *Bear Flies High* (PS–K). Illus. by Adrian Reynolds. 2009, Bloomsbury $16.99 (978-1-59990-386-6). 32pp. A bear who has always longed to fly meets four children who take him to an amusement park and have a great time. (Rev: BL 12/15/09; SLJ 2/1/10*)

296 Rosen, Michael. *Red Ted and the Lost Things* (PS–K). Illus. by Joel Stewart. 2009, Candlewick $16.99 (978-0-7636-4537-3); paper $8.99 (978-0-7636-4624-0). 40pp. A teddy bear and a stuffed crocodile at the Lost and Found bond over being abandoned and set out to find the bear's owner. (Rev: SLJ 11/1/09)

297 Rosenberg, Liz. *Tyrannosaurus Dad* (K–2). Illus. by Matthew Myers. 2011, Roaring Brook $16.99 (978-1-59643-531-5). 32pp. A young boy's Tyrannosaurus rex father turns out to be just the thing to save the day when there's bully trouble at school. (Rev: BL 4/15/11; LMC 10/11; SLJ 5/1/11)

298 Ross, Fiona. *Chilly Milly Moo* (PS–K). Illus. by author. 2011, Candlewick $15.99 (978-0-7636-5693-5). 32pp. Milly Moo, unlike the other cows, dislikes warm weather and has a special ability in cold weather — producing ice cream rather than milk. (Rev: BL 10/1/11; SLJ 11/1/11)

299 Sauer, Tammi. *Mostly Monsterly* (PS–2). Illus. by Scott Magoon. 2010, Simon & Schuster $14.99 (978-1-4169-6110-9). 40pp. A monster with a tender heart, Bernadette has trouble fitting in with her peers. ℮ Lexile AD270L (Rev: BL 7/10; LMC 11–12/10; SLJ 8/1/10)

300 Schaefer, Lola M. *Frankie Stein Starts School* (PS–1). Illus. by Kevan Atteberry. 2010, Marshall Cavendish $15.99 (978-0-7614-5656-8). 32pp. Frankie Stein angles for acceptance at the Ghoul Academy by making grotesque faces and howling like a coyote. ℮ (Rev: BLO 7/10; SLJ 10/1/10)

301 Slate, Jenny, and Dean Fleischer Camp. *Marcel the Shell with Shoes On: Things About Me* (K–2). Illus. by Amy Lind. 2011, Penguin $18.99 (978-1-59514-455-3). 40pp. Marcel, the tiny shell with shoes, takes readers on a tour of his home. ∩ (Rev: BL 11/15/11; SLJ 12/1/11)

302 Soman, David, and Jacky Davis. *The Amazing Adventures of Bumblebee Boy* (PS–2). Illus. by David Soman. 2011, Dial $16.99 (978-0-8037-3418-0). 40pp. Sam, who imagines himself the superhero Bumblebee Boy, discovers the advantages of collaboration when he's confronted by some creepy aliens and his younger brother offers to help. (Rev: BL 12/1/11; SLJ 11/1/11)

303 Sperring, Mark. *The Sunflower Sword* (PS–3). Illus. by Miriam Latimer. 2011, Andersen $16.95 (978-0-7613-7486-2). 32pp. A little knight armed with a flower charms instead of slays a giant dragon, and the two become friends in a land where dragon-human conflict was common. (Rev: BL 5/1/11; SLJ 2/1/11)

304 Spires, Ashley. *Small Saul* (PS–3). Illus. by author. 2011, Kids Can $16.95 (978-1-55453-503-3). Unpaged. Small Saul — too short to join the Navy — trains as a pirate instead, but his gentle, caring nature means he has an uncertain future. (Rev: SLJ 4/11)

305 Sturgis, Brenda Reeves. *Ten Turkeys in the Road* (PS–K). Illus. by David Slonim. 2011, Marshall Cavendish $16.99 (978-0-7614-5847-0). 32pp. Ten turkeys rehearsing circus acts block the road, holding up an impatient farmer in this colorful story that offers plenty of opportunities for counting practice. (Rev: BLO 11/15/11; LMC 1–2/12; SLJ 10/1/11)

306 Teague, David. *Franklin's Big Dreams* (PS–1). Illus. by Boris Kulikov. 2010, Hyperion $16.99 (978-1-4231-1919-7). 40pp. A beautifully illustrated story about a young boy's dreams full of dramatic construction activity in his bedroom. (Rev: BL 6/10*; SLJ 7/1/10)

307 Tegen, Katherine. *The Story of the Leprechaun* (PS–2). Illus. by Sally Anne Lambert. 2011, HarperCollins $12.99 (978-0-06-143086-2). 40pp. An industrious leprechaun shoemaker outwits a plot to steal his gold. ℮ Lexile 780L (Rev: BL 1/1–15/11; SLJ 2/1/11)

308 Thomas, Shelley Moore. *A Good Knight's Rest* (K–2). Illus. by Jennifer Plecas. 2011, Dutton $16.99 (978-0-525-42195-5). Unpaged. The Good Knight has worked hard and deserves a rest but makes the mistake of taking his three little dragon friends with him. (Rev: HB 7–8/11; SLJ 6/11)

309 Tusa, Tricia. *Follow Me* (PS–2). Illus. by author. 2011, Harcourt $16.99 (978-0-547-27201-6). 40pp. A young girl soars from a swing into the sky and travels over the Earth through a palette of colors. (Rev: BL 3/1/11; SLJ 4/11)

310 Vamos, Samantha R. *The Cazuela That the Farm Maiden Stirred* (PS–1). Illus. by Rafael Lopez. 2011, Charlesbridge $17.95 (978-1-58089-242-1). 32pp. This happy, cumulative tale involving farm animals includes many Spanish vocabulary words as it shows the process for making *arroz con leche*, or rice pudding. ALSC Notable Children's Book, 2012; Pura Belpre Illustrator Honor Book, 2012. (Rev: BL 4/15/11; SLJ 3/1/11*)

311 Viorst, Judith. *Lulu and the Brontosaurus* (1–4). Illus. by Lane Smith. 2010, Atheneum $15.99 (978-1-4169-9961-4). 128pp. Lulu demands a pet brontosaurus for her birthday and, when her parents deny her this, leaves home in search of one; when she finally happens upon one in the woods, the beast insists the girl become *his* pet instead. ℮ Lexile 910L (Rev: BL 9/1/10; LMC 1–2/11; SLJ 9/1/10)

312 Voake, Steve. *Daisy Dawson and the Secret Pond* (1–3). Illus. by Jessica Meserve. 2009, Candlewick $14.99 (978-0-7636-4009-5). 88pp. Daisy, who can communicate with animals, and her friends Boom the dog and Cyril the squirrel set out on a mission to photograph wild otters. Also in this series is *Daisy Dawson and the Big Freeze* (2010), in which Daisy rescues a lamb. (Rev: SLJ 12/1/09)

313 Watt, Melanie. *You're Finally Here!* (PS–1). Illus. by author. 2011, Hyperion/Disney $15.99 (978-1-4231-3486-2). 40pp. An enthusiastic but finicky rabbit narrates this short, amusing story, beginning by first chastising the reader for not showing up sooner. (Rev: BL 4/15/11; SLJ 3/1/11)

314 Williams, Margery. *The Velveteen Rabbit* (1–3). Illus. by Gennady Spirin. 2011, Marshall Cavendish $17.99 (978-0-7614-5848-7). 48pp. A handsome version of the classic children's story, with a tribute to the author at the end of the book. (Rev: BL 5/1/11; SLJ 5/1/11)

315 Young, Cybèle. *A Few Blocks* (PS–1). Illus. by author. 2011, Groundwood $18.95 (978-0-88899-995-5). Unpaged. Ferdie doesn't want to go to school but his older sister Viola makes it easier by making the journey an exciting fantasy involving sailing ships, knights, and dragons. (Rev: SLJ 11/1/11)

316 Ziefert, Harriet. *Bunny's Lessons* (PS–2). Illus. by Barroux. 2011, Blue Apple $16.99 (978-1-60905-028-3). 40pp. A toy rabbit describes what he has learned from his boy about emotions, responsibility, apologies, and consequences. (Rev: BL 5/1/11; SLJ 5/1/11)

317 Ziefert, Harriet. *By the Light of the Harvest Moon* (PS–2). Illus. by Mark Jones. 2009, Blue Apple $16.99 (978-193470669-5). 40pp. Under the harvest moon, the leaf people gather to celebrate fall and then fly on the wind. (Rev: BLO 11/15/09; LMC 3–4/10)

IMAGINARY ANIMALS

318 Abrahams, Peter. *Quacky Baseball* (PS–2). Illus. by Frank Morrison. 2011, HarperCollins $16.99 (978-0-06-122978-7). 32pp. The littlest duckling on the baseball team copes with anxiety and pressure as he tries to do his very best for his team. (Rev: BL 3/1/11; SLJ 2/1/11)

319 Alexander, Claire. *Small Florence: Piggy Pop Star!* (PS–1). Illus. by author. 2010, Whitman $16.99 (978-0-8075-7455-3). 32pp. Florence, a young pig in awe of her older sisters, manages to finally display her own talents when they lose their nerve during an American Idol-like audition. Lexile AD660L (Rev: BL 4/15/10; SLJ 2/1/10)

320 Alexander, Kwame. *Acoustic Rooster and His Barnyard Band* (1–3). Illus. by Tim Bowers. 2011, Sleeping Bear $15.95 (978-1-58536-688-0). 32pp. Acoustic Rooster forms a jazz band with Duck Ellington, Bee Holliday, and Pepe Ernesto Cruz to compete in the Barnyard Talent Show against the likes of Thelonius Monkey and Mules Davis in this swingin' story. (Rev: BLO 11/15/11; SLJ 11/1/11)

321 Alter, Anna. *Disappearing Desmond* (PS–2). Illus. by author. 2010, Knopf $17.99 (978-0-375-86684-5); LB $20.99 (978-0-375-96684-2). 40pp. A shy cat who prefers to disappear behind camouflage gains self-confidence when he makes friends with a gregarious rabbit. (Rev: BL 11/15/10; SLJ 9/1/10)

322 Alter, Anna. *A Photo for Greta* (PS–1). Illus. by author. 2011, Knopf $16.99 (978-0-375-85618-1); LB $19.99 (978-0-375-95618-8). 40pp. A bunny named Greta misses her photographer father when he's away on assignment but enjoys all the more the times they do spend together. (Rev: BLO 9/1/11; SLJ 8/1/11)

323 Andres, Kristina. *Elephant in the Bathtub* (K–1). Illus. by author. 2010, NorthSouth $12.95 (978-0-7358-2291-7). Unpaged. Elephant and his animal friends have an adventure in the bathtub. (Rev: SLJ 6/1/10)

324 Badescu, Ramona. *Pomelo Begins to Grow* (1–3). Trans. from French by Claudia Bedrick. Illus. by Benjamin Chaud. 2011, Enchanted Lion $16.95 (978-1-59270-111-7). Unpaged. A little elephant contends with the many concerns he has about growing up — will all his parts grow equally? Will he have to stop clowning around? (Rev: SLJ 8/1/11)

325 Baker, Keith. *No Two Alike* (PS–2). Illus. by author. 2011, Simon & Schuster $16.99 (978-1-4424-1742-7). 40pp. In rhyming text and appealing illustrations, two little red birds enjoy a snowy day and remark on how everything they see around them is unique. (Rev: BL 11/1/11*; SLJ 9/1/11)

326 Bansch, Helga. *Brava, Mimi!* (PS–2). Illus. by author. 2010, NorthSouth $16.95 (978-073582322-8). 32pp. Mimi perseveres in her desire to perform on stage despite her lack of talent and beauty. (Rev: BLO 8/10; LMC 11–12/10)

327 Bardhan-Quallen, Sudipta. *Hampire!* (K–2). Illus. by Howard Fine. 2011, HarperCollins $16.99 (978-0-06-114239-0). 32pp. The much-feared Hampire — a caped pig — turns out to be fairly harmless in this suspensefully comic barnyard tale. (Rev: BL 8/11; SLJ 8/1/11)

328 Battersby, Katherine. *Squish Rabbit* (PS–1). Illus. by author. 2011, Viking $12.99 (978-0-670-01267-1). 40pp. A lonely and fearful little bunny has trouble finding a friend until he comes across a squirrel. (Rev: BL 10/15/11; SLJ 8/1/11)

329 Battut, Eric. *The Fox and the Hen* (PS–1). Illus. by author. 2010, Boxer $16.95 (978-1-907152-02-3). 32pp. When an innocent red hen trades her first egg to a sly fox for a worm, her barnyard friends rally round, offering their own precious objects to the fox in an attempt to win back the egg. (Rev: BLO 2/1/10; SLJ 3/1/10*)

330 Battut, Eric. *Little Mouse's Big Secret* (PS–K). Illus. by author. 2011, Sterling $12.95 (978-1-4027-7462-1). 24pp. A little mouse buries an apple, keeping it a secret for himself, but over the years it grows into a tree and produces enough fruit for all the friends who wondered what he was hiding. (Rev: BL 3/15/11; SLJ 8/1/11)

331 Beaty, Andrea. *Firefighter Ted* (K–2). Illus. by Pascal Lemaitre. 2009, Simon & Schuster $15.99 (978-1-4169-2821-8). Unpaged. The good-hearted but bumbling bear last seen in *Doctor Ted* (2008) decides to become a firefighter in this funny story. (Rev: HB 9–10/09; SLJ 9/1/09)

332 Becker, Bonny. *The Sniffles for Bear* (PS–2). Illus. by Kady MacDonald Denton. 2011, Candlewick $16.99 (978-0-7636-4756-8). 32pp. Bear has a dreadful cold and will not be cheered up, even by Mouse. (Rev: BLO 9/15/11; HB 9–10/11; SLJ 8/1/11)

333 Bently, Peter. *The Great Sheep Shenanigans* (K–2). Illus. by Mei Matsuoka. 2012, Andersen $16.95 (978-076138990-3). 32pp. A wolf called Lou Pine is determined to make really tasty food out of a flock of lambs and tries various whacky disguises. (Rev: BL 4/15/12; SLJ 5/1/12)

334 Berger, Carin. *Forever Friends* (PS). Illus. by author. 2010, Greenwillow $16.99 (978-0-06-191528-4); LB $17.89 (978-0-06-191529-1). 40pp. A young rabbit and its bluebird friend are separated for a long, lonely winter but are reunited when spring arrives and the bird flies back north. (Rev: BL 3/1/10; HB 3–4/10; SLJ 3/1/10)

335 Berger, Samantha. *Martha Doesn't Share!* (PS). Illus. by Bruce Whatley. 2010, Little, Brown $16.99 (978-0-316-07367-7). Unpaged. Martha the difficult young otter learns about the value of sharing in this simple story. (Rev: HB 9–10/10; LMC 1–2/11; SLJ 10/1/10)

336 Berner, Rotraut Susanne. *Hound and Hare* (PS–2). Trans. by Shelley Tanaka. Illus. by author. 2011, Groundwood $18.95 (978-0-88899-987-0). 80pp. A new generation of hounds and hares begins to question their families' long-standing feud. (Rev: BL 6/1/11; LMC 10/11; SLJ 6/11)

337 Berry, Lynne. *Ducking for Apples* (PS–K). Illus. by Hiroe Nakata. Series: Duck. 2010, Henry Holt $16.99 (978-0-8050-8935-6). 32pp. In this cheerful story, the five little ducklings ride their bikes to an apple tree, where they gather fruit to make a pie. ℮ (Rev: BLO 7/10; SLJ 8/1/10)

338 Blackstone, Stella. *Bear's Birthday* (PS–K). Illus. by Debbie Harter. 2011, Barefoot $6.99 (978-1-84686-515-2); paper $6.99 (978-1-84686-516-9). 24pp. A bear and his friends have a busy birthday party in this lively board book. (Rev: BL 6/1/11; SLJ 6/11)

339 Bloom, Suzanne. *What About Bear?* (PS–1). Illus. by author. 2010, Boyds Mills $16.95 (978-1-59078-528-7). 32pp. Goose acts as a mediator between Bear and Little Fox, who eventually discover that they have more in common than they thought. (Rev: BL 3/15/10; SLJ 6/1/10*)

340 Bonwill, Ann. *Bug and Bear: A Story of True Friendship* (PS–K). Illus. by Layn Marlow. 2011, Marshall Cavendish $17.99 (978-0-7614-5902-6). 32pp. Bear is testy when his friend Bug annoys him on his way to naptime, and later regrets his sharp words. (Rev: BL 5/1/11; SLJ 5/1/11)

341 Boyle, Bob. *Hugo and the Really, Really, Really Long String* (PS–1). Illus. by author. 2010, Random House $15.99 (978-0-375-83423-3); LB $18.99 (978-0-375-93423-0). Unpaged. A friendly hippo decides to follow a long red thread he spies one day; his friends join him one by one, expecting a great surprise and treasure at the end. (Rev: LMC 5–6/10; SLJ 2/1/10)

342 Brett, Jan. *The Three Little Dassies* (PS–2). Illus. by author. 2010, Putnam $17.99 (978-0-399-25499-4). 32pp. In this Three Little Pigs adaptation, three fancifully dressed African rock hydraxes or dassies — Timbi, Mimibi, and Pimbi — defend their Namibian homes from a hungry eagle. (Rev: BL 9/1/10; LMC 1–2/11; SLJ 10/1/10)

343 Brooks, Erik. *Polar Opposites* (PS–2). Illus. by author. 2010, Marshall Cavendish $16.99 (978-0-7614-5685-8). 32pp. Two pen pals — an Arctic polar bear and a demure penguin from Antarctica — meet up at the Galapagos islands to share a happy vacation together despite their differences. Lexile AD170L (Rev: BL 10/1/10; LMC 1–2/11; SLJ 10/1/10)

344 Brown, Marc. *Arthur Turns Green* (K–3). Illus. by author. 2011, Little, Brown $16.99 (978-0-316-12924-4). 32pp. Arthur the aardvark is focusing on the environment but D.W. worries that she will turn green too. Lexile 580L (Rev: BL 3/1/11; SLJ 3/1/11)

345 Browne, Anthony. *Me and You* (PS–3). Illus. by author. 2010, Farrar $16.99 (978-0-374-34908-0). 32pp. The story of Goldilocks is retold here in parallel narratives — one from the baby bear's point of view — and given an urban setting and moody, evocative illustrations. (Rev: BL 9/15/10; HB 11–12/10; SLJ 11/1/10*)

346 Bunting, Eve. *Hey Diddle Diddle* (PS–2). Illus. by Mary Ann Fraser. 2011, Boyds Mills $16.95 (978-1-59078-768-7). 32pp. This catchy version of the familiar rhyme features a troupe of lively instrument-playing animals. (Rev: BL 6/1/11; SLJ 4/11)

347 Bunting, Eve. *Tweak Tweak* (PS–K). Illus. by Sergio Ruzzier. 2011, Clarion $14.99 (978-0-618-99851-7). 40pp. A little elephant on a walk with her mother learns about what makes her unique as they talk about other animals — a frog, a bird, a butterfly, a crocodile. (Rev: BL 3/1/11; SLJ 5/1/11)

348 Burkert, Rand. *Mouse and Lion* (PS–2). Illus. by Nancy Ekholm Burkert. 2011, Scholastic $17.95 (978-0-545-10147-9). 32pp. In this retelling of the classic Aesop fable the mouse plays the leading role. ALSC Notable Children's Book, 2012. (Rev: BL 12/1/11*; HB 11–12/11; LMC 1–2/12; SLJ 8/1/11*)

349 Carlson, Nancy. *Henry and the Bully* (K–2). Illus. by author. 2010, Viking $15.99 (978-0-670-01148-3). Unpaged. Young 1st-grade mouse Henry finds a way to stand up to the 2nd-grade Sam (a poodle) who is bullying him. (Rev: LMC 11–12/10; SLJ 7/1/10)

350 Carlson, Nancy. *Start Saving, Henry!* (K–2). Illus. by author. 2009, Viking $15.99 (978-0-670-01147-6). 32pp. A 7-year-old mouse named Henry really wants a Super Robot Dude, but his mother won't pay for it. Can he save enough to buy it himself? (Rev: BL 9/15/09; SLJ 10/1/09)

351 Carrer, Chiara. *Otto Carrotto* (K–3). Illus. by author. 2011, Eerdmans $16 (978-0-8028-5393-6). 26pp. A carrot-obsessed rabbit finds his singular diet has physical repercussions and decides to switch to spinach. (Rev: BL 11/1/11; SLJ 10/1/11)

352 Cash, John Carter. *The Cat in the Rhinestone Suit* (K–2). Illus. by Scott Nash. 2012, Simon & Schuster $17.99 (978-141697483-3). 32pp. A cat with a taste for sparkles has a long-standing feud with a snake called Del Moore until the cat is in danger and Del comes to the rescue; with a twangy rhythm, this colorful tale is written by the son of June Carter and Johnny Cash. (Rev: BL 4/1/12; SLJ 4/1/12)

353 Chaconas, Dori. *Cork and Fuzz: The Swimming Lesson* (PS–2). Illus. by Lisa McCue. Series: Viking Easy-to-Read. 2011, Viking $13.99 (978-0-670-01281-7). 32pp. Fuzz the possum overcomes his fear of water in order to visit his pal Cork, the muskrat, and then offers to teach Cork to climb. (Rev: HB 7–8/11; SLJ 7/11)

354 Chivers, Natalie. *Rhino's Great Big Itch!* (PS–1). Illus. by author. 2010, Good Books $16.99 (978-1-56148-684-7). 32pp. After several animals fail to help him, a friendly bird proves just the right size to help a rhinoceros with a pesky itch in the ear. (Rev: BL 5/1/10; SLJ 5/1/10)

355 Clark, Leslie Ann. *Peepsqueak!* (PS–K). Illus. by author. 2012, HarperCollins $12.99 (978-006207801-8). 32pp. Peepsqueak the newborn chick hatches with a determination to fly despite advice from Big Brown Cow, Big, Sheep, and others; after failing several times he receives some help from a kindly goose. (Rev: BL 1/1/12; SLJ 1/12)

356 Costello, David Hyde. *Little Pig Joins the Band* (PS–K). Illus. by author. 2011, Charlesbridge $14.95 (978-1-58089-264-3). 32pp. Jacob the pig is too little for any of the available instruments in the marching band, so he takes on the role of leader of his older siblings. (Rev: BL 5/1/11; SLJ 7/11)

357 Cousins, Lucy. *I'm the Best* (PS–K). Illus. by author. 2010, Candlewick $14.99 (978-0-7636-4684-4). 32pp. With exuberant bravado, a showoff dog claims to be better than all his animal friends, not realizing he's hurting their feelings until the end, when he apologizes, they forgive him, and all is well. (Rev: BL 5/1/10*; SLJ 5/1/10*)

358 Cousins, Lucy. *Maisy Goes on Vacation* (PS–K). Illus. by author. 2010, Candlewick $12.99 (978-0-7636-4752-0). Unpaged. Maisy packs her suitcase and travels to the beach with her friend Cyril, where they have fun by the ocean and then return to their hotel. (Rev: SLJ 9/1/10)

359 Craig, Lindsey. *Dancing Feet!* (PS–K). Illus. by Marc Brown. 2010, Knopf $16.99 (978-0-375-86181-9). 40pp. Vibrant collage illustrations of dancing animals enhance this book of rhythm and movement. (Rev: BL 4/1/10; SLJ 4/1/10)

360 Crimi, Carolyn. *Dear Tabby* (K–3). Illus. by David Roberts. 2011, HarperCollins $16.99 (978-0-06-114245-1). 32pp. Tabby D. Cat provides wholesome advice to a variety of different animals suffering from common emotional situations in this comic story. Lexile AD820L (Rev: BL 1/1–15/11; SLJ 2/1/11)

361 Crimi, Carolyn. *Rock 'n' Roll Mole* (K–2). Illus. by Lynn Munsinger. 2011, Dial $16.99 (978-0-8037-3166-0). 32pp. Mole is a cool rock-and-roll musician — until he has to perform in front of an audience. (Rev: BLO 10/1/11; SLJ 8/1/11)

362 Cronin, Doreen. *Rescue Bunnies* (PS–1). Illus. by Scott Menchin. 2010, HarperCollins $16.99 (978-0-06-112871-4). 32pp. A rescue bunny-in-training named Newbie learns about courage and teamwork when she helps rescue a giraffe who's stuck in the mud in this quirky, funny picture book. (Rev: BL 7/10; HB 9–10/10; SLJ 9/1/10)

363 Crummel, Susan Stevens. *Ten-Gallon Bart Beats the Heat* (K–2). Illus. by Dorothy Donohue. 2010, Marshall Cavendish $17.99 (978-0-7614-5634-6). 40pp. Dog City sheriff Bart, tired of the heat in the South, heads north to Alaska and finds new adventures — from pulling a sled to ice-fishing to panning for gold — along the way. ❂ Lexile AD510L (Rev: BL 4/15/10; SLJ 3/1/10)

364 Czekaj, Jef. *Cat Secrets* (PS–1). Illus. by author. 2011, HarperCollins $16.99 (978-0-06-192088-2). 32pp. Secretive cats are determined not to share their precious lore with non-cats and readers must prove they are real cats. ❂ (Rev: BL 12/15/10; SLJ 1/1/11)

365 Czekaj, Jef. *Hip and Hop, Don't Stop!* (PS–2). Illus. by author. 2010, Hyperion $16.99 (978-1-4231-1664-6). 40pp. Two very different wannabe rappers — a turtle and a rabbit — team up with terrific results in this lively book about sharing and working together. (Rev: BL 6/10; HB 5–6/10; LMC 8–9/10; SLJ 4/1/10)

366 D'Amico, Carmela, and Steven D'Amico. *Suki the Very Loud Bunny* (PS–1). 2011, Dutton $16.99 (978-0-525-42230-3). 32pp. A noisy young bunny's loud voice ends up saving the day when she's lost in the woods at night. (Rev: BL 2/1/11; SLJ 2/1/11)

367 Davis, Jerry, and Katie Davis. *Little Chicken's Big Day* (PS–K). Illus. by Katie Davis. 2011, Simon & Schuster $14.99 (978-1-4424-1401-3). 40pp. Little Chicken knows his mother is watching him throughout the day. (Rev: BL 3/15/11*; HB 5–6/11; SLJ 4/11)

368 DeGroat, Diane. *Ants in Your Pants, Worms in Your Plants! (Gilbert Goes Green)* (K–2). Illus. by author. 2011, HarperCollins $16.99 (978-0-06-176511-7). 32pp. Gilbert the opossum can come up with no ideas for Earth Day until his teacher mentions ants. ℮ (Rev: BL 3/15/11; SLJ 2/1/11)

369 Dempsey, Kristy. *Mini Racer* (PS–1). Illus. by Bridget Strevens-Marzo. 2010, Bloomsbury $16.99 (978-1-59990-170-1). 32pp. A group of snazzy race cars piloted by a variety of different animals fall away one by one, until only a pokey snail is left to cross the finish line. (Rev: BL 12/15/10; SLJ 1/1/11*)

370 Derom, Dirk. *Pigeon and Pigeonette* (K–2). Illus. by Sarah Verroken. 2009, Enchanted Lion $16.95 (978-1-59270-087-5). Unpaged. A small pigeon with undersize wings finds a friend to help her fly south — a big pigeon who can't see — and together they set off for warmer climes. (Rev: LMC 1–2/10; SLJ 11/1/09)

371 deRubertis, Barbara. *Kylie Kangaroo's Karate Kickers* (K–1). Illus. by R. W. Alley. Series: Animal Antics A to Z. 2011, Kane $22.60 (978-157565332-7); paper $7.95 (978-157565323-5). 32pp. A young kangaroo works hard to learn karate, eventually learning to put her faith in training and practice rather than luck. (Rev: BLO 8/11)

372 Dewdney, Anna. *Llama Llama Home with Mama* (PS). Illus. by author. 2011, Viking $17.99 (978-0-670-01232-9). Unpaged. Llama Llama's mother takes care of him when he gets sick; and when mom herself gets sick, the little llama knows exactly how to take care of her. (Rev: SLJ 9/1/11)

373 Dewdney, Anna. *Roly Poly Pangolin* (PS). Illus. by author. 2010, Viking $16.99 (978-0-670-01160-5). Unpaged. A young pangolin full of fears rolls into a tight ball at the slightest provocation, but eventually discovers how much fun it can be to make new friends; a note at the end provides information on these endangered animals. (Rev: BL 2/1/10; SLJ 2/1/10)

374 Diesen, Deborah. *The Pout-Pout Fish in the Big-Big Dark* (PS–K). Illus. by Dan Hanna. 2010, Farrar $16.99 (978-0-374-30798-1). 32pp. Mr. Fish conquers his fear of the dark and rescues Ms. Clam's lost pearl from the sea floor with the help of Miss Shimmer and Mr. Lantern. Lexile AD670L (Rev: BLO 7/10; SLJ 9/1/10)

375 DiPucchio, Kelly. *Gilbert Goldfish Wants a Pet* (PS–2). Illus. by Bob Shea. 2011, Dial $16.99 (978-0-8037-3394-7). 32pp. A lonely goldfish yearns for a pet, but after trying a dog, a mouse, and a fly, he's unsure about trying a fourth option; fortunately, a cat turns out to be just right. (Rev: BL 7/11; SLJ 7/11)

376 Dodd, Emma. *Meow Said the Cow* (PS–K). Illus. by author. 2011, Scholastic $16.99 (978-0-545-31861-7). 40pp. A cat disgruntled by a noisy rooster casts a spell on all the farm animals, swapping their voices. (Rev: BLO 8/11; LMC 11–12/11; SLJ 7/11)

377 Donaldson, Julia. *What the Ladybug Heard* (PS–1). Illus. by Lydia Monks. 2010, Henry Holt $16.99 (978-0-8050-9028-4). 32pp. A shy, silent ladybug becomes empowered to speak up and protect her farm friends when she hears bad men plotting to steal the prize cow. (Rev: BL 2/15/10; SLJ 4/1/10)

378 Dunrea, Olivier. *Old Bear and His Cub* (PS–1). Illus. by author. 2010, Philomel $16.99 (978-0-399-24507-7). 32pp. Old Bear and Little Bear reverse roles — bossy and submissive — according to who needs help most. (Rev: BL 11/1/10*; HB 1–2/11; SLJ 11/1/10*)

379 Dunrea, Olivier. *Ollie's Easter Eggs* (PS–K). Illus. by author. Series: Gossie and Friends. 2010, Houghton Mifflin $9.99 (978-0-618-53243-8). 32pp. When Ollie the gosling sees the brightly colored Easter eggs his friends have dyed, he is overcome with desire to have them all. (Rev: BL 1/1/10; SLJ 3/1/10)

380 Emberley, Ed. *The Red Hen* (PS–K). Illus. by Rebecca Emberley. 2010, Roaring Brook $17.99 (978-1-59643-492-9). 32pp. Red Hen can't find anyone to help her make a "simply splendid cake" although her friends are quite happy to help eat it in this twist on the classic tale. (Rev: BL 10/15/10; SLJ 10/1/10)

381 Erlbruch, Wolf. *Duck, Death and the Tulip* (K–3). Trans. by Catherine Chigey. Illus. by author. 2011, Gecko $17.95 (978-1-877579-02-8). 36pp. A duck becomes spooked when she realizes she's being followed by Death personified; reassuringly, the character turns out to be sensitive to her concerns, and together the two discuss the afterlife. (Rev: BLO 11/15/11; SLJ 10/1/11)

382 Ernst, Lisa Campbell. *Sylvia Jean, Scout Supreme* (PS–2). Illus. by author. 2010, Dutton $16.99 (978-0-525-47873-7). 32pp. Sylvia Jean gets a little over-enthusiastic when her Pig Scout leader challenges the troop to perform good deeds to earn a badge. (Rev: BL 12/1/09; LMC 1–2/10; SLJ 2/1/10)

383 Evans, Lezlie. *Who Loves the Little Lamb?* (PS–K). Illus. by David McPhail. 2010, Hyperion $15.99 (978-1-4231-1659-2). 32pp. Animal mothers love their children even when they are not at their best. (Rev: BL 4/15/10; SLJ 6/1/10)

384 Falconer, Ian. *Olivia Goes to Venice* (PS–1). Illus. by author. 2010, Atheneum $17.99 (978-1-4169-9674-3). 48pp. Olivia the porcine adventurer explores Venice: gondola rides, gelato, walking tours, and beautiful palazzos. (Rev: BL 9/1/10; SLJ 9/1/10)

385 Falkenstern, Lisa. *A Dragon Moves In* (K–2). Illus. by author. 2011, Marshall Cavendish $16.99 (978-0-7614-5947-7). 32pp. Initially thrilled with their discovery of a dragon hatchling, Hedgehog and Rabbit find themselves facing serious problems as their friend grows larger and larger. (Rev: BL 11/1/11; SLJ 9/1/11)

386 Finlay, Lizzie. *Little Croc's Purse* (K–3). Illus. by author. 2011, Eerdmans $14.99 (978-0-8028-5392-9).

Unpaged. Little Croc is rewarded for doing the right thing when he finds a purse full of money in this subtle character education story. e Lexile AD570L (Rev: LMC 10/11; SLJ 5/1/11)

387 Foley, Greg. *I Miss You Mouse* (PS–1). Illus. by author. 2010, Viking $12.99 (978-0-670-01238-1). Unpaged. Mouse is looking for her friend Bear and can't find him anywhere until she returns to her own house in this charming flap book. (Rev: SLJ 2/1/11)

388 Foley, Greg. *Purple Little Bird* (PS–1). Illus. by author. 2011, HarperCollins $14.99 (978-0-06-200828-2). 32pp. A purple bird limited by his own perfectionism is aided by a variety of animal friends and eventually learns to loosen up. (Rev: BL 5/1/11; SLJ 7/11)

389 Freedman, Deborah. *Blue Chicken* (PS–2). Illus. by author. 2011, Viking $15.99 (978-0-670-01293-0). 40pp. A white chicken intent on helping the artist who created her hops off the page and tips over a pot of blue paint, transforming barnyard and animals. e Lexile AD270L (Rev: BL 11/1/11*; HB 1–2/12; SLJ 9/1/11*)

390 French, Jackie. *Diary of a Baby Wombat* (K–3). Illus. by Bruce Whatley. 2010, Clarion $16.99 (978-0-547-43005-8). 32pp. Baby Wombat writes about his life and the fact that he and his mother need a new burrow in this sequel to *Diary of a Wombat* (2003). (Rev: BL 12/1/10; HB 9–10/10; SLJ 10/1/10)

391 Gay, Marie-Louise. *Caramba and Henry* (K–3). Illus. by author. 2011, Groundwood $17.95 (978-1-55498-097-0). 40pp. Caramba, the cat who cannot fly, is assigned to guard his younger brother, and ends up having to rescue him; a sequel to *Caramba* (2005). (Rev: BL 10/15/11; SLJ 11/1/11)

392 Gay, Marie-Louise. *Roslyn Rutabaga and the Biggest Hole on Earth!* (PS–1). Illus. by author. 2010, Groundwood $16.95 (978-0-88899-994-8). Unpaged. A young rabbit meets obstacles when she sets out to dig the world's biggest hole. (Rev: SLJ 9/1/10)

393 Geisert, Arthur. *Ice* (PS–2). Illus. by author. 2011, Enchanted Lion $14.95 (978-1-59270-098-1). 32pp. A group of adventurous pigs running short of water leave their sunny island in search of an iceberg in this wordless adventure. (Rev: BL 4/15/11; SLJ 5/1/11)

394 George, Lucy M. *Back to School Tortoise* (PS–2). Illus. by Merel Eyckerman. 2011, Whitman $15.99 (978-0-8075-0510-6). 24pp. An anxious tortoise dreads the first day of school in this story with a twist — the tortoise is the teacher. (Rev: BL 8/11; SLJ 7/11)

395 Glass, Beth Raisner. *Blue-Ribbon Dad* (PS–2). Illus. by Margie Moore. 2011, Abrams $14.95 (978-0-8109-9727-1). Unpaged. A young squirrel prepares a special surprise present for the dad who does so much for him. (Rev: BL 4/15/11; SLJ 5/1/11)

396 Gorbachev, Valeri. *What's the Big Idea, Molly?* (PS–2). Illus. by author. 2010, Philomel $16.99 (978-0-399-25428-4). 32pp. Molly Mouse has writer's block and she and her friends struggle to come up with a suitable birthday present for Turtle. (Rev: BL 6/10; LMC 11–12/10; SLJ 7/1/10)

397 Gormley, Greg. *Dog in Boots* (PS–1). Illus. by Roberta Angaramo. 2011, Holiday House $17.95 (978-0-8234-2347-7). 32pp. Inspired by "Puss in Boots," Dog decides to go shoe shopping but finds it more challenging than he expected. Lexile AD680L (Rev: BL 3/15/11; SLJ 3/1/11*)

398 Gravett, Emily. *Blue Chameleon* (PS–K). Illus. by author. 2011, Simon & Schuster $16.99 (978-1-4424-1958-2). 32pp. A chameleon lonely for a friend transforms himself without success until he finally finds what he's been seeking — another chameleon. (Rev: BL 3/15/11; HB 3–4/11; SLJ 3/1/11)

399 Green, Alison. *The Fox in the Dark* (K–2). Illus. by Deborah Allwright. 2010, Tiger Tales $15.95 (978-1-58925-091-8). Unpaged. Rabbit offers his den as shelter for a group of animals running from a fox; when the fox knocks, it turns out he is just as in need of shelter as they are. (Rev: SLJ 11/1/10)

400 Grey, Mini. *Three by the Sea* (PS–2). Illus. by author. 2011, Knopf $17.99 (978-0-375-86784-2); LB $20.99 (978-0-375-96784-9). 32pp. A dog, a cat, and a mouse used to sharing household duties are tested when a fox from the Winds of Change Trading Company stirs up discord. (Rev: BL 2/1/11; SLJ 4/11*)

401 Harper, Charise Mericle. *Pink Me Up* (PS–2). Illus. by author. 2010, Knopf $16.99 (978-0-375-85607-5). 40pp. When bunny Violet's mother comes down with a fever, she recruits her dad to take her to a "Pink-nic," decorating his clothing with pink so he'll fit in. (Rev: BL 4/15/10; SLJ 4/1/10)

402 Harper, Lee. *Snow! Snow! Snow!* (PS–K). Illus. by author. 2009, Simon & Schuster $14.99 (978-1-4169-8454-2). 40pp. Two puppies and their father enjoy a day frolicking in the snow in this cartoon-like, lighthearted offering. (Rev: BL 11/1/09; SLJ 10/1/09)

403 Helakoski, Leslie. *Fair Cow* (PS–2). Illus. by author. 2010, Marshall Cavendish $16.99 (978-0-7614-5684-1). 32pp. Petunia the pig helps Effie the cow primp for the state fair beauty competition in this pun-filled romp. Lexile AD430L (Rev: BL 9/1/10; LMC 1–2/11; SLJ 9/1/10)

404 Helquist, Brett. *Bedtime for Bear* (PS–1). Illus. by author. 2010, HarperCollins $16.99 (978-0-06-050205-8). Unpaged. Bear is persuaded by his raccoon friends to spend one last day playing in the snow before settling in for the winter. (Rev: BL 10/15/10; SLJ 2/1/11*)

405 Hendra, Sue. *Barry, the Fish with Fingers* (K–2). Illus. by author. 2010, Knopf $15.99 (978-0-375-85894-9); LB $18.99 (978-0-375-95894-6). Unpaged. Barry's fingers allow him to do amazing things. (Rev: LMC 11–12/10; SLJ 7/1/10)

406 Hill, Susanna Leonard. *April Fool, Phyllis!* (K–3). Illus. by Jeffrey Ebbeler. 2011, Holiday House $16.95 (978-0-8234-2270-8). 32pp. It's the first day of April and nobody believes Phyllis the groundhog when she says a blizzard is on its way; a sequel to *Punxsutawney Phyllis* (2006). (Rev: BL 3/15/11; SLJ 5/1/11)

407 Hillenbrand, Will. *Spring Is Here* (PS–2). Illus. by author. 2011, Holiday House $16.95 (978-0-8234-1602-8). 32pp. At the end of winter Mole wakes his friend Bear up from hibernation by baking a sumptuous breakfast. (Rev: BL 2/15/11; HB 3–4/11; SLJ 3/1/11)

408 Hills, Tad. *Duck and Goose Find a Pumpkin* (PS). Illus. by author. 2009, Random House $6.99 (978-037585813-0). 20pp. Duck and Goose like their friend Thistle's pumpkin and decide to find one of their own. (Rev: BL 9/15/09; SLJ 8/1/09)

409 Hills, Tad. *How Rocket Learned to Read* (K–2). Illus. by author. 2010, Random House $17.99 (978-0-375-85899-4). 40pp. A smart yellow bird enthusiastically teaches a willing dog how to read, starting with learning the alphabet. (Rev: BL 5/15/10; LMC 11–12/10; SLJ 7/1/10)

410 Hodgkinson, Jo. *The Talent Show* (K–3). Illus. by author. 2011, Andersen $16.95 (978-0-7613-7487-9). 32pp. A band composed of a bear, a crocodile, a lion, and a snake finds the perfect vocalist: a tiny red bird who is not too small after all. **e** (Rev: BL 2/15/11; SLJ 2/1/11)

411 Hodgkinson, Leigh. *Boris and the Wrong Shadow* (K–2). Illus. by author. 2009, Tiger Tales $15.95 (978-1-58925-082-6). Unpaged. Boris the cat wakes up to find that his shadow is all wrong — and that his mouse friend Vernon seems to be in possession of a cat shadow. (Rev: SLJ 9/1/09)

412 Hodgkinson, Leigh. *Introducing Limelight Larry* (PS–2). Illus. by author. 2011, Tiger Tales $15.95 (978-1-58925-102-1). Unpaged. An attention-hogging peacock tries everything to exclude his friends from this book, resulting in a comic message about the importance of sharing the spotlight. (Rev: SLJ 11/1/11)

413 Holmes, Janet A. *Me and You* (PS–K). Illus. by Judith Rossell. 2009, NorthSouth $14.95 (978-0-7358-2250-4). Unpaged. Rabbit and Mouse enjoy a day of outdoor play and togetherness. (Rev: SLJ 10/1/09)

414 Horowitz, Dave. *Duck Duck Moose* (PS–2). Illus. by author. 2009, Putnam $16.99 (978-0-399-24782-8). Unpaged. A reluctant moose follows his feathered friends south for the winter and is surprised to discover how much he likes the sunshine. (Rev: BL 9/1/09; SLJ 10/1/09)

415 Iwamura, Kazuo. *Hooray for Summer!* (PS–1). Illus. by author. 2010, NorthSouth $16.95 (978-0-7358-2285-6). 32pp. Three squirrel siblings take refuge in a cave during a thunderstorm and make friends with a rabbit and two mice. Lexile AD420L (Rev: BLO 4/15/10; HB 7–8/10; SLJ 5/1/10)

416 Jahn-Clough, Lisa. *Felicity and Cordelia: A Tale of Two Bunnies* (PS–K). Illus. by author. 2011, Farrar $16.99 (978-0-374-32300-4). 40pp. Adventuresome rabbit Felicity returns safely home after a ride in a hot air balloon, where her more cautious bunny friend Cordelia is waiting, with pie. (Rev: BL 2/15/11; SLJ 3/1/11)

417 Kaplan, Michael B. *Betty Bunny Loves Chocolate Cake* (K–3). Illus. by Stephane Jorisch. 2011, Dial $16.99 (978-0-8037-3407-4). 32pp. A chocolate-crazed young bunny has a variety of comic misadventures when she stuffs a piece of cake in her pocket. (Rev: BL 6/1/11; SLJ 6/11*)

418 Kaplan, Michael B. *Betty Bunny Wants Everything* (K–3). Illus. by Stephane Jorisch. 2012, Dial $16.99 (978-080373408-1). 32pp. Stubborn Betty throws a fit when she's told she can only have one toy at the store. (Rev: BL 2/1/12; SLJ 1/12)

419 Kasza, Keiko. *Ready for Anything!* (PS–2). Illus. by author. 2009, Putnam $16.99 (978-0-399-25235-8). 32pp. A group of animal friends consider both the best-case and worst-case scenarios before heading out on a picnic. (Rev: BL 9/15/09; SLJ 9/1/09)

420 Ketteman, Helen. *If Beaver Had a Fever* (PS–1). Illus. by Kevin O'Malley. 2011, Marshall Cavendish $16.99 (978-0-7614-5951-4). 32pp. A little bear wonders how his mom would treat a variety of sick animals. (Rev: BLO 11/15/11; LMC 1–2/12; SLJ 9/1/11)

421 Kimura, Ken. *Nine Hundred Ninety-nine Tadpoles* (PS–3). Illus. by Yasunari Murakami. 2011, NorthSouth $16.95 (978-0-7358-4013-3). 48pp. Things get too crowded in the pond when Mother and Father Frog produce 999 youngsters, and they all set off on a dangerous (and funny) journey to a bigger home. (Rev: BL 7/11; HB 7–8/11; SLJ 6/11)

422 Kirk, Daniel. *A Museum Adventure* (K–2). Illus. by author. Series: Library Mouse. 2012, Abrams $16.95 (978-141970173-3). 32pp. Mouse friends Sam and Sarah leave the library to visit a museum where they have adventures and see different kinds of art. (Rev: BLO 4/15/12)

423 Klassen, Jon. *I Want My Hat Back* (K–2). Illus. by author. 2011, Candlewick $15.99 (978-0-7636-5598-3). 40pp. A frustrated bear looking for his missing red hat asks various other animals but totally ignores the fact that his friend Rabbit has been wearing it all along. (Rev: BL 11/1/11; SLJ 8/1/11)

424 Kleven, Elisa. *Welcome Home, Mouse* (PS–K). Illus. by author. 2010, Tricycle $15.99 (978-1-58246-277-6). 32pp. A clumsy elephant apologizes for knocking down a mouse's house and builds a new one out of found materials. Lexile AD530L (Rev: BL 1/1–15/11; SLJ 9/1/10)

425 Klise, Kate. *Little Rabbit and the Meanest Mother on Earth* (1–3). Illus. by M. Sarah Klise. 2010, Harcourt $17 (978-0-15-206201-9). 32pp. Convinced he has the meanest mother on Earth, Little Rabbit suggests to a circus ringmaster that he might want to put her on display. (Rev: BLO 5/15/10; SLJ 3/1/10)

426 Kohuth, Jane. *Duck Sock Hop* (PS–K). Illus. by Jane Porter. 2012, Dial $16.99 (978-080373712-9). 32pp. Once a week the ducks get together, choose colorful socks from the box, and dance to the music! (Rev: BL 5/15/12; SLJ 6/1/12)

427 Kohuth, Jane. *Ducks Go Vroom* (PS–K). Illus. by Viviana Garofoli. 2011, Random House paper $3.99 (978-0-375-86560-2). 32pp. For beginning readers, this onomatopoeic story about a family of lively ducks visiting a goose relative uses repetition, large type, and bright cartoon illustrations. **e** (Rev: BL 12/15/10; SLJ 2/1/11)

428 Kolanovic, Dubravka. *Everyone Needs a Friend* (PS–2). Illus. by author. 2010, Price Stern Sloan $9.99 (978-0-8431-9918-5). 32pp. Jack, a lonely wolf, would like a friend, but is Walter the mouse exactly right? (Rev: BL 10/1/10; SLJ 9/1/10)

429 Koontz, Robin Michal. *The Case of the Missing Goldfish* (K–2). Illus. by author. Series: Short Tales: Furlock & Muttson Mysteries. 2010, ABDO LB $22.78 (978-1-60270-561-6). 32pp. Furry detectives Furlock and Muttson are hot on the trail of a goldfish-napper in this entertaining story. Also use *The Case of the Mystery Museum* and *The Case of the Shifting Stacks* (both 2010). (Rev: SLJ 4/1/10)

430 Korda, Lerryn. *Into the Wild* (PS). Illus. by author. Series: Playtime with Little Nye. 2010, Candlewick $7.99 (978-0-7636-4812-1). 26pp. Little Nye's friend Gracie prepares for an expedition to the edge of the yard and her friends beg to come along. (Rev: BL 4/15/10; SLJ 4/1/10)

431 Korda, Lerryn. *It's Vacation Time* (PS). Illus. by author. Series: Playtime with Little Nye. 2010, Candlewick $8.99 (978-0-7636-4813-8). Unpaged. Little Nye's friend Nella struggles to shut a bulging suitcase in this entertaining story about getting ready for vacation. (Rev: SLJ 4/1/10)

432 Krauss, Ruth. *And I Love You* (PS–1). Illus. by Steven Kellogg. 2010, Scholastic $16.99 (978-0-439-02459-4). 40pp. Originally published as *Big and Little* in 1987, this story featuring a kitten and his mother conveys the comforting message that big people love and appreciate youngsters everywhere. (Rev: BL 9/15/10; SLJ 9/1/10)

433 Landry, Leo. *Grin and Bear It* (K–3). Illus. by author. 2011, Charlesbridge $12.95 (978-1-57091-745-5). 48pp. A shy bear who knows how to write jokes and an outgoing hummingbird who knows how to deliver them

make an unlikely comic duo in this story about facing your fears. (Rev: BL 7/11; HB 9–10/11; SLJ 7/11)

434 Leeuwen, Jean Van. *Five Funny Bunnies: Three Bouncing Tales* (PS–1). Illus. by Anne Wilsdorf. 2012, Marshall Cavendish $17.99 (978-076146114-2). 32pp. In three stories five young rabbit siblings visit their grandmother, practice jumping, and enjoy storytime; with charming watercolor-and-ink illustrations. **e** (Rev: BLO 4/1/12; SLJ 4/1/12)

435 Lester, Helen. *All for Me and None for All* (PS–1). Illus. by Lynn Munsinger. 2012, Houghton Mifflin $16.99 (978-054768834-3). 32pp. A greedy pig named Gruntly learns to share when he realizes his pushy, grabby ways make him do things without thinking. (Rev: BL 3/15/12*; SLJ 5/1/12)

436 Lester, Helen. *Wodney Wat's Wobot* (PS–2). Illus. by Lynn Munsinger. 2011, Houghton Mifflin $16.99 (978-0-547-36756-9). 32pp. Young rat Wodney gets a talking robot (wobot) for his birthday that turns out to be a useful foil for the class bully Camilla. (Rev: BL 9/1/11; SLJ 8/1/11)

437 Lies, Brian. *Bats at the Ballgame* (K–2). Illus. by author. 2010, Houghton Mifflin $16.99 (978-0-547-24970-4). 32pp. In this fanciful trip to the baseball diamond, furry bats flit around the bases while their fans eat "mothdogs" and hang upside down in the stands. (Rev: BLO 7/10; SLJ 8/1/10)

438 Liwska, Renata. *Red Wagon* (PS–1). Illus. by author. 2011, Philomel $16.99 (978-0-399-25237-2). 32pp. Lucy the fox and her animal friends have a fanciful adventure on their way into town with a shopping list and her little red wagon. (Rev: BL 2/15/11*; HB 1–2/11; SLJ 2/1/11)

439 London, Jonathan. *Froggy Goes to Hawaii* (PS–1). Illus. by Frank Remkiewicz. 2011, Viking $15.99 (978-067001221-3). 32pp. Froggy has a very exciting time when he and his family visit Hawaii. (Rev: BLO 5/1/11)

440 Long, Ethan. *Chamelia* (PS–2). Illus. by author. 2011, Little, Brown $16.99 (978-031608612-7). 40pp. Bored with blending in, Chamelia the Chameleon starts dressing to stand out; eventually she realizes she can be herself and still find acceptance amongst the other lizards. (Rev: BL 4/1/11; LMC 10/11)

441 Lord, Cynthia. *Happy Birthday, Hamster* (PS–K). Illus. by Derek Anderson. 2011, Scholastic $16.99 (978-0-545-25522-6). 40pp. Convinced his friends have forgotten his birthday, a hamster doesn't notice the birthday-party-supplies shopping going on in the background; a companion to *Hot Rod Hamster* (2010) (Rev: BLO 9/1/11; SLJ 10/1/11)

442 Lord, Cynthia. *Hot Rod Hamster* (PS–K). Illus. by Derek Anderson. 2010, Scholastic $16.99 (978-0-545-03530-9). 40pp. In this lively rhymed book, a speed-demon hamster prepares for and competes in a big race. (Rev: BL 12/1/09; LMC 5–6/10; SLJ 1/1/10)

443 Loth, Sebastian. *Clementine* (PS–2). Illus. by author. 2011, NorthSouth $14.95 (978-0-7358-4009-6). 32pp. Clementine, a snail with a devotion to round things, and her friend, a snake, make two failed attempts to reach the moon using a trampoline and a slingshot before they decide on a rocket. (Rev: BL 4/1/11; SLJ 5/1/11)

444 Loth, Sebastian. *Remembering Crystal* (PS–K). Illus. by author. 2010, NorthSouth $14.95 (978-0-7358-2300-6). 64pp. A goose named Zelda mourns her turtle friend and remembers the good times they had together. (Rev: BL 8/10; LMC 10/10; SLJ 6/1/10)

445 McCarty, Peter. *Chloe* (PS–1). Illus. by author. 2012, HarperCollins $16.99 (978-006114291-8). 40pp. Rabbit Chloe and her brothers and sisters decide they'd rather rely on their creativity for fun than watch their family's new television. (Rev: BL 4/15/12*; SLJ 5/1/12*)

446 McCarty, Peter. *Henry in Love* (K–2). Illus. by author. 2010, HarperCollins $16.99 (978-0-06-114288-8); LB $17.89 (978-0-06-114289-5). 48pp. Lovestruck cat Henry shamelessly courts a pretty young bunny, resorting to all sorts of over-the-top antics in this humorous story. (Rev: BL 12/1/09; SLJ 1/1/10*)

447 McKee, David. *Elmer and Rose* (PS–1). Illus. by author. 2010, Andersen $16.95 (978-0-7613-5493-2). Unpaged. Patchwork elephant Elmer meets a pink elephant called Rose who is lost, in this story about being different. (Rev: LMC 8–9/10; SLJ 3/1/10)

448 McKee, David. *Elmer's Special Day* (PS–2). Illus. by author. 2009, Andersen $16.95 (978-0-7613-5154-2). Unpaged. The other animals are jealous of the annual parade of decorated elephants, and Elmer invites them to join in. (Rev: SLJ 10/1/09)

449 McMullan, Kate. *Bulldog's Big Day* (K–2). Illus. by Pascal Lemaitre. 2011, Scholastic $16.99 (978-0-545-17155-7). 32pp. A bulldog eager to find his place in the world tries a variety of occupations before discovering that his talent for baking cookies offers an opportunity. Lexile AD540L (Rev: BL 2/15/11*; SLJ 2/1/11)

450 McMullan, Kate. *I'm Big!* (PS–1). Illus. by Jim McMullan. 2010, HarperCollins $16.99 (978-0-06-122974-9). 40pp. A giant purple sauropod wakes up late and discovers his herd has disappeared, leaving him to face scary predators alone. (Rev: BL 10/15/10; SLJ 8/1/10)

451 McPhail, David. *Pig Pig Meets the Lion* (PS–1). Illus. by author. 2012, Charlesbridge $15.95 (978-158089358-9). 32pp. A lion that has escaped from the zoo follows Pig Pig around the house as his mother obliviously goes about her morning tasks. Lexile AD420L (Rev: BL 2/1/12; SLJ 1/12)

452 McPhail, David. *Pig Pig Returns* (PS–K). Illus. by author. 2011, Charlesbridge $16.95 (978-1-58089-356-5). 32pp. Despite his initial worries, Pig Pig enjoys cross-country travel with his aunt and uncle and has mixed feelings about coming home. (Rev: BL 5/1/11; SLJ 7/11)

453 McPhail, David. *Waddles* (PS–2). Illus. by author. 2011, Abrams $15.95 (978-0-8109-8415-8). 32pp. Waddles, a fat raccoon, pines for his friend Emily the duck during her long winter away, but celebrates their reunion each spring. (Rev: BL 2/15/11; LMC 8–9/11; SLJ 4/11)

454 Meadows, Michelle. *Hibernation Station* (PS–2). Illus. by Kurt Cyrus. 2010, Simon & Schuster $16.99 (978-1-4169-3788-3). 40pp. In this imaginative story, a train made of hollow logs rolls through the forest, collecting pajama-clad animals for their winter sleep. e Lexile 310L (Rev: BL 8/10; LMC 10/10; SLJ 7/1/10)

455 Meadows, Michelle. *Piggies in the Kitchen* (PS–2). Illus. by Ard Hoyt. 2011, Simon & Schuster $14.99 (978-1-4169-3787-6). 32pp. Piggie children take over the kitchen when their mother leaves the house, creating cookies, cake, and pie — and a disastrous mess — before cleaning up in the nick of time. (Rev: BL 2/15/11; SLJ 2/1/11)

456 Melling, David. *Don't Worry, Douglas!* (PS–1). Illus. by author. 2011, Tiger Tales $12.95 (978-1-58925-106-9). Unpaged. Douglas the bear accidentally destroys the wool hat his father gave him; in the end, he comes clean, is forgiven, and receives a new hat. (Rev: SLJ 11/1/11)

457 Melling, David. *Hugless Douglas* (PS–1). Illus. by author. 2010, Tiger Tales $15.95 (978-1-58925-098-7). Unpaged. A funny story in which a bear cub in need of a hug tries various sources that prove uncomfortable. (Rev: SLJ 10/1/10)

458 Meschenmoser, Sebastian. *Waiting for Winter* (PS–2). Illus. by author. 2009, Kane/Miller $15.99 (978-1-935279-04-4). 56pp. Young Squirrel is impatient for the arrival of snow but afraid that he will sleep through this new experience. (Rev: BL 11/1/09; LMC 1–2/10; SLJ 9/1/09)

459 Middleton, Charlotte. *Nibbles: A Green Tale* (K–2). Illus. by author. 2010, Marshall Cavendish $17.99 (978-0-7614-5791-6). 32pp. A guinea pig village nearly eats its favorite food — dandelions — into extinction in this subtle parable about overconsumption and scarcity. e (Rev: BL 5/1/10; LMC 8–9/10; SLJ 5/1/10)

460 Modarressi, Mitra. *Taking Care of Mama* (PS–2). Illus. by author. 2010, Putnam $16.99 (978-0-399-25216-7). 32pp. When Mama is in bed with a cold, Papa and the three young raccoons are initially eager to shoulder her responsibilities; a sequel to *Stay Awake, Sally* (2007). (Rev: BL 2/1/10; SLJ 4/1/10)

461 Monroe, Chris. *Sneaky Sheep* (PS–1). Illus. by author. 2010, Carolrhoda LB $16.95 (978-0-7613-5615-

8). 32pp. Two mischievous sheep, Rocky and Blossom, escape from the sheepdog, but their greener pasture proves to harbor a wolf and suddenly they need that kindly and brave dog. (Rev: BL 10/15/10; SLJ 9/1/10)

462 Moore, Inga. *A House in the Woods* (PS–2). Illus. by author. 2011, Candlewick $16.99 (978-0-7636-5277-7). 48pp. After their home is accidentally destroyed by Bear and Moose, two little pigs recruit the help of some beavers to build a new abode. (Rev: BL 12/1/11; SLJ 10/1/11)

463 Mortimer, Anne. *Pumpkin Cat* (PS–2). Illus. by author. 2011, HarperCollins $14.99 (978-0-06-187485-7). 24pp. A mouse teaches his cat friend how to plant and tend a pumpkin vine all through spring and summer; the story culminates with carving jack o'lanterns. (Rev: BLO 8/11; SLJ 7/11)

464 Moss, Miriam. *Matty in a Mess!* (PS–2). Illus. by Jane Simmons. 2010, IPG/Andersen $16.99 (978-1-84270-812-5). 32pp. Bossy, tidy Matty is always after his messy sister to clean up, but when a scary storm threatens their house, it's kind, gentle Milly who saves the day. Another book in the series is *Matty Takes Off!* (2010). (Rev: BL 1/1/10; SLJ 2/1/10)

465 Myers, Walter Dean. *Looking for the Easy Life* (K–2). Illus. by Lee Harper. 2011, HarperCollins $16.99 (978-0-06-054375-4). 40pp. Led by Uh-Huh Freddie and Oswego Pete, five monkeys on Monkey Island set out to find "the easy life" but discover that maybe a little hard work isn't so bad after all; features African American dialect and cartoon illustrations. Lexile 750L (Rev: BL 3/15/11; SLJ 2/1/11)

466 Na, Il Sung. *The Thingamabob* (PS–K). Illus. by author. 2010, Knopf $15.99 (978-0-375-86106-2). 24pp. Hilarity and confusion ensue when an innocent elephant happens upon a red umbrella in this humorous tale with compelling illustrations. (Rev: BL 2/1/10; LMC 5–6/10; SLJ 3/1/10)

467 Numeroff, Laura. *If You Give a Dog a Donut* (PS–2). Illus. by Felicia Bond. 2011, HarperCollins $16.99 (978-0-06-026683-7). 32pp. This circular story features a donut-toting dog seeking one thing after another until he ends up where he left off. (Rev: BLO 11/15/11; SLJ 10/1/11)

468 Numeroff, Laura. *Otis and Sydney and the Best Birthday Ever* (PS–1). Illus. by Dan Andreasen. 2010, Abrams $16.95 (978-0-8109-8959-7). 32pp. Best bear friends Sydney and Otis are happy to share Sydney's birthday party themselves when the party invitations go awry. (Rev: BL 9/1/10; SLJ 12/1/10)

469 Numeroff, Laura, and Nate Evans. *The Jellybeans and the Big Art Adventure* (K–2). Illus. by Lynn Munsinger. Series: The Jellybeans. 2012, Abrams $16.95 (978-141970171-9). 32pp. When Bitsy the paint-loving pig is asked to create a mural, she invites her differently talented friends along to help and pro-

vide support; the fourth installment in the series. (Rev: BLO 1/25/12; SLJ 4/1/12)

470 Numeroff, Laura, and Nate Evans. *The Jellybeans and the Big Camp Kickoff* (K–2). Illus. by Lynn Munsinger. Series: The Jellybeans. 2011, Abrams $16.95 (978-0-8109-9765-3). Unpaged. At Camp Pook-A-Woo the four animal friends with different talents and abilities all try to use them to best effect, although Nicole (a cat) is initially disappointed that there is no soccer. (Rev: SLJ 5/1/11)

471 Nyeu, Tao. *Bunny Days* (PS). Illus. by author. 2010, Dial $16.99 (978-0-8037-3330-5). 48pp. Three gentle tales of easily reparable mishaps feature a group of bunnies, a helpful bear, and familiar household appliances; quilt-like art adds atmosphere. (Rev: BL 1/1/10; SLJ 12/1/09)

472 Oldland, Nicholas. *The Busy Beaver* (PS–K). Illus. by author. 2011, Kids Can $16.95 (978-1-55453-749-5). Unpaged. An eager and previously thoughtless beaver realizes apologies are due to his animal friends who have been injured or annoyed by his chewing trees down willy-nilly. (Rev: SLJ 9/1/11)

473 Oldland, Nicholas. *Making the Moose Out of Life* (PS–2). Illus. by author. 2010, Kids Can $16.95 (978-1-55453-580-4). 32pp. A reserved and timid moose is inspired to participate more fully in life after a scary experience at sea. (Rev: SLJ 10/1/10)

474 Palatini, Margie. *Hogg, Hogg, and Hog* (K–3). Illus. by author. 2011, Simon & Schuster $15.99 (978-1-4424-0322-2). 32pp. Three trendsetting pigs head to the big city to launch the "next big thing" — OINK — but must come up with a new idea after that initial fad fizzles. (Rev: BL 2/1/11; SLJ 4/11)

475 Palatini, Margie. *Stuff* (PS–1). Illus. by Noah Z. Jones. 2011, HarperCollins $16.99 (978-0-06-171921-9). 32pp. Edward, a rabbit with more possessions than friends, finally comes to the conclusion that he'd be happier with less stuff and more company. (Rev: BL 9/15/11; SLJ 9/1/11)

476 Parenteau, Shirley. *Bears on Chairs* (PS–K). Illus. by David Walker. 2009, Candlewick $15.99 (978-0-7636-3588-6). 32pp. Four chairs and one-too-many bears create a simple, comic problem. (Rev: BL 11/1/09; SLJ 10/1/09)

477 Patricelli, Leslie. *The Patterson Puppies and the Midnight Monster Party* (PS–2). Illus. by author. 2010, Candlewick $14.99 (978-0-7636-3243-4). Unpaged. Her puppy siblings try to help Petra overcome her fear of the dark and conviction that a monster is lurking. (Rev: SLJ 5/1/10)

478 Pfister, Marcus. *Happy Birthday, Bertie!* (PS–2). Illus. by author. 2010, NorthSouth $16.95 (978-0-7358-2280-1). 32pp. Bertie the hippo eagerly anticipates his birthday party, waiting as his family decorates, bakes a cake, and invites his animal buddies over to join in the fun. (Rev: BL 1/1/10; LMC 1–2/10; SLJ 1/1/10)

479 Postgate, Daniel. *Smelly Bill: Love Stinks* (PS–1). Illus. by author. Series: Smelly Bill. 2010, Whitman $16.99 (978-0-8075-7464-5). 32pp. At the sight of poodle Peachy Snugglekins, scruffy Bill's knees go weak and he decides to clean up his act. (Rev: BL 12/1/10; LMC 1–2/11; SLJ 9/1/10)

480 Proimos, James. *Swim! Swim!* (PS). Illus. by author. 2010, Scholastic $16.99 (978-0-545-09419-1). 32pp. A lonely goldfish called Lerch thinks he's finally found a friend when a cat hops up to chat; "Lerch" is a pseudonym for James Proimos. (Rev: BL 5/15/10; LMC 10/10; SLJ 7/1/10)

481 Protopopescu, Orel. *Thelonious Mouse* (PS–2). Illus. by Anne Wilsdorf. 2011, Farrar $16.99 (978-0-374-37447-1). 32pp. Thelonious can't help making music wherever he goes, which attracts the scary attentions of Fat Cat, but eventually the two find bebop companionship at the piano. (Rev: BL 5/1/11; SLJ 8/1/11)

482 Ramos, Mario. *I Am So Strong* (K–2). Trans. from French by Jean Anderson. Illus. by author. 2011, Gecko $16.95 (978-0-9582-7877-5). Unpaged. A big bad wolf used to asserting his strength meets his match when he picks on a small creature that turns out to be a baby dragon — and his mother is not pleased. (Rev: LMC 5–6/12; SLJ 10/1/11)

483 Rayner, Catherine. *The Bear Who Shared* (PS–1). Illus. by author. 2011, Dial $16.99 (978-0-8037-3576-7). 32pp. A bear, a mouse, and a raccoon wait impatiently for a luscious fruit to ripen; when it finally falls, they share it evenly. Lexile AD400L (Rev: BL 4/1/11; SLJ 3/1/11)

484 Rayner, Catherine. *Solomon Crocodile* (PS–2). Illus. by author. 2011, Farrar $15.99 (978-0-374-38064-9). 32pp. Roughhousing Solomon the Crocodile can't find anyone to play with in the river and rejoices when one of his own turns up. (Rev: BL 12/15/11; HB 11–12/11; SLJ 11/1/11)

485 Regan, Dian Curtis. *The Snow Blew Inn* (PS–K). Illus. by Doug Cushman. 2011, Holiday House $16.95 (978-0-8234-2351-4). 32pp. An excited kitten eagerly anticipates the arrival of her cousin and aunt at the inn; but there is a blizzard and the inn is filling up with travelers — when will Abby and her mother get there and where will they sleep? Lexile AD560L (Rev: BL 10/15/11; SLJ 10/1/11)

486 Rueda, Claudia. *No* (PS). Trans. by Elisa Amado. Illus. by author. 2010, Groundwood $18.95 (978-0-88899-991-7). 44pp. Reluctant to hibernate, little bear is determined to brave out the winter cold — but realizes in the end that safe and snug is where he wants to be. (Rev: BL 11/1/10*; SLJ 9/1/10*)

487 Runton, Andy. *Owly and Wormy: Friends All Aflutter!* (PS–1). Illus. by author. 2011, Simon & Schuster $15.99 (978-1-4169-5774-4). 40pp. Owly and Wormy decide to plant flowers that will attract butterflies and then are disappointed when caterpillars turn up instead in this almost-wordless picture book about the comic book characters. ℮ (Rev: BL 2/15/11; LMC 8–9/11; SLJ 5/1/11)

488 Russell, Natalie. *Brown Rabbit in the City* (PS–1). Illus. by author. 2010, Viking $16.99 (978-0-670-01234-3). 40pp. Brown Rabbit goes to visit Little Rabbit in the city but finds her schedule totally exhausting, and the two must negotiate more time together. (Rev: BL 4/15/10; SLJ 6/1/10)

489 Russo, Marisabina. *Peter Is Just a Baby* (1–3). Illus. by author. 2012, Eerdmans $16 (978-080285384-4). 32pp. A young bear lists her own accomplishments and expresses frustration with her messy baby brother but comes to recognize that he will soon grow to become more fun. (Rev: BL 1/1/12; SLJ 1/12)

490 Russo, Marisabina. *A Very Big Bunny* (PS–1). Illus. by author. 2010, Random House $17.99 (978-0-375-84463-8); LB $20.99 (978-0-375-94463-5). 40pp. A oversize bunny and an undersize bunny become fast friends in this story about bullying and accepting differences. (Rev: BL 11/1/09; HB 1–2/10; LMC 1–2/10; SLJ 2/1/10)

491 Ruzzier, Sergio. *Hey, Rabbit!* (K–2). Illus. by author. 2010, Roaring Brook $16.99 (978-1-59643-502-5). 32pp. A rabbit surprises his woodland friends when he pulls one magical gift after another out of his suitcase. (Rev: BL 12/1/09; LMC 1–2/10; SLJ 2/1/10)

492 Ryan, Candace. *Ribbit Rabbit* (PS–1). Illus. by Mike Lowery. 2011, Walker $12.99 (978-0-8027-2180-8). 32pp. Frog and Bunny are best friends even though they sometimes have disputes over toys. (Rev: BLO 2/14/11; LMC 3–4/11; SLJ 3/1/11)

493 Ryan, Pam Muñoz. *Tony Baloney* (PS–1). Illus. by Edwin Fotheringham. 2011, Scholastic $16.99 (978-0-545-23135-0). 40pp. Middle penguin child Tony contends with the many woes and frustrations of being overlooked. Lexile AD880L (Rev: BL 2/1/11; HB 3–4/11; SLJ 2/1/11)

494 Sakai, Komako. *Mad at Mommy* (PS–1). Illus. by author. 2010, Scholastic $16.99 (978-0-545-21209-0). 40pp. A young bunny's frustration and anger with his mom — for sleeping late, for enforcing bedtimes, for not giving him what he wants — is the focus of this beautifully illustrated story. (Rev: BL 9/15/10; HB 11–12/10; SLJ 11/1/10)

495 Salley, Coleen. *Epossumondas Plays Possum* (PS–1). Illus. by Janet Stevens. 2009, Harcourt $16 (978-0-15-206420-4). 40pp. Epossumondas ignores his mother's warning and heads into the swamp alone, where he must play dead when he thinks he hears the scary loup-garou. 🎧 Lexile AD620L (Rev: BL 9/15/09; HB 9–10/09; SLJ 10/1/09*)

496 Sandall, Ellie. *Birdsong* (PS–1). Illus. by author. 2011, Egmont $16.99 (978-1-60684-193-8). 32pp. One bird after another lands on a tree branch, too involved in twittering together to notice the bough bending . . . but it is a tiny butterfly that deals the final blow. (Rev: BLO 8/11; SLJ 6/11)

497 Sattler, Jennifer. *Chick 'n' Pug* (PS–1). 2010, Bloomsbury $14.99 (978-1-59990-534-1); LB $15.89 (978-1-59990-535-8). Unpaged. A brassy little chick decides he's a lazy pug's new best friend and ably frightens off a cat threatening to usurp the limelight. (Rev: LMC 11–12/10; SLJ 11/1/10)

498 Sattler, Jennifer. *Pig Kahuna* (PS–2). Illus. by author. 2011, Bloomsbury $14.99 (978-1-59990-635-5). 32pp. An anxious young piglet faces his fear of water to save his brother's special surfboard. Lexile AD490L (Rev: BL 4/15/11; SLJ 5/1/11*)

499 Sauer, Tammi. *Mr. Duck Means Business* (PS–2). Illus. by Jeff Mack. 2011, Simon & Schuster $15.99 (978-1-4169-8522-8). 32pp. A tranquility-obsessed duck learns to be more tolerant of his friends' boisterous activities in this lively barnyard story. ℮ Lexile AD320L (Rev: BLO 1/1–15/11; LMC 5–6/11; SLJ 1/1/11)

500 Scanlon, Liz Garton. *Noodle and Lou* (PS–1). Illus. by Arthur Howard. 2011, Simon & Schuster $15.99 (978-1-4424-0288-1). 32pp. Noodle the worm's gloomy mood can only be cleared away by the efforts of his friend Lou the bird in this cheerful ode to friendship that features humorous details in the illustrations. (Rev: BL 3/1/11; SLJ 5/1/11)

501 Schachner, Judy. *Skippyjon Jones Class Action* (K–3). Illus. by author. 2011, Dutton $17.99 (978-0-525-42228-0). Unpaged. Skippyjon Jones, the Siamese who sees himself as a chihuahua, longs to go to dog obedience class in this zany story. (Rev: SLJ 7/11)

502 Schachner, Judy. *Skippyjon Jones Lost in Spice* (K–3). Illus. by author. 2009, Dutton $16.99 (978-0-525-47965-9). Unpaged. Skippyjon has a zany adventure to Mars, which includes a sock-monkey tug-of-war and the discovery that the planet is covered with chili powder. (Rev: SLJ 11/1/09)

503 Schmid, Paul. *Hugs from Pearl* (PS–K). Illus. by author. 2011, HarperCollins $14.99 (978-0-06-180434-2). Unpaged. Hug-loving Pearl the porcupine finds an inventive way to get all the affection she needs without hurting anyone. (Rev: SLJ 11/1/11)

504 Schwartz, Roslyn. *The Vole Brothers* (PS–2). Illus. by author. 2011, OwlKids $16.95 (978-1-926818-83-2). Unpaged. Two vole brothers smell a delicious slice of pizza, but discover there's stiff competition for this prize; this well-illustrated book includes lots of onomatopoeia. (Rev: LMC 1–2/12; SLJ 8/1/11)

505 Scotton, Rob. *Secret Agent Splat!* (PS–1). Illus. by author. 2012, HarperCollins $16.99 (978-0061978-71-

5). 40pp. Splat the Cat sets out to discover who's been stealing his toy ducks in this brightly illustrated, humorous story. ♪ (Rev: BLO 4/15/12; SLJ 6/1/12)

506 Scotton, Rob. *Splish, Splash, Splat!* (PS–1). Illus. by author. 2011, HarperCollins $16.99 (978-0-06-197868-5); LB $17.89 (978-0-06-197869-2). Unpaged. At-odds cat friends Splat and Spike find common ground in their shared hatred of water in this comic story. (Rev: SLJ 8/1/11)

507 Segal, John. *Pirates Don't Take Baths* (PS–K). Illus. by author. 2011, Philomel $16.99 (978-0-399-25425-3). 32pp. A stubborn young pig devises on one fantasy scenario after another in order to avoid getting a bath. (Rev: BL 7/11; SLJ 3/1/11)

508 Sendak, Maurice. *Bumble-Ardy* (PS–2). Illus. by author. 2011, HarperCollins $17.95 (978-0-06-205198-1). 40pp. A little piggy hosts a raucous birthday party for himself after his aunt goes off to work. (Rev: BL 7/11; SLJ 8/1/11*)

509 Shaw, Hannah. *School for Bandits* (PS–1). Illus. by author. 2011, Knopf $16.99 (978-0-375-86768-2); LB $19.99 (978-0-375-96768-9). 32pp. Ralph the Raccoon is just too nice and is sent off to bandit school by his well-meaning parents, who just want him to be more like the other raccoons. ℮ Lexile AD610L (Rev: BL 8/11*; SLJ 8/1/11)

510 Shea, Bob. *Oh, Daddy!* (PS–K). Illus. by author. 2010, HarperCollins $16.99 (978-0-06-173080-1). 40pp. A young hippo shows his dad how to accomplish everyday tasks such as getting dressed, watering flowers, and opening a car door. (Rev: BL 2/15/10; SLJ 4/1/10*)

511 Shields, Gillian. *When the World Was Waiting for You* (PS). Illus. by Anna Currey. 2011, Bloomsbury $14.99 (978-1-59990-531-0); LB $15.89 (978-1-59990-532-7). Unpaged. A rabbit family eagerly awaits the arrival of its newest member. (Rev: SLJ 7/11)

512 Sierra, Judy. *We Love Our School!* (PS–1). Illus. by Linda Davick. 2011, Knopf $7.99 (978-0-375-86728-6); LB $10.99 (978-0-375-96728-3). 24pp. Frog, Duck, Mouse, and Snail celebrate everything they love about their school on their first day of classes in this book with rhyming text and rebus pictures. (Rev: BL 6/1/11; SLJ 6/11)

513 Sierra, Judy. *ZooZical* (PS–2). Illus. by Marc Brown. 2011, Knopf $17.99 (978-0-375-86847-4). 40pp. A city zoo's cast of animal characters decides to put on a musical to get themselves through the dark, lonely winter. (Rev: BL 7/11; SLJ 7/11)

514 Smee, Nicola. *What's the Matter, Bunny Blue?* (PS). Illus. by author. 2010, Boxer $14.95 (978-1-906250-91-1). 32pp. With help from other animals, Bunny Blue searches for his missing grandmother. (Rev: BL 3/1/10; SLJ 4/1/10)

515 Smith, Alex T. *Foxy and Egg* (K–2). Illus. by author. 2011, Holiday House $17.95 (978-0-8234-2330-9). 32pp. Foxy has evil plans when she offers Egg a place to stay the night, but gets her comeuppance when the egg hatches not a chicken but an alligator. (Rev: BL 3/15/11; SLJ 3/1/11)

516 Smith, Alex T. *Home* (PS–2). Illus. by author. 2010, ME Media/Tiger Tales $15.95 (978-1-58925-088-8). 32pp. In this zany fantasy, four animal friends take parts of their collective home to disparate locations in order to pursue their dreams, only to realize how lonely they are without each other. (Rev: BLO 6/10; LMC 8–9/10; SLJ 5/1/10)

517 Spinelli, Eileen. *A Big Boy Now* (PS–2). Illus. by Megan Lloyd. 2012, HarperCollins $16.99 (978-006008673-2). 32pp. A young rabbit proud of his growing accomplishments gets carried away and pulls the training wheels off his bike, learning a lesson in the process. (Rev: BL 2/1/12; SLJ 1/12)

518 Spinelli, Eileen. *Buzz* (PS–1). Illus. by Vincent Nguyen. 2010, Simon & Schuster $15.99 (978-1-4169-4925-1). 32pp. A newspaper headline leads Buzz the bumblebee to doubt her flying abilities, but an emergency proves that she has no problems. (Rev: BL 6/10; LMC 10/10; SLJ 6/1/10)

519 Spinelli, Eileen. *Miss Fox's Class Earns a Field Trip* (K–3). Illus. by Anne Kennedy. 2010, Whitman $16.99 (978-0-8075-5169-1). 32pp. Miss Fox's class encounters setbacks — involving a certain visiting author — as it works toward its goal of raising $135 for a field trip to a roller coaster park in this funny book involving addition and subtraction. (Rev: BL 4/15/10; SLJ 4/1/10)

520 Spinelli, Eileen. *Miss Fox's Class Shapes Up* (K–3). Illus. by Anne Kennedy. 2011, Whitman $16.99 (978-0-8075-5171-4). 32pp. Miss Fox helps her class to become more healthy — eating properly, sleeping well, and exercising more. Lexile AD500L (Rev: BL 8/11; SLJ 7/11)

521 Stamp, Jorgen. *Flying High* (K–2). Illus. by author. 2009, Enchanted Lion $16.95 (978-1-59270-089-9). Unpaged. An ambitious and ungenerous giraffe is more appreciative of his turtle friend after his airplane crashes into the water. (Rev: LMC 11–12/09; SLJ 9/1/09)

522 Stead, Philip Christian. *A Sick Day for Amos McGee* (PS–2). Illus. by Erin E. Stead. 2010, Roaring Brook $16.99 (978-1-59643-402-8). 32pp. When the animals' favorite zookeeper is out sick with a cold, they ride the city bus to his house to take care of him. Caldecott Medal. (Rev: BL 5/1/10; LMC 8–9/10; SLJ 5/1/10)

523 Stein, David Ezra. *Interrupting Chicken* (PS–3). Illus. by author. 2010, Candlewick $16.99 (978-0-7636-4168-9). 40pp. A rooster papa attempts to read fairy tales to his young daughter, who keeps interrupting the stories — which include Hansel and Gretel and Chicken Little — to intervene and save the characters from their fates. Caldecott Honor Book. Lexile AD300L (Rev: BL 9/15/10; LMC 11–12/10; SLJ 7/1/10)

524 Stein, David Ezra. *Love, Mouserella* (PS–1). Illus. by author. 2011, Penguin $15.99 (978-0-399-25410-9). 32pp. Mouserella writes a heartfelt letter to her grandmouse in this book formatted like a letter on a pad and including drawings and photographs. (Rev: BL 11/1/11; SLJ 10/1/11)

525 Stevens, April. *Edwin Speaks Up* (PS–1). Illus. by Sophie Blackall. 2011, Random House $16.99 (978-0-375-85337-1). 40pp. A babbling baby ferret's jumbled rambles hold the key to remembering important items during the family's trip to the grocery store. (Rev: BL 5/1/11; SLJ 7/11*)

526 Stileman, Kali. *Roly-Poly Egg* (PS–2). Illus. by author. 2011, ME Media/Tiger Tales $12.95 (978-1-58925-852-5). 32pp. Splotch the bird is careless in her excitement over her new, perfect egg, and it rolls off to have scary adventures before finally returning to her intact and hatching a polka-dot blue chick; dotted lines make the egg's travels easy to follow. (Rev: BLO 5/1/11; SLJ 5/1/11)

527 Stoeke, Janet Morgan. *Pip's Trip* (PS–K). Illus. by author. 2012, Dial $16.99 (978-080373708-2). 32pp. Pip the chicken hitches a solitary ride on the farm's truck when hen pals Midge and Dot are too scared, but Pip is secretly relieved when the truck goes nowhere. Lexile AD210L (Rev: BL 1/1/12; SLJ 1/12)

528 Storms, Patricia. *The Pirate and the Penguin* (PS–2). Illus. by author. 2009, OwlKids $16.95 (978-1-897349-67-0). 32pp. A pirate and penguin, both seeking an escape from their dissatisfying lives, have a chance encounter amid the ice floes and swap identities — with hilarious, happily-ever-after results. (Rev: BL 1/1/10; LMC 1–2/10; SLJ 11/1/09)

529 Sutton, Jane. *Don't Call Me Sidney* (K–2). Illus. by Renata Gallio. 2010, Dial $16.99 (978-0-8037-2753-3). 32pp. Unhappy that his name only rhymes with "kidney," Sidney the pig experiments with being Joe until finally settling for Sid. (Rev: BL 6/10; LMC 11–12/10; SLJ 6/1/10)

530 Taylor, Sean. *Huck Runs Amuck!* (PS–3). Illus. by Peter H. Reynolds. 2011, Dial $16.99 (978-0-8037-3261-2). 48pp. Huck the goat has a huge appetite for flowers and when he finds himself in the town of North Skettyfolk, he sees flowers in unexpected places. (Rev: BL 5/1/11; SLJ 5/1/11)

531 Taylor, Sean. *The Ring Went Zing! A Story That Ends with a Kiss* (PS–2). Illus. by Jill Barton. 2010, Dial $16.99 (978-0-8037-3311-4). 40pp. A funny cumulative tale in which a frog presents his chicken love with a golden ring that falls to the ground and rolls away, followed by a growing procession of helpful animals. (Rev: LMC 11–12/10; SLJ 7/1/10)

532 Taylor, Thomas. *Little Mouse and the Big Cupcake* (PS–K). Illus. by Jill Barton. 2010, Boxer $16.95 (978-1-907152-47-4). 32pp. Little Mouse asks his animal friends to help him get a monstrous cupcake home — and they do help, but not quite as he envisaged. (Rev: BL 12/1/10; LMC 3–4/11; SLJ 12/1/10)

533 Teague, Mark. *Firehouse!* (PS–K). Illus. by author. 2010, Scholastic $16.99 (978-0-439-91500-7). 32pp. Lovable but scatterbrained bulldog Edward and his sensible cousin Judy visit a firehouse and learn about procedures there from the Dalmatian firefighters. (Rev: BL 5/15/10; SLJ 7/1/10)

534 Teckentrup, Britta. *Little Wolf's Song* (PS–2). Illus. by author. 2010, Boxer $16.95 (978-1-907152-33-7). 32pp. A young wolf impatiently waits for his voice to develop so he can join his family in howling; when he gets lost in the woods, his wish is granted. (Rev: BL 10/1/10; SLJ 11/1/10)

535 Tellegen, Toon. *Letters to Anyone and Everyone* (PS–3). Illus. by Jessica Ahlberg. 2010, Sterling $12.95 (978-1-906250-95-9). 156pp. First published in the Netherlands, this is a whimsical and compelling collection of stories in which animals communicate with each other by letter. (Rev: BL 5/15/10; LMC 5–6/10; SLJ 4/1/10)

536 Thompson, Lauren. *Leap Back Home to Me* (PS–K). Illus. by Matthew Cordell. 2011, Simon & Schuster $15.99 (978-1-4169-0664-3). 32pp. A frog encourages her young one to leap higher and higher, farther and farther, and is always there for him when he comes home. **e** (Rev: BL 4/1/11; SLJ 3/1/11)

537 Tseng, Kevin. *Ned's New Home* (PS–1). Illus. by author. 2009, Tricycle $14.99 (978-1-58246-297-4). Unpaged. Ned the worm finds himself in need of a new home when the apple he's living in begins to decompose. (Rev: LMC 1–2/10; SLJ 9/1/09)

538 Tucker, Lindy. *Porkelia: A Pig's Tale* (PS–2). Illus. by author. 2011, Charlesbridge $9.95 (978-1-934133-28-6). Unpaged. Porkelia is an ambitious pig and heads for New York City with dreams of becoming a Rockette — and it all comes true. (Rev: BL 5/1/11; SLJ 4/11)

539 Twohy, Mike. *Poindexter Makes a Friend* (PS–1). Illus. by author. 2011, Simon & Schuster $15.99 (978-1-4424-0965-1). 32pp. Shy Poindexter the pig makes friends with a bashful turtle called Shelby, and together the two read books to their stuffed animals. **e** Lexile AD740L (Rev: BL 4/1/11; SLJ 4/11*)

540 Underwood, Deborah. *A Balloon for Isabel* (PS–1). Illus. by Laura Rankin. 2010, Greenwillow $16.99 (978-0-06-177987-9). 32pp. It's graduation day and every animal will receive a balloon — except the porcupines. Can Isabel find a solution? Lexile AD510L (Rev: BL 4/15/10; SLJ 4/1/10)

541 Urbanovic, Jackie. *Sitting Duck* (PS–2). Illus. by author. 2010, HarperCollins $17.99 (978-0-06-176583-4); LB $18.89 (978-0-06-176584-1). 40pp. Max the Duck gets in over his head when he offers to babysit a rambunctious puppy. (Rev: BL 5/1/10; SLJ 5/1/10)

542 Van Lieshout, Maria. *Hopper and Wilson* (PS–2). Illus. by author. 2011, Philomel $16.99 (978-0-399-25184-9). 40pp. An elephant and a mouse set off in a boat to discover the end of the world, weather a storm, become separated, and are finally reunited. (Rev: BLO 7/11; SLJ 7/11)

543 Van Patter, Bruce. *Tucker Took It!* (PS–1). 2010, Boyds Mills $16.95 (978-1-59078-698-7). Unpaged. Tucker the goat is automatically blamed when various articles of clothing go missing on the farm, but in fact he's not eating them but rather creating a scarecrow. (Rev: LMC 5–6/10; SLJ 4/1/10)

544 Verburg, Bonnie. *The Kiss Box* (PS–K). Illus. by Henry Cole. 2011, Scholastic $16.99 (978-0-545-11284-0). 32pp. A mama bear and her little one prepare to be apart for the afternoon by talking about it and sharing kisses. (Rev: BL 12/15/11; SLJ 10/1/11)

545 Vere, Ed. *Banana!* (PS–2). Illus. by author. 2010, Henry Holt $12.99 (978-0-8050-9214-1). Unpaged. This nearly wordless book (the only words are "banana" and "please") features two monkeys, one banana, and the idea of sharing. (Rev: LMC 3–4/11; SLJ 11/1/10)

546 Villeneuve, Anne. *The Red Scarf* (K–2). Illus. by author. 2010, Tundra $17.95 (978-0-88776-989-4). 40pp. In this lively, nearly wordless, adventure, good-natured taxi driver Turpin (a white mole) finds himself taking part in a circus in his efforts to return a scarf left in his cab. (Rev: BL 1/1/10; SLJ 1/1/10)

547 Waddell, Martin. *Captain Small Pig* (PS–K). Illus. by Susan Varley. 2010, Peachtree $15.95 (978-1-56145-519-5). 32pp. Old Goat and Turkey agree to go for a row on Blue Lake with Small Pig, whose whims they indulge despite their impracticality. (Rev: BL 2/15/10*; SLJ 3/1/10)

548 Wallace, Nancy Elizabeth. *Look! Look! Look! at Sculpture* (K–3). Illus. by author. 2012, Marshall Cavendish $17.99 (978-076146132-6). 40pp. Three mice sneak into an art museum and find themselves inspired by the range of sculpture styles they see, deciding to create their own. (Rev: BL 4/15/12; SLJ 4/1/12)

549 Wallace, Nancy Elizabeth. *Pond Walk* (PS–3). Illus. by author. 2011, Marshall Cavendish $17.99 (978-0-7614-5816-6). 40pp. Buddy Bear and his mother spend a quiet day sketching and observing nature at a pond. **e** (Rev: BL 3/15/11; SLJ 4/11)

550 Walsh, Ellen Stoll. *Balancing Act* (PS–K). Illus. by author. 2010, Simon & Schuster $16.99 (978-1-4424-0757-2). 32pp. Two mice enjoying a seesaw made of a stick and a rock are joined by other animals who cause balancing problems until eventually the whole thing collapses. **e** Lexile AD110L (Rev: BL 8/10; HB 9–10/10; SLJ 8/1/10)

551 Watt, Mélanie. *Scaredy Squirrel Has a Birthday Party* (K–2). Illus. by author. 2011, Kids Can $16.95 (978-1-55453-468-5). Unpaged. Scaredy Squirrel plans to celebrate his birthday in solitary fashion as usual, but his friends have other ideas. (Rev: SLJ 5/1/11)

552 Wells, Rosemary. *Yoko Learns to Read* (PS–1). Illus. by author. 2012, Hyperion $15.99 (978-142313823-5). 32pp. The Japanese American kitten only has three books at home and they are all in Japanese — how will she learn to read English? A teacher and librarian help out. (Rev: BL 12/15/11; SLJ 2/1/12)

553 Wells, Rosemary. *Yoko's Show-and-Tell* (PS–1). Illus. by author. 2010, Hyperion $15.99 (978-1-4231-1955-5). 40pp. Against her mother's wishes, Yoko the cat brings her antique doll to school for show and tell, where the doll is tossed around and broken; fortunately, the doll is repaired and all is made well in the end. (Rev: BL 4/15/10; SLJ 7/1/10)

554 Wheeler, Lisa. *Dino-Baseball* (PS–2). Illus. by Barry Gott. 2010, Carolrhoda LB $16.95 (978-0-7613-4429-2). 32pp. The Rib-Eye Reds (carnivores) compete with the Green Sox (herbivores) in this action-packed rhyming romp. Also use *Dino-Basketball* (2011). (Rev: BL 3/1/10; SLJ 4/1/10)

555 Wheeler, Lisa. *Ugly Pie* (PS–2). Illus. by Heather Solomon. 2010, Harcourt $16 (978-0-15-216754-7). 32pp. Ol' Bear collects unwanted ingredients from his friends and bakes a delicious Ugly Pie, which his friends happily help him eat; includes a recipe. Lexile AD670L (Rev: BL 7/10; HB 7–8/10; SLJ 7/1/10)

556 Wiesner, David. *Art and Max* (K–3). Illus. by author. 2010, Clarion $17.99 (978-0-618-75663-6). 40pp. Max's artistic aspirations have unexpected results in this compelling story about two lizard friends. (Rev: BL 10/15/10*; HB 11–12/10; LMC 1–2/11; SLJ 9/1/10*)

557 Willems, Mo. *Can I Play Too?* (PS–2). Illus. by author. Series: Elephant and Piggie. 2010, Hyperion $8.99 (978-1-4231-1991-3). 64pp. Gerald the elephant and Piggie are playing catch — but can their armless new friend Snake join in? Lexile 70L (Rev: BLO 7/10; SLJ 8/1/10)

558 Willems, Mo. *Cat the Cat, Who Is That?* (PS–1). Illus. by author. 2010, HarperCollins $12.99 (978-0-06-172840-2); LB $14.89 (978-0-06-172841-9). 32pp. Readers are introduced to a bright and outgoing cast of animal characters by the likable and effervescent Cat the Cat. (Rev: BL 3/15/10; HB 5–6/10; SLJ 2/1/10)

559 Willems, Mo. *Happy Pig Day!* (PS–1). Illus. by author. Series: Elephant and Piggie. 2011, Hyperion $8.99 (978-1-4231-4342-0). 64pp. Gerald the elephant feels left out while his friend Piggie celebrates Pig Day with his porcine friends; in the end, however, Gerald realizes he can participate as well. (Rev: BL 10/15/11; SLJ 11/1/11)

560 Willems, Mo. *I Am Going!* (PS–2). Illus. by author. Series: Elephant and Piggie. 2010, Hyperion $8.99 (978-1-4231-1990-6). 64pp. Gerald the elephant gets severe separation anxiety when best friend Piggie announces she is leaving. (Rev: BL 12/15/09; SLJ 6/1/10)

561 Willems, Mo. *I Broke My Trunk!* (PS–2). Illus. by author. Series: Elephant and Piggie. 2011, Hyperion $8.99 (978-1-4231-3309-4). 64pp. Gerald the elephant tries to explain to Piggie the rather complicated story of how his trunk got broken. (Rev: BL 4/15/11; SLJ 5/1/11*)

562 Willems, Mo. *Listen to My Trumpet!* (PS–1). Illus. by author. Series: Elephant and Piggie. 2012, Hyperion $8.99 (978-142315404-4). 64pp. When Gerald the elephant summons the heart to tell Piggie her new trumpet makes an awful racket, she responds with grace and humor. (Rev: BL 2/1/12; SLJ 4/1/12*)

563 Willems, Mo. *Pigs Make Me Sneeze!* (PS–1). Illus. by author. Series: Elephant and Piggie. 2009, Hyperion $8.99 (978-1-4231-1411-6). 64pp. Convinced he must be allergic to his friend Piggie, Gerald the elephant is relieved when the doctor informs him the sniffles are only a cold. (Rev: BL 12/1/09; SLJ 12/1/09*)

564 Willems, Mo. *We Are in a Book!* (PS–2). Illus. by author. Series: Elephant and Piggie. 2010, Hyperion $8.99 (978-1-4231-3308-7). 64pp. In their latest clever adventure, Gerald the elephant and Piggie realize that they are in a book and someone is reading about them. (Rev: BL 9/15/10; LMC 3–4/11; SLJ 11/1/10*)

565 Wilson, Karma. *The Cow Loves Cookies* (PS–2). Illus. by Marcellus Hall. 2010, Simon & Schuster $16.99 (978-1-4169-4206-1). 40pp. The animals on the farm have very different tastes in food, but it's only the cow who likes cookies — why? (Rev: BL 4/15/10; LMC 8–9/10; SLJ 8/1/10)

566 Wilson, Karma. *Hogwash!* (PS–1). Illus. by Jim McMullan. 2011, Little, Brown $16.99 (978-0-316-98840-7). 40pp. A mud bath is in the future for a farmer determined to give his reluctant pigs a wash; humorous illustrations add to the fun. (Rev: BL 6/1/11; SLJ 4/11)

567 Wishinsky, Frieda. *Maggie Can't Wait* (PS–1). Illus. by Dean Griffiths. 2009, Fitzhenry & Whiteside $17.95 (978-1-55455-103-3). 32pp. A little cat girl is excited about the kitten her family is planning to adopt but this joy is deflated by her friends' lack of enthusiasm about the baby's picture. (Rev: BLO 11/15/09; SLJ 4/1/10)

568 Wood, Audrey. *Piggy Pie Po* (PS–K). Illus. by author. 2010, Harcourt $16.99 (978-0-15-202494-9). 32pp. Piggy Pie Po is a messy, rambunctious, happy-go-lucky piglet in these three rhyming and exuberant vignettes. ℮ (Rev: BL 6/10; SLJ 8/1/10)

569 Wright, Maureen. *Sleep, Big Bear, Sleep!* (PS–1). Illus. by Will Hillenbrand. 2009, Marshall Cavendish $16.99 (978-0-7614-5560-8). Unpaged. Big Bear misunderstands Old Man Winter's instructions to hibernate in this nicely illustrated story. Also use *Sneeze, Big Bear, Sneeze* (2011). (Rev: HB 1–2/10; SLJ 9/1/09)

570 Yamaguchi, Kristi. *Dream Big, Little Pig!* (PS–1). Illus. by Tim Bowers. 2011, Sourcebooks $16.99 (978-140225275-4). 32pp. Discouraged from planning a life in ballet, persistent Poppy the pig decides to become an ice-skating star. (Rev: BL 5/1/11)

571 Yamashita, Haruo. *Seven Little Mice Go to School* (PS–2). Illus. by Kazuo Iwamura. 2011, NorthSouth $16.95 (978-0-7358-4012-6). 44pp. Seven little mice nurture different fears about the first day of school, but they gain courage as they form a Mouse Train on their way through the forest. Lexile AD500L (Rev: BL 8/11; SLJ 6/11)

572 Yamashita, Haruo. *Seven Little Mice Have Fun on the Ice* (PS–1). Illus. by Kazuo Iwamura. 2011, North-South $16.95 (978-0-7358-4048-5). Unpaged. A group of clever mouse siblings finds a way to bring their mom, known as the Ice-Fishing Princess in her youth, to the ice-fishing hole, where she ably brings in a slew of fish. (Rev: SLJ 12/1/11)

573 Yee, Wong Herbert. *Mouse and Mole, Fine Feathered Friends* (K–3). Illus. by author. Series: Mouse and Mole. 2009, Houghton Mifflin $15 (978-0-547-15222-6). 48pp. Mouse and Mole contrive a unique way to attract birds so they can observe and sketch them. Also use *Mouse and Mole: A Winter Wonderland* (2010). ℮ (Rev: BL 9/15/09; SLJ 2/1/10)

574 Yee, Wong Herbert. *A Winter Wonderland* (K–3). Illus. by author. Series: Mouse and Mole. 2010, Houghton Mifflin paper $15 (978-054734152-1). 48pp. After a contrary start, Mouse and Mole come together to enjoy a snowy day. Lexile 410L (Rev: BL 11/15/10; SLJ 11/10)

575 Yolen, Jane. *How Do Dinosaurs Say I Love You?* (PS–K). Illus. by Mark Teague. 2009, Scholastic $16.99 (978-0-545-14314-1). 40pp. Parent dinosaurs forgive their children for misbehaving in various ways. Lexile AD520L (Rev: BL 11/1/09; SLJ 10/1/09)

576 Young, Ned. *Zoomer's Summer Snowstorm* (K–2). Illus. by author. 2011, HarperCollins $16.99 (978-0-06-170092-7). 32pp. A snow-cone machine overflow turns into a hot summer day delight for pooch Zoomer and his friends. (Rev: BL 4/15/11; SLJ 5/1/11)

Realistic Stories

ADVENTURE STORIES

577 Base, Graeme. *The Legend of the Golden Snail* (2–4). Illus. by author. 2010, Abrams $19.95 (978-0-8109-8965-8). 48pp. In this inventive, compassionate story, a kind-hearted little boy sets off in search of a fantastical ship, encountering many small creatures who need his help along the way. Lexile AD690L (Rev: BL 9/15/10; LMC 1–2/11; SLJ 10/1/10)

578 Crowley, Ned. *Nanook and Pryce: Gone Fishing* (PS–2). Illus. by Larry Day. 2009, HarperCollins $17.99 (978-0-06-133641-6). 32pp. Two children and their dog drift all the way around the world on a chunk of glacial ice, having many exciting experiences. (Rev: BL 9/1/09; SLJ 1/1/10)

579 Duddle, Jonny. *The Pirates Next Door* (K–2). Illus. by author. 2012, Candlewick $15.99 (978-076365842-7). 44pp. Dull-on-Sea, a town full of staid old folks, receives a comic and surprising upset when pirates move in next door to Matilda, one of the few children. (Rev: BL 2/1/12; LMC 8–9/12*; SLJ 3/12)

580 Fleming, Candace. *Clever Jack Takes the Cake* (PS–2). Illus. by G. Brian Karas. 2010, Random House $17.99 (978-0-375-84979-4). 40pp. En route to the princess's birthday party, the cake Jack baked is slowly demolished in a series of mishaps, until all he has left to give the princess is the story of his day. Fortunately, it ends up being the best gift of all. ℮ Lexile AD600L (Rev: BL 7/10*; LMC 11–12/10; SLJ 7/1/10*)

581 Garland, Michael. *Super Snow Day Seek and Find* (2–4). Illus. by author. Series: A Look Again Book. 2010, Dutton $16.99 (978-0-525-42245-7). 32pp. A young boy follows his aunt's rhymed clues to explore a winter wonderland in this story enhanced by seek-and-find illustrations. (Rev: BL 1/1–15/11; SLJ 12/1/10)

582 Hallowell, George, and Joan Holub. *Wagons Ho!* (1–3). Illus. by Lynne Avril. 2011, Whitman $16.99 (978-0-8075-8612-9). 32pp. Two parallel stories chronicle trips from Missouri to Oregon; the one featuring Jenny in 1846 takes five months while Katie's journey in 2011 takes five days. (Rev: BL 10/1/11; SLJ 8/1/11)

583 Lamb, Albert. *The Abandoned Lighthouse* (PS–2). Illus. by David McPhail. 2011, Roaring Brook $15.99 (978-1-59643-525-4). 32pp. A bear, a boy, and a dog end up at an abandoned lighthouse, where they catch some fish, eat dinner, and have a snooze, waking up just in time to get the light working again and avert a disaster. (Rev: BL 5/1/11; SLJ 6/11)

584 Lane, Adam J. B. *Stop Thief!* (K–2). Illus. by author. 2012, Roaring Brook $16.99 (978-159643693-0). 32pp. After announcing that he's too grown up for his stuffed pig, young Randall nonetheless comes to its rescue when a burglar takes off with it and conducts a dramatic chase. (Rev: BL 5/1/12; SLJ 6/1/12)

585 Meyers, Susan. *Bear in the Air* (PS–K). Illus. by Amy June Bates. 2010, Abrams $15.95 (978-0-8109-8398-4). 32pp. A baby's teddy bear has exciting adventures after being dropped out of the pram. (Rev: BL 5/1/10; LMC 10/10; SLJ 5/1/10)

586 Quattlebaum, Mary. *Pirate vs. Pirate: The Terrific Tale of a Big, Blustery Maritime Match* (PS–2). Illus.

by Alexandra Boiger. 2011, Hyperion/Disney $16.99 (978-1-4231-2201-2). 40pp. Two pirates — Bad Bart and his female counterpart Mean Mo — battle to show who is the strongest in this buccaneer romp with humor and romance. Lexile AD510L (Rev: BL 3/1/11; LMC 8–9/11; SLJ 3/1/11)

587 Stead, Philip Christian. *Jonathan and the Big Blue Boat* (PS–2). Illus. by author. 2011, Roaring Brook $16.99 (978-1-59643-562-9). 32pp. Jonathan has a series of adventures on his worldwide quest for the teddy bear his parents have taken away. (Rev: BL 6/1/11; LMC 11–12/11; SLJ 6/11)

588 Van Camp, Katie. *CookieBot! A Harry and Horsie Adventure* (PS–1). Illus. by Lincoln Agnew. 2011, HarperCollins $16.99 (978-006197445-8). 32pp. Harry and his toy horse create a robot designed to help them get into the cookie jar, but the robot runs amok. (Rev: BL 6/1/11; SLJ 6/11)

589 Van Dusen, Chris. *Randy Riley's Really Big Hit* (1–3). Illus. by author. 2012, Candlewick $15.99 (978-076364946-3). 32pp. Gifted in both science and baseball, Randy finds a way to save his town from an encroaching fireball from space. (Rev: BL 2/1/12; LMC 8–9/12; SLJ 1/12)

COMMUNITY AND EVERYDAY LIFE

590 Addasi, Maha. *Time to Pray* (K–3). Trans. by Nuha Albitar. Illus. by Ned Gannon. 2010, Boyds Mills $17.95 (978-1-59078-611-6). 32pp. Visiting her mother in the Middle East, young Yasmin learns about various Muslim traditions that she can take home with her; with parallel text in Arabic. (Rev: BLO 10/15/10; SLJ 9/1/10)

591 Alda, Arlene. *Lulu's Piano Lesson* (K–3). Illus. by Lisa Desimini. 2010, Tundra $16.95 (978-0-88776-930-6). 32pp. Lulu's piano teacher manages to circumvent the fact the young girl has not practiced all week. (Rev: BL 8/10; SLJ 7/1/10)

592 Alsdurf, Phyllis. *It's Milking Time* (K–2). Illus. by Steve Johnson. 2012, Random House $16.99 (978-037586911-2); LB $19.99 (978-037596911-9). 40pp. A young girl helps her father with the regular, twice-daily cycle of milking in this gentle, detailed story. (Rev: BL 4/1/12; SLJ 4/1/12)

593 Ashburn, Boni. *I Had a Favorite Dress* (1–3). Illus. by Julia Denos. 2011, Abrams $16.95 (978-1-4197-0016-3). 32pp. A young girl's favorite dress is constantly refashioned as she grows and grows. (Rev: BLO 8/11; SLJ 8/1/11)

594 Aylesworth, Jim. *Cock-a-Doodle-doo, Creak, Pop-pop, Moo* (PS–1). Illus. by Brad Sneed. 2012, Holiday House $16.95 (978-082342356-9). 32pp. Rhyming text and bright illustrations show life on a farm in days gone by. (Rev: BL 4/15/12; SLJ 5/1/12)

595 Barrett, Mary Brigid. *Shoebox Sam* (1–3). Illus. by Frank Morrison. 2011, Zondervan $15.99 (978-0-310-71549-8). 32pp. Two children learn the value of generosity by watching and assisting a kindly shoe-shop proprietor. (Rev: BL 7/11; SLJ 8/1/11)

596 Barton, Chris. *Shark vs. Train* (PS–1). Illus. by Tom Lichtenheld. 2010, Little, Brown $16.99 (978-0-316-00762-7). 40pp. Two boys face-off in a spirited toy chest showdown in this wacky, imaginative story. (Rev: BL 4/15/10; SLJ 4/1/10*)

597 Bloom, Suzanne. *Feeding Friendsies* (PS). Illus. by author. 2011, Boyds Mills $16.95 (978-1-59078-529-4). Unpaged. A trio of boisterous preschoolers whip up a feast featuring mud pie and raindrop soup. (Rev: SLJ 11/1/11)

598 Bottner, Barbara. *Miss Brooks Loves Books! (And I Don't)* (PS–2). Illus. by Michael Emberley. 2010, Knopf $17.99 (978-0-375-84682-3). 40pp. William Steig's *Shrek* is the book that finally interests a 1st-grade girl in reading. ❷ (Rev: BL 3/1/10; HB 5–6/10; LMC 5–6/10; SLJ 2/1/10*)

599 Bradford, Wade. *Why Do I Have to Make My Bed? A History of Messy Rooms* (K–3). Illus. by Johanna van der Sterre. 2011, Tricycle $16.99 (978-1-58246-327-8); LB $19.99 (978-1-58246-388-9). Unpaged. A boy dubious about the merits of making a bed that's only going to get messed up again gets a history lesson from his mother on bed making — and other children's chores — through the ages. (Rev: BL 1/1–15/11; SLJ 3/1/11)

600 Brennan-Nelson, Denise. *Willow and the Snow Day Dance* (K–2). Illus. by Cyd Moore. 2010, Sleeping Bear $16.95 (978-1-58536-522-7). 32pp. Willow's grumpy and elusive neighbor doesn't respond to her attempts to include him in her friendly community activities, but he does provide her (anonymously) with a recipe for a dance to make the snow fall. ❷ (Rev: BLO 1/1–15/11; SLJ 4/11)

601 Buzzeo, Toni. *Penelope Popper Book Doctor* (1–3). Illus. by Jana Christy. 2011, Upstart $17.95 (978-1-60213-054-8). Unpaged. A little girl determined to be a doctor is guided instead toward looking after damaged books in the library. (Rev: LMC 3–4/12; SLJ 11/1/11)

602 Carle, Eric. *The Artist Who Painted a Blue Horse* (PS–2). Illus. by author. 2011, Philomel $17.99 (978-0-399-25713-1). 32pp. A young boy enjoys a playful day of painting using unexpected colors for various animals in this homage to painter Franz Marc that includes an author's note about his work. (Rev: BL 10/15/11*; HB 1–2/12; LMC 3–4/12; SLJ 10/1/11)

603 Carluccio, Maria. *I'm 3! Look What I Can Do* (PS). 2010, Henry Holt $10.99 (978-0-8050-8313-2). 24pp. A young brother and sister celebrate all the things they are able to do (eat with fork and spoon, hang up my coat . . .). (Rev: BL 7/10; SLJ 8/1/10)

604 Christensen, Bonnie. *Plant a Little Seed* (PS–1). Illus. by author. 2012, Roaring Brook $17.99 (978-159643550-6). 32pp. Tells the yearlong story of a community garden, including its resident rabbits, and its harvest; facts about plants and harvest festivals are appended. (Rev: BL 4/1/12; HB 5–6/12; LMC 10/12; SLJ 8/12)

605 Clanton, Ben. *Vote for Me!* (K–2). Illus. by author. 2012, Kids Can $16.95 (978-155453822-5). 40pp. A donkey and an elephant compete for votes in this parody of the American political process. (Rev: BL 4/1/12; LMC 10/12; SLJ 4/1/12)

606 Conahan, Carolyn. *The Big Wish* (PS–2). Illus. by author. 2011, Chronicle $16.99 (978-0-8118-7040-5). 36pp. Young Molly is nurturing her dandelions in hopes of achieving a world-record-breaking wish. (Rev: BLO 8/11; SLJ 7/11)

607 Cooper, Elisha. *Farm* (PS–3). Illus. by author. 2010, Scholastic $17.99 (978-0-545-07075-1). 48pp. Cooper portrays farm life from spring through fall, showing children and adults involved in a variety of activities. (Rev: BL 2/1/10; HB 5–6/10*; LMC 5–6/10; SLJ 3/1/10)

608 Crum, Shutta. *Mine!* (PS). Illus. by Patrice Barton. 2011, Knopf $16.99 (978-0-375-86711-8). 32pp. Two very young children and a dog learn about sharing in this almost wordless funny story. (Rev: BL 7/11; SLJ 6/11*)

609 Davis, Aubrey. *A Hen for Izzy Pippik* (K–2). Illus. by Marie Lafrance. 2012, Kids Can $16.95 (978-155453243-8). 32pp. When Shaina finds a lost hen, she looks after it, its eggs, and all the subsequent offspring, bringing prosperity to the community in the process; and when the owner of the hen returns, she offers to return the hen to everyone's dismay; based on a traditional tale. (Rev: BL 2/15/12; LMC 10/12; SLJ 5/1/12)

610 Diesen, Deborah. *The Barefooted, Bad Tempered Baby Brigade* (PS–K). Illus. by Tracy Dockray. 2010, Ten Speed/Tricycle $15.99 (978-1-58246-274-5). 32pp. Pictures of rebellious babies carrying picket signs propel this funny, rhythmic story. (Rev: BL 1/1/10; SLJ 2/1/10)

611 Doyle, Malachy. *Get Happy* (PS–1). Illus. by Caroline Uff. 2011, Walker $14.99 (978-0-8027-2271-3). 32pp. Grumble less, giggle more. Doyle offers various simple tips on enjoying life and being happy. (Rev: BL 8/11; SLJ 6/11)

612 Elya, Susan Middleton. *Fire! Fuego! Brave Bomberos* (PS–1). Illus. by Dan Santat. 2012, Bloomsbury $16.99 (978-159990461-0). 40pp. This bilingual story captures a brave team of firefighters' response to an alarm call; action-packed illustrations add energy. (Rev: BL 4/15/12)

613 Formento, Alison. *This Tree Counts!* (PS–2). Illus. by Sarah Snow. 2010, Whitman $16.99 (978-0-8075-7890-2). 32pp. Formento provides a gentle science/counting lesson about the life cycle of trees along with a story about a tree-planting elementary school class. Lexile AD480L (Rev: BL 1/1/10; LMC 5–6/10; SLJ 2/1/10)

614 French, Lisa S. *The Terrible Trash Trail: Eco-Pig Stops Pollution* (PS–2). Illus. by Barry Gott. 2009, ABDO $18.95 (978-160270663-7). 32pp. Eco-Pig wakes up to find his beautiful mountaintop town has been covered in trash. (Rev: BL 2/15/10; LMC 3–4/10)

615 Garland, Sarah. *Eddie's Toolbox and How to Make and Mend Things* (K–3). Illus. by author. 2011, Frances Lincoln $17.95 (978-1-84780-053-4). 36pp. Eddie learns lots of new skills when a new family moves in next door and needs help with simple home repairs. (Rev: BL 9/1/11; SLJ 5/1/11)

616 Goodhart, Pippa. *You Choose* (K–2). Illus. by Nick Sharratt. 2012, Kane/Miller paper $7.99 (978-161067076-0). 32pp. With spreads full of pictorial options, this book challenges young children to make choices in many areas of life — to select a pet, a dream home, a mode of transportation and so forth. (Rev: BL 4/15/12; SLJ 6/1/12)

617 Graham, Bob. *A Bus Called Heaven* (K–2). Illus. by author. 2012, Walker $16.99 (978-076365893-9). 40pp. A neighborhood comes together to help young Stella bring an abandoned bus to life with paint, yard chairs, and games; when a tow truck threatens to remove the bus, the neighbors pull together again to save it. Lexile AD570L (Rev: BL 2/15/12*; HB 5–6/12; SLJ 4/1/12)

618 Guidone, Thea. *Drum City* (PS–3). Illus. by Vanessa Newton. 2010, Tricycle $15.99 (978-1-58246-308-7). 32pp. One boy beating on a pot in his backyard snowballs into an exuberant parade of rhythm and music in this catchy story. (Rev: BL 5/15/10; LMC 1–2/11; SLJ 7/1/10)

619 Guy, Ginger Foglesong. *¡Bravo!* (PS–K). Illus. by Rene King Moreno. 2010, Greenwillow $16.99 (978-006173180-8). 32pp. A young boy and girl gather seemingly unrelated objects around their yard and find enough for an impromptu musical celebration in this brightly illustrated bilingual story. (Rev: BL 11/1/10; SLJ 9/10)

620 Harper, Charise Mericle. *Henry's Heart: A Boy, His Heart, and a New Best Friend* (K–2). Illus. by author. 2011, Henry Holt $16.99 (978-080508989-9). 40pp. Heartbroken when he is denied a puppy, sad young Henry is taken to the doctor — who prescribes a dog! With factual information about the heart. Lexile AD420L (Rev: BLO 11/15/11; LMC 1–2/12; SLJ 11/11)

621 Harper, Jamie. *Miles to Go* (PS–K). Illus. by author. 2010, Candlewick $12.99 (978-0-7636-3598-5). 32pp. Preschooler Miles drives his play car down the driveway, along the street, and down the sidewalk to school. (Rev: BL 12/15/10; SLJ 5/1/11)

622 Harper, Jessica. *I Barfed on Mrs. Kenly* (K–3). Illus. by Jon Berkeley. Series: Uh-Oh, Cleo. 2010, Putnam $14.99 (978-039924673-9). 64pp. Cleo gets carsick on the way to a friend's birthday party, but Mrs. Kenley is kind about it despite the mess on her fur coat and encourages Cleo to show off her diving skills. (Rev: BLO 11/1/09; HB 3–4/10)

623 Heller, Linda. *How Dalia Put a Big Yellow Comforter Inside a Tiny Blue Box: And Other Wonders of Tzedakah* (K–3). Illus. by Stacey Dressen McQueen. 2011, Tricycle $16.99 (978-1-58246-378-0); LB $19.99 (978-1-58246-402-2). 32pp. The Jewish tradition of *tzedakah* boxes is illustrated as Dalia shows her younger brother Yossi about helping those in need. (Rev: BLO 8/11; HB 9–10/11; SLJ 7/11)

624 Hest, Amy. *When You Meet a Bear on Broadway* (PS–1). Illus. by Elivia Savadier. 2009, Farrar $16.99 (978-0-374-40015-6). 40pp. A young girl encounters a sad and lost bear cub in the middle of the city, and orchestrates a happy reunion with its mama. (Rev: BL 11/1/09*; SLJ 10/1/09)

625 Hilb, Nora, and Sharon Jennings. *Wiggle Giggle Tickle Train* (PS–K). Illus. by Nora Hilb. Photos by Marcela Cabezas Hilb. 2009, Annick $19.95 (978-1-55451-210-2); paper $8.95 (978-1-55451-209-6). Unpaged. Readers enjoy seeing a group of children playing at various games throughout the day, with appealing images paired with bouncy rhyming text. (Rev: BL 10/15/09; SLJ 12/1/09)

626 Hubbell, Patricia. *Check It Out! Reading, Finding, Helping* (PS–1). Illus. by Nancy Speir. 2011, Marshall Cavendish $16.99 (978-076145803-6). 32pp. With simple rhyming text, this book introduces the work of a children's librarian and shows how they inspire young people to read. (Rev: BLO 3/14/11; LMC 8–9/11; SLJ 3/11)

627 Hubbell, Patricia. *Snow Happy!* (PS–1). Illus. by Hiroe Nakata. 2010, Tricycle $15.99 (978-1-58246-329-2). 32pp. A group of neighborhood children enjoy a snow day in this bouncy story with dynamic illustrations. (Rev: BL 10/15/10; SLJ 10/1/10)

628 Hughes, Shirley. *Don't Want to Go!* (PS). Illus. by author. 2010, Candlewick $16.99 (978-0-7636-5091-9). 32pp. Furious at having to spend the day at a friend's house, young Lily eventually comes around and enjoys herself; when the day is done, she doesn't want to leave. (Rev: BL 10/1/10; SLJ 11/1/10*)

629 Janovitz, Marilyn. *Play Baby Play!* (PS). Illus. by author. 2012, Sourcebooks $7.99 (978-140226224-1). 24pp. A baby attends play group and enjoys playing with the other babies in this simple, rhymed story. (Rev: BLO 4/15/12; SLJ 5/1/12)

630 Javernick, Ellen. *What If Everybody Did That?* (K–2). Illus. by Collen M. Madden. 2010, Marshall Cavendish $12.99 (978-0-7614-5686-5). Unpaged. In this character education story, a boy is encouraged to think before acting impulsively through a series of scenarios. (Rev: LMC 8–9/10; SLJ 4/1/10)

631 Juster, Norton. *Neville* (PS–3). Illus. by G. Brian Karas. 2011, Random House $17.99 (978-0-375-86765-1). 32pp. A young boy anxious about starting over in a new neighborhood finds a simple way to involve the whole community in a compelling hunt for the mysterious "Neville." **❦** Lexile AD600L (Rev: BL 10/15/11*; HB 9–10/11; LMC 11–12/11; SLJ 9/1/11*)

632 Karas, G. Brian. *The Village Garage* (PS–3). Illus. by author. 2010, Henry Holt $16.99 (978-0-8050-8716-1). 32pp. This look at a village garage crew through the seasons as they deal with various challenges and use different machines. (Rev: BL 4/15/10; SLJ 6/1/10)

633 Kittinger, Jo S. *The House on Dirty-Third Street* (K–3). Illus. by Thomas Gonzalez. 2012, Peachtree $16.95 (978-156145619-2). 32pp. A young girl's prayer for her mother to keep the faith in restoring their rundown house results in the church congregation pitching in to help. (Rev: BL 2/15/12; SLJ 4/1/12)

634 Kooser, Ted. *Bag in the Wind* (1–3). Illus. by Barry Root. 2010, Candlewick $17.99 (978-076363001-0). 48pp. This thoughtful, and nicely illustrated, story about the life cycle of a simple plastic grocery bag offers messages about ecology, economy, and the importance of recycling. ☊ (Rev: BL 1/1/10; LMC 5–6/10; SLJ 1/10)

635 Kooser, Ted. *House Held Up by Trees* (K–3). Illus. by Jon Klassen. 2012, Candlewick $16.99 (978-076365107-7). 32pp. As a house abandoned by its former proud owners slowly falls apart, trees grow up around it, ultimately saving it and holding it aloft. (Rev: BL 2/15/12*; HB 3–4/12; LMC 8–9/12; SLJ 5/1/12)

636 Lee, Spike, and Tonya Lewis Lee. *Giant Steps to Change the World* (2–5). Illus. by Sean Qualls. 2011, Simon & Schuster $16.99 (978-0-689-86815-3). 40pp. With motivational quotations from various luminaries, spreads with colorful illustrations and poetic text profile people who have made significant contributions and encourage young people to follow in their footsteps. (Rev: BL 2/1/11; LMC 5–6/11; SLJ 2/1/11)

637 Lewis, J. Patrick. *The Fantastic 5 and 10¢ Store: A Rebus Adventure* (1–2). Illus. by Valorie Fisher. 2010, Random House $17.99 (978-0-375-85878-9); LB $20.99 (978-0-375-95878-6). Unpaged. This story about a store with many magical goods makes good use of rebuses and rhyming wordplay. (Rev: BL 10/1/10; LMC 1–2/11; SLJ 5/1/11)

638 London, Jonathan. *I'm a Truck Driver* (PS–1). Illus. by David Parkins. 2010, Henry Holt $12.99 (978-0-8050-7989-0). 32pp. Different kinds of trucks, from street sweepers to garbage trucks, are introduced in appealing illustrations and simple rhymes. (Rev: BL 5/1/10; SLJ 7/1/10)

639 McClure, Nikki. *To Market, to Market* (PS–3). Illus. by author. 2011, Abrams $17.95 (978-0-8109-9738-7). 40pp. Tasked with gathering the items on a shopping list, a mother and son visit one farmer's market stall after another and learn about the farmers and techniques that produced these goods. (Rev: BL 4/1/11; LMC 8–9/11; SLJ 4/11)

640 McGhee, Alison. *So Many Days* (PS–3). Illus. by Taeeun Yoo. 2010, Atheneum $15.99 (978-1-4169-5857-4). 40pp. A child and a dog explore their world as a narrator emphasizes all the opportunities that await us in life. Lexile AD420L (Rev: BL 2/1/10; SLJ 3/1/10)

641 McGowan, Michael. *Sunday Is for God* (1–3). Illus. by Steve Johnson. 2010, Random House $17.99 (978-0-375-84188-0); LB $20.99 (978-0-375-94591-5). 40pp. A young African American boy describes how he spends his Sundays, some of them enjoyable and others a bit trying, but offering opportunity for imagination. (Rev: BL 11/15/09; SLJ 1/1/10)

642 Macken, JoAnn Early. *Waiting Out the Storm* (PS–2). Illus. by Susan Gaber. 2010, Candlewick $15.99 (978-0-7636-3378-3). 32pp. With striking, impressionistic illustrations and gentle text; this book follows a mother and daughter as they retreat inside when a storm arrives and discuss how the animals manage to keep safe. (Rev: BL 1/1/10*; LMC 5–6/10; SLJ 4/1/10)

643 Manushkin, Fran. *The Belly Book* (PS). Illus. by Dan Yaccarino. 2011, Feiwel & Friends $16.99 (978-0-312-64958-6). 32pp. This playful book celebrates the human midsection — belly buttons, stomachs, perfect for belly-flopping, and so on. (Rev: BLO 11/15/11; SLJ 12/1/11)

644 Martin, Amy. *Symphony City* (1–3). Illus. by author. 2011, McSweeney's $17.95 (978-1-936365-39-5). 48pp. A young girl gets separated from her adult escort en route to a concert in the city and decides to follow the sound of music, discovering in the process that there is music everywhere. (Rev: BLO 8/11; LMC 5–6/12; SLJ 11/1/11)

645 Meng, Cece. *I Will Not Read This Book* (K–2). Illus. by Joy Ang. 2011, Clarion $16.99 (978-0-547-04971-7). 32pp. A charming reluctant reader outlines all the things he will do to avoid reading this book. (Rev: BL 9/1/11; SLJ 11/1/11)

646 Muldrow, Diane. *We Planted a Tree* (K–3). Illus. by Bob Staake. 2010, Good Books $17.99 (978-0-375-86432-2). 40pp. Nature, conservation, and family life are celebrated in this story of families around the world planting trees and the benefits these trees bring to them and to the environment. (Rev: BL 2/15/10; LMC 5–6/10; SLJ 3/1/10)

647 Murphy, Stuart J. *Freda Is Found* (PS–K). Illus. by Tim Jones Illustration. Series: Stuart J. Murphy's I See I Learn. 2011, Charlesbridge $14.95 (978-1-58089-462-3); paper $6.95 (978-1-58089-463-0). Unpaged.

This story of a young girl seeking help when she finds herself lost offers good advice on safety and decision-making. **e** (Rev: SLJ 7/11)

648 Nevius, Carol. *Soccer Hour* (1–3). Illus. by Bill Thomson. 2011, Marshall Cavendish $16.99 (978-0-7614-5689-6). 32pp. A child narrator tells readers all about what takes place at a soccer practice session in this simple story. (Rev: BL 6/1/11; SLJ 4/11)

649 Newman, Leslea. *Miss Tutu's Star* (PS–2). Illus. by Carey Armstrong-Ellis. 2010, Abrams $16.95 (978-0-8109-8396-0). 32pp. A reassuring ballet teacher coaches anxious but passionate Selena through her first recital in this colorful story told in rhyming couplets. (Rev: BL 9/1/10; LMC 11–12/10; SLJ 8/1/10)

650 Omololu, Cynthia Jaynes. *When It's Six O'Clock in San Francisco: A Trip Through Time Zones* (K–3). Illus. by Randy DuBurke. 2009, Clarion $16 (978-0-618-76827-1). 32pp. This story shows children around the world conducting activities appropriate to their time zones. (Rev: BL 9/15/09; SLJ 10/1/09)

651 Patricelli, Leslie. *Tubby* (PS). Illus. by author. 2010, Candlewick $6.99 (978-0-7636-4567-0). Unpaged. A bald, smiling baby has a wonderful time in the bathtub (barring a small incident when soap gets in an eye) in this appealing board book. Also use *Potty* (2010). (Rev: HB 1–2/11; SLJ 1/1/11)

652 Pearson, Susan. *How to Teach a Slug to Read* (K–2). Illus. by David Slonim. 2011, Marshall Cavendish $16.99 (978-0-7614-5805-0). 32pp. With appealing, cartoonish illustrations, this is a quirky guide to how to teaching slugs, with advice to read out loud, choose favorite poems, explain vocabulary, and be patient. (Rev: BLO 2/15/11; SLJ 5/1/11)

653 Peschke, Marci. *Blueberry Queen* (K–2). Illus. by Tuesday Mourning. Series: Kylie Jean. 2011, Picture Window LB $21.32 (978-1-4048-6756-7); paper $4.95 (978-1-4048-6615-7). 112pp. Kylie Jean aspires to be the Blueberry Festival Pageant queen in this story set in Texas. Also use *Drama Queen* (2011). (Rev: LMC 10/11; SLJ 7/11)

654 Piven, Hanoch. *My Best Friend Is as Sharp as a Pencil* (K–3). Illus. by author. 2010, Random House $17.99 (978-0-375-85338-8); LB $20.99 (978-0-375-95629-4). 40pp. A girl uses collages and sculptures to answer her grandmother's questions about school in this inventive story. **e** (Rev: BL 3/1/10; LMC 8–9/10; SLJ 4/1/10)

655 Plourde, Lynn. *Field Trip Day* (PS–2). Illus. by Thor Wickstrom. 2010, Dutton $16.99 (978-0-525-47994-9). 40pp. A rollicking (and quite mathematical) look at organic farming through Mrs. Shepherd's class and the vocal and wayward student named Juan. Lexile 1050 (Rev: BL 1/1/10; LMC 5–6/10; SLJ 3/1/10)

656 Polacco, Patricia. *Bun Bun Button* (PS–2). Illus. by author. 2011, Putnam $17.99 (978-0-399-25472-7). 40pp. Young Paige Darling's favorite stuffed rabbit is carried away when she attaches it to a helium balloon but the family's luck holds out and brings Bun Bun Button home. (Rev: BL 11/15/11; LMC 3–4/12; SLJ 10/1/11)

657 Reidy, Jean. *Too Purpley!* (PS–K). Illus. by Genevieve Leloup. 2010, Bloomsbury $11.99 (978-1-59990-307-1). 32pp. A little girl critiques all her outfit choices — "too matchy," "too stripey" — until she finds one that's "so comfy." (Rev: BL 1/1/10; SLJ 1/1/10)

658 Rim, Sujean. *Birdie's Big-Girl Shoes* (PS–1). Illus. by author. 2009, Little, Brown $15.99 (978-0-316-04470-7). 40pp. A young girl is excited to try on her mom's fancy shoes, until she discovers how awkward they are for playing and dancing. (Rev: BL 11/1/09*; SLJ 9/1/09)

659 Rockwell, Anne. *At the Supermarket* (PS–1). Illus. by author. 2010, Henry Holt $16.99 (978-0-8050-7662-2). 32pp. Rockwell updates her 1997 *The Supermarket,* about a young boy's shopping trip with his mother, offering new illustrations and revised text. (Rev: BLO 1/1/10; SLJ 3/1/10)

660 Rosenstiehl, Agnes. *Silly Lilly in What Will I Be Today?* (PS). Illus. by author. 2011, TOON $12.95 (978-193517908-5). 32pp. Lilly tries out a variety of occupations in this simple graphic novel for emerging readers. (Rev: BL 3/15/11; SLJ 5/1/11)

661 Rosenthal, Amy Krouse. *One Smart Cookie: Bite-Size Lessons for the School Years and Beyond* (PS–1). Illus. by Jane Dyer. 2010, HarperCollins $12.99 (978-0-06-142970-5). 40pp. A fourth volume in the series that uses cookies and baking to tie together words and life lessons. (Rev: BL 9/1/10; SLJ 9/1/10)

662 Rosenthal, Amy Krouse. *This Plus That: Life's Little Equations* (PS–3). Illus. by Jen Corace. 2011, Harper-Collins $14.99 (978-006172655-2). 40pp. A variety of familiar conceptual equations, such as barefoot + screen door + popsicles = summer! are portrayed in this light-hearted book about math and life. (Rev: BL 3/15/11*; LMC 10/11; SLJ 5/11)

663 Rosenthal, Betsy R. *Which Shoes Would You Choose?* (PS–K). Illus. by Nancy Cote. 2010, Putnam $15.99 (978-0-399-25013-2). 32pp. A simple guessing game in which Sherman wears a variety of footwear — flip-flops, hiking boots, galoshes, slippers — depending on his activities. (Rev: BL 3/1/10; SLJ 4/1/10)

664 Rosenthal, Eileen. *I Must Have Bobo!* (PS–K). Illus. by Marc Rosenthal. 2011, Simon & Schuster $14.99 (978-1-4424-0377-2). 40pp. Young Willy must cope with his cat Earl's endless fascination with his favorite sock monkey, Bobo. ℮ (Rev: BL 3/15/11; SLJ 3/1/11)

665 Schwartz, Howard. *Gathering Sparks* (PS–3). Illus. by Kristina Swarner. 2010, Roaring Brook $16.99 (978-1-59643-280-2). 32pp. In this story based on Jewish folklore, a man tells his grandson about the importance

of good deeds, which restore light and hope to the night sky. (Rev: BL 8/10; LMC 11–12/10; SLJ 8/1/10)

666 Senning, Cindy Post, and Peggy Post. *Emily's Out and About Book* (PS–1). Illus. by Leo Landry. 2009, Collins $16.99 (978-006111700-8). 32pp. Emily and her mother spend the day in town — visiting the doctor and the library, having lunch, and so forth — in this simple story that emphasizes the importance of good manners. (Rev: BL 11/1/09)

667 Shea, Bob. *Dinosaur vs. the Potty* (PS). Illus. by author. 2010, Hyperion/Disney $15.99 (978-1-4231-3339-1). 40pp. A stubborn young red dinosaur stages a spirited rebellion against the potty. (Rev: BL 10/15/10; SLJ 10/1/10)

668 Sís, Peter. *Madlenka, Soccer Star* (PS–2). Illus. by author. 2010, Farrar $16.99 (978-0-374-34702-4). 40pp. Young Madlenka dreams of being a soccer star and is willing to play with anyone and anything in this imaginative story with humorous illustrations. (Rev: BL 9/1/10; HB 11–12/10; LMC 3–4/11; SLJ 11/1/10)

669 Spinelli, Jerry. *I Can Be Anything* (PS–K). Illus. by Jimmy Liao. 2010, Little, Brown $16.99 (978-031616226-5). 32pp. A little boy considers what he might be when he grows up, in fact reviewing options available to him already (paper-plane folder, mixing-bowl licker, and so forth). (Rev: BL 1/1/10; SLJ 3/10)

670 Taback, Simms. *Postcards from Camp* (1–3). Illus. by author. 2011, Penguin $17.99 (978-0-399-23973-3). 40pp. The story of a boy's summer at camp is told through the shared correspondence between the boy and his father in this appealing book with removable pieces. (Rev: BL 7/11; SLJ 9/1/11)

671 Tafolla, Carmen. *Fiesta Babies* (PS–K). Illus. by Amy Cordova. 2010, Tricycle $12.99 (978-1-58246-319-3). 24pp. A crowd of multicultural babies participate exuberantly in the joys of a fiesta in this small, square book with bold art and a sprinkling of Spanish words. (Rev: BL 2/15/10; SLJ 3/1/10)

672 Thompson, Lauren. *Chew, Chew, Gulp!* (PS). Illus. by Jarrett J. Krosoczka. 2011, Simon & Schuster $14.99 (978-1-4169-9744-3). 32pp. This book follows four young children as they eat a variety of foods and make a variety of onomatopoeic accompanying sounds. ℮ (Rev: BL 4/15/11; SLJ 5/1/11)

673 Torrey, Richard. *Why?* (PS–2). Illus. by author. 2010, HarperCollins $16.99 (978-0-06-156170-2). 40pp. A young boy asks questions all day in this book that touches on everything from science to haircuts. (Rev: BL 4/15/10; SLJ 5/1/10)

674 Uhlberg, Myron. *A Storm Called Katrina* (1–4). Illus. by Colin Bootman. 2011, Peachtree $17.95 (978-1-56145-591-1). 40pp. Ten-year-old Louis Daniel's cornet comes in handy when his home is flooded and his family moves to the Superdome during Hurricane Katrina. (Rev: BL 9/1/11*; SLJ 9/1/11)

675 Wahl, Jan. *The Art Collector* (PS–3). Illus. by Rosalinde Bonnet. 2011, Charlesbridge $15.95 (978-1-58089-270-4). 32pp. A little boy entranced by art but disappointed by his own efforts decides to become an art collector. Lexile AD450L (Rev: BL 7/11; SLJ 7/11)

676 Warwick, Dionne, and David Freeman Wooley. *Little Man* (1–3). Illus. by Fred Willingham. 2011, Charlesbridge $19.95 (978-1-57091-731-8). Unpaged. A little African American boy in an urban neighborhood pursues his love of drums despite the lack of encouragement from others apart from his dad; comes with a CD of Dionne Warwick reading the story and drum playing by David Wooley. ❤ (Rev: SLJ 11/1/11)

677 Williams, Laura E. *The Can Man* (K–3). Illus. by Craig Orback. 2010, Lee & Low $18.95 (978-1-60060-266-5). 40pp. Tim collects and cashes in tin cans with the intention of buying himself a skateboard, but in the end gives his earnings to a homeless man. (Rev: BL 3/15/10; LMC 8–9/10; SLJ 5/1/10)

678 Wright, Michael. *Jake Goes Peanuts* (K–2). Illus. by author. 2010, Feiwel & Friends $16.99 (978-0-312-54967-1). 48pp. Jake won't eat anything but peanut butter until his parents come up with a brilliant strategy. (Rev: BL 11/15/10; LMC 11–12/10; SLJ 8/1/10)

679 Yolen, Jane, and Heidi E. Y. Stemple. *Not All Princesses Dress in Pink* (PS–1). Illus. by Anne-Sophie Lanquetin. 2010, Simon & Schuster $15.99 (978-1-4169-8018-6). Unpaged. Some princesses wear baseball jerseys and spend their time building tree houses, doing carpentry, and getting muddy, according to this book that portrays a wide variety of princess activities. (Rev: LMC 8–9/10; SLJ 6/1/10)

680 Zalben, Jane Breskin. *Baby Shower* (PS–2). Illus. by author. 2010, Roaring Brook $16.99 (978-1-59643-465-3). 32pp. Pet-obsessed Zoe dreams of young animals falling from the sky when she learns she will help with her aunt's baby shower. (Rev: BL 2/1/10*; SLJ 3/1/10)

FAMILY STORIES

681 Akin, Sara Laux. *Three Scoops and a Fig* (PS–2). Illus. by Susan Kathleen Hartung. 2010, Peachtree $15.95 (978-1-56145-522-5). 32pp. Banished from her family's Italian kitchen, little Sofia comes up with something she can efficiently contribute to celebrate the arrival of Nonna and Nonno. Lexile AD550L (Rev: BL 11/1/10; SLJ 8/1/10)

682 Andreae, Giles. *I Love My Mommy* (PS). Illus. by Emma Dodd. 2011, Hyperion/Disney $12.99 (978-1-4231-4327-7). 32pp. A toddler explains all the reasons he loves his mother in this bright oversize book. (Rev: SLJ 3/1/11)

683 Andrews, Julie, and Emma Walton Hamilton. *The Very Fairy Princess* (PS–K). Illus. by Christine Davenier. 2010, Little, Brown $16.99 (978-0-316-04050-1). 32pp. Geraldine encounters many people who doubt her true princess nature but she maintains her royalness throughout the day. ❤ (Rev: BL 4/15/10; SLJ 5/1/10)

684 Appelt, Kathi. *Brand-New Baby Blues* (PS–2). Illus. by Kelly Murphy. 2010, HarperCollins $16.99 (978-0-06-053233-8). 32pp. A young girl adjusts to the arrival of her baby brother, going from resentful to accepting. (Rev: BL 11/15/09; SLJ 2/1/10)

685 Banks, Kate. *Max's Castle* (K–2). Illus. by Boris Kulikov. 2011, Farrar $16.99 (978-0-374-39919-1). Unpaged. Often-maligned younger brother Max proves his worth to his older brothers when his skills with wordplay saves them from certain disaster in the adventure-filled fantasy world they've created. ❤ (Rev: SLJ 9/1/11)

686 Bennett, Kelly. *Dad and Pop: An Ode to Fathers and Stepfathers* (PS–2). Illus. by Paul Meisel. 2010, Candlewick $15.99 (978-0-7636-3379-0). 40pp. A young girl points out the differences and similarities between her two dads — one is a stepfather — in this positive, comforting book about blended families. (Rev: BL 2/15/10; LMC 5–6/10; SLJ 3/1/10)

687 Bennett, Kelly. *Your Daddy Was Just Like You* (PS–1). Illus. by David Walker. 2010, Putnam $16.99 (978-0-399-25258-7). 32pp. A grandmother reminisces with her grandson and his father as they look through a scrapbook. (Rev: BL 2/1/10; SLJ 3/1/10)

688 Best, Cari. *Easy as Pie* (PS–2). Illus. by Melissa Sweet. 2010, Farrar $16.99 (978-0-374-39929-0). 40pp. Young Jacob concentrates on making a peach pie for his parents' anniversary — and serves it before they all go out for dinner. (Rev: BL 2/1/10; LMC 5–6/10; SLJ 2/1/10)

689 Birdsall, Jeanne. *Flora's Very Windy Day* (K–3). Illus. by Matt Phelan. 2010, Clarion $16 (978-0-618-98676-7). 32pp. When Flora's irritating little brother Crispin is swept away by the wind, she finds she can't let him go after all. ❤ Lexile AD590L (Rev: BL 7/10*; LMC 10/10; SLJ 7/1/10)

690 Blackall, Sophie. *Are You Awake?* (PS). Illus. by author. 2011, Henry Holt $12.99 (978-0-8050-7858-9). 40pp. A little boy's mother resists his efforts to wake her up when he can't sleep. (Rev: BL 5/1/11; SLJ 6/11*)

691 Bonwill, Ann. *Naughty Toes* (PS–1). Illus. by Teresa Murfin. 2011, Tiger Tales $15.95 (978-1-58925-103-8). 32pp. Belinda seems to be a ballet natural but her sister Chloe's feet don't seem to work until she discovers tap dancing. Lexile AD560L (Rev: BLO 10/15/11; SLJ 11/1/11)

692 Borden, Louise. *Big Brothers Don't Take Naps* (PS–1). Illus. by Emma Dodd. 2011, Simon & Schuster $16.99 (978-1-4169-5503-0). 32pp. Nicholas adores his older brother James, who goes to school and no longer takes naps; Nicholas is soon to learn that he himself will soon be an older brother. (Rev: BL 6/1/11; SLJ 5/1/11)

693 Bruchac, Joseph. *My Father Is Taller Than a Tree* (PS–1). Illus. by Wendy Anderson Halperin. 2010, Dial $16.99 (978-0-8037-3173-8). 32pp. Two-page spreads featuring brief rhyming text and soft-palette illustrations celebrate close relationships between diverse fathers and sons. (Rev: BL 1/1/10; LMC 3–4/10; SLJ 3/1/10)

694 Bryne, Gayle. *Sometimes It's Grandmas and Grandpas, Not Mommies and Daddies* (PS–1). Illus. by Mary Haverfield. 2009, Abbeville $15.95 (978-0-7892-1028-9). 32pp. A young narrator explains all about what it's like being raised by grandparents. (Rev: BL 11/15/09; SLJ 1/1/10)

695 Bunting, Eve. *Will It Be a Baby Brother?* (PS–K). Illus. by Beth Spiegel. 2010, Boyds Mills $16.95 (978-1-59078-439-6). 32pp. A young boy eager for a little brother must adjust his expectations when his new sibling turns out to be a girl. (Rev: BL 10/1/10; SLJ 11/1/10)

696 Burningham, John. *There's Going to Be a Baby* (PS). Illus. by Helen Oxenbury. 2010, Candlewick $16.99 (978-0-7636-4907-4). 48pp. A young boy wonders how his life will change when the new baby arrives, and discusses this with his mother as the months pass. (Rev: BL 11/1/10*; SLJ 10/1/10*)

697 Castellucci, Cecil. *Grandma's Gloves* (K–3). Illus. by Julia Denos. 2010, Candlewick $15.99 (978-0-7636-3168-0). 32pp. A girl and her grandmother enjoy gardening together until the elderly woman dies and the girl inherits her gardening gloves. (Rev: BL 8/10; SLJ 8/1/10)

698 Child, Lauren. *I Really, Really Need Actual Ice Skates* (PS–1). Illus. by author. Series: Charlie and Lola. 2010, Dial $16.99 (978-0-8037-3451-7). Unpaged. Lola promises she will use her new ice skates if she gets them, but finds it hard to live up to this when she finds skating more difficult than expected — perhaps a scooter would have been better after all! (Rev: SLJ 1/1/11)

699 Clark, Julie Aigner. *You Are the Best Medicine* (K–3). Illus. by Jana Christy. 2010, HarperCollins $16.99 (978-0-06-195644-7). 32pp. A mother who has cancer gently tells her child about the treatment she will undergo. (Rev: BL 10/15/10; SLJ 11/1/10)

700 Clark, Karen Henry. *Sweet Moon Baby: An Adoption Tale* (PS–K). Illus. by Patrice Barton. 2010, Knopf $17.99 (978-0-375-85709-6); LB $20.99 (978-0-375-95709-3). Unpaged. The moon looks over a baby Chinese girl whose parents cannot look after her as her new family prepares for her arrival. (Rev: SLJ 1/1/11)

701 Clements, Andrew. *Because Your Mommy Loves You* (PS–2). Illus. by R. W. Alley. 2012, Clarion $16.99 (978-054725522-4). 32pp. A boy and his mother share a camping adventure in this companion to *Because Your*

Daddy Loves You (2005) that teaches preparation and self-reliance. **℮** (Rev: SLJ 4/1/12)

702 Coffelt, Nancy. *Catch That Baby!* (PS). Illus. by Scott Nash. 2011, Aladdin $16.99 (978-1-4169-9148-9). 40pp. Spirited baby Ruby takes off after his bath and leads his family on a merry chase as he resists getting dressed. (Rev: BL 5/1/11; SLJ 6/11)

703 Cora, Cat. *A Suitcase Surprise for Mommy* (PS–K). Illus. by Joy Allen. 2011, Dial $16.99 (978-0-8037-3332-9). 32pp. Little Zoran copes with separation anxiety by giving his mother a picture to take with her on a trip to New York City. (Rev: BL 2/15/11; SLJ 3/1/11)

704 Crews, Nina. *Sky-High Guy* (PS–2). Illus. by author. 2010, Henry Holt $16.99 (978-0-8050-8764-2). Unpaged. Brothers Jack and Gus work together to rescue Guy, Jack's action figure, when he gets stuck in a tree while "skydiving"; drawings on photographs blend reality and imagination. (Rev: HB 5–6/10; SLJ 4/1/10)

705 Crow, Kristyn. *The Middle-Child Blues* (K–2). Illus. by David Catrow. 2009, Putnam $16.99 (978-0-399-24735-4). Unpaged. A neglected middle child finds his niche when he whips out his guitar and starts to play the blues at the county fair. (Rev: HB 11–12/09; SLJ 11/1/09)

706 Curtis, Jamie Lee. *My Mommy Hung the Moon: A Love Story* (PS–2). Illus. by Laura Cornell. 2010, HarperCollins $16.99 (978-0-06-029016-0). 40pp. A young boy celebrates his wonderful mother in this bouncy book. Lexile AD400L (Rev: BL 11/15/10; SLJ 1/1/11)

707 De Smet, Marian. *I Have Two Homes* (PS–2). Illus. by Nynke Mare Talsma. 2012, Clavis $15.95 (978-160537102-3). 32pp. Young Nina narrates the story of her parents' divorce, from bitter separation to the new normal of her life: a positive place where she knows both love her even though they can't love each other. (Rev: BLO 5/15/12; SLJ 6/1/12)

708 Ditchfield, Christin. *"Shwatsit!"* (PS–K). Illus. by Rosalind Beardshaw. 2009, Random House $15.99 (978-0-375-84181-1); LB $18.99 (978-0-375-94351-5). Unpaged. A family tries desperately to make sense of the baby's favorite word. (Rev: SLJ 11/1/09)

709 Dorros, Arthur. *Mama and Me* (PS–K). Illus. by Rudy Gutierrez. 2011, HarperCollins $16.99 (978-0-06-058160-2). 32pp. A young girl helps her mother with basic tasks during the day, but emphasizes that she wants to do things by herself; the reason eventually becomes clear — she has been planning a party for her Mama; integrates many Spanish words and phrases. (Rev: BL 5/1/11; SLJ 5/1/11)

710 Elliott, Rebecca. *Just Because* (PS–2). Illus. by author. 2011, Lion $14.99 (978-0-7459-6267-2). Unpaged. A little boy explains all the things he loves about his older sister, even though she's mute and wheelchair-bound. (Rev: SLJ 8/1/11)

711 Evans, Kristina. *What's Special About Me, Mama?* (PS–K). Illus. by Javaka Steptoe. 2011, Disney $16.99 (978-0-7868-5274-1). 32pp. An African American mother lists her son's physical attributes and the wonderful ways in which he behaves. (Rev: BL 2/1/11; SLJ 1/1/11)

712 Fearnley, Jan. *Milo Armadillo* (K–2). Illus. by author. 2009, Candlewick $15.99 (978-0-7636-4575-5). Unpaged. Tallulah's grandmother's well-intentioned knitting efforts result in a pink armadillo toy named Milo; initially resistant, Tallulah comes to cherish her new friend. (Rev: SLJ 2/1/10)

713 Feiffer, Kate. *My Side of the Car* (K–2). Illus. by Jules Feiffer. 2011, Candlewick $16.99 (978-0-7636-4405-5). 32pp. Sadie is determined to finally get to the zoo and refuses to recognize that it is raining — definitely not on her side of the car. (Rev: BL 3/1/11; HB 3–4/11; LMC 5–6/11; SLJ 3/1/11)

714 Garland, Michael. *Grandpa's Tractor* (PS–2). Illus. by author. 2011, Boyds Mills $16.95 (978-1-59078-762-5). Unpaged. In this beautifully illustrated story, Grandpa Joe and Timmy visit the now-abandoned family farm. Lexile AD890L (Rev: SLJ 5/1/11)

715 Gibala-Broxholm, Scott. *Maddie's Monster Dad* (K–2). Illus. by author. 2011, Marshall Cavendish $16.99 (978-0-7614-5846-3). Unpaged. Fed up with her dad's busy schedule, Maddie decides to build a Monster Dad to play with her; her real Dad gets the message and makes space in his day for play. (Rev: LMC 1–2/12; SLJ 10/1/11)

716 Hardin, Melinda. *Hero Dad* (PS–1). Illus. by Bryan Langdo. 2010, Marshall Cavendish $12.99 (978-0-7614-5713-8). 24pp. A young boy enthusiastically describes his dad's "super powers" — night vision, flying, and the endurance that comes from being a soldier. e (Rev: BL 12/15/10; LMC 1–2/11; SLJ 10/1/10)

717 Hartt-Sussman, Heather. *Here Comes Hortense!* (K–2). Illus. by Georgia Graham. 2012, Tundra $17.95 (978-177049221-9). 32pp. A young boy is delighted to join his grandmother and her new husband on a trip to the theme park until he realizes that bratty young Hortense is coming too and monopolizes Nana. (Rev: BLO 4/15/12; SLJ 4/12)

718 Hodgkinson, Leigh. *Smile!* (K–2). Illus. by author. 2010, HarperCollins $16.99 (978-0-06-185269-5). Unpaged. Sunny loses her smile when told not to eat more cookies before dinner and must look for it all over the house, discovering quite a bit in her search. (Rev: SLJ 2/1/10)

719 Horrocks, Anita. *Silas' Seven Grandparents* (PS–3). Illus. by Helen Flook. 2010, Orca $19.95 (978-1-55143-561-9). 32pp. A lucky child with seven grandparents struggles to decide how to spend his time when he's invited to all of their houses at once. (Rev: BL 5/15/10; LMC 11–12/10; SLJ 9/1/10)

720 Iwai, Melissa. *Soup Day* (PS–1). Illus. by author. 2010, Henry Holt $12.99 (978-0-8050-9004-8). 32pp. On a snowy day, a young girl helps her mother choose and prepare vegetables for soup; when Dad gets home, they all share the meal together. (Rev: BL 10/15/10; SLJ 9/1/10)

721 Johnson, Angela. *Lottie Paris Lives Here* (PS–K). Illus. by Scott M. Fischer. 2011, Simon & Schuster $16.99 (978-0-689-87377-5). 32pp. Follows a day in the life of an imaginative young African American girl who lives with her Papa Pete. e (Rev: BL 8/11; SLJ 8/1/11)

722 Johnston, Tony. *My Abuelita* (1–3). Illus. by Yuyi Morales. 2009, Harcourt $16 (978-015216330-3). 32pp. With many Spanish words sprinkled throughout, a boy and his mother prepare for her day and job as a storyteller. (Rev: BL 8/09; LMC 5–6/10; SLJ 8/1/09)

723 Joosse, Barbara. *Sleepover at Gramma's House* (PS–1). Illus. by Jan Jutte. 2010, Philomel $17.99 (978-0-399-25261-7). 40pp. A little elephant packs her trunk and heads to her grandmother's cottage in the country, where the two have a delightful sleepover. (Rev: BL 5/1/10*; SLJ 6/1/10)

724 Keane, Dave. *Daddy Adventure Day* (PS–1). Illus. by Sue Ramá. 2011, Philomel $15.99 (978-0-399-24627-2). 32pp. A patient father and his overeager son share a day at the baseball stadium. Lexile AD680L (Rev: BL 2/15/11; SLJ 3/1/11)

725 Khan, Rukhsana. *Big Red Lollipop* (PS–2). Illus. by Sophie Blackall. 2010, Viking $16.99 (978-0-670-06287-4). 40pp. Pakistani American Rubina knows how to act in her new country but it's difficult to persuade her mother to adopt new customs. Charlotte Zolotow Award. (Rev: BL 2/1/10*; SLJ 3/1/10)

726 LaChanze. *Little Diva* (PS–2). Illus. by Brian Pinkney. 2010, Feiwel & Friends $16.99 (978-0-312-37010-7). 32pp. Likable, determined Nena dreams of a Broadway career like her mother's and works hard to achieve it in this picture book with detailed illustrations and a CD of the author singing and reading. (Rev: BL 3/15/10; LMC 5–6/10; SLJ 3/1/10)

727 Lawler, Janet. *A Mother's Song* (PS–K). Illus. by Kathleen Kemly. 2010, Sterling $14.95 (978-1-4027-6968-9). 24pp. A rhyming verse companion to 2006's *A Father's Song*, in which a mother encourages her daughter to enjoy nature's wonders throughout the seasons. (Rev: BL 5/1/10; SLJ 6/1/10)

728 Levine, Arthur A. *Monday Is One Day* (PS–1). Illus. by Julian Hector. 2011, Scholastic $16.99 (978-0-439-78924-0). 32pp. This book celebrates all the ways in which working parents can enjoy time with their children during the week, while anticipating the joy of the weekend. (Rev: BL 2/1/11*; SLJ 4/11)

729 Lopez, Susana. *The Best Family in the World* (PS–3). Illus. by Ulises Wensell. 2010, Kane/Miller $15.99

(978-1-935279-47-1). 28pp. Young Carlota prepares to meet her adoptive parents, imagining the most exciting possibilities. (Rev: BL 4/1/10; LMC 8–9/10; SLJ 5/1/10)

730 McAllister, Angela. *My Mom Has X-Ray Vision* (K–2). Illus. by Alex T. Smith. 2011, ME Media paper $7.95 (978-1-58925-428-2). 32pp. Matthew's mother always knows what he's doing — but how does she do it? Matthew decides to investigate. (Rev: BL 5/1/11; SLJ 4/11)

731 McDonnell, Christine. *Goyangi Means Cat* (PS–2). Illus. by Steve Johnson. 2011, Viking $16.99 (978-0-670-01179-7). 32pp. An adopted Korean girl finds life in America bewildering but bonds with the family cat. (Rev: BL 5/1/11; SLJ 7/11*)

732 Macken, JoAnn Early. *Baby Says "Moo!"* (PS). Illus. by David Walker. 2011, Hyperion/Disney $15.99 (978-1-4231-3400-8). Unpaged. Out in the car with her family, Baby constantly answers questions about various animals' sounds with "Moo!" (Rev: SLJ 3/1/11)

733 MacLachlan, Patricia. *Your Moon, My Moon: A Grandmother's Words to a Faraway Child* (PS–2). Illus. by Bryan Collier. 2011, Simon & Schuster $16.99 (978-1-4169-7950-0). 32pp. A New England grandmother reflects on the bond she feels with her African grandchild in this evocative book about family bonds spanning great distances. (Rev: BL 8/11; SLJ 8/1/11)

734 Maclear, Kyo. *Virginia Wolf* (K–2). Illus. by Isabelle Arsenault. 2012, Kids Can $16.95 (978-155453649-8). 32pp. When young Virginia awakes "feeling wolfish," her sister Vanessa sets about creating a beautiful setting full of flowers and birds to cheer her up; inspired by the relationship between Virginia Woolf and her artist sibling. (Rev: BL 2/15/12; SLJ 4/1/12*)

735 Macomber, Debbie, and Mary Lou Carney. *The Truly Terrible Horrible Sweater . . . That Grandma Knit* (PS–1). Illus. by Vincent Nguyen. 2009, HarperCollins $17.99 (978-006165093-2). 32pp. Cameron finally comes to appreciate the sweater his grandmother knitted for his birthday when she explains the importance of the pattern. **e** (Rev: BLO 11/1/09; SLJ 11/09)

736 McQuinn, Anna. *Lola Loves Stories* (PS–1). Illus. by Rosalind Beardshaw. 2010, Charlesbridge LB $15.95 (978-1-58089-258-2); paper $6.95 (978-1-58089-259-9). Unpaged. An African American girl gains inspiration from the stories her daddy reads her every night. ⌒ **e** (Rev: SLJ 7/1/10*)

737 Magenta, Emma. *Orlando on a Thursday* (PS–1). Illus. by author. 2010, Candlewick $15.99 (978-0-7636-4560-1). 32pp. Orlando's sad on Thursdays when his Mami goes to town, but his Papi keeps him happy and busy. (Rev: BL 9/1/10; SLJ 8/1/10)

738 Matthies, Janna. *The Goodbye Cancer Garden* (1–3). Illus. by Kristi Valiant. 2011, Whitman $16.99 (978-0-8075-2994-2). 32pp. Janie and her brother decide to plant a garden to represent their mom's slow triumph over breast cancer. Lexile AD660L (Rev: BL 2/15/11; SLJ 2/1/11*)

739 Medina, Meg. *Tía Isa Wants a Car* (PS–2). Illus. by Claudio Muñoz. 2011, Candlewick $15.99 (978-0-7636-4156-6). 32pp. A young Latina girl helps save money for the car her aunt so badly wants to get to the beach that reminds her of her island home; also available in Spanish. Ezra Jack Keats New Writer Award. (Rev: BL 6/1/11; HB 7–8/11; SLJ 6/11)

740 Morris, Richard. *Bye-Bye, Baby!* (PS). Illus. by Larry Day. 2009, Walker $16.99 (978-0-8027-9772-8). 40pp. Felix does not adjust well to the arrival of his baby sister and fantasizes about grim ends for her. (Rev: BL 9/15/09; SLJ 11/1/09*)

741 Nelson, Vaunda Micheaux. *Who Will I Be, Lord?* (PS–2). Illus. by Sean Qualls. 2009, Random House $16.99 (978-0-375-84342-6); LB $19.99 (978-0-375-94342-3). Unpaged. A young African American girl looking to create her future looks to the lives of her older relatives and ancestors for inspiration. (Rev: BL 11/15/09; HB 11–12/09; SLJ 10/1/09)

742 Newman, Lesléa. *Daddy, Papa, and Me* (PS). Illus. by Carol Thompson. 2009, Tricycle $7.99 (978-1-58246-262-2). Unpaged. Two fathers and their child enjoy a day full of fun in this board book. Also use *Mommy, Mama, and Me* (2009). (Rev: HB 5–6/09; SLJ 11/1/09)

743 Newman, Lesléa. *Donovan's Big Day* (PS–2). Illus. by Mike Dutton. 2011, Tricycle $15.99 (978-1-58246-332-2). 32pp. A young boy feels proud and a little nervous about his upcoming role as ring bearer in his two moms' wedding. Lexile AD1540L (Rev: BL 4/1/11; SLJ 4/11)

744 Nichols, Grace. *Whoa, Baby, Whoa!* (PS). Illus. by Eleanor Taylor. 2012, Bloomsbury $15.99 (978-159990742-0). 32pp. A baby used to being warned not to do something hears a new cry — "Go, Baby, go!" — when he ventures to take a couple of upright steps. (Rev: BL 3/1/12)

745 Norman, Geoffrey. *Stars Above Us* (K–3). Illus. by E. B. Lewis. 2009, Putnam $16.99 (978-0-399-24724-8). 32pp. A young girl, who used to be afraid of the dark, looks at the glowing stars her dad helped affix to her bedroom ceiling and thinks of him when he's away fighting in the military. (Rev: BL 9/15/09; LMC 11–12/09; SLJ 10/1/09)

746 North, Sherry. *Because I Am Your Daddy* (PS). Illus. by Marcellus Hall. 2010, Abrams $15.95 (978-0-8109-8392-2). 32pp. Daddy is shown doing fanciful things — flying his daughter to school, building a high-tech tree house — in this simple book celebrating the love between parent and child. (Rev: BL 3/1/10; SLJ 4/1/10)

747 Novak, Matt. *A Wish for You* (PS–K). Illus. by author. 2010, Greenwillow $16.99 (978-0-06-155202-1);

LB $17.89 (978-006155203-8). 32pp. Two parents get ready for and celebrate the arrival of their new baby in this lively book that celebrates birth and family. (Rev: BL 1/1/10; SLJ 3/1/10)

748 Numeroff, Laura. *What Brothers Do Best / What Sisters Do Best* (PS–K). Illus. by Lynn Munsinger. 2009, Chronicle $15.99 (978-0-8118-6545-6). Unpaged. This flip book celebrates all the good things about having a brother or sister. (Rev: BL 9/15/09; SLJ 12/1/09)

749 O'Brien, Anne Sibley. *A Path of Stars* (2–4). Illus. by author. 2012, Charlesbridge $15.95 (978-157091735-6). 40pp. Cambodian American Dara enjoys hearing her refugee grandmother's stories about the homeland, and offers comfort when she receives sad news about her brother, who still lived there. **e** Lexile 780L (Rev: BL 3/1/12)

750 Oelschlager, Vanita. *A Tale of Two Mommies* (PS–K). Illus. by Mike Blanc. 2011, Vanita $15.95 (978-098263666-4). 40pp. A young boy answers his friends' questions about living with two mommies. (Rev: BL 12/15/11)

751 Orr, Wendy. *The Princess and Her Panther* (PS–2). Illus. by Lauren Stringer. 2010, Simon & Schuster $16.99 (978-1-4169-9780-1). 40pp. A brave girl (the princess) and her younger sister (the panther) confront the "monsters" lurking outside while on a backyard camp-out. Lexile AD720L (Rev: BL 7/10; LMC 8–9/10; SLJ 7/10)

752 Parkhurst, Carolyn. *Cooking with Henry and Ellie-belly* (PS–2). Illus. by Dan Yaccarino. 2010, Feiwel & Friends $16.99 (978-0-312-54848-3). 32pp. Five-year-old Henry and his 2-year-old sister pretend they are making "raspberry-marshmallow-peanut butter waffles with barbecued banana bacon" on a television show. (Rev: BL 10/15/10; SLJ 10/1/10)

753 Paschkis, Julie. *Mooshka: A Quilt Story* (PS–2). Illus. by author. 2012, Peachtree $16.95 (978-156145620-8). 32pp. New big sister Karla discovers the joy of sharing her family's special quilt with her baby sister Hannah in this nostalgic family story. (Rev: BL 3/1/12*; HB 5–6/12; SLJ 6/1/12)

754 Peete, Holly Robinson, and Ryan Elizabeth Peete. *My Brother Charlie* (K–3). Illus. by Shane W. Evans. 2010, Scholastic $16.99 (978-0-545-09466-5). 40pp. Callie speaks lovingly — and frankly — about what it's like to have an autistic twin brother in this story of a family dealing with disability. **e** Lexile AD540L (Rev: BL 3/1/10; LMC 5–6/10; SLJ 3/1/10)

755 Pettitt, Linda, and Sharon Darrow. *Yafi's Family: An Ethiopian Boy's Journey of Love, Loss, and Adoption* (PS–2). Illus. by Jan Spivey Gilchrist. 2010, Amharic $17.95 (978-0-9797481-4-1). 32pp. In this tender international adoption story, a young Ethiopian boy and his adoptive parents reminisce about their first meeting,

and talk about the love he feels for both families. Lexile AD660L (Rev: BL 10/15/10; SLJ 1/1/11)

756 Price, Mara. *Grandma's Chocolate / El Chocolate de Abuelita* (K–2). Illus. by Lisa Fields. 2010, Arte Publico/Piñata $16.95 (978-155885587-8). 32pp. In this bilingual story, a granddaughter welcomes her grandmother's visit from Mexico, and the culturally significant gifts she brings along. (Rev: BLO 11/1/10; SLJ 1/11)

757 Proimos, James. *Todd's TV* (K–2). Illus. by author. 2010, HarperCollins $15.99 (978-0-06-170985-2). 40pp. Todd watches so much TV that the appliance has offered to adopt him; when Todd's parents realize what's happening, they finally cut back on TV in favor of family time. (Rev: BL 2/15/10; SLJ 5/1/10*)

758 Rocco, John. *Blackout* (PS–1). Illus. by author. 2011, Hyperion/Disney $16.99 (978-1-4231-2190-9). 40pp. A bored young boy gets the quality family time he seeks when the power goes out. (Rev: BL 6/1/11; SLJ 7/11*)

759 Root, Phyllis. *Creak! Said the Bed* (PS–K). Illus. by Regan Dunnick. 2010, Candlewick $15.99 (978-0-7636-2004-2). 32pp. Onomatopoeia enhances this comic rhyming cumulative tale about a creaking, groaning, overcrowded bed. (Rev: BL 3/1/10; SLJ 3/1/10)

760 Rose, Naomi C. *Tashi and the Tibetan Flower Cure* (K–3). Illus. by author. 2011, Lee & Low $18.95 (978-1-60060-425-6). 40pp. A Tibetan American girl administers a traditional flower-pollen cure when her grandfather becomes ill; the treatment process draws the community together and shows the family how much support they have in their new home. (Rev: BL 11/15/11; LMC 3–4/12; SLJ 11/1/11)

761 Roth, Carol. *All Aboard to Work — Choo-Choo!* (PS–K). Illus. by Steve Lavis. 2009, Whitman $16.99 (978-0-8075-0271-6). Unpaged. A diverse array of parents dressed for work are shown commuting aboard a train and returning home each night to shower their families with affection. (Rev: SLJ 11/1/09)

762 Sacre, Antonio. *A Mango in the Hand: A Story Told Through Proverbs* (K–3). Illus. by Sebastià Serra. 2011, Abrams $16.95 (978-0-8109-9734-9). Unpaged. Young Francisco wants mangoes for dessert on his saint day, and Papá's proverbs guide him through his efforts, teaching him about generosity; in Spanish and English. (Rev: SLJ 7/11)

763 Schubert, Leda. *Feeding the Sheep* (PS–K). Illus. by Andrea U'Ren. 2010, Farrar $16.99 (978-0-374-32296-0). 32pp. A mother explains to her little daughter all the steps involved in making a sweater, starting with feeding the sheep. (Rev: BL 3/15/10; LMC 5–6/10; SLJ 3/1/10)

764 Schubert, Leda. *The Princess of Borscht* (PS–2). Illus. by Bonnie Christensen. 2011, Roaring Brook $17.99 (978-1-59643-515-5). 32pp. When Ruthie's grandmother is in hospital and insists on having some homemade borscht, the young girl enlists some help in devising a recipe. (Rev: BL 9/15/11; SLJ 11/1/11)

765 Sheridan, Sara. *I'm Me!* (PS–K). Illus. by Margaret Chamberlain. 2011, Scholastic $17.99 (978-0-545-28222-2). 32pp. Young Imogen doesn't want to play pretend this time she visits Auntie Sara — she just wants to be herself. (Rev: BL 3/15/11; SLJ 3/1/11)

766 Siegel, Randy. *Grandma's Smile* (PS–2). Illus. by Dyanne DiSalvo. 2010, Roaring Brook $15.99 (978-1-59643-438-7). 32pp. A 6-year-old boy travels to visit his grandmother and help her locate her missing smile. (Rev: BL 7/10; SLJ 11/1/10)

767 Singer, Marilyn. *Tallulah's Solo* (PS–3). Illus. by Alexandra Boiger. 2012, Clarion $16.99 (978-054733004-4). 40pp. Though initially jealous when her brother lands a bigger ballet role than she does, Tallulah helps him rehearse and ends up celebrating his success. **e** (Rev: BLO 1/25/12; SLJ 4/1/12)

768 Sitomer, Alan Lawrence. *Daddies Do It Different* (PS–2). Illus. by Abby Carter. 2012, Hyperion $16.99 (978-142313315-5). 40pp. A young girl revels in the more chaotic but ultimately more fun ways her dad takes care of her, from dressing to bathing. (Rev: BL 2/15/12; SLJ 4/1/12)

769 Smith, Lane. *Grandpa Green* (K–2). Illus. by author. 2011, Roaring Brook $16.99 (978-1-59643-607-7). 32pp. A great-grandson celebrates his Grandpa Green's spectacular topiaries and what they convey about his long life. Caldecott Honor Book. **e** (Rev: BL 7/11; HB 9–10/11; LMC 11–12/11; SLJ 8/1/11*)

770 Stott, Ann. *I'll Be There* (PS–2). Illus. by Matt Phelan. 2010, Candlewick $14.99 (978-0-7636-4711-7). 32pp. A young son eagerly lists the things he no longer needs his mom to do for him, then asks for reassurance that she'll still be there, whether he needs her or not. (Rev: BL 2/1/11; SLJ 3/1/11)

771 Sullivan, Sarah. *Once Upon a Baby Brother* (K–3). Illus. by Tricia Tusa. 2010, Farrar $16.99 (978-0-374-34635-5). 32pp. Only when her baby brother goes away for the weekend does Lizzie realize the annoying child was actually inspiring the stories she loves to tell. (Rev: BL 5/1/10; LMC 11–12/10; SLJ 7/1/10)

772 Tillman, Nancy. *Wherever You Are: My Love Will Find You* (PS–2). Illus. by author. 2010, Feiwel & Friends $16.99 (978-031254966-4). 32pp. This sweetly reassuring rhyming picture book reinforces the message that all children are loved. (Rev: BL 9/15/10)

773 Tonatiuh, Duncan. *Dear Primo: A Letter to My Cousin* (1–3). Illus. by author. 2010, Abrams $15.95 (978-0-8109-3872-4). 32pp. Urban American Charlie exchanges letters with his Cousin Carlitos, who lives in rural Mexico; Spanish words and details of Mexican culture are integrated, and the illustrations are based on Mixtec art. (Rev: BL 2/1/10; SLJ 3/1/10)

774 Trottier, Maxine. *Migrant* (PS–2). Illus. by Isabelle Arsenault. 2011, Groundwood $18.95 (978-0-88899-975-7). 40pp. Anna's Mennonite family travels from Mexico to Canada each year to work in the fields, and the young girl imagines herself as a variety of animals in an effort to cope with the constant moving. (Rev: BL 4/1/11; LMC 10/11; SLJ 5/1/11)

775 Tuck, Justin. *Home-Field Advantage* (K–2). Illus. by Leonardo Rodriguez. 2011, Simon & Schuster $16.99 (978-1-4424-0369-7). 40pp. New York Giants defensive end Tuck offers a comic vignette from his childhood: the day he let his sisters cut his hair. Lexile AD540L (Rev: BLO 9/1/11; SLJ 9/1/11)

776 Velasquez, Eric. *Grandma's Gift* (1–3). Illus. by author. 2010, Walker $16.99 (978-080272082-5). 32pp. This companion to the autobiographical *Grandma's Records* (2001) describes young Eric's activities — including a visit to the Metropolitan Museum of Art — with his Puerto Rican grandmother during a winter break in New York City; Spanish phrases are included in the text. (Rev: BL 11/15/10; LMC 11–12/10; SLJ 10/10)

777 Wadham, Tim. *The Queen of France* (PS–3). Illus. by Kady MacDonald Denton. 2011, Candlewick $16.99 (978-0-7636-4102-3). 32pp. A young girl imagines herself the Queen of France, and considers all the ways her life might be easier before settling on being what she's most familiar with: herself. Lexile 400L (Rev: BL 4/15/11; HB 5–6/11; SLJ 2/1/11*)

778 Walton, Rick. *Baby's First Year!* (PS). Illus. by Caroline Jayne Church. 2011, Putnam $15.99 (978-0-399-25025-5). 32pp. In rhyming text and bright art, this book celebrates the key events of a baby's first year. (Rev: BL 2/15/11; SLJ 3/1/11)

779 Wells, Rosemary. *Love Waves* (PS–1). Illus. by author. 2011, Candlewick $15.99 (978-0-7636-4989-0). 32pp. A young rabbit's parents send warm thoughts — love waves — home to him while they're out at work. (Rev: BL 9/1/11; SLJ 9/1/11)

780 Wewer, Iris. *My Wild Sister and Me* (PS–2). Illus. by author. 2011, NorthSouth $16.95 (978-0-7358-4003-4). 32pp. A young boy and his older sister enjoy imaginative games together until a friend interrupts them, spoiling his day — until later. Lexile AD570L (Rev: BL 3/1/11; SLJ 3/1/11)

781 Winstanley, Nicola. *Cinnamon Baby* (PS–2). Illus. by Janice Nadeau. 2011, Kids Can $16.95 (978-1-55337-821-1). 32pp. Miriam's cinnamon bread attracts a violinist named Sebastian, and the two get married; their beautiful baby cries and cries until the smell of baking bread finally solves the problem. Lexile AD930L (Rev: BL 2/15/11; SLJ 4/11)

782 Witte, Anna. *Lola's Fandango* (K–3). Illus. by Micha Archer. 2011, Barefoot $16.99 (978-1-84686-174-1); paper $9.99 (978-1-84686-681-4). 48pp. Lola, living in the shadow of her older sister, decides to learn flamenco dancing as a way of differentiating herself from Clementina. (Rev: BL 8/11*; SLJ 12/1/11)

783 Woodson, Jacqueline. *Pecan Pie Baby* (PS–1). Illus. by Sophie Blackall. 2010, Putnam $16.99 (978-0-399-23987-8). 32pp. Gia's single-parent mother is pregnant, and Gia is jealous of the attention the pending arrival is getting. Boston Globe–Horn Book Award. Lexile AD710L (Rev: BL 8/10; HB 11–12/10; LMC 1–2/11; SLJ 10/1/10)

784 Yeh, Kat. *The Magic Brush: A Story of Love, Family, and Chinese Characters* (K–3). Illus. by Huy Voun Lee. 2011, Walker $16.99 (978-080272178-5). 40pp. A young Chinese American girl, Jasmine, is sad after the death of the grandfather who taught her calligraphy and told her stories, but she soon realizes that her younger brother would also be interested and shares what she has learned with him. (Rev: BL 12/15/10; LMC 3–4/11; SLJ 4/11)

785 Yolen, Jane. *My Father Knows the Names of Things* (PS–2). Illus. by Stephane Jorisch. 2010, Simon & Schuster $15.99 (978-1-4169-4895-7). 32pp. A young boy enumerates the amazing things that his father knows — the names of dogs, seven words that mean blue, the names of the planets — in this well-illustrated rhyming text. (Rev: BL 2/1/10; LMC 5–6/10; SLJ 3/1/10)

786 Yum, Hyewon. *There Are No Scary Wolves* (PS–K). Illus. by author. 2010, Farrar $16.99 (978-0-374-38060-1). 40pp. Balancing a young boy's imagination with reassuring scenes of everyday life, this book about seeing people as wolves capitalizes on the safety and comfort of family and the familiar. (Rev: BL 11/15/10; SLJ 10/1/10)

787 Yum, Hyewon. *The Twins' Blanket* (PS–2). Illus. by author. 2011, Farrar $16.99 (978-0-374-37972-8). 40pp. Five-year-old twin girls getting separate beds for the first time decide to divide their favorite blanket into two pieces. (Rev: BL 8/11; SLJ 8/1/11*)

788 Zia, F. *Hot, Hot Roti for Dada-ji* (1–3). Illus. by Ken Min. 2011, Lee & Low $17.95 (978-1-60060-443-0). 32pp. Grandfather Dada-ji's adventurous stories inspire young Aneel to make roti — flat, Indian bread — in this story full of Hindi culture. Lexile AD680L (Rev: BL 6/1/11; LMC 10/11; SLJ 6/11)

789 Ziefert, Harriet. *Grandma's Wedding Album* (K–3). Illus. by author. 2011, Blue Apple $17.99 (978-1-60905-058-0). 40pp. A grandmother shares her wedding album with her grandchildren; includes details of the engagement and wedding and covers wedding traditions around the world. (Rev: BLO 8/11; LMC 10/11; SLJ 6/11)

FRIENDSHIP STORIES

790 Al Abdullah, Her Majesty Queen Rania, and Kelly DiPucchio. *The Sandwich Swap* (PS–2). Illus. by Tri-

cia Tusa. 2010, Hyperion $16.99 (978-1-4231-2484-9). 32pp. Best friends Lily and Salma swap sandwiches — pita and hummus for peanut butter and jelly — and are pleasantly surprised by what they find. (Rev: BL 2/15/10; LMC 8–9/10; SLJ 4/1/10)

791 Allen, Joy. *Princess Party* (PS–K). Illus. by author. 2009, Putnam $16.99 (978-0-399-25259-4). Unpaged. Two little girls — one dressed in frills and the other wearing cowboy boots and T-shirt — host a princess party attended by diverse ethnicities wearing many styles. (Rev: SLJ 11/1/09)

792 Bateman, Teresa. *Paul Bunyan vs. Hals Halson: The Giant Lumberjack Challenge!* (PS–2). Illus. by C. B. Canga. 2011, Whitman $16.99 (978-0-8075-6367-0). 32pp. Paul Bunyan eventually succeeds in making friends with the lumberjack who has been doing his best to prove that he is better and stronger. (Rev: BL 4/15/11; SLJ 2/1/11)

793 Budnitz, Paul. *The Hole in the Middle* (PS–1). Illus. by Aya Kakeda. 2011, Hyperion/Disney $16.99 (978-1-4231-3761-0). 40pp. A self-centered young boy with a hole in his middle that leaves him feeling empty finds that the hole shrinks when he does something kind for a friend. (Rev: BL 6/1/11; SLJ 7/11)

794 Cuyler, Margery. *I Repeat, Don't Cheat!* (K–2). Illus. by Arthur Howard. 2010, Simon & Schuster $15.99 (978-1-4169-7167-2). 32pp. Jessica learns the fine line between helping her friend and letting her cheat. (Rev: BL 5/15/10; SLJ 6/1/10)

795 Demers, Dominique. *Today, Maybe* (K–3). Trans. by Sheila Fischman. Illus. by Gabrielle Grimard. 2011, Orca $19.95 (978-155469400-6). 32pp. Lovely paintings enhance this story about a young girl who is waiting for a special "someone" to turn up and dispatches visiting characters from children's literature, who include thieves, a wolf, a prince, and a witch. (Rev: BL 4/15/11)

796 DiPucchio, Kelly. *Crafty Chloe* (1–3). Illus. by Heather Ross. 2012, Atheneum $16.99 (978-144242123-3). 40pp. Unlike most of the other girls, Chloe's talent is making things, and this ability allows her to come to the rescue of an unkind classmate. **℮** (Rev: BL 12/15/11; LMC 5–6/12; SLJ 3/1/12)

797 Fagan, Cary. *Ella May and the Wishing Stone* (PS–1). Illus. by Geneviève Côté. 2011, Tundra $17.95 (978-1-77049-225-7). Unpaged. Ella May works to make amends after belittling her friends' efforts to imitate her "magical" wishing stone. (Rev: SLJ 8/1/11)

798 Harper, Charise Mericle. *Mimi and Lulu: Three Sweet Stories, One Forever Friendship* (PS–K). Illus. by author. 2009, HarperCollins $16.99 (978-0-06-17553-5). 40pp. Two friends share friction and rivalry in these three simple stories. (Rev: BL 11/15/09; SLJ 11/1/09)

799 Hudson, Cheryl Willis. *My Friend Maya Loves to Dance* (PS–3). Illus. by Eric Velasquez. 2010, Abrams $16.95 (978-0-8109-8328-1). 32pp. Vivid oil painting illustrations depict an African American girl who absolutely loves to dance. (Rev: BL 4/1/10; SLJ 6/1/10)

800 Joosse, Barbara. *Friends (Mostly)* (PS–1). Illus. by Tomaso Milian. 2010, Greenwillow $16.99 (978-0-06-088221-1). 32pp. Readers hear both sides of the story from Ruby and Henry, two friends whose relationship is sometimes rocky. (Rev: BL 10/1/10; SLJ 9/1/10)

801 Jules, Jacqueline. *Picnic at Camp Shalom* (K–3). Illus. by Deborah Melmon. 2011, Lerner/Kar-Ben $17.95 (978-0-7613-6661-4); paper $7.95 (978-0-7613-6662-1). 32pp. A misunderstanding threatens the new friendship between Carly and Sara in this Jewish camp story. Lexile AD560L (Rev: BL 6/1/11; SLJ 6/11)

802 Kirsch, Vincent. *Forsythia and Me* (PS–2). Illus. by author. 2011, Farrar $16.99 (978-0-374-32438-4). 40pp. Chester has always admired his friend Forsythia from afar but feels closer to her when she is ill and he succeeds in entertaining her. **e** Lexile AD680L (Rev: BL 1/1–15/11; LMC 5–6/11; SLJ 3/1/11)

803 Kostecki-Shaw, Jenny Sue. *Same, Same but Different* (PS–1). Illus. by author. 2011, Henry Holt $16.99 (978-0-8050-8946-2). 40pp. An American pen pal and his Indian counterpart exchange letters noting the similarities and differences in their cultures; they both, for example, enjoy climbing trees and going to school. (Rev: BLO 9/1/11; SLJ 8/1/11)

804 McGhee, Alison. *Making a Friend* (PS–K). Illus. by Marc Rosenthal. 2011, Atheneum $16.99 (978-1-4169-8998-1). 40pp. A simple story about a boy who builds a snowman, and even when it melts continues to feel its presence in his world. (Rev: BL 10/1/11; SLJ 10/1/11)

805 Mackintosh, David. *Marshall Armstrong Is New to Our School* (PS–2). Illus. by author. 2011, Abrams $16.95 (978-1-4197-0036-1). 32pp. Marshall, the new kid — and misfit — at school gains acceptance when he invites his classmates over to his house full of telescopes, instruments, and other fun gadgets. (Rev: BL 8/11; LMC 1–2/12; SLJ 8/1/11)

806 Manushkin, Fran. *Best Season Ever* (K–2). Illus. by Tammie Lyon. Series: Katie Woo. 2010, Picture Window LB $19.99 (978-1-4048-5730-8). 32pp. Katie and her friends Pedro and JoJo share their opinions about the different seasons, agreeing to disagree where necessary. (Rev: SLJ 5/1/10)

807 Moulton, Mark. *The Very Best Pumpkin* (PS–2). Illus. by Karen Good. 2010, Simon & Schuster $12.99 (978-1-4169-8288-3). 32pp. A pumpkin brings new neighbors Peter and shy Megan together in this warm book about farming. **e** Lexile AD980L (Rev: BL 8/10; SLJ 7/1/10)

808 Primavera, Elise. *Louise the Big Cheese and the Ooh-la-la Charm School* (K–2). Illus. by Diane Goode.

2012, Simon & Schuster $16.99 (978-144240599-8). 40pp. Eager for attention, Louise finds herself comically duped by a trendy new girl who purports to be from Paris. **e** (Rev: BL 2/1/12; SLJ 1/12)

809 Reid, Barbara. *Perfect Snow* (K–3). Illus. by author. 2011, Whitman $16.99 (978-0-8075-6492-9). 32pp. Scott and Jim, friends despite their different personalities, discover they can achieve a better snowman creation when they work together. (Rev: BL 10/1/11*; SLJ 8/1/11)

810 Reynolds, Peter H. *I'm Here* (PS–2). Illus. by author. 2011, Atheneum $15.99 (978-1-4169-9649-4). 32pp. A young boy who lives in his own world and feels alone even among a group of children makes an airplane out of a piece of paper and sends it off, surprised to find it returned to him by a girl. (Rev: BL 9/15/11; SLJ 10/1/11)

811 Rumford, James. *Tiger and Turtle* (1–3). Illus. by author. 2010, Roaring Brook $17.99 (978-1-59643-416-5). 32pp. A tiger and a turtle initially quarrel over a fallen flower but in the end learning an important lesson about friendship and sharing. Lexile AD950L (Rev: HB 5–6/10; LMC 5–6/10; SLJ 4/1/10)

812 Shields, Gillian. *Library Lily* (PS–1). Illus. by Francesca Chessa. 2011, Eerdmans $16 (978-0-8028-5401-8). 26pp. Young Lily loves to read and young Milly loves outdoor adventures, and together the two grow older and share their passions. (Rev: BL 11/1/11; SLJ 8/1/11)

813 Smallcomb, Pam. *I'm Not* (PS–1). Illus. by Robert Weinstock. 2011, Random House $15.99 (978-0-375-86115-4); LB $18.99 (978-0-375-96115-1). 32pp. Two friends learn to appreciate their differences in this nicely illustrated story. (Rev: BL 1/1–15/11; HB 3–4/11; SLJ 3/1/11)

814 Sydor, Colleen. *Timmerman Was Here* (K–3). Illus. by Nicolas Debon. 2009, Tundra $19.95 (978-0-88776-890-3). 32pp. A young girl is resentful of the boarder who moves into her grandfather's room, and is initially suspicious of the boarder's nocturnal activities; after her new friend departs, spring reveals that he was planting tulips around the neighborhood. (Rev: BL 11/15/09; SLJ 11/1/09)

815 Willems, Mo. *Hooray for Amanda and Her Alligator* (PS–2). Illus. by author. 2011, HarperCollins $17.99 (978-006200400-0). 72pp. Amanda's stuffed alligator is used to having her to himself and must make adjustments when she brings home a stuffed panda. Lexile AD360L (Rev: BL 4/1/11; HB 7–8/11; LMC 10/11; SLJ 5/11)

816 Wishinsky, Frieda. *You're Mean, Lily Jean!* (PS–2). Illus. by Kady MacDonald Denton. 2011, Whitman $16.99 (978-0-8075-9476-6). 32pp. Sandy always played with her little sister Carly until Lily Jean moved in next door and demoted Carly to subsidiary roles. Lexile AD350L (Rev: BL 2/1/11; SLJ 2/1/11)

HUMOROUS STORIES

817 Agee, Jon. *Mr. Putney's Quacking Dog* (K–2). Illus. by author. 2010, Scholastic $16.95 (978-0-545-16203-6). 48pp. A pun-filled book of animal jokes revolving around names. (Rev: BL 7/10; HB 7–8/10; LMC 10/10; SLJ 7/1/10)

818 Allen, Elanna. *Itsy Mitsy Runs Away* (PS–K). Illus. by author. 2011, Atheneum $16.99 (978-1-4424-0671-1). 40pp. A little girl is so fed up with bedtime that she decides to run away from home, and her kindhearted father helps her pack, reminding her just how much she will need to take with her. (Rev: BL 6/1/11; SLJ 5/1/11)

819 Asch, Frank, and Devin Asch. *The Daily Comet: Boy Saves Earth from Giant Octopus!* (2–4). Illus. by Frank Asch. 2010, Kids Can $16.95 (978-1-55453-281-0). 32pp. A science-minded boy refuses to believe the stories his tabloid editor father writes for the *Daily Comet* until he accompanies his dad on Go to Work With a Parent Day and beholds a giant octopus and other weird wonders; with effective retro illustrations. (Rev: BL 11/1/10; LMC 1–2/11; SLJ 6/11)

820 Ashman, Linda. *No Dogs Allowed* (PS–2). Illus. by Kristin Sorra. 2011, Sterling $14.95 (978-1-4027-5837-9). 32pp. This nearly wordless picture book tells the story of a restaurant with a "no dogs" policy that is forced to expand this to cover a wide range of outlandish animals brought by pet owners. (Rev: BL 9/1/11; SLJ 9/1/11)

821 Ashman, Linda. *Samantha on a Roll* (PS–1). Illus. by Christine Davenier. 2011, Farrar $16.99 (978-0-374-36399-4). 40pp. On her brand new skates for the first time, Samantha takes fast, crazy trip through town. (Rev: BL 12/1/11; SLJ 9/1/11)

822 Barnett, Mac. *Chloe and the Lion* (K–3). Illus. by Adam Rex. 2012, Hyperion $16.99 (978-142311334-8). 48pp. Author and illustrator have creative differences about their book, and it is up to Chloe, the protagonist, to set them on the right track. (Rev: BL 4/1/12; LMC 5–6/12; SLJ 4/1/12*)

823 Barnett, Mac. *Mustache!* (K–2). Illus. by Kevin Cornell. 2011, Hyperion/Disney $16.99 (978-1-4231-1671-4). 40pp. A vain king's subjects find a clever solution to their leader's unchecked narcissism. (Rev: BL 12/1/11; SLJ 9/1/11)

824 Beard, Alex. *The Jungle Grapevine* (K–2). Illus. by author. 2009, Abrams $16.95 (978-0-8109-8001-3). 48pp. An offhand remark by Turtle starts a rumor that morphs and escalates as it travels across the savanna in this amusing story paralleling a game of telephone. (Rev: BL 9/15/09; LMC 8–9/10; SLJ 9/1/09)

825 Beaty, Andrea. *Artist Ted* (PS–2). Illus. by Pascal Lemaitre. 2012, Simon & Schuster $15.99 (978-141695374-6). 32pp. Young Ted's sudden passion for art and his choice of materials (ketchup, mustard) meet less-than-appreciative reactions at home and at school. **e** Lexile AD430L (Rev: BL 2/15/12; LMC 8–9/12)

826 Bendall-Brunello, Tiziana. *I Wish I Could Read! A Story About Making Friends* (PS). Illus. by John Bendall-Brunello. 2011, Amicus LB $16.95 (978-160992109-5). 24pp. A young pig finds a book and is frustrated at his friends' inability to teach him to read but finally finds a boy who can give him what he wants. (Rev: BLO 10/15/11; SLJ 3/12)

827 Black, Michael Ian. *A Pig Parade Is a Terrible Idea* (PS–2). Illus. by Kevin Hawkes. 2010, Simon & Schuster $16.99 (978-1-4169-7922-7). 40pp. A pig parade may sound like an excellent idea, but this funny book makes clear it should be avoided. **e** Lexile AD970L (Rev: BL 8/10*; LMC 1–2/11; SLJ 12/1/10*)

828 Black, Michael Ian. *The Purple Kangaroo* (PS–2). Illus. by Peter Brown. 2010, Simon & Schuster $16.99 (978-1-4169-5771-3). 32pp. A cheeky, captivating monkey claims to be a mind-reader in this energetic story, challenging readers to put his considerable, though zany, skills to the test. Lexile AD630L (Rev: BL 1/1/10; LMC 5–6/10; SLJ 2/1/10)

829 Blackwood, Freya. *Ivy Loves to Give* (PS). Illus. by author. 2010, Scholastic $15.99 (978-0-545-23467-2). Unpaged. Ivy is immensely generous but her gifts are not always appropriate. (Rev: HB 11–12/10; SLJ 10/1/10)

830 Bliss, Harry. *Bailey* (PS–2). Illus. by author. 2011, Scholastic $16.99 (978-0-545-23344-6). Unpaged. Bailey the dog is the favorite pupil at his elementary school in this funny book with appealing cartoon illustrations. (Rev: HB 11–12/11; SLJ 9/1/11*)

831 Brennan, Eileen. *Dirtball Pete* (1–3). Illus. by author. 2010, Random House $15.99 (978-0-375-83425-7). 32pp. A mother's attempts to scrub her dirty son go for naught when his script for the school assembly is blown away and he ends up as muddy as ever. **e** (Rev: BL 7/10; LMC 11–12/10; SLJ 7/1/10)

832 Brown, Calef. *Boy Wonders* (PS–2). Illus. by author. 2011, Atheneum $16.99 (978-1-4169-7877-0). 40pp. "Is water scared of waterfalls?" "Are phones annoyed if no one calls?" Brown tackles these and other vexing questions and provides suitably appealing illustrations. (Rev: BL 6/1/11; SLJ 6/11)

833 Brown, Peter. *Children Make Terrible Pets* (PS–2). Illus. by author. 2010, Little, Brown $16.99 (978-0-316-01548-6). 40pp. In this funny role-reversal story, a young bear called Lucy comes to the difficult realization that humans do not make good pets. (Rev: BL 10/1/10; LMC 1–2/11*; SLJ 9/1/10)

49

834 Brown, Peter. *You Will Be My Friend!* (PS–2). Illus. by author. 2011, Little, Brown $16.99 (978-0-316-07030-0). Unpaged. Lucy the bear last seen in *Children Make Terrible Pets* (2010) is determined to make a new friend but many potential pals find her approach offputting. (Rev: SLJ 9/1/11)

835 Chaconas, Dori. *Don't Slam the Door!* (PS–2). Illus. by Will Hillenbrand. 2010, Candlewick $15.99 (978-0-7636-3709-5). 32pp. A funny cumulative, rhyming tale that starts with a slamming door that wakes a cat and leads to a series of chaotic events on a farm. (Rev: BL 8/10; LMC 11–12/10; SLJ 7/1/10)

836 Cox, Judy. *Pick a Pumpkin, Mrs. Millie!* (PS–2). Illus. by Joe Mathieu. 2009, Marshall Cavendish $15.99 (978-0-7614-5573-8). 32pp. Mrs. Millie, the teacher with funny language difficulties, takes her class on a field trip to a pumpkin farm. 🎧 📧 Lexile AD390L (Rev: BL 11/1/09; SLJ 9/1/09)

837 Cronin, Doreen. *M.O.M. (Mom Operating Manual)* (2–4). Illus. by Laura Cornell. 2011, Atheneum $16.99 (978-1-4169-6150-5). 56pp. A humorous guide to the care and feeding of mothers, with chapters on "Outdoor Use" and "Troubleshooting" and advice on danger signals. (Rev: BL 10/1/11; SLJ 10/1/11)

838 Cummings, Troy. *The Eensy Weensy Spider Freaks Out (Big Time)* (K–3). Illus. by author. 2010, Random House $16.99 (978-0-375-86582-4). 40pp. Eensy the spider initially decides to retire from climbing after being washed out of the waterspout, but gradually regains her nerve with help from her ladybug friend. (Rev: BL 4/1/10; LMC 8–9/10; SLJ 4/1/10)

839 Deacon, Alexis. *A Place to Call Home* (PS–1). Illus. by Viviane Schwarz. 2011, Candlewick $16.99 (978-0-7636-5360-6). Unpaged. Seven overcrowded hamster siblings set out in search of a bigger home and have many adventures — crossing a sea (a puddle), climbing a mountain (a desk), and so forth. (Rev: LMC 11–12/11; SLJ 9/1/11)

840 deGroat, Diane, and Shelley Rotner. *Homer* (1–3). Illus. by Diane deGroat. 2012, Scholastic $15.99 (978-054533272-9). 32pp. Homer the golden retriever sneaks out at night to play baseball in a contest between the Doggers and the Hounds in this funny story. (Rev: BL 3/1/12; SLJ 5/1/12)

841 Depalma, Mary Newell. *Uh-Oh!* (PS–1). Illus. by author. 2011, Eerdmans $14 (978-0-8028-5372-1). Unpaged. A young dinosaur gets himself into a series of funny "uh-oh!" situations in this nearly wordless book. (Rev: SLJ 8/1/11)

842 De Sève, Randall. *The Duchess of Whimsy: An Absolutely Delicious Fairy Tale* (K–2). Illus. by Peter de Sève. 2009, Philomel $17.99 (978-0-399-25095-8). 40pp. The Duchess of Whimsy and the Earl of Norm find common ground despite their eccentric differences

when he introduces her to grilled cheese sandwiches. (Rev: BL 10/1/09; SLJ 11/1/09)

843 DiCamillo, Kate, and Alison McGhee. *Bink and Gollie* (K–3). Illus. by Tony Fucile. 2010, Candlewick $15.99 (978-0-7636-3266-3). 96pp. Two oddball roller-skating friends — short Bink and tall Gollie — enjoy three humorous adventures in this picture book/graphic novel. Theodore Seuss Geisel Award. Lexile AD270L (Rev: BL 9/15/10; HB 1–2/11; LMC 11–12/10; SLJ 8/1/10)

844 DiCamillo, Kate, and Alison McGhee. *Two for One* (K–3). Illus. by Tony Fucile. 2012, Candlewick $15.99 (978-076363361-5). 96pp. Friends Bink and Gollie enjoy a day at the state fair, despite the mishaps they encounter. (Rev: BL 5/1/12; HB 5–6/12; SLJ 5/1/12*)

845 DiPucchio, Kelly. *Zombie in Love* (K–2). Illus. by Scott Campbell. 2011, Atheneum $12.99 (978-1-4424-0270-6). 32pp. A lonely little zombie who longs for love has no luck until the night of the Cupid's Ball. (Rev: BLO 8/11; SLJ 8/1/11)

846 Dormer, Frank W. *Socksquatch* (PS–2). Illus. by author. 2010, Henry Holt $14.99 (978-0-8050-8952-3). Unpaged. A cold-footed monster storms a castle in search of the perfect sock in this comic story. (Rev: SLJ 12/1/10)

847 Elkin, Mark. *Samuel's Baby* (PS–2). Illus. by Amy Wummer. 2010, Tricycle $15.99 (978-1-58246-301-8). Unpaged. A young boy prepares for the arrival of his baby sister by sharing his anxiety with his kindergarten class in this funny and reassuring picture book. (Rev: SLJ 7/1/10)

848 Ernst, Lisa Campbell. *The Gingerbread Girl Goes Animal Crackers* (PS–1). Illus. by author. 2011, Dutton $16.99 (978-0-525-42259-4). 32pp. Initially thrilled with a gift box of animal crackers, Gingerbread Girl unleashes considerable chaos when the animated animals are let out of their box; a sequel to *The Gingerbread Girl* (2006). (Rev: BLO 10/1/11; SLJ 12/1/11)

849 Feiffer, Kate. *But I Wanted a Baby Brother!* (K–3). Illus. by Diane Goode. 2010, Simon & Schuster $16.99 (978-1-4169-3941-2). 32pp. Instead of the baby brother he expected, Oliver is disappointed when his mom has a girl, and attempts to change the child for a baby boy. (Rev: BL 4/15/10; SLJ 6/1/10)

850 Frazee, Marla. *The Boss Baby* (K–2). Illus. by author. 2010, Simon & Schuster $16.99 (978-1-4424-0167-9). 40pp. A tyrannical baby in a suit-style onesie runs the household in corporate executive style, exhausting his weary parents. (Rev: BL 7/10; HB 7–8/10; SLJ 7/1/10*)

851 Gantos, Jack. *Three Strikes for Rotten Ralph* (1–3). Illus. by Nicole Rubel. Series: Rotten Ralph Rotten Reader. 2011, Farrar $16.99 (978-0-374-36354-3). 48pp. Rotten Ralph the cat has baseball aspirations that are subdued when he gets hit in the head, and he settles for being the team's "cat boy" instead. (Rev: BL 2/15/11; SLJ 1/1/11)

852 Gravett, Emily. *Spells* (K–3). Illus. by author. 2009, Simon & Schuster $16.99 (978-1-4169-8270-8). Unpaged. A small, ambitious frog researches a spell that will turn him into a prince, but doesn't pay sufficient attention. (Rev: LMC 11–12/09; SLJ 10/1/09*)

853 Grogan, John. *Marley Goes to School* (K–3). Illus. by Richard Cowdrey. 2009, HarperCollins $17.99 (978-0-06-156151-1); LB $18.89 (978-0-06-156152-8). Unpaged. Marley the dog follows his owner Cassie to school, where hilarity and mayhem ensue. (Rev: SLJ 11/1/09)

854 Hale, Dean. *Scapegoat: The Story of a Goat Named Oat and a Chewed-Up Coat* (K–2). Illus. by Michael Slack. 2011, Bloomsbury $16.99 (978-1-59990-468-9). Unpaged. A kindhearted neighbor intervenes on behalf of Patsy Petunia Oat the goat, who's getting unjustly blamed for Jimmy Choat's frequent misdeeds. (Rev: BL 4/15/11; LMC 10/11; SLJ 6/11)

855 Harris, Teresa E. *Summer Jackson: Grown Up* (K–3). Illus. by AG Ford. 2011, HarperCollins $16.99 (978-0-06-185757-7). Unpaged. Summer, a 7-year-old African American girl who is overeager for adult responsibilities, realizes maturity isn't all it's cracked up to be when her parents agree to let her take over their chores for a day. (Rev: SLJ 8/1/11)

856 Hassett, Ann. *Too Many Frogs!* (K–2). Illus. by John Hassett. 2011, Houghton Mifflin $16.99 (978-0-547-36299-1). 32pp. Overwhelmed by frogs emerging from her basement, Nana Quimby gets advice from neighborhood children but in the end has to solve the problem herself. (Rev: BLO 8/11; HB 7–8/11; SLJ 8/1/11)

857 Heide, Florence Parry, and Roxanne Heide Pierce. *Always Listen to Your Mother* (K–2). Illus. by Kyle M. Stone. 2010, Hyperion $15.99 (978-1-4231-1395-9). 32pp. Ernest, an obedient son of a demanding mother, finds a whole new outlook on life when spooky Vlapid and his mother move in next door. (Rev: BL 6/10; LMC 11–12/10; SLJ 7/1/10)

858 Helakoski, Leslie. *Big Chickens Go to Town* (PS–2). Illus. by Henry Cole. 2010, Dutton $16.99 (978-0-525-42162-7). 32pp. The four funny chickens accidentally hitch a ride into town in the farmer's truck and are overwhelmed by the sights in this exuberant romp full of wordplay. (Rev: BL 1/1/10; SLJ 2/1/10)

859 Himmelman, John. *Cows to the Rescue* (PS–2). Illus. by author. 2011, Henry Holt $16.99 (978-0-8050-9249-3). 32pp. When the family's car won't start, their farm animals willingly provide them with transportation to the county fair in this humorous romp. e Lexile AD510L (Rev: BLO 10/15/11; SLJ 8/1/11)

860 Himmelman, John. *Pigs to the Rescue* (PS–2). Illus. by author. 2010, Henry Holt $16.99 (978-0-8050-8683-6). 32pp. The pigs — and then the cows — overextend themselves in helping solve problems around the Greenstalk farm in this zany sequel to *Chickens to the Rescue* (2006). (Rev: BL 2/1/10; SLJ 4/1/10)

861 Holt, Kimberly Willis. *The Adventures of Granny Clearwater and Little Critter* (K–3). Illus. by Laura Huliska-Beith. 2010, Henry Holt $16.99 (978-0-8050-7899-2). 32pp. In this hyperbolic Old West tall tale, Granny and Little Critter have some run-ins with outlaws on their way west to California. Lexile AD920L (Rev: BL 11/1/10; LMC 1–2/11; SLJ 9/1/10)

862 Horowitz, Dave. *Buy My Hats!* (K–2). Illus. by author. 2010, Putnam $16.99 (978-0-399-25275-4). 32pp. Washed-up hat salesmen Frank and Carl cheer a change in the weather that makes their wares fly off the shelves in this comic story about consumer whims. (Rev: BL 6/10; LMC 11–12/10; SLJ 6/1/10)

863 Hosford, Kate. *Big Bouffant* (PS–2). Illus. by Holly Clifton-Brown. 2011, Carolrhoda $16.95 (978-0-7613-5409-3). 32pp. Bored with ordinary hairstyles, Annabelle decides to adopt a bouffant hairdo and ends up starting a school-wide trend. e Lexile AD550L (Rev: SLJ 4/11)

864 Huget, Jennifer LaRue. *The Best Birthday Party Ever* (K–1). Illus. by LeUyen Pham. 2011, Random House $16.99 (978-0-375-84763-9); LB $19.99 (978-0-375-95763-5). 32pp. A fanciful 6-year-old girl begins planning her birthday party five months in advance; comic illustrations add appeal. (Rev: BL 4/15/11; SLJ 4/11)

865 Huget, Jennifer LaRue. *How to Clean Your Room in 10 Easy Steps* (K–3). Illus. by Edward Koren. 2010, Random House $16.99 (978-0-375-84410-2). 40pp. An entertaining guide to a tiresome chore. (Rev: BL 5/15/10; LMC 8–9/10; SLJ 4/1/10)

866 Isaacs, Anne. *Dust Devil* (PS–2). Illus. by Paul O. Zelinsky. 2010, Random House $17.99 (978-0-375-86722-4). 48pp. In this tall tale sequel to 1994's *Swamp Angel,* the outsized Angelica tames a dust storm and rides off on a giant horse to defeat some desperadoes; set in 1835 Montana. e Lexile AD900L (Rev: BL 9/1/10*; LMC 1–2/11*; SLJ 9/1/10*)

867 Jarka, Jeff. *Love That Kitty! The Story of a Boy Who Wanted to Be a Cat* (PS–2). Illus. by author. 2010, Henry Holt $12.99 (978-0-8050-9053-6). 32pp. Peter decides to become a cat in this sequel to *Love That Puppy! The Story of a Boy Who Wanted to Be a Dog* (2009), and his parents patiently deal with his phases. (Rev: BL 10/1/10; SLJ 9/1/10)

868 Jeffers, Oliver. *Stuck* (PS–3). Illus. by author. 2011, Philomel $16.99 (978-0-399-25737-7). 32pp. A cumulative tale in which young Floyd throws increasingly large objects — all the way from a shoe up to a house, a fire truck, and a whale — into a tree trying to dislodge his kit. e (Rev: BL 12/1/11; LMC 5–6/12; SLJ 12/1/11)

869 Kaplan, Bruce. *Monsters Eat Whiny Children* (K–3). Illus. by author. 2010, Simon & Schuster $15.99 (978-1-4169-8689-8). 40pp. In this cautionary tale, two whiny children are kidnapped by a monster intending to eat them for dinner. Lexile AD660L (Rev: BL 8/10; SLJ 9/1/10*)

870 Könnecke, Ole. *Anton Can Do Magic* (PS–2). Illus. by author. 2011, Gecko $17.95 (978-1-8774-6737-0). Unpaged. Illustrations and text combine to tell the story of an aspiring magician with a wonky turban. (Rev: LMC 1–2/12; SLJ 10/1/11)

871 Krasnesky, Thad. *That Cat Can't Stay* (K–2). Illus. by David Parkins. 2010, Flashlight $16.95 (978-0-9799746-5-6). Unpaged. Mom loves cats and keeps taking in strays despite Dad's objections — until Dad finally comes home with a dog. (Rev: LMC 9–10/10; SLJ 5/1/10)

872 Kuskin, Karla. *A Boy Had a Mother Who Bought Him a Hat* (PS–1). Illus. by Kevin Hawkes. 2010, HarperCollins $16.99 (978-0-06-075330-6). 32pp. In this updated version of the 1976 classic, a young boy receives a series of bizarre gifts from his mother, and insists on wearing or using them all at once — a cello, a mouse, a hat, fancy shoes, skis, a Halloween mask, and an elephant. (Rev: BL 2/15/10; SLJ 3/1/10)

873 Latimer, Alex. *The Boy Who Cried Ninja* (PS–2). Illus. by author. 2011, Peachtree $15.95 (978-0-56145-579-9). 32pp. A young boy tired of getting blamed for the mischief caused by his absurd and rambunctious friends invites them all over so his parents can see the truth. Lexile AD740L (Rev: BL 4/1/11; SLJ 3/1/11)

874 Lewis, Jill. *Don't Read This Book!* (2–4). Illus. by Deborah Allwright. 2010, ME Media/Tiger Tales $15.95 (978-1-58925-094-9). 32pp. A fat, belligerent king threatens his Royal Storyteller — who seems in the midst of writing some of best-loved fairy tales of all times — in this funny fractured fairy tale. Lexile AD530L (Rev: BL 11/15/10; LMC 1–2/11; SLJ 10/1/10)

875 Lewis, Kevin. *Not Inside This House* (K–2). Illus. by David Ercolini. 2011, Scholastic $16.99 (978-043943981-7). 40pp. Livingstone Columbus Magellan Crouse's increasingly ambitious naturalist interests are not appreciated by his parents! (Rev: BLO 8/11)

876 Lloyd-Jones, Sally. *How to Get a Job — by Me, the Boss* (PS–2). Illus. by Sue Heap. 2011, Random House $17.99 (978-0-375-86664-7); LB $20.99 (978-0-375-96664-4). Unpaged. The narrator from *How to Be a Baby — By Me, the Big Sister* (2007) explains to friends and baby brother the various kinds of jobs there are (president of the world, magician, cowboy, engineer) and how to go about getting one. ℮ (Rev: SLJ 8/1/11)

877 Lum, Kate. *Princesses Are Not Perfect* (PS–3). Illus. by Sue Hellard. 2010, Bloomsbury $16.99 (978-1-59990-432-0); LB $17.89 (978-159990433-7). 32pp. Three princesses with specific talents switch roles for a day with chaotic results. (Rev: BL 12/1/09; LMC 3–4/10; SLJ 3/1/10)

878 Maccarone, Grace. *Miss Lina's Ballerinas* (PS–3). Illus. by Christine Davenier. 2010, Feiwel & Friends $16.99 (978-0-312-38243-8). 40pp. In the European city of Messina, Miss Lina has eight students (whose names all end in "ina") and must find a way to settle them down when a ninth girl — Regina — joins the class and disrupts the system of dancing in pairs. ℮ Lexile AD610L (Rev: BL 11/1/10*; SLJ 12/1/10*)

879 Maccarone, Grace. *Miss Lina's Ballerinas and the Prince* (PS–3). Illus. by Christine Davenier. 2011, Feiwel & Friends $16.99 (978-0-312-64963-0). 40pp. Miss Lina's budding ballerinas are excited when they hear a boy will be joining the class, imagining him as a prince, but the reality is somewhat different. ℮ Lexile AD790L (Rev: BL 10/15/11; SLJ 11/1/11*)

880 Milgrim, David. *Eddie Gets Ready for School* (PS–2). Illus. by author. 2011, Scholastic $8.99 (978-0-545-27329-9). 32pp. Eddie has a checklist for school days that all young readers will recognize: "Wake up." "Fall back asleep." "Wake up again." (Rev: BL 8/11; HB 7–8/11; SLJ 7/11)

881 Moser, Lisa. *Perfect Soup* (PS–1). Illus. by Ben Mantle. 2010, Random House $16.99 (978-0-375-86014-0). 40pp. Murray the mouse needs a carrot for his Perfect Soup, and there begins a cumulative tale involving everyone from a farmer to a horse, a shopkeeper, and a snowman. (Rev: BLO 12/1/10; SLJ 11/1/10)

882 Murguia, Bethanie Deeney. *Zoe Gets Ready* (PS–K). Illus. by author. 2012, Scholastic $16.99 (978-054534215-5). 40pp. It's Saturday — the day when young fashionista Zoe is allowed to choose her own clothes — and the little girl has trouble making a decision because the day offers so many possibilities. (Rev: BL 5/1/12; SLJ 6/1/12)

883 Nesbitt, Kenn. *More Bears!* (PS–2). Illus. by Troy Cummings. 2010, Sourcebooks $12.99 (978-1-4022-3835-2). Unpaged. An author tries to write a story without bears, but his young (unseen) audience disagrees with this choice and demands more bears until things get totally out of control. (Rev: LMC 1–2/11; SLJ 1/1/11)

884 O'Connor, Jane. *Fancy Nancy: Aspiring Artist* (1–3). Illus. by Robin Preiss Glasser. Series: Fancy Nancy. 2011, HarperCollins $12.99 (978-006191526-0). 32pp. Inspired by the paintings hanging in her ballet classroom, Fancy Nancy stages an exhibition. (Rev: BL 6/1/11)

885 O'Connor, Jane. *Fancy Nancy: Ooh La La! It's Beauty Day* (PS–2). Illus. by Robin Preiss Glasser. Series: Fancy Nancy. 2010, HarperCollins $12.99 (978-0-06-191525-3). Unpaged. For her mother's birthday,

Nancy converts the backyard into a spa and gives her mother a beauty treatment. (Rev: SLJ 11/1/10)

886 Offill, Jenny. *Eleven Experiments That Failed* (K–2). Illus. by Nancy Carpenter. 2011, Random House $16.99 (978-0-375-84762-2); LB $19.99 (978-0-375-95762-8). Unpaged. A young scientist undertakes a variety of ill-fated science experiments in this humorous tale rooted in scientific method. **e** (Rev: SLJ 11/1/11)

887 O'Malley, Kevin. *Animal Crackers Fly the Coop* (K–3). Illus. by author. 2010, Walker $16.99 (978-0-8027-9837-4). 40pp. In this humorous take-off of "The Bremen Town Musicians," Hen, Dog, Cat, and Cow set off to become comedians and find themselves embroiled with a bunch of robbers. (Rev: BL 2/15/10; LMC 1–2/10; SLJ 2/1/10*)

888 Orloff, Karen Kaufman. *I Wanna New Room* (PS–2). Illus. by David Catrow. 2010, Putnam $16.99 (978-0-399-25405-5). 32pp. A little boy, tired of crowding and chaos, campaigns for his own room through illustrated letters to his parents. (Rev: BL 10/15/10; LMC 3–4/11*; SLJ 12/1/10)

889 Patricelli, Leslie. *Be Quiet, Mike!* (PS–1). Illus. by author. 2011, Candlewick $14.99 (978-0-7636-4477-2). Unpaged. Young monkey Mike is constantly annoying people with his incessant drumming and banging until he creates a pots and pans drum set that changes minds. (Rev: HB 9–10/11; SLJ 8/1/11)

890 Pearce, Emily Smith. *Slowpoke* (1–3). Illus. by Scot Ritchie. 2010, Boyds Mills $16.95 (978-1-59078-705-2). 40pp. Fed up with their daughter's slow poke pace of life, toddler Fiona's parents enroll her in speed school in this comically exaggerated story about the breakneck pace of modern life. Lexile 370L (Rev: BL 10/15/10; SLJ 11/1/10)

891 Peck, Jan. *Giant Peach Yodel!* (K–3). Illus. by Barry Root. 2012, Pelican $16.99 (978-158980980-2). 32pp. Little Buddy Earl's yodeling skills save the family's reputation at the Peach Pickin' Festival in this retelling of a Russian folk tale set in the American South. (Rev: BL 4/1/12; SLJ 7/12)

892 Perry, Andrea. *The Bicklebys' Birdbath* (PS–2). Illus. by Roberta Angaramo. 2010, Atheneum $16.99 (978-1-4169-0624-7). 40pp. In this zany cumulative story, a series of animal-related mishaps concludes with a bewildered mailman in the Bicklebys' birdbath. (Rev: BL 2/1/10; LMC 3–4/10; SLJ 3/1/10)

893 Perry, John. *The Book That Eats People* (PS–3). Illus. by Mark Fearing. 2009, Tricycle $15.99 (978-1-58246-268-4). Unpaged. A panicked narrator warns readers about a hungry book that is on a rampage, eating both children and grown-ups. (Rev: SLJ 11/1/09)

894 Plourde, Lynn. *Dino Pets Go to School* (PS–1). Illus. by Gideon Kendall. 2011, Dutton $16.99 (978-0-525-42232-7). 32pp. A young boy brings his dinosaurs to Pet Day at school with unpredictable and comical results; "Dino Facts" are appended. (Rev: BL 8/11; SLJ 7/11)

895 Portis, Antoinette. *Princess Super Kitty* (PS–1). Illus. by author. 2011, HarperCollins $14.99 (978-0-06-182725-9). 40pp. Young Maggie has a creative imagination that inflates her status and her needs until she is Water Lily Hula Porpoise Princess Super Kitty of the Sea. (Rev: BL 10/15/11; SLJ 10/1/11)

896 Primavera, Elise. *Thumb Love* (PS–2). Illus. by author. 2010, Random House $16.99 (978-0-375-84481-2); LB $19.99 (978-037595182-4). 48pp. A devoted thumb-sucker devises a 12-step recovery program for fellow addicts in this humorous story. (Rev: BL 10/15/10; SLJ 10/1/10)

897 Raczka, Bob. *Fall Mixed Up* (K–3). Illus. by Chad Cameron. 2011, Carolrhoda $17.95 (978-0-7613-4606-7). 40pp. An entertaining introduction to the joys and images of autumn, with mixed-up facts that will keep children guessing. (Rev: BLO 10/1/11; LMC 1–2/12; SLJ 11/1/11)

898 Rausch, Molly. *My Cold Went on Vacation* (PS–2). Illus. by Nora Krug. 2011, Putnam $16.99 (978-0-399-25474-1). 32pp. When a young boy's cold goes away, he imagines the adventures it's having without him. (Rev: BL 1/1–15/11; SLJ 3/1/11)

899 Rennert, Laura Joy. *Buying, Training and Caring for Your Dinosaur* (K–2). Illus. by Marc Brown. 2009, Knopf $16.99 (978-0-375-83679-4). Unpaged. Various species of dinosaur are profiled in this tongue-in-cheek guide to keeping dinosaurs as pets. (Rev: BL 10/1/09; SLJ 10/1/09)

900 Robinson, Fiona. *What Animals Really Like: A New Song Composed and Conducted by Mr. Herbert Timberteeth* (1–2). Illus. by author. 2011, Abrams $15.95 (978-0-8109-8976-4). 24pp. Mr. Herbert Timberteeth has trouble getting the National Animal Choir to perform his song as it was written in this supremely silly book. (Rev: BL 9/15/11; LMC 1–2/12; SLJ 9/1/11)

901 Rosen, Michael. *Tiny Little Fly* (PS–K). Illus. by Kevin Waldron. 2010, Candlewick $15.99 (978-0-7636-4681-3). 32pp. An elephant, a tiger, and a hippo struggle mightily to catch a pesky little fly. (Rev: BL 12/15/10; HB 1–2/11; SLJ 2/1/11*)

902 Ross, Tony. *I Want a Party!* (PS–2). Illus. by author. 2011, Andersen $16.95 (978-0-7613-8089-4). 32pp. Little Princess makes great preparations for her party but forgets, alas, to send the invitations; fortunately, one friend does turn up by accident and she proves enough. (Rev: BLO 12/15/11; SLJ 10/1/11)

903 Ross, Tony. *I Want to Do It Myself! A Little Princess Story* (PS–2). Illus. by author. 2011, Andersen $16.95 (978-0-7613-7412-1). 32pp. Little Princess sets off from her castle on a solo camping trip completely ill-prepared — her friends save the day, and she returns no wiser, obstinate as ever. **e** (Rev: BL 3/15/11; SLJ 2/1/11)

904 Rubin, Adam. *Those Darn Squirrels and the Cat Next Door* (K–4). Illus. by Daniel Salmieri. 2011, Clarion $16.99 (978-0-547-42922-9). Unpaged. Grumpy old Fookwire rejoices when his pesky squirrels hatch a plan to deal with the new cat in the neighborhood; a sequel to *Those Darn Squirrels* (2008). Lexile AD810L (Rev: SLJ 5/1/11)

905 Savage, Stephen. *Where's Walrus?* (PS–K). Illus. by author. 2011, Scholastic $16.99 (978-0-439-70049-8). 32pp. An escaped zoo walrus cleverly evades capture by donning a series of funny disguises. (Rev: BL 5/1/11; SLJ 2/1/11)

906 Schmid, Paul. *Petunia Goes Wild* (PS–2). Illus. by author. 2012, HarperCollins $12.99 (978-006196334-6). 40pp. Tired of all the rules imposed on human children, Petunia decides to start living the life of a wild animal. (Rev: BLO 2/1/12; SLJ 1/12)

907 Shea, Bob. *I'm a Shark* (PS–1). Illus. by author. 2011, HarperCollins $16.99 (978-0-06-199846-1). 40pp. A shark boasts that he's not afraid of anything until someone brings up the subject of spiders. (Rev: BL 4/1/11; SLJ 4/11)

908 Sierra, Judy. *Tell the Truth, B.B. Wolf* (PS–3). Illus. by J. Otto Seibold. 2010, Knopf $16.99 (978-0-375-85620-4); LB $19.99 (978-0-375-95620-1). 40pp. The retired Big Bad Wolf receives a phone call from a librarian asking for the "true" story of how he met the three little pigs in this sequel to *Mind Your Manners, B.B. Wolf* (2007). (Rev: BL 9/15/10; HB 9–10/10; LMC 11–12/10; SLJ 7/1/10)

909 Skeers, Linda. *Tutus Aren't My Style* (PS–3). Illus. by Anne Wilsdorf. 2010, Dial $16.99 (978-0-8037-3212-4). 32pp. Outdoorsy, adventuresome Emma tries to learn how to be a ballerina when her uncle sends her a frilly pink tutu by mistake. (Rev: BLO 3/1/10; LMC 3–4/10; SLJ 2/1/10)

910 Smith, Cynthia Leitich. *Holler Loudly* (PS–2). Illus. by Barry Gott. 2010, Dutton $16.99 (978-0-525-42256-3). Unpaged. Holler's loud voice generally gets him in trouble until a tornado threatens and his hollering saves the day. (Rev: HB 1–2/11; LMC 1–2/11*; SLJ 1/1/11)

911 Smith, Lane. *It's a Book* (1–3). Illus. by author. 2010, Roaring Brook $12.99 (978-1-59643-606-0). 32pp. In this droll, tech-savvy satire, a monkey and a donkey debate and compare the merits of books versus computers. (Rev: BL 7/10; HB 9–10/10; LMC 11–12/10; SLJ 8/1/10*)

912 Smith, Linda. *The Inside Tree* (PS–2). Illus. by David Parkins. 2010, HarperCollins $16.99 (978-0-06-028241-7); LB $17.89 (978-0-06-029818-0). 32pp. Mr. Potter's life becomes more complicated when he decides to move his dog — and the tree he sleeps un-

der — inside his house. (Rev: BLO 6/10; HB 3–4/10; SLJ 1/1/10)

913 Sonnenblick, Jordan. *Dodger for Sale* (4–6). 2010, Feiwel & Friends $16.99 (978-031237795-3). 176pp. Willie, his friend Lizzie, and their blue chimpanzee pal Dodger lobby to save a patch of nearby woods while contending with leprechauns that capture Willie's little sister. (Rev: BLO 3/1/10; SLJ 5/10)

914 Stevens, Janet, and Susan Stevens Crummel. *The Little Red Pen* (PS–2). Illus. by Janet Stevens. 2011, Houghton Harcourt $16.99 (978-0-15-206432-7). 56pp. In this schoolroom take on "The Little Red Hen," a red pen falls into the trash from exhaustion after marking papers all night and is eventually rescued by the highlighter, the stapler, and other previously unhelpful occupants. (Rev: BL 3/1/11; HB 3–4/11; LMC 10/11; SLJ 3/1/11)

915 Stoeke, Janet Morgan. *The Loopy Coop Hens* (PS–1). Illus. by author. 2011, Dutton $16.99 (978-0-525-42190-0). Unpaged. A bevy of hens in awe of the rooster's ability to fly eventually discovers the truth. (Rev: HB 5–6/11; SLJ 3/1/11)

916 Stower, Adam. *Silly Doggy* (PS–2). Illus. by author. 2012, Scholastic $16.99 (978-054537323-4). 40pp. When young Lily finds a bear in her garden, she mistakes it for a (pretty useless) dog and composes a lost dog poster. (Rev: BL 4/15/12; SLJ 5/12)

917 Teague, Mark. *LaRue Across America: Postcards from the Vacation* (K–4). Illus. by author. 2011, Scholastic $16.99 (978-0-439-91502-1). Unpaged. Ike the dog is forced to shelve his summer cruise plans in exchange for a road trip with his neighbor's detestable felines; he writes letters and postcards from the road. Lexile AD900L (Rev: SLJ 2/1/11)

918 Thomas, Jan. *Here Comes the Big, Mean Dust Bunny!* (PS–2). Illus. by author. 2009, Simon & Schuster $12.99 (978-1-4169-9150-2). Unpaged. A big mean dust bunny threatens and teases the others until an incident with a cat inspires a change of heart. (Rev: SLJ 11/1/09)

919 van Mol, Sine. *Meena* (K–2). Illus. by Carianne Wijffels. 2011, Eerdmans $17 (978-0-8028-5394-3). 26pp. Three children convinced that their elderly neighbor is a witch are eventually dissuaded by her granddaughter in this picture book with humorous horror. Lexile AD340L (Rev: BL 10/15/11; SLJ 8/1/11)

920 Vernick, Audrey. *So You Want to Be a Rock Star* (K–3). Illus. by Kirstie Edmunds. 2012, Walker $16.99 (978-080272092-4); LB $17.89 (978-080272325-3). 40pp. Learn valuable skills in this humorous, reader-friendly guide to strumming an air guitar, sneering, suitable hairstyles, and autograph signing. (Rev: BL 3/1/12)

921 Waldron, Kevin. *Mr. Peek and the Misunderstanding at the Zoo* (PS–K). Illus. by author. 2010, Candlewick

$15.99 (978-0-7636-4549-6). 48pp. A group of emotionally fragile zoo animals cope with their shaky self-image when they overhear the zookeeper berating himself for gaining weight. (Rev: BL 4/1/10; LMC 10/10; SLJ 5/1/10)

922 Walton, Rick. *Mr. President Goes to School* (K–2). Illus. by Brad Sneed. 2010, Peachtree $15.95 (978-1-56145-538-6). 32pp. After a particularly hard day, the President puts on a disguise and spends time finger painting and doing the hokey pokey with elementary school students, learning a lesson about kindness and cooperation in the process. (Rev: BL 9/1/10; SLJ 10/1/10)

923 Watt, Melanie. *Chester's Masterpiece* (K–2). Illus. by author. 2010, Kids Can $18.95 (978-1-55453-566-8). 32pp. Chester the uppity cat character hides all author Watts' art supplies in this lively story. (Rev: BL 3/1/10; SLJ 4/1/10)

924 Watt, Melanie. *Have I Got a Book for You!* (PS–2). Illus. by author. 2009, Kids Can $16.95 (978-1-55453-289-6). 32pp. A wily fox makes a variety of amusing sales pitches to the reader in this entertaining book. (Rev: BL 9/15/09; LMC 11–12/09; SLJ 12/1/09)

925 Weitzman, Jacqueline. *Superhero Joe* (K–2). Illus. by Ron Barrett. 2011, Simon & Schuster $16.99 (978-1-4169-9157-1). 32pp. Young Joe dons his Cape of Confidence and zooms to the rescue of his parents (reads, gets a mop from the scary cellar so that Mom can wipe up the spilled engine oil). (Rev: BL 9/15/11; SLJ 8/1/11)

926 Willems, Mo. *Should I Share My Ice Cream?* (PS–2). Illus. by author. Series: Elephant and Piggie. 2011, Hyperion $8.99 (978-1-4231-4343-7). 64pp. Should Gerald the elephant share his totally yummy ice cream with best friend Piggie??? The decision comes too late. (Rev: BL 10/1/11; SLJ 9/1/11)

927 Willis, Jeanne. *I'm Sure I Saw a Dinosaur* (PS–3). Illus. by Adrian Reynolds. 2011, Andersen $16.95 (978-076138093-1). 32pp. A young boy's dinosaur hoax creates a thriving business for his father's ice cream shop in this light, beautifully illustrated story. (Rev: BLO 9/1/11)

928 Wilson, Tony. *The Princess and the Packet of Frozen Peas* (PS–3). Illus. by Sue deGennaro. 2012, Peachtree $16.95 (978-156145635-2). 32pp. Prince Henrik is searching for the girl of his dreams — nothing like his older brother's oversensitive bride — and he finds one who likes both hockey and camping. (Rev: BL 3/15/12; SLJ 4/1/12)

929 Wing, Natasha. *How to Raise a Dinosaur* (K–2). Illus. by Pablo Bernasconi. 2010, Running Press $16.95 (978-0-7624-3342-1). 24pp. This playful lift-the-flap guide to taking care of a pet dinosaur features practical bits of advice transferable to more ordinary pets. (Rev: BL 11/1/10; SLJ 1/1/11)

930 Yorinks, Arthur. *The Invisible Man* (PS–1). Illus. by Doug Cushman. 2011, HarperCollins $16.99 (978-0-06-156148-1). 32pp. A Brooklyn fruit merchant has a series of unfortunate experiences when he becomes invisible. (Rev: BL 1/1–15/11*; HB 1–2/11; SLJ 1/1/11)

NATURE AND SCIENCE

931 Bauer, Marion Dane. *In Like a Lion Out Like a Lamb* (PS–2). Illus. by Emily Arnold McCully. 2011, Holiday House $16.95 (978-0-8234-2238-8). 32pp. A March lion wreaks havoc in a little boy's house until he is finally persuaded to leave and sneezes out a spring lamb to take his place. (Rev: BL 3/1/11; LMC 9–10/11; SLJ 4/11)

932 Blexbolex. *Seasons* (PS–2). Trans. from French by Claudia Bedrick. Illus. by author. 2010, Enchanted Lion $19.95 (978-1-59270-095-0). Unpaged. A beautiful, thought-provoking exploration of the seasons and how they affect a landscape and the people who live there. (Rev: HB 7–8/10; SLJ 7/1/10*)

933 Brallier, Jess M. *Tess's Tree* (PS–2). Illus. by Peter H. Reynolds. 2010, HarperCollins $16.99 (978-0-06-168752-5); LB $17.89 (978-0-06-168753-2). Unpaged. A young girl organizes a touching tribute to her 175-year-old maple tree after it's damaged in a storm and must be cut down. (Rev: SLJ 2/1/10)

934 Carlstrom, Nancy White. *Mama, Will It Snow Tonight?* (PS). Illus. by Paul Tong. 2009, Boyds Mills $16.95 (978-1-59078-562-1). 32pp. A little girl and two woodland animals eagerly await the season's first snowfall (Rev: BL 9/15/09; SLJ 11/1/09)

935 Crausaz, Anne. *Seasons* (PS–2). Illus. by author. 2011, Kane/Miller $15.99 (978-1-61067-006-7). 48pp. Evocative illustrations accompanied by minimal text takes readers on a colorful tour through the many sensations of the seasons. (Rev: BLO 2/15/11; HB 5–6/11; SLJ 3/1/11)

936 Dodd, Emma. *I Love Bugs!* (PS–1). Illus. by author. 2010, Holiday House $16.95 (978-0-8234-2280-7). 32pp. Easy-to-read text celebrates the huge variety of insects and spiders in a young child's backyard. (Rev: BL 3/15/10; SLJ 6/1/10)

937 Fogliano, Julie. *And Then It's Spring* (PS–2). Illus. by Erin E. Stead. 2012, Roaring Brook $16.99 (978-159643624-4). 32pp. After planting seeds, a young boy begins to worry that green shoots will never appear. (Rev: BL 12/15/11*; HB 1–2/11; SLJ 1/12)

938 French, Vivian. *Yucky Worms* (PS–2). Illus. by Jessica Ahlberg. 2010, Candlewick $16.99 (978-0-7636-4446-8). 32pp. As they work together in the garden, a grandmother tells her young grandson all about earthworms and the good they do. (Rev: BL 5/1/10; SLJ 6/1/10*)

939 Kato, Yukiko. *In the Meadow* (PS). Trans. from Japanese by Yuki Kaneko. Illus. by Komako Sakai. 2011, Enchanted Lion $14.95 (978-1-59270-108-7). Unpaged. A young Asian girl follows a butterfly through a meadow and encounters many other insects on her brief journey. (Rev: HB 7–8/11; LMC 11–12/11; SLJ 7/11)

940 McClure, Nikki. *Mama, Is It Summer Yet?* (PS–K). Illus. by author. 2010, Abrams $17.95 (978-0-8109-8468-4). 32pp. A boy longs for summer and watches with his mother as the signs arrive. (Rev: BL 4/15/10; SLJ 4/1/10)

941 Markle, Sandra. *Butterfly Tree* (K–3). Illus. by Leslie Wu. 2011, Peachtree $16.95 (978-1-56145-539-3). 32pp. Jilly and her mother come across a strange orange cloud over Lake Erie and realize it consists of migrating monarch butterflies; includes a factual author's note. (Rev: BL 12/1/11; LMC 3–4/12; SLJ 10/1/11)

942 Messner, Kate. *Over and Under the Snow* (PS–3). Illus. by Christopher Silas Neal. 2011, Chronicle $16.99 (978-0-8118-6784-9). 44pp. A girl and her father ski through the woods, discussing the animals that live happily under the snow. (Rev: BL 12/15/11; HB 1–2/12; LMC 3–4/12*; SLJ 12/1/11)

943 Millard, Glenda. *Isabella's Garden* (PS–2). Illus. by Rebecca Cool. 2012, Candlewick $16.99 (978-076366016-1). 32pp. Folk-art illustrations accompany lyric rhymed verse in this story of a garden's progress through the seasons. (Rev: BL 5/1/12; SLJ 4/1/12)

944 Morales, Melita. *Jam and Honey* (PS). Illus. by Laura J. Bryant. 2011, Tricycle $15.99 (978-1-58246-299-8); LB $18.99 (978-1-59246-390-2). 32pp. In this story told alternately from each perspective, a girl and a honeybee learn to leave each other alone and enjoy their garden. (Rev: BL 2/15/11; SLJ 3/1/11)

945 Nargi, Lela. *The Honeybee Man* (K–3). Illus. by Krysten Brooker. 2011, Random House $17.99 (978-0-375-84980-0); LB $20.99 (978-0-375-95695-9). 40pp. In Brooklyn, N.Y., Fred keeps bees on the roof of his apartment building and releases them into the city to gather nectar. ℮ Lexile AD870L (Rev: BL 3/15/11; HB 3–4/11; SLJ 3/1/11)

946 Neubecker, Robert. *Wow! Ocean!* (PS–2). Illus. by author. 2011, Hyperion/Disney $17.99 (978-1-4231-3113-7). Unpaged. Izzy finds much to wonder at when she and her family arrive at the beach in this eye-catching book. (Rev: HB 7–8/11; SLJ 7/11)

947 Oberman, Sheldon. *The Wind That Wanted to Rest* (PS–2). Illus. by Neil Waldman. 2012, Boyds Mills $17.95 (978-159078858-5). 32pp. An angry winter wind rejected by many is calmed and befriended by a generous young girl. (Rev: BLO 4/1/12; LMC 11–12/12)

948 Pfister, Marcus. *Ava's Poppy* (PS–2). Illus. by author. 2012, NorthSouth $16.95 (978-073584057-7). 32pp. In this gentle story, a young girl befriends a beautiful poppy flower and is saddened when its petals fall

but delighted to meet a new poppy the following spring. Lexile AD500L (Rev: BL 4/15/12; LMC 8–9/12; SLJ 1/12)

949 Raschka, Chris. *Little Black Crow* (K–2). Illus. by author. 2010, Atheneum $16.99 (978-0-689-84601-4). 40pp. A little boy speculates about the life of a black crow, wondering whether it questions the universe as he does. ℮ (Rev: BL 6/10; HB 7–8/10; SLJ 7/1/10*)

950 Rose, Deborah Lee. *All of the Seasons of the Year* (PS–1). Illus. by Kay Chorao. 2010, Abrams $16.95 (978-081098395-3). 32pp. Celebrates a mother cat's love for her child throughout the year. (Rev: BL 12/1/10; SLJ 10/1/10)

951 Salas, Laura Purdie. *A Leaf Can Be . . .* (PS–2). Illus. by Violeta Dabija. 2012, Millbrook $17.95 (978-076136203-6). 32pp. Poetic text communicates the many things leaves can be, including something that captures energy, cleans the air, and is pleasing to look at. ℮ (Rev: BL 3/15/12; LMC 10/12; SLJ 3/12)

952 Siminovich, Lorena. *I Like Bugs* (PS). Illus. by author. 2010, Candlewick $6.99 (978-076364802-2). 10pp. This sturdy look-and-touch board book uses a variety of textured art effects to present close-up, eye-catching illustrations of familiar insects. (Rev: BL 5/1/10)

953 Williams, Karen Lynn. *A Beach Tail* (PS–2). Illus. by Floyd Cooper. 2010, Boyds Mills $17.95 (978-1-59078-712-0). 32pp. Eager to explore the beach but also to obey his father's order not to stray, a little boy makes a very very long tail for the lion he has drawn in the sand. (Rev: BL 4/15/10; LMC 5–6/10; SLJ 3/1/10*)

OTHER TIMES, OTHER PLACES

954 Armand, Glenda. *Love Twelve Miles Long* (2–5). Illus. by Colin Bootman. 2011, Lee & Low $17.95 (978-1-60060-245-0). 32pp. In 1820s Maryland Frederick Douglass's mother describes her thoughts as she walks 12 miles through the night to see her son on a different plantation. (Rev: BL 12/1/11; LMC 5–6/12; SLJ 11/1/11)

955 Aston, Dianna Hutts. *Dream Something Big: The Story of the Watts Towers* (K–4). Illus. by Susan L. Roth. 2011, Dial $16.99 (978-0-8037-3245-2). 40pp. Aston uses the voice of a young girl to tell the story of Simon Rodia's painstaking creation of the works of art now known as Los Angeles' Watts Towers. Lexile AD830 (Rev: BL 8/11; LMC 11–12/11; SLJ 10/1/11)

956 Bandy, Michael S., and Eric Stein. *White Water* (K–3). Illus. by Shadra Strickland. 2011, Candlewick $16.99 (978-0-7636-3678-4). 40pp. A young black boy growing up in the segregated South sneaks into town to try drinking the water from the "whites only" fountain, only to discover it's no different from the fountain for blacks; based on the author's own experience. (Rev: BL 10/15/11; LMC 3–4/12*; SLJ 9/1/11)

957 Barron, T. A. *Ghost Hands* (K–3). Illus. by William Low. 2011, Philomel $18.99 (978-039925083-5). 40pp. Auki, a young Patagonian hunter, earns a spot in the Cave of the Hands in this novel set thousands of years ago; a foreword provides facts about the cave paintings there. Lexile 510L (Rev: BL 6/1/11; SLJ 8/11)

958 Base, Graeme. *The Jewel Fish of Karnak* (K–3). Illus. by author. 2011, Abrams $19.95 (978-1-4197-0086-6). 40pp. In ancient Egypt two thieves are dispatched by the Cat Pharaoh to retrieve the stolen Jewel Fish of Karnak in this quest story that requires readers to solve puzzles. (Rev: BL 10/15/11; LMC 1–2/12; SLJ 10/1/11)

959 Bildner, Phil. *The Hallelujah Flight* (K–3). Illus. by John Holyfield. 2010, Putnam $16.99 (978-0-399-24789-7). 32pp. This inspiring story of the first African American pilot to fly across the United States is told by Thomas Allen, his young copilot. Lexile AD760L (Rev: BL 2/1/10; LMC 3–4/10; SLJ 2/1/10*)

960 Birtha, Becky. *Lucky Beans* (1–3). Illus. by Nicole Tadgell. 2010, Whitman $16.99 (978-0-8075-4782-3). 32pp. Young African American Marshall uses math to estimate how many beans there are in a huge jar and win a brand new sewing machine for his mother in this story set in the Great Depression. Lexile 600L (Rev: BL 2/1/10; HB 5–6/10; LMC 5–6/10; SLJ 2/1/10)

961 Broach, Elise. *Gumption!* (PS–K). Illus. by Richard Egielski. 2010, Atheneum $16.99 (978-1-4169-1628-4). 40pp. Young Peter and his oblivious Uncle Nigel have a thrilling safari in Africa in this clever and funny book in which the illustrations play a key role. (Rev: BL 2/1/10; LMC 5–6/10; SLJ 2/1/10)

962 Brown, Monica. *Waiting for the Biblioburro* (K–2). Illus. by John Parra. 2011, Tricycle $16.99 (978-1-58246-353-7); LB $19.99 (978-1-58246-398-8). 32pp. A young Colombian girl is inspired to write by the traveling librarian who brings books to her isolated mountain village on his burros Alfa and Beto. Lexile AD880L (Rev: BLO 8/11; HB 7–8/11; SLJ 6/11)

963 Brown, Ruth. *Gracie the Lighthouse Cat* (K–3). Illus. by author. 2011, Andersen $16.95 (978-0-7613-7454-1). 32pp. Gracie must save her kitten during a terrible storm while the lighthouse keeper's daughter is rescuing shipwrecked passengers; based on real events in 1838, this story uses text for the animals and records the human story mainly in the art. ❧ Lexile AD640L (Rev: BL 2/15/11; SLJ 2/1/11)

964 Browning, Diane. *Signed, Abiah Rose* (1–3). Illus. by author. 2010, Tricycle $15.99 (978-1-58246-311-7). 32pp. In 18th-century America young Abiah Rose, a talented artist, is told not to sign her paintings because she is not a man, and uses a small rose instead. (Rev: BL 2/15/10*; SLJ 4/1/10)

965 Casanova, Mary. *The Day Dirk Yeller Came to Town* (PS–2). Illus. by Ard Hoyt. 2011, Farrar $16.99 (978-0-

374-31742-3). 40pp. Books prove to be a town's salvation when they soothe the trigger-happy inclinations of an outlaw named Dirk Yeller in this adventure set in the Wild West. (Rev: BL 6/1/11; LMC 10/11; SLJ 7/11)

966 Costanza, Stephen. *Vivaldi and the Invisible Orchestra* (1–3). Illus. by author. 2012, Henry Holt $16.99 (978-080507801-5). 40pp. In 18th-century Venice an orphan named Candida's poems inspire Vivaldi's *The Four Seasons*. (Rev: BL 3/1/12; LMC 8–9/12; SLJ 1/12)

967 Cunnane, Kelly. *Chirchir Is Singing* (PS–1). Illus. by Jude Daly. 2011, Random House $17.99 (978-0-375-86198-7). 40pp. A young Kenyan child tries again and again to help with chores such as getting water from the well but becomes discouraged as she fails every time. (Rev: BL 9/1/11; SLJ 9/1/11)

968 Daly, Jude. *Sivu's Six Wishes* (1–3). Illus. by author. 2010, Eerdmans $16.99 (978-080285369-1). 32pp. A retelling of a Taoist tale in which an African stone carver with a yen for power discovers that he is happier as a humble artist. (Rev: BL 9/1/10; HB 9–10/10; LMC 11–12/10; SLJ 12/10)

969 Daly, Niki. *A Song for Jamela* (PS–2). Illus. by author. 2010, Frances Lincoln $16.95 (978-1-84507-871-3). 36pp. Young Jamela has an exciting day at her aunt's hair salon in South Africa. (Rev: BL 1/1–15/11; SLJ 10/1/10)

970 Evans, Shane W. *Underground* (PS–3). Illus. by author. 2011, Roaring Brook $16.99 (978-159643538-4). 32pp. With minimal text and dramatic illustrations, this effective book tells the story of a slave family's escape to the North. Coretta Scott King Illustrator Award. (Rev: BL 2/1/11; HB 1–2/11; LMC 5–6/11; SLJ 1/11)

971 Evans, Shane W. *We March* (PS–1). Illus. by author. 2012, Roaring Brook $16.99 (978-159643539-1). 32pp. A boy, a girl, and their parents wake early and travel to take part in the 1963 civil rights march on Washington, D.C. (Rev: BL 1/1/12; HB 1–2/12; LMC 3–4/12)

972 Gilani-Williams, Fawzia. *Nabeel's New Pants: An Eid Tale* (K–3). Illus. by Proiti Roy. 2010, Marshall Cavendish $15.99 (978-0-7614-5629-2). 24pp. Nabeel's wife, mother, and daughter are too busy cooking for the Eid feast to shorten his new pants in this humorous story set in Turkey. ❧ Lexile AD450L (Rev: BL 3/15/10; LMC 8–9/10; SLJ 4/1/10*)

973 Glaser, Linda. *Hannah's Way* (K–3). Illus. by Adam Gustavson. 2012, Lerner/Kar-Ben paper $7.95 (978-076135138-2). 32pp. Uprooted from Minneapolis, a young Jewish girl struggles to make friends in her new rural school in this heartwarming story set during the Great Depression. (Rev: BL 3/15/12; SLJ 4/1/12)

974 Griffin, Kitty. *The Ride: The Legend of Betsy Dowdy* (1–3). Illus. by Marjorie Priceman. 2010, Atheneum $16.99 (978-1-4169-2816-4). 40pp. In this exciting story of bravery and perseverance, a 16-year-old girl sets off on a 50-mile horseback ride when she learns the Redcoats are on their way to her North Carolina town in 1775. Lexile AD510L (Rev: BL 7/10; LMC 11–12/10; SLJ 8/1/10)

975 Grigsby, Susan. *In the Garden with Dr. Carver* (1–3). Illus. by Nicole Tadgell. 2010, Whitman $16.99 (978-0-8075-3630-8). 32pp. Dr. George Washington Carver visits a rural elementary school in Alabama and teaches the students about gardening in this picture book with evocative illustrations. Lexile 990L (Rev: BL 9/1/10; LMC 11–12/10; SLJ 10/1/10)

976 Harris, John. *Jingle Bells: How the Holiday Classic Came to Be* (2–4). Illus. by Adam Gustavson. 2011, Peachtree $16.95 (978-156145590-4). 32pp. Tells the fictionalized story of the composition of the song in 1857, when James Lord Pierpont, then living in Georgia, was homesick for his native New England winters. (Rev: BL 10/1/11; SLJ 10/1/11)

977 Harvey, Jeanne Walker. *My Hands Sing the Blues: Romare Bearden's Childhood Journey* (1–3). Illus. by Elizabeth Zunon. 2011, Marshall Cavendish $17.99 (978-0-7614-5810-4). 40pp. A fictionalized first-person narrative recounts the life of the African American collage artist who made his name during the Harlem Renaissance and whose love of the blues was reflected in his work. (Rev: BL 11/1/11; SLJ 10/1/11)

978 Hopkinson, Deborah. *The Humblebee Hunter: Inspired by the Life and Experiments of Charles Darwin and His Children* (K–2). Illus. by Jen Corace. 2010, Hyperion $16.99 (978-142311356-0). 32pp. Darwin's daughter Henrietta introduces the large family, her father's interest in science, and how they all collaborated in a bee experiment. Lexile AD610L (Rev: BL 1/1/10; LMC 8–9/10; SLJ 4/10)

979 Houston, Gloria. *Miss Dorothy and Her Bookmobile* (K–3). Illus. by Susan Condie Lamb. 2011, HarperCollins $16.99 (978-0-06-029155-6). 32pp. Dorothy's work as head of the bookmobile for a rural North Carolina area in the last century is depicted in this inspiring story. Lexile AD1090L (Rev: BL 1/1–15/11; SLJ 1/1/11)

980 Huget, Jennifer LaRue. *Thanks a LOT, Emily Post!* (PS–3). Illus. by Alexandra Boiger. 2009, Random House $16.99 (978-0-375-83853-8); LB $19.99 (978-0-375-93853-5). 40pp. Home life takes a turn for the demanding when children fed up with hearing about their behavior challenge their mother to follow Emily Post's etiquette rules herself; set in the early 1920s. (Rev: BL 9/1/09*; SLJ 10/1/09)

981 Ingalls, Ann, and Maryann Macdonald. *The Little Piano Girl: The Story of Mary Lou Williams, Jazz Legend* (1–5). Illus. by Giselle Potter. 2010, Houghton Mifflin $16 (978-0-618-95974-7). Unpaged. A fictionalized account of the African American jazz great's childhood and youth, and her amazing prowess from as early an age as 3. ℮ (Rev: LMC 8–9/10; SLJ 2/1/10)

982 Jackson, Shelley. *Mimi's Dada Catifesto* (1–4). Illus. by author. 2010, Clarion $17 (978-0-547-12681-4). 48pp. In early 20th-century Switzerland an artistic alley cat named Mimi decides to become Dada's pet; with multimedia illustrations and an author's note. (Rev: BL 6/10*; LMC 10/10; SLJ 6/1/10)

983 Johnston, Tony. *Levi Strauss Gets a Bright Idea: A Fairly Fabricated Story of a Pair of Pants* (K–3). Illus. by Stacy Innerst. 2011, Harcourt $16.99 (978-0-15-206145-6). 32pp. A tall tale about the California Gold Rush and Levi Strauss's realization that they needed better pants; with a historical note by the author. (Rev: BL 9/15/11; SLJ 8/1/11*)

984 Kay, Verla. *Hornbooks and Inkwells* (PS–3). Illus. by S. D. Schindler. 2011, Putnam $16.99 (978-0-399-23870-3). 32pp. Rhyming text presents the experiences of two brothers attending an 18th-century one-room schoolhouse. (Rev: BL 6/1/11; HB 9–10/11; LMC 11–12/11; SLJ 7/11)

985 Kay, Verla. *Whatever Happened to the Pony Express?* (K–3). Illus. by Kimberly Bulcken and Barry Root. 2010, Putnam $16.99 (978-0-399-24483-4). 32pp. Cross-country letters between a brother and sister serve as a framework for a history of the Pony Express and the forms of communication that supplanted it. (Rev: BL 5/1/10; LMC 10/10; SLJ 6/1/10)

986 Kimmel, Eric A., adapter. *Joha Makes a Wish: A Middle Eastern Tale* (1–3). Illus. by Omar Rayyan. 2010, Marshall Cavendish $17.99 (978-0-7614-5599-8). 40pp. In this tale based on Middle Eastern folklore, Joha's wishing stick, which he found on the way to Baghdad, causes nothing but trouble. ℮ Lexile AD500L (Rev: HB 5–6/10; LMC 8–9/10; SLJ 4/1/10)

987 Knapp, Ruthie. *Who Stole Mona Lisa?* (1–3). Illus. by Jill McElmurry. 2010, Bloomsbury $17.99 (978-1-59990-058-2). 32pp. This account of the Mona Lisa's eventful history, including its theft from the Louvre in 1911, is told from the perspective of the painting. ☊ Lexile AD450L (Rev: BL 11/1/10; LMC 11–12/10; SLJ 12/1/10)

988 Krensky, Stephen. *Play Ball, Jackie!* (2–4). Illus. by Joe Morse. 2011, Millbrook $16.95 (978-0-8225-9030-9). 32pp. A father and son attend the opening day baseball game of the Brooklyn Dodgers in 1947 and witness Jackie Robinson's major league debut and the attendant prejudice. ℮ Lexile 480L (Rev: BL 2/1/11; SLJ 3/1/11)

989 Lester, Alison. *Running with the Horses* (2–4). Illus. by author. 2011, NorthSouth $16.95 (978-0-7358-4002-7). Unpaged. In Vienna during World War II, 10-year-old Nina and her father, with the help of an elderly cab horse, rescue four Lippizaner stallions from the Spanish Riding School. (Rev: LMC 8–9/11; SLJ 4/11)

990 Lyons, Kelly Starling. *Ellen's Broom* (K–3). Illus. by Daniel Minter. 2012, Putnam $16.99 (978-039925003-

3). 32pp. Two former slaves joyfully legalize their marriage when the state laws are changed in Virginia, bringing with them a symbolic broom reminding them of the "jumping the broom" practice of the past. (Rev: BL 2/1/12; LMC 8–9/12; SLJ 1/12)

991 McDonnell, Patrick. *Me . . . Jane* (PS–3). Illus. by author. 2011, Little, Brown $15.99 (978-031604546-9). 40pp. With many nice details, this picture book shows Jane Goodall's journey from a young nature-loving child to a brilliant researcher in Africa. (Rev: BL 3/15/11*; HB 3–4/11; LMC 10/11; SLJ 4/11)

992 Malaspina, Ann. *Finding Lincoln* (2–4). Illus. by Colin Bootman. 2009, Whitman $16.99 (978-080752435-0). 32pp. In segregated Alabama in 1951 a librarian helps young Louis, an African American, to get access to the library and check out books about Abraham Lincoln. (Rev: BL 9/15/09; LMC 11–12/09; SLJ 8/1/09)

993 Mason, Margaret H. *These Hands* (PS–3). Illus. by Floyd Cooper. 2011, Houghton Harcourt $16.99 (978-0-547-21566-2). 32pp. An African American grandfather tells his grandson about the civil rights movement by relating personal stories of work in a bakery where his skilled hands were not allowed to touch the bread. Lexile AD680L (Rev: BL 2/1/11; LMC 10/11; SLJ 3/1/11)

994 Michelson, Richard. *Busing Brewster* (1–3). Illus. by R. G. Roth. 2010, Knopf $16.99 (978-0-375-83334-2). 32pp. In 1974 Boston two African American brothers are bused across town to a white school and a challenging year. (Rev: BL 3/15/10; LMC 8–9/10; SLJ 6/1/10)

995 Milway, Katie Smith. *The Good Garden: How One Family Went from Hunger to Having Enough* (2–4). Illus. by Sylvie Daigneault. 2010, Kids Can $18.95 (978-1-55453-488-3). 32pp. Eleven-year-old Maria Luz is put in charge of her Honduran family's garden when her father must leave home to find work. (Rev: BL 11/1/10; SLJ 10/1/10)

996 Mitchell, Margaree King. *When Grandmama Sings* (2–4). Illus. by James E. Ransome. 2012, HarperCollins $16.99 (978-0-688-17563-4). 40pp. A young African American girl accompanies her talented grandmother on a singing tour through the segregated South of the 1950s in this story that includes many lessons in prejudice and exclusion. (Rev: BL 2/1/12; HB 1–2/12; SLJ 12/1/11)

997 Moser, Lisa. *Kisses on the Wind* (K–3). Illus. by Kathryn Brown. 2009, Candlewick $15.99 (978-0-7636-3110-9). 32pp. Lydia struggles with saying goodbye to Grandma as she and her parents prepare to head west on the Oregon Trail. (Rev: BL 10/1/09; SLJ 12/1/09)

998 Napoli, Donna Jo. *The Crossing* (1–3). Illus. by Jim Madsen. 2011, Simon & Schuster $16.99 (978-1-4169-9474-9). Unpaged. Napoli provides a baby's-eye-view of the western Rockies as Sacagawea's son is carried westward in 1805. Lexile AD690L (Rev: LMC 11–12/11; SLJ 7/11)

999 Pelley, Kathleen T. *Magnus Maximus, A Marvelous Measurer* (K–3). Illus. by S. D. Schindler. 2010, Farrar $16.99 (978-0-374-34725-3). 32pp. In Victorian England, eccentric elderly Magnus Maximus is obsessed with counting and measuring until he learns there's more to life than quantification. (Rev: BL 3/15/10; LMC 5–6/10; SLJ 5/1/10)

1000 Ramsden, Ashley, reteller. *Seven Fathers* (K–3). Illus. by Ed Young. 2011, Roaring Brook $16.99 (978-1-59643-544-5). 32pp. A retelling of a Norwegian tale about a tired traveler seeking shelter for the night who is referred from one old man to his father, and from that older man to an even older one, until he eventually reaches the seventh father and receives a welcome. Lexile AD930L (Rev: BL 3/1/11; LMC 5–6/11; SLJ 3/1/11)

1001 Ramsey, Calvin A. *Ruth and the Green Book* (2–5). Illus. by Floyd Cooper. 2010, Carolrhoda $16.95 (978-0-7613-5255-6). 32pp. A young African American girl and her family head south in the 1950s, using "The Green Book" as a guide to places where black people are welcome. Lexile 810L (Rev: BL 11/1/10; LMC 1–2/11; SLJ 11/1/10*)

1002 Ramsey, Calvin A., and Bettye Stroud. *Belle, the Last Mule at Gee's Bend* (K–3). Illus. by John Holyfield. 2011, Candlewick $15.99 (978-076364058-3). 32pp. One of the mules that pulled Dr. Martin Luther King, Jr.'s casket is given license to eat out of a kindhearted woman's garden in this story full of civil rights history. (Rev: BL 9/15/11; HB 9–10/11; LMC 11–12/11; SLJ 10/11)

1003 Rawlings, Marjorie Kinnan. *The Secret River* (PS–3). Illus. by Leo Dillon. 2011, Atheneum $19.99 (978-1-4169-1179-1). 56pp. In this newly illustrated version of a 1956 award winner, young Calpurnia and her dog catch enough fish to feed her poor family and neighbors in this story of magical realism set in Depression-era Florida. Lexile AD720L (Rev: BL 12/15/10; LMC 5–6/11; SLJ 1/1/11*)

1004 Reynolds, Aaron. *Back of the Bus* (1–3). Illus. by Floyd Cooper. 2010, Philomel $16.99 (978-0-399-25091-0). 32pp. A young boy seated at the back of the bus witnesses Rosa Parks's defiance of authority. (Rev: BL 2/1/10; LMC 1–2/10; SLJ 2/1/10)

1005 Rumford, James. *Rain School* (PS–2). Illus. by author. 2010, Houghton Mifflin $16.99 (978-0-547-24307-8). 32pp. Young Thomas is eager to get to school and start learning, unaware that he will first have to help construct the building itself in this story set in Chad. (Rev: BL 9/1/10*; SLJ 10/1/10)

1006 Simpson, Lesley. *Yuvi's Candy Tree* (1–3). Illus. by Janice Lee Porter. 2011, Lerner/Kar-Ben $17.95 (978-0-7613-5651-6); paper $7.95 (978-0-7613-5652-3).

32pp. Young Yuvi relates her harrowing journey with her Ethiopian Jewish family from war-torn East Africa to Israel, aided by Operation Moses; based on a true story. (Rev: SLJ 7/11)

1007 Spinelli, Eileen. *Do You Have a Cat?* (PS–3). Illus. by Geraldo Valerio. 2010, Eerdmans $15.99 (978-0-8028-5351-6). 26pp. Paintings of cats introduce cat owners through history — from Cleopatra to Scarlatti, Queen Victoria, and Calvin Coolidge — with facts about each person. (Rev: BLO 7/10; SLJ 11/1/10)

1008 Sullivan, Sarah. *Passing the Music Down* (K–3). Illus. by Barry Root. 2011, Candlewick $16.99 (978-0-7636-3753-8). 32pp. A boy learns fiddle music from an elderly man, and the two go on to play together in this atmospheric picture book based on the relationship between musicians Melvin Wine and Jake Krack. Lexile AD800 (Rev: BL 4/15/11; HB 5–6/11; SLJ 4/11)

1009 Thong, Roseanne. *Fly Free!* (PS–3). Illus. by Eujin Kim Neilan. 2010, Boyds Mills $17.95 (978-1-59078-550-8). 32pp. Young Mai's compassion for caged sparrows outside a Buddhist temple in Vietnam results in a ripple effect that culminates with the release of the little birds. (Rev: BL 1/1/10; LMC 5–6/10; SLJ 3/1/10)

1010 Ungerer, Tomi. *Otto: The Autobiography of a Teddy Bear* (1–3). Illus. by author. 2010, Phaidon $16.95 (978-0-7148-5766-4). 36pp. An aging teddy bear reminisces on an eventful life lived through 1930s Germany and World War II. (Rev: BL 10/1/10*; HB 11–12/10; SLJ 2/1/11)

1011 Walker, Sally M. *Freedom Song: The Story of Henry "Box" Brown* (1–3). Illus. by Sean Qualls. 2012, HarperCollins $17.99 (978-0-06-058310-1). 40pp. When slave Henry Brown's wife and children are sold away, he has himself packed in a box and mailed to Pennsylvania in this fictionalized account. (Rev: BL 12/15/11; SLJ 12/1/11)

1012 Weber, Elka, reteller. *One Little Chicken* (K–2). Illus. by Elisa Kleven. 2011, Tricycle $16.99 (978-1-58246-374-2); LB $19.99 (978-1-58246-401-5). Unpaged. This story about a lost chicken that generates wealth emphasizes the importance of generosity and patience; based on a tale in the Talmud. (Rev: HB 9–10/11; SLJ 7/11)

1013 Whelan, Gloria. *The Boy Who Wanted to Cook* (K–3). Illus. by Steve Adams. Series: Tales of the World. 2011, Sleeping Bear $16.95 (978-1-58536-534-0). 32pp. Ten-year-old Pierre is told he is too young to cook in his parents' restaurant in southern France until the day he sneaks some mushrooms into a beef dish and gains a rave review. (Rev: BL 11/1/11; SLJ 10/1/11)

1014 Winter, Jeanette. *Biblioburro: A True Story from Colombia* (PS–2). Illus. by author. 2010, Simon & Schuster $16.99 (978-1-4169-9778-8). 32pp. In the Colombian jungle, a bibliophile shares his collection with those less fortunate by loading his books onto a burro

and riding to remote villages where he hosts story hour. (Rev: BL 5/1/10*; LMC 8–9/10; SLJ 6/1/10)

1015 Wiviott, Meg. *Benno and the Night of Broken Glass* (2–5). Illus. by Josee Bisaillon. 2010, Kar-Ben $17.95 (978-0-8225-9929-6); paper $7.95 (978-082259975-3). 32pp. A friendly cat watches as a Jewish Berlin neighborhood is ransacked by the Nazis on Kristallnacht; with an afterword and lists of resources. (Rev: BL 5/1/10; LMC 8–9/10; SLJ 5/1/10*)

PERSONAL PROBLEMS

1016 Beaumont, Karen. *Where's My T-R-U-C-K?* (K–2). Illus. by David Catrow. 2011, Dial $16.99 (978-0-8037-3222-3). 32pp. A little boy hunts everywhere for his lost red truck, his tantrums mounting, until Bowser the dog digs up a hole where he has hidden many treasures. (Rev: BL 11/1/11; SLJ 9/1/11)

1017 Bracken, Beth. *Too Shy for Show-and-Tell* (PS–2). Illus. by Jennifer Bell. 2011, Picture Window LB $22.65 (978-140486654-6). 32pp. Shy Sam (a giraffe) struggles to muster the courage to talk to his class for show-and-tell. (Rev: BLO 12/15/11)

1018 Cadow, Kenneth M. *Alfie Runs Away* (PS–K). Illus. by Lauren Castillo. 2010, Farrar $16.99 (978-0-374-30202-3). 40pp. Alfie is so upset when his mother decides to throw away his favorite too-small shoes, and he decides to leave home; his mother helps him pack and even includes a hug. Lexile AD360L (Rev: BL 6/10; HB 7–8/10; SLJ 6/1/10)

1019 Croza, Laurel. *I Know Here* (PS–2). Illus. by Matt James. 2010, Groundwood $18.95 (978-0-88899-923-8). 40pp. A young girl used to living in a rural setting worries about moving to the big city of Toronto. (Rev: BL 5/15/10; SLJ 10/1/10)

1020 Denise, Anika. *Bella and Stella Come Home* (PS–1). Illus. by Christopher Denise. 2010, Philomel $16.99 (978-0-399-24243-4). 40pp. With some suspicion, Bella explores her new home with her stuffed toy elephant named Stella. (Rev: BL 12/15/10; SLJ 12/1/10)

1021 Devlin, Jane. *Hattie the Bad* (PS–1). Illus. by Joe Berger. 2010, Dial $16.99 (978-0-8037-3447-0). 32pp. Hattie is just naturally bad and trying to be good just doesn't seem to work for her. (Rev: BL 2/15/10; SLJ 3/1/10)

1022 Diggs, Taye. *Chocolate Me!* (PS–2). Illus. by Shane W. Evans. 2011, Feiwel & Friends $16.99 (978-0-312-60326-7). 40pp. With his mother's help, a young African American boy learns to stand up to bullying and take pride in himself and his looks. **e** (Rev: BL 2/1/12; LMC 1–2/12; SLJ 12/1/11)

1023 DiPucchio, Kelly. *Clink* (PS–1). Illus. by Matthew Myers. 2011, HarperCollins $16.99 (978-0-06-192928-1). 32pp. An outdated robot with low self-esteem despairs of ever being purchased, until a young boy who likes simpler things picks him up and takes him home. **ℯ** (Rev: BL 4/1/11; HB 5–6/11; SLJ 3/1/11)

1024 Forler, Nan. *Bird Child* (1–3). Illus. by Francois Thisdale. 2009, Tundra $19.95 (978-0-88776-894-1). 32pp. Eliza, a child who believes in her ability to fly, uses her self-confidence to help new student Lainey, the victim of bullying. (Rev: BL 11/1/09; SLJ 9/1/09)

1025 Gleeson, Libby. *Clancy and Millie and the Very Fine House* (PS–2). Illus. by Freya Blackwood. 2010, IPG/Little Hare $16.99 (978-1-921541-19-3). 32pp. His new house seems very large and empty, and young Clancy is happy when his new friend Millie comes to play with him, building things with boxes. (Rev: BL 11/1/10; SLJ 1/1/11*)

1026 Gow, Nancy. *Ten Big Toes and a Prince's Nose* (PS–2). Illus. by Stephen Costanza. 2010, Sterling $14.95 (978-1-4027-6396-0). 32pp. An embarrassingly big-footed princess and an awkwardly big-nosed prince meet and fall in love in this reassuring tale. (Rev: BL 10/15/10; LMC 1–2/11; SLJ 11/1/10)

1027 Hobbie, Holly. *Fanny and Annabelle* (PS–3). Illus. by author. 2009, Little, Brown $16.99 (978-0-316-16688-1). 40pp. Life imitates art when Fanny writes a story about a child called Annabelle who needs the money to buy a locket for her aunt's birthday; a sequel to *Fanny* (2008). (Rev: BL 9/15/09; SLJ 12/1/09)

1028 Holmes, Janet A. *Have You Seen Duck?* (PS). Illus. by Jonathan Bentley. 2011, Scholastic $8.99 (978-0-545-22488-8). 24pp. Convinced his stuffed animal friend needs him to be there, always, a young boy embarks on a frantic search when his duck goes missing. (Rev: BL 1/1–15/11; SLJ 2/1/11)

1029 Lewis, Rose. *Orange Peel's Pocket* (PS–2). Illus. by Grace Zong. 2010, Abrams $16.95 (978-0-8109-8394-6). 32pp. An adopted Chinese child turns to the Chinese American community around her to learn about her origins. (Rev: BLO 3/1/10; SLJ 4/1/10)

1030 Lichtenheld, Tom. *Bridget's Beret* (K–2). Illus. by author. 2010, Henry Holt $16.99 (978-0-8050-8775-8). 40pp. Bridget gets "artists' block" when her trademark black beret goes missing. (Rev: BL 2/15/10*; SLJ 4/1/10)

1031 Look, Lenore. *Polka Dot Penguin Pottery* (1–3). Illus. by Yumi Heo. 2011, Random House $16.99 (978-0-375-86332-5); LB $19.99 (978-0-375-96332-2). 40pp. A young girl struggling with writer's block is taken to a pottery studio by her perceptive grandma; there, she eventually conquers her creative logjam. (Rev: BLO 8/11; SLJ 10/1/11)

1032 Lyon, George Ella. *The Pirate of Kindergarten* (PS–2). Illus. by Lynne Avril. 2010, Simon & Schuster $16.99 (978-1-4169-5024-0). 40pp. Ginny struggles with double vision until the problem is diagnosed and corrected with a temporary eye patch. **ℯ** Lexile AD580L (Rev: BL 5/1/10; LMC 8–9/10; SLJ 6/1/10)

1033 Moore, Genevieve. *Catherine's Story* (PS–3). Illus. by Karin Littlewood. 2010, Frances Lincoln $17.95 (978-1-84507-655-9). 28pp. Catherine's single-parent dad patiently guides the young girl toward realizing her full potential despite her physical and emotional limitations in this tender picture book about disabilities. (Rev: BL 1/1–15/11; SLJ 1/1/11)

1034 Primavera, Elise. *Louise the Big Cheese and the La-Di-Da Shoes* (K–2). Illus. by Diane Goode. 2010, Simon & Schuster $16.99 (978-1-4169-7181-8). Unpaged. Louise's desire for fancy shoes evaporates when she realizes how uncomfortable the shiny pumps really are. (Rev: SLJ 2/1/10)

1035 Shreeve, Elizabeth. *Oliver at the Window* (PS–K). Illus. by Candice Hartsough McDonald. 2009, Front Street $16.95 (978-1-59078-548-5). 32pp. Oliver is sad and reclusive after his parents' divorce until an unhappy new student at preschool gives him a reason to reach out. (Rev: BL 11/1/09; SLJ 10/1/09)

1036 Singer, Marilyn. *Tallulah's Tutu* (PS–2). Illus. by Alexandra Boiger. 2011, Clarion $16.99 (978-0-547-17353-5). 40pp. Devoted to the idea of having a tutu, Tallulah finds learning the basics of ballet — and the leotard — disappointing. (Rev: BL 2/15/11; SLJ 3/1/11)

1037 Soman, David, and Jacky Davis. *Ladybug Girl at the Beach* (K–1). Illus. by David Soman. 2010, Dial $16.99 (978-0-8037-3416-6). Unpaged. Lulu (aka Ladybug Girl) and her dog spend a day at the beach and find that some aspects are quite frightening. (Rev: SLJ 6/1/10)

1038 Sylvester, Kevin. *Splinters* (K–3). Illus. by author. 2010, Tundra $17.95 (978-0-88776-944-3). 40pp. Hockey team outcast Cindy receives a visit from a "fairy goaltender" in this twist on the Cinderella story that features two evil sisters, their mother (the coach), and a golden skate; a sports story with a fairy tale feel. (Rev: BL 9/1/10; SLJ 9/1/10)

1039 Willems, Mo. *Knuffle Bunny Free: An Unexpected Diversion* (PS–1). Illus. by author. 2010, HarperCollins $17.99 (978-0-0619-2957-1). 52pp. Knuffle Bunny gets left behind on an airplane to Holland in this poignant conclusion to the series. (Rev: BL 7/10; HB 9–10/10; SLJ 10/1/10*)

REAL AND ALMOST REAL ANIMALS

1040 Agee, Jon. *My Rhinoceros* (PS–2). Illus. by author. 2011, Scholastic $16.95 (978-0-545-29441-6). 32pp. A young boy is disappointed with his pet rhinoceros's limited talents, until he finds himself in a situation where only the rhino can save the day. This funny story is also available in Spanish. Lexile AD310L (Rev: BL 10/15/11; HB 11–12/11; LMC 1–2/12; SLJ 10/1/11)

1041 Antle, Bhagavan, and Thea Feldman. *Suryia and Roscoe: The True Story of an Unlikely Friendship* (PS–1). Illus. by Barry Bland. 2011, Henry Holt $16.99

(978-080509316-2). 32pp. This photoessay shares the inspiring story of an orangutan and a dog that become friends. (Rev: BL 4/15/11; SLJ 5/11)

1042 Arnosky, Jim. *At This Very Moment* (PS–3). Illus. by author. 2011, Dutton $16.99 (978-0-525-42252-5). 32pp. Young readers are invited to consider what wild animals are doing at various times throughout the day, juxtaposed against everyday human activities. (Rev: BL 5/1/11; SLJ 6/11)

1043 Balouch, Kristen. *The Little Little Girl with the Big Big Voice* (PS–2). Illus. by author. 2011, Simon & Schuster $12.99 (978-1-4424-0808-1). 32pp. A loud-mouthed little girl scares away most large animals until she comes across a lion in this lively story with vibrant illustrations. (Rev: BL 6/1/11; HB 7–8/11; SLJ 6/11)

1044 Bardoe, Cheryl. *The Ugly Duckling Dinosaur: A Prehistoric Tale* (PS–2). Illus. by Doug Kennedy. 2011, Abrams $16.95 (978-0-8109-9739-4). 32pp. A young T. rex rejected by a duck family heads into the forest and eventually finds a home. (Rev: BL 5/1/11; SLJ 4/11)

1045 Beard, Alex. *Crocodile's Tears* (2–4). Illus. by author. 2012, Abrams $17.95 (978-1-4197-0008-8). Unpaged. A rhino is curious about his friend crocodile's tears, and goes around to other endangered animals seeking an explanation; includes information on the threats the animals face. (Rev: LMC 8–9/12; SLJ 12/1/11)

1046 Beck, Carolyn. *Dog Breath* (PS–2). Illus. by Brooke Kerrigan. 2011, Fitzhenry & Whiteside $18.95 (978-155455180-4). 32pp. A young boy remembers all the good times he shared with his dog in this gentle story about loss of a pet. (Rev: BL 2/15/12; LMC 10/12)

1047 Belton, Robyn. *Herbert: The True Story of a Brave Sea Dog* (PS–2). Illus. by author. 2010, Candlewick $15.99 (978-0-7636-4741-4). 40pp. A small dog named Herbert falls overboard in a storm off New Zealand and his 12-year-old master spends the night searching, finding him after he had been in the water for 30 hours; based on a true story. (Rev: BL 5/1/10; LMC 10/10; SLJ 7/1/10)

1048 Blake, Robert J. *Little Devils* (K–3). Illus. by author. 2009, Philomel $16.99 (978-0-399-24322-6). 40pp. When their mother disappears, three Tasmanian Devil pups leave their den to find food and in the process find their mother and rescue her from a cage. (Rev: BL 11/15/09; SLJ 10/1/09)

1049 Blake, Robert J. *Painter and Ugly* (K–3). Illus. by author. 2011, Philomel $16.99 (978-0-399-24323-3). 48pp. Fast-running sled dogs Painter and Ugly are inseparable until they are sold to different owners; lonely by themselves, they find each other again during the Junior Iditarod and find a way to compete and yet be together. Lexile AD880L (Rev: BL 2/1/11; LMC 5–6/11*; SLJ 2/1/11)

1050 Blumenthal, Deborah. *The Blue House Dog* (K–3). Illus. by Adam Gustavson. 2010, Peachtree $15.95 (978-1-56145-537-9). 32pp. Remembering his own dog's death, young Cody sets about befriending a stray dog he calls Blue. (Rev: BL 7/10; LMC 1–2/11; SLJ 8/1/10)

1051 Brendler, Carol. *Winnie Finn, Worm Farmer* (PS–2). Illus. by Ard Hoyt. 2009, Farrar $15.99 (978-0-374-38440-1). Unpaged. Hoping to enter her prize earthworms in the county fair, young Winnie constructs a simple worm farm to show them off, helping her neighbors in the meantime. (Rev: LMC 11–12/09; SLJ 9/1/09)

1052 Bunting, Eve. *My Dog Jack Is Fat* (PS–1). Illus. by Michael Rex. 2011, Marshall Cavendish $16.99 (978-0-7614-5809-8). 32pp. A young boy helps his overweight dog to get fit in this lighthearted take on diet and exercise. (Rev: BL 4/15/11; SLJ 5/1/11)

1053 Burleigh, Robert. *Good-bye, Sheepie* (K–2). Illus. by Peter Catalanotto. 2010, Marshall Cavendish $16.99 (978-0-7614-5598-1). 32pp. A young boy grieves over and eventually accepts the death of his beloved dog. (Rev: BL 3/15/10; SLJ 4/1/10)

1054 Buzzeo, Toni. *Stay Close to Mama* (PS–K). Illus. by Mike Wohnoutka. 2012, Hyperion $15.99 (978-142313482-4). 32pp. An adventurous baby giraffe repeatedly risks danger as he seeks to explore his world. (Rev: BL 3/15/12; LMC 5–6/12; SLJ 1/12)

1055 Campbell, Eileen, and Judy Rand. *Charlie and Kiwi: An Evolutionary Adventure* (K–3). Illus. by Peter H. Reynolds. 2011, Atheneum $16.99 (978-1-4424-2112-7). 48pp. Charlie explores the history of the kiwi and evolution of birds in this book that blends science, history, and a bit of time travel. e Lexile AD480L (Rev: BL 6/1/11; HB 7–8/11; LMC 11–12/11; SLJ 7/11)

1056 Cantrell, Charlie, and Rachel Wagner. *A Friend for Einstein: The Smallest Stallion* (PS–2). 2011, Hyperion/Disney $16.99 (978-1-4231-4563-9). 40pp. A tiny miniature horse lonely because of his strange size finds the perfect playmate in a boxer dog named Lilly. Lexile AD780L (Rev: BL 7/11; SLJ 8/1/11)

1057 Carnesi, Monica. *Little Dog Lost: The True Story of a Brave Dog Named Baltic* (K–2). Illus. by author. 2012, Penguin $15.99 (978-039925666-0). 32pp. Based on a true story, this is a dramatic tale about a dog found floating on an iceberg toward and ultimately into the Baltic Sea. (Rev: BL 1/1/12; HB 1–2/12; SLJ 1/12)

1058 Casanova, Mary. *Utterly Otterly Night* (PS–2). Illus. by Ard Hoyt. 2011, Simon & Schuster $16.99 (978-1-4169-7562-5). Unpaged. A young otter heads out at night for some snowy fun and shows that he knows what to do when danger is near. (Rev: SLJ 11/1/11)

1059 Castillo, Lauren. *Melvin and the Boy* (PS–1). Illus. by author. 2011, Henry Holt $16.99 (978-0-8050-

8929-5). 40pp. Desperate for a pet, a young boy brings home a turtle, but soon realizes the turtle is unhappy in a house and releases him back in the park. (Rev: BL 5/1/11; SLJ 7/11)

1060 Cooper, Elisha. *Homer* (PS–2). Illus. by author. 2012, Greenwillow $16.99 (978-006201248-7). 32pp. An aging dog named Homer is content to spend his time on the porch — with food and favorite armchair — while children and younger dogs rush and play. (Rev: BL 4/15/12*)

1061 Cowen-Fletcher, Jane. *Hello, Puppy!* (PS–K). Illus. by author. 2010, Candlewick $12.99 (978-0-7636-4303-4). 32pp. A child spends time exploring her new puppy's behavior. (Rev: BL 8/10; SLJ 5/1/10)

1062 Craig, Lindsey. *Farmyard Beat* (PS). Illus. by Marc Brown. 2011, Knopf $15.99 (978-0-375-86455-1); LB $18.99 (978-0-375-96455-8). 32pp. This rhythmic and repetitive celebration of barnyard sounds features paper collage artwork. (Rev: BL 6/1/11; SLJ 7/11)

1063 Crosby, Jeff. *Wiener Wolf* (PS–2). Illus. by author. 2011, Hyperion/Disney $15.99 (978-1-4231-3983-6). Unpaged. A bored lap dog joins a pack of wolves in order to satisfy a longing for adventure and finds he has bitten off more than he can chew. (Rev: LMC 11–12/11; SLJ 6/11)

1064 Cyrus, Kurt. *Big Rig Bugs* (PS–1). Illus. by author. 2010, Walker $16.99 (978-0-8027-8674-6). 32pp. Giant, digitally enhanced illustrations show a variety of bugs devouring a sandwich discarded at a construction site. (Rev: BL 5/15/10; LMC 8–9/10; SLJ 4/1/10)

1065 Cyrus, Kurt. *The Voyage of Turtle Rex* (PS–2). Illus. by author. 2011, Houghton Harcourt $16.99 (978-0-547-42924-3). Unpaged. Follows the life of a giant prehistoric sea turtle, showing the dangers it faces and explaining its habitat. Lexile AD580L (Rev: LMC 10/11; SLJ 5/1/11*)

1066 Daly, Cathleen. *Prudence Wants a Pet* (PS–2). Illus. by Stephen Michael King. 2011, Roaring Brook $16.99 (978-1-59643-468-4). 32pp. A young girl desperate for a pet tries some novel alternatives — a car tire, a tree branch — before finally getting what she really wants. (Rev: BL 6/1/11; HB 7–8/11; SLJ 5/1/11)

1067 Davis, Anne. *No Dogs Allowed!* (PS–2). Illus. by author. 2011, HarperCollins $16.99 (978-0-06-075353-5). 32pp. Bud the cat is unhappy when his feline friend Gabby is welcoming toward a dog that turns up at their door. (Rev: BL 4/1/11; HB 7–8/11; SLJ 4/11)

1068 DiTerlizzi, Angela. *Say What?* (PS–1). Illus. by Joey Chou. 2011, Simon & Schuster $15.99 (978-1-4169-8694-2). 32pp. A little boy wonders about the noises animals make and what they really mean. ℮ (Rev: SLJ 6/11)

1069 Dockray, Tracy. *The Lost and Found Pony* (PS–2). Illus. by author. 2011, Feiwel & Friends $16.99 (978-

0-312-59259-2). 48pp. A little pony has several careers but never forgets his years belonging to a young girl; eventually the young girl, now an adult, finds him and the two are reunited. Lexile 660L (Rev: BL 6/1/11; LMC 11–12/11; SLJ 8/1/11)

1070 Dodd, Emma. *I Don't Want a Cool Cat!* (PS–1). Illus. by author. 2010, Little, Brown $15.99 (978-031603674-0). 32pp. In this funny book, a young girl enumerates the types of cats she definitely does not want — stuffy, greedy, and so forth — before settling on a playful kitten. (Rev: BL 6/10*; SLJ 7/10)

1071 Drummond, Ree. *Charlie the Ranch Dog* (PS–2). Illus. by Diane deGroat. 2011, HarperCollins $16.99 (978-0-06-199655-9). 40pp. Ranch dog Charlie, a lazy basset hound, describes his busy life even as his friend Suzie, a lively Jack Russell puppy, actually does all the work. Lexile AD440L (Rev: BL 4/1/11; LMC 10/11; SLJ 5/1/11)

1072 Ehlert, Lois. *RRRalph* (PS–3). Illus. by author. 2011, Simon & Schuster $17.99 (978-1-4424-1305-4). 40pp. A talking dog provides answers to a variety of questions using words such as "roof," "bark," and "rough;" along with guessing the words the dog will use, children will enjoy the inventive artwork. (Rev: BL 2/15/11*; SLJ 5/1/11)

1073 Esbaum, Jill. *Tom's Tweet* (K–2). Illus. by Dan Santat. 2011, Knopf $16.99 (978-0-375-85171-1); LB $19.99 (978-0-375-95171-8). Unpaged. Tom, a fat and hungry cat, ends up taking pity on a fallen baby bird called Tweet and the two become fast friends; a funny read full of wordplay. (Rev: SLJ 11/1/11)

1074 Falwell, Cathryn. *Gobble Gobble* (1–3). Illus. by author. 2011, Dawn $16.95 (978-158469-148-8); paper $8.95 (978-158469149-5). 32pp. Jenny introduces readers in rhyme to the wild turkeys that she sees around her rural home, and documents facts about the birds in a journal. Lexile 500L (Rev: BL 10/15/11; LMC 1–2/12; SLJ 12/1/11)

1075 Falwell, Cathryn. *Pond Babies* (PS–K). Illus. by author. 2011, Down East $15.95 (978-0-89272-920-3). 32pp. A mother and her young son watch the various animal babies at the local pond — a duck, a turtle, a frog, and so forth — in this book that presents questions on one page and answers on the next. (Rev: BLO 9/1/11; SLJ 8/1/11)

1076 Fischer, Scott M. *Jump!* (PS–K). Illus. by author. 2010, Simon & Schuster $14.99 (978-1-4169-7884-8). 32pp. This lively book features short rhythmic verses that depict smaller animals leaping out of the range of bigger ones — usually just in the nick of time. (Rev: BL 1/1/10; LMC 5–6/10; SLJ 2/1/10)

1077 Fleming, Candace. *Seven Hungry Babies* (PS–1). Illus. by Eugene Yelchin. 2010, Atheneum $16.99 (978-1-4169-5402-6). 40pp. The suspense builds as a frenzied mama bird returns to feed ravenous nestling after nestling in this infectious story. (Rev: BL 1/1/10; SLJ 2/1/10)

1078 Fletcher, Ashlee. *My Dog, My Cat* (PS–K). Illus. by author. 2011, Tanglewood $13.95 (978-1-933718-22-4). 32pp. A little boy contrasts behaviors and physical traits of his dog and his cat. (Rev: BL 9/1/11; SLJ 7/11)

1079 Fox, Mem. *Two Little Monkeys* (PS). Illus. by Jill Barton. 2012, Simon & Schuster $16.99 (978-141698687-4). 32pp. Two lively monkeys' escape from a hungry leopard is narrated in bouncy rhyme with a catchy refrain. e (Rev: BL 3/15/12; HB 7–8/12; LMC 5–6/12; SLJ 6/1/12)

1080 Gal, Susan. *Please Take Me for a Walk* (PS–2). Illus. by author. 2010, Knopf $15.99 (978-0-375-85863-5); LB $18.99 (978-0-375-95863-2). Unpaged. A little white terrier begs over and over for a walk, listing the things he will enjoy. (Rev: BL 4/1/10; LMC 8–9/10; SLJ 5/1/10)

1081 George, Lindsay Barrett. *Maggie's Ball* (PS). Illus. by author. 2010, Greenwillow $16.99 (978-0-06-172166-3); LB $17.89 (978-0-06-172170-0). 32pp. Maggie the dog searches all over the town for her ball in this oversize book with illustrations that show lots of potential balls for children to spot. (Rev: BL 2/15/10; SLJ 3/1/10)

1082 George, Lindsay Barrett. *That Pup!* (PS–1). Illus. by author. 2011, Greenwillow $16.99 (978-0-06-200413-0). 32pp. A puppy has fun digging up a squirrel's acorns until it meets up with the squirrel itself and the two decide to rebury them together. (Rev: BL 10/1/11; SLJ 11/1/11)

1083 Gershator, Phillis. *Who's in the Farmyard?* (PS). Illus. by Jill McDonald. 2012, Barefoot $14.99 (978-184686574-9). 24pp. Starting with the rooster, readers meet the diverse animals of the farmyard. (Rev: BL 3/1/12; SLJ 2/12)

1084 Godwin, Laura. *One Moon, Two Cats* (PS–2). Illus. by Yoko Tanaka. 2011, Atheneum $16.99 (978-1-4424-1202-6). 32pp. Paired illustrated spreads show a city cat and a country cat going about their nightly activities in very different and richly detailed settings. e (Rev: BL 10/15/11; HB 11–12/11; SLJ 8/1/11)

1085 Goodrich, Carter. *Say Hello to Zorro!* (PS–1). Illus. by author. 2011, Simon & Schuster $15.99 (978-1-4169-3893-4). Unpaged. Mr. Bud the dog does not welcome new pup Zorro to his house but the two gradually come to realize they share priorities. (Rev: SLJ 3/1/11*)

1086 Goodrich, Carter. *Zorro Gets an Outfit* (PS–1). Illus. by author. 2012, Simon & Schuster $15.99 (978-144243535-3). 48pp. Initially aghast at the prospect of wearing a costume, Zorro the pug comes around when he sees another dressed-up dog at the park. (Rev: BL 5/1/12; SLJ 4/1/12)

1087 Gorbachev, Valeri. *The Best Cat* (PS–1). Illus. by author. 2010, Candlewick $15.99 (978-0-7636-3675-3). 32pp. Siblings Jeff and Ginny have differing opinions on the family cat's diverse talents, but both agree she's the best cat there is; the illustrations add to the humor. Lexile 820 (Rev: BL 1/1/10; SLJ 3/1/10)

1088 Gore, Leonid. *Worms for Lunch?* (PS–1). Illus. by author. 2011, Scholastic $16.99 (978-0-545-24338-4). 32pp. Animals of various kinds reveal what they like to eat in simple text and illustrations with die-cuts and flaps. (Rev: BL 3/1/11; HB 3–4/11; SLJ 3/1/11)

1089 Graham-Barber, Lynda. *KokoCat, Inside and Out* (K–2). Illus. by Nancy Lane. 2012, Gryphon $16.95 (978-094071912-5). 24pp. A contented indoor cat has a scary adventure in the outdoors in this story that includes notes for adults on keeping cats safe. e (Rev: BLO 3/1/12)

1090 Gravett, Emily. *Dogs* (PS–K). Illus. by author. 2010, Simon & Schuster $15.99 (978-1-4169-8703-1). 32pp. Looks at all kinds of dogs — big, small, spotty, shabby, wrinkly — and why we love them. (Rev: BL 3/15/10; LMC 8–9/10; SLJ 3/1/10*)

1091 Greene, Stephanie. *Princess Posey and the Next-Door Dog* (K–2). Illus. by Stephanie Roth Sisson. 2011, Putnam $12.99 (978-039925463-5); paper $4.99 (978-014241939-7). 96pp. Six-year-old Posey's princess wand gives her the courage to help the big dog next door when his paw gets stuck in the fence; a beginning chapter book. e (Rev: BLO 11/15/11)

1092 Griffin, Molly Beth. *Loon Baby* (PS–2). Illus. by Anne Hunter. 2011, Houghton Mifflin $16.99 (978-0-547-25487-6). 32pp. A baby loon learns to dive during a brief panic when his mother seems to be underwater too long. (Rev: BL 2/15/11; SLJ 5/1/11)

1093 Gudeon, Adam. *Me and Meow* (PS–K). Illus. by author. 2011, HarperCollins $12.99 (978-0-06-199821-8). Unpaged. A young girl and her constant companion Meow have a fun-filled day outside in this story full of repetition. (Rev: SLJ 8/1/11)

1094 Haas, Jessie. *Bramble and Maggie: Horse Meets Girl* (1–3). Illus. by Alison Friend. 2012, Candlewick $14.99 (978-076364955-5). 56pp. A horse bored with giving riding lessons chooses a new home with a little girl named Maggie, who seems to understand. (Rev: BL 3/15/12; HB 3–4/12; SLJ 3/12)

1095 Harris, Trudy. *Say Something, Perico* (PS–2). Illus. by Cecilia Rebora. 2011, Millbrook $16.95 (978-0-7613-5231-0). 32pp. A Spanish-speaking parrot keeps being returned to the pet store by his English-speaking new owners and begins to despair of ever finding a permanent home; includes a glossary of Spanish words. Lexile AD570L (Rev: BL 12/1/11; LMC 1–2/12; SLJ 12/1/11)

1096 Havill, Juanita. *Call the Horse Lucky* (K–3). Illus. by Nancy Lane. 2010, Gryphon $15.95 (978-0-940719-

10-1). Unpaged. A young girl is instrumental in helping a neglected horse find a new, safe home. (Rev: SLJ 2/1/11)

1097 Hawkins, Emily. *Little Snow Goose* (PS). Illus. by Maggie Kneen. 2009, Dutton $16.99 (978-0-525-42166-5). 28pp. When a little fox scares a mother goose from her nest, he takes responsibility for raising her chick. (Rev: BL 11/1/09; SLJ 10/1/09)

1098 Heiligman, Deborah. *Cool Dog, School Dog* (PS–2). Illus. by Tim Bowers. 2009, Marshall Cavendish $15.99 (978-0-7614-5561-5). Unpaged. A golden retriever follows her boy to school and, despite the teacher's displeasure, soon finds a role for herself. (Rev: SLJ 9/1/09)

1099 Henkes, Kevin. *Little White Rabbit* (PS–1). Illus. by author. 2011, Greenwillow $16.99 (978-0-06-200642-4). 40pp. An imaginative little rabbit is transformed into all the things he thinks about as he hops through the forest in this simple story with humor and appealing illustrations. (Rev: BL 11/15/10; HB 1–2/11; SLJ 2/1/11*)

1100 Henrichs, Wendy. *When Anju Loved Being an Elephant* (1–3). Illus. by John Butler. 2011, Sleeping Bear $16.95 (978-1-58536-533-3). 32pp. A former circus elephant recalls the happier days of her youth living in the wild as she's moved to an elephant sanctuary. (Rev: BLO 11/15/11; SLJ 10/1/11)

1101 Hobbie, Holly. *Everything but the Horse* (PS–3). Illus. by author. 2010, Little, Brown $16.99 (978-0-316-07019-5). 32pp. Holly longs for a horse when her family moves from the city to a farm; based on the author's childhood. (Rev: BL 12/15/10; SLJ 12/1/10*)

1102 Holmes, Mary Tavener, and John Harris. *A Giraffe Goes to Paris* (1–3). Illus. by Jon Cannell. 2010, Marshall Cavendish $17.99 (978-0-7614-5595-0). 32pp. Belle the giraffe's 1826 journey to Paris from Egypt is the subject of this handsomely illustrated novel, which contains many factual details. (Rev: BL 4/1/10; LMC 8–9/10; SLJ 4/1/10)

1103 Hosta, Dar. *Doggie Do!* (PS–1). Illus. by author. 2009, Brown Dog $17.95 (978-097219674-1). 32pp. This lively picture book follows a group of playful dogs through the day, from eating and fetching to taking a snooze. (Rev: BLO 11/15/09)

1104 Hubbell, Patricia. *Horses: Trotting! Prancing! Racing!* (PS–1). Illus. by Joe Mathieu. 2011, Marshall Cavendish $17.99 (978-0-7614-5949-1). 32pp. Rhyming text introduces a wide variety of horses and their occupations, showing how we feed them and care for them. ℮ (Rev: BLO 12/15/11; SLJ 9/1/11)

1105 Huneck, Stephen. *Sally's Great Balloon Adventure* (PS–2). Illus. by author. 2010, Abrams $16.95 (978-0-8109-8331-1). 32pp. Enticed by the smell of fried chicken, Sally the lab ends up taking a solo ride in a hot air balloon. (Rev: BLO 2/1/10; SLJ 4/1/10)

1106 Isop, Laurie. *How Do You Hug a Porcupine?* (PS–1). Illus. by Gwen Millward. 2011, Simon & Schuster $15.99 (978-1-4424-1291-0). 32pp. A little boy interested in cuddling animals carefully considers how one would go about hugging a porcupine. (Rev: BL 7/11; SLJ 8/1/11)

1107 James, Simon. *George Flies South* (PS–2). Illus. by author. 2011, Candlewick $16.99 (978-0-7636-5724-6). Unpaged. Young bird George has been unwillingly to leave his nest and learn to fly, but a gust of wind carries his nest out of the tree and he is forced to take action. (Rev: HB 11–12/11; SLJ 10/1/11)

1108 Kirk, Katie. *Eli, No!* (PS–K). Illus. by author. 2011, Abrams $14.95 (978-0-8109-8964-1). 32pp. An energetic, good-natured black Lab endures many a rebuke from his human family, knowing in the end that they love him despite the mischief he creates. (Rev: BL 11/15/11; LMC 1–2/12; SLJ 11/1/11)

1109 Krilanovich, Nadia. *Chicken, Chicken, Duck!* (PS). Illus. by author. 2011, Tricycle $14.99 (978-1-58246-385-8); LB $17.99 (978-1-58246-389-6). 32pp. A bunch of barnyard animals pile into a boisterous pyramid of shapes, colors, and noises. (Rev: BL 3/1/11; SLJ 3/1/11)

1110 Kumin, Maxine. *Oh, Harry!* (K–2). Illus. by Barry Moser. 2011, Roaring Brook $16.99 (978-1-59643-439-4). 32pp. Harry the horse has various talents including opening doors, which comes in handy when pesky 6-year-old Algernon gets locked in a grain bin and is rescued, albeit not immediately. (Rev: BL 5/1/11; SLJ 5/1/11)

1111 Laminack, Lester L. *Three Hens and a Peacock* (PS–2). Illus. by Henry Cole. 2011, Peachtree $15.95 (978-1-56145-564-5). 32pp. The unexpected arrival of a rogue peacock creates jealousy amongst the other feathered creatures on a farm. Lexile AD590L (Rev: BL 4/1/11; LMC 10/11; SLJ 4/11)

1112 Lamstein, Sarah. *Big Night for Salamanders* (K–3). Illus. by Carol Benioff. 2010, Boyds Mills $17.95 (978-1-932425-98-7). 32pp. On a warm, rainy spring night, a young boy and his parents help spotted salamanders cross a dangerous road. (Rev: BL 2/15/10; LMC 8–9/10; SLJ 3/1/10)

1113 Levine, Ellen. *Seababy* (PS–3). Illus. by Jon Van Zyle. 2012, Walker $16.99 (978-080279808-4). 32pp. A baby sea otter separated from his mother during a storm is cared for at a rehabilitation center and taught how to look after himself before being released into the wild. (Rev: BL 4/15/12)

1114 Lewin, Betsy. *Where Is Tippy Toes?* (PS–K). Illus. by author. 2010, Simon & Schuster $16.99 (978-1-4169-3808-8). Unpaged. Where does Tippy Toes the cat spend his time? Readers lift the flaps to follow his adventures. (Rev: LMC 11–12/10; SLJ 9/1/10)

1115 Lindbergh, Reeve. *Homer the Library Cat* (PS–1). Illus. by Anne Wilsdorf. 2011, Candlewick $15.99 (978-0-7636-3448-3). 32pp. A cat used to the quiet life falls out a window and goes searching for a calm place to hang out; the perfect spot turns out to be the library. (Rev: BL 10/1/11; SLJ 12/1/11)

1116 Lobel, Anita. *Nini Lost and Found* (PS–1). Illus. by author. 2010, Knopf $15.99 (978-0-375-85880-2). 40pp. Overly adventurous tabby cat Nini goes exploring and finds the night world scarier than she expected. (Rev: BL 8/10*; HB 11–12/10; SLJ 9/1/10)

1117 Lobel, Gillian. *Moonshadow's Journey* (K–1). Illus. by Karin Littlewood. 2009, Whitman $16.99 (978-080755273-5). 32pp. A young swan learns about the dangers of migration in this story of family support and survival. (Rev: BLO 11/15/09; SLJ 8/1/09)

1118 Long, Ethan. *Bird and Birdie in a Fine Day* (PS–1). Illus. by author. 2010, Tricycle $14.99 (978-1-58246-321-6). Unpaged. Cartoon characters Bird and Birdie enjoy a beautiful morning, a wonderful afternoon, and a marvelous evening together. (Rev: BL 3/1/10; SLJ 4/1/10)

1119 Lord, Janet. *Where Is Catkin?* (PS). Illus. by Julie Paschkis. 2010, Peachtree $16.95 (978-1-56145-523-2). 32pp. Folk-style artwork full of hidden details will engage readers in this story of a cat hunting for other animals. (Rev: BL 2/15/10; SLJ 4/1/10)

1120 Luxbacher, Irene. *Mattoo, Let's Play!* (PS–2). Illus. by author. 2010, Kids Can $16.95 (978-1-55453-424-1). 32pp. Young Ruby is too rough for her cat Mattoo, and it is only when she pretends to tame him in the jungle that she discovers how cuddly he can be. (Rev: BLO 4/15/10; SLJ 5/1/10)

1121 Lyon, Tammie. *Olive and Snowflake* (PS–1). Illus. by author. 2011, Marshall Cavendish $16.99 (978-0-7614-5955-2). Unpaged. When her parents say Snowflake must go to obedience school, Olive worries that — like her dog — she will have to sit, stay, and generally learn to behave. **e** (Rev: LMC 3–4/12; SLJ 9/1/11)

1122 McAllister, Angela. *Little Mist* (PS–1). Illus. by Sarah Fox-Davies. 2011, Knopf $16.99 (978-0-375-86788-0); LB $19.99 (978-0-375-96788-7). 32pp. A young snow leopard feels very small when he follows his mama out of their cave for the first time. (Rev: BL 4/1/11; SLJ 3/1/11)

1123 McCully, Emily Arnold. *Wonder Horse: The True Story of the World's Smartest Horse* (PS–2). Illus. by author. 2010, Henry Holt $16.99 (978-0-8050-8793-2). 32pp. This fascinating novel is based on the true story of a former slave, Bill "Doc" Key, who became a veterinarian after the Civil War and taught a very clever horse the alphabet, colors, and counting. (Rev: BL 4/15/10*; LMC 8–9/10; SLJ 6/1/10*)

1124 McDonnell, Christine. *Dog Wants to Play* (PS–K). Illus. by Jeff Mack. 2009, Viking $15.99 (978-0-670-

01126-1). 32pp. When one barnyard animal after another turns down a puppy's invitation to play, he finally finds the perfect companion: a little boy. (Rev: BL 11/1/09; SLJ 9/1/09)

1125 McKinlay, Meg. *Duck for a Day* (2–4). Illus. by Leila Rudge. 2012, Candlewick $12.99 (978-076365784-0). 96pp. Neighbors Abby and Noah quibble over who will be allowed to bring their teacher's pet duck home for a night; when the duck escapes it takes teamwork to bring him home. (Rev: BL 4/15/12; HB 5–6/12; SLJ 8/12)

1126 Markle, Sandra. *Race the Wild Wind: A Story of the Sable Island Horses* (K–3). Illus. by Layne Johnson. 2011, Walker $17.99 (978-0-8027-9766-7). 32pp. Markle tells the story of the wild horses that live on Nova Scotia's Sable Island, focusing on a leading stallion that learns how to survive in the harsh climate. (Rev: BL 7/11; LMC 10/11; SLJ 7/11)

1127 Martin, Bill. *Ten Little Caterpillars* (PS–K). Illus. by Lois Ehlert. 2011, Simon & Schuster $17.99 (978-1-4424-3385-4). 40pp. Brightly hued botanical illustrations — complete with labels — add appeal to the simple, rhymed story of ten caterpillars' adventures in a field of flowers and the process of metamorphosis. (Rev: BL 7/11; SLJ 8/1/11)

1128 Meade, Holly. *If I Never Forever Endeavor* (PS–2). Illus. by author. 2011, Candlewick $15.99 (978-0-7636-4071-2). 32pp. A little bird mulls over the pros and cons of leaving the nest and testing its flying abilities in this beautifully illustrated book. (Rev: BL 4/15/11; LMC 5–6/11; SLJ 5/1/11)

1129 Meadows, Michelle. *Itsy-Bitsy Baby Mouse* (PS–1). Illus. by Matthew Cordell. 2012, Simon & Schuster $15.99 (978-141693786-9). 40pp. A tiny baby mouse gets lost and has a scary time before finding his way home with the help of an older mouse. (Rev: BL 3/15/12; SLJ 2/12)

1130 Minor, Wendell. *My Farm Friends* (PS–K). Illus. by author. 2011, Putnam $16.99 (978-0-399-24477-3). 32pp. Barnyard animals are portrayed through sweetly quirky rhymes and lively, comic illustrations. (Rev: BL 1/1–15/11; SLJ 2/1/11)

1131 Murphy, Yannick. *Baby Polar* (PS–K). Illus. by Kristen Balouch. 2009, Clarion $16 (978-0-618-99850-0). 32pp. A baby polar bear lost in a snowstorm mistakes his mother for a warm snow cave. (Rev: BL 11/15/09; SLJ 11/1/09)

1132 Na, Il Sung. *A Book of Sleep* (K–2). Illus. by author. 2009, Knopf $15.99 (978-0-375-86223-6); LB $18.99 (978-0-375-96223-3). 24pp. A watchful owl oversees a forest filled with animals at rest in this evocative tale. (Rev: BL 11/1/09*; SLJ 11/1/09*)

1133 Na, Il Sung. *Snow Rabbit, Spring Rabbit: A Book of Changing Seasons* (PS–K). Illus. by author. 2011, Knopf $15.99 (978-0-375-86786-6); LB $18.99 (978-0-

375-96786-3). 24pp. A rabbit, her coat white for winter, watches other animals' preparations for and behavior during winter, before welcoming the spring as her own coat changes color. ℮ Lexile 450L (Rev: BL 1/1–15/11; SLJ 2/1/11*)

1134 Nelson, Jessie, and Karen Leigh Hopkins. *Labracadabra* (K–2). Illus. by Deborah Melmon. 2011, Viking $14.99 (978-0-670-01251-0). 36pp. Zach is kind of disappointed with his new (rescued) dog Larry until Larry's tail seems to exhibit magical abilities. (Rev: SLJ 8/1/11)

1135 Nelson, Marilyn. *Snook Alone* (K–3). Illus. by Timothy Basil Ering. 2010, Candlewick $16.99 (978-0-7636-2667-9). 48pp. A monk, Abba Jacob, and his loyal and devoted terrier Snook become separated during a storm in this emotive story. Lexile AD890L (Rev: BL 6/10*; HB 1–2/11; LMC 11–12/10; SLJ 10/1/10*)

1136 Newton, Jill. *Crash Bang Donkey!* (PS–2). Illus. by author. 2010, Whitman $16.99 (978-0-8075-1330-9). 32pp. Farmer Gruff is wakened from his badly needed slumber by a rambunctious musical donkey in this rhythmic story in which the pair finally find mutual benefits in a life together. (Rev: BL 2/1/10; SLJ 2/1/10)

1137 North, Sherry. *Champ's Story: Dogs Get Cancer Too!* (1–3). Illus. by Kathleen Rietz. 2010, Sylvan Dell $16.95 (978-1-60718-077-7); paper $8.95 (978-1-60718-088-3). 32pp. Cody sees his dog through treatment for cancer, and then Champ in turn provides care and comfort to Cody after he hurts his ankle. ℮ (Rev: LMC 1–2/11; SLJ 10/1/10)

1138 Noullet, Georgette. *Bed Hog* (PS–1). Illus. by David Slonim. 2011, Marshall Cavendish $12.99 (978-0-7614-5823-4). 24pp. A sweet-eyed beagle goes padding from one bed to another, looking for space to settle down; eventually he finds it in a young boy's room. (Rev: BL 4/15/11; SLJ 4/11)

1139 Numeroff, Laura. *What Puppies Do Best* (PS–2). Illus. by Lynn Munsinger. 2011, Chronicle $14.99 (978-0-8118-6601-9). Unpaged. This simple book showcases life as a puppy — chasing balls, digging holes, learning to sit, giving and getting kisses. (Rev: SLJ 10/1/11)

1140 O'Hair, Margaret. *My Kitten* (K–2). Illus. by Tammie Lyon. 2011, Marshall Cavendish $15.99 (978-0-7614-5811-1). 32pp. A little girl describes and sometimes imitates her kitten's behavior in this well-illustrated book. (Rev: BL 5/1/11; SLJ 5/1/11)

1141 Ohora, Zachariah. *Stop Snoring, Bernard!* (PS–2). Illus. by author. 2011, Henry Holt $16.99 (978-0-8050-9002-4). 32pp. An otter with a snoring problem is banished by his peers at the zoo and tries unsuccessfully to find somewhere else to sleep; eventually the other otters realize they miss him and welcome him back. Lexile AD370L (Rev: BL 4/1/11; LMC 5–6/11; SLJ 3/1/11)

1142 Pelley, Kathleen T. *Raj the Bookstore Tiger* (K–3). Illus. by Paige Keiser. 2011, Charlesbridge $15.95 (978-1-58089-230-8). 32pp. Raj, a bookstore cat who thinks he's a tiger, copes with injured self-esteem when a new employee's pet insists he's a "plain old kitty cat." Lexile AD740L (Rev: BL 2/15/11; SLJ 3/1/11)

1143 Peters, Lisa Westberg. *Frankie Works the Night Shift* (PS–K). Illus. by Jennifer Taylor. 2010, Greenwillow $16.99 (978-0-06-009095-1). 32pp. Frankie the cat chases mice for a living in this funny story with a strong counting component. (Rev: BL 4/15/10; SLJ 2/1/10)

1144 Raschka, Chris. *Hip Hop Dog* (PS–2). Illus. by Vladimir Radunsky. 2010, HarperCollins $16.99 (978-0-06-123963-2). 32pp. An unwanted urban dog turns street-smart and learns to rap in this positive, colorful book about making the best of a bad situation. (Rev: BL 1/1/10; HB 3–4/10; SLJ 3/1/10)

1145 Raye, Rebekah. *Bear-ly There* (1–3). Illus. by author. 2009, Tilbury $16.95 (978-0-88448-314-4). 32pp. Young Charlie and his family work together to discourage a bear from invading their territory in this well-illustrated novel. (Rev: BL 1/1/10; SLJ 2/1/10)

1146 Reed, Lynn Rowe. *Basil's Birds* (PS–1). Illus. by author. 2010, Marshall Cavendish $17.99 (978-0-7614-5627-8). 32pp. Birds build a nest on school janitor Basil's head, and he becomes quite devoted to the little hatchlings. (Rev: BL 5/15/10; SLJ 3/1/10)

1147 Reed, Lynn Rowe. *Roscoe and the Pelican Rescue* (PS–2). Illus. by author. 2011, Holiday House $14.95 (978-0-8234-2352-1). 32pp. A young boy's trip to the beach is spoiled by the Deepwater Horizon drilling disaster but his work rescuing oil-covered pelicans and other creatures is rewarding. Lexile AD810L (Rev: BL 6/1/11; LMC 11–12/11; SLJ 7/11)

1148 Richardson, Justin, and Peter Parnell. *Christian, the Hugging Lion* (K–3). Illus. by Amy June Bates. 2010, Simon & Schuster $16.99 (978-1-4169-8662-1). Unpaged. Tells the story of Ace and John, who buy a lion at Harrods department store in London and raise it in an apartment until it becomes too big and must be moved to Kenya; based on a true story. (Rev: LMC 8–9/10; SLJ 6/1/10)

1149 Ritz, Karen. *Windows with Birds* (PS–2). Illus. by author. 2010, Boyds Mills $16.95 (978-1-59078-656-7). 32pp. A cat learns to adjust to his new surroundings when his family moves from a large house to an apartment. (Rev: BL 2/15/10; LMC 8–9/10; SLJ 3/1/10)

1150 Roberton, Fiona. *Wanted: The Perfect Pet* (PS–3). Illus. by author. 2010, Putnam $16.99 (978-0-399-25461-1). 32pp. A lonely duck answers a little boy's ad seeking canine companionship, and the two manage to get on surprisingly well. (Rev: BL 7/10; LMC 10/10; SLJ 7/1/10)

1151 Robey, Katharine Crawford. *Where's the Party?* (PS–2). Illus. by Kate Endle. 2011, Charlesbridge

$15.95 (978-1-58089-268-1); paper $6.95 (978-1-58089-269-8). 32pp. Kate wakes to birdsong announcing a "Par-ty!" and follows the sounds to a brook where there are new ducklings; includes information on the 10 birds featured. (Rev: BLO 8/11; SLJ 6/11)

1152 Root, Phyllis. *Scrawny Cat* (PS–2). Illus. by Alison Friend. 2011, Candlewick $16.99 (978-0-7636-4164-1). Unpaged. A scared and lonely stray cat finds a new home with a woman who is also lonely. (Rev: HB 11–12/11; SLJ 12/1/11)

1153 Rosenthal, Eileen. *I'll Save You Bobo!* (PS–1). Illus. by Marc Rosenthal. 2012, Atheneum $14.99 (978-144240378-9). 40pp. Willy (a boy) is fed up with his pesky cat Earl and writes a jungle story featuring his stuffed monkey Bobo facing many dangers, but this exercise proves salutary and the two come to an understanding. **e** (Rev: SLJ 4/1/12*)

1154 Rostoker-Gruber, Karen. *Bandit's Surprise* (PS–1). Illus. by Vincent Nguyen. 2010, Marshall Cavendish $16.99 (978-0-7614-5623-0). 32pp. Bandit the cat copes with change when his owner brings home a fuzzy gray kitten. (Rev: BL 4/1/10; SLJ 3/1/10*)

1155 Rostoker-Gruber, Karen. *Ferret Fun* (PS–1). Illus. by Paul Rátz de Tagyos. 2011, Marshall Cavendish $17.99 (978-0-7614-5817-3). 32pp. Two ferrets, Fudge and Einstein, are frightened of a visiting house cat, but Marvel turns out to be OK and even has useful talents. (Rev: BL 3/15/11; LMC 8–9/11; SLJ 4/11*)

1156 Samuels, Barbara. *The Trucker* (PS–K). Illus. by author. 2010, Farrar $16.99 (978-0-374-37804-2). 40pp. Disappointed to receive a cat instead of the toy truck he wants, vehicle-obsessed Leo quickly discovers his new pet is actually the best play companion ever. (Rev: BL 4/15/10; SLJ 5/1/10*)

1157 Sayre, April Pulley. *If You're Hoppy* (PS–1). Illus. by Jackie Urbanovic. 2011, Greenwillow $16.99 (978-0-06-156634-9). 40pp. A rhyming twist on "If You're Happy and You Know It," presenting animals that are hoppy, floppy, flappy, slimy, and so forth. (Rev: BL 3/1/11; SLJ 1/1/11)

1158 Schmid, Paul. *A Pet for Petunia* (PS–2). Illus. by author. 2011, HarperCollins $12.99 (978-0-06-196331-5). 40pp. Petunia is obsessed with her stuffed toy skunk and determined to have a real one, despite her parents' adamant refusals. (Rev: BL 5/1/11; SLJ 5/1/11*)

1159 Sherry, Kevin. *Acorns Everywhere!* (PS). Illus. by author. 2009, Dial $16.99 (978-0-8037-3256-8). 32pp. A manic squirrel feverishly gathers and buries acorns, and then has trouble remembering where he hid them. (Rev: BL 9/15/09; SLJ 10/1/09)

1160 Singer, Marilyn. *What Is Your Dog Doing?* (PS–1). Illus. by Kathleen Habbley. 2011, Atheneum $12.99 (978-1-4169-7931-9). 32pp. Simple wordplay and rhymed text add appeal to this book depicting dogs of all different walks of life. **e** (Rev: BL 7/11; SLJ 6/11)

1161 Spinelli, Eileen. *Do You Have a Dog?* (K–2). Illus. by Geraldo Valerio. 2011, Eerdmans $16 (978-0-8028-5387-5). 26pp. Eleven historical figures and their dogs are portrayed in this light blend of history and canine affection told in rhyme. (Rev: BLO 10/15/11; LMC 3–4/12; SLJ 11/1/11)

1162 Stein, David Ezra. *Pouch!* (PS–K). Illus. by author. 2009, Putnam $15.99 (978-0-399-25051-4). 32pp. A young kangaroo has his first alarming adventure outside his mother's pouch. (Rev: BL 9/15/09*; HB 11–12/09; SLJ 9/1/09)

1163 Stephens, Helen. *Fleabag* (PS–1). Illus. by author. 2010, Henry Holt $16.99 (978-0-8050-7975-2). 32pp. A flea-ridden stray dog makes a new friend in this story about loyal friends. (Rev: BL 4/15/10; SLJ 7/1/10)

1164 Stewart, Paul. *In the Dark of the Night* (1–3). Illus. by Tim Vyner. 2009, Frances Lincoln $17.95 (978-1-84507-764-8). Unpaged. A wolf cub, Cub-of-Mine, accompanies his father out into the night and learns all about the importance of the moon and the wolf song. (Rev: LMC 3–4/10; SLJ 12/1/09)

1165 Thompson, Lauren. *Wee Little Bunny* (PS–1). Illus. by John Butler. Series: Wee Little. 2010, Simon & Schuster $14.99 (978-1-4169-7937-1). 32pp. A baby bunny has some brave adventures in the big woods: chasing a dragonfly, encountering a grumpy porcupine, and eventually returning home to tell his mom all about it. (Rev: BL 1/1/10; SLJ 2/1/10)

1166 Underwood, Deborah. *Granny Gomez and Jigsaw* (PS–2). Illus. by Scott Magoon. 2010, Hyperion $16.99 (978-078685216-1). 40pp. When Granny Gomez's spirited pet pig outgrows her house, she builds him a barn, missing his companionship until she breaks out her camping gear and joins him there; this quirky, offbeat story features bright illustrations. (Rev: BL 1/1/10; LMC 8–9/10)

1167 Vischer, Frans. *Fuddles* (PS–2). Illus. by author. 2011, Aladdin $15.99 (978-1-4169-9155-7). 32pp. Bored with his everyday routine, Fuddles the cat escapes into the wide world only to find that it is a pretty scary place. **e** Lexile 500L (Rev: BL 4/1/11; LMC 8–9/11; SLJ 4/11)

1168 Voake, Charlotte. *Ginger and the Mystery Visitor* (PS–2). Illus. by author. 2010, Candlewick $15.99 (978-0-7636-4865-7). 40pp. Ginger and the kitten are outraged when a neighborhood cat decides to invade their house, especially at mealtimes. (Rev: HB 11–12/10; SLJ 10/1/10)

1169 Wahman, Wendy. *A Cat Like That* (PS–1). Illus. by author. 2011, Henry Holt $16.99 (978-0-8050-8942-4). 32pp. A condescending cat explains all the bad things humans do and what it takes to be a cat's best friend. (Rev: BL 5/1/11; SLJ 6/11)

1170 Walsh, Barbara. *Sammy in the Sky* (K–3). Illus. by Jamie Wyeth. 2011, Candlewick $16.99 (978-0-7636-

4927-2). 32pp. A young girl's family helps her to cope when the family dog passes away. Lexile AD740L (Rev: BL 8/11; LMC 11–12/11; SLJ 8/1/11*)

1171 Wardlaw, Lee. *Won Ton: A Cat Tale Told in Haiku* (K–3). Illus. by Eugene Yelchin. 2011, Henry Holt $16.99 (978-0-8050-8995-0). 40pp. A cynical and feisty stray cat gets adopted, and slowly learns to love his new home in this story told from the cat's perspective in a series of senryu poems — similar to haiku but reflective of personality and behavior rather than the natural world. ALSC Notable Children's Book, 2012. ∩ (Rev: BL 2/1/11*; HB 3–4/11; LMC 5–6/11*; SLJ 2/1/11*)

1172 Wild, Margaret. *Harry and Hopper* (PS–2). Illus. by Freya Blackwood. 2011, Feiwel & Friends $16.99 (978-0-312-64261-7). 32pp. Young Harry slowly learns to accept the fact that his dog Hopper was killed in an accident in this touching story about grief. Lexile AD690L (Rev: BL 2/1/11*; HB 1–2/11; SLJ 4/11*)

1173 Wild, Margaret. *Puffling* (PS–2). Illus. by Julie Vivas. 2009, Feiwel & Friends $16.99 (978-0-312-56570-1). 32pp. A baby puffin hatches and grows under the care of his loving parents, eager to grow strong enough to leave his parents and start his own life; the lovely illustrations show the puffling's progress. (Rev: BL 9/15/09*; LMC 10/09; SLJ 12/1/09)

1174 Willems, Mo. *City Dog, Country Frog* (PS–2). Illus. by Jon J Muth. 2010, Hyperion $17.99 (978-1-4231-0300-4). 64pp. In spring City Dog gets to go to the country and makes friends with a frog; the two play together over successive visits, but come winter Country Frog is gone and a lonely City Dog must wait for the next spring to make a new friend. ALSC Notable Children's Book, 2011. Lexile AD490L (Rev: BL 3/15/10*; HB 7–8/10; SLJ 5/1/10*)

1175 Wilson, Karma. *What's in the Egg, Little Pip?* (K–2). Illus. by Jane Chapman. 2010, Simon & Schuster $16.99 (978-1-4169-4204-7). 40pp. Penguin Little Pip is jealous of the egg her parents are protecting so carefully in this third book in the series that features warm, realistic illustrations. ℮ (Rev: BL 2/1/11; SLJ 2/1/11)

1176 Wright, Johanna. *Bandits* (PS–1). Illus. by author. 2011, Roaring Brook $16.99 (978-1-59643-583-4). 32pp. Expressive illustrations add appeal to this story of "bandits" — raccoons — roaming a neighborhood after dark. (Rev: BL 9/1/11*; SLJ 8/1/11)

1177 Yolen, Jane. *The Day Tiger Rose Said Goodbye* (PS–3). Illus. by Jim LaMarche. 2011, Random House $16.99 (978-0-375-86663-0); LB $19.99 (978-0-375-96663-7). 32pp. An old cat's last day on earth is documented in this sensitive story. ℮ (Rev: BL 7/11; LMC 1–2/12*; SLJ 8/1/11)

1178 Young, Judy. *A Pet for Miss Wright* (PS–3). Illus. by Andrea Wesson. 2011, Sleeping Bear $15.95 (978-1-58536-509-8). 32pp. A lonely writer tries one pet after another, eventually settling on a dog who watches, lis-

tens, and learns to retrieve the dictionary and thesaurus. (Rev: BL 4/1/11; SLJ 5/1/11)

1179 Ziefert, Harriet. *My Dog Thinks I'm a Genius* (PS–2). Illus. by Barroux. 2011, Blue Apple $16.99 (978-1-60905-059-7). Unpaged. A boy who loves making paintings of his dog discovers that the dog has artistic abilities all his own. (Rev: SLJ 9/1/11)

SCHOOL STORIES

1180 Bergman, Mara. *Lively Elizabeth! What Happens When You Push* (PS–1). Illus. by Cassia Thomas. 2010, Whitman $16.99 (978-0-8075-4702-1). 32pp. One child's push leads to a disastrous domino effect, lots of blame, and plenty of regret. (Rev: BL 10/1/10; SLJ 9/1/10)

1181 Buzzeo, Toni. *Adventure Annie Goes to Kindergarten* (PS–K). Illus. by Amy Wummer. 2010, Dial $16.99 (978-0-8037-3358-9). 32pp. Plucky Annie may have difficulty following the kindergarten rules but when two students get lost she is the one who leaps to the rescue. (Rev: BL 5/1/10; LMC 8–9/10; SLJ 5/1/10)

1182 Cook, Lisa Broadie. *Peanut Butter and Homework Sandwiches* (K–2). Illus. by Jack E. Davis. 2011, Putnam $16.99 (978-0-399-24533-6). 32pp. Martin has a difficult week at school when a substitute teacher replaces the cool Mr. Elliot. (Rev: BL 8/11; LMC 11–12/11; SLJ 7/11)

1183 Cox, Judy. *Carmen Learns English* (PS–2). Illus. by Angela Dominguez. 2010, Holiday House $16.95 (978-0-8234-2174-9). 32pp. A young Spanish-speaking girl adjusts to learning English with the guidance of a helpful teacher. Lexile AD620L (Rev: BL 8/10; LMC 3–4/11; SLJ 9/1/10)

1184 Gall, Chris. *Substitute Creacher* (K–2). Illus. by author. 2011, Little, Brown $16.99 (978-0-316-08915-9). 40pp. A classroom of rambunctious kids is faced with a slimy, tentacled substitute teacher, who spins terrifying tales about previous students who misbehaved. (Rev: BL 6/1/11; LMC 10/11; SLJ 7/11)

1185 Grandits, John. *Ten Rules You Absolutely Must Not Break If You Want to Survive the School Bus* (K–3). Illus. by Michael Allen Austin. 2011, Clarion $16.99 (978-0-618-78822-4). 32pp. This tongue-in-cheek book features a big brother laying down 10 school bus survival rules for his younger brother, who manages to break all of them in one day and live to tell the tale. (Rev: BL 7/11; LMC 10/11*; SLJ 7/11*)

1186 Grigsby, Susan. *First Peas to the Table* (1–3). Illus. by Nicole Tadgell. 2012, Whitman $16.99 (978-080752452-7). 32pp. A teacher successfully uses a vegetable garden as an opportunity to discuss the life and accomplishments of Thomas Jefferson. (Rev: BL 3/15/12; LMC 8–9/12; SLJ 2/12)

1187 Gutman, Dan. *Miss Child Has Gone Wild!* (1–3). Illus. by Jim Paillot. Series: My Weirder School. 2011, HarperCollins LB $15.89 (978-006196917-1); paper $3.99 (978-006196916-4). 112pp. A.J. and his friends — now in 3rd grade at Ella Mentry School — enjoy a field trip to the zoo in this first volume in a new series. Lexile 600L (Rev: BLO 11/15/11)

1188 Husband, Amy. *Dear Teacher* (K–2). Illus. by author. 2010, Sourcebooks paper $8.99 (978-1-4022-4268-7). 24pp. Young Michael composes a series of extravagantly inventive excuses for his absence on the first day back at school. (Rev: BL 8/10; LMC 11–12/10; SLJ 8/1/10)

1189 Loewen, Nancy. *The Last Day of Kindergarten* (PS–K). Illus. by Sachiko Yoshikawa. 2011, Marshall Cavendish $16.99 (978-0-7614-5807-7). Unpaged. A young girl reflects on her year in kindergarten and her forthcoming graduation. (Rev: SLJ 3/1/11)

1190 Lorenz, Albert. *The Exceptionally, Extraordinarily Ordinary First Day of School* (2–4). Illus. by author. 2010, Abrams $15.95 (978-0-8109-8960-3). Unpaged. An imaginative young boy eager for an ordinary, unremarkable school describes his old one — full of quirky characters, animals everywhere, crazy field trips — with much detail and aplomb in this surreal story full of humor. (Rev: SLJ 11/1/10)

1191 McCourt, Lisa. *Ready for Kindergarten, Stinky Face?* (PS–K). Illus. by Cyd Moore. 2010, Scholastic paper $3.99 (978-0-545-11518-6). 32pp. A young boy's wild anxieties about the first day of school are calmly put to rest by his patient mother in this reassuring story. (Rev: BL 8/10; SLJ 9/1/10)

1192 Milord, Susan. *Happy 100th Day* (K–2). Illus. by Mary Newell DePalma. 2011, Scholastic $16.99 (978-043988281-1). 40pp. Graham dreads the 100th Day of School, which coincides with his birthday, when he learns he must read 100 books by then. Lexile AD650L (Rev: BLO 1/1–15/11; SLJ 2/11)

1193 Morton, Carlene. *The Library Pages* (K–3). Illus. by Valeria Docampo. 2010, Upstart $17.95 (978-1-60213-045-6). Unpaged. While out on maternity leave, the school librarian receives a DVD showing her students "helping" around the library by reshelving everything and making repairs with glitter tape; the librarian is horrified until everyone yells "April Fool!" (Rev: LMC 11–12/10; SLJ 9/1/10)

1194 O'Connor, Jane. *Fancy Nancy: Poet Extraordinaire!* (1–3). Illus. by Robin Preiss Glasser. Series: Fancy Nancy. 2010, HarperCollins $12.99 (978-006189643-9). 32pp. Fancy Nancy is inspired by her class poetry unit but finds herself unable to get started writing. (Rev: BL 4/15/10)

1195 Portis, Antoinette. *Kindergarten Diary* (PS–1). Illus. by author. 2010, HarperCollins $12.99 (978-0-06-145691-6). 32pp. Annalina confides her early fears about kindergarten and how it took only a month before she realized she was enjoying herself. (Rev: BL 5/15/10; HB 7–8/10; SLJ 7/1/10)

1196 Poydar, Nancy. *No Fair Science Fair* (K–3). Illus. by author. 2011, Holiday House $14.95 (978-0-8234-2269-2). 32pp. Otis's efforts at attracting birds earn a "Stick-withit-Prize" from the science fair judges. Lexile AD420L (Rev: BL 3/1/11; SLJ 3/1/11)

1197 Preller, James. *A Pirate's Guide to First Grade* (PS–1). Illus. by Greg Ruth. 2010, Feiwel & Friends $16.99 (978-0-312-36928-6). 48pp. An imaginative young boy narrates his first day in 1st grade using dynamic pirate lingo. ℰ Lexile AD690L (Rev: BL 8/10; LMC 8–9/10; SLJ 8/1/10*)

1198 Primavera, Elise. *Louise the Big Cheese and the Back-to-School Smarty-Pants* (K–2). Illus. by Diane Goode. 2011, Simon & Schuster $16.99 (978-1-4424-0600-1). Unpaged. Louise enters 2nd grade determined to make straight A's, but things don't work out as planned. (Rev: SLJ 6/11*)

1199 Pulver, Robin. *Thank You, Miss Doover* (1–3). Illus. by Stephanie Roth Sisson. 2010, Holiday House $16.95 (978-0-8234-2046-9). 32pp. Young Jack struggles to learn how to write a thank-you letter in this funny book with cartoonlike illustrations. Lexile GN540L (Rev: BL 11/15/10; LMC 3–4/11; SLJ 10/1/10)

1200 Quackenbush, Robert. *First Grade Jitters* (K–1). Illus. by Yan Nascimbene. 2010, HarperCollins $16.99 (978-0-06-077632-9). 32pp. A boy needs reassurance from his friends before starting 1st grade in this updated version of the 1982 classic. ℰ (Rev: BLO 7/10; SLJ 7/1/10)

1201 Rockwell, Anne. *First Day of School* (K–2). Illus. by Lizzy Rockwell. 2011, HarperCollins $16.99 (978-0-06-050191-4). 40pp. A diverse group of kids prepare for their first day of school by recalling how they got through last year's first day. (Rev: BL 8/11; SLJ 9/1/11)

1202 Urdahl, Catherine. *Polka-Dot Fixes Kindergarten* (PS–K). Illus. by Mai S. Kemble. 2011, Charlesbridge $16.95 (978-1-57091-737-0); paper $7.95 (978-1-57091-738-7). 32pp. Starting kindergarten is stressful for Polka-Dot, and even Grandpa's emergency kit doesn't help her cope with classmate Liz; Polka-Dot finds her own solution in the end. (Rev: BL 8/11; SLJ 7/11)

1203 Vernick, Audrey. *Is Your Buffalo Ready for Kindergarten?* (PS–K). Illus. by Daniel Jennewein. 2010, HarperCollins $16.99 (978-0-06-176275-8). 32pp. A young buffalo does his best to behave in a kindergarten class full of children also learning the rules in this funny story. (Rev: BL 8/10; SLJ 6/1/10)

1204 Wells, Rosemary. *Hands Off, Harry!* (PS–K). Illus. by author. 2011, HarperCollins $14.99 (978-0-

06-192112-4). 40pp. A young boy having a hard time respecting others' personal space learns a different way of behaving. (Rev: BL 5/1/11; SLJ 7/11)

1205 Winters, Kay. *This School Year Will Be the Best!* (K–2). Illus. by Renee Andriani. 2010, Dutton $16.99 (978-0-525-42775-4). 32pp. When a teacher asks her young students to share their hopes for the coming year, the responses are satisfyingly diverse. (Rev: BL 5/1/10; SLJ 8/1/10)

1206 Wortche, Allison. *Rosie Sprout's Time to Shine* (PS–1). Illus. by Patrice Barton. 2011, Knopf $17.99 (978-037586721-7); LB $20.99 (978-037596721-4). 40pp. Rosie has always been jealous of overly confident and successful Violet, but she discovers she herself can shine when a gardening project — and a chance to be generous — come along. (Rev: BLO 12/15/11; LMC 3–4/12; SLJ 1/12)

TRANSPORTATION AND MACHINES

1207 Biggs, Brian. *Everything Goes: On Land* (K–2). Illus. by author. 2011, HarperCollins $14.99 (978-0-06-195809-0). 56pp. A busy look at city streets crowded with vehicles of all kinds, as Dad answers young Henry's many questions about modes of transportation. (Rev: BL 11/1/11; SLJ 11/1/11)

1208 Clement, Nathan. *Job Site* (PS–1). Illus. by author. 2011, Boyds Mills $16.95 (978-1-59078-769-4). Unpaged. A community park takes shape as a bulldozer, excavator, loader, and other heavy machinery work according to the instructions of the boss. (Rev: SLJ 5/1/11)

1209 Cuyler, Margery. *The Little Dump Truck* (PS–1). Illus. by Bob Kolar. 2009, Henry Holt $12.99 (978-0-8050-8281-4). 32pp. A contented dump truck and its driver, Hard Hat Pete, are busy at a construction site in this rhyming story with digital art. (Rev: BL 9/15/09; SLJ 11/1/09)

1210 de Roo, Elena. *The Rain Train* (PS–1). Illus. by Brian Lovelock. 2011, Candlewick $15.99 (978-0-7636-5313-2). 32pp. A little boy enjoys a trip on a train through a rainy night — that all turns out to be a dream. (Rev: BL 5/1/11; SLJ 6/11)

1211 London, Jonathan. *A Plane Goes Ka-Zoom!* (PS). Illus. by Denis Roche. 2010, Henry Holt $15.99 (978-0-8050-8970-7). 32pp. A family visits an air show, watches activities at an airport, and then takes a ride in a plane. (Rev: BL 9/1/10; SLJ 11/1/10)

1212 McMullan, Kate. *I'm Fast!* (PS–1). Illus. by Jim McMullan. 2012, HarperCollins $16.99 (978-006192085-1). 40pp. A train and a red sports car engage in a (not too) exciting battle of speed. (Rev: BL 12/15/11; HB 1–2/12; SLJ 1/12)

1213 Mandel, Peter. *Jackhammer Sam* (K–2). Illus. by David Catrow. 2011, Roaring Brook $16.99 (978-1-

59643-034-1). 40pp. Sam is proud of his jackhammer's vibrations and bounces along to the rhythm as he sends people flying. (Rev: BL 11/15/11; HB 11–12/11; SLJ 11/1/11)

1214 Meltzer, Lynn. *The Construction Crew* (PS–K). Illus. by Carrie Eko-Burgess. 2011, Henry Holt $12.99 (978-0-8050-8884-7). 40pp. A construction crew demolishes an old building and builds a house in this simple story with rhyming text and colorful illustrations. (Rev: BL 12/1/11; SLJ 12/1/11)

1215 Niemann, Christoph. *That's How!* (PS–1). Illus. by author. 2011, HarperCollins $16.99 (978-0-06-201963-9). Unpaged. An imaginative little boy pictures the mysterious mechanisms — which usually involve animals — behind various construction machines and vehicles. (Rev: BL 7/1/11; SLJ 5/1/11)

1216 Sarcone-Roach, Julia. *Subway Story* (1–3). Illus. by author. 2011, Knopf $16.99 (978-0-375-85859-8). Unpaged. A fascinating story of a New York City subway car named Jessie, who works for decades before being recycled as part of an artificial reef in the Atlantic. (Rev: HB 11–12/11*; LMC 11–12/11; SLJ 9/1/11)

1217 Stein, Peter. *Cars Galore* (PS–1). Illus. by Bob Staake. 2011, Candlewick $15.99 (978-0-7636-4743-8). 32pp. Using illustrations and rhyming text, Stein presents a variety of cars of different shapes, sizes, and characteristics, including one that runs on air. (Rev: BL 3/1/11; HB 3–4/11; SLJ 2/1/11)

1218 Suen, Anastasia. *Road Work Ahead* (PS–K). Illus. by Jannie Ho. 2011, Viking $15.99 (978-0-670-01288-6). 32pp. A boy, his mother, and their dog have a delay-filled journey to Grandma's house, allowing them to enjoy all the details of construction work. (Rev: BL 9/15/11; SLJ 10/1/11)

1219 Sutton, Sally. *Demolition* (PS–2). Illus. by Brian Lovelock. 2012, Candlewick $15.99 (978-076365830-4). 32pp. A team of construction and demolition machines tear down an old parking garage and create an attractive city park. (Rev: BL 2/15/12; SLJ 6/1/12*)

1220 Viva, Frank. *Along a Long Road* (PS–1). Illus. by author. 2011, Little, Brown $16.99 (978-0-316-12925-1). 40pp. Spare text accompanies continuous woodcut-style illustrations in this paean to cycling. (Rev: BL 5/1/11; SLJ 6/11*)

1221 Williams, Treat. *Air Show!* (PS–2). Illus. by Robert Neubecker. 2010, Hyperion $16.99 (978-1-4231-1185-6). 40pp. Their father flies young Ellie and Gill to an air show where they see all kinds of aircraft. (Rev: BL 6/10; HB 9–10/10; SLJ 7/1/10)

1222 Zimmerman, Andrea. *Train Man* (PS–K). Illus. by David Clemesha. 2012, Henry Holt $14.99 (978-080507991-3). 32pp. Two young boys who enjoy playing with a toy train set are taken on a fun ride on a zoo train. (Rev: BL 3/1/12; SLJ 5/1/12)

Graphic Novels

1223 Barnett, Mac. *Oh No! (Or How My Science Project Destroyed the World)* (K–3). Illus. by Dan Santat. 2010, Hyperion/Disney $16.99 (978-1-4231-2312-5). Unpaged. Things get out of control when a girl builds a robot for the science fair in this fast-paced graphic novel. (Rev: LMC 11–12/10; SLJ 7/1/10)

1224 Cammuso, Frank. *The Dragon Players* (2–4). Illus. by author. Series: Knights of the Lunch Table. 2009, Scholastic paper $9.99 (978-043990323-3). 128pp. Artie and his Camelot Middle School friends enter a robot contest, vying against the bully called Horde; Merlin offers advice and the Ladies of the Lunch stir a boiling pot. (Rev: BL 11/15/09; SLJ 1/10)

1225 Cosentino, Ralph. *Wonder Woman: The Story of the Amazon Princess* (1–3). Illus. by author. 2011, Viking $16.99 (978-067006256-0). 40pp. Tells the story of Wonder Woman's origins and transformation into a superhero capable of destroying villains. (Rev: BLO 3/14/11; SLJ 5/1/11)

1226 Coudray, Philippe. *Benjamin Bear in Fuzzy Thinking* (K–2). Trans. by Leigh Stein. Illus. by author. 2011, TOON $12.95 (978-193517912-2). 32pp. Funny comic strip stories for emerging readers feature a bear with unusual thought processes. Lexile GN20L (Rev: BL 10/15/11; HB 11–12/11; LMC 1–2/12; SLJ 11/1/11)

1227 Dunklee, Annika. *My Name Is Elizabeth!* (PS–1). Illus. by Matthew Forsythe. 2011, Kids Can $14.95 (978-1-55453-560-6). Unpaged. A young girl fed up with nicknames shouts out her name preference — Elizabeth! (Rev: LMC 1–2/12; SLJ 10/1/11)

1228 Hayes, Geoffrey. *Benny and Penny in the Toy Breaker* (PS–2). Illus. by author. 2010, Raw Junior/TOON $12.95 (978-1-935179-07-8). 32pp. Mouse siblings Benny and Penny unite to protect their toys from their boisterous cousin Bo when he comes to visit; the cartoon illustrations will attract new readers. (Rev: BL 3/15/10; SLJ 7/1/10)

1229 Hayes, Geoffrey. *Patrick in a Teddy Bear's Picnic and Other Stories* (K–2). Illus. by author. 2011, TOON $12.95 (978-193517909-2). 32pp. Patrick the bear has a variety of adventures in this comic book full of lovable, dynamic illustrations; suitable for beginning readers. (Rev: BL 4/15/11; SLJ 7/1/11)

1230 Johnson, R. Kikuo. *The Shark King* (2–4). Illus. by author. 2012, TOON $12.95 (978-193517916-0). 40pp. The shape-shifting shark god Kamohoalii has a child with a young human woman, and the child has trouble fitting in with the people of his village; a graphic novel for early readers. (Rev: BL 3/15/12*; HB 7–8/12; LMC 10/12; SLJ 5/1/12)

1231 Knight, Hilary, and Steven Kroll. *Nina in That Makes Me Mad!* (PS–2). Illus. by Hilary Knight. 2011, TOON $12.95 (978-193517910-8). 32pp. On one side of each two-page spread, expressive young Nina exclaims about a variety of different things that make her mad; the opposite side is a funny comic strip illustrating the girl's complaint. Lexile GN160L (Rev: BL 10/15/11; LMC 1–2/12; SLJ 11/1/11)

1232 Kochalka, James. *Johnny Boo and the Happy Apples* (K–3). Illus. by author. 2009, Top Shelf $9.95 (978-160309041-4). 40pp. Little ghost Johnny Boo wants big muscles and hears that Happy Apples will supply these, but the apples are hard to acquire. The fourth adventure in this series is *Johnny Boo and the Mean Little Boy* (2010). (Rev: BL 10/15/09)

1233 Le Gall, Frank. *Freedom!* (2–4). Trans. by Carol Klio Burrell. Illus. by Flore Balthazar. 2012, Lerner/Graphic Universe LB $29.27 (978-076137884-6); paper $6.95 (978-076138546-2). 48pp. A bored kitten named Miss Annie has gentle adventures, including venturing out of an open window, in this simple graphic novel. **e** (Rev: BL 2/15/12; LMC 5–6/12; SLJ 5/1/12)

1234 Lechner, John. *Sticky Burr: The Prickly Peril* (K–3). Illus. by author. 2009, Candlewick $15.99 (978-076364145-0); paper $6.99 (978-076364580-9). 56pp. Scurvy Burr, irritated by the general acceptance of the nicer Spiny Burr, decides to take over Burr Village with the help of exiled Burweena. (Rev: BL 11/15/09; SLJ 11/09)

1235 Long, Ethan. *Rick and Rack and the Great Outdoors* (1–3). Illus. by author. 2010, Blue Apple $10.99 (978-160905034-4). 40pp. This lively graphic novel for beginning readers comprises three short, comic stories about a raccoon and moose and their adventures in the forest. (Rev: BL 10/15/10)

1236 Luciani, Brigitte. *A Hubbub* (K–3). Trans. by Edward Gauvin. Illus. by Eve Tharlet. Series: Mr. Badger and Mrs. Fox. 2010, Lerner/Graphic Universe $25.26 (978-076135626-4); paper $6.95 (978-076135632-5). 32pp. The Badger and Fox families introduced in *The Meeting* (2010) have blended together, although Ginger Fox has trouble adjusting to her badger stepbrothers. (Rev: BL 12/15/10; SLJ 11/10)

1237 Luciani, Brigitte. *The Meeting* (K–3). Trans. by Carol Klio Burrell. Illus. by Eve Tharlet. Series: Mr. Badger and Mrs. Fox. 2010, Lerner/Graphic Universe LB $25.26 (978-0-7613-5625-7); paper $6.95 (978-0-7613-5631-8). 32pp. Two families — foxes and badgers — share the same burrow, with some opposition from the children. Also use *What a Team!* (2011). (Rev: BL 3/15/10*; LMC 8–9/10; SLJ 5/10)

1238 McGuiness, Dan. *Pilot and Huxley: The First Adventure* (2–4). Illus. by author. 2010, Scholastic paper $7.99 (978-054526504-1). 64pp. Pilot and Huxley have a series of daring and zany adventures in this funny graphic novel. Lexile GN400L (Rev: BL 12/15/10; LMC 5–6/11; SLJ 3/1/11)

1239 McGuiness, Dan. *Pilot and Huxley: The Next Adventure* (1–3). Illus. by author. 2011, Scholastic paper $8.99 (978-054526845-5). 64pp. Pilot and Huxley find themselves in an alternate holiday universe where Santa Claus is evil and zombies are friendly. (Rev: BL 10/15/11; SLJ 11/1/11)

1240 Pilkey, Dav. *Super Diaper Baby 2: The Invasion of the Potty Snatchers* (1–3). Illus. by author. 2011, Scholastic $9.99 (978-054517532-6). 192pp. George and Harold, in trouble because of their earlier comic book about poop, decided to do a book about pee. (Rev: BL 9/15/11; SLJ 1/12)

1241 Smith, Jeff. *Little Mouse Gets Ready* (PS–K). Illus. by author. 2009, Raw Junior/TOON $12.95 (978-193517901-6). 32pp. A little mouse gets dressed to go to the barn with his mother, struggling with buttonholes and tucking in tags in this funny graphic novel. (Rev: BL 8/09; LMC 11–12/09; SLJ 11/09)

1242 Spiegelman, Nadja. *Zig and Wikki in Something Ate My Homework* (K–2). Illus. by Trade Loeffler. 2010, Raw Junior/TOON $12.95 (978-193517902-3). 40pp. Aliens Zig and Wikki are dispatched to Earth in search of specimens for their class zoo in this zany, science-infused story. (Rev: BL 3/15/10; SLJ 7/10)

1243 Spiegelman, Nadja. *Zig and Wikki in The Cow* (1–3). Illus. by Trade Loeffler. 2012, TOON $12.95 (978-193517915-3). 40pp. Aliens Zig and Wikki must get eaten by a cow in order to reclaim their missing spaceship in this sequel to 2010's *Zig and Wikki in Something Ate My Homework*. (Rev: BL 3/15/12; LMC 10/12; SLJ 5/1/12)

1244 Tukel, Onur. *Little Friends* (K–2). Illus. by author. 2012, Marshall Cavendish $14.99 (978-076146260-6). 64pp. Friends Louisa and Sara have an on-again off-again relationship with a neighboring boy named Barry. (Rev: BL 4/15/12; LMC 11–12/12; SLJ 6/1/12)

1245 Venable, Colleen. *And Then There Were Gnomes* (2–4). Illus. by Stephanie Yue. Series: Guinea Pig, Pet Shop Private Eye. 2010, Lerner/Graphic Universe LB $27.93 (978-076134599-2); paper $6.95 (978-076135480-2). 48pp. Sasspants the detective guinea pig and her wannabe assistant Hamisher the Hamster believe a ghost is the culprit in the case of the missing pet shop mice. This volume is followed by *The Ferret's a Foot* and *Fish You Were Here* (both 2011). Lexile GN220L (Rev: BLO 6/10)

1246 Venable, Colleen. *Hamster and Cheese* (1–3). Illus. by Stephanie Yue. Series: Guinea Pig, Pet Shop Private Eye. 2010, Lerner/Graphic Universe LB $27.93 (978-0-7613-4598-5); paper $6.95 (978-0-7613-5479-6). 48pp. Guinea pig Sasspants and other animals at the pet shop investigate the theft of Mr. Venezi's sandwiches. (Rev: BL 3/15/10; LMC 10/10; SLJ 5/10)

Stories About Holidays and Holy Days

GENERAL AND MISCELLANEOUS

1247 Callahan, Sean. *The Leprechaun Who Lost His Rainbow* (K–3). Illus. by Nancy Cote. 2009, Whitman $16.99 (978-0-8075-4454-9). Unpaged. A charming leprechaun named Roy G. Biv asks for Colleen's help in bringing an end to the St. Patrick's Day rain. (Rev: SLJ 11/1/09)

1248 Compestine, Ying Chang. *The Runaway Wok: A Chinese New Year Tale* (K–3). Illus. by Sebastià Serra. 2011, Dutton $16.99 (978-0-525-42068-2). 32pp. A desperately poor Chinese family comes upon a magical wok that allows them to share their good luck with their neighbors on Chinese New Year. ℮ (Rev: BL 1/1–15/11; SLJ 2/1/11)

1249 Cox, Judy. *Cinco de Mouse-O!* (K–2). Illus. by Jeffrey Ebbeler. 2010, Holiday House $16.95 (978-0-8234-2194-7). 32pp. Mouse enjoys the festivities on Cinco de Mayo despite the relentless Cat and the dangers from exuberant humans. (Rev: BL 2/15/10; LMC 8–9/10; SLJ 4/1/10)

1250 Holub, Joan. *Groundhog Weather School* (PS–3). Illus. by Kristin Sorra. 2009, Putnam $16.99 (978-0-399-24659-3). 32pp. Groundhog realizes the importance of correct weather prediction and opens a school. (Rev: BL 11/15/09; SLJ 11/1/09)

1251 Jalali, Reza. *Moon Watchers: Shirin's Ramadan Miracle* (2–4). Illus. by Anne Sibley O'Brien. 2010, Tilbury $16.95 (978-0-88448-321-2). 32pp. Disappointed because she is too young to fast, 9-year-old Shirin instead focuses on learning about Ramadan and doing good deeds. (Rev: BL 6/10; LMC 11–12/10; SLJ 9/1/10)

1252 Lin, Grace. *Thanking the Moon: Celebrating the Mid-Autumn Moon Festival* (PS–3). Illus. by author. 2010, Knopf $16.99 (978-0-375-86101-7). 32pp. A Chinese American family celebrates the traditional festival of the mid-autumn moon in this nicely illustrated book with cultural information. ℮ (Rev: BL 9/15/10; LMC 1–2/11; SLJ 9/1/10)

1253 May, Eleanor. *The Best Mother's Day Ever* (K–2). Illus. by M. H. Pilz. 2010, Kane paper $5.95 (978-1-57565-299-3). 32pp. Lucy, who has a bad record with efforts to please her mother, asks her friend Diego to help and they plan a Mexican Mother's Day, with predictable results but a happy ending. (Rev: BL 2/15/10; SLJ 3/1/10)

1254 Miller, Pat. *Squirrel's New Year's Resolution* (PS–1). Illus. by Kathi Ember. 2010, Whitman $16.99 (978-0-8075-7591-8). 32pp. Squirrel learns what resolutions are but can't immediately think of one worth making. (Rev: BL 10/15/10; LMC 11–12/10; SLJ 10/1/10)

1255 Robert, Na'ima B. *Ramadan Moon* (K–3). Illus. by Shirin Adl. 2009, Frances Lincoln $17.95 (978-1-84507-922-2). 32pp. This book about the Islamic holiday follows a Muslim family through the rituals of the month. (Rev: BL 11/15/09; SLJ 12/1/09)

1256 Washington, Donna L. *Li'l Rabbit's Kwanzaa* (PS–K). Illus. by Shane W. Evans. 2010, HarperCollins paper $12.99 (978-006072816-8). 32pp. A young rabbit rallies the family's animal friends to help his sick Granna celebrate the holiday; includes "The Nguzo Saba — The Seven Principles of Kwanzaa." (Rev: BL 11/1/10; HB 11–12/10; SLJ 10/10)

BIRTHDAYS

1257 Avraham, Kate Aver. *What Will You Be, Sara Mee?* (PS–3). Illus. by Anne Sibley O'Brien. 2010, Charlesbridge $16.95 (978-1-58089-210-0); paper $7.95 (978-158089211-7). 32pp. This story of a Korean American girl's lively first birthday party is narrated by her older brother, Chong. (Rev: BL 2/1/10; SLJ 2/1/10)

1258 Janni, Rebecca. *Every Cowgirl Needs a Horse* (K–2). Illus. by Lynne Avril. 2010, Dutton $16.99 (978-0-525-42164-1). 32pp. Wannabe cowgirl Nellie Sue makes the best of disappointment when she receives a bike — not the horse she wanted — for her birthday. Lexile AD650L (Rev: BL 2/1/10; LMC 3–4/10; SLJ 2/1/10)

1259 McClatchy, Lisa. *Dear Tyrannosaurus Rex* (K–2). Illus. by John Manders. 2010, Random House $16.99 (978-0-375-85608-2); LB $19.99 (978-0-375-95608-9). 40pp. Erin attempts to entice a local museum's T-rex to her 6th birthday party by explaining all the treats in store — including the hokey pokey, the trampoline, and pin-the-tail-on-the-dinosaur. ℮ (Rev: BLO 8/10; SLJ 12/1/10)

1260 McNamara, Margaret. *George Washington's Birthday: A Mostly True Tale* (K–3). Illus. by Barry Blitt. 2012, Random House $17.99 (978-037584499-7). 40pp. Wry illustrations add appeal to this story of 7-year-old George, who ends up spending his birthday chopping down a cherry tree, throwing rocks across the Rappahannock, and more, while believing his family has forgotten the celebration. ℮ (Rev: BL 2/1/12; HB 1–2/12; LMC 5–6/12; SLJ 1/12)

1261 Ross, Tony. *I Want Two Birthdays!* (PS–2). Illus. by author. 2010, Andersen $16.95 (978-0-7613-5495-6). 32pp. Little Princess becomes too greedy about birthdays and it takes an "unbirthday" to make the day special again. Lexile AD590L (Rev: BL 2/1/10; LMC 8–9/10; SLJ 3/1/10)

1262 Schoenherr, Ian. *Don't Spill the Beans!* (PS). Illus. by author. 2010, Greenwillow $16.99 (978-0-06-172457-2); LB $17.89 (978-0-06-172458-9). 32pp. Bear has a difficult time hiding the fact that it's his birthday from his animal friends. (Rev: BL 2/1/10; SLJ 1/1/10*)

CHRISTMAS

1263 Brett, Jan. *Home for Christmas* (K–3). Illus. by author. 2011, Putnam $17.99 (978-039925653-0). 32pp. A young troll runs away from his family seeking a less demanding place to live but finds, just in time for Christmas, that home is best. (Rev: BL 10/15/11; SLJ 10/1/11)

1264 Buck, Nola. *A Christmas Goodnight* (PS–K). Illus. by Sarah Jane Wright. 2011, HarperCollins $12.99 (978-006166491-5). 24pp. A Christmas bedtime book in which a young boy bids goodnight to all the characters in a manger scene. (Rev: BL 10/15/11; HB 11–12/11; SLJ 10/1/11)

1265 Clark, Mary Higgins. *The Magical Christmas Horse* (PS–1). Illus. by Wendell Minor. 2011, Simon & Schuster $17.99 (978-141699478-7). 40pp. A young Arizona boy reminisces about the wonderful Christmas he shared with his Connecticut grandparents, and wishes his younger brother could experience one like it. (Rev: BL 10/1/11; SLJ 10/1/11)

1266 Cole, Brock. *The Money We'll Save* (1–3). Illus. by author. 2011, Farrar $16.99 (978-037435011-6). 40pp. Penny-pinching Pa's plan to raise a turkey to eat for Christmas dinner goes spectacularly awry in this comic story set in 19th-century New York City. (Rev: BL 12/1/11; HB 11–12/11; SLJ 10/1/11)

1267 dePaola, Tomie. *Strega Nona's Gift* (K–2). Illus. by author. 2011, Penguin $16.99 (978-039925649-3). 32pp. At Christmas time, Big Anthony finds himself so enticed by Strega Nona's cooking that he eats a pot of turnips intended for the goat, and the goat retaliates by eating his blanket; meantime Strega Nona sends out nighttime gifts. ♫ ℮ (Rev: BL 12/15/11; HB 11–12/11; SLJ 10/1/11)

1268 Dunrea, Olivier. *A Christmas Tree for Pyn* (PS–2). Illus. by author. 2011, Philomel $16.99 (978-039924506-0). 32pp. A young girl pining for her own Christmas tree finally breaks through to her distant father when she gets lost in the snowy woods; in the end, she receives both a tree and the affection she craves. Lexile AD700L (Rev: BL 10/15/11; HB 11–12/11; SLJ 10/1/11*)

1269 Fackelmayer, Regina. *The Gifts* (PS–3). Illus. by Christa Unzner. 2009, NorthSouth $16.95 (978-073582265-8). 32pp. In this quiet story, a generous young girl is rewarded for her good deeds when a kind-hearted man and a boy decorate her Christmas tree for her. (Rev: BL 11/1/09; HB 11–12/09)

1270 Ghigna, Charles. *I See Winter* (PS). Illus. by Ag Jatkowska. 2011, Picture Window $21.32 (978-140486588-4); paper $4.95 (978-140486850-2). 24pp. From subtle changes in the weather and landscape to preparations for Christmas, this book celebrates winter in simple, poetic text. (Rev: BLO 11/15/11)

1271 Jay, Alison. *The Nutcracker* (K–3). Illus. by author. 2010, Dial $16.99 (978-080373285-8). 40pp. Nostalgic illustrations grace this retelling of the classic story about the nutcracker soldier who becomes a prince. (Rev: BL 10/15/10; HB 11–12/10)

1272 Kimmel, Eric A. *The Spider's Gift: A Ukrainian Christmas Story* (K–2). Illus. by Katya Krenina. 2010, Holiday House $16.95 (978-082341743-8). 32pp. Katrusya's impoverished family cuts down a small pine tree for Christmas and decorates it with buttons, but spiders nesting in the tree give them an unexpected present. Lexile AD500L (Rev: BL 8/10; SLJ 10/1/10)

1273 Kladstrup, Kristin. *The Gingerbread Pirates* (PS–2). Illus. by Matt Tavares. 2009, Candlewick $16.99 (978-076363223-6). 32pp. A group of pirate-shaped gingerbread cookies come to life in a daring attempt to save themselves from being eaten by Santa. (Rev: BL 9/15/09; HB 11–12/09; SLJ 10/09)

1274 Lester, Helen. *Tacky's Christmas* (PS–2). Illus. by Lynn Munsinger. 2010, Houghton Mifflin $16.99 (978-054717208-8). 32pp. Tacky's Santa costume convinces penguin hunters to put down their guns and spare his friends. (Rev: BL 10/15/10; HB 11–12/10; SLJ 10/10)

1275 Lewis, Anne Margaret. *What Am I? Christmas* (PS–K). Illus. by Tom Mills. Series: My Look and See Holiday Book. 2011, Whitman $9.99 (978-080758958-8). 24pp. This Christmas flap-book with rhyming text presents readers with a series of short, guessable, what am I queries. (Rev: BL 11/1/11; SLJ 10/1/11)

1276 Light, Steve. *The Christmas Giant* (PS–1). Illus. by author. 2010, Candlewick $15.99 (978-076364692-9). 32pp. A giant and an elf collaborate to grow the perfect Christmas tree in this story with brief text but detailed illustrations. (Rev: BL 10/15/10; HB 11–12/10)

1277 Lloyd-Jones, Sally. *Song of the Stars: A Christmas Story* (PS–1). Illus. by Alison Jay. 2011, Zondervan $15.99 (978-031072291-5). 32pp. Nature and the animals welcome the birth of the baby Jesus in this alliterative text with rich illustrations and spare, poetic language. (Rev: BL 11/1/11; SLJ 10/1/11)

1278 McGinley, Phyllis. *The Year Without a Santa Claus* (K–3). Illus. by John Manders. 2010, Marshall Cavendish $16.99 (978-076145799-2). 40pp. New illustrations grace this update of McGinley's rhyming story, originally published in 1957, about how children react when Santa decides to take a vacation. Lexile AD810L (Rev: BLO 11/15/10; HB 11–12/10; SLJ 10/10)

1279 Martin, Ruth. *Santa's on His Way* (PS–K). Illus. by Sophy Williams. 2011, Candlewick $12.99 (978-076365555-6). 14pp. Santa, the elves, and the reindeer rush around getting ready for Christmas Eve in this story with "changing pictures" that involve lifting flaps. (Rev: BLO 10/15/11; SLJ 10/11)

1280 Milgrim, David. *Santa Duck and His Merry Helpers* (PS–1). Illus. by author. 2010, Putnam $12.99 (978-039925473-4). 32pp. Nicholas Duck ponders on the real meaning of Christmas when his siblings try to help him with his duties for Santa. (Rev: BL 12/1/10; HB 11–12/10; SLJ 10/10*)

1281 Noble, Trinka Hakes. *A Christmas Spider's Miracle* (K–3). Illus. by Stephen Costanza. 2011, Sleeping Bear $16.95 (978-158536602-6). 32pp. Sensing the dire state of a poor family's Christmas, a kind spider covers their spare Christmas tree with shimmering, woven designs; based on a Ukrainian legend. (Rev: BLO 11/15/11; SLJ 10/1/11)

1282 Park, Linda Sue. *The Third Gift* (K–2). Illus. by Bagram Ibatoulline. 2011, Clarion $16.99 (978-054720195-5). 32pp. A boy and his father wander the landscape, collecting precious sap — myrrh — to be sold to the Wise Men, who have a special birth to attend. (Rev: BL 10/15/11; SLJ 10/1/11)

1283 Pfister, Marcus. *Snow Puppy* (PS–1). Trans. by NordSud Verlag. Illus. by author. 2011, NorthSouth $16.95 (978-0-7358-4031-7). 32pp. A kindhearted man who returns a puppy lost in the snow is invited to share Christmas with the pup's family. (Rev: BL 10/1/11; SLJ 11/1/11)

1284 Pulver, Robin. *Christmas Kitten, Home at Last* (PS–2). Illus. by Layne Johnson. 2010, Whitman $16.99 (978-080751157-2). 32pp. Santa, who apparently is allergic to cats, matches a stray kitten picked up on Christmas Eve with a little girl who will love him. (Rev: BL 10/15/10)

1285 Rawlinson, Julia. *Fletcher and the Snowflake Christmas* (PS–1). Illus. by Tiphanie Beeke. Series: Fletcher. 2010, Greenwillow $16.99 (978-006199033-5). 32pp. Fletcher the fox and his animal friends worry that Santa won't be able to find the rabbits' new burrow. Lexile AD810L (Rev: BL 12/1/10; HB 11–12/10; SLJ 10/10)

1286 Rees, Douglas. *Jeannette Claus Saves Christmas* (PS–2). Illus. by Olivier Latyk. 2010, Simon & Schuster $16.99 (978-141692686-3). 40pp. Santa's hip daughter Jeanette saves the day when a few ne'er-do-well reindeer escape their harness on Christmas Eve. (Rev: BL 11/15/10; HB 11–12/10; SLJ 10/10)

1287 Sacre, Antonio. *La Noche Buena: A Christmas Story* (2–4). Illus. by Angela Dominguez. 2010, Abrams $16.95 (978-081098967-2). 32pp. Visiting her grandmother in Miami's Little Havana, young New Englander Nina learns to appreciate new Christmas traditions. (Rev: BL 10/15/10; HB 11–12/10)

1288 Shannon, David. *It's Christmas, David!* (PS–1). Illus. by author. 2010, Scholastic $16.99 (978-054514311-0). 32pp. Christmas is coming and seems to bring equal amounts of joy and misery for rambunctious young David. (Rev: BL 9/15/10; HB 11–12/10; SLJ 10/10)

1289 Slegers, Liesbet. *The Child in the Manger* (PS–2). Illus. by author. 2010, Clavis $15.95 (978-160537084-2). 32pp. Simple text and illustrations tell the story of Christ's birth. (Rev: BL 10/15/10; SLJ 10/10)

1290 Smith, Maggie. *Christmas with the Mousekins: A Story with Crafts, Recipes, Poems and More!* (K–3). Illus. by author. 2010, Knopf $15.99 (978-037583330-4). 40pp. A quaint mouse family busies itself getting ready for Christmas in this activity book with charming illustrations, recipes, and directions for crafts. **e** (Rev: BL 9/15/10; HB 11–12/10)

1291 Thompson, Lauren. *The Christmas Magic* (PS–1). Illus. by Jon J Muth. 2009, Scholastic $16.99 (978-043977497-0). 40pp. A lonely, rather scrawny Santa readies his sleigh, gifts, and reindeer, waiting for the magic to arrive before setting out to bring joy to children around the world. (Rev: BL 11/1/09; HB 11–12/09; SLJ 10/09)

1292 Thompson, Lauren. *One Starry Night* (PS–1). Illus. by Jonathan Bean. 2011, Simon & Schuster $16.99 (978-068982851-5). 32pp. Parent-child animal pairs make their way to the manger to behold baby Jesus in this serene retelling of the story. (Rev: BL 11/15/11; HB 11–12/11; SLJ 10/1/11*)

1293 Trumbauer, Lisa. *The Great Reindeer Rebellion* (PS–2). Illus. by Jannie Ho. 2009, Sterling $14.95 (978-140274462-4). 28pp. When the reindeer go on strike, Santa struggles to fill his sled-team with other animals. (Rev: BL 11/15/09; SLJ 10/09)

EASTER

1294 Brett, Jan. *The Easter Egg* (PS–K). Illus. by author. 2010, Putnam $17.99 (978-0-399-25238-9). 32pp. Hoppi the rabbit's hopes of winning the Easter egg competition are derailed when he heeds a mother robin's cry for help; in the end, his generosity is commended. (Rev: BL 12/1/09; LMC 1–2/10; SLJ 2/1/10)

1295 Mackall, Dandi Daley. *The Story of the Easter Robin* (PS–2). Illus. by Anna Vojtech. 2010, Zondervan $15.99 (978-031071331-9). 24pp. Two Easter stories are intertwined in this warm novel — that of Tressa, who worries about the robin's eggs on the window ledge, and that of a small brown robin that pulled a thorn from Jesus's crown. (Rev: BL 2/15/10)

1296 Mortimer, Anne. *Bunny's Easter Egg* (PS–K). Illus. by author. 2010, HarperCollins $12.99 (978-0-06-126664-2). 32pp. Busy Bunny is exhausted after hiding all but one of her Easter eggs and takes it into her basket while she has a rest; and overnight it hatches into a downy little duckling. (Rev: BL 3/15/10; SLJ 1/1/10)

1297 Thomas, Jan. *The Easter Bunny's Assistant* (PS–K). Illus. by author. 2012, HarperCollins $12.99 (978-006169286-4). 40pp. Skunk gets so excited about dyeing Easter eggs with his bunny friend that he loses control of his stink in this funny book with directions for making colored eggs. (Rev: BL 1/1/12; SLJ 1/12)

1298 Vail, Rachel. *Piggy Bunny* (PS–2). Illus. by Jeremy Tankard. 2012, Feiwel & Friends $14.99 (978-031264988-3). 32pp. A little pig determined to be the Easter Bunny gets a lift from a creative grandma who orders him a costume. (Rev: BL 1/1/12; SLJ 1/12)

1299 Vainio, Pirkko. *Who Hid the Easter Eggs?* (PS–1). Illus. by author. 2011, NorthSouth $16.95 (978-0-7358-2304-4). 32pp. A squirrel named Harry persuades a jackdaw to try to replace the Easter eggs he has stolen, and reassures Jack that he will soon have his own eggs to look after. Lexile AD580L (Rev: BLO 1/1–15/11; SLJ 5/1/11)

HALLOWEEN

1300 Cox, Judy. *Haunted House, Haunted Mouse* (K–2). Illus. by Jeffrey Ebbeler. 2011, Holiday House $16.95 (978-0-8234-2315-6). 32pp. Mouse ends up in a pickle when he dives into a trick-or-treater's goody bag and gets carried along to a haunted house. Lexile AD460L (Rev: BL 10/15/11; SLJ 10/1/11)

1301 Demas, Corinne. *Halloween Surprise* (PS–1). Illus. by R. W. Alley. 2011, Walker $12.99 (978-0-8027-8612-8). 32pp. A young girl's two cats watch and react as she tries out many different Halloween costume possibilities before hitting on a perfect, creative solution. (Rev: BLO 7/11; SLJ 8/1/11)

1302 Fraser, Mary Ann. *Heebie-Jeebie Jamboree* (PS–2). Illus. by author. 2011, Boyds Mills $15.95 (978-1-59078-857-8). 32pp. At Halloween Sam and his sister Daphne, dressed as a ghost and a witch, attend the festivities at the cemetery. (Rev: BL 9/1/11; SLJ 9/1/11)

1303 Montijo, Rhode. *The Halloween Kid* (PS–2). Illus. by author. 2010, Simon & Schuster $12.99 (978-1-4169-3575-9). 32pp. When Goodie Goblins arrive in town to steal candy, the courageous Halloween Kid saves the day. **e** (Rev: BL 9/1/10; LMC 10/10; SLJ 7/1/10)

1304 Pamintuan, Macky. *Twelve Haunted Rooms of Halloween* (PS–2). Illus. by author. 2011, Sterling $14.95 (978-1-4027-7935-0). Unpaged. This Halloween take on "The Twelve Days of Christmas" involving a bear's visit to a haunted house features detailed illustrations with an "I Spy" element that will keep readers occupied. (Rev: SLJ 9/1/11)

1305 Rohmann, Eric. *Bone Dog* (PS–2). Illus. by author. 2011, Roaring Brook $16.99 (978-1-59643-150-8). 32pp. A boy's beloved dog passes away but is reanimated as a bone dog on Halloween, just in time to save him from a graveyard full of skeletons. (Rev: BL 11/15/11; SLJ 7/11*)

1306 Sharratt, Nick. *What's in the Witch's Kitchen?* (1–3). Illus. by author. 2011, Candlewick $12.99 (978-0-7636-5224-1). Unpaged. This appealing flap book full of choices takes readers on a tour through a witch's kitchen and some of the favorite ingredients; the illustrations are full of Halloween images. (Rev: SLJ 8/1/11)

1307 Thomas, Jan. *Pumpkin Trouble* (PS–K). Illus. by author. 2011, HarperCollins $9.99 (978-0-06-169284-0). 40pp. Duck ends up trapped inside the jack-o-lantern he carved to surprise his friends Pig and Mouse. (Rev: BL 9/1/11; SLJ 6/11)

1308 Walker, Sally M. *Druscilla's Halloween* (PS–3). Illus. by Lee White. 2009, Carolrhoda LB $16.95 (978-0-8225-8941-9). 32pp. Before the days of brooms, witches used to sneak up and frighten children on Halloween; elderly Drusilla's knees creak too loudly and she seeks a silent form of transportation. (Rev: BL 9/15/09; SLJ 9/1/09)

1309 Yee, Wong Herbert. *Mouse and Mole, a Perfect Halloween* (K–2). Illus. by author. Series: Mouse and Mole. 2011, Houghton Mifflin $14.99 (978-0-547-55152-4). Unpaged. Friends Mouse and Mole prepare for Halloween and explore their fears about the holiday. (Rev: SLJ 9/1/11)

JEWISH HOLY DAYS

1310 Glaser, Linda. *Hoppy Passover!* (PS–K). Illus. by Daniel Howarth. 2011, Whitman $15.99 (978-0-8075-3380-2). 24pp. Bunnies Violet and Simon celebrate Passover with their family in this warm family story, a sequel to *Hoppy Hanukkah!* (2009). (Rev: BL 2/1/11; SLJ 2/1/11)

1311 Goldin, Barbara Diamond. *Cakes and Miracles: A Purim Tale* (PS–3). Illus. by Jaime Zollars. 2010, Marshall Cavendish $17.99 (978-0-7614-5701-5). Unpaged. A newly edited and illustrated edition of the 1991 publication about young, blind Hershel who discovers new abilities during the Jewish holiday of Purim. (Rev: SLJ 10/1/10)

1312 Newman, Leslea. *A Sweet Passover* (K–3). Illus. by David Slonim. 2012, Abrams $16.95 (978-081099737-0). 40pp. Miriam loves Passover at Grandma and Grandpa's house but by the eighth day she is sick of eating matzah; includes a recipe for matzah brei and a glossary. (Rev: BL 2/15/12; SLJ 4/1/12)

THANKSGIVING

1313 Manushkin, Fran. *Katie Saves Thanksgiving* (K–2). Illus. by Tammie Lyon. Series: Katie Woo. 2010, Picture Window LB $19.99 (978-1-4048-5988-3); paper $3.95 (978-1-4048-6367-5). 32pp. Katie is able to save her family's Thanksgiving through thoughtfulness, generosity, and neighborliness. (Rev: SLJ 3/1/11)

VALENTINE'S DAY

1314 Choldenko, Gennifer. *A Giant Crush* (K–3). Illus. by Melissa Sweet. 2011, Putnam $16.99 (978-0-399-24352-3). 32pp. A young bunny too shy to declare his affection hides little presents for Cami to find, until a friend tells him he must speak up. (Rev: BL 12/1/11; SLJ 11/1/11)

1315 Elliot, Laura Malone. *A String of Hearts* (K–3). Illus. by Lynn Munsinger. 2010, HarperCollins $16.99 (978-0-06-000085-1). 32pp. Mary Ann, a young squirrel, helps her bear friend Sam come up with the perfect things to write on Tiffany's valentine and Sam comes to realize Mary Ann's true value. Lexile AD510L (Rev: BLO 12/1/10; SLJ 1/1/11)

1316 Friedman, Laurie. *Ruby Valentine Saves the Day* (PS–1). Illus. by Lynne Avril. 2010, Carolrhoda $16.95 (978-0-7613-4213-7). 32pp. Ruby Valentine and her cockatoo move their Valentine's Day party to town when snow prevents their guests from attending. ✪ Lexile AD540L (Rev: BL 1/1–15/11; SLJ 12/1/10)

1317 Manushkin, Fran. *No Valentines for Katie* (K–2). Illus. by Tammie Lyon. Series: Katie Woo. 2010, Picture Window LB $19.99 (978-1-4048-5986-9); paper $3.95 (978-1-4048-6365-1). 32pp. Katie is so involved in making a valentine that she forgets to put her name in the box. (Rev: SLJ 3/1/11)

1318 Petersen, David. *Snowy Valentine* (PS–1). Illus. by author. 2011, HarperCollins $14.99 (978-0-06-146378-5). 32pp. In hopes of finding an ideal gift for his wife Lily, Jasper Bunny spends Valentine's Day visiting friends and seeking advice — and ends up with a perfect but unintended present. (Rev: BL 12/15/11; SLJ 11/1/11)

Books for Beginning Readers

1319 Arnold, Tedd. *Buzz Boy and Fly Guy* (PS–2). Illus. by author. Series: Fly Guy. 2010, Scholastic paper $5.99 (978-054522274-7). 32pp. Buzz creates a book in which his pet fly is now the size of a man and can speak, having adventures with a dragon and pirates. (Rev: BL 9/1/10; SLJ 10/10)

1320 Arnold, Tedd. *Fly Guy Meets Fly Girl!* (K–2). Illus. by author. Series: Fly Guy. 2010, Scholastic $5.99 (978-0-545-11029-7). 30pp. Fly Guy meets Fly Girl in this offbeat love story; but can they leave Buzz and Liz? (Rev: SLJ 6/1/10)

1321 Arnold, Tedd. *Fly Guy vs. the Fly Swatter!* (PS–2). Series: Fly Guy. 2011, Scholastic $6.99 (978-0-545-31286-8). 30pp. Fly Guy accidentally gets taken along on a school trip to a fly swatter factory in this 10th book in the series. (Rev: SLJ 9/1/11)

1322 Arnold, Tedd. *I Spy Fly Guy!* (1–3). Illus. by author. Series: Fly Guy. 2009, Scholastic $5.99 (978-0-545-11028-0). 32pp. Fly Guy has a narrow escape when he hides in the garbage can during a game of hide-and-seek. ∩ (Rev: BLO 11/1/09; SLJ 12/1/09)

1323 Arnold, Tedd. *Ride, Fly Guy, Ride!* (PS–2). Illus. by author. Series: Fly Guy. 2012, Scholastic paper $6.99 (978-054522276-1). 32pp. Fly Guy has a wild time when he is blown out the car window and into a passing truck — then a boat, a train, and an airplane — with Buzz and his dad in hot pursuit. (Rev: BL 3/1/12)

1324 Benjamin, A. H. *Jumping Jack* (1–2). Illus. by Garry Parsons. Series: I Am Reading. 2009, Kingfisher paper $3.99 (978-0-7534-6297-3). 48pp. When Jack's grandmother cooks him a breakfast of jumping beans, suddenly he's bouncing and flying everywhere he goes until his clever grandma solves the problem by baking him leaden brownies. (Rev: BLO 11/15/09; LMC 5–6/10; SLJ 2/1/10)

1325 Björkman, Steve. *Dinosaurs Don't, Dinosaurs Do* (PS–1). Illus. by author. Series: I Like to Read. 2011, Holiday House $14.95 (978-0-8234-2355-2). Unpaged. Simple text and humorous illustrations introduce some basics of good behavior. (Rev: SLJ 11/1/11)

1326 Blackaby, Susan. *Brownie Groundhog and the February Fox* (1–3). Illus. by Carmen Segovia. 2011, Sterling $14.95 (978-1-4027-4336-8). 24pp. A hungry fox and a clever groundhog become unlikely friends when they discover what they have in common: a longing for spring. (Rev: BLO 12/15/10; LMC 3–4/11; SLJ 2/1/11*)

1327 Bunting, Eve. *Frog and Friends* (1–2). Illus. by Josée Masse. Series: I Am a Reader! 2011, Sleeping Bear $9.95 (978-1-58536-548-7); paper $3.99 (978-1-58536-689-7). 37pp. In three chapters about Frog and his friends a strange round object appears on the pond and causes some consternation; regifting gains acceptance; and an uninvited hippo visits. (Rev: SLJ 10/1/11)

1328 Bunting, Eve. *Frog and Friends: Best Summer Ever* (1–3). Illus. by Josée Masse. Series: I Am a Reader! 2012, Sleeping Bear $9.95 (978-158536550-0); paper $3.99 (978-158536691-0). 48pp. In three simple stories, Frog compares himself to a bat, goes on vacation with more friends than expected, and learns about the stars. (Rev: BLO 5/15/12; SLJ 10/11)

1329 Capucilli, Alyssa Satin. *Scat, Cat!* (K–1). Illus. by Paul Meisel. 2010, HarperCollins $16.99 (978-0-06-117754-5). 32pp. In this simple book for beginning readers, a lost cat who is shooed away all day eventually finds a porch to curl up on — and is welcomed inside by a young boy in the morning. ℯ (Rev: BL 12/15/10; SLJ 10/1/10)

1330 Catrow, David. *Funny Lunch* (K–2). Illus. by author. 2010, Scholastic $6.99 (978-0-545-05747-9). Unpaged. A cat and dog short-order cook duo fill their customers' orders creatively and imaginatively in this funny story. In the third book, *Best in Show* (2011), Max enters a canine talent contest. (Rev: SLJ 7/1/10)

1331 Cuyler, Margery. *Tick Tock Clock* (PS–K). Illus. by Robert Neubecker. Series: I Can Read. 2012, HarperCollins $16.99 (978-006136309-2). 32pp. Children can reinforce their time-telling skills with this simple account of twins' activities at various times during the day. (Rev: BL 1/1/12; SLJ 1/12)

1332 Day, Alexandra. *Carl and the Baby Duck* (PS–1). Illus. by author. Series: My Readers. 2011, Macmillan $15.99 (978-0-312-62484-2); paper $3.99 (978-0-312-62485-9). 32pp. Friendly rottweiler Carl helps Mama Duck search for her missing offspring. (Rev: BL 6/1/11; SLJ 5/1/11)

1333 Egan, Tim. *Dodsworth in London* (K–2). Illus. by author. Series: Dodsworth. 2009, Houghton Mifflin $15 (978-0-547-13816-9). Unpaged. Dodsworth and his duck friend become separated on a trip to London when there is some confusion with the Queen's duck. Lexile 260L (Rev: HB 11–12/09; SLJ 1/1/10)

1334 Egan, Tim. *Dodsworth in Rome* (K–2). Illus. by author. Series: Dodsworth. 2011, Houghton Mifflin $14.99 (978-0-547-39006-2). Unpaged. Dodsworth and his bouncy, wayward duck take a trip to Rome to see the Sistine Chapel, eat pizza, and take coins from the Trevi Fountain. (Rev: HB 5–6/11; SLJ 4/11)

1335 Farley, Robin. *Mia and the Too Big Tutu* (PS–1). Illus. by Aleksey Ivanov and Olga Ivanov. Series: I Can Read!: My First Shared Reading. 2010, HarperCollins $16.99 (978-0-06-173302-4); LB $3.99 (978-0-06-173301-7). 32pp. Mia the cat is so excited about going to dance class that she accidentally takes her older sister's tutu. (Rev: SLJ 10/1/10)

1336 Feldman, Thea. *Harry Cat and Tucker Mouse: Tucker's Beetle Band* (1–3). Illus. by Olga Ivanov and Aleksey Ivanov. Series: My Readers. 2011, Square Fish $15.99 (978-0-312-62575-7); paper $3.99 (978-0-312-62576-4). 32pp. Chester the Cricket is called in to play drums for a beetle band that's been disturbing his friends' slumber. ℯ Lexile 500L (Rev: SLJ 5/1/11)

1337 Galan, Ana. *Who Wears Glasses?* (K–2). Illus. by Seb Burnett. 2010, Scholastic paper $3.99 (978-0-545-21020-1). Unpaged. Rhyming text and illustrations reveal animals wearing all kinds of glasses. (Rev: SLJ 9/1/10)

1338 Gilman, Grace. *Dixie* (K–1). Illus. by Sarah McConnell. Series: I Can Read! 2011, HarperCollins $16.99 (978-0-06-171914-1); paper $3.99 (978-0-06-171913-4). 32pp. A loving little dog tries to derail her owner's involvement in the school play. (Rev: BL 6/1/11; SLJ 6/11)

1339 Green, Jessica. *Scratch Kitten Goes to Sea* (2–4). Illus. by Mitch Vane. 2010, IPG/Little Hare paper $6.99 (978-192127244-8). 81pp. A kitten named Scratch hopes to make a life aboard a sailing ship, but his adventures with mice bring his downfall; the first in a series of beginning chapter books. Lexile 600L (Rev: BL 1/1/10)

1340 Griffiths, Andy. *The Big Fat Cow That Goes Kapow* (2–3). Illus. by Terry Denton. 2009, Feiwel & Friends $14.99 (978-0-312-36788-6). 123pp. Ten zany short stories featuring Seuss-like rhymes and cheeky illustrations are collected in this book for beginning readers. Lexile 380L (Rev: SLJ 1/1/10*)

1341 Hapka, Catherine. *Pony Scouts: Back in the Saddle* (PS–2). Illus. by Anne Kennedy. Series: I Can Read! 2011, HarperCollins $16.99 (978-0-06-125539-7); paper $3.99 (978-0-06-125541-0). 32pp. After falling off her pony during a riding lesson, Annie must decide whether or not to get back on in this simple book for beginning readers. (Rev: SLJ 9/1/11)

1342 Hapka, Catherine. *Runaway Ponies!* (K–2). Illus. by Anne Kennedy. Series: Pony Scouts I Can Read. 2012, HarperCollins $16.99 (978-006208669-3); paper $3.99 (978-006208667-9). 32pp. Meg is spending the weekend at Jill's and her absentmindedness results in all five ponies getting out of the stable, posing the girls a challenge. ∩ (Rev: BL 4/1/12)

1343 Hartnett, Sonya. *Sadie and Ratz* (K–3). Illus. by Ann James. 2012, Candlewick $14.99 (978-076365315-6). 64pp. Clever Hannah blames her hands, which she's named Sadie and Ratz, whenever she does something wrong, which happens regularly when she's near her irritating younger brother. (Rev: BL 5/1/12; SLJ 4/1/12*)

1344 Hayes, Geoffrey. *A Poor Excuse for a Dragon* (PS–2). Illus. by author. Series: Step into Reading. 2011, Random House $12.99 (978-0-375-87180-1); paper $3.99 (978-0-375-86867-2). 48pp. A kind young dragon struggling with ferocity is awarded a job guarding a castle. e (Rev: BL 8/11; LMC 11–12/11; SLJ 6/11)

1345 Hays, Anna Jane. *Spring Surprises* (PS–1). Illus. by Hala Wittwer Swearingen. Series: Step Into Reading. 2010, Random House paper $3.99 (978-037585840-6). 24pp. Celebrates the arrival of spring in rhyming text suitable for beginning readers. (Rev: BL 2/1/10)

1346 Heller, Alyson. *Time for T-Ball* (PS–1). Illus. by Steve Björkman. Series: After-School Sports Club. 2010, Aladdin paper $3.99 (978-141699412-1). 32pp. Caleb regrets heckling his teammates when he himself does poorly at T-ball practice. (Rev: BL 4/1/10)

1347 Hill, Susan. *Black Beauty and the Thunderstorm* (1–3). Illus. by Bill Farnsworth. Series: My Readers. 2011, Square Fish $15.99 (978-0-312-64705-6); paper $3.99 (978-0-312-64721-6). 48pp. Black Beauty tells some of the events of his life, including when he rescued his owner's daughter's cat during a thunderstorm. (Rev: SLJ 6/11)

1348 Kann, Victoria. *Pinkalicious: Pink Around the Rink* (PS–2). Illus. by author. Series: I Can Read! 2010, HarperCollins $16.99 (978-0-06-192880-2); paper $3.99 (978-0-06-192879-6). 32pp. Pinkalicious brightens her new white ice skates with a pink magic marker, that unfortunately bleeds onto the ice, highlighting all the places she has fallen. (Rev: SLJ 1/1/11)

1349 Kertell, Lynn Maslen. *Cupcake Surprise!* (PS–1). Illus. by Sue Hendra. Series: Scholastic Reader. 2012, Scholastic paper $3.99 (978-054538269-4). 32pp. Siblings Jack and Anna bake cupcakes for their dad's birthday and have several surprises in the process. (Rev: BLO 2/27/12)

1350 Kuenzler, Lou. *The Ugly Egg* (1–3). Illus. by David Hitch. Series: I Am Reading. 2009, Kingfisher paper $3.99 (978-0-7534-6284-3). 48pp. When a kind-hearted puffin longing for offspring finds and hatches a dragon egg, the other birds are scornful — until the dragon's nest-warming skills are realized and embraced. (Rev: BLO 11/15/09; SLJ 2/1/10)

1351 Kvasnosky, Laura McGee. *Zelda and Ivy: The Big Picture* (1–3). Illus. by author. 2010, Candlewick $14.99 (978-0-7636-4180-1). 48pp. A movie starring Secret Agent Fox inspires the fox siblings to do some sleuthing of their own in this episodic book for beginning readers. (Rev: HB 9–10/10; SLJ 9/1/10)

1352 Lewis, J. Patrick. *Tugg and Teeny* (K–2). Illus. by Christopher Denise. 2011, Sleeping Bear $9.95 (978-1-58536-514-2); paper $3.99 (978-158536685-9). 40pp. Tugg the gorilla and Teeny the monkey share three simple adventures in which they explore music, art, and poetry. (Rev: BL 3/15/11; SLJ 5/1/11)

1353 Lin, Grace. *Ling and Ting: Not Exactly the Same!* (1–2). Illus. by author. 2010, Little, Brown $14.99 (978-0-316-02452-5). 48pp. Twin sisters Ling and Ting may look alike but they prove in these six short chapters that they are in fact quite different. Lexile 390L (Rev: BL 5/1/10*; LMC 8–9/10; SLJ 7/1/10*)

1354 McCully, Emily Arnold. *Late Nate in a Race* (PS–1). Illus. by author. Series: I Like to Read. 2012, Holiday House $14.95 (978-082342421-4). 24pp. Nate is a mouse who is chronically slow but surprises everybody, including himself, on race day. (Rev: BL 2/15/12; SLJ 4/1/12)

1355 McMullan, Kate. *Pearl and Wagner: Four Eyes* (K–2). Illus. by R. W. Alley. 2010, Dial $15.99 (978-0-8037-3086-1). 40pp. Friends and a teacher help Wagner the mouse adjust to the fact that he needs to wear glasses. (Rev: HB 9–10/10; LMC 1–2/11; SLJ 9/1/10)

1356 McNamara, Margaret. *The Garden Project* (PS–1). Illus. by Mike Gordon. 2010, Aladdin paper $3.99 (978-141699171-7). 32pp. A class of 1st-graders plants and tends a small vegetable garden in this story for beginning readers. (Rev: BLO 7/10)

1357 McPhail, David. *Boy, Bird, and Dog* (PS–1). Illus. by author. Series: I Like to Read. 2011, Holiday House $14.95 (978-0-8234-2346-0). Unpaged. Simple text and humorous illustrations introduce the concept of up and down as a boy, a bird, and a dog, enjoy a tree house. (Rev: SLJ 11/1/11)

1358 Manushkin, Fran. *Katie in the Kitchen* (K–2). Illus. by Tammie Lyon. 2010, Capstone LB $19.99 (978-1-4048-5724-7). 32pp. Frustrated that no one will let her help with household jobs, young Katie Woo decides to cook dinner — with predictably chaotic results. Lexile 380L (Rev: BLO 7/10; SLJ 5/1/10)

1359 Manushkin, Fran. *Katie Woo Has the Flu* (K–2). Illus. by Tammie Lyon. 2011, Capstone $19.99 (978-140486518-1); paper $3.95 (978-140486854-0). 32pp. Sick with the flu, Katie misses the fun and friends she enjoys at school. (Rev: BLO 12/15/11)

1360 Meisel, Paul. *See Me Run* (PS–1). Illus. by author. Series: I Like to Read. 2011, Holiday House $14.95 (978-0-8234-2349-1). Unpaged. Simple text and humorous illustrations describe dogs having a wonderful time at the dog park. (Rev: SLJ 11/1/11)

1361 Minarik, Else Holmelund. *Little Bear and the Marco Polo* (K–1). Illus. by Dorothy Doubleday. Series: I Can Read. 2010, HarperCollins $16.99 (978-0-06-085485-0); paper $3.99 (978-0-06-085487-4). 32pp. Little Bear learns about his grandfather's seafaring life and the fact that there are bears of different kinds around the world. (Rev: HB 9–10/10; SLJ 8/1/10)

1362 Morris, Jennifer E. *Please Write Back!* (PS–1). Illus. by author. 2010, Scholastic paper $3.99 (978-0-545-11506-3). Unpaged. A young crocodile sends his grandma a simple letter, and eagerly awaits her response. (Rev: SLJ 4/1/10)

1363 O'Connor, Jane. *Every Day Is Earth Day* (K–2). Illus. by Robin Preiss Glasser. Series: Fancy Nancy. 2010, HarperCollins $16.99 (978-006187327-0); paper $3.99 (978-006187326-3). 32pp. Fancy Nancy learns to balance her newfound environmental zeal with tolerance when her family resists her new rules. e (Rev: BLO 6/10)

1364 O'Connor, Jane. *Fancy Nancy and the Fabulous Fashion Boutique* (1–3). Illus. by Robin Preiss Glasser. Series: Fancy Nancy. 2010, HarperCollins $17.99 (978-006123592-4). 32pp. Fancy Nancy grapples with kindness, instant gratification, and generosity as she has a fashion yard sale and plans for her little sister's birthday party. ☊ (Rev: BL 11/15/10)

1365 Parish, Herman. *Amelia Bedelia Bakes Off* (1–3). Illus. by Lynn Sweat. 2010, Greenwillow $17.99 (978-0-06-084358-8); LB $18.89 (978-0-06-084359-5). 64pp. Amelia Bedelia sets out to enter her famed baked goods in a bake-off, but her literal interpretations nearly get her in trouble. (Rev: SLJ 2/1/11)

1366 Parish, Herman. *Amelia Bedelia's First Apple Pie* (PS–2). Illus. by Lynne Avril. 2010, Greenwillow $16.99 (978-0-06-196409-1); LB $17.89 (978-0-06-196410-7). Unpaged. With her usual over-literal interpretations, Amelia accompanies her grandmother to the farmer's market to buy ingredients for a pie. (Rev: SLJ 12/1/10)

1367 Parish, Herman. *Amelia Bedelia's First Day of School* (K–2). Illus. by Lynne Avril. 2009, Greenwillow $16.99 (978-0-06-154455-2); LB $17.89 (978-0-06-154456-9). 32pp. Amelia's first day of school is full of funny misunderstandings. (Rev: BL 9/15/09; SLJ 11/1/09)

1368 Parish, Herman. *Amelia Bedelia's First Field Trip* (1–3). Illus. by Lynne Avril. 2011, Greenwillow $16.99 (978-0-06-196413-8); LB $17.89 (978-0-06-196414-5). 32pp. Comic literalist Amelia Bedelia enjoys a class trip to a farm, where she "tosses salad," "shakes a leg," and looks forward to a swim in the "car pool" on the way home. (Rev: SLJ 9/1/11)

1369 Ries, Lori. *Aggie Gets Lost* (K–2). Illus. by Frank W. Dormer. 2011, Charlesbridge $12.95 (978-1-57091-633-5). 48pp. After a boy and his family have tried everything to find their dog, their blind neighbor suggests a different approach. (Rev: SLJ 8/1/11)

1370 Ries, Lori. *Aggie the Brave* (1–3). Illus. by Frank W. Dormer. 2010, Charlesbridge $12.95 (978-1-57091-635-9). 48pp. Ben worries about his dog Aggie while she is being spayed, and looks after her when she comes home. Lexile AD230L (Rev: BLO 11/15/10; HB 9–10/10; LMC 1–2/11; SLJ 8/1/10*)

1371 Rylant, Cynthia. *Annie and Snowball and the Surprise Day* (K–2). Illus. by Sucie Stevenson. 2012, Simon & Schuster $15.99 (978-141693944-3). 40pp. Annie, her pet rabbit, and her dad share a pleasant day in the country. (Rev: BLO 4/1/12)

1372 Rylant, Cynthia. *Brownie and Pearl Get Dolled Up* (PS). Illus. by Brian Biggs. Series: Brownie and Pearl. 2010, Simon & Schuster $13.99 (978-1-4169-8631-7). 24pp. Brownie and her cat Pearl have a great time dressing to the nines. (Rev: BLO 4/15/10; SLJ 4/1/10)

1373 Rylant, Cynthia. *Brownie and Pearl Grab a Bite* (PS–1). Illus. by Brian Biggs. Series: Brownie and Pearl. 2011, Simon & Schuster $13.99 (978-1-4169-8634-8). 24pp. Brownie and her cat Pearl forage in the refrigerator and pantry to assemble a tasty snack for themselves. (Rev: BL 9/1/11; SLJ 8/1/11)

1374 Rylant, Cynthia. *Brownie and Pearl Hit the Hay* (PS–1). Illus. by Brian Biggs. Series: Brownie and Pearl. 2011, Simon & Schuster $13.99 (978-1-4169-8635-5). Unpaged. Brownie and her cat Pearl enjoy a bath, snack, and story before heading off to bed together. e (Rev: SLJ 9/1/11)

1375 Rylant, Cynthia. *Brownie and Pearl Step Out* (PS–K). Illus. by Brian Biggs. Series: Brownie and Pearl.

2010, Simon & Schuster $12.99 (978-1-4169-8632-4). 24pp. Suffering a moment of shyness when arriving at a friend's party, Brownie relies on her gregarious cat Pearl to lead the way. Also use *Brownie and Pearl See the Sights* (2010). (Rev: BL 12/1/09; SLJ 2/1/10)

1376 Rylant, Cynthia. *Mr. Putter and Tabby Clear the Decks* (K–2). Illus. by Arthur Howard. Series: Mr. Putter and Tabby. 2010, Harcourt $15 (978-0-15-206715-1). Unpaged. On a hot summer day Mr. Putter and his cat Tabby join Mrs. Teaberry and her mischievous dog Zeke on a sightseeing boat cruise. (Rev: SLJ 10/1/10)

1377 Rylant, Cynthia. *Mr. Putter and Tabby Ring the Bell* (K–2). Illus. by Arthur Howard. Series: Mr. Putter and Tabby. 2011, Harcourt $14.99 (978-0-15-205071-9). 44pp. It's fall and Mr. Putter thinks back to his happy days at school, inspiring him and Mrs. Teaberry to take their pets to an unexpectedly unruly "show-and-tell." (Rev: BL 10/1/11; SLJ 8/1/11)

1378 Rylant, Cynthia. *Mr. Putter and Tabby Spill the Beans* (K–2). Illus. by Arthur Howard. 2009, Harcourt $15 (978-0-15-205070-2). 44pp. Mr. Putter is in for more fun than he expected when he goes to a bean cookery class with Mrs. Teaberry. (Rev: BL 8/09; SLJ 12/1/09)

1379 Schneider, Josh. *Tales for Very Picky Eaters* (K–3). Illus. by author. 2011, Clarion $14.99 (978-0-547-14956-1). 48pp. An inventive Dad tries everything imaginable to get his very picky son to eat, weaving complex, giggle-inducing fantasies; an easy-reading chapter book. (Rev: BL 5/1/11; SLJ 6/11)

1380 Scieszka, Jon. *The Spooky Tire* (K–2). Illus. by David Shannon and Loren Long. Series: Jon Scieszka's Trucktown. Ready-to-Roll. 2009, Simon & Schuster LB $13.89 (978-1-4169-4153-8); paper $3.99 (978-1-4169-4142-2). Unpaged. A cement truck rummaging through a junkyard for a new tire on a dark and stormy night gets spooked by an ominous voice. (Rev: SLJ 11/1/09)

1381 Sias, Ryan. *Zoe and Robot: Let's Pretend* (PS–2). Illus. by author. 2011, Blue Apple $10.99 (978-160905063-4). 40pp. A young girl tries in vain to get a robot to understand imaginative play in this graphic novel for beginning readers. (Rev: BL 6/1/11)

1382 Silverman, Erica. *Spring Babies* (K–2). Illus. by Betsy Lewin. Series: Cowgirl Kate and Cocoa. 2010, Houghton Harcourt $15 (978-0-15-205396-3). 40pp. Cowgirl Kate and her talking horse help with the arrival of a new calf, and Cocoa learns to accept a new puppy. ☊ Lexile 360L (Rev: BL 1/1/10; HB 5–6/10; SLJ 6/1/10)

1383 Spinner, Stephanie. *Paddywack* (K–3). Illus. by Daniel Howarth. Series: Step into Reading. 2010, Random House paper $3.99 (978-0-375-86186-4). 48pp. Paddywack the horse and Jane come to a better understanding when she learns the importance of rewarding him with treats. (Rev: SLJ 6/1/10)

1384 Surgal, Jon. *Have You Seen My Dinosaur?* (PS–2). Illus. by Joe Mathieu. Series: Beginner Books. 2010, Random House $8.99 (978-0-375-85639-6); LB $12.99 (978-0-375-95639-3). Unpaged. A young boy searches high and low for his beloved dinosaur, not realizing that his pet is following him the whole way. (Rev: SLJ 5/1/10)

1385 Umansky, Kaye. *Alien Alby* (1–2). Illus. by Sophie Rohrbach. Series: I Am Reading. 2010, Kingfisher paper $3.99 (978-075343005-7). 48pp. In this wacky book for beginning readers full of wordplay, a young alien misses his pet Squee, who's been banished from the bed after refusing to wipe his paws. (Rev: BL 8/10)

1386 Urbanovic, Jackie. *Ducks in a Row* (K–2). Illus. by author and Joe Mathieu. Series: I Can Read! 2011, HarperCollins $16.99 (978-0-06-186438-4); paper $3.99 (978-0-06-186437-7). 32pp. Max the Duck feels unwanted until his demanding aunts stop in on their way south, and soon he longs to get back to his relaxing life. (Rev: SLJ 3/1/11)

1387 Wallace, Rich. *Benched* (2–4). Illus. by Jimmy Holder. Series: Kickers. 2010, Knopf $12.99 (978-037585756-0); LB $15.99 (978-037595756-7). 128pp. Ben's behavior at school deteriorates as he faces problems at home, and he finds himself in trouble on the soccer field; with soccer tips. ☾ (Rev: BL 1/1–15/11)

1388 Watts, Frances. *The Greatest Sheep in History* (2–4). Illus. by Judy Watson. Series: Ernie & Maud. 2011, Eerdmans paper $5.99 (978-0-8028-5374-5). 86pp. Superhero-in-training Ernie and his sheep sidekick Maud attend a superhero convention that turns out to pose superhero challenges. Lexile 910L (Rev: BL 7/11; SLJ 7/11)

1389 Weeks, Sarah. *Mac and Cheese* (K–2). Illus. by Jane Manning. Series: I Can Read. 2010, HarperCollins $16.99 (978-0-06-117079-9). 32pp. Two feline friends who couldn't be more different share an adventure when the wind blows away Macaroni's hat in this book for beginning readers. ☾ Lexile 510L (Rev: BL 12/15/10; SLJ 9/1/10)

1390 Weiss, Ellen, and Mel Friedman. *Porky and Bess* (K–3). Illus. by Marsha Winborn. Series: Step into Reading. 2010, Random House $12.99 (978-0-375-85458-3); paper $3.99 (978-0-375-96113-7). 48pp. A slovenly bachelor pig and a tidy cat with three kittens become friends despite their differences in this whimsical book for beginning readers. Lexile 410L (Rev: BL 1/1/10; LMC 5–6/10; SLJ 1/1/10)

1391 Willems, Mo. *Let's Say Hi to Friends Who Fly!* (PS–1). Illus. by author. 2010, HarperCollins $12.99 (978-0-06-172842-6); LB $14.89 (978-0-06-172846-4). 32pp. In this bright book for beginning readers, Cat the Cat and her similarly named animal friends have high-flying adventures in the sky. (Rev: BL 1/1/10; HB 5–6/10; SLJ 2/1/10)

1392 Yorinks, Arthur. *Flappy and Scrappy* (K–2). Illus. by Aleksey Ivanov and Olga Ivanov. Series: I Can Read! 2011, HarperCollins $16.99 (978-0-06-205117-2). 48pp. In this book for beginning readers, dogs Flappy and Scrappy are always there for each other. (Rev: SLJ 3/1/11)

Fiction for Older Readers

General

1393 Abrahams, Peter. *Robbie Forester and the Outlaws of Sherwood Street* (5–8). 2012, Philomel $16.99 (978-039925502-1). 320pp. Robyn, a 7th-grader, receives a charm bracelet as thanks for a good deed and finds that she has special powers that help in her mission to fight injustice in her Brooklyn neighborhood. ℮ (Rev: BL 2/1/12; LMC 8–9/12)

1394 Almond, David. *My Name Is Mina* (4–7). 2011, Delacorte $15.99 (978-0-385-74073-9); LB $18.99 (978-037598964-3). 304pp. This prequel to *Skellig* (1998) explores the life of homeschooled Mina, who lives next door to Michael, and her imaginative fascination with language and nature. (Rev: BL 9/15/11*; SLJ 11/1/11)

1395 Appelt, Kathi. *Keeper* (4–7). Illus. by August Hall. 2010, Simon & Schuster $16.99 (978-1-4169-5060-8). 416pp. Ten-year-old Keeper believes her absent mother is a mermaid and sets off in a boat, in the company of her dog and a seagull, to find her. ∩ Lexile 770L (Rev: BL 6/10; HB 9–10/10; LMC 10/10; SLJ 7/10)

1396 Babbitt, Natalie. *The Moon Over High Street* (3–5). 2012, Scholastic $15.95 (978-054537636-5). 160pp. Joe, 12 and an aspiring astronomer, goes to live with his aunt in a small Ohio town, where the richest man in town sees promise in the orphan and offers him a promising future as a businessman. (Rev: BL 3/15/12; HB 5–6/12; LMC 8–9/12; SLJ 4/12; VOYA 6/12)

1397 Banerjee, Anjali. *Seaglass Summer* (4–6). 2010, Random House $15.99 (978-038573567-4); LB $18.99 (978-038590555-8). 176pp. Aspiring veterinarian Poppy, 11, learns some important lessons while helping her uncle Sanjay at his vet practice. ℮ Lexile 590L (Rev: BL 3/1/10; LMC 8–9/10; SLJ 6/10)

1398 Beard, Darleen Bailey. *Annie Glover Is Not a Tree Lover* (3–6). Illus. by Heather Maione. 2009, Farrar $15.99 (978-0-374-30351-8). 120pp. Despite her initial mortification at her grandmother's histrionic behavior, 9-year-old Annie, her best friend, and her grandma rally their town together to save a historic elm tree. (Rev: LMC 1–2/10; SLJ 11/09)

1399 Bell, Juliet. *Kepler's Dream* (5–7). 2012, Putnam $16.99 (978-039925645-5). 256pp. Ella goes to live with her estranged grandmother in Albuquerque while her mother is being treated for cancer and finds herself learning about family history and investigating a mystery. (Rev: BL 5/15/12*; LMC 11–12/12; SLJ 5/1/12)

1400 Bennet, Olivia. *The Allegra Biscotti Collection* (5–8). Illus. Series: The Allegra Biscotti Collection. 2010, Sourcebooks paper $8.99 (978-1-4022-4391-2). 256pp. Eighth-grader Emma adopts an alter ego, Allegra Biscotti, to represent her fashion designs for the likes of *Vogue* in this entertaining book full of Emma's sketches. Also use *Who What Wear*. (Rev: BL 12/15/10; SLJ 12/1/10)

1401 Blexbolex. *People* (4–12). Trans. from French by Claudia Bedrick. Illus. by author. 2011, Enchanted Lion $19.95 (978-1-59270-110-0). Unpaged. A stimulating look at the similarities and differences in our lives, pairing, for example, a contortionist and a plumber, a bystander and a rescuer, a partygoer and a hermit. (Rev: HB 9–10/11; SLJ 9/1/11)

1402 Boyce, Frank Cottrell. *The Unforgotten Coat* (3–6). Illus. by Carl Hunter. 2011, Candlewick $15.99 (978-0-7636-5729-1). 112pp. Two Mongolian immigrant boys turn to kindhearted Julie, 12, for help in navigating the culture in their new home near Liverpool, England. (Rev: BL 9/1/11; SLJ 11/1/11)

1403 Brown, Jason Robert, and Dan Elish. *Thirteen* (5–7). 2008, HarperCollins $15.99 (978-006078749-3); LB $16.89 (978-006078750-9). 208pp. In this humorous coming-of-age story, Evan finds himself relocated halfway across the country — from comfortable New York City to the middle of Indiana — and grappling with the social terrain of his new school and preparations for his bar mitzvah speech. (Rev: BL 9/1/08)

1404 Cabot, Meg. *Blast from the Past* (3–5). Series: Allie Finkle's Rules for Girls. 2010, Scholastic $15.99 (978-054504048-8). 240pp. When her school field trip group merges with people from her old school, Allie contends with their meanness by being true to herself. ⌒ e Lexile 840L (Rev: BLO 10/15/10)

1405 Cheng, Andrea. *Where Do You Stay?* (4–7). 2011, Boyds Mills $17.95 (978-1-59078-707-6). 134pp. After Jerome's mother dies, the 11-year-old goes to live with an aunt and cousins, struggling to adjust to his new setting with the help of a homeless man who shares his love of music. Lexile 590L (Rev: BL 3/15/11; SLJ 5/11)

1406 Christopher, Lucy. *Flyaway* (5–8). 2011, Scholastic $16.99 (978-0-545-31771-9). 336pp. Thirteen-year-old Isla's deep connection with birds and nature helps her when her father is in the hospital and she befriends a boy with leukemia. ⌒ e Lexile HL580L (Rev: BL 8/11*; SLJ 12/1/11*; VOYA 8/11)

1407 Clark, Catherine. *How Not to Run for President* (5–8). 2012, Egmont $15.99 (978-160684101-3). 192pp. After he saves a candidate's life, Aidan is brought along on the campaign trail, where he learns firsthand how the fickle media game works. e Lexile 600L (Rev: BL 2/1/12; LMC 3–4/12; SLJ 1/12)

1408 Cooper, Ilene. *Angel in My Pocket* (5–8). 2011, Feiwel & Friends $16.99 (978-0-312-37014-5). 288pp. A magical coin travels from middle-schooler Bette to three classmates who also are suffering a variety of problems in this novel about friendship, magic, and transformation. Lexile 810L (Rev: BLO 2/15/11; LMC 5–6/11; SLJ 3/1/11; VOYA 6/11)

1409 Cuevas, Michelle. *The Masterwork of a Painting Elephant* (3–7). Illus. by Ed Young. 2011, Farrar $15.99 (978-0-374-34854-0). 144pp. An artistic elephant named Birch and a boy abandoned as a baby, Pigeon Jones, become fast friends and travel together in search of their loved ones. (Rev: BL 9/1/11; SLJ 12/1/11)

1410 Dionne, Erin. *Notes from an Accidental Band Geek* (5–8). 2011, Dial $16.99 (978-0-8037-3564-4). 304pp. Ambitious 9th-grader Elsie has her heart set on becoming a French horn player in an orchestra and is surprised to find that she actually enjoys playing the melliphone in the school's marching band despite her initial resistance. (Rev: BL 11/1/11; SLJ 10/1/11)

1411 Dionne, Erin. *The Total Tragedy of a Girl Named Hamlet* (4–7). 2010, Dial $16.99 (978-0-803-73298-8). 304pp. It's not easy for socially uncertain 8th-grader Hamlet when her genius 7-year-old sister Desdemona starts attending her middle school; however an audi-

tion for *A Midsummer Night's Dream* reveals Hamlet's acting abilities. e Lexile 750L (Rev: BL 1/1/10; LMC 5–6/10; SLJ 2/10)

1412 Dutton, Sandra. *Mary Mae and the Gospel Truth* (4–6). 2010, Houghton Mifflin $15 (978-0-547-24966-7). 144pp. Ten-year-old Mary Mae touches off a family debate over science versus religion when her interest in fossils worries her devout mother. e Lexile 680L (Rev: BL 6/10; SLJ 7/10)

1413 Edgar, Elsbeth. *The Visconti House* (4–7). 2011, Candlewick $16.99 (978-0-7636-5019-3). 304pp. Laura, who wants to fit in in her 8th-grade class, and Leon, a new student, become friends as they work together to unravel the history of Laura's supposedly haunted house; set in Australia. e Lexile 650L (Rev: BL 2/1/11; SLJ 2/1/11; VOYA 4/11)

1414 Fraustino, Lisa Rowe. *The Hole in the Wall* (5–8). 2010, Milkweed $16.95 (978-157131696-7). 280pp. Strip mining has ruined their environment and 11-year-old twins Sebby and Barbara wonder if some of the strange things they are seeing are real in this novel that blends ecology and science fiction. (Rev: BL 12/15/10; LMC 3–4/11)

1415 Frazier, Sundee T. *Brendan Buckley's Sixth-Grade Experiment* (4–6). 2012, Delacorte $16.99 (978-038574050-0); LB $19.99 (978-037598949-0). 288pp. Biracial, science-savvy Brendan is now in middle school and dealing with his growing feelings for new girl Morgan, his changing friendship with Khal, and problems with his African American father. ⌒ e (Rev: BLO 2/1/12; LMC 3–4/12; SLJ 1/12)

1416 Fredericks, Mariah. *Life* (5–8). Series: In the Cards. 2008, Simon & Schuster $16.99 (978-068987658-5). 262pp. Syd narrates this well-written stand-alone volume in a tarot-reading series as the three best friends seek answers about their daily lives. Lexile NC560L (Rev: BL 9/1/08; SLJ 8/08)

1417 Friedman, Laurie. *Mallory's Super Sleepover* (3–5). Illus. by Jennifer Kalis. Series: Mallory. 2011, Darby Creek $15.95 (978-082258887-0). 160pp. Mallory struggles to plan a 10th birthday sleepover that will please both her friends and her parents. (Rev: BL 12/15/11)

1418 Friend, Catherine. *Barn Boot Blues* (4–7). 2011, Marshall Cavendish $16.99 (978-0-7614-5930-9). 144pp. Twelve-year-old Taylor is miserable when her family moves from Minneapolis to a rural farm, but her innate sense of humor helps her make new friends at school. e (Rev: HB 11–12/11; LMC 1–2/12; SLJ 12/1/11)

1419 Friesen, Jonathan. *The Last Martin* (5–7). 2011, Zondervan $14.99 (978-0-310-72080-5). 264pp. Convinced that he is about to die because of a family curse, 13-year-old Martin starts to exhibit increasingly reckless behavior but also finds himself making new friends who try to help him; a story full of humor. ℮ (Rev: SLJ 5/11*)

1420 Gidwitz, Adam. *A Tale Dark and Grimm* (4–7). 2010, Dutton $16.99 (978-0-525-42334-8). 256pp. Capitalizing on the gruesome nature of many of the Grimm tales, Gidwitz puts long-suffering Hansel and Gretel through a series of torturous scenarios en route to their happy ending. (Rev: BL 11/15/10; HB 1–2/11; LMC 1–2/11; SLJ 11/1/10*)

1421 Givner, Joan. *Ellen's Book of Life* (5–8). 2008, Groundwood $17.95 (978-088899853-8). 208pp. When Ellen's mother dies, Ellen seeks out her birth mother and is introduced to Judaism in this multilayered first-person narrative, the third in a series. (Rev: BL 10/15/08; SLJ 1/1/09)

1422 Golds, Cassandra. *The Museum of Mary Child* (5–8). 2009, Kane/Miller $16.99 (978-1-935279-13-6). 329pp. Sad teen Heloise, who longs for love, finds a doll under the floorboards of her bedroom and runs away from home when her unloving godmother threatens it. Lexile 840L (Rev: BLO 8/09; LMC 1–2/10; SLJ 12/09)

1423 Graff, Lisa. *Double Dog Dare* (3–5). 2012, Philomel $16.99 (978-039925516-8). 304pp. Two 4th-graders vying for news anchor position in the media club enter a school-sanctioned dare contest, only to discover that their troubled family lives mean they'd be better off as friends than rivals. (Rev: BL 3/15/12; LMC 10/12; SLJ 4/1/12)

1424 Greene, Stephanie. *Happy Birthday, Sophie Hartley* (3–5). 2010, Clarion $16 (978-0-547-25128-8). 128pp. Eager for attention, Sophie grandly tells her friends that she will be getting a baby gorilla for her 10th birthday — and then must face the consequences. (Rev: BLO 5/15/10; SLJ 7/1/10)

1425 Greenwald, Lisa. *My Life in Pink and Green* (4–7). 2009, Abrams $16.95 (978-0-8109-8352-6). 272pp. Twelve-year-old Lucy's family's pharmacy is in serious financial trouble until Lucy has the idea to turn part of it into an eco-spa. ℮ Lexile 680L (Rev: BL 2/15/09; SLJ 4/1/09)

1426 Greenwald, Sheila. *Watch Out, World — Rosy Cole Is Going Green!* (3–5). Illus. by author. 2010, Farrar $15.99 (978-0-371-36280-5). 112pp. Rosy's efforts for the school's "Keep It Green" fair involve keeping 2,000 worms in a dresser drawer. Lexile 760L (Rev: BL 2/15/10; LMC 5–6/10; SLJ 4/1/10)

1427 Grimes, Nikki. *Almost Zero* (2–4). Illus. by R. Gregory Christie. 2010, Putnam $10.99 (978-039925177-1). 128pp. Dyamonde is annoyed when her mother refuses to buy her a new pair of shoes, but when a classmate's apartment is destroyed she is determined to help. Lexile 630L (Rev: BLO 11/1/10; HB 11–12/10; SLJ 1/11)

1428 Gutman, Dan. *The Talent Show* (4–7). 2010, Simon & Schuster $15.99 (978-1-4169-9003-1). 224pp.

A small Kansas town decides to hold a talent show to renew their spirits after a destructive tornado; however, even as the show takes place and the students have picked a favorite another tornado affects the outcome. ℮ Lexile 800L (Rev: BL 6/10; LMC 11–12/10; SLJ 8/10)

1429 Harkrader, Lisa. *The Adventures of Beanboy* (4–7). Illus. by author. 2012, Houghton Mifflin $9.99 (978-054755078-7). 240pp. Thirteen-year-old Tucker's creation of a superhero sidekick for a comic book competition leads to a big boost in his own confidence in and out of school. ℮ Lexile 670L (Rev: BL 3/1/12; SLJ 2/12*)

1430 Hawkins, Aaron R. *The Year Money Grew on Trees* (5–8). 2010, Houghton Mifflin $16 (978-0-547-27977-0). 304pp. Fourteen-year-old Jackson learns a lot about farming — and about himself — when his manipulative neighbor promises him the deed to her son's apple orchard — if he can sell $8,000 worth of fruit in the first year. ℮ Lexile 810L (Rev: BL 9/15/10; LMC 3–4/11; SLJ 10/1/10)

1431 Henson, Heather. *Dream of Night* (4–8). 2010, Simon & Schuster $15.99 (978-1-4169-4899-5). 224pp. Twelve-year-old Shiloh slowly learns to trust others with the help of her foster mother and Dream of Night, a horse that has also suffered and that offers its own perspective. ℮ Lexile 470L (Rev: BLO 4/15/10; LMC 8–9/10; SLJ 4/10)

1432 Hermes, Patricia. *Emma Dilemma, the Nanny, and the Best Horse Ever* (3–5). 2011, Marshall Cavendish $15.99 (978-0-7614-5905-7). 144pp. Emma's favorite horse is to be sold, and her best friend, Luisa, is moving away. What else can go wrong? ℮ Lexile 550L (Rev: BL 4/1/11; SLJ 3/1/11)

1433 Hershey, Mary. *Love and Pollywogs from Camp Calamity* (3–5). 2010, Random House $15.99 (978-0-385-73744-9); LB $18.99 (978-0-385-90666-1). 224pp. Fourth-grader Effie's much-awaited week at Camp Wickitawa doesn't go according to plan when she discovers her older sister will be there too, and that she suffers totally unexpected homesickness. (Rev: SLJ 6/1/10)

1434 Hiaasen, Carl. *Chomp* (5–8). 2012, Knopf $16.99 (978-037586842-9); LB $19.99 (978-037596842-6). 304pp. A reality TV show called "Expedition Survival" sparks an exciting environmental adventure when the star disappears in the Everglades. ⌒ ℮ Lexile 800L (Rev: BL 11/15/11; HB 3–4/12; LMC 5–6/12*; SLJ 3/12*)

1435 Holt, Kimberly Willis. *Piper Reed, Campfire Girl* (3–5). Illus. by Christine Davenier. 2010, Henry Holt $15.99 (978-080509006-2). 160pp. Fifth-grader Piper takes pity on a classmate after he embarrasses himself on a weekend camping trip; the fourth installment in this chapter book series. ℮ Lexile 530L (Rev: BL 1/1–15/11)

1436 Horvath, Polly. *Northward to the Moon* (5–8). 2010, Random House LB $20.99 (978-0-375-96110-6). 256pp. Jane recounts her family's varied experiences as, after their stepfather is fired from his teaching job, they travel back from Saskatchewan to Massachusetts in this sequel to *My One Hundred Adventures* (2008). ♫ ℮ Lexile 750L (Rev: BL 11/15/09; HB 1–2/10; LMC 3–4/10; SLJ 2/10)

1437 Hyde, Natalie. *Saving Arm Pit* (3–6). 2011, Fitzhenry & Whiteside paper $9.95 (978-1-55455-151-4). 136pp. A baseball team in a challenged town called Harmony Point starts a feverish letter-writing campaign in hopes of keeping their beloved postmaster coach on the job. (Rev: LMC 1–2/12; SLJ 10/1/11*)

1438 Ignatow, Amy. *The Long-Distance Dispatch Between Lydia Goldblatt and Julie Graham-Chang* (4–6). Illus. by author. Series: The Popularity Papers. 2011, Abrams $15.95 (978-0-8109-9724-0). Julie copes with making her own way in junior high when Lydia's mother gets a job in London in this believable story told through shared letters and e-mails. (Rev: BL 4/15/11; SLJ 7/11)

1439 Ignatow, Amy. *Research for the Social Improvement and General Betterment of Lydia Goldblatt and Julie Graham-Chang* (3–6). Illus. by author. Series: The Popularity Papers. 2010, Abrams $15.95 (978-0-8109-8421-9). 208pp. Fifth-graders Lydia and Julie decide to launch a social investigation into the lives of their school's popular girls so they will be more prepared for junior high. (Rev: BL 3/1/10; SLJ 4/10; VOYA 8/10)

1440 Ignatow, Amy. *Words of (Questionable) Wisdom from Lydia Goldblatt and Julie Graham-Chang* (3–6). Illus. by author. Series: The Popularity Papers. 2011, Abrams $15.95 (978-141970063-7). 208pp. Twelve-year-old best friends Lydia and Julie record their lives as they deal with challenges ranging from plagiarism to a friend's mother's death. (Rev: BLO 11/15/11; SLJ 4/10)

1441 Johnson, Peter. *The Amazing Adventures of John Smith, Jr. AKA Houdini* (5–7). 2012, HarperCollins $15.99 (978-006198890-5). 176pp. Thirteen-year-old John "Houdini" Smith writes a novel that describes his life in Providence, Rhode Island, his family problems, and his efforts to make money raking leaves. ℮ Lexile 950L (Rev: BL 1/12; SLJ 4/12*)

1442 Jukes, Mavis. *The New Kid* (2–5). 2011, Knopf $14.99 (978-0-375-85879-6); LB $17.99 (978-0-375-95879-3). 288pp. Carson Blum, an adopted child and nearly 9 years old, moves with his dad to California and must deal with missing his grandparents and friends along with meeting students at his new public school. (Rev: BL 12/15/11; HB 1–2/12; SLJ 12/1/11)

1443 Kelley, Jane. *Nature Girl* (4–6). 2010, Random House $16.99 (978-0-375-85634-1); LB $19.99 (978-0-375-95634-8). 256pp. Unsettled by spending a technology-free summer in Vermont and missing her best friend Lucy, 12-year-old urban girl Megan takes off on the Appalachian Trail with only her dog for company. ℮ Lexile 590L (Rev: BL 4/1/10; SLJ 3/10)

1444 Koss, Amy Goldman. *The Not-So-Great Depression* (5–7). 2010, Roaring Brook paper $9.99 (978-1-59643-613-8). 272pp. When her divorced mother is laid off, 14-year-old Jacki and her siblings face losing their privileged private-school life; the subtitle, *In Which the Economy Crashes, My Sister's Plans Are Ruined, My Mom Goes Broke, My Dad Grows Vegetables, and I Do Not Get a Hamster*, fills in some of the rest of the story. ℮ Lexile 810L (Rev: BL 3/15/10; HB 5–6/10; LMC 5–6/10; SLJ 5/10)

1445 Kowitt, H. N. *The Loser List* (4–7). Illus. by author. 2011, Scholastic $9.99 (978-0-545-24004-8). 224pp. Seventh-grader Danny Shine finds himself in trouble when he ends up on the Loser List in the girls' bathroom, and then befriends a bully in detention. Lexile 480L (Rev: BL 3/15/11; LMC 10/11; SLJ 4/11)

1446 Kowitt, H. N. *Revenge of the Loser* (4–7). Illus. by author. 2012, Scholastic paper $9.99 (978-054539926-5). 240pp. Jealous 7th-grader Danny finally finds a flaw in seemingly perfect new kid Ty but his attempts to exploit it go off track; the diary-style narrative is peppered with cartoons. (Rev: BLO 5/15/12; SLJ 6/12)

1447 Kurtz, Jane. *Lanie* (3–5). Illus. by Robert Papp. 2010, American Girl paper $6.95 (978-1-59369-682-5). 108pp. Outdoorsy, scientifically inclined Lanie, 10, misses her friend Dakota, who is away in Indonesia, but enjoys exploring her backyard with her favorite aunt. The second book in the series is *Lanie's Real Adventures* (2010), in which her environmental gardening methods are challenged. (Rev: SLJ 7/1/10)

1448 Lainez, Rene Colato. *My Shoes and I* (2–4). Illus. by Fabrico Vanden Broeck. 2010, Boyds Mills $16.95 (978-1-59078-385-6). 32pp. Mario gains strength and inspiration from a new pair of shoes as he and his papa undertake a long, challenging journey to join his mother in the United States. Lexile AD330L (Rev: BL 2/1/10; LMC 5–6/10; SLJ 3/1/10)

1449 Leavitt, Lindsey. *Princess for Hire* (5–8). 2010, Hyperion $16.99 (978-142312192-3). 256pp. Fifteen-year-old Desi is offered a chance to escape her humdrum life — to "sub" for real princesses — but soon learns this is harder than it seems. Lexile 670L (Rev: BLO 3/1/10; SLJ 5/10)

1450 Lieb, Josh. *I Am a Genius of Unspeakable Evil and I Want to Be Your Class President* (5–7). 2009, Penguin $15.99 (978-1-59514-240-5). 304pp. Overweight, apparently slow but secretly genius 7th-grader Oliver Watson takes on his arch nemesis — his father — by running for class president, a move secretly motivated by a desire for Dad's affection. ♫ ℮ Lexile 780L (Rev: BL 10/15/09; SLJ 10/09; VOYA 12/09)

1451 Look, Lenore. *Alvin Ho: Allergic to Dead Bodies, Funerals, and Other Fatal Circumstances* (2–4). Illus. by LeUyen Pham. 2011, Random House $15.99 (978-037586831-3); LB $18.99 (978-037596831-0). 176pp. Perennially worried Chinese American 2nd-grader Alvin prepares himself to attend his grandfather's best friend's funeral in this humorous take on death and funerals. ☊ ℮ Lexile 600L (Rev: BL 10/15/11; HB 9–10/11)

1452 Look, Lenore. *Ruby Lu, Star of the Show* (2–4). Illus. by Stef Choi. 2011, Simon & Schuster $15.99 (978-1-4169-1775-5). 137pp. Ruby's father loses his job just as she is starting 3rd grade, causing many changes in her life. ℮ Lexile 620L (Rev: BL 2/1/11; HB 3–4/11; SLJ 3/1/11)

1453 Lord, Cynthia. *Touch Blue* (4–7). 2010, Scholastic $16.99 (978-0-545-03531-6). 192pp. When the state of Maine threatens to close an island school for lack of pupils, the families take in foster children, and 11-year-old Tess must adjust to the arrival of 13-year-old Aaron. ☊ Lexile 750L (Rev: BL 8/10; HB 11–12/10; SLJ 9/1/10)

1454 MacDonald, Anne Louise. *Seeing Red* (5–8). 2009, Kids Can $17.95 (978-1-55453-291-9); paper $8.95 (978-1-55453-292-6). 224pp. Thirteen-year-old Frankie wonders if he has supernatural powers as he discovers new talents — for working with horses and disabled children, helping injured birds, and making friends. (Rev: BL 3/1/09; LMC 10/09; SLJ 8/09)

1455 McGhee, Alison. *Julia Gillian (and the Dream of the Dog)* (4–6). Illus. by Drazen Kozjan. 2010, Scholastic $16.99 (978-0-545-03351-0). 327pp. While dealing with the myriad problems of middle school, Julia also must face the fact that her aging dog is reaching the end of his life. Lexile 810L (Rev: HB 9–10/10; SLJ 8/10)

1456 McLean, Dirk. *Curtain Up!* (1–4). Illus. by France Brassard. 2010, Tundra $17.95 (978-0-88776-899-6). 40pp. McLean provides many details of a musical production through the eyes of Amaya, a young girl who lands a role. (Rev: BL 11/1/10; SLJ 10/1/10)

1457 MacLean, Jill. *The Present Tense of Prinny Murphy* (5–8). 2010, Fitzhenry & Whiteside paper $11.95 (978-1-55455-145-3). 230pp. In Fiddler's Cove, Newfoundland, Prinny Murphy faces many challenges — an alcoholic mother who no longer lives at home, a distant father, loss of her best friend, bullying — but when she reads Virginia Euwer Wolff's *Make Lemonade* she recognizes a kindred spirit and resolves to conquer her problems. Lexile 700L (Rev: BL 12/15/10; LMC 11–12/10; SLJ 7/10; VOYA 8/10)

1458 Mankell, Henning. *When the Snow Fell* (5–8). Trans. from Swedish by Laurie Thompson. 2009, Delacorte $15.99 (978-0-385-73497-4); LB $18.99 (978-0-385-90491-9). 256pp. Now almost 14, Joel becomes a hero when he rescues an old man from freezing to death in this third volume about the appealing young Swede. (Rev: BL 10/1/09*; SLJ 12/09)

1459 Mass, Wendy. *Finally* (4–7). 2010, Scholastic $16.99 (978-0-545-05242-9). 304pp. Rory's long-nurtured dreams about what she'll do when she turns 12 turn out to be full of pitfalls in this light, funny story about confidence and insecurity. ☊ (Rev: BL 2/1/10; SLJ 7/10)

1460 Mass, Wendy. *Thirteen Gifts* (4–7). 2011, Scholastic $16.99 (978-0-545-31003-1). 352pp. This story of Tara's summer in Willow Falls combines magic, mystery, and quirky characters. ☊ ℮ Lexile 720L (Rev: BL 8/11; SLJ 9/1/11*)

1461 Messner, Kate. *The Brilliant Fall of Gianna Z* (4–7). 2009, Bloomsbury $16.99 (978-0-8027-9842-8). 198pp. Seventh-grader Gianna must complete a science assignment in order to compete in the cross-country running sectionals but life keeps interfering. (Rev: BL 8/09; SLJ 12/09)

1462 Mitton, Tony. *The Storyteller's Secrets* (4–6). Illus. by Peter Bailey. 2010, Random House $15.99 (978-0-385-75190-2); LB $18.99 (978-0-385-75191-9). 128pp. Twins Toby and Tess are fascinated by the verse adaptations of European folklore told by a mysterious old man in this richly illustrated book. (Rev: BL 6/10; LMC 10/10; SLJ 6/10)

1463 Moranville, Sharelle Byars. *The Hop* (4–6). Illus. by Niki Daly. 2012, Hyperion $16.99 (978-142313736-8). 288pp. A timid toad and a nature-loving girl work together in different ways to save a patch of woods from destruction in this contemporary novel with an element of fantasy. (Rev: BL 3/15/12; LMC 5–6/12; SLJ 3/12)

1464 Myers, Walter Dean. *Amiri and Odette* (4–8). Illus. by Javaka Steptoe. 2009, Scholastic $17.99 (978-059068041-7). 40pp. Overtones of urban youth, hip-hop, and Shakespeare abound in this colorfully illustrated, modern-day version in verse of the ballet Swan Lake. (Rev: BL 12/1/08; LMC 5–6/09; SLJ 1/1/09; VOYA 10/09)

1465 Myers, Walter Dean. *Checkmate* (5–8). 2011, Scholastic $16.99 (978-0-439-91627-1). 144pp. Zander and his middle-school friends in Harlem intervene when their chess-star classmate Sidney is caught trying to buy drugs. (Rev: BL 9/1/11; SLJ 10/1/11)

1466 Orlev, Uri. *The Song of the Whales* (5–8). Trans. by Hillel Halkin. 2010, Houghton Mifflin $16 (978-054725752-5). 112pp. Living in Jerusalem, Mikha'el becomes close to his grandfather and joins him on nightly dream journeys; as the old man's health fails he passes his ability as a dream master on to his grandson. (Rev: BL 3/1/10*; SLJ 5/10)

1467 Palmer, Robin. *Yours Truly, Lucy B. Parker: Girl vs. Superstar* (5–7). 2010, Putnam $15.99 (978-0-399-25489-5). 224pp. Plagued by family, friendship, and puberty problems, 12-year-old Lucy writes to Dr. Maude, a famous psychologist, for advice about handling her complicated life. Lexile 1080L (Rev: BL 6/10; LMC 8–9/10; SLJ 4/10)

1468 Paratore, Coleen Murtagh. *Sweet and Sunny* (3–4). 2010, Scholastic $16.99 (978-0-545-07582-4). 178pp. Plucky African American Sunny copes with many problems as she continues her quest to create a national Kid's Day. (Rev: SLJ 5/1/10)

1469 Parry, Rosanne. *Heart of a Shepherd* (4–7). 2009, Random House $15.99 (978-0-375-84802-5); LB $18.99 (978-0-375-94802-2). 176pp. In this heartwarming faith-based coming-of-age story, 11-year-old Brother learns a lot about ranching in eastern Oregon — and himself — when his courageous father is deployed to Iraq. ☊ ℯ (Rev: BL 2/15/09; HB 5–6/09*; SLJ 3/1/09)

1470 Paulsen, Gary. *Notes from the Dog* (4–7). 2009, Random House $15.99 (978-0-385-73845-3); LB $18.99 (978-0-385-90730-9). 133pp. Fourteen-year-old Finn overcomes his shyness as he befriends his new neighbor, 24-year-old breast cancer survivor Johanna, who inspires him with her enthusiasm for life. ℯ Lexile 760L (Rev: BL 8/09; LMC 11–12/09; SLJ 9/09; VOYA 10/09)

1471 Peirce, Lincoln. *Big Nate on a Roll* (3–6). Illus. by author. Series: Big Nate. 2011, HarperCollins $12.99 (978-0-06-194438-3); LB $14.89 (978-0-06-194439-0). 216pp. Sixth-grader Nate aims to beat newcomer Artur — Mr. Perfect — and win the scouts' fundraising drive and the accompanying prize of a skateboard. (Rev: HB 9–10/11; SLJ 10/1/11)

1472 Perl, Erica S. *When Life Gives You O.J.* (4–6). 2011, Knopf $15.99 (978-0-375-85924-3); LB $18.99 (978-0-375-95924-0). 208pp. Ten-year-old Zelly agrees to look after a practice dog — an orange juice container — while she waits for the real thing. ℯ (Rev: BL 6/1/11; SLJ 9/1/11)

1473 Potter, Ellen. *The Humming Room* (4–7). 2012, Feiwel & Friends $16.99 (978-031264438-3). 192pp. Sent to live with an estranged uncle on a remote island, 12-year-old orphan Roo finds a frail cousin named Phillip, a wild boy, and a walled-off and abandoned garden; inspired by Frances Hodgson Burnett's *The Secret Garden*. ℯ Lexile 800L (Rev: BL 2/1/12*; LMC 8–9/12; SLJ 5/1/12)

1474 Preller, James. *Justin Fisher Declares War!* (3–5). 2010, Scholastic $15.99 (978-054503301-5). 144pp. Snarky middle-school class clown Justin learns how to go for laughs without alienating his peers in this coming-of-age story. (Rev: BLO 10/15/10; SLJ 12/1/10)

1475 Railsback, Lisa. *Noonie's Masterpiece* (3–5). Illus. by Sarajo Frieden. 2010, Chronicle $18.99 (978-08118-6654-5). 208pp. Fourth-grade artist Noonie has been through a "blue period" since her mother's death but now hopes that a "purple period" will bring her archaeologist father home — especially if she wins the

art contest. Lexile 660L (Rev: BL 5/1/10; LMC 8–9/10; SLJ 7/10)

1476 Ray, Delia. *Here Lies Linc* (5–8). 2011, Knopf $16.99 (978-0-375-86757-6); LB $19.99 (978-037596756-6). 304pp. Eager to impress his new classmates, formerly home-schooled 12-year-old Linc throws himself into the Adopt-a-Grave project and finds out some unexpected facts about his own family. (Rev: BL 9/1/11; SLJ 9/1/11)

1477 Rayburn, Tricia. *Ruby's Slippers* (4–7). 2010, Aladdin paper $6.99 (978-1-4169-8701-7). 352pp. A Wizard of Oz-inspired tale in which 7th-grader Ruby is swept from her rural Kansas home to a new life in Florida filled with new electronics and culture, a grandmother, and typical middle school politics. ℯ Lexile 790L (Rev: BL 6/10; LMC 11–12/10)

1478 Resau, Laura. *Star in the Forest* (4–8). 2010, Delacorte $14.99 (978-0-385-73792-0). 160pp. After her father is deported to Mexico as an illegal immigrant, 11-year-old Zitlally turns to her trailer-park neighbor Crystal and the two girls care for an abandoned dog that Zitlally believes holds the key to her father's return. ℯ Lexile 780L (Rev: BL 2/1/10*; HB 3–4/11; LMC 5–6/10; SLJ 2/10)

1479 Rhodes, Jewell Parker. *Ninth Ward* (5–8). 2010, Little, Brown $15.99 (978-0-316-04307-6). 160pp. Plucky 12-year-old Lanesha, who lives in New Orleans's Ninth Ward, draws on her special gifts when Hurricane Katrina arrives. ☊ (Rev: BL 5/1/10; LMC 10/10; SLJ 8/10)

1480 Rising, Janet. *The Word on the Yard* (4–6). Series: The Pony Whisperer. 2010, Sourcebooks paper $6.99 (978-1-4022-3952-6). 208pp. Teenager Pia navigates her new school and tension with her dad's girlfriend by spending time with her horse; in a supernatural twist, she discovers a mysterious statue that allows her to hear her horse's thoughts. The first volume in a series. (Rev: BL 6/10; SLJ 9/1/10)

1481 Rocklin, Joanne. *One Day and One Amazing Morning on Orange Street* (3–6). 2011, Abrams $16.95 (978-0-8109-9719-6). 224pp. The last remaining orange tree on an empty lot is precious to the residents of its Southern California neighborhood, and when it is threatened they come together to face their myriad problems. ℯ Lexile 830L (Rev: BL 3/15/11; HB 7–8/11; SLJ 5/11*)

1482 Schaefer, Laura. *The Secret Ingredient* (4–7). Illus. 2011, Simon & Schuster $15.99 (978-1-4424-1959-9). 240pp. Annie, 14 and in her last summer before high school, gets her friends to help her compete in a scone baking contest to win a vacation in London; a sequel to *The Teashop Girls* (2008). ℯ Lexile 710L (Rev: BL 6/1/11; SLJ 8/11)

1483 Schroeder, Lisa. *It's Raining Cupcakes* (4–7). 2010, Simon & Schuster $15.99 (978-1-4169-9084-0). 224pp. As her mother opens a cupcake shop, 12-year-old Isabel longs to travel and pins her hopes on a baking contest; with recipes. **e** Lexile 640L (Rev: BLO 2/15/10; SLJ 2/10)

1484 Schroeder, Lisa. *Sprinkles and Secrets* (4–7). 2011, Simon & Schuster $15.99 (978-1-4424-2263-6). 224pp. Sophie's dreams of becoming an actress are on the verge of coming true, but can she appear in a commercial advertising the competitor to her best friend Isabel's shop? A sequel to *It's Raining Cupcakes* (2010). (Rev: SLJ 10/1/11)

1485 Senzai, N. H. *Shooting Kabul* (4–7). 2010, Simon & Schuster $16.99 (978-1-4424-0194-5). 272pp. Fadi's little sister Mariam is lost when the family flees Afghanistan in July 2001, and they continue to search for her even as they deal with a new life in the United States and the backlash after September 11. **e** Lexile 800L (Rev: BL 6/10; LMC 10/10; SLJ 6/10; VOYA 8/10)

1486 Silberberg, Alan. *Milo: Sticky Notes and Brain Freeze* (5–8). Illus. by author. 2010, Simon & Schuster $15.99 (978-1-4169-9430-5). 288pp. The death of 12-year-old Milo's mother overshadows all the normal trials and tribulations of middle school in this novel that interweaves humor and pain. **e** (Rev: HB 11–12/10; LMC 11–12/11; SLJ 9/1/10*)

1487 Simon, Coco. *Alexis and the Perfect Recipe* (4–6). Series: Cupcake Diaries. 2011, Simon & Schuster paper $5.99 (978-144242901-7). 160pp. Alexis, who loves organization and planning, gets a little haphazard when she develops a major crush on Emma's brother Matt. (Rev: BL 1/1/12)

1488 Springstubb, Tricia. *What Happened on Fox Street* (4–7). 2010, HarperCollins $15.99 (978-0-06-198635-2). 224pp. Although she still misses her dead mother, 10-year-old Mo is fairly happy with life on Fox Street until the summer her friend Mercedes seems to change and her father receives an interesting offer for their house. ∩ **e** (Rev: BL 9/1/10*; HB 9–10/10; SLJ 9/1/10)

1489 Tashjian, Janet. *My Life as a Book* (4–7). Illus. by Jake Tashjian. 2010, Henry Holt $16.99 (978-0-8050-8903-5). 224pp. Derek spends a summer at reading camp and, to his surprise, learns to love books. (Rev: BL 8/10*; LMC 8–9/10; SLJ 8/10)

1490 Vail, Rachel. *Justin Case: School, Drool, and Other Daily Disasters* (3–5). Illus. by Matthew Cordell. 2010, Feiwel & Friends $16.99 (978-0-312-53290-1). 256pp. Third-grader Justin shares in his diary his worries about coping at school and at home (making friends, gym class, his self-confident younger sister, his beloved stuffed animal). (Rev: BL 3/1/10; LMC 5–6/10; SLJ 5/1/10)

1491 Vernick, Audrey. *Water Balloon* (4–7). 2011, Clarion $16.99 (978-0-547-59554-2). 310pp. Thirteen-year-old Marley is having a tough summer — her parents have separated and she must move into her father's

home; her friends seem to have changed — until she meets a new boy who offers friendship and maybe more. **e** Lexile 630L (Rev: SLJ 10/1/11*; VOYA 10/11)

1492 Wells, Rosemary, and Secundino Fernandez. *My Havana: Memories of a Cuban Boyhood* (3–5). Illus. by Peter Ferguson. 2010, Candlewick $17.99 (978-0-7636-4305-8). 72pp. This fictionalized account of the life of Cuban architect Secundino Fernandez captures the uncertainty and upheaval he faced as he moved from Cuba to Spain, back to Cuba, and then — fleeing the Castro regime in the late 1950s — to New York. (Rev: BL 8/10; SLJ 9/1/10)

1493 Wells, Tina. *The Secret Crush* (4–8). Illus. by Michael Segawa. Series: Mackenzie Blue. 2010, HarperCollins $10.99 (978-0-06-158311-7). 226pp. Seventh-grader Mackenzie Blue hopes to catch the attention of cute Landon, and the school's forthcoming rock-and-roll musical seems a good opportunity. **e** (Rev: SLJ 5/10)

1494 Weyn, Suzanne. *Empty* (5–8). 2010, Scholastic $17.99 (978-054517278-3). 192pp. In this dystopian story, three teens struggle to survive in a world thrown into chaos by global warming and lack of petroleum. (Rev: BL 10/15/10; LMC 3–4/11; SLJ 1/1/11)

1495 Wight, Eric. *Frankie Pickle and the Pine Run 3000* (2–4). Illus. by author. 2010, Simon & Schuster $9.99 (978-1-4169-6485-8). 112pp. When Frankie doesn't do well enough at knot-tying to qualify for the Possum Scout badge, he tries his hand at model car racing instead. Lexile 600L (Rev: BL 2/1/10; SLJ 2/1/10)

1496 Williams, Maiya. *The Fizzy Whiz Kid* (5–8). 2010, Abrams $16.95 (978-081098347-2). 288pp. Suddenly plunked down among the children of movie stars, producers, and makeup artists, midwesterner Mitchell wins over his new classmates when he lands a spot in a TV commercial. (Rev: BL 3/1/10; SLJ 5/10)

1497 Winters, Ben H. *The Secret Life of Ms. Finkleman* (5–8). 2010, HarperCollins $16.99 (978-0-06-196541-8). 256pp. Brainy 7th-grader Bethesda investigates her music teacher and uncovers an unsuspected past as a punk rocker, resulting in an unusual school concert. Lexile 910L (Rev: BL 11/15/10; LMC 3–4/11; SLJ 11/1/10)

1498 Wolitzer, Meg. *The Fingertips of Duncan Dorfman* (5–8). 2011, Dutton $16.99 (978-0-525-42304-1). 256pp. Three middle-school students learn about themselves as they spend time at the Youth Scrabble Tournament. **e** (Rev: BL 9/15/11; LMC 1–2/12; SLJ 9/1/11)

1499 Woods, Brenda. *Saint Louis Armstrong Beach* (4–7). 2011, Penguin $16.99 (978-0-399-25507-6). 144pp. When Hurricane Katrina arrives, 12-year-old clarinet-playing Saint Louis Armstrong Beach makes plans to get the dog he loves, Shadow, to safety. **e** Lexile 660L (Rev: BL 11/15/11; HB 11–12/11; LMC 1–2/12*; SLJ 10/1/11*)

1500 Wynne-Jones, Tim. *Rex Zero: The Great Pretender* (4–7). Series: Rex Zero. 2010, Farrar $16.99 (978-0-374-36260-7). 224pp. Rex, now 12, is unhappy that his family has moved across town yet determined to start middle school with his old friends, however difficult that may be; set in 1963 Ottawa against a backdrop of civil rights turmoil. ℮ Lexile 610L (Rev: BL 12/1/10; HB 11–12/10; SLJ 10/1/10)

1501 Yee, Lisa. *Warp Speed* (4–7). 2011, Scholastic $16.99 (978-0-545-12276-4). 214pp. Marley, a shy wallflower geek who loves Star Trek and suffers bullying, must chart a new course for himself when his speed and agility catch the coach's eye and Marley becomes a star athlete. Lexile HL620L (Rev: BL 2/15/11; HB 3–4/11; SLJ 5/11)

Adventure and Mystery

1502 Adam, Paul. *Max Cassidy: Escape from Shadow Island* (5–9). 2009, HarperCollins $16.99 (978-0-06-186323-3). 295pp. Max Cassidy, a British 14-year-old escape artist who still performs despite the fact that his mother is accused of murdering his father; sets out to prove her innocence in this fast-paced novel full of tension. (Rev: SLJ 4/10; VOYA 4/10)

1503 Aguiar, Nadia. *Secrets of Tamarind* (5–8). 2011, Feiwel & Friends $16.99 (978-0-312-38030-4). 384pp. The Nelson children first seen in *The Lost Island of Tamarind* (2008) return to the magical island to save it from environmental disaster in this blend of adventure and fantasy. ℮ Lexile 860L (Rev: BL 7/11; SLJ 9/1/11)

1504 Allison, Jennifer. *The Bones of the Holy* (5–8). Series: Gilda Joyce Psychic Investigator. 2011, Dutton $16.99 (978-052542212-9). 288pp. Teen sleuth Gilda uses her perceptive powers to investigate a spooky and sinister past her mother's prospective new husband seems to be hiding. ∩ (Rev: BL 5/1/11; SLJ 6/12)

1505 Andrews, Jan. *When Apples Grew Noses and White Horses Flew: Tales of Ti-Jean* (2–6). Illus. by Dušan Petričić. 2011, Groundwood $16.95 (978-0-88899-952-8). 70pp. Canadian folk hero Ti-Jean is featured in three comic tales of trickery, valor, and disguise. (Rev: HB 7–8/11; LMC 10/11; SLJ 8/11)

1506 Angleberger, Tom. *Horton Halfpott, or, The Fiendish Mystery of Smugwick Manor, or, The Loosening of M'Lady Luggertuck's Corset* (3–6). Illus. by author. 2011, Abrams $14.95 (978-0-8109-9715-8). 213pp. In 19th-century England a kitchen boy named Horton becomes embroiled in romance and mystery when a diamond is stolen at Smugwick Manor. ∩ ℮ (Rev: BL 5/1/11; LMC 8–9/11; SLJ 6/11)

1507 Arrigan, Mary. *Rabbit Girl* (4–6). 2011, Frances Lincoln paper $8.95 (978-184780156-2). 224pp.

A mysterious portrait ties Mallie Kelly to the era in which it was drawn — London during the blitz — in this quirky novel that brings past and present together. (Rev: BL 1/1/12; SLJ 2/12)

1508 Avi. *Murder at Midnight* (5–8). 2009, Scholastic $17.99 (978-0-545-08090-3). 272pp. In this compelling companion to *Midnight Magic* (2009) set in Italy in 1490, Mangus the magician and his young servant Fabrizio race against the clock as they strive to uncover a traitor. ∩ (Rev: BL 8/09; LMC 1–2/10; SLJ 10/09)

1509 Baccalario, Pierdomenico. *Star of Stone* (5–9). Trans. from Italian by Leah D. Janeczko. Series: Century Quartet. 2010, Random House $16.99 (978-0-375-85896-3); LB $19.99 (978-0-375-95896-0). 304pp. Harvey, Elettra, Mistral, and Sheng are led all around Manhattan by tricky clues left by an eccentric professor in this action-packed sequel to *Ring of Fire* (2009). Also use *City of Wind* (2011). ∩ ℮ (Rev: SLJ 11/1/10)

1510 Balliett, Blue. *The Danger Box* (5–7). 2010, Scholastic $16.99 (978-0-439-85209-8). 320pp. When isolated, myopic Zoomy, 12, receives a mysterious box of "treasures" from his alcoholic father, curious things begin to happen. ∩ ℮ Lexile 750L (Rev: BL 10/1/10; LMC 3–4/11; SLJ 9/1/10*)

1511 Bancks, Tristan. *Mac Slater Hunts the Cool* (5–8). 2010, Simon & Schuster $15.99 (978-1-4169-8574-7). 224pp. Is Mac truly cool? He feels like an outsider at his Australian school, but when he enters a contest to come up with the next cool trend, he gets a chance to prove that outsiders can be cool too. Lexile 690L (Rev: BL 4/1/10; LMC 8–9/10; SLJ 3/10)

1512 Bancks, Tristan. *Mac Slater vs. the City* (5–8). 2011, Simon & Schuster $15.99 (978-1-4169-8576-1). 192pp. Eighth-grader Mac and his friend Paul are excited to travel to New York City to compete in a Coolhunter competition but find more challenges than expected. (Rev: BLO 3/25/11; SLJ 4/11)

1513 Barnett, Mac. *The Case of the Case of Mistaken Identity* (4–6). Illus. by Adam Rex. Series: Brixton Brothers. 2009, Simon & Schuster $14.99 (978-1-4169-7815-2). 192pp. Twelve-year-old gumshoe Steve Brixton gets mixed up with a ring of undercover crime-fighting librarians as he hunts for an invaluable quilt in this funny series opener. ∩ Lexile 590L (Rev: BL 10/15/09; LMC 11–12/09; SLJ 3/10)

1514 Barnett, Mac. *The Ghostwriter Secret* (3–6). Illus. by Adam Rex. Series: Brixton Brothers. 2010, Simon & Schuster $14.99 (978-1-4169-7817-6). 240pp. Detective agency operator Steve Brixton, 12, becomes embroiled in a kidnapping scheme when he sets out in search of his hero, mystery author MacArthur Bart. ∩ ℮ Lexile 690L (Rev: SLJ 12/1/10)

1515 Barnett, Mac. *It Happened on a Train* (4–6). Illus. by Adam Rex. Series: Brixton Brothers. 2011, Simon & Schuster $15.99 (978-141697819-0). 288pp. Seventh-grader Steve Brixton's short-lived retirement from sleuthing is interrupted when he discovers a mystery on a train trip through California. (Rev: BL 11/1/11)

1516 Barrett, Tracy. *The Case That Time Forgot* (4–6). Series: Sherlock Files. 2010, Henry Holt $15.99 (978-0-8050-8046-9). 160pp. Xena and Xander, descendants of Sherlock himself, help a classmate called Karim to find an ancient Egyptian amulet in this story full of modern technology and old-fashioned codes and sleuthing. ⏺ ⅇ Lexile 700L (Rev: BL 5/1/10; SLJ 7/10)

1517 Beauregard, Lynda. *In Search of the Fog Zombie: A Mystery About Matter* (3–5). Illus. by Der-shing Helmer. Series: Summer Camp Science Mysteries. 2012, Lerner/Graphic Universe LB $29.27 (978-076135689-9); paper $6.95 (978-076138544-8). 48pp. Science and mystery are combined in this graphic novel set in a summer camp (with a rumored zombie) and including information about solids, liquids, gases, and so forth. ⅇ (Rev: BL 3/15/12; SLJ 5/1/12)

1518 Beil, Michael D. *The Mistaken Masterpiece* (5–8). Series: The Red Blazer Girls. 2011, Knopf $16.99 (978-0-375-86740-8); LB $19.99 (978-037596740-5). 320pp. The Red Blazer Girls are asked to investigate the ownership of a family heirloom, and discover more than they bargained for. ⏺ ⅇ (Rev: BL 5/1/11; SLJ 8/11)

1519 Beil, Michael D. *The Vanishing Violin* (5–8). Series: The Red Blazer Girls. 2010, Knopf $16.99 (978-0-375-86103-1); LB $19.99 (978-0-375-96103-8). 336pp. The four Red Blazer Girls — Sophie, Margaret, Becca, and Leigh Ann — must solve various violin-related mysteries at St. Veronica's School. ⏺ ⅇ (Rev: BL 7/10; SLJ 8/10)

1520 Bonk, John J. *Madhattan Mystery* (5–8). 2012, Walker $16.99 (978-080272349-9). 304pp. Twelve-year-old Lexi and her younger brother Kevin overhear details about stolen jewels while staying in New York City with their aunt; a wild chase through subway tunnels and parks ensues. ⅇ Lexile 790L (Rev: BL 5/1/12*; LMC 10/12; SLJ 5/1/12)

1521 Boyce, Frank Cottrell. *Chitty Chitty Bang Bang Flies Again* (3–6). Illus. by Joe Berger. 2012, Candlewick $15.99 (978-076365957-8). 192pp. In this funny sequel to the original Ian Fleming (1964) story, the 21st-century British Tooting family find themselves owning an aging camper van that suddenly sprouts wings and carries them off to adventure. ⅇ Lexile 710L (Rev: BL 2/1/12; LMC 8–9/12; SLJ 3/12*)

1522 Bransford, Nathan. *Jacob Wonderbar for President of the Universe* (4–6). Illus. by C. S. Jennings. 2012, Dial $15.99 (978-080373538-5). 224pp. Jacob Wonderbar's bid to be elected president of the universe meets various obstacles including dirty politics and threats to Earth's survival. (Rev: BL 3/15/12; SLJ 6/12)

1523 Brezenoff, Steve. *The Burglar Who Bit the Big Apple* (3–6). Illus. by C. B. Canga. Series: Field Trip

Mysteries. 2010, Stone Arch LB $23.99 (978-1-4342-2139-1); paper $5.95 (978-1-4342-2771-3). 88pp. Sixth-grade friends Cat, Sam, Egg, and Gum solve a satisfying mystery while on a class trip to New York City. Also use *The Zombie Who Visited New Orleans* (2010). Lexile 500L (Rev: SLJ 1/1/11)

1524 Brezenoff, Steve. *The Zoo with the Empty Cage* (3–6). Illus. by C. B. Canga. Series: Field Trip Mysteries. 2009, Stone Arch LB $23.99 (978-1-4342-1610-6). 88pp. Edward G. Garrison (Egg) and his friends in the Science Club search for the rare and endangered Island Foxes that have gone missing from the zoo. Also use *The Painting That Wasn't There* (2009). (Rev: LMC 1–2/10; SLJ 2/1/10)

1525 Broach, Elise. *Missing on Superstition Mountain* (3–5). Illus. by Antonio Caparo. Series: Superstition Mountain. 2011, Henry Holt $15.99 (978-0-8050-9047-5). 272pp. Fascinated by Superstition Mountain, three young brothers new to Arizona ignore their parents' warnings and investigate; the first volume in a series. (Rev: BL 5/1/11; SLJ 7/11)

1526 Broad, Michael. *Ghost Diamond!* (2–4). Illus. by author. Series: Agent Amelia. 2011, Darby Creek $22.60 (978-0-7613-8056-6); paper $5.95 (978-0-7613-8060-3). 143pp. Elementary school mastermind Amelia solves three short cases using ingenious gadgetry and always staying one step ahead of her too-curious mother. Also use *Zombie Cows!* (2011). ⅇ (Rev: LMC 3–4/12; SLJ 8/1/11)

1527 Buckley, Michael. *M Is for Mama's Boy* (4–7). Illus. by Ethen Beavers. Series: NERDS. 2010, Abrams $14.95 (978-0-8109-8986-3). 288pp. The 5th-grade NERDS team is back to deal with more outrageous behavior by supervillain Simon. ⏺ Lexile 780L (Rev: BL 9/15/10; LMC 1–2/11; SLJ 12/1/10)

1528 Buckley, Michael. *NERDS: National Espionage, Rescue, and Defense Society* (4–7). Illus. by Ethen Beavers. Series: NERDS. 2009, Abrams $14.95 (978-0-8109-4324-7). 306pp. Former cool kid Jackson Jones now finds himself among the school's nerd population, but he soon learns that the unassuming geeks whom he so recently delighted in tormenting are actually members of a top-secret spy ring that is attempting to stop the insidious Dr. Jigsaw from destroying the world. The third volume in the series is *The Cheerleaders of Doom* (2011). ⏺ Lexile 760L (Rev: BL 10/15/09; LMC 1–2/11; SLJ 12/09)

1529 Butler, Dori Hillestad. *The Case of the Fire Alarm* (2–4). Illus. by Jeremy Tugeau. Series: The Buddy Files. 2010, Whitman $14.99 (978-080750913-5); paper $4.99 (978-080750935-7). 128pp. Buddy happily takes a break from being a therapy dog to solve a mystery in this satisfying story. Also use *The Case of the Missing Family* (2010). ⅇ Lexile 480L (Rev: BL 1/1–15/11)

1530 Butler, Dori Hillestad. *The Case of the Library Monster* (1–3). Illus. by Jeremy Tugeau. Series: The

Buddy Files. 2011, Whitman $14.99 (978-080750914-2). 128pp. Buddy the dog detective decides to investigate the case of the blue skink that's been skulking around the school library. (Rev: BLO 3/25/11)

1531 Butler, Dori Hillestad. *The Case of the Lost Boy* (1–3). Illus. by Jeremy Tugeau. Series: The Buddy Files. 2010, Whitman $14.99 (978-0-8075-0910-4). 128pp. After being adopted from the dog pound, golden retriever Buddy — formerly known as King — works to solve the mystery of why his old family gave him up. ℮ Lexile 450L (Rev: BL 1/1/10; LMC 5–6/10; SLJ 2/1/10)

1532 Cadenhead, MacKenzie. *Sally's Bones* (4–6). Illus. by T. S. Spookytooth. 2011, Sourcebooks paper $6.99 (978-1-4022-5943-2). 176pp. Sally Simplesmith, 11 and still mourning for her mother, is adopted by a lovable skeleton dog that she must then protect from false accusations. (Rev: BL 9/15/11; SLJ 12/1/11)

1533 Carman, Patrick. *Floors* (4–7). 2011, Scholastic $16.99 (978-0-545-25519-6). 272pp. Charged with taking care of the magical Whippet Hotel, Leo and his dad must protect the place from a foreboding future hinted at by mysterious clues. ℮ Lexile 870L (Rev: BL 10/15/11; SLJ 11/1/11)

1534 Chari, Sheela. *Vanished* (4–7). 2011, Hyperion/Disney $16.99 (978-1-4231-3163-2). 240pp. East Indian American Neela, 11, gets embroiled in a mystery when her grandmother's prized veena (a traditional Indian instrument) is stolen. (Rev: BL 9/1/11; SLJ 12/1/11)

1535 Cheshire, Simon. *Treasure of Dead Man's Lane and Other Case Files* (4–7). Illus. by R. W. Alley. Series: Saxby Smart, Private Detective. 2010, Roaring Brook $16.99 (978-159643475-2). 208pp. Schoolboy sleuth Saxby solves three challenging mysteries with the help of his sidekicks in this book that underlines the clues. ℮ (Rev: BL 5/15/10*; SLJ 7/10)

1536 Child, Lauren. *Ruby Redfort: Look into My Eyes* (5–8). Illus. 2012, Candlewick $16.99 (978-076365120-6). 400pp. Brilliant 13-year-old Ruby is hired to crack codes for a secret crime-fighting organization in this multilayered, fast-paced novel. ⌒ ℮ Lexile 800L (Rev: BL 2/15/12; LMC 8–9/12; SLJ 4/12; VOYA 4/12)

1537 Clements, Andrew. *Fear Itself* (4–6). Illus. by Adam Stower. Series: Benjamin Pratt and the Keepers of the School. 2011, Atheneum $14.99 (978-141693887-3). 224pp. In this followup to 2010's *We the Children*, sleuths Ben and Jill befriend a retired janitor and solve some maritime clues that help them in their desperate fight to save their school. ⌒ ℮ Lexile 800L (Rev: BL 9/15/10; SLJ 9/1/10)

1538 Clements, Andrew. *We the Children* (4–6). Illus. by Adam Stower. Series: Benjamin Pratt and the Keepers of the School. 2010, Atheneum $14.99 (978-141693886-6). 160pp. Sixth-grader Benjamin is adjusting to his parents' separation when he and his friend Jill uncover a string of clues in their quest to save their historic school from nefarious developers. (Rev: BL 3/15/10; HB 5–6/10; SLJ 5/10)

1539 Collard, Sneed B. *The Governor's Dog Is Missing* (4–7). Series: Slate Stephens Mysteries. 2011, Bucking Horse $16 (978-098444601-8). 176pp. Slate and Daphne, both 12, investigate the disappearance of Cat, the governor of Minnesota's dog. (Rev: BL 5/1/11; SLJ 6/11)

1540 Collard, Sneed B. *Hangman's Gold* (4–7). Series: Slate Stephens Mysteries. 2011, Bucking Horse $16 (978-098444602-5). 208pp. Crime-solving duo Slate and Daphne return with a Wild West mystery involving cowboy art and missing gold. (Rev: BL 1/1/12; SLJ 1/12)

1541 Conly, Jane Leslie. *Murder Afloat* (5–8). 2010, Hyperion/Disney $17.99 (978-142310416-2). 176pp. In the 1870s privileged 14-year-old Benjamin is kidnapped and put to work aboard an oyster ship in this suspenseful high seas adventure. (Rev: BL 12/1/10; HB 11–12/10; LMC 1–2/11; SLJ 3/1/11)

1542 Corriveau, Art. *Thirteen Hangmen* (5–7). 2012, Abrams $16.95 (978-141970159-7). 352pp. Transported during the night on his 13th birthday, Tony finds himself in the company of 13-year-old boys from throughout Boston's history, tasked with solving a dynamic mystery. (Rev: BL 5/1/12; LMC 11–12/12; SLJ 9/12)

1543 Coven, Wanda. *Heidi Heckelbeck Has a Secret* (1–3). Illus. by Priscilla Burris. 2012, Simon & Schuster $14.99 (978-144244087-6); paper $4.99 (978-144243565-0). 128pp. After being home-schooled, Heidi starts 2nd grade at a public school and meets with trouble on her very first day; for new chapter-book readers. (Rev: BL 2/15/12; SLJ 6/1/12)

1544 Cox, Judy. *The Case of the Purloined Professor* (4–7). Illus. by Omar Rayyan. 2009, Marshall Cavendish $16.99 (978-076145544-8). 256pp. Rat brothers Ishbu and Frederick team up to find a missing scientist in this adventure-filled story. Lexile 710L (Rev: BL 9/15/09; LMC 11–12/09; SLJ 11/09)

1545 Crocker, Carter. *Last of the Gullivers* (5–7). 2012, Philomel $16.99 (978-039924231-1). 240pp. Twelve-year-old orphan Michael is a boy headed for trouble until he finds purpose when he discovers a village full of Lilliputians and is entrusted with their care. ℮ Lexile 750L (Rev: BL 2/1/12; HB 9–10/12; SLJ 2/12)

1546 Cronin, Doreen. *The Trouble with Chickens* (3–5). Illus. by Kevin Cornell. Series: J. J. Tully Mysteries. 2011, HarperCollins $14.99 (978-0-06-121532-2); LB $15.89 (978-0-06-121533-9). 128pp. J. J. Tully, retired search-and-rescue dog, undertakes a search for two missing chickens and meets unexpected challenges in this funny whodunit. ℮ Lexile 570L (Rev: BL 2/1/11; HB 3–4/11; SLJ 2/1/11)

1547 Doyle, Bill, and David Borgenicht. *Everest* (4–8). Illus. by Yancey Labat. Series: Worst-Case Scenario Ultimate Adventure. 2011, Chronicle $12.99 (978-0-8118-7123-5). 204pp. Readers are invited to participate in the decision-making process in this choose-your-own-adventure style story of a team trying to summit Mount Everest. ℮ (Rev: SLJ 6/11)

1548 Eames, Brian. *The Dagger Quick* (4–7). 2011, Simon & Schuster $15.99 (978-1-4424-2311-4). 320pp. Kitto, a 12-year-old with a clubfoot, finds himself setting out to sea with his long-lost pirate uncle in this fast-paced adventure set in the 17th century. ℮ Lexile 690L (Rev: LMC 11–12/11; SLJ 8/11)

1549 Elish, Dan. *The School for the Insanely Gifted* (4–6). 2011, HarperCollins $15.99 (978-0-06-113873-7). 304pp. Eleven-year-old Daphna, student at a school for geniuses, sets off with her friends to find her missing mother. (Rev: BL 9/15/11; SLJ 8/11)

1550 Evans, Lissa. *Horten's Miraculous Mechanisms* (4–7). 2012, Sterling $14.95 (978-140279806-1). 272pp. Diminutive 10-year-old Stuart Horten has moved with his family to his father's hometown, and soon discovers mysterious old coins that offer clues to the disappearance long ago of his great-uncle Tony, a magician. (Rev: BL 4/1/12)

1551 Feinstein, John. *Change-Up: Mystery at the World Series* (5–8). 2009, Knopf $16.99 (978-0-375-85636-5); LB $19.99 (978-0-375-95636-2). 336pp. What is Nationals pitcher Norbert Doyle hiding? Teen sports reporters Stevie and Susan Carol investigate. ⌢ Lexile 770L (Rev: BL 9/1/09; SLJ 9/09; VOYA 6/09)

1552 Frazier, Angie. *The Mastermind Plot* (4–7). 2012, Scholastic $16.99 (978-054520864-2). 240pp. Zanna hopes to get closer to her detective uncle while in Boston, and fulfill her dream of becoming a real sleuth in this mystery set in 1904; a sequel to *The Midnight Tunnel* (2011). (Rev: BL 5/1/12; SLJ 2/12)

1553 Frazier, Angie. *The Midnight Tunnel* (4–7). 2011, Scholastic $16.99 (978-0-545-20862-8). 288pp. In New Brunswick at the turn of the 20th century, 11-year-old Suzanna (Zanna) Snow prefers sleuthing to working at her family's inn; however, her famous detective uncle's efforts to solve a mysterious disappearance disappoint her. ℮ Lexile 800L (Rev: BL 2/1/11; LMC 5–6/11; SLJ 4/11)

1554 Freeman, Martha. *The Case of the Diamond Dog Collar* (2–4). Series: First Kids Mystery. 2011, Holiday House $16.95 (978-082342337-8). 144pp. The president's dog has a fancy new collar and one of the gems is missing. Could it be a diamond? First Daughters Cammie, 10, and Tessa, 7, investigate. Lexile 630L (Rev: BL 10/15/11; LMC 3–4/12)

1555 Freeman, Martha. *The Case of the Rock 'n' Roll Dog* (2–4). Series: First Kids Mystery. 2010, Holiday House $16.95 (978-0-8234-2267-8). 128pp. First Daughter Cammie, 10, and her younger sister Tessa investigate when items go missing from the White House. Lexile 580L (Rev: BL 11/1/10; SLJ 11/1/10)

1556 Freeman, Martha. *The Case of the Ruby Slippers* (2–4). Series: First Kids Mystery. 2012, Holiday House $16.95 (978-082342409-2). 124pp. First daughters Tessa and Cammie swing into action when Dorothy's real ruby slippers disappear from the Smithsonian. (Rev: BL 5/1/12; SLJ 5/1/12)

1557 Freeman, Martha. *Who Stole Grandma's Million-Dollar Pumpkin Pie?* (3–6). Series: Chickadee Court Mystery. 2009, Holiday House $16.95 (978-0-8234-2215-9). 209pp. Alex and Yasmeen, 11, are hot on the trail of their grandma's secret, prizewinning pumpkin pie recipe in this lively mystery. Lexile 760L (Rev: SLJ 1/1/10)

1558 Garretson, Dee. *Wildfire Run* (4–7). Series: Danger's Edge. 2010, HarperCollins $16.99 (978-006195347-7). 272pp. In this action-packed story, the president's son and two friends are marooned at Camp David when a series of natural disasters overwhelms the security system. (Rev: BL 10/15/10; SLJ 9/1/10)

1559 Gibbs, Stuart. *Belly Up* (5–7). 2010, Simon & Schuster $15.99 (978-1-4169-8731-4). 304pp. Who is responsible for the death of the zoo's star hippo? Twelve-year-old Teddy and Summer, daughter of the zoo owner, investigate in this fast-paced story full of humor and animal facts. ℮ Lexile 820L (Rev: BL 5/1/10; LMC 10/10; SLJ 5/10)

1560 Gibbs, Stuart. *Spy School* (4–7). 2012, Simon & Schuster $15.99 (978-144242182-0). 304pp. Twelve-year-old Ben achieves his lifelong wish when he leaves his middle school for the CIA's secretive Academy of Espionage — only to find that a life of spying isn't all it's cracked up to be. (Rev: BL 3/15/12; SLJ 2/12)

1561 Giles, Stephen M. *The Death (and Further Adventures) of Silas Winterbottom* (5–7). Series: The Death (and Further Adventures) of Silas Winterbottom. 2010, Sourcebooks $12.99 (978-1-4022-4090-4). 240pp. When rich, elderly Uncle Silas invites three 12-year-old prospective heirs to his estate, the three very different cousins — Adele, Milo, and Isabella — become closer as they recognize that his intentions are far from benign. ℮ Lexile 830L (Rev: BL 9/15/10; LMC 11–12/10)

1562 Golding, Julia. *Cat O'Nine Tails* (5–8). Series: Cat Royal Adventures. 2009, Roaring Brook $16.99 (978-159643445-5). 400pp. Cat and her friends are kidnapped and pressed into service in the British Navy and must use guile and courage to survive as they travel to the New World, where Cat becomes engaged to a Creek Indian. Lexile 760L (Rev: BL 11/1/09; SLJ 11/09; VOYA 2/10)

1563 Gordon, Amy. *Twenty Gold Falcons* (4–7). 2010, Holiday House $16.95 (978-0-8234-2252-4). 216pp. Aiden's finding it hard to adjust to her new life in the city of Gloria until she learns about 20 missing gold coins and sets out to find them with some newly made friends. Lexile 710L (Rev: BL 5/1/10; LMC 11–12/10; SLJ 8/10)

1564 Grabenstein, Chris. *The Smoky Corridor* (5–8). Series: Haunted Places Mystery. 2010, Random House $16.99 (978-0-375-86511-4); LB $19.99 (978-0-375-96511-1). 336pp. Zach Jennings, the boy who can communicate with ghosts, starts 6th grade at a new school and discovers that its many challenges include a brain-eating zombie and a host of ghosts guarding a cemetery. e Lexile 690L (Rev: BLO 12/1/10; SLJ 7/10)

1565 Grant, Katy. *Hide and Seek* (5–8). 2010, Peachtree $15.95 (978-1-56145542-3). 227pp. Chase, 14, enjoys geocaching (using a GPS to locate hidden items) and exploring in the Arizona mountains with his dog; one day he stumbles on two abducted boys and becomes embroiled in their plight. Lexile 700L (Rev: BL 10/1/10; LMC 11–12/10; SLJ 9/1/10)

1566 Graves, Keith. *The Orphan of Awkward Falls* (5–8). Illus. by author. 2011, Chronicle $16.99 (978-0-8118-7814-2). 338pp. When 12-year-old Josephine Cravitz and her family move to Awkward Falls, she becomes the target of a mad cannibal escaped from the town's Asylum for the Dangerously Insane; a complex, suspenseful story with light humor and horror. (Rev: BLO 11/15/11; LMC 1–2/12; SLJ 10/1/11)

1567 Gustafson, Scott. *Eddie: The Lost Youth of Edgar Allan Poe* (3–6). Illus. by author. 2011, Simon & Schuster $15.99 (978-1-4169-9764-1). 208pp. Gustafson imagines an episode in young Poe's childhood, in which he relies on the help of animals — including a raven — to clear his name after being falsely accused of property destruction. (Rev: BL 9/1/11; SLJ 12/1/11)

1568 Gutman, Dan. *Mission Unstoppable* (5–8). Illus. Series: The Genius Files. 2011, HarperCollins $16.99 (978-0-06-182764-8); LB $17.89 (978-0-06-182765-5). 256pp. Twin geniuses Coke and Pepsi McDonald, 12, are pursued by nefarious government agents while on a cross-country road trip with their parents. e (Rev: BL 12/1/10; LMC 8–9/11; SLJ 3/1/11)

1569 Hahn, Mary Downing. *Closed for the Season: A Mystery Story* (5–8). 2009, Clarion $16 (978-0-547-08451-0). 182pp. Thirteen-year-old Logan's search for a murderer leads him and his new friend Arthur to an eerie, abandoned amusement park in this well-executed mystery. ∩ e Lexile 670L (Rev: LMC 10/09; SLJ 9/09; VOYA 10/09)

1570 Hahn, Mary Downing. *The Ghost of Crutchfield Hall* (4–7). 2010, Clarion $17 (978-0-547-38560-0). 160pp. Florence goes to live at her great-aunt's house, realizing too late that the house is haunted by the malicious ghost of her cousin Sophia, who died suspiciously. ∩ e Lexile 680L (Rev: BL 10/1/10; LMC 1–2/11; SLJ 8/10)

1571 Harvey, Jacqueline. *Alice-Miranda at School* (2–4). 2011, Delacorte $14.99 (978-0-385-73993-1); LB $17.99 (978-0-385-90811-5). 272pp. Alice-Miranda, seven and a quarter years old, starts at her posh new prep school and immediately sets about solving all manner of mysteries large and small. (Rev: LMC 10/11; SLJ 4/11)

1572 Hiaasen, Carl. *Scat* (5–8). 2009, Knopf $16.99 (978-037583486-8); LB $19.99 (978-037593486-5). 384pp. Nick and Marta team up to solve the real cause of their high school biology teacher's disappearance in this well-paced, conservation-themed read set in the Florida Everglades. ∩ Lexile 810L (Rev: BL 11/1/08; HB 1–2/09; SLJ 1/1/09*)

1573 Higgins, Jack, and Justin Richards. *Death Run* (5–8). Series: Rich and Jade. 2008, Putnam $16.99 (978-039925081-1). 272pp. Teenage twins Rich and Jade travel around the world with their secret-agent dad in this action-packed, fast-paced sequel to 2007's *Sure Fire*. e Lexile HL660L (Rev: BL 9/1/08; SLJ 12/08; VOYA 8/08)

1574 Higgins, Jack, and Justin Richards. *First Strike* (5–8). Series: Rich and Jade. 2010, Putnam $16.99 (978-039925240-2). 240pp. When two disparate sets of villains invade the White House with designs on stealing nuclear launch codes, the British twins Rich and Jade and their secret-agent father again save the day. (Rev: BLO 6/10; VOYA 8/10)

1575 Higgins, Jack, and Justin Richards. *Sharp Shot* (5–8). Series: Rich and Jade. 2009, Putnam $16.99 (978-0-399-25239-6). 240pp. In this action-packed volume, the third in a series, twins Jade and Rich find themselves on a dangerous mission to thwart an evil plot after they're attacked by one of their secret agent dad's old enemies. Lexile HL730L (Rev: BLO 11/1/09; SLJ 3/10)

1576 Higgins, Simon. *Moonshadow: Rise of the Ninja* (4–7). 2010, Little, Brown $15.99 (978-0-316-05531-4). 336pp. Moonshadow is forced to test his skills as a ninja when Silver Wolf's warriors attack in this story set in Japan in the time of the samurai. Lexile 840L (Rev: BL 6/10; LMC 8–9/10; SLJ 8/10)

1577 Horowitz, Anthony. *The Greek Who Stole Christmas* (4–7). Series: A Diamond Brothers Mystery. 2008, Penguin paper $7.99 (978-014240375-4). 144pp. Amid the Christmas noise and bustle, Diamond brothers Nick and Tim bumble their way through protecting a dazzling young pop star who has received death threats. e Lexile 630L (Rev: BL 11/1/08; SLJ 8/09)

1578 Horvath, Polly. *Mr. and Mrs. Bunny — Detectives Extraordinaire!* (3–6). Illus. by Sophie Blackall. 2012, Random House $16.99 (978-037586755-2); LB $19.99 (978-037596755-9). 256pp. When Madeline's hopelessly anachronistic parents go missing, the dutiful 5th-grader who can communicate with animals enlists the help of neighboring detectives Mr. and Mrs. Bunny to bring them home. ⌒ **e** Lexile 730L (Rev: BL 2/15/12*; HB 1–2/12; LMC 5–6/12; SLJ 2/12)

1579 Jackson, Melanie. *The Big Dip* (4–7). 2009, Orca paper $9.95 (978-1-55469-178-4). 109pp. Fifteen-year-old Joe's little sister is kidnapped soon after Joe witnessed a man shot to death at an amusement park; Joe investigates in this suspenseful novel suitable for reluctant readers. (Rev: BL 2/1/10; LMC 5–6/10; SLJ 11/09)

1580 Jacobson, Jennifer Richard. *Small as an Elephant* (4–7). 2011, Candlewick $15.99 (978-0-7636-4155-9). 288pp. Abandoned in Maine by his bipolar mother, 11-year-old Jack sets out for his Boston home determined to escape detection by adults. ⌒ **e** Lexile 790L (Rev: BL 6/1/11; HB 3–4/11; SLJ 4/11; VOYA 2/11)

1581 Kelly, Katy. *Melonhead and the Undercover Operation* (3–5). Illus. by Gillian Johnson. 2011, Delacorte $12.99 (978-0-385-73659-6); LB $15.99 (978-0-385-90618-0). 256pp. Melonhead and his fellow FBI Junior Special Agent Sam investigate whether a neighbor is one of the Ten Most Wanted criminals. (Rev: BL 11/1/11; SLJ 11/1/11)

1582 Kennedy, Emma. *Wilma Tenderfoot: The Case of the Frozen Hearts* (4–7). 2011, Dial $16.99 (978-080373540-8). 352pp. Wilma Tenderfoot, a 10-year-old orphan servant, finally gets the chance to try her sleuthing skills when she meets a famous detective. **e** (Rev: BL 11/15/11; LMC 1–2/12)

1583 Klise, Kate. *Till Death Do Us Bark* (3–6). Illus. by M. Sarah Klise. Series: 43 Old Cemetery Road. 2011, Harcourt $15 (978-054740036-5). 144pp. In this third installment in the humorous mystery series, Seymour's newly adopted, barking wolfhound leads him into a puzzle involving an inheritance. **e** Lexile 710L (Rev: BL 1/1–15/11)

1584 Korman, Gordon. *Framed* (5–7). Series: Swindle. 2010, Scholastic $16.99 (978-0-545-17849-5). 240pp. A Super Bowl ring has gone missing and Griffin's retainer is found in its place. He and his friends try to clear his name in this follow-up to *Swindle* (2008) and *Zoobreak* (2009). ⌒ Lexile 730L (Rev: LMC 11–12/10; SLJ 9/1/10)

1585 Korman, Gordon. *Zoobreak* (4–7). 2009, Scholastic $16.99 (978-054512499-7). 240pp. When Savannah finds her missing pet monkey Cleo at a floating animal zoo, she and her friends plan a rescue mission; a sequel to *Swindle* (2008). ⌒ **e** Lexile 700L (Rev: BL 11/1/09; LMC 11–12/09; SLJ 11/09; VOYA 10/09)

1586 Krieg, Jim. *Griff Carver, Hallway Patrol* (4–7). 2010, Penguin $15.99 (978-1-59514-276-4). 240pp. Thirteen-year-old Griff Carver fights crime as part of the Safety Patrol at Rampart Middle School, disciplining everyone from the principal on down in this humorous spoof of a police procedural that includes a hall-

pass counterfeiting ring. ⌒ **e** Lexile 710L (Rev: BL 5/1/10*; HB 5–6/10; LMC 3–4/10; SLJ 3/10)

1587 Kuhlman, Evan. *Brother from a Box* (4–6). Illus. by Iacopo Bruno. 2012, Atheneum $16.99 (978-144242658-0). 304pp. Matthew's computer-genius father creates a robotic twin brother for him that proves such a success that unsavory characters seek to steal him; this multilayered story is full of action and humor. **e** (Rev: BLO 4/1/12; LMC 8–9/12; SLJ 6/12)

1588 Lacey, Josh. *Island of Thieves* (4–7). 2012, Houghton Mifflin $15.99 (978-054776327-9). 240pp. Tom and his shifty Uncle Harvey hunt for lost treasure in Peru and find themselves almost immediately in danger in this exciting, fast-paced story. ⌒ **e** Lexile 640L (Rev: BL 5/1/12*; LMC 8–9/12; SLJ 6/12)

1589 LaFevers, R. L. *The Basilisk's Lair* (2–5). Illus. by Kelly Murphy. Series: Nathaniel Fludd, Beastologist. 2010, Houghton Mifflin $15 (978-0-547-23867-8). 160pp. Young Nate's beastology skills are tested when he goes off to West Africa with his Aunt Phil in pursuit of a highly dangerous escaped basilisk. (Rev: BL 5/15/10; SLJ 7/1/10)

1590 Lafevers, R. L. *The Flight of the Phoenix* (2–5). Illus. by Kelly Murphy. Series: Nathaniel Fludd, Beastologist. 2009, Houghton Mifflin $16 (978-0-547-23865-4). 144pp. Nathaniel's parents are declared lost at sea in 1926 and he goes to live with his father's cousin, finding himself in training as a beastologist. ⌒ (Rev: BL 10/1/09; LMC 1–2/10; SLJ 9/1/09)

1591 LaFevers, R. L. *Theodosia and the Eyes of Horus* (5–8). Illus. by Yoko Tanaka. Series: Theodosia. 2010, Houghton Mifflin $16 (978-0-547-22592-0). 384pp. Supernaturally talented Theodosia, 11, copes with her difficult family while using her knowledge of Egyptian lore to stymie the evil powers of the Arcane Order of the Black Sun. (Rev: BLO 2/1/10; SLJ 7/10)

1592 LaFevers, R. L. *Theodosia and the Last Pharaoh* (5–8). Illus. by Yoko Tanaka. Series: Theodosia. 2011, Houghton Mifflin $16.99 (978-054739018-5). 400pp. Endeavoring to return a priceless Egyptian artifact, 11-year-old Theodosia and her cat Isis arouse interest as soon as they arrive in Cairo. (Rev: BL 5/1/11)

1593 LaFevers, R. L. *Theodosia and the Staff of Osiris* (5–8). Series: Theodosia. 2008, Houghton Mifflin $16 (978-061892764-7). 400pp. Brainy 11-year-old Theodosia solves the puzzles of misplaced mummies and ancient curses — all the while coping with a conniving grandmother and a father in prison — in this witty first-person tale set in Edwardian England. ⌒ **e** Lexile 750L (Rev: BL 11/15/08; SLJ 12/08)

1594 LaFevers, R. L. *The Unicorn's Tale* (2–5). Illus. by Kelly Murphy. Series: Nathaniel Fludd, Beastologist. 2011, Houghton Mifflin $14.99 (978-054748277-4). 160pp. Nate and Aunt Phil nurse a sick unicorn and continue the search for information about Nate's parents. Lexile 730L (Rev: BL 4/1/11)

1595 Lawrence, Caroline. *The Case of the Deadly Desperados* (4–6). Series: Western Mysteries. 2012, Putnam $16.99 (978-039925633-2). 272pp. In 1862 Nevada Territory 12-year-old Pinky Pinkerton finds his foster parents scalped in their cabin, and flees to the silver mining town of Virginia City pursued by a trio of baddies who want a mysterious legacy from his father. ∩ e (Rev: BL 2/15/12*; HB 5–6/12; SLJ 3/12; VOYA 4/12)

1596 Leach, Sara. *Count Me In* (4–6). 2011, Orca paper $9.95 (978-1-55469-404-4). 164pp. Tabitha, her three hateful cousins, and her aunt find themselves stranded in the woods with a hungry bear and a raging river in this survival story suitable for reluctant readers. e Lexile 560L (Rev: SLJ 11/1/11)

1597 Levy, Elizabeth. *Diamonds and Danger: A Mystery at Sea* (4–6). Illus. by Mordicai Gerstein. 2010, Roaring Brook $16.99 (978-159643462-2). 160pp. Eleven-year-old mystery lover Philippa and her parents live on a large cruise ship, and Philippa investigates questions surrounding the new captain and his son Philip; includes lots of details of life at sea. (Rev: BL 11/1/10; LMC 1–2/11; SLJ 11/1/10)

1598 Lewman, David. *The Case of the Mystery Meat Loaf* (4–7). Series: Club CSI. 2012, Simon & Schuster $15.99 (978-144244646-5); paper $5.99 (978-144243394-6). 160pp. When the whole school swim team comes down with food poisoning, three middle-grade sleuths kick into action to figure out the cause and the culprit. e (Rev: BLO 4/1/12; SLJ 4/12)

1599 London, C. Alexander. *We Are Not Eaten by Yaks* (5–8). Series: An Accidental Adventure. 2011, Philomel $12.99 (978-0-399-25487-1). 240pp. When their mother goes missing, 11-year-old twins Oliver and Celia journey with their father to Tibet, where they encounter many dangerous adventures. ∩ Lexile 760L (Rev: BL 1/1–15/11; SLJ 4/11)

1600 McCaughrean, Geraldine. *The Death-Defying Pepper Roux* (5–8). 2010, HarperCollins LB $17.89 (978-0-06-183666-4). 336pp. Believing his aunt's prediction that he will die at the age of 14, young Pepper Roux first runs away to sea and then has a series of exciting adventures; set in France. ∩ Lexile 920L (Rev: BL 11/1/09*; HB 1–2/10; LMC 5–6/10; SLJ 1/10)

1601 MacDonald, Bailey. *The Secret of the Sealed Room: A Mystery of Young Benjamin Franklin* (5–8). 2010, Simon & Schuster $16.99 (978-1-4169-9760-3). 208pp. A young Benjamin Franklin helps 14-year-old Patience, a runaway indentured servant who is suspected of murder. e Lexile 1050L (Rev: BL 12/1/10; SLJ 1/1/11)

1602 McDonald, Megan. *Judy Moody, Girl Detective* (3–5). Illus. by Peter H. Reynolds. 2010, Candlewick $15.99 (978-0-7636-3450-6). 192pp. Ardent Nancy Drew fan Judy Moody, a 3rd-grader, investigates the mystery of the missing police dog. ∩ e Lexile 570L (Rev: BL 9/1/10; SLJ 8/1/10)

1603 Maddox, Jake. *Blizzard!* (5–9). Illus. by Sean Tiffany. Series: A Jake Maddox Sports Story. 2009, Stone Arch LB $23.99 (978-1-4342-1206-1). 72pp. Two teen boys are on their way to an awards dinner when a catastrophic blizzard challenges their survival skills; suitable for reluctant readers, this easy-reading novel includes large black-and-white illustrations. (Rev: SLJ 6/1/09)

1604 Maddox, Jake. *Shipwreck!* (5–9). Illus. by Sean Tiffany. Series: A Jake Maddox Sports Story. 2009, Stone Arch LB $23.99 (978-1-4342-1207-8). 72pp. When their whale-watching boat sinks, three teens must use their wits to survive sweltering heat, storms, and even a shark attack; suitable for reluctant readers, this easy-reading novel includes large black-and-white illustrations. (Rev: SLJ 6/1/09)

1605 Maddox, Jake, and Lisa Trumbauer. *Kart Crash* (4–7). Illus. by Sean Tiffany. Series: A Jake Maddox Sports Story. 2008, Stone Arch $16.95 (978-143420777-7). 72pp. Austin learns the value of teamwork and determination in this fast-paced tale set on the go-kart track. Lexile 470L (Rev: BL 11/15/08)

1606 Malaghan, Michael. *Greek Ransom* (4–7). 2010, Andersen paper $9.99 (978-1-84270-786-9). 272pp. When their archaeologist parents are kidnapped on a Greek island, Nick and Callie must rescue them in an action-packed adventure that includes hidden treasure, exciting chases, and even an earthquake and a monster. (Rev: BL 4/15/10; SLJ 2/10)

1607 Margolin, Phillip, and Ami Margolin Rome. *Vanishing Acts* (4–7). 2011, HarperCollins $16.99 (978-006188556-3). 176pp. Nancy Drew protégée Madison Kincaid, 12, solves two missing-person cases — one in collaboration with her attorney father — while coping with junior high in Portland, Oregon. (Rev: BL 5/1/11; SLJ 2/12)

1608 Margolis, Leslie. *Girl's Best Friend* (5–8). Series: Maggie Brooklyn Mystery. 2010, Bloomsbury $14.99 (978-1-59990-525-9). 272pp. Twelve-year-old Maggie, a Nancy Drew fan, solves the mystery of disappearing dogs in Park Slope, Brooklyn, and then tackles missing money in this lighthearted novel. e Lexile 620L (Rev: HB 9–10/10; LMC 10/10; SLJ 12/1/10)

1609 Mass, Wendy. *The Candymakers* (4–6). 2010, Little, Brown $16.99 (978-0-316-00258-5). 464pp. Four children gather at a candy factory in a contest to create a new candy sensation in this character-driven mystery with echoes of *Charlie and the Chocolate Factory*. ∩ e Lexile 740L (Rev: BL 11/15/10; HB 11–12/10; SLJ 11/1/10)

1610 Milway, Alex. *The Curse of Mousebeard* (4–7). Series: Mousehunter Trilogy. 2010, Little, Brown $15.99 (978-0-316-07744-6). 368pp. In this followup to 2009's *The Mousehunter*, Emiline and her friends find themselves in the lost land of mice known as Norgammon as they seek a way to free Mousebeard from his curse. **e** (Rev: BLO 5/15/10; SLJ 6/10)

1611 Mitchelhill, Barbara. *Storm Runners* (4–8). 2008, Andersen paper $9.95 (978-184270640-4). 217pp. In this thrilling read, global warming turns out to be a conspiracy masterminded by villains, and it's up to 10-year-old Ally and her older sister to save the next city on the bad guys' "hit list"— Edinburgh, Scotland. Lexile 630L (Rev: BL 11/1/08)

1612 Mone, Gregory. *Fish* (3–5). 2010, Scholastic $16.99 (978-0-545-11632-9). 256pp. A young boy named Fish reluctantly trades his Irish farm life for a trip aboard a pirate ship and becomes embroiled in adventure and mystery. (Rev: BL 7/10; LMC 11–12/10; SLJ 9/1/10)

1613 Montgomery, Lewis B. *The Case of the Diamonds in the Desk* (1–3). Illus. by Amy Wummer. Series: Milo and Jazz Mysteries. 2012, Kane LB $22.60 (978-157565392-1); paper $6.95 (978-157565391-4). 96pp. Milo finds diamonds in his school desk, and he and Jazz swing into investigative mode. **e** (Rev: BL 2/15/12)

1614 Montgomery, Lewis B. *The Case of the Missing Moose* (2–4). Illus. by Amy Wummer. Series: Milo and Jazz Mysteries. 2011, Kane $22.60 (978-157565331-0); paper $6.95 (978-157565322-8). 96pp. Away at summer camp, Milo is able to solve a sports mystery with the help of Jazz, who is staying at a girls' camp on the same lake and shows up in the nick of time. Also use *The Case of the July 4th Jinx* (2010). (Rev: BL 5/1/11)

1615 Moodie, Craig. *Into the Trap* (4–8). 2011, Roaring Brook $15.99 (978-1-59643-585-8). 208pp. An action-packed story set off the coast of Maine and featuring 12-year-old Eddie, who enlists a summer visitor to help in catching the person who has been stealing his family's lobsters. **e** Lexile 600L (Rev: BL 7/11; SLJ 8/11)

1616 Moulton, Erin E. *Flutter: The Story of Four Sisters and One Incredible Journey* (4–7). 2011, Philomel $16.99 (978-0-399-25515-1). 208pp. Guided by Vermont folklore, Maple, 9, and her sister Dawn undertake a daring trek into the heart of the mountains to gather water from a mysterious well, hoping to save their premature baby sister's life. (Rev: BLO 5/1/11; SLJ 7/11)

1617 Muller, Rachel Dunstan. *Squeeze* (5–8). 2010, Orca paper $9.95 (978-1-55469-324-5). 166pp. Four teens embark on a caving expedition with disastrous results in this suspenseful story full of betrayal and teen drama. **e** Lexile HL640L (Rev: BL 11/1/10; SLJ 10/1/10)

1618 Newsome, Richard. *The Billionaire's Curse* (4–6). Illus. by Jonny Duddle. Series: The Archer Legacy. 2010, HarperCollins $16.99 (978-0-06-194490-1). 352pp. In this action-packed story, 13-year-old Gerald, an Australian, inherits money from an English great-aunt — along with a letter charging him with solving the mystery of her death. **e** Lexile 730L (Rev: BL 5/1/10; LMC 11–12/10; SLJ 7/10)

1619 Newsome, Richard. *The Emerald Casket* (4–6). Illus. by Jonny Duddle. Series: The Archer Legacy. 2011, HarperCollins $16.99 (978-0-06-194492-5). 359pp. Gerald, a 13-year-old Australian billionaire, and his friends Ruby and Sam visit India to seek a casket full of gems in this fast-paced second installment in the series that features the evil Mason Green. **e** Lexile 660L (Rev: BL 4/1/11; SLJ 8/11)

1620 O'Connor, Barbara. *The Fantastic Secret of Owen Jester* (4–6). 2010, Farrar $15.99 (978-0-374-36850-0). 168pp. Mischievous Owen contends with his rival Viola's distaste for his pet frog — and struggles to keep his fantastic two-passenger submarine a secret from her. **e** Lexile 770L (Rev: BL 9/15/10; HB 11–12/10; LMC 1–2/11; SLJ 10/1/10*)

1621 Odyssey, Shawn Thomas. *The Wizard of Dark Street* (4–7). 2011, Egmont $16.99 (978-1-60684-143-3). 352pp. Blending fantasy and mystery, this book set in 1877 New York City follows 12-year-old Oona, who has decided to become a detective rather than follow in her wizard family's footsteps — until her wizard uncle is attacked. Lexile 890L (Rev: BL 7/11; SLJ 9/1/11)

1622 Peterson, P. J. *Wild River* (4–7). 2009, Delacorte $14.99 (978-0-385-73724-1); LB $17.99 (978-0-385-90656-2). 120pp. When a kayaking trip with his older brother turns dangerous, 12-year-old Ryan must make life-or-death decisions in this exciting, harrowing tale. **e** Lexile 420L (Rev: BL 8/09; SLJ 9/09)

1623 Potter, Ellen. *The Kneebone Boy* (4–8). 2010, Feiwel & Friends $16.99 (978-0-312-37772-4). 288pp. Otto, Lucia, and Max Hardscrabble, three idiosyncratic children, have many adventures while looking for their long-absent mother in a British seaside town. **e** Lexile 850L (Rev: BL 9/15/10; HB 9–10/10; LMC 11–12/10; SLJ 9/1/10)

1624 Promitzer, Rebecca. *The Pickle King* (5–8). 2010, Scholastic $17.99 (978-0-545-17087-1). 416pp. A complex, multilayered novel in which 11-year-old Bea and her friends investigate a mystery involving a ghost. ∩ Lexile 880L (Rev: BL 2/1/10; LMC 3–4/10; SLJ 6/10)

1625 Pullman, Philip. *Two Crafty Criminals! And How They Were Captured by the Daring Detectives of the New Cut Gang* (3–6). Illus. by Martin Brown. 2012, Knopf $16.99 (978-037587029-3); LB $19.99 (978-037597029-0). 320pp. In Victorian London, the New Cut Gang, led by 11-year-old Benny Kaminsky, solves two mysteries involving counterfeiting and theft. ∩ **e** (Rev: BL 4/1/12; HB 5–6/12; LMC 10/12; SLJ 5/12)

1626 Reiss, Kathryn. *A Bundle of Trouble* (4–7). Illus. by Sergio Giovine. 2011, American Girl $10.95 (978-159369753-2); paper $6.95 (978-159369754-9).

165pp. In early 20th-century New York during a rash of kidnappings, Rebecca becomes suspicious of some of the people she meets in her neighborhood. (Rev: BL 5/1/11)

1627 Richards, Justin. *Thunder Raker* (3–5). Illus. by Jim Hansen. Series: Agent Alfie. 2010, HarperCollins paper $6.99 (978-000727357-7). 112pp. Mistakenly enrolled in spy school. Alfie ends up triumphing over tough assignments and quirky teachers to save the day. (Rev: BL 1/1–15/11)

1628 Riel, Jorn. *The Shipwreck* (4–6). Illus. by Helen Cann. Series: Inuk Quartet. 2011, Barefoot paper $12.99 (978-184686335-6). 112pp. A young Viking boy, Leiv, is shipwrecked off the coast of Greenland and finds a new home with an Inuit community, discovering a liking for their rejection of violence. (Rev: BLO 11/15/11; SLJ 11/11)

1629 Riordan, Rick. *The Maze of Bones* (4–8). Series: The 39 Clues. 2008, Scholastic $12.99 (978-054506039-4); LB $12.99 (978-054509054-4). 224pp. Part adventure story, part online gaming platform, this book kicks off a ten-title series with the story of orphans Amy and Dan, who decipher clues and puzzles in their round-the-world quest. ∩ ℮ Lexile 610L (Rev: BL 10/15/08; LMC 5–6/09; SLJ 11/1/08*)

1630 Rollins, James. *Jake Ransom and the Howling Sphinx* (5–8). 2011, HarperCollins $16.99 (978-0-06-147382-1). 370pp. An evil mummified creature delivers an ominous message to siblings Jake and Kady, who must fight for their lives in this fast-paced archaeological time-travel thriller. ∩ ℮ Lexile 700L (Rev: LMC 11–12/11; SLJ 10/1/11; VOYA 8/11)

1631 Roy, Ron. *January Joker* (1–3). Illus. by John Steven Gurney. Series: Calendar Mysteries. 2009, Random House LB $11.99 (978-0-375-95661-4); paper $4.99 (978-0-375-85661-7). 96pp. Seven-year-old twins Bradley and Brian and friends Nate and Lucy (younger siblings and cousins of the characters in the A to Z Mystery series) investigate strange lights in the backyard and decided that aliens have landed. (Rev: LMC 11–12/09; SLJ 12/1/09)

1632 Runholt, Susan. *Adventure at Simba Hill* (5–8). 2011, Viking $16.99 (978-0-670-01201-5). 288pp. Fourteen-year-old friends Kari and Lucas accompany Kari's archaeologist uncle to Kenya, where they solve a mystery involving disappearing artifacts. ℮ Lexile 870L (Rev: BL 5/1/11; SLJ 7/11)

1633 Selfors, Suzanne. *Smells Like Treasure* (4–7). 2011, Little, Brown $15.99 (978-0-316-04399-1). 416pp. Homer Winslow Pudding, 12, faces a challenger for his uncle's place in the society of Legends, Objects, Secrets, and Treasures (LOST) and hopes his basset hound, Dog, will help him prevail. A sequel to *Smells Like Dog* (2010). (Rev: BL 5/1/11; SLJ 9/1/11*)

1634 Shelton, Dave. *A Boy and a Bear in a Boat* (3–5). Illus. by author. 2012, Random House $16.99 (978-038575248-0); LB $19.99 (978-038575249-7). 304pp. A boy and a bear aboard a small boat in the middle of a very large sea experience boredom, bickering, and fear. (Rev: BL 5/15/12*; LMC 10/12)

1635 Sherry, Maureen. *Walls Within Walls* (4–7). Illus. by Adam Stower. 2010, HarperCollins $16.99 (978-0-06-176700-5). 348pp. When three young siblings move into a luxurious Manhattan apartment, they discover that their new home is full of clues that may reveal a treasure. ℮ Lexile 770L (Rev: BL 9/15/10; LMC 3–4/11; SLJ 10/1/10)

1636 Smith, Roland. *Eruption* (5–8). Series: Storm Runners. 2012, Scholastic $16.99 (978-054508174-0). 160pp. While in Mexico pursuing a missing circus act, Chase and his dad end up a hair too close to an erupting volcano and a few wild animals. (Rev: BL 3/15/12)

1637 Smith, Roland. *I, Q* (5–8). Series: I, Q. 2008, Sleeping Bear paper $8.95 (978-158536325-4). 293pp. Q and Angela's musician parents have recently married, sentencing the two teens to a yearlong band tour enlivened by mysterious stalkers who may be related to Angela's dead mother, who worked for the Secret Service.. Lexile HL660L (Rev: BL 10/15/08; SLJ 12/08)

1638 Smith, Roland. *Storm Runners* (5–8). Series: Storm Runners. 2011, Scholastic $16.99 (978-0-545-08175-7). 160pp. Chase, 13, is well prepared for the challenges posed by a hurricane, a bus accident, and escaped zoo animals in this exciting, fast read. (Rev: BL 4/15/11; SLJ 4/11)

1639 Sobol, Donald J. *Encyclopedia Brown, Super Sleuth* (3–6). Illus. by James Bernardin. 2009, Dutton $15.99 (978-052542100-9). 96pp. Ten short mysteries engage venerable sleuth Encyclopedia Brown in this new collection; the solutions are in the back of the book. (Rev: BLO 11/15/09)

1640 Soup, Cuthbert. *A Whole Nother Story* (3–6). Illus. by Jeffrey Stewart Timmins. 2010, Bloomsbury $16.99 (978-159990435-1). 272pp. A scientist and his three children and psychic dog are on the run from spies and government agents who want to steal their time machine in this adventure laced with humor. (Rev: BL 11/15/09; LMC 3–4/10; SLJ 1/10)

1641 Stewart, Trenton Lee. *The Extraordinary Education of Nicholas Benedict* (4–6). Illus. by Diana Sudyka. 2012, Little, Brown $17.99 (978-031617619-4). 480pp. At his new orphanage 9-year-old Nicholas, who has an ugly nose and narcolepsy, learns to avoid the vicious bullies known as the Spiders and discovers a mystery that may change his life. ∩ ℮ Lexile 900L (Rev: BL 2/1/12*; HB 3–4/12; LMC 8–9/12; SLJ 4/12; VOYA 4/12)

1642 Suma, Nova Ren. *Dani Noir* (5–8). 2009, Simon & Schuster $15.99 (978-1-4169-7564-9). 272pp. Thirteen-year-old Dani's main enjoyment is watching noir films at the local art theater, and these fuel her imagination to the point that she suspects an older teen, Jackson, of two-timing his girlfriend. Her resulting investigation teachers her about life and herself. (Rev: BL 11/1/09; LMC 11–12/09; SLJ 12/09)

1643 Turnage, Sheila. *Three Times Lucky* (4–6). 2012, Dial $16.99 (978-080373670-2). 320pp. A murder, a kidnapping, and lots of unanswered questions about family histories set the scene for this satisfying mystery featuring 11-year-old protagonist Mo. ⌒ ℮ Lexile 560L (Rev: BL 5/1/12*; HB 7–8/12; LMC 11–12/12; SLJ 6/12; VOYA 8/12)

1644 Van Draanen, Wendelin. *Sammy Keyes and the Night of Skulls* (5–8). 2011, Knopf $15.99 (978-037586108-6); LB $18.99 (978-037596108-3). 272pp. Junior high sleuth Sammy and her friends find themselves in the midst of a mystery in a graveyard on Halloween night. (Rev: BL 10/1/11)

1645 Van Draanen, Wendelin. *Sammy Keyes and the Wedding Crasher* (5–8). 2010, Knopf $16.99 (978-037586107-9); LB $19.99 (978-037596107-6). 304pp. Starting 8th grade Sammy is shocked to find herself suspected of making threats against her history teacher; she also must cope with her nemesis Heather and her duties as a reluctant bridesmaid. ⌒ ℮ Lexile 750L (Rev: BL 12/15/10; VOYA 2/11)

1646 Van Draanen, Wendelin. *Sinister Substitute* (3–5). Illus. by Stephen Gilpin. Series: The Gecko and Sticky. 2010, Knopf $12.99 (978-037584378-5); LB $15.99 (978-037594572-4). 208pp. Middle school superhero Dave, aka the Gecko, and his sidekick Sticky — an actual gecko — set out to thwart a sinister bad guy who's disguised himself as a substitute teacher in this energetic adventure story. ⌒ Lexile 860L (Rev: BL 1/1/10)

1647 Van Tol, Alex. *Gravity Check* (4–6). Series: Orca Sports. 2011, Orca paper $9.95 (978-155469349-8). 176pp. Five riders on a British Columbia bike trail discover a clandestine pot farm in this tense thriller for reluctant readers. (Rev: BL 9/1/11)

1648 Voelkel, J&P. *The End of the World Club* (4–6). Series: Jaguar Stones. 2010, Egmont $16.99 (978-1-60684-072-6). 416pp. Max and Lola travel to Spain to retrieve a magical stone needed to save Max's parents from the Maya Lords of Death. ⌒ ℮ Lexile 760L (Rev: BL 2/1/11; LMC 5–6/11; SLJ 1/1/11)

1649 Walden, Mark. *Dreadnought* (5–8). Series: H.I.V.E. 2011, Simon & Schuster $16.99 (978-144242186-8). 304pp. When an especially villainous classmate hijacks the villain school's airborne defense platform, Otto and his friends come to the rescue. ℮ Lexile 1000L (Rev: BL 4/15/11)

1650 Walden, Mark. *Escape Velocity* (5–8). Series: H.I.V.E. 2011, Simon & Schuster $16.99 (978-144242185-1). 352pp. Otto, who is still learning to use his newfound abilities, must break into MI6 in order to rescue Dr. Nero from H.O.P.E. — the Hostile Operative Prosecution Executive. Also use *Rogue* (2011). ℮ Lexile 990L (Rev: BL 6/1/11)

1651 Warner, Gertrude Chandler. *The Clue in the Recycling Bin* (2–4). Illus. by Robert Papp. Series: Boxcar Children. 2011, Whitman $14.99 (978-080751208-1). 128pp. Volunteering at a recycling center, the Alden children stumble upon a string of break-ins involving reclaimed metal. (Rev: BL 5/1/11)

1652 Warner, Gertrude Chandler. *The Dog-Gone Mystery* (2–5). Illus. by Robert Papp. Series: Boxcar Children. 2009, Whitman LB $14.99 (978-0-8075-1658-4); paper $4.99 (978-0-8075-1657-7). 120pp. When two dogs disappear from their dog Watch's obedience class, the four Alden children swing into action. (Rev: SLJ 12/1/09)

1653 Warner, Gertrude Chandler. *The Pumpkin Head Mystery* (2–4). Illus. by Robert Papp. Series: Boxcar Children. 2010, Whitman $14.99 (978-080756668-8); paper $4.99 (978-080756669-5). 128pp. The Boxcar Children attempt to dispel the bad luck stalking their grandparents' friends' farm. ℮ Lexile 430L (Rev: BL 1/1–15/11)

1654 Warner, Gertrude Chandler. *The Spy in the Bleachers* (2–5). Illus. by Robert Papp. Series: Boxcar Children. 2010, Whitman $14.99 (978-080757606-9); paper $4.99 (978-080757607-6). 128pp. The four siblings investigate when it seems someone is stealing players' signals and relaying them to the other team. (Rev: BL 5/1/10)

1655 Watson, Geoff. *Edison's Gold* (4–7). 2010, Egmont $15.99 (978-160684094-8). 320pp. Tom Edison IV, the great-great-grandson of the esteemed inventor, hatches a plan to restore his family's fortune by creating gold in this action-filled mystery involving a secret society and a descendant of Nikola Tesla. Lexile 880L (Rev: BL 11/1/10; LMC 1–2/11; SLJ 1/1/11)

1656 Watson, Jude. *In Too Deep* (4–7). Series: 39 Clues. 2009, Scholastic $12.99 (978-054506046-2); LB $12.99 (978-054509064-3). 208pp. Amy and Dan travel to Australia searching for clues to their parents' disappearance while battling threats from humans and animals in this sixth installment in the series. ⌒ ℮ Lexile 550L (Rev: BL 1/1/10)

1657 Watson, Stephanie. *Elvis and Olive: Super Detectives* (3–6). Series: Elvis & Olive. 2010, Scholastic $15.99 (978-054515148-1). 240pp. The quite different preteen friends Natalie and Annie (the series uses their code names) start a successful detective agency. (Rev: BLO 11/1/10; LMC 8–9/10; SLJ 8/10)

1658 Weeks, Sarah. *Pie* (3–6). 2011, Scholastic $16.99 (978-0-545-27011-3). 192pp. After her beloved aunt Polly's death, 10-year-old Alice and her friend Charlie investigate the disappearance of Polly's cat and the destruction of her famous bakery; a chapter book set in 1955. (Rev: BL 9/1/11; SLJ 9/1/11*)

1659 Wildavsky, Rachel. *The Secret of Rover* (4–7). 2011, Abrams $16.95 (978-0-8109-9710-3). 368pp. Katie and David, 12-year-old twins whose parents invented a secret spying device, find themselves embroiled in political intrigue. (Rev: BL 5/1/11; SLJ 4/11*)

1660 Wilkins, Kay. *A Scaly Tale* (4–7). Illus. by Ailin Chambers. Series: Ripley's Bureau of Investigation. 2010, Ripley paper $4.99 (978-189395152-5). 128pp. After a half-man, half-reptile creature is spotted in the Florida Everglades, Ripley's Bureau of Investigation sends a team with special powers to look into the matter. ☊ Lexile 820L (Rev: BL 9/1/10)

1661 Winters, Ben H. *The Mystery of the Missing Everything* (5–8). 2011, HarperCollins $16.99 (978-0-06-196544-9). 272pp. Eighth-grader Bethesda Fielding investigates a missing sports trophy in this sequel to *The Secret Life of Ms. Finkleman* (2010). (Rev: BL 10/1/11; SLJ 10/1/11)

Animal Stories

1662 Altbacker, E. J. *Shark Wars* (4–6). 2011, Penguin $12.99 (978-1-59514-376-1). 256pp. Young reef shark Gray is banished from his clan, or shiver, and must find a new home and battle to protect it. ☊ ☞ (Rev: LMC 10/11; SLJ 8/11)

1663 Applegate, Katherine. *The One and Only Ivan* (3–6). Illus. by Patricia Castelao. 2012, HarperCollins $16.99 (978-006199225-4). 320pp. A bored gorilla named Ivan makes his elephant friend Stella an improbable promise in this first-person story based on real life. ☞ (Rev: BL 2/15/12; HB 1–2/12; SLJ 1/12)

1664 Arnosky, Jim. *Slow Down for Manatees* (1–3). Illus. by author. 2010, Putnam $16.99 (978-0-399-24170-3). 32pp. A pregnant manatee injured by a motorboat is rehabilitated at an aquarium in this touching story that examines the real threats boaters pose to the animals. Lexile AD860L (Rev: BL 3/1/10; HB 5–6/10; LMC 3–4/10; SLJ 2/1/10)

1665 Behrens, Andy. *The Fast and the Furriest* (2–5). 2010, Knopf $15.99 (978-0-375-85922-9); LB $18.99 (978-0-375-95922-6). 224pp. A funny story about 12-year-old Kevin's sudden interest in competition when his dog shows skill in agility courses. ☊ ☞ Lexile 660L (Rev: BL 2/1/10; SLJ 3/10)

1666 Blom, Jen J. *Possum Summer* (4–7). Illus. by Omar Rayyan. 2011, Holiday House $17.95 (978-0-8234-2331-6). 160pp. Eleven-year-old Princess ("P") misses her father when he is stationed in Iraq, and ignoring his advice about wild animals she rescues a baby possum on their Oklahoma ranch. (Rev: BL 5/1/11; SLJ 6/11)

1667 Cole, Henry. *A Nest for Celeste: A Story About Art, Inspiration, and the Meaning of Home* (2–5). Illus. by author. 2010, HarperCollins $16.99 (978-0-06-170410-9); LB $17.89 (978-0-06-170411-6). 352pp. In this story set in 1821 Louisiana, Celeste the mouse's life improves when John James Audubon and his assistant move into her house, offering her protection from rats and other dangers. (Rev: BL 2/15/10; LMC 3–4/10; SLJ 3/1/10)

1668 Duncan, Lois. *Movie for Dogs* (4–6). 2010, Scholastic $16.99 (978-054510854-6). 208pp. Andi and her brother Bruce collaborate on a dog-themed movie; do they have a chance at Hollywood? ☊ (Rev: BLO 5/15/10; VOYA 6/10)

1669 Edwards, Julie Andrews, and Emma Walton Hamilton. *Little Bo in Italy: The Continued Adventures of Bonnie Boadicea* (1–3). Illus. by Henry Cole. 2010, HarperCollins $19.99 (978-006008908-5). 112pp. Little Bo the cat and her master Billy have a European adventure when the yacht they're working on visits Rome and Pisa. (Rev: BL 2/1/11)

1670 Ganny, Charlee. *Chihuawolf: A Tail of Mystery and Horror* (3–6). Illus. by Nicola Slater. 2011, Sourcebooks paper $6.99 (978-1-4022-5940-1). 144pp. A privileged Chihuahua named Paco has everything he needs in life except romance, and sets his sights on a beautiful Afghan hound named Natasha, which poses many challenges. (Rev: BL 10/1/11; LMC 1–2/12; SLJ 9/1/11)

1671 Ibbotson, Eva. *One Dog and His Boy* (3–6). 2012, Scholastic $16.99 (978-054535196-6). 288pp. Ten-year-old Hal is overjoyed when his wealthy parents finally agree to get him a dog — until he discovers that it is merely a weekend rental. ☊ (Rev: BL 3/1/12; HB 5–6/12; LMC 5–6/12; SLJ 3/12)

1672 Jennings, Patrick. *Guinea Dog* (3–5). 2010, Egmont $15.99 (978-1-60684-053-5). 192pp. Fifth-grader Rufus is disappointed when his mother brings him a guinea pig rather than a dog, but he names him Fido and is surprised by the rodent's doglike talents. Lexile 600L (Rev: BL 6/10; LMC 10/10; SLJ 9/1/10)

1673 Kehret, Peg. *Ghost Dog Secrets* (5–7). 2010, Dutton $16.99 (978-0-525-42178-8). 192pp. The ghost of an abused dog helps 6th-grader Rusty locate and save other abused dogs in this slightly creepy story with a strong, believable protagonist. Lexile 730L (Rev: BL 10/1/10; LMC 1–2/11; SLJ 9/1/10; VOYA 8/10)

1674 Korman, Gordon. *Showoff* (3–6). Series: Swindle. 2012, Scholastic $16.99 (978-054532059-7). 256pp. Luthor the clumsy Doberman wreaks havoc at a Dog Show, before Griffin Bing — the Man with the Plan — intervenes and succeeds in transforming him into a success. ☊ ☞ Lexile 740L (Rev: BL 1/1/12; SLJ 5/1/12)

1675 Kurtz, Chris. *The Pup Who Cried Wolf* (3–5). Illus. by Guy Francis. 2010, Bloomsbury $15.99 (978-1-

59990-497-9); paper $5.99 (978-159990492-4). 160pp. Lobo, a New York City Chihuahua who longs to run wild with wolves, gets a reality check when he gets to Yellowstone. Lexile 630L (Rev: BL 5/15/10; LMC 10/10; SLJ 9/1/10)

1676 Lester, Alison. *The Sea Rescue* (2–4). Illus. by Roland Harvey. Series: Horse Crazy. 2009, Chronicle paper $4.99 (978-0-8118-6940-9). 64pp. Horseback-riding friends Bonnie and Sam get caught in a storm and aid in the rescue of drowning men in this chapter book set in the Australian bush. Also use *The Royal Show* (2009). (Rev: SLJ 1/1/10)

1677 Lowry, Lois. *Bless This Mouse* (3–6). Illus. by Eric Rohmann. 2011, Houghton Harcourt $15.99 (978-0-547-39009-3). 160pp. A colony of church mice, led by Mouse Mistress Hildegarde, face challenges from an exterminator and from the cats and other pets expected to attend the Blessing of the Animals. ⋒ **e** Lexile 690L (Rev: BL 3/1/11; SLJ 3/1/11)

1678 Meddaugh, Susan. *Martha on the Case* (1–3). Adapted by Jamie White. Series: Martha Speaks. 2010, Houghton Harcourt paper $5.99 (978-0-547-21055-1). 108pp. Talking dog Martha helps investigate crimes in two lively stories. (Rev: SLJ 7/1/10)

1679 Mills, Claudia. *Mason Dixon: Pet Disasters* (3–6). Illus. by Guy Francis. 2011, Knopf $12.99 (978-0-375-86873-3); LB $15.99 (978-0-375-96873-0). 176pp. Mason, 9, resists all attempts to get him to bond with a pet until his friend Brody introduces him to a three-legged dog. Lexile 780L (Rev: SLJ 11/1/11)

1680 Murphy, Jill. *Dear Hound* (3–5). Illus. by author. 2010, Walker $14.99 (978-0-8027-2190-7). 192pp. Foxes help Alfie, a timid (but large) deerhound puppy, to reunite at last with his beloved family after many adventures. (Rev: BL 8/10; LMC 10/10; SLJ 9/1/10)

1681 Nolan, Lucy. *Home on the Range* (2–4). Illus. by Mike Reed. Series: Down Girl and Sit. 2010, Marshall Cavendish $14.99 (978-0-7614-5649-0). 54pp. City dogs Down Girl and Sit accompany their owners on a trip to a dude ranch and have many adventures. (Rev: SLJ 5/1/10)

1682 Orr, Wendy. *Lost! A Dog Called Bear* (2–4). Illus. by Susan Boase. 2011, Henry Holt $15.99 (978-080508931-8); paper $5.99 (978-080509381-0). 112pp. Logan's coping with his parents' divorce and a move to the city when his dog gets lost — at the same time, Hannah's parents won't let her have a dog so she works at an animal shelter; the two meet and become friends. (Rev: BL 9/15/11; LMC 11–12/11)

1683 Paley, Jane. *Hooper Finds a Family: A Hurricane Katrina Dog's Survival Tale* (3–7). Illus. 2011, HarperCollins $15.99 (978-0-06-201103-9). 144pp. A personable yellow Lab orphaned by Hurricane Katrina narrates this inspiring story about adjusting to new sur-

roundings in New York City. **e** Lexile 540L (Rev: BL 7/11; SLJ 7/11)

1684 Platt, Chris. *Astra* (3–6). 2010, Peachtree $15.95 (978-156145541-6). 160pp. Lily, 13, is forbidden to ride after her mother's death on the trail, but when she is given ownership of her mother's horse Astra she starts training for the Tevis Cup Endurance Race. Lexile 730L (Rev: BL 9/1/10; LMC 3–4/11; SLJ 3/1/11)

1685 Platt, Chris. *Storm Chaser* (4–6). 2009, Peachtree $14.95 (978-156145496-9). 178pp. On her family's Nevada dude ranch, 13-year-old Jessie must train her favorite horse, Storm Chaser, for possible sale to the despised Ariel. (Rev: BLO 11/1/09; SLJ 10/09)

1686 Pyron, Bobbie. *A Dog's Way Home* (4–7). 2011, HarperCollins $16.99 (978-0-06-198674-1); LB $17.89 (978-0-06-198673-4). 320pp. Told in alternating chapters by Abby, an 11-year-old girl, and Tam, a beloved dog trying to find his way home after the accident in which they both were injured, this tense story ends happily. ⋒ (Rev: BL 2/15/11; SLJ 4/11; VOYA 4/11)

1687 Salisbury, Graham. *Zoo Breath* (3–5). Illus. by Jacqueline Rogers. Series: Calvin Coconut. 2010, Random House $12.99 (978-0-385-73704-3); LB $18.99 (978-0-385-90642-5). 160pp. In his campaign to be allowed to keep the family dog despite Streak's bad breath, Calvin investigates the problem for his school assignment. **e** (Rev: SLJ 12/1/10)

1688 Schwartz, Virginia Frances. *Nutz!* (3–5). Illus. by Christina Leist. 2012, Orca paper $12.95 (978-189658087-6). 144pp. Fat, jealous cat Amos watches disdainfully as his human, Tyler, 10, fawns over their household's newest pet, an injured baby squirrel named Nutz. (Rev: BL 3/1/12; SLJ 4/1/12)

1689 Smiley, Jane. *A Good Horse* (4–8). 2010, Knopf $16.99 (978-037586229-8); LB $19.99 (978-037596228-8). 256pp. Thirteen-year-old Abby worries that her colt Jack might be the offspring of a stolen mare at the same time that she is dealing with the sale of her prized Black George. **e** (Rev: BL 10/15/10; HB 11–12/10; SLJ 12/1/10)

1690 Stauffacher, Sue. *Gator on the Loose!* (4–6). Illus. by Priscilla Lamont. Series: Animal Rescue Team. 2010, Knopf $12.99 (978-0-375-85847-5); LB $15.99 (978-0-375-95847-2). 160pp. Ten-year-old Keisha, daughter of mixed-race parents, helps in her family's animal rescue business, finding suitable homes for animals including an alligator. ⋒ **e** Lexile 740L (Rev: BL 4/1/10; LMC 8–9/10; SLJ 8/10)

1691 Stauffacher, Sue. *Hide and Seek* (3–5). Illus. by Priscilla Lamont. Series: Animal Rescue Team. 2010, Knopf $12.99 (978-0-375-85849-9); LB $15.99 (978-0-375-95849-6). 160pp. Ten-year-old Keisha Carter and her family come to the rescue when an inquisitive deer gets a plastic pumpkin stuck on its head. ⋒ (Rev: BL 12/1/10; SLJ 12/1/10)

1692 Townsend, Wendy. *The Sundown Rule* (4–7). 2011, Namelos $18.95 (978-1-60898-099-4). 128pp. Louise's father is on assignment in Brazil and she must live with relatives in a housing development, far from the woods and the animals that Louise so loves. Lexile 750L (Rev: SLJ 4/11)

1693 Voigt, Cynthia. *Young Fredle* (3–5). Illus. by Louise Yates. 2011, Knopf $16.99 (978-0-375-86457-5); LB $19.99 (978-0-375-96457-2). 224pp. Led astray by his sweet tooth, a young kitchen mouse finds himself cast out into the dangers of the world at large and has many scary adventures before finding his way home. ∩ **e** Lexile 840L (Rev: BL 1/1–15/11; HB 3–4/11; SLJ 2/1/11)

1694 Wallace, Sandra Neil. *Little Joe* (3–5). Illus. by Mark Elliott. 2010, Knopf $15.99 (978-0-375-86097-3); LB $18.99 (978-0-375-96097-0). 192pp. Nine-year-old Eli's father and grandfather coach him as he raises his first calf for market in this story set in rural Pennsylvania. **e** Lexile 710L (Rev: BL 7/10; HB 9–10/10; SLJ 8/10)

1695 Wells, Ken. *Rascal: A Dog and His Boy* (5–8). Illus. by Christian Slade. 2010, Knopf $16.99 (978-037586652-4); LB $19.99 (978-037596652-1). 208pp. A playful beagle puppy named Rascal learns how to be an alert, responsive dog when his young owner, Meely, is in danger, in this novel set in the Louisiana bayou. Lexile 720L (Rev: BL 9/1/10; LMC 1–2/11)

Ethnic Groups

1696 Ada, Alma Flor, and Gabriel Zubizarreta. *Dancing Home* (4–6). 2011, Atheneum $14.99 (978-1-4169-0088-7). 160pp. Margie, 10, tries to hide her Mexican background until her cousin Lupe arrives in California and Margie slowly learns to appreciate her heritage. **e** Lexile 960L (Rev: BL 7/11; SLJ 7/11)

1697 Barnes, Derrick. *We Could Be Brothers* (5–8). 2010, Scholastic $17.99 (978-054513573-3). 176pp. African American 8th-graders Robeson and Pacino come from different backgrounds but recognize their common aims as they confront Tariq, a threatening classmate. Lexile HL600L (Rev: BL 11/15/10; VOYA 4/11)

1698 Cervantes, Jennifer. *Tortilla Sun* (4–7). 2010, Chronicle $16.99 (978-0-8118-7015-3). 224pp. Izzy, 12, spends a summer in New Mexico with her grandmother and learns about her father and her cultural heritage. (Rev: BLO 5/1/10; LMC 8–9/10; SLJ 6/10)

1699 Cheng, Andrea. *Only One Year* (2–4). Illus. by Nicole Wong. 2010, Lee & Low $16.95 (978-1-60060-252-8). 104pp. Nine-year-old Sharon and her younger sister are devastated when their parents decided to send their 2-year-old brother to spend a year in China with his grandparents. (Rev: BL 2/15/10; LMC 8–9/10; SLJ 4/1/10)

1700 Colon, Edie. *Good-bye, Havana! Hola, New York!* (1–3). Illus. by Raúl Colón. 2011, Simon & Schuster $16.99 (978-1-4424-0674-2). 32pp. Chronicles 6-year-old Gabriella's first year in New York after her parents flee Castro's Cuba. (Rev: BL 9/1/11; SLJ 9/1/11)

1701 Han, Jenny. *Clara Lee and the Apple Pie Dream* (2–4). Illus. by Julia Kuo. 2011, Little, Brown $14.99 (978-0-316-07038-6). 150pp. Korean American Clara Lee conquers her fear of public speaking and shyness about her heritage and runs for Little Miss Apple Pie. Lexile 600L (Rev: BL 12/1/10; HB 3–4/11; LMC 1–2/11*; SLJ 2/1/11)

1702 Krishnaswami, Uma. *The Grand Plan to Fix Everything* (4–6). Illus. by Abigail Halpin. 2011, Atheneum $16.99 (978-1-4169-9589-0). 272pp. Eleven-year-old Dini is initially sad when she hears her family is moving to India for two years, but also hopeful that she will get to meet her favorite Bollywood star. (Rev: BL 9/1/11; SLJ 5/11)

1703 Lai, Thanhha. *Inside Out and Back Again* (4–7). 2011, HarperCollins $15.99 (978-0-06-196278-3). Based on the author's own childhood experiences, this novel in verse tells the story of 10-year-old Hà and her journey with her mother and brothers from Vietnam to rural Alabama, where she faces many challenges. ALSC Notable Children's Book, 2012; National Book Award for Young People's Literature; Newbery Honor Book; Pura Belpre Illustrator Honor Book, 2012. **e** Lexile 800L (Rev: BL 1/1–15/11*; HB 3–4/11; SLJ 3/1/11*)

1704 Lin, Grace. *Dumpling Days* (3–6). 2012, Little, Brown $15.99 (978-031612590-1). 264pp. Pacy and her family travel to their homeland, Taiwan, to celebrate Grandma's birthday, and Pacy finds challenges, a love for dumplings, and a growing understanding of her heritage. ∩ **e** (Rev: BL 1/1/12; HB 3–4/12; LMC 1–2/12*)

1705 Lo, Ginnie. *Auntie Yang's Great Soybean Picnic* (K–2). Illus. by Beth Lo. 2012, Lee & Low $18.95 (978-160060442-3). 32pp. Chinese sisters in Indiana in the 1950s joyously discover a soybean farm and start a tradition of an annual celebration picnic. (Rev: BL 4/15/12*; LMC 11–12/12; SLJ 6/1/12*)

1706 Shang, Wendy Wan-Long. *The Great Wall of Lucy Wu* (4–6). 2011, Scholastic $17.99 (978-0-545-16215-9). 320pp. Chinese American Lucy's plans for a terrific year in 6th grade go awry when her great-aunt arrives from China and moves into her bedroom; slowly she comes to appreciate the traditions her aunt brings with her. Lexile 700L (Rev: BL 2/15/11; SLJ 2/1/11)

Family Stories

1707 Almond, David. *Slog's Dad* (4–7). Illus. by Dave McKean. 2011, Candlewick $15.99 (978-0-7636-4940-1). 58pp. A young boy grieving after his father's death meets a stranger he believes to be his dad returned with his legs intact. (Rev: BL 3/15/11; SLJ 5/11; VOYA 6/11)

1708 Alvarez, Julia. *How Tía Lola Ended Up Starting Over* (4–7). Series: Tía Lola. 2011, Knopf $15.99 (978-037586914-3); LB $18.99 (978-037596914-0). 160pp. Tía Lola starts a bed-and-breakfast with the help of the children, but it seems that someone wants the business to fail; who can be wishing them ill in this mystery set in Vermont and featuring Latino families? (Rev: BL 11/1/11)

1709 Alvarez, Julia. *How Tía Lola Learned to Teach* (4–7). Series: Tía Lola. 2010, Knopf $15.99 (978-0-375-86460-5); LB $18.99 (978-0-375-96460-2). 144pp. In this sequel to *How Tía Lola Came to (Visit) Stay* (2001), Miguel and Juanita's Dominican aunt is teaching at their school and worrying about her soon-to-expire visa. ◑ (Rev: BL 12/1/10; HB 1–2/11; LMC 3–4/11; SLJ 11/1/10)

1710 Alvarez, Julia. *How Tía Lola Saved the Summer* (4–7). Series: Tía Lola. 2011, Knopf $15.99 (978-0-375-86727-9); LB $18.99 (978-037596727-6). 160pp. Tía Lola saves the day when three unwelcome girls and their father visit Miguel's Vermont farmhouse, creating a summer camp atmosphere. (Rev: BL 5/1/11; SLJ 7/11)

1711 Bateson, Catherine. *Magenta McPhee* (3–6). 2010, Holiday House $16.95 (978-0-8234-2253-1). 176pp. Magenta goes online to find a dating match for her lonely, divorced father in this funny, realistic story about a teen who writes fantasies. Lexile 640L (Rev: BL 3/1/10; HB 5–6/10; SLJ 3/10)

1712 Birdsall, Jeanne. *The Penderwicks at Point Mouette* (4–7). 2011, Knopf $16.99 (978-0-375-85851-2); LB $19.99 (978-037595851-9). 304pp. Father, his new wife, and young son are away in England and Rosalind is in New Jersey, so Skye finds herself in an unaccustomed role as OAP (oldest available Penderwick) when the three younger sisters go to Maine with Aunt Claire. (Rev: BL 5/1/11; SLJ 7/11)

1713 Blume, Judy. *Friend or Fiend? with the Pain and the Great One* (1–4). Illus. by James Stevenson. 2009, Delacorte $12.99 (978-038573308-3); LB $16.99 (978-038590327-1). 128pp. Third-grader Abigail (the Great One) and her brother Jacob (the Pain) have adventures including a visit to relatives in New York and celebrating their cat Fuzzy's birthday. ◑ ℮ Lexile 360L (Rev: BL 4/15/09; SLJ 5/1/09)

1714 Bredsdorff, Bodil. *Eidi* (4–6). Trans. from Danish by Kathryn Mahaffy. Series: The Children of Crow Cove. 2009, Farrar $16.99 (978-0-374-31267-1). 138pp. This installment in the series tells the story of Eidi, a young girl who leaves her home after the birth of her stepbrother, only to find herself caring for a young orphan who is being abused his stepfather. ALSC Notable Children's Book, 2010. Lexile 810L (Rev: BL 9/1/09*; HB 11–12/09; SLJ 12/09)

1715 Cameron, Ann. *Spunky Tells All* (2–4). Illus. by Lauren Castillo. Series: Julian and Huey. 2011, Farrar $15.99 (978-0-374-38000-7). 128pp. Spunky the dog narrates this story about the difficulty of communicating with humans and what happens when his family adopts a cat; an illustrated chapter book. (Rev: BL 11/1/11; SLJ 11/1/11*)

1716 Compestine, Ying Chang. *Crouching Tiger* (K–3). Illus. by Yan Nascimbene. 2011, Candlewick $16.99 (978-0-7636-4642-4). 40pp. Vinson is initially scornful by his Chinese grandfather's tai chi, but comes to recognize that the old man is respected for his prowess. (Rev: BL 12/15/11; HB 1–2/12; SLJ 12/1/11)

1717 Couloumbis, Audrey. *Jake* (3–6). 2010, Random House $15.99 (978-037585630-3); LB $18.99 (978-037595630-0). 176pp. When his mother breaks her leg, 10-year-old Jake finds himself in the care of his paternal grandfather. ℮ (Rev: BL 9/1/10; SLJ 10/10)

1718 Couloumbis, Audrey. *Lexie* (3–5). Illus. by Julia Denos. 2011, Random House $15.99 (978-0-375-85632-7); LB $18.99 (978-0-375-95632-4). 200pp. Lexie, 10, is looking forward to spending time at her family's Jersey beach house with her recently divorced dad until she discovers he is bringing his girlfriend and her sons. ℮ Lexile 600L (Rev: HB 7–8/11; SLJ 7/11)

1719 Cox, Judy. *Nora and the Texas Terror* (2–4). Illus. by Amanda Haley. 2010, Holiday House $15.95 (978-0-8234-2283-8). 96pp. When 3rd-grader Nora's uncle loses his job, he and his family — including Nora's annoying cousin Ellie — move to live with them in Oregon. Lexile 450L (Rev: BL 12/15/10; SLJ 12/1/10)

1720 Davies, Jacqueline. *The Bell Bandit* (3–6). Series: Lemonade War. 2012, Houghton Mifflin $15.99 (978-054756737-2). 192pp. Siblings Evan and Jessie investigate the disappearance of the family's bell as they spend Christmas and New Year's at Grandma's house in the aftermath of a devastating fire. ◑ (Rev: BL 4/1/12; LMC 8–9/12)

1721 Draper, Sharon M. *The Birthday Storm* (2–4). 2009, Scholastic $14.99 (978-0-545-07152-9). 112pp. Sassy and her family travel to Florida to celebrate their grandma's birthday, but a hurricane is arriving at the same time — and the local sea turtles are in danger. (Rev: BL 11/15/09; SLJ 11/1/09)

1722 Elliott, Zetta. *Bird* (4–8). Illus. by Shadra Strickland. 2008, Lee & Low $19.95 (978-1-60060-241-2). 48pp. Bird, an African American boy struggling with his brother's death from drugs, finds solace in drawing and the understanding of his uncle in this novel in verse. ALSC Notable Children's Book, 2009. (Rev: BL 11/1/08; LMC 3–4/09)

1723 Ellison, Elizabeth Stow. *Flight* (4–8). 2008, Holiday House $16.95 (978-082342128-2). 245pp. Caught between her unresponsive, oblivious parents and her older brother Evan who's coping with a learning disability, 12-year-old Samantha struggles to advocate for Evan and eventually discovers that her mother is hiding her own disability — that she cannot read. Lexile 710L (Rev: BLO 11/1/08; SLJ 11/1/08)

1724 Fosberry, Jennifer. *My Name Is Not Alexander* (1–3). Illus. by Mike Litwin. 2011, Sourcebooks $16.99 (978-1-4022-5433-8). 32pp. A young narrator imagines himself as one historical personality after another — complete with lavish costumes. (Rev: BL 5/1/11; SLJ 6/11)

1725 Frazier, Sundee T. *The Other Half of My Heart* (4–6). 2010, Delacorte $16.99 (978-0-385-73440-0); LB $19.99 (978-0-385-90446-9). 304pp. Biracial twins Keira and Minna, 11, experience life differently because of their different skin tones and personalities, and entering the Miss Black Pearl Pre-Teen competition underlines this. ◖ ℮ Lexile 750L (Rev: BL 8/10*; LMC 10/10; SLJ 7/10; VOYA 6/10)

1726 Glatt, Lisa, and Suzanne Greenberg. *Abigail Iris: The Pet Project* (2–4). Illus. by Joy Allen. 2010, Walker $14.99 (978-0-8027-8657-9). 176pp. Abigail Iris is upset that her sister is allergic to her new kitten and feels jealous of her three friends who have no siblings. (Rev: SLJ 4/1/10)

1727 Hermes, Patricia. *Emma Dilemma, the Nanny, and the Secret Ferret* (2–4). 2010, Marshall Cavendish $15.99 (978-0-7614-5650-6). 144pp. Young Emma sneaks her pet ferret Marmaduke along on the family vacation, with predictably chaotic results. ℮ Lexile 540L (Rev: SLJ 4/1/10)

1728 Hirsch, Odo. *Darius Bell and the Glitter Pool* (4–7). 2010, Kane/Miller $15.99 (978-193527965-5). 240pp. Broke and desperate, Darius's once wealthy family has nothing to give to the community as its annual thank you, until an earthquake reveals a hidden cave that may provide the answer; set in Australia. Lexile 770L (Rev: BL 9/1/10; LMC 3–4/11)

1729 Holm, Jennifer L. *The Trouble with May Amelia* (3–6). Illus. by Adam Gustavson. 2011, Simon & Schuster $15.99 (978-1-4169-1373-3). 204pp. May Amelia, a Finnish American 13-year-old, shows her inner strength as she copes with criticism from family and community in this sequel to the Newbery Honor Book; set in 1900 Washington state. ◖ ℮ Lexile 690L (Rev: BL 3/1/11; HB 5–6/11; SLJ 4/11)

1730 Jones, Marcia Thornton. *Ratfink* (3–5). Illus. by C. B. Decker. 2010, Dutton $16.99 (978-0-525-42066-8). 224pp. Fifth-grader Logan slowly learns to accept and even appreciate his aging, forgetful, and embarrassing Grandpa, who actually ends up helping him deal with problems at school and at home. ℮ Lexile 630L (Rev: BL 12/15/09*; SLJ 2/10)

1731 Kehret, Peg. *Runaway Twin* (5–8). 2009, Dutton $16.99 (978-0-525-42177-1). 197pp. Thirteen-year-old Sunny Skyland leaves her Nebraska foster home for Washington state on a quest to find the twin sister from whom she was separated ten years before. Lexile 740L (Rev: BLO 8/09; SLJ 12/09; VOYA 12/09)

1732 Kennedy, Marlane. *The Dog Days of Charlotte Hayes* (4–7). 2009, Greenwillow $15.99 (978-0-06-145241-3); LB $16.89 (978-0-06-145242-0). 144pp. Eleven-year-old Charlotte, no dog lover, nonetheless works to find a better home for the St. Bernard her family neglects. ℮ Lexile 790L (Rev: BL 2/15/09; SLJ 4/1/09)

1733 Kerley, Barbara. *The Extraordinary Mark Twain (According to Susy)* (2–5). Illus. by Edwin Fotheringham. 2010, Scholastic $17.99 (978-0-545-12508-6). 48pp. Thirteen-year-old Susy Clemens decides to set the world straight on her father (Twain) in this unusual book that features pages of Susy's (often misspelled) journal. (Rev: BL 12/1/09; LMC 5–6/10; SLJ 1/1/10*)

1734 LaFleur, Suzanne. *Eight Keys* (4–7). 2011, Random House $16.99 (978-0-385-74030-2); LB $19.99 (978-038590833-7). 224pp. Twelve-year-old orphan Elise is having trouble adapting to middle school when she discovers keys to rooms that her late father designed, which help her cope. (Rev: BL 9/1/11; SLJ 8/11)

1735 Leal, Ann Haywood. *A Finders-Keepers Place* (4–6). 2010, Henry Holt $16.99 (978-0-8050-8882-3). 272pp. In this moving family drama set in the 1970s, Esther, 11, realizes in view of her mother's manic depression that it's up to her to find her missing younger sister and then to search for their absent father. (Rev: BL 11/1/10; SLJ 1/1/11)

1736 Little, Kimberley Griffiths. *The Healing Spell* (5–8). 2010, Scholastic $17.99 (978-0-545-16559-4). 368pp. A healer in the Louisiana bayou gives 12-year-old Livie a spell to help coax her mother out of a coma. Lexile 800L (Rev: BL 6/10; LMC 8–9/10; SLJ 11/1/10)

1737 Lytton, Deborah. *Jane in Bloom* (5–8). 2009, Dutton $16.99 (978-0-525-42078-1). 182pp. When 12-year-old Jane's "perfect" older sister Lizzie dies of anorexia, Jane's parents separate and the girl is left to cope by herself — which she does with the aid of a babysitter, a puppy, a digital camera, and a new friend. ℮ Lexile HL540L (Rev: BL 2/15/09; SLJ 5/1/09)

1738 McDonough, Yona Zeldis. *The Cats in the Doll Shop* (2–5). Illus. by Heather Maione. 2011, Viking $14.99 (978-0-670-01279-4). 128pp. In 1915 Anna, 11, welcomes her cousin Trudie from Russia; Trudie is shy and withdrawn until her love of cats helps her to adjust; a sequel to *The Doll Shop Downstairs* (2009). ℮ (Rev: BL 12/1/11; LMC 3–4/12; SLJ 12/1/11)

1739 McKinnon, Hannah Roberts. *The Properties of Water* (4–7). 2010, Farrar $16.99 (978-0-0374-36145-). 169pp. When her older sister Marni is paralyzed in a diving accident, 12-year-old Lacey's life is turned upside down. (Rev: BL 11/1/10; SLJ 12/1/10)

1740 MacLachlan, Patricia. *Kindred Souls* (3–5). 2012, HarperCollins $14.99 (978-006052297-1). 128pp. When Jake's grandfather is hospitalized, the boy makes the old man's dream of rebuilding the sod house where he was born a reality. (Rev: BL 1/12; HB 1–2/12; SLJ 4/1/12)

1741 Martin, Ann M. *Ten Rules for Living with My Sister* (3–6). 2011, Feiwel & Friends $16.99 (978-0-312-36766-4). 240pp. When their grandfather moves in, 9-year-old Pearl and 13-year-old Lexie have to share a room and find a way to get along. ℮ Lexile 790L (Rev: BL 8/11; HB 9–10/11; SLJ 10/1/11; VOYA 10/11)

1742 Monninger, Joseph. *Wish* (5–8). 2010, Delacorte $17.99 (978-0-385-73941-2); LB $20.99 (978-0-385-90788-0). 190pp. Fifteen-year-old Bee sets out to give her little brother Tommy, an 11-year-old with cystic fibrosis, the experience of a lifetime — a chance to swim with sharks. ℮ (Rev: BL 12/1/10*; SLJ 1/1/11)

1743 Murphy, Sally. *Pearl Verses the World* (2–4). Illus. by Heather Potter. 2011, Candlewick $14.99 (978-0-7636-4821-3). 73pp. Lonely young Pearl doesn't fit in at school and longs to be at home with her mother and grandmother, who unfortunately is dying; Pearl recounts her life in non-rhyming verse. (Rev: HB 9–10/11; SLJ 9/1/11)

1744 Nielsen, Susin. *Dear George Clooney, Please Marry My Mom* (5–8). 2010, Tundra $18.95 (978-0-88776-977-1). 240pp. Fed up with her phony new stepmom, and her mother's out-of-control dating, 12-year-old Violet decides that George Clooney would be the perfect dad replacement. ℮ (Rev: BL 9/1/10; SLJ 9/1/10; VOYA 10/10)

1745 Pennypacker, Sara. *Clementine and the Family Meeting* (2–4). Illus. by Marla Frazee. 2011, Hyperion/Disney $14.99 (978-1-4231-2356-9). 160pp. Third-grader Clementine copes with mixed feelings when her parents announce there's a new baby on the way. (Rev: BL 7/11; SLJ 8/1/11)

1746 Rocklin, Joanne. *The Five Lives of Our Cat Zook* (3–6). 2012, Abrams $16.95 (978-141970192-4). 240pp. When their beloved cat Zook falls ill, 10-year-old Oona explains to her younger brother that Zook has only used five of his nine lives — and then explains them all. (Rev: BL 3/15/12*; SLJ 4/12)

1747 Rosenthal, Betsy R. *Looking for Me* (4–7). 2012, Houghton Mifflin $15.99 (978-054761084-9). 176pp.

The fourth of 12 children in a Jewish family in 1936 Baltimore, 11-year-old Edith finds it difficult to establish her own identity. ℮ (Rev: BL 4/15/12; SLJ 4/12)

1748 Snyder, Laurel. *Penny Dreadful* (3–6). Illus. by Abigail Halpin. 2010, Random House $16.99 (978-0-375-86199-4); LB $19.99 (978-0-375-96199-1). 320pp. When wealthy Penelope Grey's father quits his job, the family is forced to move to a less-opulent Tennessee farm house, where Penny has the freedom she's always wanted. ♫ ℮ Lexile 740L (Rev: BL 10/1/10*; LMC 1–2/11; SLJ 1/1/11)

1749 Soetoro-ng, Maya. *Ladder to the Moon* (3–5). Illus. by Yuyi Morales. 2011, Candlewick $16.99 (978-0-7636-4570-0). 48pp. A golden ladder takes young Suhaila and her deceased Grandma Annie on a journey to the moon, where they meet people in need of help; written by Barack Obama's half-sister, this mystical story is a tribute to their mother. Lexile AD830L (Rev: BL 3/1/11*; LMC 8–9/11; SLJ 4/11)

1750 Spinelli, Eileen. *The Dancing Pancake* (3–6). Illus. by Joanne Lew-Vriethoff. 2010, Knopf $12.99 (978-0-375-85870-3); LB $15.99 (978-0-375-95870-0). 256pp. After her parents separate, Bindi, 11, moves with her mother into an apartment over the cafe that her aunt owns, where Bindi finds new friends and understanding. ℮ Lexile 440L (Rev: BL 4/1/10; LMC 8–9/10; SLJ 5/10)

1751 Spinelli, Jerry. *Jake and Lily* (4–6). 2012, HarperCollins $15.99 (978-006028135-9). 352pp. Twins Jake and Lily, 11, cope with growing up and losing the closeness they've shared since birth. (Rev: BL 2/15/12; HB 5–6/12; SLJ 6/12)

1752 Springstubb, Tricia. *Mo Wren, Lost and Found* (4–6). Illus. by Heather Ross. 2011, HarperCollins $15.99 (978-0-06-199039-7). 256pp. After their mother's death, 10-year-old Mo and her younger sister Dottie must move to the other side of town, attend a new school, and start a new life in an apartment above their father's new business. (Rev: BL 9/1/11*; SLJ 11/1/11)

1753 Summers, Laura. *Desperate Measures* (4–7). 2011, Putnam $16.99 (978-0-399-25616-5). 250pp. Vicky, 13, her mentally disabled twin sister Rhianna, and their younger brother Jamie run away to their aunt's cottage to avoid being split up by the foster care system. (Rev: LMC 11–12/11; SLJ 7/11)

1754 Warner, Sally. *Happily Ever Emma* (2–4). Illus. by Jamie Harper. 2010, Viking $14.99 (978-0-670-01084-4). 144pp. Third-grader Emma is unhappy to learn that her divorced mother is dating, but feels very guilty when she deliberately fails to pass on a message. ℮ Lexile 790L (Rev: BL 12/15/10; SLJ 1/1/11)

1755 Whittemore, Jo. *Odd Girl In* (5–7). 2011, Simon & Schuster paper $6.99 (978-1-4424-1284-2). 234pp. Unruly Alex, 12, and her older twin brothers are enrolled in a good behavior program after one prank too many, and, despite the various challenges, the whole experience turns out well in this novel full of humor. ☻ (Rev: SLJ 3/1/11)

1756 Yee, Lisa. *Aloha, Kanani* (3–5). Illus. by Sarah Davis. 2011, American Girl $12.95 (978-1-59369-840-9); paper $6.95 (978-159369839-3). 120pp. Kanani, a 10-year-old Hawaiian girl, finds herself less content with her island life when her cousin Rachel arrives from New York City with suitcases of clothes and a dislike of swimming and surfing. (Rev: BL 5/1/11; SLJ 8/11)

1757 Yee, Lisa. *Bobby the Brave (Sometimes)* (2–4). Illus. by Dan Santat. 2010, Scholastic $15.99 (978-0-545-05594-9). 160pp. Bobby worries that his unathletic nature and asthma disappoint his former-football-star dad; he's reassured when he that sees Dad struggles with things like cooking and sewing. ☻ Lexile 690L (Rev: BL 12/1/10; HB 9–10/10; SLJ 8/1/10)

Fantasy and the Supernatural

1758 Abela, Deborah. *The Ghosts of Gribblesea Pier* (3–6). 2011, Farrar $15.99 (978-0-374-36239-3). 240pp. On her 12th birthday, Aurelie learns a secret about ghosts that may help her stop a greedy villain from demolishing her family's amusement park. ☻ (Rev: LMC 1–2/12; SLJ 11/1/11)

1759 Alexander, R. C. *Unfamiliar Magic* (5–8). 2010, Random House $17.99 (978-0-375-85854-3). 368pp. Desi, a young witch whose mother has left on a mysterious quest, must fend for herself with only a cat in human form for companionship. Lexile 650L (Rev: BLO 4/15/10; LMC 8–9/10; SLJ 4/10)

1760 Anderson, M. T. *The Empire of Gut and Bone* (5–8). Series: Norumbegan Quartet. 2011, Scholastic $17.99 (978-0-545-13884-0). 336pp. In the land of New Norumbega, Brian and Gregory plead with the lazy, snooty inhabitants — who live inside an alien body — to resist the Thusser invasion of Vermont; the third volume in the series. (Rev: BL 5/1/11; SLJ 7/11)

1761 Anderson, M. T. *The Suburb Beyond the Stars* (5–8). Series: Norumbegan Quartet. 2010, Scholastic $17.99 (978-0-545-13882-6). 240pp. Brian and Gregory discover that Prudence is missing, a strange suburb has appeared near her Vermont home, time is not working properly, and the Thussers threaten destruction; a sequel to *The Game of Sunken Places* (2004). Lexile 620L (Rev: BL 6/10; LMC 11–12/10; SLJ 7/10)

1762 Appelbaum, Susannah. *The Tasters Guild* (4–7). Illus. by Jennifer Taylor. Series: Poisons of Caux. 2010, Knopf $16.99 (978-0-375-85174-2); LB $19.99 (978-0-375-95174-9). 384pp. In this exciting second installment, Poison Ivy and her friends battle new dangers as they work to save King Verdigris. (Rev: BL 11/15/10; SLJ 8/10)

1763 Arbuthnott, Gill. *The Keeper's Tattoo* (5–8). 2010, Scholastic $17.99 (978-0-545-17166-3). 432pp. In a land called Archipelago, 15-year-old Nyssa and her twin brother bear tattoos that hold the secret to the ancient cult of the Keepers; but her brother is being held by the cruel Alaric, and Nyssa must rescue him. ☻ Lexile 790L (Rev: BLO 5/25/10; LMC 10/10; SLJ 7/10)

1764 Armstrong, Alan. *Looking for Marco Polo* (4–7). Illus. by Tim Jessell. 2009, Random House $16.99 (978-0-375-83321-2); LB $19.99 (978-0-375-93321-9). 304pp. Eleven-year-old Mark hears many stories about famed explorer Marco Polo when recovering from an asthma attack while searching for his missing father in the Gobi Desert. Lexile 830L (Rev: BL 8/09; SLJ 12/09)

1765 Baggott, Julianna. *The Ever Breath* (4–6). 2009, Delacorte $16.99 (978-0-385-73761-6); LB $19.99 (978-0-385-90676-0). 240pp. After their father goes missing, twins Truman and Camille follow a secret passageway to the Breath World and encounter unusual creatures as they look for the Ever Breath, a magical stone that maintains balance between worlds. ☻ Lexile 680L (Rev: BL 10/1/09; LMC 11–12/09; SLJ 1/10)

1766 Baker, E. D. *The Dragon Princess* (5–8). Series: Tales of the Frog Princess. 2008, Bloomsbury $16.99 (978-159990194-7). 250pp. In hopes of controlling an unfortunate flaw — she turns into a dragon whenever she's upset — 15-year-old princess Millie appeals to the Blue Witch for help in this lighthearted tale. ♫ ☻ Lexile 820L (Rev: BLO 11/15/08; VOYA 12/08)

1767 Baker, E. D. *Fairy Lies* (5–8). Series: Wings: A Fairy Tale. 2012, Bloomsbury $16.99 (978-159990550-1). 256pp. Half-fairy Tamisin's half-goblin boyfriend Jak endeavors to rescue her when she's kidnapped by King Oberon in this fast-paced sequel to *Wings: A Fairy Tale* (2008). (Rev: LMC 3–4/12; SLJ 3/12; VOYA 2/12)

1768 Barnhill, Kelly. *The Mostly True Story of Jack* (5–8). 2011, Little, Brown $16.99 (978-0-316-05670-0). 323pp. Dumped with his aunt and uncle, Jack — who has considered himself virtually invisible up till now — soon realizes that there is something strange going on in Hazelwood, Iowa, and he is suddenly the center of attention. ♫ ☻ Lexile 740L (Rev: BL 8/11*; LMC 10/11; SLJ 9/1/11; VOYA 8/11)

1769 Barnholdt, Lauren. *Hailey Twitch and the Campground Itch* (2–4). Illus. by Suzanne Beaky. Series: Hailey Twitch. 2011, Sourcebooks paper $6.99 (978-1-4022-2446-1). 144pp. Hailey enjoys a camping vacation with family and friends, but her sprite friend Maybelle's magic seems to be misfiring. (Rev: SLJ 7/11)

1770 Barnholdt, Lauren. *Hailey Twitch Is Not a Snitch* (2–4). Illus. by Suzanne Beaky. Series: Hailey Twitch. 2010, Sourcebooks paper $9.99 (978-140222444-7). 160pp. Second-grader Hailey takes responsibility for the havoc created by Maybelle, a sprite who lives in

Hailey's dollhouse and is determined to prove that she is not a total follower of rules. Also use *Hailey Twitch and the Great Teacher Switch* (2010). (Rev: BL 7/10; LMC 8–9/10)

1771 Barron, T. A. *Doomraga's Revenge* (5–8). Series: Merlin's Dragon Trilogy. 2009, Philomel $16.99 (978-0-399-25212-9). 256pp. The powerful dragon Basil tackles threats to Avalon while Merlin is preoccupied with personal woes; the middle volume in the trilogy. The trilogy conclusion is *Ultimate Magic* (2010). (Rev: BL 9/1/09; SLJ 9/09)

1772 Barry, Dave, and Ridley Pearson. *The Bridge to Never Land* (4–6). Series: Never Land. 2011, Hyperion/Disney $18.99 (978-1-4231-3865-5). 448pp. Sarah and Aidan find themselves in danger when they follow clues to the origins of Peter Pan. ☊ (Rev: BL 7/11; SLJ 9/1/11)

1773 Barry, Dave, and Ridley Pearson. *Peter and the Sword of Mercy* (4–6). Illus. by Greg Call. Series: Starcatchers. 2009, Hyperion/Disney $18.99 (978-1-4231-2134-3). 516pp. This action-packed adventure set in 1901 involves Peter and Molly's daughter Wendy and a magical sword that once belonged to Charlemagne. ℯ Lexile 710L (Rev: BL 2/1/10; LMC 5–6/10; SLJ 3/10; VOYA 2/10)

1774 Bauer, A. C. E. *Come Fall* (4–7). 2010, Random House $15.99 (978-0-375-85825-3). 240pp. Misfits Salman, Lu, and Blos become friends in 7th grade and deal with bullies, dysfunctional homes, and other problems with some input from Puck, Oberon, and Titania in this fantasy inspired by *A Midsummer Night's Dream.* ℯ (Rev: BL 7/10; LMC 10/10; SLJ 9/1/10)

1775 Bauer, Marion Dane. *The Golden Ghost* (2–3). Illus. by Peter Ferguson. 2011, Random House $12.99 (978-0-375-86649-4); LB $15.99 (978-0-375-96649-1). 96pp. A canine ghost awaits Delsie and her friend Todd as they investigated an abandoned house. ℯ (Rev: BL 3/15/11; SLJ 4/11)

1776 Bauer, Marion Dane. *The Very Little Princess* (2–4). Illus. by Elizabeth Sayles. 2010, Random House $12.99 (978-0-375-85691-4); LB $15.99 (978-0-375-95691-1). 128pp. Visiting her grandmother for the first time, 10-year-old Zoey discovers a tiny china doll that comes to life and starts ordering her around. (Rev: BL 11/15/09; LMC 3–4/10; SLJ 4/1/10)

1777 Bell, Hilari. *Crown of Earth* (5–8). Series: The Shield, Sword, and Crown. 2009, Simon & Schuster $16.99 (978-1-4169-0598-1). 272pp. In this fast-paced stand-alone sequel to *Sword of Waters* (2008), Prince Edoran endeavors to save the life of the hostage Weasel by enlisting the help of his friend Arisa. Lexile 880L (Rev: SLJ 10/09)

1778 Bell, Hilari. *The Goblin Gate* (5–8). Series: The Goblin Wood. 2010, HarperCollins $16.99 (978-0-06-165102-1). 384pp. Jeriah goes off in search of the spell that will open the gate to the otherworld and release his brother; the sequel to 2003's *The Goblin Wood.* ℯ Lexile 750L (Rev: HB 9–10/10; SLJ 10/1/10)

1779 Benz, Derek, and J. S. Lewis. *Grey Griffins: The Brimstone Key* (5–8). Series: The Clockwork Chronicles. 2010, Little, Brown $15.99 (978-0-316-04522-3). 353pp. Max, Harley, Natalia, and Ernie, four children with superpowers, enter middle school at Iron Bridge Academy, where they will train to fight against the forces of evil, including a threat known as the Clockwork King; a sequel series to the Grey Griffins. Lexile 770L (Rev: BLO 4/15/10; LMC 8–9/10; SLJ 8/10; VOYA 10/10)

1780 Berkeley, Jon. *The Hidden Boy* (3–6). Series: Bell Hoot Fables. 2010, HarperCollins $16.99 (978-0-06-168758-7). 262pp. Thinking they've won a vacation, members of the Flint family find themselves instead in a very strange place — suddenly minus son Theo — and Bea must find her little brother. Lexile 800L (Rev: BL 12/1/09; LMC 3–4/10; SLJ 4/10)

1781 Berry, Julie Gardner. *The Rat Brain Fiasco* (3–6). Illus. by Sally Faye Gardner. Series: Splurch Academy for Disruptive Boys. 2010, Grosset & Dunlap paper $6.99 (978-0-448-45359-0). 199pp. Troublemaker Cody Mack is sent off to a supposed reformatory boarding school but soon discovers it is in fact run by monsters with evil intentions toward the students; part prose narrative and part graphic novel, this book mixes humor and suspense. ℯ Lexile 510L (Rev: SLJ 11/1/10)

1782 Booraem, Ellen. *Small Persons with Wings* (5–7). 2011, Dial $16.99 (978-0-8037-3471-5). 304pp. When Mellie's family inherits a dilapidated inn, they find it swarming with fairy-like beings who are desperate to regain a magical moonstone. ℯ Lexile 660L (Rev: BL 1/1–15/11; HB 3–4/11; LMC 11–12/11; SLJ 1/1/11*)

1783 Bozarth, Jan. *Kerka's Book* (3–5). Illus. by Andrea Burden. Series: Fairy Godmother Academy. 2009, Random House LB $10.99 (978-0-375-95183-1); paper $7.99 (978-0-375-85183-4). 224pp. Kerka, soon to turn 13 and training as a fairy godmother, meets many magical creatures when she ventures into the world of Aventurine. (Rev: BLO 11/15/09; SLJ 1/10)

1784 Breitrose, Prudence. *Mousenet* (3–6). Illus. by Stephanie Yue. 2011, Hyperion/Disney $16.99 (978-142312489-4). 400pp. Megan, whose uncle has just invented the world's smallest computer, is befriended by a group of mice eager to use the computer to improve their own society — and even the planet. ℯ (Rev: BL 10/15/11; SLJ 1/12)

1785 Briggs, Andy. *Rise of the Heroes* (5–8). Series: Hero.com. 2009, Walker paper $7.99 (978-0-8027-9503-8). 251pp. Downloading superpowers including flight and laser vision proves irresistible to four teens who find their new abilities challenging at first. Lexile 780L (Rev: BL 8/09; SLJ 9/09)

1786 Bruchac, Joseph. *Dragon Castle* (5–8). 2011, Dial $16.99 (978-0-8037-3376-3). 352pp. A 15-year-old Slovakian prince, Rashko, must contend with the arrival of a rogue army when his parents are away and finds himself relying on the power of an ancestor who slayed a dragon. ℮ Lexile 850L (Rev: BLO 8/11; HB 9–10/11; LMC 1–2/12*; SLJ 8/11)

1787 Buckingham, Royce. *The Dead Boys* (5–8). 2010, Putnam $16.99 (978-0-399-25222-8). 203pp. Arriving in a Washington town where his mother will work at a nuclear plant, 12-year-old Teddy finds that his new friends are all dead and there is a menacing sycamore tree next door. ℮ Lexile 850L (Rev: SLJ 11/1/10)

1788 Burt, Marissa. *Storybound* (4–7). 2012, HarperCollins $16.99 (978-006202052-9). 416pp. Una Fairchild, 12, is magically transported to the Land of Story where she finds mystery and danger. (Rev: BL 3/15/12; SLJ 8/12)

1789 Buzbee, Lewis. *Bridge of Time* (5–8). 2012, Feiwel & Friends $17.99 (978-031238257-5). 304pp. Best friends Lee Jones and Joan Lee, 8th-graders who discover their respective parents are divorcing, wish they could go back to an earlier, better time — and get more than they bargained for. ℮ (Rev: BL 4/1/12; SLJ 5/1/12)

1790 Carman, Patrick. *Things That Go Bump in the Night* (4–6). Series: 3:15 Season One. 2011, Scholastic $12.99 (978-0-545-38475-9). 162pp. Ten chilling stories — each with an audio introduction and a video conclusion, available online — feature young teens in tense situations; requires Internet access or smart phone app. (Rev: LMC 1–2/12; SLJ 11/1/11)

1791 Carroll, Michael. *The Ascension: A Super Human Clash* (5–8). Series: Super Human. 2011, Philomel $16.99 (978-0-399-25624-0). 378pp. Villain Krodin returns in this second installment in the series and is conquered by the teenage superheroes after plenty of struggle and fast-paced action. Lexile 680L (Rev: SLJ 8/11)

1792 Catanese, P. W. *Dragon Games* (5–8). Series: The Books of Umber. 2010, Simon & Schuster $16.99 (978-1-4169-7521-2). 373pp. Lord Umber and his ward Happenstance travel to Sarnica in an attempt to sate an unquenchable thirst for knowledge about dragons and a disregard for looming danger. ⌒ ℮ Lexile 740L (Rev: SLJ 7/10)

1793 Chapman, Linda, and Steve Cole. *Be a Genie in Six Easy Steps* (3–5). 2009, HarperCollins $16.99 (978-0-06-125219-8). 326pp. Four new stepsiblings are adjusting to life together in the English countryside when they discover a book that can teach them how to become genies, with predictably unpredictable results. A sequel is *The Last Phoenix* (2010). Lexile 590L (Rev: BL 5/15/09; SLJ 12/09)

1794 Choldenko, Gennifer. *No Passengers Beyond This Point* (5–8). 2011, Dial $16.99 (978-0-8037-3534-7). 288pp. Three children sent to live in Colorado find themselves in a disconcerting alternate reality, and their determination to support each other is what pulls them through. ⌒ ℮ (Rev: BL 2/1/11; HB 1–2/11; LMC 5–6/11; SLJ 2/1/11; VOYA 4/11)

1795 Churchyard, Kathleen. *Bye for Now: A Wisher's Story* (4–7). 2011, Egmont $15.99 (978-1-60684-190-7). 272pp. Robin, 11, is not enjoying her birthday and wishes she could be someone else; the next day she wakes up in London in the body of 11-year-old Fiona, who has quite a different life — but is it better? ℮ (Rev: BL 9/1/11; SLJ 12/1/11)

1796 Clayton, Emma. *The Whisper* (5–8). 2012, Scholastic $17.99 (978-054531772-6). 320pp. Telepathic twins Mika and Ellie endeavor to halt the evil that is dividing the population into the poor on one side of The Wall and the megalomaniacs on the other side in this sequel to *The Roar* (2009). (Rev: BL 3/1/12; SLJ 3/12)

1797 Cody, Matthew. *The Dead Gentleman* (5–8). 2011, Knopf $15.99 (978-037585596-2); LB $18.99 (978-037595596-9). 288pp. A time-traveling device enables Tommy, a 1901 street urchin, to contact modern-day teen Jezebel; the two unite their strengths to save the world from zombies. (Rev: BL 2/1/12; SLJ 3/12)

1798 Cody, Matthew. *Powerless* (5–8). 2009, Knopf $15.99 (978-0-375-85595-5); LB $18.99 (978-0-375-95595-2). 288pp. When Daniel, 12, arrives in Noble's Green he soon learns that all the other kids have superpowers that they will lose when they turn 13. Can Daniel use his intelligence to prevent this? ⌒ ℮ Lexile 800L (Rev: BL 10/15/09; LMC 11–12/09; SLJ 1/10)

1799 Cohagan, Carolyn. *The Lost Children* (4–6). 2010, Aladdin $16.99 (978-1-4169-8616-4). 320pp. In this complex fantasy, lonely 12-year-old Josephine is transported to another realm — a medieval world that draws on the energy of children — where she discovers unknown strengths with her new friends Ida and Fargus. ℮ Lexile 740L (Rev: BL 1/1/10; LMC 5–6/10; SLJ 3/10)

1800 Cole, Steve. *Z. Rex* (5–8). Series: The Hunting. 2009, Philomel $16.99 (978-0-399-25253-2). 276pp. Scottish teenager Adam has to rely on himself when his dad leaves for a business trip and all manner of scary thugs — including a man-eating dinosaur — show up at his house. (Rev: BL 8/09; LMC 11–12/09; SLJ 10/09)

1801 Colfer, Eoin. *The Atlantis Complex* (5–8). Series: Artemis Fowl. 2010, Hyperion $17.99 (978-142312819-9). 368pp. In this seventh title in the series, Artemis combats global warming while struggling to overcome a serious case of the Atlantis Complex, an affliction that causes OCD, paranoia, and multiple personalities. ⌒ ℮ Lexile 900L (Rev: BL 10/1/10; VOYA 12/10)

1802 Colfer, Eoin. *The Time Paradox* (4–8). Series: Artemis Fowl. 2008, Hyperion $17.99 (978-1-4231-0836-

8). 391pp. Artemis travels back in time to retrieve a substance that will cure his mother's disease. ☊ **ℓ** Lexile 780L (Rev: SLJ 10/1/08; VOYA 10/08)

1803 Collodi, Carlo. *Pinocchio* (3–5). Trans. by Claude Sartirano. Illus. by Quentin Greban. 2010, NorthSouth $19.95 (978-073582324-2). 88pp. A carefully abridged and nicely illustrated version of the story about a puppet whose nose betrays him. (Rev: BL 1/1–15/11)

1804 Coman, Carolyn. *The Memory Bank* (4–6). Illus. by Rob Shepperson. 2010, Scholastic $16.99 (978-0-545-21066-9). 288pp. The full-page pen-and-ink and pencil drawings enhance this complex story about Hope Scroggins, who tries to find her younger sister Honey and ends up at the Memory Bank, where memories and dreams are sorted and stored. Lexile 730L (Rev: BL 11/1/10*; LMC 11–12/10; SLJ 12/1/10)

1805 Cook, Eileen. *Wishes for Beginners* (3–5). Series: Fourth Grade Fairy. 2011, Simon & Schuster paper $6.99 (978-1-4169-9812-9). 146pp. Willow, a 4th-grader honing her secret fairy powers, has high hopes of becoming friends with the popular Miranda until her own magic abilities seem to fail her. **ℓ** Lexile 670L (Rev: SLJ 7/11)

1806 Coombs, Kate. *The Runaway Dragon* (5–8). 2009, Farrar $16.99 (978-0-374-36361-1). 304pp. With powerful friends in tow, 16-year-old Princess Meg courageously pursues her dragon, Laddy, through the far reaches of an enchanted forest while dodging the evil witch Malison in this sequel to *The Runaway Princess* (2006). **ℓ** Lexile 780L (Rev: BL 9/1/09; HB 9–10/09; SLJ 9/09)

1807 Cowing, Sue. *You Will Call Me Drog* (5–8). 2011, Carolrhoda $16.95 (978-076136076-6). 288pp. A possessed puppet that won't come off a boy's hand turns out to be a good thing, helping him to stick up for himself. (Rev: BL 9/15/11; LMC 1–2/12; SLJ 2/12)

1808 Crilley, Paul. *Rise of the Darklings* (5–8). Series: Invisible Order. 2010, Egmont $16.99 (978-160684031-3); LB $19.99 (978-160684064-1). 352pp. A fast-paced, multilayered fantasy in which 12-year-old Emily Snow — used to selling watercress on the streets of Victorian London — finds herself in the middle of an ancient war. ☊ Lexile 650L (Rev: BLO 5/15/10; LMC 1–2/11; SLJ 10/10)

1809 Crum, Shutta. *Thomas and the Dragon Queen* (3–5). Illus. by Lee Wildish. 2010, Knopf $15.99 (978-0-375-8570-34); LB $18.99 (978-0-375-95703-1). 272pp. A diminutive 12-year-old named Thomas, who has managed to qualify as a knight, sets out to rescue a princess from a dragon. (Rev: BL 7/10; LMC 10/10; SLJ 8/1/10*)

1810 Dakin, Glenn. *The Society of Unrelenting Vigilance* (5–7). Series: Candle Man. 2009, Egmont $15.99 (978-1-60684-015-3); LB $18.99 (978-1-60684-047-4). 304pp. Young Theo discovers he has the ability to melt

people into puddles in this contemporary fast-paced adventure story with a Victorian feel. (Rev: BL 10/15/09; HB 1–2/10; LMC 11–12/09; SLJ 10/09)

1811 Dale, Anna. *Magical Mischief* (4–6). 2011, Bloomsbury $16.99 (978-1-59990-629-4); paper $7.99 (978-159990630-0). 304pp. When the magic in his bookstore gets out of hand, Mr. Hardbattle and his friends Miss Quint and 13-year-old Arthur look for a new home for it. (Rev: BL 5/1/11; SLJ 9/1/11)

1812 De Quidt, Jeremy. *The Toymaker* (5–8). 2010, Random House $16.99 (978-0-385-75180-3). 368pp. Orphaned young Mathias finds a piece of paper that holds a valuable secret and must elude his various pursuers in this eerie adventure. **ℓ** Lexile 710L (Rev: BL 7/10*; HB 9–10/10; LMC 11–12/10; SLJ 10/1/10)

1813 de Saint-Exupéry, Antoine. *The Little Prince* (4–8). Trans. from French by Richard Howard. Illus. by author. 2009, Houghton Mifflin $35 (978-0-547-26069-3). 64pp. This effective pop-up presentation will attract new readers to the classic story. (Rev: BL 12/15/09; SLJ 3/10)

1814 Diamand, Emily. *Raiders' Ransom* (4–8). Series: Raiders' Ransom. 2009, Scholastic $17.99 (978-0-545-14297-7). 352pp. In the early 23rd century, when global warming has put much of Great Britain underwater and at risk from attack by marauding Raiders, 13-year-olds Lilly and Zeph are from opposing tribes but must join forces to rescue the kidnapped daughter of the prime minister. Also use *Flood and Fire* (2011). ☊ Lexile 720L (Rev: BL 12/1/09; LMC 11–12/09; SLJ 12/09)

1815 DiTerlizzi, Tony. *A Hero for WondLa* (5–8). Illus. by author. 2012, Simon & Schuster $17.99 (978-141698312-5). 464pp. Eva Nine, 12, who was raised underground by a robot, finds her way to New Attica, a seeming utopia; but she soon discovers a sinister underbelly. ☊ **ℓ** (Rev: BL 3/15/12; SLJ 6/12; VOYA 6/12)

1816 D'Lacey, Chris. *Gruffen* (K–2). Illus. by Adam Stower. Series: The Dragons of Wayward Crescent. 2009, Scholastic $9.99 (978-0-545-16815-1). 104pp. Nine-year-old Liz's mom makes her a dragon called Gruffen to protect her from a "monster" in her room; Gruffen gets off to a rocky start but eventually solves the problem. Lexile 700L (Rev: HB 1–2/10; LMC 11–12/09; SLJ 5/1/10)

1817 Dowell, Frances O'Roark. *Falling In* (4–7). 2010, Simon & Schuster $16.99 (978-1-4169-5032-5). 272pp. Middle-schooler Isabelle Bean suddenly finds herself in an alternate world in which a frightening witch might be her grandmother Grete. ☊ **ℓ** Lexile 850L (Rev: BL 1/1/10*; LMC 5–6/10; SLJ 4/10)

1818 Doyle, Bill. *Attack of the Shark-Headed Zombie* (3–5). Illus. by Scott Altmann. Series: Stepping Stones. 2011, Random House LB $12.99 (978-037596675-0); paper $4.99 (978-037586675-3). 112pp. Compelled to take jobs in order to afford new bikes, Henry and Keats sign up to clean a disheveled and spooky mansion; all manner of paranormal adventures ensue in this action-packed beginning chapter book. ℰ Lexile 480L (Rev: BL 4/15/11; LMC 10/11)

1819 Drago, Ty. *The Undertakers: Rise of the Corpses* (4–7). 2011, Sourcebooks paper $10.99 (978-1-4022-4785-9). 480pp. Gifted with the ability to see zombies, 12-year-old Will joins the Undertakers, a group determined to thwart the zombies' evil plans. (Rev: BL 5/1/11; SLJ 7/11)

1820 Duey, Kathleen. *Silence and Stone* (3–5). Illus. by Sandara Tang. Series: The Faeries' Promise. 2010, Simon & Schuster $15.99 (978-1-4169-8456-6); paper $4.99 (978-1-4169-8457-3). 109pp. Fairy Alida tells a lie in order to escape from the castle where she has been confined for decades. (Rev: SLJ 9/1/10)

1821 Ebbitt, Carolyn Q. *The Extra-Ordinary Princess* (5–8). 2009, Bloomsbury $16.99 (978-1-59990-340-8). 320pp. A younger, overlooked princess is thrust into the spotlight when an evil uncle tries to take over Gossling, leaving her to rescue her older siblings and save the kingdom. (Rev: BL 5/15/09; LMC 1–2/10; SLJ 9/09)

1822 Else, Barbara. *The Traveling Restaurant: Jasper's Voyage in Three Parts* (4–7). 2012, Gecko $17.95 (978-187757903-5). 295pp. When the powerful Lady Gall sets Jasper's family in her sights, the 12-year-old sets off on an epic search involving aspects of fantasy, time travel, mystery, and seafaring. (Rev: BLO 4/1/12; HB 5–6/12; SLJ 3/12)

1823 Epstein, Adam Jay, and Andrew Jacobson. *The Familiars* (4–6). Illus. by Bobby Chiu. Series: The Familiars. 2010, HarperCollins $16.99 (978-0-06-196108-3). 368pp. A streetwise cat finds himself posing as an assistant to a boy magician and must persuade other "familiars" that he is the genuine thing. ℰ Lexile 920L (Rev: BL 6/1/10; SLJ 8/10)

1824 Epstein, Adam Jay, and Andrew Jacobson. *Secrets of the Crown* (4–6). Illus. by Peter Chan and Kei Acedera. Series: The Familiars. 2011, HarperCollins $16.99 (978-0-06-196111-3). 384pp. With human magic gone, three animals — Aldwyn the cat, Skylar the blue jay, and Gilbert the tree frog — set out to wrest control of the Shifting Fortress from the evil rabbit Paksahara and restore the status quo. ℰ Lexile 930L (Rev: BLO 11/15/11; SLJ 8/11; VOYA 12/11)

1825 Evans, Nate. *Meet the Beast* (2–4). Illus. by Vince Evans. 2010, Sourcebooks paper $4.99 (978-1-4022-4050-8). 128pp. Nine-year-old Zeke and his little sister receive a tiny monster named Otto, who causes some problems but is also useful at discouraging bullies; this early chapter book is highly illustrated and occasionally jumps into graphic novel format. (Rev: BL 11/1/10; SLJ 3/1/11)

1826 Fagan, Deva. *The Magical Misadventures of Prunella Bogthistle* (4–8). 2010, Henry Holt $16.99

(978-0-8050-8743-7). 272pp. Prunella isn't very successful as a witch, but during her quest to find the Mirable Chalice, she finds that she has other talents; plenty of details about life as a witch make this an entertaining read. Lexile 640L (Rev: LMC 8–9/10; SLJ 6/10; VOYA 6/10)

1827 Flanagan, John. *Halt's Peril* (5–8). Series: Ranger's Apprentice. 2010, Philomel $17.99 (978-039925207-5). 320pp. In this ninth installment in the series, Will and Horace defy danger and save Halt by trusting each other and working together. ∩ ℰ Lexile 800L (Rev: BL 9/15/10)

1828 Flanagan, John. *The Kings of Clonmel* (5–8). Series: Ranger's Apprentice. 2010, Philomel $17.99 (978-039925206-8). 368pp. Halt, Will, and Horace work against a cult religion called the Outsiders and they discover secrets from Halt's past in this eighth installment in the series. ∩ Lexile 830L (Rev: BLO 6/10; VOYA 6/10)

1829 Flanagan, John. *The Lost Stories* (5–8). Series: Ranger's Apprentice. 2011, Philomel $17.99 (978-039925618-9). 352pp. A collection of nine stories that give the back story to the Ranger's Apprentice series. ∩ ℰ (Rev: BL 11/15/11; SLJ 4/12)

1830 Flanagan, John. *The Outcasts* (5–9). Series: Brotherband Chronicles. 2011, Philomel $18.99 (978-039925619-6). 432pp. In an alternate Scandinavia called Skandia outcasts Hal, Stig, and other 16-year-olds undertake military training and compete with each other in races at sea. ∩ ℰ (Rev: BL 11/15/11*; SLJ 2/12)

1831 Flanagan, John. *The Siege of Macindaw* (4–8). Series: Ranger's Apprentice. 2009, Philomel $17.99 (978-039925033-0). 304pp. Will, Horace, and a healer band together with the Skandians to reclaim Castle Macindaw and rescue Alyss in this sixth installment in the series. Also use *The Emperor of Nihon-Ja* (2011). ∩ ℰ Lexile 850L (Rev: BLO 4/15/09)

1832 Fletcher, Charlie. *Silvertongue* (5–8). Series: Stoneheart Trilogy. 2009, Hyperion $16.99 (978-1-4231-0179-6). 480pp. In this final book in the trilogy, George, 13, and Edie, 12, employ their newfound gifts — and receive help from statues come to life — in the fight against the Walker, the Last Knight, and the Ice Devil. (Rev: SLJ 6/1/09; VOYA 4/09)

1833 Funke, Cornelia. *Ghost Knight* (4–6). Trans. by Oliver Latsch. Illus. by Andrea Offermann. 2012, Little, Brown $16.99 (978-031605614-4). 352pp. Boarding school newcomer Jon's homesickness vanishes when he's confronted by fearsome ghosts in this exciting story set in Salisbury, England. ∩ ℰ (Rev: BL 3/1/12; HB 5–6/12; LMC 8–9/12; SLJ 7/12)

1834 Galante, Cecilia. *Willa Bean's Cloud Dreams* (2–4). Illus. by Kristi Valiant. Series: Little Wings. 2011, Random House LB $12.99 (978-037596947-8); paper $4.99 (978-037586947-1). 112pp. Willa Bean is a young cupid who looks a bit different from the norm, and is nervous about her ability to fly. **e** (Rev: BL 12/15/11)

1835 Gardner, Lyn. *Out of the Woods* (3–7). Illus. by Mini Grey. 2010, Random House $17.99 (978-0-385-75154-4); LB $20.99 (978-0-385-75156-8). 320pp. Poking fun at well-known fairy tale tropes, this story features an evil witch, a magic pipe, and three plucky sisters who are ready to face any challenge; a sequel to 2006's *Into the Woods*. (Rev: BLO 2/1/10; HB 3–4/10; SLJ 6/10)

1836 George, Jessica Day. *Tuesdays at the Castle* (4–8). 2011, Bloomsbury $16.99 (978-1-59990-644-7). 232pp. Princess Celie, 11, lives in a magical castle that has the power to change itself at will; it also has its favorite people and it comes to the aid of Celie when her parents are in danger. **e** Lexile 860L (Rev: LMC 1–2/12; SLJ 11/1/11)

1837 Gibbs, Stuart. *The Last Musketeer* (5–8). 2011, HarperCollins $16.99 (978-0-06-204838-7). 256pp. On a trip to Paris 14-year-old Greg is whisked back to 1615 France, where he meets young Aramis, Porthos, and Athos and has adventures including a struggle against Richelieu. Lexile 700L (Rev: BL 10/15/11; LMC 1–2/12; SLJ 10/1/11)

1838 Gliori, Debi. *Witch Baby and Me* (4–6). Illus. by author. Series: Witch Baby and Me. 2010, IPG/Corgi paper $7.99 (978-055255676-7). 247pp. Nine-year-old Lily is aware that her baby sister Daisy has unusual powers and seeks to curb their wayward effects. **e** (Rev: BLO 12/1/10; SLJ 9/1/10)

1839 Gliori, Debi. *Witch Baby and Me After Dark* (3–5). Illus. by author. 2010, IPG/Corgi paper $7.99 (978-055255678-1). 208pp. Nine-year-old Lily struggles to keep her baby sister (who's really a witch) in disguise in this British Halloween story. The fourth installment in the series is *Witch Baby and Me on Stage* (2011). **e** (Rev: BL 9/1/10; SLJ 9/1/10)

1840 Golding, Julia. *Mines of the Minotaur* (5–8). Series: The Companions Quartet. 2008, Marshall Cavendish $16.99 (978-0-7614-5302-4). 269pp. This installment in the series features Connie, a 13-year-old who has a gift for communicating with mythical creatures. (Rev: SLJ 10/1/08; VOYA 6/08)

1841 Grabenstein, Chris. *The Black Heart Crypt* (5–8). Series: Haunted Mystery. 2011, Random House $16.99 (978-037586900-6); LB $19.99 (978-037596900-3). 336pp. Thirteen-year-old Zack and his friends face vengeful ghosts on Halloween in this scary fourth book in the series. **e** (Rev: BL 8/11; SLJ 2/12)

1842 Haberdasher, Violet. *Knightley Academy* (4–8). Series: Knightley Academy. 2010, Simon & Schuster $15.99 (978-1-4169-9143-4). 469pp. Orphan Henry Grim becomes the first commoner to attend the pres-

tigious Knightley Academy, which trains police and other public authorities in the Britonian Isles, and soon uncovers a plot to start war. **e** Lexile 860L (Rev: BL 2/15/10; SLJ 4/10)

1843 Haberdasher, Violet. *The Secret Prince* (5–8). Series: Knightley Academy. 2011, Aladdin $16.99 (978-1-4169-9145-8). 256pp. Back at Knightley Academy and studying for their knighthood, Henry and his friends start a secret battle society and Henry learns about his parents and his destiny. Lexile 830L (Rev: BL 7/11; LMC 10/11; SLJ 8/11)

1844 Hardinge, Frances. *Fly Trap* (5–8). 2011, HarperCollins $16.99 (978-0-06-088044-6). 592pp. Orphan Mosca, her goose, and con man Eponymous Clent journey to the city of Toll, which is divided into the parallel towns of Toll-by-Day and the scary Toll-by-Night. (Rev: BL 3/15/11; HB 5–6/11; SLJ 6/11; VOYA 6/11)

1845 Hardy, Janice. *The Shifter* (5–8). Series: The Healing Wars. 2009, HarperCollins $16.99 (978-0-06-174704-5); LB $17.89 (978-0-06-176177-5). 384pp. Fifteen-year-old Nya and her younger sister have the ability to remove pain, but Nya's gift is more tenuous and puts her in danger. **e** Lexile 630L (Rev: BL 10/15/09; HB 11–12/09; SLJ 1/10)

1846 Harper, Suzanne. *A Gaggle of Goblins* (4–6). Series: Unseen World of Poppy Malone. 2011, Greenwillow $16.99 (978-0-06-199607-8). 304pp. Poppy Malone, 9-year-old daughter of paranormal investigators, is skeptical of such shenanigans until her family moves to Texas and Poppy meets a goblin in the attic of their house. (Rev: BL 5/1/11; SLJ 11/1/11)

1847 Harris, Lewis. *A Taste for Red* (4–6). 2009, Clarion $16 (978-054714462-7). 176pp. Sixth-grader Svetlana, unsettled by a move, becomes convinced she's a vampire because she sleeps under the bed, has heightened senses, and eats only red foods; but then she meets teacher Ms. Larch, who has a vile odor and an evil smile. (Rev: BL 9/1/09; LMC 10/09; SLJ 9/09)

1848 Harrison, Michelle. *Thirteen Treasures* (5–8). 2010, Little, Brown $15.99 (978-0-316-04148-5). 368pp. Tanya, a 13-year-old whose sleep has been disrupted by fairies, is sent to stay with her grandmother at Elvesden Manor and there uncovers dark secrets that place her in danger. **e** Lexile 770L (Rev: BL 4/1/10; SLJ 4/10)

1849 Hartley, A. J. *Darwen Arkwright and the Peregrine Pact* (5–8). Illus. by Emily Osborne. 2011, Penguin $16.99 (978-1-59514-409-6). 448pp. Darwen, 11, receives a mysterious mirror that acts as a portal to another dimension full of battle and magic; his new friend Alexandra helps him make sense of all the mayhem. **e** Lexile 810L (Rev: BLO 10/15/11; SLJ 12/1/11)

1850 Hashimoto, Meika. *The Magic Cake Shop* (3–5). Illus. by Josée Masse. 2011, Random House $15.99 (978-0-375-86822-1); LB $18.99 (978-0-375-96822-8). 176pp. Sent to stay with her Uncle Simon, young

Emma triumphs over this loathsome relative with the help of a baker who has some magical abilities. (Rev: BL 10/15/11; SLJ 12/1/11)

1851 Haskell, Merrie. *The Princess Curse* (5–8). 2011, HarperCollins $16.99 (978-0-06-200813-8). 336pp. Based on the fairy tale about the dancing princesses, this story set in 15th-century Romania involves 13-year-old Reveka, apprentice to a herbalist, who tries to break the curse on the princesses of Sylvania. ℮ Lexile 790L (Rev: BL 10/15/11; SLJ 12/1/11)

1852 Hawes, Jason, and Grant Wilson. *Ghost Hunt: Chilling Tales of the Unknown* (4–8). 2010, Little, Brown $16.99 (978-0-316-09959-2). 304pp. Stories of ghost investigations by the Atlantic Paranormal Society are paired with discussion of the techniques used. Also use *Ghost Hunt 2: More Chilling Tales of the Unknown* (2011). ℮ (Rev: SLJ 11/1/10; VOYA 12/10)

1853 Haworth, Danette. *The Summer of Moonlight Secrets* (4–7). 2010, Walker $16.99 (978-0-8027-9520-5). 240pp. Allie Jo, who lives at a rundown hotel, befriends resident skateboarder Chase and the two spend a summer helping Tara, a girl who is part sea creature and is in danger. Lexile 610L (Rev: BL 6/10; LMC 8–9/10; SLJ 7/10)

1854 Hayter, Rhonda. *The Witchy Worries of Abbie Adams* (4–6). 2010, Dial $16.99 (978-0-8037-3468-5). 256pp. Fifth-grader Abbie, one of a long line of witches and trying to keep her talents hidden, is surprised when her new kitten turns out to be a young Thomas Edison. How to reverse the process? ℮ Lexile 1170L (Rev: BL 2/15/10; LMC 5–6/10; SLJ 4/10)

1855 Henderson, Jason. *Vampire Rising* (5–8). Series: Alex Van Helsing. 2010, HarperTeen $16.99 (978-006195099-5). 224pp. When he is sent to school in Switzerland, 14-year-old Alex Van Helsing learns that vampires are real and that his family has been participating in a vampire-hunting agency called the Polidorium since 1821. ℮ Lexile HL780L (Rev: BL 3/1/10; SLJ 5/10; VOYA 6/10)

1856 Henderson, Jason. *Voice of the Undead* (5–8). Series: Alex Van Helsing. 2011, HarperTeen $16.99 (978-0-06-195101-5). 304pp. Vampire hunter Alex Van Helsing has another exciting adventure, this time involving Ultravox, a vampire with special vocal gifts. (Rev: BL 5/1/11; SLJ 9/1/11)

1857 Higgins, F. E. *The Eyeball Collector* (5–8). 2009, Feiwel & Friends $14.99 (978-0-312-56681-4). 272pp. Young Hector Fitzbaudly seeks revenge for his father's death, setting out to track down the evil, one-eyed Gulliver Truepin. ℮ Lexile 950L (Rev: BL 9/15/09; HB 9–10/09; LMC 1–2/10; SLJ 11/09)

1858 Higgins, F. E. *The Lunatic's Curse* (5–8). 2011, Feiwel & Friends $15.99 (978-031256682-1). 352pp. Rex's quest to solve his father's death leads him to the insane asylum on Lake Beluarum in this page-turner

that includes an evil stepmother, steampunk aspects, and cannibalism. ℮ Lexile 810L (Rev: BL 8/11; LMC 11–12/11; SLJ 3/12)

1859 Higgins, Simon. *The Nightmare Ninja* (5–8). Series: Moonshadow. 2011, Little, Brown $15.99 (978-0-316-05533-8). 369pp. Moonshadow contends with the altered emotional state of his former rival, now comrade, Snowhawk as he continues to dodge the evil advances of Silver Wolf's underlings; the second book in the series. (Rev: SLJ 9/1/11)

1860 Hoffman, Nina Kiriki. *Thresholds* (5–7). 2010, Viking $15.99 (978-0-670-06319-2). 256pp. Maya moves with her family to Oregon after her best friend's death and the 7th-grader becomes fascinated with her mysterious neighbors, eventually discovering the portal into a fantastical realm they are guarding. ℮ Lexile 630L (Rev: BL 8/10; LMC 10/10; SLJ 9/1/10)

1861 Holt, K. A. *Brains for Lunch: A Zombie Novel in Haiku?!* (5–8). Illus. by Gahan Wilson. 2010, Roaring Brook $15.99 (978-1-59643-629-9). 96pp. Irreverent, sometimes gross, haiku tell the humorous story of a middle school populated by zombies, humans, and blood-sucking chupacabras. (Rev: BL 6/10; LMC 11–12/10; SLJ 10/1/10)

1862 Holub, Joan, and Suzanne Williams. *Athena the Brain* (4–6). Series: Goddess Girls. 2010, Simon & Schuster paper $5.99 (978-1-4169-8271-5). 176pp. Young Athena, 12, is taken aback when she is informed that she is a daughter of Zeus and must attend a goddess (and godboy) school on Mount Olympus. ℮ Lexile 710L (Rev: BLO 3/1/10; SLJ 4/10)

1863 Hood, Ann. *Angel of the Battlefield* (3–6). Illus. by Karl Kwasny. Series: Treasure Chest. 2011, Grosset & Dunlap $16.99 (978-044845471-9). 192pp. Reeling from their parents' divorce, twins Maisie and Felix, 12, arrive at a historic Rhode Island mansion, where a room full of artifacts transports them back to 1836 where they meet Clara Barton. ℮ (Rev: BLO 10/15/11; LMC 3–4/12)

1864 Horowitz, Anthony. *Return to Groosham Grange: The Unholy Grail* (5–8). 2009, Philomel $16.99 (978-0-399-25063-7). 214pp. In this funny and somewhat spooky tale, David competes with a new student to earn Groosham Grange's top prize, the magical cup known as the Unholy Grail; a sequel to *Groosham Grange* (2008). Lexile 690L (Rev: BL 8/09; SLJ 9/09; VOYA 8/09)

1865 Howell, Troy. *The Dragon of Cripple Creek* (5–8). 2011, Abrams $19.95 (978-0-8109-9713-4). 304pp. Kat, 12, falls into an abandoned mine chute in Colorado and discovers not only gold but an ancient dragon guarding the hoard; Kat inadvertently starts a 21st-century gold rush even as she seeks to protect the dragon and the environment. (Rev: BL 5/1/11; SLJ 7/11)

1866 Hunter, Erin. *Island of Shadows* (5–8). Series: Seekers: Return to the Wild. 2012, HarperCollins $16.99 (978-006199634-4). 304pp. Bears Toklo, Lusa, and Kallik, missing their former companion Ujurak, encounter many dangers as they make a difficult journey home in this first volume in a new series that is a companion to the Seeker books. (Rev: BL 1/1/12)

1867 Hunter, Erin. *Sign of the Moon* (5–8). Series: Warriors, Omen of the Stars. 2011, HarperCollins $16.99 (978-006155518-3). 352pp. Jayfeather prepares for a dangerous journey that will reveal truth about the final battle as clan disputes continue; the fourth installment in this series. (Rev: BL 9/1/11)

1868 Ibbotson, Eva. *The Ogre of Oglefort* (4–6). 2011, Dutton $16.99 (978-0-525-42382-9). 256pp. A quirky story about a depressed ogre, a princess, and would-be rescuers who all find a satisfying but unexpected ending. 𝖊 Lexile 910L (Rev: BL 7/11; HB 7–8/11; LMC 11–12/11; SLJ 8/11)

1869 Iggulden, Conn. *Tollins: Explosive Tales for Children* (3–6). Illus. by Lizzy Duncan. 2009, HarperCollins $16.99 (978-0-06-173098-6). 176pp. Three interlinked stories feature Tollins — winged creatures bigger than fairies; a young Tollin named Sparkler has several adventures, including one in which he saves his people from being used in fireworks production. (Rev: BL 2/15/10*; SLJ 2/1/10)

1870 Ita, Sam. *Frankenstein: A Pop-Up Book* (4–7). Illus. by author. 2010, Sterling $26.95 (978-1-4027-5865-2). 8pp. With pop-up features, this abridged graphic novel version is effectively scary. (Rev: BL 12/15/10; SLJ 9/1/10)

1871 Jacques, Brian. *Doomwyte* (5–8). Illus. by David Elliot. Series: Redwall. 2008, Philomel $23.99 (978-039924544-2). 400pp. In this latest installment in the series, two contemptible new villains are thwarted in their quest for the jeweled eyes of the Great Doomwyte Idol. 𝛀 Lexile 860L (Rev: BL 9/1/08)

1872 Jacques, Brian. *The Rogue Crew* (5–8). Illus. by Sean Rubin. Series: Redwall. 2011, Philomel $23.99 (978-039925416-1). 400pp. Wearat returns to exact revenge in this satisfying, action-packed final installment of the Redwall series. (Rev: BL 5/1/11)

1873 Jacques, Brian. *The Sable Quean* (5–8). Illus. by Sean Charles Rubin. Series: Redwall. 2010, Philomel $23.99 (978-039925164-1). 416pp. Buckler and other courageous Redwall creatures prepare to battle the evil Sable Quean when the abbey's young inhabitants start disappearing. 𝛀 (Rev: BLO 12/1/09; VOYA 12/09)

1874 Jenkins, Emily. *Invisible Inkling* (2–4). Illus. by Harry Bliss. 2011, HarperCollins $14.99 (978-0-06-180220-1). 160pp. A small creature called an Inkling helps Hank navigate 4th grade and its bullies when his best friend moves away. 𝖊 Lexile 570L (Rev: BL 6/1/11; HB 7–8/11; SLJ 7/11)

1875 Johnson-Shelton, Nils. *The Invisible Tower* (5–8). Series: Otherworld Chronicles. 2012, HarperCollins $16.99 (978-006207086-9). 352pp. Ordinary kid Artie Kingfisher, 12, learns that he is actually King Arthur brought back to life in the 21st century and that he must save the world from disaster. 𝛀 𝖊 (Rev: BL 3/1/12; SLJ 3/12; VOYA 2/12)

1876 Jonell, Lynne. *Hamster Magic* (1–3). Illus. by Brandon Dorman. 2010, Random House LB $15.99 (978-0-375-96660-6). 112pp. Four siblings adjusting to living in the country get way more than they bargained for when they come across a hamster prepared to grant their wishes. (Rev: BL 12/1/10; LMC 1–2/11; SLJ 1/1/11)

1877 Jones, Allan. *Fair Wind to Widdershins* (4–6). Illus. by Gary Chalk. Series: The Six Crowns. 2011, Greenwillow $15.99 (978-006200626-4). 176pp. Trundle the hedgehog and his friends continue their quest to find the notorious Crowns while keeping themselves safe from Captain Grizzletusk in this second installment in the series. Lexile 830L (Rev: BLO 10/15/11; SLJ 3/1/12)

1878 Jones, Allan. *Fire over Swallowhaven* (4–6). Illus. by Gary Chalk. Series: The Six Crowns. 2012, Greenwillow $15.99 (978-006200629-5). 160pp. Trundle, Esmeralda, and Jack's mission to find the third crown in the nest of the phoenix is interrupted by a call to battle. (Rev: BL 3/15/12)

1879 Jones, Allan. *Trundle's Quest* (4–6). Illus. by Gary Chalk. Series: The Six Crowns. 2011, Greenwillow $15.99 (978-0-06-200623-3). 176pp. Trundle the hedgehog's simple life as a lamplighter ends abruptly when Esmeralda, a Romany hedgehog, appears on the scene convinced that Trundle can help her find the Six Crowns of the Badgers of Power. Lexile 860L (Rev: BL 3/1/11; SLJ 5/1/11)

1880 Joyce, William, and Laura Geringer. *Nicholas St. North and the Battle of the Nightmare King* (3–5). Illus. by William Joyce. Series: The Guardians. 2011, Atheneum $14.99 (978-144243048-8). 240pp. Nicholas St. North defends the village of Santoff Claussen from the Nightmare King and his evil Fearlings, and then must seek five other Guardians to continue the fight in this first installment in the series. (Rev: BL 11/1/11)

1881 Kaye, Marilyn. *Here Today, Gone Tomorrow* (5–8). Series: Gifted. 2009, Kingfisher paper $7.99 (978-0-7534-6310-9). 224pp. When her classmates begin mysteriously disappearing, clairvoyant Emily battles low self-esteem and bullying and uses her talents to save them. Lexile HL610L (Rev: BL 11/1/09; SLJ 10/09)

1882 Kelley, Jane. *The Girl Behind the Glass* (3–5). 2011, Random House $16.99 (978-0-375-86220-5); LB $19.99 (978-0-375-96220-2). 192pp. Hannah, 11, is the only member of her family who can sense the spirit of the girl who died in her house 80 years earlier. (Rev: BL 9/1/11; SLJ 9/1/11)

1883 Kennedy, Kim. *Misty Gordon and the Mystery of the Ghost Pirates* (4–7). Illus. by Greg Call. 2010, Abrams $15.95 (978-0-8109-9357-0). 218pp. Eleven-year-old Misty finds an old diary that draws her into secrets of the past in this mystery involving ghosts and pirates. ☻ Lexile 780L (Rev: BL 9/1/10; LMC 1–2/11; SLJ 10/1/10)

1884 Kent, Derek Taylor. *Scary School, by Derek the Ghost* (3–6). Illus. by Scott M. Fischer. 2011, Harper-Collins $15.99 (978-006196092-5). 256pp. A series of comic and intriguing vignettes from Scary School — a place where monsters and humans learn together. ☻ (Rev: BL 7/11; LMC 11–12/11)

1885 Kessler, Liz. *Emily Windsnap and the Siren's Secret* (4–7). Illus. by Natacha Ledwidge. 2010, Candlewick $15.99 (978-0-7636-4374-4). 240pp. Emily helps to resolve a dispute between the merpeople of Shiprock and human developers, and in the process finds some lost sirens and solves a mystery. ☻ Lexile 590L (Rev: BLO 3/1/10; SLJ 4/10)

1886 Kessler, Liz. *A Year Without Autumn* (4–7). 2011, Candlewick $15.99 (978-0-7636-5595-2). 304pp. A ride in an old elevator transports 12-year-old Jenni into the future and provides unhappy news about her best friend Autumn's little brother; Jenni manages to return to the present and avert the accident that was in store. ☻ (Rev: BLO 11/15/11; LMC 1–2/12; SLJ 12/1/11)

1887 Kirby, Matthew J. *Icefall* (5–8). 2011, Scholastic $17.99 (978-0-545-27424-1). 336pp. In Viking times, Princess Solveig and her siblings are sent to a fortress on a fjord for safety during a war but soon realize that there is a traitor in their midst. ⌒ ☻ (Rev: BL 11/15/11; SLJ 11/1/11; VOYA 10/11)

1888 Klimo, Kate. *The Dragon in the Library* (4–6). Illus. by John Shroades. Series: Dragon Keepers. 2010, Random House $15.99 (978-0-375-85591-7); LB $18.99 (978-0-375-95591-4). 224pp. Dragon Keeper cousins Jesse and Daisy discover that their friend Professor Andersson — and their newly grumpy dragon Emmy — are both in danger in this installment that also introduces a magical library. ☻ (Rev: BL 5/15/10; SLJ 9/1/10)

1889 Klimo, Kate. *The Dragon in the Sea* (4–6). Illus. by John Shroades. Series: Dragon Keepers. 2012, Random House $15.99 (978-037587065-1); LB $18.99 (978-037597065-8). 224pp. Jesse, Daisy, and their dragon Emmy head underwater to rescue a newly discovered dragon egg from the snatches of a sea monster. (Rev: BL 5/15/12)

1890 Kloepfer, John. *The Zombie Chasers* (4–7). Illus. by Steve Wolfhard. Series: The Zombie Chasers. 2010, HarperCollins $15.99 (978-0-06-185304-3). 224pp. This is a gruesomely humorous — and graphically illustrated — story of a zombified neighborhood in which only Zack, Rice, Zoe, and Madison are normal and must defend themselves against the hungry crowd.

Also use *Undead Ahead* (2011). ☻ Lexile 760L (Rev: BL 4/15/10; LMC 11–12/10; SLJ 11/1/10)

1891 Knudsen, Michelle. *The Princess of Trelian* (4–7). 2012, Candlewick $16.99 (978-076365062-9). 448pp. Meg struggles to clear her dragon's name after a rash of attacks plague Lourin. (Rev: BL 3/15/12; HB 5–6/12; VOYA 6/12)

1892 Korman, Gordon. *The Medusa Plot* (5–8). Series: The 39 Clues: Cahills vs. Vespers. 2011, Scholastic $12.99 (978-054529839-1). 224pp. Amy and Dan Cahill combine their talents to rescue captured friends and family from the evil Vespers. ⌒ ☻ (Rev: BL 11/1/11; SLJ 4/12)

1893 Lairamore, Dawn. *Ivy and the Meanstalk* (5–8). 2011, Holiday House $16.95 (978-0-8234-2392-7). 240pp. Princess Ivy and her dragon friend Elridge struggle to set things right by returning a magical harp to the giant's widow in this fractured take on Jack and the Beanstalk. (Rev: BL 10/1/11; LMC 1–2/12; SLJ 9/1/11)

1894 Lairamore, Dawn. *Ivy's Ever After* (5–8). 2010, Holiday House $16.95 (978-0-8234-2261-6). 320pp. A well-meaning but somewhat cowardly dragon rescues a young, independent-minded princess from marrying an evil man. Lexile 980L (Rev: BL 5/15/10; SLJ 8/10)

1895 Lasky, Kathryn. *Daughters of the Sea: Hannah* (4–8). 2009, Scholastic $16.99 (978-0-439-78310-1). 320pp. Orphan Hannah, 15, gets a job as a scullery maid in 19th-century Boston, meets a young artist who seems to have an incredible understanding of her, and on a trip to the coast starts to recognize how she reacts to the presence of water. ☻ Lexile 800L (Rev: BL 9/1/09; SLJ 10/09; VOYA 2/10)

1896 Lasky, Kathryn. *Felix Takes the Stage* (2–4). Illus. by Stephen Gilpin. Series: The Deadlies. 2010, Scholastic $15.99 (978-054511681-7). 160pp. A family of recluse spiders flee their comfortable home in the Los Angeles symphony hall just ahead of the exterminator. The second book in the series is *Spiders on the Case* (2011), in which spiders foil humans who are stealing rare books from the Boston Public Library. ☻ Lexile 660L (Rev: BL 5/1/10)

1897 Lasky, Kathryn. *Lone Wolf* (5–8). Series: Wolves of the Beyond. 2010, Scholastic $15.99 (978-0-545-09310-1). 240pp. A young wolf with a defective paw is adopted by a mother grizzly bear who teaches him various skills in this first installment in the series. ⌒ ☻ Lexile 890L (Rev: BL 12/1/09; LMC 3–4/10; SLJ 3/10)

1898 Lasky, Kathryn. *Lucy* (5–8). Series: Daughters of the Sea. 2012, Scholastic $17.99 (978-043978-312-5). 312pp. Seventeen-year-old Lucy, who has been brought up in New York City by a minister and his ambitious wife, spends the summer in Bar Harbor, Maine, in 1899 and finds out about her sisters, her mother, and her affinity for the sea. ☻ (Rev: BLO 4/15/12)

1899 Lasky, Kathryn. *Shadow Wolf* (5–8). Series: Wolves of the Beyond. 2010, Scholastic $16.99 (978-0-545-09312-5). 272pp. Deformed wolf Faolan struggles to accept his lot as a lowly "gnaw wolf" even as a rival challenges him at every turn. ℯ Lexile 870L (Rev: BL 12/1/10; SLJ 1/1/11)

1900 Law, Ingrid. *Scumble* (5–8). 2010, Dial $16.99 (978-0-8037-3307-7). 416pp. It's Ledge's turn to acquire an unusual power on his 13th birthday in this companion to *Savvy* (2008), and his new ability to create havoc has unwelcome results. ∩ (Rev: BL 7/10*; HB 9–10/10; SLJ 9/1/10)

1901 Lawson, Julie. *Ghosts of the Titanic* (5–8). 2012, Holiday House $16.95 (978-082342423-8). 169pp. Parallel plots and a neat time-travel sequence splice the stories of modern-day class clown Kevin with that of young 1912 seamen Angus, who's been given the grim job of recovering the *Titanic* victims' bodies, in this complex story. (Rev: BL 2/15/12; LMC 11–12/12)

1902 Leeuwen, Joke van . *Eep!* (4–8). Trans. by Bill Nagelkerke. Illus. by author. 2012, Gecko paper $7.95 (978-187757907-3). 152pp. A childless couple's discovery and stewardship of an odd bird-girl bonds them to others who've cared for the creature in this touching, quirky tale. (Rev: BL 3/1/12*; HB 5–6/12; SLJ 3/12)

1903 Levine, Gail Carson. *Fairies and the Quest for Never Land* (3–5). Illus. by David Christiana. Series: Disney Fairies. 2010, Disney $18.99 (978-1-4231-0935-8). 224pp. In this modern day sequel, Peter Pan returns to whisk one of Wendy Darling's descendants away to Never Land, where she finds unexpected adventures. (Rev: BLO 5/15/10; SLJ 8/1/10)

1904 Levine, Gail Carson. *A Tale of Two Castles* (4–6). 2011, HarperCollins $16.99 (978-0-06-122965-7); LB $17.89 (978-0-06-122966-4). 336pp. Twelve-year-old Elodie finds herself working for a curmudgeonly dragon who teaches her to solve mysteries. ∩ ℯ Lexile 630L (Rev: BL 3/15/11; HB 5–6/11; SLJ 4/11)

1905 Lewis, Josh. *Super Chicken Nugget Boy and the Furious Fry* (2–4). Illus. by Douglas Holgate. Series: Super Chicken Nugget Boy. 2010, Hyperion/Disney $16.99 (978-1-4231-1491-8); paper $4.99 (978-1-4231-1492-5). 144pp. When Fern Goldberg falls into a vat of green liquid, his skin starts turning green whenever he comes into condiments such as ketchup. A sequel is *Super Chicken Nugget Boy and the Pizza Planet People* (2011). (Rev: LMC 11–12/10; SLJ 6/1/10)

1906 Littlewood, Kathryn. *Bliss* (3–6). 2012, HarperCollins $16.99 (978-006208423-1). 384pp. When their parents go away, the Bliss children are entrusted with keeping the magical recipes safe, but temptation proves too much and the results are unfortunate. ℯ (Rev: BL 2/1/12; SLJ 2/12; VOYA 12/11)

1907 Lovric, Michelle. *The Undrowned Child* (5–7). 2011, Delacorte $17.99 (978-0-385-73999-3); LB $20.99 (978-0-385-90814-6). 464pp. Eleven-year-old Teo, an orphan adopted by two scientists, finds herself taking part in a battle to save 1899 Venice from destruction in this fantasy full of historical detail. ℯ Lexile 830L (Rev: BL 6/1/11; LMC 11–12/11; SLJ 8/11*)

1908 Lubar, David. *My Rotten Life: Nathan Abercrombie, Accidental Zombie* (4–6). 2009, Starscape paper $5.99 (978-076531634-9). 160pp. A social outcast's life turns around thanks to "Hurt-Be-Gone," an experimental drug that renders him a half-dead zombie but has some hidden advantages. (Rev: BL 9/15/09)

1909 MacLachlan, Patricia. *Waiting for the Magic* (3–5). Illus. by Amy June Bates. 2011, Atheneum $15.99 (978-1-4169-2745-7). 160pp. A family suffering disruptions finds some healing when they adopt four dogs and a cat and slowly realize that they can understand the animals' speech. ℯ Lexile 420L (Rev: BL 8/11; LMC 11–12/11; SLJ 10/1/11*)

1910 McMann, Lisa. *The Unwanteds* (4–7). 2011, Simon & Schuster $16.99 (978-1-4424-0768-8). 400pp. In a dystopian land named Quill, Unwanted 13-year-olds with artistic abilities are purged from society; Alex, declared an Unwanted, finds himself in the magical land of Artime, where he learns new skills and worries about his twin brother Aaron, one of the Wanted. (Rev: BLO 9/1/11; SLJ 8/11)

1911 McNamee, Eoin. *The Ring of Five* (5–7). 2010, Random House $16.99 (978-0-385-73731-9). 352pp. Unhappy young Danny Caulfield gets a chance to go to boarding school and is surprised to find himself at Wilson's Academy of the Devious Arts where he is trained to protect the Upper World from the Lower World. ℯ Lexile 740L (Rev: BL 6/10; LMC 10/10; SLJ 6/10)

1912 Malone, Marianne. *The Sixty-Eight Rooms* (4–6). Illus. by Gina Triplett. 2010, Random House $16.99 (978-0-375-85710-2); LB $19.99 (978-0-375-95710-9). 288pp. Ruthie and her friend Jack discover a way to shrink themselves so they can explore the 68 intricate Thorne Rooms at Chicago's Art Institute. A sequel is *Stealing Magic* (2012). ∩ ℯ Lexile 730L (Rev: BL 1/1/10; LMC 3–4/10; SLJ 2/10)

1913 Marrone, Amanda. *The Multiplying Menace* (4–7). 2010, Aladdin paper $5.99 (978-1-4169-9033-8). 288pp. Twelve-year-old Maggie's somewhat unpredictable magical talents cause her difficulties until she's sent to live with her grandmother and hones her skills. ℯ Lexile 760L (Rev: BL 8/10; LMC 10/10; SLJ 8/10)

1914 Meloy, Colin. *Wildwood* (4–8). Illus. by Carson Ellis. 2011, HarperCollins $16.99 (978-0-06-202468-8). 560pp. Twelve-year-old Prue enters the Wilderness in search of her brother, who's been abducted by crows, in this richly imagined fantasy. (Rev: BL 7/11; SLJ 8/11*)

1915 Messer, Stephen. *Windblowne* (4–7). 2010, Random House $16.99 (978-0-375-86195-6). 304pp. Hoping to become a better kite-maker, Oliver seeks help from his Uncle Gilbert and his talking red kite; together they work to save the trees that support their treehouse village. Lexile 760L (Rev: BL 5/15/10; LMC 8–9/10; SLJ 6/10)

1916 Milford, Kate. *The Boneshaker* (5–8). 2010, Clarion $17 (978-0-547-24187-6). 384pp. In 1913 Arcane, Missouri, 13-year-old Natalie is suspicious of the owner of a traveling medicine show who has many mysterious machines; but everyone else seems to be taken in by him. ⌒ e Lexile 900L (Rev: BL 5/15/10*; LMC 10/10; SLJ 6/10)

1917 Miller, Christopher, and Allan Miller. *Hunter Brown and the Secret of the Shadow* (4–7). Series: Codebearers. 2008, Warner $13.99 (978-159317328-9). 366pp. Pranksters Stretch and Hunter are transported to fantastical Solandra, where they must fight amongst the Codebearers, battling evil and following the wisdom contained in a mysterious book. (Rev: BLO 11/1/08; SLJ 3/1/09)

1918 Millet, Lydia. *The Fires Beneath the Sea* (4–6). Series: The Dissenters. 2011, Big Mouth $17.99 (978-1-931520-71-3). 256pp. Thirteen-year-old Cara's mother has disappeared, and a sea otter has been communicating with Cara; with her brothers Cara sets out on a quest that involves danger, evil, and ecological concerns. e Lexile 780L (Rev: SLJ 8/11)

1919 Mlynowski, Sarah. *Fairest of All* (4–6). Series: Whatever After. 2012, Scholastic $14.99 (978-054540330-6). 192pp. Abby and her brother Jonah enter Snow White's world via a mysterious mirror, and find themselves wrestling with whether to intercede between her and the poison apple. e Lexile 400L (Rev: BL 4/1/12)

1920 Moskowitz, Hannah. *Zombie Tag* (5–8). 2011, Roaring Brook $15.99 (978-1-59643-720-3). 240pp. Zombie tag is just a game until 12-year-old Will's older brother Graham suddenly comes back to life. (Rev: BL 12/15/11; SLJ 12/1/11)

1921 Mull, Brandon. *Seeds of Rebellion* (5–8). Series: Beyonders. 2012, Aladdin $19.99 (978-141699794-8). 512pp. Jason succeeds in traveling from Colorado back to Lyrian in this action-packed story and joins with Rachel and Galloran to fight the evil that is lurking. ⌒ e (Rev: BL 2/1/12; SLJ 3/12)

1922 Mull, Brandon. *A World Without Heroes* (4–7). Series: Beyonders. 2011, Simon & Schuster $19.99 (978-1-4169-9792-4). 464pp. Jason, 14, is transported into an alternate world called Lyrian where he meets another young American, Rachel, and the two set out on a quest to overthrow the evil emperor and find their way home. ⌒ e Lexile 710L (Rev: BL 2/15/11; SLJ 3/1/11; VOYA 8/11)

1923 Nesbet, Anne. *The Cabinet of Earths* (4–7). 2012, HarperCollins $16.99 (978-006196313-1). 272pp. Full

of mystery and magic, this book tells of 13-year-old Maya's relocation, with her family, to Paris, where she struggles to keep watch over her young brother while finding herself enchanted by the magical Cabinet of Earths. e Lexile 800L (Rev: BL 1/1/12; HB 1–2/12; SLJ 5/1/12; VOYA 12/11)

1924 Newbery, Linda. *Lucy and the Green Man* (4–6). 2010, Random House $16.99 (978-0-385-75204-6); LB $19.99 (978-0-385-75207-7). 224pp. Lucy's grandfather's mysterious and magical friend Lob comes to live with his granddaughter — the only one who believed he existed — after Grandpa passes away. Lexile 650L (Rev: BL 11/15/10; LMC 5–6/11; SLJ 1/1/11)

1925 Newbound, Andrew. *Ghoul Strike!* (5–8). 2010, Scholastic $16.99 (978-054522938-8). 320pp. Twelve-year-old ghost hunter Alannah Malarra is out of her depth when she faces spirits from another dimension and must call in reinforcements. (Rev: BL 10/15/10; SLJ 1/1/11)

1926 Nimmo, Jenny. *The Secret Kingdom* (4–7). 2011, Scholastic $16.99 (978-0-439-84673-8). 224pp. Charlie Bone introduces this tale of his ancestor Timoken the Red King, who, with his sister Zobayda, finds himself in an action-packed fantasy adventure. (Rev: BL 10/1/11; SLJ 9/1/11)

1927 Nix, Garth. *Lord Sunday* (5–8). Series: Keys to the Kingdom. 2010, Scholastic $17.99 (978-043970090-0). 320pp. Arthur and his allies meet with great hardship and eventually triumph over the diabolical Lord Sunday in this series conclusion. ⌒ e Lexile 980L (Rev: BL 4/15/10)

1928 Nix, Garth, and Sean Williams. *Troubletwisters* (4–7). 2011, Scholastic $16.99 (978-054525897-5). 304pp. When their house mysteriously explodes, twins Jaide and Jack, 12, are sent to live with their previously unknown Grandma X, where they discover they have unusual talents, and that a power named The Evil is lurking. (Rev: BL 9/15/11)

1929 Noël, Alyson. *Radiance* (5–8). Series: Riley Bloom. 2010, Square Fish paper $7.99 (978-0-312-62917-5). 192pp. When Riley crosses over into the afterlife, she must adapt to her surroundings by relying on Bodhi, her well-intentioned guide. ⌒ e Lexile 1120L (Rev: LMC 3–4/11; SLJ 9/1/10)

1930 Noël, Alyson. *Shimmer* (5–8). Series: Riley Bloom. 2011, Square Fish paper $7.99 (978-0-312-64825-1). 192pp. Riley, a dead 12-year-old who is now a Soul Catcher, works with her mentor Bodhi to control the antics of vengeful Rebecca, who died during a slave revolt in 1733. (Rev: BL 5/1/11; SLJ 4/11)

1931 Norcliffe, James. *The Boy Who Could Fly* (5–8). 2010, Egmont $16.99 (978-1-60684-084-9). 304pp. Michael accepts an offer that allows him to fly, and to escape the miserable home for unwanted children where he lives, but is he really better off? Lexile 700L (Rev: BL 7/10; HB 9–10/10; SLJ 4/11)

1932 Nylund, Eric. *The Resisters* (5–8). 2011, Random House $16.99 (978-0-375-86856-6); LB $19.99 (978-0-375-96856-3). 212pp. Twelve-year-old Ethan learns that his understanding of the world has been false and that adults are all subject to mind control; only prepubescent children are safe and can resist. ☊ ℮ Lexile 720L (Rev: BL 3/15/11; LMC 10/11; SLJ 7/11)

1933 O'Dell, Kathleen. *The Aviary* (5–8). 2011, Knopf $15.99 (978-0-375-85605-1); LB $18.99 (978-037595605-8). 352pp. At the turn of the 20th century in Maine, solitary 11-year-old Clara discovers that there is a link between the birds in the aviary in the rose garden and the supposed drowning of five children some years before. (Rev: BL 10/1/11; SLJ 11/1/11)

1934 Oliver, Lauren. *Liesl and Po* (4–7). Illus. by Kei Acedera. 2011, HarperCollins $16.99 (978-0-06-201451-1). 308pp. A young apothecary's apprentice accidentally switches a box of magic with a vessel containing Liesl's father's ashes, leading to an adventure full of ghosts. ☊ ℮ Lexile 830L (Rev: BL 9/1/11; SLJ 11/1/11*)

1935 Oz, Amos. *Suddenly in the Depths of the Forest* (4–7). Trans. from Hebrew by Sondra Silverston. 2011, Houghton Mifflin $15.99 (978-0-547-55153-1). 144pp. A multilayered story about two children — Maya and Matti — who set out despite their fears to find out why their village has been cursed and all the animals have disappeared; an allegorical fable about tolerance and redemption. ℮ Lexile NC1260L (Rev: BL 2/15/11; HB 5–6/11; LMC 10/11*; SLJ 5/11; VOYA 4/11)

1936 Paterson, Katherine, and John Paterson. *The Flint Heart* (3–6). Illus. by John Rocco. 2011, Candlewick $19.99 (978-0-7636-4712-4). 304pp. The Patersons adapt Eden Philpott's 1910 story about two siblings — Charles and Unity — struggling to rescue their father from the domineering grasp of a cursed piece of flint; the action-packed text is enhanced by striking illustrations. (Rev: BL 9/1/11; SLJ 8/1/11*)

1937 Patten, E. J. *Return to Exile* (5–8). Illus. by John Rocco. Series: Hunter Chronicles. 2011, Simon & Schuster $16.99 (978-1-4424-2032-8). 512pp. Twelve-year-old Sky and his family have moved back to the small town of Exile, Sky's Uncle Phineas has disappeared, and Sky appears to be being targeted by monsters. ℮ Lexile 800L (Rev: BL 10/15/11; LMC 5–6/12; SLJ 12/1/11)

1938 Paver, Michelle. *Oath Breaker* (5–9). Series: Chronicles of Ancient Darkness. 2009, HarperCollins $16.99 (978-0-06-072837-3); LB $17.89 (978-0-06-072838-0). 292pp. When Torak's friend is murdered by a soul-eater, he sets out to get revenge in this fifth book in the series. Lexile 660L (Rev: SLJ 8/09; VOYA 2/09)

1939 Peck, Richard. *Secrets at Sea* (4–7). Illus. by Kelly Murphy. 2011, Dial $16.99 (978-0-8037-3455-5). 272pp. In the late 19th century Helena and her mouse siblings must conquer their fears as they accompany the Cranston family (whose house they live in) on an ocean voyage to Europe, meeting many new mice and people as they travel. (Rev: BL 9/1/11; SLJ 9/1/11)

1940 Poe, Edgar Allan. *Edgar Allan Poe's Tales of Death and Dementia* (5–8). Illus. by Gris Grimly. 2009, Simon & Schuster $18.99 (978-1-4169-5025-7). 136pp. A highly illustrated adaptation of four of Poe's thrillingly macabre stories. (Rev: BL 9/1/09; SLJ 9/09)

1941 Pogue, David. *Abby Carnelia's One and Only Magical Power* (3–6). Illus. by Antonio Caparo. 2010, Roaring Brook $15.99 (978-159643384-7). 288pp. Abby's discovery that she has a perplexing — and totally useless — magical power leads her to Camp Cadabra and some surprising discoveries. ☊ (Rev: BL 5/15/10; LMC 5–6/10; SLJ 5/10)

1942 Prineas, Sarah. *Found* (4–7). Illus. by Antonio Caparo. Series: The Magic Thief. 2010, HarperCollins $16.99 (978-0-06-137593-4). 368pp. In the third book in the series, Conn is on the run after escaping from prison and heads for Dragon Mountain in an effort to save Wellmet from bad magic. Lexile 730L (Rev: LMC 8–9/10)

1943 Quimby, Laura. *The Carnival of Lost Souls* (5–8). 2010, Abrams $16.95 (978-081098980-1). 352pp. Orphaned Jack Carr, a Houdini aficionado, is happy to find a home with Professor Hawthorne but unhappy surprises await him. (Rev: BL 10/15/10; LMC 1–2/11; SLJ 12/1/10)

1944 Reeve, Philip. *No Such Thing as Dragons* (4–7). 2010, Scholastic $16.99 (978-0-545-22224-2). 192pp. A mute boy named Ansel apprenticed to a fraudulent dragon hunter is much surprised to discover that dragons do in fact exist — and are simply hungry animals. ℮ (Rev: BL 8/10; LMC 11–12/10; SLJ 9/1/10)

1945 Renner, Ellen. *Castle of Shadows* (4–7). 2012, Houghton Mifflin $15.99 (978-054774446-9). 400pp. In a fantastic kingdom in the 1850s Princess Charlie, 11, sets out to find her missing mother and finds mystery and adventure. (Rev: BL 3/15/12; SLJ 4/12*)

1946 Rex, Adam. *Cold Cereal* (4–7). Illus. by author. 2012, HarperCollins $16.99 (978-006206002-0). 432pp. A funny and complex fantasy involving humor, secret experiments, parallel stories, and engaging characters both fairy and real. (Rev: BL 2/1/12; SLJ 2/12*)

1947 Rich, Susan, ed. *Half-Minute Horrors* (5–8). 2009, HarperCollins $12.99 (978-0-06-183379-3). 160pp. A collection of varied short horror stories by more than 70 authors. Lexile 720L (Rev: BL 9/15/09; HB 1–2/10; SLJ 1/10)

1948 Richter, Jutta. *The Cat: Or, How I Lost Eternity* (5–8). Trans. by Anna Brailovsky. Illus. by Rotraut Susanne Berner. 2007, Milkweed $14 (978-157131676-9). 63pp. Eight-year-old Christine is late for school every day because a talking alley cat waylays her and together they discuss everything from math to eternity. Batchelder Honor Book, 2008. Lexile 720L (Rev: BL 3/1/08; SLJ 2/08)

1949 Riley, James. *Half Upon a Time* (5–9). 2010, Simon & Schuster $15.99 (978-1-4169-9593-7). 388pp. Good-hearted but clumsy Jack and a sassy punk princess set off on a memorable quest to locate her mother, Snow White, in this zany fractured fairy tale. ℮ (Rev: LMC 1–2/11; SLJ 3/1/11)

1950 Riordan, Rick. *The Lost Hero* (4–8). Series: Heroes of Olympus. 2010, Hyperion/Disney $18.99 (978-142311339-3). 560pp. Teen demigods Piper, Leo, and Jason meet up at Camp Half-Blood and are sent on an urgent quest that takes them across the United States in three days. ∩ ℮ Lexile 660L (Rev: BLO 10/1/10; HB 1–2/11; LMC 5–6/11; SLJ 2/1/11)

1951 Riordan, Rick. *The Red Pyramid* (5–8). Series: The Kane Chronicles. 2010, Hyperion $17.99 (978-1-4231-1338-6). 528pp. Carter, 14, and Sadie, 12, discover they are descended from Egyptian royalty as they hone their newly evident magical talents while searching for their Egyptologist father, who disappeared after releasing an enemy god from the Rosetta Stone. ∩ ℮ Lexile 650L (Rev: BL 5/15/10*; HB 7–8/10; LMC 10/10; SLJ 6/10)

1952 Riordan, Rick. *The Son of Neptune* (5–8). Series: Heroes of Olympus. 2011, Hyperion $19.99 (978-1-4231-4059-7). 544pp. In this sequel to *The Lost Hero* (2010), Percy Jackson finds himself in Camp Jupiter, a modern refuge for demigods, where he makes friends with Hazel and Frank and together they set off to free Thanatos (Death) and then tackle bigger challenges. ∩ ℮ (Rev: BLO 10/1/11; SLJ 12/1/11)

1953 Riordan, Rick. *The Throne of Fire* (5–8). Series: The Kane Chronicles. 2011, Hyperion $18.99 (978-1-4231-4056-6). 464pp. Carter and Sadie must revive the sun god Ra in order to stop Apophis, the snake god of Chaos, from wreaking destruction. (Rev: BL 5/1/11; SLJ 6/11*)

1954 Roberts, Laura Peyton. *Green* (5–8). 2010, Delacorte $16.99 (978-0-385-73558-2). 272pp. Thirteen-year-old Lily succeeds her grandmother as Keeper of the Green Clan's gold in this clever, leprechaun-filled story. ℮ Lexile 720L (Rev: BL 12/1/09; LMC 1–2/10; SLJ 2/10)

1955 Rodda, Emily. *The Wizard of Rondo* (4–7). 2009, Scholastic $16.99 (978-0-545-11516-2). 400pp. Cousins Leo and Mimi return to the land of Rondo to find a missing wizard and in the process have a confrontation with the evil Blue Queen. (Rev: BL 10/1/09; SLJ 12/09)

1956 Russell, Christine, and Christopher Russell. *The Quest of the Warrior Sheep* (4–7). 2011, Sourcebooks paper $6.99 (978-1-4022-5511-3). 224pp. After a silver object falls from the sky, five sheep set off to contact the sheep god Aries and return the object — which they're convinced is an ancient relic — while pursued by their owners, a few reporters, and a couple of crooks. Also in this series is *The Warrior Sheep Go West* (2011). ℮ Lexile 660L (Rev: BLO 2/14/11; SLJ 5/11)

1957 Rutkoski, Marie. *The Cabinet of Wonders* (5–8). Series: The Kronos Chronicles. 2008, Farrar $16.95 (978-0-374-31026-4). 272pp. Sprinkled with tidbits of Bohemian history, this volume set in an alternate European Renaissance follows 12-year-old Petra as she works with the Roma to retrieve her father's eyes from an evil prince. ∩ ℮ Lexile 720L (Rev: BL 7/08; HB 1–2/09; SLJ 10/1/08)

1958 Rutkoski, Marie. *The Celestial Globe* (5–8). Series: The Kronos Chronicles. 2010, Farrar $16.99 (978-0-374-31027-1). 304pp. British spy John Dee helps Petra escape Prince Rodolfo, and subsequently enrolls her in magic classes instead of returning her home. Lexile 640L (Rev: BLO 4/15/10; SLJ 4/10)

1959 Rutkoski, Marie. *The Jewel of the Kalderash* (5–8). Series: Kronos Chronicles. 2011, Farrar $16.99 (978-037433678-3). 336pp. Petra embarks on a daring quest to find who created the Gray Men, so she can free her father from this curse in this fast-paced series conclusion. ℮ Lexile 680L (Rev: BL 10/15/11)

1960 Sage, Angie. *Darke* (5–8). Illus. by Mark Zug. Series: Septimus Heap. 2011, HarperCollins $17.99 (978-006124242-7). 656pp. Jenna and Septimus's 14th birthday celebration is interrupted when a new Darke Domaine opens up and the two — along with Beetle — are called to save the day; the 6th installment in the series. (Rev: BL 5/1/11)

1961 Sage, Angie. *Syren* (3–6). Illus. by Mark Zug. Series: Septimus Heap. 2009, HarperCollins $17.99 (978-006088210-5); LB $18.89 (978-006088211-2). 640pp. Wolf Boy is away on a mission while Septimus and his dragon fly off to bring Princess Jenna and the others back from the Harbor; all does not go as planned. (Rev: BL 11/15/09; SLJ 11/09)

1962 Salvatore, R. A., and Geno Salvatore. *The Stowaway* (5–8). Series: Stone of Tymora. 2008, Mirrorstone $17.95 (978-078695094-2). 304pp. In this fantastical maritime tale, young orphan Maimum uses a magical stone to fend off pirates, beasts, and demons. ℮ (Rev: BL 11/15/08)

1963 San Souci, Robert D. *Haunted Houses* (4–6). Illus. by Kelly Murphy. 2010, Henry Holt $16.99 (978-0-8050-8750-5). 288pp. Ten creepy haunted house stories feature haunted houses, ghosts, spiders, and other scary situations. ℮ Lexile 900L (Rev: BL 9/1/10; LMC 11–12/10; SLJ 9/1/10)

1964 Sanders, Stephanie S. *Villain School: Good Curses Evil* (3–6). 2011, Bloomsbury $15.99 (978-1-59990-610-2). 224pp. Young villains threatening to give up their family's legacy and turn benevolent are given a reeducation in this boarding school story with a supernatural twist. ℮ Lexile 710L (Rev: BL 10/15/11; LMC 3–4/12; SLJ 9/1/11)

1965 Saunders, Kate. *Beswitched* (5–8). 2011, Delacorte $16.99 (978-0-385-74075-3); LB $19.99 (978-037598967-4). 256pp. On her way to boarding school in England, 12-year-old Flora finds herself transported back to 1935 and discovers that her new dorm mates have summoned her. (Rev: BL 11/1/11*; SLJ 12/1/11)

1966 Sazaklis, John. *Royal Rodent Rescue* (1–4). Illus. by Art Baltazar. Series: DC Super Pets! 2011, Picture Window LB $22.65 (978-1-4048-6307-1); paper $4.95 (978-1-4048-6622-5). 56pp. Streaky the Super-Cat saves the queen's prized hamster from an evil cat in this action-packed story with integral illustrations. (Rev: SLJ 6/11)

1967 Schlitz, Laura Amy. *The Night Fairy* (2–5). Illus. by Angela Barrett. 2010, Candlewick $16.99 (978-0-7636-3674-6). 128pp. Injured by a bat, a young night fairy named Flory must learn to live in a scary new daylight world and finds many unexpected friends. ⋒ Lexile 630L (Rev: BL 1/1/10*; HB 3–4/11; LMC 5–6/10; SLJ 4/1/10*)

1968 Sensel, Joni. *The Farwalker's Quest* (5–8). 2009, Bloomsbury $16.99 (978-1-59990-272-2). 400pp. Not long before the Namingfest in which Ariel expects to be selected as an apprentice Healtouch, Ariel and her friend Zeke find a telling dart that alters their futures. Lexile 660L (Rev: BL 2/15/09; SLJ 4/1/09)

1969 Sensel, Joni. *The Timekeeper's Moon* (5–8). 2010, Bloomsbury $16.99 (978-1-59990-457-3). 336pp. In the future without technology or books introduced in *The Farwalker's Quest* (2009), Ariel and her guardian, Scarl, follow a mysterious map, aware that success is vital. Lexile 700L (Rev: BLO 2/1/10; LMC 5–6/10; SLJ 3/10)

1970 Skelton, Matthew. *The Story of Cirrus Flux* (4–7). 2010, Delacorte $17.99 (978-0-385-73381-6); LB $20.99 (978-0-385-90398-1). 304pp. In this suspenseful fantasy set in 18th-century London and featuring steampunk-style gadgets, orphan Cirrus must protect a magical token left by his father. ⋒ (Rev: BL 2/1/10; HB 5–6/10; LMC 5–6/10; SLJ 3/10)

1971 Smith, Clete Barrett. *Aliens on Vacation* (5–8). Illus. by Christian Slade. 2011, Hyperion/Disney $16.99 (978-1-4231-3363-6). 272pp. Scrub is not pleased to find himself spending a summer at his eccentric grandmother's Washington State bed and breakfast, where he soon discovers things are not at all what they seem. (Rev: BL 5/1/11; SLJ 7/11)

1972 Smith, Jennifer E. *The Storm Makers* (4–7). Illus. by Brett Helquist. 2012, Little, Brown $16.99 (978-031617958-4). 372pp. Twelve-year-olds Ruby and Simon move with their parents to a Wisconsin farm during a terrible drought, and discover that Simon's strange ties to the weather suggest he may be a very powerful Storm Maker. (Rev: BL 4/1/12; LMC 8–9/12; SLJ 6/12)

1973 Sniegoski, Tom. *Quest for the Spark, vol. 1* (4–7). Illus. by Jeff Smith. Series: Bone. 2011, Scholastic $22.99 (978-054514101-7); paper $10.99 (978-054514102-4). 224pp. Tom Elm, 12, teams up with a motley crew after he receives a vision telling him to use his necklace to defeat the Nacht, a rogue dragon, in this (illustrated) text addition to the Bone graphic novel series. Lexile 790L (Rev: BL 1/1–15/11; SLJ 3/11)

1974 Sniegoski, Tom. *Quest for the Spark, vol. 2* (4–7). Illus. by Jeff Smith. Series: Bone. 2012, Scholastic $22.99 (978-054514103-1); paper $10.99 (978-054514104-8). 224pp. Twelve-year-old Tom proves himself a competent quest leader by obtaining a piece of the Spark that will defeat the evil Nacht. (Rev: BL 2/15/12)

1975 Spratt, R. A. *The Adventures of Nanny Piggins* (3–6). Illus. by Dan Santat. 2010, Little, Brown $15.99 (978-0-316-06819-2). 256pp. Parsimonious Mr. Green hires a candy-loving, former circus star pig as nanny to his three children, much to their glee. (Rev: BL 8/10*; LMC 10/10; SLJ 8/10)

1976 St. John, Lauren. *The Elephant's Tale* (5–8). Series: Legend of the Animal Healer. 2010, Dial $16.99 (978-0-8037-3291-9). 221pp. Eleven-year-old Martine, who can communicate with and heal animals, faces the possible loss of her grandmother's South African animal sanctuary in this action-filled final volume in the series. ℮ Lexile 880L (Rev: SLJ 7/10)

1977 St. John, Lauren. *The Last Leopard* (4–7). 2009, Dial $16.99 (978-0-8037-3342-8). 208pp. In this third volume about a girl with a gift for healing animals, 11-year-old Martine is on a safari with her grandmother, and she and her best friend Ben must search for an elusive white leopard in grave danger from those who hunt it for its mystical powers. ℮ Lexile 920L (Rev: BL 2/15/09; SLJ 5/1/09)

1978 Stanley, Diane. *The Silver Bowl* (5–8). 2011, HarperCollins $16.99 (978-0-06-157543-3). 320pp. A young scullery maid chooses to share the visions she's been keeping silent when foretold events seem to threaten the royal family she works for. Lexile 700L (Rev: BL 4/15/11; SLJ 7/11*)

1979 Stephens, John. *The Emerald Atlas* (4–7). Series: The Books of Beginning. 2011, Knopf $17.99 (978-0-375-86870-2); LB $20.99 (978-0-375-96870-9). 419pp. Siblings Kate, Michael, and Emma have lived in a series of orphanages since their parents disappeared, and now they discover they can travel through time and must deal with both good and evil. ∩ ℮ (Rev: BL 3/1/11; HB 3–4/11; LMC 5–6/11; SLJ 6/11*)

1980 Stephens, Sarah Hines. *Midway Monkey Madness* (1–4). Illus. by Art Baltazar. Series: DC Super Pets! 2011, Picture Window LB $22.65 (978-1-4048-6305-7); paper $4.95 (978-1-4048-6619-5). 56pp. Beppo the Super-Monkey saves the day from a malevolent giant gorilla in this action-packed story with integral illustrations. (Rev: SLJ 6/11)

1981 Stevermer, Caroline. *Magic Below Stairs* (4–6). 2010, Dial $16.99 (978-0-8037-3467-8). 208pp. Ten-year-old orphan Frederick, who is surreptitiously guarded by an elf, is selected as a servant and later apprentice to a wizard. (Rev: BL 6/10; SLJ 7/10)

1982 Stewart, Paul. *The Immortals* (5–8). Illus. by Chris Riddell. Series: Edge Chronicles. 2010, Random House $19.99 (978-037583743-2); LB $22.99 (978-037593743-9). 688pp. In this concluding volume in the exciting series, Nate Quarter flees for his life from the phraxmines of the Eastern Woods. ℮ (Rev: BL 10/1/10)

1983 Stewart, Paul. *Legion of the Dead* (4–6). Illus. by Chris Riddell. Series: Barnaby Grimes. 2010, Random House $16.99 (978-038575131-5); LB $19.99 (978-038575132-2). 240pp. Victorian-era zombies must be overcome by the hero — dogged young Barnaby — in this cheerfully gruesome historical horror romp. The fourth installment is *Phantom of Blood Alley* (2010). (Rev: BL 2/1/10)

1984 Stine, R. L. *Goosebumps Wanted: The Haunted Mask* (3–6). 2012, Scholastic $15.99 (978-054541793-8). 240pp. When 12-year-old Lu-Ann puts on a mask that she finds at the bottom of a trunk, it sticks to her skin and she seems suddenly filled with rage; at the same time, her friend Devin is struggling with sinister vines in a Halloween pumpkin patch; a 20th-anniversary, suitably spooky issue. ℮ (Rev: BL 4/15/12)

1985 Stratton, Allan. *The Grave Robber's Apprentice* (5–8). 2012, HarperCollins $16.99 (978-006197608-7). 288pp. Grave robber Hans becomes aware of his royal heritage in this complex fantasy. (Rev: BL 5/15/12*; SLJ 3/12)

1986 Stringer, Helen. *The Midnight Gate* (5–8). 2011, Feiwel & Friends $17.99 (978-0-312-38764-8). 384pp. Paranormally gifted Belladonna and her friend Steve tackle a dangerous assignment involving a trip to the Land of the Dead. (Rev: BL 5/1/11; SLJ 5/11)

1987 Stringer, Helen. *Spellbinder* (5–8). 2009, Feiwel & Friends $17.99 (978-0-312-38763-1). 384pp. The friendly, benevolent ghosts who populate Belladonna Johnson's world begin to disappear, and the 12-year-old enters the Land of the Dead to find out why. ∩ ℮ Lexile 840L (Rev: BL 10/15/09; SLJ 10/09; VOYA 2/10)

1988 Tanner, Lian. *Museum of Thieves* (4–7). 2010, Delacorte $17.99 (978-0-385-73905-4); LB $20.99 (978-0-385-90768-2). 312pp. In a world where children are chained to their parents until a separation ceremony, 12-year-old Goldie manages to escape and finds herself playing an important role. ∩ (Rev: BL 10/1/10; SLJ 10/1/10)

1989 Toft, Di. *Wolven* (4–8). 2010, Scholastic $16.99 (978-0-545-17109-0). 336pp. Twelve-year-old Nat is devoted to his unconventional-looking dog, and is astonished when it suddenly morphs into a human boy. Lexile 860L (Rev: BLO 6/10; LMC 11–12/10; SLJ 8/10)

1990 Townley, Roderick. *The Door in the Forest* (5–8). 2011, Knopf $16.99 (978-0-375-85601-3); LB $19.99 (978-0-375-95601-0). 256pp. Fourteen-year-old Daniel, who cannot lie, and Emily, who has magical powers, travel from their town — which is being occupied by soldiers — to a mysterious nearby island. ℮ Lexile 600L (Rev: BL 3/1/11; HB 3–4/11; SLJ 3/1/11)

1991 Trafton, Jennifer. *The Rise and Fall of Mount Majestic* (3–6). Illus. by Brett Helquist. 2010, Dial $16.99 (978-0-8037-3375-6). 344pp. Apathetic 10-year-old Persimmony's life gets more exciting when she finds herself embroiled in a quest to ensure her island's continued well-being; satisfying the tempestuous king, who's 12 years old, adds plenty of comedy to the story. ℮ Lexile 930L (Rev: BL 1/1–15/11; LMC 3–4/11; SLJ 3/1/11*)

1992 Trivas, Tracy. *The Wish Stealers* (4–7). 2010, Simon & Schuster $16.99 (978-1-4169-8725-3). 288pp. A girl named Griffin Penshine receives a box of stolen wishes — pennies dredged from a fountain — and attempts to reunite each one with its owner in order to escape misfortune. ℮ Lexile 710L (Rev: BLO 11/15/09; LMC 10/10; SLJ 3/10)

1993 Ullman, Barb Bentler. *Whistle Bright Magic* (3–6). Series: A Nutfolk Tale. 2010, HarperCollins $16.99 (978-0-06-188286-9). 224pp. Zelly and her mother move to Plunkit after Zelly's grandmother dies, and Zelly yearns for her absent father while helping the Nutfolk save their community from developers; a sequel to *The Fairies of Nutfolk Wood* (2006). Lexile 850L (Rev: BLO 2/1/10; SLJ 2/10)

1994 Umansky, Kaye. *Clover Twig and the Magical Cottage* (4–7). Illus. by Johanna Wright. 2009, Roaring Brook $16.99 (978-1-59643-507-0). 304pp. In this funny, clever tale, 11-year-old Clover gets work cleaning a witch's magical cottage and finds herself protecting the cottage from the witch's evil sister. Lexile 550L (Rev: BL 8/09; HB 9–10/09; LMC 11–12/09; SLJ 9/09)

1995 Ursu, Anne. *Breadcrumbs* (4–6). 2011, HarperCollins $16.99 (978-0-06-201505-1). 336pp. A shard of glass from an enchanted mirror causes 10-year-old Hazel's friend Jack to be imprisoned by an evil Snow Queen and Hazel must enter a magic wood to rescue him in this richly imagined fantasy featuring several fairy tale tropes. ∩ **e** (Rev: BL 11/15/11; HB 1–2/12; SLJ 11/1/11*)

1996 Valente, Catherynne M. *The Girl Who Circumnavigated Fairyland in a Ship of Her Own Making* (5–8). Illus. by Ana Juan. 2011, Feiwel & Friends $16.99 (978-0-312-64961-6). 256pp. This quirky, imaginative story features 12-year-old September, who is carried off to Fairyland, where she has some wild and wonderful adventures among the unusual and sometimes sinister inhabitants there. ∩ Lexile 920 (Rev: BL 4/15/11; HB 5–6/11; LMC 10/11; SLJ 5/11; VOYA 6/11)

1997 Van Cleve, Kathleen. *Drizzle* (5–8). 2010, Dial $16.99 (978-0-8037-3362-6). 358pp. Polly, an 11-year-old who can communicate with plants, lives on a rhubarb farm where it rains at the same time every Monday; when the rains stop, Polly must use her powers of logic and communication to solve the problem. ∩ Lexile 650L (Rev: BL 3/1/10; SLJ 4/10)

1998 van Eekhout, Greg. *Kid Vs. Squid* (4–7). 2010, Bloomsbury $16.99 (978-1-59990-489-4). 256pp. When a girl steals a shrunken head from the Museum of the Strange and Curious, Thatcher and Trudy chase the thief and end up saving a cursed civilization; a lighthearted fantasy full of humor. (Rev: BL 5/15/10; LMC 8–9/10; SLJ 7/10)

1999 Vernon, Ursula. *Attack of the Ninja Frogs* (2–5). Illus. by author. Series: Dragonbreath. 2010, Dial $12.99 (978-0-8037-3365-7). 206pp. Young dragon Danny and his friend Wendell the iguana travel with exchange student Suki to mythical Japan to seek a way to stop ninja frogs from attacking Suki. (Rev: SLJ 7/1/10)

2000 Vernon, Ursula. *Curse of the Were-Wiener* (2–5). Illus. by author. Series: Dragonbreath. 2010, Dial $12.99 (978-080373469-2). 208pp. In this zany horror story for young readers, Danny Dragonbreath must help his friend Wendell the iguana when a hot dog bites him and he starts to turn into a were-wiener. (Rev: BL 10/15/10)

2001 Vernon, Ursula. *Lair of the Bat Monster* (3–5). Illus. by author. Series: Dragonbreath. 2011, Dial $12.99 (978-080373525-5). 208pp. Danny gets kidnapped by a giant bat monster of legend, and his friend Wendell must rescue him in this lively graphic novel. (Rev: BLO 2/14/11)

2002 Wagner, Hilary. *Nightshade City* (5–8). Illus. by Omar Rayyan. Series: Nightshade Chronicles. 2010, Holiday House $17.95 (978-0-8234-2285-2). 320pp. A city of intelligent rats prepares to overthrow its oppressive ruler. Lexile 800L (Rev: BL 9/15/10; LMC 3–4/11; SLJ 1/1/11; VOYA 12/10)

2003 Wagner, Hilary. *The White Assassin* (5–8). Illus. by Omar Rayyan. Series: Nightshade Chronicles. 2011, Holiday House $17.95 (978-0-8234-2333-0). 256pp. Nightshade City's residents work to keep themselves safe from Billycan's devious and conniving ways in this fast-paced sequel to *Nightshade City* (2010). (Rev: BLO 10/15/11; SLJ 10/1/11)

2004 Walsh, Pat. *The Crowfield Curse* (5–8). 2010, Scholastic $16.99 (978-0-545-22922-7). 336pp. In England in 1347, 14-year-old orphaned William comes across a hobgoblin and discovers he himself has magical powers, which must be put to good use; this suspenseful story is full of medieval details. ∩ Lexile 840L (Rev: BL 10/15/10; LMC 11–12/10; SLJ 9/1/10*)

2005 Walsh, Pat. *The Crowfield Demon* (5–8). 2012, Scholastic $16.99 (978-054531769-6). 368pp. In this sequel to *The Crowfield Curse* (2010), young William — who can see into the spirit world — must deal with a fallen angel threatening Crowfield Abbey and all therein. **e** (Rev: BLO 4/1/12; SLJ 5/1/12) [800L]

2006 Ward, David. *Between Two Ends* (4–6). 2011, Abrams $16.95 (978-081099714-1). 304pp. Twelve-year-old Yeats travels into "The Arabian Nights" to stop the source of his family's present malaise before it harms everyone. (Rev: BL 5/1/11)

2007 Wells, Kitty. *Paw Power* (2–4). Illus. by Joanna Harrison. Series: Pocket Cats. 2011, Random House $13.99 (978-0-385-75201-5); LB $16.99 (978-0-385-75202-2). 208pp. One of Maddy's ceramic cat figurines comes to life to help her deal with the school bully in this sensitive, accessible story. The third volume in the series is *Feline Charm* (2011). **e** (Rev: BLO 1/1–15/11; SLJ 3/1/11)

2008 Wells, Kitty. *Shadow Magic* (2–4). Illus. by Joanna Harrison. Series: Pocket Cats. 2011, Random House $13.99 (978-0-385-75200-8). 202pp. An aloof ceramic cat figurine gives Maddy the ability to be invisible, which enables her to spy on her secretive cousin who's come to live with the family for awhile. (Rev: SLJ 9/1/11)

2009 Wells, Rosemary. *On the Blue Comet* (5–8). Illus. by Bagram Ibatoulline. 2010, Candlewick $16.99 (978-0-7636-3722-4). 336pp. The crash of 1929 hits 11-year-old Oscar's family hard and the young model train devotee, longing for his old set, discovers a magical train that allows him to visit different times and places. ∩ (Rev: BL 7/10; HB 9–10/10; LMC 11–12/10; SLJ 9/1/10)

2010 Welsh, M. L. *Mistress of the Storm: A Verity Gallant Tale* (4–8). 2011, Random House $16.99 (978-0-385-75244-2); LB $19.99 (978-0-385-75245-9). 320pp. Twelve-year-old Verity's life takes a turn for the eventful when she uncovers family secrets that lead to a confrontation with a powerful witch. **e** Lexile 750L (Rev: LMC 11–12/11; SLJ 10/1/11*; VOYA 6/11)

2011 West, Jacqueline. *The Shadows* (4–6). Illus. by Poly Bernatene. Series: Books of Elsewhere. 2010, Dial $16.99 (978-0-8037-3440-1). 256pp. When the family moves to a big Victorian house, 11-year-old Olive's emotionally absent parents leave her to explore the mysteries of the old paintings, and an odd pair of glasses that allow her to step inside the art. Also use *Spellbound* (2011). ⌒ ℮ (Rev: BL 6/10; LMC 10/10; SLJ 5/10)

2012 Wharton, Thomas. *The Shadow of Malabron* (5–8). 2009, Candlewick $16.99 (978-0-7636-3911-2). 400pp. A motorcycle crash transports a boy to a magical realm where all the world's stories originate in this imaginative, well-conceived novel about the battle between good and evil. ℮ Lexile 830L (Rev: BL 2/15/10; LMC 1–2/10; SLJ 11/09)

2013 Willingham, Bill. *Down the Mysterly River* (4–7). Illus. by Mark Buckingham. 2011, Starscape $15.99 (978-0-7653-2792-5). 336pp. Max, Boy Scout and sleuth, finds himself and three talking animals in a forest, being chased by the mysterious and sinister Blue Cutters. (Rev: BLO 9/1/11; SLJ 12/1/11)

2014 Wilson, N. D. *The Chestnut King* (4–7). Series: 100 Cupboards. 2010, Random House $16.99 (978-0-375-83885-9); LB $19.99 (978-0-375-93885-6). 496pp. In this trilogy conclusion, young Henry finally meets the Chestnut King, who can help him to defeat the evil witch Nimiane. ⌒ ℮ Lexile 670L (Rev: BLO 2/1/10; SLJ 6/10)

2015 Wilson, N. D. *The Dragon's Tooth* (5–8). Series: Ashtown Burials. 2011, Random House $16.99 (978-0-375-86439-1). 496pp. Cyrus and Antigone struggle to rescue their brother Dan from the clutches of Dr. Phoenix, who is performing experiments on him, in this fast-paced fantasy involving an ancient secret society. ⌒ Lexile 640L (Rev: BL 10/15/11*; SLJ 11/1/11*)

2016 Winkler, Henry, and Lin Oliver. *Zero to Hero* (3–6). Series: Ghost Buddy. 2012, Scholastic $17.99 (978-054529887-2). 176pp. Billy Broccoli, rising 6th-grader, has a lot to cope with: a new home (his mother has remarried), a new school, and a ghost, who in fact turns out to be quite useful. ⌒ ℮ Lexile 800L (Rev: BL 12/15/11; LMC 5–6/12; SLJ 4/1/12)

2017 Wrede, Patricia C. *Across the Great Barrier* (5–8). Series: Frontier Magic. 2011, Scholastic $16.99 (978-0-545-03343-5). 352pp. In the second volume of this series set in an alternate Wild West, 18-year-old Eff decides against magic school and joins an expedition to the wilderness beyond the Great Barrier. (Rev: BL 9/1/11; SLJ 9/1/11)

2018 Yep, Laurence. *City of Ice* (5–8). Series: City Trilogy. 2011, Tor $16.99 (978-0-7653-1925-8). 384pp. Scirye and her companions travel to the Arctic Circle in their quest to stop the evil Mr. Roland and dragon Badik from acquiring magical power; the sequel to *City of Fire* (2009). ℮ Lexile 890L (Rev: BL 6/1/11; SLJ 6/11)

2019 Zahler, Diane. *Princess of the Wild Swans* (4–7). Illus. by Yvonne Gilbert. 2012, HarperCollins $16.99

(978-006200492-5). 224pp. When tasked with making shirts from stinging nettles for each of her five brothers to free them from a curse, 12-year-old Princess Meriel rues her distaste for sewing; based on Grimm's "The Six Swans." (Rev: BL 3/1/12; SLJ 3/12)

2020 Zahler, Diane. *The Thirteenth Princess* (4–7). 2010, HarperCollins $15.99 (978-0-06-182498-2). 256pp. Zita learns that she is a king's daughter and that her 12 sisters are under a magic spell. ⌒ Lexile 850L (Rev: BL 12/15/09; LMC 8–9/10; SLJ 3/10)

Friendship Stories

2021 Barden, Stephanie. *Cinderella Smith* (2–4). Illus. by Diane Goode. 2011, HarperCollins $14.99 (978-0-06-196423-7). 160pp. "Cinderella" Smith navigates the ever-changing waters of elementary school friendships and her predisposition for losing shoes at inopportune times. ℮ Lexile 670L (Rev: BL 4/1/11; HB 5–6/11; SLJ 7/11)

2022 Barrows, Annie. *Doomed to Dance* (1–3). Illus. by Sophie Blackall. Series: Ivy and Bean. 2009, Chronicle $14.99 (978-0-8118-6266-0). 136pp. Disappointed at being cast as squids in their first ballet recital, friends Ivy and Bean figure out a way to get out of performing without letting anyone down in this sixth volume in the series. ⌒ ℮ Lexile 530L (Rev: BL 11/1/09; HB 1–2/10; SLJ 1/1/10)

2023 Barrows, Annie. *No News Is Good News* (1–3). Illus. by Sophie Blackall. Series: Ivy and Bean. 2011, Chronicle $14.99 (978-081186693-4). 128pp. After starting a neighborhood newspaper, Ivy and Bean find themselves in the midst of controversy. ⌒ (Rev: BL 12/15/11; HB 1–2/12)

2024 Baskin, Nora Raleigh. *The Summer Before Boys* (5–8). 2011, Simon & Schuster $15.99 (978-1-4169-8673-7). 196pp. When her mother is deployed to Iraq, Julia, 12, moves in with her friend Eliza's family but the girls' close bond is threatened by Julia's crush on a boy. ℮ Lexile 720L (Rev: BL 3/1/11; HB 5–6/11; SLJ 4/11)

2025 Bowe, Julie. *My Best Frenemy* (3–6). Series: Friends for Keeps. 2010, Dial $16.99 (978-0-8037-3501-9). 240pp. Fourth-grader Ida May describes her confusion as she tries to choose her friends, especially in the face of a challenging game of truth or dare. (Rev: BLO 5/15/10; SLJ 7/1/10)

2026 Cabot, Meg. *Glitter Girls, and the Great Fake Out* (3–5). Series: Allie Finkle's Rules for Girls. 2010, Scholastic $15.99 (978-054504047-1). 208pp. Allie ditches her friends in favor of a popular birthday party, and — even worse — lies to them in the process. ⌒ ℮ Lexile 830L (Rev: BLO 3/1/10; HB 5–6/10)

2027 Cotler, Steve. *Cheesie Mack Is Not a Genius or Anything* (4–6). Illus. by Adam McCauley. 2011, Random House $15.99 (978-0-375-86437-7); LB $18.99 (978-0-375-96437-4). 240pp. Ronald (aka "Cheesie") Mack tells readers about the summer after fifth grade when he and his friend Georgie solve a mystery and have many interesting experiences. ℮ Lexile 770L (Rev: BL 4/1/11; HB 5–6/7; SLJ 3/1/11)

2028 Dee, Barbara. *This Is Me from Now On* (5–8). 2010, Aladdin paper $5.99 (978-141699414-5). 272pp. Seventh-grader Evie is fascinated by the new girl next door, who lives totally by her own rules. ℮ (Rev: BLO 11/15/10)

2029 DeLaCroix, Alice. *The Best Horse Ever* (3–5). Illus. by Ronald Himler. 2010, Holiday House $15.95 (978-0-8234-2254-8). 80pp. Abby's new horse leads to friendship troubles in this accessible early chapter book. Lexile 510L (Rev: BL 3/15/10; SLJ 6/1/10)

2030 English, Karen. *Nikki and Deja: The Newsy News Newsletter* (1–3). Illus. by Laura Freeman. 2010, Clarion $15 (978-0-547-22247-9). 96pp. African American girls Nikki and Deja struggle with the boundaries between news and gossip while deciding what to print in their neighborhood newsletter. ℮ Lexile 680L (Rev: SLJ 2/1/10)

2031 English, Karen. *Wedding Drama* (1–3). Illus. by Laura Freeman. Series: Nikki and Deja. 2012, Clarion $14.99 (978-054761564-6). 112pp. A class lottery for the chance to attend their teacher's upcoming wedding drives a wedge between African American friends Nikki and Deja. ℮ (Rev: BL 2/15/12; LMC 11–12/12)

2032 Friedman, Laurie. *Happy New Year, Mallory!* (2–5). Illus. by Jennifer Kalis. Series: Mallory. 2009, Carolrhoda $15.95 (978-082258883-2). 176pp. Appendicitis ruins 9-year-old Mallory's planned New Year's reunion with her friends from summer camp. Lexile 710L (Rev: BL 9/15/09)

2033 Greene, Stephanie. *Princess Posey and the Perfect Present* (K–2). Illus. by Stephanie Roth Sisson. 2011, Putnam $12.99 (978-0-399-25462-8). 96pp. First-grader Posey is hurt when her friend's teacher gift outshines her own. ⌒ ℮ (Rev: BL 3/1/11; HB 3–4/11; SLJ 8/1/11)

2034 Greenwald, Lisa. *Sweet Treats and Secret Crushes* (5–8). 2010, Abrams $16.95 (978-0-8109-8990-0). 291pp. It's Valentine's Day, and a snowstorm promises to ruin the romantic plans of 13-year-old BFFs Olivia, Kate, and Georgia, but distributing fortune cookies to neighbors in the Brooklyn, New York, apartment building brings unexpected benefits. (Rev: BL 9/15/10; SLJ 12/1/10)

2035 Harper, Charise Mericle. *Just Grace and the Double Surprise* (2–4). Illus. by author. Series: Just Grace. 2011, Houghton Mifflin $14.99 (978-0-547-37026-2). 176pp. Grace, 8, navigates two big changes in her life: her best friend Mimi's family adopts a baby boy instead of the expected girl, and her parents say yes to getting a dog. Lexile 720L (Rev: HB 9–10/11; SLJ 8/1/11)

2036 Harper, Charise Mericle. *Just Grace and the Terrible Tutu* (2–4). Illus. by author. Series: Just Grace. 2011, Houghton Mifflin $15 (978-0-547-15224-0). 176pp. Friends Grace and Mimi, 8, put their heads together to entertain Lily, a spirited 4-year-old with an endless supply of tutus; but the experience makes Mimi worry about the forthcoming arrival of a newly adopted little sister. ℮ Lexile 820L (Rev: BL 1/1–15/11; HB 1–2/11; SLJ 4/11)

2037 House, Silas, and Neela Vaswani. *Same Sun Here* (5–8). 2012, Candlewick $15.99 (978-076365684-3). 228pp. Twelve-year-old Meena, an immigrant from India living in Chinatown, New York, with her struggling parents, and 12-year-old River, an unemployed Kentucky coal miner's son, become pen pals and through letters and e-mails share their problems and aspirations. ℮ Lexile 890L (Rev: BL 3/1/12; LMC 8–9/12; SLJ 4/12*)

2038 Impey, Rose. *Best Friends!* (4–6). Series: The Sleepover Club. 2009, HarperCollins paper $6.99 (978-000726494-0). 123pp. The four Sleepover Club girls — Frankie, Kenny, Lyndz, and Fliss — are determined to beat the mean girls in the school competition; the first volume in a British series. (Rev: BL 11/1/09)

2039 Leader, Jessica. *Nice and Mean* (5–7). 2010, Aladdin paper $6.99 (978-1-4169-9160-1). 272pp. Middle-schoolers Sachi and Marina are very different and get off to a bad start when they work together on a video project. ℮ Lexile 680L (Rev: BL 7/10; LMC 11–12/10)

2040 McTighe, Carolyn. *How to Ruin Your Life and Other Lessons School Doesn't Teach You* (3–6). 2010, Red Deer paper $9.95 (978-088995401-4). 112pp. PJ and Katie's long friendship is jeopardized when Katie beats PJ in a practice run. (Rev: BL 11/15/10; SLJ 12/10)

2041 Magoon, Kekla. *Camo Girl* (5–8). 2011, Simon & Schuster $15.99 (978-1-4169-7804-6). 224pp. Biracial 6th-grader Ella, an outsider unhappy with her skin tone, is pleased when popular Bailey moves to town and befriends her, but anxious to keep her friendship with the troubled Z. ℮ Lexile 600L (Rev: BL 2/1/11; LMC 11–12/11; SLJ 1/1/11)

2042 Martin, Ann M. *The Summer Before* (4–6). 2010, Scholastic $16.99 (978-054516093-3). 224pp. This in-depth prequel to the popular Babysitters Club series provides plenty of character development for each of the four main characters. (Rev: BL 4/1/10)

2043 Moss, Marissa. *Amelia's BFF* (3–5). Illus. by author. Series: Amelia's Notebooks. 2011, Simon & Schuster $9.99 (978-1-4424-0376-5). Unpaged. Amelia finds herself caught in the middle between two friends vying for the title of her BFF. (Rev: SLJ 6/11)

2044 Moss, Marissa. *Amelia's Boy Survival Guide* (4–7). Illus. by author. Series: Amelia's Notebooks. 2012, Simon & Schuster $9.99 (978-144244084-5). 80pp. After starting off 8th grade with confidence, Amelia finds herself reeling from an unexpected crush. (Rev: BLO 4/1/12)

2045 Myracle, Lauren. *Luv Ya Bunches* (4–6). Series: Flower Power. 2009, Abrams $15.95 (978-081094211-0). 240pp. Four 10-year-old girls — each named after a flower and of different ethnicities — navigate the shoals of 5th grade in this story told through straight narrative, instant messages, blog posts, and even a video script. (Rev: BL 9/15/09*; LMC 1–2/11; SLJ 11/09)

2046 Myracle, Lauren. *Oopsy Daisy* (4–6). Series: Flower Power. 2012, Abrams $16.95 (978-141970019-4). 384pp. The four 5th-grade friends return to help each other through life's ups and downs, including Violet coping with her mom's return from the hospital, Yasamin's conflicts with her parents, and Project Teacherly Lurve, a matchmaking scheme. (Rev: BL 2/15/12)

2047 Myracle, Lauren. *Violet in Bloom* (4–6). Series: Flower Power. 2010, Abrams $15.95 (978-0-8109-8983-2). 352pp. The three friends from 2009's *Luv Ya Bunches* are back on a quest to replace their cafeteria's snack food with healthier fare while each dealing with her own concerns. Lexile 700L (Rev: BL 10/1/10; SLJ 12/1/10)

2048 Pennypacker, Sara. *Clementine, Friend of the Week* (2–4). Illus. by Marla Frazee. Series: Clementine. 2010, Hyperion $14.99 (978-1-4231-1355-3). 176pp. The pressure is on when 3rd-grader Clementine is chosen to be Friend of the Week. (Rev: BL 10/1/10; SLJ 7/1/10)

2049 Urban, Linda. *Hound Dog True* (3–6). 2011, Harcourt $15.99 (978-0-547-55869-1). 176pp. Scared of starting classes in a new school, shy 5th-grader Mattie takes comfort in the fact that her uncle is a custodian there, but eventually learns that making friends is up to her. (Rev: BL 9/1/11; SLJ 10/1/11*)

2050 Walliams, David. *Mr. Stink* (4–7). Illus. by Quentin Blake. 2010, Penguin $15.99 (978-159514332-7). 272pp. Twelve-year-old Chloe befriends a smelly tramp despite her mother's crusade to clean up the streets in this funny British book. ⏵ ℮ Lexile 730L (Rev: BL 11/15/10*; LMC 1–2/11; SLJ 1/1/11)

2051 Willner-Pardo, Gina. *The Hard Kind of Promise* (5–7). 2010, Clarion $16 (978-0-547-24395-5). 208pp. In kindergarten Sarah and Marjorie promised to be friends forever, but by 7th grade Marjorie's oddness jeopardizes Sarah's chances for popularity. ℮ Lexile 670L (Rev: BL 8/10; HB 7–8/10; SLJ 8/10)

Graphic Novels

2052 Aguirre, Jorge. *Giants Beware!* (2–5). Illus. by Rafael Rosado. 2012, First Second paper $14.99 (978-159643582-7). 208pp. Young tomboy Claudette is determined to do her civil duty and slay a giant, but this proves to be more problematic than she expected. (Rev: BL 3/15/12; HB 9–10/12; LMC 10/12; SLJ 5/1/12*)

2053 Alley, Zoe. *There's a Princess in the Palace* (3–5). Illus. by R. W. Alley. 2010, Roaring Brook $19.99 (978-159643471-4). 40pp. Cinderella, Sleeping Beauty, Snow White, the frog prince, and the princess and the pea all are featured in this fractured, comic book retelling. (Rev: BL 8/10; HB 9–10/10; LMC 11–12/10; SLJ 9/10)

2054 Baltazar, Art, and Franco. *Billy Batson and the Magic of Shazam: Mr. Mind over Matter* (3–5). Illus. by Byron Vaughns. 2011, DC Comics paper $12.99 (978-140122993-1). 144pp. Witty text and unified themes add cross-generational appeal to this updated take on Captain Marvel. (Rev: BL 6/1/11)

2055 Beka. *Dance Class: So, You Think You Can Hip-Hop?* (4–8). Illus. by Crip. 2012, Papercutz $9.99 (978-159707254-0). 48pp. A graphic novel in which dance students compete for the lead role in *Sleeping Beauty* while at the same time swooning over KT, the hip-hop teacher. (Rev: BL 3/15/12; LMC 10/12)

2056 Cammuso, Frank. *The Battling Bands* (3–5). Illus. by author. Series: Knights of the Lunch Table. 2011, Scholastic paper $10.99 (978-043990318-9). 128pp. Artie and his friends want to start a rock band but first have to find the Singing Sword. Lexile GN260L (Rev: BL 10/15/11)

2057 Chad, Jon. *Leo Geo and His Miraculous Journey Through the Center of the Earth* (3–6). Illus. by author. 2012, Roaring Brook $15.99 (978-159643661-9). 40pp. This squat but wide graphic novel offers narrator Leo Geo a chance to illustrate his adventures as he tunnels through the Earth and delivers facts about geology (and the occasional monster and other surprises). (Rev: BL 2/15/12; LMC 5–6/12; SLJ 2/12)

2058 Chantler, Scott. *The Sign of the Black Rock* (4–7). Illus. by author. Series: Three Thieves. 2011, Kids Can $17.95 (978-155453416-6); paper $8.95 (978-155453417-3). 112pp. Dessa and her fugitive friends spend a rainy night at the Black Rock Inn, evading detection by the Queen's soldiers, also guests at the inn, who've been sent to capture her; this second installment in the series focuses in part on the innkeeper and his shady activities. Lexile GN510L (Rev: BL 10/15/11; SLJ 11/1/11)

2059 Clamp. *Cardcaptor Sakura, vol. 1* (3–8). Illus. by author. 2010, Dark Horse paper $19.99 (978-159582522-3). 576pp. Three previously published volumes in the series about 4th-grader Sakura and her efforts to save the universe are collected in this remastered and newly translated volume. (Rev: BLO 1/1–15/11)

2060 Conway, Gerry. *Crawling with Zombies* (3–6). Illus. by Paulo Henrique. 2010, Papercutz $10.99 (978-159707220-5); paper $6.99 (978-159707219-9). 64pp. This graphic novel brings the Hardy Boys detectives of the 1950s up-to-date with a story of zombie-like behavior among the teenagers of Bayport. (Rev: BLO 2/15/11; SLJ 5/1/11)

2061 Cosentino, Ralph. *Superman: The Story of the Man of Steel* (1–3). Illus. by author. 2010, Viking $16.99 (978-0-670-06285-0). 40pp. This action-packed book serves as a fine introduction to the superhero and his origins; includes retro cartoon art in bold primary colors. Lexile 1430 (Rev: BL 1/1/10; SLJ 5/10)

2062 Dahl, Michael. *The Man Behind the Mask* (3–5). Illus. by Dan Schoening. Series: DC Super Heroes: Batman. 2009, Stone Arch LB $25.32 (978-1-4342-1563-5); paper $5.95 (978-1-4342-1730-1). 56pp. Batman faces the villain responsible for his parents' deaths in this fast-moving graphic novel. Also use *My Frozen Valentine* (2009). (Rev: SLJ 1/1/10)

2063 Davis, Jim. *The Curse of the Cat People* (2–5). Illus. by author. Series: Garfield & Co. 2011, Papercutz $7.99 (978-1-59707-267-0). 32pp. Garfield finds himself in ancient Egypt and meets Neferkitty and some cats that want him to be their new pharaoh. Also use *Fish to Fry* (2011), in which Garfield is in court for crimes against fishkind. (Rev: SLJ 7/1/11)

2064 de Saint-Exupéry, Antoine, and Joann Sfar. *The Little Prince* (5–9). Illus. by Joann Sfar. 2010, Houghton Mifflin $19.99 (978-054733802-6). 112pp. A respectful graphic-novel retelling of Saint-Exupery's classic about a stranded pilot and a little boy who discuss matters of life and love. e (Rev: BL 9/15/10*; SLJ 11/10; VOYA 12/10)

2065 Deutsch, Barry. *Hereville: How Mirka Got Her Sword* (3–6). Illus. by author. 2010, Abrams $15.95 (978-081098422-6). 144pp. Mirka, an 11-year-old Orthodox Jewish girl with a longing for adventure, is challenged when a talking pig arrives in the village. (Rev: BL 10/15/10; HB 11–12/10; LMC 1–2/11)

2066 Eaton, Maxwell. *The Flying Beaver Brothers and the Evil Penguin Plan* (2–4). Illus. by author. 2012, Knopf LB $12.99 (978-037596447-3); paper $6.99 (978-037586447-6). 96pp. Two beavers must stop penguins from an evil plot to destroy their island by turning it into a frosty resort. (Rev: BL 1/12; LMC 3–4/12; SLJ 3/1/12)

2067 Emerson, Sharon. *Zebrafish* (5–8). Illus. by Renee Kurilla. 2010, Simon & Schuster $16.99 (978-1-4169-9525-8). 128pp. Led by purple-haired Vita — the only one with any musical abilities — the members of a middle-school rock band prepare for a performance that will bring donations for the fight against cancer. (Rev: BL 3/15/10; LMC 10/10; SLJ 5/10)

2068 Everheart, Chris. *Shadow Cell Scam* (4–8). Illus. by Arcana Studio. Series: The Recon Academy. 2009, Stone Arch $25.32 (978-1-4342-1166-8). 64pp. Working together, four superpower-endowed teens confront danger and adversity when they're sent to protect the launch of a Navy spy satellite in this thrilling graphic novel. (Rev: LMC 10/09; SLJ 9/09)

2069 Fearing, Mark. *Earthling!* (3–6). Illus. by author. 2012, Chronicle $22.99 (978-081187106-8); paper $12.99 (978-145210906-0). 248pp. Bud accidentally gets on the wrong bus and ends up in an intergalactic school, where he must hide his earthling status or risk arousing suspicion. (Rev: BL 3/15/12; LMC 8–9/12; SLJ 9/12; VOYA 6/12)

2070 Friesen, Ray. *Piranha Pancakes* (3–5). Illus. by author. 2010, Don't Eat Any Bugs paper $9.95 (978-098023143-4). 100pp. Melville and Tbyrd are back in another volume of zany stories full of wordplay and bold illustrations. (Rev: BL 4/15/11)

2071 Giarrusso, Chris. *G-Man: Learning to Fly* (3–5). Illus. by author. 2010, Image paper $9.99 (978-160706270-7). 96pp. A spirited young boy commandeers his family's magic blanket for a bit of lively fun in this superpowered collection of funny adventures. (Rev: BL 12/15/10)

2072 Gownley, Jimmy. *The Meaning of Life . . . and Other Stuff* (3–7). Illus. by author. Series: Amelia Rules! 2011, Atheneum paper $10.99 (978-141698612-6). 160pp. This seventh book in the Amelia Rules series finds the protagonist on the verge of puberty and yearning for simpler times. (Rev: BL 9/15/11)

2073 Gownley, Jimmy. *True Things (Adults Don't Want Kids to Know)* (3–7). Illus. by author. Series: Amelia Rules! 2010, Atheneum paper $10.99 (978-141698609-6). 176pp. In this sixth Amelia offering, Amelia contends with a powerful crush, her aunt dating her teacher, and increasing tension between her family and friends. (Rev: BL 10/15/10; SLJ 1/1/11)

2074 Gownley, Jimmy. *The Tweenage Guide to Not Being Unpopular* (3–7). Illus. by author. Series: Amelia Rules! 2010, Atheneum paper $10.99 (978-141698608-9). 192pp. Amelia and her friend Rhonda are determined to avoid unpopularity in middle school, though their popularity crusade hits some obstacles. (Rev: BL 3/15/10; SLJ 5/10)

2075 Hale, Shannon, and Dean Hale. *Rapunzel's Revenge* (5–8). Illus. by Nathan Hale. 2008, Bloomsbury $18.99 (978-1-59990-070-4). 144pp. In the Wild West, a girl called Rapunzel eventually escapes from a prison in a magic tree and uses her hair to gain revenge against the woman who kept her real mother a slave. ALSC Notable Children's Book, 2009. (Rev: BL 9/1/08; HB 11–12/08; LMC 11–12/08*; SLJ 9/08)

2076 Hatke, Ben. *Zita the Spacegirl* (3–6). Illus. by author. 2011, Roaring Brook $17.99 (978-159643695-4); paper $10.99 (978-159643446-2). 188pp. Joseph is abducted when he and Zita open a portal to an alien dimension, and Zita must follow and rescue him, experiencing many adventures. (Rev: BL 12/15/10; LMC 3–4/11; SLJ 1/1/11)

2077 Holm, Jennifer L., and Matthew Holm. *Babymouse: Mad Scientist* (3–5). Illus. by Jennifer L. Holm. Series: Babymouse. 2011, Random House LB $12.99 (978-037596574-6); paper $6.99 (978-037586574-9). 96pp. Babymouse discovers an amoeba named Squish while working on her science fair project. (Rev: BL 9/15/11)

2078 Holm, Jennifer L., and Matthew Holm. *Babymouse Burns Rubber* (4–6). Illus. by Jennifer L. Holm. Series: Babymouse. 2010, Random House LB $12.99 (978-037595713-0); paper $5.99 (978-037585713-3). 96pp. Babymouse's dreams of driving a race car come true when her friend Wilson helps her build a soapbox derby car. (Rev: BL 1/1/10)

2079 Holm, Jennifer L., and Matthew Holm. *Cupcake Tycoon* (4–6). Illus. by Jennifer L. Holm. Series: Babymouse. 2010, Random House LB $12.99 (978-037596573-9); paper $6.99 (978-037586573-2). 96pp. Babymouse participates in a library fundraiser after she accidentally sets off the sprinkler system and ruins some books; the 13th installment in the series. (Rev: BL 10/15/10)

2080 Holm, Jennifer L., and Matthew Holm. *Super Amoeba* (3–5). Illus. by Jennifer L. Holm. Series: Squish. 2011, Random House LB $12.99 (978-037593783-5); paper $6.99 (978-037584389-1). 96pp. The first volume in a new humorous series about an amoeba named Squish who imitates his favorite superhero in an effort to stop bullies from tormenting his friends. (Rev: BL 3/15/11; LMC 10/11; SLJ 7/11)

2081 Holm, Jennifer L., and Matthew Holm. *A Very Babymouse Christmas* (3–5). Illus. by Jennifer L. Holm. Series: Babymouse. 2011, Random House LB $12.99 (978-037596779-5); paper $6.99 (978-037586779-8). 96pp. Babymouse is determined to get the new Whiz Bang, an electronic gadget, for Christmas and is willing to take on Santa to get it. **e** (Rev: BLO 12/15/11; HB 11–12/11; SLJ 10/1/11)

2082 Kibuishi, Kazu. *Copper* (5–8). 2010, Graphix paper $12.99 (978-0-545-09893-9). 96pp. A collection of funny short stories, in graphic novel format, featuring a boy named Copper and his fraidy-cat talking dog Fred; with author comments on how he creates comic strips. (Rev: BL 12/1/09; LMC 3–4/10; SLJ 5/10)

2083 Kibuishi, Kazu. *The Last Council* (4–7). Illus. by author. Series: Amulet. 2011, Scholastic paper $10.99 (978-054520887-1). 224pp. Emily and her friends arrive in the cloud city of Cielis and find themselves in a contest for a seat on the Guardian Council. Lexile GN400L (Rev: BL 10/15/11)

2084 Kibuishi, Kazu. *The Stonekeeper's Curse* (4–7). Series: Amulet. 2009, Graphix $21.99 (978-0-439-84682-0). 224pp. This sequel to *The Stonekeeper* (2007) has Emily and Navin searching for a remedy that will save their mother from poison, even as the evil Elf King is in pursuit. The third volume in the series is *The Cloud Searchers* (2010). (Rev: BL 10/15/09; LMC 1–2/10; SLJ 11/09)

2085 Kim, Susan, and Laurence Klavan. *City of Spies* (4–7). Illus. by Pascal Dizin. 2010, First Second paper $16.99 (978-1-59643-262-8). 172pp. Evelyn and her friend Tony expose Nazi spies in this story set in New York in 1942. (Rev: BL 3/15/10*; LMC 8–9/10; SLJ 5/10)

2086 Kipling, Rudyard, and Lewis Helfand. *Kim* (5–8). Illus. by Rakesh Kumar. 2011, Campfire paper $9.99 (978-938002842-2). 72pp. The classic story of the boy who becomes a spy is presented in graphic-novel format with accessible text and colorful illustrations. (Rev: BL 1/1–15/11; LMC 5–6/11)

2087 Krosoczka, Jarrett J. *Lunch Lady and the Bake Sale Bandit* (2–4). Illus. by author. 2010, Knopf LB $12.99 (978-037596729-0); paper $6.99 (978-037586729-3). 96pp. Who is stealing bake sale goods? The Lunch Lady, Dee, Hector, and Terrence go head-to-head with a notorious bandit. (Rev: BL 2/15/11)

2088 Krosoczka, Jarrett J. *Lunch Lady and the Summer Camp Shakedown* (3–5). Illus. by author. 2010, Knopf LB $12.99 (978-0-375-96095-6); paper $6.99 (978-0-375-86095-9). 96pp. Lunch Lady is working as cook at the summer camp Hector, Dee, and Terrence are attending, and together they tackle the mysterious Scum Monster. **e** Lexile GN390L (Rev: BLO 6/10; SLJ 7/10)

2089 Labatt, Mary. *Witches' Brew* (2–4). Illus. by Jo Rioux. Series: Sam and Friends. 2011, Kids Can $16.95 (978-155453472-2); paper $7.95 (978-155453473-9). 96pp. Three strange women move into the neighborhood with pets including toads and a black cat. Could they be witches? Sam the sheepdog detective and his human friends investigate. (Rev: BL 5/1/11)

2090 Langridge, Roger. *The Muppet Show Comic Book: Family Reunion* (3–6). Illus. by Amy Mebberson. 2010, Boom! paper $9.99 (978-160886587-1). 112pp. This deftly illustrated book captures all the distinct personalities of the Muppets, and reworks some favorite sketches. (Rev: BL 11/15/10)

2091 Loux, Matthew. *The Truth About Dr. True* (3–6). Illus. by author. Series: Salt Water Taffy. 2009, Oni paper $5.95 (978-193496404-0). 96pp. Adventure and mystery — involving a 19th-century murder and an unusual ghost — await Jack and Benny when they spend the summer in a small Maine seaside town. The fourth volume in the series is *Caldera's Revenge* (2011). (Rev: BL 1/1/10)

2092 McCranie, Stephen. *Mal and Chad: The Biggest, Bestest Time Ever!* (2–5). Illus. by author. 2011, Philomel paper $9.99 (978-039925221-1). 224pp. Child genius Mal and his dog Chad have a variety of shape-shifting, time-travel adventures even as Mal tackles the usual concerns of a 4th-grader. (Rev: BL 5/1/11)

2093 Mendes, Melissa. *Freddy Stories* (2–4). Illus. by author. 2011, Hand Thumb paper $10 (978-098359421-5). 112pp. A hoodie-wearing girl named Freddy stars in a series of short stories featuring her everyday adventures with her dog, her fractured but loving family, and her imagination. (Rev: BLO 2/28/12)

2094 Mucci, Tim. *The Odyssey* (5–8). Illus. by Emanuel Tenderini. 2010, Sterling paper $7.95 (978-1-4027-3155-6). 128pp. This graphic novel emphasizes Odysseus's various adventures on his journey home — with Circe, Calypso, the cyclops, the sirens, and so forth. (Rev: BL 4/15/10*; LMC 10/10; SLJ 7/10)

2095 Neel, Julien. *Secret Diary* (4–7). Trans. by Carol Klio Burrell. Illus. by author. 2012, Lerner/Graphic Universe LB $27.93 (978-076138776-3); paper $8.95 (978-076138868-5). 48pp. Lou, 12, contends with her shiftless single mom, the mean girls at school, and her timidity about dating in this appealing graphic novel. **e** (Rev: BL 3/15/12; LMC 11–12/12; SLJ 7/1/12)

2096 Nickel, Scott. *The Incredible Rockhead vs. Papercut* (2–4). Illus. by C. S. Jennings. Series: Graphic Sparks. 2010, Stone Arch LB $22.65 (978-143421976-3). 40pp. In this quirky superhero comic, Chip Stone (a rock) faces off against the dangerous and unpredictable Papercut. Lexile GN240L (Rev: BLO 9/1/10)

2097 Nykko. *The Master of Shadows* (4–7). Trans. by Carol Kilo Burrell. Illus. by Bannister. Series: Else-Where Chronicles. 2009, Graphic Universe LB $27.93 (978-076134461-2); paper $6.95 (978-076134744-6). 48pp. Max, Rebecca, Theo, and Noah must tackle the Master of Shadows in their continuing search for a way to escape the strange world of ElseWhere. (Rev: BL 4/15/09; LMC 10/09; SLJ 5/09) [741.5]

2098 O'Connor, George. *Athena: Grey-Eyed Goddess* (5–9). Illus. by author. 2010, Roaring Brook $16.99 (978-159643649-7); paper $9.99 (978-159643432-5). 80pp. A graphic-novel retelling of the myths involving Athena, the Greek goddess of wisdom and war. (Rev: BL 5/1/10; SLJ 5/10)

2099 O'Malley, Kevin. *Desk Stories* (1–3). Illus. by author. 2011, Whitman $16.99 (978-0-8075-1562-4). 32pp. Six short graphic-novel stories depict richly imagined comic scenarios involving school desks. (Rev: BL 8/11; LMC 1–2/12; SLJ 8/1/11)

2100 Parker, Jake. *Rescue on Tankium3* (3–6). Illus. by author. 2011, Scholastic $21.99 (978-054511716-6); paper $10.99 (978-054511717-3). 146pp. Galactic Security Agent Missile Mouse battles an evil king on a distant galaxy, dodging peril at every turn in this lively graphic novel. (Rev: BL 4/15/11; LMC 10/11; SLJ 3/11)

2101 Phelan, Matt. *The Storm in the Barn* (5–8). 2009, Candlewick $24.99 (978-0-7636-3618-0). 208pp. In 1937 Kansas 11-year-old Jack faces many challenges — bullies, a sister with problems, and above all the hardships of the Dust Bowl — to which he may have a solution. (Rev: BL 8/09*; LMC 11–12/09; SLJ 9/09)

2102 Pilkey, Dav. *The Adventures of Ook and Gluk, Kung-Fu Cavemen from the Future* (2–4). Illus. by author. 2010, Scholastic $9.99 (978-054517530-2). 176pp. In this wacky graphic novel, two young Stone Age cavemen travel to the year 2222 and learn kung fu in order to save their own time from an evil corporation. **e** Lexile GN420L (Rev: BL 9/15/10; LMC 1–2/11; SLJ 11/10)

2103 Renier, Aaron. *The Unsinkable Walker Bean* (5–8). Illus. by author. 2010, First Second paper $13.99 (978-159643453-0). 208pp. Exciting action rules in this imaginative story of courageous young Walter's dangerous quest to return a pearl skull to the witches on the Mango Islands. (Rev: BL 6/1/10*; LMC 3–4/11; SLJ 9/10; VOYA 6/10)

2104 Reynolds, Aaron. *Big Hairy Drama* (3–5). Illus. by Neil Numberman. Series: Joey Fly, Private Eye. 2010, Henry Holt $16.99 (978-080508243-2); paper $9.99 (978-080509110-6). 128pp. Joey Fly and his sidekick Sammy Stingtail (a scorpion) investigate the disappearance of stage star Greta Divawing, a butterfly. (Rev: BL 12/15/10; SLJ 1/11)

2105 Robbins, Trina. *The Drained Brains Caper* (4–7). Illus. by Tyler Page. Series: Chicagoland Detective Agency. 2010, Lerner/Graphic Universe LB $29.27 (978-076134601-2); paper $6.95 (978-076135635-6). 64pp. New to summer school, Megan, 13, soon becomes suspicious about the principal's motives and seeks help from computer genius Raf. The second volume is *The Maltese Mummy* (2011). Lexile GN390L (Rev: BL 9/15/10; LMC 1–2/11; SLJ 11/10)

2106 Roman, Dave. *Astronaut Academy: Zero Gravity* (5–8). 2011, First Second paper $9.99 (978-1-59643-620-6). 187pp. Child space hero Hakata Soy enrolls in Astronaut Academy and meets danger in his first term when a robot doppelganger is sent to kill him. (Rev: BL 6/11; LMC 8–9/11; SLJ 5/11)

2107 Rosa, Don. *The Life and Times of Scrooge McDuck* (5–8). Illus. by author. 2010, Boom! $24.99 (978-1-60886-538-3). 127pp. Rosa tells the story of Scrooge McDuck's origins in Scotland, exploits in America, and success in Africa, rendering him the world's richest duck and introducing many famous characters along the way. (Rev: BL 3/15/10*; SLJ 5/10)

2108 Santat, Dan. *Sidekicks* (3–6). Illus. by author. 2011, Scholastic $24.99 (978-0-439-29811-7); paper $12.99 (978-0-439-29819-3). 224pp. Middle-aged superhero Captain Amazing is looking for a new sidekick, and his pets Roscoe and Fluffy both seek the job — leading to new adventures. (Rev: BL 4/15/11; HB 7–8/11; LMC 10–11/11*; SLJ 7/1/11)

2109 Schweizer, Chris. *Tricky Coyote Tales* (2–4). Illus. by Chad Thomas. Series: Tricky Journeys. 2011, Lerner LB $27.93 (978-076136601-0); paper $6.95 (978-076137859-4). 64pp. In this book that blends graphic novel format with running text, readers help a hungry coyote decide how to react to a variety of animals. e (Rev: BL 10/15/11; LMC 1–2/12)

2110 Shaw, Murray, and M. J. Cosson. *Sherlock Holmes and a Scandal in Bohemia* (4–6). Illus. by Sophie Rohrbach. Series: On the Case with Holmes and Watson. 2010, Lerner LB $26.60 (978-076136185-5); paper $6.95 (978-076136197-8). 48pp. This engaging graphic novel adaptation of the classic tale involving a blackmail plot against the king of Bohemia includes a section explaining Holmes's reasoning; the first in a series. Lexile GN600L (Rev: BL 11/15/10)

2111 Shiga, Jason. *Meanwhile* (4–9). Illus. by author. 2010, Abrams $15.95 (978-0-8109-8423-3). 80pp. A mad scientist asks a boy to test one of three inventions in this choose-your-own-adventure graphic novel. (Rev: BL 1/1/10*; SLJ 3/10)

2112 Sonneborn, Scott. *Shell Shocker* (2–4). Illus. by Dan Schoening. Series: DC Super Heroes. 2011, Stone Arch LB $25.32 (978-1-4342-2615-0); paper $5.95 (978-1-4342-3092-8). 56pp. The Flash (aka police scientist Barry Allen) prevents a series of catastrophes in this fast-paced chapter book. (Rev: BL 7/11; SLJ 6/11)

2113 Spires, Ashley. *Binky the Space Cat* (2–4). Illus. by author. 2009, Kids Can $16.95 (978-155453309-1). 64pp. A humorous story about Binky the cat's adventurous spirit and conflicting love for his humans. (Rev: BL 8/09; LMC 10/09; SLJ 11/09)

2114 Spires, Ashley. *Binky to the Rescue* (2–4). Illus. by author. 2010, Kids Can $16.95 (978-155453502-6). 64pp. A zany graphic novel about a house cat who imagines himself in a space station. (Rev: BL 10/15/10; SLJ 11/10)

2115 Spires, Ashley. *Binky Under Pressure* (2–4). Illus. by author. 2011, Kids Can $16.95 (978-155453504-0); paper $8.95 (978-155453767-9). 64pp. Binky, an imaginative cat with aspirations to living in a space station, is not pleased when a new cat named Gracie arrives in his abode. (Rev: BL 9/15/11; SLJ 11/1/11)

2116 TenNapel, Doug. *Cardboard* (5–8). Illus. by author. 2012, Scholastic $24.99 (978-054541872-0); paper $12.99 (978-054541873-7). 288pp. A jobless father's meager birthday gift — a cardboard box that the two fashion into a boxer — comes alive for his son and mayhem ensues. (Rev: BL 3/15/12; HB 7–8/12; LMC 11–12/12; SLJ 9/12; VOYA 6/12)

2117 TenNapel, Doug. *Ghostopolis* (5–8). Illus. by author. 2010, Scholastic $24.99 (978-0-545-21027-0); paper $14.99 (978-0-545-21028-7). 288pp. When Frank Gallows of the Supernatural Immigration Task Force accidentally transports him to the afterlife, young Garth Hale discovers he has hitherto unknown powers and is in danger from the sinister ruler of Ghostopolis. Lexile GN300L (Rev: BL 3/15/10; SLJ 7/10; VOYA 2/10)

2118 Twain, Mark, and Jean David Morvan, et al. *The Adventures of Tom Sawyer* (5–8). Illus. by Severine Lefebvre. Series: Papercutz' Classics Illustrated Deluxe. 2009, Papercutz $17.95 (978-159707152-9); paper $13.95 (978-159707153-6). Bold manga-style illustrations enhance this adaptation that preserves the plot twists and tenor of the original story. (Rev: BL 1/1/10; SLJ 1/10)

2119 Varon, Sara. *Bake Sale* (5–8). Illus. by author. 2011, First Second $19.99 (978-159643740-1); paper $16.99 (978-159643419-6). 160pp. Cupcake, who runs a bakery and plays in a band, is thrilled when his friend Eggplant invites him to go to Istanbul and meet his idol, Turkish Delight. (Rev: BL 9/15/11; LMC 1–2/12; SLJ 11/1/11)

2120 Wagner, Josh. *Sky Pirates of Neo Terra* (4–7). Illus. by Camilla D'Errico. 2010, Image paper $17.99 (978-160706324-7). 128pp. Billy sets out to thwart the Witch Queen's evil plans by rescuing her mechanic — his friend Ricket's dad. (Rev: BLO 1/1–15/11)

2121 Weigel, Jeff. *Thunder from the Sea: Adventure on Board the HMS Defender* (3–5). Illus. by author. 2010, Putnam $17.99 (978-0-399-25089-7). 48pp. Twelve-year-old Jack Hoyton enlists in the Royal Navy during the time of the Napoleonic Wars in this exciting graphic novel. e (Rev: BL 4/15/10; SLJ 8/1/10)

2122 Young, Frank. *Oregon Trail: The Road to Destiny* (3–6). Illus. by David Lasky. 2011, Sasquatch paper $14.95 (978-157061649-5). 128pp. Rebecca, 11, chronicles her family's journey along the Oregon Trail in this historical graphic novel that includes lots of discomforts and hardships and the occasional tragedy. (Rev: BLO 11/15/11; SLJ 1/12)

Growing into Maturity

Family Problems

2123 Atkinson, Elizabeth. *I, Emma Freke* (4–7). 2010, Carolrhoda $16.95 (978-0-7613-5604-2). 232pp. Twelve-year-old Emma, tall and uncertain, learns a lot about herself when she is invited to a family reunion of the father she has never met. (Rev: BL 11/1/10; SLJ 2/1/11*)

2124 Auch, M. J. *Guitar Boy* (5–8). 2010, Henry Holt $16.99 (978-0-8050-9112-0). 272pp. When his mother suffers a brain injury and his father throws him out, 13-year-old Travis's love of guitars and music helps him to survive and even contribute to restoring his family. ∩ Lexile 750L (Rev: BL 11/1/10; LMC 11–12/10; SLJ 9/1/10)

2125 Bauer, Marion Dane. *Shelter from the Wind* (5–9). 2010, Marshall Cavendish $16.99 (978-0-7614-5687-2). 112pp. Originally published in 1975, this is a story of a girl coming to terms with upheaval in her family including alcoholism, divorce, and remarriage. (Rev: LMC 8–9/10)

2126 Clifton, Lutricia. *Freaky Fast Frankie Joe* (4–6). 2012, Holiday House $16.95 (978-082342367-5). 248pp. Twelve-year-old Frankie Joe is uprooted from a Texas trailer park when his mother is arrested, and must adjust to life in Illinois with the father he never met, a stepmother, and four half brothers. (Rev: BL 4/15/12; LMC 8–9/12; SLJ 5/1/12)

2127 Connor, Leslie. *Crunch* (5–8). 2010, HarperCollins $16.99 (978-0-06-169229-1); LB $17.89 (978-0-06-169233-8). 336pp. When his parents are stranded on vacation, 14-year-old Dewey must help his older sister look after their three younger siblings and at the same time run their dad's bicycle repair shop and solve the mystery of missing parts. Lexile HL490L (Rev: BL 4/1/10; HB 7–8/10; LMC 11–12/10; SLJ 5/10)

2128 DeFelice, Cynthia. *Wild Life* (4–7). 2011, Farrar $16.99 (978-0-374-38001-4). 192pp. When his parents are posted to Iraq, 12-year-old Erik is sent to his grandparents in North Dakota; unhappy there, he strikes out on his own with his newly adopted dog and manages to survive a time in the wilderness. Lexile 860L (Rev: BLO 6/21/11; LMC 10/11; SLJ 6/11)

2129 Derby, Sally. *Kyle's Island* (5–8). 2010, Charlesbridge $16.95 (978-1-58089-316-9). 192pp. Heartbroken that this will be the last summer at his family's lake cottage — his parents have just divorced — 13-year-old Kyle spends much of his time nursing his anger and fishing with an elderly neighbor who helps him deal with his unhappiness. Lexile 670L (Rev: BL 12/15/09; LMC 5–6/10; SLJ 1/10)

2130 De Vries, Maggie. *Somebody's Girl* (3–6). Series: Orca Young Readers. 2011, Orca paper $7.95 (978-1-55469-383-2). 164pp. Martha, a difficult 9-year-old, is upset when she learns her adoptive parents are having a baby. ❢ (Rev: LMC 10/11; SLJ 7/11)

2131 Galante, Cecilia. *Willowood* (3–6). 2010, Simon & Schuster $16.99 (978-1-4169-8022-3). 272pp. Lily, 11, struggles to adjust to life in a new city, finding friendship in unexpected places as her busy mother works long hours. ❢ Lexile 630L (Rev: BLO 5/15/10; LMC 5–6/10; SLJ 3/10)

2132 Jackson, Alison. *Eggs over Evie* (4–6). Illus. by Tuesday Mourning. 2010, Henry Holt $16.99 (978-0-8050-8294-4). 224pp. Thirteen-year-old Evie starts off the summer reeling from the news that her new stepmother is expecting a baby, but gains confidence and perspective from a cooking class and her handsome class partner. (Rev: BL 12/15/10; LMC 3–4/11; SLJ 1/1/11*)

2133 Jones, Traci L. *Silhouetted by the Blue* (5–8). 2011, Farrar $16.99 (978-0-374-36914-9). 208pp. Serena, an African American 7th-grader, must finally ask for help when her father does not recover from his depression after her mother's death. Lexile 720L (Rev: BL 6/1/11; HB 7–8/11; SLJ 8/11*)

2134 LaFleur, Suzanne. *Love, Aubrey* (4–7). 2009, Random House $15.99 (978-038573774-6); LB $18.99 (978-038590686-9). 272pp. When her mother disappears after her father and sister die in a car accident, 11-year-old Aubrey struggles to cope. ∩ (Rev: BL 8/09*; SLJ 9/09)

2135 Little, Kimberley Griffiths. *Circle of Secrets* (4–6). 2011, Scholastic $17.99 (978-0-545-16561-7). 336pp. Shelby, 11, goes to live in the Louisiana bayou with her estranged mother and together they try to resolve conflicts in this story with a mysterious ghost angle. (Rev: BL 12/1/11; SLJ 12/1/11*)

2136 McKay, Hilary. *Caddy's World* (4–7). 2012, Simon & Schuster $16.99 (978-144244105-7). 272pp. In this prequel to the series about the Casson family, 12-year-old Caddy is thrown for a loop when her newest sibling, Rose, is born prematurely and her mother decamps for the hospital, leaving her father to look after the family. ❢ Lexile 770L (Rev: BL 5/1/12*; HB 3–4/12; SLJ 3/12*; VOYA 2/12)

2137 Mason, Simon. *Moon Pie* (5–8). 2011, Random House $16.99 (978-038575235-0); LB $19.99 (978-038575237-4). 336pp. Martha, 11, looks after her little brother Tug after her mother's death as her father struggles with his drinking. ❢ (Rev: BL 11/15/11; HB 11–12/11)

2138 Newman, John. *Mimi* (4–7). 2011, Candlewick $15.99 (978-0-7636-5415-3). 192pp. Mimi's mother was killed in an accident and everyone in the family — even the dog — is having trouble dealing with this; the fact that Mimi was adopted from China is mentioned in passing. (Rev: BLO 9/1/11; SLJ 9/1/11)

2139 Nicholls, Sally. *Season of Secrets* (5–8). 2011, Scholastic $16.99 (978-0-545-21825-2). 240pp. Sisters Hannah and Molly are sent to live with their grandparents in northern England after their mother's death, and there they cope very differently with their grief, Molly increasingly absorbed in an inner world. ❢ Lexile 620L (Rev: BL 12/15/10; HB 1–2/11; LMC 5–6/11; SLJ 2/1/11)

2140 O'Connor, Sheila. *Sparrow Road* (5–8). 2011, Putnam $16.99 (978-0-399-25458-1). 247pp. Raine, 12, ends up meeting her estranged father when she accompanies her mother to a remote artists' retreat for the summer. ℮ Lexile 530L (Rev: BL 7/11*; LMC 10/11; SLJ 7/11)

2141 Sheinmel, Courtney. *All the Things You Are* (5–8). 2011, Simon & Schuster $15.99 (978-1-4169-9717-7). 256pp. Twelve-year-old Carly's mother is arrested for embezzling, and this has an impact on the whole family, particularly affecting Carly's school life. (Rev: BLO 6/21/11; SLJ 7/11)

2142 Sherrard, Valerie. *Tumbleweed Skies* (3–6). 2010, Fitzhenry & Whiteside paper $11.95 (978-155455113-2). 153pp. In the summer of 1954, 10-year-old Ellie must go to live with her cold and distant grandmother in Saskatchewan while her salesman father hits the road. (Rev: BL 5/15/10*; LMC 11–12/10; SLJ 3/1/11*)

2143 Snyder, Zilpha Keatley. *William S. and the Great Escape* (5–7). 2009, Simon & Schuster $16.99 (978-1-4169-6763-7). 224pp. In a small California town during the Great Depression, the four youngest Baggett siblings flee their coarse, abusive family for their aunt's house after sister Janey's guinea pig is flushed down the toilet. ∩ ℮ Lexile 980L (Rev: BL 7/09; LMC 11–12/09; SLJ 10/09)

2144 Watson, Renée. *What Momma Left Me* (5–8). 2010, Bloomsbury $16.99 (978-1-59990-446-7). 240pp. African American Serenity, 13, tells how she and her brother cope when they go to live with their grandparents after their mother dies and their father disappears. (Rev: BL 5/1/10; LMC 10/10; SLJ 8/10; VOYA 8/10)

2145 Wilson, Jacqueline. *Cookie* (4–7). Illus. by Nick Sharratt. 2009, Roaring Brook $16.99 (978-1-59643-534-6). 336pp. Beauty Cookson and her mother flee the abusive, boorish yet wealthy Mr. Cookson and start a new life of their own in this endearing tale of redemption. ∩ Lexile 680L (Rev: BL 9/1/09; LMC 11–12/09; SLJ 10/09)

Personal Problems

2146 Allen, Crystal. *How Lamar's Bad Prank Won a Bubba-Sized Trophy* (5–8). 2011, HarperCollins $16.99 (978-0-06-199272-8). 288pp. Bowling is an important anchor in the difficult life of 13-year-old African American Lamar, but it threatens to undercut his best efforts in this humorous novel about young teen love and emotions. ∩ ℮ Lexile 550L (Rev: BL 3/1/11; SLJ 2/1/11; VOYA 4/11)

2147 Amato, Mary. *Invisible Lines* (5–8). Illus. by Antonio Caparo. 2009, Egmont $15.99 (978-1-60684-010-8); LB $18.99 (978-1-60684-043-6). 352pp. Soccer and science are safe havens for 7th-grader Trevor, who lives in a grim housing project but attends a school for the

privileged and has trouble fitting in. Lexile 650L (Rev: BL 11/1/09; SLJ 11/09)

2148 Axelrod, Amy. *Your Friend in Fashion, Abby Shapiro* (5–7). Illus. by author. 2011, Holiday House $17.95 (978-0-8234-2340-8). 256pp. In 1959, 11-year-old Abby has a hard time making the transition from girlhood to womanhood, and leans on her close-knit Jewish extended family for support and guidance while sharing her problems in letters to Jackie Kennedy. Lexile 710L (Rev: BL 4/15/11; SLJ 4/11)

2149 Bauer, Joan. *Close to Famous* (5–8). 2011, Viking $16.99 (978-0-670-01282-4). 256pp. Slow learner and talented baker Foster, 12, and her mother flee her mother's abusive boyfriend to start a new life in West Virginia, where she learns to read and gets the chance to market her baked goods. YALSA Best Fiction for Young Adults, 2012. ℮ Lexile 540L (Rev: BL 1/1–15/11; HB 1–2/11; LMC 5–6/11; SLJ 3/1/11)

2150 Bial, Raymond. *Chigger* (4–7). 2012, Motes paper $14 (978-193489438-5). 220pp. In the late 1950s straight-laced Luke's family learns to open up and trust rebellious girl Chigger when confronted with evidence of the girl's emotional needs. (Rev: BLO 3/15/12; SLJ 8/12)

2151 Block, Francesca Lia. *House of Dolls* (3–6). Illus. by Barbara McClintock. 2010, HarperCollins $15.99 (978-0-06-113094-6); LB $22.47 (978-0-06-113095-3). 80pp. Emotionally neglected Madison takes her frustration out on her dolls, sending the boys off to "war" and depriving the girls of their beautiful dresses until her grandmother comes to the rescue; gorgeous, detailed illustrations enhance the story. (Rev: BL 3/15/10*; HB 7–8/10; SLJ 6/10)

2152 Boelts, Maribeth. *The PS Brothers* (4–6). 2010, Harcourt $15 (978-0-547-34249-8). 144pp. Friends Russell and Shawn long to have a dog to protect them from bullies and their efforts to raise money lead them to discover an illegal dog-fighting ring. ℮ Lexile 810L (Rev: BL 12/15/10; SLJ 11/1/10)

2153 Clements, Andrew. *Troublemaker* (5–8). Illus. by Mark Elliott. 2011, Atheneum $16.99 (978-1-4169-4930-5). 160pp. When his older brother Mitchell gets out of jail a changed character, 6th-grader Clay also decides to reform, but finds it harder than expected. ∩ Lexile 730L (Rev: BL 6/1/11; HB 7–8/11; LMC 1–2/12; SLJ 7/11)

2154 Cooper, Ilene. *Look at Lucy!* (2–4). Illus. by David Merrell. 2009, Random House LB $11.99 (978-0-375-95558-7); paper $4.99 (978-0-375-85558-0). 112pp. Bobby enters his beagle, Lucy, in a pet shop "spokes-pet" contest even though he must overcome his fear of public speaking in order to do so. (Rev: SLJ 10/1/09)

2155 Corriveau, Art. *How I, Nicky Flynn, Finally Get a Life (and a Dog)* (4–7). 2010, Abrams $16.95 (978-081098298-7). 272pp. The gift of a former seeing-eye dog coaxes depressed 11-year-old Nicky Flynn to meet people and explore his new Boston neighborhood. Lexile 670L (Rev: BL 3/1/10; LMC 11–12/10; SLJ 5/10)

2156 Day, Karen. *A Million Miles from Boston* (5–8). 2011, Random House $15.99 (978-0-385-73899-6); LB $18.99 (978-0-385-90763-7). 224pp. Lucy, 12, contends with her dad's new girlfriend, the shifting social landscape, and a pesky boy from back home who's popped up at their summer vacation home in Maine. (Rev: BL 3/15/11; LMC 10/11; SLJ 6/11)

2157 Donovan, Gail. *What's Bugging Bailey Blecker?* (4–6). 2011, Dutton $16.99 (978-0-525-42286-0). 208pp. Set adrift in a new school, Bailey gains maturity by dealing with the loss of a pet, a disappointing party, and an outbreak of head lice. ℮ Lexile 670L (Rev: BL 2/15/11; HB 3–4/11; SLJ 2/1/11)

2158 Fogelin, Adrian. *Summer on the Moon* (5–8). 2012, Peachtree $15.95 (978-156145626-0). 240pp. Socko, 13, and his mother move from the gritty inner city to the suburbs, where they will look after an elderly relative, but the situation there is not as simple or satisfactory as they hoped. Lexile 630L (Rev: BL 4/15/12*; LMC 11–12/12; SLJ 7/12)

2159 Gephart, Donna. *Olivia Bean, Trivia Queen* (4–7). 2012, Delacorte $16.99 (978-038574052-4); LB $19.99 (978-037598952-0). 288pp. Olivia's desire to see her father, who now lives in California, fuels her determination to compete in "Kids' Week" on *Jeopardy*; then her father will really appreciate her? (Rev: BL 5/15/12; SLJ 3/12)

2160 Gervay, Susanne. *I Am Jack* (3–6). Illus. by Cathy Wilcox. 2009, Tricycle $14.99 (978-1-58246-286-8). 128pp. Eleven-year-old Jack is being bullied and having dreadful headaches, but his home life is problematic and it is his friend Anna who initiates change in his life. (Rev: BLO 11/15/09; SLJ 2/1/10)

2161 Graff, Keir. *The Other Felix* (4–6). 2011, Roaring Brook $16.99 (978-1-59643-655-8). 176pp. A young boy coping with nightmares and disengaged parents meets another boy who knows how to fight off monsters. (Rev: BLO 9/15/11; SLJ 12/1/11)

2162 Grant, Vicki. *Hold the Pickles* (5–8). Series: Orca Currents. 2012, Orca LB $16.95 (978-155469921-6); paper $9.95 (978-155469920-9). 112pp. A puny 15-year-old eager for a chance to earn some money dresses up as a hot dog at a food fair, making him a prime target for bullies; for reluctant readers, this action-packed story also involves a mystery. ℮ Lexile HL580L (Rev: BL 3/1/12; LMC 8–9/12; SLJ 5/1/12)

2163 Grimes, Nikki. *Planet Middle School* (5–8). 2011, Bloomsbury $15.99 (978-1-59990-284-5). 150pp. African American Joylin, 12, copes with changes to her body and social relationships as she goes through puberty. (Rev: BL 9/15/11; SLJ 12/1/11*)

2164 Helget, Nicole, and Nate LeBoutillier. *Horse Camp* (5–8). 2012, Egmont $15.99 (978-160684351-2). 304pp. Twins Percy and Penny, 12, grudgingly adjust to farm life with their uncle in Minnesota after their mother is arrested. (Rev: BL 5/15/12*; SLJ 6/12)

2165 Henkes, Kevin. *Junonia* (4–6). Illus. by author. 2011, HarperCollins $15.99 (978-0-06-196417-6); LB $16.89 (978-0-06-196418-3). 192pp. Nearly 10 years old, Alice is unsettled when she and her parents go to Sanibel as usual in February but things are not the same as always — as she likes them to be. ☊ (Rev: BL 3/1/11*; HB 5–6/11; LMC 10/11; SLJ 6/11)

2166 Hiranandani, Veera. *The Whole Story of Half a Girl* (4–6). 2012, Delacorte $16.99 (978-038574128-6); LB $19.99 (978-037598995-7). 224pp. Half Jewish, half Hindi Sonia contends with many challenges when her father loses his job and she must leave her private school and attend the local middle school. ℮ (Rev: BL 1/1/12; LMC 11–12/12; SLJ 2/12)

2167 Hobbs, Valerie. *The Last Best Days of Summer* (4–8). 2010, Farrar $16.99 (978-0-374-34670-6). 192pp. Twelve-year-old Lucy is tugged in two directions — she wants to join the "in" crowd at school and yet she does not want to abandon her neighbor Eddie, who has Down syndrome and will be attending the same school. ℮ Lexile 570L (Rev: BL 4/1/10*; LMC 5–6/10; SLJ 4/10)

2168 Houtman, Jacqueline Jaeger. *The Reinvention of Edison Thomas* (5–8). 2010, Front Street $17.95 (978-1-59078-708-3). 192pp. Eddy is bright and loves science and inventing but has great difficulty getting along with the other students and is often the butt of pranks. Lexile 780L (Rev: BL 4/1/10; LMC 10/10; SLJ 6/10)

2169 Howe, James. *Addie on the Inside* (5–8). 2011, Atheneum $16.99 (978-1-4169-1384-9). 224pp. Seventh grade brings a combination of challenges for Addie Carle in this verse companion to *The Misfits* (2001) and *Totally Joe* (2005). ℮ (Rev: BL 6/1/11; SLJ 8/11*)

2170 Hurwitz, Michele Weber. *Calli Be Gold* (4–6). 2011, Random House $15.99 (978-0-385-73970-2); LB $18.99 (978-0-385-90802-3). 208pp. Calli, a quiet and thoughtful 11-year-old, resists her parents' efforts to mold her as another of the family's overachievers. ℮ (Rev: BL 3/15/11; SLJ 6/11)

2171 Krech, R.W. *Love Puppies and Corner Kicks* (5–8). 2010, Dutton $16.99 (978-0-525-42197-9). 192pp. American Andrea DiLorenzo, 13, moves to Scotland and initially has trouble making friends and is distressed when her stutter returns; however, her soccer skills help her overcome her loneliness and adjust to her new life. ℮ Lexile 530L (Rev: LMC 1–2/10; SLJ 4/10)

2172 Ludwig, Trudy. *Confessions of a Former Bully* (3–5). Illus. by Beth Adams. 2010, Tricycle $15.99 (978-1-58246-309-4). 48pp. Recording her experiences in her notebook, bully Katie slowly learns to correct her bad behavior when she's referred to the school counselor. Lexile 810L (Rev: BL 9/1/10; LMC 3–4/11; SLJ 8/1/10)

2173 Margolis, Leslie. *Girls Acting Catty* (4–6). 2009, Bloomsbury $15.99 (978-1-59990-237-1). 208pp. Sixth-grader Annabelle faces many challenges: a group of mean girls at school, her mother's forthcoming marriage, her cute future stepbrother, her first bra . . . . The third book in the series is *Everybody Bugs Out* (2011). ◯ (Rev: SLJ 12/09)

2174 Millard, Glenda. *The Naming of Tishkin Silk* (4–6). Illus. by Patrice Barton. 2009, Farrar $15.99 (978-0-374-35481-7). 112pp. Since his baby sister died and his mother has been in hospital, Griffin Silk has had to cope with making the difficult transition from home-schooling to public school. Lexile 930L (Rev: BL 11/1/09; LMC 11–12/09; SLJ 12/1/09)

2175 Morris, Taylor. *Blowout* (5–8). Illus. by Anne Keenan Higgins. Series: Hello, Gorgeous! 2011, Grosset & Dunlap paper $6.99 (978-044845526-6). 224pp. Mickey, 13, is sure her ship has come in when she gets a job working at her mother's salon, but she finds getting in with the popular crowd isn't as easy as she'd hoped. (Rev: BL 4/1/11)

2176 Moulton, Erin E. *Tracing Stars* (4–6). 2012, Philomel $16.99 (978-039925696-7). 224pp. Rising 6th-grader Indie Lee sets out to reclaim her missing pet lobster and become the kind of girl who won't embarrass her popular sister over the course of one short summer. (Rev: BL 5/15/12*; HB 7–8/12; LMC 11–12/12; SLJ 6/12)

2177 Musgrove, Marianne. *Lucy the Good* (3–5). Illus. by Cheryl Orsini. 2010, Henry Holt $16.99 (978-0-8050-9051-2). 177pp. Seven-year-old Lucy attempts to control her bad behavior when her Dutch great-aunt comes to visit them in Australia. ℮ Lexile 570L (Rev: BL 10/1/10; HB 11–12/10; SLJ 11/1/10)

2178 Myracle, Lauren. *Ten* (3–5). Series: Winnie Years. 2011, Dutton $16.99 (978-0-525-42356-0). 272pp. This volume follows Winnie's life from her 10th birthday through her 11th and the various challenges she faces with humor and courage. ℮ (Rev: BL 6/1/11; SLJ 9/1/11)

2179 Palacio, R. J. *Wonder* (5–8). 2012, Knopf $15.99 (978-037586902-0); LB $18.99 (978-037596902-7). 320pp. Augie Pullman, a 10-year-old with facial abnormalities who has been homeschooled, is sent to a private school in Manhattan with repercussions for himself and others. ◯ ℮ (Rev: BL 2/1/12*; HB 7–8/12; SLJ 2/12*)

2180 Patron, Susan. *Lucky for Good* (3–6). Illus. by Erin McGuire. Series: Lucky's Hard Pan Trilogy. 2011, Atheneum $16.99 (978-1-4169-9058-1). 224pp. Lucky, now 11, copes with a challenge to her mother's cafe and her friends' problems with some help from the people of Hard Pan, California; the last volume in the trilogy

that began with *The Higher Power of Lucky* (2006). ◯ Lexile 980L (Rev: BL 6/1/11; HB 7–8/11; SLJ 8/11)

2181 Patterson, Nancy Ruth. *Ellie Ever* (3–5). Illus. by Patty Weise. 2010, Farrar $15.99 (978-0-374-32108-6). 128pp. After losing everything in the hurricane that killed her father, Ellie and her mother move to a horse farm, and Ellie attends a school where a false rumor spreads that she is a princess. Lexile 820L (Rev: BL 9/1/10; HB 9–10/10; LMC 11–12/10; SLJ 9/1/10)

2182 Paulsen, Gary. *Crush: The Theory, Practice, and Destructive Properties of Love* (5–8). Series: Liar, Liar. 2012, Random House $12.99 (978-038574230-6); LB $15.99 (978-037599054-0). 176pp. Too scared to ask Tina Zabinski for a date, 14-year-old Kevin decides to investigate how relationships work and launches a series of often ill-fated romance projects, including a speed dating night at school; a companion to *Liar, Liar* and *Flat Broke* (both 2011). ◯ ℮ (Rev: BL 4/15/12; HB 5–6/12; LMC 10/12; SLJ 4/12)

2183 Paulsen, Gary. *Flat Broke: The Theory, Practice and Destructive Properties of Greed* (5–8). Series: Liar, Liar. 2011, Random House $12.99 (978-0-385-74002-9); LB $15.99 (978-0-385-90818-4). 128pp. When his allowance is cut off because of his behavior in *Liar Liar* (2011), 14-year-old Kevin schemes up some clever ways to make money that don't always go over so well with his customers. ◯ ℮ Lexile 810L (Rev: BL 6/1/11; HB 9–10/11; SLJ 7/11)

2184 Paulsen, Gary. *Liar, Liar* (5–8). Series: Liar, Liar. 2011, Random House $12.99 (978-038574001-2); LB $15.99 (978-038590817-7). 128pp. Fourteen-year-old Kevin lies to make life easier until he finally gets in too deep and has to work out a way to extricate himself. ◯ (Rev: BL 3/1/11; HB 3–4/11; LMC 8–9/11; SLJ 9/11)

2185 Paulsen, Gary. *Paintings from the Cave: Three Novellas* (5–9). 2011, Random House $15.99 (978-0-385-74684-7); LB $18.99 (978-0-385-90921-1). 162pp. Lonely children trying to overcome abuse or neglect use various strategies in these three stories that reflect the author's own difficult childhood. ℮ Lexile 880L (Rev: LMC 5–6/12; SLJ 12/1/11)

2186 Preller, James. *Bystander* (5–8). 2009, Feiwel & Friends $16.99 (978-0-312-37906-3). 240pp. Seventh-grader Eric moves to a new town and is quickly befriended by the charismatic school bully, prompting him to question the morality of his own bystander status. ℮ Lexile HL600L (Rev: BL 10/1/09; LMC 10/09; SLJ 1/10; VOYA 2/10)

2187 Reinhardt, Dana. *The Summer I Learned to Fly* (5–8). 2011, Random House $15.99 (978-0-385-73954-2); LB $18.99 (978-0-385-90792-7). 224pp. In the summer of 1986, 13-year-old Drew (aka Birdie) finally finds a friend in runaway Emmett, and he helps her cope with the fact that her widowed mother is dating. ◯ ℮ Lexile 750L (Rev: BL 6/1/11; HB 7–8/11; LMC 11–12/11; SLJ 6/11; VOYA 6/11)

2188 Richter, Jutta. *Beyond the Station Lies the Sea* (3–6). Trans. by Anna Brailovsky. 2009, Milkweed $14 (978-157131690-5). 96pp. Hoping to get to the sea, homeless 9-year-old Niner and his older friend Cosmos sell Niner's guardian angel to a rich woman, with predictably grim consequences. **e** Lexile 580L (Rev: BL 9/15/09; HB 9–10/09; LMC 3–4/10; SLJ 11/09; VOYA 2/10)

2189 Sawyer, Kim Vogel. *Katy's Debate* (5–8). Series: Katy Lambright. 2010, Zondervan paper $9.99 (978-0-310-71923-6). 204pp. Katy, a Mennonite, is adjusting to high school and enjoying the debating team when she learns her father is considering remarriage. Can she dissuade him? In *Katy's Homecoming* (2011), Katy struggles to find a balance between her modest religion and popularity at school. *Katy's Decision* (2011) is the fourth book in the series. (Rev: SLJ 8/11)

2190 Sternberg, Julie. *Like Pickle Juice on a Cookie* (2–4). Illus. by Matthew Cordell. 2011, Abrams $14.95 (978-0-8109-8424-0). 122pp. Eleanor copes with her long-time babysitter Bibi's departure to Florida and learns to adjust to a new one in this early chapter book. Gryphon Award. **e** Lexile 440L (Rev: BL 2/15/11; HB 5–6/11; LMC 8–9/11; SLJ 4/11)

2191 Stone, Phoebe. *The Boy on Cinnamon Street* (4–7). 2012, Scholastic $16.99 (978-054521512-1). 240pp. Diminutive 7th-grader Louise, who has suffered tragedy in her life and lives with her grandparents, finds herself opening up when her friend Reni helps her with the mystery of a secret admirer. **e** Lexile 720L (Rev: BL 3/1/12*; HB 1–2/12; LMC 3–4/12; SLJ 1/12; VOYA 2/12)

2192 Stout, Shawn K. *Fiona Finkelstein, Big-Time Ballerina!!* (2–4). Illus. by Angela Martini. 2009, Aladdin $14.99 (978-1-4169-7927-2). 176pp. Missing her absent mother, ballerina wannabe Fiona, 9, bravely overcomes her stage fright with the help of her kind dad. (Rev: BL 9/15/09; SLJ 1/1/10)

2193 Tan, Shaun. *Lost and Found: Three by Shaun Tan* (5–10). Illus. by author. 2011, Scholastic $21.99 (978-0-545-22924-1). 128pp. A beautifully illustrated collection of three stories first published in Australia and dealing with loss. (Rev: BL 4/1/11; HB 5–6/11; SLJ 4/11*)

2194 Tracy, Kristen. *Camille McPhee Fell Under the Bus . . . .* (3–5). 2009, Delacorte $16.99 (978-0-385-73687-9); LB $19.99 (978-0-385-90633-3). 293pp. Camille, a 4th-grader whose best friend has moved away and whose parents' marriage is troubled, reacts by isolating herself. (Rev: BL 8/09; SLJ 11/1/09*)

2195 Tracy, Kristen. *The Reinvention of Bessica Lefter* (4–7). 2011, Delacorte $15.99 (978-0-385-73688-6); LB $18.99 (978-0-385-90634-0). 320pp. Eager to shuck off her elementary school persona, Bessica decides on a series of brash and ill-fated attempts to change her

appearance in time for the beginning of 6th grade. **e** Lexile 570L (Rev: BL 1/1–15/11; SLJ 3/1/11)

2196 Walliams, David. *The Boy in the Dress* (4–7). Illus. by Quentin Blake. 2009, Penguin $15.99 (978-1-59514-299-3). 240pp. British 12-year-old Dennis discovers he's interested in fashion — and enjoys wearing dresses — in this funny story that includes some slapstick moments but also some difficult ones with his father and brother. (Rev: BL 11/1/09; SLJ 12/09)

2197 Weissman, Elissa Brent. *Nerd Camp* (4–6). 2011, Atheneum $15.99 (978-1-4424-1703-8). 272pp. Nerdy 10-year-old Gabe tries to hide his intellectual abilities from cool Zack, who's about to become his stepbrother. (Rev: BL 5/1/11; SLJ 6/11)

2198 Young, Karen Romano. *Doodlebug* (3–5). Illus. by author. 2010, Feiwel & Friends $14.99 (978-0-312-56156-7). 112pp. Twelve-year-old Dodo believes her family's move from Southern California to San Francisco is related to her own ADD-related school problems, and starts a notebook documenting her life and problems. (Rev: BL 9/15/10; SLJ 1/1/11)

Physical and Emotional Problems

2199 Draper, Sharon M. *Out of My Mind* (5–8). 2010, Simon & Schuster $16.99 (978-1-4169-7170-2). 304pp. Intelligent 10-year-old Melody, who has cerebral palsy, describes the frustrations of her life, which are somewhat alleviated when she gets a specially adapted computer and can interact with students in a regular classroom. ∩ **e** Lexile 700L (Rev: BL 1/1/10*; HB 3–4/10; LMC 5–6/10; SLJ 3/10)

2200 Erskine, Kathryn. *Mockingbird* (4–7). 2010, Philomel $15.99 (978-0-399-25264-8). 240pp. Ten-year-old Caitlin, who has Asperger's syndrome and recently lost her older brother in a school shooting, struggles to find closure. National Book Award. ∩ **e** Lexile 630L (Rev: BL 2/15/10; HB 3–4/10; LMC 5–6/10; SLJ 4/10)

2201 Lafaye, A. *Water Steps* (4–7). 2009, Milkweed $16.95 (978-1-57131-687-5); paper $6.95 (978-1-57131-686-8). 188pp. Terrified of water since seeing her family drown as a little girl, 11-year-old Kyna finds she must spend the summer at Lake Champlain with her adoptive parents, who are trying to help her overcome her fears. ∩ Lexile 790L (Rev: BL 3/15/09; SLJ 9/09)

2202 Selznick, Brian. *Wonderstruck* (4–8). Illus. by author. 2011, Scholastic $29.99 (978-0-545-02789-2). 640pp. Two parallel stories set 50 years apart involve lonely children who've lost their hearing and run off to New York City to discover themselves; Ben's story unfolds in text, Rose's in pictures. Lexile 830L (Rev: BL 8/11*; HB 9–10/11; SLJ 8/11*; VOYA 10/11)

2203 Shreve, Susan. *The Lovely Shoes* (5–8). 2011, Scholastic $16.99 (978-0-439-68049-3). 256pp. In 1950s Ohio 14-year-old Franny, a girl with a curled-in foot and clunky orthopedic shoes — and a beautiful, fashion-obsessed mother, goes to Italy to see shoe designer Salvatore Ferragamo and finds the attention she deserves. Lexile 1030L (Rev: HB 9–10/11; SLJ 10/1/11)

2204 White, Andrea. *Window Boy* (5–8). 2008, Bright Sky $17.95 (978-193397914-4). 256pp. Twelve-year-old Sam invents a relationship with his hero Winston Churchill to help him cope with cerebral palsy and a difficult family life in 1968 England. Lexile 700L (Rev: BLO 8/08; SLJ 10/1/08)

Historical Fiction and Foreign Lands

General and Miscellaneous

2205 Abdul-Jabbar, Kareem, and Raymond Obstfeld. *What Color Is My World? The Lost History of African-American Inventors* (3–6). Illus. by Ben Boos. 2012, Candlewick $17.99 (978-076364564-9). 44pp. Using the framework of a fictional story about young twins helping a handyman work on their home, this book presents information on 16 often-unknown African American inventors. (Rev: BL 2/1/12; SLJ 2/12)

2206 Bourke, Pat. *Yesterday's Dead* (5–8). 2012, Second Story paper $11.95 (978-192692032-0). 232pp. In the face of the 1918 flu epidemic, doctor's aide Meredith, 13, must find a way to stay healthy as one adult after another contracts the flu. (Rev: BLO 3/15/12; SLJ 4/12; VOYA 6/12)

2207 Couloumbis, Audrey, and Akila Couloumbis. *War Games: A Novel Based on a True Story* (4–7). 2009, Random House $16.99 (978-0-375-85628-0); LB $19.99 (978-0-375-95628-7). 224pp. In Greece in 1941, adventuresome Petros and his family must hide their ties to America when a Nazi commandant comes to live at their house. ℮ Lexile 710L (Rev: BL 10/1/09; HB 11–12/09; LMC 11–12/09; SLJ 10/09)

2208 Harlow, Joan Hiatt. *Secret of the Night Ponies* (4–6). 2009, Simon & Schuster $16.99 (978-141690783-1). 336pp. In 1965 Newfoundland 13-year-old Jessie participates in three daring rescues — of shipwreck victims, an abused orphan, and a herd of wild ponies. ℮ Lexile 670L (Rev: BL 11/1/09; SLJ 11/09)

2209 Hughes, Susan. *The Island Horse* (3–5). Illus. by Alicia Quist. 2012, Kids Can $16.95 (978-155453592-7). 160pp. Reeling from the death of her mother, Ellie, 9, channels her grief into a crusade to protect her island's wild ponies in this moving story set in the 1800s. (Rev: BL 3/15/12; SLJ 4/1/12)

2210 Kerz, Anna. *The Gnome's Eye* (4–7). 2010, Orca paper $9.95 (978-1-55469-195-1). 224pp. Theresa, 10, describes her Yugoslav family's journey from an Austrian refugee camp to Toronto, Canada, where Theresa

struggles to make the transition to a new language, a new school, and a new culture in the early 1950s. ℮ Lexile 650L (Rev: BL 5/15/10; LMC 11–12/10; SLJ 8/10)

2211 Lottridge, Celia Barker. *The Listening Tree* (4–8). 2011, Fitzhenry & Whiteside paper $11.95 (978-1-55455-052-4). 154pp. Nine-year-old Ellen, new to city life, gains the courage to talk to strangers when she overhears plans to evict her neighbors in this Depression story set in Canada. Lexile 1240 (Rev: BL 4/15/11; SLJ 5/11; VOYA 4/11)

2212 Spradlin, Michael P. *Keeper of the Grail* (5–8). Series: The Youngest Templar. 2008, Putnam $17.99 (978-0-399-24763-7). 248pp. Fourteen-year-old Tristan, who has been raised by monks, becomes a squire to a Templar knight and finds himself journeying to the Holy Land and returning with the Holy Grail; an action-packed, first-person narrative. Also use *Trail of Fate* (2009) and *Orphan of Destiny* (2010). ∩ Lexile 830L (Rev: BL 9/15/08; LMC 1–2/09; SLJ 2/1/09)

2213 Thomason, Mark. *Moonrunner* (4–8). 2009, Kane/Miller $15.95 (978-1-935279-03-7). 217pp. In 1890s Australia, Casey, 12, copes with a difficult transition to a new home by befriending a spirited wild stallion that he decides to save from captivity at all costs. Lexile 620L (Rev: BL 4/15/09; SLJ 6/1/09)

Africa

2214 Atinuke. *Anna Hibiscus* (1–3). Illus. by Lauren Tobia. 2010, Kane/Miller paper $5.99 (978-193527973-0). 112pp. A beginning chapter book set in modern Africa, this tells stories about Anna and her twin younger brothers Double and Trouble. Also in this series is *Anna Hibiscus' Song* (2011). Boston Globe–Horn Book Honor Award. ∩ Lexile 670L (Rev: BLO 12/1/10; LMC 1–2/11)

2215 Atinuke. *Good Luck, Anna Hibiscus!* (1–3). Illus. by Lauren Tobia. 2011, Kane/Miller paper $5.99 (978-1-61067-007-4). 112pp. African child Anna Hibiscus prepares for her first trip to Canada to visit her grandmother. Also use *Have Fun, Anna Hibiscus!* (2011), which tells the story of her snowy time in Canada. (Rev: HB 5–6/11; SLJ 8/1/11)

2216 Atinuke. *The No. 1 Car Spotter* (2–5). Illus. by Warwick Johnson Cadwell. 2011, Kane/Miller paper $5.99 (978-161067051-7). 112pp. When a Corolla is abandoned near his isolated African village, Oluwalase figures out a way to make it run, and the village is able to bring its goods to market for the first time. (Rev: BL 10/1/11; LMC 3–4/12)

2217 McKissack, Patricia C. *Never Forgotten* (4–8). Illus. by Leo Dillon. 2011, Random House $18.99 (978-0-375-84384-6). 48pp. Full of magical realism, this is the wrenching story, told in free verse, of a father left behind in West Africa after his son is taken to America in a slave ship. (Rev: BL 9/1/11*; SLJ 9/1/11*)

Asia

2218 Ellis, Deborah. *No Ordinary Day* (4–7). 2011, Groundwood $16.95 (978-1-55498-134-2). 144pp. Valli, a poor Indian orphan who has a fear of lepers, is horrified to hear that she herself has the disease. (Rev: BL 11/1/11*; SLJ 9/1/11*)

2219 Kang, Hildi. *Chengli and the Silk Road Caravan* (4–6). 2011, Tanglewood $14.95 (978-1-933718-54-5). 200pp. In 7th-century China, 13-year-old Chengli sets out on an adventure along China's Silk Road in a quest to learn more about the father he never knew. (Rev: BLO 10/1/11; LMC 1–2/12; SLJ 10/1/11)

2220 Lloyd, Alison. *Year of the Tiger* (5–8). 2010, Holiday House $16.95 (978-0-8234-2277-7). 208pp. In ancient China two 12-year-old boys from different backgrounds become friends amid turbulent times. Lexile 600L (Rev: BL 4/15/10; LMC 10/10; SLJ 6/10)

2221 Malaspina, Ann. *Yasmin's Hammer* (2–5). Illus. by Doug Chayka. 2010, Lee & Low $18.95 (978-1-60060-359-4). 40pp. Yasmin struggles to raise money so she and her sister can attend school in Dhaka, Bangladesh. (Rev: BL 5/15/10; LMC 10/10; SLJ 7/1/10)

2222 Peet, Mal, and Elspeth Graham. *Cloud Tea Monkeys* (2–4). Illus. by Juan Wijngaard. 2010, Candlewick $15.99 (978-0-7636-4453-6). 56pp. Friendly monkeys come to young Tashi's aid when her mother is too ill to work in the tea plantation in the Himalayas. (Rev: BL 2/15/10; LMC 8–9/10; SLJ 4/1/10)

2223 Perkins, Mitali. *Bamboo People* (5–8). 2010, Charlesbridge $16.95 (978-1-58089-328-2). 288pp. Contemporary Burma is seen through the perspectives of two protagonists — 15-year-old Chiko, reluctant soldier and son of an imprisoned doctor, and Tu Reh, a Karenni refugee. ∩ Lexile 680L (Rev: BL 5/15/10; HB 7–8/10; LMC 11–12/10; SLJ 11/1/10*)

2224 Reedy, Trent. *Words in the Dust* (5–8). 2011, Scholastic $17.99 (978-0-545-26125-8). 266pp. Learning to read and the unexpected opportunity to have her cleft palate repaired give 13-year-old Afghani Zulaikha a new outlook on life. ∩ Lexile 670L (Rev: BL 1/1–15/11; LMC 5–6/11; SLJ 2/1/11)

2225 Rocco, John. *Fu Finds the Way* (3–5). Illus. by author. 2009, Hyperion $16.99 (978-1-4231-0965-5). 40pp. Young Fu averts a deadly duel by impressing a great warrior with his mastery of the tea ceremony in this handsome picture book. (Rev: BLO 1/1/10; LMC 3–4/10; SLJ 10/1/09)

2226 Russell, Ching Yeung. *Tofu Quilt* (3–6). 2009, Lee & Low $16.95 (978-160060423-2). 136pp. A novel in free verse about a young girl determined to be a writer,

who struggles with societal restrictions in 1960s Hong Kong. **℮** (Rev: BL 11/1/09; SLJ 10/09)

2227 Say, Allen. *The Boy in the Garden* (K–2). Illus. by author. 2010, Houghton Mifflin $17.99 (978-0-547-21410-8). 32pp. The ancient Japanese folk tale about a crane that turns into a woman is revisited in this quiet, evocative story about young Jori. **℮** (Rev: BL 9/1/10; HB 9–10/10; LMC 5–6–11*; SLJ 10/1/10)

2228 Sheth, Kashmira. *Boys Without Names* (4–7). 2010, HarperCollins $15.99 (978-0-06-185760-7). 320pp. Eleven-year-old Gopal's rural family cannot make ends meet and heads for Mumbai where the boy looks for work only to find himself a captive in a soul-crushing sweatshop. **℮** Lexile 670L (Rev: BL 11/15/09; SLJ 1/10)

2229 Smith, Icy. *Half Spoon of Rice: A Survival Story of the Cambodian Genocide* (4–7). Illus. by Sopaul Nhem. 2010, East West Discovery Press $19.95 (978-0-9821675-8-8). 44pp. Nine-year-old Nat relates his shocking experiences after the Khmer Rouge force millions to leave Phnom Penh and work in the fields; a moving picture book for older readers. (Rev: BL 12/15/09; LMC 5–6/10; SLJ 12/09)

2230 Starke, Ruth. *Noodle Pie* (5–7). 2010, Kane/Miller $15.99 (978-1-935279-25-9). 200pp. Andy, an 11-year-old Australian boy, keeps a diary during his visit to Vietnam, the place of his father's birth, recording all the interesting cultural differences and the fun he has with his cousin Minh as they work to revamp the family's restaurant. Lexile 770L (Rev: BLO 3/15/10; LMC 8–9/10; SLJ 5/10)

Europe

2231 Barrow, Randi. *Saving Zasha* (4–7). 2011, Scholastic $16.99 (978-0-545-20632-7). 240pp. In Russia at the end of World War II, a young boy finds a beautiful German shepherd in the woods, and becomes determined to shield the dog from the anti-German sentiment that is running rampant. ∩ (Rev: BL 2/1/11; SLJ 4/11)

2232 Clark, Kathy. *Guardian Angel House* (5–8). Series: Holocaust Remembrance. 2009, Second Story paper $14.95 (978-1-897187-58-6). 200pp. Two Jewish sisters — 12-year-old Susan and 6-year-old Vera — find a safe haven from the Nazis in the Guardian Angel House, a Catholic convent in Budapest; based on the experiences of the author's aunt. (Rev: SLJ 2/10; VOYA 2/10)

2233 Davis, Tony. *Future Knight* (2–4). Illus. by Gregory Rogers. 2009, Delacorte $12.99 (978-038573800-2); LB $15.99 (978-038590706-4). 160pp. In 1409 Roland Wright, 10-year-old son of a blacksmith, aspires to become a knight; this story is full of details of the time. (Rev: BL 11/15/09; SLJ 8/09)

2234 Greene, Jacqueline Dembar. *The Secret Shofar of Barcelona* (1–3). Illus. by Doug Chayka. 2009, Lerner/

Kar-Ben LB $17.95 (978-0-8225-9915-9); paper $7.95 (978-0-8225-9944-9). 32pp. A brave Jew who stays loyal to his faith in post-Inquisition Spain contrives clever ways to continue celebrating his religious traditions in this inspiring story. (Rev: BL 11/15/09; LMC 11–12/09; SLJ 10/1/09)

2235 Hartnett, Sonya. *The Midnight Zoo* (5–8). Illus. by Andrea Offermann. 2011, Candlewick $16.99 (978-0-7636-5339-2). 208pp. Caged animals share their horrors with Romany brothers Andrej, 12, and Tomas, 9, who are fleeing a German attack in World War II. ∩ ℮ Lexile 940L (Rev: BL 8/11; HB 9–10/11; LMC 11–12/11; SLJ 9/1/11; VOYA 10/11)

2236 Marsden, Carolyn. *Take Me with You* (4–7). 2010, Candlewick $14.99 (978-0-7636-3739-2). 176pp. In Italy after World War II best friends Pina and Susanna, both 11, are still at the orphanage and hoping for eventual adoption even if it means separation. (Rev: BL 1/1/10*; LMC 5–6/10; SLJ 3/10)

2237 Meyer, Susan Lynn. *Black Radishes* (4–7). 2010, Delacorte $16.99 (978-0-385-73881-1); LB $19.99 (978-0-385-90748-4). 240pp. In World War II France, young Gustave, a Jew, takes personal risks to help the Resistance. Sydney Taylor Honor Award. (Rev: BL 12/15/10; SLJ 1/1/11)

2238 Mitchell, Jack. *The Ancient Ocean Blues* (5–8). 2008, Tundra paper $9.95 (978-088776832-3). 128pp. In 63 B.C. Greece, teenager Marcus Oppius arrives in Athens on an espionage mission for Julius Caesar. ℮ Lexile 800L (Rev: BLO 11/15/08; SLJ 5/1/09)

2239 Morpurgo, Michael. *An Elephant in the Garden* (4–8). 2011, Feiwel & Friends $16.99 (978-0-312-59369-8). 208pp. On the eve of the Allied bombing of Dresden in 1945, Lizzie and her family rescue a zoo elephant named Marlene and together they flee toward the west. (Rev: BL 10/1/11; SLJ 9/1/11)

2240 Parry, Rosanne. *Second Fiddle* (5–8). 2011, Random House $16.99 (978-0-375-86196-3); LB $19.99 (978-0-375-96196-0). 240pp. In 1990 Berlin, three 8th-grade American girls rescue a soldier beaten by Soviet officers and plot to get him safely to Paris. ∩ ℮ Lexile 810L (Rev: BL 4/15/11; SLJ 3/1/11)

2241 Richardson, Nan. *The Pearl* (3–5). Illus. by Alexandra Young. 2011, Umbrage $17.95 (978-1-884167-24-9). Unpaged. This Russian Cinderella story set in the 18th century involves a wealthy, music-loving man and a peasant girl with a lovely voice and features beautiful illustrations and lyrical text. (Rev: SLJ 8/1/11)

2242 Shefelman, Janice Jordan. *Anna Maria's Gift* (3–5). Illus. by Robert Papp. 2010, Random House $12.99 (978-0-375-85881-9); LB $15.99 (978-0-375-95881-6). 112pp. Three girls contend with love, loss, and jealousy at an orphanage in 1715 Venice, where they receive violin instruction from Antonio Vivaldi. ℮ Lexile 470L (Rev: BL 4/15/10; LMC 8–9/10; SLJ 4/1/10)

2243 Tak, Bibi Dumon. *Soldier Bear* (4–8). Trans. by Laura Watkinson. Illus. by Philip Hopman. 2011, Eerdmans $13 (978-0-8028-5375-2). 144pp. Based on a true story, this engaging novel is about a bear called Voytek that served in the Polish army in World War II and boosts morale while also carrying live ammunition. ℮ Lexile 780L (Rev: BL 10/15/11; HB 11–12/11; LMC 1–2/12; SLJ 11/1/11)

2244 Thompson, Kate. *Most Wanted* (3–5). Illus. by Jonny Duddle. 2010, HarperCollins $15.99 (978-0-06-173037-5). 128pp. A baker's son finds himself in charge of the mad ruler's horse in this action-packed story based on the emperor Caligula. (Rev: BL 10/15/10; HB 1–2/11; LMC 1–2/11; SLJ 11/1/10)

2245 Thor, Annika. *The Lily Pond* (4–6). Trans. by Linda Schenck. 2011, Delacorte $16.99 (978-038574039-5); LB $19.99 (978-038590838-2). 224pp. Thirteen-year-old Stephie, an Austrian Jewish refugee, adjusts to life in the Swedish city of Gothenburg and makes friends while worrying about her parents in Vienna. ∩ (Rev: BL 12/1/11; HB 1–2/12; SLJ 1/12)

2246 Watts, Irene N., reteller. *Clay Man: The Golem of Prague* (5–8). Illus. by Kathryn E. Shoemaker. 2009, Tundra $19.95 (978-0-88776-880-4). 96pp. Told from the perspective of pensive 13-year-old Jacob, the story of the magical golem who protected the Jews of 16th-century Prague is illustrated in striking black-and-white drawings. ℮ Lexile 780L (Rev: BLO 12/1/09; SLJ 3/10)

Great Britain and Ireland

2247 Avi. *Crispin: The End of Time* (5–8). 2010, HarperCollins $16.99 (978-0-06-174080-0); LB $17.89 (978-0-06-174082-4). 240pp. Still heading for Iceland, Crispin leaves Troth at a convent that needs a healer and continues on alone, soon finding himself in danger from a group of traveling musicians. ∩ ℮ Lexile 690L (Rev: BL 4/15/10; HB 7–8/10; SLJ 6/10)

2248 Buzbee, Lewis. *The Haunting of Charles Dickens* (5–8). Illus. by Greg Ruth. 2010, Feiwel & Friends $17.99 (978-0-312-38256-8). 368pp. Twelve-year-old Meg searches the streets of 1862 London for her missing brother Orion, accompanied by a family friend, the famed author Charles Dickens. ℮ Lexile 910L (Rev: BL 11/1/10; LMC 1–2/11; SLJ 11/1/10; VOYA 2/11)

2249 Cushman, Karen. *Alchemy and Meggy Swann* (4–8). 2010, Clarion $16 (978-0-547-23184-6). 176pp. In Elizabethan England, 13-year-old Meggy, who needs sticks to walk, arrives in London to work with the father who abandoned her years before; as she adapts to city life she also comes to believe that her father is in serious trouble and determines to save him. ∩ (Rev: BL 3/1/10*; LMC 10/10; SLJ 4/10)

2250 Deedy, Carmen Agra, and Randall Wright. *The Cheshire Cheese Cat: A Dickens of a Tale* (4–6). Illus. by Barry Moser. 2011, Peachtree $16.95 (978-1-56145-595-9). 228pp. In Ye Old Cheshire Cheese Inn in 19th-century London, a cat named Skilley befriends a mouse named Pip and protects the mice and a raven from a hungry alley cat, all under the amused eyes of customer Charles Dickens. ∩ Lexile 740L (Rev: BLO 3/1/12; SLJ 9/1/11*)

2251 Lasky, Kathryn. *Hawksmaid: The Untold Story of Robin Hood and Maid Marian* (5–8). 2010, Harper-Collins $16.99 (978-0-06-000071-4). 304pp. The back story for Robin Hood's Maid Marian is explored in this inspiring story of a young girl who uses her falconry skills to steal from the rich. **e** Lexile 780L (Rev: BL 5/15/10; LMC 5–6/10; SLJ 7/10)

2252 McKay, Hilary. *Wishing for Tomorrow* (3–6). Illus. by Nick Maland. 2010, Simon & Schuster $16.99 (978-1-4424-0169-3). 273pp. More than a hundred years after publication of Frances Hodgson Burnett's *A Little Princess,* this sequel tells the story of what happens after Sara Crewe leaves the Select Seminary for Young Ladies. ∩ Lexile 800L (Rev: HB 1–2/10; LMC 8–9/10; SLJ 3/10)

2253 Morris, Gerald. *The Adventures of Sir Gawain the True* (3–5). Illus. by Aaron Renier. Series: Knights' Tales. 2011, Houghton Mifflin $14.99 (978-054741855-1). 128pp. Sir Gawain eventually learns the essence of courtliness and courtesy in this irreverent fractured tale. **e** Lexile 770L (Rev: BL 4/1/11)

2254 Nelson, Mary Elizabeth. *Catla and the Vikings* (5–8). 2012, Orca paper $9.95 (978-145980057-1). 192pp. In northern England in 1066, 13-year-old Catla survives a Viking attack and journeys to a neighboring town to warn the citizens, facing her fears as she goes. **e** Lexile 640L (Rev: BL 4/15/12; LMC 10/12; SLJ 6/12)

2255 Updale, Eleanor. *Johnny Swanson* (4–6). 2011, Random House $16.99 (978-0-385-75198-8); LB $19.99 (978-0-385-75199-5). 384pp. Eleven-year-old Johnny ends up solving a murder and acquitting his mother in this inspiring hard-luck mystery set in 1929 England. **e** Lexile 740L (Rev: BL 5/1/11; HB 3–4/11; SLJ 3/1/11)

2256 Woelfle, Gretchen. *All the World's a Stage: A Novel in Five Acts* (4–7). Illus. by Thomas Cox. 2011, Holiday House $16.95 (978-0-8234-2281-4). 176pp. When he is caught picking pockets, 12-year-old Kit is offered a chance to redeem himself by working as a stage hand, and participates in the construction of the Globe Theatre in this atmospheric story set in Elizabethan England. (Rev: BL 4/15/11; HB 5–6/11; LMC 10/11; SLJ 5/11)

2257 Wood, Maryrose. *The Hidden Gallery* (4–6). Illus. by Jon Klassen. Series: The Incorrigible Children of Ashton Place. 2011, HarperCollins $15.99 (978-0-06-179112-3). 320pp. Governess Penelope contends with the challenges of taking care of her wolf-like young charges in London, where they attract mischief and spread mayhem wherever they go. ∩ **e** Lexile 960L (Rev: BL 2/1/11*; SLJ 3/1/11)

2258 Wood, Maryrose. *The Mysterious Howling* (4–6). Illus. by Jon Klassen. Series: The Incorrigible Children of Ashton Place. 2010, HarperCollins $15.99 (978-0-06-179105-5). 267pp. Penelope, 15, is hired as governess for three feral children that Lord Frederick has determined must become civilized in time for the estate's Christmas party; set in 19th-century England. ∩ **e** Lexile 1000L (Rev: BL 12/15/09*; HB 5–6/10; SLJ 5/10)

2259 Wood, Maryrose. *The Unseen Guest* (4–7). Series: The Incorrigible Children of Ashton Place. 2012, HarperCollins $15.99 (978-006179118-5). 240pp. The three children raised by wolves threaten to undo their years of training by nanny Penelope and return to the wild. ∩ **e** (Rev: BL 3/15/12*; SLJ 4/12; VOYA 4/12)

Latin America and Caribbean

2260 Engle, Margarita. *Wild Book* (5–8). Illus. 2012, Harcourt $16.99 (978-054758131-6). 144pp. Dyslexic Josefa comes to understand the freeing power of words in this story set in 1912 Cuba; based on the life of the author's grandmother. **e** (Rev: BL 3/1/12; LMC 11–12/12; SLJ 3/12)

2261 Ryan, Pam Muñoz. *The Dreamer* (4–8). Illus. by Peter Sís. 2010, Scholastic $17.99 (978-0-439-26970-4). 384pp. Ryan imagines the young life of the poet Pablo Neruda, who was shy, afraid of his demanding father, and interested in nature and the lives of the indigenous Indians of Chile. ∩ Lexile 650L (Rev: BL 2/1/10*; HB 3–4/10; LMC 3–4/10; SLJ 4/10)

Middle East

2262 Abdel-Fattah, Randa. *Where the Streets Had a Name* (5–8). 2010, Scholastic $17.99 (978-0-545-17292-9). 304pp. Thirteen-year-old Palestinian Hayaat faces checkpoints and curfews when she travels from Bethlehem to Jerusalem in search of some soil she hopes will bring relief to her sick grandmother. ∩ Lexile 740L (Rev: BL 10/1/10; HB 1–2/11; LMC 1–2/11; SLJ 11/1/10; VOYA 4/10)

2263 Akbarpour, Ahmad. *Good Night, Commander* (5–8). Illus. by Morteza Zahedi. 2010, Groundwood $17.95 (978-0-88899-989-4). 24pp. Childlike illustrations accompany this account of a young Iranian boy's devastating wartime experiences. (Rev: BL 5/1/10; LMC 8–9/10; SLJ 5/1/10)

2264 Pal, Erika. *Azad's Camel* (1–3). Illus. by author. 2010, Frances Lincoln $17.95 (978-1-84507-982-6). 40pp. A reluctant young camel jockey discovers his camel can talk and together the two plan their escape from the grueling, dangerous sport. Lexile AD450L (Rev: BL 9/1/10; SLJ 9/1/10)

United States

NATIVE AMERICANS

2265 Edwardson, Debby Dahl. *Blessing's Bead* (5–8). 2009, Farrar $16.99 (978-0-374-30805-6). 192pp. Two narratives — the first set in 1917 and the second in 1989 — tell the stories of Inupiaq Eskimo teenagers and the quite different challenges they face. (Rev: BL 10/15/09*; LMC 11–12/09; SLJ 11/09)

2266 Howard, Ellen. *The Crimson Cap* (5–8). 2009, Holiday House $16.95 (978-0-8234-2152-7). 192pp. Eleven-year-old Pierre Talon finds himself living with the Hasinai Indians after setting out on an ill-fated mission with explorer La Salle. Lexile 720L (Rev: BLO 12/1/09; LMC 1–2/10; SLJ 11/09)

THE REVOLUTION

2267 Anderson, Laurie Halse. *Forge* (5–8). 2010, Simon & Schuster $16.99 (978-1-4169-6144-4). 2pp. In this sequel to 2008's *Chains,* recently freed slave Curzon, 15, is on the run during the time of the American Revolution, eventually joining the army to battle the British at Saratoga. ⌐ ℮ Lexile 820L (Rev: BL 9/15/10; HB 11–12/10; LMC 1–2/11; SLJ 10/1/10)

2268 Calkhoven, Laurie. *Daniel at the Siege of Boston, 1776* (4–7). Series: Boys of Wartime. 2010, Dutton $16.99 (978-052542144-3). 176pp. Twelve-year-old Daniel finds the courage to reveal a traitor to General Washington in this coming-of-age story set in Revolutionary War-era America. Lexile 710L (Rev: BL 2/1/10; LMC 5–6/10)

2269 Giff, Patricia Reilly. *Storyteller* (4–7). 2010, Random House $15.99 (978-0-375-83888-0); LB $18.99 (978-0-375-93888-7). 176pp. While staying with an aunt, Elizabeth uncovers the story of an 18th-century ancestor whose dramatic Revolutionary War experiences culminated in the Battle of Oriskany. ℮ Lexile HL610L (Rev: BL 9/15/10; LMC 1–2/11; SLJ 11/1/10)

2270 Gregory, Kristiana. *Cannons at Dawn: The Second Diary of Abigail Jane Stewart* (4–8). Series: Dear America. 2011, Scholastic $12.99 (978-0-545-21319-6); LB $16.99 (978-0-545-28088-4). 256pp. Abigail and her family follow the Continental Army after their Valley Forge home burns down and the 13-year-old matures as the war progresses. ℮ (Rev: SLJ 7/11)

2271 Pryor, Bonnie. *Captain Hannah Pritchard: The Hunt for Pirate Gold* (5–8). Series: Historical Fiction Adventures. 2011, Enslow LB $27.93 (978-0-7660-3817-2). 160pp. Still disguised as Jack, Hannah Pritchard leads her crew on missions for the Continental navy while searching for lost pirate treasure in this final installment in the trilogy set during the American Revolution. (Rev: BLO 10/15/11; SLJ 2/12; VOYA 12/11)

2272 Woodruff, Elvira. *George Washington's Spy* (4–6). 2010, Scholastic $16.99 (978-0-545-10487-6). 230pp. Ten-year-old Matt and his younger sister travel back in time with some friends and become embroiled in the American Revolution as they learn about both sides in the conflict. (Rev: LMC 3–4/11; SLJ 12/1/10)

THE YOUNG NATION, 1789–1861

2273 Buckey, Sarah Masters. *Meet Marie-Grace* (4–6). Illus. by Christine Kornacki. 2011, American Girl $12.95 (978-159369651-1); paper $6.95 (978-159369652-8). 120pp. Reserved Massachusetts girl Marie-Grace is able to handle the boisterous nature of 1853 New Orleans with the help of a new friend, Cécile, who is black. ℮ Lexile 750L (Rev: BL 10/15/11; SLJ 4/1/12)

2274 Cooper, Afua. *My Name Is Henry Bibb: A Story of Slavery and Freedom* (5–8). 2009, Kids Can $16.95 (978-1-55337-813-6). 160pp. Based on a true story, this gritty first-person account of Henry Bibb, the son of a black woman and a white plantation owner in 19th-century Kentucky, depicts the cruelty, humiliation, and yearning for freedom that was part of a slave's daily experience. Lexile 800L (Rev: BL 8/09; LMC 11–12/09; SLJ 10/09)

2275 Cooper, Afua. *My Name Is Phillis Wheatley: A Story of Slavery and Freedom* (5–8). 2009, Kids Can $16.95 (978-1-55337-812-9). 152pp. Set in Senegal, Boston, and London, this first-person account tells the fictionalized true story of Phillis Wheatley, the 18th-century slave who became a renowned poet. Lexile 790L (Rev: BL 9/1/09; SLJ 10/09)

2276 Hyatt, Patricia Rusch. *The Quite Contrary Man: A True American Tale* (K–3). Illus. by Kathryn Brown. 2011, Abrams $16.95 (978-0-8109-4065-9). 32pp. In early 19th-century New England, Joseph Palmer refuses to shave his beard as the law requires and is eventually sent to jail in this story of an independent spirit. Lexile AD840L (Rev: BL 4/1/11; LMC 8–9/11; SLJ 3/1/11)

2277 Myers, Anna. *The Grave Robber's Secret* (4–7). 2011, Walker $16.99 (978-0-8027-2183-9). 224pp. In 19th-century Philadelphia, 12-year-old Robby Hare has helped his father to rob graves, but he suspects that actual murder may be afoot when a boarder called Mr. Burke moves in; loosely based on the murders that took place in Edinburgh, Scotland, in the early 1800s. ℮ Lexile 650L (Rev: BL 4/15/11; LMC 3–4/11; SLJ 3/1/11)

2278 Nolen, Jerdine. *Eliza's Freedom Road: An Underground Railroad Diary* (4–7). 2011, Simon & Schuster $14.99 (978-1-4169-5814-7). 160pp. House slave Eliza, 12, describes in her diary her escape from a cruel master with the help of the Underground Railroad, and records some of the stories she has heard and read; set in 1855. ℮ Lexile 670L (Rev: BLO 1/1–15/11; SLJ 2/1/11)

2279 Olson, Tod. *How to Get Rich in the California Gold Rush: An Adventurer's Guide to the Fabulous Riches Discovered in 1848* (4–8). Illus. by Scott Allred. 2008, National Geographic $16.95 (978-142630315-9); LB $25.90 (978-142630316-6). 48pp. In this fictional story set in factual historical context, three young men head west to become gold barons and reach the conclusion that they're better off seeking their fortune in other ways. Lexile NC990L (Rev: BL 10/15/08; SLJ 12/08*; VOYA 2/09)

2280 Platt, Kin. *A Mystery for Thoreau* (5–8). 2008, Farrar $16 (978-037435337-7). 176pp. In mid-19th-century Concord, Massachusetts, teen journalist Oliver Puckle investigates a murder near Thoreau's cabin at Walden Pond; both humorous and melodramatic, this novel conveys much about the time and place. (Rev: BL 11/1/08; SLJ 12/08; VOYA 12/08)

PIONEERS AND WESTWARD EXPANSION

2281 Galbraith, Kathryn O. *Arbor Day Square* (PS–3). Illus. by Cyd Moore. 2010, Peachtree $16.95 (978-1-56145-517-1). 32pp. A girl and her father decide to plant trees in their frontier prairie town, kicking off an annual Arbor Day tradition in this charming story. (Rev: BL 4/15/10; SLJ 4/1/10)

2282 Ketchum, Liza. *Newsgirl* (4–7). 2009, Viking $16.99 (978-0-670-01119-3). 336pp. Set in 1851 San Francisco, this is the story of 12-year-old Amelia, who dresses as a boy to sell newspapers and eventually becomes a news item herself. Lexile 640L (Rev: BL 9/15/09; SLJ 9/09)

2283 Naylor, Phyllis Reynolds. *Emily's Fortune* (3–5). Illus. by Ross Collins. 2010, Delacorte $14.99 (978-0-385-73616-9); LB $17.99 (978-0-385-90589-3). 160pp. A lively story in which newly orphaned Emily, now an heiress, travels (with her turtle Rufus and new friend Jackson) west by stagecoach to her aunt's home and must outsmart the evil Victor en route. (Rev: BL 4/15/10; LMC 10/10; SLJ 6/1/10*)

2284 Patron, Susan. *Behind the Masks: The Diary of Angeline Reddy* (4–8). Series: Dear America. 2012, Scholastic $12.99 (978-054530437-5). 304pp. In California in 1880, 14-year-old Angeline investigates her father's disappearance and meets a variety of obstacles, including a ghost and a gang of vigilantes. (Rev: BL 12/15/11; SLJ 1/12; VOYA 12/11)

2285 Rose, Caroline. *May B* (3–7). 2012, Random House $15.99 (978-158246393-3); LB $18.99 (978-158246412-1). 240pp. May, 11, a housemaid to a young family in a Kansas sod house in the late 1870s, struggles to survive when the husband and wife leave her alone to care for the house. ℮ Lexile 680L (Rev: BL 1/1/12; HB 1–2/12; LMC 3–4/12)

2286 Yolen, Jane. *Elsie's Bird* (K–3). Illus. by David Small. 2010, Philomel $17.99 (978-0-399-25292-1).

40pp. Elsie and her father leave Boston after Elsie's mother dies and head for Nebraska, where the city-loving girl feels alone and scared until her pet canary escapes and Elsie must brave the prairie to retrieve him. Lexile AD890L (Rev: BL 8/10; HB 9–10/10; LMC 1–2/11*; SLJ 9/1/10*)

THE CIVIL WAR

2287 Calkhoven, Laurie. *Will at the Battle of Gettysburg, 1863* (4–7). Series: Boys of Wartime. 2011, Dutton $16.99 (978-0-525-42145-0). 227pp. Twelve-year-old Will lives in Gettysburg and dreams of being a drummer boy in the Union Army until the war comes right to his doorstep. ℮ (Rev: SLJ 3/1/11)

2288 Kluger, Jeffrey. *Freedom Stone* (5–7). 2011, Philomel $16.99 (978-039925214-3). 320pp. Young slave Lillie struggles to clear her father's name and gain freedom for herself, her brother, and her mother with the help of a magical stone from Africa. ℮ Lexile 1030L (Rev: BL 2/1/11*; LMC 5–6/11; SLJ 6/11)

2289 Myers, Laurie. *Escape by Night: A Civil War Adventure* (3–5). Illus. by Amy June Bates. 2011, Henry Holt $14.99 (978-0-8050-8825-0). 128pp. When Tommy, the son of a Presbyterian minister in Georgia during the Civil War, returns a soldier's journal to its rightful owner, he discovers the man is a Yankee in disguise, and he must make a difficult decision. (Rev: BL 4/15/11; LMC 11–12/11; SLJ 6/11)

2290 Polacco, Patricia. *Just in Time, Abraham Lincoln* (3–5). Illus. by author. 2011, Putnam $17.99 (978-0-399-25471-0). 48pp. Video gamers Michael and Derek find themselves unexpectedly involved in the battle of Antietam when they dress as Union soldiers. Lexile 570L (Rev: BL 2/1/11; LMC 5–6/11*; SLJ 3/1/11)

2291 Schwabach, Karen. *The Storm Before Atlanta* (5–8). 2010, Random House $16.99 (978-0-375-85866-6); LB $19.99 (978-0-375-95866-3). 320pp. Jeremy dreams of glory when he joins the Union Army, but as the war progresses and he meets an escaped slave, Dulcie, and a Confederate soldier named Charlie, reality sets in. ℮ (Rev: BL 1/1–15/11; SLJ 2/1/11)

RECONSTRUCTION TO WORLD WAR II, 1865–1941

2292 Avi. *City of Orphans* (5–8). Illus. by Greg Ruth. 2011, Simon & Schuster $16.99 (978-1-4169-7102-3). 368pp. Newsboy Maks, 13, contends with filthy living conditions, poverty, and the predicament of his sister, who's been falsely accused of stealing a watch from the Waldorf Hotel in this tense story set in 1893 New York City. ∩ ℮ Lexile HL570L (Rev: BL 8/11*; HB 9–10/11; LMC 11–12/11; SLJ 8/11)

2293 Bolden, Tonya. *Finding Family* (4–7). 2010, Bloomsbury $15.99 (978-1-59990-318-7). 176pp.

In Charleston, West Virginia, at the turn of the 20th century, 12-year-old African American Delana learns that many of the stories she was told about her family were pure fiction. (Rev: BL 9/1/10*; LMC 10/10; SLJ 9/1/10)

2294 Bond, Victoria, and T. R. Simon. *Zora and Me* (5–8). 2010, Candlewick $16.99 (978-0-7636-4300-3). 192pp. The fictionalized story of Zora Neale Hurston's childhood is told by her best friend Carrie, 10, as they play together and overhear adult secrets in Eatonville, Florida. ∩ ℮ Lexile 860L (Rev: BL 10/15/10*; LMC 11–12/10; SLJ 11/1/10)

2295 Brown, Irene Bennett. *Before the Lark* (5–9). 2011, Texas Tech Univ. paper $18.95 (978-089672727-4). 204pp. Cleft-lip sufferer Jocey, 12, contends with bullying and poverty, eventually discovering the empowerment that comes with self-sufficiency in this story set in 19th-century Missouri; a new edition of an award-winning book first published in 1981. (Rev: BLO 10/15/11)

2296 Choldenko, Gennifer. *Al Capone Shines My Shoes* (5–8). 2009, Dial $17.99 (978-0-8037-3460-9). 288pp. In *Al Capone Does My Shirts* (2004), 12-year-old Moose benefited from his acquaintance with the famous gangster; now Capone is demanding help in return. ∩ ℮ Lexile 620L (Rev: BL 9/1/09; HB 9–10/09; SLJ 9/09; VOYA 10/09)

2297 Crowley, James. *Starfish* (4–8). 2010, Hyperion $16.99 (978-1-4231-2588-4). 352pp. Beatrice and Lionel, young Blackfoot Nation children, run away from their boarding school in the early 1900s and hide in the Montana mountains. ℮ (Rev: BL 6/10; LMC 11–12/10; VOYA 12/10)

2298 Forrester, Sandra. *Leo and the Lesser Lion* (3–6). 2009, Knopf $16.99 (978-037585616-7); LB $19.99 (978-037595616-4). 304pp. Young Bayliss decides to become a nun after she survives the swimming accident that killed her older brother in 1932 Alabama but her resolve is tested when two homeless girls take over Leo's bedroom. ℮ Lexile 870L (Rev: BL 11/1/09; LMC 10/09; SLJ 11/09)

2299 Fusco, Kimberly Newton. *The Wonder of Charlie Anne* (5–8). 2010, Knopf $16.99 (978-0-375-86104-8). 256pp. When Charlie Anne's mother dies in the Depression era, cousin Mirabel comes to live with the family and life becomes even tougher; however, a friendship with an African American neighbor — despite the disapproval of bigoted neighbors — brings her comfort. ∩ Lexile 970L (Rev: BL 9/1/10; LMC 11–12/10; SLJ 10/1/10*)

2300 Giff, Patricia Reilly. *R My Name Is Rachel* (4–7). 2011, Random House $15.99 (978-0-375-83889-7); LB $18.99 (978-0-375-93889-4). 176pp. Three formerly city children are left to fend for themselves on an isolated farm in upstate New York when their father must leave to work near Canada during the Great Depression;

Rachel, 12, takes solace in her correspondence with an old neighbor. ∩ ℮ Lexile 550L (Rev: BLO 1/12; HB 11–12/11; LMC 5–6/12; SLJ 11/1/11)

2301 Harlow, Joan Hiatt. *Firestorm!* (4–7). 2010, Simon & Schuster $16.99 (978-141698485-6). 336pp. Poppy, a 12-year-old pickpocket, and Justin, 13-year-old son of a wealthy jeweler, become unlikely friends and manage a daring escape from the Great Chicago Fire of 1871; an Afterword distinguishes between fiction and fact. Lexile 660L (Rev: BL 11/15/10; SLJ 2/1/11)

2302 Hobbs, Valerie. *Maggie and Oliver, or, a Bone of One's Own* (3–6). Illus. by Jennifer Thermes. 2011, Henry Holt $15.99 (978-0-8050-9294-3). 192pp. Oliver, a dog abandoned after the death of its owner, and Maggie, an orphaned street urchin, find each other in this initially bleak but ultimately optimistic story set in early-20th-century Boston. (Rev: BL 11/1/11; SLJ 10/1/11)

2303 Holm, Jennifer L. *Turtle in Paradise* (4–6). 2010, Random House $16.99 (978-0-375-83688-6); LB $19.99 (978-0-375-93688-3). 208pp. Turtle, 11, is sent to live with relatives in Key West when her mother's new employer turns out to be anti-children in this Depression-era story based on the experiences of the author's great-grandmother. Newbery Honor Book. ∩ ℮ Lexile 610L (Rev: BL 4/15/10*; LMC 8–9/10; SLJ 4/10)

2304 Klise, Kate. *Stand Straight, Ella Kate: The True Story of a Real Giant* (K–3). Illus. by M. Sarah Klise. 2010, Dial $16.99 (978-0-8037-3404-3). 32pp. This first-person account is based on the true story of Ella Kate Ewing, born in 1872, who was more than 7 feet tall at the age of 17 and who chose to appear in museum and circus exhibits as a career. Lexile AD640L (Rev: BL 6/10*; LMC 10/10; SLJ 6/1/10)

2305 Korman, Gordon. *Unsinkable* (5–8). Series: Titanic. 2011, Scholastic paper $5.99 (978-0-545-12331-0). 176pp. A young Irish pickpocket named Paddy finds himself aboard the *Titanic* in this tense historical adventure, the first installment in a series. The second volume is *Collision Course* (2011). Also use *S.O.S.* (2011). ∩ ℮ Lexile 820L (Rev: BLO 8/11; SLJ 9/1/11)

2306 LaFaye, A. *Walking Home to Rosie Lee* (2–4). Illus. by Keith D. Shepherd. 2011, Cinco Puntos $16.95 (978-1-933693-97-2). 32pp. At the end of the Civil War, a young slave boy named Gabe heads north in search of his mother, who was sold and sent away from him. (Rev: BL 11/1/11; SLJ 9/1/11)

2307 Larson, Kirby. *The Friendship Doll* (4–6). 2011, Delacorte $15.99 (978-0-385-73745-6); LB $18.99 (978-0-385-90667-8). 202pp. One of the 58 dolls Japan presented to the United States in 1927, Miss Kanagawa, has an inspiring influence on each of the girls she lives with. ℮ Lexile 760L (Rev: BL 7/11; LMC 1–2/12; SLJ 8/11)

2308 Latham, Irene. *Leaving Gee's Bend* (5–8). 2010, Putnam $16.99 (978-0-399-25179-5). 240pp. Ten-year-old African American Ludelphia sets out on a dangerous journey to get help for her ailing mother in 1932. Lexile 700L (Rev: BL 2/1/10; LMC 1–2/10; SLJ 1/10; VOYA 2/10)

2309 Lemna, Don. *Out in Left Field* (4–7). Illus. by Matt Collins. 2012, Holiday House $16.95 (978-082342313-2). 224pp. Eleven-year-old Donald has a miserable time in 1947 and into 1948, starting with a humiliating flop in baseball and continuing through other misadventures in this funny sequel to *When the Sergeant Came Marching Home* (2008). (Rev: BL 4/1/12)

2310 Lowry, Lois. *Like the Willow Tree: The Diary of Lydia Amelia Pierce* (4–7). Illus. Series: Dear America. 2011, Scholastic $12.99 (978-0-545-14469-8); LB $16.99 (978-0-545-26556-0). 224pp. Eleven-year-old Lydia and her brother are sent to live with the Shakers at Sabbathday Lake, Maine, when their parents die in the influenza epidemic of 1918. Lexile 830L (Rev: BL 12/1/10; SLJ 2/1/11)

2311 McCaughrean, Geraldine. *The Glorious Adventures of the Sunshine Queen* (5–8). 2011, HarperCollins $16.99 (978-0-06-200806-0). 336pp. In the 1890s, 12-year-old Cissy and two friends have great adventures on a Missouri River paddle steamer when they are pulled out of school because of a diphtheria outbreak. ⌂ Lexile 950L (Rev: BL 4/1/11; HB 5–6/11; SLJ 7/11; VOYA 6/11)

2312 Murphy, Claire Rudolf. *Marching with Aunt Susan: Susan B. Anthony and the Fight for Women's Suffrage* (3–6). Illus. by Stacey Schuett. 2011, Peachtree $16.95 (978-1-56145-593-5). 36pp. In 1896 Bessie is not allowed to go hiking with her father and brothers and decides to go to a women's suffrage meeting instead; there she meets Susan B. Anthony and is drawn into the movement. (Rev: BL 12/1/11; LMC 5–6/12*; SLJ 9/1/11)

2313 Pinkney, Andrea Davis. *Bird in a Box* (4–7). 2011, Little, Brown $16.99 (978-0-316-07403-2). 245pp. Three young boxing fans facing personal challenges come together at the Mercy Home for Negro Orphans and are inspired by the great Joe Louis's victories during the Great Depression. ⌂ e (Rev: BL 4/15/11; HB 5–6/11; LMC 10/11; SLJ 3/1/11)

2314 Swain, Gwenyth. *Hope and Tears: Ellis Island Voices* (5–8). Illus. 2012, Boyds Mills $17.95 (978-159078765-6). 96pp. Fictionalized personal histories in the form of letters, diary entries, poems, and monologues and dialogues — accompanied by a factual commentary — provide lots of information about the experiences of immigrants arriving at Ellis Island. (Rev: BL 4/15/12; HB 5–6/12; SLJ 5/12)

2315 Tarshis, Lauren. *I Survived the Shark Attacks of 1916* (3–7). Illus. by Scott Dawson. Series: I Survived. 2010, Scholastic $16.99 (978-0-545-20688-4). 87pp.

Based on the New Jersey shark attacks of 1916, this story follows of group of boys who play pranks on each other, doubting the existence of the shark — until they see it for themselves. Lexile 610L (Rev: SLJ 12/1/10)

2316 Taylor, Sarah Stewart. *Amelia Earhart: This Broad Ocean* (4–7). Illus. by Ben Towle. 2010, Hyperion $17.99 (978-1-4231-1337-9). 96pp. Young Grace, who wants to be a reporter one day, is entranced by Earhart and her bravery in this graphic novel presentation of a portion of Earhart's life. (Rev: BL 3/15/10*; LMC 8–9/10; SLJ 5/10)

2317 Tubb, Kristin O'Donnell. *Selling Hope* (5–8). 2010, Feiwel & Friends $16.99 (978-031261122-4). 224pp. As Halley's Comet approaches in 1910, imaginative 13-year-old Hope sells "anti-comet" pills with the help of a young Buster Keaton. (Rev: BL 11/15/10*; SLJ 12/1/10)

2318 Vanderpool, Clare. *Moon over Manifest* (5–8). 2010, Delacorte $16.99 (978-0-385-73883-5); LB $19.99 (978-0-385-90750-7). 351pp. Twelve-year-old Abilene arrives in Manifest, Kansas, in 1936 hoping to learn more about her father, and a box of mementos prompts her to set out on a journey of discovery. Newbery Medal. ⌂ e (Rev: BL 10/15/10*; LMC 5–6/11; SLJ 11/1/10)

2319 Ylvisaker, Anne. *The Luck of the Buttons* (4–6). 2011, Candlewick $15.99 (978-0-7636-5066-7). 240pp. Twelve-year-old Tugs Button's fortunes begin to change when she wins a three-legged race and a Brownie camera in this small-town Iowa story set during the Great Depression. Lexile 730L (Rev: BL 4/15/11; HB 3–4/11; SLJ 4/11)

WORLD WAR II AND AFTER

2320 Abbott, Tony. *Lunch-Box Dream* (5–8). 2011, Farrar $16.99 (978-0-374-34673-7). 192pp. Two families — one white and one black — traveling through the South in 1959 are brought together by unlikely circumstances in this tense story. (Rev: BL 7/11; SLJ 9/1/11)

2321 Brandeis, Gayle. *My Life with the Lincolns* (5–7). 2010, Henry Holt $16.99 (978-0-8050-9013-0). 256pp. In the summer of 1966, intelligent 12-year-old Mina Edelmann believes that she is the reincarnation of one of Abraham Lincoln's sons as she learns about racism and watches the civil rights movement. ⌂ e Lexile 840L (Rev: BL 2/15/10; LMC 5–6/10; SLJ 3/10)

2322 Celenza, Harwell. *Duke Ellington's Nutcracker Suite* (2–5). Illus. by Don Tate. 2011, Charlesbridge $19.95 (978-1-57091-700-4). 32pp. A fascinating, fictionalized account of Duke Ellington's re-creation of Tchaikovsky's Nutcracker Suite with Billy Strayhorn; includes CD. (Rev: BL 11/1/11; SLJ 11/1/11)

2323 Conkling, Winifred. *Sylvia and Aki* (4–6). 2011, Tricycle $16.99 (978-1-58246-337-7); LB $19.99 (978-1-58246-438-1). 160pp. Two parallel narratives set in the 1940s follow the lives of Sylvia Mendez, a Mexican American girl whose father sues Orange County, California, in hopes of getting his daughter into school there, and of Aki, a Japanese American girl who misses her home when her family is moved to an internment camp in Arizona. ℮ (Rev: BLO 11/15/11; SLJ 6/11)

2324 Fawcett, Katie Pickard. *To Come and Go Like Magic* (5–8). 2010, Knopf $15.99 (978-0-375-85846-8); LB $18.99 (978-0-375-95846-5). 256pp. A new teacher nurtures 12-year-old Chili Sue Mahoney's desire to leave the depressed town of Mercy Hill, in the Appalachian hills of Kentucky; set in the 1970s. ℮ (Rev: BL 3/1/10; SLJ 2/10; VOYA 4/10)

2325 Fitzmaurice, Kathryn. *A Diamond in the Desert* (5–8). 2012, Viking $16.99 (978-067001292-3). 256pp. A young boy at a Japanese internment camp in 1942 gets so caught up in building a baseball diamond that he abandons his younger sister, which has serious consequences. (Rev: BL 3/15/12; LMC 8–9/12; SLJ 2/12)

2326 Fixmer, Elizabeth. *Saint Training* (5–7). 2010, Zondervan $14.99 (978-0-310-72018-8). 256pp. In the turbulent 1960s, 6th-grader Mary Clare is the oldest in a large Catholic family and decides that sainthood will be her — and her family's — salvation. ℮ (Rev: BL 11/15/10; SLJ 11/1/10)

2327 Flores-Galbis, Enrique. *Ninety Miles to Havana* (5–8). 2010, Roaring Brook $16.99 (978-1-59643-168-3). 304pp. A fictionalized account of the author's experience of coming to America from Cuba in the 1960s, when he was separated from his parents and placed in a camp in Miami. Lexile 790L (Rev: BL 5/1/10; LMC 8–9/10; SLJ 8/10; VOYA 12/10)

2328 Gantos, Jack. *Dead End in Norvelt* (5–8). 2011, Farrar $15.99 (978-0-374-37993-3). 352pp. Grounded for the entire summer, spirited Jack, 11, finds himself helping to write obituaries and coping with small-town life full of eccentric people in this funny and thoughtful story set in 1962. Newbery Medal. ∩ ℮ Lexile 920L (Rev: BL 8/11; HB 9–10/11; LMC 11–12/11; SLJ 9/1/11)

2329 Geisert, Bonnie. *Prairie Winter* (3–6). 2009, Houghton Mifflin $16 (978-0-618-68588-2). 224pp. A fierce winter on the Great Plains in the 1950s means that 6th-grader Rachel and her sisters can move into town and attend school without interruption, a change that is both thrilling and worrying. ℮ Lexile 720L (Rev: BL 11/1/09; SLJ 1/10; VOYA 12/09)

2330 Haworth, Danette. *Me and Jack* (3–6). 2011, Walker $16.99 (978-0-8027-9453-6). 240pp. When 6th-grader Josh and his Air Force recruiter father move to the Pennsylvania mountains, the boy must defend his newly acquired and much loved dog from accusations by the hostile local residents; set during the Vietnam War. (Rev: BL 4/1/5/11; SLJ 5/11)

2331 Jones, Traci L. *Finding My Place* (5–8). 2010, Farrar $16.99 (978-0-374-33573-1). 208pp. In mid-1970s Denver, Tiphanie starts her freshman year as the only black girl in her school and discovers that there are other outsiders. ℮ Lexile 750L (Rev: BL 4/15/10; LMC 8–9/10; SLJ 6/10)

2332 Larson, Kirby. *The Fences Between Us: The Diary of Piper Davis* (4–7). Series: Dear America. 2010, Scholastic $12.99 (978-0-545-22418-5); LB $16.99 (978-0-545-26232-3). 317pp. Thirteen-year-old Piper describes in her diary the many changes that take place in her life starting in December 1941. (Rev: BL 7/10; SLJ 12/1/10; VOYA 10/10)

2333 Levine, Kristin. *The Lions of Little Rock* (5–8). 2012, Putnam $16.99 (978-039925644-8). 304pp. In 1958 Little Rock, Arkansas, 13-year-old Marlee, who is already struggling with acute shyness, must deal with the fact that her best friend is thrown out of school because she is a light-skinned black. ∩ (Rev: BL 1/1/12; SLJ 1/12)

2334 Lieurance, Suzanne. *The Lucky Baseball: My Story in a Japanese-American Internment Camp* (3–6). Series: Historical Fiction Adventures. 2009, Enslow LB $27.93 (978-0-7660-3311-5). 160pp. Twelve-year-old Harry Yakamoto relies on baseball to sustain him through the hardship of his family's internment camp experience in the early 1940s. (Rev: BL 9/1/09; SLJ 1/10)

2335 McMullan, Margaret. *Sources of Light* (5–8). 2010, Houghton Mifflin $16 (978-054707659-1). 240pp. A young African American girl copes with racial tensions when her mother moves the family from Pennsylvania to Jackson, Mississippi, after her father's death in Vietnam in 1962. ℮ Lexile 840L (Rev: BL 4/15/10; HB 5–6/10; SLJ 5/10; VOYA 8/10)

2336 Noe, Katherine Schlick. *Something to Hold* (4–7). 2011, Clarion $16.99 (978-0-547-55813-4). 256pp. In the early 1960s Kitty, 11, contends with being one of few white children on an Indian reservation, struggling to make friends while learning about discrimination; includes a map, author's note, glossary, and pronunciation guide. (Rev: BL 10/1/11; SLJ 11/1/11)

2337 Peck, Richard. *A Season of Gifts* (5–8). 2009, Dial $16.99 (978-0-8037-3082-3). 176pp. Spunky, rifle-toting Grandma Dowdel, last seen in *A Long Way from Chicago* (1998) and *A Year Down Yonder* (2000), intervenes in the life of a weak-kneed preacher's son in this tale of neighborly kindness set in 1958 small-town Illinois. ∩ Lexile 690L (Rev: BL 8/09*; HB 9–10/09; SLJ 10/09; VOYA 12/09)

2338 Pinkney, Andrea Davis. *With the Might of Angels: The Diary of Dawnie Rae Johnson, Hadley, Virginia, 1954* (5–8). Illus. Series: Dear America. 2011, Scholastic $12.99 (978-0-545-29705-9). 336pp. Dawnie Rae chronicles her life in her diary: she's 12 and has been chosen to integrate an all-white school in her town in

1954 while also facing difficulties at home. ∩ ℮ (Rev: BL 9/1/11; SLJ 9/1/11)

2339 Scattergood, Augusta. *Glory Be* (3–6). 2012, Scholastic $16.99 (978-054533180-7). 208pp. In 1964, 11-year-old Gloriana faces an obstacle to her usual birthday pool party — desegregation, which has the led the town to close the pool indefinitely. ℮ (Rev: BL 1/12; LMC 3–4/12; SLJ 2/12)

2340 Shank, Marilyn Sue. *Child of the Mountains* (4–7). 2012, Delacorte $16.99 (978-038574079-1); LB $19.99 (978-037598969-8). 272pp. In rural Appalachia in 1953, Lydia, 11, confides in her diary as she struggles to come to terms with her brother's death from cystic fibrosis and her mother's stint in jail. ℮ (Rev: BL 4/15/12; LMC 8–9/12; SLJ 5/1/12)

2341 Sherman, M. Zachary. *A Time for War* (4–6). Illus. by Fritz Casas. Series: Bloodlines. 2011, Stone Arch LB $23.32 (978-1-4342-2558-0); paper $6.95 (978-1-4342-3097-3). 88pp. In World War II, paratrooper Michael Donovan escapes death and finds he is braver than he thought; nonfiction sections and illustrations add information to the dramatically presented text. (Rev: BL 6/1/11; SLJ 8/11)

2342 Shimko, Bonnie. *The Private Thoughts of Amelia E. Rye* (5–8). 2010, Farrar $16.99 (978-0-374-36131-0). 192pp. Abandoned by her father before birth and feeling unloved by her mother, Amelia finds a friend in Fancy Nelson, a feisty girl who is the first African American in Amelia's class; set in upstate New York in the 1960s. ℮ Lexile 790L (Rev: BL 4/15/10*; LMC 5–6/10; SLJ 4/10)

2343 Smiley, Jane. *The Georges and the Jewels* (4–8). Illus. by Elaine Clayton. 2009, Knopf $16.99 (978-0-375-86227-4); LB $19.99 (978-0-375-96227-1). 256pp. Twelve-year-old Abby cares for her family's horses as a way of escaping isolation, family drama, and her father's strict religious views in 1960s California. ℮ Lexile 970L (Rev: BL 9/15/09; HB 11–12/09; SLJ 10/09)

2344 Stanley, Diane. *Saving Sky* (5–8). 2010, HarperCollins $15.99 (978-0-06-123905-2). 199pp. Living on a New Mexico ranch, 7th-grader Sky is isolated from the terrorism affecting the nation until her friend Kareem finds himself under suspicion. (Rev: BL 6/10*; SLJ 9/1/10)

2345 Stone, Phoebe. *The Romeo and Juliet Code* (5–8). 2011, Scholastic $16.99 (978-0-545-21511-4). 300pp. Eleven-year-old Felicity is sent from London to relatives in Maine to protect her from bombardment by the Germans; she becomes friends with adoptee Derek and together they solve a family mystery. (Rev: BL 1/1–15/11; HB 3–4/11; LMC 5–6/11; SLJ 2/1/11)

2346 Tarshis, Lauren. *I Survived Hurricane Katrina, 2005* (3–6). Illus. by Scott Dawson. Series: I Survived. 2011, Scholastic $16.99 (978-054520689-1); paper $4.99 (978-054520696-9). 112pp. Eleven-year-old Barry Tucker's family is trapped during the storm in this story of heroic behavior. (Rev: BL 2/1/11)

2347 Tooke, Wes. *King of the Mound: My Summer with Satchel Paige* (5–7). 2012, Simon & Schuster $15.99 (978-144243346-5). 160pp. Recovering from a bout with polio that has left him with a leg brace, 12-year-old Nick is happy to help with odd jobs at the North Dakota stadium where his father is catcher, and to meet the great Satchel Paige. (Rev: BL 2/15/12; SLJ 2/12)

2348 Wallace, Rich. *War and Watermelon* (5–8). 2011, Viking $15.99 (978-0-670-01152-0). 192pp. In 1969, 12-year-old Brody longs to make the football team, goes to Woodstock, and mediates between his older brother and his father on the subject of Vietnam; presented in a first-person, diary format. ℮ Lexile 630L (Rev: BL 7/11; LMC 11–12/11; SLJ 7/11)

2349 Watson, Renee. *A Place Where Hurricanes Happen* (2–5). Illus. by Shadra Strickland. 2010, Random House $17.99 (978-0-375-85609-9). 40pp. In alternating free-verse voices, four young friends from the same New Orleans neighborhood describe their experiences during and after Hurricane Katrina. (Rev: BL 5/15/10; LMC 11–12/10; SLJ 6/1/10)

2350 Wiles, Deborah. *Countdown* (5–7). Series: Sixties Trilogy. 2010, Scholastic $17.99 (978-0-545-10605-4). 377pp. A girl coming of age during the Cold War in suburban Maryland copes with ordinary family drama and strife at school along with the pervasive atmosphere of fear during the Cuban missile crisis; includes period newspaper clippings, posters, ads, and other ephemera. ∩ Lexile 800L (Rev: BL 5/1/10*; HB 11–12/11; LMC 10/10; SLJ 7/10)

2351 Williams-Garcia, Rita. *One Crazy Summer* (4–7). 2010, Amistad $15.99 (978-0-06-076088-5); LB $16.89 (978-0-06-076089-2). 224pp. African American Delphine, 11, and her younger sisters are sent from Brooklyn to visit the mother who abandoned them and moved to California; there they find little welcome and spend time at a community center run by the Black Panthers. Newbery Honor Book; Scott O'Dell Award for Historical Fiction. ∩ ℮ Lexile 750L (Rev: BL 2/1/10*; HB 3–4/10; LMC 3–4/10; SLJ 3/10)

2352 Wittlinger, Ellen. *This Means War!* (5–8). 2010, Simon & Schuster $16.99 (978-1-4169-7101-6). 224pp. After her best friend Lowell abandons her for the company of boys, 10-year-old Juliet befriends Polly, and the girls become intent on challenging the boys to increasingly risky and dangerous tests of will in this story set during the Cold War. Lexile 740L (Rev: BL 2/1/10; HB 5–6/10; SLJ 4/10)

2353 Yep, Laurence. *The Star Maker* (3–5). 2011, HarperCollins $15.99 (978-0-06-025315-8); LB $16.89 (978-0-06-025316-5). 112pp. In 1950s San Francisco 8-year-old Chinese American Artie succeeds in meeting a foolish fireworks promise with the help of his Uncle Chester. Lexile 530L (Rev: BL 11/15/10; SLJ 2/1/11)

Humorous Stories

2354 Anderson, M. T. *Agent Q, or the Smell of Danger!* (4–7). Illus. by Kurt Cyrus. Series: Pals in Peril. 2010, Simon & Schuster $16.99 (978-1-4169-8640-9). 294pp. Crime-fighting teens Lily, Jasper, and Katie are trying to get home to New Jersey after their adventures in Delaware, but the evil Autarch has other things in mind. ❺ (Rev: BL 9/15/10*; SLJ 11/1/10)

2355 Anderson, M. T. *Zombie Mommy* (5–8). Illus. by Kurt Cyrus. Series: Pals in Peril. 2011, Simon & Schuster $16.99 (978-144243068-6). 240pp. Lily, Katie, Drgnan, and Jasper Dash, Boy Technonaut must save Lily's mother, who has been possessed by a zombie with ambitions. Lexile 710L (Rev: BL 10/15/11; HB 11–12/11)

2356 Basye, Dale E. *Blimpo: The Third Circle of Heck* (4–7). Illus. by Bob Dob. Series: Heck. 2010, Random House $16.99 (978-037585676-1); LB $19.99 (978-037595676-8). 464pp. Milton Fauster, 11, must help his sister Marlo, who is training as Satan's secretary, and his friend Virgil, who is consigned to the circle for overweight children, in this third installment in the humorous series. (Rev: BLO 2/15/10)

2357 Basye, Dale E. *Rapacia: The Second Circle of Heck* (4–7). Illus. by Bob Dob. Series: Heck. 2009, Random House $16.99 (978-0-375-84077-7); LB $19.99 (978-0-375-94077-4). 362pp. Marlo joins other young shoplifters in the second circle of Heck, where he is taunted by cool stuff he can never have. ∩ (Rev: BL 5/15/11; SLJ 8/09)

2358 Basye, Dale E. *Snivel: The Fifth Circle of Heck* (4–7). Illus. by Bob Dob. Series: Heck. 2012, Random House $16.99 (978-037586834-4); LB $19.99 (978-037596834-1). 448pp. Deceased Milton and Marlo Fauster save the world from Nikola Tesla's nefarious plot to come back to life. ❺ (Rev: BL 3/15/12; SLJ 3/12; VOYA 10/12)

2359 Bean, Raymond. *Rippin' It Old School* (3–5). 2010, AmazonEncore paper $9.95 (978-1-935597-08-7). 176pp. After the wild success of his first invention (in 2008's *Sweet Farts*, 10-year-old millionaire Keith is struggling to come up with his next big thing, and coping with the jealousy of family and friends. (Rev: BL 9/15/10; SLJ 5/11)

2360 Beaty, Andrea. *Attack of the Fluffy Bunnies* (3–6). Illus. by Dan Santat. 2010, Abrams $12.95 (978-0-8109-8416-5). 192pp. Two twins use their knowledge of horror movies to predict the sequence of events when their summer camp is taken over by giant warrior rab-

bits. ❺ Lexile 790L (Rev: BL 5/1/10; LMC 11–12/10; SLJ 7/1/10)

2361 Bolger, Kevin. *Zombiekins* (4–6). Illus. by Aaron Blecha. 2010, Penguin paper $10.99 (978-159514177-4). 208pp. Chaos and hilarity ensue when 4th-grader Stanley returns from a trip to Dementedyville with a possessed stuffed animal whose bite turns schoolmates into zombies. ❺ Lexile 880L (Rev: BL 6/10; SLJ 10/10)

2362 Bruel, Nick. *Bad Kitty for President* (3–5). Illus. by author. 2012, Roaring Brook $13.99 (978-159643669-5). 144pp. Annoyed with all the strays in town, Bad Kitty decides to run for president of the Neighborhood Cat Coalition in this book full of details of voter registration, debate coaching, and media interviews. (Rev: BL 3/15/12; SLJ 4/1/12)

2363 Bruel, Nick. *Bad Kitty vs. Uncle Murray: The Uproar at the Front Door* (2–4). Illus. by author. 2010, Roaring Brook $13.99 (978-1-59643-596-4). 160pp. Poor Uncle Murray has been left in charge of Bad Kitty and Poor Puppy and his good nature is sorely tried. (Rev: SLJ 8/1/10)

2364 Castle, M. E. *Popular Clone* (4–7). 2012, Egmont $15.99 (978-160684232-4). 320pp. Socially inept and bullied scientific genius Fisher is frustrated when he clones himself so he can stay home and play video games while his clone attends school, and it turns out that Fisher Two becomes popular. ∩ ❺ (Rev: BL 1/1/12)

2365 Devillers, Julia, and Jennifer Roy. *Trading Faces* (4–7). 2008, Simon & Schuster $16.99 (978-1-4169-7531-1). 300pp. Middle school twins Emma and Payton have very different social lives — one is popular while the other is brainy — and switch places with interesting results. ❺ Lexile HL460L (Rev: SLJ 5/1/09)

2366 Draper, Sharon M. *The Dazzle Disaster Dinner Party* (2–4). 2010, Scholastic $15.99 (978-0-545-07154-3). 144pp. Ambitious 4th-grader Sassy decides to hold a dinner party for her class, but things do not go quite as planned. Lexile 530L (Rev: BL 12/15/10; SLJ 1/1/11)

2367 Fleming, Candace. *The Fabled Fifth Graders of Aesop Elementary School* (3–5). 2010, Random House $15.99 (978-0-375-86334-9); LB $18.99 (978-0-375-96334-6). 176pp. The intrepid Mr. Jupiter steps up to educate the gang of rowdy 5th-graders in this zany story packed with fable-related hyperbole, a sequel to *The Fabled Fourth Graders of Aesop Elementary School* (2007). ❺ Lexile 660L (Rev: BL 9/1/10; HB 9–10/10; SLJ 9/1/10)

2368 Foley, Lizzie K. *Remarkable* (3–7). 2012, Dial $16.99 (978-080373706-8). 304pp. Ordinary enough to be unsuitable for the town of Remarkable's School for the Remarkably Gifted, 10-year-old Jane Doe is the only student in the public school until the trouble-making Grimlet twins and a pirate captain arrive and lead her in a series of adventures. (Rev: BL 3/15/12*; HB 3–4/12; LMC 10/12; SLJ 4/12)

2369 Gifford, Peggy. *Moxy Maxwell Does Not Love Practicing the Piano (But She Does Love Being in Recitals)* (3–5). Photos by Valorie Fisher. 2009, Random House $12.99 (978-0-375-84488-1); LB $15.99 (978-0-375-96688-0). 177pp. Ten-year-old Moxy prepares for her recital — planning and constructing her clothes to the extent that she has no time for actual rehearsal. (Rev: BL 12/15/09; SLJ 11/1/09)

2370 Gosselink, John. *The Defense of Thaddeus A. Ledbetter* (4–7). 2010, Abrams $14.95 (978-0-8109-8977-1). 240pp. Mastermind and social misfit Thaddeus, 12, spends his time writing a "Prison Diary" and campaigning for his release from unfair In-school Suspension. Lexile 970L (Rev: BL 11/1/10; LMC 1–2/11; SLJ 11/1/10; VOYA 12/10)

2371 Grant, Michael. *The Call* (5–8). Series: The Magnificent 12. 2010, HarperCollins $16.99 (978-006183366-3). 224pp. An ordinary, fearful 12-year-old finds himself pitted against the Pale Queen in this tongue-in-cheek story about overcoming phobias; the first installment in a series. Also use *The Trap*. e Lexile 710L (Rev: BL 11/15/10*)

2372 Green, D. L. *Zeke Meeks vs. the Putrid Puppet Pals* (2–4). Illus. by Josh Alves. 2012, Capstone $21.32 (978-140486803-8); paper $5.95 (978-140487223-3). 128pp. Lighthearted gross-out humor adds appeal to this story of 3rd-grader Zeke, who deals with minor annoyances at home — an embarrassing dog, an annoying sister — and a felt finger puppet fad gripping his elementary school. (Rev: BL 3/15/12; LMC 5–6/12)

2373 Griffiths, Andy. *Killer Koalas from Outer Space: And Lots of Other Very Bad Stuff That Will Make Your Brain Explode* (4–7). Illus. by Terry Denton. 2011, Feiwel & Friends $12.99 (978-0-312-36789-3). 176pp. Often gross and silly, this collection of short stories, verse, and cartoons featuring "Very Bad" characters — everything from zombie kittens, killer koalas, and inadequate adults — will captivate its intended audience. (Rev: BL 11/1/11; SLJ 10/1/11)

2374 Harper, Charise Mericle. *Just Grace and the Snack Attack* (2–4). Illus. by author. Series: Just Grace. 2009, Houghton Mifflin $15 (978-0-547-15223-3). 176pp. Grace's research into flavored potato chips prompts speculation about various apparently unrelated aspects of her life. Lexile 940L (Rev: BL 3/15/10; HB 11–12/09; SLJ 12/1/09)

2375 Kelly, Katy. *Melonhead and the Big Stink* (3–5). Illus. by Gillian Johnson. 2010, Delacorte $14.99 (978-0-385-73658-9); LB $17.99 (978-0-385-90617-3). 224pp. Adam "Melonhead" and his friend Sam, rising 5th-graders, do their very best to behave in order to

travel to New York to see the smelly "titan arum" that only blooms every seven years. (Rev: BLO 4/15/10; SLJ 7/1/10)

2376 Kimmel, Elizabeth Cody. *The Reinvention of Moxie Roosevelt* (5–7). 2010, Dial $16.99 (978-0-8037-3303-9). 256pp. Thirteen-year-old Moxie decides to reinvent herself when she heads off to boarding school, eventually realizing that it's easiest to just be herself. Lexile 780L (Rev: BL 6/10; LMC 1–2/11; SLJ 7/10)

2377 Kinard, Kami. *The Boy Project (Notes and Observations of Kara McAllister)* (5–8). Illus. by author. 2012, Scholastic $12.99 (978-054534515-6). 272pp. Kara employs scientific method to help figure out the best way to land a date, documenting her progress on note cards. e (Rev: BL 3/1/12; SLJ 2/12)

2378 Kinney, Jeff. *Diary of a Wimpy Kid: Cabin Fever* (5–8). Illus. by author. 2011, Abrams $12.95 (978-141970223-5). 224pp. It's the month between Thanksgiving and Christmas, and Greg is tired of having to behave for Santa, especially when the adults in his life are so unreasonable. (Rev: BLO 11/1/11)

2379 Kinney, Jeff. *Diary of a Wimpy Kid: The Ugly Truth* (5–8). Illus. by author. 2010, Abrams $13.95 (978-081098491-2). 224pp. Charging headlong toward puberty, Greg Heffley suffers a series of mortifying tween social gaffes. Lexile 1000L (Rev: BLO 11/1/10; SLJ 5/11)

2380 Krulik, Nancy. *Trouble Magnet* (2–4). Illus. by Aaron Blecha. Series: George Brown, Class Clown. 2010, Grosset & Dunlap paper $4.99 (978-0-448-45368-2). 128pp. A 4th-grader suffering from a case of enormous belches struggles to control the behavior when he arrives at his new school. (Rev: SLJ 7/1/10)

2381 Lowry, Lois. *The Birthday Ball* (3–5). Illus. by Jules Feiffer. 2010, Houghton Mifflin $16 (978-0-547-23869-2). 192pp. Princess Patricia's 16th birthday — and the time to choose between unappealing suitors — is looming and she takes refuge in disguising herself as a peasant girl and attending the village school. ∩ e Lexile 870L (Rev: BL 3/10*; HB 3–4/10; SLJ 3/10)

2382 Luper, Eric. *Jeremy Bender vs. the Cupcake Cadets* (3–6). 2011, HarperCollins $15.99 (978-0-06-201512-9). 240pp. After 6th-grader Jeremy damages his father's beloved antique motorboat, he and his friend Slater dress up as girls and hope to win the prize money in a model-sailboat race organized by the Cupcake Cadet club. (Rev: BL 5/1/11; SLJ 6/11)

2383 McDonald, Megan. *Cloudy with a Chance of Boys* (4–6). Series: Sisters Club. 2011, Candlewick $15.99 (978-0-7636-4615-8). 272pp. Is 12-year-old Stevie ready for a boyfriend? She struggles with this idea even as her older sister Alex admires a student named Scott and her younger sister Joey prefers frogs; the third book in the series. ∩ e Lexile 500L (Rev: BL 3/15/11; SLJ 3/1/11)

2384 McDonald, Megan. *Stink and the Midnight Zombie Walk* (K–3). Illus. by Peter H. Reynolds. Series: Stink. 2012, Candlewick $12.99 (978-076365692-8). 160pp. The book release party for a zombie thriller attracts a lot of attention in this early chapter book. ◌ (Rev: BL 2/1/12)

2385 McDonald, Megan. *Stink and the Ultimate Thumb-Wrestling Smackdown* (2–4). Illus. by Peter H. Reynolds. Series: Stink. 2011, Candlewick $12.99 (978-076364346-1). 144pp. After flunking gym class, Stink tries thumb-wrestling before deciding to take up karate; lively graphics and wordplay add to the fun. (Rev: BL 1/1–15/11)

2386 McDonald, Megan. *Stink: Solar System Superhero* (2–4). Illus. by Peter H. Reynolds. Series: Stink. 2010, Candlewick $12.99 (978-0-7636-4321-8). 118pp. When 2nd-grader Stink learns that Pluto has been demoted to a dwarf planet, he sets out to restore its status in this entertaining and informative story. ◌ Lexile 930 (Rev: BL 1/1/10; SLJ 2/1/10)

2387 Nesbo, Jo. *Doctor Proctor's Fart Powder* (4–7). Illus. by Mike Lowery. Series: Doctor Proctor's Fart Powder. 2010, Simon & Schuster $14.99 (978-1-4169-7972-2). 160pp. Dr. Proctor's loud but non-smelly invention launches Nilly into outer space at the beginning of this humorous, action-packed story in which bad people try to steal this wondrous product; set in Norway. Also use *Bubble in the Bathtub*. ◌ Lexile 830L (Rev: BL 1/1/10; SLJ 2/10)

2388 Nesbo, Jo. *Who Cut the Cheese?* (4–7). Trans. by Tara F. Chance. Illus. by Mike Lowery. Series: Doctor Proctor's Fart Powder. 2012, Aladdin $15.99 (978-144243307-6). 464pp. In this sequel to *Doctor Proctor's Fart Powder* (2010), Nilly, Lisa, and Dr. Procter apply their zany inventions to the burgeoning crises threatening Norway. ℮ Lexile 770L (Rev: BL 1/1/12; LMC 5–6/12; SLJ 6/12)

2389 Norriss, Andrew. *I Don't Believe It, Archie!* (2–5). Illus. by Hannah Shaw. 2012, Random House $12.99 (978-038575250-3); LB $15.99 (978-038575251-0). 128pp. Prone to misadventure, young Archie's stories are never believed in this funny British import. ℮ (Rev: BL 3/1/12*; HB 3–4/12; LMC 3–4/12; SLJ 3/12)

2390 O'Malley, Kevin. *Once Upon a Royal Super Baby* (3–5). Illus. by Scott Goto. 2010, Walker $16.99 (978-0-8027-2164-8). 32pp. A boy and girl bicker over their creative writing assignment, the girl imagining a sweet royal baby who can talk to birds while the boy gives him superpowers, a motorcycle, and sunglasses. (Rev: BL 11/1/10; LMC 11–12/10; SLJ 9/1/10)

2391 Paulsen, Gary. *Lawn Boy Returns* (5–8). Series: Lawn Boy. 2010, Random House $12.99 (978-0-385-74662-5); LB $15.99 (978-0-385-90899-3). 101pp. The enterprising 12-year-old's lawn business grows into a monster and his hippie stockbroker gets him involved in risky high finance — and then there's the sponsorship

of a boxer — when all he really wants is to play with the other kids. ◌ ℮ Lexile 920L (Rev: BLO 6/16/10; HB 7–8/10; SLJ 6/10)

2392 Paulsen, Gary. *Masters of Disaster* (4–6). 2010, Random House $12.99 (978-0-385-73997-9); LB $15.99 (978-0-385-90816-0). 112pp. Three boys set out to prove their mettle by undertaking progressively more dangerous dares in this zany and often gross chapter book. ◌ ℮ (Rev: BL 10/1/10; LMC 1–2/11; SLJ 11/1/10)

2393 Peirce, Lincoln. *Big Nate: In a Class by Himself* (3–6). Illus. by author. Series: Big Nate. 2010, HarperCollins $12.99 (978-0-06-194434-5); LB $14.89 (978-0-06-194435-2). 224pp. Reacting to a fortune cooking message, 6th-grader Nate sets out to excel all day and instead merely succeeds in racking up a series of detentions. (Rev: BL 3/1/10; SLJ 4/10)

2394 Pinkwater, Daniel. *Adventures of a Cat-Whiskered Girl* (5–8). 2010, Houghton Mifflin $16 (978-0-547-22324-7). 282pp. Fourteen-year-old Audrey, who resembles a cat, has a series of chaotic and wacky adventures around the Hudson river town of Poughkeepsie, encountering characters from other realms, dimensions, and places. (Rev: BL 5/15/10; HB 5–6/10; SLJ 8/10)

2395 Raschka, Chris. *Seriously, Norman!* (5–8). Illus. by author. 2011, Scholastic $17.95 (978-0-545-29877-3). 352pp. Twelve-year-old Norman's tutor Balthazar Birdsong assigns him, along with kite flying, to read the dictionary, inspiring some interesting vocabulary in this quirkily amusing book. (Rev: BL 9/15/11; SLJ 11/1/11)

2396 Rees, Douglas. *Uncle Pirate to the Rescue* (3–6). Illus. by Tony Auth. 2010, Simon & Schuster paper $5.99 (978-1-4169-7505-2). 112pp. Wilson's elementary school class comes to the rescue when his swashbuckling uncle goes missing at sea in this funny sequel to *Uncle Pirate* (2008). Lexile 570L (Rev: SLJ 3/10)

2397 Scieszka, Jon, ed. *Guys Read: Funny Business* (4–7). Illus. by Adam Rex. 2010, HarperCollins $16.99 (978-0-06-196374-2); paper $5.99 (978-0-06-196373-5). 256pp. A collection of humorous stories by well-known writers that will appeal to boys. ℮ (Rev: BL 10/1/10*; SLJ 10/1/10; VOYA 2/11)

2398 Seegert, Scott. *How to Grow Up and Rule the World* (5–8). Illus. by John Martin. 2010, Egmont $13.99 (978-1-60684-013-9). 200pp. The comically sinister Vordak provides dazzling insights into the mind of an evil genius in this giggle-worthy personal development book, featuring tips on wardrobe, social behavior, housing, and death traps. Lexile NC1140L (Rev: BL 9/1/10; SLJ 12/1/10)

2399 Sherman, Deborah. *The BEDMAS Conspiracy* (5–7). 2011, Fitzhenry & Whiteside paper $9.95 (978-1-55455-181-1). 172pp. Cousins Adam and Daniela are determined to win the middle school talent show with their rock band despite their respective deficiencies. Lexile 660L (Rev: LMC 3–4/12; SLJ 12/1/11)

2400 Skye, Obert. *Wonkenstein: The Creature from My Closet* (4–7). Illus. by author. 2011, Henry Holt $12.99 (978-0-8050-9268-4). 240pp. Twelve-year-old Rob is uninterested in books and they pile up in his closet — until the day a strange being emerges from the heap, appearing to be a combination of Willy Wonka and Frankenstein, complicating Rob's all-too-average life. Lexile 860L (Rev: BL 10/15/11; SLJ 9/1/11)

2401 Stadler, Alexander. *Invasion of the Relatives* (2–4). Illus. by author. Series: Julian Rodriguez. 2009, Scholastic $15.99 (978-0-439-91967-8). 144pp. The fuss and bother surrounding Thanksgiving nearly drives Julian (er, First Officer Julian Rodriguez, space traveler) over the edge, and he expresses his discontent through his computer. (Rev: BL 11/15/09; SLJ 3/1/10)

2402 Trueit, Trudi. *Mom, There's a Dinosaur in Beeson's Lake* (3–5). Illus. by Jim Paillot. Series: Secrets of a Lab Rat. 2010, Simon & Schuster $14.99 (978-1-4169-7593-9). 145pp. Ten-year-old Scab McNally faces many difficult situations in this funny book, including swimming lessons that may reveal his fear of the water. (Rev: SLJ 5/1/10)

2403 Vande Velde, Vivian. *8 Class Pets + 1 Squirrel ÷ 1 Dog = Chaos* (2–4). Illus. by Steve Björkman. 2011, Holiday House $15.95 (978-0-8234-236-4-). 67pp. This zany story captures the mounting chaos that is unleashed when a squirrel wakes up a sleeping dog, which leads to an all-out pursuit into and through the halls of an elementary school, adding new animals as they go; the animals all speak, using very different styles that add to the fun. Lexile 740L (Rev: BL 10/15/11; SLJ 12/1/11)

2404 Van Draanen, Wendelin. *The Power Potion* (3–6). Illus. by Stephen Gilpin. Series: The Gecko and Sticky. 2010, Knopf $12.99 (978-037584379-2); LB $15.99 (978-037594573-1). 240pp. Dave and his sidekick gecko swap a villain's mysterious potion for a presumably inert substitute, which turns out to cause incapacitating diarrhea; the fourth book in the series. (Rev: BLO 4/15/10)

2405 Venuti, Kristin Clark. *The Butler Gets a Break* (4–7). Series: Bellweather Tales. 2010, Egmont $15.99 (978-1-60684-087-0). 224pp. Hospitalized with a broken leg, Benway the butler hears about the escapades of the Bellweathers and worries that he may lose his job; a sequel to *Leaving the Bellweathers* (2009). (Rev: BL 11/1/10; SLJ 11/1/10)

2406 Venuti, Kristin Clark. *Leaving the Bellweathers* (4–7). Series: Bellweather Tales. 2009, Egmont $15.99 (978-160684006-1). 256pp. Butler Tristan Benway is looking forward to ending his tenure with the eccentric Bellweathers and starts a memoir about their outrageous behaviors. ∩ (Rev: BL 9/15/09; HB 11–12/09; SLJ 9/09)

School Stories

2407 Adderson, Caroline. *Star of the Week* (2–4). Illus. by Ben Clanton. 2012, Kids Can $15.95 (978-155453578-1). 128pp. It's Jasper's turn to be Star of the Week but he finds himself upstaged left and right in this appealing chapter book. (Rev: BL 3/1/12; LMC 10/12; SLJ 3/12)

2408 Angleberger, Tom. *The Strange Case of Origami Yoda* (4–6). Illus. by author. 2010, Abrams $12.95 (978-0-8109-8425-7). 160pp. Sixth-grader Tommy vacillates between belief and disbelief when a classmate comes to school with a origami finger puppet that seems to dispense sage advice. ∩ e Lexile 760L (Rev: BL 5/1/10; SLJ 5/10)

2409 Barshaw, Ruth McNally. *Ellie McDoodle: New Kid in School* (4–7). Illus. by author. 2008, Bloomsbury $12.99 (978-159990238-8). 176pp. In 6th grade at a new school Ellie McDoodle tackles finding friends, horrible school lunches, and various other trials and tribulations recounted through sketches, cartoons, and engaging text. Also use *Ellie McDoodle: Best Friends Fur-Ever* (2010). Lexile 510L (Rev: BLO 8/08)

2410 Becker, Bonny. *The Magical Ms. Plum* (2–4). Illus. by Amy Portnoy. 2009, Knopf $12.99 (978-0-375-85637-2); LB $15.99 (978-0-375-95637-9). 112pp. A talented teacher and her magical closet supply the children in her class with exactly what they need. e Lexile 670L (Rev: BL 11/1/09; LMC 11/09; SLJ 11/1/09)

2411 Butcher, Kristin. *Cheat* (5–8). 2010, Orca LB $16.95 (978-1-55469-275-0); paper $9.95 (978-1-55469-274-3). 112pp. Eager for acclaim, school newspaper reporter Laurel is disappointed when her story about school cheating is poorly received. (Rev: BL 12/15/10; SLJ 2/1/11)

2412 Buyea, Rob. *Because of Mr. Terupt* (4–6). 2010, Delacorte $16.99 (978-038573882-8); LB $19.99 (978-038590749-1). 208pp. A group of 5th-graders with diverse problems learn a lot from a new teacher in this novel told from several perspectives. (Rev: BL 10/15/10; LMC 5–6/11*; SLJ 12/1/10*)

2413 Cooper, Rose. *Gossip from the Girls' Room* (5–8). 2011, Delacorte $12.99 (978-0-385-73947-4); LB $15.99 (978-0-385-90791-0). 200pp. Sixth-grader Sophia's attempts to bring down a popular girl at school by posting gossipy blogs go awry. e (Rev: BL 1/1–15/11; SLJ 3/1/11)

2414 Daneshvari, Gitty. *Class Is Not Dismissed!* (4–7). Series: School of Fear. 2010, Little, Brown $16.99 (978-0-316-03328-2). 320pp. In this lighthearted followup to 2009's *School of Fear*, the four phobia-ridden students return to take another stab at curing their unreasonable and paralyzing fears and together investigate who is stealing from their school. (Rev: BL 10/1/10; SLJ 9/1/10)

2415 Danneberg, Julie. *The Big Test* (1–3). Illus. by Judy Love. 2011, Charlesbridge $16.95 (978-1-58089-360-2); paper $6.95 (978-1-58089-361-9). 32pp. Mrs. Hartwell's class gets lots of practice before the day of the dreaded standardized test. (Rev: BL 8/11; SLJ 7/11)

2416 Davies, Jacqueline. *The Lemonade Crime* (3–5). 2011, Houghton Mifflin $15.99 (978-0-547-27967-1). 160pp. Siblings Jessie and Evan (of 2007's *The Lemonade War*) are now in the same 4th-grade class and bond over a trial seeking justice about the missing proceeds from the lemonade stand. (Rev: BL 5/1/11; SLJ 8/11)

2417 Devillers, Julia. *New Girl in Town* (3–5). Illus. by Paige Pooler. Series: Liberty Porter, First Daughter. 2010, Simon & Schuster $15.99 (978-1-4169-9128-1). 194pp. First daughter Liberty doesn't sacrifice her ideals in order to win friends when she starts at her new school in Washington, D.C. (Rev: SLJ 9/1/10)

2418 Durand, Hallie. *Just Desserts* (2–4). Illus. by Christine Davenier. 2010, Atheneum $15.99 (978-1-4169-6387-5). 208pp. Third-grader Dessert is inspired by lessons on the American Revolution to start a club to fight back against annoying siblings, but her good efforts backfire. (Rev: BLO 8/10; LMC 10/10; SLJ 6/1/10)

2419 Feldman, Jody. *The Seventh Level* (5–8). 2010, Greenwillow $16.99 (978-0-06-195105-3). 304pp. Eager for acceptance into his middle school's secret society, the Legend, Travis is thrilled when he begins receiving the clues and puzzles that, if solved, will grant him admittance. **e** Lexile 630L (Rev: BL 5/1/10; SLJ 10/1/10)

2420 Friedman, Laurie. *Mallory Goes Green* (2–5). Illus. by Jennifer Kalis. Series: Mallory. 2010, Carolrhoda $15.95 (978-082258885-6). 160pp. Mallory's enthusiasm for the environment tends to alienate classmates and adults until she realizes she must take another approach. The 14th book in the series is *Mallory in the Spotlight* (2010) in which a starring role calls friendship tension. (Rev: BL 2/15/10)

2421 Gephart, Donna. *How to Survive Middle School* (5–8). 2010, Delacorte $15.99 (978-038573793-7); LB $18.99 (978-038590701-9). 256pp. Used to being bullied and grieving the loss of his best friend Elliott, 13-year-old David Greenberg finds a new ally in Sophie who boosts his popularity by promoting his YouTube videos. **e** (Rev: BL 3/1/10; SLJ 6/10)

2422 Graff, Lisa. *Sophie Simon Solves Them All* (3–5). Illus. by Jason Beene. 2010, Farrar $14.99 (978-0-374-37125-8). 112pp. In pursuit of an advanced graphing calculator, friendless whiz-kid Sophie begins charging her classmates for solving their problems in this

amusing story. **e** Lexile 680L (Rev: BL 9/15/10; HB 11–12/10; LMC 11–12/10; SLJ 9/1/10)

2423 Greene, Stephanie. *Princess Posey and the First Grade Parade* (K–2). Illus. by Stephanie Roth Sisson. 2010, Putnam $12.99 (978-0-399-25167-2). 96pp. Posey has many anxieties about starting 1st grade in this early chapter book. (Rev: BL 7/10; LMC 10/10; SLJ 6/1/10)

2424 Greenwald, Tommy. *Charlie Joe Jackson's Guide to Not Reading* (4–7). Illus. by J. P. Coovert. 2011, Roaring Brook $14.99 (978-1-59643-691-6). 224pp. Middle-schooler Charlie Joe goes to great lengths to avoid reading, although he is partial to some kinds of books — checkbooks, comic books, and Facebook. (Rev: BL 5/1/11; SLJ 8/11)

2425 Grimes, Nikki. *Rich* (2–4). Illus. by R. Gregory Christie. 2009, Putnam $10.99 (978-039925176-4). 112pp. Dyamonde and Free befriend a new classmate, Damaris, who is homeless and living in a shelter. ∩ **e** (Rev: BL 11/1/09)

2426 Gutman, Dan. *Miss Laney Is Zany!* (3–5). Illus. by Jim Paillot. Series: My Weird School Daze. 2010, HarperCollins LB $15.89 (978-0-06-155417-9); paper $3.99 (978-0-06-155415-5). 104pp. A.J.'s new game-show-loving speech teacher comes up with a way to solve the school's financial woes in this beginning chapter book with lots of wordplay. (Rev: SLJ 9/1/10)

2427 Holmes, Sara Lewis. *Operation Yes* (5–8). 2009, Scholastic $16.99 (978-054510795-2). 256pp. Miss Loupe uses improv acting in her 6th-grade class at an Air Force base school, and she is rewarded by her students' loyal support when her brother goes missing in Afghanistan. ∩ (Rev: BL 9/15/09*; HB 11–12/09; SLJ 11/09)

2428 Lowry, Lois. *Gooney Bird on the Map* (2–4). Illus. by Middy Thomas. 2011, Houghton Mifflin $15.99 (978-0-547-55622-2). 128pp. Gooney Bird comes up with a plan to make staying home for spring break more fun than going on vacation. (Rev: BL 11/1/11; SLJ 10/1/11)

2429 McElligott, Matthew, and Larry Tuxbury. *Benjamin Franklinstein Lives!* (4–7). Illus. by Matthew McElligott. Series: Benjamin Franklinstein. 2010, Putnam $12.99 (978-0-399-25229-7). 128pp. Science whiz Victor's expectations of winning the school science fair are dashed when a lightning strike revives a dormant Ben Franklin, who had been in secret suspended animation. A sequel is *Benjamin Franklinstein Meets the Fright Brothers* (2011). **e** Lexile 590L (Rev: BL 9/1/10; LMC 11–12/10; SLJ 11/1/10)

2430 MacLachlan, Patricia. *Word After Word After Word* (2–5). 2010, HarperCollins $14.99 (978-0-06-027971-4); LB $15.89 (978-0-06-027972-1). 128pp. Fourth-grader Lucy comes to understand the power of poetry when a visiting author spends time in her class. ℮ (Rev: BL 3/15/10*; SLJ 7/1/10)

2431 McMullan, Kate. *School! Adventures at the Harvey N. Trouble Elementary School* (1–4). Illus. by George Booth. 2010, Feiwel & Friends $12.99 (978-0-312-37592-8). 160pp. Heading for school each morning Ron Faster — always in a hurry — is ready to deal with music teacher Doremi Fasollatido and Janitor Iquit. (Rev: LMC 8–9/10; SLJ 8/1/10)

2432 Messner, Kate. *Marty McGuire* (2–4). Illus. by Brian Floca. 2011, Scholastic $15.99 (978-0-545-14244-1); paper $5.99 (978-0-545-14246-5). 144pp. An active, nature-loving young girl is reluctantly cast as the princess in the school play and learns a little about drama and improvisation. ♫ Lexile 660L (Rev: BL 6/1/11; LMC 10–11/11; SLJ 12/1/11)

2433 Millard, Glenda. *Layla, Queen of Hearts* (4–6). Illus. by Patrice Barton. 2010, Farrar $15.99 (978-0-374-34360-6). 112pp. Third-grader Layla is at a loss for who to bring to school for Senior Citizens' Day, until she meets charming and scatterbrained Miss Amelie. Lexile 900L (Rev: BLO 3/1/10; SLJ 6/1/10)

2434 Mills, Claudia. *Fractions = Trouble!* (2–3). Illus. by G. Brian Karas. 2011, Farrar $15.99 (978-0-374-36716-9). 116pp. Third-grader Wilson has difficulty with fractions and grudgingly accepts tutoring while fretting about his science fair project. (Rev: SLJ 6/11)

2435 Mongredien, Sue. *Be My Valentine* (4–6). Series: The Sleepover Club. 2010, IPG/Lion paper $6.99 (978-000727705-6). 128pp. Two mean girls exploit Fliss's crush on Ryan in a hurtful Valentine's Day prank, and her friends plan revenge. (Rev: BLO 11/15/09)

2436 Moss, Marissa. *The Vampire Dare!* (2–4). Illus. by author. 2011, Simon & Schuster paper $5.99 (978-144241737-3). 80pp. Fourth-grader Daphne fills her journal with doodles and musings about coming up with the perfect vampire outfit for Costume Day. (Rev: BL 5/1/11)

2437 Myers, Walter Dean. *The Cruisers* (5–8). 2010, Scholastic $15.99 (978-0-439-91626-4). 123pp. The four low-achieving 8th-grade creators of *The Cruiser* alternative newspaper are assigned the roles of peacekeepers during a Civil War unit with interesting results; set in a Harlem school for the gifted and talented. ♫ Lexile 810L (Rev: BL 9/1/10*; LMC 1–2/11; SLJ 10/1/10)

2438 Patterson, James, and Chris Tebbetts. *Middle School, the Worst Years of My Life* (3–6). Illus. by Laura Park. 2011, Little, Brown $15.99 (978-0-316-10187-5). 288pp. Middle school misfit Rafe decides to break every rule in the school's code of conduct and spends his time pulling fire alarms, painting graffiti, and so forth until he is finally expelled and the frustrated adults con-

sider an alternative arts school. (Rev: BL 9/15/11; SLJ 11/1/11*)

2439 Peirce, Lincoln. *Big Nate Strikes Again* (3–6). Series: Big Nate. 2010, HarperCollins $13.99 (978-0-06-194436-9); LB $14.89 (978-0-06-194437-6). 215pp. Big Nate must cope with the unbearable Gina, an A-plus student who keeps showing up where he doesn't want her in school. Lexile 430L (Rev: BL 2/1/11; HB 11–12/10; SLJ 12/1/10)

2440 Peschke, Marci. *Daisy's Summer Essay* (2–4). Illus. by M. H. Pilz. Series: Growing Up Daisy. 2011, ABDO LB $25.65 (978-161641114-5). 80pp. Mexican American Daisy Martinez gets help from her *abuela* and creates an excellent show-and-tell project for her 4th-grade class in this first installment in a new series that also includes *Daisy's Fall Festival, Daisy's Field Trip Adventure,* and *Daisy for President* (all 2011). (Rev: BL 5/1/11)

2441 Polacco, Patricia. *The Junkyard Wonders* (2–5). Illus. by author. 2010, Philomel $17.99 (978-0-399-25078-1). 48pp. A creative teacher inspires a classroom of slow learners, insisting that her students have as much potential as anyone else. Lexile 660L (Rev: BL 5/1/10; LMC 10/10; SLJ 7/1/10)

2442 Rylander, Chris. *The Fourth Stall* (4–7). 2011, HarperCollins $15.99 (978-0-06-199496-8). 320pp. Sixth-graders Mac and Vince run a successful business helping fellow students with everything from tests to defense against bullies, but find their friendship tested when they confront a real challenge. (Rev: BL 2/15/11; LMC 5–6/11; SLJ 9/1/11; VOYA 12/11)

2443 Rylander, Chris. *The Fourth Stall, Part II* (4–7). 2012, HarperCollins $15.99 (978-006199630-6). 240pp. Expert problem-solvers Mac and Vince continue to build their advice business (conducted from the washroom) even as their classmates' dilemmas get more and more complex. (Rev: BL 3/1/12; VOYA 12/11)

2444 Salisbury, Graham. *Kung Fooey* (3–5). Illus. by Jacqueline Rogers. Series: Calvin Coconut. 2011, Random House $12.99 (978-0-385-73963-4); LB $15.99 (978-0-385-90797-2). 144pp. Calvin is curious about his new classmate Benny who makes various claims that seem unlikely, but also worries when class bully Tito picks on Benny; the sixth installment in the series set in Hawaii. Also use *Dog Heaven* (2010). ℮ (Rev: SLJ 8/1/11)

2445 Schoenberg, Jane. *The One and Only Stuey Lewis: Stories from the Second Grade* (2–3). Illus. by Cambria Evans. 2011, Farrar $16.99 (978-0-374-37292-7). 128pp. Second-grader Stuey contends with familiar school troubles and triumphs in these four short stories. (Rev: BLO 8/11; LMC 11–12/11; SLJ 8/1/11)

2446 Simon, Coco. *The Cupcake Cure* (4–6). Series: Cupcake Diaries. 2011, Simon & Schuster paper $5.99 (978-144242275-9). 160pp. Four girls form a bond during the early days of middle school as they navigate prickly social situations together. (Rev: BL 5/1/11)

2447 Starkey, Scott. *How to Beat the Bully Without Really Trying* (3–6). 2012, Simon & Schuster $15.99 (978-144241685-7). 272pp. New student Rodney is immediately picked on by the resident bully but gains stature when a stray baseball knocks Josh out cold. (Rev: BL 1/1/12; SLJ 4/12)

2448 Stewart, Kiera. *Fetching* (5–8). 2011, Hyperion/Disney $16.99 (978-1-4231-3845-7). 304pp. Olivia applies dog training principles to the "pack" of mean cliquish kids at her middle school, but finds that the results are not quite what she expected. e Lexile 740L (Rev: BL 10/15/11; SLJ 11/1/11; VOYA 12/11)

2449 Stine, R. L. *It's the First Day of School . . . Forever!* (4–6). 2011, Feiwel & Friends $15.99 (978-0-312-64954-8). 192pp. Artie's first day at middle school does not go well, and the boy relives the same disastrous events over and over — but is it all a bad dream? ∩ e (Rev: BL 8/11; LMC 11–12/11; SLJ 8/1/11*)

2450 Thomson, Melissa. *Keena Ford and the Secret Journal Mix-Up* (1–3). Illus. by Frank Morrison. 2010, Dial $15.99 (978-0-8037-3465-4). 128pp. Second-grader Keena, an African American living in Washington, D.C., faces difficult choices when Tiffany threatens to share Keena's personal diary with the whole school. e Lexile 780L (Rev: BL 11/15/10; SLJ 10/1/10)

2451 Tracy, Kristen. *Bessica Lefter Bites Back* (4–7). 2012, Delacorte $16.99 (978-038574069-2); LB $19.99 (978-037598961-2). 272pp. Bessica's iffy social standing goes from bad to worse when her friend lets fly a rumor about a nasty foot fungus even as she must work out a strategy for sharing mascot duty. e Lexile 550L (Rev: BL 2/15/12; LMC 8–9/12; SLJ 3/12; VOYA 4/12)

2452 Trueit, Trudi. *Scab for Treasurer?* (2–5). Illus. by Jim Paillot. Series: Secrets of a Lab Rat. 2011, Aladdin $14.99 (978-1-4169-7594-6); paper $4.99 (978-141696113-0). 160pp. In a bid to become 4th-grade class president, Scab pledges to eat any food his classmates bring him. ∩ e Lexile 490L (Rev: BL 7/11; SLJ 7/11)

2453 Wardlaw, Lee. *101 Ways to Bug Your Friends and Enemies* (5–8). 2011, Dial $16.99 (978-0-8037-3262-9). 288pp. Eighth grade proves challenging to "Sneeze" Wyatt as he attends some classes at high school, falls for Hayley who unfortunately is in love with someone else, and a golfer bullies him. e Lexile 600L (Rev: BLO 10/15/11; SLJ 10/1/11)

2454 Warner, Sally. *EllRay Jakes Is a Rock Star!* (2–4). Illus. by Jamie Harper. Series: EllRay Jakes. 2011, Viking $14.99 (978-0-670-01158-2). 117pp. EllRay is eager to have something to bring for show and tell and borrows his geologist dad's crystals without permission

— only to find himself in a tight spot when the crystals go missing. e (Rev: SLJ 9/1/11)

2455 Warner, Sally. *EllRay Jakes Is Not a Chicken!* (2–4). Illus. by Jamie Harper. 2011, Viking $14.99 (978-0-670-06243-0). 144pp. EllRay struggles to be good at school, even in the face of bullies, lest his father cancel their upcoming trip to Disneyland. (Rev: BL 6/1/11; LMC 10/11; SLJ 8/1/11)

2456 Winerip, Michael. *Adam Canfield: The Last Reporter* (5–8). 2009, Candlewick $16.99 (978-0-7636-2342-5). 384pp. Featuring teen journalist Adam and his coeditor sidekick Jennifer, this third installment in a series builds upon themes of enterprise, journalistic ethics, and budding romance. ∩ Lexile 710L (Rev: BLO 10/15/09; SLJ 10/09; VOYA 12/09)

2457 Winston, Sherri. *President of the Whole Fifth Grade* (3–6). 2010, Little, Brown $15.99 (978-0-316-11432-5). 288pp. Brianna is so eager to become class president (and later rich and famous) that she jeopardizes her relationship with her friends. e Lexile 730L (Rev: BL 12/1/10; LMC 1–2/11; SLJ 12/1/10)

2458 Wong, Janet S. *Me and Rolly Maloo* (2–4). Illus. by Elizabeth Buttler. 2010, Charlesbridge $15.95 (978-1-58089-158-5). 128pp. Popular 4th-grader Rolly asks the nerdy Jenna, a math whiz, to provide the answers in the upcoming test; which girl is the cheater? Lexile 740L (Rev: BL 6/10; LMC 1–2/11; SLJ 11/1/10)

2459 Yoo, David. *The Detention Club* (5–8). 2011, HarperCollins $16.99 (978-0-06-178378-4). 304pp. Sixth-grader Peter's zany scheme to boost his faltering popularity lands him in detention in this humorous story about the challenges of middle school. e Lexile 880L (Rev: BL 8/11; HB 9–10/11; SLJ 10/1/11)

2460 Zucker, Naomi. *Callie's Rules* (4–7). 2009, Egmont $15.99 (978-160684027-6). 240pp. Callie, 11, is a smart kid who tries to understand what's necessary to fit in in middle school but feels compelled, along with her family, to take a stand when her school decides to ban "satanic" Halloween celebrations. A sequel is *Write On, Callie Jones* (2010). (Rev: BL 9/1/09; SLJ 8/09)

Science Fiction

2461 Arntson, Steven. *The Wikkeling* (5–8). Illus. by Daniela Jaglenka Terrazzini. 2011, Running Press $18 (978-0-7624-3903-4). 256pp. In the dystopian city of the Addition, Henrietta and her friends Gary and Rose are being menaced by a yellow creature called the Wikkeling that gives them headaches. (Rev: BL 5/1/11; SLJ 5/11)

2462 Boyce, Frank Cottrell. *Cosmic* (4–7). 2010, HarperCollins $16.99 (978-0-06-183683-1). 320pp. Twelve-year-old Liam is so big that he's often mistaken for an adult, and he decides to capitalize on this and enter the Greatest Dad Ever Contest to win a flight into space. ∩ **e** Lexile 670L (Rev: BL 11/15/09*; HB 3–4/10; LMC 3–4/10; SLJ 2/10)

2463 Carman, Patrick. *The Dark Planet* (5–8). Illus. by Squire Broel. Series: Atherton. 2009, Little, Brown $16.99 (978-0-316-16674-4). 350pp. In the action-driven conclusion to this trilogy, Edgar seeks answers about himself as he desperately works to save the homeland of his friend, Dr. Harding. ∩ (Rev: SLJ 10/09; VOYA 10/09)

2464 Carroll, Michael. *Super Human* (5–8). 2010, Philomel $16.99 (978-0-399-25297-6). 336pp. Four teens with superpowers challenge the Helotry's plans to resurrect an ancient warrior. **e** Lexile 690L (Rev: BL 5/1/10; LMC 10/10; SLJ 7/10; VOYA 8/10)

2465 Chase, Max. *Alien Attack* (3–5). Illus. Series: Star Fighters. 2012, Bloomsbury paper $5.99 (978-159990850-2). 128pp. Peri, a student at the Intergalactic Force Academy, and Diesel, a half-Martian, escape an invasion of aliens and challenge them from their high-tech spaceship; an action-packed story full of sci fi treats. (Rev: BL 5/15/12; LMC 10/12)

2466 Dallimore, Jan. *Captain Cal and the Garbage Planet* (1–4). Illus. by Richard Morden. 2010, Picture Window LB $14.99 (978-1-4048-5509-0). 56pp. Captain Cal and his capable team save a distant galaxy from drowning in garbage in this zany, lighthearted tale. Also use *Captain Cal and the Robot Army* (2010). (Rev: BL 2/15/10; LMC 1–2/10; SLJ 2/1/10)

2467 DiTerlizzi, Tony. *The Search for Wondla* (5–8). 2010, Simon & Schuster $17.99 (978-1-4169-8310-1). 496pp. Eva Nine, 12, who has been raised by a robot in an underground home, finally gets to see the real world and finds it a dangerous place full of bizarre creatures; features many rich illustrations and, using a Webcam, readers can access additional information on Eva Nine's world. ∩ Lexile 760L (Rev: BL 9/1/10; LMC 11–12/10; SLJ 8/10)

2468 Dunn, Mark. *The Age of Altertron* (4–7). Series: The Calamitous Adventures of Rodney and Wayne, Cosmic Repairboys. 2009, McAdam paper $12.95 (978-0-59692-345-4). 150pp. In an alternate 1956 the town of Pitcherville is facing numerous strange calamities that 13-year-old twins Rodney and Wayne attempt to resolve with the aid of a physics teacher; the first installment in a zany series. (Rev: LMC 3–4/10; SLJ 2/10)

2469 Fagan, Deva. *Circus Galacticus* (4–7). 2011, Harcourt $16.99 (978-054758136-1). 304pp. Frustrated orphan Trix joins a circus that tours the universe in a spaceship and learns to navigate new relationships and explore her past. (Rev: BL 11/15/11; SLJ 1/12; VOYA 12/11)

2470 Fergus, Maureen. *Ortega* (5–8). 2010, Kids Can $16.95 (978-1-55453-474-6). 224pp. A gorilla named Ortega has been raised in a laboratory and given the ability to speak, but when he is asked to attend middle school, things go awry. Lexile 1040L (Rev: LMC 10/10; SLJ 7/10)

2471 Haddix, Margaret Peterson. *Sabotaged* (5–8). Series: The Missing. 2010, Simon & Schuster $16.99 (978-141695424-8). 384pp. Siblings Jonah and Katherine are sent back in time to help a missing child in the mysterious Roanoke Colony, but things do not go as planned. ∩ **e** (Rev: BL 10/1/10; SLJ 7/10)

2472 Haddix, Margaret Peterson. *Sent* (5–8). Series: The Missing. 2009, Simon & Schuster $15.99 (978-1-4169-5422-4). 313pp. In this suspenseful sequel to 2008's *Found,* Chip, Jonah, Katherine, and Alex arrive in 15th-century England through the magic of time travel, and struggle to save Princes Edward and Richard from their fates while watching history unfold. (Rev: BL 8/09; SLJ 10/09)

2473 Haddix, Margaret Peterson. *Torn* (4–6). Series: The Missing. 2011, Simon & Schuster $15.99 (978-141698980-6). 352pp. Time travelers Jonah and Katherine are in peril on Henry Hudson's ill-fated 1611 expedition, unsure that they can preserve history and get back home. (Rev: BL 9/1/11)

2474 Hall, Teri. *Away* (5–8). 2011, Dial $16.99 (978-0-8037-3502-6). 240pp. In this sequel to *The Line* (2010), Rachel is struggling to adapt to living among the Others and continues to search for father, who she now learns is still alive. (Rev: BLO 9/15/11; SLJ 12/1/11)

2475 Hall, Teri. *The Line* (5–8). 2010, Dial $16.99 (978-0-803-73466-1). 228pp. Rachel lives with her mother on an estate close to the Line, which separates the Unified States from the territory called Away; when she hears a plaintive recording from Away, Rachel feels compelled to act. **e** Lexile 760L (Rev: BL 2/1/10; LMC 3–4/10; SLJ 4/10)

2476 Heath, Jack. *Remote Control* (5–8). 2010, Scholastic $17.99 (978-0-545-07591-6). 326pp. Genetically engineered teen agent Six of Hearts faces a crime lord and the ChaosSonic corporation as he battles to rescue his kidnapped clone-brother Kyntak; a sequel to *The Lab* (2008). **e** Lexile 840L (Rev: BL 4/15/10; SLJ 4/10)

2477 Hulme, John, and Michael Wexler. *The Split Second* (5–8). Series: The Seems. 2008, Bloomsbury $16.99 (978-159990130-5). 300pp. In this followup to 2007's *The Glitch in Sleep,* 13-year-old Becker Drane sets about using his talents to save a fantastical world beset by horrifying storms. ∩ **e** Lexile 1030L (Rev: BL 10/15/08; SLJ 1/1/09; VOYA 2/09)

2478 Hurd, Thacher. *Bongo Fishing* (3–6). 2011, Henry Holt $16.99 (978-0-8050-9100-7). 240pp. A friendly, pop culture-loving alien takes earthling Jason on an entertaining intergalactic adventure that also includes a mysterious character called Dr. Zimburger. Lexile 740L (Rev: BL 2/15/11; LMC 5–6/11; SLJ 2/1/11)

2479 Jennings, Patrick. *Invasion of the Dognappers* (4–6). 2012, Egmont $15.99 (978-160684287-4). 208pp. Despite the adults' incredulity that aliens are stealing the dogs, young Logan and his friends form the Intergalactic Canine Rescue Unit. (Rev: BL 5/15/12; LMC 8–9/12; SLJ 4/12)

2480 Lupica, Mike. *The Batboy* (5–8). 2010, Philomel $17.99 (978-0-399-25000-2). 256pp. Fourteen-year-old Brian gets permission to become a bat boy for the Detroit Tigers despite his mother's misgivings. (Rev: BL 1/1/10; SLJ 4/10)

2481 Lyga, Barry. *Archvillain* (4–7). 2010, Scholastic $16.99 (978-0-545-19649-9). 192pp. A plasma storm brings 6th-grader Kyle, already confident and smart, additional strength and intellect, plus the ability to fly; however, to Kyle's dismay, the storm also produces an annoying rival — superpower-endowed Mighty Mike. Lexile 740L (Rev: BL 9/15/10; LMC 11–12/10; SLJ 10/1/10)

2482 Lyga, Barry. *The Mad Mask* (4–7). 2012, Scholastic $17.99 (978-054519651-2). 240pp. Determined to prove that his rival Might Mike is an alien with sinister designs on the world, 12-year-old Kyle (aka the Azure Avenger) teams up with Mad Mask in this fast-paced superhero spoof; a sequel to *Archvillain* (2010). Lexile 810L (Rev: BL 1/1/12; SLJ 3/12)

2483 Lynch, Chris. *Prime Evil* (5–8). Series: Cyberia. 2010, Scholastic $16.99 (978-0-545-02795-3). 148pp. Zane's ability to communicate with animals saves the day when he is sent to Primeval Ranch and must deal with strangely hostile animals and the machinations of the evil Dr. Gristle; the final volume in the trilogy, following *Cyberia* (2009) and *Monkey See, Monkey Don't* (2010). (Rev: BL 1/1–15/11; SLJ 2/1/11)

2484 McKissack, Patricia C., and Fredrick L. McKissack, et al. *Clone Codes* (4–7). 2010, Scholastic $16.99 (978-0-439-92983-7). 192pp. In 2170, 13-year-old Leanna learns about slaves in the Civil War and realizes that her own life is similar; she is not a human being but an enslaved clone. Lexile 680L (Rev: BL 1/1/10; LMC 3–4/10; SLJ 2/10)

2485 Matas, Carol. *The Edge of When* (5–8). 2012, Fitzhenry & Whiteside paper $12.95 (978-155455198-9). 230pp. In three separate but linked stories first published 30 years ago and now updated, 12-year-old Rebecca is transported into the future, at one point to 2050 where a postapocalyptic society is kidnapping healthy children from the past. (Rev: BL 3/15/12)

2486 Myklusch, Matt. *Jack Blank and the Imagine Nation* (4–7). Series: Jack Blank Adventures. 2010, Aladdin $16.99 (978-1-4169-9561-6). 480pp. Jack Blank fits right in at St. Barnaby's Home for the Hopeless, Abandoned, Forgotten, and Lost until he destroys a zombie robot and is taken to the Imagine Nation to hone his superpowers and save the world. ∩ Lexile 780L (Rev: BL 7/10; LMC 10/10; SLJ 9/1/10)

2487 Myklusch, Matt. *The Secret War* (5–8). Series: Jack Blank Adventures. 2011, Aladdin $16.99 (978-1-4169-9564-7). 554pp. In this second complex volume in the series, Jack must deal with a dangerous computer virus while battling the spyware parasite in his own body. (Rev: BLO 9/15/11; LMC 11–12/11; SLJ 11/1/11; VOYA 12/11)

2488 Russell, David O., and Andrew Auseon. *Alienated* (5–8). 2009, Simon & Schuster $16.99 (978-1-4169-8298-2). 352pp. Best friends Gene and Vince have fun publishing a tabloid focusing on extraterrestrials until things turn serious and they find themselves embroiled in an intergalactic war. ℮ Lexile 780L (Rev: BL 11/15/09; SLJ 1/10)

2489 Scieszka, Jon, and Francesco Sedita. *Spaceheadz #1* (3–5). Illus. by Shane Prigmore. Series: SPHDZ. 2010, Simon & Schuster $14.99 (978-1-4169-7951-7). 160pp. Michael's first day of 5th grade gets weird when he's partnered with two kids claiming to be from another planet in this zany space adventure story. Books 2 and 3 were published in 2010 and 2011, respectively. Lexile 580L (Rev: BL 4/1/10; LMC 8–9/10; SLJ 9/1/10*)

2490 Teague, Mark. *The Doom Machine* (4–7). 2009, Scholastic $17.99 (978-0-545-15142-9). 384pp. Set in the 1950s, this zany science fiction yarn follows town troublemaker Jack on an intergalactic journey of discovery to save his uncle's invention from the grips of aliens. Lexile 610L (Rev: BL 10/15/09; HB 1–2/10; LMC 11–12/09; SLJ 10/09; VOYA 10/09)

2491 van Eekhout, Greg. *The Boy at the End of the World* (5–8). 2011, Bloomsbury $16.99 (978-1-59990-524-2). 256pp. The only human survivor of a Life Ark in this post-apocalyptic story, Fisher has instinctive knowledge of many things and sets out to explore his environment in the company of a robot he calls Click. (Rev: BL 5/1/11; SLJ 9/1/11)

Short Stories and Anthologies

2492 Benedictus, David. *Return to the Hundred Acre Wood* (2–4). Illus. by Mark Burgess. 2009, Dutton $19.99 (978-0-525-42160-3). 160pp. A collection of new stories about Christopher Robin and his friends. ∩ ℮ Lexile 940L (Rev: BL 11/1/09; SLJ 1/1/10)

2493 Book Wish Foundation. *What You Wish For: A Book for Darfur* (5–8). 2011, Putnam $17.99 (978-0399-25454-3). With a foreword by Mia Farrow and contributions by authors including Alexander McCall Smith, Jane Yolen, Naomi Shihab Nye, and Cynthia Voigt, this is a collection of stories and poems that focus on young people's aspirations, created to benefit the refugees of Darfur. ℮ (Rev: BL 10/1/11*; LMC 1–2/12; SLJ 11/1/11; VOYA 2/12)

2494 Bradman, Tony, ed. *Under the Weather: Stories About Climate Change* (4–7). 2010, Frances Lincoln $16.95 (978-1-84507-930-7). 215pp. This multicultural selection of short stories examines how climate change is affecting people in different parts of the world. (Rev: BL 1/1–15/11; SLJ 1/1/11) [808.83936]

2495 Hurwitz, Johanna, ed. *I Fooled You: Ten Stories of Tricks, Jokes, and Switcheroos* (4–6). 2010, Candlewick $16.99 (978-0-7636-3789-7); paper $6.99 (978-0-7636-4877-0). 192pp. David Adler, Michelle Knudsen, and Megan McDonald are among the 10 authors represented in this diverse collection. (Rev: LMC 5–6/10; SLJ 3/10)

2496 Kibuishi, Kazu, ed. *Explorer: The Mystery Boxes* (4–8). Illus. 2012, Abrams $19.95 (978-141970010-1); paper $10.95 (978-141970009-5). 128pp. An anthology of short graphic works all centering on the theme of a mysterious box and its contents. (Rev: BL 2/15/12; HB 5–6/12; LMC 8–8/12; SLJ 3/1/12*; VOYA 4/12)

2497 O'Malley, Kevin. *Backpack Stories* (2–4). Illus. by author. 2009, Whitman $16.99 (978-0-8075-0504-5). 32pp. Ranging in tone from zany to touching, this book of four short stories is centered around backpacks. (Rev: BL 9/15/09; LMC 10/09; SLJ 9/1/09)

2498 Tellegen, Toon. *Far Away Across the Sea* (K–4). Trans. by Martin Cleaver. Illus. by Jessica Ahlberg. 2010, Boxer $12.95 (978-1-907152-37-5). 160pp. Bright watercolor illustrations enhance this collection of short and quirky animal stories. (Rev: BL 10/15/10; LMC 11–12/10; SLJ 11/1/10)

2499 Van Allsburg, Chris, ed. *The Chronicles of Harris Burdick: 14 Amazing Authors Tell the Tales* (3–7). Illus. by editor. 2011, Houghton Mifflin $24.99 (978-0-547-54810-4). 228pp. Well-known authors present stories inspired by the illustrations in Van Allsburg's *The Mysteries of Harris Burdick*. YALSA Best Fiction for Young Adults, 2012. ℮ Lexile 840L (Rev: BL 9/1/11; HB 9–10/11; SLJ 8/11; VOYA 10/11)

2500 Weiss, M. Jerry, and Helen S. Weiss, eds. *This Family Is Driving Me Crazy: Ten Stories About Surviving Your Family* (5–8). 2009, Putnam $17.99 (978-0-399-25040-8). 240pp. Gordon Korman, Jack Gantos, Walter Dean Myers, and Nancy Springer are among the authors represented in this collection of varied stories with themes including forgiveness, self-discovery, and compassion in the face of adversity. Lexile 830L (Rev: BL 10/1/09; LMC 11/09; SLJ 10/09; VOYA 2/10)

Sports Stories

2501 Aronson, Sarah. *Beyond Lucky* (4–7). 2011, Dial $16.99 (978-0-8037-3520-0). 256pp. Soccer looms more important on Ari's radar than his forthcoming bar mitzvah, and he is convinced that the trading card he has found will bring him luck. (Rev: BL 9/1/11; SLJ 8/11)

2502 Barber, Tiki, and Paul Mantell. *Goal Line* (4–7). Illus. 2011, Simon & Schuster $15.99 (978-141699095-6). 176pp. Ronde Barber copes with a case of sibling envy after his twin brother's summer growth spurt in this football-fueled family story. ℮ Lexile 760L (Rev: BLO 8/11)

2503 Barber, Tiki, and Ronde Barber, et al. *Red Zone* (4–7). 2010, Simon & Schuster $15.99 (978-141696860-3). 176pp. The Eagles junior-high football team manages to make it to the state championship despite an outbreak of chicken pox. ℮ Lexile 790L (Rev: BL 9/1/10)

2504 Bowen, Fred. *Hardcourt Comeback* (4–7). Series: Fred Bowen Sports Story. 2010, Peachtree paper $5.95 (978-156145516-4). 144pp. Basketball star Brett's confidence is shaken when he misses an easy shot and his uneasiness spreads to other areas. (Rev: BL 4/15/10; SLJ 5/10)

2505 Bowen, Fred. *Throwing Heat* (3–5). 2010, Peachtree paper $5.95 (978-156145540-9). 136pp. Fastballer Jack, an 8th-grader, learns to control his pitching in this book for baseball fans. (Rev: BL 9/1/10; SLJ 10/1/10)

2506 Bowen, Fred. *Touchdown Trouble* (3–5). 2009, Peachtree paper $5.95 (978-1-56145-497-6). 128pp. Sam's football team must make a difficult decision when it is revealed that their winning score was the result of an illegal fifth-down play; includes an account of a similar situation in a famous 1940 Cornell-Dartmouth game. Lexile 660L (Rev: BL 9/1/09; SLJ 1/10)

2507 Choat, Beth. *Soccerland* (5–8). Series: The International Sports Academy. 2010, Marshall Cavendish $16.99 (978-0-7614-5724-4). 231pp. Soccer phenom Flora struggles to adjust when she goes from her tiny Maine town to a prestigious soccer camp where her talents aren't as exceptional and the culture is cutthroat. (Rev: BLO 8/10; SLJ 11/1/10)

2508 Coy, John. *Eyes on the Goal* (4–6). Series: 4 for 4. 2010, Feiwel & Friends $16.99 (978-0-312-37330-6). 176pp. The four friends first seen in *Top of the Order* (2009) are now headed for soccer camp where they finally manage to get on the same team. ℮ Lexile 530L (Rev: BLO 2/1/10; LMC 5–6/10; SLJ 4/10)

2509 Garza, Xavier. *Maximilian and the Mystery of the Guardian Angel* (3–6). Illus. by author. 2011, Cinco Puntos paper $12.95 (978-193369398-9). 160pp. Aspiring Mexican wrestler Maximilian, 11, finally meets his hero, El Àngel, and comes face-to-face with the scary villains who want to end his winning streak; in both English and Spanish. (Rev: BLO 1/25/12; SLJ 1/12)

2510 Gassman, Julie. *You Can't Spike Your Serves* (2–4). Illus. by Jorge Santillan. Series: Victory School Superstars. 2011, Stone Arch LB $25.32 (978-1-4342-2231-2). 56pp. Super-talented athlete Alicia hatches a plan to help out a friend at a disadvantaged school in this sports story. (Rev: BL 9/1/11; SLJ 6/11)

2511 Gratz, Alan. *Fantasy Baseball* (5–8). 2011, Dial $16.99 (978-0-8037-3463-0). 304pp. Twelve-year-old Alex finds himself joining an odd baseball league populated by characters from classic children's literature and fairy tales in this multilayered fantastical story. e Lexile 730L (Rev: BLO 1/1–15/11; SLJ 4/11)

2512 Gunderson, Jessica. *Don't Break the Balance Beam!* (2–4). Illus. by Jorge Santillan. Series: Sports Illustrated Kids: Victory School Superstars. 2011, Capstone LB $25.32 (978-1-4342-2057-8); paper $5.95 (978-1-4342-2807-9). 56pp. At the Victory School for Super Athletes, Kenzie — who excels on the balance beam — triumphs over athletic humiliation; an early chapter book. Lexile 440L (Rev: BL 1/1–15/11; LMC 3–4/11; SLJ 1/1/11)

2513 Gutman, Dan. *Roberto and Me* (4–6). Series: Baseball Card Adventure. 2010, HarperCollins $15.99 (978-006123484-2); LB $16.89 (978-006123485-9). 192pp. Young Stosh travels back in time in an attempt to save baseball star Roberto Clemente's life in this adventure and takes a surprising twist halfway through. ⌒ e Lexile 580L (Rev: BL 1/1/10; VOYA 8/10)

2514 Gutman, Dan. *Ted and Me* (5–8). 2012, HarperCollins $15.99 (978-006123487-3). 208pp. Charged with going back in time to warn FDR of the impending attack of Pearl Harbor, Stosh meets Ted Williams and gets some solid baseball advice. ⌒ e Lexile 630L (Rev: BLO 4/1/12)

2515 Hicks, Betty. *Doubles Troubles* (2–4). Illus. by Simon Gane. Series: Gym Shorts. 2010, Roaring Brook $15.99 (978-159643489-9). 64pp. Henry learns the importance of being kind and gracious in this story of competition on the tennis court and cooperation on a history project. e Lexile 540L (Rev: BL 3/15/10)

2516 Higgins, M. G. *Power Hitter* (4–6). Series: Travel Team. 2012, Lerner/Darby Creek LB $27.93 (978-076138324-6); paper $7.95 (978-076138539-4). 128pp. Sammy Perez's prized slugging ability seems to evaporate when the team switches to wooden bats; for reluctant readers. (Rev: BL 4/15/12; SLJ 4/12)

2517 Kew, Trevor. *Sidelined* (5–8). Series: Sports Stories. 2011, Orca $9.95 (978-155277550-9); LB $16.95 (978-155277551-6). 128pp. Marjan copes with competitive jealousy when her talented friend Vicky lands a

spot on an elite soccer team in this story set in Vancouver. (Rev: BLO 8/11)

2518 Knudson, Mike. *Raymond and Graham: Bases Loaded* (3–5). Illus. by Stacy Curtis. Series: Raymond and Graham. 2010, Viking $14.99 (978-0-670-01205-3). 155pp. Baseball pals Raymond and Graham contend with obstacles on the path to their team winning the Little League Championship in this story presented in slightly larger-than-usual font; a sequel to *Raymond and Graham Rule the School* (2008). (Rev: SLJ 2/1/10)

2519 Lupica, Mike. *Million-Dollar Throw* (5–8). 2009, Philomel $17.99 (978-0-399-24626-5). 244pp. Thirteen-year-old Nate Brodie, star quarterback of the school football team, gets a chance to solve his family's money problems when he is selected for the million-dollar football toss during halftime at a pro football game. ⌒ e Lexile 960L (Rev: BL 9/1/09; SLJ 12/09; VOYA 12/09)

2520 Lupica, Mike. *Shoot-Out* (4–6). Series: Comeback Kids. 2010, Philomel $10.99 (978-039924718-7). 165pp. Accustomed to winning, Jack has a difficult time when he moves to a new school and his soccer team loses its first match. ⌒ Lexile 920L (Rev: BL 9/1/10; SLJ 9/10)

2521 Lupica, Mike. *The Underdogs* (5–8). 2011, Philomel $17.99 (978-039925001-9). 256pp. When his economically depressed town cuts funding for his football program, 12-year-old Will Tyler swings into action and revives the team. (Rev: BL 9/1/11)

2522 Messner, Kate. *Sugar and Ice* (5–7). 2010, Walker $16.99 (978-0-8027-2081-8). 288pp. When Russian skating coach Andrei Grosheva offers 12-year-old farm girl Claire a scholarship to train with the elite in Lake Placid, she encounters a world of mean girls on ice, where competition is everything. (Rev: BL 9/1/10; SLJ 12/1/10)

2523 Mills, Claudia. *Basketball Disasters* (3–6). Illus. by Guy Francis. 2012, Knopf $12.99 (978-037586875-7); LB $15.99 (978-037596875-4). 176pp. Persuaded to join the basketball team by his best friend, Mason has a hard time coping with a serious losing streak and his dad's misguided coaching. e (Rev: BL 2/1/12; LMC 3–4/12)

2524 Northrop, Michael. *Plunked* (5–8). 2012, Scholastic $16.99 (978-054529714-1). 256pp. Formerly bold and brassy 6th-grader Jack struggles to recover his pluck after being struck in the head by a baseball. e Lexile 640L (Rev: BL 3/1/12; LMC 8–9/12; SLJ 4/12; VOYA 6/12)

2525 Ripken, Cal, Jr. *Hothead* (5–8). 2011, Hyperion/Disney $16.99 (978-1-4231-4000-9). 135pp. Gifted — and frustrated by family woes — 7th-grade shortstop Connor finally learns to control his temper when it threatens to derail his sports career. ⌒ e Lexile 810L (Rev: BL 2/15/11; SLJ 4/11)

2526 Ritter, John H. *The Desperado Who Stole Baseball* (5–8). 2009, Philomel $17.99 (978-0-399-24664-7). 272pp. In the 1880s, 12-year-old Jack Dillon — self-proclaimed baseball whiz — and outlaw Billy the Kid play in a key game in which a California mining town competes against the Chicago White Stockings; a rollicking prequel to *The Boy Who Saved Baseball* (2003). ♫ Lexile 750L (Rev: BL 2/15/09; SLJ 4/1/09)

2527 Ross, Jeff. *The Drop* (4–7). Series: Orca Sports. 2011, Orca paper $9.95 (978-1-55469-392-4). 168pp. For reluctant readers, this is an exciting snowboarding adventure story set in the mountains of British Columbia. (Rev: BL 7/11; SLJ 8/11)

2528 Scaletta, Kurtis. *Jinxed!* (2–4). Illus. by Eric Wight. Series: Topps League. 2012, Abrams $15.95 (978-141970286-0); paper $5.95 (978-141970261-7). 112pp. Hired as a bat boy for the summer, Chad enjoys the hard work and seeks to help a shortstop who think he is jinxed. **e** (Rev: BLO 5/15/12; LMC 11–12/12)

2529 Sherman, M. Zachary. *Impulse* (5–8). Illus. by Caio Majado. Series: Tony Hawk's 900 Revolution. 2011, Capstone LB $25.32 (978-1-4342-3203-8); paper $6.95 (978-1-4342-3452-0). 128pp. Fourteen-year-old foster child Dylan, aka Slider, contends with the mysterious disappearance of his admired older brother in this skateboard-fueled thriller with magical elements; this series appeals to reluctant readers. Lexile 660L (Rev: BLO 8/11; LMC 1–2/12; SLJ 12/1/11; VOYA 10/11)

2530 Smith, Charles R. *Winning Words: Sports Stories and Photographs* (5–8). Illus. by author. 2008, Candlewick $17.99 (978-076361445-4). 80pp. This short story collection from sportswriter Smith interprets some of sport's best themes, including confidence, determination, and motivation, and includes photographs that add interest. Lexile 620L (Rev: BL 9/1/08; SLJ 8/08)

2531 Spring, Debbie. *Breathing Soccer* (5–8). 2008, Thistledown $10.95 (978-189723542-3). 140pp. Asthmatic soccer buff Lisa, 12, gains inspiration from stories of athletes overcoming physical struggles in this believable, happy-ending tale. (Rev: BLO 8/08; SLJ 1/1/09)

2532 Wallace, Rich. *Ball Hogs* (3–5). Illus. by Jimmy Holder. Series: Kickers. 2010, Knopf $12.99 (978-0-375-85754-6); LB $15.99 (978-0-375-95754-3). 128pp. Fourth-grader Ben copes with an arrogant teammate in this soccer story. Also use *Fake Out* (2010) and *Game-Day Jitters* (2011). (Rev: SLJ 9/1/10)

2533 Wallace, Rich. *Sports Camp* (4–6). 2010, Knopf $15.99 (978-0-375-84059-3); LB $18.99 (978-0-375-94059-0). 160pp. Riley, 11, struggles to fit in at a summer athletics camp despite being one of the youngest and lackluster at basketball and softball. Lexile 730L (Rev: BL 3/1/10; SLJ 4/10)

Fairy Tales

2534 Alderson, Brian. *Thumbelina* (K–2). Illus. by Bagram Ibatoulline. 2009, Candlewick $17.99 (978-0-7636-2079-0). 40pp. Detailed realistic paintings enhance this retelling of the familiar story about a diminutive girl and her adventures. (Rev: BLO 11/1/09; LMC 1–2/10; SLJ 12/1/09)

2535 Elya, Susan Middleton. *Rubia and the Three Osos* (PS–2). Illus. by Melissa Sweet. 2010, Hyperion/Disney $15.99 (978-1-4231-1252-5). 40pp. With Spanish words sprinkled throughout, this retelling of Goldilocks set in the Southwest includes a glossary. Lexile AD450L (Rev: BLO 8/10; SLJ 10/1/10) [394.2]

2536 Gardner, Carol. *Princess Zelda and the Frog* (PS–2). Illus. 2011, Feiwel & Friends $16.99 (978-0-312-60325-0). 40pp. Two bulldogs, one dressed as a princess and one as a frog, add considerable humor to this retelling of the traditional story about a frog that turns into a prince. Lexile AD700L (Rev: BLO 8/11; SLJ 6/11) [398.2]

2537 Grimm, Jacob, and Wilhelm Grimm. *Snow White* (1–4). Illus. by Quentin Greban. 2009, NorthSouth $16.95 (978-0-7358-2257-3). 32pp. This faithful retelling features effective illustrations. (Rev: BLO 11/1/09; LMC 11–12/09; SLJ 11/1/09) [398.2]

2538 Manna, Anthony L., and Soula Mitakidou. *The Orphan: A Cinderella Story from Greece* (1–4). Illus. by Giselle Potter. 2011, Random House $16.99 (978-0-375-86691-3). 40pp. Mother Nature helps a Greek girl to meet the prince (in church) and escape a life of drudgery with her stepmother and stepsisters. **℮** (Rev: BL 10/15/11; HB 11–12/11; LMC 11–12/11; SLJ 9/1/11) [398.2]

2539 Peck, Jan, and David Davis. *The Green Mother Goose: Saving the World One Rhyme at a Time* (PS–1).

Illus. by Carin Berger. 2011, Sterling $14.95 (978-1-4027-6525-4). 32pp. Thirty familiar fairy tales are given eco-conscious facelifts in this nicely illustrated collection. Lexile 1140 (Rev: BL 4/15/11; LMC 10/11; SLJ 5/1/11) [811]

2540 Piumini, Roberto, reteller. *Goldilocks and the Three Bears* (2–4). Illus. by Valentina Salmaso. Series: Storybook Classics. 2009, Picture Window LB $25.32 (978-1-4048-5499-4). 32pp. A simple retelling with friendly looking bears, this will appeal to newly independent readers; includes discussion questions, a glossary, and advice on writing fairy tales. (Rev: LMC 1–2/10; SLJ 1/1/10) [398.22]

2541 *Rapunzel: Based on the Original Story by the Brothers Grimm* (K–3). Illus. by Sarah Gibb. 2011, Whitman $16.99 (978-0-8075-6804-0). 32pp. Beautifully detailed collage illustrations add appeal to this somewhat softened and sentimentalized version of Rapunzel. (Rev: BL 5/1/11; SLJ 4/11) [398.2]

2542 Sabuda, Robert. *Beauty and the Beast* (1–4). Illus. by author. 2010, Simon & Schuster $29.99 (978-141696079-9). 12pp. Complex, dynamic pop-ups enhance the familiar story. (Rev: BL 12/15/10) [398.2]

2543 Seabrooke, Brenda. *Wolf Pie* (1–3). Illus. by Liz Callen. 2010, Clarion $16 (978-0-547-04403-3). 48pp. In this fractured fairy tale, Wilfong the wolf fails to blow down the Pygg brothers' nice brick house and instead camps outside, eventually becoming their friend and protector. (Rev: LMC 10/10; SLJ 8/1/10) [398.2]

2544 Singer, Marilyn. *Mirror Mirror: A Book of Reversible Verse* (2–5). Illus. by Josée Masse. 2010, Dutton $16.99 (978-0-525-47901-7). 32pp. Clever "reverso" wordplay provides a new angle on some well-loved fairy tales as different pairs of perspectives are offered in verse. Lexile 1040 (Rev: BL 1/1/10*; HB 3–4/10; LMC 5–6/10; SLJ 1/1/10*) [811]

2545 Spirin, Gennady. *Little Red Riding Hood* (K–2). Illus. by author. 2010, Marshall Cavendish $17.99 (978-0-7614-5704-6). 32pp. A handsomely illustrated version that is close to the original and features images

inspired by 17th-century Holland. (Rev: BL 11/1/10; LMC 11–12/10; SLJ 9/1/10) [398.2]

2546 *Three Little Pigs* (PS–1). Illus. by Bernadette Watts. 2012, NorthSouth $16.95 (978-073584058-4). 32pp. With dramatic, warm artwork, this is a retelling of the classic tale about the pigs being tormented by a wolf. (Rev: BL 1/1/12; LMC 8–9/12; SLJ 1/12) [398.2]

Folklore

General

2547 Davis, David. *Fandango Stew* (PS–4). Illus. by Ben Galbraith. 2011, Sterling $14.95 (978-1-4027-6527-8). 32pp. This frontier version of the familiar "Stone Soup" tale features two hard-up hombres, Slim and his grandson Luis, who make a delicious pot of soup from one lowly fandango bean. Lexile AD820L (Rev: BL 3/15/11; LMC 8–9/10; SLJ 4/11) [398.2]

2548 Husain, Shahrukh. *The Wise Fool: Fables from the Islamic World* (1–5). Illus. by Micha Archer. 2011, Barefoot $19.99 (978-1-846-86226-7). 64pp. A retelling of 22 folktales about Mulla Nasreddin Hoca, a wise man remembered for his insightful and humorous stories. (Rev: BL 11/15/11; SLJ 9/1/11) [398.2]

2549 Yolen, Jane, and Heidi E. Y. Stemple. *The Barefoot Book of Dance Stories* (1–4). Illus. by Helen Cann. 2010, Barefoot $23.99 (978-1-84686-219-9). 96pp. Eight dance-based folktales and fables from around the world are collected in this beautifully illustrated book that includes notes about the style and steps of each dance (waltz, polka, reels, and so forth). (Rev: BL 1/1–15/11; SLJ 12/1/10) [792.8]

Africa

2550 Onyefulu, Ifeoma. *The Girl Who Married a Ghost and Other Tales from Nigeria* (2–5). Illus. by Julia Cairns. 2010, Frances Lincoln $15.95 (978-1-84780-176-0). 112pp. A collection of stories that reflect the concerns and dreams of the peoples of Nigeria. (Rev: BL 12/15/10; SLJ 3/1/11) [398.2]

Asia

China

2551 Maddern, Eric. *The King and the Seed* (K–3). Illus. by Paul Hess. 2009, Frances Lincoln $16.95 (978-1-84507-926-0). 28pp. Young Jack's honesty is rewarded with appointment as heir to the throne in this handsome retelling of a Chinese Mandarin story, featuring detailed watercolor and colored pencil illustrations. (Rev: BL 1/1/10; SLJ 1/1/10) [398.20951]

India

2552 McDermott, Gerald. *Monkey: A Trickster Tale from India* (PS–2). Illus. by author. 2011, Harcourt $16.99 (978-0-15-216596-3). 32pp. This Buddhist trickster tale, in which Crocodile and Monkey vie for superiority, is enhanced by McDermott's signature illustrations. (Rev: BL 4/15/11; HB 5–6/11; SLJ 4/11*) [398.2]

Japan

2553 Henrichs, Wendy. *I Am Tama, Lucky Cat: A Japanese Legend* (K–3). Illus. by Yoshiko Jaeggi. 2011, Peachtree $16.95 (978-1-56145-589-8). 32pp. Describes the origins of the beckoning cat and how it came to be a symbol of good luck. (Rev: BLO 11/15/11; SLJ 12/1/11) [398.2]

2554 Macdonald, Margaret Read, reteller. *The Boy from the Dragon Palace: A Folktale from Japan* (PS–3). Illus. by Sachiko Yoshikawa. 2011, Whitman $16.99 (978-0-8075-7513-0). Unpaged. A greedy flower seller realizes his personal fortunes are tied to the kindness he expresses towards others in this richly illustrated folktale. (Rev: HB 11–12/11; LMC 1–2/12; SLJ 8/1/11) [398.2]

Europe

Central and Eastern Europe

2555 Aylesworth, Jim. *The Mitten* (PS–2). Illus. by Barbara McClintock. 2009, Scholastic $16.99 (978-0-439-92544-0). 32pp. In this retelling of a beloved Ukrainian tale, a young boy's lost mitten becomes a warm refuge for a variety of woodland animals. (Rev: BL 11/1/09*; LMC 11–12/09; SLJ 12/1/09*) [398.2]

Germany

2556 Coombs, Kate. *Hans My Hedgehog: A Tale from the Brothers Grimm* (K–3). Illus. by John Nickle. 2012, Atheneum $16.99 (978-141691533-1). 40pp. Half hedgehog, half human, Hans seeks understanding and acceptance in an enchanted woodland, where he proves adept at breaking spells and giving guidance. (Rev: BL 1/1/12; LMC 5–6/12; SLJ 1/12) [398.2]

2557 Morpurgo, Michael. *The Pied Piper of Hamelin* (3–6). Illus. by Emma Chichester Clark. 2011, Candlewick $16.99 (978-0-7636-4824-4). 64pp. In this attractive retelling narrated by an orphan who uses a crutch, Hamelin is a town with a vast divide between the lives of rich and poor, and the rats are shown invading every inch. (Rev: BL 1/1/12; HB 1–2/12; SLJ 11/1/11) [398.2]

Great Britain and Ireland

2558 Artell, Mike. *Jacques and de Beanstalk* (PS–2). Illus. by Jim Harris. 2010, Dial $16.99 (978-0-8037-2816-5). 32pp. In this Cajun adaptation of the classic story, Jacques is depicted as a hard-working youngster lured by the smarmy magic bean man; a glossary provides help with the dialect. (Rev: BLO 2/1/10; SLJ 4/1/10) [398.2]

2559 Bunting, Eve. *Finn McCool and the Great Fish* (1–3). Illus. by Zachary Pullen. 2010, Sleeping Bear $16.95 (978-1-58536-366-7). 32pp. In this story, Ireland's mythological giant seeks wisdom from a salmon. (Rev: BL 4/1/10; SLJ 4/1/10) [398.2]

2560 MacDonald, Margaret Read. *Too Many Fairies: A Celtic Tale* (K–2). Illus. by Susan Mitchell. 2010, Marshall Cavendish $17.99 (978-0-7614-5604-9). 32pp. In this Scottish-Irish folktale an old woman who hates housework initially welcomes some helpful fairies but soon finds their noise too irritating — at which point

the fairies undo all their good work. (Rev: BL 4/15/10; LMC 8–9/10; SLJ 4/1/10) [398.2]

2561 Matthews, John. *Arthur of Albion* (4–8). Illus. by Pavel Tatarnikov. 2008, Barefoot $24.99 (978-184686049-2). 96pp. This compendium includes ten Arthurian legends ranging from familiar to obscure and interspersed with background information. (Rev: BLO 10/15/08) [398.2]

2562 San Souci, Robert D. *Robin Hood and the Golden Arrow* (1–3). Illus. by E. B. Lewis. 2010, Scholastic $17.99 (978-0-439-62538-8). 32pp. Robin Hood dons a disguise to trick the sheriff and win a contest designed to trap him. (Rev: BL 10/15/10; LMC 1–2/11; SLJ 10/1/10) [398.2]

Greece and Italy

2563 Gray, Luli. *Ant and Grasshopper* (PS–2). Illus. by Giuliano Ferri. 2011, Simon & Schuster $16.99 (978-1-4169-5140-7). 32pp. In this retelling, cautious Ant prepares carefully for winter while happy-go-lucky Grasshopper prefers to play the fiddle and sing, and the two eventually find they are in fact in harmony. (Rev: BL 2/15/11; SLJ 2/1/11*) [398.2]

2564 Hartman, Bob. *Mr. Aesop's Story Shop* (K–3). Illus. by Jago. 2011, IPG/Lion $14.99 (978-074596915-2). 48pp. Aesop himself relates 10 familiar fables from his spot in the marketplace in this well-illustrated collection. (Rev: BL 8/11) [398]

2565 Hoberman, Mary Ann. *You Read to Me, I'll Read to You: Very Short Fables to Read Together* (1–4). Illus. by Michael Emberley. 2010, Little, Brown $16.99 (978-0-316-04117-1). 32pp. Designed for two voices, this collection features 13 Aesop fables retold in verse and accompanied by lively illustrations. ℮ Lexile AD330L (Rev: BL 1/1–15/11; SLJ 4/11) [811]

2566 Lowry, Amy. *Fox Tails: Four Fables from Aesop* (K–2). Illus. by author. 2012, Holiday House $16.95 (978-082342400-9). 32pp. Four fables featuring foxes are melded into one in this subtly humorous introduction to Aesop's works for young people. (Rev: BL 2/15/12*; LMC 8=912; SLJ 4/1/12) [398.2]

2567 Morrison, Toni, and Slade Morrison. *The Tortoise or the Hare* (PS–2). Illus. by Joe Cepeda. 2010, Simon & Schuster $16.99 (978-1-4169-8334-7). 32pp. In this Aesop rewrite, a fast hare and a ponderous tortoise announce that it's not about whether you win or lose, it's about being friends and good sports. (Rev: BL 11/1/10; LMC 11–12/10; SLJ 10/1/10) [398.2]

2568 Naidoo, Beverley, reteller. *Aesop's Fables* (1–4). Illus. by Piet Grobler. 2011, Frances Lincoln $18.95 (978-1-84780-007-7). 52pp. Sixteen fables are portrayed in an African setting in this vivid collection that includes a few words from varied African languages. (Rev: SLJ 11/1/11*) [398.2]

2569 O'Malley, Kevin. *The Great Race* (K–2). Illus. by author. 2011, Walker $16.99 (978-0-8027-2158-7). 32pp. In an entertaining twist on the tortoise vs. hare story, grumpy Nate Tortoise challenges arrogant Lever Lapin to a race and beats him while he's busy signing autographs. (Rev: BL 4/1/11; LMC 10/11; SLJ 5/1/11) [398.2]

2570 Percy, Graham, reteller. *The Ant and the Grass-hopper* (1–3). Illus. by reteller. Series: Aesop's Fables. 2009, The Child's World LB $27.07 (978-1-60253-201-4). 32pp. Aesop's well-loved fable about the busy ant and the lazy grasshopper gets an update for younger readers. Also use *The Lion and the Mouse* (2009). (Rev: LMC 3–4/10; SLJ 1/1/10) [398.2]

2571 Sharpe, Leah Marinsky, reteller. *The Goat-Faced Girl: A Classic Italian Folktale* (2–4). Illus. by Jane Marinsky. 2009, Godine $16.95 (978-1-56792-393-3). 32pp. A beautiful but lazy princess learns her lesson when her adoptive mother, a sorceress, gives her the head of a goat to teach her a lesson about the value of beauty. (Rev: SLJ 1/1/10*) [398.2]

Scandinavia

2572 Yolen, Jane. *Sister Bear: A Norse Tale* (K–2). Illus. by Linda Graves. 2011, Marshall Cavendish $17.99 (978-076145958-3). 32pp. On their way to visit the King of Denmark, Halva and her dancing bear succeed in dealing with a pesky band of trolls. (Rev: BLO 11/15/11; SLJ 10/1/11) [398.2]

Spain and Portugal

2573 Kimmel, Eric A. *Medio Pollito: A Spanish Tale* (K–2). Illus. by Valeria Docampo. 2010, Marshall Cavendish $17.99 (978-0-7614-5705-3). 32pp. The half-chick of the traditional folk tale (he has one leg, one eye, one wing . . .) sets off for Madrid and has various adventures with help from friends he meets along the way. (Rev: BL 9/1/10; LMC 1–2/11; SLJ 9/1/10) [398.2094]

Jewish Folklore

2574 Kimmelman, Leslie. *The Little Red Hen and the Passover Matzah* (PS–1). Illus. by Paul Meisel. 2010, Holiday House $16.95 (978-0-8234-1952-4). 32pp. In this version of The Little Red Hen, the plucky protagonist exclaims "Oy gevalt!" as Passover approaches and "What chutzpah!" when her lazy friends show up to the seder dinner she's had to make by herself. (Rev: BL 2/1/10; HB 5–6/10; SLJ 3/1/10*) [398.2]

2575 Stampler, Ann Redisch, reteller. *The Rooster Prince of Breslov* (1–3). Illus. by Eugene Yelchin. 2010, Clarion $16.99 (978-0-618-98974-4). 32pp. The well-loved Yiddish folktale about an unlikely old man who cures a prince who is behaving like a rooster is presented with bright illustrations. Lexile AD790L (Rev: HB 9–10/10; LMC 1–2/11; SLJ 10/1/10*)

Middle East

2576 Tarnowska, Wafa'. *The Arabian Nights* (4–8). Illus. by Carole Hénaff. 2010, Barefoot $24.99 (978-1-84686-122-2). 128pp. Eight of Scheherazade's tales — including Aladdin but also ones that will not be familiar to most children — are presented with evocative illustrations. (Rev: BL 1/1–15/11; SLJ 2/1/11*) [398.2]

North America

Canada

2577 Kimmel, Eric A. *The Flying Canoe: A Christmas Story* (1–3). Illus. by Daniel San Souci. 2011, Holiday House $16.95 (978-082341730-8). 32pp. In this French-Canadian tale, a group of fur traders are spirited away to Montreal via a flying canoe on the night before Christmas. (Rev: BL 9/15/11; SLJ 10/1/11) [398.2]

Mythology

General and Miscellaneous

2578 Malam, John. *Dragons* (4–7). Series: Mythologies. 2010, Black Rabbit LB $28.50 (978-1-59566-982-7). 32pp. Malam looks at dragons, with and without wings, in legends around the world; with color illustrations and many sidebars, this book is aimed at reluctant readers. Also use *Fairies* (2010), *Giants,* and *Monsters* (both 2012). (Rev: LMC 10/10; SLJ 4/1/10) [398.24]

2579 Ollhoff, Jim. *Indian Mythology* (4–7). Series: The World of Mythology. 2011, ABDO LB $27.07 (978-1-61714-722-7). 32pp. With chapters on Brahma, Vishnu, Shiva, and Kali, this is a clear introduction to Hindu gods and goddesses. (Rev: BL 2/1/12; SLJ 12/1/11) [398.20954]

2580 Ollhoff, Jim. *Japanese Mythology* (4–7). Series: The World of Mythology. 2011, ABDO LB $27.07 (978-1-61714-723-4). 32pp. With chapters on Amaterasu, O-Kuni-Nushi, and Jimmu, this is a clear introduction to Japanese gods and goddesses. (Rev: BL 2/1/12; SLJ 12/1/11) [398.20952]

2581 Ollhoff, Jim. *Mayan and Aztec Mythology* (4–7). Series: The World of Mythology. 2011, ABDO LB $27.07 (978-1-61714-724-1). 32pp. This appealing introduction to the mythology and legends of the Mayan and Aztec cultures features concise text and eye-catching illustrations and reproductions. (Rev: BL 2/1/12; SLJ 12/1/11) [972.81]

2582 Ollhoff, Jim. *Middle Eastern Mythology* (4–7). Series: The World of Mythology. 2011, ABDO LB $27.07 (978-1-61714-725-8). 32pp. This appealing introduction to the mythology and legends of the Middle East provides information on various Mesopotamian and Canaanite gods and goddesses. (Rev: BL 2/1/12; SLJ 12/1/11) [398.20939]

2583 Williams, Marcia. *Ancient Egypt: Tales of Gods and Pharaohs* (3–5). Illus. by author. 2011, Candlewick $16.99 (978-0-7636-5308-8). 48pp. This blend of ancient Egyptian history and mythology features several short tales and comic-strip illustrations with period elements. (Rev: BL 10/1/11; SLJ 9/1/11) [398.2]

Classical

2584 Bryant, Megan E. *Oh My Gods! A Look-It-Up Guide to the Gods of Mythology* (4–7). Series: Mythlopedia. 2010, Franklin Watts LB $39 (978-1-6063-1026-7). 128pp. An irreverent, highly graphic volume that succeeds in conveying lots of information in an entertaining manner; with a useful map of ancient Greece, pronunciation guides, and a list of top 10 things to know about each divine being. Companion volumes are *All in the Family! A Look-It-Up Guide to the In-Laws, Outlaws, and Offspring of Mythology* (2009), *She's All That! A Look-It-Up Guide to the Goddesses of Mythology* and *What a Beast! A Look-It-Up Guide to the Monsters and Mutants of Mythology* (both 2010). (Rev: BL 10/1/09; LMC 3–4/10) [398.2]

2585 DiPrimio, Pete. *The Sphinx* (4–7). Illus. Series: Monsters in Myth. 2010, Mitchell Lane LB $21.50 (978-158415931-5). 48pp. This volume explores the role of the Sphinx in Greek and Egyptian mythology. (Rev: BL 6/1/11) [398.2209182]

2586 Karas, G. Brian. *Young Zeus* (1–4). Illus. by author. 2010, Scholastic $17.99 (978-0-439-72806-5). 48pp. An irreverent, lively account of Zeus's early life, telling how he came to rule heaven and earth. Lexile AD570L (Rev: BL 2/1/10; HB 3–4/10; LMC 5–6/10; SLJ 2/1/10*) [398.2]

2587 Kelly, Sophia. *What a Beast: A Look-It-Up Guide to the Monsters and Mutants of Mythology* (4–7). Illus. Series: Mythlopedia. 2009, Scholastic LB $39 (978-160631028-1); paper $13.95 (978-160631060-1). 128pp. Greek and Roman mythology is given a fresh, modern spin in this irreverent guide to the multidimensional beasts of legend. (Rev: BL 3/1/10; LMC 3–4/10*) [398.2]

2588 Napoli, Donna Jo. *Treasury of Greek Mythology: Classic Stories of Gods, Goddesses, Heroes and Monsters* (4–7). Illus. by Christina Balit. 2011, National Geographic $24.95 (978-1-4263-0844-4); LB $33.90 (978-1-4263-0845-1). 192pp. This large, eye-catching volume introduces 25 major characters in Greek mythology, outlining each one's origins, realm of power, and legendary story lines; the lyrical text is enhanced by humor and helpful back matter. (Rev: BL 12/1/11; SLJ 10/1/11*) [398.2]

2589 O'Connor, George. *Zeus: King of the Gods* (5–9). Series: Olympians. 2010, First Second paper $9.99 (978-1-59643-431-8). 78pp. The first of a series of graphic novels based on mythology, this is a good intro-duction to Zeus and his circle. (Rev: BL 1/1/10; LMC 8–9/10; SLJ 3/10) [741.5]

2590 Orr, Tamra. *The Sirens* (4–7). Illus. 2010, Mitchell Lane LB $21.50 (978-158415930-8). 48pp. This volume explores the importance of the sirens in mythologies around the Mediterranean. (Rev: BL 6/1/11) [398.20938]

2591 Townsend, Michael. *Amazing Greek Myths of Wonder and Blunders* (2–4). Illus. by author. 2010, Dial $14.99 (978-080373308-4). 160pp. An engaging graphic-novel version of some well-known myths, offering an accessible glimpse of the ancient world with touches of contemporary humor. (Rev: BL 1/1/10; LMC 11–12/10; SLJ 1/10; VOYA 6/10) [398.2]

2592 Tracy, Kathleen. *Cerberus* (4–7). Illus. Series: Monsters in Myth. 2010, Mitchell Lane LB $21.50 (978-158415924-7). 48pp. This volume explores the mythological importance of the three-headed dog. (Rev: BL 6/1/11) [398.20938]

Poetry

General

2593 Adoff, Arnold. *Roots and Blues: A Celebration* (4–8). Illus. by R. Gregory Christie. 2011, Clarion $17.99 (978-054723554-7). 96pp. In prose and poetry, Adoff explores the history of the blues from the days of slavery to the present. (Rev: BL 2/15/11*; LMC 1–2/11; SLJ 2/1/11*) [811]

2594 Crawley, Dave. *Reading, Rhyming, and 'Rithmetic* (1–3). Illus. by Liz Callen. 2010, Boyds Mills $17.95 (978-1-59078-565-2). 32pp. A humorous collection of 20 poems about all aspects of school life. (Rev: LMC 8–9/10; SLJ 4/1/10) [811]

2595 Dakos, Kalli. *A Funeral in the Bathroom: And Other School Bathroom Poems* (3–5). Illus. by Mark Beech. 2011, Whitman $14.99 (978-0-8075-2675-0). 48pp. A collection of poems on an unusual topic: activities that take place in a school bathroom (including the funeral for a goldfish). (Rev: LMC 1–2/12; SLJ 8/1/11) [811]

2596 Durango, Julia. *Under the Mambo Moon* (3–5). Illus. by Fabricio VandenBroeck. 2011, Charlesbridge $12.95 (978-1-57091-723-3). 48pp. Poems celebrate the Latin American people, music, and dance that young Marisol sees and hears at her father's record store. Lexile 840L (Rev: BL 6/1/11; SLJ 7/11) [811]

2597 Gaiman, Neil. *Instructions* (K–3). Illus. by Charles Vess. 2010, HarperCollins $14.99 (978-006196030-7). 40pp. A poetic guide to navigating fairy tales and returning home again. (Rev: BLO 6/10; VOYA 10/10) [821]

2598 George, Kristine O'Connell. *Emma Dilemma: Big Sister Poems* (PS–3). Illus. by Nancy Carpenter. 2011, Clarion $16.99 (978-0-618-42842-7). 48pp. Big sister Jessica finds her little sister Emma a source of joy and extreme annoyance, as expressed in 34 evocative poems. (Rev: BL 5/1/11; SLJ 2/1/11*) [811]

2599 Gerstein, Mordicai. *Dear Hot Dog: Poems About Everyday Stuff* (K–3). Illus. by author. 2011, Abrams $16.95 (978-0-8109-9732-5). 32pp. Topics from falling asleep to eating spaghetti are captured in this accessible collection. (Rev: BL 12/15/11; LMC 1–2/12*; SLJ 10/1/11) [811]

2600 Heard, Georgia, ed. *The Arrow Finds Its Mark: A Book of Found Poems* (3–6). Illus. by Antoine Guilloppe. 2012, Roaring Brook $16.99 (978-159643665-7). 48pp. An interesting anthology of "found" poems — from lists, advertisement, signs, tweets — that show poetry existing wherever you look. (Rev: BL 4/1/12; LMC 5–6/12; SLJ 4/12) [811]

2601 Hines, Anna Grossnickle. *Peaceful Pieces: Poems and Quilts About Peace* (2–5). Illus. by author. 2011, Henry Holt $16.99 (978-0-8050-8996-7). 32pp. Beautiful quilts provide a backdrop for poems about peace and tolerance. (Rev: BL 1/1–15/11*; LMC 5–6/11; SLJ 2/1/11) [811]

2602 Hoberman, Mary Ann. *The Tree That Time Built: A Celebration of Nature, Science, and Imagination* (3–7). 2009, Sourcebooks $19.99 (978-1-4022-2517-8). 222pp. A well-chosen selection of classic and contemporary poems that contemplate various aspects of the natural world. (Rev: BL 12/15/09; LMC 1–2/10; SLJ 1/10) [811]

2603 Hoberman, Mary Ann, ed. *Forget-Me-Nots: Poems to Learn by Heart* (3–5). Illus. by Michael Emberley. 2012, Little, Brown $19.99 (978-031612947-3). 144pp. One hundred and twenty-three accessible, memorizable poems are collected in this appealing volume that features some of poetry's biggest names. (Rev: BL 4/1/12; HB 5–6/12; LMC 8–9/12; SLJ 6/1/12) [811]

2604 Hopkins, Lee Bennett, selector. *Amazing Faces* (2–5). Illus. by Chris Soentpiet. 2010, Lee & Low $18.95 (978-1-60060-334-1). 40pp. A collection of multicultural poems celebrating human emotions, with contributions from authors including Joseph Bruchac, Pat Mora, Jane Yolen, and Langston Hughes, and illustrated with rich watercolors. (Rev: BL 4/15/10; LMC 10/10; SLJ 5/10) [811]

2605 Hopkins, Lee Bennett, selector. *I Am the Book* (2–5). Illus. by Yayo. 2011, Holiday House $16.95 (978-0-8234-2119-0). 32pp. Thirteen poems by writers including Naomi Shihab Nye, Jane Yolen, and Karla Kuskin celebrate the pleasures of books and reading. (Rev: BL 3/1/11; SLJ 4/11) [811]

2606 Jackson, Rob. *Weekend Mischief* (2–5). Illus. by Mark Beech. 2010, Boyds Mills $17.95 (978-1-59078-494-5). 32pp. A young boy's weekend is captured in this collection of 20 lively poems full of humor. (Rev: LMC 5–6/10; SLJ 4/1/10) [811]

2607 Janeczko, Paul B., selector. *A Foot in the Mouth: Poems to Speak, Sing, and Shout* (4–7). Illus. by Chris Raschka. 2009, Candlewick $17.99 (978-0-7636-0663-3). 64pp. Appealing poems ranging from evocative to nonsensical are chosen for their suitability to be read aloud and organized into useful categories. (Rev: BL 2/15/09*; HB 3–4/09; SLJ 3/1/09*; VOYA 2/10) [811]

2608 Judd, Jennifer Cole, and Laura Wynkoop, eds. *An Eyeball in My Garden: And Other Spine-Tingling Poems* (4–6). Illus. by Johan Olander. 2010, Marshall Cavendish $15.99 (978-0-7614-5655-1). 64pp. Forty-four creepy poems run the gamut from comic to downright eerie in this illustrated collection. ❢ (Rev: LMC 1–2/11; SLJ 11/1/10) [811]

2609 Katz, Susan. *The President's Stuck in the Bathtub: Poems About the Presidents* (2–5). Illus. by Robert Neubecker. 2012, Clarion $17.99 (978-054718221-6). 64pp. Interesting and often comic bits of presidential trivia are collected in this appealing collection of poems with cartoon illustrations. ❢ (Rev: BL 1/1/12; LMC 10/12; SLJ 9/12) [811]

2610 Lawson, JonArno. *Think Again* (5–8). Illus. by Julie Morstad. 2010, Kids Can $16.95 (978-1-55453-423-4). 64pp. Forty-eight poems look at the uncertainty and poignancy of first love. (Rev: BL 3/15/10; LMC 8–9/10) [811]

2611 Lewis, J. Patrick. *The House* (4–7). Illus. by Roberto Innocenti. 2009, Creative Education $19.95 (978-1-56846-201-1). 64pp. This unusual picture book for older children uses poetry and arresting images to present the passing of time from the perspective of a house. (Rev: BL 12/15/09; LMC 3–4/10; SLJ 1/10) [811]

2612 Lewis, J. Patrick. *Skywriting: Poems to Fly* (4–7). Illus. by Laslo Kubinyi. 2010, Creative Editions $17.95 (978-156846203-5). 32pp. This anthology of poems celebrates the adventure of flight, examining scenes in history from the myth of Icarus to the modern day. (Rev: BL 11/15/10; LMC 1–2/11; SLJ 11/1/10) [811.54]

2613 Mitton, Tony. *Rumble, Roar, Dinosaur! More Prehistoric Poems with Lift-the-Flap Surprises!* (PS–2).

Illus. by Lynne Chapman. 2010, Kingfisher $12.99 (978-0-7534-1932-8). Unpaged. This interactive book of poems combines playful poems with appealing illustrations. (Rev: SLJ 5/1/10) [811]

2614 Myers, Walter Dean, and Christopher Myers. *We Are America: A Tribute from the Heart* (4–8). 2011, HarperCollins $16.99 (978-0-06-052308-4). 40pp. Fourteen short, free-verse poems explore key events and figures in American history ranging from Tecumseh and Abraham Lincoln to Jimi Hendrix and Barbara Jordan. (Rev: BL 5/1/11; SLJ 5/11) [811]

2615 Nelson, Marilyn. *Sweethearts of Rhythm: The Story of the Greatest All-Girl Swing Band in the World* (5–8). Illus. by Jerry Pinkney. 2009, Dial $21.99 (978-0-8037-3187-5). 80pp. Nelson offers up accessible, rhythmic poems that pay homage to an all-female New Orleans jazz band — the Sweethearts of Rhythm — from the 1940s in this lively, beautifully illustrated book. (Rev: BL 10/15/09; HB 11–12/09; LMC 11–12/09; SLJ 10/09; VOYA 12/09) [811]

2616 Raczka, Bob. *Lemonade: And Other Poems Squeezed from a Single Word* (2–5). Illus. by Nancy Doniger. 2011, Roaring Brook $16.99 (978-1-59643-541-4). 48pp. Word puzzles combine with short pitty verses in this fascinating collection of 22 poems. (Rev: BL 12/15/10*; HB 3–4/11; LMC 5–6/11; SLJ 5/11) [811]

2617 Salas, Laura Purdie. *BookSpeak! Poems About Books* (2–5). Illus. by Josee Bisaillon. 2011, Clarion $16.99 (978-054722300-1). 32pp. This quirky collection of diverse poems looks at all the aspects of books, from plot to cover and index. (Rev: BLO 11/15/11) [811]

2618 Shange, Ntozake. *We Troubled the Waters* (4–8). Illus. by Rod Brown. 2009, Amistad $16.99 (978-0-06-133735-2); LB $17.89 (978-0-06-133737-6). 32pp. This is a moving collection of unflinching poems portraying the brutality of racism, with stark artwork. (Rev: BL 10/1/09*; SLJ 12/09) [811]

2619 Shapiro, Sheryl, and Simon Shapiro. *Better Together* (PS–1). Illus. by Dušan Petričić. 2011, Annick $19.95 (978-1-55451-279-9); paper $8.95 (978-1-55451-278-2). 32pp. Combinations of different everyday substances, foods, people, and even activities are explored in 13 funny poems. (Rev: BL 6/1/11; SLJ 7/11) [811]

2620 Shields, Carol Diggory. *Someone Used My Toothbrush! And Other Bathroom Poems* (PS–3). Illus. by Paul Meisel. 2010, Dutton $16.99 (978-0-525-47937-6). 40pp. Everything from brushing teeth to doing icky chores is presented in this playful collection of bathroom poems. (Rev: BL 4/1/10; LMC 8–9/10; SLJ 5/1/10) [811]

2621 Singer, Marilyn. *A Stick Is an Excellent Thing: Poems Celebrating Outdoor Play* (PS–1). Illus. by LeUyen

Pham. 2012, Clarion $16.99 (978-054712493-3). 40pp. This collection of infectious poems celebrating outdoor play is enhanced by bright, colorful illustrations and an engaging layout. (Rev: BL 1/1/12; HB 1–2/12; SLJ 1/12) [811]

2622 Sklansky, Amy E. *Out of This World: Poems and Facts About Space* (3–5). Illus. by Stacey Schuett. 2012, Knopf $17.99 (978-037586459-9); LB $20.99 (978-037596459-6). 40pp. Twenty diverse poems accompanied by attractive digital illustrations treat the subjects of space travel and astronomy. (Rev: BL 4/1/12; LMC 8–9/12; SLJ 4/1/12) [811]

2623 Stevenson, Robert Louis. *A Child's Garden of Verses* (PS–5). Illus. by Barbara McClintock. 2011, HarperCollins $17.99 (978-0-06-028228-8). 80pp. McClintock's blend of charming spot art and full-page illustrations will attract new readers to the poems originally published in 1885. (Rev: HB 7–8/11; SLJ 8/1/11) [811]

2624 Swaim, Jessica. *Scarum Fair* (2–4). Illus. by Carol Ashley. 2010, Boyds Mills $17.95 (978-1-59078-590-4). 32pp. A collection of spookily humorous poems about the weird offerings at the tents and booths of Scarum Fair. (Rev: BLO 10/15/10; LMC 1–2/11; SLJ 11/1/10) [811]

2625 Yolen, Jane, and Andrew Fusek Peters, eds. *Switching on the Moon* (PS–1). Illus. by G. Brian Karas. 2010, Candlewick $21.99 (978-0-7636-4249-5). 95pp. An elegant anthology of 60 bedtime poems by writers including Tennyson, Plath, Langston Hughes, and Lee Bennett Hopkins. (Rev: BL 10/1/10; HB 11–12/10; SLJ 10/1/10*) [398.6]

African American Poetry

2626 Grady, Cynthia. *I Lay My Stitches Down* (4–7). Illus. by Michele Wood. 2012, Eerdmans $17 (978-080285386-8). 34pp. Drawing from the structures and discipline of a quilt, these free-verse poems — each consisting of 10 lines of 10 syllables — explore various aspects of the African American experience. (Rev: BL 2/1/12; HB 1–2/12; LMC 5–6/12; SLJ 1/12) [1.3.2.2]

2627 Greenfield, Eloise. *The Great Migration: Journey to the North* (2–4). Illus. by Jan Spivey Gilchrist. 2010, HarperCollins $16.99 (978-0-06-125921-0). 32pp. Free verse poems tell the story of the migration of a million African Americans from the rural South to the industrial North between 1915 and 1930, and eloquently express their hopes and regrets. **e** Lexile 730L (Rev: BL 2/1/11*; HB 1–2/11; SLJ 4/11*) [811]

2628 Hughes, Langston. *I, Too, Am America* (K–4). Illus. by Bryan Collier. 2012, Simon & Schuster $16.99 (978-144242008-3). 40pp. Hughes's famous poem is accompanied by inspiring, evocative illustrations; with

an illustrator's note about the role of Pullman porters. (Rev: BL 4/1/12; LMC 10/12*; SLJ 6/1/12) [811]

2629 Johnson, Dinah. *Black Magic* (PS–2). Illus. by R. Gregory Christie. 2010, Henry Holt $15.99 (978-0-8050-7833-6). 32pp. A young African American girl considers all the best things about the color black. (Rev: BL 2/1/10*; LMC 1–2/10; SLJ 2/1/10) [811]

2630 Shange, Ntozake. *Freedom's a-Callin Me* (4–7). Illus. by Rod Brown. 2012, HarperCollins $16.99 (978-0-06-133741-3). 32pp. Poems and paintings capture the danger, strife, and hope experienced by those who strove to escape from slavery via the Underground Railroad. (Rev: BL 2/1/12; HB 1–2/12; SLJ 12/1/11) [811]

2631 Smith, Hope Anita. *Mother Poems* (4–7). Illus. by author. 2009, Henry Holt $16.95 (978-0-8050-8231-9). 80pp. In simple free-verse poems, a young African American girl expresses her love for her mother, and the loss she feels upon her death. (Rev: BL 2/15/09; SLJ 4/1/09) [811]

Animals

2632 Blackaby, Susan. *Nest, Nook and Cranny* (3–6). Illus. by Jamie Hogan. 2010, Charlesbridge $15.95 (978-1-58089-350-3). 60pp. A collection of diverse poems about animals and their habitats. (Rev: BL 2/1/10; LMC 11–12/10; SLJ 3/10) [811]

2633 Bulion, Leslie. *At the Sea Floor Café: Odd Ocean Critter Poems* (5–8). Illus. by Leslie Evans. 2011, Peachtree $14.95 (978-1-56145-565-2). 45pp. Eighteen poems provide compelling glimpses into the lives of some of the more interesting and bizarre marine creatures. (Rev: LMC 11–12/11; SLJ 4/11) [811]

2634 Ehlert, Lois. *Lots of Spots* (PS–1). Illus. by author. 2010, Simon & Schuster $17.99 (978-1-4424-0289-8). 40pp. Collages and brief poems accompany illustrations of animals that sport spots. (Rev: BL 4/15/10; LMC 5–6/10; SLJ 8/1/10)

2635 Elliott, David. *In the Sea* (PS–2). Illus. by Holly Meade. 2012, Candlewick $16.99 (978-076364498-7). 32pp. Twenty different marine creatures are presented alongside simple odes to their habits and habitats. (Rev: BL 2/1/12*; SLJ 4/1/12) [811]

2636 Elliott, David. *In the Wild* (PS–2). Illus. by Holly Meade. 2010, Candlewick $16.99 (978-0-7636-4497-0). 32pp. With woodcut illustrations, this is a collection of short poems celebrating wild animals. (Rev: BL 7/10; LMC 11–12/10; SLJ 7/1/10*) [811]

2637 Franco, Betsy. *A Dazzling Display of Dogs* (K–3). Illus. by Michael Wertz. 2011, Tricycle $16.99 (978-1-58246-343-8). 40pp. All aspects of dogs are explored in these 34 funny, energetic, concrete poems. (Rev: BL 12/15/10; HB 1–2/11; SLJ 1/1/11*) [811]

2638 Gibson, Amy. *Around the World on Eighty Legs* (PS–3). Illus. by Daniel Salmieri. 2011, Scholastic $18.99 (978-0-439-58755-6). 56pp. Poems full of humor and wordplay introduce animals around the world, organized by continent. (Rev: BL 2/1/11; HB 3–4/11; SLJ 2/1/11) [811]

2639 Gottfried, Maya. *Our Farm: By the Animals of Farm Sanctuary* (K–3). Illus. by Robert Rahway Zakanitch. 2010, Knopf $17.99 (978-0-375-86118-5). 40pp. Abused farm animals at a shelter describe their happy lives in this handsome collection of poems. **e** (Rev: BL 3/1/10; LMC 3–4/10; SLJ 1/1/10) [811]

2640 Hauth, Katherine B. *What's for Dinner? Quirky, Squirmy Poems from the Animal World* (2–5). Illus. by David Clark. 2011, Charlesbridge $16.95 (978-1-57091-471-3); paper $7.95 (978-157091472-0). 48pp. Twenty-nine fun poems focus on the different ways the world's animals get their dinner. **e** (Rev: BL 2/15/11; LMC LMC 10/11; SLJ 3/1/11) [811]

2641 Lewis, J. Patrick. *What's Looking at You, Kid?* (PS–1). Illus. by Renee Graef. 2012, Sleeping Bear $14.95 (978-158536793-1). 32pp. Bright illustrations provide clues to lively rhymed riddles about animals and insects. (Rev: BLO 4/15/12; SLJ 5/1/12) [818]

2642 MacLachlan, Patricia, and Emily MacLachlan Charest. *I Didn't Do It* (PS–3). Illus. by Katy Schneider. 2010, HarperCollins $16.99 (978-0-06-135833-3); LB $17.89 (978-0-06-135834-0). Unpaged. Fourteen free poems are told from the dogs' perspective and convey doggy complaints and joys. (Rev: SLJ 10/1/10) [811]

2643 Mitton, Tony. *Gnash, Gnaw, Dinosaur! Prehistoric Poems with Lift-the-Flap Surprises!* (PS–3). Illus. by Lynne Chapman. 2009, Kingfisher $12.99 (978-0-7534-6226-3). Unpaged. A variety of different dinosaurs are accompanied by short, well-executed rhymes describing their habits in this brightly illustrated volume for budding dino buffs. (Rev: SLJ 11/1/09) [811]

2644 Prelutsky, Jack. *The Carnival of the Animals by Camille Saint-Saëns* (1–4). Illus. by Mary GrandPré. 2010, Knopf $19.99 (978-0-375-86458-2); LB $22.99 (978-0-375-96458-9). Unpaged. Poems composed to accompany Saint-Saëns' beloved orchestral work are collected here; a CD of the music and Prelutsky's readings is included. (Rev: SLJ 12/1/10*) [811]

2645 Rosen, Michael J. *The Hound Dog's Haiku and Other Poems for Dog Lovers* (2–4). Illus. by Mary Azarian. 2011, Candlewick $17.99 (978-0-7636-4499-4). 56pp. Beautiful woodcut illustrations enhance this collection of dog-related poetry. (Rev: BL 8/11; HB 9–10/11; LMC 11–12/11; SLJ 8/11) [811]

2646 Swinburne, Stephen R. *Ocean Soup: Tide-Pool Poems* (1–3). Illus. by Mary Peterson. 2010, Charlesbridge $16.95 (978-1-58089-200-1); paper $7.95 (978-1-58089-201-8). 32pp. Tide-pool animals are introduced in first-person verse accompanied by factual information and illustrations in this large-format book. (Rev: BL 1/1/10; SLJ 4/1/10) [811]

2647 Yolen, Jane. *An Egret's Day* (3–6). Illus. 2010, Boyds Mills $17.95 (978-1-59078-650-5). 32pp. This collection of photographs and short poems presents a look at the great egret's habitat, habits, and unique life. (Rev: BL 1/1/10; LMC 5–6/10; SLJ 3/1/10) [811]

Haiku

2648 Raczka, Bob. *Guyku: A Year of Haiku for Boys* (1–3). Illus. by Peter H. Reynolds. 2010, Houghton Harcourt $16.99 (978-0-547-24003-9). Unpaged. Addressing the seasons in order, this collection of haiku poetry celebrates the activities typical of boys in the outdoors. (Rev: BL 6/1/10; HB 11–12/10; LMC 5–6/11*; SLJ 9/1/10*) [811]

Holidays

2649 Brown, Calef. *Hallowilloween: Nefarious Silliness from Calef Brown* (2–5). Illus. by author. 2010, Houghton Harcourt $16.99 (978-0-547-21540-2). Unpaged. A collection of nonsense verse about zombies, werewolves, and other things Halloween, with suitably wacky illustrations. (Rev: SLJ 8/1/10*) [811]

Humorous Poetry

2650 Hopkins, Lee Bennett, ed. *Dizzy Dinosaurs: Silly Dino Poems* (K–2). Illus. by Barry Gott. Series: I Can Read! 2011, HarperCollins $16.99 (978-0-06-135839-5); paper $3.99 (978-0-06-135841-8). 48pp. Humorous poems about dinosaurs by writers including Marilyn Singer, Douglas Florian, and Rebecca Kai Dotlich are targeted at newly independent readers. (Rev: HB 3–4/11; SLJ 5/1/11) [811]

2651 Katz, Alan. *Poems I Wrote When No One Was Looking* (3–5). Illus. by Edward Koren. 2011, Simon & Schuster $17.99 (978-1416935186). 160pp. This book of comically irreverent poems covers such topics as changing a diaper, spelling mistakes, and embarrassing situations. **e** (Rev: BL 1/1/10; LMC 1–2/12; SLJ 11/1/11) [811]

2652 Kinerk, Robert. *Oh, How Sylvester Can Pester! And Other Poems More or Less About Manners* (PS–2). Illus. by Drazen Kozjan. 2011, Simon & Schuster $16.99 (978-1-4169-3362-5). 32pp. Full of wordplay, these 20 funny poems focus on etiquette. (Rev: BL 2/15/11; HB 3–4/11; SLJ 3/1/11) [811]

2653 Lear, Edward. *His Shoes Were Far Too Tight* (2–5). Ed. by Daniel Pinkwater. Illus. by Calef Brown. 2011, Chronicle $16.99 (978-0-8118-6792-4). 40pp. Ten poems showcasing Lear's talent for absurdity are collected in this brightly illustrated book. (Rev: BL 6/1/11; LMC 10/11; SLJ 6/11) [821]

2654 Levine, Gail Carson. *Forgive Me, I Meant to Do It: False Apology Poems* (2–5). Illus. by Matthew Cordell. 2012, HarperCollins $15.99 (978-006178725-6). 80pp. Borrowing from William Carlos Williams' poem "This Is Just to Say," Levine creates a collection of lighthearted poems poking fun in various directions including fairy tales. (Rev: BL 3/1/12*; HB 3–4/12; SLJ 2/12) [811]

2655 Prelutsky, Jack. *I've Lost My Hippopotamus* (2–4). Illus. by Jackie Urbanovic. 2012, Greenwillow $18.99 (978-006201457-3). 144pp. More than 100 diverse poems full of funny wordplay focus on many topics. (Rev: BL 12/15/11; SLJ 2/1/12*) [811]

2656 Prelutsky, Jack, selector. *There's No Place Like School* (K–3). Illus. by Jane Manning. 2010, HarperCollins $16.99 (978-0-06-082338-2); LB $17.89 (978-0-06-082339-9). 32pp. A collection of 18 short, humorous poems by writers including Lee Bennett Hopkins, Carol Diggory Shields, and Prelutsky himself. (Rev: SLJ 7/1/10) [811]

2657 Rasmussen, Halfdan. *A Little Bitty Man: And Other Poems for the Very Young* (PS–K). Trans. from Danish by Marilyn Nelson and Pamela Espeland. Illus. by Kevin Hawkes. 2011, Candlewick $15.99 (978-0-7636-2379-1). 32pp. This illustrated collection contains 13 of the Danish poet Rasmussen's nonsense poems. (Rev: BL 9/15/11; HB 9–10/11; SLJ 8/1/11*) [831]

2658 Silverstein, Shel. *Every Thing On It* (2–7). Illus. by author. 2011, HarperCollins $19.99 (978-0-06-199816-4). 208pp. This posthumous Silverstein collection features drawings and poems taken from the author's personal archive and never previously published. (Rev: BL 9/1/11; SLJ 9/1/11*) [811]

2659 Wheeler, Lisa. *Spinster Goose: Twisted Rhymes for Naughty Children* (K–3). Illus. by Sophie Blackall. 2011, Simon & Schuster $16.99 (978-1-4169-2541-5). 41pp. Naughty characters from various nursery rhymes and children's stories are sent to live with the crooked Spinster Goose (sister of Mother Goose) in these dark-

ly funny rhymes. (Rev: BL 2/15/11; HB 5–6/11; SLJ 3/1/11) [811]

Nature and the Seasons

2660 Cooling, Wendy. *All the Wild Wonders: Poems of Our Earth* (2–5). Illus. by Piet Grobler. 2010, Frances Lincoln $19.95 (978-1-84780-073-2). 48pp. John Milton, William Blake, and Ogden Nash are among the more than 30 poets represented in this anthology of poems about nature and the environment. (Rev: BL 11/1/10; SLJ 1/1/11) [811]

2661 Coombs, Kate. *Water Sings Blue* (1–4). Illus. by Meilo So. 2012, Chronicle $16.99 (978-081187284-3). 32pp. Beautiful watercolor illustrations accompany a range of poems celebrating underwater and seashore life. (Rev: BL 4/15/12*; HB 7–8/12; LMC 8–9/12*; SLJ 5/1/12*) [811]

2662 Davies, Nicola. *Outside Your Window: A First Book of Nature* (PS–2). Illus. by Mark Hearld. 2012, Candlewick $19.99 (978-076365549-5). 108pp. A large-format, poetic introduction to the seasons and the related changes in nature. (Rev: BL 4/1/12; SLJ 4/1/12) [808.81]

2663 Florian, Douglas. *Poetrees* (3–6). Illus. by author. 2010, Simon & Schuster $16.99 (978-1-4169-8672-0). 48pp. Striking, atmospheric illustrations enhance this poetic celebration of trees that is full of wordplay. (Rev: BL 3/1/10; HB 3–4/10; LMC 5–6/10; SLJ 2/1/10) [811]

2664 Florian, Douglas. *UnBEElievables: Honeybee Poems and Paintings* (2–5). Illus. by author. 2012, Simon & Schuster $16.99 (978-144242652-8). 32pp. This collection of informative poems explores the world of honeybees — their social order, hive structure, pollination, and threats facing them. (Rev: BL 4/1/12; HB 3–4/12; LMC 8–9/12*; SLJ 2/12) [811]

2665 Hopkins, Lee Bennett, ed. *Sharing the Seasons: A Book of Poems* (2–5). Illus. by David Diaz. 2010, Simon & Schuster $21.99 (978-1-4169-0210-2). 88pp. With 48 poems — 12 for each season — this well-illustrated collection represents the works of well-known writers including Carl Sandburg, Joseph Bruchac, and Hopkins himself. (Rev: BL 3/1/10*; LMC 3–4/10; SLJ 6/1/10) [811]

2666 Mordhorst, Heidi. *Pumpkin Butterfly: Poems from the Other Side of Nature* (2–5). Illus. by Jenny Reynish. 2009, Boyds Mills $16.95 (978-1-59078-620-8). 32pp. Twenty-three poems about nature are varied in both form and subject. (Rev: BL 11/1/09; LMC 1–2/10; SLJ 12/09) [811]

2667 Sidman, Joyce. *Dark Emperor and Other Poems of the Night* (3–6). Illus. by Rick Allen. 2010, Houghton Mifflin $16.99 (978-0-547-15228-8). 32pp. Poetry and science are combined with rich illustrations in this collection of diverse poems about life in the woods at night. Newbery Honor Book. ℮ (Rev: BL 6/1/10*; HB 9–10/10; LMC 1–2/11; SLJ 8/10) [811]

2668 Sidman, Joyce. *Swirl by Swirl: Spirals in Nature* (PS–3). Illus. by Beth Krommes. 2011, Houghton Mifflin $16.99 (978-0-547-31583-6). 40pp. A fascinating look at spirals in nature, with informative and lyrical free-verse text and eye-catching scratchboard illustrations. (Rev: BL 9/1/11*; SLJ 9/1/11*) [811]

2669 Sidman, Joyce. *Ubiquitous: Celebrating Nature's Survivors* (2–5). Illus. by Beckie Prange. 2010, Houghton Mifflin $17 (978-0-618-71719-4). 40pp. Beautifully illustrated, this collection of poetry and prose conveys factual information and playful imagery about organisms ranging from bacteria to coyotes to humans. ℮ (Rev: BL 1/1/10*; SLJ 3/1/10*) [811]

2670 Singer, Marilyn. *A Full Moon Is Rising* (2–4). Illus. by Julia Cairns. 2011, Lee & Low $19.95 (978-1-60060-364-8). 48pp. Seventeen poems follow a full moon as it rises around the globe. (Rev: BL 5/1/11; SLJ 6/11) [811]

Biography

Adventurers and Explorers

Collective

2671 Cummins, Julie. *Women Explorers: Perils, Pistols, and Petticoats* (4–7). Illus. by Cheryl Harness. 2012, Dial $17.99 (978-080373713-6). 48pp. This tribute to female explorers focuses on 10 fearless and brilliant adventurers virtually unheard of in the history books. (Rev: BL 3/1/12; SLJ 3/12) [920]

2672 Hagglund, Betty. *Epic Treks* (5–9). Illus. by Peter Bull. Series: Epic Adventure. 2011, Kingfisher $19.99 (978-0-7534-6668-1). 64pp. An exciting account of explorers' expeditions — including those of Lewis and Clark, Stanley and Livingston, and Amundsen and Scott, and the less-known Burke and Wills — with many graphics and technical details. (Rev: BL 11/1/11; SLJ 11/1/11) [920]

2673 Mooney, Carla. *Explorers of the New World: Discover the Golden Age of Exploration* (3–7). Illus. by Tom Casteel. Series: Build It Yourself. 2011, Nomad paper $15.95 (978-1-936313-44-0). 120pp. With chapters focusing on Columbus, Cabot, Magellan, and the Spanish conquistadors, this volume gives an overview of the men who discovered and later explored the New World. (Rev: SLJ 9/1/11) [910.9]

2674 Mundy, Robyn, and Nigel Rigby. *Epic Voyages* (5–9). Illus. Series: Epic Adventure. 2011, Kingfisher $19.99 (978-0-7534-6574-5). 64pp. Magellan, Cook, Shackleton, Heyerdahl, and the more recent Chichester are the focus of this large-format volume full of gripping accounts and color photographs. (Rev: BL 11/1/11; SLJ 5/11) [910.4]

2675 Phelan, Matt. *Around the World* (4–7). Illus. by author. 2011, Candlewick $24.99 (978-076363619-7). 240pp. In graphic novel form, Phelan tells the story of three 19th-century adventurers inspired by Verne's *Around the World in Eighty Days*: Thomas Stevens, a bicyclist; reporter Nellie Bly; and retired sea captain Joshua Slocum. (Rev: BL 9/15/11*; HB 11–12/11; LMC 1–2/12; SLJ 9/1/11) [920]

2676 Stone, Tanya Lee. *Almost Astronauts: 13 Women Who Dared to Dream* (5–8). 2009, Candlewick $24.99 (978-0-7636-3611-1). 144pp. The story of the 13 women who fought to prove they were just as qualified, intelligent, and brave as the men who were training as astronauts in the early 1960s. ALSC Notable Children's Book, 2010; YALSA Excellence in Nonfiction for Young Adults Award Finalist, 2010; Amelia Bloomer Book List, 2010; Sibert Medal Winner, 2010. ∩ (Rev: BL 2/15/09; HB 3–4/09; LMC 8–9/09; SLJ 3/1/09*; VOYA 2/09) [920]

Individual

EARHART, AMELIA

2677 Burleigh, Robert. *Night Flight: Amelia Earhart Crosses the Atlantic* (1–4). Illus. by Wendell Minor. 2011, Simon & Schuster $16.99 (978-1-4169-6733-0). 40pp. Amelia Earhart's white-knuckle flight across the Atlantic in 1932 is described in spare, lyrical free verse text and gouache and watercolor illustrations. Lexile AD500L (Rev: BL 2/1/11*; HB 3–4/11; LMC 5–6/11; SLJ 2/1/11) [921]

2678 Fleming, Candace. *Amelia Lost: The Life and Disappearance of Amelia Earhart* (4–7). Illus. 2011, Random House $18.99 (978-0-375-84198-9); LB $21.99 (978-0-375-94598-4). 128pp. Fleming uses twin narratives — one a biographical overview of Earhart's life and the other the drama of her final flight — to create a compelling and suspenseful account. Lexile 930L (Rev: BL 12/1/10; HB 3–4/11; LMC 8–9/11*; SLJ 3/1/11*) [921]

HUDSON, HENRY

2679 Weaver, Janice. *Hudson* (3–6). Illus. by David Craig. 2010, Tundra $22.95 (978-0-88776-814-9). 48pp. A dramatic account of Henry Hudson's often unsuccessful explorations and his abandonment by a mutinous crew. (Rev: BL 6/1/10*; LMC 3–4/11; SLJ 9/1/10) [921]

QUIMBY, HARRIET

2680 Whitaker, Suzanne George. *The Daring Miss Quimby* (1–3). Illus. by Catherine Stock. 2009, Holiday House $16.95 (978-082341996-8). 32pp. The story of Harriet Quimby, the first American woman to earn a pilot's license. (Rev: BL 8/09; LMC 3–4/10; SLJ 8/1/09) [921]

RIDE, SALLY

2681 Riddolls, Tom. *Sally Ride: The First American Woman in Space* (5–8). Illus. 2010, Crabtree LB $31.93 (978-077872541-1). 112pp. Chronicling her life from youth to adulthood, this biography presents a straightforward and clearly written portrait of astronaut Sally Ride. (Rev: BL 1/1–15/11) [911]

SMITH, ELINOR

2682 Brown, Tami Lewis. *Soar, Elinor!* (2–4). Illus. by Francois Roca. 2010, Farrar $16.99 (978-0-374-37115-9). 40pp. Introduces the life of Elinor Smith, who became a licensed pilot at the age of 16 in 1928 and went on to become a test pilot. Lexile AD780L (Rev: BL 12/15/10; LMC 1–2/11; SLJ 11/1/10) [921]

Artists, Composers, Entertainers, and Writers

Collective

2683 Cotter, Charis. *Born to Write: The Remarkable Lives of Six Famous Authors* (4–8). 2009, Annick $24.95 (978-1-55451-192-1); paper $14.95 (978-1-55451-191-4). 168pp. E. B. White, C. S. Lewis, and Madeleine L'Engle are among the authors featured in this interesting volume that discusses the writers that inspired them. (Rev: BL 12/15/09; SLJ 12/09) [920]

2684 Raczka, Bob. *Before They Were Famous: How Seven Artists Got Their Start* (4–7). Illus. 2010, Millbrook LB $25.26 (978-0-7613-6077-3). 32pp. Durer, Michelangelo, Gentileschi, Sargent, Paul Klee, Picasso, and Salvador Dali are the artists featured here, each with a page devoted to their childhood plus early artwork and several other works including a self-portrait. (Rev: BL 11/1/10; LMC 3–4/11; SLJ 1/1/11) [920]

Artists

CLOSE, CHUCK

2685 Close, Chuck. *Face Book* (5–8). Illus. 2012, Abrams $18.95 (978-141970163-4). 64pp. Portrait artist Chuck Close offers insight into his creative process and how he has dealt with disability; with 14 beautifully reproduced works that can be mixed and matched. (Rev: BL 3/15/12; HB 5–6/12) [921]

DA VINCI, LEONARDO

2686 Augarde, Steve. *Leonardo da Vinci* (4–8). Illus. by Leo Brown. Series: Lifelines. 2009, Kingfisher $16.99 (978-0-7534-6174-7). 64pp. This book opens with an illustrated, diary-style narrative in which a fictional 10-year-old apprentice to Leonardo da Vinci reveals

glimpses into the artist's personality, process, and intellect; the second half of the book looks at everyday life in the Renaissance and details of da Vinci's work. (Rev: BL 11/1/09; SLJ 1/10) [921]

DAVE THE POTTER

2687 Hill, Laban Carrick. *Dave the Potter: Artist, Poet, Slave* (K–3). Illus. by Bryan Collier. 2010, Little, Brown $16.99 (978-0-316-10731-0). 40pp. This picture book chronicles the life of Dave, an unusual 19th-century slave who was a skilled and prolific potter. (Rev: BL 11/1/10; LMC 11–12/10; SLJ 8/1/10*) [921]

FRAZEE, MARLA

2688 Llanas, Sheila Griffin. *Marla Frazee* (3–5). Illus. Series: Children's Illustrators. 2012, ABDO LB $16.95 (978-161783246-8). 24pp. This volume explores the life from childhood of the illustrator who has earned two Caldecott Honors. (Rev: BL 5/1/12; SLJ 5/1/12) [921]

GUYTON, TYREE

2689 Shapiro, J. H. *Magic Trash: A Story of Tyree Guyton and His Art* (2–4). Illus. by Vanessa Brantley-Newton. 2011, Charlesbridge $15.95 (978-1-58089-385-5). 32pp. A picture-book biography of the artist who sees art in all kinds of everyday environments. (Rev: BL 11/1/11; SLJ 11/1/11) [921]

KAHLO, FRIDA

2690 Novesky, Amy. *Me, Frida* (1–3). Illus. by David Diaz. 2010, Abrams $16.95 (978-0-8109-8969-6). 32pp. Imaginative illustrations enliven this picture-book biography of Frida Kahlo, emphasizing how she came into her own as an artist after moving to San Francisco with her husband Diego Rivera. (Rev: BL 11/1/10; LMC 11–12/10; SLJ 12/1/10) [921]

LICHTENSTEIN, ROY

2691 Rubin, Susan Goldman. *Whaam! The Art and Life of Roy Lichtenstein* (4–7). Illus. 2008, Abrams $18.95 (978-081099492-8). 48pp. With many reproductions of his works and thoughtful, engaging text, this eye-catching book offers a portrait of Roy Lichtenstein and his diverse artistic achievements. Lexile 1030L (Rev: BL 11/1/08; HB 1–2/09; SLJ 10/1/08) [921]

MONET, CLAUDE

2692 Maltbie, P. I. *Claude Monet: The Painter Who Stopped the Trains* (3–5). Illus. by Jos. A. Smith. 2010, Abrams $18.95 (978-0-8109-8961-0). 32pp. This picture book tells the story of how Monet's son's love for trains inspired his father to create wonderful Impressionist scenes at Paris's first train station. (Rev: BL 11/1/10; LMC 11–12/10; SLJ 10/1/10) [921]

MORAN, THOMAS

2693 Judge, Lita. *Yellowstone Moran: Painting the American West* (1–3). Illus. by author. 2009, Viking $16.99 (978-0-670-01132-2). 32pp. In 1871 artist Thomas Moran joined an expedition to the West, documenting his journey in paint and his journal. (Rev: BL 11/1/09; LMC 11–12/09; SLJ 9/1/09) [921]

NOGUCHI, ISAMU

2694 Hale, Christy. *The East-West House: Noguchi's Childhood in Japan* (3–6). Illus. by author. 2009, Lee & Low $17.95 (978-1-60060-363-1). 32pp. A biography of Isamu Noguchi, Japanese American artist, sculptor, and landscape architect, focusing on his boyhood in Japan and his problems with being biracial. (Rev: BL 11/1/09; LMC 11–12/09; SLJ 9/1/09) [921]

PICASSO, PABLO

2695 Penrose, Antony. *The Boy Who Bit Picasso* (2–4). Illus. 2011, Abrams $16.95 (978-0-8109-9728-8). 48pp. The author recalls episodes shared with Picasso — his parents were friends of the artist — in this visually pleasing book that includes photographs taken by Penrose's mother. Lexile 800L (Rev: BL 6/1/11; SLJ 6/11) [709.2]

PINKNEY, JERRY

2696 Llanas, Sheila Griffin. *Jerry Pinkney* (3–5). Illus. Series: Children's Illustrators. 2012, ABDO LB $16.95 (978-161783247-5). 24pp. Portrays Pinkney's life from childhood, including his struggle with dyslexia, and his success as an award-winning illustrator. (Rev: BL 5/1/12; SLJ 5/1/12) [921]

RIVERA, DIEGO

2697 Marin, Guadalupe Rivera. *My Papa Diego and Me / Mi papa Diego y yo: Memories of My Father and His Art / Recuerdos de mi padre y su arte* (2–4). Illus. by Diego Rivera. 2009, Children's Book Press $17.95 (978-089239228-5). 32pp. This bilingual biography pairs 13 Diego Rivera paintings with his daughter's recollections about these works and their creation. (Rev: BL 11/1/09; HB 11–12/09; LMC 11/09) [921]

2698 Tonatiuh, Duncan. *Diego Rivera: His World and Ours* (1–3). Illus. by author. 2011, Abrams $16.95 (978-0-8109-9731-8). 40pp. In addition to introducing the artist and his work, this volume speculates about what Rivera would paint if he were alive today. (Rev: BL 5/1/11; SLJ 4/11) [921]

SAY, ALLEN

2699 Say, Allen. *Drawing from Memory* (4–7). Illus. by author. 2011, Scholastic $17.99 (978-0-545-17686-6). 64pp. Say tells the story of his creative awakening in words and illustrations, beginning with his childhood in World War II Japan. Lexile HL560L (Rev: BL 8/11*; SLJ 9/1/11*) [921]

SCHULZ, CHARLES

2700 Gherman, Beverly. *Sparky: The Life and Art of Charles Schulz* (4–8). Illus. 2010, Chronicle $16.99 (978-0-8118-6790-0). 128pp. A graphic-format biography of the creator of *Peanuts,* with many excerpts from the comic strip. (Rev: BL 6/10; SLJ 8/10; VOYA 6/10) [921]

SELZNICK, BRIAN

2701 Llanas, Sheila Griffin. *Brian Selznick* (3–5). Illus. Series: Children's Illustrators. 2012, ABDO LB $16.95 (978-161783248-2). 24pp. Covers Selznick's love of books as a child and his progression to become the acclaimed artist he is today. (Rev: BL 5/1/12; SLJ 5/1/12) [921]

TRAYLOR, BILL

2702 Tate, Don. *It Jes' Happened: When Bill Traylor Started to Draw* (2–4). Illus. by R. Gregory Christie. 2012, Lee & Low $17.95 (978-160060260-3). 32pp. Born into slavery and freed at the end of the Civil War, Bill Traylor started to draw at the age of 85 in 1939, producing moving works until his death in 1949. (Rev: BL 5/15/12*; HB 5–6/12; LMC 11–12/12; SLJ 6/1/12*) [921]

WARHOL, ANDY

2703 Christensen, Bonnie. *Fabulous! A Portrait of Andy Warhol* (3–6). Illus. by author. 2011, Henry Holt $16.99 (978-080508753-6). 40pp. An inspiring profile of Warhol as a boy facing many challenges who nonetheless went on to become a success. (Rev: BL 6/1/11; HB 7–8/11; LMC 10/11; SLJ 5/11) [921]

YOUNG, ED

2704 Young, Ed, and Libby Koponen. *The House Baba Built: An Artist's Childhood in China* (3–5). Illus. by Ed Young. 2011, Little, Brown $17.99 (978-0-316-07628-9). 48pp. Young's illustrations and Koponen's text tell the story of the artist's childhood in Shanghai as World War II grew closer. (Rev: BL 9/1/11*; SLJ 9/1/11*) [921]

Composers

BOULOGNE, JOSEPH

2705 Cline-Ransome, Lesa. *Before There Was Mozart: The Story of Joseph Boulogne, Chevalier de Saint-George* (1–3). Illus. by James E. Ransome. 2011, Random House $17.99 (978-0-375-83600-8); LB $20.99 (978-0-375-93621-0). 40pp. Mozart contemporary Joseph Boulogne rose from his obscure West Indian half-French, half-slave background to become a noted musical protégé. Lexile 1110L (Rev: BL 2/15/11; HB 3–4/11; LMC 5–6/11; SLJ 2/1/11) [921]

Entertainers

ALONSO, ALICIA

2706 Bernier-Grand, Carmen T. *Alicia Alonso: Prima Ballerina* (5–8). Illus. by Raúl Colón. 2011, Marshall Cavendish $19.99 (978-0-7614-5562-2). 64pp. Cuban ballerina Alicia Alonso's success in overcoming personal disability is chronicled in this free-verse biography. (Rev: BL 9/1/11*; SLJ 9/1/11) [921]

ARMSTRONG, LOUIS

2707 Weinstein, Muriel Harris. *Play, Louis, Play! The True Story of a Boy and His Horn* (3–5). Illus. by Frank Morrison. 2010, Bloomsbury $15.99 (978-159990375-0). 128pp. Explores Louis Armstrong's childhood from the point of view of his first cornet, bought from a pawn shop. (Rev: BL 2/1/11; LMC 3–4/11; SLJ 4/11) [921]

BAKER, JOSEPHINE

2708 Winter, Jonah. *Jazz Age Josephine* (K–3). Illus. by Marjorie Priceman. 2012, Atheneum $16.99 (978-141696123-9). 40pp. This picture-book biography introduces the dancer and describes her accomplishments and the considerable obstacles she faced. (Rev: BL 11/1/11*) [921]

BEYONCÉ

2709 Bednar, Chuck. *Beyoncé* (5–8). Series: Transcending Race in America. 2010, Mason Crest $22.95 (978-1-4222-1607-1). 64pp. Beyoncé Knowles is of African American and Creole descent, and this biography explains how she feels her background has influenced her life. Lexile 1180L (Rev: LMC 3–4/10; SLJ 1/10) [921]

BIEBER, JUSTIN

2710 Bieber, Justin. *Justin Bieber: First Step 2 Forever: My Story* (4–8). 2010, HarperCollins $21.99 (978-0-06-203974-3). 240pp. Bieber tells the story of his rise to stardom and includes many photographs of himself. e (Rev: SLJ 1/1/11; VOYA 2/11) [921]

DYLAN, BOB

2711 Golio, Gary. *When Bob Met Woody: The Story of the Young Bob Dylan* (3–5). Illus. by Marc Burckhardt. 2011, Little, Brown $17.99 (978-031611299-4). 40pp. The young Bob Zimmerman's fortune-changing trip from Minnesota to New York City to visit his idol Woody Guthrie is encapsulated in this biography that includes useful back matter. (Rev: BL 3/1/11; LMC 10/11) [921]

FITZGERALD, ELLA

2712 Orgill, Roxane. *Skit-Scat Raggedy Cat: Ella Fitzgerald* (2–4). Illus. by Sean Qualls. 2010, Candlewick $17.99 (978-0-7636-1733-2). 48pp. Ella Fitzgerald's rise from poverty to fame is chronicled in this compelling story full of jazz-infused language. (Rev: BL 6/10; LMC 11–12/10; SLJ 7/1/10) [921]

HENDRIX, JIMI

2713 Golio, Gary. *Jimi: Sounds Like a Rainbow: A Story of the Young Jimi Hendrix* (3–5). Illus. by Javaka Steptoe. 2010, Clarion $16.99 (978-0-618-85279-6). 32pp. This picture-book biography focuses on Jimi's childhood and early interest in music. (Rev: BL 11/1/10; LMC 1–2/11*; SLJ 9/1/10*) [921]

HENSON, JIM

2714 Krull, Kathleen. *Jim Henson: The Guy Who Played with Puppets* (4–7). Illus. by Steve Johnson. 2011, Random House $16.99 (978-0-375-85721-8); LB $19.99 (978-037595721-5). 40pp. A portrait of the creator of the Muppets, with details of his first job on TV at the age of 16. (Rev: BL 11/1/11; SLJ 10/1/11) [921]

HEPBURN, AUDREY

2715 Cardillo, Margaret. *Just Being Audrey* (1–3). Illus. by Julia Denos. 2011, HarperCollins $16.99 (978-0-06-185283-1). 32pp. This well-organized biography offers a glimpse into the life of the beautiful and famously kind actress. (Rev: BL 12/1/10; SLJ 4/11) [921]

HOUDINI, HARRY

2716 Biskup, Agnieszka. *Houdini: The Life of the Great Escape Artist* (2–4). Illus. by Pat Kinsella. Series: American Graphic. 2011, Capstone LB $29.32 (978-142965474-6). 32pp. Presents Houdini's various feats in graphic-novel format and includes an account of his death. (Rev: BL 3/15/11) [921]

2717 Carlson, Laurie M. *Harry Houdini for Kids: His Life and Adventures with 21 Magic Tricks and Illusions* (4–8). Illus. 2009, Chicago Review paper $16.95 (978-1-55652-782-1). 144pp. This attractive biography full of illustrations and sidebars also includes 21 simple tricks. e (Rev: BL 2/15/09; SLJ 4/1/09) [921]

2718 MacLeod, Elizabeth. *Harry Houdini* (2–3). Illus. by John Mantha. Series: Kids Can Read. 2009, Kids Can $14.95 (978-1-55453-298-8); paper $3.95 (978-1-55453-299-5). 32pp. This accessible biography concentrates on the renowned magician's most sensational feats. (Rev: SLJ 1/1/10) [921]

2719 Weaver, Janice. *Harry Houdini: The Legend of the World's Greatest Escape Artist* (4–7). Illus. by Chris Lane. 2011, Abrams $18.95 (978-1-4197-0014-9). 48pp. Covers Houdini's life and career as well as his interest in exposing fake mediums; historical sidebars add interest. (Rev: BL 12/1/11; LMC 3–4/12; SLJ 11/1/11*) [921]

JACKSON, MICHAEL

2720 Collins, Terry. *King of Pop: The Story of Michael Jackson* (4–7). Illus. by Michael Byers. 2012, Capstone LB $29.99 (978-142966015-0); paper $7.95 (978-142967994-7). 32pp. Though it omits the more controversial aspects of Jackson's life, this biography does include information about Jackson's turbulent early life. (Rev: BL 3/15/12) [921]

2721 Krohn, Katherine. *Michael Jackson: Ultimate Music Legend* (4–6). 2010, Lerner LB $26.60 (978-0-7613-5762-9). 48pp. Covering some of the unhappier aspects, Krohn gives a concise account of the performer's life, with emphasis on his childhood and the Jackson 5 and then on his later career and personal life. (Rev: BL 2/1/11; SLJ 5/10) [921]

2722 Pratt, Mary K. *Michael Jackson: King of Pop* (5–8). Series: Lives Cut Short. 2009, ABDO LB $32.79 (978-1-60453-788-8). 112pp. From his childhood through performing in the Jackson 5, then going solo, and the various controversies of his later life, this is a balanced profile of the performer who died at the age of 50. (Rev: BL 2/1/10; SLJ 3/10) [921]

JAY-Z

2723 Gunderson, Jessica. *Jay-Z: Hip-Hop Icon* (5–7). Illus. by Pat Kinsella. Series: American Graphic. 2012, Capstone LB $29.99 (978-142966017-4); paper $7.95

(978-142967993-0). 32pp. This evenhanded graphic-novel biography of Jay-Z focuses on the less glamorous aspects of stardom, showing readers the hard work and shrewd decision making it takes to succeed. (Rev: BL 3/15/12) [921]

LADY GAGA

2724 Heos, Bridget. *Lady Gaga* (5–8). Illus. 2011, Rosen LB $26.50 (978-143583574-0). 48pp. This biography chronicles Gaga's fairly conventional childhood growing up in Manhattan and documents her fast rise to fame. (Rev: BL 4/1/11) [921]

LAWRENCE, JENNIFER

2725 Krohn, Katherine. *Jennifer Lawrence: Star of The Hunger Games* (4–7). Illus. 2012, Lerner LB $26.60 (978-076138642-1); paper $8.95 (978-076138665-0). 48pp. Hunger Games star Jennifer Lawrence's meteoric rise to fame is captured in this colorful biography that looks at her life chronologically and includes many quotations and photographs. e Lexile 900L (Rev: BL 2/1/12; SLJ 1/12) [921]

LEDGER, HEATH

2726 Watson, Stephanie. *Heath Ledger: Talented Actor* (5–8). Series: Lives Cut Short. 2009, ABDO LB $32.79 (978-1-60453-789-5). 112pp. The brief life story of the Australian actor who died at the age of 28. (Rev: SLJ 3/10) [921]

M. I. A.

2727 Peppas, Lynn. *M. I. A.* (5–8). Illus. Series: Superstars! 2010, Crabtree LB $26.60 (978-077877249-1). 32pp. An interesting profile of the British rap star who came to prominence with the soundtrack of *Slumdog Millionaire*. (Rev: BL 6/1/11) [921]

MARCEAU, MARCEL

2728 Spielman, Gloria. *Marcel Marceau: Master of Mime* (2–5). Illus. by Manon Gauthier. 2011, Lerner/Kar-Ben $17.95 (978-0-7613-3961-8); paper $7.95 (978-0-7613-3962-5). Unpaged. A life of the French mime who was active in the Resistance in World War II and later studied in Paris. (Rev: LMC 11–12/11; SLJ 10/1/11) [921]

MILLS, FLORENCE

2729 Schroeder, Alan. *Baby Flo: Florence Mills Lights Up the Stage* (K–3). Illus. by Cornelius Van Wright. 2012, Lee & Low $18.95 (978-160060410-2). 40pp. African American singer and dancer Florence Mills first appeared on stage at the age of 3; the story of this woman who became famous during the Harlem Renaissance will fascinate young readers. (Rev: BL 5/15/12; LMC 10/12; SLJ 6/1/12) [921]

MOZART, MARIA ANNA

2730 Rusch, Elizabeth. *For the Love of Music: The Remarkable Story of Maria Anna Mozart* (1–3). Illus. by Steve Johnson. 2011, Tricycle $16.99 (978-1-58246-326-1). 32pp. A handsomely illustrated life of Mozart's older sister Maria Anna, also a piano virtuoso. (Rev: BL 11/1/10; HB 1–2/11; LMC 10/11; SLJ 1/1/11) [921]

ODETTA

2731 Alcorn, Stephen, and Samantha Thornhill. *Odetta: The Queen of Folk* (2–4). Illus. by Stephen Alcorn. 2010, Scholastic $17.99 (978-0-439-92818-2). 40pp. A spirited introduction to the life and career of folk singer and civil rights activist Odetta, from her birth in 1930 Alabama. (Rev: BL 11/1/10*; LMC 1–2/11; SLJ 11/1/10) [921]

REINHARDT, DJANGO

2732 Christensen, Bonnie. *Django: World's Greatest Jazz Guitarist* (3–6). Illus. by author. 2009, Roaring Brook $17.99 (978-1-59643-422-6). 32pp. Tells the story of how the famous jazz guitar player triumphed over a horrible hand injury. (Rev: BL 11/1/09*; LMC 11–12/09; SLJ 9/1/09*) [921]

SARG, TONY

2733 Sweet, Melissa. *Balloons over Broadway: The True Story of the Puppeteer of Macy's Parade* (K–2). Illus. by author. 2011, Houghton Mifflin $16.99 (978-0-547-19945-0). 40pp. Chronicles the life of Tony Sarg, a boy fascinated with puppets and gadgetry from a young age, and his role in creating the famous Thanksgiving Day parade. (Rev: BL 9/15/11*; SLJ 9/1/11*) [921]

SHAKUR, TUPAC

2734 Harris, Ashley Rae. *Tupac Shakur: Multi-Platinum Rapper* (5–8). Series: Lives Cut Short. 2009, ABDO LB $32.79 (978-1-60453-791-8). 112pp. Focusing on the achievements of a life tragically cut short, this appealing book reveals that Shakur was a gifted student in high school. (Rev: SLJ 3/10) [921]

SMITH, WILL

2735 Miles, Liz. *Will Smith* (3–6). Series: Culture in Action. 2010, Heinemann-Raintree $28.21 (978-1-4109-3397-3). 32pp. With eye-catching photographs and high-interest information, this is a useful biography of the rap star. Lexile 770L (Rev: LMC 3–4/10) [921]

STEFANI, GWEN

2736 Raum, Elizabeth. *Gwen Stefani* (3–6). Series: Culture in Action. 2010, Heinemann-Raintree $28.21 (978-1-4109-3395-9). 32pp. Everything a reluctant (or avid) reader needs to know about the singer-songwriter, fashion designer, and actress and her successes. Lexile 750L (Rev: LMC 3–4/10) [921]

SWIFT, TAYLOR

2737 Reusser, Kayleen. *Taylor Swift* (3–6). Illus. Series: Day by Day with . . . 2010, Mitchell Lane LB $25.70 (978-158415857-8). 32pp. Plenty of color photographs add appeal to this biography of country star Taylor Swift. (Rev: BL 6/1/11) [921]

WINFREY, OPRAH

2738 Weatherford, Carole Boston. *Oprah: The Little Speaker* (1–3). Illus. by London Ladd. 2010, Marshall Cavendish $17.99 (978-0-7614-5632-2). 32pp. This picture-book biography focuses on the first six years of Oprah's life, with her grandmother on a pig farm in Mississippi. (Rev: BL 3/15/10; SLJ 4/1/10) [921]

Writers

BARRIE, JAMES

2739 Yolen, Jane. *Lost Boy: The Story of the Man Who Created Peter Pan* (2–4). Illus. by Steve Adams. 2010, Dutton $17.99 (978-0-525-47886-7). 40pp. A compelling and handsome biography of Scotsman James Barrie, with many quotations. (Rev: BL 6/10; LMC 11–12/10; SLJ 7/1/10*) [921]

BRUCHAC, JOSEPH

2740 Parker-Rock, Michelle. *Joseph Bruchac: An Author Kids Love* (3–5). Series: Authors Kids Love. 2009, Enslow LB $23.93 (978-0-7660-3060-9). 48pp. With lengthy quotations, this profile touches on Bruchac's childhood and struggle to come to terms with his Native American heritage. (Rev: SLJ 11/1/09) [921]

CISNEROS, SANDRA

2741 Warrick, Karen Clemens. *Sandra Cisneros: Inspiring Latina Author* (5–8). Series: Latino Biography Library. 2009, Enslow $31.93 (978-0-7660-3162-3). 128pp. The story of the Mexican American author, the challenges she faced growing up, and how her books reflect her life. (Rev: SLJ 4/10) [921]

DICKENS, CHARLES

2742 Hopkinson, Deborah. *A Boy Called Dickens* (3–5). Illus. by John Hendrix. 2012, Random House $17.99 (978-037586732-3); LB $20.99 (978-037596732-0). 40pp. This fictionalized account of young Charles Dickens's life emphasizes his hard childhood and eventual return to school. (Rev: BL 12/15/11*; HB 1–2/12; LMC 3–4/12; SLJ 1/12) [921]

2743 Manning, Mick, and Brita Granstrom. *Charles Dickens: Scenes from an Extraordinary Life* (3–5). Illus. by Mick Manning. 2011, Frances Lincoln $18.95 (978-184780187-6). 48pp. Using a graphic-novel approach, this simple picture-book biography features first-person passages as well as third-person factual narrative. (Rev: BL 1/1/12; SLJ 1/12) [921]

HURSTON, ZORA NEALE

2744 Fradin, Dennis B., and Judith Bloom Fradin. *Zora! The Life of Zora Neale Hurston* (4–6). Illus. 2012, Clarion $17.99 (978-054700695-6). 192pp. The tumultuous life of African American writer Zora Neale Hurston is chronicled in this inspiring biography. (Rev: BL 2/1/12; HB 11–12/12; VOYA 4/12) [921]

NERUDA, PABLO

2745 Brown, Monica. *Pablo Neruda: Poet of the People* (1–3). Illus. by Julie Paschkis. 2011, Henry Holt $16.99 (978-0-8050-9198-4). 32pp. This handsome picture-book biography portrays the at-times turbulent life of the Chilean poet. Lexile AD970L (Rev: BL 1/1–15/11; HB 3–4/11; LMC 5–6/11; SLJ 2/1/11) [921]

PARK, LINDA SUE

2746 Parker-Rock, Michelle. *Linda Sue Park: An Author Kids Love* (3–5). Series: Authors Kids Love. 2009, Enslow LB $23.93 (978-0-7660-3158-6). 48pp. Park discusses her writing and researching process in this clearly written, interview-based biography. (Rev: SLJ 11/1/09) [921]

ROWLING, J. K.

2747 Peterson-Hilleque, Victoria. *J. K. Rowling: Extraordinary Author* (5–8). Series: Essential Lives. 2010, ABDO LB $32.79 (978-1-61613-517-1). 112pp. This volume describes Rowling's youth and personal life as well as her career, giving information on her efforts to get Harry Potter published, her success, and some of the key characters. (Rev: SLJ 3/1/11) [921]

SCIESZKA, JON

2748 Scieszka, Jon. *Knucklehead: Tall Tales and Mostly True Stories of Growing Up Scieszka* (4–7). 2008, Viking $16.99 (978-0-670-01106-3). 96pp. Scieszka's entertaining autobiography tells a story of growing up one of six irreverent brothers in Flint, Michigan. 🎧 (Rev: BL 9/1/08; HB 11–12/08; LMC 1–2/09; SLJ 10/1/08*; VOYA 12/08) [921]

SEUSS, DR.

2749 Guillain, Charlotte. *Dr. Seuss* (K–3). Illus. Series: Read and Learn Author Biographies. 2012, Heinemann LB $22 (978-143295959-3). 24pp. For early elementary readers, this simple biography uses a question-and-answer format to introduce students to the works and life of Dr. Seuss. (Rev: BLO 3/1/12; LMC 10/12) [921]

STOWE, HARRIET BEECHER

2750 Sonneborn, Liz. *Harriet Beecher Stowe* (5–8). Series: Leaders of the Civil War Era. 2009, Chelsea House $30 (978-1-60413-302-8). 112pp. Enhanced by a mix of illustrations, period documents, photographs, and concise sidebars, this book provides a balanced look at the author who inspired many to support abolitionism. (Rev: LMC 10/09) [921]

TWAIN, MARK

2751 Burleigh, Robert. *The Adventures of Mark Twain by Huckleberry Finn* (2–4). Illus. by Barry Blitt. 2010, Simon & Schuster $17.99 (978-0-689-83041-9). 48pp. With the expected colorful narration, Huck Finn tells the story of his creator Mark Twain's life; the humorous, old-fashioned illustrations enhance this picture-book biography and inform readers. Lexile AD750L (Rev: BL 2/15/11; SLJ 3/1/11*) [921]

WARREN, MERCY OTIS

2752 Woelfle, Gretchen. *Write On, Mercy! The Secret Life of Mercy Otis Warren* (2–5). Illus. by Alexandra Wallner. 2012, Boyds Mills $16.95 (978-159078822-6). 40pp. A profile of the woman who, at the time of the Revolution, wrote patriotic plays and poems as well as a three-volume history. (Rev: BL 4/15/12; LMC 11–12/12; SLJ 5/12) [921]

WILHEIM, LILY RENEE

2753 Robbins, Trina. *Lily Renee, Escape Artist: From Holocaust Survivor to Comic Book Pioneer* (4–7). Illus. by Anne Timmons. 2011, Lerner LB $29.27 (978-076136010-0); paper $7.95 (978-076138114-3). 96pp. With helpful back matter that provides historical context, this is the story of a Jewish girl who escapes from Germany in 1939 and goes on to become a cartoonist in America. 🅔 Lexile GN510L (Rev: BL 10/15/11; LMC 3–4/12; SLJ 11/1/11; VOYA 12/11) [921]

YACCARINO, DAN

2754 Yaccarino, Dan. *All the Way to America: The Story of a Big Italian Family and a Little Shovel* (PS–3). Illus. by author. 2011, Knopf $16.99 (978-0-375-86642-5). 40pp. Yaccarino tells the story of four generations of his family, starting with his great-grandfather, who came to the United States from Italy with a little shovel and a devotion to hard work and enjoying life. (Rev: BL 3/1/11; SLJ 3/1/11*) [921]

Contemporary and Historical Americans

Collective

2755 Brown, Monica. *Side by Side / Lado a lado: The Story of Dolores Huerta and Cesar Chavez / La historia de Dolores Huerta y César Chávez* (2–4). Illus. by Joe Cepeda. 2010, HarperCollins $16.99 (978-006122781-3). 32pp. The parallel stories of workers' rights advocates César Chávez and Dolores Huerta are presented in this brightly illustrated bilingual book. (Rev: BL 11/1/10; SLJ 11/10) [920]

2756 Freedman, Russell. *Abraham Lincoln and Frederick Douglass: The Story Behind an American Friendship* (5–9). Illus. 2012, Clarion $18.99 (978-054738562-4). 128pp. This attractive title offers a glimpse into the respectful friendship that grew between Frederick Douglass and Abraham Lincoln after Emancipation. (Rev: BL 2/1/12*; HB 5–6/12; SLJ 5/1/12*; VOYA 4/12) [920]

2757 George-Warren, Holly. *The Cowgirl Way: Hats Off to America's Women of the West* (5–8). Illus. 2010, Houghton Mifflin $18 (978-0-618-73738-3). 112pp. With many photographs, posters, quotes, and other elements, this is a comprehensive account of the activities of cowgirls on the western frontier. e Lexile 1180L (Rev: BL 8/10; HB 7–8/10; SLJ 7/10; VOYA 6/10) [920]

2758 Obama, Barack. *Of Thee I Sing: A Letter to My Daughters* (K–3). Illus. by Loren Long. 2010, Knopf $17.99 (978-0-375-83527-8); LB $20.99 (978-0-375-93527-5). 40pp. Obama uses the framework of a letter to his daughters to introduce 13 famous Americans who exemplify various virtues. (Rev: BLO 11/15/10*; SLJ 1/1/11) [920]

2759 Rosenberg, Aaron. *The Civil War: One Event, Six People* (4–6). Illus. Series: Profiles. 2011, Scholastic paper $6.99 (978-054523756-7). 160pp. This collective biography introduces six key players in the Civil War — Abraham Lincoln, Frederick Douglass, Clara Barton, George McClellan, Robert E. Lee, and Mathew Brady — and looks at their importance and influence. (Rev: BL 6/1/11; SLJ 6/11) [920]

2760 Waldman, Neil. *A Land of Big Dreamers: Voices of Courage in America* (3–5). Illus. by author. 2011, Millbrook $16.95 (978-0-8225-6810-0). 32pp. Thirteen Americans who have shown courage in the face of adversity are represented here in quotations, brief facts, and portraits. (Rev: BL 2/15/11; SLJ 3/1/11) [973]

2761 Winter, Jonah. *Wild Women of the Wild West* (3–5). Illus. by Susan Guevara. 2011, Holiday House $16.95 (978-0-8234-1601-1). 40pp. Calamity Jane, Belle Starr, and Annie Oakley are among the 15 women profiled here for their contributions on the western frontier. (Rev: BL 12/1/11; SLJ 11/1/11) [920]

African Americans

BRIDGES, RUBY

2762 Donaldson, Madeline. *Ruby Bridges* (3–6). Illus. 2009, Lerner LB $27.93 (978-0-7613-4220-5). 48pp. Tells the story of the first African American student to attend a newly integrated school in New Orleans in 1960, with information on Bridges's recent activism. (Rev: BL 2/1/10; SLJ 9/1/09) [921]

DESMOND, VIOLA

2763 Warner, Jody Nyasha. *Viola Desmond Won't Be Budged!* (2–4). Illus. by Richard Rudnicki. 2010, Groundwood $18.95 (978-0-88899-779-1). Unpaged. This book tells the story of a Canadian black woman who refused to move her seat in a movie theater in 1946. (Rev: BL 11/15/10; LMC 1–2/11; SLJ 12/1/10) [921]

DOUGLASS, FREDERICK

2764 Cline-Ransome, Lesa. *Words Set Me Free: The Story of Young Frederick Douglass* (2–4). Illus. by James E. Ransome. 2012, Simon & Schuster $16.99 (978-141695903-8). 32pp. This picture-book biography of Frederick Douglass emphasizes how learning to read enhanced his life. (Rev: BL 3/15/12) [921]

2765 Sterngass, John. *Frederick Douglass* (5–8). Series: Leaders of the Civil War Era. 2009, Chelsea House $30 (978-1-60413-306-6). 112pp. Enhanced by a mix of illustrations, period documents, photographs, and concise sidebars, this book provides a balanced look at the eloquent man who galvanized many in the fight against slavery. (Rev: LMC 10/09) [921]

HOLMES, BENJAMIN C.

2766 Sherman, Pat. *Ben and the Emancipation Proclamation* (1–3). Illus. by Floyd Cooper. 2010, Eerdmans $16.99 (978-0-8028-5319-6). 32pp. Tells the story of Benjamin Holmes, who surreptitiously learned to read while a young slave, and displayed this talent when a fellow slave prison inmate acquired a copy of the newspaper containing Lincoln's Emancipation Proclamation. (Rev: BL 2/15/10; LMC 10/10; SLJ 2/1/10) [921]

JACKSON, JESSE

2767 Linde, Barbara. *Jesse Jackson* (2–5). Illus. Series: Civil Rights Crusaders. 2011, Gareth Stevens LB $22.60 (978-143395682-9). 24pp. Covers Jackson's involvement in civil rights, his campaign for president, and his subsequent political work. (Rev: BL 10/1/11) [921]

KING, MARTIN LUTHER, JR.

2768 Watkins, Angela Farris. *My Uncle Martin's Big Heart* (PS–2). Illus. by Eric Velasquez. 2010, Abrams $18.95 (978-0-8109-8975-7). 32pp. Dr. Martin Luther King's niece tells the happy, gentle story of her relationship with her famous uncle. Lexile AD820L (Rev: BL 9/1/10; LMC 1–2/11; SLJ 10/1/10) [323.092]

2769 Watkins, Angela Farris. *My Uncle Martin's Words for America* (K–4). Illus. by Eric Velasquez. 2011, Abrams $19.95 (978-1-4197-0022-4). 40pp. Referring to key words used in his speeches, Martin Luther King Jr.'s niece describes her uncle's beliefs and work. (Rev: BLO 1/12; SLJ 10/1/11) [921]

NORTHUP, SOLOMON

2770 Fradin, Judith Bloom, and Dennis B. Fradin. *Stolen into Slavery: The True Story of Solomon Northup, Free Black Man* (5–8). Illus. 2012, National Geographic $18.95 (978-142630937-3); LB $27.90 (978-142630938-0). 128pp. Drawing on his memoir, this dramatic story tells of free black man Northup's ordeal

after he was kidnapped and sold into slavery in 1841. **e** (Rev: BL 2/1/12; SLJ 4/12) [921]

PARKS, ROSA

2771 Kittinger, Jo S. *Rosa's Bus: The Ride to Civil Rights* (2–5). Illus. by Steven Walker. 2010, Boyds Mills $17.95 (978-1-59078-722-9). 40pp. The life of Rosa Parks is framed by the story of the bus on which she famously refused to give up her seat. (Rev: BL 11/15/10; SLJ 12/1/10) [323.1196]

SHELTON, PAULA YOUNG

2772 Shelton, Paula Young. *Child of the Civil Rights Movement* (2–4). Illus. by Raúl Colón. 2009, Random House $17.99 (978-0-375-84314-3); LB $20.99 (978-0-375-95414-6). 40pp. The daughter of Andrew Young provides a memoir of her childhood experiences as a witness to the civil rights movement, including the exuberant march from Selma to Montgomery. Lexile AD960L (Rev: BL 2/1/10*; LMC 3–4/10; SLJ 12/1/09*) [323.1196]

TRUTH, SOJOURNER

2773 Horn, Geoffrey M. *Sojourner Truth: Speaking Up for Freedom* (4–7). Illus. Series: Voices for Freedom: Abolitionist Views. 2009, Crabtree LB $30.60 (978-077874824-3). 64pp. With many images and clear text, this is an attractive profile of the woman who fought for the rights of her people. (Rev: BL 2/1/10) [921]

2774 Pinkney, Andrea Davis. *Sojourner Truth's Step-Stomp Stride* (K–3). Illus. by Brian Pinkney. 2009, Hyperion $16.99 (978-0-7868-0767-3). 32pp. A dramatic portrait of the freed slave and her passion for abolition, emphasizing the power of speech and energy. (Rev: BL 11/15/09; LMC 5–6/10; SLJ 12/1/09*) [921]

TUBMAN, HARRIET

2775 Malaspina, Ann. *Harriet Tubman* (5–8). Series: Leaders of the Civil War Era. 2009, Chelsea House $30 (978-1-60413-303-5). 112pp. Enhanced by a mix of illustrations, period documents, photographs, and concise sidebars, this book provides a balanced look at the courageous woman who led so many to freedom. (Rev: LMC 10/09) [921]

Hispanic Americans

CHAVEZ, CESAR

2776 Adler, David A., and Michael S. Adler. *A Picture Book of Cesar Chavez* (1–4). Illus. by Marie Olofsdotter. 2010, Holiday House $17.95 (978-0-8234-2202-9). 32pp. A thorough and balanced overview of the life of the activist for migrant farm workers. (Rev: BL 7/10; LMC 3–4/11; SLJ 8/1/10) [921]

HUERTA, DOLORES

2777 Van Tol, Alex. *Dolores Huerta: Voice for the Working Poor* (5–8). Illus. Series: Crabtree Ground-breakers Biographies. 2010, Crabtree LB $31.93 (978-077872536-7). 112pp. Dolores Huerta's lifetime of advocacy for farm safety and environmental conscience is portrayed here in clear language and many black-and-white photographs. (Rev: BL 1/1–15/11; VOYA 12/10) [921]

2778 Warren, Sarah. *Dolores Huerta: A Hero to Migrant Workers* (K–3). Illus. by Robert Casilla. 2012, Marshall Cavendish $17.99 (978-076146107-4). 32pp. Dolores Huerta's fight for the rights of migrant workers begins in the classroom, where her students are too hungry and sick to learn. (Rev: BL 4/15/12; LMC 11–12/12; SLJ 5/1/12) [921]

Historical Figures and Important Contemporary Americans

BLY, NELLIE

2779 Macy, Sue. *Bylines: A Photobiography of Nellie Bly* (5–7). 2009, National Geographic $19.95 (978-1-4263-0513-9); LB $28.90 (978-1-4263-0514-6). 64pp. This well-researched photobiography of reporter Nellie Bly weaves together maps, period photographs, artifacts, and illuminating captions to paint a memorable portrait. (Rev: BL 8/09; SLJ 10/09) [921]

BROWN, JOHN

2780 Hendrix, John. *John Brown: His Fight for Freedom* (5–8). 2009, Abrams $18.95 (978-0-8109-3798-7). 40pp. Bold illustrations enhance this picture book for older readers that covers the famed abolitionist's life, ideals, and sometimes questionable actions. (Rev: BL 10/15/09*; LMC 3–4/10; SLJ 11/09) [921]

DAVIS, JEFFERSON

2781 Aretha, David. *Jefferson Davis* (5–8). Series: Leaders of the Civil War Era. 2009, Chelsea House $30 (978-1-60413-297-7). 112pp. Enhanced by a mix of illustrations, period documents, photographs, and concise sidebars, this book provides a balanced look at the leader of the Confederacy. (Rev: LMC 10/09) [921]

FRANKLIN, BENJAMIN

2782 Schroeder, Alan. *Ben Franklin: His Wit and Wisdom from A–Z* (1–3). Illus. by John O'Brien. 2011, Holiday House $16.95 (978-0-8234-1950-0). 32pp. An

attractive, alphabetical tour of Benjamin Franklin's life providing snippets of information about his inventions, personal life, politics, and public service. (Rev: BL 4/15/11; HB 5–6/11; SLJ 4/11) [921]

HALVORSEN, GAIL S.

2783 Tunnell, Michael O. *Candy Bomber: The Story of the Berlin Airlift's "Chocolate Pilot"* (4–7). 2010, Charlesbridge $18.95 (978-1-58089-336-7); paper $9.95 (978-1-58089-337-4). 110pp. The inspiring story of Lt. Gail S. Halvorsen, who brought joy to the children of West Berlin in 1948, when the city was isolated and short of all supplies. Lexile 1130L (Rev: BL 6/10*; HB 9–10/10; SLJ 7/10) [943]

HANCOCK, JOHN

2784 Raatma, Lucia. *A Signer for Independence: John Hancock* (5–8). Series: We the People. 2009, Compass Point LB $26.65 (978-0-7565-4122-4). 48pp. Accessible and well-illustrated, with a useful timeline, this book provides a balanced look at John Hancock. (Rev: LMC 10/09) [921]

JACKSON, STONEWALL

2785 Doak, Robin S. *Confederate General: Stonewall Jackson* (4–8). Series: We the People. 2009, Compass Point LB $26.65 (978-0-7565-4110-1). 48pp. Doak provides a balanced overview of the life and career of the enigmatic general, with a timeline and well-chosen illustrations. (Rev: LMC 10/09) [921]

2786 Koestler-Grack, Rachel A. *Stonewall Jackson* (5–8). Series: Leaders of the Civil War Era. 2009, Chelsea House $30 (978-1-60413-299-1). 112pp. Enhanced by a mix of illustrations, period documents, photographs, and concise sidebars, this book provides an even-handed profile of the general responsible for some significant military victories. (Rev: LMC 10/09) [921]

KENNEDY, EDWARD M.

2787 McElroy, Lisa Tucker. *Ted Kennedy: A Remarkable Life in the Senate* (4–7). Series: Gateway Biographies. 2009, Lerner LB $25.26 (978-0-7613-4457-5). 48pp. A useful resource for report writers, this biography has all the facts about the late senator's life and political service. (Rev: SLJ 8/09) [921]

KEY, FRANCIS SCOTT

2788 Kulling, Monica. *Francis Scott Key's Star-Spangled Banner* (1–3). Illus. by Richard Walz. Series: Step into Reading. 2012, Random House paper $3.99 (978-037586725-5). 48pp. For beginning readers, this is a simple portrait of Key's life and the War of 1812. ℮ (Rev: BL 12/15/11; SLJ 4/1/12) [921]

KNOX, HENRY

2789 Silvey, Anita. *Henry Knox: Bookseller, Soldier, Patriot* (2–5). Illus. by Wendell Minor. 2010, Clarion $17.99 (978-0-618-27485-7). 40pp. This biography tells the little-known story of Henry Knox's journey to procure heavy artillery to defend Boston in 1776, **e** (Rev: BL 9/1/10*; SLJ 12/1/10) [921]

LAFFITE, JEAN

2790 Rubin, Susan Goldman. *Jean Laffite: The Pirate Who Saved America* (1–4). Illus. by Jeff Himmelman. 2012, Abrams $18.95 (978-081099733-2). 48pp. Tells the story of the Jewish pirate born in Saint-Domingue, who settled in New Orleans, playing a role in the War of 1812, and became a respected businessman. (Rev: BL 3/15/12; SLJ 5/1/12) [921]

WEBSTER, NOAH

2791 Shea, Pegi Deitz. *Noah Webster: Weaver of Words* (4–7). Illus. by Monica Vachula. 2009, Boyds Mills $18.95 (978-1-59078-441-9). 40pp. This is a large-format, illustrated biography of Webster (1758–1843), who was a man of many interests but is best known for his dictionary of the American language. Lexile 1000L (Rev: BL 11/15/09; LMC 5–6/10; SLJ 11/09) [921]

Native Americans

BLACK ELK

2792 Nelson, S. D. *Black Elk's Vision: A Lakota Story* (5–8). 2010, Abrams $19.95 (978-0-8109-8399-1). 48pp. A look at the life of the Lakota medicine man who fought in the Battle of Little Bighorn and later traveled with Buffalo Bill's Wild West show before being injured at the massacre at Wounded Knee. (Rev: BL 3/15/10*; SLJ 4/10) [921]

JOSEPH, CHIEF

2793 Biskup, Agnieszka. *Thunder Rolling Down the Mountain: The Story of Chief Joseph and the Nez Perce* (4–7). Illus. by Rusty Zimmerman. Series: American Graphic. 2011, Capstone LB $29.32 (978-142965472-2). 32pp. A graphic novel account of the life of the Nez Perce leader and his efforts on behalf of his people. (Rev: BL 6/1/11) [921]

JUMPER, BETTY MAE

2794 Annino, Jan Godown. *She Sang Promise: The Story of Betty Mae Jumper: Seminole Tribal Leader* (2–5). Illus. by Lisa Desimini. 2010, National Geographic $17.95 (978-1-4263-0592-4); LB $26.90 (978-1-4263-0593-1). 48pp. Betty Mae Jumper, daughter of a French trapper and a Seminole woman, conquered many challenges to become a leader of the Seminole tribe. (Rev: LMC 3–4/10; SLJ 4/1/10) [921]

POKIAK-FENTON, MARGARET

2795 Jordan-Fenton, Christy, and Margaret Pokiak-Fenton. *Fatty Legs* (4–8). Illus. by Liz Amini-Holmes. 2010, Annick $21.95 (978-1-55451-247-8); paper $12.95 (978-1-55451-246-1). 106pp. This autobiography tells the moving story of a young Inuvialuit girl whose desire to learn to read led her to spend two years in a church-run school that tried to erase the students' identities; set in the 1940s. (Rev: SLJ 12/1/10) [921]

2796 Jordan-Fenton, Christy, and Margaret Pokiak-Fenton. *A Stranger at Home: A True Story* (3–6). Illus. by Liz Amini-Holmes. 2011, Annick $21.95 (978-1-55451-362-8); paper $12.95 (978-1-55451-361-1). 124pp. In this sequel to *Fatty Legs* (2010), Pokiak-Fenton recalls her return to her Inuit village after two years being educated by priests and nuns, and her realization that she has forgotten her own language and is now regarded as an outsider. (Rev: SLJ 12/1/11) [921]

TINGLE, TIM

2797 Tingle, Tim. *Saltypie: A Choctaw Journey from Darkness into Light* (3–5). Illus. by Karen Clarkson. 2010, Cinco Puntos $17.95 (978-1-933693-67-5). 40pp. Choctaw storyteller Tingle reflects on his life, recounting the bravery with which his family faced the racism and discrimination that colored their daily life. (Rev: BL 5/1/10; LMC 11–12/10; SLJ 5/1/10) [921]

ZITKALA-SA

2798 Capaldi, Gina, and Q. L. Pearce. *Red Bird Sings: The Story of Zitkala-Sa, Native American Author, Musician, and Activist* (2–4). Illus. by Gina Capaldi. 2011, Carolrhoda $17.95 (978-076135257-0). 32pp. In the late 1800s, a young Sioux girl opted to head east with missionaries instead of staying on the reservation, and her musical skills helped her in her fight for Native American rights; draws on semi-autobiographical stories. (Rev: BL 11/1/11) [921]

Presidents

ADAMS, JOHN AND ABIGAIL

2799 Adler, David A., and Michael S. Adler. *A Picture Book of John and Abigail Adams* (1–3). Illus. by Ronald Himler. Series: Picture Book Biography. 2010, Holiday House $17.95 (978-082342007-0). 32pp. An introduction to the public and private lives of the second president and his wife. (Rev: BL 2/1/10) [921]

GRANT, ULYSSES S.

2800 Crompton, Samuel Willard. *Ulysses S. Grant* (5–8). Series: Leaders of the Civil War Era. 2009, Chelsea House $30 (978-1-60413-301-1). 112pp. Enhanced by a mix of illustrations, period documents, photographs, and concise sidebars, this book provides a balanced look at the most successful leader of the Union Army and president of the United States. (Rev: LMC 10/09) [921]

JEFFERSON, THOMAS

2801 Miller, Brandon Marie. *Thomas Jefferson for Kids: His Life and Times with 21 Activities* (5–8). Illus. 2011, Chicago Review paper $16.95 (978-1-56976-348-3). 144pp. Age-appropriate activities (dancing a reel, making a simple microscope) extend this balanced biography that covers personal and political aspects of Jefferson. (Rev: BLO 9/15/11; SLJ 10/1/11) [921]

KENNEDY FAMILY

2802 Krull, Kathleen. *The Brothers Kennedy: John, Robert, Edward* (2–4). Illus. by Amy June Bates. 2010, Simon & Schuster $16.99 (978-1-4169-9158-8). 40pp. Profiles the three brothers who became politicians and their mutual support, legacy, and tragedy. (Rev: BL 3/15/10; LMC 8–9/10; SLJ 3/1/10) [921]

KENNEDY, JOHN FITZGERALD

2803 Rappaport, Doreen. *Jack's Path of Courage* (2–5). Illus. by Matt Tavares. 2010, Hyperion/Disney $17.99 (978-1-4231-2272-2). 48pp. This picture-book biography covers JFK's life from childhood and features memorable quotations and striking illustrations. Lexile AD780L (Rev: BL 12/15/10; HB 11–12/10; SLJ 10/1/10) [921]

LINCOLN, ABRAHAM

2804 Kalman, Maira. *Looking at Lincoln* (K–3). Illus. by author. 2012, Penguin $17.99 (978-039924039-3). 32pp. A young girl recalls facts about Abraham Lincoln's influence on the country as she wonders aloud about aspects of his personal and family life. (Rev: BL 1/12; HB 1–2/12; LMC 8–9/12; SLJ 9/12) [921]

2805 Krull, Kathleen, and Paul Brewer. *Lincoln Tells a Joke: How Laughter Saved the President (and the Country)* (2–4). Illus. by Stacy Innerst. 2010, Harcourt $16 (978-0-15-206639-0). 40pp. Emphasizes Lincoln's use of humor to cope with tense and difficult situations. (Rev: BL 2/15/10; HB 5–6/10; SLJ 3/1/10*) [921]

OBAMA, BARACK

2806 Abramson, Jill. *Obama: The Historic Journey* (4–7). Illus. 2009, The New York Times $24.95 (978-0-670-01208-4). 96pp. Striking photographs, informative text drawing on reports from the *New York Times,* and

careful explanation of political terms combine to make this a useful and educational biography of the president. (Rev: SLJ 8/09; VOYA 6/09) [921]

2807 Krensky, Stephen. *Barack Obama* (5–9). Illus. 2009, DK $14.99 (978-0-7566-5804-5); paper $5.99 (978-0-7566-5805-2). 128pp. With the usual DK visual format, this is an attractive portrait of Obama's life, placing his background and experience in historical context. (Rev: BL 4/1/10; SLJ 4/10) [921]

2808 von Zumbusch, Amelie. *Barack Obama's Family Tree: Roots of Achievement* (3–5). Illus. Series: Making History: The Obamas. 2010, Rosen LB $21.25 (978-143589390-0). 24pp. Introduces Obama's family history and discusses the influence of his parents and grandparents. (Rev: BL 6/10; LMC 10/10) [921]

2809 Weatherford, Carole Boston. *Obama: Only in America* (3–5). Illus. by Robert T. Barrett. 2010, Marshall Cavendish $17.99 (978-0-7614-5641-4). 48pp. Illustrated with paintings and featuring lyrical prose and excerpts from speeches, this admiring portrait covers the key events in Obama's life. (Rev: BL 5/1/10; LMC 8–9/10; SLJ 4/10) [921]

2810 Zeiger, Jennifer. *Barack Obama* (4–6). Illus. Series: Cornerstones of Freedom. 2012, Scholastic LB $30 (978-053123050-3); paper $8.95 (978-053128150-5). 64pp. With a map ("What Happened Where"), a timeline, and a list of influential individuals, this biography covers Ôbama's life through the beginning of his reelection bid. (Rev: BL 4/15/12) [921]

REAGAN, RONALD

2811 Burgan, Michael. *Ronald Reagan: A Photographic Story of a Life* (5–8). Illus. Series: DK Biography. 2011, DK $14.99 (978-0-7566-7075-7); paper $5.99 (978-0-7566-7074-0). 128pp. A visual introduction to the life of the actor who became president. ℮ (Rev: BL 6/1/11; SLJ 11/1/11) [921]

ROOSEVELT, FRANKLIN D.

2812 Krull, Kathleen. *A Boy Named FDR: How Franklin D. Roosevelt Grew Up to Change America* (3–5). Illus. by Steven Johnson and Lou Fancher. 2011, Knopf $17.99 (978-0-375-85716-4); LB $20.99 (978-0-375-95716-1). Unpaged. Franklin Roosevelt's childhood and young adulthood are described in this picture-book biography that takes readers up to 1924; an epilogue explains his achievements and legacy. (Rev: BL 1/1–15/11; LMC 5–6/11; SLJ 2/1/11) [921]

WASHINGTON, GEORGE

2813 Keating, Frank. *George: George Washington, Our Founding Father* (2–4). Illus. by Mike Wimmer. 2012, Simon & Schuster $16.99 (978-141695482-8). 32pp. A picture-book biography with full-page paintings and selections from his "Rules of Civility and Decent Behavior in Company and Conversation." (Rev: BL 12/15/11; SLJ 1/12) [921]

First Ladies and Other Women

BARTON, CLARA

2814 Krensky, Stephen. *Clara Barton* (5–7). Illus. Series: DK Biography. 2011, DK $14.99 (978-0-7566-7279-9); paper $5.99 (978-0-7566-7278-2). 128pp. A life of the woman who nursed the wounded on the battlefields of the Civil War and founded the American Red Cross. e (Rev: BLO 7/11; SLJ 9/1/11) [921]

EDMONDS, SARAH EMMA

2815 Jones, Carrie. *Sarah Emma Edmonds Was a Great Pretender: The True Story of a Civil War Spy* (2–4). Illus. by Mark Oldroyd. 2011, Carolrhoda $17.95 (978-0-7613-5399-7). 32pp. Sarah Emma Edmonds disguised herself as a boy and ran away from her abusive father in the 1850s; this inspiring picture book tells her courageous story. Lexile 780L (Rev: BL 4/15/11; HB 7–8/11; SLJ 4/11) [921]

2816 Moss, Marissa. *Nurse, Soldier, Spy: The Story of Sarah Edmonds, a Civil War Hero* (2–5). Illus. by John Hendrix. 2011, Abrams $18.95 (978-0-8109-9735-6). 48pp. This interesting biography presents short vignettes in the life of Sarah Emma Edmonds, a Canadian woman who lived most of her life as a man, including a stint in the Union Army during the Civil War. (Rev: BL 5/1/11; SLJ 5/1/11) [921]

GRANDIN, TEMPLE

2817 Montgomery, Sy. *Temple Grandin: How the Girl Who Loved Cows Embraced Autism and Changed the World* (4–8). Illus. 2012, Houghton Mifflin $17.99 (978-054744315-7). 160pp. A fascinating account of how Temple Grandin's autism has allowed her to design facilities that are substantially less threatening to livestock. (Rev: BL 3/15/12; SLJ 4/12*) [921]

LAZARUS, EMMA

2818 Glaser, Linda. *Emma's Poem: The Voice of the Statue of Liberty* (K–3). Illus. by Claire A. Nivola. 2010, Houghton Mifflin $16 (978-0-547-17184-5). 32pp. Moving free verse and detailed mixed-media paintings illustrate the life of Emma Lazarus, who grew up rich but became a champion for poor immigrants. (Rev: BL 2/1/10; SLJ 3/1/10) [921]

2819 Silverman, Erica. *Liberty's Voice: The Story of Emma Lazarus* (1–3). Illus. by Stacey Schuett. 2011, Dutton $17.99 (978-0-525-47859-1). 32pp. Silverman chronicles the life of the humanitarian who was motivated by her empathy toward Russian Jews to write

the poem that appears on the Statue of Liberty. Lexile AD810L (Rev: BL 1/1–15/11; SLJ 2/1/11) [921]

LEWIS, IDA

2820 Moss, Marissa. *The Bravest Woman in America: The Story of Ida Lewis* (K–3). Illus. by Andrea U'Ren. 2011, Tricycle $16.99 (978-1-58246-369-8); LB $19.99 (978-158246400-8). 32pp. Lighthouse keeper's daughter Ida Lewis, born in 1842, grows up to fill her father's shoes and rescues many from the sea in her long career. Lexile AD810L (Rev: BL 7/11; HB 7–8/11; LMC 5–6/11; SLJ 7/11) [921]

LOW, JULIETTE GORDON

2821 Corey, Shana. *Here Come the Girl Scouts!* (1–4). Illus. by Hadley Hooper. 2012, Scholastic $17.99 (978-054534278-0). 40pp. Tells the story of the formation of Girl Scouts in the United States through a picture-book profile of founder Juliette Gordon Low. (Rev: BL 1/1/12; LMC 8–9/12; SLJ 2/12) [921]

2822 Wadsworth, Ginger. *First Girl Scout: The Life of Juliette Gordon Low* (4–7). Illus. 2011, Clarion $17.99 (978-0-547-24394-8). 224pp. An appealing account of the life of the woman known as Daisy who came from a privileged background, was partially deaf, and founded the Girl Scout movement in the United States. e (Rev: BL 12/1/11; HB 11–12/11; SLJ 10/1/11) [921]

OBAMA, MICHELLE

2823 Hopkinson, Deborah. *Michelle* (K–3). Illus. by A. G. Ford. 2009, HarperCollins $17.99 (978-0-06-182739-6); LB $18.89 (978-0-06-182743-3). 32pp. An admiring account of the life of the woman who was born on Chicago's South Side, worked hard to become a success, and became First Lady in 2009. (Rev: BL 11/1/09; SLJ 12/1/09) [921]

2824 Mattern, Joanne. *Michelle Obama* (2–4). Series: A Robbie Reader. What's So Great About . . . ? 2010, Mitchell Lane LB $18.50 (978-1-58415-833-2). 32pp. For early readers, this book covers Michelle Obama's youth and family and her personal and professional achievements. (Rev: BL 6/10; LMC 8–9/10; SLJ 5/1/10) [921]

2825 Weatherford, Carole Boston. *Michelle Obama: First Mom* (2–4). Illus. by Robert T. Barrett. 2010, Marshall Cavendish $17.99 (978-0-7614-5640-7). 32pp. Michelle Obama's domestic side is highlighted in this profile illustrated with sepia-toned oil paintings. (Rev: BL 10/15/10; LMC 11–12/10; SLJ 11/1/10) [921]

SCIDMORE, ELIZA

2826 Zimmerman, Andrea. *Eliza's Cherry Trees: Japan's Gift to America* (1–3). Illus. by Ju Hong Chen. 2011, Pelican $16.99 (978-1-58980-954-3). 32pp. The story of Eliza Scidmore, a photographer and author who was the first woman to have an important job at the National

Geographic Society, and her efforts to bring beautiful Japanese flowering cherry trees to Washington, D.C. Lexile AD670L (Rev: BL 7/11; SLJ 6/11) [975.3]

SOTOMAYOR, SONIA

2827 Gitlin, Martin. *Sonia Sotomayor: Supreme Court Justice* (5–8). Series: Essential Lives. 2010, ABDO LB $32.79 (978-1-61613-518-8). 112pp. After covering Sotomayor's youth and education, this volume looks at her legal career and explains some of the legal issues in sidebars. (Rev: SLJ 3/1/11) [921]

2828 McElroy, Lisa Tucker. *Sonia Sotomayor: First Hispanic U.S. Supreme Court Justice* (5–8). Illus. 2010, Lerner LB $26.60 (978-0-7613-5861-9). 48pp. This concise, straightforward biography provides an introduction to the first Hispanic Supreme Court justice. Lexile 940L (Rev: BL 6/10; SLJ 5/10) [921]

2829 Winter, Jonah. *Sonia Sotomayor: A Judge Grows in the Bronx / La juez que crecio en el Bronx* (K–3). Illus. by Edel Rodriguez. 2009, Atheneum $16.99 (978-

144240303-1). 40pp. This bilingual biography focuses on the triumphs and achievements of Supreme Court justice Sonia Sotomayor. (Rev: BL 12/15/09) [921]

TAYLOR, ANNIE EDSON

2830 Van Allsburg, Chris. *Queen of the Falls* (3–5). Illus. by author. 2011, Houghton Mifflin $18.99 (978-0-547-31581-2). 40pp. The fascinating story of the woman who in 1901, at the age of 62, decided to tackle the Niagara Falls in a barrel, seeking funds to keep herself out of the poorhouse. Lexile 1060L (Rev: BL 1/1–15/11; HB 3–4/11; SLJ 3/1/11*)

VAN LEW, ELIZABETH

2831 Vander Hook, Sue. *Civil War Spy: Elizabeth Van Lew* (5–8). Series: We the People. 2009, Compass Point LB $26.65 (978-0-7565-4104-0). 48pp. Accessible and well-illustrated, with a useful timeline, this book gives readers a balanced look at the canny female spy who provided the Union with key information during the Civil War. (Rev: LMC 10/09) [921]

Scientists, Inventors, Naturalists, and Business Figures

Collective

2832 McClafferty, Carla Killough. *Tech Titans: One Frontier, Six Bios* (5–7). Illus. 2012, Scholastic paper $6.99 (978-054536577-2). 144pp. Bill Gates, Steve Jobs, Mark Zuckerberg, Larry Page, Sergey Brin, and Jeff Bezos — the men behind Windows, Apple, Facebook, Google, and Amazon — are profiled here. Lexile 1010L (Rev: BL 4/15/12; LMC 10/12) [920]

2833 Venezia, Mike. *Steve Jobs and Steve Wozniak: Geek Heroes Who Put the Personal in Computers* (2–4). Illus. by author. Series: Getting to Know the World's Greatest Inventors and Scientists. 2010, Scholastic LB $28 (978-0-531-23730-4). 32pp. With cartoons, images, and accessible large-font text, this is a good introduction to two computer greats. (Rev: BL 5/1/10; SLJ 7/1/10) [920]

2834 Young, Jeff C. *Inspiring African-American Inventors: Nine Extraordinary Lives* (5–8). Illus. Series: Great Scientists and Famous Inventors. 2009, Enslow LB $33.27 (978-159845080-4). 128pp. Nine African American inventors are profiled here, with details of their inventions and links to relevant Web sites. (Rev: BL 2/1/10; VOYA 4/10) [920]

Individual

BAER, RALPH

2835 Wyckoff, Edwin Brit. *The Guy Who Invented Home Videos Games: Ralph Baer and His Awesome Invention* (3–5). Illus. 2010, Enslow $22.60 (978-076603450-1). 32pp. Readers learn about the radio repairman who fled Nazi Germany and went on to develop video games. (Rev: BL 3/1/11) [921]

BANNEKER, BENJAMIN

2836 Maupin, Melissa. *Benjamin Banneker* (4–6). Illus. Series: Journey to Freedom. 2009, Child's World LB $28.50 (978-160253117-8). 32pp. The life and accomplishments of African American inventor, astronomer, and activist Benjamin Banneker are presented with a timeline and a glossary. (Rev: BL 2/1/10; LMC 5–6/10) [921]

BEZOS, JEFF

2837 Robinson, Tom. *Jeff Bezos: Amazon.com Architect* (5–8). Illus. Series: Publishing Pioneers. 2009, ABDO LB $22.95 (978-160453759-8). 112pp. This positive, informative biography of Amazon founder Jeff Bezos focuses on business innovation. (Rev: BL 12/1/09) [921]

BOMBARDIER, JOSEPH-ARMAND

2838 Older, Jules. *Snowmobile: Bombardier's Dream Machine* (4–6). Illus. by Michael Lauritano. 2012, Charlesbridge $14.95 (978-158089334-3); paper $6.95 (978-158089335-0). 64pp. The inspiring story of the inventor of the snowmobile features line drawings and an accessible yet detailed look at the invention. (Rev: BL 3/15/12; SLJ 4/12) [921]

CANNON, ANNIE JUMP

2839 Gerber, Carole. *Annie Jump Cannon, Astronomer* (3–5). Illus. by Christina Wald. 2011, Pelican $16.99 (978-1-58980-911-6). 32pp. Groundbreaking female astronomer Annie Jump Cannon developed a spectral classification system and a mnemonic device still used by astronomers today; this picture-book biography accurately depicts the hurdles female scientists faced in the late 1800s. (Rev: BL 10/15/11; SLJ 12/1/11) [921]

CARSON, RACHEL

2840 Lawlor, Laurie. *Rachel Carson and Her Book That Changed the World* (2–4). Illus. by Laura Beingessner. 2012, Holiday House $16.95 (978-082342370-5). 32pp. A moving picture-book tribute to the scientific and ethical contributions that Rachel Carson made to the world. Lexile 890L (Rev: BL 2/15/12; HB 7–8/12; LMC 8–9/12; SLJ 4/1/12) [921]

2841 Scherer, Glenn, and Marty Fletcher. *Who on Earth Is Rachel Carson? Mother of the Environmental Movement* (4–7). Series: Scientists Saving the Earth. 2009, Enslow LB $31.93 (978-1-59845-116-0). 112pp. Readers gain insight into the environmental climate of the 1970s, and the importance of Carson, who strove to raise awareness and end pesticide-related threats to wildlife. (Rev: SLJ 1/10; VOYA 2/10) [921]

CARVER, GEORGE WASHINGTON

2842 Marzollo, Jean. *The Little Plant Doctor: A Story About George Washington Carver* (K–3). Illus. by Ken Wilson-Max. 2011, Holiday House $16.95 (978-0-8234-2325-5). 32pp. An old Missouri tree narrates this picture-book biography, explaining the care the young Carver took with plants and the challenges he faced. (Rev: BL 3/15/11; SLJ 6/11) [921]

COLT, SAMUEL

2843 Wyckoff, Edwin Brit. *The Man Behind the Gun: Samuel Colt and His Revolver* (3–5). Illus. Series: Genius at Work! Great Inventor Biographies. 2010, Enslow LB $22.60 (978-076603446-4). 32pp. Wyckoff chronicles Colt's lifelong interest in things that go bang, and the way in which mass production contributed to his revolver's success. (Rev: BL 3/1/11) [921]

CORWIN, JEFF

2844 Corwin, Jeff. *Jeff Corwin: A Wild Life: The Authorized Biography* (4–8). 2009, Puffin paper $5.99 (978-0-14-241403-3). 100pp. Wildlife biologist Jeff Corwin traces the roots of his love of nature and animals in this lively, adventure-rich autobiography. (Rev: BL 12/1/09; SLJ 12/1/09) [921]

CURIE, MARIE AND PIERRE

2845 Lin, Yoming S. *The Curies and Radioactivity* (3–5). Illus. Series: Eureka! 2011, Rosen LB $21.25 (978-144885033-4). 24pp. Traces the lives of Marie and Pierre Curie and their important scientific work. (Rev: BL 12/1/11) [921]

DARWIN, CHARLES

2846 Krull, Kathleen. *Charles Darwin* (5–8). Illus. by Boris Kulikov. Series: Giants of Science. 2010, Viking $15.99 (978-0-670-06335-2). 128pp. An engaging profile of the famous scientist, covering his life from child-

hood and explaining his theories. (Rev: BL 12/1/10*; HB 1–2/11; SLJ 3/1/11) [921]

2847 Wood, A. J. *Charles Darwin and the Beagle Adventure* (5–8). 2009, Candlewick $19.99 (978-0-7636-4538-0). 30pp. Creatively designed to look like Charles Darwin's journal, this book shares a wealth of information about Darwin's journey on the *HMS Beagle* . (Rev: LMC 1–2/10; SLJ 10/09*) [921]

DIEMER, WALTER

2848 McCarthy, Meghan. *Pop! The Invention of Bubble Gum* (1–3). Illus. by author. 2010, Simon & Schuster $15.99 (978-1-4169-7970-8). 40pp. A humorous profile of Walter Diemer, the inventor of bubble gum, who was a young accountant in Philadelphia in the 1920s; includes facts about gum. (Rev: BL 4/15/10; HB 5/1/10; LMC 8–9/10; SLJ 5/1/10*) [921]

EARLE, SYLVIA

2849 Reichard, Susan E. *Who on Earth Is Sylvia Earle? Undersea Explorer of the Ocean* (4–7). Series: Scientists Saving the Earth. 2009, Enslow LB $31.93 (978-1-59845-118-4). 112pp. An interesting biography of the scientist devoted to underwater exploration and the protection of this environment from threats including oil pollution. (Rev: SLJ 1/10; VOYA 2/10) [921]

EDISON, THOMAS

2850 Brown, Don. *A Wizard from the Start: The Incredible Boyhood and Amazing Inventions of Thomas Edison* (1–3). Illus. by author. 2010, Houghton Mifflin $16 (978-0-547-19487-5). 32pp. Edison's boyhood and adolescence are the focus of this inspiring biography, which chronicles Edison's trials at school and hard work as a "news butch" before becoming an inventor. Lexile AD940L (Rev: BL 6/10; SLJ 4/1/10*) [921]

FIBONACCI, LEONARDO

2851 D'Agnese, Joseph. *Blockhead: The Life of Fibonacci* (3–5). Illus. by John O'Brien. 2010, Henry Holt $16.99 (978-0-8050-6305-9). 40pp. A beautifully illustrated, lighthearted yet informative introduction to the mathematician's childhood, love of numbers, and famous sequence. ♫ Lexile AD570L (Rev: BL 1/1/10; HB 5–6/10; LMC 8–9/10; SLJ 3/1/10) [921]

FORD, HENRY

2852 Mitchell, Don. *Driven: A Photobiography of Henry Ford* (4–7). 2010, National Geographic $18.95 (978-1-4263-0155-1); LB $27.90 (978-1-4263-0156-8). 64pp. With many photographs and quotations, this is a fine portrait of the founder of the automobile company, frankly discussing his social views, ideals, and character flaws. (Rev: BL 6/10; HB 5–6/10; SLJ 4/10; VOYA 6/10) [338.7]

187

FOSSEY, DIAN

2853 Kushner, Jill Menkes. *Who on Earth Is Dian Fossey? Defender of the Mountain Gorillas* (4–7). Illus. Series: Scientists Saving the Earth. 2009, Enslow LB $31.93 (978-159845117-7). 112pp. Fossey's work with mountain gorillas is the main focus of this profile that includes information on careers in environmental science and activism. (Rev: BL 2/15/10; SLJ 1/10; VOYA 2/10) [921]

GOODALL, JANE

2854 Winter, Jeanette. *The Watcher: Jane Goodall's Life with the Chimps* (2–4). Illus. by author. 2011, Random House $17.99 (978-0-375-86774-3); LB $20.99 (978-0-375-96774-0). 48pp. Winter emphasizes Goodall's early passion for nature in this account of her progress to becoming an internationally recognized expert on chimpanzees and the threats they face. (Rev: BL 3/1/11*; HB 3–4/11; LMC 8–9/11; SLJ 4/11) [921]

KELLOGG, W. K.

2855 Wyckoff, Edwin Brit. *The Cornflake King: W. K. Kellogg and His Amazing Cereal* (3–5). Illus. Series: Genius at Work! Great Inventor Biographies. 2010, Enslow LB $22.60 (978-076603448-8). 32pp. Wyckoff chronicles Kellogg's early career and his accidental invention of the popular breakfast food. (Rev: BL 3/1/11) [921]

LORENZ, KONRAD

2856 Greenstein, Elaine. *The Goose Man: The Story of Konrad Lorenz* (K–2). Illus. by author. 2010, Clarion $16 (978-0-547-08459-6). 32pp. Animal behaviorist Konrad Lorenz's childhood love of animals led to his Nobel Prize-winning research on geese. (Rev: BL 12/15/09; LMC 8–9/10; SLJ 2/1/10) [921]

MCCOY, ELIJAH

2857 Kulling, Monica. *All Aboard! Elijah McCoy's Steam Engine* (1–3). Illus. by Bill Slavin. Series: Great Idea. 2010, Tundra $17.95 (978-088776945-0). 32pp. A simple introduction to the life and achievements of McCoy, a black inventor born in 1843 who faced many challenges. (Rev: BL 8/10; SLJ 8/10) [921]

MERIAN, MARIA

2858 Engle, Margarita. *Summer Birds: The Butterflies of Maria Merian* (K–3). Illus. by Julie Paschkis. 2010, Henry Holt $16.99 (978-0-8050-8937-0). 32pp. Maria Merian disproved the popular belief that butterflies

were "beasts of the devil" in the 17th century; this inspiring story shows the young scientist and artist pursuing her passions. (Rev: BL 3/15/10*; LMC 5–6/10; SLJ 7/1/10) [921]

ROTHSCHILD, WALTER

2859 Judge, Lita. *Strange Creatures: The Story of Walter Rothschild and His Museum* (1–3). Illus. by author. 2011, Hyperion/Disney $17.99 (978-1-4231-1389-8). 40pp. Lord Walter Rothschild's lifelong fascination with exotic animals spawned one of the most extensive collections of rare and fascinating animals in the world by the time he was 24 years old. Lexile AD950L (Rev: BL 2/15/11; SLJ 2/1/11) [595]

SANTOS-DUMONT, ALBERTO

2860 Griffin, Victoria. *The Fabulous Flying Machines of Alberto Santos-Dumont* (1–3). Illus. by Eva Montanari. 2011, Abrams $16.95 (978-1-4197-0011-8). 32pp. First flyer Alberto Santos-Dumont's high-society Paris life and his rivalry with Louis Bleriot are documented in this account that also covers his friend Cartier's invention of the wristwatch. (Rev: BL 10/15/11; LMC 1–2/12*; SLJ 9/1/11) [921]

SIKORSKY, IGOR

2861 Wyckoff, Edwin Brit. *Helicopter Man: Igor Sikorsky and His Amazing Invention* (3–5). Illus. Series: Genius at Work! Great Inventor Biographies. 2010, Enslow LB $22.60 (978-076603445-7). 32pp. Wyckoff chronicles Sikorsky's devotion to his dream of building a successful helicopter. (Rev: BL 3/1/11) [921]

WALTON, SAM

2862 Blumenthal, Karen. *Mr. Sam: How Sam Walton Built Wal-Mart and Became America's Richest Man* (5–8). Illus. 2011, Viking $17.99 (978-0-670-01177-3). 160pp. A frank profile of the Oklahoma-born man who had a profound influence on the retail face of America — and beyond. **ℰ** (Rev: BL 6/1/11; HB 7–8/11; LMC 11–12/11; SLJ 7/11) [381]

WANG, VERA

2863 Dakers, Diane. *Vera Wang: A Passion for Bridal and Lifestyle Design* (5–8). Illus. Series: Crabtree Groundbreakers Biographies. 2010, Crabtree LB $31.93 (978-077872535-0). 112pp. Chronicling life from youth to adulthood, this biography presents a straightforward and clearly written portrait of fashion great Vera Wang. Lexile NC1210L (Rev: BL 1/1–15/11) [921]

Sports Figures

Collective

2864 Berman, Len. *The Twenty-five Greatest Baseball Players of All Time* (5–8). Illus. 2010, Sourcebooks $16.99 (978-140223886-4). 138pp. Twenty-five of baseball's greatest are profiled in short chapters emphasizing career statistics and triumphs over challenges. (Rev: BL 9/1/10; SLJ 1/1/11; VOYA 12/10) [920]

2865 Stout, Glenn. *Baseball Heroes* (3–6). Illus. 2010, Houghton Mifflin paper $5.99 (978-054741708-0). 128pp. Hank Greenburg, Jackie Robinson, Fernando Valenzuela, and Ila Borders are profiled in this inspiring, well-written book about overcoming obstacles. (Rev: BL 9/1/10) [920]

2866 Stout, Glenn. *Yes, She Can! Women's Sports Pioneers* (4–7). 2011, Houghton Mifflin paper $5.99 (978-0-547-41725-7). 128pp. Profiles women from different backgrounds and eras who made their name in various sports, from Gertrude Eberle through Julie Krone and Danica Patrick. e (Rev: BL 5/1/11; SLJ 7/11) [920]

Baseball

AARON, HANK

2867 Morrison, Jessica. *Hank Aaron: Home Run Hero* (5–8). Illus. Series: Crabtree Groundbreakers Biographies. 2010, Crabtree LB $31.93 (978-077872538-1). 112pp. Morrison covers Hammerin' Hank's life from childhood and his move from the Negro Leagues to major-league baseball. Lexile 1080L (Rev: BL 1/1–15/11) [921]

2868 Tavares, Matt. *Henry Aaron's Dream* (2–4). Illus. by author. 2010, Candlewick $16.99 (978-0-7636-3224-

3). 40pp. In this effective biography, Tavares describes Aaron's youth and the many challenges he faced in achieving his dream of playing major league baseball. (Rev: BL 2/15/10; LMC 5–6/10; SLJ 1/1/10*) [921]

CLEMENTE, ROBERTO

2869 Perdomo, Willie. *¡Clemente!* (1–3). Illus. by Bryan Collier. 2010, Henry Holt $16.99 (978-0-8050-8774-1). 40pp. Tells the story of Clemente's life from the perspective of a boy named for him. (Rev: BL 2/15/10; LMC 5–6/10; SLJ 4/1/10) [921]

DOBY, LARRY

2870 Crowe, Chris. *Just as Good: How Larry Doby Changed America's Game* (1–3). Illus. by Mike Benny. 2012, Candlewick $32 (978-076365026-1). 32pp. The first African American to play in the American League, Larry Doby was instrumental in securing a championship for the Cleveland Indians in the 1948 World Series. Lexile AD690L (Rev: BL 2/1/12; LMC 5–6/12; SLJ 1/12) [921]

GEHRIG, LOU

2871 Buckley, James, Jr. *Lou Gehrig: Iron Horse of Baseball* (5–8). Series: Sterling Biographies. 2010, Sterling $12.95 (978-1-4027-7151-4). 124pp. Details of Gehrig's life and personality are placed in historical context and enhanced by an appealing layout, plentiful images, and first-person accounts. (Rev: BL 5/1/10; LMC 8–9/10) [921]

GREENBERG, HANK

2872 Sommer, Shelley. *Hammerin' Hank Greenberg: Baseball Pioneer* (4–7). 2011, Calkins Creek $17.95 (978-1-59078-452-5). 132pp. Pioneering Jewish baseball player Hank Greenberg overcame considerable prejudice in his time on the diamond during the 1930s and 1940s. (Rev: BL 3/1/11; SLJ 4/11; VOYA 8/11) [921]

LINCECUM, TIM

2873 Boone, Mary. *Tim Lincecum* (2–4). Illus. Series: Robbie Reader Contemporary Biographies. 2011, Mitchell Lane LB $25.70 (978-161228058-5). 32pp. A profile of the pitcher who led the San Francisco Giants to a World Series championship in 2010. (Rev: BL 12/1/11) [921]

MANLEY, EFFA

2874 Vernick, Audrey. *She Loved Baseball: The Effa Manley Story* (1–3). Illus. by Don Tate. 2010, HarperCollins $16.99 (978-0-06-134920-1). 32pp. The life of the African American who became the first woman to be inducted into the Baseball Hall of Fame and, with her husband, founded the Negro League team that became the Newark Eagles. (Rev: BL 9/1/10; SLJ 11/1/10*) [921]

PIKE, LIPMAN

2875 Michelson, Richard. *Lipman Pike: America's First Home Run King* (2–4). Illus. by Zachary Pullen. 2011, Sleeping Bear $16.95 (978-1-58536-465-7). 32pp. Evoking the spirit of baseball's early years in the 1860s, this picture book tells the story of a young Jewish boy who ran fast and was a strong hitter. (Rev: BL 3/1/11; LMC 11–12/11; SLJ 5/1/11) [921]

ROBINSON, JACKIE

2876 Robinson, Sharon. *Jackie's Gift: A True Story of Christmas, Hanukkah, and Jackie Robinson* (K–3). Illus. by E. B. Lewis. 2010, Viking $16.99 (978-067001162-9). 32pp. When young Steve Satlow, whose family bucked the trend and welcomed the African American Robinsons into their neighborhood, mentions that they do not have a Christmas tree, young Jackie Robinson goes to get one — unaware that the Satlows are Jewish. (Rev: BL 2/1/11; SLJ 10/10) [921]

2877 Teitelbaum, Michael. *Jackie Robinson: Champion for Equality* (5–8). Series: Sterling Biographies. 2010, Sterling $12.95 (978-1-4027-7148-4). 128pp. Details of Robinson's life and personality are placed in historical context and enhanced by an appealing layout, plentiful images, and first-person accounts. (Rev: LMC 8–9/10) [921]

RUTH, BABE

2878 Fischer, David. *Babe Ruth: Legendary Slugger* (5–8). Series: Sterling Biographies. 2010, Sterling $12.95 (978-1-4027-7147-7). 128pp. Details of Ruth's life and personality are placed in historical context and enhanced by an appealing layout, plentiful images,

and first-person accounts. Lexile 1080L (Rev: LMC 8–9/10) [921]

WAGNER, HONUS

2879 Yolen, Jane. *All Star! Honus Wagner and the Most Famous Baseball Card Ever* (1–3). Illus. by Jim Burke. 2010, Philomel $17.99 (978-0-399-24661-6). 32pp. Yolen tells the story of Honus Wagner, who seemed an unlikely candidate to become a baseball star. (Rev: BL 2/15/10; LMC 3–4/10; SLJ 3/1/10*) [921]

WILLIAMS, TED

2880 Tavares, Matt. *There Goes Ted Williams: The Greatest Hitter Who Ever Lived* (2–5). Illus. by author. 2012, Candlewick $16.99 (978-076362789-8). 40pp. An admiring portrait of the baseball star that nonetheless mentions his legendary temper in an author's note. (Rev: BLO 2/15/12; HB 1–2/12; LMC 8–9/12; SLJ 1/12) [921]

Basketball

BIRD, SUE

2881 Boone, Mary. *Sue Bird* (2–4). Illus. Series: Robbie Reader Contemporary Biographies. 2011, Mitchell Lane LB $25.70 (978-161228062-2). 32pp. This profile begins with a career highlight and then provides details of the early life and determination of the Seattle Storm basketball star. (Rev: BL 12/1/11) [921]

JAMES, LEBRON

2882 Gagne, Tammy. *LeBron James* (1–3). Illus. Series: Day by Day With. 2010, Mitchell Lane $25.70 (978-158541858-5). 32pp. The talents and positive qualities of the basketball star are presented here in this approachable, well-designed book. (Rev: BL 9/1/10) [921]

ROSE, DERRICK

2883 Sandler, Michael. *Derrick Rose* (3–5). Illus. Series: Basketball Heroes Making a Difference. 2012, Bearport LB $23.93 (978-161772439-8). 24pp. This positive biography focuses on the charity work of basketball great Derrick Rose. (Rev: BL 4/1/12) [921]

WADE, DWYANE

2884 DiPrimio, Pete. *Dwyane Wade* (2–4). Illus. Series: Robbie Reader Contemporary Biographies. 2011, Mitchell Lane LB $25.70 (978-161228063-9). 32pp. With career statistics and a chronology, this is a profile of the Miami Heat player who grew up in a tough neighborhood of Chicago. (Rev: BL 12/1/11) [921]

Boxing

ALI, MUHAMMAD

2885 Myers, Walter Dean. *Muhammad Ali: The People's Champion* (1–3). Illus. by Alix Delinois. 2010, Collins $16.99 (978-0-06-029131-0); LB $17.89 (978-0-06-029132-7). 40pp. With quotations and a brisk pace, this is a simple picture-book biography of the prize fighter. (Rev: BL 11/1/09; SLJ 2/1/10) [921]

2886 Timblin, Stephen. *Muhammad Ali: King of the Ring* (5–8). Series: Sterling Biographies. 2010, Sterling $12.95 (978-1-4027-7152-1). 124pp. Details of Ali's life and personality are placed in historical context and enhanced by an appealing layout, plentiful images, and first-person accounts. (Rev: BL 5/1/10; LMC 8–9/10) [921]

JOHNSON, JACK

2887 Smith, Charles R. *Black Jack: The Ballad of Jack Johnson* (1–3). Illus. by Shane W. Evans. 2010, Roaring Brook $16.99 (978-1-59643-473-8). 40pp. Tells the story of the first African American heavyweight boxing champion, who faced racial prejudice in the early 20th century. (Rev: BL 4/1/10*; LMC 8–9/10; SLJ 7/1/10) [921]

LOUIS, JOE

2888 De La Peña, Matt. *A Nation's Hope: The Story of Boxing Legend Joe Louis* (1–3). Illus. by Kadir Nelson. 2011, Dial $17.99 (978-0-8037-3167-7). 40pp. Joe Louis's epic fight against German Max Schmeling at Yankee Stadium in 1938 is portrayed in dramatic text and effective illustrations. (Rev: BL 2/1/11*; HB 1–2/11; LMC 5–6/11; SLJ 2/1/11*)

Football

FITZGERALD, LARRY

2889 Sandler, Michael. *Larry Fitzgerald* (2–4). Illus. Series: Football Heroes Making a Difference. 2010, Bearport $22.61 (978-193608758-7). 24pp. Sandler describes the life and achievements of the Arizona Cardinals star along with his efforts to give back to the community. (Rev: BL 9/1/10) [921]

GONZALEZ, TONY

2890 Sandler, Michael. *Tony Gonzalez* (2–4). Illus. Series: Football Heroes Making a Difference. 2010, Bearport LB $22.61 (978-193608761-7). 24pp. Sandler describes the life and achievements of the record-setting

NFL star along with his foundation's efforts to help sick children. (Rev: BL 9/1/10) [921]

JOHNSON, CHRIS

2891 Orr, Tamra. *Chris Johnson* (2–4). Illus. Series: Robbie Reader Contemporary Biographies. 2011, Mitchell Lane LB $25.70 (978-161228064-6). 32pp. This profile of the running back for the Tennessee Titans starts off with a career highlight that draws readers in. (Rev: BL 12/1/11) [921]

MANNING, PEYTON

2892 Sandler, Michael. *Peyton Manning* (2–4). Illus. Series: Football Heroes Making a Difference. 2011, Bearport LB $22.61 (978-161772311-7). 24pp. Discusses significant moments in the football career of quarterback Peyton Manning and examines his charity work, including his role in beginning the PeyBack Foundation. (Rev: BL 11/1/11) [921]

2893 Wilner, Barry. *Peyton Manning: A Football Star Who Cares* (3–6). Illus. Series: Superstar Athletes. 2011, Enslow $23.93 (978-076603774-8). 48pp. This profile celebrates Manning's humanitarian causes while also providing plenty of football fodder. (Rev: BL 9/1/11) [921]

PETERSON, ADRIAN

2894 Sandler, Michael. *Adrian Peterson* (2–4). Illus. Series: Football Heroes Making a Difference. 2010, Bearport LB $22.61 (978-1-936087-59-4). 24pp. Sandler describes the life and achievements of the Minnesota Vikings star along with his efforts to give back to the community. (Rev: BL 9/1/10; SLJ 6/1/10) [921]

POLAMALU, TROY

2895 Sandler, Michael. *Troy Polamalu* (2–4). Illus. Series: Football Heroes Making a Difference. 2011, Bearport LB $22.61 (978-161772312-4). 24pp. Looks at the life and career of the football player and at his work with mentally disabled children. (Rev: BL 11/1/11) [921]

ROMO, TONY

2896 Sandler, Michael. *Tony Romo* (2–4). Illus. Series: Football Heroes Making a Difference. 2010, Bearport $22.61 (978-1-936087-60-0). 24pp. Sandler describes the life and achievements of the Dallas Cowboys star along with his efforts to give back to the community. (Rev: BL 9/1/10; SLJ 6/1/10) [921]

SANCHEZ, MARK

2897 Sandler, Michael. *Mark Sanchez* (2–4). Illus. Series: Football Heroes Making a Difference. 2011, Bearport LB $22.61 (978-161772310-0). 24pp. Looks at the life and career of the football player and at his work with inner-city and diabetic children. (Rev: BL 11/1/11) [921]

Tennis

ASHE, ARTHUR

2898 Hubbard, Crystal. *Game Set Match Champion Arthur Ashe* (4–7). Illus. by Kevin Belford. 2010, Lee & Low $19.95 (978-1-60060-366-2). 48pp. The African American tennis champion's early challenges, successes on the court, and social activism are documented in this picture-book biography. (Rev: BL 10/15/10; LMC 3–4/11; SLJ 3/1/11) [921]

WILLIAMS, VENUS AND SERENA

2899 Bailey, Diane. *Venus and Serena Williams: Tennis Champions* (5–8). Illus. Series: Sports Families. 2010, Rosen LB $26.50 (978-143583552-8). 48pp. Bailey tells the story of the sisters' childhood in California and their famous rivalry on the courts. (Rev: BL 9/1/10) [921]

Track and Field

COACHMAN, ALICE

2900 Malaspina, Ann. *Touch the Sky: Alice Coachman, Olympic High Jumper* (2–4). Illus. by Eric Velasquez. 2012, Whitman $16.99 (978-080758035-6). 32pp. First female African American Olympic gold medalist Alice Coachman's struggle from poverty and hardship to stardom is chronicled in this inspiring biography. (Rev: BL 2/1/12; LMC 8–9/12; SLJ 4/1/12) [921]

OWENS, JESSE

2901 Gigliotti, Jim. *Jesse Owens: Gold Medal Hero* (5–8). Series: Sterling Biographies. 2010, Sterling $12.95 (978-1-4027-7149-1). 128pp. Details of Owens's life and personality are placed in historical context and enhanced by an appealing layout, plentiful images, and first-person accounts. Lexile 1040L (Rev: LMC 8–9/10) [921]

THORPE, JIM

2902 Labrecque, Ellen. *Jim Thorpe: An Athlete for the Ages* (5–8). Series: Sterling Biographies. 2010, Sterling $12.95 (978-1-4027-7150-7). 124pp. Details of Thorpe's life and personality are placed in historical context and enhanced by an appealing layout, plentiful images, and first-person accounts. (Rev: BL 5/1/10; LMC 8–9/10) [921]

2903 Schuman, Michael A. *Jim Thorpe: "There's No Such Thing as 'Can't'"* (5–8). Series: Americans — The Spirit of a Nation. 2009, Enslow LB $31.93 (978-0-7660-3021-3). 128pp. A dramatic introduction draws readers into this informative and accessible account of Thorpe's life and achievements. (Rev: LMC 11–12/09; SLJ 9/09) [921]

Miscellaneous Sports

ANDERSON, TILLIE

2904 Stauffacher, Sue. *Tillie the Terrible Swede: How One Woman, a Sewing Needle, and a Bicycle Changed History* (K–3). Illus. by Sarah McMenemy. 2011, Knopf $17.99 (978-0-375-84442-3); LB $20.99 (978-0-375-94442-0). 40pp. Tells the story of a Swedish American woman who defied gender barriers and became a famous bicycle racer, even wearing a scandalous pants outfit. Lexile 760L (Rev: BL 2/1/11; HB 3–4/11; LMC 10/11; SLJ 2/1/11) [921]

WOODS, TIGER

2905 Roberts, Jeremy. *Tiger Woods: Golf's Master* (5–8). Illus. Series: USA Today Lifeline Biographies. 2008, Lerner LB $33.26 (978-158013569-6). 112pp. Newsy sidebars, photographs, personal stories, and historical context enrich this well-designed biography that also provides thorough descriptions of golf and its gear. (Rev: BL 9/1/08; LMC 3–4/09; SLJ 11/1/08) [921]

World Figures

Individual

ALEXANDER THE GREAT

2906 Demi. *Alexander the Great* (4–7). Illus. by author. 2010, Marshall Cavendish $19.99 (978-0-7614-5700-8). 59pp. The story of the infamous Macedonian conquerer is presented in this concise, beautifully illustrated book. ℮ (Rev: BL 9/15/10; LMC 1–2/11; SLJ 10/1/10) [921]

AUNG SAN SUU KYI

2907 Rose, Simon. *Aung San Suu Kyi* (4–7). Illus. Series: Remarkable People. 2011, Weigl LB $27.13 (978-161690833-1); paper $12.95 (978-161690834-8). 24pp. An admiring, informative profile of the Myanmar activist who won the Nobel Prize. (Rev: BL 9/15/11) [921]

CLEOPATRA

2908 Blackaby, Susan. *Cleopatra: Egypt's Last and Greatest Queen* (5–8). Series: Sterling Biographies. 2009, Sterling $12.95 (978-1-4027-6540-7); paper $5.95 (978-1-4027-5710-5). 124pp. A useful and engaging biography for report writers or anyone interested in the renowned queen and her times. (Rev: SLJ 8/09) [921]

2909 Shecter, Vicky Alvear. *Cleopatra Rules! The Amazing Life of the Original Teen Queen* (4–7). 2010, Boyds Mills $17.95 (978-1-59078-718-2). 176pp. Using irreverent teenspeak that will not appeal to all readers, Schecter presents detailed information in a layout full of sidebars and illustrations. Lexile 880L (Rev: BL 10/1/10; LMC 11–12/10; SLJ 10/1/10; VOYA 12/10) [921]

ELIZABETH I, QUEEN OF ENGLAND

2910 Hollihan, Kerrie Logan. *Elizabeth I, the People's Queen: Her Life and Times: 21 Activities* (4–8). Illus. 2011, Chicago Review paper $16.95 (978-1-56976-349-0). 144pp. The life and times of England's Queen Elizabeth I are given plenty of historical and political context in this well-organized book that includes 21 activities. (Rev: LMC 10/11; SLJ 5/11) [921]

GENGHIS KHAN

2911 Nardo, Don. *Genghis Khan and the Mongol Empire* (5–9). Series: World History. 2011, Gale/Lucent $33.45 (978-1-4205-0326-5). 96pp. An accessible portrait of Genghis Khan, his military reforms, his conquests in western Asia, and his legacy. ℮ (Rev: SLJ 7/11) [921]

JOAN OF ARC

2912 Demi. *Joan of Arc* (3–5). Illus. by author. 2011, Marshall Cavendish $19.99 (978-0-7614-5953-8). 56pp. An elegant picture-book biography portraying the brief but significant life of Joan of Arc, patron saint of France. (Rev: BL 9/1/11; SLJ 10/1/11) [921]

KAMKWAMBA, WILLIAM

2913 Kamkwamba, William, and Bryan Mealer. *The Boy Who Harnessed the Wind* (1–3). Illus. by Elizabeth Zunon. 2012, Dial $16.99 (978-080373511-8). 32pp. In a remote, impoverished Malawi village, 14-year-old Kamkwamba constructed a windmill out of salvaged materials and brought electricity to his neighbors. ⌒ ℮ (Rev: BL 2/15/12; SLJ 1/12) [921]

KORCZAK, JANUSZ

2914 Bogacki, Tomek. *The Champion of Children: The Story of Janusz Korczak* (4–7). Illus. by author. 2009,

Farrar $17.99 (978-0-374-34136-7). 40pp. A brave doctor who gave up his medical practice to found a Jewish orphanage in Poland during World War II and to accompany the children to Treblinka is profiled in this stark but inspiring story. (Rev: BL 10/1/09; LMC 11–12/09; SLJ 12/09) [921]

KOUANCHAO, MALICHANSOUK

2915 Youme. *Mali Under the Night Sky: A Lao Story of Home* (PS–3). Illus. by author. 2010, Cinco Puntos $17.95 (978-1-933693-68-2). 40pp. This is the story of the childhood of Laotian American artist Malichansouk Kouanchao, whose family flees the civil war in Laos and ends up spending time in jail. (Rev: BL 1/1–15/11; LMC 5–6/11; SLJ 11/1/10) [921]

KUBLAI KHAN

2916 Krull, Kathleen. *Kubla Khan: The Emperor of Everything* (3–5). Illus. by Robert Byrd. 2010, Viking $17.99 (978-0-670-01114-8). 48pp. In this vividly illustrated book, Kubla Khan, the first emperor of the Yuan dynasty, matures to enlightened adulthood and ascends the throne. (Rev: BL 7/10; HB 11–12/10; LMC 1–2/11; SLJ 10/1/10*) [921]

MAATHAI, WANGARI

2917 Johnson, Jen Cullerton. *Seeds of Change: Planting a Path to Peace* (2–4). Illus. by Sonia Lynn Sadler. 2010, Lee & Low $18.95 (978-1-60060-367-9). 40pp. This inspiring story of Nobel Peace Prize laureate Wangari Maathai's environmental activism discusses her education and love of nature in poetic text with colorful illustrations. Lexile 820L (Rev: BL 6/10; LMC 11–12/10; SLJ 4/1/10) [921]

2918 Napoli, Donna Jo. *Mama Miti: Wangari Maathai and the Trees of Kenya* (K–3). Illus. by Kadir Nelson. 2010, Simon & Schuster $16.99 (978-1-4169-3505-6). 40pp. Vibrant collage artwork enhances this picturebook biography of the simple and successful conservation movement Maathai founded in Kenya. (Rev: BL 2/15/10; LMC 5–6/10; SLJ 2/1/10) [921]

NIVOLA, CLAIRE A.

2919 Nivola, Claire A. *Orani: My Father's Village* (2–5). Illus. by author. 2011, Farrar $16.99 (978-0-374-35657-6). Unpaged. The author reminisces about her childhood spent in a small Sardinian village in this nostalgic memoir with evocative illustrations. SLJ Best Nonfiction Books of 2011; Horn Book Best Nonfiction Books of 2011. Lexile NC1080L (Rev: HB 9–10/11; SLJ 6/11*) [945]

SENDLER, IRENA

2920 Rubin, Susan Goldman. *Irena Sendler and the Children of the Warsaw Ghetto* (3–6). Illus. by Bill Farnsworth. 2011, Holiday House $18.95 (978-0-8234-2251-7). 32pp. Rubin tells the inspiring story of a young Catholic social worker who risked her life to protect Warsaw Jews from the Nazis. (Rev: BL 4/15/11; LMC 10/11; SLJ 5/11) [940.53]

2921 Vaughan, Marcia. *Irena's Jars of Secrets* (4–7). Illus. by Ron Mazellan. 2011, Lee & Low $18.95 (978-1-60060-439-3). 40pp. A picture-book profile of Irena Sendler, a Polish Catholic social worker who helped save nearly 2,500 children in the Warsaw Ghetto from deportation to the death camps in the early 1940s. Lexile 1040L (Rev: BL 12/1/11; LMC 5–6/12; SLJ 11/1/11) [921]

SON THI ANH, TUYET

2922 Skrypuch, Marsha Forchuk. *Last Airlift: A Vietnamese Orphan's Rescue from War* (4–8). Illus. 2012, Pajama $17.95 (978-098694954-8). 120pp. Tells the story of 8-year-old Son Thi Anh Tuyet, a Vietnamese orphan whose suffering had included polio, who was on the last Canadian flight out of Saigon in 1975. Lexile 670L (Rev: BL 4/15/12; HB 9–10/12; SLJ 4/12) [921]

WILLIAM, PRINCE, AND MIDDLETON, KATE

2923 Doeden, Matt. *Prince William and Kate: A Royal Romance* (5–8). Illus. 2011, Lerner LB $26.60 (978-076138029-0). 48pp. Tells the story of Kate and William's individual lives and their relationship, ending with their wedding day; with many photographs and a timeline. (Rev: BL 11/1/11) [921]

The Arts and Language

Art and Architecture

General and Miscellaneous

2924 Bingham, Jane. *Graffiti* (5–7). Illus. Series: Culture in Action. 2009, Raintree LB $28.21 (978-1-4109-3401-7); paper $7.99 (978-1-4109-3418-5). 32pp. Bingham traces the history of graffiti back to cave walls and describes (with examples) modern forms and the pitfalls of indulging in this activity. (Rev: LMC 3–4/10; SLJ 2/10) [751.7]

2925 Bingham, Jane. *Michelangelo* (3–6). Series: Culture in Action. 2010, Heinemann-Raintree $28.21 (978-1-4109-3402-4). 32pp. A high-interest introduction to Michelangelo's work with activities that reinforce literacy and knowledge of the arts. Lexile 770L (Rev: LMC 3–4/10) [709.2]

2926 *Children's Book of Art: An Introduction to the World's Most Amazing Paintings and Sculptures* (5–8). Illus. 2009, DK $24.99 (978-0-7566-5511-2). 144pp. This well-designed, large-format volume includes everything from artist profiles to style analysis to how-to instructions. (Rev: BLO 10/1/09; SLJ 10/09) [700]

2927 Guéry, Anne, and Olivier Dussutour. *Alphab'art* (1–4). 2009, Frances Lincoln $19.95 (978-1-84780-013-8). 60pp. This fascinating artistic tour of the alphabet challenges readers to find the individual letters in diverse works of art — some familiar and some lesser-known; the back matter provides context. (Rev: BLO 11/15/09; SLJ 1/10) [421.1]

2928 Hosack, Karen. *Buildings* (4–8). Illus. Series: What Is Art? 2008, Raintree LB $27.50 (978-1-4109-3165-8). 32pp. Hosack introduces a number of kinds of buildings — public spaces, private residences, memorials, and so forth — and discusses their function and form; a bright layout and well-chosen illustrations add appeal. (Rev: SLJ 3/1/09) [720]

2929 Hosack, Karen. *Drawings and Cartoons* (4–8). Illus. Series: What Is Art? 2008, Raintree LB $27.50 (978-1-4109-3163-4). 32pp. Drawings from Michelangelo to modern-day are on display here, accompanied by a paragraph disclosing their purpose and posing questions about their style. (Rev: SLJ 3/1/09) [741]

2930 Laroche, Giles. *What's Inside? Fascinating Structures Around the World* (4–8). Illus. by author. 2009, Houghton Mifflin $17 (978-0-618-86247-4). Unpaged. This handsome, fact-filled volume looks at both the exteriors and interiors (with people going about activities) of 14 structures ranging from tombs, temples, and castles to skyscrapers and the Sydney Opera House. (Rev: BL 2/15/09; SLJ 5/1/09) [720]

2931 McCully, Emily Arnold. *The Secret Cave: Discovering Lascaux* (1–3). Illus. by author. 2010, Farrar $16.99 (978-0-374-36694-0). 40pp. The 1940 discovery of the striking cave paintings at Lascaux by French schoolboys is the focus of this dramatically illustrated picture book. (Rev: BL 11/1/10; LMC 11–12/10; SLJ 10/1/10*) [944]

2932 Miles, Liz. *Photography* (3–6). Series: Culture in Action. 2010, Heinemann-Raintree $28.21 (978-1-4109-3400-0). 32pp. Covering everything from the first cameras to today's photojournalists, this title also offers activities that reinforce literacy skills and understanding of the arts. Lexile 780L (Rev: LMC 3–4/10) [771.3]

2933 Monet, Claude. *Monet's Impressions* (K–3). Illus. by author. 2009, Chronicle $15.99 (978-0-8118-7056-6). 48pp. Reproductions of 16 Monet works are presented alongside quotations and snippets of the artist's letters. (Rev: BLO 11/1/09; LMC 1–2/10; SLJ 11/1/09) [759.4]

2934 *My Art Book: Amazing Art Projects Inspired by Masterpieces* (3–6). 2011, DK $15.99 (978-0-7566-7582-0). 80pp. A visually appealing volume of projects associated with 14 famous works of art; they range from the cave paintings of Lascaux to Warhol's pop art and include a variety of materials and techniques. (Rev: SLJ 8/11) [745.5]

2935 Ogier, Susan. *Objects and Meanings* (5–8). Series: Step-Up Art and Design. 2010, Cherrytree LB $27.10 (978-1-84234-573-3). 32pp. With plenty of photographs, this volume looks at the artistic techniques involved in everything from still life and trompe l'oeil to folk art and using found objects. Also use *People in Action, A Sense of Place,* and *Talking Textiles* (all 2010). (Rev: LMC 10/10; SLJ 5/10) [700]

2936 Raczka, Bob. *Action Figures: Paintings of Fun, Daring, and Adventure* (3–5). Illus. 2009, Millbrook LB $25.26 (978-0-7613-4140-6). 32pp. Eighteen action-packed paintings by well-known artists represent different styles and eras (from 1450 to 1962), and are accompanied by informative and interesting captions. (Rev: BL 11/1/09; SLJ 10/1/09) [704.9]

2937 Serres, Alain. *And Picasso Painted Guernica* (4–8). Trans. by Rosalind Price. 2011, Allen & Unwin $24.99 (978-1-74175-994-5). 52pp. This handsome volume explores Picasso's major mural documenting the destruction of Guernica during the Spanish Civil War, and illustrates the evolution of his art. Lexile 900L (Rev: SLJ 1/1/11*)

2938 Tomecek, Stephen M. *Art and Architecture* (4–7). Illus. 2010, Chelsea House LB $35 (978-1-60413-168-0). 174pp. Twenty-five accessible experiments illustrate important concepts in art or architecture ranging from the practical — testing stress on metal, how an arch supports a load — to the more artistic — mixing pigments, how image depth affects perspective. (Rev: SLJ 11/1/10) [701.03]

2939 Wenzel, Angela. *Thirteen Art Mysteries Children Should Know* (5–7). Illus. 2011, Prestel $14.95 (978-3-7913-7044-6). 48pp. In chronological order, this volume presents 13 mysteries of the art world, including questions about the Mona Lisa, a Raphael painting, van Gogh's ear, and the identity of graffiti artist Banksy. (Rev: BL 11/1/11; SLJ 10/1/11) [759]

Communication

General and Miscellaneous

2940 Marcovitz, Hal. *Bias in the Media* (5–8). 2010, Gale/Lucent LB $32.45 (978-1-4205-0224-4). 112pp. With chapters titled "Why Are the Media Biased?," "The Cable Wars," "Citizens as Journalists: Bias in the Blogosphere," "Pockets of Bias," and "Are There Unbiased Media?," this is a useful introduction to assessing the media. (Rev: SLJ 2/1/11) [302.23097]

Codes and Ciphers

2941 Bell-Rehwoldt, Sheri. *Speaking Secret Codes* (4–7). Series: Edge Books: Making and Breaking Codes. 2010, Capstone LB $26.65 (978-1-4296-4569-0). 32pp. Readers learn about spoken codes and how to work with codes, with activities and photographs. Lexile 770L (Rev: SLJ 1/1/11) [302.2]

2942 Blackwood, Gary. *Mysterious Messages: A History of Codes and Ciphers* (5–8). 2009, Dutton $16.99 (978-0-525-47960-4). 176pp. This well-written history clearly explains the ins and outs of codes and ciphers and includes many interesting examples and stories. (Rev: BL 10/15/09; LMC 11–12/09; SLJ 12/09) [652]

2943 Gilbert, Adrian. *Codes and Ciphers* (3–6). Series: Spy Files. 2009, Firefly paper $6.95 (978-1-55407-573-7). 32pp. The Morse code, Navajo code talkers, cipher machines, and secret writing and microdots are among the codes and ciphers described in this volume that also includes historical information and exercises. (Rev: SLJ 4/10) [652]

2944 Gregory, Jillian. *Breaking Secret Codes* (4–7). Series: Edge Books: Making and Breaking Codes. 2010, Capstone LB $26.65 (978-1-4296-4568-3). 32pp.

Gregory looks at various kinds of codes and the methods used to break them. Also use *Making Secret Codes* (2010). Lexile 830L (Rev: SLJ 1/1/11) [652]

Reading, Speaking, and Writing

Books, Printing, Libraries, and Schools

2945 Anderson, Judith. *Education for All* (4–7). Series: Working for Our Future. 2010, Black Rabbit LB $28.50 (978-1-59771-193-7). 32pp. This volume explains why the United Nations chose education for all as one of its eight Millennium Development goals and looks at the various reasons why children do not go to school. (Rev: BL 6/10; LMC 10/10; SLJ 4/10) [370]

2946 Cefrey, Holly. *Researching People, Places and Events* (5–8). Series: Digital and Information Literacy. 2010, Rosen LB $26.50 (978-1-4358-5317-1). 48pp. Providing helpful information and advice for undertaking research projects on the Internet, this guide offers tips on the difference between primary and secondary sources, evaluating sources, and avoiding plagiarism. (Rev: LMC 1–2/10; SLJ 3/10) [001.4]

2947 Cornwall, Phyllis. *Put It All Together* (3–6). Illus. Series: Super Smart Information Strategies. 2010, Cherry Lake LB $27.07 (978-1-60279-643-0). 32pp. Presents advice on presenting the results of research, with emphasis on organization and considering both purpose and audience. (Rev: LMC 8–9/10; SLJ 6/10) [372.1]

2948 Donovan, Sandy. *Bob the Alien Discovers the Dewey Decimal System* (2–4). Illus. by Martin Haake. Series: In the Library. 2010, Picture Window LB $25.32 (978-1-4048-5757-5). 24pp. A librarian introduces a well-mannered alien in search of information about spiders to the basics of the Dewey Decimal system. Also use

Bored Bella Learns About Fiction and Nonfiction and *Karl and Carolina Uncover the Parts of a Book* (both 2010). (Rev: LMC 11–12/10; SLJ 4/1/10) [025.4]

2949 Fontichiaro, Kristin. *Go Straight to the Source* (3–6). Illus. Series: Super Smart Information Strategies. 2010, Cherry Lake LB $27.07 (978-1-60279-640-9). 32pp. Describes how to use primary sources — images, objects, and documents — effectively and how to tie them in with secondary sources. (Rev: SLJ 6/10) [020]

2950 Green, Julie. *Write It Down* (3–6). Illus. Series: Super Smart Information Strategies. 2010, Cherry Lake LB $27.07 (978-1-60279-645-4). 32pp. Describes how to find the key information in your research and the use of highlighting, sticky notes, tables, and so forth in enhancing note-taking. (Rev: SLJ 6/10) [371.3]

2951 Guillain, Charlotte. *My First Day at a New School* (K–2). Illus. Series: Growing Up. 2011, Heinemann LB $22 (978-1-4329-4796-5). 24pp. Using simple vocabulary and large color photographs, this reassuring book gives new students a sense of what to expect from their first day at school. (Rev: BL 7/11; SLJ 6/11) [371.002]

2952 Hughes, Susan. *Off to Class: Incredible and Unusual Schools Around the World* (3–7). Illus. 2011, OwlKids $12.95 (978-1-926818-85-6). 64pp. A fascinating look at schools ranging from tent schools in Haiti to schools in caves in China, boat schools, e-mail schools, and more. (Rev: BL 11/1/11; SLJ 9/1/11) [371]

2953 King, M. G. *Librarian on the Roof! A True Story* (K–3). Illus. by Stephen Gilpin. 2010, Whitman $16.99 (978-080754512-6). 32pp. The inspiring story of a spunky Texas librarian who held a rooftop vigil to raise money for her library. (Rev: BL 8/10; LMC 11–12/10; SLJ 10/10) [027.4764]

2954 Myron, Vicki, and Brett Witter. *Dewey the Library Cat: A True Story* (4–8). 2010, Little, Brown $15.99 (978-0-316-06871-0). 224pp. A kindhearted librarian takes pity when she finds a freezing kitten in the library's book return in this children's adaptation that focuses on Dewey's everyday adventures. (Rev: BL 5/15/10; LMC 8–9/10; SLJ 6/10) [636.80092]

2955 Pascaretti, Vicki, and Sara Wilkie. *Team Up Online* (3–6). Illus. Series: Super Smart Information Strategies. 2010, Cherry Lake LB $27.07 (978-1-60279-644-7). 32pp. Discusses the best ways of collaborating online on research projects and provides exercises and checklists. (Rev: SLJ 6/10) [025.04]

2956 Rabbat, Suzy. *Find Your Way Online* (3–6). Illus. Series: Super Smart Information Strategies. 2010, Cherry Lake LB $27.07 (978-1-60279-639-3). 32pp. Provides advice on effective research on the Internet, looking specifically at narrowing searches and using subject directories and subscription databases. (Rev: SLJ 6/10) [004.1]

2957 Truesdell, Ann. *Find the Right Site* (3–6). Illus. Series: Super Smart Information Strategies. 2010, Cherry Lake LB $27.07 (978-1-60279-638-6). 32pp. Provides advice on evaluating the content of Web sites. (Rev: SLJ 6/10) [025.042]

Signs and Symbols

2958 Heller, Lora. *Sign Language ABC* (PS–2). Illus. by author. 2012, Sterling $14.95 (978-140276392-2). 32pp. A clear and accessible guide to the American Sign Language alphabet. (Rev: BL 12/15/11; SLJ 2/1/12) [419]

Words and Grammar

2959 Amoroso, Cynthia. *Hold Your Horses! (And Other Peculiar Sayings)* (1–3). Illus. by Mernie Gallagher-Cole. Series: Sayings and Phrases. 2011, Child's World LB $25.64 (978-160253681-4). 24pp. A variety of familiar idioms are presented in context and with humorous illustrations. Also use *I'm All Thumbs! (And Other Odd Things We Say)*, *It's a Long Shot! (And Other Strange Sayings)*, and *That's the Last Straw! (And Other Weird Things We Say)* (all 2011). (Rev: BL 4/15/11) [428.1]

2960 Cleary, Brian P. *But and For, Yet and Nor: What Is a Conjunction?* (2–4). Illus. by Brian Gable. Series: Words Are CATegorical. 2010, Millbrook $15.95 (978-082259153-5). 32pp. An appealing introduction to the use of conjunctions, with entertaining illustrations. (Rev: BL 2/1/10) [425]

2961 Cleary, Brian P. *Cool! Whoa! Ah and Oh! What Is an Interjection?* (2–4). Illus. by Brian Gable. Series: Words Are CATegorical. 2011, Millbrook $16.95 (978-158013594-8). 32pp. Frenetic illustrations support the many examples of different kinds of interjections. Also use *Thumbtacks, Earwax, Lipstick, Dipstick: What Is a Compound Word?* (2011). (Rev: BL 2/1/11) [428.2]

2962 Edwards, Wallace. *The Cat's Pajamas* (4–7). Illus. by author. 2010, Kids Can $18.95 (978-1-55453-308-4). Unpaged. Rich illustrations depicting animals acting out idioms make clear that these 26 figures of speech cannot be taken literally. Lexile AD820L (Rev: SLJ 2/1/11) [428]

2963 Heinrichs, Ann. *Interjections* (2–4). Illus. by Dan McGeehan. Series: Language Rules! 2010, Child's World LB $27.07 (978-1-60253-428-5). 24pp. This lively title offers tips and examples of how to use interjections. (Rev: BL 10/1/10; SLJ 12/1/10) [428.2]

2964 Lunge-Larsen, Lise. *Gifts from the Gods: Ancient Words and Wisdom from Greek and Roman Mythology* (4–6). Illus. by Gareth Hinds. 2011, Houghton Mifflin $18.99 (978-0-547-15229-5). 96pp. Seventeen everyday words and phrases (Achilles' heel, Pandora's box, victory) with roots in classical mythology are examined here, with excerpts from children's books and relevant illustrations. (Rev: BL 11/1/11; SLJ 10/1/11) [401]

2965 Oelschlager, Vanita. *Life Is a Bowl Full of Cherries: A Book of Food Idioms and Silly Pictures* (K–3). Illus. by Robin Hegan. 2011, Vanita $15.95 (978-098263663-3); paper $8.95 (978-098263662-6). 40pp. Visual representations of food-related puns and idioms ("food for thought") are presented in bright spreads, with brief explanations. (Rev: BL 5/1/11) [440]

2966 Ogburn, Jacqueline K. *Little Treasures: Endearments from Around the World* (PS–3). Illus. by Chris Raschka. 2012, Houghton Mifflin $16.99 (978-054742862-8). 32pp. Readers learn loving terms in 14 languages, including English, Spanish, Hindi, and Chinese. e (Rev: BL 12/15/11; SLJ 1/12) [808.88]

2967 PatrickGeorge. *A Drove of Bullocks: A Compilation of Animal Group Names* (3–6). Illus. by author. 2011, PatrickGeorge paper $12.99 (978-0-9562558-0-8). Unpaged. An imaginatively presented collection of fascinating collective names for groups of animals and birds. Also use *A Filth of Starlings: A Compilation of Bird and Aquatic Animal Group Names* (2011). (Rev: SLJ 7/11)

Writing and Speaking

2968 Hershenhorn, Esther. *S Is for Story: A Writer's Alphabet* (3–6). Illus. by Zachary Pullen. 2009, Sleeping Bear $17.95 (978-1-58536-439-8). 40pp. An alphabetical celebration of books and writing. (Rev: BL 10/1/09; SLJ 3/10) [808.3]

2969 Mack, Jim. *Journals and Blogging* (3–6). Illus. Series: Culture in Action. 2009, Raintree LB $28.21 (978-1-4109-3406-2); paper $7.99 (978-1-4109-3423-9). 32pp. An appealing introduction to writing journals and blogs, with information on Internet etiquette and safety and on well-known practitioners of these arts. (Rev: LMC 3–4/10; SLJ 2/10) [808]

2970 Minden, Cecilia, and Kate Roth. *How to Write a News Article* (2–4). Illus. Series: Language Arts Explorer Junior: Writing. 2012, Cherry Lake LB $24.21 (978-161080308-3). 24pp. A step-by-step guide to producing a simple news story, with useful examples and checklist. Also use *How to Write a How-To* (2012). (Rev: BL 3/15/12) [808]

2971 Raum, Elizabeth. *Poetry* (3–6). Series: Culture in Action. 2010, Heinemann-Raintree $28.21 (978-1-4109-3404-8). 32pp. A high-interest introduction to poetry and the joys of writing and reading it, with activities designed to build literacy and understanding of the arts. Lexile 800L (Rev: LMC 3–4/10) [808.1]

2972 Rosinsky, Natalie M. *Write Your Own Graphic Novel* (4–8). 2008, Compass Point LB $24.95 (978-075653856-9). 64pp. Rosinsky introduces such helpful concepts as storyboarding, editing, and peer collaboration while providing photos of young writers at work and referencing familiar graphic novels. Lexile 1010L (Rev: BL 11/1/08; SLJ 3/1/09) [741.5]

2973 St. John, Amanda. *Bridget and Bo Build a Blog* (2–4). Illus. by Katie McDee. Series: Writing Builders. 2012, Norwood LB $25.27 (978-159953507-4). 32pp. Nine-year-old Bo teaches his friend Bridget how to build and write a blog in this story full of helpful hints and ideas for topics. (Rev: BL 4/1/12*) [808]

Music

General

2974 *Children's Book of Music: An Introduction to the World's Most Amazing Music and Its Creators* (3–6). 2010, DK $24.99 (978-0-7566-6734-4). 142pp. This broad, chronological survey of music looks at musical history, famous composers and musicians, musical instruments, and so forth, and features a visually appealing layout full of photographs and sidebars. (Rev: LMC 3–4/11*; SLJ 1/1/11) [780.9]

2975 Crossingham, John. *Learn to Speak Music: A Guide to Creating, Performing, and Promoting Your Songs* (5–8). Illus. by Jeff Kulak. 2009, OwlKids paper $17.95 (978-1-897349-65-6). 96pp. An attractive overview of the basics of music with advice on writing music, forming a band, dealing with stage fright, and so forth. (Rev: BL 11/1/09; LMC 1–2/10; SLJ 11/09) [782.42]

2976 Mack, Jim. *Hip-Hop* (3–6). Series: Culture in Action. 2010, Heinemann-Raintree $28.21 (978-1-4109-3393-5). 32pp. A high-interest introduction to the various forms of hip-hop music and its history, with activities that reinforce literacy and understanding. Lexile 870L (Rev: LMC 3–4/10) [793.3]

2977 Miles, Liz. *Making a Recording* (3–6). Illus. Series: Culture in Action. 2009, Raintree LB $28.21 (978-1-4109-3392-8); paper $7.99 (978-1-4109-3409-3). 32pp. An appealing introduction to recording music, with information on history, techniques, and well-known practitioners of these arts. (Rev: LMC 3–4/10; SLJ 2/10) [781.49]

2978 Miles, Liz. *The Orchestra* (3–6). Series: Culture in Action. 2010, Heinemann-Raintree $28.21 (978-1-4109-3394-2). 32pp. Introduces the structure of an orchestra, what it's like to play in one, and the kinds of music they play, with activities that are designed to reinforce understanding and literacy. Lexile 840L (Rev: LMC 3–4/10) [784.2]

Ballads and Folk Songs

2979 Crews, Nina. *The Neighborhood Sing-Along* (PS–1). Illus. by author. 2011, Greenwillow $17.99 (978-0-06-185063-9). 64pp. Urban cityscape photographs of multicultural children add appeal to this collection of songs and rhymes. (Rev: BL 4/15/11; HB 5–6/11; SLJ 4/11) [782.42]

2980 Goembel, Ponder. *Animal Fair* (PS–K). Illus. by author. 2010, Marshall Cavendish $12.99 (978-0-7614-5642-1). 24pp. With detailed, humorous illustrations, this is a retelling of the children's nonsense folk song. (Rev: BL 3/1/10; SLJ 4/1/10) [782.42]

2981 Katz, Alan. *Mosquitoes Are Ruining My Summer! And Other Silly Dilly Camp Songs* (3–5). Illus. by David Catrow. Series: Silly Dilly. 2011, Simon & Schuster $16.99 (978-1-4169-5568-9). 32pp. Familiar children's songs are given new lyrics describing the woes and wonders of summer camp. (Rev: BL 4/15/11; SLJ 7/11) [782.42]

2982 Lyon, George Ella. *Which Side Are You On? The Story of a Song* (3–5). Illus. by Christopher Cardinale. 2011, Cinco Puntos $17.95 (978-1-933693-96-5). 40pp. The story of the composition of the famed labor rights song "Which Side Are You On?" is presented here against a backdrop of mining company thugs, striking workers, and violence. ♫ (Rev: BL 11/15/11; HB 1–2/12; LMC 5–6/12; SLJ 11/1/11) [782.42]

2983 Norworth, Jack. *Take Me Out to the Ball Game* (PS–K). Illus. by Amiko Hirao. Series: Children's Favorite Activity Songs. 2011, Imagine $17.95 (978-1-

202

936140-26-8). 16pp. Text and illustrations present the familiar song; an accompanying CD contains songs by Carly Simon, with modified lyrics and a note about Jackie Robinson. (Rev: BL 3/1/11; SLJ 7/11) [782.42]

2984 Stotts, Stuart. *We Shall Overcome: The Song That Changed the World* (5–8). Illus. by Terrance Cummings. 2010, Houghton Mifflin LB $18 (978-0-547-18210-0). 80pp. Stotts reviews the history of the song that inspired, encouraged, and comforted those involved in the U.S. civil rights movement; includes a CD with a Pete Seeger recording. Lexile 1080L (Rev: BL 11/1/09; LMC 1–2/10; SLJ 2/10) [782.42162]

2985 Ward, Jennifer. *There Was an Old Monkey Who Swallowed a Frog* (PS–2). Illus. by Steve Gray. 2010, Marshall Cavendish $16.99 (978-076145580-6). 32pp. A funny cumulative tale about a monkey's strange diet in the jungle. (Rev: BL 3/15/10; LMC 8–9/10) [782.42]

Holidays

2986 Long, Laurel. *The Twelve Days of Christmas* (1–3). Illus. by author. 2011, Dial $16.99 (978-080373357-2). 32pp. Handsome paintings conceal hidden gifts in this new interpretation of the traditional carol. (Rev: BL 10/15/11; SLJ 10/1/11) [782.42]

2987 Ray, Jane. *The Twelve Days of Christmas* (PS–3). Illus. by author. 2011, Candlewick $16.99 (978-076365735-2). 32pp. In the early 20th century, a young woman's small row house fills up with gifts, starting with a partridge in a pear tree and growing ever more abundant. (Rev: BL 10/1/11; SLJ 10/1/11) [782.42]

Musical Instruments

2988 Ganeri, Anita. *Pianos and Keyboards* (4–6). Illus. Series: How the World Makes Music. 2011, Black Rabbit LB $28.50 (978-159920479-6). 32pp. Introduces keyboard instruments from around the world — from the familiar piano and organ to the less common hurdy-gurdy and celeste — with illustrations and clear text. (Rev: BL 10/1/11) [786]

2989 Salzmann, Mary Elizabeth. *What in the World Is a Clarinet?* (K–3). Illus. Series: Musical Instruments. 2012, ABDO LB $25.65 (978-161783203-1). 24pp. A simple introduction to the clarinet, its structure, how it is played, and its role in music. (Rev: BL 4/1/12) [788.6]

2990 Storey, Rita. *The Violin and Other Stringed Instruments* (3–5). Illus. Series: Let's Make Music. 2009, Smart Apple Media LB $19.95 (978-159920212-9).

32pp. This visually appealing book introduces the violin, the guitar, and other stringed instruments and explains how they make music and how they are used. (Rev: BL 11/1/09) [787]

Singing Games and Songs

2991 Allen, Nancy Kelly. *"Happy Birthday": The Story of the World's Most Popular Song* (1–3). Illus. by Gary Undercuffler. 2010, Pelican $16.99 (978-1-58980-675-7). Unpaged. Tells the story of the sisters who wrote the familiar song in the late 19th century, initially with the title "Good Morning to All." (Rev: SLJ 5/1/10) [782.42]

2992 Cabrera, Jane. *The Wheels on the Bus* (PS–1). Illus. by author. 2011, Holiday House $16.95 (978-0-8234-2350-7). 32pp. Hyenas, flamingos, crocodiles, and bush babies are among the animals in this jungle version of the familiar song. (Rev: BL 10/1/11; SLJ 9/1/11) [782.42]

2993 Dylan, Bob. *Man Gave Names to All the Animals* (PS–2). Illus. by Jim Arnosky. 2010, Sterling $17.95 (978-1-4027-6858-3). 32pp. Realistic pencil and acrylic illustrations enhance this updated version of the 1979 Bob Dylan song. (Rev: BL 10/15/10; SLJ 9/1/10) [782.42]

2994 Emberley, Rebecca, and Ed Emberley. *If You're a Monster and You Know It* (PS–K). Illus. by Rebecca Emberley. 2010, Scholastic $16.99 (978-0-545-21829-0). 32pp. Neon-bright monsters are on parade in this boisterous adaptation of the familiar children's song "If You're Happy and You Know It"; a downloadable CD is available on the publisher's Web site. (Rev: BL 9/15/10; SLJ 9/1/10*) [782.42]

2995 Jackson, Jill, and Sy Miller. *Let There Be Peace on Earth: And Let It Begin with Me* (PS–2). Illus. by David Diaz. 2009, Tricycle $18.99 (978-158246285-1). 32pp. The lyrics to the popular children's song are given a picture-book update in this book featuring a history of the song, biographical notes on the husband-wife team that created it, information about peace symbols, and musical notations. (Rev: BL 9/15/09; SLJ 12/09) [782.42164]

2996 Katz, Karen. *The Babies on the Bus* (PS). Illus. by author. 2011, Henry Holt $14.99 (978-0-8050-9011-6). Unpaged. Boisterous illustrations add appeal to this baby-themed take on "The Wheels on the Bus." (Rev: SLJ 6/11) [782.42]

2997 Long, Ethan. *The Croaky Pokey!* (PS–1). Illus. by author. 2011, Holiday House $14.95 (978-0-8234-2291-3). Unpaged. A rousing version of "Hokey Pokey" featuring a pond full of lively, dancing frogs and a pesky fly. (Rev: SLJ 3/1/11) [782.42]

2998 Quattlebaum, Mary. *Jo MacDonald Had a Garden* (PS–1). Illus. by Laura J. Bryant. 2012, Dawn $16.95 (978-158469164-8); paper $8.95 (978-158469165-5). 32pp. In this follow-up to *Jo MacDonald Saw a Pond* (2011), Jo and her cousin Mike plant and care for a vegetable garden. Lexile AD550L (Rev: BLO 4/15/12; LMC 10/12; SLJ 6/1/12) [782.42]

2999 Quattlebaum, Mary. *Jo MacDonald Saw a Pond* (PS–1). Illus. by Laura J. Bryant. 2011, Dawn paper $16.95 (978-1-58469-151-8). 32pp. This updated take on "Old McDonald's Farm" features the farmer's granddaughter discovering a pond and describing eight of its inhabitants; end notes present facts and activities. (Rev: BL 11/1/11; SLJ 12/1/11) [782.42]

Performing Arts

Dance

3000 Ancona, George. *¡Olé! Flamenco* (5–8). Photos by author. 2010, Lee & Low $19.95 (978-1-60060-361-7). Unpaged. A photo-essay about the Spanish art form that incorporates dance, music, and song, explaining its history and traditions and following a group of young people who are studying flamenco in Santa Fe, New Mexico. (Rev: BL 12/1/10; HB 1–2/11; LMC 5–6/11; SLJ 1/1/11) [793.3]

3001 Bingham, Jane. *Ballet* (4–8). Series: Dance. 2009, Heinemann LB $31.43 (978-1-4329-1374-8). 48pp. A colorful overview of the origins and evolution of ballet, with discussion of the various skills required, the rigorous training, and the complexities of staging a ballet. (Rev: LMC 3–4/09)

3002 Greenberg, Jan, and Sandra Jordan. *Ballet for Martha: Making Appalachian Spring* (2–4). Illus. by Brian Floca. 2010, Roaring Brook $17.99 (978-159643338-0). 48pp. The process of artistic creation is the focus of this book, which provides a glimpse into the collaboration of composer, choreographer, and artist that gave rise to the ballet *Appalachian Spring* in 1944. Lexile AD710L (Rev: BL 7/10*; HB 7–8/10; LMC 10/10; SLJ 8/10) [792.8]

3003 Mellow, Mary Kate, and Stephanie Troeller. *Ballet for Beginners* (1–4). 2010, Imagine $14.95 (978-1-936140-01-5). 80pp. Prima Princessa introduces young readers to the movements seen in ballet and shows them around the School of American Ballet and the classes held there. (Rev: BL 2/1/10; SLJ 4/10) [792.8]

3004 Nelson, Marilyn. *Beautiful Ballerina* (K–3). Illus. by Susan Kuklin. 2009, Scholastic $17.99 (978-0-545-08920-3). 32pp. A poem and photographs put readers on the stage with ballerinas from the Dance Theatre of Harlem. (Rev: BL 11/1/09; SLJ 11/1/09) [792.8]

3005 Underwood, Deborah. *Ballroom Dancing* (3–6). Series: Culture in Action. 2010, Heinemann-Raintree $28.21 (978-1-4109-3398-0). 32pp. Is ballroom dancing art or sport? This and other questions are addressed in this well-illustrated title with activities designed to build literacy and understanding of the arts. Lexile 710L (Rev: LMC 3–4/10) [793.3]

3006 Williams, Ann-Marie. *Learn to Speak Dance: A Guide to Creating, Performing and Promoting Your Moves* (5–8). Illus. by Jeff Kulak. 2011, OwlKids $22.95 (978-1-926818-88-7); paper $14.95 (978-1-926818-89-4). 96pp. A large-format introduction to styles of dance — ballet, ballroom, flamenco, and so forth — with discussion of choreography, preparing for performances, stage fright, and other aspects. (Rev: BL 11/1/11; SLJ 7/11) [792.8]

Motion Pictures, Radio, and Television

3007 Miles, Liz. *Movie Special Effects* (3–6). Series: Culture in Action. 2010, Heinemann-Raintree $28.21 (978-1-4109-3399-7). 32pp. A high-interest introduction to the special effects used in movies, with activities that reinforce literacy and understanding. Lexile 920L (Rev: LMC 3–4/10) [778.5]

Theater and Play Production

3008 Krensky, Stephen. *Lizzie Newton and the San Francisco Earthquake* (3–5). Illus. by Jeremy Tugeau. Series: History Speaks. 2010, Millbrook LB $27.93 (978-0-8225-9031-6). 48pp. Ten-year-old Lizzie sets out to find her parents after the 1906 San Francisco earthquake in this partly fictionalized story that is accompanied by a readers' theater script designed for six or more parts. Lexile 410L (Rev: BL 1/1–15/11; SLJ 12/1/10) [979]

3009 Underwood, Deborah. *Staging a Play* (3–6). Illus. Series: Culture in Action. 2009, Raintree LB $28.21 (978-1-4109-3396-6); paper $7.99 (978-1-4109-3413-0). 32pp. An appealing introduction to stage production, with information on the roles of the director, actors, set and light and sound technicians, costume and makeup experts, and so forth. (Rev: LMC 3–4/10; SLJ 2/10) [792.02]

History and Geography

History and Geography in General

Miscellaneous

3010 Moore, Christopher. *From Then to Now: A Short History of the World* (5–8). Illus. by Andrej Krystofor-ski. 2011, Tundra $25.95 (978-0-88776-540-7). 176pp. Moore offers a broad and fascinating overview of developments in human history from hunter-gatherers to industrialization and the modern, interconnected world. (Rev: BL 5/1/11; SLJ 5/11) [909]

3011 Sloan, Christopher. *Mummies: Dried, Tanned, Sealed, Drained, Frozen, Embalmed, Stuffed, Wrapped, and Smoked . . . and We're Dead Serious* (4–7). Illus. 2010, National Geographic $17.95 (978-1-4263-0695-2); LB $26.90 (978-1-4263-0696-9). 48pp. Mummies from around the world are profiled in this fascinating book featuring plenty of close-up photographs. (Rev: BLO 10/15/10; LMC 3–4/11; SLJ 12/1/10) [393]

Paleontology and Dinosaurs

3012 Abramson, Andra Serlin, and Jason Brougham, et al. *Inside Dinosaurs* (4–6). Illus. by Jason Brougham. 2010, Sterling $16.95 (978-1-4027-7074-6); paper $9.95 (978-1-4027-7778-3). 49pp. Gatefold features enhance this boldly colored overview of dinosaurs' internal workings. (Rev: LMC 1–2/11; SLJ 12/1/10*) [567.9]

3013 Bardoe, Cheryl. *Mammoths and Mastodons: Titans of the Ice Age* (4–7). Illus. 2010, Abrams $18.95 (978-0-8109-8413-4). 48pp. Two boys discover a perfectly preserved frozen baby mammoth in this story, which offers a glimpse into the lives of these Ice Age giants as well as an introduction to the science of paleontology. Orbis Pictus Honor Award for Outstanding Nonfiction for Children, 2011. (Rev: BL 3/15/10; SLJ 4/10) [569]

3014 Barry, Frances. *Let's Look at Dinosaurs: A Flip-the-Flap Book* (PS–1). Illus. by author. 2011, Candlewick $12.99 (978-0-7636-5354-5). 32pp. With flaps and fold-outs, this wide-format book answers many questions about dinosaurs, taking care to distinguish between fact and conjecture. Lexile 567.9 (Rev: BL 9/1/11; SLJ 8/1/11) [567.9]

3015 Burnie, David. *Dinosaurs* (4–6). Illus. Series: Navigators. 2010, Kingfisher $12.99 (978-0-7534-6414-4). 48pp. Answers many questions about dinosaurs with detailed, lifelike images and concise text organized in eye-catching spreads. (Rev: BL 9/1/10; SLJ 10/1/10) [567.9]

3016 Hartland, Jessie. *How the Dinosaur Got to the Museum* (K–3). Illus. by author. 2011, Blue Apple $17.99 (978-1-60905-090-0). 40pp. The journey of a diplodocus skeleton from discovery to the halls of the Smithsonian is recounted in double-page spreads that show the contributions of various experts. (Rev: BL 11/1/11; SLJ 11/1/11*) [567.913]

3017 Judge, Lita. *Born to Be Giants: How Baby Dinosaurs Grew to Rule the World* (2–4). Illus. by author. 2010, Roaring Brook $17.99 (978-159643443-1). 48pp. Profiling eight species of dinosaur, this book looks at the babies and how they matured. (Rev: BL 3/1/10; LMC 5–6/10; SLJ 5/10) [500]

3018 Leedy, Loreen. *My Teacher Is a Dinosaur: And Other Prehistoric Poems, Jokes, Riddles, and Amazing Facts* (2–5). Illus. by author. 2010, Marshall Cavendish $17.99 (978-0-7614-5708-4). 48pp. A lighthearted tour of prehistoric life with an excellent timeline. (Rev: BL 11/1/10; SLJ 1/1/11) [550]

3019 Lessem, Don. *The Ultimate Dinopedia: The Most Complete Dinosaur Reference Ever* (3–6). Illus. by Franco Tempesta. 2010, National Geographic $24.95 (978-142630164-3); LB $34.90 (978-142630165-0). 272pp. This comprehensive dinosaur encyclopedia includes phonetic spellings and etymological guides along with striking illustrations. Also available as an iPad app. (Rev: BL 12/15/10; LMC 5–6/11) [567.9]

3020 McGowan, Chris. *Dinosaur Discovery: Everything You Need to Be a Paleontologist* (3–6). Illus. by Erica Lyn Schmidt. 2011, Simon & Schuster $17.99 (978-1-4169-4764-6). 48pp. Thirteen dinosaurs are briefly highlighted in this book that presents paleontology-related activities — taking molds of teeth, creating mummified skin, and so forth. ℮ Lexile 870L (Rev: BL 6/1/11; LMC 11–12/11; SLJ 7/11) [560]

3021 Macleod, Elizabeth. *Monster Fliers: From the Time of the Dinosaurs* (K–3). Illus. by John Bindon. 2010, Kids Can $16.95 (978-1-55453-199-8). 32pp. Nineteen different dinosaurs are described and illustrated in this engaging book that includes comparative sizes and a timeline. (Rev: BL 3/15/10; LMC 8–9/10; SLJ 4/1/10) [567.918]

3022 Manning, Mick, and Brita Granstrom. *Woolly Mammoth* (K–3). Illus. by Brita Granstrom. 2009, Frances Lincoln $16.95 (978-1-84507-860-7). 32pp. Rhyming couplets describe the life of a mammoth while sidebars provide more-detailed information for older readers. (Rev: BL 11/15/09; LMC 3–4/10; SLJ 1/1/10) [569.67]

3023 Naish, Darren. *Dinosaurs Life Size* (5–7). Illus. 2010, Barron's $14.99 (978-0-7641-6378-4). 80pp. A large-format eye-catching book full of dinosaur facts and pictures of life-size dinosaur parts — jaws, eyes, and claws and so forth — plus fold-out pages including a timeline. (Rev: LMC 3–4/11; SLJ 12/1/10) [567.9]

3024 O'Hearn, Michael. *Triceratops vs. Stegosaurus: When Horns and Plates Collide* (3–5). Illus. Series: Edge Bks. Dinosaur Wars. 2009, Capstone LB $25.32 (978-1-4296-3938-5). 32pp. A triceratops goes head-to-head with a stegosaurus in this attention-grabbing title focusing on the dinosaurs' defenses, weapons, attack styles, and who would likely win in a face-off. Among other titles in the series are *Spinosaurus vs. Giganotosaurus: Battle of the Giants* and *Allosaurus vs. Brachiosaurus: Might Against Height* (both 2009). (Rev: LMC 11–12/10; SLJ 6/1/10) [567.915]

3025 Ray, Deborah Kogan. *Dinosaur Mountain: Digging into the Jurassic Age* (4–6). Illus. by author. 2010, Farrar $16.99 (978-0-374-31789-8). 40pp. With readable text and interesting illustrations, Ray tells the exciting story of the "Bone Wars" of the late 19th century and Earl Douglass's discovery of Utah's Dinosaur Mountain. (Rev: BL 2/1/10; LMC 5–6/10; SLJ 5/10) [567.90973]

3026 Sloan, Christopher. *Baby Mammoth Mummy: Frozen in Time: A Prehistoric Animal's Journey into the 21st Century* (5–8). Illus. 2011, National Geographic $17.95 (978-1-4263-0865-9); LB $26.90 (978-142630866-6). 48pp. Tells the story of the discovery in Siberia of the baby mammoth called Lyuba, and discusses what scientists have learned about her world. (Rev: BL 11/15/11; SLJ 12/1/11) [569]

3027 West, David. *Velociraptors and Other Raptors and Small Carnivores* (3–5). Illus. Series: Dinosaurs! 2010, Gareth Stevens LB $26.60 (978-143394224-2). 32pp. Computer-enhanced illustrations give this guide to the razor-toothed velociraptors plenty of immediate appeal. (Rev: BL 10/1/10) [567.912]

Anthropology, Prehistoric Life, and Evolution

3028 Loxton, Daniel. *Evolution: How We and All Living Things Came to Be* (3–8). Illus. by author and Jim W. W. Smith. 2010, Kids Can $18.95 (978-1-55453-430-2). 56pp. Helpful images and question-and-answer sections enhance this accessible presentation of the theory of evolution and the evidence that supports it. (Rev: BLO 2/15/10; LMC 8–9/10; SLJ 5/10) [576.8]

3029 Nicolson, Cynthia Pratt. *Totally Human: Why We Look and Act the Way We Do* (3–6). Illus. by Dianne Eastman. 2011, Kids Can $16.95 (978-1-55453-569-9). 40pp. This quirky history of human behavior goes back to the dawn of life to explain some of humanity's weirdest impulses and traits. (Rev: BL 2/15/11; LMC 10/11; SLJ 10/1/11) [576.8]

3030 Prap, Lila. *Dinosaurs?!* (K–3). Illus. by author. 2010, NorthSouth $16.95 (978-0-7358-2284-9). Unpaged. A flock of chickens are astonished to think they might be descended from dinosaurs in this humorous and informative look at evolution. (Rev: LMC 10/10; SLJ 3/1/10) [567.9]

3031 Pringle, Laurence. *Billions of Years, Amazing Changes: The Story of Evolution* (5–8). Illus. by Steve Jenkins. 2011, Boyds Mills $17.95 (978-1-59078-723-6). 96pp. A fascinating, colorful presentation of man's discoveries over time about evolution, with clear explanation of the four core principles plus examples of natural selection and many images. Lexile 1000L (Rev: BL 12/1/11; HB 1–2/12; LMC 1–2/12*; SLJ 12/1/11*) [596.8]

Archaeology

3032 Aronson, Marc, and Mike Parker Pearson, Riverside Project. *If Stones Could Speak: Unlocking the Secrets of Stonehenge* (4–6). 2010, National Geographic $17.95 (978-1-4263-0599-3); LB $26.90 (978-1-4263-0600-6). 64pp. This is a fascinating account of recent archaeological discoveries at Stonehenge, with information on the site and its history and on the science of investigating ancient places. Orbis Pictus Honor Award for Outstanding Nonfiction for Children, 2011. Lexile 1070L (Rev: BL 2/1/10*; HB 5–6/10; LMC 3–4/10; SLJ 3/10) [936.2]

3033 Capek, Michael. *Easter Island* (5–8). Series: Unearthing Ancient Worlds. 2008, Lerner LB $30.60 (978-0-8225-7583-2). 80pp. This volume focuses on the statues of Easter Island, exploring their discovery and significance. (Rev: SLJ 10/1/08)

3034 Compoint, Stephane. *Buried Treasures: Uncovering Secrets of the Past* (5–8). Illus. 2011, Abrams $19.95 (978-0-8109-9781-3). 80pp. Suitable mainly for browsing, this volume features eye-catching photographs of discoveries around the world and shots of scientists at work. (Rev: BL 6/1/11; SLJ 7/11) [930.1]

3035 Hartland, Jessie. *How the Sphinx Got to the Museum* (2–4). Illus. by author. 2010, Blue Apple $17.99 (978-1-60905-032-0). 40pp. The life story of Egypt's seven-ton Sphinx is presented in this visually appealing book, which traces the monument's journey from its construction to its current home in New York City's Metropolitan Museum of Art. Lexile AD1120L (Rev: BL 10/1/10*; LMC 3–4/11; SLJ 1/1/11*) [932]

3036 Huey, Lois Miner. *American Archaeology Uncovers the Dutch Colonies* (5–8). Series: American Archaeology. 2009, Marshall Cavendish LB $21.95 (978-0-7614-4263-9). 64pp. Fascinating artifacts and field research bring the Dutch colonies to life in this visually appealing book that includes dig techniques and glimpses at excavation sites. Also use *American Archaeology Uncovers the Vikings, American Archaeology Uncovers the Earliest English Colonies, American Archaeology Uncovers the Westward Movement,* and *American Archaeology Uncovers the Underground Railroad* (all 2009). e (Rev: BL 10/1/09; LMC 3–4/10; SLJ 2/1/10) [974.7]

World History

General

3037 Albee, Sarah. *Poop Happened! A History of the World from the Bottom Up* (4–6). Illus. by Robert Leighton. 2010, Walker LB $20.89 (978-0-8027-9825-1); paper $15.99 (978-0-8027-2077-1). 176pp. A fascinating review of sanitation across the ages, from ancient Egypt and Greece to the problems astronauts face in space; with information on diseases such as cholera and plague. (Rev: BL 2/15/10; LMC 8–9/10; SLJ 5/10) [363.72]

3038 Beccia, Carlyn. *The Raucous Royals: Test Your Royal Wits: Crack Codes, Solve Mysteries, and Deduce Which Royal Rumors Are True* (4–7). Illus. by author. 2008, Houghton Mifflin $17 (978-061889130-6). 64pp. Beccia encourages critical thinking in this book that examines the rumors and mystery surrounding eleven royal figures including Richard II, Catherine the Great, Prince Dracula, and Marie Antoinette. (Rev: BL 10/15/08; SLJ 12/08) [929.7]

3039 Corrigan, Jim. *The 1900s Decade in Photos: A Decade of Discovery* (4–9). Series: Amazing Decades in Photos. 2010, Enslow LB $27.93 (978-0-7660-3129-6). 64pp. With many color photographs and illustrations and simple text, this volume covers events around the world in the first decade of the 20th century. Other titles in this series include *The 1910s Decade in Photos: A Decade That Shook the World, The 1920s Decade in Photos: The Roaring Twenties,* and *The 1930s Decade in Photos: Depression and Hope.* and continue on through the beginning of the 21st century. (Rev: LMC 3–4/10) [973.911]

3040 Guiberson, Brenda Z. *Disasters: Natural and Man-Made Catastrophes Through the Centuries* (5–8). 2010, Henry Holt $18.99 (978-0-8050-8170-1). 240pp. Guiberson presents compelling accounts of 10 well-known disasters including the sinking of the *Titanic,* the Great Chicago Fire, the 1918 flu pandemic, and Hurricane Katrina. (Rev: BL 5/15/10; HB 7–8/10; LMC 8–9/10; SLJ 6/10) [904]

3041 MacDonald, Fiona. *Top 10 Worst Ruthless Warriors You Wouldn't Want to Know!* (4–7). Illus. by David Antram. 2012, Gareth Stevens LB $26.60 (978-143396685-9). 32pp. The exploits of Genghis Khan, Alexander the Great, and Japanese warrior Yoshitsune, among others, are portrayed in this lively and irreverent history that is not for the faint-hearted. Also use *Top 10 Worst Wicked Rulers You Wouldn't Want to Know!* — which introduces Robespierre, Ivan the Terrible, and others. (Rev: BL 4/15/12; SLJ 6/12) [920]

3042 Mooney, Carla. *The Industrial Revolution: Investigate How Science and Technology Changed the World with 25 Projects* (4–7). Illus. by Jen Vaughn. Series: Build It Yourself. 2011, Nomad $21.95 (978-1-936313-81-5); paper $15.95 (978-1-936313-80-8). 128pp. This illustrated title introduces the great minds that gave rise to the Industrial Revolution and showcases their innovations; includes 25 very varied projects. (Rev: BL 12/1/11; SLJ 1/12) [338.0973]

3043 Murrell, Deborah. *Gladiator* (4–7). Series: Qeb Warriors. 2010, Black Rabbit LB $28.50 (978-1-59566-736-6). 32pp. This volume gives arresting descriptions of the lives, battle tactics, and weapons of Roman centurions and Greek hoplites, with maps and eye-catching illustrations. (Rev: LMC 1–2/10)

3044 Price, Sean Stewart. *The Kids' Guide to Lost Cities* (3–5). Illus. Series: Kids' Guides. 2011, Capstone LB $26.65 (978-142966009-9). 32pp. Machu Picchu and Pompeii are among the lost cities discussed in this historical survey. (Rev: BL 2/15/12) [930.1]

3045 Ross, Stewart. *Into the Unknown: How Great Explorers Found Their Way by Land, Sea, and Air* (4–8). Illus. by Stephen Biesty. 2011, Candlewick $19.99 (978-0-7636-4948-7). 96pp. A handsome and informative overview of 14 important journeys of exploration, starting in 340 B.C. with Pytheas the Greek's voyage to the Arctic Circle and ending in 1969 with Neil Armstrong and Buzz Aldrin's landing on the moon. Boston Globe–Horn Book Award. (Rev: BL 7/11; HB 5–6/11; LMC 10/11; SLJ 5/11*) [910.9]

Ancient History

General and Miscellaneous

3046 Apte, Sunita. *The Aztec Empire* (3–5). Series: True Book Ancient Civilizations. 2009, Children's Press LB $26 (978-0-531-25227-7). 48pp. Taking care to distinguish between fact and legend, this attractive volume discusses the Aztec empire's people and culture and the ruins that reveal information about them. (Rev: LMC 1–2/10; SLJ 12/1/09) [972]

3047 Croy, Anita, ed. *Ancient Aztec and Maya* (5–9). Series: Facts at Your Fingertips. 2010, Black Rabbit LB $35.65 (978-1-933834-58-0). 64pp. After presenting historical facts about the Aztec and Mayan civilizations, this volume goes on to look at specific sites and the cultures of these peoples. (Rev: LMC 3–4/10) [972]

3048 Galloway, Priscilla, and Dawn Hunter. *Adventures on the Ancient Silk Road* (5–8). 2009, Annick $24.95 (978-1-55451-198-3); paper $14.95 (978-1-55451-197-6). 168pp. The ancient trade route is brought to life in accounts of three travelers many years apart: the monk Xuanzang, the conqueror Genghis Khan, and the merchant Marco Polo. (Rev: BL 1/1/10; SLJ 12/09) [950]

3049 Jestice, Phyllis G. *Ancient Persian Warfare* (3–6). Series: Ancient Warfare. 2010, Gareth Stevens LB $26 (978-1-4339-1973-2). 32pp. In chapters on foot soldiers, fighting with horses, weapons and armor, and war at sea, this volume looks at the armies of ancient Persia and the famous leaders of the time. (Rev: SLJ 6/10) [355.02]

3050 Maloy, Jackie. *The Ancient Maya* (3–5). Series: True Book Ancient Civilizations. 2009, Children's Press LB $26 (978-0-531-25229-1). 48pp. Taking care to distinguish between fact and legend, this attractive volume discusses the ancient Maya's culture and the ruins that reveal information about them. (Rev: LMC 1–2/10; SLJ 12/1/09) [972]

3051 Miller, Reagan. *Communication in the Ancient World* (5–7). Illus. Series: Life in the Ancient World. 2011, Crabtree LB $19.95 (978-077871733-1); paper $8.95 (978-077871740-9). 32pp. This accessible book explores the development of writing, counting, and calendars in various cultures — Rome, South America, Egypt, Japan — around the ancient world. (Rev: BL 10/1/11; LMC 9–10/12) [302.2]

3052 Newman, Sandra. *The Inca Empire* (3–5). Series: True Book Ancient Civilizations. 2009, Children's Press LB $26 (978-0-531-25228-4). 48pp. Taking care to distinguish between fact and legend, this attractive volume discusses the Inca people and culture and the ruins that reveal information about them. (Rev: BL 10/1/09; LMC 1–2/10; SLJ 12/1/09) [985]

3053 Price, Massoume. *Ancient Iran* (4–8). Illus. Series: Culture of Iran Youth Series. 2008, Anahita $19.95 (978-0-9809714-0-8). 72pp. After a brief discussion of Iran today, this well-illustrated volume gives a chronological overview of the peoples and culture of ancient Iran. (Rev: SLJ 3/1/09) [935]

3054 Raum, Elizabeth. *What Did the Vikings Do for Me?* (4–7). Illus. Series: Linking Past to Present. 2010, Heinemann LB $29 (978-143293745-4). 32pp. This intriguing overview of Viking history and culture also explains their legacy in aspects including language, justice, and the role of women. (Rev: BL 10/1/10; LMC 1–2/11) [948]

Egypt and Mesopotamia

3055 Adamson, Heather. *Ancient Egypt: An Interactive History Adventure* (3–5). Illus. 2009, Capstone LB $27.98 (978-142963415-1). 112pp. In this engaging history book with a choose-your-own-adventure twist, readers select which role they'd like to play in ancient Egypt, from slave to pharaoh. (Rev: BL 7/10; LMC 1–2/10) [932]

3056 Croy, Anita, ed. *Ancient Egypt* (5–9). Series: Facts at Your Fingertips. 2010, Black Rabbit LB $35.65 (978-1-933834-54-2). 64pp. After presenting historical facts about ancient Egypt before and after the pharaohs, this volume goes on to look at specific sites of importance — Abu Simbel, Thebes, Memphis, and so forth. Also use *Ancient Mesopotamia* (2010). (Rev: LMC 3–4/10) [932.222]

3057 England, Victoria. *Top 10 Worst Things About Ancient Egypt You Wouldn't Want to Know* (4–7). Illus. by David Antram. 2012, Gareth Stevens LB $26.60 (978-143396688-0). 32pp. Starvation, irascible pharaohs, and drudging stone cutting and hauling work are a few of the things ancient Egyptians had to endure; this lively and irreverent history book will appeal to browsers and reluctant readers. (Rev: BL 4/15/12; SLJ 6/12) [932]

3058 Hollar, Sherman. *Ancient Egypt* (5–8). Series: Ancient Civilizations. 2011, Britannica Educational LB $31.70 (978-1-61530-523-0). 88pp. This slim volume offers an accessible introduction to the culture, religion, architecture, and inventions of ancient Egypt. e (Rev: SLJ 12/1/11) [932]

3059 Jestice, Phyllis G. *Ancient Egyptian Warfare* (3–6). Illus. Series: Ancient Warfare. 2010, Gareth Stevens LB $26 (978-1-4339-1971-8). 32pp. In chapters on foot soldiers, fighting with horses, weapons and armor, and war at sea, this volume looks at the armies of ancient Egypt and the famous leaders of the time. (Rev: SLJ 6/10) [355.0]

Greece

3060 Anderson, Michael, ed. *Ancient Greece* (5–8). Series: Ancient Civilizations. 2011, Britannica Educational LB $31.70 (978-1-61530-513-1). 88pp. This slim volume offers an accessible introduction to the culture, religion, architecture, and inventions of ancient Greece. *e* (Rev: SLJ 12/1/11) [938]

3061 Caper, William. *Ancient Greece: An Interactive History Adventure* (3–5). Illus. 2009, Capstone LB $29.32 (978-142963417-5). 112pp. In this engaging history book with a choose-your-own-adventure twist, readers select which role they'd like to play in ancient Greece, from slave to philosopher. (Rev: BL 7/10) [938]

3062 Croy, Anita, ed. *Ancient Greece* (5–9). Series: Facts at Your Fingertips. 2010, Black Rabbit LB $35.65 (978-1-933834-55-9). 64pp. Crete, Mycenai, Sparta, Olympia, and Athens are among the sites described in this overview of the history and culture of ancient Greece. (Rev: LMC 3–4/10) [938]

3063 Martell, Hazel Mary, and Cleo Kuhtz. *Ancient Greek Civilization* (5–8). Series: Ancient Civilizations and Their Myths and Legends. 2010, Rosen LB $26.50 (978-1-4042-8033-5). 48pp. This volume introduces daily life in ancient Greece and describes religion, agriculture, government, trade, clothing, entertainment, and so forth, at the same time retelling some of the best-known myths. (Rev: LMC 1–2/10) [292.13]

3064 Rice, Rob S. *Ancient Greek Warfare* (3–6). Series: Ancient Warfare. 2010, Gareth Stevens LB $26 (978-1-4339-1972-5). 32pp. In chapters on fortress cities, war on land, and war at sea, this volume looks at the armies of ancient Greece and at the life and achievements of Alexander the Great. (Rev: SLJ 6/10) [355.02]

Rome

3065 Anderson, Michael, ed. *Ancient Rome* (5–8). Series: Ancient Civilizations. 2011, Britannica Educational LB $31.70 (978-1-61530-522-3). 88pp. This slim volume offers an accessible introduction to the culture, religion, architecture, and inventions of ancient Rome. *e* (Rev: SLJ 12/1/11) [937]

3066 Croy, Anita, ed. *Ancient Rome* (5–9). Series: Facts at Your Fingertips. 2010, Black Rabbit LB $35.65 (978-1-933834-56-6). 64pp. From the birth of Rome through the peak of imperial power to the later empire, this well-illustrated volume provides easy access to facts and looks at different areas of the Roman Empire in some detail. (Rev: LMC 3–4/10) [937]

3067 Hanel, Rachael. *Ancient Rome: An Interactive History Adventure* (3–5). Illus. 2009, Capstone LB $29.32 (978-142963416-8). 112pp. In this engaging history book with a choose-your-own-adventure twist, readers select which role they'd like to play in ancient Rome, from slave to senator. (Rev: BL 7/10) [937]

3068 Matthews, Rupert. *100 Things You Should Know About Gladiators* (3–6). Illus. Series: Remarkable Man and Beast: Facing Survival. 2010, Mason Crest LB $19.95 (978-142221970-6). 48pp. With plenty of lively photographs and illustrations woven together with cohesive text, this is a useful introduction to gladiators. (Rev: BL 10/15/10; LMC 3–4/11; SLJ 2/1/11) [796.8]

3069 Rice, Rob S. *Ancient Roman Warfare* (3–6). Series: Ancient Warfare. 2010, Gareth Stevens LB $26 (978-1-4339-1974-9). 32pp. In chapters on building an empire, weapons and equipment, camps, and war at sea, this volume looks at the armies of ancient Rome and the famous leaders of the time. (Rev: SLJ 6/10) [355.0]

Middle Ages

3070 Allen, Kathy. *The Horrible, Miserable Middle Ages: The Disgusting Details About Life During Medieval Times* (4–8). Series: Fact Finders: Disgusting History. 2010, Capstone LB $25.32 (978-1-4296-3958-3). 32pp. Allen concentrates on the grosser side of medieval life, describing poor sanitation, rotten food, bugs, medical horrors, and so forth. Lexile 850L (Rev: LMC 11–12/10) [940.1]

3071 Lassieur, Allison. *The Middle Ages: An Interactive History Adventure* (3–5). 2009, Capstone $27.98 (978-142963418-2). 112pp. In this engaging history book with a choose-your-own-adventure twist, readers select which role they'd like to play in the Middle Ages, from peasant to medieval knight. (Rev: BL 7/10; LMC 1–2/10) [940.1]

World War I

3072 Murphy, Jim. *Truce: The Day the Soldiers Stopped Fighting* (5–8). 2009, Scholastic $19.99 (978-0-545-13049-3). 144pp. The famous Christmas Truce on the western front in December 1914 is explained in this well-written book that features sepia illustrations and discussion of changing attitudes throughout this long war. (Rev: BL 10/15/09*; HB 11–12/09; LMC 1–2/10; SLJ 11/09) [940.4]

3073 Swain, Gwenyth. *World War I* (4–6). Illus. Series: You Choose. 2012, Capstone $31.32 (978-142966020-4); paper $6.95 (978-142967997-8). 112pp. This choose-your-own-adventure story emphasizes the choices that had to be made in World War I — a nurse in Belgium must decide whether to stay at her hospital, a British teen can enlist or wait until he is called up, and so forth. (Rev: BL 5/15/12) [940.3]

World War II

3074 Burgan, Michael. *Refusing to Crumble: The Danish Resistance in World War II* (5–8). Series: Taking a Stand. 2010, Compass Point LB $31.99 (978-0-7565-4298-6). 64pp. An introduction to the Danish response to the Nazi invasion in 1940, giving the reasons for surrender and highlighting the actions of the underground resistance, brave Danes who worked to save Jews and sabotage the Germans. Lexile 970L (Rev: LMC 11–12/10; VOYA 8/10)

3075 Gitlin, Martin. *World War II on the Home Front* (4–5). Illus. Series: You Choose. 2012, Capstone $31.32 (978-142966019-8); paper $6.95 (978-142967998-5). 112pp. This choose-your-own-adventure story emphasizes the politically loaded decisions that had to be made while living on the home front during World War II. (Rev: BL 5/15/12) [973.91]

3076 Graham, Ian. *You Wouldn't Want to Be a World War II Pilot! Air Battles You Might Not Survive* (4–8). Illus. by David Antram. Series: You Wouldn't Want to Be. 2009, Franklin Watts LB $29 (978-0-531-21326-1). 32pp. This appealing volume provides facts and ex-amples of the dangers of flying in World War II. Lexile IG910L (Rev: LMC 1–2/10)

3077 Levy, Debbie. *The Year of Goodbyes: A True Story of Friendship, Family, and Farewells* (5–8). Illus. 2010, Hyperion $16.99 (978-142312901-1). 144pp. Based on a poetry album created by the author's mother in 1938 as the Jewish family waited for U.S. visas while their German friends disappeared around them. Lexile 910L (Rev: BL 2/15/10; SLJ 5/10)

3078 Ruelle, Karen Gray, and Deborah Durland DeSaix. *The Grand Mosque of Paris: A Story of How Muslims Rescued Jews During the Holocaust* (3–6). Illus. by Karen Gray Ruelle. 2009, Holiday House $17.95 (978-082342159-6). 40pp. This inspiring book describes how the Muslims of Paris threw their Grand Mosque open to Jews during the Nazi occupation and saved many lives. (Rev: BL 11/15/09; LMC 1–2/10; SLJ 10/09) [940.53]

3079 Seiple, Samantha. *Ghosts in the Fog: The Untold Story of Alaska's WWII Invasion* (5–8). Illus. 2011, Scholastic $16.99 (978-0-545-29654-0). 224pp. Seiple gives us a fascinating and well-researched account of the Japanese invasion and occupation of Alaska in June 1942, including information about the detention of Native Americans. (Rev: BL 12/1/11; LMC 1–2/12; SLJ 11/1/11; VOYA 10/11) [940.54]

3080 Wood, Douglas. *Franklin and Winston: A Christmas That Changed the World* (5–8). Illus. by Barry Moser. 2011, Candlewick $16.99 (978-076363383-7). 40pp. In December 1941, Churchill and FDR met and became friends during a tense time, discussing strategies that would have lasting consequences. (Rev: BL 9/15/11*; SLJ 10/1/11) [940.53]

Geographical Regions

Africa

General

3081 Opini, Bathseba, and Richard B. Lee. *Africans Thought of It: Amazing Innovations* (3–6). Illus. Series: We Thought of It. 2011, Annick LB $21.95 (978-1-55451-277-5); paper $11.95 (978-1-55451-276-8). 48pp. Looks at inventions by Africans in fields as varied as hunting, agriculture, medicine, sports, and the arts. (Rev: LMC 3–4/12; SLJ 10/1/11) [960]

Central and Eastern Africa

3082 Bojang, Ali Brownlie. *Sudan in Our World* (5–8). Series: Countries in Our World. 2010, Smart Apple Media $28.50 (978-1-59920-434-5). 32pp. Bojang covers Sudan's geography, people, culture, economy, government, and future, with frank discussion of the poverty and fighting that have plagued the country. (Rev: SLJ 12/1/10) [962.4]

3083 Reynolds, Jan. *Only the Mountains Do Not Move: A Maasai Story of Culture and Conservation* (2–5). Illus. 2011, Lee & Low $18.95 (978-1-60060-333-4). 40pp. Reynolds offers a glimpse into the daily life of a Maasai village in northern Kenya, showing all the ways it has adapted to political, cultural, and environmental challenges. (Rev: BL 9/1/11; SLJ 10/1/11) [305.896]

3084 Roth, Susan L., and Cindy Trumbore. *The Mangrove Tree: Planting Trees to Feed Families* (3–7). Illus. by Susan L. Roth. 2011, Lee & Low $19.95 (978-1-60060-459-1). 40pp. In simple cumulative verse, this picture book tells the story of Japanese American biologist Gordon Sato's project to plant mangrove trees in Eritrea and help the surrounding community. (Rev: BL 5/1/11; SLJ 5/1/11*) [577.69]

Southern Africa

3085 Bojang, Ali Brownlie. *South Africa in Our World* (5–8). Series: Countries in Our World. 2010, Smart Apple Media $28.50 (978-1-59920-444-4). 32pp. Bojang covers South Africa's geography, people, culture, economy, government, and future, with frank discussion of such topics as apartheid and AIDS. (Rev: SLJ 12/1/10) [968.06]

Western Africa

3086 Taylor, Dereen. *Nigeria* (4–7). Illus. Series: A World of Food. 2010, Oliver LB $24.95 (978-193454514-0). 32pp. This book presents an overview of Nigeria's cuisine, complete with simple recipes, colorful illustrations, and plenty of cultural context. (Rev: BL 4/1/10; LMC 10/10) [394.1]

Asia

India

3087 Ejaz, Khadija. *Recipe and Craft Guide to India* (4–7). Illus. 2010, Mitchell Lane LB $24.50 (978-158415938-4). 64pp. Cultural and culinary projects introduce readers to many aspects of India. (Rev: BL 1/1–15/11; LMC 1–2/11*) [641.5954]

Japan

3088 Malam, John. *You Wouldn't Want to Be a Ninja Warrior! A Secret Job That's Your Destiny* (3–5). Illus. by David Antram. 2012, Scholastic LB $29 (978-053120873-1); paper $9.95 (978-053120948-6). 32pp.

Malam looks at the training and weapons of the average ninja, and the skills they needed to develop. (Rev: BL 2/15/12; SLJ 4/12) [355.5]

3089 Mofford, Juliet Haines. *Recipe and Craft Guide to Japan* (4–7). Illus. 2010, Mitchell Lane LB $24.50 (978-158415933-9). 64pp. Cultural and culinary projects introduce readers to many aspects of Japan. (Rev: BL 1/1–15/11; LMC 1–2/11*) [641.5952]

Other Asian Lands

3090 Behnke, Alison. *Angkor Wat* (5–8). Series: Unearthing Ancient Worlds. 2008, Lerner LB $30.60 (978-0-8225-7585-6). 80pp. This volume focuses on the ruins of Angkor Wat, thoroughly explaining the archaeological science that fueled the discoveries and providing color maps, illustrations, and photos. (Rev: SLJ 10/1/08)

3091 Fordyce, Deborah. *Afghanistan* (3–6). Series: Welcome to My Country. 2010, Marshall Cavendish LB $19.95 (978-1-60870-149-0). 48pp. An overview of the geography, history, government, economy, people, culture, and diet of Afghanistan. (Rev: SLJ 12/1/10) [958.1]

3092 Harris, Nathaniel. *Burma (Myanmar)* (4–6). Series: Global Hotspots. 2010, Marshall Cavendish $12.99 (978-0-7614-4758-0). 32pp. An introduction to the turbulent history of Myanmar, ending with a discussion of contemporary problems. (Rev: SLJ 4/10) [959.1]

3093 Kwek, Karen, and Jameel Haque. *Pakistan* (3–6). 2010, Marshall Cavendish LB $19.95 (978-1-60870-158-2). 48pp. An overview of the geography, history, government, economy, people, culture, and diet of Pakistan. (Rev: SLJ 12/1/10) [954.91]

3094 Sobol, Richard. *The Life of Rice: From Seedling to Supper* (3–6). Illus. 2010, Candlewick $17.99 (978-0-7636-3252-6). 40pp. A photographer travels around Thailand, documenting the cultural and agricultural importance of rice. (Rev: BL 10/15/10; LMC 11–12/10; SLJ 9/1/10) [633.1]

3095 Sobol, Richard. *The Mysteries of Angkor Wat: Exploring Cambodia's Ancient Temple* (4–6). Photos by Richard Sobol. Series: Traveling Photographer. 2011, Candlewick $17.99 (978-0-7636-4166-5). 48pp. Full of beautiful photographs, this is a fascinating account of the history and mystery surrounding the ancient Cambodian temple. (Rev: LMC 11–12/11; SLJ 8/11) [959.6]

3096 Winter, Jeanette. *Nasreen's Secret School: A True Story from Afghanistan* (2–4). Illus. by author. 2009, Simon & Schuster $16.99 (978-1-4169-9437-4). 40pp. When her father is abducted by the Taliban and her mother disappears, Nasreen goes to live with her grand-

mother and attends a secret school. **e** Lexile AD630L (Rev: BL 9/15/09*; HB 11–12/09; LMC 10/09; SLJ 9/1/09) [371.823]

Europe

France

3097 LaRoche, Amelia. *Recipe and Craft Guide to France* (4–7). Illus. Series: World Crafts and Recipes. 2010, Mitchell Lane LB $24.50 (978-158415936-0). 64pp. Cultural and culinary projects introduce readers to many aspects of France. (Rev: BL 1/1–15/11; LMC 1–2/11*) [641.5941]

Great Britain and Ireland

3098 Losure, Mary. *The Fairy Ring; or, Elsie and Frances Fool the World* (5–8). Illus. 2012, Candlewick $16.99 (978-076365670-6). 192pp. Losure tells the story of two cousins who as girls in early-20th-century England posed with paintings of fairies and convinced many, including Arthur Conan Doyle, that they were real. ∩ **e** Lexile 940L (Rev: BL 3/1/12*; HB 3–4/12*; SLJ 5/12; VOYA 2/12) [398]

3099 Rubbino, Salvatore. *A Walk in London* (1–3). Illus. by author. 2011, Candlewick $16.99 (978-0-7636-5272-2). 40pp. A young girl describes her tour of London with her mother, with details of all the places they visit; captions to the illustrations in this large-format book provide key information. (Rev: BL 5/1/11; SLJ 6/11) [942.1]

Greece and Italy

3100 Lamprell, Klay. *Not-for-Parents Rome: Everything You Ever Wanted to Know* (4–7). Illus. 2011, Lonely Planet paper $14.99 (978-174220818-3). 96pp. More a source of trivia and amusement than a guidebook, this is nonetheless informative and directed at young visitors to the city; includes many photographs, maps, and images. (Rev: BL 12/1/11) [914.5632]

Spain and Portugal

3101 Croy, Anita. *Spain* (4–8). Series: Countries of the World. 2010, National Geographic LB $27.90 (978-1-4263-0633-4). 64pp. In addition to giving an overview of the country's geography, people, culture, history, government, economy, and climate, this volume includes special features such as "The Wild West — in Spain!" and "The Real El Cid." (Rev: BL 4/1/10; SLJ 4/10) [946]

The Middle East

General

3102 Marx, Trish. *Sharing Our Homeland: Palestinian and Jewish Children at Summer Peace Camp* (3–6). Illus. by Cindy Karp. 2010, Lee & Low $19.95 (978-1-58430-250-5). 48pp. A Muslim girl and a Jewish boy share and learn to appreciate each other's cultures while at summer peace camp. (Rev: BL 5/15/10; LMC 1–2/11; SLJ 10/1/10) [915.69406]

Other Middle Eastern Lands

3103 Wilkes, Sybella. *Out of Iraq: Refugees' Stories in Words, Paintings and Music* (5–9). Illus. 2010, Evans Brothers $17.99 (978-0-237-53930-6). 70pp. A variety of compelling interviews conducted with artists, journalists, teachers, children, and young adults show a moving picture of the humanitarian implications of the 2003 invasion of Iraq. (Rev: SLJ 11/1/10) [305.9]

North and South America (Excluding the United States)

North and South America

3104 Harrison, David L. *Mammoth Bones and Broken Stones: The Mystery of North America's First People* (4–6). Illus. by Richard Hilliard. 2010, Boyds Mills $18.95 (978-159078561-4). 46pp. Harrison looks at our fragments of knowledge about the earliest inhabitants of North America, asking when they arrived and who arrived first, and documenting the artifacts they left behind. Lexile 1040L (Rev: BLO 11/15/10; LMC 3–4/11; SLJ 12/1/10) [970.01]

3105 Mann, Charles C. *Before Columbus: The Americas of 1491* (5–8). 2009, Simon & Schuster $24.99 (978-1-4169-4900-8). 117pp. This clearly written and designed history of pre-Columbian America includes brightly colored illustrations and sidebars that illuminate what for many is a misunderstood period of history. (Rev: BL 9/1/09*; LMC 11–12/09; SLJ 9/09*) [970.01]

Canada

3106 Boudreau, Hélène. *Life in a Fishing Community* (2–4). Series: Learn About Rural Life. 2009, Crabtree LB $26.60 (978-0-7787-5072-7); paper $8.95 (978-0-7787-5085-7). 32pp. Life in the rural fishing community of Lunenburg, Nova Scotia, is described along with the work involved in fishing and the kinds of fish caught, with information about fishing around the world. (Rev: SLJ 2/1/10) [639.2]

3107 Enzoe, Pete, and Mindy Willet. *The Caribou Feed Our Soul* (3–6). Illus. Series: Land Is Our Storybook. 2011, Fitzhenry & Whiteside $16.95 (978-1-897252-67-3). 26pp. The author, a Chipewyan Dene, describes his efforts to protect the caribou of Canada's Northwest Territories and discusses traditional tales and rituals. (Rev: BL 7/11; LMC 10/11; SLJ 6/11) [639]

3108 Walker, Sally M. *Blizzard of Glass: The Halifax Explosion of 1917* (5–8). Illus. 2011, Henry Holt $18.99 (978-0-8050-8945-5). 160pp. With many archival photographs and compelling narrative, this book tells the story of the explosion of a munitions ship in Halifax harbor in Canada in 1917 following a collision with another vessel; almost 2,000 people were killed. (Rev: BL 11/1/11; SLJ 10/1/11) [971.6]

Mexico

3109 Somervill, Barbara A. *It's Cool to Learn About Countries: Mexico* (3–6). Series: Social Studies Explorer. 2010, Cherry Lake LB $29.93 (978-1-60279-833-5). 48pp. Readers learn about the geography, population, government, and culture of Mexico; includes a recipe, an art project, and a few activities. (Rev: SLJ 1/1/11) [972]

Central America

3110 Crandell, Rachel. *Hands of the Rain Forest: The Emberá People of Panama* (1–3). Illus. 2009, Henry Holt $16.99 (978-0-8050-7990-6). 32pp. A photo-essay introducing the lifestyle and traditions of the Emberá people of Panama, with maps and a timeline. (Rev: BL 11/15/09; LMC 11–12/09; SLJ 11/1/09) [972.87]

South America

3111 Aronson, Marc. *Trapped: How the World Rescued 33 Miners from 2,000 Feet Below the Chilean Desert* (4–8). Illus. 2011, Atheneum $16.99 (978-1-4169-1397-9). 144pp. A gripping story of the mine disaster in 2010 and the massive effort to rescue the survivors, with information on geology and mining techniques. (Rev: BL 9/1/11*; SLJ 8/11*) [363.11]

3112 Franchino, Vicky. *It's Cool to Learn About Countries: Brazil* (3–6). Series: Social Studies Explorer. 2010, Cherry Lake LB $29.93 (978-1-60279-827-4). 48pp. Readers learn about the geography, population, government, and culture of Brazil; includes a recipe, an art project, and a few activities. (Rev: SLJ 1/1/11) [981]

Polar Regions

3113 Baker, Stuart. *Climate Change in the Antarctic* (3–6). Illus. 2009, Marshall Cavendish LB $19.95 (978-076144438-1). 32pp. With chapters on the effects of climate change on the topography, plants, and animals of the Antarctic, this well-illustrated slim volume will be attractive to reluctant readers. (Rev: BL 2/15/10; LMC 3–4/10) [508.3398]

3114 Wade, Rosalyn. *Polar Worlds* (4–7). Illus. Series: Insiders. 2011, Simon & Schuster $16.99 (978-144243275-8). 64pp. Three-D illustrations draw readers into this overview of the Arctic and Antarctic regions and their topography and flora and fauna, with discussion of exploration, survival measures, and environmental threats. (Rev: BL 12/1/11) [919]

United States

General History and Geography

3115 Croy, Elden. *United States* (4–8). Series: Countries of the World. 2010, National Geographic LB $27.90 (978-1-4263-0632-7). 64pp. In addition to giving an overview of the country's geography, people, culture, history, government, economy, and climate, this volume includes special features such as "Mississippi Flyway" and "Go West, Young Man!" (Rev: BL 4/1/10; SLJ 4/10) [973]

3116 Uschan, Michael V. *Protests and Riots* (5–8). Series: American History. 2010, Gale/Lucent LB $33.45 (978-1-4205-0278-7). 112pp. Primary source quotes and period photographs enhance this overview of key protests throughout American history. (Rev: SLJ 4/11) [973]

Historical Periods

NATIVE AMERICANS

3117 Bjornlund, Lydia. *The Trail of Tears: The Relocation of the Cherokee Nation* (5–8). Series: American History. 2010, Gale/Lucent LB $33.45 (978-1-4205-0211-4). 104pp. Primary source quotations and period photographs enhance this account of the tragic journey of the Cherokee away from their homeland. (Rev: SLJ 4/11) [975.004]

3118 Cunningham, Kevin, and Peter Benoit. *The Inuit* (3–5). Illus. Series: A True Book: American Indian. 2011, Scholastic LB $28 (978-053120760-4); paper $6.95 (978-053129302-7). 48pp. Introduces the Inuit people and their history, clothing, diet, survival skills,

society, and so forth. Also use *The Comanche, The Navajo,* and *The Zuni* (all 2011). (Rev: BL 9/15/11) [979.8004]

3119 Dennis, Yvonne Wakim, and Arlene Hirschfelder. *A Kid's Guide to Native American History: More Than 50 Activities* (4–6). Illus. by Gail Rattray. 2009, Chicago Review paper $16.95 (978-155652802-6). 256pp. This collection of activities, crafts, recipes, and games illustrates the regional differences between Native American tribes, and looks at their present lives and customs; includes extensive back matter. (Rev: BL 1/1/10; LMC 11–12/10; SLJ 11/09) [970.004]

3120 Noble, Trinka Hakes. *The People of Twelve Thousand Winters* (2–5). Illus. by Jim Madsen. Series: Tales of the World. 2012, Sleeping Bear $16.95 (978-158536529-6). 32pp. Full of details of daily life, this account of Lenni Lenape life in an area now part of New Jersey features 10-year-old Walking Turtle, who worries about the fate of his younger cousin, Little Talk, who is disabled. (Rev: BL 5/1/12; SLJ 5/1/12) [974.004]

3121 Zimmerman, Dwight Jon. *Saga of the Sioux: An Adaptation of Dee Brown's Bury My Heart at Wounded Knee* (5–8). Illus. 2011, Henry Holt $18.99 (978-0-8050-9364-3). 240pp. This adaptation of Dee Brown's classic work provides a short history of the Sioux tribe and examines the events leading up to the Wounded Knee massacre. (Rev: BL 10/1/11; LMC 11–12/11; SLJ 9/1/11; VOYA 8/11) [978]

DISCOVERY AND EXPLORATION

3122 Perritano, John. *Spanish Missions* (3–7). Series: A True Book. 2010, Children's Press LB $26 (978-0-531-20575-4). 48pp. A look at Spanish mission buildings, with beautiful color photographs and discussion of their history and the impact of the missions on the Native Americans. Lexile 950L (Rev: BL 11/15/10; LMC 8–9/10) [266.27]

COLONIAL PERIOD

3123 McNeese, Tim. *Colonial America: 1543–1763* (5–8). Illus. Series: Discovering U.S. History. 2010, Chelsea House $35 (978-1-60413-349-3). 136pp. Covering more than 200 years, this is a satisfying survey of social and political developments in colonial America, with illustrations, maps, photographs, and interesting sidebar features. **ℯ** (Rev: LMC 11–12/10; SLJ 8/10) [973.2]

3124 Marsico, Katie. *The Doctor* (3–5). Illus. Series: Colonial People. 2011, Marshall Cavendish LB $20.95 (978-1-60870-412-5). 48pp. Explores the lives of the doctors of the colonial period and the kinds of techniques they had at their disposal. (Rev: BL 12/1/11; SLJ 12/1/11) [610.69]

3125 Petersen, Christine. *The Glassblower* (3–5). Illus. Series: Colonial People. 2011, Marshall Cavendish LB $20.95 (978-1-60870-413-2). 48pp. Explores the lives and importance of the glassblowers who made a variety of key products in the colonial period. (Rev: BL 12/1/11; SLJ 12/1/11) [666]

3126 Petersen, Christine. *The Tanner* (3–5). Illus. Series: Colonial People. 2011, Marshall Cavendish LB $20.95 (978-1-60870-418-7). 48pp. Explores the lives of the tanners who made a variety of products from leather in the colonial period. Other volumes in this series include *The Tailor* (2011). (Rev: BL 12/1/11; SLJ 12/1/11) [675]

3127 Waxman, Laura Hamilton. *Who Were the Accused Witches of Salem? And Other Questions About the Witchcraft Trials* (3–6). Illus. Series: Six Questions of American History. 2012, Lerner LB $30.60 (978-076135225-9). 48pp. Six thoughtful questions about the Salem Witch trials are considered with reference to the historical and cultural context; includes informative back matter. (Rev: BL 2/1/12; SLJ 3/12) [133.4]

REVOLUTIONARY PERIOD

3128 Allen, Kathy. *The First American Flag* (1–3). Illus. by Siri Weber Feeney. 2009, Picture Window LB $23.99 (978-140485541-0). 32pp. Allen bursts the legend of Betsy Ross and tells the real story of the creation of the flag. (Rev: BL 3/1/10) [929.9]

3129 Blair, Margaret Whitman. *Liberty or Death: The Surprising Story of Runaway Slaves Who Sided with the British During the American Revolution* (5–8). 2010, National Geographic $18.95 (978-1-4263-0590-0); LB $27.90 (978-1-4263-0591-7). 64pp. Using personal quotes and anecdotes, Blair tells the unhappy story of the runaway slaves who were promised freedom if they fought for the British during the Revolution. Lexile 1160L (Rev: BL 1/1/10*; LMC 5–6/10; SLJ 3/10) [973.3]

3130 Castrovilla, Selene. *Upon Secrecy* (4–7). Illus. by Jeff Crosby and Shelley Ann Jackson. 2009, Boyds Mills $17.95 (978-1-59078-573-7). 32pp. This illustrated book provides a well-written, slightly fictionalized history of the Culper Spy Ring, a New York City organization instrumental in Washington's ultimate defeat of the British. (Rev: LMC 11–12/09; SLJ 10/09) [973.3]

3131 Crawford, Laura. *The American Revolution from A to Z* (3–5). Illus. by Judith Hierstein. 2009, Pelican $15.95 (978-1-58980-515-6). Unpaged. Suitable for browsing, this alphabet book covers many topics relating to the American Revolution, from prominent characters and events to the less familiar (Betty Zane and the Battle of the Kegs, for example). (Rev: LMC 1/1/10*; SLJ 1/1/10) [973.3]

3132 Isaacs, Sally Senzell. *Colonists and Independence* (4–6). Illus. Series: All About America. 2011, Kingfisher LB $19.89 (978-0-7534-6581-3); paper $9.99 (978-0-7534-6513-4). 32pp. With many photographs, paintings, maps, and primary documents, this overview of the colonial settlers and the struggle for independence will be useful for report writers. (Rev: BL 9/1/11; SLJ 8/11) [973]

3133 McNeese, Tim. *Revolutionary America 1764–1789* (5–8). Series: Discovering U.S. History. 2010, Chelsea House $35 (978-1-60413-350-9). 136pp. McNeese provides a succinct overview of the key events and issues of this period of turmoil, with a chronology and timeline plus illustrations and primary sources. (Rev: LMC 11–12/10) [973.3]

3134 Malaspina, Ann. *Phillis Sings Out Freedom: The Story of George Washington and Phillis Wheatley* (2–4). Illus. by Susan Keeter. 2010, Whitman $16.99 (978-0-8075-6545-2). 32pp. Malaspina interweaves the story of Washington's revolutionary efforts with the life and poetry of Phillis Wheatley, a slave who was eventually freed by her owners. (Rev: BL 9/1/10; LMC 11–12/10; SLJ 10/1/10) [973.4]

3135 Mortensen, Lori. *Writing the U.S. Constitution* (1–3). Illus. by Siri Weber Feeney. 2009, Picture Window LB $23.99 (978-140485540-3). 32pp. Mortensen provides clear explanations of the concepts underlying the Constitution and places the process of creating it in historical context. Also use *Paul Revere's Ride* (2009). (Rev: BL 3/1/10) [342.7302]

3136 Murphy, Jim. *The Crossing: How George Washington Saved the American Revolution* (5–8). 2010, Scholastic $21.99 (978-0-439-69186-4). 96pp. With many quotations, illustrations, maps, and reproductions, plus clear text, this is an appealing account of Washington's efforts to whip a ragtag army into shape and his various triumphs and failures. (Rev: BL 11/15/10*; SLJ 12/1/10*) [973.3]

3137 Waxman, Laura Hamilton. *What Are the Articles of Confederation? And Other Questions About the Birth of the United States* (3–6). Illus. Series: Six Questions of American History. 2012, Lerner LB $30.60 (978-076135330-0). 48pp. Six thoughtful questions about the Articles of Confederation are considered with reference to the historical and cultural context; includes informative back matter. (Rev: BL 2/1/12) [342.7302]

THE YOUNG NATION, 1789–1861

3138 Jurmain, Suzanne. *Worst of Friends: Thomas Jefferson, John Adams and the True Story of an American Feud* (1–3). Illus. by Larry Day. 2011, Dutton $16.99 (978-0-525-47903-1). Unpaged. The tumultuous friendship between Thomas Jefferson and John Adams is portrayed in this fascinating picture book. (Rev: BL 12/1/11*; LMC 3–4/12; SLJ 11/1/11*) [973.4]

3139 Kerley, Barbara. *Those Rebels, John and Tom* (2–4). Illus. by Edwin Fotheringham. 2012, Scholastic $17.99 (978-054522268-6). 48pp. Thomas Jefferson and John Adams' divergent approaches to politics and philosophy are presented in this entertaining look at how our founding fathers excelled at compromise. (Rev: BL 12/1/11*; LMC 3–4/12; SLJ 9/12) [973.4]

3140 McNeese, Tim. *Early National America: 1790–1850* (5–8). Illus. Series: Discovering U.S. History. 2010, Chelsea House $35 (978-1-60413-351-6). 136pp. A satisfying survey of social and political developments in the early years of the United States, with illustrations, maps, photographs, and interesting sidebar features. **ℯ** (Rev: LMC 11–12/10; SLJ 8/10) [973]

PIONEER LIFE AND WESTWARD EXPANSION

3141 Brown, Don. *Gold! Gold from the American River!* (2–4). Illus. by author. 2011, Roaring Brook $17.99 (978-159643223-9). 64pp. With quotations, maps, cartoon figures, and revealing vignettes about the lives of miners, this volume covers the California gold rush and the people involved. Lexile 1010L (Rev: BL 12/1/10; SLJ 2/1/11) [979.4]

3142 Domnauer, Teresa. *Life in the West* (2–4). Series: A True Book: Westward Expansion. 2010, Children's Press LB $26 (978-0-531-20583-9). 48pp. This volume answers such questions as "Why did so many people choose to move west?" and "What kinds of chores did pioneer children do?" as it explores life on ranches and the prairie. Also use *Westward Expansion* (2010). (Rev: LMC 8–9/10; SLJ 4/1/10) [978]

3143 Friedman, Mel. *The California Gold Rush* (2–4). Series: A True Book: Westward Expansion. 2010, Children's Press LB $26 (978-0-531-20581-5). 48pp. This volume answers such questions as "Why was travel to California so dangerous?" and "What was life like in a gold-mining camp?" as it explores life during the gold rush. (Rev: SLJ 4/1/10) [979.4]

3144 Ratliff, Tom. *You Wouldn't Want to Be a Pony Express Rider! A Dusty, Thankless Job You'd Rather Not Do* (3–5). Illus. by Mark Bergin. 2012, Scholastic LB $29 (978-053120872-4); paper $9.95 (978-053120947-9). 32pp. Ratliff presents a frank look at the life of a Pony Express rider and its many challenges. (Rev: BL 2/15/12) [383]

3145 Schwartz, Heather E. *Foul, Filthy American Frontier: The Disgusting Details About the Journey Out West* (4–8). Series: Fact Finders: Disgusting History. 2010, Capstone LB $25.32 (978-1-4296-3957-6). 32pp. Allen concentrates on the grosser side of life on the American frontier, describing poor sanitation, rotten food, bugs, medical horrors, and so forth. (Rev: LMC 11–12/10)

3146 Sheinkin, Steve. *Which Way to the Wild West?* (5–9). Illus. by Tim Robinson. 2009, Flash Point $19.95 (978-1-59643-321-2). 260pp. Useful for both research-ers and browsers, this is a fact-filled but lively history of just what went on in the West. Lexile 940L (Rev: HB 9–10/09; LMC 10/09; SLJ 9/09)

3147 Spradlin, Michael P. *Off Like the Wind! The First Ride of the Pony Express* (2–5). Illus. by Layne Johnson. 2010, Walker $17.99 (978-0-8027-9652-3). 40pp. A dramatic account of the exploits of the riders who faced many dangers as they delivered the mail. (Rev: BL 1/1/10; LMC 1–2/10; SLJ 2/1/10) [383]

3148 Staton, Hilarie N. *Cowboys and the Wild West* (4–6). Illus. Series: All About America. 2011, Kingfisher LB $19.89 (978-0-7534-6582-0); paper $9.99 (978-0-7534-6510-3). 32pp. With many photographs, paintings, maps, and primary documents, this overview of the lives of cowboys and other residents of the Wild West will be useful for report writers. (Rev: BL 9/1/11; SLJ 8/11) [978]

3149 Todras, Ellen H. *Wagon Trains and Settlers* (4–6). Illus. Series: All About America. 2011, Kingfisher paper $9.99 (978-0-7534-6511-0). 32pp. With many photographs, paintings, maps, and primary documents, this overview of the lives of pioneers will be useful for report writers. (Rev: BL 9/1/11; SLJ 8/11) [973.8]

3150 Walker, Paul Robert. *Gold Rush and Riches* (4–6). Illus. Series: All About America. 2011, Kingfisher LB $19.89 (978-0-7534-6584-4); paper $9.99 (978-0-7534-6512-7). 32pp. With many photographs, paintings, maps, and primary documents, this overview of the lives of men and women who headed west during the gold rush will be useful for report writers. (Rev: BL 9/1/11; SLJ 8/11) [978]

THE CIVIL WAR

3151 Johnson, Jennifer. *Gettysburg: The Bloodiest Battle of the Civil War* (4–6). Series: 24/7 Goes to War: On the Battlefield. 2009, Franklin Watts LB $27 (978-0-531-25528-5); paper $7.95 (978-0-531-25453-0). 64pp. The battle of Gettysburg is condensed into this slim though information-packed book that features soldiers' personal experiences as well as notes on battle strategy. (Rev: SLJ 2/10) [973]

3152 McNeese, Tim. *The Civil War Era 1851–1865* (5–8). Series: Discovering U.S. History. 2010, Chelsea House $35 (978-1-60413-352-3). 136pp. McNeese provides a succinct overview of the key events and issues of the Civil War, with a chronology and timeline plus illustrations and primary sources. (Rev: LMC 11–12/10) [973.7]

3153 Mountjoy, Shane. *Causes of the Civil War: The Differences Between the North and South* (5–8). Series: The Civil War: A Nation Divided. 2009, Chelsea House $35 (978-1-60413-036-2). 136pp. This volume looks at the political scene in the early 19th century and the rivalries that led to the outbreak of war. (Rev: SLJ 10/09) [973.711]

3154 Mountjoy, Shane. *Technology and the Civil War* (5–8). Series: The Civil War: A Nation Divided. 2009, Chelsea House $35 (978-1-60413-037-9). 136pp. In chapters covering railroads and the telegraph, weapons, ironclads, submarines, medicine, and photography, this volume documents the advances made during the war. (Rev: SLJ 8/09) [973.7301]

3155 Slavicek, Louise Chipley. *Women and the Civil War* (5–8). Series: The Civil War: A Nation Divided. 2009, Chelsea House $35 (978-1-60413-040-9). 128pp. Chapters cover women's roles as nurses, spies, soldiers, and scouts, and look at their work in the camps and on the home front in both North and South; there is also discussion of the situation of African American women. (Rev: SLJ 8/09) [973.7301]

RECONSTRUCTION TO THE KOREAN WAR, 1865–1950

3156 Bolden, Tonya. *FDR's Alphabet Soup: New Deal America, 1932–1939* (5–8). 2010, Knopf LB $22.99 (978-0-375-95214-2). 144pp. A lively review of FDR's presidency and in particular of the provisions of the New Deal and the impact it had on the American people. (Rev: BL 12/1/09; LMC 1–2/10; SLJ 1/10) [900]

3157 Brill, Marlene Targ. *Annie Shapiro and the Clothing Workers' Strike* (2–4). Illus. by Jamel Akib. 2010, Millbrook LB $27.93 (978-1-58013-672-3). 48pp. This well-researched book tells the inspiring story of Hannah "Annie" Shapiro, the Russian girl who led a walkout at a Chicago clothing factory in 1910; includes a reader's theater section. (Rev: BL 10/1/10; LMC 1–2/11*; SLJ 12/1/10) [331.892]

3158 Garland, Sherry. *Voices of the Dust Bowl* (4–7). Illus. by Judith Hierstein. Series: Voices of History. 2012, Pelican $16.99 (978-158980964-2). 40pp. Sixteen moving first-person narratives convey how the drought and dust storms of the 1930s affected people in all walks of lives — even Bonnie and Clyde. (Rev: BL 5/15/12; LMC 10/12; SLJ 7/12) [973.917]

3159 Gonzales, Doreen. *The Secret of the Manhattan Project* (5–8). Illus. Series: Stories in American History. 2012, Enslow LB $31.93 (978-076603954-4). 128pp. Placing events in clear historical context, this is a compelling account of the development and deployment of the atomic bomb. (Rev: BL 4/1/12*; SLJ 4/12) [355.8]

3160 Graham, Ian. *You Wouldn't Want to Work on the Hoover Dam! An Explosive Job You'd Rather Not Do* (3–5). Illus. by David Antram. 2012, Scholastic LB $29 (978-053120871-7); paper $9.95 (978-053120946-2). 32pp. With cartoons and breezy text, this is a good introduction to the building of the Hoover Dam, the dangers involved, and the fact that few jobs were available during the Depression. (Rev: BL 2/15/12; SLJ 4/12) [627]

3161 McNeese, Tim. *The Gilded Age and Progressivism 1891–1913* (5–8). Series: Discovering U.S. History. 2010, Chelsea House $35 (978-1-60413-355-4). 136pp. McNeese provides a succinct overview of the key events and issues of this period of industrial progress and expanded immigration, with a chronology and timeline plus illustrations and primary sources. **e** (Rev: LMC 11–12/10; SLJ 8/10) [973]

3162 Marrin, Albert. *Years of Dust: The Story of the Dust Bowl* (5–8). 2009, Dutton $22.99 (978-0-525-42077-4). 128pp. This is a moving explanation of the nature of the Dust Bowl and its impact on agriculture and the population that lived there; personal accounts add depth, as do numerous sidebars and a warning about future events like this. (Rev: BL 8/09*; LMC 10/09; SLJ 8/09) [978]

3163 Nardo, Don. *Migrant Mother: How a Photograph Defined the Great Depression* (5–8). Illus. Series: Captured History. 2011, Compass Point $33.99 (978-075654397-6). 64pp. Dorothea Lange's photograph of a Depression-era farm worker serves as the anchor for a discussion of the Great Depression and Lange's contributions. (Rev: BL 4/1/11; LMC 10/11) [973.917]

3164 Rosenstock, Barb. *The Camping Trip That Changed America: Theodore Roosevelt, John Muir, and Our National Parks* (1–3). Illus. by Mordicai Gerstein. 2012, Dial $16.99 (978-080373710-5). 32pp. Theodore Roosevelt's inspirational camping trip with John Muir gave rise to the establishment of the national park system; this readable book chronicles the adventure. (Rev: BL 12/15/11; HB 1–2/12; LMC 8–9/12; SLJ 9/12)

3165 Sandler, Martin W. *The Dust Bowl Through the Lens: How Photography Revealed and Helped Remedy a National Disaster* (5–9). 2009, Walker $19.99 (978-0-8027-9547-2). 96pp. Sandler tells the devastating story of the American dust bowl through a series of photo-essays including period quotations and concise, engaging captions. (Rev: BL 11/1/09; HB 1–2/10; LMC 10/09; SLJ 10/09; VOYA 8/09) [973.917022]

3166 Sandler, Martin W. *The Impossible Rescue: The True Story of an Amazing Arctic Adventure* (5–8). Illus. 2012, Candlewick $22.99 (978-076365080-3). 176pp. The death-defying 1897–1898 rescue of nearly 300 sailors trapped in winter ice on Alaska's Point Barrow is described in this dramatic tale. (Rev: BL 5/15/12*; HB 9–10/12; SLJ 9/12; VOYA 8/12) [979.803]

3167 Staton, Hilarie N. *The Industrial Revolution* (4–6). Illus. Series: All About America. 2012, Kingfisher LB $19.89 (978-075346712-1); paper $9.99 (978-075346670-4). 32pp. In chapters such as "The First Mills," "Canals and Factories," and "Mass Production," Staton reviews technological developments in the United States from colonial times through the mid-1900s. (Rev: BL 4/15/12; SLJ 3/12) [338.0973]

3168 Van Rynbach, Iris, and Pegi Deitz Shea. *The Taxing Case of the Cows: A True Story About Suffrage*

(1–3). Illus. by Emily Arnold McCully. 2010, Clarion $16.99 (978-0-547-23631-5). 32pp. In 19th-century Connecticut sisters Abby and Julia Smith refuse to pay their taxes on the grounds that they are not allowed to vote. (Rev: BL 12/1/10; HB 1–2/11; LMC 5–6/11; SLJ 12/1/10) [324.6]

3169 Wadsworth, Ginger. *Camping with the President* (3–5). Illus. by Karen Dugan. 2009, Boyds Mills $16.95 (978-159078497-6). 32pp. Intricately tinted watercolor illustrations enliven this account of Teddy Roosevelt's 1903 camping trip in Yosemite with naturalist John Muir. (Rev: BL 9/15/09; LMC 11–12/09) [973.91]

3170 Winter, Jonah. *Born and Bred in the Great Depression* (2–4). Illus. by Kimberly Bulcken Root. 2011, Random House $17.99 (978-037586197-0); LB $20.99 (978-037596197-7). 40pp. The author describes his father's childhood in East Texas during the 1930s, the youngest of eight children. ❁ (Rev: BL 11/15/11; HB 1–2/12; SLJ 1/12) [976.4]

THE 1950s TO THE PRESENT

3171 Aretha, David. *Sit-Ins and Freedom Rides* (5–8). Series: Civil Rights Movement. 2009, Morgan Reynolds LB $28.95 (978-1-59935-098-1). 128pp. Aretha offers a detailed, well-illustrated look at the grassroots efforts of the early 1960s, with personal anecdotes, a helpful timeline, and lists of additional resources. (Rev: BL 2/1/10; SLJ 9/09) [323.1196]

3172 Bausum, Ann. *Marching to the Mountaintop: How Poverty, Labor Fights, and Civil Rights Set the Stage for Martin Luther King, Jr.'s Final Hours* (5–8). Illus. 2012, National Geographic $19.95 (978-142630939-7); LB $28.90 (978-142630940-3). 112pp. With succinct text, use of primary resources, gripping photographs, and attractive design, this is an compelling account — suitable for research and for browsing — of the 1968 Memphis sanitation workers strike and the death of Martin Luther King, Jr. ❁ (Rev: BL 2/1/12; LMC 8–9/12; SLJ 3/12) [323.092]

3173 McNeese, Tim. *Modern America: 1964–Present* (5–8). Illus. Series: Discovering U.S. History. 2010, Chelsea House $35 (978-1-60413-361-5). 144pp. Covering American history from LBJ through Obama, this is a satisfying survey of social and political developments with illustrations, maps, photographs, and interesting sidebar features. ❁ (Rev: SLJ 8/10) [973.92]

3174 Niven, Felicia Lowenstein. *Fabulous Fashions of the 1970s* (4–7). Illus. Series: Fabulous Fashions of the Decades. 2011, Enslow LB $23.93 (978-076603826-4). 48pp. Looks at all aspects of fashion in the 1970s, from men's and women's clothing to hairstyles, accessories, and pop culture. (Rev: BL 4/1/12; VOYA 10/10) [746.9]

Regions

MIDWEST

3175 Brezina, Corona. *Indiana: Past and Present* (3–6). Series: The United States: Past and Present. 2010, Rosen LB $26.50 (978-1-4358-3521-4). 48pp. Includes chapters on the geography, history, government, economy, and people of Indiana, with a timeline and "Indiana at a Glance." (Rev: SLJ 6/10) [977.2]

3176 Brill, Marlene Targ, and Elizabeth Kaplan. *Minnesota* (3–6). Series: It's My State! 2010, Marshall Cavendish LB $21.95 (978-1-60870-054-7). 80pp. This accessible survey covers geography, history, people and culture, government, and the economy and includes an introductory "quick look" and information about the state song, seal, and so forth. (Rev: SLJ 2/1/11) [917.76]

3177 Coury, Tina Nichols. *Hanging Off Jefferson's Nose: Growing Up on Mount Rushmore* (4–6). Illus. by Sally Wern Comport. 2012, Dial $16.99 (978-080373731-0). 40pp. Tells the fascinating story of the creation of Mount Rushmore; the project was started by Gutzon Borglum but finished by his son Lincoln, who is the focus of this book. (Rev: BL 4/15/12; SLJ 7/12) [730.92]

3178 Johnson, Robin. *What's in the Midwest?* (3–6). Illus. Series: All Around the U.S. 2011, Crabtree LB $19.95 (978-077871823-9); paper $8.95 (978-077871829-1). 32pp. Covers the history, geography, climate, industry, and culture of the midwestern United States, looking both at the rural areas and the cities of 12 states. (Rev: BL 10/1/11) [917.7]

3179 Kenney, Karen Latchana. *Mount Rushmore* (2–4). Illus. by Judith A. Hunt. Series: Our Nation's Pride. 2011, ABDO LB $28.50 (978-1-61641-153-4). 32pp. Kenney describes how Mount Rushmore was created and its importance as a symbol today. (Rev: SLJ 7/11) [978.3]

3180 Peterson, Sheryl. *Wisconsin* (3–8). Series: This Land Called America. 2010, Creative Education $28.50 (978-1-58341-802-4). 32pp. History, culture, and geography are all covered in this attractive slim volume that provides the vital facts report writers need. (Rev: LMC 8–9/10) [977.5]

MOUNTAIN STATES

3181 Aldridge, Rebecca. *The Hoover Dam* (5–8). Series: Building America: Then and Now. 2009, Chelsea House $35 (978-1-60413-069-0). 120pp. This book about the Hoover Dam includes illustrative maps, primary source documents, Web sites, a timeline, and glossary. (Rev: LMC 10/09) [627]

3182 Altman, Linda Jacobs, and Stephanie Fitzgerald. *Colorado* (3–6). Series: It's My State! 2010, Marshall

Cavendish LB $21.95 (978-1-60870-046-2). 80pp. This accessible survey covers geography, history, people and culture, government, and the economy and includes an introductory "quick look," a recipe, and information about the state song, seal, and so forth. (Rev: SLJ 2/1/11) [978.8]

NORTHEAST

3183 Bjorklund, Ruth, and Stephanie Fitzgerald. *Massachusetts* (3–6). Series: It's My State! 2010, Marshall Cavendish LB $21.95 (978-1-60870-053-0). 80pp. This accessible survey covers geography, history, people and culture, government, and the economy and includes an introductory "quick look" and information about the state song, seal, and so forth. (Rev: SLJ 2/1/11) [917.44]

3184 Burgan, Michael. *Fort McHenry* (4–6). Series: Symbols of American Freedom. 2009, Chelsea Clubhouse $30 (978-1-60413-520-6). 48pp. Plenty of photographs, drawings, diagrams, and historical anecdotes enhance this portrait of the construction and history of Fort McHenry. (Rev: SLJ 4/10) [975.26]

3185 Hankins, Chelsey. *The Lincoln Memorial* (3–6). Series: Symbols of American Freedom. 2009, Chelsea Clubhouse $30 (978-1-60413-518-3). 48pp. With clear, simple language, this book looks at the history and contemporary importance of the Lincoln Memorial and includes photographs and excerpts from speeches as well as tips on making a successful visit. (Rev: LMC 3–4/10; SLJ 3/1/10) [975.3]

3186 Kenney, Karen Latchana. *Ellis Island* (2–4). Illus. by Judith A. Hunt. Series: Our Nation's Pride. 2011, ABDO LB $28.50 (978-1-61641-150-3). 32pp. Kenney looks at the history and importance of Ellis Island. (Rev: SLJ 7/11) [304.8]

3187 Kenney, Karen Latchana. *The White House* (2–4). Illus. by Judith A. Hunt. Series: Our Nation's Pride. 2011, ABDO LB $28.50 (978-1-61641-154-1). 32pp. Kenney describes how the site was chosen for the White House, the history of the building and the people who have lived and worked there, and what it's like to visit it. (Rev: SLJ 7/11) [975.3]

3188 McCurdy, Michael. *Walden Then and Now: An Alphabetical Tour of Henry Thoreau's Pond* (5–8). Illus. by author. 2010, Charlesbridge $16.95 (978-158089253-7). 32pp. "C is for the cabin Henry built with his own hands." This handsome book explores Walden Pond in Thoreau's time and today. (Rev: BL 9/1/10; LMC 1–2/11; SLJ 9/10) [818]

3189 Mann, Elizabeth. *Statue of Liberty: A Tale of Two Countries* (4–6). Illus. by Alan Witschonke. Series: Wonders of the World. 2011, Mikaya $22.95 (978-1-931414-43-2). 48pp. This well-researched book chronicles the development, delivery, and worldwide impact of the Statue of Liberty. (Rev: BLO 11/15/11; LMC 11–12/11; SLJ 8/11) [974.7]

3190 Rau, Dana Meachen. *The Northeast* (3–5). Illus. Series: A True Book. 2012, Scholastic LB $28 (978-053124851-5); paper $6.95 (978-053128326-4). 48pp. History, people, geography, economy, and challenges are all covered in this overview of the 11 northeastern states that includes bright photographs, maps, and a timeline. (Rev: BL 4/1/12; LMC 10/12) [974]

3191 Staib, Walter, and Jennifer Fox. *A Feast of Freedom: Tasty Tidbits from the City Tavern* (3–6). Illus. by Fernando Juarez. 2010, Running Press $15.95 (978-0-7624-3598-2). 48pp. The City Tavern in Philadelphia has been the venue for many political and business meetings over the years, and this picture book presents 14 vignettes — covering a private meeting between Washington and Lafayette, the writing of the Constitution, and so forth — plus a recipe and information on the tavern today. (Rev: LMC 11–12/10; SLJ 8/10) [973.3]

3192 Staton, Hilarie. *Ellis Island* (4–6). Series: Symbols of American Freedom. 2009, Chelsea Clubhouse $30 (978-1-60413-519-0). 48pp. Tells the story of Ellis Island's importance as a first stage for many immigrants arriving in the United States, describes how its role has changed over the years, and explains its symbolism both for young researchers and students planning visits of their own. Also in this series: *Independence Hall* (2009). (Rev: SLJ 5/10) [304.8]

3193 Staton, Hilarie. *The Statue of Liberty* (3–6). Series: Symbols of American Freedom. 2009, Chelsea Clubhouse $30 (978-1-60413-516-9). 48pp. With clear, simple language, this book looks at the history and contemporary importance of the statue and includes photographs and excerpts from speeches as well as tips on making a successful visit. (Rev: LMC 3–4/10; SLJ 3/1/10) [974.7]

3194 Todras, Ellen H. *The Gettysburg Battlefield* (3–6). Series: Symbols of American Freedom. 2009, Chelsea Clubhouse $30 (978-1-60413-514-5). 48pp. With photographs and excerpts from speeches, this book explains the importance of this battlefield and provides tips for those planning a visit. (Rev: LMC 3–4/10; SLJ 3/1/10)

3195 Tougas, Joe. *New York* (3–8). Series: This Land Called America. 2010, Creative Education $28.50 (978-1-58341-785-0). 32pp. History, culture, and geography are all covered in this attractive slim volume that provides the vital facts report writers need. (Rev: LMC 8–9/10) [974.7]

3196 Yezerski, Thomas F. *Meadowlands: A Wetlands Survival Story* (1–3). Illus. by author. 2011, Farrar $17.99 (978-0-374-34913-4). 40pp. With lovely ink-and-watercolor illustrations, Yezerski traces the history of the Meadowlands, a wetlands area within sight of New York City that once was home to the Lenni Lenape and was gradually industrialized until conservation initiatives were finally implemented. (Rev: BL 3/1/11; LMC 5–6/11; SLJ 3/1/11) [577.6]

PACIFIC STATES

3197 Feinstein, Stephen. *Hawai'i Volcanoes National Park* (4–8). Illus. Series: America's National Parks: Adventure, Explore, Discover. 2009, Enslow LB $33.27 (978-1-59845-094-1). 128pp. Links to Web sites add to the information provided here on the Hawaiian park and its geology and ecology, as well as its history and myths associated with it. Lexile 870 (Rev: SLJ 9/09)

3198 Gendell, Megan. *The Spanish Missions of California* (3–7). Series: A True Book. 2010, Children's Press LB $26 (978-0-531-20577-8). 48pp. An interesting survey of the history and structure of the Spanish mission buildings and their importance to society 500 years ago. (Rev: LMC 8–9/10) [979.4]

3199 Gish, Melissa. *Washington* (3–8). Series: This Land Called America. 2010, Creative Education $28.50 (978-1-58341-800-0). 32pp. History, culture, and geography are all covered in this attractive slim volume that provides the vital facts report writers need. (Rev: LMC 8–9/10) [979.7]

SOUTH

3200 Bailey, Diane. *Tennessee: Past and Present* (3–6). Series: The United States: Past and Present. 2010, Rosen LB $26.50 (978-1-4358-3522-1). 48pp. Includes chapters on the geography, history, government, economy, and people of Tennessee, with a timeline and "Tennessee at a Glance." (Rev: SLJ 6/10) [976.8]

3201 Kostyal, K. M. *1776: A New Look at Revolutionary Williamsburg* (4–8). 2009, National Geographic $27.90 (978-1-4263-0518-4). 48pp. The history of Williams-

burg, Virginia, is told from the perspectives of a variety of period characters, who focus on everything from food and dress to slavery. (Rev: BL 10/15/09; LMC 11–12/09; SLJ 11/1/09) [973.3]

3202 Suben, Eric. *The Spanish Missions of Florida* (3–7). Series: A True Book. 2010, Children's Press LB $26 (978-0-531-20578-9). 48pp. A look at Spanish mission buildings in Florida, with beautiful color photographs and discussion of their history and the impact of the missions on the Native Americans. Lexile 910L (Rev: LMC 8–9/10) [975.9]

SOUTHWEST

3203 Gendell, Megan. *The Spanish Misssions of Texas* (3–7). Series: A True Book. 2010, Children's Press LB $26 (978-0-531-20580-8). 48pp. A look at the Spanish mission buildings of Texas, with beautiful color photographs and discussion of their history and their impact of the missions on the Native Americans. Lexile 940L (Rev: LMC 8–9/10) [976.4]

3204 Lynch, Wayne, and Aubrey Lang. *Sonoran Desert* (5–8). Series: Our Wild World Ecosystems. 2009, NorthWord $16.95 (978-1-58979-389-7). 64pp. The fascinating flora, fauna, topography, and climate of America's Sonoran Desert are described in chatty, well-written text and an abundance of eye-catching illustrations and color photographs. (Rev: SLJ 10/09) [77.5409791]

3205 Lyon, Robin. *The Spanish Missions of Arizona* (3–7). Series: A True Book. 2010, Children's Press LB $26 (978-0-531-20576-1). 48pp. A look at the Spanish mission buildings of Arizona, with beautiful color photographs and discussion of their history and the impact of the missions on the Native Americans. Also use *The Spanish Missions of New Mexico* (2010). Lexile 930L (Rev: LMC 8–9/10) [979.1]

Social Institutions and Issues

Business and Economics

General

3206 Chapman, Garry, and Gary Hodges. *Coffee* (5–8). Illus. Series: World Commodities. 2010, Black Rabbit LB $28.50 (978-159920584-7). 32pp. Explores the cultural, environmental, and political story of coffee. (Rev: BL 10/1/10; LMC 5–6/11) [338.1]

3207 Cipriano, Jeri. *How Do Mortgages, Loans, and Credit Work?* (5–8). Illus. Series: Economics in Action. 2010, Crabtree LB $26.60 (978-077874445-0); paper $8.95 (978-077874456-6). 32pp. Covers interest rates and borrowing and lending in general, with particular attention to credit cards. (Rev: BLO 8/10) [332.7]

3208 Heinrichs, Ann. *The Great Recession* (4–7). Series: Cornerstones of Freedom. 2011, Scholastic LB $30 (978-053125035-8); paper $8.95 (978-053126560-4). 64pp. This visually appealing volume offers straightforward, age-appropriate information on the economic crisis of the first decade of the 21st century and its causes and impact on U.S. residents. (Rev: BL 10/1/11) [330.973]

3209 Johanson, Paula. *Making Good Choices About Fair Trade* (5–8). Series: Green Matters. 2010, Rosen LB $29.95 (978-1-4358-5315-7). 64pp. A thought-provoking introduction to international trade and the ways in which consumers can encourage fair trade practices, with real-life examples and discussion of labor laws. (Rev: BL 10/1/09; LMC 1–2/10) [381.3]

3210 Larson, Jennifer S. *What Can You Do with Money?: Earning, Spending, and Saving* (K–2). Series: Exploring Economics. 2010, Lerner LB $25.26 (978-0-7613-3910-6). 32pp. An easy-to-read introduction to earning and spending money, with explanations of the nature of income and goods and services. Also use *What Is Money, Anyway? Why Dollars and Coins Have Value* (2010). (Rev: SLJ 8/1/10) [331.2]

3211 Mattern, Joanne. *The Mars Family: M and M Mars Candy Makers* (2–4). Illus. Series: Food Dudes. 2011, ABDO LB $25.65 (978-161613560-7). 32pp. This business profile explores the family legacy of the Mars company, which got its start when founder Franklin Mars began experimenting with candy while recovering from polio. (Rev: BL 4/1/11) [338.7]

3212 Rau, Dana Meachen. *Saving Money* (2–4). Series: Money and Banks. 2010, Gareth Stevens LB $22 (978-1-4339-3386-8). 24pp. A clear introduction to ways of saving money, from piggy banks to savings accounts and even stocks. Also use *Spending Money*, and *What Is a Bank?* (both 2010). (Rev: SLJ 6/1/10)

Consumerism

3213 Larson, Jennifer S. *Who's Buying? Who's Selling? Understanding Consumers and Producers* (K–2). Series: Exploring Economics. 2010, Lerner LB $25.26 (978-0-7613-3912-0). 32pp. The concept of exchanging money for goods or services is explored in chapters on consumers, producers, vendors, supply and demand, and bartering. (Rev: SLJ 8/1/10) [381]

Money-Making Ideas and Budgeting

3214 Larson, Jennifer S. *Do I Need It? Or Do I Want It? Making Budget Choices* (K–2). Illus. 2010, Lerner LB $25.62 (978-076133914-4). 32pp. Young readers learn about the options they have regarding money — including donating it, saving it, and spending it right away — in this introduction to simple money management. (Rev: BL 4/1/10; LMC 5–6/10) [332.024]

3215 Salzmann, Mary Elizabeth. *Money for School* (2–4). Illus. Series: Your Piggy Bank: A Guide to Spending and Saving for Kids! 2010, ABDO LB $27.07 (978-1-61641-031-5). 24pp. Readers learn about money basics and help young Mason decide how to manage the little bit he has for school. Other titles in this series include *Money for Toys* and *Money for Food* (2011). (Rev: SLJ 5/1/11) [332.024]

Ecology and Environment

General

3216 Anderson, Judith. *Sustaining the Environment* (4–7). Series: Working for Our Future. 2010, Black Rabbit LB $28.50 (978-1-59771-198-2). 32pp. This volume explains why the United Nations chose sustaining the environment as one of its eight Millennium Development goals and looks at the various obstacles challenging this mission. (Rev: BL 6/1/10; LMC 10/10; SLJ 4/10)

3217 Apte, Sunita. *Eating Green* (4–7). Series: Going Green. 2010, Bearport LB $25.27 (978-1-59716-965-3). 32pp. Things people can do to lessen damage to the environment are discussed in this book series, which is supported with a Web site featuring additional information and activities. (Rev: LMC 1–2/10)

3218 Arnold, Caroline. *A Warmer World: From Polar Bears to Butterflies, How Climate Change Affects Wildlife* (3–7). Illus. by Jamie Hogan. 2012, Charlesbridge $16.95 (978-158089266-7); paper $7.95 (978-158089267-4). 32pp. Global warming's challenges to the animal kingdom are the focus of this cautionary book. **e** (Rev: BL 2/15/12; LMC 11–12/12; SLJ 4/1/12) [363.738]

3219 Bailey, Jacqui. *What's the Point of Being Green?* (4–6). Illus. by Jan McCafferty. 2010, Barron's paper $12.99 (978-0-7641-4427-1). 96pp. Answering questions such as "Why are trees important?" and "How did it get so bad?," this appealing book presents many environmental challenges and explains what we can do to ameliorate the problems. (Rev: LMC 11–12/10; SLJ 8/10)

3220 Caduto, Michael J. *Catch the Wind, Harness the Sun: 22 Super-Charged Science Projects for Kids* (5–8). Illus. 2011, Storey $26.95 (978-1-60342-971-9); paper $16.95 (978-1-60342-794-4). 224pp. Focusing on energy conservation and global warming, this book collects 22 empowering projects that can be undertaken by young people concerned about the environment. **e** (Rev: BL 5/1/11; SLJ 7/11*) [333.79]

3221 Cole, Joanna. *The Magic School Bus and the Climate Challenge* (2–4). Illus. by Bruce Degen. 2010, Scholastic $16.99 (978-0-590-10826-3). 48pp. Ms. Frizzle takes her class on a global tour that demonstrates the effects of climate change. (Rev: BL 2/15/10; LMC 5–6/10; SLJ 2/1/10)

3222 Farrell, Courtney. *Keeping Water Clean* (3–7). Series: Language Arts Explorer: Save the Planet. 2010, Cherry Lake LB $27.07 (978-1-60279-659-1). 32pp. Students are given a mission at the beginning of the book and must use creative thinking and problem solving to gather facts as they travel on a virtual trip researching water conservation. (Rev: LMC 8–9/10; SLJ 4/10) [363.7394]

3223 Goldsworthy, Steve. *The Top 10 Ways You Can Travel Green* (3–5). Illus. Series: Being Green. 2010, Weigl LB $28.55 (978-161690085-4); paper $12.95 (978-161690086-1). 32pp. Helpful and innovative suggestions for making transportation more green are sandwiched between a history of green travel and a look at what the future may hold. (Rev: BL 3/1/11) [333.79]

3224 Gutman, Dan, ed. *Recycle This Book: 100 Top Children's Book Authors Tell You How to Go Green* (5–9). 2009, Random House paper $5.99 (978-0-385-73721-0). 267pp. In brief essays (and a poem) Laurie Halse Anderson, Lois Lowry, Rick Riordan, and 97 other authors children will recognize describe what they do to help the earth; some serious, some lighthearted, these pieces are grouped by location (home, school, community, and so forth) and usually include a practical suggestion. (Rev: LMC 5–6/09; SLJ 8/09) [640]

3225 Hanel, Rachael. *Climate Fever: Stopping Global Warming* (5–8). Series: Green Generation. 2010, Compass Point LB $31.99 (978-0-7565-4246-7). 64pp. Well organized and clearly written, this book is part of a series explaining about steps people can take to adjust their consumption and ease environmental impact, encouraging readers to spur change in their own communities. (Rev: LMC 1–2/10)

3226 Hirsch, Rebecca E. *Protecting Our Natural Resources* (3–7). Series: Language Arts Explorer: Save the Planet. 2010, Cherry Lake LB $27.07 (978-1-60279-661-4). 32pp. Students are given a mission at the beginning of the book and must use creative thinking and problem solving to gather facts as they travel on a virtual trip through the various ways to protect natural resources. (Rev: LMC 8–9/10; SLJ 4/10) [333.72]

3227 Hollyer, Beatrice. *Our World of Water: Children and Water Around the World* (2–4). Illus. 2009, Henry Holt $16.95 (978-080508941-7). 48pp. Six stories of how different countries use and appreciate water are collected in this book, which features child narrators and color photographs. (Rev: BL 11/1/09; SLJ 8/1/09) [363.6]

3228 Jakab, Cheryl. *Global Warming* (4–7). Series: Global Issues. 2009, Smart Apple Media LB $28.50 (978-1-59920-451-2). 32pp. Offering a global perspective, this volume covers warmer temperatures, declining ice cover, changing seasons and rainfall patterns, and the migration that will be caused by all these changes. (Rev: SLJ 2/10) [363.738]

3229 Jakubiak, David J. *What Can We Do About Acid Rain?* (3–5). Series: Protecting Our Planet. 2011, Rosen LB $21.25 (978-1-4488-4984-0); paper $8.25 (978-1-4488-5116-4). 24pp. This broad overview discusses what acid rain is, how it forms, and the harm it does to the environment, and looks at what can be done to prevent it — and the successes achieved so far. ℰ (Rev: BL 2/15/12; SLJ 11/1/11) [363.738]

3230 Jakubiak, David J. *What Can We Do About Deforestation?* (3–5). Series: Protecting Our Planet. 2011, Rosen LB $21.25 (978-1-4488-4986-4); paper $8.25 (978-1-4488-5119-5). 24pp. This broad overview discusses the importance of trees and the harm that deforestation does to the environment, and looks at what can be done to reverse the damage. Also use *What Can We Do About Toxins in the Environment?* (2011). ℰ (Rev: BL 2/15/12; SLJ 11/1/11) [634.9]

3231 Johnson, J. Angelique. *The Eco-Student's Guide to Being Green at School* (2–4). Illus. by Kyle Poling. Series: Point it Out! Tips for Green Living. 2010, Picture Window LB $25.99 (978-140486027-8). 24pp. Explores the various rooms in a school and the actions students can take to improve the eco-friendliness. (Rev: BL 3/1/11; LMC 3–4/11) [640]

3232 Kelsey, Elin. *Not Your Typical Book About the Environment* (4–6). Illus. by Clayton Hanmer. 2010, OwlKids $22.95 (978-189734979-3); paper $10.95 (978-189734984-7). 64pp. This colorful book with comic-style illustrations describes how many options there are for consumers, looking at four areas in particular: fashion, food, technology, and energy. (Rev: BL 6/10; LMC 10/10; SLJ 6/10) [304.2]

3233 Kirk, Ellen. *Human Footprint* (3–7). Illus. 2011, National Geographic paper $6.95 (978-1-4263-0767-6). 32pp. Based on a National Geographic documentary and subtitled "Everything You Will Eat, Use, Wear, Buy, and Throw Out in your Lifetime," this attractive book looks at the average American's consumption. (Rev: BL 7/11; SLJ 6/11) [304.2]

3234 Langley, Andrew. *Avoiding Hunger and Finding Water* (5–8). Illus. Series: The Environment Challenge. 2011, Raintree LB $32 (978-141094298-2). 48pp. Famine and drought are the main focuses of this effective volume that also covers population growth, climate change, pollution, and so forth. (Rev: BL 2/15/12) [363.8]

3235 Langley, Andrew. *Bridging the Energy Gap* (5–8). Illus. Series: The Environment Challenge. 2011, Raintree LB $32 (978-141094297-5); paper $8.99 (978-141094304-0). 48pp. Langley explains the current sources of our energy, alternative options, and the importance of conserving energy. (Rev: BL 2/15/12) [333.79]

3236 McKenzie, Precious. *Cleaning Up the Earth* (1–3). Illus. Series: Green Earth Discovery Library. 2011, Rourke paper $7.95 (978-161741768-9). 24pp. After explaining pollution and global warming, this book discusses how young people can help to achieve progress. (Rev: BL 2/15/12; LMC 5–6/12) [363.7]

3237 McKenzie, Precious. *Our Organic Garden* (1–3). Illus. Series: Green Earth Discovery Library. 2011, Rourke paper $7.95 (978-161741767-2). 24pp. Introduces the principles of organic gardening and explains the benefits of this approach. (Rev: BL 2/15/12; LMC 5–6/12) [635.0]

3238 Mason, Paul. *How Big Is Your Clothing Footprint?* (5–9). Series: Environmental Footprints. 2010, Marshall Cavendish LB $28.50 (978-0-7614-4410-7). 32pp. Fibers (natural and artificial), cleaning techniques, fashion, shipping, and other aspects of the clothes we wear are discussed in this useful title. Other volumes in the series include *How Big Is Your Energy Footprint?, How Big Is Your Food Footprint?,* and *How Big Is Your Water Footprint?* (all 2010). (Rev: LMC 5–6/10; SLJ 11/1/09) [391]

3239 Metz, Lorijo. *What Can We Do About Invasive Species?* (3–5). Illus. Series: Protecting Our Planet. 2009, PowerKids LB $21.25 (978-140428084-7). 24pp. Providing information on a variety of invasive species from around the world — from camels and rabbits to kudzu — this book offers a thought-provoking glimpse into the consequences of human activities. (Rev: BL 2/15/10) [577]

3240 Minden, Cecilia. *Reduce, Reuse, and Recycle* (3–7). Series: Language Arts Explorer: Save the Planet. 2010, Cherry Lake LB $27.07 (978-1-60279-662-1). 32pp. Students are given a mission at the beginning of the book and must use creative thinking and problem solving to gather facts as they travel on a virtual trip through the various ways to minimize waste. (Rev: LMC 8–9/10; SLJ 4/10) [363.72]

3241 Morgan, Sally. *Ozone Hole* (3–5). Illus. Series: Earth SOS. 2009, Black Rabbit LB $28.50 (978-159771224-8). 32pp. Discusses the causes — natural and resulting from human activity — of the hole in the ozone layer and explains its importance using clear language and many visuals. (Rev: BL 2/15/10) [577.27]

3242 Munro, Roxie. *EcoMazes: Twelve Earth Adventures* (1–3). Illus. by author. 2010, Sterling $14.95 (978-1-4027-6393-9). 40pp. Twelve vibrantly colored ecosystem mazes from different biomes around the world present a variety of landforms, wildlife, and ecological facts. (Rev: BL 6/10; SLJ 6/1/10*) [577]

3243 Parr, Todd. *The Earth Book* (PS–1). Illus. by author. 2010, Little, Brown $9.99 (978-0-316-04265-9). 40pp. Simple, accessible actions (turning off the tap when brushing teeth, using both sides of the paper) that protect the planet are the focus of this attractive book. (Rev: BL 3/1/10; SLJ 3/1/10) [333.72]

3244 Simon, Seymour. *Global Warming* (3–5). Illus. 2010, HarperCollins $17.99 (978-0-06-114250-5); LB $18.89 (978-0-06-114251-2). 32pp. A clear, comprehensive guide to the causes and effects of global warming and climate change, with many effective photographs. (Rev: BL 2/15/10; SLJ 3/1/10) [363.738]

3245 Spilsbury, Richard. *Climate Change Catastrophe* (4–8). Series: Can the Earth Survive? 2010, Rosen LB $26.50 (978-1-4358-5354-6). 48pp. With case studies and suggested strategies for the future, this volume looks at global warming problems around the world and the impact on everyday life. Additional titles in this series by this author are *Deforestation Crisis* and *Threats to Our Water Supply* (both 2010). (Rev: LMC 3–4/10; SLJ 1/10) [363.738]

3246 Suzuki, David, and Kathy Vanderlinden. *You Are the Earth: Know Your World So You Can Help Make It Better* (4–8). Illus. by Wallace Edwards. 2011, Greystone paper $16.95 (978-1-55365-476-6). 144pp. This wide-ranging survey discusses the importance of clean air, water, and soil and the interrelatedness of the sun's energy and plant, animal, and human life, with information on creation myths plus activities and experiments. (Rev: BL 3/1/11; SLJ 3/1/11*) [577]

3247 Thomas, Keltie. *Animals That Changed the World* (4–8). Illus. 2010, Annick $21.95 (978-1-55451-243-0); paper $12.95 (978-1-55451-242-3). 112pp. A fascinating look at the ways in which animals impact life on earth and human history; the cat, dog, beaver, pigeon, and horse are profiled, and expressions involving

animals are explained. (Rev: LMC 5–6/11; SLJ 1/1/11) [590]

3248 Webb, Barbara L. *What Does Green Mean?* (1–3). Illus. 2011, Rourke paper $7.95 (978-161741973-7). 24pp. This accessible offering gives young readers a chance to understand what it means to be "green," and examines a variety of actions that make this an achievable goal. (Rev: BL 2/15/12) [333.7]

3249 Welsbacher, Anne. *Earth-Friendly Design* (4–8). Illus. Series: Saving Our Living Earth. 2008, Lerner LB $30.60 (978-082257564-1). 72pp. A straightforward look at the life cycle of the products we use daily (including vehicles and houses), examining how innovative thinking can lead to greener solutions. (Rev: BL 12/1/08; VOYA 12/08) [745.2]

3250 Wilson, Janet. *Our Earth: How Kids Are Saving the Planet* (2–5). Illus. by author. 2010, Second Story $18.95 (978-1-897187-84-5). 32pp. Wilson profiles young people around the world who have made significant contributions to solving environmental problems. (Rev: BL 1/1–15/11; SLJ 6/11) [333.72092]

Cities

3251 Jakab, Cheryl. *Sustainable Cities* (4–7). Series: Global Issues. 2009, Smart Apple Media LB $28.50 (978-1-59920-454-3). 32pp. This volume discusses the factors that lead to unsustainable urban growth and the transportation and construction changes that could improve the situation. (Rev: SLJ 2/10) [307.76]

3252 Kent, Peter. *Peter Kent's City Across Time: From the Stone Age to the Distant Future* (2–4). Illus. by author. 2010, Kingfisher $16.99 (978-0-7534-6400-7). 48pp. An engaging look at how an imaginary European city evolved from the Stone Age to the 21st century, with detailed cross-section illustrations. (Rev: BL 5/1/10; SLJ 6/10) [307.76]

Garbage and Waste Recycling

3253 Bergen, Lara. *Don't Throw That Away! A Lift-the-Flap Book About Recycling and Reusing* (PS–K). Illus. by Betsy Snyder. Series: Little Green Books. 2009, Simon & Schuster paper $6.99 (978-141697517-5). 14pp. Many simple and creative repurposing projects are presented in this lively book, which features bright illustrations against a paper-bag-brown background. (Rev: BLO 1/1/10) [363.72]

3254 Morgan, Sally. *Waste and Recycling* (1–3). Series: Helping Our Planet. 2011, Cherrytree LB $28.50 (978-1-84234-608-2). 32pp. This book offers readers plenty of practical advice for reducing the amount of waste a household creates. (Rev: SLJ 8/1/11) [363.72]

3255 Spilsbury, Richard. *Waste and Recycling Challenges* (4–8). Series: Can the Earth Survive? 2010, Rosen LB $26.50 (978-1-4358-5355-3). 48pp. With case studies and suggested strategies for the future, this volume looks at waste disposal problems around the world and the impact on everyday life. (Rev: LMC 3–4/10; SLJ 1/10) [363.72]

3256 Winter, Jonah. *Here Comes the Garbage Barge!* (1–3). Illus. by Red Nose Studio. 2010, Random House LB $17.99 (978-0-375-95218-0). 40pp. This book tells the true story of a gigantic barge of garbage from Islip, NY, that was turned away from port after port all the way to Belize before finally turning back to its original home in 1987. Lexile AD670L (Rev: BL 2/15/10; LMC 3–4/10; SLJ 1/1/10*)

Pollution

3257 Ball, Jacqueline A. *Traveling Green* (2–5). Illus. Series: Going Green. 2009, Bearport LB $25.27 (978-159716964-6). 32pp. With many statistics and photographs, this is a good introduction to the types of transport that are kindest to the environment, explaining the dangers posed by pollution. (Rev: BL 2/15/10; LMC 1–2/10) [790.1]

3258 Benoit, Peter. *The BP Oil Spill* (3–5). Series: A True Book: Disasters. 2011, Children's Press LB $28 (978-0-531-20630-0); paper $6.95 (978-0-531-28999-0). 48pp. Benoit examines the disaster and its aftermath and provides photographs, maps, timelines, and statistics. (Rev: LMC 3–4/12; SLJ 11/1/11) [363.738]

3259 Bouler, Olivia. *Olivia's Birds: Saving the Gulf* (3–6). Illus. by author. 2011, Sterling $14.95 (978-1-4027-8665-5). 32pp. Eleven-year-old Olivia's striking illustrations of birds fill the pages of this book, alongside her inspiring story of donating her artwork to help the Gulf recover from the 2010 oil spill. (Rev: BL 5/1/11; SLJ 6/11) [598]

3260 Bridges, Andrew. *Clean Air* (5–8). Series: Sally Ride Science. 2009, Roaring Brook paper $6.99 (978-1-59643-576-6). 40pp. A look at the importance of clean air and the ways in which it is threatened by human activity. Lexile 740 (Rev: SLJ 9/09) [363.739]

3261 Coad, John. *Reducing Pollution* (4–9). Series: Why Science Matters. 2009, Heinemann-Raintree $32.86 (978-1-4329-2483-6). 56pp. Illustrating science's role in everyday life, this volume offers a comprehensive overview of the causes and consequences of pollution, and what we can do to reduce it. (Rev: LMC 11–12/09) [363.73]

3262 Geiger, Beth. *Clean Water* (5–8). Series: Sally Ride Science. 2009, Roaring Brook paper $6.99 (978-1-59643-577-3). 40pp. A look at the importance of clean water and the ways in which it is threatened by human activity. Lexile 740 (Rev: SLJ 9/09)

3263 Landau, Elaine. *Oil Spill! Disaster in the Gulf of Mexico* (3–5). Illus. 2011, Millbrook LB $25.26 (978-0-7613-7485-5). 32pp. Tells the story of the 2010 oil spill, the struggle to stop the leak, and the impact on the environment, with a final chapter titled "What's to Be Done?" ℮ Lexile 780L (Rev: BL 3/1/11*; SLJ 4/11) [363.738]

3264 Morgan, Sally. *Pollution* (1–3). Series: Helping Our Planet. 2011, Cherrytree LB $28.50 (978-1-84234-607-5). 32pp. Morgan looks at the sources of air and water pollution, the impact of oil spills, dumping, and farming, and steps we can take to limit pollution. (Rev: SLJ 8/1/11) [363]

3265 Person, Stephen. *Saving Animals from Oil Spills* (3–5). Illus. Series: Rescuing Animals from Disasters. 2011, Bearport LB $25.27 (978-161772288-2). 32pp. Looks at the impact on wildlife of such disasters as the *Exxon Valdez* spill in Alaska and the Deepwater Horizon explosion in the Gulf, introducing the people who risk their lives to save animals and the techniques they use. (Rev: BL 10/1/11) [628.1]

Population

3266 Anderson, Judith. *Ending Poverty and Hunger* (4–7). Series: Working for Our Future. 2010, Black Rabbit LB $28.50 (978-1-59771-195-1). 32pp. This volume explains why the United Nations chose eliminating poverty and hunger as one of its eight Millennium Development goals and looks at the various reasons why children are deprived of these basics and what can be done to improve the situation. (Rev: BL 6/1/10; LMC 10/10; SLJ 4/10)

3267 Barber, Nicola. *Coping with Population Growth* (5–8). Illus. Series: Environment Challenge. 2011, Raintree LB $32 (978-141094296-8); paper $8.99 (978-141094303-3). 48pp. This book looks at the importance of population growth to our world and at the relationship between population and food supply, poverty, pollution, education, and so forth. (Rev: BL 2/15/12) [304.6]

3268 McLeish, Ewan. *Population Explosion* (4–8). Series: Can the Earth Survive? 2010, Rosen LB $26.50 (978-1-4358-5356-0). 48pp. With case studies and suggested strategies for the future, this volume looks at population problems around the world and the impact on everyday life. (Rev: LMC 3–4/10; SLJ 1/10) [363.9]

Government and Politics

United Nations and International Affairs

3269 Anderson, Judith. *An Equal Chance for Girls and Women* (4–7). Series: Working for Our Future. 2010, Black Rabbit LB $28.50 (978-1-59771-196-8). 32pp. This volume explains why the United Nations chose equal opportunity for girls and women as one of its eight Millennium Development goals and looks at the various reasons why girls are deprived of opportunity and what can be done to improve the situation. (Rev: BL 6/10; LMC 10/10; SLJ 4/10) [323.3]

3270 Head, Honor. *Famous Spies* (5–8). Series: Spies and Spying. 2010, Smart Apple Media $28.50 (978-1-59920-358-4). 32pp. Different types of espionage are explored in readable, eye-catching profiles with sidebars covering technology and codes. (Rev: LMC 1–2/10)

3271 Smith, David J. *This Child, Every Child: A Book About the World's Children* (4–7). Illus. by Shelagh Armstrong. Series: CitizenKid. 2011, Kids Can $18.95 (978-1-55453-466-1). 36pp. The impact of the 1989 United Nations Convention on the Rights of the Child is outlined in this accessible, well-researched and thought-provoking volume. Lexile 1020L (Rev: BL 4/15/11; LMC 10/11; SLJ 5/1/11) [305.23]

United States

Civil Rights

3272 Brimner, Larry Dane. *Birmingham Sunday* (5–8). 2010, Boyds Mills LB $17.95 (978-1-59078-613-0). 48pp. This highly illustrated and moving account of the bombing in 1963 Alabama that killed four young girls places the tragedy in context of the civil rights turmoil of the time. Lexile NC1190L (Rev: BL 2/1/10; LMC 8–9/10; SLJ 4/10) [323.1196]

3273 Deutsch, Stacia, and Rhody Cohon. *Hot Pursuit: Murder in Mississippi* (5–8). Illus. by Craig Orback. 2010, Lerner/Kar-Ben $17.95 (978-0-7613-3955-7). 40pp. A dramatic fictional story about civil rights activists who were murdered in Mississippi in 1964 is intertwined with informational chapters providing background context. (Rev: BL 4/1/10; LMC 8–9/10) [323.092]

3274 Grant, Reg. *Slavery: Real People and Their Stories of Enslavement* (4–7). 2009, DK $24.99 (978-0-7566-5169-5). 192pp. The history of slavery around the world and information about its continued practice today is accompanied by firsthand accounts of people involved in slavery. (Rev: BL 7/09; LMC 11–12/09; SLJ 8/09) [306.362]

3275 Hinton, KaaVonia. *Brown v. Board of Education of Topeka, Kansas, 1954* (5–8). Series: Monumental Milestones: Great Events of Modern Times. 2010, Mitchell Lane LB $29.95 (978-1-58415-738-0). 48pp. Useful for research, this slim volume provides facts and biographical sketches key to this important ruling and supplies the necessary background to fully understand the issues involved. (Rev: BL 2/1/10; LMC 5–6/10; SLJ 1/10)

3276 Pinkney, Andrea Davis. *Sit-In: How Four Friends Stood Up by Sitting Down* (2–4). Illus. by Brian Pinkney. 2010, Little, Brown $16.99 (978-0-316-07016-4). 40pp. When four young black men sat down at a whites-only lunch counter in Greensboro, North Carolina, their courage helped set the ball rolling toward integration. (Rev: BL 2/1/10*; LMC 10/10; SLJ 4/1/10*) [323.1196]

3277 Slade, Suzanne. *Climbing Lincoln's Steps: The African American Journey* (2–5). Illus. by Colin Bootman. 2010, Whitman $16.99 (978-0-8075-1204-3).

32pp. Using the Lincoln Memorial as a backdrop, this attractive picture book touches on key events in civil rights history — from the Emancipation Proclamation to the election of President Obama. (Rev: BL 9/15/10; LMC 11–12/10; SLJ 8/1/10) [305.800973]

Crime and Criminals

3278 Earnest, Peter, and Suzanne Harper. *The Real Spy's Guide to Becoming a Spy* (4–8). Illus. by Bret Bertholf. 2009, Abrams $16.95 (978-0-8109-8329-8). 144pp. This guide to spying covers skills and training, tactics, jargon, and true-life stories. (Rev: SLJ 10/09; VOYA 12/09) [27.1200]

3279 Gardner, Robert. *Who Forged This Document? Crime-Solving Science Projects* (3–7). Illus. Series: Who Dunnit? Forensic Science Experiments. 2010, Enslow LB $23.93 (978-0-7660-3246-0). 48pp. With experiments and Who Dunnit sections, this book explores techniques to identify handwriting, inks, paper, counterfeit money, and forgeries. Also use *Who Can Solve the Crime? Science Projects Using Detective Skills* (2010). (Rev: LMC 3–4/10; SLJ 7/10) [363.25]

3280 Gardner, Robert. *Whose Bones Are These? Crime-Solving Science Projects* (4–6). Illus. Series: Who Dunnit? Forensic Science Experiments. 2010, Enslow LB $23.93 (978-0-7660-3248-4). 48pp. After an introduction discussing science fairs and the scientific method, Gardner discusses various aspects of using bodies, blood, and other evidence to solve crimes and offers a related project for each. Also use *Whose Fingerprints Are These?* (2010). (Rev: LMC 3–4/10; SLJ 5/10) [614]

3281 Graham, Ian. *Forensic Technology* (4–7). Illus. Series: New Technology. 2011, Black Rabbit LB $34.25 (978-159920532-8). 48pp. Describes the technology being used in investigating, deaths, fires and explosions, fakes and forgeries, and computer crimes, as well as the importance of print evidence and DNA profiling. (Rev: BL 10/15/11) [363.25]

3282 Higgins, Melissa. *The Night Dad Went to Jail: What to Expect When Someone You Love Goes to Jail* (K–3). Illus. by Wednesday Kirwan. Series: Life's Challenges. 2011, Capstone LB $25.32 (978-140486679-9). 24pp. Policemen, social workers, and support groups are among the factors introduced in this explanation of what happens when someone has to go to jail. (Rev: BL 10/1/11) [362.82]

3283 Spilsbury, Richard. *Bones Speak! Solving Crimes from the Past* (5–9). 2009, Enslow $23.93 (978-0-7660-3377-1). 48pp. Spilsbury provides a thorough overview of all things forensic, covering everything from insect evidence to careers in this field. (Rev: LMC 11–12/09; SLJ 11/1/09) [363.2]

3284 Stiefel, Chana. *Fingerprints: Dead People Do Tell Tales* (5–7). Illus. Series: True Forensic Crime Stories.

2011, Enslow LB $31.93 (978-076603689-5). 104pp. Looking at what makes fingerprints unique, how they are located, and the ways in which criminals try to hide their fingerprints, this is a useful volume for young researchers. (Rev: BL 10/1/11) [363.25]

Elections and Political Parties

3285 Nelson, Robin, and Sandy Donovan. *Getting Elected: A Look at Running for Office* (3–5). Illus. Series: How Does Government Work? 2012, Lerner LB $27.93 (978-076136519-8). 40pp. Using a fictional mayor as a framework, this volume covers the ins and outs of conducting a successful political campaign; includes photographs of actual elections. **e** (Rev: BL 4/1/12) [324.70973]

3286 Tracy, Kathleen. *The Historic Fight for the 2008 Democratic Presidential Nomination: The Clinton View* (5–8). Series: Monumental Milestones. 2009, Mitchell Lane LB $29.95 (978-1-58415-731-1). 48pp. A brief biography of Hillary Clinton accompanies a detailed account of the campaign to win the Democratic presidential nomination. (Rev: BL 4/1/09; SLJ 4/1/09) [973.931092]

Federal Government and Agencies

3287 Anderson, Dale. *The FBI Files: Successful Investigations* (5–8). Series: The FBI Story. 2009, Mason Crest LB $22.95 (978-1-4222-0561-7). 64pp. Anderson reviews several FBI success stories using accessible text full of illustrations. Also use *The FBI and White-Collar Crime, The FBI and Organized Crime,* and *The FBI and Civil Rights* (all 2009). (Rev: LMC 5–6/10) [363.25]

3288 Crewe, Sabrina. *A History of the FBI* (5–8). Series: The FBI Story. 2009, Mason Crest LB $22.95 (978-1-4222-0563-1). 64pp. A succinct, highly illustrated account of the FBI's creation and significant achievements over the years. Also use *The FBI and Crimes Against Children* (2009) and other volumes in this series. (Rev: LMC 5–6/10; SLJ 4/10) [363.25]

3289 Price, Sean Stewart. *U.S. Presidents* (3–8). Illus. by Eldon Doty. Series: Truth and Rumors. 2010, Capstone LB $25.32 (978-1-4296-3952-1). 32pp. Did John Quincy Adams give an interview while naked? Was Jimmy Carter attacked by a rabbit? Price answers these and other questions and ends with a final chapter on how to tell the difference between fact and fiction. (Rev: LMC 11–12/10) [923.173]

3290 Thomas, William David. *How to Become an FBI Agent* (5–8). Series: The FBI Story. 2009, Mason Crest LB $22.95 (978-1-4222-0571-6). 64pp. Readers learn about the process of applying to the FBI and the training that successful applicants receive. (Rev: LMC 5–6/10) [363.25]

Social Problems and Solutions

3291 O'Brien, Anne Sibley, and Perry Edmond O'Brien. *After Gandhi* (4–7). Illus. by Anne Sibley O'Brien. 2009, Charlesbridge $15.95 (978-1-58089-129-5). 192pp. Subtitled *One Hundred Years of Nonviolent Resistance,* this volume looks at Gandhi's legacy through the work of activists such as Martin Luther King, Jr., Nelson Mandela, and Cesar Chavez. (Rev: BL 2/15/09; SLJ 2/1/09)

3292 O'Neal, Claire. *Ways to Help in Your Community* (5–7). Series: How to Help: A Guide to Giving Back. 2010, Mitchell Lane LB $29.95 (978-1-58415-921-6). 48pp. Hosting a block party, organizing a neighborhood yard sale, feeding the hungry at a soup kitchen, and getting involved at your local library are among the approachable suggestions for volunteering in this well-organized book; lists of online resources are appended. Also use *Volunteering in Your School* (2010). (Rev: BL 4/1/11; SLJ 2/1/11) [361.3]

3293 Raatma, Lucia. *Citizenship* (4–6). Illus. Series: Cornerstones of Freedom. 2012, Scholastic LB $30 (978-053123064-0); paper $8.95 (978-053128164-2). 64pp. With many photographs and sidebars, Raatma explores the basics of becoming a U.S. citizen and some of the issues of current controversy. (Rev: BL 4/15/12) [323.60973]

3294 Reusser, Kayleen. *Celebrities Giving Back* (5–7). Series: How to Help: A Guide to Giving Back. 2010, Mitchell Lane LB $29.95 (978-1-58415-922-3). 48pp. Bono, Jimmy Carter, and Miley Cyrus are among the celebrities covered in this survey of the charitable activities of famous people. (Rev: BL 4/1/11; SLJ 2/1/11) [361.7]

3295 Robinson, J. Dennis. *Striking Back: The Fight to End Child Labor Exploitation* (5–8). Series: Taking a Stand. 2010, Compass Point LB $31.99 (978-0-7565-4297-9). 64pp. After an overview of child labor, this volume describes some of the dangers children faced and the movement to stop this exploitation, highlighting Mother Jones and others who had the courage to fight. Lexile 1000L (Rev: LMC 11–12/10; VOYA 8/10) [331.3]

3296 Sanders, Lynn Bogen. *Social Justice: How You Can Make a Difference* (4–7). Series: Take Action. 2009, Capstone LB $25.32 (978-1-4296-2798-6). 32pp. Step-by-step instructions guide readers through formulating a plan of action, and profiles of activist teens describe their goals and strategies. (Rev: SLJ 5/1/09) [303.372]

3297 Saul, Laya. *Ways to Help Disadvantaged Youth* (5–7). Series: How to Help: A Guide to Giving Back. 2010, Mitchell Lane LB $29.95 (978-1-58415-918-6). 48pp. Drives to collect books, toys, or school supplies and becoming involved in tutoring are among the approachable suggestions for volunteering in this well-organized book; lists of online resources are appended. (Rev: BL 4/1/11; SLJ 2/1/11) [362.74]

3298 Schwartz, Heather E. *Political Activism: How You Can Make a Difference* (4–7). Series: Take Action. 2009, Capstone LB $25.32 (978-1-4296-2799-3). 32pp. Personal profiles and practical advice are the hallmarks of books in this appealing series. (Rev: BL 4/1/09; SLJ 5/1/09) [322.40973]

3299 Solway, Andrew. *Graphing Immigration* (4–8). Illus. Series: Real World Data. 2010, Raintree LB $28.21 (978-143292617-5); paper $7.99 (978-143292626-7). 32pp. Solway uses charts, graphs, and tables — as well as interesting sidebars and photographs — to present trends in immigration and associated problems. (Rev: BL 2/1/10; SLJ 6/10) [304.802]

3300 Suvanjieff, Ivan, and Dawn Gifford Engle. *Peace-Jam: A Billion Simple Acts of Peace* (5–10). 2008, Puffin paper $16.99 (978-0-14-241234-3). 208pp. This volume introduces the Nobel Peace laureates who are active in the work of the PeaceJam Foundation and describes their activism along with efforts by young people to support their causes. (Rev: SLJ 5/1/09; VOYA 12/08) [303.6]

3301 Wilson, Janet. *One Peace: True Stories of Young Activists* (4–7). Illus. by author. 2008, Orca $19.95 (978-1-55143-892-4). 48pp. In double-page spreads featuring children's poems, artwork, photos, and quotations, this picture book for older readers tells the stories of activists ages 8 to 15, who have often experienced atrocities. (Rev: BL 1/1/09; SLJ 2/1/09) [327.1]

Religion and Holidays

General and Miscellaneous

3302 Alexander, Cecil. *All Things Bright and Beautiful* (PS–2). Illus. by Ashley Bryan. 2010, Atheneum $16.99 (978-1-4169-8939-4). 40pp. Cecil Alexander's well-known 19th-century hymn is presented here in a rich collages, with the musical score at the end. (Rev: BL 3/1/10*; LMC 8–9/10; SLJ 4/1/10) [264.23]

3303 Delval, Marie-Hélène. *Images of God for Young Children* (K–3). Illus. by Barbara Nascimbeni. 2011, Eerdmans $16.50 (978-0-8028-5391-2). 90pp. A nicely illustrated introduction to the concept that God can be found everywhere. (Rev: BL 4/15/11; SLJ 4/11) [231]

3304 dePaola, Tomie. *Let the Whole Earth Sing Praise* (PS–K). Illus. by author. 2011, Putnam $15.99 (978-0-399-25478-9). 32pp. A biblically inspired celebration of all aspects of the natural world, drawing on the art of the Otomi people of Puebla, Mexico. (Rev: BL 3/1/11; LMC 5–6/11; SLJ 3/1/11) [231.7]

3305 Levete, Sarah. *Death* (3–6). Illus. 2009, Rosen LB $26.50 (978-143585351-5). 48pp. Levete provides an overview of death and mourning traditions in religions around the world. (Rev: BL 4/1/10; LMC 1–2/10; SLJ 12/09) [203]

3306 O'Connor, Frances. *The History of Islam* (5–8). Series: Understanding Islam. 2009, Rosen LB $29.25 (978-1-4358-5064-4). 64pp. After looking at the origins of Islam, this volume distinguishes between Sunnis and Shiites, discusses the Koran, describes Islam's spread through the world, and gives an overview of the practice of Islam today. (Rev: LMC 10/09*) [297.09]

3307 *What Do You Believe? Religion and Faith in the World Today* (5–8). Illus. 2011, DK $16.99 (978-075667228-7). 96pp. The major world religions are introduced here — along with minor religions, spiritual movements, and atheism — with discussion of religious practices, morality, science and Creationism, and other related aspects. (Rev: BL 6/1/11) [200]

Bible Stories

3308 Delval, Marie-Hélène. *The Bible for Young Children* (K–3). Illus. by Jean-Claude Gotting. 2010, Eerdmans $16.50 (978-0-8028-5383-7). 88pp. This attractively illustrated book presents nine Bible stories adapted for young readers. (Rev: BL 11/15/10; SLJ 3/1/11) [220.9]

3309 Grimes, Nikki. *Voices of Christmas* (3–6). Illus. by Eric Velasquez. 2009, Zondervan $16.99 (978-031071192-6). 32pp. A rich, lyrical telling of the Nativity story, giving voice to characters ranging from Mary and Joseph to Herod and the innkeeper. (Rev: BL 11/15/09; HB 11–21/09; SLJ 10/09) [232.92]

3310 Jules, Jacqueline. *Miriam in the Desert* (K–3). Illus. by Natascia Ugliano. 2010, Lerner/Kar-Ben $17.95 (978-076134494-0); paper $8.95 (978-076134496-4). 32pp. The story of Moses's strong, comforting sister Miriam is given a warm, positive treatment in this updated Bible story. (Rev: BL 11/15/10) [222]

Holidays and Holy Days

General and Miscellaneous

3311 Anderson, Sheila. *Kwanzaa* (PS–K). Illus. by Holli Conger. Series: Cultural Holidays. 2009, ABDO LB $18.95 (978-160270604-0). 32pp. A simple, brightly illustrated introduction to the customs and meaning of Kwanzaa. (Rev: BLO 11/1/09) [394.2612]

3312 Barner, Bob. *The Day of the Dead / El día de los muertos* (PS–1). Trans. by Teresa Mlawer. Illus. by author. 2010, Holiday House $16.95 (978-082342214-2). 32pp. Bright pastel illustrations and bilingual text describe the joy and festivity of the Mexican celebration. (Rev: BL 9/15/10; LMC 1–2/11) [394.264]

3313 Blackwell, Amy Hackney. *Lent, Yom Kippur, and Other Atonement Days* (5–8). Series: Holidays and Celebrations. 2010, Knopf $19.99 (978-1-60413-100-0). 112pp. The customs of Lent, Yom Kippur, and the Buddhist holiday Rains Retreat are detailed and given historical context in this illustrated book. (Rev: BL 11/15/09; SLJ 1/10) [202]

3314 Bullard, Lisa. *Marco's Cinco de Mayo* (K–2). Illus. by Holli Conger. Series: Holidays and Special Days. 2012, Millbrook LB $23.93 (978-076135082-8); paper $6.95 (978-076138580-6). 24pp. A Mexican American boy explains the traditions of Cinco de Mayo and shows how his family celebrates. **e** (Rev: BL 4/1/12; SLJ 4/1/12) [972]

3315 Craats, Rennay. *Columbus Day: Observing the Day Christopher Columbus Came to the Americas* (3–6). Illus. Series: American Celebrations. 2010, Weigl LB $27.13 (978-160596775-2); paper $11.95 (978-160596933-6). 24pp. History, rituals, and symbols are among the topics covered in this accessible introduction to the holiday. (Rev: BL 1/1–15/11) [394.264]

3316 Dickmann, Nancy. *Ramadan and Id-ul-Fitr* (PS–1). Illus. Series: Holidays and Festivals. 2010, Acorn LB $21.50 (978-1-4329-4049-2); paper $5.99 (978-1-4329-4068-3). 24pp. With clear, simple text and effective illustrations, Dickmann introduces Islam's holy month and the celebration that takes place at its end. Lexile 230L (Rev: BL 11/15/10; SLJ 12/1/10) [297.3]

3317 Foran, Jill. *Martin Luther King Jr. Day: Recognizing the Life and Work of Martin Luther King Jr.* (3–5). Illus. Series: American Celebrations. 2010, Weigl LB $27.13 (978-160596772-1); paper $11.95 (978-160596779-0). 24pp. History, rituals, and symbols are among the topics covered in this accessible introduction to the holiday. (Rev: BL 1/1–15/11) [394.26]

3318 Hamilton, Lynn. *Presidents' Day: Honoring the Accomplishments of All U.S. Presidents* (3–5). Illus. Series: American Celebrations. 2010, Weigl LB $27.13 (978-160596773-8); paper $11.95 (978-160596931-2). 24pp. Describes the ways in which this holiday celebrates the history of the nation and its presidents. (Rev: BL 1/1–15/11) [394.261]

3319 Landau, Elaine. *What Is St. Patrick's Day?* (K–2). Series: I Like Holidays! 2011, Enslow LB $21.26 (978-0-7660-3704-5); paper $6.95 (978-1-59845-291-4). 24pp. This straightforward overview for young children provides some cultural and historical background about St. Patrick's Day, and includes colorful photographs of

contemporary celebrations and an activity. (Rev: SLJ 11/1/11) [394.2]

3320 Murray, Julie. *Ramadan* (K–3). Series: Holidays. 2011, ABDO LB $25.65 (978-1-61783-041-9). 24pp. A simple introduction to the holiday and its traditions, with large photographs. (Rev: SLJ 12/1/11) [297]

3321 Rissman, Rebecca. *Martin Luther King, Jr. Day* (PS–K). Illus. Series: Holidays and Festivals. 2010, Heinemann LB $21.50 (978-143294055-3). 24pp. An introduction for very young children to the importance of this holiday and to the life of the man it honors. (Rev: BL 2/1/11) [394.261]

3322 Tait, Leia. *Cinco de Mayo: Celebrating Mexican History and Culture* (3–5). Illus. Series: American Celebrations. 2010, Weigl LB $27.13 (978-160596776-9); paper $11.95 (978-160596934-3). 24pp. History, rituals, and symbols are among the topics covered in this accessible introduction to the Mexican holiday. (Rev: BL 1/1–15/11) [394.262]

3323 Tokunbo, Dimitrea. *The Sound of Kwanzaa* (PS–2). Illus. by Lisa Cohen. 2009, Scholastic $16.99 (978-054501865-4). 32pp. The rituals and celebrations of Kwanzaa are presented along with a pronunciation guide and a recipe. (Rev: BL 11/1/09; LMC 1–2/10; SLJ 10/09) [394.261]

Christmas

3324 Farmer, Jacqueline. *O Christmas Tree: Its History and Holiday Traditions* (1–4). Illus. by Joanne Friar. 2010, Charlesbridge $16.95 (978-158089238-4); paper $7.95 (978-158089239-1). 32pp. The history of the Christmas tree custom, from pagan and early Christian practices through current times, is the focus of this colorful book. (Rev: BL 9/1/10; HB 11–12/10; SLJ 10/10) [394.2663]

3325 Isadora, Rachel. *Twelve Days of Christmas* (1–3). Illus. by author. 2010, Putnam $16.99 (978-039925073-6). 32pp. Using text and rebuses, with bright collages, this picture book sets the traditional carol in Africa. (Rev: BL 10/15/10; HB 11–12/10; SLJ 10/10) [782.42]

3326 Mora, Pat. *A Piñata in a Pine Tree: A Latino Twelve Days of Christmas* (PS–3). Illus. by Magaly Morales. 2009, Clarion $16 (978-061884198-1). 32pp. With a pronunciation guide and a glossary, this adaptation of "The Twelve Days of Christmas" introduces many elements of Latino holiday celebrations. (Rev: BL 11/1/09; HB 11–12/09; SLJ 10/09) [782.42]

Easter

3327 Merrick, Patrick. *Easter Bunnies* (1–3). Illus. Series: Our Holiday Symbols. 2010, Child's World LB $24.21 (978-160253333-2). 24pp. Merrick explains the history and sometimes puzzling origins of the Easter Bunny. (Rev: BLO 3/1/10) [394.2667]

Halloween

3328 Lewis, Anne Margaret. *What Am I? Halloween* (PS–2). Illus. by Tom Mills. Series: My Look and See Holiday Book. 2011, Whitman $9.99 (978-0-8075-8959-5). Unpaged. "I can float through the air/and I like to shout, BOO!/What am I? What could I be?" Questions like this are answered on flaps: "I am a spooky ghost/on Halloween./That's me!" (Rev: SLJ 9/1/11) [394.2646]

Jewish Holy Days and Celebrations

3329 Bernhard, Durga. *Around the World in One Shabbat: Jewish People Celebrate the Sabbath Together* (K–3). Illus. by author. 2011, Jewish Lights $18.99 (978-1-58023-433-7). 32pp. The rituals of Shabbat are explained through a series of vignettes showing Jewish families around the world. ℮ (Rev: BL 4/15/11; SLJ 5/1/11) [296.4]

3330 Rosen, Michael J. *Chanukah Lights* (2–5). Illus. by Robert Sabuda. 2011, Candlewick $34.99 (978-076365533-4). 16pp. An intricate pop-up tour of the global Festival of Lights, this fragile yet engrossing volume will require adult participation for complete enjoyment and understanding. (Rev: BLO 10/15/11; HB 11–12/11; SLJ 10/1/11)

3331 Ziefert, Harriet. *Passover: Celebrating Now, Remembering Then* (PS–3). Illus. by Karla Gudeon. 2010, Blue Apple $17.99 (978-160905020-7). 40pp. Contrasting history, tradition, and contemporary practice, this is a handsome account of the Passover celebration. (Rev: BL 4/15/10) [296.4]

Thanksgiving

3332 Colman, Penny. *Thanksgiving: The True Story* (5–8). Illus. 2008, Henry Holt $18.95 (978-080508229-6). 144pp. Colman presents a fascinating look at the origins, customs, and foods of America's Thanksgiving, drawing on survey responses as well as historical research. (Rev: BL 9/1/08; HB 11–12/08; SLJ 11/1/08; VOYA 8/08) [394.2649]

Valentine's Day

3333 Lynette, Rachel. *Let's Throw a Valentine's Day Party* (2–4). Illus. Series: Holiday Parties. 2011, Rosen LB $21.25 (978-144882570-7). 24pp. A useful, compact guide to holding a party, with suggestions for games, food, and decorations. (Rev: BL 12/15/11) [793.2]

3334 Speechley, Greta. *Valentine Crafts* (2–4). Illus. 2010, Gareth Stevens LB $28 (978-143393600-5). 32pp. A variety of everyday materials are employed in a dozen Valentine's Day craft projects. (Rev: BLO 11/15/10) [745.594]

Prayers

3335 Brooks, Jeremy. *Let There Be Peace: Prayers from Around the World* (PS–3). Illus. by Jude Daly. 2009, Frances Lincoln $16.95 (978-184507530-9). 32pp. A collection of prayers from a variety of religions and countries are presented with beautiful illustrations. (Rev: BL 11/15/09) [242.82]

3336 Jordan, Deloris. *Baby Blessings: A Prayer for the Day You Are Born* (PS–K). Illus. by James E. Ransome. 2010, Simon & Schuster $16.99 (978-1-4169-5362-3). 32pp. A simple celebration of life as an African American baby grows to kindergarten age in an atmosphere of faith and love. (Rev: BL 11/15/09; SLJ 12/1/09) [242]

3337 Paterson, Katherine. *Brother Sun, Sister Moon: Saint Francis of Assisi's Canticle of the Creatures* (2–5). Illus. by Pamela Dalton. 2011, Chronicle $17.99 (978-0-8118-7734-3). 36pp. Brother Francis's words celebrating the natural world are reimagined and enhanced with lush cut paper illustrations. ℮ Lexile 740L (Rev: BL 8/11*; SLJ 7/11*)

3338 Piper, Sophie. *The Lion Book of Prayers to Read and Know* (2–4). Illus. by Anthony Lewis. 2010, Lion $12.99 (978-0-7459-6147-7). 96pp. Prayers from a variety of sources — including an 18th-century New England sampler — are illustrated in this accessible book for young readers. (Rev: SLJ 2/1/10) [242.8]

3339 Warren, Rick. *The Lord's Prayer* (PS–2). Illus. by Richard Jesse Watson. 2011, Zondervan $16.99 (978-031071086-8). 40pp. This handsome volume provides a good, accessible interpretation of the Lord's Prayer in the King James version with line-by-line commentary. (Rev: BL 11/15/10; SLJ 2/11) [226.9]

Social Groups

Ethnic Groups

3340 Keedle, Jayne. *Americans from the Caribbean and Central America* (4–8). Series: New Americans. 2010, Marshall Cavendish LB $35.64 (978-0-7614-4302-5). 80pp. Part of a series that looks at the experiences of recent immigrants, this book discusses the challenges that new arrivals face and the impact they have on society; the citizenship process is explained and personal accounts add impact. Also use by this author *Mexican Americans* and *West African Americans* (2010). (Rev: LMC 3–4/10; SLJ 2/10)

3341 Morrison, Jessica. *Military* (4–7). Illus. 2011, Weigl LB $20.99 (978-161690661-0); paper $14.95 (978-161690665-8). 48pp. African Americans who played pivotal roles in America's wars, from the Revolution to Iraq and Afghanistan are portrayed in this inspiring title. (Rev: BL 2/1/12)

3342 Nelson, Kadir. *Heart and Soul: The Story of America and African Americans* (3–7). Illus. by author. 2011, HarperCollins $19.99 (978-0-06-173074-0). 108pp. An elderly African American woman narrates the story of her people's struggle to be accepted and free in America in this compelling portrait with evocative full-page paintings. Coretta Scott King Author Award. ◯ ℯ Lexile 1050L (Rev: BL 8/11*; HB 11–12/11; SLJ 9/1/11*) [973]

3343 Pokiak, James, and Mindy Willett. *Proud to Be Inuvialuit / Quviahuktunga Inuvialuugama* (3–5). Photos by Tessa Macintosh. Illus. Series: The Land Is Our Storybook. 2010, Fifth House $16.95 (978-1-897252-59-8). 26pp. Pokiak presents his people and their way of life today, showing a modern whale harvest and explaining how ancient traditions have been retained. (Rev: BL 10/15/10; LMC 11–12/10; SLJ 5/11) [971.9]

3344 Walker, Paul Robert. *A Nation of Immigrants* (4–6). Illus. Series: All About America. 2012, Kingfisher LB $19.89 (978-075346713-8); paper $9.99 (978-075346671-1). 32pp. Illustrations, archival reproductions, and photographs add appeal to this survey of the various waves of immigrants to the United States from the earliest people to cross the land bridge from Siberia to the census of 2010. (Rev: BL 4/15/12; SLJ 3/12) [304.8]

3345 Weatherford, Carole Boston. *The Beatitudes: From Slavery to Civil Rights* (2–4). Illus. by Tim Ladwig. 2010, Eerdmans $16.99 (978-0-8028-5352-3). 32pp. Weatherford uses the Beatitudes as the framework for a rich picture-book history of the African American experience, from slavery through the civil rights movement to the inauguration of Barack Obama. (Rev: BL 2/1/10; SLJ 3/1/10) [323.0973]

3346 Weiss, Gail Garfinkel. *Americans from Russia and Eastern Europe* (5–8). Series: New Americans. 2009, Marshall Cavendish LB $24.95 (978-0-7614-4310-0). 80pp. This volume provides an overview of immigration past and present from these regions, providing census data and population maps and charts as well as discussing these immigrants' contributions to American culture. (Rev: LMC 3–4/10; SLJ 2/10) [305.8991]

Terrorism

3347 Brown, Don. *America Is Under Attack: September 11, 2001: The Day the Towers Fell* (3–5). Series: Actual Times. 2011, Roaring Brook $16.99 (978-1-59643-694-7). Unpaged. This balanced, straightforward account covers the events from the hijacking of the planes to the collapse of the towers. ALSC Notable Children's Book, 2012. Lexile 840L (Rev: HB 11–12/11; LMC 1–2/12; SLJ 9/1/11*) [973.931]

3348 Burgan, Michael. *Terrorist Groups* (5–7). Series: Terrorism. 2010, Compass Point LB $27.99 (978-0-7565-4311-2). 48pp. After providing a definition of terrorism, Burgan looks at various terrorist groups past and present: the IRA, Irgun, Fatah, ETA, Farc, Tamil Tigers, Hezbollah, Aum Shinrikyo, Hamas, and al-Qaeda. Lexile 990L (Rev: LMC 11–12/10) [363.325]

3349 Ching, Jacqueline. *Cyberterrorism* (5–8). Series: Doomsday Scenarios: Separating Fact from Fiction. 2010, Rosen LB $29.25 (978-1-4358-3565-8). 64pp. After describing cyberterrorists and their techniques, this volume describes some worst-case scenarios, assesses the scope of the threat, and looks at ways of fighting back. (Rev: LMC 11–12/10) [363.325]

3350 Nardo, Don. *The History of Terrorism* (5–7). Series: Terrorism. 2010, Compass Point LB $27.99 (978-0-7565-4310-5). 48pp. A broad, well-illustrated survey of terrorism through time, looking at the governments, groups, and individuals that have sought to achieve their goals through violence and the various strategies they have used. (Rev: LMC 11–12/10) [363.3]

Personal Development

Behavior

General

3351 Andrews, Beth. *Why Are You So Scared? A Child's Book About Parents with PTSD* (1–4). Illus. by Katherine Kirkland. 2011, Magination $14.95 (978-143381045-9); paper $9.95 (978-143381044-2). 32pp. This book provides accessible information for children whose parents are coping with post-traumatic stress disorder. (Rev: BL 11/1/11) [616.85]

3352 Buchholz, Rachel. *How to Survive Anything: Shark Attack, Lightning, Embarrassing Parents, Pop Quizzes, and Other Perilous Situations* (4–8). Illus. by Chris Philpot. 2011, National Geographic paper $14.95 (978-1-4263-0774-4). 208pp. Full of humor, this survival guide covers everything from truly dangerous situations to public humiliation. (Rev: BLO 8/11; SLJ 7/11) [646.7]

3353 Chassé, Jill D. *The Babysitter's Survival Guide: Fun Games, Cool Crafts, and How to Be the Best Babysitter in Town* (5–10). Illus. by Jessica Secheret. 2010, Sterling $12.95 (978-1-40274-654-3). 108pp. With information on how to assess job opportunities, this helpful guide offers plenty of activity ideas, advice for coping with difficult behaviors, and general tips on running a business. (Rev: SLJ 9/1/10) [649]

3354 Cindrich, Sharon. *A Smart Girl's Guide to Style: How to Have Fun with Fashion, Shop Smart, and Let Your Personal Style Shine Through* (4–7). Illus. by Shannon Laskey. Series: Be Your Best. 2010, American Girl paper $9.95 (978-1-59369-648-1). 119pp. With a light and breezy tone, this book outlines plenty of fashion dos and don'ts in chapters that define the difference between fashion and style, lay out the basics, and give shopping and storage advice. (Rev: SLJ 7/10) [562]

3355 Fox, Annie. *Real Friends vs the Other Kind* (5–8). Series: Middle School Confidential. 2009, Free Spirit paper $9.99 (978-1-57542-319-7). 90pp. The intricacies of middle school friendships, allegiances, and romances are examined here, with advice from real tweens about handing difficult situations. (Rev: SLJ 8/09) [177.62]

3356 Graves, Sue. *But Why Can't I?* (PS–1). Illus. by Desideria Guicciardini. Series: Our Emotions and Behavior. 2011, Free Spirit $12.99 (978-1-57542-376-0). 25pp. Simple plot lines and real-life scenarios make this a useful discussion-starter about rules and their purpose in keeping us safe and healthy. Also use *I'm Not Happy, Not Fair, Won't Share,* and *Who Feels Scared?* (all 2011). (Rev: SLJ 8/1/11) [152.4]

3357 Guillain, Charlotte. *My First Sleepover* (K–2). Illus. Series: Growing Up. 2011, Heinemann LB $22 (978-1-4329-4802-3). 24pp. This reassuring book gives readers a sense of what to expect on their first sleepover. (Rev: BL 7/11; SLJ 6/11) [793.2]

3358 Jackson, Donna M. *What's So Funny? Making Sense of Humor* (3–7). Illus. by Ted Stearn. 2011, Viking $16.99 (978-067001244-2). 64pp. Jackson looks at the origins of humor, the physiology of laughter, animals and humor, and various other aspects of being funny. (Rev: BLO 8/11; SLJ 7/11) [152.4]

3359 Ljungkvist, Laura. *Follow the Line to School* (PS–1). Illus. by author. Series: Follow the Line. 2011, Viking $16.99 (978-0-670-01226-8). 32pp. As readers follow the line through this book, they are introduced to the various parts of a bright, well-equipped school and answer a variety of questions. (Rev: BL 8/11; HB 9–10/11; SLJ 7/11) [371]

3360 Lundsten, Apry. *A Smart Girl's Guide to Parties: How to Be a Great Guest, Be a Happy Hostess, and Have Fun at Any Party* (4–7). Illus. by Angela Martini. Series: Be Your Best. 2010, American Girl paper $9.95 (978-1-59369-645-0). 96pp. With a light and breezy tone, this book outlines party etiquette for both hosts and guests at affairs formal and informal, with advice on invitations, gifts, and so forth. (Rev: SLJ 7/10)

3361 Marshall, Shelley. *Super Ben's Brave Bike Ride: A Book About Courage* (PS–K). Illus. by Ben Mahan. Series: Character Education with Super Ben and Molly the Great. 2010, Enslow $21.26 (978-0-7660-3515-7). 24pp. Young bear Ben finds the courage to get to his friend Molly the rabbit's house alone when his mother is busy, wearing his cape to bolster his confidence. Also use *Super Ben's Dirty Hands: A Book About Healthy Habits* (2010). (Rev: LMC 3/1/10; SLJ 5/1/10) [179]

3362 Moss, Wendy L. *Being Me: A Kid's Guide to Boosting Confidence and Self-Esteem* (5–8). Illus. 2011, Magination $14.95 (978-143380883-8); paper $9.95 (978-143380884-5). 112pp. "Stand Up for Yourself" and "Hang Out with a Group" are two of the chapters in this book full of helpful and practical advice for building social confidence. (Rev: BL 1/1–15/11; SLJ 3/1/11) [155.4]

3363 Naik, Anita. *Read the Signals: The Body Language Handbook* (4–8). Series: Really Useful Handbooks. 2009, Crabtree LB $29.27 (978-0-7787-4388-0); paper $9.95 (978-0-7787-4401-6). This positive, often humorous book provides information on handling and interpreting a variety of tricky social situations — from bullying to shyness to flirtation — presented in digestible, bullet-point format. (Rev: BL 4/1/09; LMC 10/09; SLJ 6/1/09) [153.6]

3364 Orr, Tamra. *Ways to Help the Elderly* (5–8). Series: How to Help: A Guide to Giving Back. 2010, Mitchell Lane LB $21.50 (978-1-58415-915-5). 48pp. Using real-life examples, this thoughtful book suggests many ways in which children can help elderly people. (Rev: SLJ 12/1/10) [305.26]

3365 Spinelli, Eileen, and Jerry Spinelli. *Today I Will: A Year of Quotes, Notes, and Promises to Myself* (5–8). Illus. by Julia Rothman. 2009, Knopf $15.99 (978-0-375-84057-9); LB $18.99 (978-0-375-96230-1). 384pp. In this page-a-day advice book, the Spinellis offer accessible, often humorous quotes, advice, and affirmations from celebrities, historical figures, and popular literature. (Rev: BL 11/15/09; SLJ 10/09) [082]

3366 Szpirglas, Jeff. *You Just Can't Help It! Your Guide to the Wild and Wacky World of Human Behavior* (3–6). Illus. by Josh Holinaty. 2011, OwlKids $22.95 (978-1-926818-07-8); paper $12.95 (978-1-926818-08-5). 64pp. Plenty of hip trivia and an eye-catching layout add appeal to this book that explores the instincts behind human impulses and behavior. (Rev: LMC 8–9/11; SLJ 6/11; VOYA 2/11) [599.9]

3367 Zelinger, Laurie. *A Smart Girl's Guide to Liking Herself — Even on the Bad Days* (4–6). Illus. by Jennifer Kalis. Series: Be Your Best. 2012, American Girl paper $9.95 (978-159369943-7). 96pp. The importance of high self-esteem is underlined in this guide that in-

cludes quizzes and advice on how to shake off negative feelings. (Rev: BL 4/15/12; SLJ 7/12) [155.43]

Etiquette

3368 Arnold, Tedd, and Joe Berger, et al. *Manners Mash-Up: A Goofy Guide to Good Behavior* (2–4). Illus. by Tedd Arnold. 2011, Dial $16.99 (978-0-8037-3480-7). 40pp. Fourteen well-known children's book illustrators each present an amusing spread showing how to behave properly. (Rev: BL 1/1–15/11; HB 7–8/11; SLJ 3/1/11) [395.1]

3369 Jakubiak, David J. *A Smart Kid's Guide to Online Bullying* (2–5). Illus. Series: Kids Online. 2009, Rosen LB $21.25 (978-1-4042-8114-1). 24pp. This practical guide includes plenty of smart advice for kids who find themselves dealing with cyberbullies. (Rev: BL 4/1/10; SLJ 3/1/10) [302.3]

3370 Verdick, Elizabeth. *Don't Behave Like You Live in a Cave* (4–6). Illus. by Steve Mark. Series: Laugh and Learn. 2010, Free Spirit paper $8.95 (978-1-57542-353-1). 120pp. A humorous, practical guide to good behavior, setting realistic goals, and exercise and nutrition, using a cartoon Cave Boy and Cave Girl as examples of poor etiquette. (Rev: SLJ 1/1/11) [395.1]

Family Relationships

3371 Ajmera, Maya, and Sheila Kincade, et al. *Our Grandparents: A Global Album* (PS–1). 2010, Charlesbridge $16.95 (978-1-57091-458-4); paper $7.95 (978-1-57091-459-1). Unpaged. Multicultural youngsters and grandparents are shown engaging in simple, joyful activities together in this book celebrating the important bridge between generations. (Rev: LMC 11–12/10; SLJ 2/1/10)

3372 Crist, James J., and Elizabeth Verdick. *Siblings: You're Stuck with Each Other, So Stick Together* (3–6). Illus. by Steve Mark. Series: Laugh and Learn. 2010, Free Spirit $8.95 (978-157542336-4). 128pp. Following information on the relationship between siblings (birth order and so forth), this book presents advice on avoiding friction and forging friendship. (Rev: BL 4/15/10; SLJ 6/10) [306.875]

3373 Fakhrid-Deen, Tina. *Let's Get This Straight: The Ultimate Handbook for Youth with LGBTQ Parents* (5–10). 2010, Seal $15.95 (978-1-58005-333-4). 174pp. This insightful book discusses the various challenges children with LGBTQ parents will face and offers excerpts from interviews, questionnaires, and a good list of resources. (Rev: SLJ 3/1/11) [306.8]

3374 Fox, Annie. *What's Up with My Family?* (5–8). Series: Middle School Confidential. 2010, Free Spirit paper $9.99 (978-1-57542-333-3). 96pp. Stories of children in difficult family situations alternate with advice for dealing with family issues and staying positive; a blend of fictional graphic novel stories and practical advice. (Rev: LMC 8–9/10; SLJ 4/10) [646.7]

3375 Hoffman, Mary. *The Great Big Book of Families* (PS–2). Illus. by Ros Asquith. 2011, Dial $16.99 (978-0-8037-3516-3). 40pp. A compendium that celebrates all types of families and shows the many differences in the ways in which we live. (Rev: BL 3/15/11; LMC 10/11*; SLJ 5/1/11*) [306.85]

3376 Ollhoff, Jim. *Beginning Genealogy: Expert Tips to Help You Trace Your Own Ancestors* (3–6). Series: Your Family Tree. 2010, ABDO LB $18.95 (978-1-61613-460-0). 32pp. A helpful guide for young readers to family trees, the meanings of last names, and how to get started researching your background. Also use *Collecting Primary Records, DNA: Window to the Past: How Science Can Help Untangle Your Family Roots, Exploring Immigration: Discovering the Rich Heritage of America's Immigrants, Filling the Family Tree: Interviewing Relatives to Discover Facts and Stories,* and *Using Your Research: How to Check Your Facts and Use Your Information* (all 2010). (Rev: SLJ 3/1/11) [929.1]

3377 Rotner, Shelley, and Sheila M. Kelly. *I'm Adopted!* (PS–K). Illus. by Shelley Rotner. 2011, Holiday House $16.95 (978-0-8234-2294-4). 32pp. Simple text with age-appropriate scenarios and close-up photographs showing a variety of conventional and unconventional families are features of this exploration of what adoption is and how it works. (Rev: BLO 9/1/11; SLJ 9/1/11) [362.734]

3378 Schuette, Sarah L. *Adoptive Families* (PS–2). Series: My Family. 2009, Capstone LB $18.65 (978-1-4296-3977-4). 24pp. For very young readers, this book presents adoptive families of various ethnicities. Also use *Blended Families, Foster Families,* and *Single-Parent Families* (all 2009). (Rev: LMC 11–12/10; SLJ 5/1/10) [306.87]

3379 Simons, Rae. *Blended Families* (5–8). Illus. Series: The Changing Face of Modern Families. 2009, Mason Crest $22.95 (978-1-4222-1492-3). 64pp. This book about blended families provides statistics, information, and advice through graphs, newspaper articles, and questions for discussion. Also use *Grandparents Raising Kids* and *Single Parents.* (Rev: LMC 5–6/10; SLJ 3/10)

3380 Stewart, Sheila. *What Is a Family?* (5–8). Illus. Series: The Changing Face of Modern Families. 2009, Mason Crest $22.95 (978-1-4222-1528-9). 64pp. Exploring what, exactly, makes a family a family, this book provides statistics, information, and advice through graphs, newspaper articles, and questions for discussion. Also use *Celebrity Families.* (Rev: LMC 5–6/10; SLJ 3/10)

Personal Problems and Relationships

3381 Rechner, Amy. *The In Crowd: Dealing with Peer Pressure* (5–8). Series: What's the Issue? 2009, Compass Point $27.99 (978-0-7565-1891-2). 48pp. A compelling mix of direct quotes, real-life scenarios, quizzes, and short glossaries enhance this book about coping with peer pressure; suitable for reluctant readers. (Rev: LMC 10/09; SLJ 10/09) [303.3]

3382 Schwartz, John. *Short: Walking Tall When You're Not Tall at All* (4–8). 2010, Flash Point $16.99 (978-1-59643-323-6). 144pp. Short himself, journalist Schwartz explores various aspects of the importance of height (in terms of popularity, business success, and so forth); provides information on such topics as genetics and growth hormones; and takes aim at the media in this funny book that's part memoir, part self-help book. (Rev: BL 2/15/10; LMC 5–6/10; SLJ 3/10) [921]

3383 Shapiro, Ouisie. *Bullying and Me: Schoolyard Stories* (4–7). Illus. by Steven Vote. 2010, Whitman $16.99 (978-0-8075-0921-0). 32pp. A baker's dozen of stories describe physical abuse, verbal abuse, and online bullying, each followed by advice on how to deal with such situations. Lexile 740L (Rev: BL 8/10; LMC 11–12/10*; SLJ 10/1/10) [371.5]

Careers

General and Miscellaneous

3384 Cohn, Jessica. *Animator* (4–6). Series: Cool Careers: Cutting Edge. 2010, Gareth Stevens LB $26 (978-1-4339-1953-4). 32pp. Explains the roles that animators play in cinematography and includes a "Career Fact File" that gives the career outlook, earnings, and training needed. (Rev: SLJ 8/10) [791.43]

3385 Crabtree, Marc. *Meet My Neighbor, the News Camera Operator* (K–3). Illus. Series: Meet My Neighbor. 2012, Crabtree LB $21.27 (978-077874560-0). 24pp. A Toronto cameraman gets ready for work, conducts interviews, and edits in the studio in this simple, colorful introduction. Also use *Meet My Neighbor, the Librarian* (2012). (Rev: BL 5/15/12) [777.092]

3386 Dolan, Edward F. *Careers in the U.S. Air Force* (5–8). Series: Military Service. 2009, Marshall Cavendish $24.95 (978-0-7614-4205-9). 80pp. This straightforward guide to the U.S. Air Force covers everything from training to joining requirements to salary; part of a recommended series that covers other branches of service. (Rev: BL 10/1/09; SLJ 3/10) [358.40023]

3387 Horn, Geoffrey M. *FBI Agent* (4–8). Illus. Series: Cool Careers: Helping Careers. 2008, Gareth Stevens LB $24 (978-083689193-5). 32pp. What *do* FBI agents do? This book answers the question with facts about the training and responsibilities plus information on key cases. Lexile 760L (Rev: BL 10/15/08) [363.250973]

3388 Marsico, Katie. *Working at the Library* (K–2). Series: 21st Century Junior Library. 2009, Cherry Lake LB $27.07 (978-1-60279-511-2). 24pp. Employees from librarians to shelvers to custodians are presented in this concise portrayal of what goes on at a library; suitable for beginning readers. (Rev: SLJ 2/1/10) [027]

3389 Marsico, Katie. *Working at the Post Office* (K–2). Series: 21st Century Junior Library. 2009, Cherry Lake LB $27.07 (978-1-60279-512-9). 24pp. Marsico presents an overview of all the functions undertaken at a post office; suitable for beginning readers. (Rev: SLJ 2/1/10) [383]

3390 Owen, Ruth. *Building Green Places: Careers in Planning, Designing, and Building* (5–8). Illus. Series: Green-Collar Careers. 2011, Crabtree LB $31.93 (978-077874852-6). 64pp. Looks at careers that involve designing and constructing eco-friendly buildings, cities, and parks. (Rev: BL 2/15/12) [720]

3391 Swinburne, Stephen R. *Whose Shoes? A Shoe for Every Job* (PS–2). Illus. by author. 2010, Boyds Mills $16.95 (978-159078569-0). 32pp. Readers guess a person's vocation based on the shoes he or she is wearing. (Rev: BL 2/1/10; HB 5–6/10; LMC 5–6/10) [331.702]

3392 Sylvester, Kevin. *Game Day: Meet the People Who Make It Happen* (5–8). 2010, Annick $21.95 (978-1-55451-251-5); paper $12.95 (978-1-55451-250-8). 136pp. Sylvester looks beyond the athletes to explore the roles of people behind the scenes of professional sports — a mechanic, a game scheduler, an umpire, a Zamboni driver, and so forth. **e** (Rev: BL 2/1/11; SLJ 1/1/11; VOYA 12/10) [796]

Arts and Entertainment

3393 Hambleton, Vicki, and Cathleen Greenwood. *So, You Want to Be a Writer? How to Write, Get Published, and Maybe Even Make It Big!* (5–8). 2012, Beyond Words $17.99 (978-158270359-6); paper $9.99 (978-158270353-4). 192pp. From "What's It Like to Be a Writer" to "How to Get Published: Creating a Proposal" and "Writing as a Career: You Mean I Can Get Paid for That?," this is a thorough overview of the writing process, covering all formats and genres and providing many examples. (Rev: BL 4/1/12; LMC 8–9/12) [808]

3394 Hasan, Heather. *How to Produce, Release, and Market Your Music* (5–8). Illus. Series: Garage Bands. 2012, Rosen LB $12.95 (978-144885658-9). 64pp. Everything you need to know about making it in the music world, from initial recording through booking shows, establishing copyright, marketing strategies, and use of social media. (Rev: BL 4/1/12) [780.23]

3395 Marsico, Katie. *Choreographer* (4–7). Illus. Series: Cool Arts Careers. 2011, Cherry Lake $18.95 (978-161080136-2). 32pp. Bright photos add appeal to this career guide, which gives readers a sense of what's required to be a professional choreographer. (Rev: BL 10/1/11) [792.82]

Engineering, Technology, and Trades

3396 Jozefowicz, Chris. *Video Game Developer* (4–6). Series: Cool Careers: Cutting Edge. 2010, Gareth Stevens LB $26 (978-1-4339-1958-9). 32pp. Explains the roles of video game developers and the tools of the trade and includes a "Career Fact File" that gives the career outlook, earnings, and training needed. (Rev: SLJ 8/10) [794.8]

3397 Thomas, William David. *Environmental Engineer* (4–6). Series: Cool Careers: Cutting Edge. 2010, Gareth Stevens LB $26 (978-1-4339-1956-5). 32pp. Explains the roles that environmental engineers play in keeping our world as clean and unpolluted as possible and includes a "Career Fact File" that gives the career outlook, earnings, and training needed. (Rev: SLJ 8/10) [628]

Police and Fire Fighters

3398 Crabtree, Marc. *Meet My Neighbor, the Police Officer* (K–3). Illus. Series: Meet My Neighbor. 2012, Crabtree LB $21.27 (978-077874561-7). 24pp. This accessible book follows a real police officer around on the job as she attends a meeting, stakes out a speed trap, and makes an arrest. (Rev: BL 5/15/12) [363.2]

3399 Goldish, Meish. *Firefighters to the Rescue* (3–5). Illus. Series: Work of Heroes: First Responders in Action. 2011, Bearport LB $25.27 (978-161772284-4). 32pp. With information on training and gear, this is an overview of a fire fighter's job, with accounts of various notable incidents. (Rev: BL 10/1/11) [363.37023]

3400 Nolan, Janet. *The Firehouse Light* (K–3). Illus. by Marie Lafrance. 2010, Tricycle $15.99 (978-1-58246-298-1). 32pp. Traces the evolution of firefighting equipment through the decades as a single four-watt bulb continues to glow for more than 100 years; based on a true story. Lexile AD990L (Rev: BL 6/10; SLJ 9/1/10*) [363.3]

Science

3401 Gaffney, Timothy R. *Storm Scientist: Careers Chasing Severe Weather* (4–8). Series: Wild Science Careers. 2009, Enslow LB $31.93 (978-0-7660-3050-3). 112pp. Full of tales of hard work and engaging action, this book presents an in-depth look at the real life, skills, and even salary expectations of scientists studying severe weather. (Rev: SLJ 10/09) [551.5023]

3402 Thomas, William David. *Marine Biologist* (4–6). Series: Cool Careers: Cutting Edge. 2010, Gareth Stevens LB $26 (978-1-4339-1957-2). 32pp. Explains the roles that marine biologists play in studying marine life in the oceans, lakes, and rivers and includes a "Career Fact File" that gives the career outlook, earnings, and training needed. (Rev: SLJ 8/10) [578.7]

3403 Willett, Edward. *Disease-Hunting Scientist: Careers Hunting Deadly Diseases* (4–8). Series: Wild Science Careers. 2009, Enslow LB $31.93 (978-0-7660-3052-7). 112pp. Full of real-life tales of hard work and engaging action, this book presents an in-depth look at the everyday activities, skills, and even salary expectations of scientists studying deadly epidemics. (Rev: SLJ 10/09) [614.4023]

Transportation

3404 Marsico, Katie. *Working at the Airport* (K–2). Series: 21st Century Junior Library. 2009, Cherry Lake LB $27.07 (978-1-60279-510-5). 24pp. Employees from baggage handlers to pilots are presented in this concise portrayal of what goes on at an airport; suitable for beginning readers. (Rev: SLJ 2/1/10) [387.7]

Health and the Human Body

Alcohol, Drugs, and Smoking

3405 Bailey, Jacqui. *Taking Action Against Drugs* (5–8). Series: Taking Action. 2010, Rosen LB $26.50 (978-1-4358-5492-5). 48pp. Bailey discusses the dangers of illegal drugs and the reasons why people choose to take them, along with their social and physical effects. (Rev: LMC 1–2/10)

Disabilities, Physical and Mental

3406 Stefanski, Daniel. *How to Talk to an Autistic Kid* (2–6). Illus. 2011, Free Spirit $12.99 (978-1-57542-365-4). 48pp. Stefanski, an autistic 14-year-old, offers an insider's take on what it's like to have autism, and how others can make those with the affliction feel included and accepted. (Rev: BL 4/15/11; SLJ 6/11) [618.92]

3407 Verdick, Elizabeth, and Elizabeth Reeve. *The Survival Guide for Kids with Autism Spectrum Disorders (and Their Parents)* (4–8). Illus. by Nick Kobyluch. 2012, Free Spirit paper $16.99 (978-157542385-2). 240pp. This straightforward book provides background information on autism and famous people who have suffered from autism, and gives guidance on improving life at home and at school. (Rev: BL 4/15/12; SLJ 5/1/12; VOYA 6/12) [618.92]

Disease and Illness

3408 Anderson, Judith. *Fighting Disease* (4–7). Series: Working for Our Future. 2010, Black Rabbit LB $28.50 (978-1-59771-194-4). 32pp. This volume explains why the United Nations chose fighting disease as one of its eight Millennium Development goals and looks at the various reasons why people are deprived of good medical care and what can be done to improve the situation. (Rev: BL 6/10; LMC 10/10; SLJ 4/10) [362.196]

3409 Anonymous . *Quicksand: HIV/AIDS In Our Lives* (4–7). 2009, Candlewick $16.99 (978-076361589-5). 112pp. Part Q&A, part memoir, this book provides frank and supportive information about HIV/AIDS, dispelling myths in an age-appropriate manner. (Rev: BL 12/1/09; LMC 11–12/09; SLJ 11/09) [616.97]

3410 Beccia, Carlyn. *I Feel Better with a Frog in My Throat: History's Strangest Cures* (1–4). Illus. by author. 2010, Houghton Mifflin $17 (978-0-547-22570-8). 48pp. This guide to folk remedies offers readers the challenge of deciding which possible cure *really* works, with answers revealed at the end of the book. (Rev: BL 10/1/10; LMC 5–6/11; SLJ 11/1/10) [615.8]

3411 Chilman-Blair, Kim, and John Taddeo. *Medikidz Explain HIV* (5–8). Series: Superheroes on a Medical Mission. 2010, Rosen LB $29.25 (978-143589458-7). 40pp. Using cartoon illustrations and a graphic novel format, this volume — and the Medikidz superheroes — explain the HIV virus and its dangers. Also use *Medikidz Explain Swine Flu, Medikidz Explain Depression,* and *Medikidz Explain Sleep Apnea* (all 2010). (Rev: BL 3/15/11; SLJ 5/1/11) [614.5]

3412 Chilman-Blair, Kim, and John Taddeo. *What's Up with Ella? Medikidz Explain Diabetes* (4–6). Illus. Series: Superheroes on a Medical Mission. 2010, Rosen LB $29.95 (978-143583538-2). 40pp. A young girl is taken on a tour of the pancreas in this light, superhero-inspired take on type 1 diabetes. (Rev: BL 3/15/10) [618.92]

3413 Chilman-Blair, Kim, and John Taddeo. *What's Up with Max? Medikidz Explain Asthma* (4–7). Series: Superheroes on a Medical Mission. 2010, Rosen LB $29.25 (978-1-4358-3534-4). 40pp. Multicultural young "superheroes" explain about asthma and its treatment and show readers around the relevant parts of the body. Also use *What's Up with Pam? Medikidz Explain Childhood Obesity, What's Up with Paulina? Medikidz Explain Food Allergies,* and *What's Up with Sean? Medikidz Explain Scoliosis* (all 2010) (Rev: LMC 10/10) [616.2]

3414 Cunningham, Kevin. *Pandemics* (3–5). Illus. Series: A True Book: Disasters. 2011, Scholastic LB $28 (978-053125423-3); paper $6.95 (978-053126628-1). 48pp. With statistics and Web resources, this volume covers everything from influenza to smallpox, cholera, and plague. (Rev: BL 11/15/11) [614.4]

3415 Jurmain, Suzanne. *The Secret of the Yellow Death: A True Story of Medical Sleuthing* (5–8). 2009, Houghton Mifflin $19 (978-0-618-96581-6). 112pp. As compelling as good fiction, this well-illustrated true story chronicles the fascinating methods used by scientists to discover the cause of yellow fever. (Rev: BL 9/15/09; HB 11–12/09; LMC 1–2/10; SLJ 9/09) [614.5]

3416 Landau, Elaine. *Chickenpox* (1–3). Series: Head-to-Toe Health. 2009, Marshall Cavendish $19.95 (978-0-7614-3498-6). 32pp. The causes, symptoms, and experience of chickenpox are portrayed in this straightforward and useful guide. Also use *Food Allergies* (2009). (Rev: SLJ 1/1/10) [616.9]

3417 Markle, Sandra. *Leukemia: True Survival Stories* (5–8). Series: Powerful Medicine. 2010, Lerner LB $27.93 (978-0-8225-8700-2). 48pp. Arresting full-color photographs, cross-sections, and personal stories are combined with facts about procedures and information about the medical personnel involved. (Rev: LMC 11–12/10) [616.99]

3418 Reingold, Adam. *Smallpox: Is It Over?* (4–7). Illus. 2010, Bearport LB $25.27 (978-193608802-7). 32pp. This well-organized book presents a clear and balanced view of smallpox, from the biology of the virus itself, to symptoms, to its long and eventful history and purported "defeat" in 1980. (Rev: BL 10/1/10) [614.5]

Doctors and Medicine

3419 Donovan, Sandy. *Does an Apple a Day Keep the Doctor Away? And Other Questions About Your Health and Body* (4–6). Illus. by Colin W. Thompson. Series: Is That a Fact? 2010, Lerner LB $26.60 (978-0-8225-9084-2). 40pp. Familiar sayings and old wives' tales about health are unraveled and examined with humor and eye-catching illustrations. Also use *Does It Really Take Seven Years to Digest Swallowed Gum? And Other Questions You've Always Wanted to Ask* (2010). (Rev: LMC 5–6/10; SLJ 7/10) [610]

3420 Gorman, Jacqueline Laks. *Dentists* (K–2). Illus. Series: People in My Community. 2010, Gareth Stevens LB $22.60 (978-143393800-9). 24pp. A simple introduction to the work dentists do and what young children can expect on dental visits. (Rev: BL 3/15/11) [617.6]

3421 Guillain, Charlotte. *Visiting the Dentist* (PS–2). Series: Growing Up. 2011, Heinemann LB $22 (978-1-4329-4804-7); paper $6.49 (978-1-4329-4814-6). 24pp. This book for early readers answers such questions as "What Happens When I Go In?" and "Why Does the Dentist Wear a Mask and Gloves?" — and of course "Will Going to the Dentist Hurt?" (Rev: SLJ 6/11) [617.6]

The Human Body

General

3422 Basher, Simon, and Dan Green. *Human Body: A Book with Guts* (5–8). Illus. by Simon Basher. 2011, Kingfisher $14.99 (978-075346628-5); paper $8.99 (978-075346501-1). 128pp. An irreverent and entertaining look at the inner workings of the human body with Basher's cartoon illustrations. (Rev: BL 3/1/11) [612]

3423 Bruhn, Aron. *Inside Human Body* (4–6). Illus. by Joel Ito and Kathleen Kemly. 2010, Sterling $16.95 (978-1-4027-7091-3); paper $9.95 (978-1-4027-7779-0). 49pp. Gatefold features enhance this boldly colored overview of humans' internal workings. (Rev: LMC 1–2/11; SLJ 12/1/10*) [612]

3424 Donovan, Sandy. *Hawk and Drool: Gross Stuff in Your Mouth* (4–8). Illus. by Michael Slack. Series: Gross Body Science. 2010, Lerner LB $29.27 (978-0-8225-8966-2). 48pp. Cavities, canker sores, bacteria, and saliva are among the gross items causing smelly breath that are discussed here with close-up pictures. (Rev: LMC 1–2/10)

3425 Harris, Robie H. *Who Has What? All About Girls' Bodies and Boys' Bodies* (PS–2). Illus. by Nadine Bernard Westcott. 2011, Candlewick $15.99 (978-0-7636-2931-1). 32pp. Young Nellie and Gus are at the beach with their parents and they explore the ways in which girls' and boys' bodies are different, and the same. (Rev: BL 9/1/11*; HB 11–12/11; SLJ 10/1/11*) [612.6]

3426 Hibbert, Clare. *I'm Tired and Other Body Feelings* (PS–2). Illus. by Simona Dimitri. Series: Feelings. 2011, Amicus LB $16.95 (978-160753175-3). 24pp. A simple guide to how it feels to be tired, hungry, sick, dizzy, and so forth, with relevant illustrations and text in speech balloons. (Rev: BL 10/1/11) [152.4]

3427 Hirschmann, Kris. *Reflections of Me: Girls and Body Image* (5–8). Series: What's the Issue? 2009,

Compass Point $27.99 (978-0-7565-4132-3). 48pp. A compelling mix of direct quotes, real-life scenarios, quizzes, and short glossaries enhance this book about girls' body image problems; suitable for reluctant readers. (Rev: LMC 10/09; SLJ 10/09) [155.3]

3428 Levy, Joel. *Phobiapedia: All the Things We Fear the Most!* (3–6). Illus. 2011, Scholastic paper $8.99 (978-054534929-1). 80pp. An intriguing survey of 50-plus phobias, ranging from the well-known arachnophobia to the strange lutraphobia (fear of otters), with interesting facts about origins and etymology. (Rev: BL 12/1/11) [616.85]

3429 Macnair, Patricia. *Everything You Need to Know About the Human Body* (3–5). Illus. 2011, Kingfisher $12.99 (978-075346686-5). 160pp. This overview provides clear, well-illustrated information on the various body parts and systems. (Rev: BL 11/1/11) [612]

3430 Pinnington, Andrea, and Penny Lamprell. *My Body* (K–2). Illus. Series: Discover More. 2012, Scholastic $7.99 (978-054534514-9). 32pp. A useful and interesting introduction to the parts of the body (hair, skin, breathing, blood) and the senses. (Rev: BL 4/15/12) [612]

3431 Simon, Seymour. *The Human Body* (4–7). Illus. 2008, HarperCollins $19.99 (978-006055541-2); LB $20.89 (978-006055542-9). 64pp. Drawing on earlier books, Simon presents a detailed overview of the human body with vivid illustrations and clear captions. (Rev: BL 10/15/08; HB 9–10/08; SLJ 11/1/08) [612]

3432 Zoehfeld, Kathleen Weidner. *Human Body* (K–2). Illus. Series: Scholastic Reader. 2010, Scholastic paper $3.99 (978-054523752-9). 32pp. For beginning readers, this is a clear introduction to basic body parts (skin, senses, and so forth). Lexile 630L (Rev: BL 1/1–15/11) [612]

Circulatory System

3433 Corcoran, Mary K. *The Circulatory Story* (2–4). Illus. by Jef Czekaj. 2010, Charlesbridge $17.95 (978-1-58089-208-7); paper $7.95 (978-1-58089-209-4). 44pp. Providing a humorous, accessible survey of the human circulatory system, Corcoran narrates as an eye-catching green imp goes tubing down a girl's bloodstream, making comical observations along the way. Lexile 850L (Rev: BL 1/1/10; LMC 10/10; SLJ 4/1/10) [612.1]

3434 Markle, Sandra. *Faulty Hearts: True Survival Stories* (5–8). Series: Powerful Medicine. 2010, Lerner LB $27.93 (978-0-8225-8699-9). 48pp. Arresting full-color photographs, cross-sections, and personal stories are combined with facts about procedures and information about the medical personnel involved, (Rev: LMC 11–12/10; VOYA 10/10) [612.1]

Nervous System

3435 Stewart, Melissa. *You've Got Nerve! The Secrets of the Brain and Nerves* (2–4). Illus. by Janet Hamlin. Series: Gross and Goofy Body. 2010, Marshall Cavendish LB $20.95 (978-076144157-1). 48pp. Detailed, compelling facts about the human and animal brains and nervous systems are presented in this clearly organized book. (Rev: BL 9/1/10) [612.8]

Senses

3436 Markle, Sandra. *Lost Sight: True Survival Stories* (5–8). Series: Powerful Medicine. 2010, Lerner LB $27.93 (978-0-8225-8701-9). 48pp. Arresting full-color photographs, cross-sections, and personal stories are combined with facts about procedures and information about the medical personnel involved, (Rev: BL 10/1/10; LMC 11–12/10) [612.8]

3437 Parker, Vic. *Having a Hearing Test* (K–2). Illus. Series: Growing Up. 2011, Heinemann LB $22 (978-143294799-6). 24pp. This reassuring book gives readers a sense of what to expect from a hearing test. (Rev: BL 7/11) [617.8]

Skeletal-Muscular System

3438 Clements, Andrew. *The Handiest Things in the World* (PS–2). Illus. by Raquel Jaramillo. 2010, Atheneum $16.99 (978-1-4169-6166-6). 48pp. A simple celebration of all the things our hands can do and the tools we use with them. (Rev: BL 3/1/10; LMC 10/10; SLJ 5/1/10) [612]

3439 Jenkins, Steve. *Bones: Skeletons and How They Work* (2–5). Illus. by author. 2010, Scholastic $16.99 (978-0-545-04651-0). 48pp. Human and animal skeletons are explored in often humorous detail using concise text and cut-paper collages, with many comparisons and several gatefolds. (Rev: BL 5/15/10; HB 7–8/10; LMC 10/10; SLJ 7/10) [612]

3440 Stewart, Melissa. *Give Me a Hand: The Secrets of Hands, Feet, Arms, and Legs* (2–4). Illus. by Janet Hamlin. Series: Gross and Goofy Body. 2010, Marshall Cavendish LB $20.95 (978-076144158-8). 48pp. Covering arms, legs, and feet in addition to hands, this is an interesting introduction to the function of human and animal body appendages. (Rev: BL 9/1/10) [591.4]

Skin and Hair

3441 Stewart, Melissa. *Here We Grow: The Secrets of Hair and Nails* (2–4). Illus. by Janet Hamlin. Series: Gross and Goofy Body. 2010, Marshall Cavendish LB $20.95 (978-076144172-4). 48pp. Covering facial and body hair, nail, melanin, and so forth, this is an interesting introduction to the function of these organs in humans and animals. Also use *The Skin You're In: The Secrets of Skin* (2010). (Rev: BL 9/1/10) [612.7]

3442 Sutherland, Adam. *Body Decoration* (5–8). Illus. Series: On the Radar: Street Style. 2012, Lerner LB $26.60 (978-076137769-6). 32pp. With a history of body decoration since ancient times, this is an interesting survey of the various forms that are popular today. (Rev: BLO 3/15/12; SLJ 4/1/12) [391.6]

Hygiene, Physical Fitness, and Nutrition

3443 Barraclough, Sue. *Wash and Clean* (2–4). Illus. 2012, Black Rabbit LB $24.25 (978-159771310-8). 24pp. Healthy human habits are compared with those of animals in this informative volume with chapter titles such as "Biting and Chewing" and "Hands, Nails, Claws." (Rev: BL 4/1/12) [613]

3444 Edwards, Hazel, and Goldie Alexander. *Talking About Your Weight* (4–7). Illus. Series: Healthy Living. 2010, Gareth Stevens LB $26 (978-143393655-5). 32pp. Loaded topics such as eating disorders and obesity are presented in a clear, nonjudgmental fashion with emphasis on making better choices. (Rev: BL 4/1/10) [613]

3445 Mar, Jonathan, and Grace Norwich. *The Body Book for Boys* (5–8). Illus. by Ming Sung Ku. 2010, Scholastic paper $8.99 (978-054523751-2). 128pp. This straightforward book presents information on subjects of concern to middle-school boys, from hygiene to the opposite sex. (Rev: BL 12/1/10) [613]

3446 Simons, Rae. *I Eat When I'm Sad: Food and Feelings* (3–5). Illus. Series: Kids and Obesity. 2010, Mason Crest $19.95 (978-142221714-6); paper $7.95 (978-142221902-7). 48pp. This well-designed book takes a nonjudgmental and constructive look at the factors that motivate children to overeat. (Rev: BL 10/1/10; LMC 3–4/11) [616.85]

3447 Sullivan, Jaclyn. *What's in Your Chicken Nugget?* (3–5). Illus. Series: What's in Your Fast Food? 2012, Rosen LB $21.25 (978-144886208-5); paper $8.25 (978-144886375-4). 24pp. Books in this series explore the true contents of foods popular with children, explaining the science behind preservatives, fillers, and fats. ℮ (Rev: BL 4/1/12; LMC 10/12) [641.6]

3448 Thornhill, Jan. *Who Wants Pizza? The Kids' Guide to the History, Science and Culture of Food* (5–8). 2010, Maple Tree paper $10.95 (978-1-897349-97-7). 64pp. Taking pizza as an example, this appealingly busy and well-illustrated book discusses the nutrients that food provides to the body and looks at various scientific (the chemistry of fertilizers, for example) and cultural as-

pects (a Bushman eating caterpillars) of food. (Rev: BL 12/1/10; LMC 11–12/10) [641.3]

3449 Tuminelly, Nancy. *Super Simple Bend and Stretch* (1–3). Illus. Series: Super Simple Exercise. 2011, ABDO LB $27.07 (978-161714959-7). 32pp. Introduces basic exercises as well as the benefits of healthy eating, and recommends tracking weekly progress. (Rev: BL 12/1/11) [613.7]

3450 Vestergaard, Hope. *Potty Animals: What to Know When You've Gotta Go!* (PS). Illus. by Valeria Petrone. 2010, Sterling $14.95 (978-1-4027-5996-3). 32pp. A colorful cast of animals illustrate different aspects of hygiene, cleanliness, privacy, and communication in this appealing guide to the potty. (Rev: BL 3/15/10; SLJ 5/1/10) [649.62]

3451 Watson, Stephanie. *Mystery Meat: Hot Dogs, Sausages, and Lunch Meats: The Incredibly Disgusting Story* (4–7). Illus. Series: Disgusting Food. 2011, Rosen LB $26.50 (978-1-4488-1268-4). 48pp. Discusses the ingredients of "mystery meats" and the impact they can have on our bodies and minds, with some eye-catchingly off-putting photographs. (Rev: BL 4/1/11; SLJ 6/11) [664]

Safety and Accidents

3452 Hurley, Michael. *Surviving the Wilderness* (4–7). Series: Extreme Survival. 2011, Heinemann LB $33.50 (978-1-4109-3972-2). 56pp. Hurley explores the dangers posed in the mountains, forest, outback, desert, jungle, and wilderness as well as those we face at sea, and offers survival tips and advice. (Rev: SLJ 8/11) [613.6]

3453 Kyi, Tanya Lloyd. *Fifty Poisonous Questions: A Book with Bite* (4–7). Illus. by Ross Kinnaird. 2011, Annick $21.95 (978-1-55451-281-2); paper $12.95 (978-1-55451-280-5). 110pp. This luridly illustrated volume offers considerable information on poisons of all kinds, with humorous illustrations, interesting sidebars, and "Foul Facts." (Rev: LMC 11–12/11; SLJ 9/1/11) [615.9]

3454 Long, Denise. *Survivor Kid: A Practical Guide to Wilderness Survival* (5–8). Illus. 2011, Chicago Review paper $12.95 (978-156976708-5). 144pp. Personal anecdotes bolster the sensible advice presented here about staying safe in the woods. ℮ (Rev: BL 6/1/11) [613.6]

3455 Miller, Edward. *Fireboy to the Rescue! A Fire Safety Book* (K–2). Illus. by author. 2010, Holiday House $16.95 (978-0-8234-2222-7). 32pp. Flashy, cut-paper-style artwork enhances this superhero-inspired take on fire safety, which includes plenty of practical advice. Lexile AD640L (Rev: BL 1/1/10; SLJ 2/1/10) [628.9]

Sex Education and Reproduction

Babies

3456 Anderson, Judith. *Healthy Mothers* (4–7). Series: Working for Our Future. 2010, Black Rabbit LB $28.50 (978-1-59771-197-5). 32pp. This volume explains why the United Nations chose promoting healthy mothers as one of its eight Millennium Development goals. (Rev: BL 6/10; LMC 10/10; SLJ 4/10) [306.874.]

Sex Education and Puberty

3457 Katz, Anne. *Girl in the Know: Your Inside-and-Out Guide to Growing Up* (4–8). Illus. by Monika Melny-chuk. 2010, Kids Can $18.95 (978-1-55453-303-9). 112pp. A straightforward, conversational, and wide-ranging introduction to the physical and emotional changes that accompany puberty. (Rev: BL 4/1/10; LMC 8–9/10; SLJ 5/10) [613]

3458 Larimore, Walt. *The Ultimate Guys' Body Book: Not-So-Stupid Questions About Your Body* (5–8). Illus. by Guy Francis. 2012, Zondervan paper $7.99 (978-031072323-3). 192pp. Answering such questions as "I've got BO — what's a guy to do?" and "My acne is scary! What's wrong with my face?," this book offers a Christian perspective on puberty. (Rev: BL 4/15/12; SLJ 5/1/12; VOYA 6/12) [613]

Physical and Applied Sciences

General Science

Miscellaneous

3459 Brake, Mark. *Really, Really Big Questions About Space and Time* (4–7). Illus. by Nishant Choksi. 2010, Kingfisher $16.99 (978-075346502-8). 64pp. Presents lighthearted and thoughtful answers to questions children ask about space and time, with a section on "How to Think Like a Scientist and Apply the Scientific Method." (Rev: BL 11/1/10; LMC 3–4/11) [523.1]

3460 Bryson, Bill. *A Really Short History of Nearly Everything* (5–8). Illus. 2009, Delacorte $19.99 (978-0-385-73810-1). 176pp. A junior edition of his popular book for adults, this volume tackles many scientific topics with humor and cheer. e Lexile 1190L (Rev: BL 11/15/09; SLJ 2/10) [900]

3461 Parker, Steve. *What About . . . Science and Technology?* (5–8). Illus. Series: Answering Q&A Questions. 2009, Mason Crest $19.95 (978-1-4222-1565-4). 40pp. Using a question-and-answer format, two-page spreads look at subjects ranging from matter and magnetism to sound and transportation. (Rev: SLJ 4/10) [500]

3462 Richardson, Gillian. *Kaboom! Explosions of All Kinds* (4–7). 2009, Annick $22.95 (978-1-55451-204-1); paper $12.95 (978-1-55451-203-4). 83pp. Loud noises of all kinds are covered here — natural explosions (in the earth and outer space, in plants and animals) and manmade explosions (dynamite, fireworks, internal combustion engine, and so forth). (Rev: BL 12/1/09; SLJ 12/09) [541]

3463 Weakland, Mark. *Bubbles Float, Bubbles Pop* (1–3). Illus. Series: Science Starts. 2011, Capstone LB $25.99 (978-142965250-6); paper $7.95 (978-142966141-6). 32pp. A succinct guide to the nature of bubbles and how they are formed. (Rev: BL 4/1/11; LMC 10/11) [530.4]

Experiments and Projects

3464 Bardhan-Quallen, Sudipta. *Kitchen Science Experiments: How Does Your Mold Garden Grow?* (4–7). Illus. by Edward Miller. Series: Mad Science. 2010, Sterling $12.95 (978-140272413-8). 64pp. Eighteen activities introduce basics of biology and chemistry through recipes that can be used in everyday kitchens. (Rev: BL 12/1/10; LMC 5–6/11; SLJ 2/1/11) [579]

3465 Bardhan-Quallen, Sudipta. *Nature Science Experiments: What's Hopping in a Dust Bunny?* (4–6). Illus. by Edward Miller. 2010, Sterling LB $12.95 (978-1-4027-2412-1). 64pp. Diverse experiments, some of which require specialized equipment, mostly involve everyday objects and are presented in clear text with scientific explanations. (Rev: SLJ 9/1/10) [570.78]

3466 Benbow, Ann, and Colin Mably. *Awesome Animal Science Projects* (2–4). Illus. by Tom LaBaff. Series: Real Life Science Experiments. 2009, Enslow LB $23.93 (978-0-7660-3148-7). 48pp. Focuses on easy experiments that illustrate characteristics of backyard animals and animal behavior, answering questions such as "What Seeds Do Different Birds Like?" and "Are Earthworms Attracted to Light?" (Rev: BL 8/09; SLJ 1/1/10) [590.78]

3467 Brown, Jordan D. *Crazy Concoctions: A Mad Scientist's Guide to Messy Mixtures* (4–7). Illus. by Anthony Owsley. 2012, Imagine $14.95 (978-193614051-0). 80pp. For budding scientists with a love of glop and viscosity, this volume proposes a number of experiments involving such ingredients as cornstarch and raisins and with names such as "bogus barf." (Rev: BL 2/15/12; SLJ 4/12) [540.76]

3468 Burns, Loree Griffin. *Citizen Scientists: Be a Part of Scientific Discovery from Your Own Backyard* (3–6).

Illus. by Ellen Harasimowicz. 2012, Henry Holt $19.99 (978-080509062-8); paper $12.99 (978-080509517-3). 80pp. Shows young readers various scientific studies they can do around the year in the backyard involving butterflies, birds, frogs, and ladybugs; with excellent photographs. (Rev: BL 4/1/12; HB 5–6/12; SLJ 7/12) [590.72]

3469 Calhoun, Yael. *Plant and Animal Science Fair Projects, Revised and Expanded Using the Scientific Method* (5–8). Series: Science Projects Using the Scientific Method. 2010, Enslow LB $34.60 (978-0-7660-3421-1). 160pp. With a focus on the basics of scientific investigation, this well-organized and attractive volume gives an overview of the topic and provides experiments that support various hypotheses. (Rev: LMC 8–9/10; SLJ 9/1/10) [570.78]

3470 Connolly, Sean. *The Book of Potentially Catastrophic Science: 50 Experiments for Daring Young Scientists* (5–8). Illus. 2010, Workman $13.95 (978-0-7611-5687-1). 256pp. Each chapter of this compelling book presents a scientific milestone, starting with Stone Age tools and ending with the Hadron Collider, and provides the historical context and related activities. (Rev: BL 6/10; HB 3–4/11; SLJ 9/1/10) [507.8]

3471 Gardner, Robert. *Genetics and Evolution Science Fair Projects, Revised and Expanded Using the Scientific Method* (5–8). Series: Biology Science Projects Using the Scientific Method. 2010, Enslow LB $34.60 (978-0-7660-3422-8). 160pp. With a focus on the basics of scientific investigation, this well-organized and attractive volume gives an overview of the topic and provides experiments that support various hypotheses. (Rev: LMC 8–9/10; SLJ 9/1/10) [576.078]

3472 Margles, Samantha. *Mythbusters Science Fair Book* (4–8). Illus. 2011, Scholastic paper $9.99 (978-054523745-1). 128pp. A collection of science projects that answer common questions (can we believe the five-second rule?) using proper scientific methods. (Rev: BL 4/15/11) [507.8]

3473 Spangler, Steve. *Naked Eggs and Flying Potatoes: Unforgettable Experiments That Make Science Fun* (3–6). Illus. 2010, Greenleaf paper $14.95 (978-160832060-8). 160pp. With experiments organized under headings such as "The Power of Air" and "Gooey Wonders," this volume presents child-friendly projects that may require adult help. (Rev: BL 12/1/10; SLJ 12/1/10) [507.8]

Astronomy

General

3474 Carson, Mary Kay. *Far-Out Guide to Asteroids and Comets* (4–6). Illus. Series: Far-Out Guide to the Solar System. 2010, Enslow LB $23.93 (978-0-7660-3188-3); paper $7.95 (978-1-59845-191-7). 48pp. A lively and well-illustrated introduction to asteroids and comets and their threats to Earth. (Rev: SLJ 12/1/10) [523.44]

3475 DeCristofano, Carolyn Cinami. *A Black Hole Is Not a Hole* (4–6). Illus. by Michael Carroll. 2012, Charlesbridge $9.99 (978-157091783-7). 80pp. With humor, lively text, and dramatic illustrations, this book introduces important information about black holes in an appealing and understandable fashion. ⌒ (Rev: BL 2/1/12*; LMC 11–12/12; SLJ 4/12*) [523.8]

3476 Fox, Karen C. *Older Than the Stars* (2–6). Illus. by Nancy Davis. 2010, Charlesbridge $15.95 (978-1-57091-787-5). Unpaged. The formation of the universe is broken down into small, accessible bits of information in this lively book full of eye-catching illustrations. (Rev: LMC 11–12/10; SLJ 2/1/10) [523.1]

3477 Hicks, Terry Allan. *Earth and the Moon* (4–8). Series: Space! 2010, Marshall Cavendish LB $32.79 (978-0-7614-4254-7). 64pp. After an overview of Earth and its moon, Hicks looks at our growing understanding over time and the missions to explore our moon. Also use *Saturn* (2010). ℮ (Rev: LMC 3–4/10; SLJ 2/10) [525]

3478 Scott, Elaine. *Space, Stars, and the Beginning of Time: What the Hubble Telescope Saw* (5–8). Illus. 2011, Clarion $17.99 (978-0-547-24189-0). 66pp. This inspiring tribute to the Hubble Space Telescope features a discussion of the history of astronomy, and how the Hubble contributed to our understanding of the universe. (Rev: HB 3–4/11; SLJ 3/1/11) [522]

3479 Sherman, Josepha. *Asteroids, Meteors, and Comets* (5–7). Series: Space! 2009, Marshall Cavendish LB $22.95 (978-0-7614-4252-3). 64pp. Good for research, this volume presents facts clearly and concisely with many photos and other illustrations. (Rev: LMC 3–4/10; SLJ 2/10) [523]

3480 Weakland, Mark. *The Lonely Existence of Asteroids and Comets* (3–5). Illus. by Carlos Aon. Series: Adventures in Science. 2012, Capstone $29.99 (978-142967546-8); paper $7.95 (978-142967987-9). 32pp. Weakland uses a graphic-novel format to explore the small bodies that zoom around in space. (Rev: BL 3/15/12; LMC 11–12/12) [523.44]

3481 Williams, Brian. *What About . . . the Universe?* (5–8). Illus. Series: Answering Q&A Questions. 2009, Mason Crest $19.95 (978-1-4222-1566-1). 40pp. Using a question-and-answer format, two-page spreads look at subjects ranging from the Big Bang to space missions and the solar system. (Rev: SLJ 4/10) [520]

Earth

3482 Carson, Mary Kay. *Far-Out Guide to Earth* (4–6). Illus. Series: Far-Out Guide to the Solar System. 2010, Enslow LB $23.93 (978-0-7660-3182-1); paper $7.95 (978-1-59845-183-2). 48pp. A lively and well-illustrated introduction to our planet with information on the technology used to study it. (Rev: SLJ 12/1/10) [525]

3483 Gilpin, Dan. *Planet Earth* (3–5). Illus. by Peter Bull. Series: Explorers. 2011, Kingfisher $10.99 (978-075346591-2). 32pp. An inviting mix of text, sidebars, captions, fact lists, and more add read-appeal to this well-illustrated book about Earth, its position in space, and its geology, environment, and inhabitants. (Rev: BL 2/15/12) [550]

3484 Goldsmith, Mike. *Earth: The Life of Our Planet* (4–7). Illus. by Mark A. Garlick. 2011, Kingfisher $17.99 (978-075346625-4). 48pp. This broad overview of the big events that have shaped Earth's climate and topography begins with the planet's formation and ends with space exploration and possibilities for the future. (Rev: BLO 10/15/11; LMC 5–6/12) [550]

3485 Wells, Robert E. *What's So Special About Planet Earth?* (1–3). Illus. by author. 2009, Whitman $16.99 (978-0-8075-8815-4). 32pp. In a lighthearted fashion, Wells explores the benefits of living on Earth and compares conditions here with those on the other planets. (Rev: BL 9/15/09; LMC 11–12/09; SLJ 9/1/09) [525]

Moon

3486 Ross, Stewart. *Moon: Science, History, and Mystery* (4–6). 2009, Scholastic LB $18.99 (978-0-545-12732-5). 128pp. An oversize, information-packed book celebrating the moon's history, mythology, influence on culture generally, and human exploration. (Rev: LMC 11–12/09; SLJ 12/09) [523.3]

Planets

3487 Allyn, Daisy. *Jupiter: The Largest Planet* (K–2). Illus. Series: Our Solar System. 2010, Gareth Stevens LB $22.60 (978-1-4339-3821-4); paper $8.15 (978-1-4339-3822-1). 24pp. Bright images and clear information about Jupiter are presented in a small, square format. Lexile 420 (Rev: BL 1/1–15/11; SLJ 11/1/10) [523.45]

3488 Arlon, Penelope, and Tory Gordon Harris. *Planets* (3–5). Illus. Series: Discover More. 2012, Scholastic paper $12.99 (978-054533028-2). 80pp. A visually appealing overview of the planets, with information on related aspects such as asteroids and space travel plus the ability to download a digital book that offers interactivity and links to other features. (Rev: BL 3/1/12; SLJ 4/1/12) [523.4]

3489 Bjorklund, Ruth. *Venus* (4–8). Series: Space! 2010, Marshall Cavendish LB $32.79 (978-0-7614-4251-6). 64pp. In chapters covering the discovery of Venus, its features, missions to the planet, and handy quick facts, this accessible title features useful, well-presented material. ℮ (Rev: LMC 3–4/10; SLJ 2/10) [523.42]

3490 Capaccio, George. *Jupiter* (4–8). Series: Space! 2010, Marshall Cavendish LB $32.79 (978-0-7614-4244-8). 64pp. Capaccio looks at the physical features of Jupiter, the history of its discovery and what we have since learned about it, and speculates about future mis-

sions. Also use *The Sun* and *Neptune* (both 2010). ℮ (Rev: LMC 3–4/10; SLJ 2/10) [523.45]

3491 Carson, Mary Kay. *Far-Out Guide to Jupiter* (4–6). Illus. 2010, Enslow LB $23.93 (978-0-7660-3184-5); paper $7.95 (978-1-59845-186-3). 48pp. A lively and well-illustrated introduction to the planet and its moons. Also use *Far-Out Guide to the Icy Dwarf Planets* (2010). (Rev: SLJ 12/1/10) [523.45]

3492 Colligan, L. H. *Mercury* (4–8). Series: Space! 2010, Marshall Cavendish LB $32.79 (978-0-7614-4239-4). 64pp. Colligan looks at how planets were formed, the history of Mercury's discovery and what we have since learned about it, and speculates about its future importance. ℮ (Rev: LMC 3–4/10; SLJ 2/10) [523.41]

3493 James, Lincoln. *Mercury: The Iron Planet* (K–2). Illus. Series: Our Solar System. 2010, Gareth Stevens LB $22.6 (978-143393827-6). 24pp. Bright images and clear information about Mercury are presented in a small, square format. Lexile 420 (Rev: BL 1/1–15/11; SLJ 11/1/10) [523.41]

3494 Lew, Kristi. *The Dwarf Planet Pluto* (4–8). Series: Space! 2010, Marshall Cavendish LB $32.79 (978-0-7614-4243-1). 64pp. The author discusses Pluto's composition, its new status as a dwarf planet, missions to Pluto, and pertinent facts. ℮ (Rev: LMC 3–4/10; SLJ 2/10) [523.482]

3495 McGranaghan, John. *Meet the Planets* (2–4). Illus. by Laurie Allen Klein. 2011, Sylvan Dell $16.95 (978-1-60718-123-1); paper $8.95 (978-1-60718-133-0). Unpaged. A lighthearted introduction to the planets, with cartoonish caricatures and plenty of facts and information on science and astronomy. ℮ (Rev: LMC 11–12/11; SLJ 7/11) [523.4]

3496 Miller, Ron. *Seven Wonders of the Gas Giants and Their Moons* (5–8). Illus. Series: Seven Wonders. 2011, 21st Century LB $33.26 (978-0-7613-5449-9). 80pp. Saturn's rings, the great red spot of Jupiter, and the auroras of Saturn are among the seven wonders explored in this interesting volume. Also use *Seven Wonders of the Rocky Planets and Their Moons* (2011). ℮ (Rev: BL 3/1/11; SLJ 2/1/11) [523.4]

3497 Roza, Greg. *Uranus: The Ice Planet* (K–2). Illus. Series: Our Solar System. 2010, Gareth Stevens LB $22.60 (978-143393842-9). 24pp. Bright images and clear information about Uranus are presented in a small, square format. Lexile 420 (Rev: BL 1/1–15/11; SLJ 11/1/10) [523.47]

3498 Sherman, Josepha. *Neptune* (5–7). Series: Space! 2009, Marshall Cavendish LB $22.95 (978-0-7614-4246-2). 64pp. Good for research, this volume presents facts clearly and concisely with many photos and other illustrations. (Rev: SLJ 2/10) [523.4]

3499 Sherman, Josepha. *Uranus* (4–8). Series: Space! 2010, Marshall Cavendish LB $32.79 (978-0-7614-

4248-6). 64pp. The author discusses the discovery of this planet, mysteries surrounding it, Voyager 2's expedition, and other key facts in this easily understood volume. Also use *Mars* (2010). ℮ (Rev: LMC 3–4/10; SLJ 2/10) [523.47]

Solar System

3500 Farndon, John. *Exploring the Solar System* (4–9). Series: Why Science Matters. 2009, Heinemann-Raintree $32.86 (978-1-4329-2484-3). 56pp. This appealing guide to the solar system emphasizes the importance of scientific understanding to everyday life. (Rev: LMC 11–12/09) [523.4]

3501 Goldsmith, Mike. *Solar System* (1–3). Illus. Series: Discover Science. 2010, Kingfisher $9.99 (978-075346447-2). 56pp. This lively solar system overview contains plenty of glossy photos, intriguing facts, activities, and comprehensive back matter. (Rev: BL 10/1/10; LMC 11–12/10) [523.2]

3502 Tourville, Amanda Doering. *Exploring the Solar System* (4–7). Illus. Series: Let's Explore Science. 2010, Rourke LB $32.79 (978-161590323-8). 48pp. With information on the sun and moon, planets, comets, and asteroids, this is an introduction to the solar system and how scientists study it. (Rev: BL 9/1/10) [523.2]

3503 Trammel, Howard K. *The Solar System* (3–5). Illus. Series: True Book: Space. 2010, Children's Press LB $26 (978-053116898-1). 48pp. A beautifully illustrated introduction to the solar system with fascinating sidebars. (Rev: BL 11/1/09*; LMC 1–2/10) [523.2]

Stars

3504 Abramson, Andra Serlin, and Mordecai-Mark Mac Low. *Inside Stars* (5–8). Illus. 2011, Sterling paper $9.95 (978-140278162-9). 48pp. A dramatic presentation of information about the Big Bang, the formation and death of stars, the sun, and so forth, with many photographs and gatefolds. (Rev: BL 11/1/11) [523.8]

3505 Aguilar, David A. *Super Stars: The Biggest, Hottest, Brightest, Most Explosive Stars in the Milky Way* (4–8). 2010, National Geographic LB $25.90 (978-1-4263-0602-0). 48pp. An exciting, engaging look at different types of stars (for example, G Stars, planetary nebulae, and brown dwarfs), with beautiful photographs and art. Lexile NC1160L (Rev: BL 4/15/10; LMC 8–9/10; SLJ 4/10) [523.8]

3506 Croswell, Ken. *The Lives of Stars* (5–8). Illus. 2009, Boyds Mills $19.95 (978-159078582-9). 75pp. Using easy-to-understand language and striking im-

ages, Croswell describes the different kinds of stars and how they are formed, live, and eventually die. (Rev: BLO 11/1/09; LMC 11–12/09; SLJ 11/09) [523.8]

3507 Forest, Christopher. *The Kids' Guide to the Constellations* (3–5). Illus. Series: Kids' Guides. 2011, Capstone LB $26.65 (978-142966007-5). 32pp. With "Fun Facts" and "Gazing Guides," this is an accessible introduction focusing on 11 constellations and explaining the myths associated with them. (Rev: BL 2/15/12) [523.8]

3508 Kim, F. S. *Constellations* (3–5). Illus. Series: True Book: Space. 2010, Children's Press LB $26 (978-053116895-0); paper $6.95 (978-053122802-9). 48pp. Science, history, and mythology are all covered in this well-illustrated and clearly explained introduction to the constellations, who discovered them, and their importance today. (Rev: BL 11/1/09*; LMC 1–2/10) [523.8]

3509 Miller, Ron. *Seven Wonders Beyond the Solar System* (5–8). Series: Seven Wonders. 2011, 21st Century LB $33.26 (978-0-7613-5454-3). 80pp. Miller discusses how stars and galaxies are formed and looks at significant nebulas and superclusters as well as the search for an Earthlike planet; readers are challenged to choose an eighth wonder. ℮ (Rev: BL 3/1/11; SLJ 2/1/11) [523.8]

3510 Than, Ker. *Stars* (3–5). Illus. Series: True Book: Space. 2010, Children's Press LB $26 (978-053116899-8); paper $6.95 (978-053122806-7). 48pp. A beautifully illustrated introduction to the life of stars, what happens when they die, and how and why we study them. (Rev: BL 11/1/09*; LMC 1–2/10) [523.8]

Sun and the Seasons

3511 Esbaum, Jill. *Everything Spring* (PS–K). Series: Picture the Seasons. 2010, National Geographic paper $5.95 (978-1-4263-0607-5). 16pp. A variety of young animals experience the joys of spring in this simple book full of photographs. (Rev: LMC 8–9/10; SLJ 5/1/10) [508.2]

3512 Hicks, Terry Allan. *Why Do Leaves Change Color?* (2–4). Series: Tell Me Why, Tell Me How. 2010, Marshall Cavendish LB $20.95 (978-0-7614-4827-3). 32pp. With chapters such as "A Sign of the Times" and "The Colors of Life," this volume introduces essential concepts in easy-to-read text and lots of helpful illustrations. (Rev: BL 3/1/11; SLJ 2/1/11) [575.5]

3513 James, Lincoln. *The Sun: Star of the Solar System* (K–2). Illus. Series: Our Solar System. 2010, Gareth Stevens LB $22.60 (978-143393848-1). 24pp. Bright images and clear information about the sun are presented in a small, square format. Lexile 420 (Rev: BL 1/1–15/11; SLJ 11/1/10) [523.7]

3514 Pfeffer, Wendy. *The Longest Day: Celebrating the Summer Solstice* (1–3). Illus. by Linda Bleck. 2010, Dutton $17.99 (978-0-525-42237-2). 40pp. For young readers, this is an introduction to the summer solstice, how it has been celebrated through the centuries, and the differences in time zones; with activities. (Rev: BL 4/15/10; SLJ 6/1/10) [394.263]

3515 Rau, Dana Meachen. *Seasons* (PS–2). Series: Bookworms. Natures Cycles. 2009, Marshall Cavendish $15.95 (978-0-7614-4098-7). 24pp. The concept of how the Earth's tilt results in different seasons in different parts of the world is captured in this simple book suitable for beginning readers. (Rev: LMC 1–2/10; SLJ 4/1/10) [508.2]

3516 Wells, Robert E. *Why Do Elephants Need the Sun?* (2–4). Illus. by author. 2010, Whitman $16.99 (978-0-8075-9081-2). 32pp. Playful illustrations enhance this exploration of the sun's importance to everything on Earth, covering photosynthesis, gravity, and nuclear fusion as well as the sun's impact on weather and water. (Rev: BL 9/15/10*; LMC 11–12/10; SLJ 10/1/10) [599.67]

Biological Sciences

General

3517 Jackson, Cari. *Alien Invasion: Invasive Species Become Major Menaces* (4–6). Illus. Series: Current Science. 2009, Gareth Stevens LB $31 (978-1-4339-2057-8). 48pp. Invasive species from around the world — plants and animals — are profiled in this engaging title, which focuses on humankind's role in spreading or maintaining the problem. (Rev: SLJ 4/10) [577]

3518 Rau, Dana Meachen. *Food Chains* (PS–2). Illus. Series: Bookworms. Natures Cycles. 2009, Marshall Cavendish $15.95 (978-0-7614-4095-6). 24pp. The concept of how energy is transferred from food to animals to crops and back again is captured in this simple book suitable for beginning readers. (Rev: LMC 1–2/10; SLJ 4/1/10) [577]

3519 Schwartz, David M., and Yael Schy. *What in the Wild? Mysteries of Nature Concealed . . . and Revealed* (2–4). Photos by Dwight Kuhn. Series: In the Wild. 2010, Tricycle $16.99 (978-1-58246-310-0). 44pp. Readers are challenged to guess the identity of natural objects presented in color photographs accompanied by brief verses; the answers are hidden behind flaps. (Rev: BL 9/15/10; SLJ 9/1/10) [508]

Animal Life

General

3520 Burnie, David. *How Animals Work: Why and How Animals Do the Things They Do* (5–8). Illus. 2010, DK $24.99 (978-0-7566-5897-7). 192pp. This highly visual, oversize volume covers everything from animal anatomy, locomotion, diet, and habitat to evolution and communication. (Rev: BL 9/1/10; SLJ 12/1/10) [571.1]

3521 de la Bedoyere, Camilla. *Wild Animals* (3–6). Illus. Series: Ripley's Believe It or Not! Twists. 2010, Mason Crest LB $19.95 (978-142221835-8). 48pp. Characteristics of wild animals are introduced through a lively blend of conversational text, snappy sidebars, and innovative design elements, with a focus on the unusual. Lexile IG1010L (Rev: BL 4/15/11) [590]

3522 Fielding, Beth. *Animal Tails* (2–4). Illus. 2011, Charlesbridge $14.95 (978-0-9797455-8-4). 36pp. Fielding explores the wide variety of kinds of animal tails and their different functions — balancing, warning, swimming, wagging, and so forth. Lexile NC1060L (Rev: BLO 8/11; SLJ 10/1/11) [573.9]

3523 Gleason, Carrie. *Animal Rights Activist* (5–8). Series: Get Involved! 2009, Crabtree LB $26.60 (978-0-7787-4693-5); paper $8.95 (978-0-7787-4705-5). 32pp. Gleason explains animal rights and the nature of activism before discussing vegetarianism, animal testing, factory farming, and so forth, and giving tips on what young people can do to protect animals. (Rev: SLJ 2/10) [179]

3524 Grayson, Robert. *Military* (4–7). Series: Working Animals. 2010, Marshall Cavendish LB $19.95 (978-1-60870-164-3). 64pp. Describes the varied roles that animals — ranging from rats and pigeons to dogs, dolphins, and horses — have played in military operations. (Rev: SLJ 12/1/10) [355.424]

3525 Grubman, Steve, and Jill Davis. *Orangutans Are Ticklish: Fun Facts from an Animal Photographer* (2–4). Illus. by Steve Grubman. 2010, Random House $16.99 (978-0-375-85886-4); LB $19.99 (978-0-375-95886-1). 40pp. Large, clearly focused photographs accompany fascinating facts about wild animals. (Rev: BL 8/10; SLJ 8/1/10) [590.22]

3526 Haven, Kendall. *Animal Mummies* (4–8). 2010, Scholastic $19.99 (978-0-545-03460-9). 112pp. A fascinating overview of the practice of mummifying animals, with large, eye-catching photographs. (Rev: LMC 10/10)

3527 Hile, Lori. *Animal Survival* (4–7). Series: Extreme Survival. 2011, Heinemann LB $33.50 (978-1-4109-3973-9). 56pp. Hile tells stories of animals that have beaten the odds and survived disasters. (Rev: SLJ 8/11)

3528 Ipcizade, Catherine. *Big Predators* (K–2). Series: Big. 2009, Capstone LB $21.32 (978-1-4296-3316-1). 24pp. Simple text and eye-catching, close-up photographs describe predators in action — big, bigger, and biggest — in this wide-format photoessay. (Rev: LMC 3–4/10; SLJ 2/1/10) [591.5]

3529 Laidlaw, Rob. *On Parade: The Hidden World of Animals in Entertainment* (3–6). 2010, Fitzhenry & Whiteside $19.95 (978-1-55455-143-9). 53pp. An interesting, and sad, look at how animals are abused in circuses, on movies and TV programs, in zoos, and in sporting events, with suggestions for animal sanctuaries and other improvements. (Rev: BL 2/1/11; SLJ 3/1/11; VOYA 2/11) [636.088]

3530 Marrin, Albert. *Little Monsters: The Creatures That Live on Us and in Us* (4–7). Illus. 2011, Dutton $19.99 (978-052542262-4). 160pp. Not for the faint of heart, this book discusses — and shows in graphic detail — parasites that live on or in the human body (leeches, tapeworms, and so forth). (Rev:) [578.6]

3531 Martin, Claudia. *Farming* (4–7). Series: Working Animals. 2010, Marshall Cavendish LB $19.95 (978-1-60870-162-9). 64pp. Animals' varied roles in agriculture are described in this attractive, informative book. Also use *Helpers* (2010), about animals that help the blind and deaf. (Rev: SLJ 12/1/10) [636]

3532 Mezzanotte, Jim. *Police* (4–7). Series: Working Animals. 2010, Marshall Cavendish LB $19.95 (978-1-60870-166-7). 64pp. Animals' varied roles in police operations — search-and-rescue, tracking, bomb sniffing, and so forth — are described in this attractive, informative book. (Rev: SLJ 12/1/10) [363.2]

3533 Pittau, Francesco, and Bernadette Gervais. *Out of Sight* (K–2). Illus. by authors. 2010, Chronicle $19.99 (978-0-8118-7712-1). 16pp. This large, lift-the-flap and pop-up book features a wide range of hidden animals. (Rev: SLJ 2/1/11*) [590]

3534 Ruurs, Margriet. *Amazing Animals: The Remarkable Things That Creatures Do* (2–4). Illus. by W. Allan Hancock. 2011, Tundra $17.95 (978-0-88776-973-3). 32pp. Suited for browsing more than research, this highly illustrated volume introduces 44 animals from around the world and their interesting characteristics and behaviors. (Rev: BL 5/1/11; SLJ 6/11) [591.5]

3535 Silverman, Buffy. *Can an Old Dog Learn New Tricks? And Other Questions About Animals* (4–6). Illus. by Colin W. Thompson. Series: Is That a Fact? 2010, Lerner LB $26.60 (978-0-8225-9083-5). 40pp.

Familiar sayings and old wives' tales about animals are unraveled and examined with humor and eye-catching illustrations. (Rev: LMC 5–6/10; SLJ 7/10) [590]

3536 Webb, Sophie. *Far from Shore: Chronicles of an Open Ocean Voyage* (4–6). Illus. by author. 2011, Houghton Mifflin $17.99 (978-0-618-59729-1). 80pp. Webb documents her research work with dolphins in the Pacific Ocean and the many other birds and animals she saw during a four-month trip, with notes on scientific methods and research techniques. (Rev: BL 9/1/11; HB 9–10/11; LMC 1–2/12; SLJ 9/1/11) [591.77]

Amphibians and Reptiles

GENERAL AND MISCELLANEOUS

3537 Hutchinson, Mark. *Reptiles* (4–7). Illus. Series: Insiders. 2011, Simon & Schuster $16.99 (978-144243276-5). 64pp. With dramatic 3-D illustrations, this volume offers a general overview of reptiles and then focuses on 12 specific animals, exploring their anatomy, behavior, and other characteristics. (Rev: BL 9/15/11; LMC 1–2/12) [597.9]

ALLIGATORS AND CROCODILES

3538 Bodden, Valerie. *Crocodiles* (K–2). Illus. Series: Amazing Animals. 2010, Creative Education $16.95 (978-158341806-2). 24pp. A simple overview of the characteristics of crocodiles, with eye-catching photographs. (Rev: BL 7/10) [597.98]

3539 Hamilton, Sue. *Attacked by a Crocodile* (4–7). Series: Close Encounters of the Wild Kind. 2010, ABDO LB $27.07 (978-1-60453-929-5). 32pp. Exciting stories and graphic photographs add high-interest appeal to the information about crocodiles and advice on avoiding and surviving such an attack. (Rev: LMC 10/10; SLJ 5/10) [597.98]

3540 Riggs, Kate. *Alligators* (K–3). Illus. Series: Amazing Animals. 2012, Creative Education LB $17.95 (978-160818104-9). 24pp. For new or reluctant readers, this is a good introduction to the alligator's physical characteristics, habitat, and behavior, and includes a story from folklore explaining why alligators and dogs don't get along. (Rev: BL 3/1/12) [599.98]

FROGS AND TOADS

3541 Markle, Sandra. *The Case of the Vanishing Golden Frogs: A Scientific Mystery* (4–6). Illus. 2011, Millbrook LB $29.27 (978-0-7613-5108-5). 48pp. One scientist's crusade against a fungus killing off Panamanian golden frogs is described in this attractive volume. (Rev: BL 9/15/11*; SLJ 11/1/11*) [597.8]

3542 Markle, Sandra. *Hip-Pocket Papa* (K–3). Illus. by Alan Marks. 2010, Charlesbridge $15.95 (978-1-57091-708-0). 32pp. Markle introduces the life and characteristics of the hip-pocket frog of Australia's temperate rainforest — and the role of the father — in this beautifully illustrated picture book. Lexile AD1060L (Rev: BL 1/1/10; LMC 10/10; SLJ 3/1/10) [597.8]

3543 Pringle, Laurence. *Frogs! Strange and Wonderful* (2–5). Illus. by Meryl Henderson. 2012, Boyds Mills $16.95 (978-159078371-9). 32pp. With clear writing and beautiful watercolor illustrations, this book offers extensive information on frogs and toads, covering everything from anatomy, habitat, location, and diet to sounds, metamorphosis, and conservation. Lexile 980L (Rev: BL 4/15/12; LMC 11–12/12; SLJ 7/12) [597.8]

3544 Stewart, Melissa. *A Place for Frogs* (K–3). Illus. by Higgins Bond. 2010, Peachtree $16.95 (978-1-56145-521-8). Unpaged. A richly illustrated tour of frogs' life, endangered status, and measures we can take to save them. (Rev: SLJ 5/1/10) [597.8]

3545 Turner, Pamela S. *The Frog Scientist* (5–9). Photos by Andy Comins. Series: Scientists in the Field. 2009, Houghton Mifflin $18 (978-0-618-71716-3). 58pp. Why are frog populations disappearing at an alarming rate? This fascinating book recounts the research of African American biologist Tyrone Hayes and explains the advances he has made in this environmentally sensitive field. Lexile 950L (Rev: BL 8/09*; HB 9–10/09; SLJ 9/09) [597.8]

LIZARDS

3546 Bishop, Nic. *Lizards* (2–4). Illus. by author. 2010, Scholastic $17.99 (978-0-545-20634-1). 48pp. Wildlife photographer Nic Bishop presents a compelling look at the lizard world in this book that includes plenty of succinct scientific information. (Rev: BL 12/1/10*; HB 11–12/10; SLJ 10/1/10*) [597.95]

3547 Collard, Sneed B. *Lizards* (4–7). Illus. 2012, Charlesbridge $16.95 (978-158089324-4); paper $7.95 (978-158089325-1). 48pp. A clear, well-designed introduction to lizards and their life cycle, habitats, diets, and so forth, with plenty of close-up photographs. ℮ (Rev: BL 1/1/12; LMC 11–12/12; SLJ 5/12) [597.95]

3548 Crump, Marty. *Mysteries of the Komodo Dragon: The Biggest, Deadliest Lizard Gives Up Its Secrets* (3–5). Illus. 2010, Boyds Mills $18.95 (978-159078757-1). 40pp. With fascinating facts, lively text, and color photographs, this volume describes the life of the lizard, scientific study of the animal, and conservation efforts. (Rev: BL 11/1/10; LMC 1–2/11; SLJ 11/1/10) [597.95]

3549 Gish, Melissa. *Komodo Dragons* (5–8). Illus. Series: Living Wild. 2011, Creative Education LB $23.95 (978-160818080-6). 48pp. Gish looks at komodo dragons' habitats, physical characteristics, behaviors, relationships with humans, endangered status, and role in folklore. (Rev: BL 12/1/11) [597.95]

SNAKES

3550 Hamilton, Sue. *Bitten by a Rattlesnake* (4–7). Series: Close Encounters of the Wild Kind. 2010, ABDO LB $27.07 (978-1-60453-930-1). 32pp. Exciting stories and graphic photographs add high-interest appeal to the information about these snakes and advice on avoiding and surviving such an attack. (Rev: LMC 10/10; SLJ 5/10) [597.96]

Animal Behavior and Anatomy

GENERAL

3551 Allman, Toney. *Animal Life in Groups* (5–8). Series: Animal Behavior. 2009, Chelsea House $32.95 (978-1-60413-142-0). 110pp. Examining the reasons why animals choose to live in groups, this volume discusses safety in numbers and various ways animals can cooperate, looking in particular at colonies, schools and flocks, herds, predator groups, and primate societies. (Rev: LMC 11–12/09) [591.5]

3552 Barner, Bob. *Animal Baths* (PS–K). Illus. by author. 2011, Chronicle $15.99 (978-1-4521-0056-2). Unpaged. Barner illustrates how a variety of animals clean themselves. ℮ (Rev: LMC 3–4/12; SLJ 12/1/11) [591.5]

3553 Berkes, Marianne. *Going Home: The Mystery of Animal Migration* (K–2). Illus. by Jennifer DiRubbio. 2010, Dawn $16.95 (978-1-58469-126-6); paper $8.95 (978-158469127-3). 32pp. Poems relate various animals' migratory experiences and are supported by extensive back matter including maps. (Rev: BLO 2/15/10; LMC 10/10; SLJ 5/1/10) [591.56]

3554 Carney, Elizabeth. *Great Migrations: Whales, Wildebeests, Butterflies, Elephants, and Other Amazing Animals on the Move* (3–5). Illus. 2010, National Geographic $18.95 (978-142630700-3); LB $27.90 (978-142630701-0). 48pp. The migration stories of eight diverse animals, ranging from army ants to Mali elephants, are presented in this attractive book with maps, facts, and clear text. (Rev: BL 12/15/10) [591.56]

3555 Dale, Jay. *Top 10 Minibeasts* (3–6). Illus. Series: Deadly and Incredible Animals. 2012, Black Rabbit LB $27.10 (978-159920411-6). 32pp. This books looks at the 10 deadliest small animals, starting with the Japanese giant hornet and counting down through spiders, bees, worms, and scorpions. (Rev: BLO 3/1/12) [595]

3556 de la Bedoyere, Camilla. *100 Things You Should Know About Nocturnal Animals* (4–6). Illus. Series: 100 Things You Should Know About. 2009, Mason Crest $19.95 (978-1-4222-1523-4). 48pp. Good for browsers, this volume looks at the distinctive senses of nocturnal animals (sight, smell, and so forth) and provides photographs, quizzes, activities, and brain teasers. (Rev: LMC 5–6/10; SLJ 2/10) [591.5]

3557 de la Bedoyere, Camilla. *Smartest and Silliest* (2–5). Illus. Series: Animal Opposites. 2010, Black Rabbit LB $27.10 (978-159566761-8). 32pp. A fascinating, well-designed introduction to animal intelligence in all its amazing forms. (Rev: BLO 3/14/11; LMC 5–6/11) [590]

3558 Eamer, Claire. *Spiked Scorpions and Walking Whales: Modern Animals, Ancient Animals, and Water* (4–6). 2009, Annick $19.95 (978-1-55451-206-5); paper $9.95 (978-1-55451-205-8). 100pp. Four categories of animals that bridge the gap between terrestrial and aquatic are explored in this adaptation-focused book. (Rev: BLO 11/5/09; SLJ 2/10; VOYA 6/10) [591.3]

3559 Goldstein, Natalie. *Animal Hunting and Feeding* (5–8). Series: Animal Behavior. 2009, Chelsea House $32.95 (978-1-60413-143-7). 110pp. Examining the ways in which animals hunt and feed, this volume discusses waiting for food, sharing and taking, plant-eating animals, generalists and specialists, and scavengers and decomposers. (Rev: LMC 11–12/09) [591.5]

3560 Hulbert, Laura. *Who Has These Feet?* (PS–2). Illus. by Erik Brooks. 2011, Henry Holt $16.99 (978-0-8050-8907-3). 42pp. Animals' feet and their function are the focus of this well-illustrated book that uses a guessing game format. (Rev: BL 8/11; LMC 11–12/11; SLJ 9/1/11) [590]

3561 Jenkins, Steve, and Robin Page. *How to Clean a Hippopotamus: A Look at Unusual Animal Partnerships* (K–3). Illus. by Steve Jenkins. 2010, Houghton Mifflin $16 (978-0-547-24515-7). 32pp. A compelling, close-up look at symbiotic relationships between animals. ℮ Lexile GN950L (Rev: BL 3/15/10*; SLJ 4/1/10*) [591.7]

3562 Jenkins, Steve, and Robin Page. *Time for a Bath* (K–3). Illus. by Steve Jenkins. 2011, Houghton Mifflin $12.99. (978-0-547-25037-3). 24pp. Well, how do animals take baths? Eye-catching illustrations show various surprising techniques. Also use *Time to Sleep* (2011). ℮ (Rev: LMC 10/11; SLJ 6/11) [591.56]

3563 Jenkins, Steve, and Robin Page. *Time to Eat* (PS–3). Illus. by Steve Jenkins. 2011, Houghton Mifflin $12.99 (978-0-547-25032-8). 24pp. This small, square book with beautiful collage illustrations explores the eating habits of a variety of animals, including a baby blue whale, an anaconda, and an ostrich. (Rev: BL 2/15/11*; SLJ 5/1/11) [591.5]

3564 Kenney, Karen Latchana. *Animal Tracks* (PS–2). Illus. Series: Our Animal World. 2011, Amicus $16.95 (978-160753142-5). 24pp. For beginning readers, this simple text with photographs discusses animal tracks and what they tell us. (Rev: BL 10/15/11) [591.47]

3565 McPhee, Margaret. *Show-Offs* (2–4). Illus. Series: Animal Planet: Weird and Wonderful. 2011, Kingfisher $12.99 (978-075346722-0). 64pp. Looks at the how different animals use posture, plumage, movements, and

so forth to attract and repel other animals. (Rev: BL 10/1/11) [591]

3566 Markle, Sandra. *Animal Heroes: True Rescue Stories* (4–7). 2009, Lerner LB $29.27 (978-0-8225-7884-0). 64pp. A compelling collection of stories of animals saving human lives — from a dog on September 11, 2001, to a gorilla, a cat, and dolphins; with factual information about each animal. (Rev: BL 7/08; LMC 3–4/09) [636.088]

3567 Marsh, Laura. *Amazing Animal Journeys* (2–4). Illus. 2010, National Geographic LB $11.90 (978-1-4263-0742-3); paper $3.99 (978-1-4263-0741-6). 48pp. Zebras, red crabs, and walruses are featured in this colorful account of unusual animal migrations. (Rev: BL 12/1/10; LMC 5–6/11; SLJ 3/1/11) [591.56]

3568 Miller, Debbie S. *Survival at 40 Below* (2–4). Illus. by Jon Van Zyle. 2010, Walker $17.99 (978-0-8027-9815-2); LB $18.89 (978-080279816-9). 40pp. Arctic animals' fascinating techniques and adaptations for winter survival are the focus of this nicely illustrated book. (Rev: BL 12/1/09; LMC 1–2/10; SLJ 1/1/10) [591.75]

3569 Morlock, Lisa. *Track That Scat!* (K–3). Illus. by Carrie Anne Bradshaw. 2012, Sleeping Bear $15.95 (978-158536536-4). 32pp. Finn and her dog explore the woods, noting — and sometimes stepping in — a variety of different animal droppings. (Rev: BL 4/15/12; LMC 11–12/12; SLJ 5/1/12) [591.47]

3570 Schaefer, Lola M. *Just One Bite* (PS–2). Illus. by Geoff Warning. 2010, Chronicle $17.99 (978-081186473-2). 40pp. Using life-size illustrations (sometimes showing only a part of a head), this colorful, large-format book shows 11 animals — from earthworm up to sperm whale — and how much they eat in just one bite. (Rev: BL 11/1/10; LMC 1–2/11; SLJ 11/10) [591.5]

3571 Schueller, Gretel H., and Sheila K. Schueller. *Animal Migration* (5–8). Series: Animal Behavior. 2009, Chelsea House $32.95 (978-1-60413-127-7). 110pp. Examining how and why animals migrate, this volume discusses birds, whales and other marine animals, animals that migrate on foot, sea turtles and salmon, and so forth. (Rev: LMC 11–12/09) [591.5]

3572 Thimmesh, Catherine. *Friends: True Stories of Extraordinary Animal Friendships* (4–8). Illus. 2011, Houghton Mifflin $16.99 (978-0-547-39010-9). 32pp. Thirteen short real-life stories of unlikely animal friendships — a basset hound and an owl, for example. (Rev: BL 9/1/11; SLJ 7/11) [591.5]

BABIES

3573 Bredeson, Carmen. *Baby Animals of the Seashore* (K–3). Illus. Series: Nature's Baby Animals. 2011, Enslow LB $21.26 (978-076603565-2). 24pp. With clear information and close-up photographs, this title introduces king penguin chicks, harbor seal pups, and other baby animals. (Rev: BL 5/1/11) [591.769]

3574 Feldman, Thea. *Baby Animals* (K–3). Illus. 2012, Kingfisher paper $3.99 (978-075346754-1). 32pp. From puppies and kittens to a wide range of species, this book for beginning readers introduces baby animals and associated vocabulary. (Rev: BL 4/1/12) [591.3]

3575 Owen, Ruth. *Squirrel Kits* (K–3). Illus. Series: Wild Baby Animals. 2011, Bearport LB $19.96 (978-161772160-1). 24pp. Using simple text and bright photographs, this volume introduces baby squirrels, what they eat, and how they learn to live on their own. Also use *Skunk Kits, Raccoon Cubs,* and *Polar Bear Cubs* (2011). (Rev: BL 7/11) [599.36]

3576 Reasoner, Charles. *Animal Babies!* (PS). Illus. by author. 2011, Rourke $5.99 (978-161236054-6). 10pp. For the very young, this is a simple, sturdy introduction to animal babies. (Rev: BLO 12/15/11) [591.3]

CAMOUFLAGE

3577 Kenney, Karen Latchana. *How Animals Hide* (PS–2). Illus. Series: Our Animal World. 2011, Amicus $16.95 (978-160753143-2). 24pp. For beginning readers, this simple text with photographs discusses animal camouflage techniques. (Rev: BL 10/15/11) [591.47]

3578 Schwartz, David M., and Yael Schy. *Where Else in the Wild? More Camouflaged Creatures Concealed . . . and Revealed* (1–4). Photos by Dwight Kuhn. 2009, Tricycle $16.99 (978-1-58246-283-7). Unpaged. Eleven well-camouflaged creatures are introduced by way of poetry and photography in this nicely designed, interactive book. (Rev: BL 10/15/09; LMC 3–4/10; SLJ 10/1/09) [591.47]

COMMUNICATION

3579 Davies, Nicola. *Talk, Talk, Squawk!* (3–5). Illus. by Neal Layton. 2011, Candlewick $14.99 (978-0-7636-5088-9). 64pp. Explores ways in which animals communicate with each other using colors, patterns, smells, movements, vibrations, sounds, and electricity. Lexile NC1220L (Rev: BL 11/15/11; HB 1–2/12; LMC 3–4/12; SLJ 11/1/11) [591.59]

DEFENSES

3580 Jenkins, Steve. *Never Smile at a Monkey* (K–3). Illus. by author. 2009, Houghton Mifflin $16 (978-0-618-96620-2). Unpaged. Animals can be dangerous — and this fascinating book explores how 18 animals react to perceived threats. (Rev: BL 10/15/09; LMC 3–4/10*; SLJ 9/1/09*) [591.6]

3581 Kenney, Karen Latchana. *Spiny Animals* (PS–2). Illus. Series: Our Animal World. 2011, Amicus $16.95 (978-160753144-9). 24pp. For beginning readers, this simple text with photographs discusses the defense

mechanisms of animals like sea urchins and porcupines. (Rev: BL 10/15/11) [591.47]

HOMES

3582 Ham, Catherine. *Step Inside! A Look Inside Animal Homes* (K–3). Illus. 2012, EarlyLight $14.95 (978-098320142-7). 32pp. Compelling photographs accompany rhymed poems about a variety of animal homes, from treetop nests to underground burrows. ❧ (Rev: BL 3/15/12) [591.56]

3583 Phillips, Dee. *Chipmunk's Hole* (K–3). Illus. Series: Hole Truth! Underground Animal Life. 2012, Bearport LB $23.93 (978-161772407-7). 24pp. Readers learn about the lives, habitat, diet, and life cycle of eastern chipmunks. (Rev: BL 4/1/12) [599.36]

REPRODUCTION

3584 Cusick, Dawn, and Joanne O'Sullivan. *Animal Eggs: An Amazing Clutch of Mysteries and Marvels!* (3–5). Illus. 2011, EarlyLight $14.95 (978-0-9797455-3-9). 48pp. This informative and highly illustrated survey takes a conversational approach to unveiling the marvels and mysteries of eggs — amphibian, reptile, insect, and bird. Lexile NC1010L (Rev: BL 4/15/11; SLJ 4/11) [591.468]

3585 Kenney, Karen Latchana. *Who Lays Eggs?* (PS–2). Illus. Series: Our Animal World. 2011, Amicus $16.95 (978-160753146-3). 24pp. For beginning readers, this simple text with photographs discusses animals that lay eggs such as birds, spiders, and crocodiles. (Rev: BL 10/15/11) [591.4]

Animal Species

GENERAL AND MISCELLANEOUS

3586 Burnie, David. *Mammals* (3–6). Illus. Series: Navigators. 2011, Kingfisher $12.99 (978-075346610-0). 48pp. An illustrated overview of mammals, from deserts and rain forests to grasslands and frozen tundra, with information on life cycles, habitats, diet, and homes. (Rev: BL 12/15/11) [599]

3587 Cohn, Scotti. *Big Cat, Little Kitty* (PS–3). Illus. by Susan Detwiler. 2011, Sylvan Dell $16.95 (978-1-60718-124-8); paper $8.95 (978-1-60718-134-7). Unpaged. Cohn describes the similarities and differences between domestic and wild cats, exploring the various habitats of the latter. ❧ (Rev: LMC 11–12/11; SLJ 8/1/11) [599.75]

3588 de la Bedoyere, Camilla. *Why Why Why — Are Orangutans Hairy?* (4–6). Illus. 2009, Mason Crest $18.95 (978-142221570-8). 32pp. Goofy and accessible, this book uses cartoons and sketches — as well as facts — to answer questions about mammals. (Rev: BL 1/1/10) [599]

3589 Eamer, Claire. *Lizards in the Sky: Animals Where You Least Expect Them* (3–5). Illus. 2010, Annick $21.95 (978-155451265-2); paper $12.95 (978-155451264-5). 104pp. This interesting volume with close-up photographs presents brief profiles of birds and spiders that live underwater, shrimp living in the desert, climbing fish, and other animals with unusual characteristics. (Rev: BL 12/1/10; LMC 3–4/11; SLJ 12/1/10) [591.4]

3590 Ganeri, Anita. *Meerkat* (PS–2). Series: A Day in the Life: Desert Animals. 2011, Heinemann LB $22 (978-1-4329-4773-6); paper $6.49 (978-1-4329-4782-8). 24pp. Answering questions such as "What do meerkats look like?" and "What do meerkats do during the day?," Ganeri presents the physical characteristics and life of this desert animal. (Rev: SLJ 6/11) [599.74]

3591 George, Jean Craighead. *The Buffalo Are Back* (3–5). Illus. by Wendell Minor. 2010, Dutton $16.99 (978-0-525-42215-0). 32pp. A stirring history of the American buffalo, from Native Americans' sustainable herd management techniques, to mass slaughter, to 20th-century preservation efforts. (Rev: BL 4/15/10; SLJ 7/1/10) [599.64]

3592 Gish, Melissa. *Bison* (5–8). Illus. Series: Living Wild. 2011, Creative Education LB $23.95 (978-1-60818-077-6). 48pp. Gish looks at the bison's habitats, physical characteristics, behaviors, relationships with humans, protected status, importance to Native Americans, and status as a symbol of the American West. (Rev: BL 12/1/11; SLJ 11/1/11) [599.64]

3593 Halls, Kelly Milner. *Wild Horses: Galloping Through Time* (4–7). Illus. by Mark Hallet. 2008, Darby Creek $18.95 (978-1-58196-065-5). 72pp. Gorgeous photographs and clear text tell the history of horses and document the presence of wild horses worldwide. (Rev: BLO 7/29/08; SLJ 10/1/08) [599.665]

3594 Joubert, Beverly, and Dereck Joubert. *African Animal Alphabet* (K–3). Photos by Beverly Joubert. 2011, National Geographic $16.95 (978-1-4263-0781-2); LB $26.90 (978-1-4263-0782-9). 48pp. With alliterative text, facts, and eye-catching full-color photographs, this is an appealing alphabetical introduction to African animals from antelope to zebra. (Rev: SLJ 5/1/11) [591.96]

3595 Otfinoski, Steven. *Raccoons* (4–6). 2010, Marshall Cavendish LB $20.95 (978-0-7614-4841-9). 46pp. This volume covers the animal's habitat, diet, reproduction, life span, adaptability, and relationship with humans. (Rev: SLJ 1/1/11) [599.76]

3596 *Savage SAFARI: EXTREME ENCOUNTERS wITH ANIMAL WARRIORS* (2–5). Illus. 2010, Kingfisher $14.99 (978-0-7534-6456-4). 48pp. Lions, wild dogs, eagles, cheetahs, elephants, cobras, and leopards are among the animals profiled in this overview of the many fierce animals found in Africa. (Rev: BL 6/10; LMC 10/10; SLJ 6/10) [591.4]

3597 Schlaepfer, Gloria G. *Hyenas* (4–6). 2010, Marshall Cavendish LB $20.95 (978-0-7614-4838-9). 48pp. This volume covers the animal's habitat, diet, reproduction, life span, adaptability, and the dangers it faces. (Rev: SLJ 1/1/11) [599.74]

APE FAMILY

3598 Gibbons, Gail. *Gorillas* (K–3). Illus. by author. 2011, Holiday House $17.95 (978-0-8234-2236-4). 32pp. A concise and appealing introduction to gorillas and their lives in Africa. Lexile AD820L (Rev: BL 4/15/11; SLJ 4/11) [599.884]

3599 McLeese, Don. *Gorillas* (1–3). Illus. Series: Eye to Eye with Endangered Species. 2010, Rourke LB $27.07 (978-161590274-3). 24pp. With eye-catching photographs, this book looks at gorillas' lives and the threats they face. (Rev: BL 3/1/11) [599.884]

3600 Pimm, Nancy Roe. *Colo's Story: The Life of One Grand Gorilla* (4–6). Series: The Columbus Zoo Books for Young Readers. 2011, Columbus Zoo and Aquarium $18.95 (978-0-9841554-4-6); paper $8.95 (978-0-9841554-5-3). 78pp. The inspiring story of Colo, the first gorilla born in captivity, is told in this interesting book that shows changes in zoo management and primate conservation since the 1950s. (Rev: SLJ 7/11) [599.884]

3601 Riggs, Kate. *Gorillas* (K–3). Illus. Series: Amazing Animals. 2012, Creative Education LB $17.95 (978-160818107-0). 24pp. For new or reluctant readers, this is a good introduction to the gorilla's physical characteristics, habitat, and behavior, and includes a story from folklore explaining why all they do is eat and sleep. (Rev: BL 3/1/12) [599.884]

3602 Sayre, April Pulley. *Meet the Howlers!* (PS–2). Illus. by Woody Miller. 2010, Charlesbridge $16.95 (978-1-57091-733-2). 32pp. Full-bleed illustrations and a monkey-call refrain enhance this accessible introduction to howler monkeys. (Rev: BL 3/15/10; SLJ 3/1/10) [599.8]

BATS

3603 Gerber, Carole. *Little Red Bat* (1–3). Illus. by Christina Wald. 2010, Sylvan Dell $16.95 (978-1-60718-069-2); paper $8.95 (978-160718-080-7). 32pp. An endearing little bat ponders whether to fly south for the winter or stay put as she considers preparations her woodland friends have made for winter in this informational book with a fictional feel. (Rev: BL 4/15/10; LMC 11–12/10; SLJ 6/1/10) [599.4]

3604 Stewart, Melissa. *A Place for Bats* (PS–3). Illus. by Higgins Bond. 2012, Peachtree $16.95 (978-156145624-6). 32pp. Introduces the bats of North America with photographs and information on habitat and threats to their survival. (Rev: BL 2/1/12; SLJ 5/1/12) [599.4]

BEARS

3605 Arnold, Caroline. *A Polar Bear's World* (K–2). Illus. by author. Series: Animals. 2010, Capstone LB $25.32 (978-140485743-8). 24pp. This book presents engaging information about polar bears — how far they can swim without stopping, for example — with effective artwork. (Rev: BL 9/15/10) [599.786]

3606 Bodden, Valerie. *Polar Bears* (K–2). Illus. Series: Amazing Animals. 2010, Creative Company $16.95 (978-158341811-6). 24pp. A simple overview of the characteristics of polar bears, with eye-catching photographs. (Rev: BL 7/10) [599.786]

3607 Guiberson, Brenda Z. *Moon Bear* (PS–3). Illus. by Ed Young. 2010, Henry Holt $16.99 (978-0-8050-8977-6). 32pp. Guiberson portrays the life of the Southeast Asian moon bear and explains the threats that it faces; with eye-catching illustrations and an informative author's note. Lexile AD780L (Rev: BL 1/1/10; SLJ 4/1/10*) [599.78]

3608 Hamilton, Sue. *Mauled by a Bear* (4–7). Series: Close Encounters of the Wild Kind. 2010, ABDO LB $27.07 (978-1-60453-932-5). 32pp. Exciting stories and graphic photographs add high-interest appeal to the information about bears and advice on avoiding and surviving such an attack. (Rev: LMC 10/10; SLJ 5/10) [599.7]

3609 McAllister, Ian, and Nicholas Read. *The Salmon Bears: Giants of the Great Bear Rainforest* (5–8). Illus. by Ian McAllister. 2010, Orca paper $18.95 (978-155469205-7). 89pp. Introduces grizzly, black, and spirit bears as they experience the seasons in the Great Bear Rainforest of British Columbia, and their relationship with the salmon in the rivers. (Rev: BL 6/10; SLJ 7/10) [599.78]

3610 Newman, Mark. *Polar Bears* (K–3). Photos by author. 2010, Henry Holt $16.99 (978-0-8050-8999-8). Unpaged. Appealing photographs and simple text introduce the lives of polar bears — physical characteristics, life cycle, and so forth — and discuss the challenges they face as their habitat is disappearing. (Rev: HB 1–2/11; LMC 5–6/11; SLJ 2/1/11) [599.786]

3611 Rosing, Norbert. *Polar Bears* (3–5). Illus. 2010, Firefly $19.95 (978-1-55407-599-7); paper $9.95 (978-155407623-9). 56pp. Close-up photographs with informative captions show the lives of polar bears through the four seasons. (Rev: BL 12/1/10; SLJ 2/1/11) [599.786]

BIG CATS

3612 de la Bedoyere, Camilla. *100 Things You Should Know About Big Cats* (3–6). Illus. Series: Remarkable Man and Beast: Facing Survival. 2010, Mason Crest LB $19.95 (978-142221965-2). 48pp. With plenty of lively photographs and illustrations woven together with cohesive text, this is a useful introduction to big cats. (Rev: BL 10/15/10; LMC 3–4/11) [599.75]

3613 Eszterhas, Suzi. *Cheetah* (PS–2). Illus. Series: Eye on the Wild. 2012, Frances Lincoln $15.99 (978-184780301-6). 28pp. With beautiful photographs, this large-format book follows cheetah cubs and shows their close bonds with their mothers. (Rev: BL 4/15/12; LMC 11–12/12; SLJ 5/1/12) [599.759]

3614 Hamilton, Sue. *Ambushed by a Cougar* (4–7). Series: Close Encounters of the Wild Kind. 2010, ABDO LB $27.07 (978-1-60453-928-8). 32pp. Exciting stories and graphic photographs add high-interest appeal to the information about cougars and advice on avoiding and surviving such an attack. (Rev: LMC 10/10; SLJ 5/10) [599.73]

3615 Hatkoff, Craig, and Juliana Hatkoff, et al. *Leo the Snow Leopard: The True Story of an Amazing Rescue* (1–3). 2010, Scholastic $17.99 (978-0-545-22927-2). Unpaged. The story of an orphaned snow leopard that is rescued from the mountains in Pakistan and finds a home at the Bronx Zoo. (Rev: BL 10/15/10; SLJ 10/1/10) [599.75]

3616 Joubert, Beverly, and Dereck Joubert. *Face to Face with Leopards* (3–6). Series: Face to Face with Animals. 2009, National Geographic $16.95 (978-1-4263-0636-5); LB $25.90 (978-1-4263-0637-2). 32pp. The story of the two authors meeting a days-old leopard cub is illustrated with ample close-up photographs. (Rev: SLJ 11/09) [599.75]

3617 Joubert, Beverly, and Dereck Joubert. *Face to Face with Lions* (4–8). Illus. by author. 2008, National Geographic $16.95 (978-142630207-7). 32pp. Lions' biology, habitat, diet, and reproduction are vividly portrayed in this photographic guide that also provides engaging firsthand experiences, Lexile 820L (Rev: BL 11/15/08) [599.757]

3618 Macken, JoAnn Early. *Cougars* (K–2). Series: Animals That Live in the Mountains. 2010, Weekly Reader LB $22 (978-1-4339-2411-8). 24pp. Close-up photographs and bright backgrounds enliven this book about the life and habitat of cougars. (Rev: SLJ 8/1/10) [599.75]

3619 Montgomery, Sy. *Saving the Ghost of the Mountain: An Expedition Among Snow Leopards in Mongolia* (4–7). Photos by Nic Bishop. Series: Scientists in the Field. 2009, Houghton Mifflin $18 (978-0-618-91645-0). 74pp. This compelling and thoughtful account of an (ultimately unsuccessful) expedition to find a snow leopard features eye-catching photographs and a handsome layout. (Rev: BLO 8/09; HB 11–12/09; SLJ 10/09) [599.75]

3620 Otfinoski, Steven. *Jaguars* (4–6). Series: Animals Animals. 2010, Marshall Cavendish LB $20.95 (978-0-7614-4839-6). 48pp. This volume covers the animal's habitat, diet, reproduction, life span, adaptability, and relationship with humans. (Rev: SLJ 1/1/11) [599.75]

3621 Riggs, Kate. *Cheetahs* (K–3). Illus. Series: Amazing Animals. 2011, Creative Education $16.95 (978-158341988-5). 24pp. Riggs provides clear, interesting facts enhanced by large, eye-catching photographs and retells an African folktale about cheetahs' tear lines. (Rev: BL 4/15/11) [599.75]

COYOTES, FOXES, AND WOLVES

3622 Ganeri, Anita. *Fennec Fox* (PS–2). Series: A Day in the Life: Desert Animals. 2011, Heinemann LB $22 (978-1-4329-4771-2); paper $6.49 (978-1-4329-4780-4). 24pp. "What do fennec foxes look like?" Ganeri answers this and other basic questions and provides large photographs. (Rev: BLO 3/14/11; SLJ 6/11) [599.776]

3623 Green, Emily. *Wolves* (K–2). Illus. Series: Backyard Wildlife. 2011, Children's Press LB $21.95 (978-160014563-6). 24pp. A simple introduction with simple text and bright photographs that will appeal to emerging readers. (Rev: BL 6/1/11) [599.773]

3624 McLeese, Don. *Gray Wolves* (1–3). Illus. Series: Eye to Eye with Endangered Species. 2010, Rourke LB $27.07 (978-161590271-2). 24pp. With eye-catching photographs, this book looks at gray wolves' lives and the threats they face. (Rev: BL 3/1/11) [599.733]

3625 Read, Tracy C. *Exploring the World of Coyotes* (4–6). Series: Exploring the World of . . . 2011, Firefly $16.95 (978-1-55407-795-3); paper $6.95 (978-1-55407-795-3). 24pp. Introduces the physical characteristics, mating choices, communication, and family life of coyotes. (Rev: SLJ 8/11) [599.7]

DEER FAMILY

3626 Ganeri, Anita. *Arabian Oryx* (PS–2). Series: A Day in the Life: Desert Animals. 2011, Heinemann LB $22 (978-1-4329-4769-9); paper $6.49 (978-1-4329-4778-1). 24pp. Answering questions such as "What do Arabian oryxes look like?" and "What do Arabian oryxes do at night?," Ganeri presents the physical characteristics and life of this desert animal. (Rev: SLJ 6/11) [599.6]

3627 Kawa, Katie. *Fawns* (PS–K). Illus. Series: Cute and Cuddly: Baby Animals. 2011, Gareth Stevens LB $22.60 (978-143395542-6). 24pp. A very simple book featuring brief text and adorable photographs of baby deer, with basic information about their lives. (Rev: BL 2/15/12) [599.65]

3628 Urbigkit, Cat. *Path of the Pronghorn* (2–4). Illus. by Mark Gocke. 2010, Boyds Mills $17.95 (978-159078756-4). 32pp. This large-format volume with excellent color photographs and clear text introduces readers to the habitat and habits of pronghorn antelope, the fastest land mammals in North America. Lexile AD1100L (Rev: BL 12/15/10; SLJ 11/1/10) [599.63]

3629 Zobel, Derek. *Deer* (PS–1). Series: Blastoff! Readers: Backyard Wildlife. 2010, Bellwether Media LB

$15.95 (978-1-60014-440-0). 24pp. With chapters including "What Are Deer?," "What Deer Look Like," and "Food and Seasons," this is a very simple introduction for early readers. (Rev: SLJ 1/1/11) [599.65]

ELEPHANTS

3630 de la Bedoyere, Camilla. *100 Things You Should Know About Elephants* (3–6). Illus. Series: Remarkable Man and Beast: Facing Survival. 2010, Mason Crest LB $19.95 (978-142221968-3). 48pp. With plenty of lively photographs and illustrations woven together with cohesive text, this is a useful introduction to elephants. (Rev: BL 10/15/10; LMC 3–4/11) [599.67]

3631 Lewin, Ted, and Betsy Lewin. *Balarama: A Royal Elephant* (2–5). Illus. by Ted Lewin. 2009, Lee & Low $19.95 (978-1-60060-265-8). 56pp. The Lewins describe their encounters with Indian parade elephants; with facts about the elephants and their training. (Rev: BL 11/15/09; LMC 11–12/09; SLJ 9/1/09) [636.9670954]

3632 Marsh, Laura. *Elephants* (K–3). Series: Great Migrations. 2010, National Geographic LB $11.90 (978-1-4263-0744-7); paper $3.99 (978-1-4263-0743-0). 48pp. Focusing on African elephants, this volume discusses their habitat and diet, their migration patterns, and the dangers they face. (Rev: SLJ 3/1/11) [599.67]

3633 Zimmer, Tracie Vaughn. *Cousins of Clouds: Elephant Poems* (K–3). Illus. by Megan Halsey. 2011, Clarion $16.99 (978-0-618-90349-8). 32pp. Elephants' biology, behavior, and importance in ancient mythology are described in text, poems, and mixed-media collages. (Rev: BL 4/15/11; SLJ 4/11) [599.67]

MARSUPIALS

3634 Green, Emily. *Opossums* (K–2). Illus. Series: Backyard Wildlife. 2011, Children's Press LB $21.95 (978-160014561-2). 24pp. A simple introduction with simple text and bright photographs that will appeal to emerging readers. (Rev: BL 6/1/11) [599.2]

3635 Heos, Bridget. *What to Expect When You're Expecting Joeys: A Guide for Marsupial Parents (and Curious Kids)* (1–3). Illus. by Stéphane Jorisch. 2011, Millbrook LB $25.26 (978-0-7613-5859-6). 32pp. This humorous and informative book provides information on marsupial babies. ℮ (Rev: LMC 3–4/12; SLJ 10/1/11) [599.2]

RODENTS

3636 Green, Emily. *Beavers* (K–2). Illus. Series: Backyard Wildlife. 2011, Children's Press LB $21.95 (978-160014560-5). 24pp. A simple introduction with simple text and bright photographs that will appeal to emerging readers. Also use *Porcupines* (2011). (Rev: BL 6/1/11) [599.37]

3637 Lunis, Natalie. *Capybara: The World's Largest Rodent* (2–4). Illus. Series: More SuperSized. 2010, Bearport LB $22.61 (978-193608731-0). 24pp. Large glossy photos and clear, concise text make an accessible introduction to the world's largest rodent. (Rev: BL 4/1/10) [599.35]

SHEEP AND GOATS

3638 Kawa, Katie. *Lambs* (PS–K). Illus. Series: Cute and Cuddly: Baby Animals. 2011, Gareth Stevens LB $22.60 (978-143395546-4). 24pp. A very simple book featuring brief text and adorable photographs of baby sheep, with basic information about their lives. (Rev: BL 2/15/12) [636.3]

3639 Macken, JoAnn Early. *Bighorn Sheep* (K–2). Series: Animals That Live in the Mountains. 2010, Weekly Reader LB $22 (978-1-4339-2409-5). 24pp. Close-up photographs and bright backgrounds enliven this book about the life and habitat of bighorn sheep. Also use *Mountain Goats* (2010). (Rev: SLJ 8/1/10) [599.649]

Birds

GENERAL AND MISCELLANEOUS

3640 Berendt, John. *My Baby Blue Jays* (PS–3). Illus. by author. 2011, Viking $16.99 (978-0-670-01290-9). 32pp. The author documents in words and photographs the blue jays that built a nest on the balcony of his New York apartment, and the ensuing eggs and growing baby birds. (Rev: BL 5/1/11; SLJ 5/1/11) [598.8]

3641 Gish, Melissa. *Hummingbirds* (5–8). Illus. Series: Living Wild. 2011, Creative Education LB $23.95 (978-160818078-3). 48pp. Gish looks at hummingbirds' habitats, physical characteristics, behaviors, relationships with humans, and symbolic importance in some cultures. (Rev: BL 12/1/11) [598.7]

3642 Larson, Jeanette, and Adrienne Yorinks. *Hummingbirds: Facts and Folklore from the Americas* (4–6). Illus. by Adrienne Yorinks. 2011, Charlesbridge $16.95 (978-1-58089-332-9); paper $8.95 (978-1-58089-333-6). 64pp. Interweaving facts, folklore, collage artwork, and extensive back matter, this volume gives readers a good overview of these birds and their anatomy, flight, habitat, diet, migration, and predators. ℮ (Rev: BL 3/1/11; LMC 10/11; SLJ 3/1/11) [598.7]

3643 Montgomery, Sy. *Kakapo Rescue: Saving the World's Strangest Parrot* (4–7). Illus. by Nic Bishop. 2010, Houghton Mifflin $18 (978-061849417-0). 80pp. The quest to save New Zealand's endangered Kakapo parrot is the focus of this inspiring conservation book. (Rev: BL 4/15/10*; SLJ 6/10) [639.9]

3644 Munro, Roxie. *Hatch!* (PS–3). Illus. by author. 2011, Marshall Cavendish $17.99 (978-0-7614-5882-1). 40pp. Readers guess the identities of birds based on pictures of their eggs in this volume that provides

facts on birds including the great horned owl, emperor penguin, ostrich, and bald eagle. (Rev: BL 3/15/11; HB 5–6/11; LMC 8–9/11; SLJ 5/1/11) [598]

3645 Rebman, Renee C. *Vultures* (3–5). Illus. Series: Animals Animals. 2011, Marshall Cavendish LB $20.95 (978-076144880-8). 48pp. Rebman examines the vulture's anatomy, scavenging habits, flight, and life cycle, with discussion of threats to their long-term survival. (Rev: BL 10/15/11) [598.9]

3646 Sill, Cathryn. *About Hummingbirds: A Guide for Children* (K–3). Illus. by John Sill. Series: About . . . 2011, Peachtree $16.95 (978-1-56145-588-1). Unpaged. Simple text and bright watercolor illustrations introduce these fascinating birds and their characteristics. (Rev: SLJ 9/1/11) [598.7]

3647 Stockdale, Susan. *Bring on the Birds* (PS–1). Illus. by author. 2011, Peachtree $15.95 (978-1-56145-560-7). 32pp. A rhyming, brightly illustrated introduction to familiar and exotic birds, focusing on 21 diverse species. (Rev: BL 3/15/11; LMC 8–9/11; SLJ 4/11) [598]

3648 Vogel, Carole Garbuny. *The Man Who Flies with Birds* (4–8). 2009, Lerner/Kar-Ben $18.95 (978-0-8225-7643-3). 64pp. This is the fascinating story of Yossi Leshem, an Israeli ornithologist whose research on bird migration resulted in air space restrictions that reduce the number of bird-airplane collisions. (Rev: HB 11–12/09; LMC 1–2/10; SLJ 12/09) [598.0956]

3649 Wolf, Sallie. *The Robin Makes a Laughing Sound: A Birder's Journal* (4–8). Illus. by author. 2010, Charlesbridge $11.95 (978-1-58089-318-3). 43pp. The author's journal — with sketches, watercolors, poems, and notes — documents bird visitors throughout the year, from geese to woodpeckers, robins, and cardinals. (Rev: SLJ 6/10) [598]

DUCKS, GEESE, AND SWANS

3650 Kawa, Katie. *Ducklings* (PS–K). Illus. Series: Cute and Cuddly: Baby Animals. 2011, Gareth Stevens LB $22.60 (978-143395538-9). 24pp. A very simple book featuring brief text and adorable photographs of baby ducks, with basic information about their lives. (Rev: BL 2/15/12) [598.4]

EAGLES, HAWKS, AND OTHER BIRDS OF PREY

3651 Arnosky, Jim. *Thunder Birds: Nature's Flying Predators* (2–5). Illus. by author. 2011, Sterling $14.95 (978-1-4027-5661-0). 32pp. Arnosky introduces a variety of birds of prey with succinct text, large paintings, and pencil drawings in this attractive volume with fold-out pages. (Rev: BL 6/1/11; SLJ 6/11*) [598.153]

3652 Lunis, Natalie. *Peregrine Falcon: Dive, Dive, Dive!* (1–3). Illus. Series: Blink of an Eye: Superfast Animals! 2010, Bearport LB $22.61 (978-193608793-8). 24pp.

Clear action photographs enhance this profile of the world's fastest animal. (Rev: BL 10/1/10) [598.9]

3653 Macken, JoAnn Early. *Golden Eagles* (K–2). Series: Animals That Live in the Mountains. 2010, Weekly Reader LB $22 (978-1-4339-2413-2). 24pp. Close-up photographs and bright backgrounds enliven this book about the life and habitat of golden eagles. (Rev: SLJ 8/1/10) [598.9]

3654 Riggs, Kate. *Eagles* (K–3). Illus. Series: Amazing Animals. 2012, Creative Education LB $17.95 (978-160818106-3). 24pp. For new or reluctant readers, this is a good introduction to the eagle's physical characteristics, habitat, and behavior, and includes a story from folklore explaining why people respect eagles. (Rev: BL 3/1/12) [598.9]

GULLS AND OTHER SEA BIRDS

3655 Dunning, Joan. *Seabird in the Forest: The Mystery of the Marbled Murrelet* (K–3). Illus. 2011, Boyds Mills $17.95 (978-1-59078-715-1). 32pp. A fascinating, lyrical account of the life of a Pacific Coast seabird that chooses to nest and raise its young far inland. (Rev: BL 4/15/11; SLJ 5/1/11) [598]

3656 Lewin, Ted. *Puffling Patrol* (2–4). Illus. by Betsy Lewin. 2012, Lee & Low $19.95 (978-160060424-9). 56pp. On an island off the coast of Iceland, two children volunteer to help fledgling puffins that took the wrong direction and have become stranded in town; handsome illustrations add appeal to the natural drama. Lexile 910L (Rev: BL 4/1/12; LMC 11–12/12; SLJ 7/12) [598.3]

3657 Metz, Lorijo. *Discovering Seagulls* (3–5). Series: Along the Shore. 2011, Rosen LB $21.25 (978-1-4488-4995-6). 24pp. A clear introduction that provides information on habitat, physical characteristics, diet, relationship with humans, and so forth. e (Rev: SLJ 12/1/11) [598.3]

OWLS

3658 Curtis, Jennifer Keats. *Baby Owl's Rescue* (3–4). Illus. by Laura Jacques. 2009, Sylvan Dell $16.95 (978-1-934359-95-2); paper $8.95 (978-1-607180-40-1). Unpaged. A baby owl is lucky enough to be blown out of its nest and into the backyard of young Maddie and Max, whose mother is a wildlife rehabilitator and teaches them how to treat the bird. (Rev: LMC 1–2/10; SLJ 12/1/09) [598.9]

3659 Gish, Melissa. *Owls* (5–8). Illus. Series: Living Wild. 2011, Creative Education LB $23.95 (978-160818081-3). 48pp. Gish looks at owls' habitats, physical characteristics, behaviors, relationships with

humans, protected status, and role in folklore. (Rev: BL 12/1/11) [598.9]

PENGUINS

3660 Bodden, Valerie. *Penguins* (K–2). Illus. Series: Amazing Animals. 2010, Creative Company/Creative Education LB $16.95 (978-158341810-9). 24pp. A simple overview of the characteristics of penguins, with eye-catching photographs. (Rev: BL 7/10) [598.47]

3661 London, Jonathan. *Little Penguin: The Emperor of Antarctica* (PS–2). Illus. by Julie Olson. 2011, Marshall Cavendish $17.99 (978-0-7614-5954-5). Unpaged. Two penguins take turns caring for their fluffy hatchling in this sweet and informative look at the birds' family life. e (Rev: LMC 1–2/12; SLJ 9/1/11) [598]

3662 Marzollo, Jean. *Pierre the Penguin: A True Story* (PS–2). Illus. by Laura Regan. 2010, Sleeping Bear $15.95 (978-1-58536-485-5). Unpaged. A biologist at the California Academy of Sciences helps an African penguin who loses his feathers and becomes alienated from the other penguins. (Rev: SLJ 8/1/10) [598.47]

3663 Momatiuk, Yva, and John Eastcott. *Face to Face with Penguins* (3–6). Photos by authors. Series: Face to Face with Animals. 2009, National Geographic $16.95 (978-1-4263-0561-0); LB $25.90 (978-1-4263-0562-7). 32pp. With beautiful photographs, this attractive volume looks at the nesting habits, diet, and social lives of penguins, as well as the threats to their survival. (Rev: SLJ 11/09) [598.47]

3664 Sill, Cathryn. *About Penguins: A Guide for Children* (PS–2). Illus. by John Sill. 2009, Peachtree $15.95 (978-1-56145-488-4). 48pp. Covering 17 species of penguins, this beautifully illustrated book describes key characteristics. (Rev: BL 9/15/09; SLJ 9/1/09) [598.47]

Conservation of Endangered Species

3665 Barker, David. *Top 50 Reasons to Care About Great Apes* (5–8). Series: Top 50 Reasons to Care About Endangered Animals. 2010, Enslow LB $31.93 (978-0-7660-3456-3). 104pp. Readers learn about apes' biology and habitat, behavior, and threats to their survival; activities in which young people can contribute to apes' welfare are listed. (Rev: LMC 3–4/10) [599.88]

3666 Christopherson, Sara Cohen. *Top 50 Reasons to Care About Marine Turtles* (5–8). Series: Top 50 Reasons to Care About Endangered Animals. 2010, Enslow LB $31.93 (978-0-7660-3455-6). 104pp. Threats to marine turtles' survival are the main focus of this volume that also discusses the animals' biology, habitat, and behavior. Also use *Top 50 Reasons to Care About Whales and Dolphins* (2010). (Rev: LMC 3–4/10) [597.928]

3667 Firestone, Mary. *Top 50 Reasons to Care About Elephants* (5–8). Series: Top 50 Reasons to Care About Endangered Animals. 2010, Enslow LB $31.93 (978-0-7660-3454-9). 104pp. Readers learn about elephants' biology and habitat, behavior, and threats to their survival; activities in which young people can contribute to elephant welfare are listed. Also in this series by this author are *Top 50 Reasons to Care About Giant Pandas, Top 50 Reasons to Care About Rhinos,* and *Top 50 Reasons to Care About Tigers* (all 2010). (Rev: LMC 3–4/10) [599.67]

3668 Hirsch, Rebecca E. *Helping Endangered Animals* (3–7). Series: Language Arts Explorer: Save the Planet. 2010, Cherry Lake LB $27.07 (978-1-60279-658-4). 32pp. Students are given a mission at the beginning of the book and must use creative thinking and problem solving to gather facts as they travel on a virtual trip researching the plight of animals including pandas and elephants. (Rev: LMC 8–9/10; SLJ 4/10) [591.68]

3669 Hirsch, Rebecca E. *Top 50 Reasons to Care About Polar Bears* (5–8). Series: Top 50 Reasons to Care About Endangered Animals. 2010, Enslow LB $31.93 (978-0-7660-3458-7). 104pp. Threats to polar bears' survival are the main focus of this volume that also discusses the animals' biology, habitat, and behavior. (Rev: LMC 3–4/10) [599.74]

3670 Jenkins, Martin. *Can We Save the Tiger?* (2–4). Illus. by Vicky White. 2011, Candlewick $16.99 (978-0-7636-4909-8). 56pp. A beautifully illustrated book about extinct and endangered animals and humans' impact on their environment past and future. ALSC Notable Children's Book, 2012. Lexile 970L (Rev: BLO 2/14/11; SLJ 3/1/11*) [333.9]

3671 Martin, Jacqueline Briggs. *The Chiru of High Tibet: A True Story* (1–3). Illus. by Linda Wingerter. 2010, Houghton Harcourt $17.99 (978-0-618-58130-6). 40pp. One researcher's quest to protect the endangered chiru (small antelope) of Tibet is chronicled in this inspiring story. ℮ (Rev: HB 9–10/10; LMC 3–4/11*; SLJ 10/1/10) [599.64]

3672 Morgan, Sally. *Animal Rescue* (1–3). Series: Helping Our Planet. 2011, Cherrytree LB $28.50 (978-1-84234-606-8). 32pp. Morgan introduces the kinds of animals that are endangered, the reasons for their status, and what can be done to protect them. (Rev: SLJ 8/1/11) [333.95]

3673 Silhol, Sandrine, and Gaelle Guerive. *Extraordinary Endangered Animals* (5–8). Illus. by Marie Doucedame. 2011, Abrams $24.95 (978-1-4197-0034-7). 160pp. Two-page spreads introduce species in six geographical groupings and describe habitat, location, feeding, hibernation, reproduction, and adaptations to the environment; with maps, large photographs, and

discussion of threats to survival. (Rev: BL 11/15/11; LMC 3–4/12; SLJ 11/1/11) [333.95]

Insects and Arachnids

GENERAL AND MISCELLANEOUS

3674 Arnosky, Jim. *Creep and Flutter: The Secret World of Insects and Spiders* (3–5). Illus. by author. 2012, Sterling $14.95 (978-140277766-0). 40pp. With six fold-out pages, this large-format book is an informative and well-illustrated exploration of a variety of insects and spiders. (Rev: BL 4/15/12; SLJ 4/1/12) [595.7]

3675 *Ask a Bug* (2–5). Illus. 2011, DK $9.99 (978-075667230-0). 48pp. Many frequently asked questions about insects — "why do crickets sing" and "why don't spiders get stuck to their own webs," for example — are answered in this appealing and informative book that will attract browsers. ℮ (Rev: BLO 3/14/11; LMC 10/11) [595.7]

3676 Baker, Nick. *Bug Zoo* (2–4). Illus. 2010, DK $12.99 (978-0-7566-6166-3). 64pp. Baker showing how to catch and care for 13 different kinds of common insects is the focus of this compelling book with close-up photos and clear instructions. (Rev: BLO 10/1/10; SLJ 7/1/10) [500]

3677 Beccaloni, George. *Biggest Bugs Life-Size* (3–7). Illus. 2010, Firefly $19.95 (978-155407699-4). 88pp. Thirty-five bugs of unusual sizes are presented in this fascinating book full of close-up photographs. (Rev: BL 12/1/10; SLJ 12/1/10) [595.714]

3678 Bodden, Valerie. *Crickets* (K–1). Illus. Series: Creepy Creatures. 2011, Creative Education $16.95 (978-158341993-9). 24pp. A basic introduction to crickets and their anatomy and behavior. (Rev: BL 4/1/11; LMC 8–9/11) [595.7]

3679 Burris, Judy, and Wayne Richards. *The Secret Lives of Backyard Bugs* (4–6). Illus. 2011, Storey $24.95 (978-1-60342-985-6); paper $14.95 (978-1-60342-563-6). 128pp. Lightning bugs, ladybugs, dragonflies, stick insects, bees, cicadas, aphids, and luna moths are among the bugs covered in this attractive volume that also outlines a garden's seasonal cycles and the life cycles of plants, soil, and insects and spiders. ℮ (Rev: LMC 11–12/11; SLJ 11/1/11) [595.7]

3680 Glaser, Linda. *Not a Buzz to Be Found: Insects in Winter* (2–4). Illus. by Jaime Zollars. 2011, Millbrook LB $25.26 (978-0-7613-5644-8). 32pp. Glaser explores the wintertime state of 12 insects including the monarch butterfly, woolly bear caterpillar, and the praying mantis. (Rev: BL 11/1/11; SLJ 11/1/11) [595.7]

3681 Gleason, Carrie. *Feasting Bedbugs, Mites, and Ticks* (3–6). Illus. Series: Creepy Crawlies. 2010,

Crabtree LB $26.60 (978-0-7787-2500-8); paper $8.95 (978-0-7787-2507-7). 32pp. With plenty of close-up color photographs, this title explores the characteristics of tiny insects that share our environment. (Rev: BL 10/1/10; SLJ 2/1/11) [614.4]

3682 Hansen, Amy S. *Bugs and Bugsicles: Insects in the Winter* (2–4). Illus. by Robert Clement Kray. 2010, Boyds Mills $17.95 (978-1-59078-269-9); paper $11.95 (978-1-59078-763-2). 32pp. How do insects survive winter? A colorful answer to this question, exploring the lives of insects including a praying mantis, a ladybug, a monarch butterfly, and a woolly bear caterpillar. (Rev: BL 3/1/10; LMC 5–6/10; SLJ 4/1/10) [595.714]

3683 Johnson, Jinny. *Insects and Creepy-Crawlies* (3–5). Illus. by Peter Bull. Series: Explorers. 2011, Kingfisher $10.99 (978-075346592-9). 32pp. An inviting mix of text, sidebars, captions, fact lists, and more add read-appeal to this well-illustrated book about insects and their habitats. (Rev: BL 2/15/12) [595.7]

3684 Markle, Sandra. *Mites: Master Sneaks* (4–7). Illus. Series: Arachnid World. 2012, Lerner LB $29.27 (978-076135046-0). 48pp. With large color photographs and concise text, this book introduces the life cycle, characteristics, and behavior of the mite. (Rev: BL 3/1/12; SLJ 2/12) [595.4]

3685 Markle, Sandra. *Ticks: Dangerous Hitchhikers* (3–5). Illus. 2011, Lerner LB $29.27 (978-076135041-5). 48pp. With close-up photographs, this volume introduces ticks, their anatomy, life cycle, and diet, and the dangers they pose to humans and pets. (Rev: BL 4/1/11) [595.4]

3686 Munro, Roxie. *Busy Builders* (K–3). Illus. by author. 2012, Marshall Cavendish $17.99 (978-076146105-0). 40pp. An oversize exploration of eight insects and one spider and the structures they build as their homes. (Rev: BL 4/15/12; HB 5–6/12; LMC 11–12/12; SLJ 5/1/12) [595.7156]

3687 Pringle, Laurence. *Cicadas! Strange and Wonderful* (2–4). Illus. by Meryl Henderson. 2010, Boyds Mills $16.95 (978-159078673-4). 32pp. An attractive picture-book introduction to these insects and their life cycle, habitat, and behavior. (Rev: BL 12/1/10; LMC 1–2/11*; SLJ 1/11) [595.7]

3688 Voake, Steve. *Insect Detective* (PS–1). Illus. by Charlotte Voake. 2010, Candlewick $16.99 (978-0-7636-4447-5). 32pp. Portrays a variety of familiar insects communicating with each other, building homes, eating, and defending themselves from predators, and encourages young readers to observe the natural world. (Rev: BL 5/1/10; LMC 10/10; SLJ 6/1/10*) [595.7]

3689 Werner, Sharon, and Sarah Forss. *Bugs by the Numbers* (4–6). 2011, Blue Apple $19.99 (978-1-60905-061-0). Unpaged. Interesting facts about insects

are combined with counting features in this visually appealing book with several liftable flaps. (Rev: SLJ 7/11) [595.7]

3690 Young, Karen Romano. *Bug Science: 20 Projects and Experiments About Arthropods: Insects, Arachnids, Algae, Worms, and Other Small Creatures* (4–8). Illus. by David Goldin. Series: Science Fair Winners. 2009, National Geographic LB $24.90 (978-1-4263-0520-7); paper $12.95 (978-1-4263-0519-1). 80pp. Divided into workshops that focus on specific bugs, this is an appealing compendium of projects that are properly documented and explained. (Rev: SLJ 3/10; VOYA 4/10) [595.7]

ANTS

3691 Nirgiotis, Nicholas. *Killer Ants* (2–5). Illus. by Emma Stevenson. 2009, Holiday House $17.95 (978-0-8234-2034-6). 32pp. Army ants, driver ants, and fire ants are among the dangerous varieties discussed in this informative, eye-catching volume. (Rev: BL 9/15/09; LMC 1–2/10; SLJ 9/1/09) [595.79]

BEES AND WASPS

3692 Hamilton, Sue. *Swarmed by Bees* (4–7). Series: Close Encounters of the Wild Kind. 2010, ABDO LB $27.07 (978-1-60453-933-2). 32pp. Exciting stories and graphic photographs add high-interest appeal to the information about bees and advice on avoiding and surviving such an attack. (Rev: LMC 10/10; SLJ 5/10) [595.79]

3693 Rotner, Shelley, and Anne Woodhull. *The Buzz on Bees: Why Are They Disappearing?* (1–3). Illus. by Shelley Rotner. 2010, Holiday House $16.95 (978-0-8234-2247-0). 32pp. Emphasizing bees' importance to humans, this bright, readable book about Colony Collapse Disorder offers advice on ways to attract and assist the pollinators. (Rev: BL 5/15/10; LMC 11–12/10; SLJ 6/1/10) [638]

BEETLES

3694 Gibbons, Gail. *Ladybugs* (K–3). Illus. by author. 2012, Holiday House $17.95 (978-082342368-2). 32pp. With concise text and colorful art, this is an accessible and informative introduction to the ladybug and its anatomy, diet, life cycle, habitat, defenses, and threats to survival. (Rev: BL 4/15/12; LMC 8–9/12; SLJ 4/1/12) [595.76]

3695 Jenkins, Steve. *The Beetle Book* (3–5). Illus. by author. 2012, Houghton Mifflin $16.99 (978-054768084-2). 40pp. With bright illustrations and accessible snippets of fact and trivia, this title offers readers a bug's-eye view of the dazzling world of beetles. (Rev: BL 4/1/12*; LMC 10/12*; SLJ 4/12*) [595.76]

CATERPILLARS, BUTTERFLIES, AND MOTHS

3696 Aston, Dianna Hutts. *A Butterfly Is Patient* (2–4). Illus. by Sylvia Long. 2011, Chronicle $16.99 (978-0-8118-6479-4). 40pp. A handsome presentation showing butterflies and their metamorphosis, camouflage, protective mechanisms, wonderful patterns, and other characteristics. Lexile AD1040L (Rev: BLO 7/11; LMC 11–12/11*; SLJ 7/11*) [595.78]

3697 Lawrence, Ellen. *A Butterfly's Life* (1–3). Illus. Series: Animal Diaries: Life Cycles. 2012, Bearport LB $23.93 (978-161772413-8). 24pp. A young boy's diary entries follow butterflies as they mate, migrate away, and return the next summer; with photographs, maps, and illustrations. (Rev: BL 4/1/12) [595.78]

3698 Marsh, Laura. *Butterflies* (K–3). Series: Great Migrations. 2010, National Geographic LB $11.90 (978-1-4263-0740-9); paper $3.99 (978-1-4263-0739-3). 48pp. Focusing on the monarch butterfly, this volume discusses their incredible migrations, the reasons why they undertake these long trips, and the dangers they face. (Rev: LMC 5/1/11; SLJ 3/1/11) [595.7]

3699 Simon, Seymour. *Butterflies* (2–4). Illus. 2011, HarperCollins $17.99 (978-006191493-5). 32pp. Simon uses the story of the monarch butterfly to draw children into this exploration of the world of moths and butterflies, encouraging participation in activities relating to these insects. (Rev: BL 10/15/11*) [595.78]

3700 Singer, Marilyn. *Caterpillars* (2–4). Illus. 2011, Charlesbridge $14.95 (978-0-9797455-7-7). 40pp. Rhymed text guides readers through a brightly illustrated exploration of caterpillars. (Rev: BLO 8/11; SLJ 11/1/11) [595.78]

SPIDERS AND SCORPIONS

3701 Ganeri, Anita. *Scorpion* (PS–2). Series: A Day in the Life: Desert Animals. 2011, Heinemann LB $22 (978-1-4329-4776-7); paper $6.49 (978-1-4329-4785-9). 24pp. Answering questions such as "What do scorpions look like?" and "What do scorpions do at night?," Ganeri presents the physical characteristics and life of this desert animal. (Rev: SLJ 6/11) [595.4]

3702 Lasky, Kathryn. *Silk and Venom: Searching for a Dangerous Spider* (5–8). Photos by Christopher G. Knight. 2011, Candlewick $16.99 (978-0-7636-4222-8). 64pp. A scientist's research trips to study the dangerous brown recluse spider are documented in this compelling book, which includes plenty of photographs and factual material about spiders. Lexile 1050L (Rev: BL 2/15/11; HB 3–4/11; LMC 5–6/11; SLJ 3/1/11) [595.4]

3703 Markle, Sandra. *Wind Scorpions: Killer Jaws* (4–7). Illus. Series: Arachnid World. 2012, Lerner LB $29.27 (978-076135048-4). 48pp. With large color photographs and concise text, this book introduces the life cycle, characteristics, and behavior of the wind scorpion. Also use *Tarantulas: Supersized Predators* (2012). e (Rev: BL 3/1/12; SLJ 2/12) [595.4]

3704 Otfinoski, Steven. *Scorpions* (3–5). Illus. Series: Animals Animals. 2011, Marshall Cavendish LB $20.95 (978-076144878-5). 48pp. With good photographs and clear text, this volume looks at the scorpion's anatomy and sting, its dangerous mating habits, its predatory nature, and its relationship with humans. (Rev: BL 10/15/11) [595.4]

Marine and Freshwater Life

GENERAL AND MISCELLANEOUS

3705 Bang, Molly, and Penny Chisholm. *Ocean Sunlight: How Tiny Plants Feed the Seas* (K–3). Illus. by Molly Bang. 2012, Scholastic $18.99 (978-054527322-0). 48pp. The sun narrates this interesting and accessible book, which explains how ocean plankton captures energy, creates food, and lays the foundation of a whole ecosystem. (Rev: BL 5/15/12*; HB 5–6/12; LMC 8–9/12; SLJ 6/1/12) [571.4]

3706 Becker, Helaine. *The Big Green Book of the Big Blue Sea* (3–5). Illus. by Willow Dawson. 2012, Kids Can $15.95 (978-155453746-4); paper $9.95 (978-155453747-1). 80pp. After discussing the ocean and its vulnerability to pollution and other changes, Becker looks at marine life and various strategies for survival, providing illustrative experiments. (Rev: BL 2/15/12; LMC 10/12; SLJ 6/1/12) [577.7]

3707 Blake, Carly. *Why Why Why — Do Dolphins Squeak?* (4–6). Illus. 2009, Mason Crest LB $18.95 (978-142221581-4). 32pp. Goofy and accessible, this book uses cartoons and sketches — as well as facts — to answer questions about dolphins and whales. (Rev: BL 1/1/10) [599.53]

3708 Johnson, Rebecca L. *Journey into the Deep: Discovering New Ocean Creatures* (5–8). 2010, Millbrook $31.93 (978-0-7613-4148-2). 64pp. Documenting the Census of Marine Life, which was conducted between 2000 and 2001, this book provides facts, pithy quotes, and vivid photographs captured from the mission. Lexile 920L (Rev: BL 12/1/10; LMC 1–2/11; SLJ 10/1/10) [591.77]

3709 Moore, Heidi. *Ocean Food Chains* (4–7). Series: Protecting Food Chains. 2010, Heinemann LB $32 (978-1-4329-3859-8); paper $8.99 (978-1-4329-3866-6). 48pp. With chapter headings that ask questions such as "What Are the Producers in Oceans?" and "What Are the Decomposers in Oceans?," this volume explores food chains within an ocean habitat and discusses why we need to protect them. (Rev: SLJ 11/1/10) [577.7]

3710 Parker, Steve. *Ocean and Sea* (4–7). Illus. Series: Scholastic Discover More. 2012, Scholastic paper $15.99 (978-054533022-0). 112pp. In five chapters — "All About Oceans," "Oceans of the World," "Life in the Ocean," "People and Oceans," and "Oceans Under Threat" — this attractive print book offers bright images and succinct text; an accompanying digital companion, *Shark Spotter*, offers additional detail on that species and includes videos. (Rev: BL 3/1/12) [551.46]

3711 Rizzo, Johnna. *Oceans: Dolphins, Sharks, Penguins, and More!* (4–7). 2010, National Geographic $14.95 (978-1-4263-0686-0). 64pp. This large-format volume full of eye-catching photographs and easy-to-find factoids covers 15 types of marine animals and will inspire browsers to investigate further. (Rev: BLO 6/10; LMC 10/10; SLJ 6/10) [551.46]

CORALS AND JELLYFISH

3712 Chin, Jason. *Coral Reefs* (K–3). Illus. by author. 2011, Roaring Brook $16.99 (978-1-59643-563-6). 32pp. Facts about coral reefs are presented alongside a story about a young girl studying them. (Rev: BL 8/11; HB 9–10/11; LMC 11–12/11; SLJ 10/1/11) [577.7]

3713 Metz, Lorijo. *Discovering Jellyfish* (3–5). Series: Along the Shore. 2011, Rosen LB $21.25 (978-1-4488-4997-0). 24pp. A clear introduction that provides information on habitat, physical characteristics, diet, predators, and so forth. ℮ (Rev: SLJ 12/1/11)

DOLPHINS AND PORPOISES

3714 Riggs, Kate. *Dolphins* (K–3). Illus. Series: Amazing Animals. 2011, Creative Education $16.95 (978-158341989-2). 24pp. Riggs provides clear, interesting facts enhanced by large, eye-catching photographs and retells a Greek myth about dolphins' relationship with humans. (Rev: BL 4/15/11) [599.53]

FISH

3715 Stewart, Melissa. *A Place for Fish* (K–3). Illus. by Higgins Bond. 2011, Peachtree $16.95 (978-1-56145-562-1). 32pp. Rich illustrations showcase a variety of endangered fishes in their native habitats, and the text emphasizes in simple language the threats that humans pose; "Fascinating Fish Facts" and vocabulary words are included. Lexile AD940L (Rev: BL 4/15/11; SLJ 3/1/11) [597.17]

3716 Turner, Pamela S. *Project Seahorse* (5–8). Illus. by Scott Tuason. Series: Scientists in the Field. 2010, Houghton Mifflin $18 (978-0-547-20713-1). 64pp. Sea horses and the scientists who study these beguiling creatures are the focus of this book, which contains the story of fishermen and biologists working together to protect a reef where they live. (Rev: BL 7/10; HB 9–10/10; SLJ 8/10) [596]

MOLLUSKS, SPONGES, STARFISH

3717 Cerullo, Mary M., and Clyde F. E. Roper. *Giant Squid: Searching for a Sea Monster* (4–6). Illus. 2012, Capstone LB $26.86 (978-142967541-3); paper $8.95 (978-142968023-3). 48pp. This title describes undersea expeditions to learn about the mysterious giant squid, and documents what little we do know about them. (Rev: BL 3/15/12; SLJ 5/1/12) [594]

3718 Halfmann, Janet. *Star of the Sea: A Day in the Life of a Starfish* (K–2). Illus. by Joan Paley. 2011, Henry Holt $16.99 (978-0-8050-9073-4). Unpaged. Readers learn about the characteristics and life of a starfish or sea star in this beautifully illustrated book. (Rev: LMC 10/11; SLJ 7/11) [593.9]

3719 Newquist, H. P. *Here There Be Monsters: The Legendary Kraken and the Giant Squid* (5–8). Illus. 2010, Houghton Mifflin $18 (978-0-547-07678-2). 80pp. Explores the history and mystery of the giant squid, with many illustrations, historical maps, and scientific facts. (Rev: BL 9/1/10; HB 11–12/10; SLJ 9/1/10) [594]

SEA MAMMALS

3720 Harvey, Jeanne Walker. *Astro the Steller Sea Lion* (1–3). Illus. by Shennen Bersani. 2010, Sylvan Dell $16.95 (978-1-60718-076-0); paper $8.95 (978-1-60718-087-6). Unpaged. An orphaned sea lion raised at California's Marine Mammal Center returns to his laboratory home each time his handlers try to release him. (Rev: BL 11/1/2010; LMC 1–2/11*; SLJ 9/1/10) [599.79]

3721 Kawa, Katie. *Baby Seals* (PS–K). Illus. Series: Cute and Cuddly: Baby Animals. 2011, Gareth Stevens LB $22.60 (978-143395534-1). 24pp. A very simple book featuring brief text and adorable photographs of baby seals, with basic information about their habits and habitat. ℮ (Rev: BL 2/15/12) [599.79]

3722 Lourie, Peter. *The Manatee Scientists: Saving Vulnerable Species* (4–7). Illus. Series: Scientists in the Field. 2011, Houghton Mifflin $18.99 (978-0-547-15254-7). 80pp. Lourie looks at research scientists' work on manatees around the world, where these mammals face quite different dangers depending on the environment and priorities of the human population. (Rev: BL 5/1/11; SLJ 7/11) [599.55092]

3723 Person, Stephen. *Walrus: Tusk, Tusk* (3–5). Illus. Series: Built for Cold: Arctic Animals. 2011, Bearport LB $25.27 (978-161772133-5). 32pp. Dramatic photographs add appeal to this book, which explores the biology, habitat, and threats facing walruses. (Rev: BL 4/1/11) [599.79]

3724 Read, Tracy C. *Exploring the World of Seals and Walruses* (4–6). Series: Exploring the World of . . . 2011, Firefly $16.95 (978-1-55407-784-7); paper $6.95 (978-1-55407-784-7). 24pp. Introduces the physical characteristics, habitat, family life, and behaviors of these sea mammals. (Rev: SLJ 8/11) [599.79]

3725 Rebman, Renee C. *Walruses* (3–5). Illus. Series: Animals Animals. 2011, Marshall Cavendish LB $20.95 (978-076144881-5). 48pp. Rebman examines the walrus's anatomy, diet, and life cycle, with discussion of threats to long-term survival. (Rev: BL 10/15/11) [599.79]

SHARKS

3726 Bodden, Valerie. *Sharks* (K–2). Illus. Series: Amazing Animals. 2010, Creative Company/Creative Education LB $16.95 (978-158341812-3). 24pp. A simple overview of the characteristics of sharks, with eye-catching photographs. (Rev: BL 7/10) [597.3]

3727 Brusha, Joe. *Top 10 Deadliest Sharks* (4–7). Illus. by Anthony Spay. 2010, Silver Dragon paper $9.99 (978-098275072-8). 200pp. Facts about sharks are presented along with assessments of their threats to humans. (Rev: BL 3/15/11) [741.5]

3728 Hamilton, Sue. *Eaten by a Shark* (4–7). Series: Close Encounters of the Wild Kind. 2010, ABDO LB $27.07 (978-1-60453-931-8). 32pp. Exciting stories and graphic photographs add high-interest appeal to the information about sharks and advice on avoiding and surviving such an attack. (Rev: LMC 10/10; SLJ 5/10) [597.3]

3729 Smith, Miranda. *Sharks* (4–7). Illus. Series: Kingfisher Knowledge. 2010, Kingfisher paper $8.99 (978-075346405-2). 64pp. An eye-catching overview of sharks' physical characteristics, habit, diet, and behavior, with spreads on *Jaws* and on shark attacks as well as information on their history and myths about these animals. (Rev: BL 2/15/10; SLJ 9/1/08) [597.3]

WHALES

3730 Lourie, Peter. *Whaling Season: A Year in the Life of an Arctic Whale Scientist* (4–8). Series: Scientists in the Field. 2009, Houghton Mifflin $18 (978-0-618-77709-9). 80pp. Lourie follows the work of Arctic whale scientist John Craighead George (son of the well-known children's author) in this fascinating account of George's everyday work, the research process, his subjects, and his ways of relaxing at the end of the day. Lexile NC1150L (Rev: BL 12/1/09*; SLJ 2/10) [599.5]

3731 Marsh, Laura. *Whales* (K–3). Series: Great Migrations. 2010, National Geographic LB $11.90 (978-1-4263-0746-1); paper $3.99 (978-1-4263-0745-4). 48pp. Focusing on sperm whales, this volume discusses their anatomy and diet, their migration patterns, and the dangers they face. (Rev: SLJ 3/1/11) [599.5]

3732 Riggs, Kate. *Killer Whales* (K–3). Illus. Series: Amazing Animals. 2012, Creative Education LB $17.95 (978-160818109-4). 24pp. For new or reluctant readers, this is a good introduction to the killer whale's physical characteristics, habitat, and behavior, and includes a story from Canadian folklore. (Rev: BL 3/1/12) [599.53]

Microscopes and Microbiology

3733 Brown, Jordan D. *Micro Mania: A Really Close-Up Look at Bacteria, Bedbugs and the Zillions of Other Gross Little Creatures That Live In, On and All Around You!* (4–6). 2009, Imagine $19.95 (978-0-9823064-2-0). 80pp. Close-up gross-out photographs of bacteria, microbes, fungi, and other parasites are presented here along with information about the scientists who study them plus some activities. Lexile 1010L (Rev: SLJ 3/10) [500]

Oceanography

GENERAL

3734 Hynes, Margaret. *Oceans and Seas* (4–6). Illus. by Thomas Bayley. Series: Navigators. 2010, Kingfisher $12.99 (978-0-7534-6415-1). 48pp. This attractive volume introduces all aspects of the marine environment, covering everything from tides and waves to pollution, preservation, marine archaeology, and future threats and opportunities. (Rev: BL 9/1/10; SLJ 10/1/10) [551.46]

CURRENTS, TIDES, AND WAVES

3735 Mara, Wil. *How Do Waves Form?* (2–4). Series: Tell Me Why, Tell Me How. 2010, Marshall Cavendish LB $20.95 (978-0-7614-4829-7). 32pp. With information on such topics as the relationship between wind and waves and how tsunamis are formed, this volume introduces essential concepts in easy-to-read text and lots of helpful illustrations. (Rev: BL 3/1/11; SLJ 2/1/11) [551.46]

3736 Spilsbury, Louise, and Richard Spilsbury. *Sweeping Tsunamis* (3–6). Series: Awesome Forces of Nature. 2010, Heinemann LB $29 (978-1-4329-3785-0). 32pp. "Where do tsunamis happen?" "Who helps when tsunamis happen?" These and other questions are answered — and case studies look at famous events — in this eye-catching volume. (Rev: LMC 11–12/10; SLJ 9/1/10) [551.46]

SEASHORES AND TIDAL POOLS

3737 Wilson, Hannah. *Seashore* (PS–1). Illus. by Simon Mendez. Series: Flip the Flaps. 2010, Kingfisher $9.99 (978-0-7534-6445-8). 18pp. With a single question-and-answer flap per spread, this appealing book presents various types of seashore with large-font text and realistic paintings. (Rev: BL 2/1/11; SLJ 4/11) [551.458]

UNDERWATER EXPLORATION

3738 Mallory, Kenneth. *Adventure Beneath the Sea: Living in an Underwater Science Station* (5–8). Illus. by Brian Skerry. 2010, Boyds Mills $18.95 (978-159078607-9). 48pp. This readable book describes life in an underwater science station on a reef off the Florida Keys, with discussion of the training required, the living conditions, and the tasks performed. (Rev: BL 12/1/10; LMC 1–2/11; SLJ 11/1/10) [551.46]

Pets

GENERAL AND MISCELLANEOUS

3739 Hamilton, Lynn. *Ferret* (3–5). Illus. Series: My Pet. 2009, Weigl LB $26 (978-160596096-8). 32pp. Facts about ferrets, including "Ferret Firsts," are combined with tips on choosing and caring for these animals. (Rev: BL 4/1/10) [636.976]

3740 Love, Ann, and Jane Drake. *Talking Tails: The Incredible Connection Between People and Their Pets* (4–6). Illus. by Bill Slavin. 2010, Tundra $22.95 (978-0-88776-884-2). 80pp. Human-animal relationships from familiar (dogs and cats) to less common (reptiles, for example) are explored, with information on body language and pet care. (Rev: BL 4/15/10; SLJ 3/10) [636.088]

3741 Niven, Felicia Lowenstein. *Learning to Care for Small Mammals* (2–4). Series: Beginning Pet Care with American Humane. 2010, Enslow LB $23.93 (978-0-7660-3195-1). 48pp. After a brief history of small mammals (rabbits, ferrets, and so forth), this book describes the environment you need to provide for them and the various problems and challenges you will face. (Rev: SLJ 3/1/11) [636.9]

3742 Silverstein, Alvin, and Virginia Silverstein, et al. *Poison Dart Frogs* (3–5). Illus. Series: Far-Out and Unusual Pets. 2012, Enslow LB $23.93 (978-076603881-3). 48pp. Factual information on these frogs is combined with tips on keeping one as a pet and discussion of their pros and cons in the home. (Rev: BL 4/15/12) [639.3]

3743 Silverstein, Alvin, and Virginia Silverstein, et al. *Rats* (3–5). Illus. Series: Far-Out and Unusual Pets. 2012, Enslow LB $23.93 (978-076603882-0). 48pp. Factual information on rats is combined with tips on keeping one as a pet and discussion of their pros and cons in the home. (Rev: BL 4/15/12) [636.935]

3744 Tracy, Kathleen. *The Hamster in Our Class* (1–3). Illus. 2012, Mitchell Lane LB $25.70 (978-158415980-3). 32pp. Solid information on hamster care is woven into a simple story about a class caring for its pet, Hamlet. (Rev: BL 4/1/12) [636.935]

3745 Urbigkit, Cat. *The Guardian Team: On the Job with Rena and Roo* (K–3). Illus. 2011, Boyds Mills $16.95 (978-1-59078-770-0). 32pp. The fascinating story of an orphaned wild burro (Roo) and a puppy (Rena), the runt of the litter, who bond with each other as they are trained to guard the sheep on a Wyoming ranch; a companion to *Brave Dogs, Gentle Dogs* (2005). (Rev: BL 12/1/11; LMC 5–6/12; SLJ 10/1/11) [636.737]

CATS

3746 Bearce, Stephanie. *Care for a Kitten* (3–6). Series: A Robbie Reader. How to Convince Your Parents You Can. 2010, Mitchell Lane LB $18.50 (978-1-58415-803-5). 32pp. For beginning readers, this book outlines the pros and cons of getting a kitten and provides tips on preparing the house. (Rev: SLJ 5/1/10) [636.8]

3747 Whitehead, Sarah. *How to Speak Cat!* (4–8). 2008, Scholastic paper $6.99 (978-0-545-02079-4). 96pp. Amply illustrated, this book offers advice on building a relationship with a pet cat through body language cues and mutual respect. (Rev: SLJ 6/1/09) [599.75]

DOGS

3748 Adams, Michelle Medlock. *Care for a Puppy* (3–6). Series: A Robbie Reader. How to Convince Your Parents You Can. 2010, Mitchell Lane LB $18.50 (978-1-58415-802-8). 32pp. For beginning readers, this book outlines the pros and cons of getting a puppy and offers a chapter titled "Perfecting the Puppy Pitch to Your Parents." (Rev: SLJ 5/1/10) [636.7]

3749 Bial, Raymond. *Rescuing Rover: Saving America's Dogs* (4–7). Illus. 2011, Houghton Mifflin $16.99 (978-0-547-34125-5). 80pp. Cruelty to animals, puppy mills, dogfighting, dog rescue services, and animal shelters are all discussed in this wide-ranging survey that also includes a personal account of adopting a rescue dog. Lexile NC1230L (Rev: BL 6/1/11; LMC 1–2/12; SLJ 7/11) [636.08]

3750 Bozzo, Linda. *Guide Dog Heroes* (2–4). Series: Amazing Working Dogs with American Humane. 2010, Enslow LB $23.93 (978-0-7660-3198-2). 48pp. With large, simple text and many photographs, this book starts with a true story and follows with information on guide dog breeds, training, working tasks, and status as heroes. Also use *Police Dog Heroes* and *Service Dog Heroes* (both 2010). (Rev: SLJ 3/1/11) [362.4]

3751 Fetty, Margaret. *Seizure-Alert Dogs* (3–5). Illus. Series: Dog Heroes. 2009, Bearport LB $25.27 (978-159716865-6). 32pp. Describes how dogs can help people anticipate and deal with seizures. (Rev: BL 11/1/09) [362.196]

3752 Gewirtz, Elaine Waldorf. *The Chihuahua* (4–8). Illus. Series: Our Best Friends. 2011, Eldorado Ink LB $34.95 (978-193290475-8). 112pp. An attractive introduction to these small dogs and their pros and cons as pets. (Rev: BL 4/15/11) [636.76]

3753 Gewirtz, Elaine Waldorf. *Fetch This Book: Train Your Dog to Do Almost Anything* (4–8). Series: Our Best Friends. 2010, Eldorado Ink $34.95 (978-1-932904-60-4). 112pp. In clearly written chapters such as "What Your Dog Thinks About Training," "Establishing Who's in Charge," and "Making Your Dog a Champion," this is a practical guide to dog training from the basics to advanced opportunities in service roles. (Rev: BL 8/10*; SLJ 9/1/10) [636.7]

3754 Goldish, Meish. *Baghdad Pups* (3–5). Illus. Series: Dog Heroes. 2011, Bearport LB $25.27 (978-1-61772-150-2). 32pp. The dogs that work with soldiers in war zones are the focus here. Also use *Prison Puppies* (2011), about dogs trained by inmates for various tasks. (Rev: BL 5/1/11; SLJ 6/11) [956.7044]

3755 Goldish, Meish. *Pest-Sniffing Dogs* (3–5). Illus. Series: Dog Heroes. 2012, Bearport LB $25.27 (978-161772454-1). 32pp. Dogs trained to detect bed bugs, termites, and more are the focus of this title, which includes information on the dogs' training regimen and visually appealing photographs. (Rev: BL 4/15/12) [636.73]

3756 Houston, Dick. *Bulu: African Wonder Dog* (5–8). 2010, Random House LB $18.99 (978-0-375-94720-9). 336pp. The true story of an African terrier with an unusual personality and a protective attitude toward other animals. Lexile 700L (Rev: BL 3/15/10; LMC 8–9/10; SLJ 5/10) [636.7]

3757 Hubbell, Patricia. *Shaggy Dogs, Waggy Dogs* (PS–2). Illus. by Donald Wu. 2011, Marshall Cavendish $17.99 (978-0-7614-5957-6). Unpaged. A rhymed celebration of all things doggy. ℮ (Rev: SLJ 9/1/11) [636.7]

3758 Laidlaw, Rob. *No Shelter Here: Making the World a Kinder Place for Dogs* (3–6). Illus. 2012, Pajama $21.95 (978-098694955-5). 64pp. Laidlaw provides solid advice on caring for a dog, but the emphasis here is on how dogs are mistreated and on the work of "Dog Champions" who are seeking better conditions for all dogs. (Rev: BL 4/15/12; LMC 11–12/12; SLJ 4/12) [636.7]

3759 Lendroth, Susan. *Calico Dorsey: Mail Dog of the Mining Camps* (PS–3). Illus. by Adam Gustavson. 2010, Tricycle $16.99 (978-1-58246-318-6); LB $19.99 (978-1-58246-367-4). Unpaged. In 1885 California a border collie named Dorsey is trained to deliver mail to miners across the desert. (Rev: BL 10/15/10; LMC 3–4/11; SLJ 9/1/10) [636.7]

3760 McCarthy, Meghan. *The Incredible Life of Balto* (2–4). Illus. by author. 2011, Knopf $16.99 (978-0-375-84460-7). 40pp. This nonfiction picture book tells the story of the sled dog who delivered anti-diptheria serum

to Nome, Alaska, in 1925 and became famous in the process. (Rev: BL 7/11; SLJ 6/11) [636.73]

3761 Morn, September. *The Doberman Pinscher* (4–7). Illus. Series: Our Best Friends. 2011, Eldorado Ink LB $34.95 (978-193290477-2). 112pp. An attractive introduction to these popular dogs and their pros and cons as pets. (Rev: BL 4/15/11) [636.73]

3762 Patent, Dorothy Hinshaw. *Saving Audie: A Pit Bull Puppy Gets a Second Chance* (2–4). Illus. by William Munoz. 2011, Walker $17.99 (978-0-8027-2272-0). 40pp. A pit bull formerly part of NFL star Michael Vick's dogfighting ring undergoes rehabilitation and finds a happy home with a family in San Francisco. (Rev: BL 3/1/11; SLJ 5/1/11*) [636.755]

3763 Prap, Lila. *Doggy Whys?* (2–4). Illus. by author. 2011, NorthSouth $14.95 (978-0-7358-4014-0). 40pp. "Why do dogs wag their tails?" Prap answers these and other doggy questions with humor and facts, describing particular breeds and their pros and cons. (Rev: BL 6/1/11; LMC 8–9/11; SLJ 5/1/11) [636.7]

3764 Schweitzer, Karen. *The Cocker Spaniel* (4–7). Illus. Series: Our Best Friends. 2011, Eldorado Ink LB $34.95 (978-193290476-5). 112pp. An attractive introduction to these dogs and their pros and cons as pets. (Rev: BL 4/15/11) [636.752]

3765 Stamper, Judith Bauer. *Eco Dogs* (3–5). Illus. Series: Dog Heroes. 2011, Bearport LB $25.27 (978-1-61772-152-6). 32pp. A fascinating look at dogs that work with wildlife scientists to help endangered animals and habitats. (Rev: BL 5/1/11; SLJ 6/11) [636.7]

3766 Weatherford, Carole Boston. *First Pooch: The Obamas Pick a Pet* (PS–2). Illus. by Amy June Bates. 2009, Marshall Cavendish $16.99 (978-0-7614-5636-0). 32pp. The story of the Obamas' dog Bo is given a family focus and enhanced with plenty of facts about other presidential pets and promises. (Rev: BL 11/15/09; LMC 5–6/10; SLJ 12/1/09) [973.932]

3767 Wheeler, Jill C. *Portuguese Water Dogs* (3–5). Illus. 2010, ABDO LB $16.95 (978-160453784-0). 24pp. A concise introduction to the current White House canine incumbent, with information on anatomy, personality, and so forth. Also use *Boston Terriers, Welsh Corgis,* and *Weimaraners* (all 2010). (Rev: BL 9/1/10) [636.73]

FISH

3768 Niven, Felicia Lowenstein. *Learning to Care for Fish* (2–4). Series: Beginning Pet Care with American Humane. 2010, Enslow LB $23.93 (978-0-7660-3193-7). 48pp. After a brief history of fish, this book describes the environment you need to provide to pet fish and the various problems and challenges you will face. (Rev: SLJ 3/1/11) [639.34]

HORSES AND PONIES

3769 Lewin, Ted. *Stable* (K–3). Illus. by author. 2010, Roaring Brook $17.99 (978-1-59643-467-7). 40pp. Evocative watercolor illustrations enhance this passage-of-time story about Brooklyn's Kensington stable, which has been in use since the 1800s. (Rev: BL 10/15/10; LMC 1–2/11; SLJ 10/1/10) [636.1]

3770 Scanlan, Lawrence. *The Big Red Horse: The Story of Secretariat and the Loyal Groom Who Loved Him* (4–8). Photos by Raymond Woolfe. 2010, HarperTrophy paper $7.99 (978-0-00-639352-8). 170pp. Prized racehorse Secretariat's inspiring story is portrayed in this biography, which features a variety of compelling anecdotes and black-and-white pictures. (Rev: SLJ 3/1/11)

3771 Wilsdon, Christina. *For Horse-Crazy Girls Only: Everything You Want to Know About Horses* (3–8). Illus. by Alecia Underhill. 2010, Feiwel & Friends $14.99 (978-0-312-60323-6). 150pp. A lighthearted survey of all things horse, from horse jokes and lore to information on markings and ailments to practical tips on working with horses. (Rev: SLJ 4/11) [636.1]

Zoos and Marine Aquariums

3772 Bleiman, Andrew, and Chris Eastland. *Zoo Borns! Zoo Babies from Around the World* (PS–3). Photos by authors. 2010, Simon & Schuster $12.99 (978-1-4424-1272-9). 160pp. With appealing photographs and simple first-person text, this book introduces baby animals including a hyena, a mongoose, an ocelot, and a fennec fox. (Rev: SLJ 10/1/10) [591.3]

3773 Halls, Kelly Milner, and William Sumner. *Saving the Baghdad Zoo: A True Story of Hope and Heroes* (4–7). Illus. by William Sumner. 2010, Greenwillow $17.99 (978-0-06-177202-3). 64pp. American soldiers work together with Iraqi citizens to protect and provide for the animals of the Baghdad zoo in this inspiring story of cooperation. (Rev: BL 2/15/10; SLJ 6/10) [590.73]

3774 Komiya, Teruyuki. *More Life-Size Zoo* (PS–2). Trans. by Junko Miyakoshi. Illus. by Toshimitsu Matsuhashi. 2010, Seven Footer $18.95 (978-1-934734-19-3). 48pp. In this sequel to *Life-Size Zoo* (2009), Komiya offers up more vivid life-size photographs, fold-outs, and quirky facts for a variety of zoo animals. (Rev: BLO 8/10; SLJ 9/1/10) [591.4]

Botany

Foods and Farming

GENERAL

3775 Arlon, Penelope, and Tory Gordon Harris. *Farm* (PS–K). Illus. Series: Discover More. 2012, Scholastic $7.99 (978-054536571-0). 32pp. This print picture book offers an overview of types of farms and the animals and equipment found there, and is supported by a digital companion with additional features. (Rev: BLO 3/1/12) [630]

3776 Reilly, Kathleen M. *Food: 25 Amazing Projects Investigate the History and Science of What We Eat* (4–6). Illus. by Farah Rizvi. 2010, Nomad paper $15.95 (978-1-934670-59-0). 124pp. Activities reinforce the information presented on food in general and around the world, farming, packaging, and healthy choices. (Rev: SLJ 2/1/11) [641.3]

3777 Vogel, Julia. *Local Farms and Sustainable Food* (3–7). Series: Language Arts Explorer: Save the Planet. 2010, Cherry Lake LB $27.07 (978-1-60279-660-7). 32pp. Students are given a mission at the beginning of the book and must use creative thinking and problem solving to gather facts as they travel on a virtual trip through the process of growing and distributing organic food. (Rev: LMC 8–9/10; SLJ 4/10) [630]

FARMS, RANCHES, AND FARM ANIMALS

3778 Bailer, Darice. *Donkeys* (3–5). Illus. 2011, Marshall Cavendish LB $20.95 (978-0-7614-4875-4). 48pp. Bailer looks at how and why we keep donkeys, their anatomy and life cycle, abuse of donkeys, and the relationship between donkeys and people. (Rev: BL 10/15/11; SLJ 11/1/11) [636.1]

3779 Katz, Jon. *Meet the Dogs of Bedlam Farm* (K–2). Photos by author. 2011, Henry Holt $16.99 (978-0-8050-9219-6). 32pp. With many pictures and appealing text, Katz introduces the four dogs that live with him on an upstate New York farm, and the jobs that they do each day. Lexile AD600L (Rev: BL 2/1/11; LMC 5–6/11; SLJ 3/1/11*) [636.7]

FOODS

3780 Ancona, George. *Come and Eat!* (PS–1). Illus. 2011, Charlesbridge $16.95 (978-1-58089-366-4); paper $7.95 (978-1-58089-367-1). 48pp. A lively overview of food customs around the world, with appetizing color photographs. (Rev: BL 6/1/11; SLJ 7/11) [394.1]

3781 Butterworth, Chris. *How Did That Get in My Lunchbox? The Story of Food* (K–3). Illus. by Lucia Gaggiotti. 2011, Candlewick $12.99 (978-0-7636-5005-6). 32pp. Butterworth presents an appealing tour of a typical child's lunch and the origins of the ingredients. (Rev: BL 4/15/11; HB 3–4/11; LMC 8–9/11; SLJ 4/11) [641.3]

3782 Nelson, Robin. *From Cocoa Bean to Chocolate* (K–3). Illus. Series: Start to Finish: Food. 2012, Lerner LB $23.93 (978-076136560-0). 24pp. Bold, full-page photographs add appeal to this account of how cocoa beans get turned into chocolate, starting with the farmer and ending with the wrapper. Also use *From Peanut to Peanut Butter* (2012). (Rev: BL 5/15/12) [664]

3783 Sylver, Adrienne. *Hot Diggity Dog: The History of the Hot Dog* (K–3). Illus. by Elwood H. Smith. 2010, Dutton $16.99 (978-0-525-47897-3). 32pp. So who did invent the hot dog and who propagated it? This overview covers early origins in ancient Rome, popularity in Europe, star role in the United States, and role as astronaut food. (Rev: BL 4/15/10; SLJ 6/1/10) [641.3]

3784 Taus-Bolstad, Stacy. *From Milk to Ice Cream* (K–3). Illus. Series: Start to Finish: Food. 2012, Lerner LB $23.93 (978-076139177-7). 24pp. Bold, full-page photographs add appeal to this account of how milk gets turned into ice cream. *From Grass to Milk* explains how the grass a cow eats becomes nutritious milk (2012). (Rev: BL 5/15/12) [637]

FRUITS

3785 Ziefert, Harriet. *One Red Apple* (PS–2). Illus. by Karla Gudeon. 2009, Blue Apple $16.99 (978-1-934706-67-1). Unpaged. Follows the life of an apple from harvest to store, to picnic, to seed, and to sapling and tree. (Rev: SLJ 11/1/09) [583.73]

VEGETABLES

3786 Sayre, April Pulley. *Rah, Rah, Radishes! A Vegetable Chant* (PS–1). Photos by author. 2011, Simon & Schuster $14.99 (978-1-4424-2141-7). 32pp. A celebration of all things vegetable, with attractive photographs and rhyming text. (Rev: BL 5/1/11; SLJ 6/11*) [641.3]

Leaves and Trees

3787 Preus, Margi. *CelebriTrees: Historic and Famous Trees of the World* (2–5). Illus. by Rebecca Gibbon. 2011, Henry Holt $16.99 (978-0-8050-7829-9). 40pp. An interesting history of 14 trees around the world that are important for their size, longevity, or as witness of important historical or cultural events. Lexile 1020L (Rev: BL 5/1/11; HB 3–4/11; SLJ 2/1/11) [582.16]

Plants

3788 Mooney, Carla. *Sunscreen for Plants* (4–7). Illus. Series: A Great Idea! Going Green. 2009, Norwood LB $18.95 (978-159953344-5). 48pp. Discusses how exposure to the sun affects plants and posits potential inventions that could reduce the problem of sun damage. (Rev: BL 2/15/10) [632]

Seeds

3789 Galbraith, Kathryn O. *Planting the Wild Garden* (PS–3). Illus. by Wendy Anderson Halperin. 2011, Peachtree $15.95 (978-1-56145-563-8). 32pp. This celebration of seed dispersal encourages wonder and appreciation for all the ways nature ensures new generations of flowers. Lexile AD490L (Rev: BL 4/15/11; LMC 11–12/11; SLJ 6/11) [581.467]

3790 Peterson, Cris. *Seed Soil Sun: Earth's Recipe for Food* (K–3). Photos by David R. Lundquist. 2010, Boyds Mills $17.95 (978-1-59078-713-7). Unpaged. The roles of seeds, soil, and sunlight are explained along with the mechanism of photosynthesis in this attractive and accessible book. (Rev: BL 11/1/10; LMC 1–2/11; SLJ 11/1/10) [581.4]

Chemistry

3791 Aloian, Molly. *Mixtures and Solutions* (3–5). Series: Why Chemistry Matters. 2009, Crabtree LB $26.60 (978-0-7787-4243-2). 32pp. A slim introduction to the various types of mixtures and solutions, how they are formed, and how we use them. (Rev: LMC 8–9/09) [541.34]

3792 Brent, Lynnette. *Acids and Bases* (3–5). Series: Why Chemistry Matters. 2009, Crabtree LB $26.60 (978-0-7787-4239-5). 32pp. A slim introduction to the properties of acids and bases, explaining how they exist in our bodies and in the environment. Also use *Chemical Changes, States of Matter,* and *Elements and Compounds* (all 2009). (Rev: LMC 8–9/09) [546.24]

Geology and Geography

Earth and Geology

3793 Gardner, Robert. *Planet Earth Science Fair Projects, Revised and Expanded Using the Scientific Method* (5–8). Series: Earth Science Projects Using the Scientific Method. 2010, Enslow LB $34.60 (978-0-7660-3423-5). 160pp. With a focus on the basics of scientific investigation, this well-organized and attractive volume gives an overview of the topic and provides experiments that support various hypotheses. (Rev: LMC 8–9/10) [550]

3794 Gilpin, Dan. *Planet Earth: What Planet Are You On?* (5–8). Illus. by Simon Basher. 2010, Kingfisher paper $8.99 (978-0-7534-6412-0). 128pp. Geological features of the Earth (such as the core, crust, and volcanoes) are personified as cartoon characters in this informational and entertaining overview of earth science. (Rev: BL 5/15/10; LMC 8–9/10) [550]

3795 Twist, Clint, and Lisa Regan, et al. *Extreme Earth* (3–6). Illus. Series: Ripley's Believe It or Not! Twists. 2010, Mason Crest LB $19.95 (978-142221829-7). 48pp. The basics of earth science are introduced through a lively blend of conversational text, snappy sidebars, and innovative design elements, with a focus on record-breaking earthquakes, hurricanes, volcanic explosions, and so on. Lexile IG1100L (Rev: BL 4/15/11) [550]

Earthquakes and Volcanoes

3796 Aronin, Miriam. *Earthquake in Haiti* (3–5). Series: Code Red. 2010, Bearport LB $25.27 (978-1-936088-66-9). 32pp. This picture book tells the story of the 2010 disaster, referring frequently to the experiences of two survivors, and describes the ongoing recovery efforts. Lexile 910L (Rev: LMC 5–6/11; SLJ 5/1/11)

3797 Benoit, Peter. *The Haitian Earthquake of 2010* (3–5). Illus. Series: A True Book: Disasters. 2011, Scholastic LB $28 (978-053125420-2); paper $6.95 (978-053126625-0). 48pp. With statistics and Web resources, this volume covers the disaster and the aftermath. (Rev: BL 11/15/11) [972.94]

3798 Mara, Wil. *Why Do Earthquakes Happen?* (2–4). Series: Tell Me Why, Tell Me How. 2010, Marshall Cavendish LB $20.95 (978-0-7614-4826-6). 32pp. With easy-to-read text and lots of helpful illustrations, this volume introduces essential concepts relating to tectonic plates and seismic waves. (Rev: BL 3/1/11; SLJ 2/1/11) [551.22]

3799 Person, Stephen. *Devastated by a Volcano!* (3–5). Illus. Series: Disaster Survivors. 2010, Bearport LB $25.27 (978-193608750-1). 32pp. Firsthand accounts bring immediacy to the factual information on the causes and characteristics of volcanic eruptions and our efforts to predict them. (Rev: BL 4/1/10; LMC 10/10) [551.21]

3800 Spilsbury, Louise, and Richard Spilsbury. *Shattering Earthquakes* (3–6). Series: Awesome Forces of Nature. 2010, Heinemann LB $29 (978-1-4329-3784-3). 32pp. "What happens in an earthquake?" "Can earthquakes be predicted?" These and other questions are answered — and case studies look at famous tremors — in this eye-catching volume. (Rev: LMC 11–12/10; SLJ 9/1/10) [551.22]

3801 Stewart, Melissa. *Inside Earthquakes* (5–8). Illus. by Cynthia Shaw. Series: Inside. 2011, Sterling $16.95 (978-140275877-5); paper $9.95 (978-140278163-6). 48pp. A dramatic presentation of information about what causes earthquakes and their impact on the population and environment, with many photographs and gatefolds. (Rev: BL 11/1/11) [551.22]

3802 Stewart, Melissa. *Inside Volcanoes* (5–8). Illus. by Cynthia Shaw. Series: Inside. 2011, Sterling $16.95

(978-140275876-8); paper $9.95 (978-140278164-3). 48pp. A dramatic presentation of information about the different kinds of volcanoes and eruptions and their impact on the population and environment, with many photographs and gatefolds. (Rev: BL 11/1/11) [551.21]

Icebergs and Glaciers

3803 Love, Donna. *The Glaciers Are Melting!* (PS–1). Illus. by Shennen Bersani. 2011, Sylvan Dell $16.95 (978-1-6071-8126-2); paper $8.95 (978-1-6071-8136-1). Unpaged. Presents facts about climate change as animals discuss their worries about the melting glaciers and what can be done about it. **e** Lexile AD680L (Rev: LMC 11–12/11; SLJ 8/1/11) [551.31]

Physical Geography

General and Miscellaneous

3804 Casil, Amy Sterling. *The Creation of Canyons* (5–9). Series: Land Formation: The Shifting, Moving, Changing Earth. 2010, Rosen LB $29.95 (978-1-4358-5296-8). 64pp. Part of a series that addresses how landforms are created and the ways in which scientists seek to understand them, this volume includes useful examples and provides interesting career information. (Rev: LMC 1–2/10)

Deserts

3805 Ceceri, Kathy. *Discover the Desert: The Driest Place on Earth* (4–6). Illus. by Samuel Carbaugh. Series: Discover Your World. 2009, Nomad paper $16.95 (978-1-9346704-6-0). 112pp. A large-format look at deserts and their topography and human and animal inhabitants, with information on famous explorers and preparations you need to make for a desert expedition. (Rev: BL 2/15/10; SLJ 3/10) [910.9154]

3806 Donald, Rhonda Lucas. *Deep in the Desert* (1–3). Illus. by Sherry Neidigh. 2011, Sylvan Dell $16.95 (978-1-60718-125-5); paper $8.95 (978-1-60718-135-4). Unpaged. Donald offers new lyrics for well-known children's songs, describing the desert and the animals that live there; includes facts and activities. **e** (Rev: LMC 11–12/11; SLJ 7/11) [577.54]

3807 Silverman, Buffy. *Desert Food Chains* (4–7). Series: Protecting Food Chains. 2010, Heinemann LB $32 (978-1-4329-3856-7); paper $8.99 (978-1-4329-3863-5). 48pp. With chapter headings that ask questions such

as "What Are the Producers in Deserts?" and "What Are the Decomposers in Deserts?," this volume explores species and food chains in deserts and discusses why we need to protect them. (Rev: SLJ 11/1/10) [577.5]

Forests and Rain Forests

3808 Ganeri, Anita. *Rainforests* (3–5). Illus. by Peter Bull. Series: Explorers. 2011, Kingfisher $10.99 (978-075346590-5). 32pp. An inviting mix of text, sidebars, captions, fact lists, and more add read-appeal to this well-illustrated book about rain forests and the flora and fauna found there. (Rev: BL 2/15/12) [577.34]

3809 Moore, Heidi. *Rain Forest Food Chains* (4–7). Series: Protecting Food Chains. 2010, Heinemann LB $32 (978-1-4329-3860-4); paper $8.99 (978-1-4329-3867-3). 48pp. With chapter headings that ask questions such as "What Are the Producers in Rain Forests?" and "What Are the Decomposers in Rain Forests?," this volume explores species and food chains within rain forests and discusses why we need to protect them. (Rev: SLJ 11/1/10) [577.3]

3810 Simon, Seymour. *Tropical Rainforests* (2–5). Illus. 2010, HarperCollins $16.99 (978-0-06-114253-6); LB $17.89 (978-006114254-3). 32pp. This visually appealing book provides oversize text and excellent color photographs of the flora and fauna of tropical rain forests, some of the products that originate there, and the problem of their destruction. (Rev: BL 10/15/10; SLJ 9/1/10) [578.734]

Prairies and Grasslands

3811 Lunde, Darrin. *After the Kill* (2–4). Illus. by Catherine Stock. 2011, Charlesbridge $16.95 (978-1-57091-743-1); paper $7.95 (978-1-57091-744-8). Unpaged. A grisly and vivid account of predators and prey on the Serengeti Plain. **e** (Rev: HB 7–8/11; SLJ 7/11) [599.7]

3812 Sill, Cathryn. *Grasslands* (2–5). Illus. by John Sill. Series: About Habitat. 2011, Peachtree $16.95 (978-156145559-1). 48pp. Sills introduces the environment, plants, and animals found in grasslands around the world using appealing illustrations and accessible text. (Rev: BL 4/15/11) [577.4]

Rocks, Minerals, and Soil

3813 Franchino, Vicky. *Junior Scientists: Experiment with Soil* (3–5). Illus. Series: Science Explorer Junior. 2010, Cherry Lake LB $27.07 (978-160279837-3). 32pp. Beginning with an overview of the scientific method, this book features soil experiments done with everyday materials. (Rev: BL 10/1/10; LMC 3–4/11) [631]

3814 Green, Dan, and Simon Basher. *Rocks and Minerals: A Gem of a Book!* (5–8). Illus. by Simon Basher. 2009, Kingfisher paper $8.99 (978-075346314-7). 128pp. Friendly cartoon characters narrate this informative introduction to rocks, gems, crystals, fossils, and so forth. (Rev: BL 9/15/09; SLJ 10/09) [500]

3815 Tomecek, Stephen M. *Rocks and Minerals* (1–3). Illus. by Kyle Poling. Series: Jump into Science. 2010, National Geographic $16.95 (978-4-4263-0538-2); LB $25.90 (978-1-4263-0539-9). 32pp. Part geology, part examination of rocks' cultural significance throughout the world, this picture book offers interesting facts with plenty of colorful computer graphics. (Rev: BL 1/1–15/11; SLJ 4/11) [552]

Mathematics

General

3816 Adler, David A. *Fractions, Decimals, and Percents* (3–5). Illus. by Edward Miller. 2010, Holiday House $16.95 (978-082342199-2). 32pp. Using the framework of a county fair, this brightly illustrated book shows how to move comfortably between fractions, decimals, and percents. (Rev: BL 3/1/10) [513.2]

3817 Adler, David A. *Mystery Math: A First Book of Algebra* (2–4). Illus. by Edward Miller. 2011, Holiday House $16.95 (978-0-8234-2289-0). 32pp. A haunted house setting and comic-creepy premise add appeal to this algebra book for beginners. (Rev: BL 10/1/11; SLJ 9/1/11) [512]

3818 Arroyo, Sheri L. *How Crime Fighters Use Math* (4–6). Series: Math in the Real World. 2009, Chelsea Clubhouse $28 (978-1-60413-602-9). 32pp. Measurement, estimation, data analysis, and problem solving are all used in this examination of crime-fighting activities. (Rev: SLJ 3/10)

3819 Cleary, Brian P. *A Fraction's Goal — Parts of a Whole* (K–3). Illus. by Brian Gable. Series: Math Is CATegorical. 2011, Millbrook $16.95 (978-082257881-9). 32pp. Uses humor and charts to introduce fractions (parts of pizzas and groups of people) and their usefulness. (Rev: BL 10/1/11) [513.2]

3820 Dugan, Christine. *Pack It Up: Surface Area and Volume* (3–5). Illus. 2012, Teacher Created Materials paper $8.99 (978-143333461-0). 32pp. Readers are invited to practice their understanding of surface area and volume in this story about a family moving. Also use *Tonight's Concert: Using Data and Graphs, A Sense of Art: Perimeter and Area,* and *Hurricane Hunters: Measures of Central Tendency* (all 2012). (Rev: BL 5/15/12) [510]

3821 Ellis, Julie. *Pythagoras and the Ratios* (4–7). Illus. by Phyllis Hornung Peacock. 2010, Charlesbridge $16.95 (978-1-57091-775-2); paper $7.95 (978-1-57091-776-9). 32pp. An entertaining picture book that explains ratios as young Pythagoras establishes that Octavius's pipes are the wrong length to make melodious music. (Rev: LMC 10/10; SLJ 2/10) [516.2]

3822 Hense, Mary. *How Astronauts Use Math* (4–8). Illus. Series: Math in the Real World. 2009, Chelsea Clubhouse $28 (978-1-60413-610-4). 32pp. A look at how astronauts use math in their everyday activities. Also use *How Fighter Pilots Use Math* (2009). (Rev: SLJ 4/10) [629.45]

3823 Hyland, Tony. *Multiplying and Dividing at the Bake Sale* (3–5). Illus. Series: Real World Math. 2010, Capstone $25.32 (978-142965244-5). 32pp. Corey and his grandfather bake muffins for the school bake sale, and Corey works out how much money is made; the fictional story is followed by a problem-solving activity. (Rev: BL 1/1–15/11; LMC 3–4/11) [641.8]

3824 Noonan, Diana. *Collecting Data in Animal Investigations* (3–5). Illus. Series: Real World Math. 2010, Capstone LB $25.32 (978-142965237-7). 32pp. A class of 4th-graders collect data on animals they see in the park and organize the information in diagrams, charts, and graphs; the fictional stories are followed by a problem-solving activity. (Rev: BL 1/1–15/11; LMC 3–4/11) [590.72]

3825 Orr, Tamra. *Wildfires* (5–8). Illus. Series: Real World Math: Natural Disasters. 2012, Cherry Lake LB $27.07 (978-161080329-8). 32pp. Math problems ranging in difficulty are integrated into this account of wildfires and their causes and impact. (Rev: BL 4/1/12) [363.37]

3826 Yoder, Eric, and Natalie Yoder. *Sixty-five Short Mysteries You Solve with Math!* (3–6). Series: One Minute Mysteries. 2010, Science, Naturally paper $9.95 (978-0-9678020-0-8). 176pp. One-page scenarios set in the home, outdoors, and at camp and sports fields present real-world problems that involve math skills and some creative thought. **e** (Rev: LMC 10/10; SLJ 1/1/11) [793.74]

Geometry

3827 Leedy, Loreen. *Seeing Symmetry* (1–4). Illus. by author. 2012, Holiday House $17.95 (978-082342360-6). 32pp. This engaging, large-format book introduces different kinds of symmetry with clear explanations and examples; includes activities. (Rev: BL 4/15/12; HB 7–8/12; LMC 11–12/12*; SLJ 4/1/12) [516]

Mathematical Puzzles

3828 Larochelle, David. *1+1=5: And Other Unlikely Additions* (K–3). Illus. by Brenda Sexton. 2010, Sterling $14.95 (978-1-4027-5995-6). Unpaged. This arithmetic book challenges foregone conclusions about simple number problems by presenting creative scenarios where one plus one doesn't equal two. (Rev: BL 9/15/10; LMC 11–12/10; SLJ 9/1/10) [513.2]

3829 Slade, Suzanne. *What's the Difference? An Endangered Animal Subtraction Story* (1–3). Illus. by Joan Waites. 2010, Sylvan Dell $16.95 (978-1-60718-070-8); paper $8.95 (978-1-60718-081-4). Unpaged. Part math practice, part animal interest book, this volume introduces 12 endangered species with a rhyming math word problem, a picture, and a paragraph about its population in the wild. (Rev: LMC 10/10; SLJ 6/1/10) [591.68]

Numbers and Number Systems

3830 Schwartz, Joanne. *City Numbers* (3–7). Illus. by Matt Beam. 2011, Groundwood $18.95 (978-1-55498-081-9). 60pp. An unusual look at numbers of all kinds seen in an urban landscape. (Rev: BL 6/1/11; LMC 11–12/11; SLJ 5/1/11) [971.3]

Time, Clocks, and Calendars

3831 Adler, David A. *Time Zones* (2–4). Illus. by Edward Miller. 2010, Holiday House $16.95 (978-0-8234-2201-2). 32pp. Discusses the need for time zones and the history behind the division of the world into 24 zones; with charts, maps, and photographs. (Rev: BL 12/15/10; SLJ 9/1/10) [389]

3832 Bernhard, Durga. *While You Are Sleeping: A Lift-the-Flap Book of Time Around the World* (PS–3). Illus. by author. 2011, Charlesbridge $14.95 (978-1-57091-473-7). 24pp. Flaps are used to show how time zones work, with illustrations of different activities taking place in different countries around the world. Lexile NC480L (Rev: BL 4/15/11; HB 5–6/11; SLJ 3/1/11) [389]

3833 Jenkins, Steve. *Just a Second* (4–7). Illus. by author. 2011, Houghton Mifflin $16.99 (978-061870896-3). 40pp. Jenkins explores time, looking at the amazing things that can take place in a second, a minute, an hour, a month, and a year. (Rev: BL 11/1/11) [529]

Weights and Measures

3834 Adamson, Thomas K., and Heather Adamson. *How Do You Measure Length and Distance?* (PS–2). Series: Measure It! 2010, Capstone LB $25.99 (978-1-4296-4456-3). 32pp. This visually appealing book guides readers through the ways we measure and the tools we use. Also in this series: *How Do You Measure Liquids?*, *How Do You Measure Time?*, and *How Do You Measure Weight?* (Rev: SLJ 4/11) [530.8]

3835 Adler, David A. *Perimeter, Area, and Volume: A Monster Book of Dimensions* (2–4). Illus. by Edward Miller. 2012, Holiday House $16.95 (978-082342290-6). 32pp. Appealing monsters guide young readers through the principles of dimensions, showing how to measure area and calculate volume. (Rev: BL 3/15/12; LMC 8–9/12; SLJ 4/1/12) [516]

3836 Robbins, Ken. *For Good Measure: The Ways We Say How Much, How Far, How Heavy, How Big, How Old* (4–7). 2010, Flash Point $17.99 (978-1-59643-344-1). 48pp. Robbins takes an unusual, highly illustrated approach to explaining various measurements, including the metric system. (Rev: BLO 4/1/10; HB 5–6/10; LMC 5–6/10; SLJ 4/10) [510]

Meteorology

General

3837 Cassino, Mark, and Jon Nelson. *The Story of Snow: The Science of Winter's Wonder* (2–4). Illus. by Nora Aoyagi. 2009, Chronicle $16.99 (978-0-8118-6866-2). 34pp. Dazzling close-up photographs enhance this book about snow crystals and their beautiful diversity. (Rev: BL 12/1/09*; LMC 1–2/10; SLJ 11/1/09) [551.57]

Storms

3838 Bailer, Darice. *Why Does It Thunder and Lightning?* (2–4). Series: Tell Me Why, Tell Me How. 2010, Marshall Cavendish LB $20.95 (978-0-7614-4825-9). 32pp. Answering such questions as "What Makes Thunderstorm Clouds?" and "How Does a Thunderstorm Begin?," this volume introduces essential concepts in easy-to-read text and lots of helpful illustrations. (Rev: BL 3/1/11; SLJ 2/1/11) [551.55]

3839 Benoit, Peter. *Hurricane Katrina* (3–5). Illus. Series: A True Book: Disasters. 2011, Scholastic LB $28 (978-053125421-9); paper $6.95 (978-053126626-7). 48pp. With statistics and Web resources, this volume covers the disaster and the aftermath. (Rev: BL 11/15/11) [976.3]

3840 Carson, Mary Kay. *Inside Hurricanes* (5–8). Illus. 2010, Sterling $16.95 (978-140275880-5); paper $9.95 (978-140277780-6). 48pp. Inventive, eye-catching fold-outs and dramatic photographs enhance this engaging book about hurricanes. (Rev: BL 10/1/10; LMC 1–2/11; SLJ 12/1/10*) [551.552]

3841 Carson, Mary Kay. *Inside Tornadoes* (4–6). 2010, Sterling $16.95 (978-1-4027-5879-9); paper $9.95 (978-1-4027-7781-3). 49pp. Gatefold features enhance this boldly colored overview of tornadoes, how they are formed, and their destructive force. Also use *Inside Hurricanes* (2010). (Rev: SLJ 12/1/10*) [551.55]

3842 Fradin, Judith Bloom, and Dennis B. Fradin. *Tornado! The Story Behind These Twisting, Turning, Spinning, and Spiraling Storms* (4–6). Illus. 2011, National Geographic $16.95 (978-1-4263-0779-9); LB $26.90 (978-1-4263-0780-5). 64pp. Eyewitness stories, newspaper reports, photographs, and statistics make this an exciting and informative survey of U.S. tornadoes through the years. Lexile 1120L (Rev: BL 7/11; LMC 3–4/12*; SLJ 10/1/11) [551.55]

3843 Oxlade, Chris. *Why Why Why — Do Tornadoes Spin?* (4–6). Illus. 2009, Mason Crest $18.95 (978-142221586-9). 32pp. Goofy and accessible, this book uses cartoons and sketches — as well as facts — to answer questions about tornadoes. (Rev: BL 1/1/10) [551.55]

3844 Raum, Elizabeth. *Can You Survive Storm Chasing? An Interactive Survival Adventure* (3–5). Series: You Choose: Survival. 2011, Capstone LB $30.65 (978-1-4296-6587-2); paper $6.95 (978-1-4296-7347-1). 112pp. In this choose-your-own adventure with many endings, readers' decisions will govern their ultimate survival. (Rev: SLJ 12/1/11) [613.6]

3845 Rebman, Renee C. *How Do Tornadoes Form?* (2–4). Series: Tell Me Why, Tell Me How. 2010, Marshall Cavendish LB $20.95 (978-0-7614-4828-0). 32pp. With easy-to-read text and lots of helpful illustrations, this volume introduces essential concepts relating to the formation of tornadoes. (Rev: SLJ 2/1/11) [551.55]

3846 Spilsbury, Louise, and Richard Spilsbury. *Howling Hurricanes* (3–6). Series: Awesome Forces of Nature. 2010, Heinemann LB $29 (978-1-4329-3781-2). 32pp. "Where do hurricanes happen?" "Can people prepare for hurricanes?" These and other questions are answered — and case studies look at famous storms — in this eye-catching volume. (Rev: LMC 11–12/10; SLJ 9/1/10) [551.55]

3847 Stewart, Melissa. *Inside Lightning* (5–8). Illus. by Cynthia Shaw. Series: Inside. 2011, Sterling $16.95 (978-140275878-2). 48pp. A dramatic presentation of information about what causes lightning and its impact on the population and environment, with many photographs and gatefolds. (Rev: BL 11/1/11*) [551.55]

3848 Zelch, Patti R. *Ready, Set . . . WAIT! What Animals Do Before a Hurricane* (PS–3). Illus. by Connie McLennan. 2010, Sylvan Dell $16.95 (978-1-60718-072-2); paper $8.95 (978-1-60718-083-8). Unpaged. Compares human and animal preparations for an approaching storm. (Rev: BL 12/1/10; SLJ 9/1/10) [591.512]

Water

3849 Lyon, George Ella. *All the Water in the World* (PS–K). Illus. by Katherine Tillotson. 2011, Atheneum $15.99 (978-1-4169-7130-6). 40pp. Simple text and appealing illustrations introduce the water cycle and what we can do to save water and keep it clean. (Rev: BL 3/15/11*; HB 5–6/11; LMC 10/11*; SLJ 5/1/11*) [551.48]

3850 Rau, Dana Meachen. *Water* (PS–2). Illus. Series: Bookworms. Nature's Cycles. 2009, Marshall Cavendish $15.95 (978-0-7614-4099-4). 24pp. The concept of how water goes from liquid to vapor to clouds to rain and back again is captured in this simple book suitable for beginning readers. (Rev: SLJ 4/1/10) [508.2]

Weather

3851 Gardner, Robert. *Weather Science Fair Projects, Revised and Expanded Using the Scientific Method* (5–8). Series: Earth Science Projects Using the Scientific Method. 2010, Enslow LB $34.60 (978-0-7660-3424-2). 160pp. With a focus on the basics of scientific investigation, this well-organized and attractive volume gives an overview of the topic and provides experiments that support various hypotheses. (Rev: LMC 8–9/10) [551.63]

3852 Gibbons, Gail. *It's Snowing!* (K–3). Illus. by author. 2011, Holiday House $17.95 (978-0-8234-2237-1). 32pp. The formation of snowflakes, typical locations of snowstorms, record snowfalls, and definitions of various degrees of severity are all presented here, along with illustrations of how we behave before, during, and after snowstorms. (Rev: BL 9/15/11; SLJ 11/1/11) [551.57]

Physics

General

3853 Cook, Trevor. *Experiments with States of Matter* (3–7). Series: Science Lab. 2009, Rosen LB $25.25 (978-1-4358-2805-6). 32pp. A variety of science experiments using simple materials from around the house; each one illustrates a key concept pertaining to the varying states of matter. (Rev: LMC 11–12/09) [530.4]

3854 Mason, Adrienne. *Motion, Magnets, and More: The Big Book of Primary Science* (K–2). Illus. by Claudia Davila. 2011, Kids Can $18.95 (978-155453707-5). 128pp. Materials, structures, states of matter, and forces of motion are covered in this well-illustrated volume that includes experiments that reinforce basic concepts. (Rev: BL 12/1/11; LMC 1–2/12) [500.2]

3855 Solway, Andrew. *Sports Science* (4–9). Series: Why Science Matters. 2009, Heinemann-Raintree $32.86 (978-1-4329-2480-5). 56pp. Geared towards illuminating science's role in our everyday lives, this title provides a thorough, well-researched look at the science of sports. (Rev: LMC 11–12/09)

3856 Taylor-Butler, Christine. *Think Like a Scientist in the Gym* (3–5). Illus. Series: Science Explorer Junior. 2011, Cherry Lake LB $27.07 (978-161080163-8). 32pp. Using the gym and sports as a framework, this book demonstrates how running, throwing, jumping, breathing, and so forth involve principles of physics; with related experiments. (Rev: BL 12/1/11) [507.8]

Energy and Motion

General

3857 Drummond, Allan. *Energy Island: How One Community Harnessed the Wind and Changed Their World* (1–3). Illus. by author. 2011, Farrar $16.99 (978-0-374-32184-0). 40pp. The inspiring story of the Danish island of Samsø's successful efforts to become energy independent, a project started by a visionary teacher and supported by his students and then the whole population. Lexile AD920L (Rev: BL 3/1/11*; LMC 5–6/11; SLJ 3/1/11*) [333.9]

3858 Farrell, Courtney. *Using Alternative Energies* (3–7). Series: Language Arts Explorer: Save the Planet. 2010, Cherry Lake LB $27.07 (978-1-60279-663-8). 32pp. Students are given a mission at the beginning of the book and must use creative thinking and problem solving to gather facts as they travel on a virtual trip researching solar power, wind power, and other alternatives. (Rev: LMC 8–9/10) [333.79]

3859 Gray, Susan H. *Experiments with Motion* (4–6). Illus. Series: True Book: Experiments. 2011, Scholastic LB $28 (978-053126346-4). 48pp. Readers learn about laws governing motion and scientific investigation before tackling experiments using everyday materials. (Rev: BL 12/1/11) [531]

3860 Jakab, Cheryl. *Renewable Energy* (4–7). Series: Global Issues. 2009, Smart Apple Media LB $28.50 (978-1-59920-453-6). 32pp. Offering a global perspective, this volume discusses the benefits of renewable energy and the various challenges the technology faces. (Rev: SLJ 2/10) [333.79]

3861 Leedy, Loreen. *The Shocking Truth About Energy* (K–3). Illus. by author. 2010, Holiday House $17.95 (978-0-8234-2220-3). 32pp. An imaginary bolt of energy named Erg narrates this accessible, engaging book, which offers an introduction to basic energy concepts, explaining the various forms, how they are generated, and pros and cons of each alternative. (Rev: BL 4/15/10; LMC 10/10; SLJ 5/1/10) [333.79]

3862 McLeish, Ewan. *Challenges to Our Energy Supply* (4–8). Series: Can the Earth Survive? 2010, Rosen

LB $26.50 (978-1-4358-5357-7). 48pp. With case studies and suggested strategies for the future, this volume looks at energy shortages around the world and the impact on everyday life. (Rev: LMC 3–4/10; SLJ 1/10) [333.79]

Nuclear Energy

3863 Benoit, Peter. *Nuclear Meltdowns* (3–5). Illus. 2011, Scholastic LB $28 (978-053125422-6); paper $6.95 (978-053126627-4). 48pp. With statistics and Web resources, this volume covers everything from how power plants to work to the accidents at Three Mile Island and Chernobyl. (Rev: BL 11/15/11) [363.17]

3864 Jakubiak, David J. *What Can We Do About Nuclear Waste?* (3–5). Illus. Series: Protecting Our Planet. 2011, Rosen LB $21.25 (978-144884983-3). 24pp. After a basic description of how nuclear energy works, this book looks at our choices for storing and disposing of dangerous nuclear waste. e (Rev: BL 2/15/12) [363.72]

Magnetism and Electricity

3865 Solway, Andrew. *Generating and Using Electricity* (4–9). Series: Why Science Matters. 2009, Heinemann-Raintree $32.86 (978-1-4329-2481-2). 56pp. This appealing guide offers a look at the key role electricity plays in our lives. (Rev: LMC 11–12/09) [537]

Simple Machines

3866 Walker, Sally M., and Roseann Feldmann. *Put Wheels and Axles to the Test* (3–5). Illus. Series: How Do Simple Machines Work? 2011, Lerner LB $27.93 (978-076135326-3). 40pp. With chapters titled "Work," "Machines," "Friction," "Parts of a Wheel and Axle," and "Gears," this book explains concepts and provides simple experiments. (Rev: BL 12/1/11) [621.8078]

3867 Yasuda, Anita. *Explore Simple Machines! 25 Great Projects, Activities, Experiments* (2–4). Illus. by Bryan Stone. Series: Explore Your World. 2011, Nomad paper $12.95 (978-193631382-2). 96pp. Levers, inclined planes, pulleys, screws, wedges, and wheels and axles are introduced and then demonstrated in kid-friendly projects (a crane, a drawbridge, a whirligig, and so forth). (Rev: BL 12/1/11) [621.8]

Space Exploration

3868 Bortz, Fred. *Seven Wonders of Space Technology* (5–8). Illus. 2011, Lerner LB $33.26 (978-076135453-6). 80pp. Observatories, satellites, the International Space Station, and the Mars Rovers are among the pieces of space technology covered in this volume that also looks at the future. (Rev: BL 3/1/11) [629.4]

3869 Nardo, Don. *Destined for Space: Our Story of Exploration* (3–5). Illus. 2012, Capstone LB $31.86 (978-142967540-6); paper $8.95 (978-142968024-0). 64pp. The history of space exploration is narrated in simple text accompanied by bright illustrations. (Rev: BLO 2/27/12) [629.45]

Technology, Engineering, and Industry

General and Miscellaneous Industries and Inventions

3870 Arato, Rona. *Design It! The Ordinary Things We Use Every Day and the Not-So-Ordinary Ways They Came to Be* (4–6). Illus. by Claudia Newell. 2010, Tundra paper $20.95 (978-0-88776-846-0). 72pp. The inspiration and design behind many commonly used and taken-for-granted objects are explored in this well-organized volume that asks readers to consider function, usability, ergonomics, aesthetics and environmental impact of objects. (Rev: LMC 3–4/11; SLJ 1/1/11) [745.2]

3871 Becker, Helaine. *What's the Big Idea: Inventions That Changed Life on Earth* (3–6). Illus. by Steve Attoe. 2009, Maple Tree $29.95 (978-189734960-1); paper $19.95 (978-189734961-8). 96pp. This appealing, conversational book looks at inventions throughout history that met various human needs, looking in particular at design and at high-interest facts; suitable for browsing. (Rev: BL 2/1/10; LMC 3–4/10*) [609]

3872 Bodden, Valerie. *Carousels* (K–3). Illus. Series: Thrill Rides. 2012, Creative Education $17.95 (978-160818112-4). 24pp. A history of merry-go-rounds, with beautiful photographs and emphasis on the fact that even the smallest children are allowed aboard. (Rev: BL 4/1/12) [791.06]

3873 Boothroyd, Jennifer. *From Marbles to Video Games: How Toys Have Changed* (K–3). Illus. Series: Comparing Past and Present. 2011, Lerner LB $25.26 (978-076136746-8); paper $7.95 (978-076137841-9). 32pp. Charting the evolution of toys from jacks to Pokémon, this book provides readers with many thought-provoking comparisons as it examines changes in materials, marketing, and habits. (Rev: BL 10/1/11) [790.1]

3874 Gates, Phil. *Nature Got There First: Inventions Inspired by Nature* (3–6). Illus. 2010, Kingfisher $16.99 (978-075346410-6). 64pp. Gates explores similarities between nature and technology in this attractive volume suitable for browsing. (Rev: BL 9/1/10; LMC 11–12/10) [508]

3875 Kent, Peter. *Technology* (4–7). Illus. Series: Navigators. 2009, Kingfisher $12.99 (978-075346307-9). 48pp. For browsers and those interested in learning about exciting technologies — everything from new developments in computers and electronics to nanotechnology, wave farming, and superstructures, this is a well-designed informative volume. (Rev: BLO 11/1/09; LMC 1–2/10) [500]

3876 Lee, Dora. *Biomimicry: Inventions Inspired by Nature* (3–6). Illus. by Margot Thompson. 2011, Kids Can $18.95 (978-1-55453-467-8). 40pp. A fascinating, large-format and well-illustrated survey of facets of nature that have inspired human inventions and may do so in the future, organized in such chapters as "Medical Marvels" and "Magic Materials"; suitable for browsing. (Rev: BL 9/15/11; SLJ 11/1/11) [608]

3877 *Nylon* (K–1). Illus. Series: Investigate Materials. 2012, Nomad $16.95 (978-193631397-6). 24pp. A clean, spare layout and bright photographs add appeal to this exploration of where nylon comes from and how it's used. (Rev: BL 4/1/12)

3878 Rau, Dana Meachen. *Fireworks* (2–4). Illus. Series: Surprising Science. 2010, Marshall Cavendish LB $20.95 (978-076144868-6). 24pp. Discusses the history of fireworks and how they are made, and includes safety information. (Rev: BL 4/1/11; LMC 8–9/11) [662]

3879 Ye, Ting-Xing. *The Chinese Thought of It: Amazing Inventions and Innovations* (5–8). Illus. 2009, Annick LB $19.95 (978-155451196-9); paper $9.95 (978-155451195-2). 48pp. Famous inventions from 37 centuries of Chinese history are presented in this well-organized book. (Rev: BLO 11/15/09) [609.51]

Aeronautics and Airplanes

3880 Benoit, Peter. *The Hindenburg Disaster* (3–5). Series: A True Book: Disasters. 2011, Children's Press LB $28 (978-0-531-20626-3); paper $6.95 (978-0-531-28995-2). 48pp. Benoit examines the disaster and provides a history of airships, photographs, maps, and statistics. (Rev: LMC 3–4/12; SLJ 11/1/11) [363.124]

3881 Finkelstein, Norman H. *Three Across: The Great Transatlantic Air Race of 1927* (5–8). Illus. 2008, Boyds Mills $17.95 (978-159078462-4). 136pp. Finkelstein focuses on the first three fliers to make it across the Atlantic Ocean in this interesting account that conveys the flavor of the Roaring Twenties. (Rev: BL 9/1/08; LMC 11–12/08; SLJ 11/1/08; VOYA 12/08) [629.130]

3882 Mooney, Carla. *Pilotless Planes* (5–7). Illus. Series: A Great Idea. 2010, Norwood LB $25.27 (978-1-59953-381-0). 48pp. An interesting account of the development and potential uses of "drones" in military and civilian situations. (Rev: BL 11/1/10; SLJ 1/1/11) [623.74]

3883 Parker, Vic. *My First Trip on an Airplane* (K–2). Illus. Series: Growing Up. 2011, Heinemann LB $22 (978-1-4329-4801-6). 24pp. This reassuring book gives first-time plane passengers a sense of what to expect on the ground and in the air. (Rev: BL 7/11; SLJ 6/11) [387.7]

3884 Verstraete, Larry. *Surviving the Hindenburg* (3–5). Illus. by David Geister. 2012, Sleeping Bear $16.95 (978-158536787-0). 32pp. The true story of the Hindenburg disaster is told here from the perspective of 14-year-old cabin boy Werner Franz, and includes detailed illustrations. (Rev: BL 4/1/12; LMC 11–12/12; SLJ 8/12) [363.12]

Building and Construction

General

3885 Barker, Geoff. *Incredible Skyscrapers* (5–7). Illus. Series: Superstructures. 2010, Amicus LB $19.95 (978-160753133-3). 32pp. Sky-scraping structures from around the world are profiled in this book, which offers technical explanations of the engineering feats required in building such a structure. (Rev: BL 7/11) [720]

3886 Goldish, Meish. *Amazing Amusement Park Rides* (1–5). Illus. Series: So Big Compared to What? 2011, Bearport LB $22.61 (978-161772304-9). 24pp. A look at amazing structures around the world, with colorful photographs, statistics, and size comparisons. (Rev: BL 1/1/12; SLJ 2/12) [791.06]

3887 Goldish, Meish. *Spectacular Skyscrapers* (1–5). Illus. Series: So Big Compared to What? 2011, Bearport LB $22.61 (978-161772303-2). 24pp. With dramatic photographs, statistics, and size comparisons, this volume introduces some of the tallest buildings in the world and provides historical context. (Rev: BL 1/1/12; SLJ 2/12) [720]

3888 Graham, Ian. *Amazing Stadiums* (5–7). Series: Superstructures. 2010, Amicus LB $28.50 (978-1-60753-131-9). 32pp. With discussion of stadiums past and future, this book looks at nine specific structures around the world and gives information on the architects and the challenges they faced. (Rev: BL 7/11; SLJ 11/1/10) [725]

3889 Graham, Ian. *Fabulous Bridges* (5–7). Series: Superstructures. 2010, Amicus LB $28.50 (978-1-60753-132-6). 32pp. With discussion of bridges past and future, this book looks at nine specific structures around the world and gives information on the architects and the challenges they faced. Also use *Tremendous Tunnels* (2010). (Rev: BL 7/11; SLJ 11/1/10) [624.2]

3890 Sandler, Michael. *Freaky-Strange Buildings* (1–5). Illus. Series: So Big Compared to What? 2011, Bearport LB $22.61 (978-161772305-6). 24pp. Unusual structures featured here include the Burj Al Arab Hotel in Dubai, which resembles the sail of an Arab boat, and the Guggenheim Museum in Bilboa, Spain. Also use *Stupendous Sports Stadiums* (2011). (Rev: BL 1/1/12; SLJ 2/12) [720]

3891 Wearing, Judy, and Tom Riddolls. *Golden Gate Bridge* (4–7). Illus. Series: Structural Wonders. 2009, Weigl LB $18.20 (978-160596136-1). 32pp. Looks at the history, construction, and design of the bridge, with period photographs and information on key individuals. (Rev: BL 9/15/09; SLJ 11/09) [624.2]

Houses

3892 Laroche, Giles. *If You Lived Here: Houses of the World* (K–3). Illus. by author. 2011, Houghton Mifflin $16.99 (978-0-547-23892-0). 32pp. Attractive cut-paper collages invite readers to explore 16 very different kinds of homes around the world. e Lexile NC1170L (Rev: BL 10/15/11; HB 9–10/11; SLJ 9/1/11*) [392.3]

Clothing, Textiles, and Jewelry

3893 Shaffer, Jody Jensen. *Blue Jeans Before the Store* (1–3). Illus. by Dan McGeehan. Series: Before the Store. 2012, Child's World LB $28.50 (978-160973628-6). 32pp. This well-designed title encourages readers to consider how a pair of jeans is made — from how the cotton is grown, to the fabric created at the textile mill, to the sewing in a factory, and eventually the selling in a store. (Rev: BL 4/1/12) [338.47687]

Computers and Automation

3894 Cindrich, Sharon. *A Smart Girl's Guide to the Internet* (3–7). Illus. by Ali Douglass. 2009, American Girl paper $9.95 (978-1-59369-599-6). 96pp. This colorful and appealing volume is subtitled *How to Connect with Friends, Find What You Need, and Stay Safe Online* and provides relevant guidance to games, blogs, games, music, and so forth along with quizzes, lists, and other features. (Rev: LMC 1–2/10) [004.67]

3895 Graham, Ian. *Robot Technology* (4–7). Illus. Series: New Technology. 2011, Black Rabbit LB $34.25 (978-159920533-5). 48pp. Describes the kinds of robots being used in various environments (space, military, factories, hospitals) and the technology evolutions taking place. (Rev: BL 10/15/11) [629.8]

3896 Truesdell, Ann. *Get to the Right Site* (3–5). Illus. Series: Information Explorer Junior. 2012, Cherry Lake LB $27.07 (978-161080365-6). 32pp. This research-friendly guide provides solid advice on how to evaluate Web sites. (Rev: BL 4/1/12) [025.042]

Electronics

3897 Oxlade, Chris. *Gaming Technology* (4–7). Illus. Series: New Technology. 2011, Black Rabbit LB $34.25 (978-159920531-1). 48pp. An attractive (if soon dated) introduction to the technology used in creating video games. (Rev: BL 10/15/11) [794.8]

Television, Motion Pictures, Radio, and Recording

3898 Hirschmann, Kris. *HDTV: High Definition Television* (4–6). Series: Great Idea. 2010, Norwood LB $25.27 (978-1-59953-379-7). 48pp. Hirschmann looks at the development of high-definition television, how it works, and how it changes the way we watch TV, with "Did You Know" boxes, photographs, and useful Web sites. (Rev: SLJ 1/1/11) [384.55]

3899 Kinney, Jeff. *The Wimpy Kid Movie Diary: How Greg Heffley Went Hollywood* (4–8). Illus. 2010, Abrams $14.95 (978-081099616-8). 208pp. Kinney offers a behind-the-scenes glimpse at the making of *Diary of a Wimpy Kid: The Movie* in this engrossing book. Lexile 1000L (Rev: BLO 3/15/10) [791.43]

Transportation

General

3900 Askew, Amanda. *Loaders* (PS–2). Illus. Series: Mighty Machines. 2010, Firefly paper $5.95 (978-155407706-9). 24pp. How loaders work — and why we use them — are explored in this clear early reader. Also use *Cranes* and *Diggers* (both 2010). (Rev: BL 10/15/10) [621.8]

3901 Ganeri, Anita. *Things That Go* (K–2). Illus. by Mark Bergin. Series: Flip the Flaps. 2010, Kingfisher $9.99 (978-0-7534-6409-0). 18pp. With a single question-and-answer flap per spread, this appealing book presents various kinds of transportation with large-font text. (Rev: BL 2/1/11; SLJ 4/11) [629]

3902 Gifford, Clive. *Things That Go* (3–5). Illus. by Peter Bull. Series: Explorers. 2011, Kingfisher $10.99 (978-075346593-6). 32pp. An inviting mix of text, sidebars, captions, fact lists, and more add read-appeal to this well-illustrated book about vehicles including cars, planes, boats, and rockets. (Rev: BL 2/15/12)

3903 Isaacs, Sally Senzell. *Stagecoaches and Railroads* (4–6). Illus. Series: All About America. 2012, Kingfisher LB $19.89 (978-075346696-4); paper $9.99 (978-075346516-5). 32pp. In 13 highly illustrated spreads, this informative book looks at the transportation system that made it possible to develop the West — steamboats, stagecoaches, and of course the railroads. (Rev: BL 4/15/12; SLJ 3/12) [388]

Automobiles and Trucks

3904 Bearce, Stephanie. *All About Electric and Hybrid Cars and Who's Driving Them* (4–7). Series: Tell Your Parents. 2010, Mitchell Lane LB $29.95 (978-1-58415-763-2). 64pp. With photographs and graphics, this is an attractive introduction to the mechanics and benefits of hybrid and electric cars. (Rev: BL 10/1/09; LMC 1–2/10)

3905 Benjamin, Daniel. *Prius* (4–6). Series: Green Cars. 2010, Marshall Cavendish LB $19.95 (978-1-60870-011-0). 48pp. Benjamin introduces the technology used in the Toyota hybrid and discusses the environmental benefits of this eco-friendly car. (Rev: SLJ 1/1/11) [629.22]

3906 Economy, Peter. *New Car Design* (1–3). Illus. Series: We Both Read. 2010, Treasure Bay $9.95 (978-160115243-5); paper $4.99 (978-160115244-2). 44pp. Designed to be shared between a child and a parent or tutor, this book features an appealing overview of the process of car design. (Rev: BLO 8/10) [629.222]

3907 Lew, Kristi. *Volt* (4–6). Series: Green Cars. 2010, Marshall Cavendish LB $19.95 (978-1-60870-013-4). 48pp. Lew reviews the battery technology used in the Chevrolet Volt and the future of electric cars. (Rev: SLJ 1/1/11) [629.22]

3908 Murphy, John. *The Eisenhower Interstate System* (5–8). Series: Building America: Then and Now. 2009, Chelsea House $35 (978-1-60413-067-6). 120pp. This book about the Eisenhower Interstate System includes illustrative maps, primary source documents, Web sites, a timeline, and glossary. (Rev: LMC 10/09)

3909 Power, Bob. *Dodge Vipers* (3–6). Illus. Series: Wild Wheels. 2011, Gareth Stevens LB $26.60 (978-143395822-9). 32pp. With a V-10 engine, the Viper is one the fastest cars available today; learn all about the car's history, horsepower, and track performance here. Also use *Ferraris, Maseratis,* and *Lamborghinis* (all 2011). (Rev: BL 12/1/11) [629.222]

3910 Rau, Dana Meachen. *Cars* (PS–1). Series: Bookworms. We Go! 2009, Marshall Cavendish $15.95 (978-0-7614-4078-9). 24pp. A very basic introduction to cars and trucks and their uses, suitable for beginning readers. (Rev: SLJ 4/1/10) [629.22]

3911 Swanson, Jennifer. *How Hybrid Cars Work* (4–6). Illus. by Glen Mullaly. Series: How Things Work. 2011, Child's World LB $18.95 (978-160973217-2). 32pp. Cartoon characters — a caveman and a robot — narrate this overview of the technology and environmental benefits involved in hybrid cars. (Rev: BL 10/1/11*) [629.222]

3912 Warhol, Tom. *Aptera* (4–6). Series: Green Cars. 2010, Marshall Cavendish LB $19.95 (978-1-60870-008-0). 48pp. Warhol looks at the technology used in the Aptera, a futuristic car that appeared in a Star Trek movie. (Rev: SLJ 1/1/11) [629.22]

3913 Zabludoff, Marc. *Ebox* (4–6). Series: Green Cars. 2010, Marshall Cavendish LB $19.95 (978-1-60870-009-7). 48pp. Zabludoff reviews the technology used in the eBox and the future of electric cars. (Rev: SLJ 1/1/11) [629.22]

Railroads

3914 Rau, Dana Meachen. *Trains* (PS–1). Series: Bookworms. We Go! 2009, Marshall Cavendish $15.95 (978-0-7614-4081-9). 24pp. A very basic introduction to trains and their uses, suitable for beginning readers. (Rev: SLJ 4/1/10) [625.2]

3915 Steele, Philip. *Trains: The Slide-Out, See-Through Story of World-Famous Trains and Railroads* (K–6). Illus. by Sebastian Quigley and Nicholas Forder. Series: Legendary Journeys. 2010, Kingfisher $19.99 (978-

0-7534-6465-6). 30pp. Readers explore railroads in spreads covering the history, some of the most famous trains, and even the architecture of key stations; with photographs, diagrams, maps, and interactive features. (Rev: BL 12/15/10; SLJ 5/1/11) [385.09]

3916 Zimmermann, Karl. *The Stourbridge Lion: America's First Locomotive* (1–3). Illus. by Steven Walker. 2012, Boyds Mills $16.95 (978-159078859-2). 32pp. Tells the story of the first locomotive, brought to America from England, to haul coal from the Pennsylvania coalfields to the canals. (Rev: BL 4/1/12; LMC 11–12/12; SLJ 8/12) [388]

Ships, Boats, and Lighthouses

3917 Benoit, Peter. *The Titanic Disaster* (3–5). Illus. Series: True Book: Disasters. 2011, Children's Press LB $26 (978-0-531-20627-0); paper $6.95 (978-0-531-28996-9). 48pp. A clear account of the disaster, covering the construction of the vessel, the safety measures, and the mistakes made by the crew. (Rev: BL 4/1/11; SLJ 11/1/11) [910.916]

3918 Burgan, Michael. *Titanic* (3–8). Illus. by Eldon Doty. Series: Truth and Rumors. 2010, Capstone LB $25.32 (978-1-4296-3951-4). 32pp. Burgan clarifies certain aspects of the construction and final voyage of the *Titanic*, answering questions like "Was the *Titanic* disaster predicted before 1912?" and "Did an officer kill a passenger?," and finishes with a chapter on how to tell the difference between fact and fiction. (Rev: LMC 11–12/10) [910.45]

3919 Cerullo, Mary M. *Shipwrecks: Exploring Sunken Cities Beneath the Sea* (5–8). 2009, Dutton $18.99 (978-0-525-47968-0). 64pp. Cerullo looks at two well-preserved shipwrecks, describing the sinkings themselves, the state of the wrecks today which are home to a variety of marine life, and the technology used to explore these environments. (Rev: BL 12/1/09; SLJ 1/10; VOYA 12/09) [930.1028]

3920 Denenberg, Barry. *Titanic Sinks!* (5–8). Illus. 2011, Viking $19.99 (978-067001243-5). 80pp. Blending fact and fiction, this oversize volume infuses real information about the sinking with imagined sensationalistic newspaper articles, written by a victim of the disaster, that add energy and drama. (Rev: BL 10/15/11*; HB 3–4/12; LMC 3–4/12; SLJ 11/11) [910.9163]

3921 Gunderson, Jessica. *Your Life as a Cabin Attendant on the Titanic* (3–6). Illus. by Rachel Dougherty. Series: The Way It Was. 2012, Picture Window LB $25.99 (978-140487158-8); paper $7.95 (978-140487248-6). 32pp. Follows the experiences of a 20-year-old cabin attendant, one of only 18 female stewards, as the *Titanic* sails toward its doom. (Rev: BL 4/15/12) [910.9163]

3922 Hopkinson, Deborah. *Titanic: Voices from the Disaster* (4–8). Illus. 2012, Scholastic $17.99 (978-

054511674-9). 304pp. With diagrams, maps, charts, and period photographs, this account also draws on survivor letters as well as newspaper and other reports. ∩ (Rev: BL 12/1/11; HB 3–4/12; LMC 5–6/12; SLJ 2/12*; VOYA 4/12) [910.9163]

3923 Lassieur, Allison. *Can You Survive the Titanic? An Interactive Survival Guide Adventure* (3–5). Series: You Choose: Survival. 2011, Capstone LB $30.65 (978-1-4296-6586-5); paper $6.95 (978-1-4296-7351-8). 112pp. In this choose-your-own adventure offering, readers make choices in a number of situations that ultimately determine whether or not they would have survived the shipwreck; in the process they learn details of the ship, the circumstances, and the social differences among passengers. (Rev: HB 3–4/12; SLJ 12/1/11) [910.9163]

3924 Rau, Dana Meachen. *Boats* (PS–1). Series: Bookworms. We Go! 2009, Marshall Cavendish $15.95 (978-0-7614-4076-5). 24pp. A very basic introduction to boats and their uses, suitable for beginning readers. (Rev: SLJ 4/1/10) [623.82]

3925 Wishinsky, Frieda. *Remembering the Titanic* (2–4). Illus. Series: Scholastic Reader. 2012, Scholastic paper $3.99 (978-054535844-6). 32pp. Archival photographs, reproductions, and underwater images of the wreck add drama to this account. (Rev: BL 3/1/12) [910.916]

Weapons, Submarines, and the Armed Forces

3926 Alvarez, Carlos. *AC-130H/U Gunships* (4–6). Illus. Series: Military Machines. 2010, Children's Press LB $19.95 (978-160014493-6). 24pp. A dynamic layout and plenty of action shots enhance this detailed, technical profile of the enormous air force plane that acts as a shield for ground troops; suitable for reluctant readers. Also use *AH-1W Super Cobras, MH-53E Sea Dragons,* and *Strykers* (all 2010). (Rev: BL 11/15/10) [623.74]

3927 Bodden, Valerie. *Tanks* (2–4). Illus. Series: Built for Battle. 2012, Creative Education LB $17.95 (978-160818129-2). 24pp. This volume looks at the history of tanks, some famous tanks, how they perform in battle, and their parts and crews. (Rev: BL 4/1/12) [623.7]

3928 Boos, Ben. *Swords: An Artist's Devotion* (4–7). Illus. by author. 2008, Candlewick $24.99 (978-076363148-2). 96pp. In this large-format book, masterfully crafted swords used by everyone from peasants to sultans and in many countries over many centuries are illustrated and described in detail. (Rev: BLO 11/1/08; SLJ 10/1/08) [623.4]

3929 Goldish, Meish. *Coast Guard: Civilian to Guardian* (4–7). Illus. Series: Becoming a Soldier. 2010, Bearport LB $22.61 (978-193608812-6). 24pp. Recent recruits' journeys from enlistment through placement, conditioning, training, and graduation are presented in this true-to-life book that doesn't gloss over the rigors of military life. (Rev: BL 10/1/10) [363.28]

3930 Goldish, Meish. *Horses, Donkeys, and Mules in the Marines* (3–5). Illus. 2012, Bearport LB $23.93 (978-161772453-4). 24pp. Explores the roles of animals in the Marine Corps over the years, the training they undergo, and their current missions. (Rev: BLO 3/1/12) [359.9]

3931 Hamilton, John. *Navy SEALs* (4–6). Illus. Series: United States Armed Forces. 2011, ABDO LB $18.95 (978-161783067-9). 32pp. Introduces the Navy SEALs and their training and equipment, with some of their history and an account of the raid on Osama bin Laden's compound and other missions. (Rev: BL 10/1/11) [359.9]

3932 Peppas, Lynn. *Powerful Armored Vehicles* (2–4). Illus. Series: Vehicles on the Move. 2011, Crabtree LB $26.60 (978-077872750-7). 32pp. This detail-rich title provides readers with photographs of armored vehicles of various nations. Also use *Military Helicopters: Flying into Battle, Fighter Jets: Defending the Skies,* and *Aircraft Carriers: Runways at Sea* (all 2012). (Rev: BL 3/1/12) [623.74]

3933 Schwartz, Heather E. *Women of the U.S. Air Force: Aiming High* (3–7). Series: Snap: Women in the U.S. Armed Forces. 2011, Capstone LB $26.65 (978-1-4296-5449-4). 32pp. A real-life story of a female Air Force recruit adds personal appeal to this title that explores women's history and growing presence and importance in the U.S. Air Force. Also use *Women of the U.S. Navy: Making Waves* (2011). (Rev: SLJ 6/11) [358.4]

Recreation

Crafts

General and Miscellaneous

3934 Bell-Rehwoldt, Sheri. *The Kids' Guide to Duct Tape Projects* (3–5). Illus. 2011, Capstone LB $26.65 (978-142966010-5). 32pp. The title says it all: here are step-by-step instructions for a variety of practical projects. (Rev: BL 2/15/12) [745.5]

3935 Gillman, Claire, and Sam Martin. *The Kids' Winter Fun Book* (3–5). Illus. 2011, Barron's paper $12.99 (978-076414726-5). 128pp. This is a comprehensive guide to cold-weather activities, with ideas divided into four sections: crafting, outdoor play, indoor play, and feasting. (Rev: BL 12/15/11; SLJ 1/12) [745.5]

3936 Henry, Sally, and Trevor Cook. *Eco-Crafts* (4–8). Photos by authors. Series: Make Your Own Art. 2011, Rosen LB $25.25 (978-1-4488-1582-1); paper $11.75 (978-1-4488-1611-8). 32pp. Craft projects here — glow jars, a bird feeder, cat bookends, and so forth — feature natural or reused materials or support wildlife in some way. Also recommended in this series: *Making Mosaics* (2011). (Rev: SLJ 7/11) [745.5]

3937 Icanberry, Mark. *LooLeDo: Extraordinary Projects from Ordinary Objects* (K–3). Illus. 2010, LooLeDo $12.95 (978-189332712-2). 96pp. The creator of the Web site LooLeDo presents 31 easy-to-follow, well-illustrated projects using household and recycled materials. (Rev: BLO 11/15/10) [746.5]

3938 Mooney, Carla. *Amazing African Projects You Can Build Yourself* (4–7). Illus. by Megan Stearns. Series: Build It Yourself. 2010, Nomad paper $15.95 (978-1-9346704-1-5). Unpaged. Full of information about all aspects of Africa, this volume includes 25 projects — such as a mask, a basket, and rock paintings — made with everyday materials. e Lexile IG930L (Rev: SLJ 10/1/10) [745.5096]

3939 Oldham, Todd. *Kid Made Modern* (3–6). Illus. 2009, AMMO $22.95 (978-1-934429-36-5). 192pp. In addition to acquainting readers with modern design, this book includes a variety of child-friendly craft projects, including paper lanterns and jewelry, that require varying levels of skill. (Rev: BL 12/15/09; SLJ 2/10) [700]

3940 Ross, Kathy. *One-of-a-Kind Stamps and Crafts* (3–6). Illus. by Nicole in den Bosch. 2010, Millbrook $25.26 (978-0-8225-9216-7); paper $7.95 (978-1-58013-885-7). 48pp. Offers clear instructions on creating 20 stamps using beads, buttons, foam shapes, coins, and so forth. (Rev: SLJ 4/1/10) [761]

American Historical Crafts

3941 Mooney, Carla. *George Washington: 25 Great Projects You Can Build Yourself* (4–7). Illus. by Samuel Carbaugh. Series: Build It Yourself. 2010, Nomad paper $15.95 (978-1-934670-63-7). 121pp. Part Washington biography, part colonial crafts book, this volume provides plenty of historical information while also giving clear instructions for activities such as making swords and wigs. (Rev: BL 3/1/11; SLJ 3/1/11) [973.4]

Clay and Other Modeling Crafts

3942 Cuxart, Bernadette. *Modeling Clay Animals: Easy-to-Follow Projects in Simple Steps* (1–4). Illus. 2010, Barron's paper $9.99 (978-0-7641-4579-7). 96pp. Cuxart introduces a few basic shapes that can be repeated to form different animals in this clear guide. (Rev: BL 12/15/10; SLJ 12/1/10) [731.42]

Drawing and Painting

3943 Bergin, Mark. *How to Draw Pets* (4–7). Illus. Series: How to Draw. 2011, Rosen LB $25.25 (978-144884511-8). 32pp. Cats, dogs, and rabbits are among the animals featured in this slim volume that shows how to use pencils, ink, charcoal, and pastels. (Rev: BL 11/1/11) [743.6]

3944 Clay, Kathryn. *How to Draw Mythical Creatures* (4–6). Illus. by Anne Timmons. 2009, Capstone $25.32 (978-142962307-0). 32pp. Mermaids, dragons, pixies, unicorns — all these and more are presented with black-and-white sketches followed by a full-color illustration; useful for relatively experienced young artists. (Rev: BLO 11/15/09) [743]

3945 Gonyea, Mark. *A Book About Color* (2–5). Illus. by author. 2010, Henry Holt $19.99 (978-0-8050-9055-0). 96pp. An introduction to primary and secondary colors, the color wheel, and properties such as warmth. (Rev: BL 2/15/10; HB 5–6/10; SLJ 3/1/10) [700]

3946 Hart, Christopher. *You Can Draw Cartoon Animals: A Simple Step-by-Step Drawing Guide* (2–6). Illus. by author. Series: Just for Kids! 2009, Walter Foster paper $12.99 (978-1-60058-611-8). 120pp. Simple instructions help readers learn to draw a variety of wild and domestic animals. (Rev: SLJ 4/10) [741.5]

3947 Kesselring, Susan. *Five Steps to Drawing Faces* (3–6). Illus. by Dana Regan. 2011, Child's World LB $25.64 (978-160973197-7). 32pp. This straightforward drawing book helps children draw a variety of different faces and expressions. (Rev: BL 11/1/11) [743.4]

3948 LaBaff, Stephanie. *Draw Aliens and Space Objects in 4 Easy Steps: Then Write a Story* (3–5). Illus. by Tom LaBaff. Series: Drawing in 4 Easy Steps. 2012, Enslow LB $23.93 (978-076603841-7). 48pp. A wildly imaginative gallery of astronauts, aliens, robots, spacecraft is combined with advice on incorporating the images into a story. (Rev: BL 4/1/12) [743]

3949 Lee, Frank. *Telling the Story in Your Graphic Novel* (4–6). Illus. Series: How to Draw Your Own Graphic Novel. 2012, Rosen LB $12.30 (978-144886453-9). 32pp. This series volume helps readers to conceive story lines and create drama suitable for graphic novels. (Rev: BL 3/15/12) [741.5]

3950 Masiello, Ralph. *Ralph Masiello's Farm Drawing Book* (1–4). Illus. by author. Series: Drawing Book. 2012, Charlesbridge $16.95 (978-157091537-6); paper $7.95 (978-157091538-3). 32pp. Clear instructions for drawing farm animals and fixtures are appended with bits of folk trivia, songs, information, and farm crafts. e (Rev: BL 12/15/11) [743.6]

3951 Masiello, Ralph. *Ralph Masiello's Robot Drawing Book* (2–5). Illus. by author. 2011, Charlesbridge $16.95 (978-1-57091-535-2); paper $7.95 (978-157091536-9).

32pp. Step-by-step directions for drawing ten colorful robots. (Rev: BLO 7/11; SLJ 8/1/11) [743]

3952 Peot, Margaret. *Inkblot: Drip, Splat, and Squish Your Way to Creativity* (4–6). Illus. by author. 2011, Boyds Mills $19.95 (978-1-59078-720-5). 56pp. A large-format introduction to creating inkblot art and using them to develop ideas. (Rev: BL 5/1/11; SLJ 5/11*) [751.4]

3953 Roza, Greg. *Drawing Dracula* (3–6). Illus. Series: Drawing Movie Monsters Step-by-Step. 2010, Windmill LB $25.65 (978-1-61533-015-7); paper $12.85 (978-1-61533-021-8). 24pp. Straightforward step-by-step instructions teach readers how to recreate the famous vampire. Also use *Drawing Frankenstein, Drawing Godzilla,* and *Drawing King Kong* (2010). e (Rev: SLJ 5/11) [743]

3954 Sikorski, Joy, and Nick Sunday. *How to Draw a Happy Witch and 99 Things That Go Bump in the Night* (K–3). Illus. by Joy Sikorski. 2011, Sterling paper $9.95 (978-1-4027-5708-2). 96pp. This drawing book includes instructions for Halloween-inspired items (a witch, a jack-o-lantern) within a story about a nighttime expedition visit through wetlands and on to a jazz club. (Rev: BL 11/1/11; SLJ 10/1/11) [741.2]

Masks and Mask Making

3955 Henry, Sally, and Trevor Cook. *Making Masks* (4–8). Photos by authors. Series: Make Your Own Art. 2011, Rosen LB $25.25 (978-1-4488-1583-8); paper $11.75 (978-1-4488-1613-2). 32pp. Color photographs and clear instructions add appeal to this book detailing a variety of creative mask projects. (Rev: SLJ 7/11) [731.785]

Paper Crafts

3956 Castleforte, Brian. *Papertoy Monsters: 50 Cool Papertoys You Can Make Yourself!* (4–7). Illus. by Robert James. 2011, Workman paper $16.95 (978-0-7611-5882-0). 231pp. Fifty different paper craft projects are contained within this punch-out-and-assemble collection. (Rev: BL 12/15/10; SLJ 4/11) [745]

3957 Henry, Sally, and Trevor Cook. *Origami* (4–8). Photos by authors. Series: Make Your Own Art. 2011, Rosen LB $25.25 (978-1-4488-1586-9); paper $11.75 (978-1-4488-1619-4). 32pp. Color photographs and clear instructions detail a variety of origami projects such as a bird, a lotus flower, a windmill, and a butterfly. Also use *Papier-Mâché* (2011). (Rev: SLJ 7/11) [745.592]

3958 Jackson, Paul. *Origami Toys: That Tumble, Fly, and Spin* (4–6). Illus. by author. Photos by Avi Valdman. 2010, Gibbs Smith paper $19.99 (978-1-4236-0524-9). 128pp. Clear diagrams guide readers through creating origami objects with moving parts; projects are rated by difficulty. (Rev: SLJ 4/10) [736.9]

3959 Jackson, Paul, and Miri Golan. *Origami Zoo: 25 Fun Paper Animal Creations!* (1–6). Illus. by Paul Jackson. Photos by Avi Valdman. 2011, Gibbs Smith paper $19.99 (978-1-4236-2016-7). 128pp. Clear illustrations add appeal to this collection of 25 different origami projects involving animals (koalas, monkeys, and butterflies, for example), which vary in difficulty from very simple to challenging. (Rev: SLJ 5/1/11) [736]

3960 Ransom, Candice. *Scrapbooking Just for You! How to Make Fun, Personal, Save-Them-Forever Keepsakes* (4–9). Illus. 2010, Sterling $14.95 (978-1-4027-4096-1). 120pp. Plenty of innovative ideas for a variety of different scrapbooking projects — including magnets, frames, and cards — are collected in this well-designed title that also has instructions for hosting a scrapbooking party. (Rev: BLO 11/15/10; SLJ 6/10) [745.5]

Sewing and Needle Crafts

3961 Plumley, Amie Petronis, and Andria Lisle. *Sewing School: 21 Sewing Projects Kids Will Love to Make* (3–6). Photos by Justin Fox Burks. 2010, Storey paper $16.95 (978-1-60342-578-0). 144pp. This attractive, large-format volume presents child-friendly projects that teach children various skills and increase in sophistication as the book progresses. (Rev: BL 12/15/10; SLJ 2/1/11) [646.2]

Toys and Dolls

3962 Henry, Sally, and Trevor Cook. *Making Puppets* (4–8). Photos by authors. Series: Make Your Own Art. 2011, Rosen LB $25.25 (978-1-4488-1584-5); paper $11.75 (978-1-4488-1615-6). 32pp. Color photographs and clear instructions add appeal to this book detailing a variety of creative puppet projects. (Rev: BL 12/15/11; SLJ 7/11) [791.5]

Hobbies

General and Miscellaneous

3963 Champion, Neil. *Finding Your Way* (4–7). Illus. 2010, Amicus LB $28.50 (978-1-60753-038-1). 32pp. Plenty of interactive quizzes and eye-catching photographs enhance this survival guide with an emphasis on navigation techniques — both technological and natural. (Rev: BL 10/1/10; SLJ 11/1/10) [613.6]

3964 Kenney, Karen Latchana. *Cool Holiday Parties: Perfect Party Planning for Kids* (3–6). Illus. Series: Cool Parties. 2011, ABDO LB $27.07 (978-1-61714-974-0). 32pp. Bright photographs and practical advice enhance this activity-filled book about holiday party planning. Other titles in this series include *Cool Family Parties, Cool Slumber Parties,* and *Cool Theme Parties* (all 2011). (Rev: SLJ 12/1/11) [793.2]

3965 Latno, Mark. *The Paper Boomerang Book: Build Them, Throw Them, and Get Them to Return Every Time* (5–8). 2010, Chicago Review paper $12.95 (978-1-56976-282-0). 128pp. Everything you need to know about boomerangs and their construction and use, with a surprising depth of kid-friendly physics. **e** (Rev: SLJ 7/10; VOYA 12/10) [629.133]

3966 Ralston, Birgitta. *Snow Play: How to Make Forts and Slides and Winter Campfires, Plus the Coolest Loch Ness Monster and 23 Other Brrrilliant Projects in the Snow* (4–12). Photos by Vegard Fimland. 2010, Artisan $14.95 (978-1-57965-405-4). 112pp. Ralston presents a variety of compelling snow projects, ranging from small ornaments to an LED-illuminated birthday cake to a snow cave. (Rev: SLJ 4/11) [796.9]

3967 Trusty, Brad, and Cindy Trusty. *The Kids' Guide to Balloon Twisting* (4–8). Illus. Series: Kids' Guides. 2012, Capstone LB $26.65 (978-142965444-9). 32pp.

A variety of twisted-balloon projects are presented with easy-to-follow directions. (Rev: BL 9/1/11) [745.594]

Cooking

3968 Barker, Geoff. *Mexico* (3–6). Series: A World of Food. 2010, Clara House $24.95 (978-1-934545-13-3). 32pp. With color photographs, information on the country's history, agriculture, and culture, this book covers Mexican holidays and provides simple recipes suitable for this age group. (Rev: LMC 10/10; SLJ 5/10) [641.3]

3969 Blaxland, Wendy. *Mexican Food* (5–8). Illus. Series: I Can Cook! 2012, Smart Apple Media LB $28.50 (978-1-59920-668-4). 32pp. Introduces the food of Mexico, with appealing recipes and clear photographs, along with information on the culture and geography of the country. Also in this series, use *Chinese Food, French Food,* and *Middle Eastern Food* (all 2011). (Rev: BL 1/1/12; SLJ 12/1/11) [641.5956]

3970 Blaxland, Wendy. *Middle Eastern Food* (5–8). Illus. Series: I Can Cook! 2011, Black Rabbit LB $28.50 (978-159920672-1). 32pp. With recipes that will need adult supervision, this book places Middle Eastern food and ingredients in historical and cultural perspective. (Rev: BL 1/1/12) [641.5956]

3971 Deen, Paula, and Martha Nesbit. *Paula Deen's Cookbook for the Lunch-Box Set* (3–6). Illus. by Susan Mitchell. 2009, Simon & Schuster $21.99 (978-1-4169-8268-5). 192pp. With recipes for bake sales, sleepovers, pool parties, and more, this is a cookbook with an old-fashioned appeal. (Rev: SLJ 12/09) [641]

3972 La Penta, Marilyn. *Way Cool Drinks* (2–5). Illus. Series: Yummy Tummy Recipes. 2011, Bearport LB

$22.61 (978-161772163-2). 24pp. Slushies, smoothies, and shakes feature large in this guide to drinks with names like "Red Lava Volcano." (Rev: BL 10/1/11) [641.8]

3973 Llewellyn, Claire, and Clare O'Shea. *Cooking with Fruits and Vegetables* (5–8). Series: Cooking Healthy. 2011, Rosen LB $27.95 (978-1-4488-4844-7). 48pp. Basic cooking terms and techniques are defined and illustrated in this accessible guide to cooking fruits and vegetables. Also use *Cooking with Meat and Fish* (2011). (Rev: SLJ 12/1/11) [641.3]

3974 Mattern, Joanne. *Recipe and Craft Guide to China* (4–7). Illus. Series: World Crafts and Recipes. 2010, Mitchell Lane LB $24.50 (978-158415937-7). 64pp. Mattern looks at foods and crafts found in various geographic regions around China, with recipes and activities; a glossary and vocabulary words are included. (Rev: BL 1/1/10) [641.591]

3975 Mendez, Sean. *One World Kids Cookbook: Easy, Healthy and Affordable Family Meals* (5–8). 2011, Interlink $20 (978-1-56656-866-1). 96pp. Recipes from around the world are presented alongside snippets of trivia and relevant food proverbs. (Rev: SLJ 12/1/11) [641.5]

3976 Orr, Tamra. *The Food of China* (4–7). Illus. Series: Flavors of the World. 2011, Marshall Cavendish LB $21.95 (978-160870234-3). 64pp. Introduces the five major cuisines of China, the kinds of foods that are eaten and the way they are cooked, and festive dishes, with recipes and photographs. (Rev: BL 10/1/11) [394.1]

3977 Price, Pam. *Cool Pet Treats: Easy Recipes for Kids to Bake* (3–6). Illus. 2010, ABDO LB $17.95 (978-160453777-2). 32pp. This guide to cooking up treats for pets features plenty of basic cooking information and advice about equipment and ingredients. (Rev: BL 10/1/10) [636.7]

Gardening

3978 Barker, David. *Compost It* (3–7). Series: Language Arts Explorer: Save the Planet. 2010, Cherry Lake LB $27.07 (978-1-60279-656-0). 32pp. Students are given a mission at the beginning of the book and must use creative thinking and problem solving to gather facts as they travel on a virtual trip researching how gardeners create and use compost. (Rev: LMC 8–9/10; SLJ 4/10) [631.8]

3979 Gourley, Robbin. *First Garden: The White House Garden and How It Grew* (1–4). Illus. by author. 2011, Clarion $16.99 (978-0-547-48224-8). 48pp. With recipes and gardening tips, this engaging volume traces the history of growing food at the White House, from John Adams to Michelle Obama. (Rev: BL 4/15/11; LMC 10/11; SLJ 6/11) [712.09753]

3980 Hengel, Katherine. *Cool Basil from Garden to Table: How to Plant, Grow, and Prepare Basil* (3–6). Illus. Series: Cool Garden to Table. 2012, ABDO LB $27.07 (978-161783182-9). 32pp. Accessible guidance on planting, growing, harvesting, and eating basil is presented clearly, with six recipes. (Rev: BL 4/1/12) [583]

3981 Hirsch, Rebecca E. *Growing Your Own Garden* (3–7). Series: Language Arts Explorer: Save the Planet. 2010, Cherry Lake LB $27.07 (978-1-60279-657-7). 32pp. Readers use creative thinking and problem solving to gather facts as they travel on a virtual trip researching vegetable gardening. (Rev: LMC 8–9/10; SLJ 4/10) [635]

3982 Leavitt, Amie Jane. *A Backyard Vegetable Garden for Kids* (4–7). Illus. Series: Gardening for Kids. 2008, Mitchell Lane LB $20.95 (978-158415634-5). 48pp. Young people learn to reap the rewards of their very own backyard garden — or container garden — in this helpful volume that offers simple, practical advice. (Rev: BL 10/15/08) [635]

Magic

3983 Becker, Helaine. *Magic Up Your Sleeve: Amazing Illusions, Tricks, and Science Facts You'll Never Believe* (4–7). Illus. by Claudia Dávila. 2010, Maple Tree paper $10.95 (978-1-897349-76-2). 64pp. Thirty sleights of hand incorporating various scientific properties are collected in this clear, easy-to-follow book. (Rev: BLO 5/15/10; SLJ 4/10) [793.8]

3984 Tremaine, Jon. *Pocket Tricks* (4–6). Illus. by Mark Turner. 2010, Black Rabbit LB $28.50 (978-159566853-0). 32pp. A book of simple magic tricks with items you might find in your pocket. Also use *Paper Tricks, Magical Illusions,* and *Magic with Numbers* (all 2010). (Rev: BL 5/1/11) [793.8]

Model Making

3985 Kenney, Sean. *Cool Robots* (K–4). Illus. 2010, Henry Holt $12.99 (978-0-8050-8763-5). 32pp. LEGO aficionado Kenney shows off some of his most inspiring creations and provides instructions, tips, and designs. Also use *Cool City* (2011). (Rev: BLO 8/10; SLJ 11/1/10) [629.8]

Photography and Filmmaking

3986 Sullivan, George. *Click Click Click! Photography for Children* (5–8). Illus. 2012, Prestel $14.95 (978-379137079-8). 96pp. A brief history of photography begins this user-friendly guide to getting started taking effective, well-composed pictures. (Rev: BL 1/1/12; SLJ 2/12) [771]

Stamp, Coin, and Other Types of Collecting

3987 Reid, Margarette S. *Lots and Lots of Coins* (K–3). Illus. by True Kelley. 2011, Dutton $16.99 (978-0-525-47879-9). 32pp. A boy and his father share their interest in coin collecting and the history of money in this appealing book. (Rev: BL 2/15/11; SLJ 3/1/11) [737.4]

Jokes, Puzzles, Riddles, Word Games

Jokes and Riddles

3988 Boynton, Sandra. *Amazing Cows! A Book of Bovinely Inspired Misinformation* (2–4). Illus. by author. 2010, Workman paper $9.95 (978-0-7611-6214-8). 80pp. With wordplay, knock-knock jokes, limericks, ads, anecdotes, and more, this is a silly celebration of all things bovine. (Rev: BL 2/15/11; SLJ 4/11) [636.2]

3989 Dahl, Michael. *Chuckle Squad: Jokes About Classrooms, Sports, Food, Teachers, and Other School Subjects* (K–3). Illus. by Anne Haberstroh. Series: Michael Dahl Presents Super Funny Joke Books. 2011, Picture Window LB $23.99 (978-140485773-5); paper $6.95 (978-140486370-5). 80pp. Full of humorous illustrations, this is an accessible book of jokes on all topics relating to schools. Lexile AD360L (Rev: BLO 1/1–15/11) [818]

3990 Lewis, J. Patrick. *Spot the Plot: A Riddle Book of Book Riddles* (K–2). Illus. by Lynn Munsinger. 2009, Chronicle $15.99 (978-0-8118-4668-4). Unpaged. Challenges young readers to identify books based on scenarios such as a pumpkin coach pulled by mice, a princess with unbelievably long hair, and a spider that weaves words into her web. (Rev: HB 11–12/09; LMC 1–2/10; SLJ 11/1/09) [811]

3991 Rosenberg, Pam. *Sports Jokes* (2–5). Illus. by Mernie Gallagher-Cole. 2010, Child's World LB $22.79 (978-160253521-3). 24pp. Where do ghosts go swimming? Why is tennis such a noisy game? Plenty of humorous wordplay is on offer in this zany joke book full of cartoon-style illustrations. Also use *Space Jokes, Doctor Jokes,* and *Holiday Jokes* (all 2010). (Rev: BL 12/15/10) [818]

3992 Teitelbaum, Michael. *Halloween Howlers: Frightfully Funny Knock-Knock Jokes* (PS–2). Illus. by Jannie Ho. 2011, HarperCollins $6.99 (978-006180891-3). 16pp. Interactive features add to the fun in this spooky collection of Halloween knock-knock jokes. (Rev: BLO 9/15/11) [818]

Puzzles

3993 Brookes, Olivia. *Uncover History* (K–2). Illus. by Peter Kent. Series: Hide-and-Seek Visual Adventures. 2010, Windmill LB $22.80 (978-1-60754-653-5). 24pp. Concise fact-filled text and detailed illustrations of buildings of the past with cutaway walls showing the activities inside make this seek-the-hidden-object book informative and entertaining. Also use *Uncover Nature* and *Uncover Technology* (both 2010). (Rev: LMC 11–12/10; SLJ 6/1/10) [909]

3994 Chedru, Delphine. *Spot It Again!* (K–2). Illus. by author. 2011, Abrams $14.95 (978-081099736-3). 40pp. Sixteen eye-catching seek-and-find illustrations, some behind flaps, conceal abstract animal shapes. (Rev: BLO 6/15/11; SLJ 5/11) [793.73]

3995 Marzollo, Jean. *I Spy an Apple* (K–2). Photos by Walter Wick. Series: Scholastic Reader. 2011, Scholastic $3.99 (978-054522095-8). 32pp. For beginning readers, this I Spy teaches words and visual recognition in bright photographs of objects. (Rev: BLO 7/11) [793.73]

3996 Marzollo, Jean. *I Spy an Egg in a Nest* (K–2). Photos by Walter Wick. Series: Scholastic Reader. 2011, Scholastic paper $3.99 (978-054522093-4). 32pp. For beginning readers, this I Spy book combines simple phrases with eye-catching photographs. (Rev: BL 1/1–15/11) [793.73]

3997 Raffin, Deborah. *Mitzi's World: Seek and Discover More Than 150 Details in 15 Works of Folk Art* (K–3). Illus. by Jane Wooster Scott. 2009, Abrams $17.95

(978-0-8109-8004-4). 32pp. A black-and-white dog explores diverse American scenes full of objects to discover. (Rev: BLO 11/1/09; LMC 3–4/10; SLJ 9/1/09) [793.73]

3998 Sheppard, Kate. *Animal I Spy: What Can You Spot?* (PS). Illus. by author. 2010, Kingfisher $6.99 (978-0-7534-6395-6). 18pp. This find-and-seek board book combines challenging clues and dynamic illustrations in six different animal-related spying games. (Rev: BL 5/1/10; SLJ 6/1/10) [590]

3999 Staake, Bob. *Look! A Book! A Zany Seek-and-Find Adventure* (PS–3). Illus. by author. 2011, Little, Brown $16.99 (978-0-316-11862-0). 40pp. Easy-to-read rhyming text offers clues to the searching and counting tasks on each page. (Rev: BL 2/15/11; SLJ 2/1/11*) [793.73]

4000 Wick, Walter. *Can You See What I See? Treasure Ship* (K–3). Illus. by author. Series: Can You See What I See? 2010, Scholastic $13.99 (978-043902643-7). 40pp. Shipwrecks and beach combing are the focus of this addition to the popular series. Also use *Can You See What I See? Toyland Express* (2011). (Rev: BLO 2/1/10)

310

Mysteries, Monsters, Curiosities, and Trivia

4001 Arnosky, Jim. *Monster Hunt: Exploring Mysterious Creatures with Jim Arnosky* (2–5). Illus. by author. 2011, Hyperion/Disney $16.99 (978-1-4231-3028-4). 32pp. Arnosky looks at mysterious creatures from the Loch Ness Monster to the prehistoric carcharodon; large, realistic paintings accompany the narrative. Lexile NC1090L (Rev: BL 6/1/11; LMC 11–12/11; SLJ 7/11) [001.944]

4002 Belanger, Jeff. *What It's Like to Climb Mount Everest, Blast Off into Space, Survive a Tornado, and Other Extraordinary Stories* (5–8). Illus. 2011, Sterling paper $9.95 (978-140276711-1). 136pp. First-person accounts describe a variety of exciting, extreme adventures in this compilation that will appeal to reluctant readers. Lexile 1250 (Rev: BL 4/15/11) [179]

4003 *The Book of Why? 50 Questions and All the Answers* (K–3). Illus. by Kath Grimshaw. 2010, Kingfisher paper $7.99 (978-0-7534-6396-3). 64pp. Answers to pressing questions such as why elephants have trunks and why your legs look shorter underwater are presented in this eye-catching book. Also use *The Book of How* (2010). (Rev: BL 4/1/10; SLJ 9/1/10) [500]

4004 Doft, Tony. *Nostradamus* (3–6). Illus. Series: Unexplained. 2011, Children's Press LB $21.95 (978-160014584-1). 24pp. This appealing survey of theories and stories pertaining to Nostradamus will appeal to reluctant readers. Lexile 710L (Rev: BL 4/15/11) [133.3092]

4005 Donovan, Sandy. *Does It Really Take Seven Years to Digest Swallowed Gum? And Other Questions You've Always Wanted to Ask* (4–6). Illus. 2010, Lerner LB $26.60 (978-082259085-9). 40pp. This book applies science to the investigation of childhood myths, including whether a penny on a railroad track can derail a train and if it's really possible to swing in a circle over a swingset. (Rev: BL 4/1/10; LMC 5–6/10; SLJ 7/10) [610]

4006 Erickson, Justin. *Alien Abductions* (3–6). Illus. Series: Unexplained. 2011, Children's Press LB $21.95 (978-160014582-7). 24pp. This appealing survey of theories and stories pertaining to alien abductions will appeal to reluctant readers. Lexile 780L (Rev: BL 4/15/11) [001.942]

4007 Halls, Kelly Milner. *Alien Investigation: Searching for the Truth About UFOs and Aliens* (5–8). Illus. by Rick C. Spears. 2012, Millbrook $20.95 (978-076136204-3). 64pp. Halls explores reports of alien encounters, with interviews of witnesses and discussion of hoaxes. ❷ (Rev: BL 4/1/12; LMC 10/12*; VOYA 6/12) [001.942]

4008 Helstrom, Kraig. *Crop Circles* (3–6). Illus. Series: Unexplained. 2011, Children's Press LB $21.95 (978-160014583-4). 24pp. Reluctant readers will be attracted to this account of various hoaxes. (Rev: BL 4/1/11; SLJ 4/11) [001.94]

4009 Hirschmann, Kris. *Demons* (5–8). Illus. Series: Monsters and Mythical Creatures. 2011, ReferencePoint $26.95 (978-160152147-7). 80pp. Demons and evil spirits' prevalence throughout world cultures is explored here, with eye-catching illustrations and discussion of topics such as exorcism and demonic possession. (Rev: BL 8/11; SLJ 4/11) [133.4]

4010 Howe, John. *Lost Worlds* (4–6). Illus. by author. 2009, Kingfisher $16.99 (978-0-7534-6107-5). 96pp. Real and legendary "lost worlds" — the Garden of Eden, Pompeii, Atlantis, and Camelot, for example — are the focus of this attractive volume that mixes history and myth. (Rev: BL 11/1/09; LMC 1–2/10; SLJ 6/10) [813.6]

4011 Hubbard, Ben. *Top 10 Biggest* (3–6). 2010, Crabtree LB $26.60 (978-0-7787-7487-7); paper $8.95 (978-0-7787-7508-9). 32pp. A nice variety of natural and man-made records — from the biggest hamburger and food fight to the biggest flower, swimming pool, and tomb — are covered in this browsable volume. (Rev: SLJ 7/10) [152.14]

4012 Jones, Jen. *Cancer, Scorpio, and Pisces: All About the Water Signs* (4–6). Illus. Series: Zodiac Fun. 2009, Capstone LB $26.65 (978-1-4296-4015-2). 32pp. A light introduction to the water signs of the zodiac, with a personality profile, compatibility with other signs, and sketches of celebrities. Also use *Gemini, Libra, and Aquarius: All About the Air Signs* (2010). (Rev: BLO 3/1/10; LMC 11–12/10; SLJ 4/10) [133.5]

4013 Kerns, Ann. *Wizards and Witches* (4–7). Illus. Series: Fantasy Chronicles. 2009, Lerner LB $27.93 (978-0-8225-9983-8). 48pp. Kerns touches on everything from King Arthur's court to Middle Earth in her tour of primarily European and American witches and wizards. (Rev: BL 10/1/09; LMC 11–12/09; SLJ 1/10) [133.4]

4014 Krull, Kathleen. *Big Wig: A Little History of Hair* (3–6). Illus. by Peter Malone. 2011, Scholastic $18.99 (978-0-439-67640-3). 48pp. A broad survey, full of bizarre facts, of hairstyles and head coverings through the ages. (Rev: BL 9/1/11; LMC 10/11; SLJ 7/11) [391.5]

4015 Kyi, Tanya Lloyd. *Fifty Underwear Questions: A Bare-All History* (4–7). Illus. by Ross Kinnaird. 2011, Annick $21.95 (978-155451353-6); paper $12.95 (978-155451352-9). 116pp. Everything you wanted to know about underwear through the ages, with some fascinating pieces of trivia — all delivered with humor and even some games. (Rev: BL 12/15/11; SLJ 2/12) [391.4]

4016 Law, Stephen. *Really, Really Big Questions About the Weird, the Wonderful, and Everything Else* (5–8). Illus. by Nishant Choksi. 2009, Kingfisher $16.99 (978-0-75346-309-3). 64pp. What is nothing? Is my mind my brain? How important is happiness? Is time travel possible? These are only a few of the questions posed here as Law tackles some weighty problems in an accessible manner. (Rev: BL 12/15/09; LMC 1–2/10; SLJ 1/10) [100]

4017 Marks, Jennifer L. *Aries, Leo, and Sagittarius: All About the Fire Signs* (4–6). Illus. Series: Zodiac Fun. 2009, Capstone LB $26.65 (978-1-4296-4014-5). 32pp. A light introduction to the fire signs of the zodiac, with a personality profile, compatibility with other signs, and sketches of celebrities. (Rev: LMC 11–12/10; SLJ 4/10) [133.5]

4018 Michels, Troy. *Atlantis* (3–6). Illus. Series: Unexplained. 2011, Children's Press LB $21.95 (978-160014585-8). 24pp. This appealing survey of theories and stories pertaining to the lost continent will appeal to reluctant readers. Lexile 800L (Rev: BL 4/15/11) [001.94]

4019 Murphy, Glenn. *How Loud Can You Burp? More Extremely Important Questions (and Answers!)* (4–7). Illus. by Mike Phillips. 2009, Flash Point paper $10.99 (978-1-59643-506-3). 284pp. Bizarre and often funny questions gleaned from Murphy's Web site are answered in a casual and engaging manner in this com-

pendium of facts and trivia. (Rev: BLO 8/21/09; SLJ 10/09) [500]

4020 Murphy, Glenn. *Stuff That Scares Your Pants Off! A Book of Scary Things (and How to Avoid Them)* (4–8). Illus. by Mike Phillips. 2011, Roaring Brook paper $14.99 (978-1-59643-633-6). 192pp. This reassuring and humorous book examines the fears we harbor about wild animals, natural disasters, doctors, dentists, snakes, spiders, and so forth. ℮ Lexile 1210L (Rev: LMC 5–6/11; SLJ 9/1/11) [001.9]

4021 Owen, Ruth. *Top 10 Fastest* (3–6). Series: Crabtree Contact. 2010, Crabtree LB $26.60 (978-0-7787-7488-4); paper $8.95 (978-0-7787-7509-6). 32pp. A nice variety of natural and man-made records — from the fastest car and motorbike to the fastest growing plant and fastest mammal — are covered in this browsable volume. (Rev: SLJ 7/10) [531]

4022 Pearce, Q. L. *Ghost Hunters* (5–7). Illus. Series: Mysterious Encounters. 2011, Kidhaven LB $27.50 (978-073775290-8). 48pp. Case studies, historical facts, and scientific explorations ground this satisfying book about haunted houses and the people who investigate them. (Rev: BL 8/11) [133.1]

4023 Reinhart, Matthew, and Robert Sabuda. *Dragons and Monsters* (2–5). Illus. by authors. Series: Encyclopedia Mythologica. 2011, Candlewick $29.99 (978-0-7636-3173-4). 12pp. Grotesque and fearsome monsters from myths and traditions around the world are depicted in this beautifully executed pop-up book. (Rev: BL 9/1/11; HB 5–6/11; SLJ 8/1/11*) [398]

4024 Rosenthal, Amy Krouse. *The Wonder Book* (2–4). Illus. by Paul Schmid. 2010, HarperCollins $17.99 (978-0-06-142974-3). 80pp. Puns, poems, palindromes, puzzles, and quirky kid-friendly questions abound in this light compendium made for browsing. (Rev: BL 1/1/10; SLJ 3/1/10)

4025 Schroeder, Andreas. *Duped! True Stories of the World's Best Swindlers* (4–7). Illus. by Remy Simard. 2011, Annick $21.95 (978-155451351-2); paper $12.95 (978-155451350-5). 144pp. With graphic-novel flair, this is a lighthearted but informative exploration of hoaxes in modern times. (Rev: BL 12/15/11; SLJ 1/12) [364.16]

4026 Tibballs, Geoff. *Ripley's Believe It or Not! Enter If You Dare!* (5–7). 2010, Ripley Entertainment $28.95 (978-1-893951-63-1). 254pp. A compendium of odd information organized in such chapters as "Animal Antics," "Extreme Sports," "Incredible Feats," "Fantastic Food," and "Amazing Science." (Rev: BL 11/1/10; SLJ 12/1/10) [031.02]

4027 Williams, Dinah. *Monstrous Morgues of the Past* (4–6). Illus. Series: Scary Places. 2011, Bearport LB $25.27 (978-161772149-6). 32pp. This effective book describes 11 morgues that were the site of hair-raising stories. (Rev: BL 3/15/11) [133.1]

Sports and Games

General and Miscellaneous

4028 Bell-Rehwoldt, Sheri. *The Kids' Guide to Jumping Rope* (4–8). Illus. Series: Kids' Guides. 2012, Capstone LB $26.65 (978-142965443-2). 32pp. A variety of jump rope tricks and rhymes are presented with easy-to-follow directions. (Rev: BL 9/1/11) [796.2]

4029 Catel, Patrick. *Surviving Stunts and Other Amazing Feats* (4–7). Series: Extreme Survival. 2011, Heinemann LB $33.50 (978-1-4109-3969-2). 56pp. Catel describes amazing feats performed by stuntmen and daredevils. (Rev: SLJ 8/11) [613.6]

4030 Gifford, Clive. *Golf: From Tee to Green — The Essential Guide for Young Golfers* (5–8). Illus. 2010, Kingfisher $16.99 (978-075346399-4). 64pp. This informative guide covers everything from gear and techniques to clothing and the achievements of golfing greats. (Rev: BL 9/1/10) [796.352]

4031 Gigliotti, Jim. *Barefoot Waterskiing* (5–8). Illus. Series: Extreme Sports. 2011, Child's World LB $27.07 (978-160973177-9). 32pp. This extreme sports offering boasts dynamic photographs alongside historical and safety information about barefoot waterskiing. (Rev: BL 1/1/12) [797.3]

4032 Green, Sara. *Cheerleading Camp* (4–7). Illus. Series: Kick, Jump, Cheer! 2011, Children's Press LB $22.95 (978-160014647-3). 24pp. This breezy book offers a behind-the-scenes glimpse into what takes place at cheerleading camp. (Rev: BL 10/1/11) [791.6]

4033 Hamilton, S. L. *White Water* (4–6). Illus. Series: Xtreme Sports. 2010, ABDO LB $25.65 (978-161613006-0). 32pp. With plenty of exciting photographs, Hamilton introduces the thrills of white-water canoeing, kayaking, and rafting. (Rev: BL 9/1/10) [796.04]

4034 Hile, Kevin. *Video Games* (5–8). Series: Technology 360. 2009, Gale/Lucent $32.45 (978-1-4205-0170-4). 104pp. An attractive and informative look at video games and how they are created, with discussion of their history and impact on culture plus a glossary and lists of material for further research. (Rev: BL 4/1/10; LMC 8–9/10) [794.8]

4035 Hile, Lori. *Surviving Extreme Sports* (4–7). Series: Extreme Survival. 2011, Heinemann LB $33.50 (978-1-4109-3968-5). 56pp. Starting with a chapter titled "Are You Nuts!?," Hile tells stories of extreme sports including diving, skateboarding, mountaineering, and skydiving. (Rev: SLJ 8/11) [796.046]

4036 Price, Sean Stewart. *The Kids' Guide to Pro Wrestling* (3–5). Illus. Series: Kids' Guides. 2011, Capstone LB $26.65 (978-142966008-2). 32pp. Pro wrestling trivia, history, information, and even some choice moves are presented here. (Rev: BL 2/15/12) [796.812]

4037 Ross, Stewart. *Sports Technology* (4–7). Illus. Series: New Technology. 2011, Black Rabbit LB $34.25 (978-159920534-2). 48pp. Technology's importance in all aspects of sports — equipment, judging and timing, surfaces and stadiums, clothing, machinery, training and cheating — is discussed in this attractive book. (Rev: BL 10/15/11) [688.76]

4038 Woods, Bob. *Snowmobile Racers* (4–6). Illus. Series: Kid Racers. 2010, Enslow LB $23.93 (978-076603487-7). 48pp. Reluctant readers will enjoy the illustrations and information on the equipment and techniques of safe snowmobile racing. (Rev: BL 9/1/10) [796.94]

Automobile Racing

4039 Pimm, Nancy Roe. *The Daytona 500: The Thrill and Thunder of the Great American Race* (5–8). Series: Spectacular Sports. 2011, Millbrook $29.27 (978-0-7613-6677-5). 64pp. This visually appealing book features lots of information about the early days of NASCAR racing, including tragedies and rivalries. ℮ (Rev: BL 3/1/11; SLJ 5/11) [796.7]

Baseball

4040 Bildner, Phil. *The Unforgettable Season: The Story of Joe DiMaggio, Ted Williams, and the Record-Setting Summer of '41* (2–4). Illus. by S. D. Schindler. 2011, Putnam $16.99 (978-0-399-25501-4). 32pp. A handsome tribute to the talents of the baseball greats of 1941. Lexile AD980L (Rev: BLO 5/1/11; HB 5–6/11; SLJ 3/1/11*) [796.357]

4041 Bowen, Fred. *No Easy Way: The Story of Ted Williams and the Last .400 Season* (1–3). Illus. by Charles S. Pyle. 2010, Dutton $16.99 (978-0-525-47877-5). 32pp. A picture-book celebration of the baseball great, his lasting dreams, and his determination to win. (Rev: BL 12/15/09; LMC 3–4/10; SLJ 1/1/10) [921]

4042 Buckley, James, Jr. *Ultimate Guide to Baseball* (4–7). Illus. by Mike Arnold. Series: Scholastic Ultimate Guides. 2010, Scholastic LB $30 (978-0-531-20750-5). 160pp. An appealing review of key events, teams, athletes, slang, and all other aspects of baseball. (Rev: BL 6/10; SLJ 5/10; VOYA 8/10) [796.357]

4043 Goodman, Michael E. *The Story of the Boston Red Sox* (5–8). Illus. 2011, Creative Education LB $23.95 (978-160818034-9). 48pp. The star-studded history of the Boston Red Sox is chronicled in this statistics-filled title rife with archival and contemporary photographs. (Rev: BL 2/1/12)

4044 Goodman, Michael E. *The Story of the San Francisco Giants* (5–8). Illus. 2011, Creative Education LB $23.95 (978-160818055-4). 48pp. The city-hopping history of the San Francisco Giants is chronicled in this statistics-filled title rife with archival and contemporary photographs. (Rev: BL 2/1/12)

4045 LeBoutillier, Nate. *The Story of the Los Angeles Dodgers* (5–8). Illus. 2011, Creative Education LB $23.95 (978-160818045-5). 48pp. The city-hopping history of the Los Angeles Dodgers is chronicled in this statistics-filled title rife with archival and contemporary photographs. (Rev: BL 2/1/12)

4046 Teitelbaum, Michael. *Baseball* (4–7). Illus. Series: Innovation in Sports. 2008, Cherry Lake LB $18.95 (978-160279255-5). 32pp. Teitelbaum tells the story of baseball by focusing not on the athletes but on the development of the rules, equipment, and training and profiling lesser-known figures — such as the man who invented box scoring — who made important contributions. (Rev: BL 9/1/08) [796.357]

4047 Tocher, Timothy. *Odd Ball: Hilarious, Unusual, and Bizarre Baseball Moments* (3–6). Illus. by Stacy Curtis. 2011, Marshall Cavendish $15.99 (978-0-7614-5813-5). 64pp. A fascinating and humorous collection of baseball trivia. (Rev: BL 4/15/11; SLJ 6/11) [796.357]

4048 Vernick, Audrey. *Brothers at Bat: The True Story of An Amazing All-Brother Baseball Team* (1–3). Illus. by Steven Salerno. 2012, Clarion $16.99 (978-054738557-0). 40pp. The true story of a passionate baseball-playing New Jersey family — the Acerras — whose children form their own semipro team in 1938 and became the longest-running all-brother team in history. Lexile AD780L (Rev: BL 4/15/12*; HB 3–4/12; LMC 10/12; SLJ 4/12) [796.35709749]

Basketball

4049 Macy, Sue. *Basketball Belles: How Two Teams and One Scrappy Player Put Women's Hoops on the Map* (3–5). Illus. by Matt Collins. 2011, Holiday House $16.95 (978-0-8234-2163-3). 32pp. The first all-female intercollegiate basketball game is described from the perspective of Stanford's Agnes Morley, a guard in the historic game against Berkeley in 1896. (Rev: BL 3/15/11*; LMC 8–9/11; SLJ 4/11) [796.3]

4050 Silverman, Steve. *The Story of the Indiana Pacers* (5–8). Illus. Series: The NBA: A History of Hoops. 2010, Creative Education $23.95 (978-158341946-5). 48pp. With plenty of action-packed photographs this volume tells the story of this team, its key players, and best games. (Rev: BL 9/1/10) [796.323]

4051 Stewart, Mark. *The Georgetown Hoyas* (4–7). Illus. Series: Team Spirit: College Basketball. 2010, Norwood LB $26.60 (978-159953364-3). 48pp. A look at the history of university's basketball team, the key players and coaches, uniform, and so forth, with lots of photographs and statistics. (Rev: BL 9/1/10) [796.323]

4052 Yancey, Diane. *Basketball* (5–10). Series: Science Behind Sports. 2011, Gale/Lucent LB $33.45 (978-1-4205-0293-0). 112pp. This volume looks at all aspects of the sport, focusing in particular on the physics involved and the mental attitude required for success. ℮ (Rev: SLJ 9/1/11) [796.3]

Bicycles

4053 Robinson, Laura. *Cyclist Bikelist: The Book for Every Rider* (4–6). Illus. by Ramon K. Perez. 2010, Tundra paper $17.95 (978-088776784-5). 80pp. Vivid, cartoon-style illustrations and a wealth of practical advice enhance this comprehensive guide for young cyclists that covers equipment, safety, and so forth. (Rev: BL 6/10; SLJ 9/1/10) [796.6]

Camping and Backpacking

4054 George, Jean Craighead, and Twig C. George. *Pocket Guide to the Outdoors: Based on My Side of the Mountain* (5–8). 2009, Dutton paper $9.99 (978-0-525-42163-4). 138pp. This companion piece to George's *My Side of the Mountain* provides information on identifying edible plants, building shelters, catching fish, orienteering, and so forth. (Rev: SLJ 3/10; VOYA 6/10)

Football

4055 Frisch, Aaron. *New York Giants* (K–3). Illus. Series: Super Bowl Champions. 2011, Creative Company $16.95 (978-160818023-3). 24pp. For young children, this is a visually appealing profile of the New York Giants, with short, straightforward text and a child-friendly glossary. This 18-volume series covers other teams around the country. (Rev: BL 2/1/11) [796.332]

4056 Latimer, Clay. *VIP Pass to a Pro Football Game: From the Locker Room to the Press Box* (2–4). Illus. Series: Sports Illustrated Kids: Game Day. 2011, Capstone LB $26.65 (978-142965461-6). 32pp. Readers learn about all aspects of a pro game, introducing the people involved and the actions that take place. (Rev: BLO 3/14/11) [796.332]

4057 LeBoutillier, Nate. *The Story of the Chicago Bears* (5–8). Illus. 2009, Creative Education LB $22.95 (978-158341750-8). 48pp. With eye-catching photographs and a pleasing design and interesting text, this is a fascinating history of a football team. (Rev: BL 10/1/09*) [796.323]

4058 Stewart, Mark, and Mike Kennedy. *Touchdown: The Power and Precision of Football's Perfect Play* (5–8). 2009, Lerner LB $27.93 (978-0-8225-8751-4). 64pp. Full of action photographs, trading cards, and period prints, this engaging book provides a history of American football, its heroes, bloopers, and most thrilling moments. (Rev: BL 9/1/09; SLJ 1/10) [796.33]

4059 Thomas, Keltie. *How Football Works* (3–5). Illus. by Stephen MacEachern. 2010, OwlKids $22.95 (978-189734987-8); paper $12.95 (978-189734988-5). 64pp. History, rules, equipment, players, and famous games are all covered here with photographs and information packaged in small bites. (Rev: BL 11/1/10; SLJ 3/1/11) [796.332]

Horsemanship

4060 Dowdy, Penny. *Dressage* (3–5). Illus. Series: Horsing Around. 2009, Crabtree LB $26.60 (978-077874978-3). 32pp. Featuring plenty of action photos and a layout evocative of barns and stables, this book communicates the importance of a strong connection between horse and rider, highlighting some famous competitors. (Rev: BL 1/1/10) [798.2]

4061 Johnson, Robin. *Show Jumping* (3–5). Illus. Series: Horsing Around. 2009, Crabtree LB $26.60 (978-077874979-0). 32pp. Featuring plenty of action photos and a layout evocative of barns and stables, this book looks at the training, skills, and rituals of show jumping, highlighting some famous riders and horses. Also use *Rodeo* (2009). (Rev: BL 1/1/10) [798.2]

Ice Hockey

4062 Stewart, Mark, and Mike Kennedy. *Score! The Action and Artistry of Hockey's Magnificent Moment* (5–8). Illus. 2010, Millbrook LB $29.27 (978-0-8225-8753-8). 64pp. Not for beginning players, this is a book about strategy and technique, with information about key players. ℮ (Rev: BL 9/1/10; SLJ 4/11) [796.355]

Motor Bikes and Motorcycles

4063 Sandler, Michael. *Mighty MotoXers* (3–6). Illus. Series: X-Moves. 2009, Bearport LB $16.96 (978-159716951-6). 24pp. Sandler highlights the history, equipment, and thrills of motocross racing, providing gravity-defying photographs. (Rev: BL 1/1/10) [796.7]

Self-Defense

4064 Ellis, Carol. *Judo and Jujitsu* (5–7). Illus. 2011, Marshall Cavendish LB $20.95 (978-076144933-1).

48pp. This grounded title offers information about the history, practice, and philosophy of judo and jujitsu. (Rev: BL 2/1/12; SLJ 4/12)

4065 Haney-Withrow, Anna. *Tae Kwon Do* (5–7). Illus. 2011, Marshall Cavendish LB $20.95 (978-076144940-9). 48pp. This grounded title offers information about the history, practice, and philosophy of tae kwon do. (Rev: BL 2/1/12; SLJ 4/12)

4066 Mack, Gail. *Kickboxing* (5–7). Illus. 2011, Marshall Cavendish LB $20.95 (978-076144936-2). 48pp. This grounded title offers information about the history, practice, and philosophy of kickboxing. (Rev: BL 2/1/12; SLJ 4/12)

Snowboarding

4067 Sandler, Michael. *Cool Snowboarders* (3–6). Illus. Series: X-Moves. 2009, Bearport LB $16.96 (978-159716949-3). 24pp. With dramatic photographs, Sandler offers an overview of the history of snowboarding, the thrills of the sport, and the amazing accomplishments of the champions. (Rev: BL 1/1/10) [796.939]

4068 Schwartz, Heather E. *Snowboarding* (5–10). Series: Science Behind Sports. 2011, Gale/Lucent LB $33.45 (978-1-4205-0322-7). 104pp. After reviewing the history of snowboarding, this book discusses training and other preparations, glides and turns, jumps and rails, and aerial moves before looking at psychological aspects. e (Rev: SLJ 9/1/11) [796.9]

Soccer

4069 Capucilli, Alyssa Satin. *My First Soccer Game* (PS–K). Illus. by Leyah Jensen. 2011, Simon & Schuster $9.99 (978-144242747-1). 14pp. This board book offers a simple introduction to the basics of soccer (Rev: BLO 8/11; SLJ 12/11) [796.334]

4070 Gifford, Clive. *My First Soccer Book* (2–5). Illus. 2012, Kingfisher $12.99 (978-075346783-1). 48pp. Covering equipment, the field, and rules first, this book then looks at preparation and basic skills and provides many helpful photographs and tips. (Rev: BL 5/15/12; LMC 10/10; SLJ 6/1/12) [796.334]

4071 Gifford, Clive. *Soccer Players and Skills* (3–6). Series: Spotlight on Soccer. 2010, Rosen LB $23.95 (978-1-61532-611-2); paper $10 (978-1-61532-612-9). 32pp. The different roles and skill sets of various soccer field positions are discussed in depth. Also use (all 2010) *Soccer Rules and Regulations, Teamwork in Soccer,* and *The Business of Soccer,* which discusses the management of soccer teams and franchising. (Rev: SLJ 2/1/11) [796.334]

4072 Kennedy, Mike, and Mark Stewart. *Soccer in Asia* (2–4). Illus. Series: Smart About Sports: Soccer. 2011, Norwood LB $21.27 (978-159953448-0). 24pp. Plenty of bright, clearly focused photographs add appeal to this survey of soccer's influence and importance in Asian culture, with details of history, stadiums, player statistics, and so forth. Also use *Soccer in the British Isles, Soccer in Africa,* and *Soccer in South America* (all 2011). (Rev: BL 7/11; LMC 11–12/11) [796.334095]

4073 Stewart, Mark, and Mike Kennedy. *Goal! The Fire and Fury of Soccer's Greatest Moment* (5–8). 2010, Millbrook LB $27.93 (978-0-8225-8754-5). 64pp. Famous goals are the main focus of this book that also explores the history of the game and the scoring rules. (Rev: BL 3/1/10; SLJ 5/10) [796.334]

Surfing

4074 Sandler, Michael. *Super Surfers* (3–6). Illus. Series: X-Moves. 2009, Bearport $16.95 (978-159716953-0). 24pp. Sandler highlights the history, equipment, and thrills of surfing, providing photographs of daring feats. (Rev: BL 1/1/10) [797.3]

Author and Illustrator Index

Authors and illustrators are arranged alphabetically by last name, followed by book titles — which are also arranged alphabetically — and the text entry number. Book titles may refer to those that appear as a main entry or as an internal entry mentioned in the annotation. Fiction titles are indicated by (F) following the entry number.

Title Index

This index contains both main entry titles and internal titles cited within entries. References are to entry numbers, not page numbers. Fiction titles are indicated by (F) following the entry number.

385

Subject/Grade Level Index

All entries are listed by subject and then according to grade level suitability (see the key at the foot of pages for grade level designations). Subjects are arranged alphabetically and subject heads may be subdivided into nonfiction (e.g., "Airplanes") and fiction (e.g., "Airplanes — Fiction"). References to entries are by entry number, not page number.

Architecture
See also Building and construction
IJ: 2928, 2930

Architecture — Experiments and projects
IJ: 2938

Arctic
See also Inuit
PI: 3568   IJ: 3166

Arizona
I: 3205

Armed forces
See also Fighter pilots; and individual branches, e.g., Air Force (U.S.)
I: 3931

Armstrong, Louis
PI: 2707

Art
See also Drawing and painting; and names of individuals, e.g., Monet, Claude
P: 2933   PI: 2927, 2936   I: 2925, 2934   IJ: 2926, 2935, 2937, 2939

Art — Biography
P: 2687, 2690, 2693, 2698, 2915   PI: 2688, 2689, 2692, 2695, 2696, 2697, 2701, 2702, 2704   I: 2694, 2703   IJ: 2684, 2685, 2686, 2691, 2699

Art — Experiments and projects
IJ: 2938

Art — Fiction
P: 556, 602, 675, 825, 884, 964, 968, 977, 1030   PI: 1475

Art Institute of Chicago — Fiction
I: 1912

Art thefts — Fiction
P: 987

Arthur, King
IJ: 2561

Artificial reefs — Fiction
P: 1216

Ashe, Arthur
IJ: 2898

Asia
See also specific countries, e.g., Afghanistan

Asian Americans
See specific groups, e.g., Afghan Americans

Asperger's syndrome — Fiction
IJ: 2200

Asteroids
PI: 3480   I: 3474   IJ: 3479, 3499

Asthma
IJ: 3413

Astronauts
IJ: 3822

Astronauts — Biography
IJ: 2676, 2681

Astronomy
See also specific bodies, e.g., Asteroids
P: 3501   IJ: 3478, 3481

Athena (Greek deity) — Fiction
I: 1862   IJ: 2098

Athletes
See specific sports, e.g., Baseball — Biography; and names of athletes, e.g., Ashe, Arthur

Atlantis
I: 4018

Atomic bomb
IJ: 3159

Aung San Suu Kyi
IJ: 2907

Australia — Fiction
P: 84, 178   PI: 1676   IJ: 1413, 1511, 2213, 2230

Authors — Biography
P: 2749, 2754   PI: 2739, 2740, 2742, 2743, 2746, 2751   I: 2744   IJ: 2683, 2741, 2747, 2748, 2750

Authors — Fiction
P: 1178   I: 2226

Autism
PI: 3406   IJ: 3407

Autism — Fiction
P: 754   IJ: 2296

Automobile travel — Fiction
PI: 917   IJ: 1436

Automobiles
P: 3906, 3910   I: 3905, 3907, 3909, 3911, 3912, 3913

Automobiles — Biography
IJ: 2852

Automobiles — Fiction
P: 621, 1212, 1217

Autumn
P: 13

Autumn — Fiction
P: 897

Aviation
See also Airplanes; Airships
IJ: 3881

Aztecs
PI: 3046   IJ: 3047

Aztecs — Mythology
IJ: 2581

B

Babies — Fiction
P: 23, 58, 610, 629, 671, 695, 696, 702, 740, 744, 747, 778, 781, 783, 847, 849, 850

Babysitting
IJ: 3353

Babysitting — Fiction
P: 541, 628   PI: 2190

Bacteria
I: 3733

Baer, Ralph
PI: 2835

Baghdad (Iraq)
IJ: 3773

Baker, Josephine
P: 2708

Baking
See also specific baking products, e.g., Cupcakes

Baking — Fiction
P: 661, 688   PI: 1850   IJ: 1483, 2149

Ballet
P: 3004   PI: 3002, 3003   IJ: 3001

Ballet — Biography
IJ: 2706

Ballet — Fiction
P: 232, 246, 269, 649, 691, 767, 878, 879, 909, 1036, 1335, 2022   PI: 2192   IJ: 1464

Balloon twisting
IJ: 3967

Ballroom dancing
I: 3005

Bands (music)
IJ: 3394

Bangladesh — Fiction
PI: 2221

Banneker, Benjamin
I: 2836

Bar mitzvah — Fiction
IJ: 1403

Barber, Ronde — Fiction
IJ: 2502

Barber, Tiki — Fiction
IJ: 2502

Barges
P: 3256

Barrie, James
PI: 2739

Barton, Clara
IJ: 2814

P = Primary; PI = Primary-Intermediate; I = Intermediate; IJ = Intermediate-Junior High

Barton, Clara — Fiction
I: 1863

Baseball
P: 2983,
4048 **PI:** 4040 **I:** 4047 **IJ:** 4042,
4043, 4044, 4045, 4046

Baseball — Biography
P: 2869, 2870, 2874, 2879,
4041 **PI:** 2868, 2873, 2875,
2880 **I:** 2865 **IJ:** 2864, 2867, 2871,
2872, 2877, 2878

Baseball — Fiction
P: 318, 589, 724 **PI:** 988, 2505,
2518, 2528 **I:** 1437, 2334, 2513,
2516, 2523 **IJ:** 1551, 2325, 2347,
2480, 2511, 2514, 2524, 2526

Basketball
PI: 4049 **IJ:** 4050, 4051, 4052

Basketball — Biography
P: 2882 **PI:** 2881, 2883, 2884

Basketball — Fiction
IJ: 2504

Bathrooms — Poetry
P: 2620

Baths and bathing — Fiction
P: 323, 507, 651

Bats (animal)
P: 3603, 3604

Beaches
See also Seashores

Beaches — Fiction
P: 953, 1037

Bearden, Romare — Fiction
P: 977

Beards — Fiction
P: 2276

Bears
See also specific types, e.g., Polar bears
P: 3607 **IJ:** 3608, 3609

Bears — Fiction
P: 264, 281, 1145 **IJ:** 2243

Bears — Folklore
P: 2535

Beauty contests — Fiction
P: 653

Beauty shops — Fiction
P: 885

Beavers
P: 3636

Beavers — Fiction
P: 179

Bedtime books
P: 114, 117, 118, 119, 121, 122, 123,
125, 127, 128, 129, 130, 135, 137, 139,
140, 141, 142, 143, 146, 148, 150, 152,
153, 154, 157, 159, 160, 164, 1264

Bedtime books — Fiction
P: 113, 115, 116, 120, 124, 126, 131,
132, 133, 136, 138, 145, 147, 149, 151,
155, 156, 158, 161, 162, 163, 165, 167,
168, 209

Bedtime books — Poetry
P: 2625

Bees
IJ: 3692

Bees — Fiction
P: 944, 945

Bees — Poetry
PI: 2664

Beetles
PI: 3695

Behavior
See also Animal behavior; Etiquette
P: 3356 **I:** 3366

Behavior — Fiction
P: 35, 316, 575, 630, 661, 666, 980,
1021, 1204 **PI:** 2177

Belongings — Fiction
P: 475

Berlin (Germany) — Fiction
IJ: 2240

Berlin Airlift
IJ: 2783

Beyoncé
IJ: 2709

Bezos, Jeff
IJ: 2837

Bibb, Henry — Fiction
IJ: 2274

Bible
P: 3308, 3310

Bicycle racing — Biography
P: 2904

Bicycles
I: 4053

Bicycles — Fiction
P: 1220 **IJ:** 2127

Bieber, Justin
IJ: 2710

Big Bang theory
PI: 3476

Big cats
See also individual species, e.g., Lions
P: 3587 **I:** 3612

Bilingualism — Fiction
P: 1095, 1183

Biography
See also under specific occupations,
e.g., Art; specific sports, e.g., Baseball; and cultural groups, e.g., African
Americans

Biography — Collective
P: 2758 **PI:** 2760, 2761 **I:** 2673,
2759, 2865 **IJ:** 2671, 2672, 2674,
2683, 2684, 2756, 2832, 2834, 2864,
2866

Biology
See also Marine biology
IJ: 3545

Biology — Poetry
PI: 2669

Bird, Sue
PI: 2881

Birds
See also specific birds, e.g., Eagles
P: 3644, 3647, 3655 **IJ:** 3649

Birds — Fiction
P: 47, 1055, 1073, 1077, 1107, 1118,
1128, 1146, 1151, 1295

Birds — Migration
IJ: 3648

Birds of prey
See also specific birds, e.g., Eagles
PI: 3651

Birmingham (AL)
IJ: 3272

Birth order — Fiction
P: 705

Birthdays — Fiction
P: 338, 396, 468, 478, 551, 659, 864,
1257, 1258, 1259, 1260, 1261, 1262,
1375 **PI:** 1417, 1424, 1721

Bison
PI: 3591 **IJ:** 3592

Black Elk
IJ: 2792

Black holes
I: 3475

Black Panther Party — Fiction
IJ: 2351

Blackouts (electric) — Fiction
P: 758

Blind — Fiction
P: 1311

Blizzards — Fiction
P: 485 **IJ:** 1603

Blogs
PI: 2973 **I:** 2969

Blogs — Fiction
IJ: 2413

Blue jays
P: 3640

Blues (music) — Poetry
IJ: 2593

Bly, Nellie
IJ: 2779

Board books
P: 55, 3253

Boarding schools — Fiction
I: 2252

Boats
See Ships and boats

Body image
IJ: 3427

Body language
IJ: 3363

Bombardier, Joseph-Armand
I: 2838

Books and reading
PI: 2948   I: 2968

Books and reading — Fiction
P: 221, 225, 409, 539, 552, 598, 601,
626, 645, 652, 736, 812, 826, 911, 924,
962, 965, 1014   IJ: 1457, 1489

Books and reading — Poetry
PI: 2605, 2617

Books for beginning readers
P: 3388, 3389, 3404, 3515, 3518, 3538,
3564, 3574, 3577, 3581, 3585, 3606,
3660, 3726, 3850, 3900, 3910, 3914,
3924   I: 3746, 3748

**Books for beginning readers —
Fiction**
P: 427, 660, 851, 1319, 1320, 1321,
1322, 1324, 1325, 1326, 1327, 1328,
1329, 1330, 1332, 1335, 1336, 1337,
1338, 1341, 1342, 1343, 1344, 1345,
1346, 1347, 1348, 1349, 1350, 1351,
1352, 1353, 1354, 1355, 1356, 1357,
1358, 1359, 1360, 1361, 1362, 1363,
1364, 1365, 1366, 1368, 1369, 1370,
1371, 1372, 1373, 1374, 1375, 1376,
1377, 1378, 1379, 1380, 1381, 1382,
1383, 1384, 1385, 1386, 1389, 1390,
1391, 1392, 1531   PI: 1230, 1340,
1387, 1388, 1676

**Books for beginning readers —
Poetry**
P: 2650

Boomerangs
IJ: 3965

Boots — Fiction
P: 41

Borglum, Lincoln
I: 3177

Boston (MA) — Fiction
P: 994   I: 2302

Boulogne, Joseph
P: 2705

Bowling — Fiction
IJ: 2146

Boxing — Biography
P: 2885, 2887, 2888   IJ: 2886

Boxing — Fiction
IJ: 2313

Boy Scouts of America
See Scouts and scouting

Boys — Poetry
P: 2648

Brain and nervous system
PI: 3435

Brain injury — Fiction
IJ: 2124

Brazil
I: 3112

Bridges
IJ: 3889

Bridges, Ruby
I: 2762

British Columbia
IJ: 3609

Brooklyn (NY) — Fiction
IJ: 1393

Brothers and sisters — Fiction
P: 493, 689, 698, 748, 752, 767, 771,
1343   IJ: 1420, 1723, 2153, 2296

Brown, Henry — Fiction
P: 1011

Brown, John
IJ: 2780

Brown v. Board of Education
IJ: 3275

Bruchac, Joseph
PI: 2740

Bubbles
P: 3463

Budgeting
PI: 3215

Building and construction
See also Architecture; Construction
equipment; and types of buildings,
e.g., Skyscrapers
PI: 3886, 3890   IJ: 2928, 2930

**Building and construction —
Fiction**
P: 150, 240, 1208, 1214, 1218

Bullies and bullying
IJ: 3383

Bullies and bullying — Fiction
P: 297, 349, 1024   PI: 1874, 2007,
2172, 2455   I: 2160, 2447   IJ: 1501,
2186, 2448

Bulls — Fiction
P: 260

Bunyan, Paul — Fiction
P: 792

Burma
See Myanmar (Burma)

Butlers — Fiction
IJ: 2405

Butterflies and moths
See also Monarch butterflies
P: 3697, 3698   PI: 3696, 3699, 3699

C

California
See also Gold Rush (California)
I: 3198

California — Fiction
IJ: 2282

Cambodia — Fiction
IJ: 2229

**Cambodian Americans —
Fiction**
PI: 749

Camels — Fiction
P: 2264

Camps and camping
PI: 2981   I: 3102

Camps and camping — Fiction
P: 670   PI: 1433, 1517   I: 2197,
2360, 2533

Canada — Biography
PI: 2763   I: 2838

Canada — Fiction
IJ: 1500, 2210, 2211

Canada — Folklore
P: 2577

Cancer — Fiction
P: 699, 738   IJ: 1470, 2067

Candy — Fiction
I: 1609

Cannon, Annie Jump
PI: 2839

Canoes and canoeing
I: 4033

Capone, Al — Fiction
IJ: 2296

Capybaras
PI: 3637

Careers
P: 3385, 3388, 3389, 3398,
3404   I: 3384, 3396, 3397,
3402   IJ: 2975, 3290, 3386, 3387,
3390, 3392, 3395, 3401, 3403, 3545

Careers — Fiction
P: 1, 876

Caribou
I: 3107

Carnivals — Poetry
PI: 2624

P = Primary; PI = Primary-Intermediate; I = Intermediate; IJ = Intermediate-Junior High

Carols
See Christmas — Songs and carols

Carson, Rachel
PI: 2840   IJ: 2841

Cartoons and cartooning
IJ: 2929

**Cartoons and cartooning —
Biography**
IJ: 2700, 2753

Carver, George Washington
P: 2842

**Carver, George Washington —
Fiction**
P: 975

Castles — Fiction
P: 196

Caterpillars
PI: 3700

Caterpillars — Fiction
P: 1127

Catholicism — Fiction
IJ: 2326

Cats
P: 3587   I: 3746   IJ: 2954, 3747

Cats — Fiction
P: 5, 81, 241, 411, 851, 871, 923, 963,
1007, 1067, 1070, 1073, 1078, 1084,
1087, 1089, 1093, 1114, 1115, 1116,
1119, 1120, 1140, 1142, 1143, 1149,
1152, 1153, 1154, 1155, 1156, 1167,
1168, 1169, 1171, 1177, 1284, 1329,
1373, 1374, 1669   PI: 917, 982, 1233,
1339, 1667, 1688, 1738, 1966, 2115,
2362, 2363   I: 1746, 2250   IJ: 1948

Cats — Folklore
P: 2553

Cattle
PI: 3988

Cattle — Fiction
P: 298

Cave paintings
P: 2931

Cave paintings — Fiction
P: 957

Caving — Fiction
IJ: 1617

Celebrities
IJ: 3294

Cerebral palsy — Fiction
IJ: 2199, 2204

Chad — Fiction
P: 1005

Chameleons — Fiction
P: 398

Charity
IJ: 3294

Charity — Fiction
P: 623   IJ: 2067

Chavez, Cesar
PI: 2755, 2776

Cheating — Fiction
IJ: 2411

Cheerleading
IJ: 4032

Cheetahs
P: 3613, 3621

Chemistry
PI: 3791, 3792

Cherokee Indians
IJ: 3117

Cherry trees
P: 2826

Chess — Fiction
IJ: 1465

Chicago Bears (football team)
IJ: 4057

Chicago Fire (1871) — Fiction
IJ: 2301

Chickenpox
P: 3416

Chickens — Fiction
P: 609, 858, 1111

Child labor
IJ: 3295

Children — Rights
IJ: 3271, 3288

Children's rights
See Children — Rights

Chile
IJ: 3111

Chile — Fiction
IJ: 2261

China
IJ: 3879

China — Cookbooks
IJ: 3974, 3976

China — Fiction
I: 2219   IJ: 2220

China — Folklore
P: 2551

Chinese Americans — Fiction
P: 784, 806, 1029, 1031, 1252,
1313, 1317, 1353, 1358, 1705,
1716   PI: 1451, 1452, 1699,
2353   I: 1706

Chinese New Year — Fiction
P: 1248

Chinese tea ceremony — Fiction
PI: 2225

Chipmunks
P: 3583

Chiru
P: 3671

Chocolate
P: 3782

Choices — Fiction
P: 616

Choreography
IJ: 3395

Christian life — Fiction
P: 741   I: 1412   IJ: 1469, 2189,
2343

Christmas
P: 2987, 3325, 3326   I: 3309

Christmas — Fiction
P: 5, 1263, 1264, 1265, 1266, 1267,
1268, 1269, 1270, 1271, 1272, 1273,
1274, 1275, 1276, 1277, 1278, 1279,
1280, 1281, 1282, 1283, 1284, 1285,
1286, 1288, 1289, 1290, 1291, 1292,
1293   PI: 1287

Christmas — Folklore
P: 2577

Christmas — Songs and carols
P: 2986

Christmas trees
PI: 3324

Christmas truce (1914)
IJ: 3072

Churchill, Winston — Fiction
IJ: 2204

Cicadas
PI: 3687

Cinco de Mayo
P: 3314   PI: 3322

Cinco de Mayo — Fiction
P: 1249

Circles — Fiction
P: 73

Circulatory system
See also Heart
PI: 3433   IJ: 3434

Circuses — Fiction
P: 546

Cisneros, Sandra
IJ: 2741

Cities and city life
See also Extinct cities; and names of
specific cities, e.g., New York (NY)
PI: 3252

Cities and city life — Fiction
P: 11

Citizenship
I: 3293

City Tavern (Philadelphia, PA)
I: 3191

Civil rights
See also Human rights; Women's rights
PI: 3276, 3277, 3345   **IJ:** 3171, 3172, 3272, 3273

Civil rights — Biography
P: 2768   **PI:** 2763, 2767, 2769, 2771, 2772   **IJ:** 2886

Civil rights — Fiction
P: 1002, 1004   **IJ:** 2321

Civil rights — Poetry
IJ: 2618

Civil War (U.S.)
See also names of specific battles, e.g., Gettysburg, Battle of; and names of individuals, e.g., Lincoln, Abraham
IJ: 3152, 3153, 3154, 3155

Civil War (U.S.) — Biography
PI: 2815, 2816   **I:** 2759   **IJ:** 2765, 2775, 2781, 2785, 2786, 2800, 2814, 2831

Civil War (U.S.) — Fiction
PI: 2289   **IJ:** 2291

Civilization
I: 4010

Clarinets
P: 2989

Clay
PI: 3942

Clay modeling
PI: 3942

Clemente, Roberto
P: 2869

Clemente, Roberto — Fiction
I: 2513

Cleopatra
IJ: 2909

Climate change
P: 3803   **PI:** 3221   **I:** 3113
IJ: 3245

Clinton, Hillary Rodham
IJ: 3286

Clocks
See Time and clocks

Clones and cloning — Fiction
IJ: 2364, 2484

Close, Chuck
IJ: 2685

Clothing and dress
See also Fashion; Shoes
P: 3893   **IJ:** 3238, 3354

Clothing and dress — Fiction
P: 41, 593, 657, 882

Clouds — Fiction
P: 259

Clumsiness — Fiction
P: 424

Coachman, Alice
PI: 2900

Coast Guard (U.S.)
IJ: 3929

Cocoa beans
P: 3782

Codes and ciphers
I: 2943   **IJ:** 2941, 2942, 2944

Coffee
IJ: 3206

Coin collecting
P: 3987

Cold War — Fiction
IJ: 2352

Collections and collecting
See also specific types of collecting, e.g., Coin collecting

Collective nouns
I: 2967

Colombia — Fiction
P: 962, 1014

Colonial period (U.S.)
See also specific colonies, e.g., Roanoke Colony
PI: 3124, 3125, 3126   **I:** 3132   **IJ:** 3036, 3123, 3201

Colonial period (U.S.) — Biography
P: 2782

Color
P: 38, 62, 64, 68   **PI:** 3945

Color — Fiction
P: 45, 63, 100, 388

Colorado
I: 3182

Colt, Samuel
PI: 2843

Columbus Day
I: 3315

Comas — Fiction
IJ: 1736

Comets
PI: 3480   **I:** 3474   **IJ:** 3479, 3499

Coming of age — Fiction
PI: 1474   **I:** 2166   **IJ:** 1403, 1458, 2129, 2327

Communication
IJ: 3051

Communication — Fiction
P: 824

Community life — Fiction
P: 600, 617   **I:** 1437, 1481

Comparisons — Fiction
P: 48

Compost
I: 3978

Compost — Fiction
P: 19

Computers — Biography
PI: 2833   **IJ:** 2832

Concept books
P: 26, 29, 31, 32, 37, 44, 46, 51, 56

Concept books — Color
P: 59, 60, 61, 65, 66, 67

Concept books — Measurement
P: 3834

Concept books — Opposites
P: 33

Concept books — Size and shape
P: 71, 74, 75, 77, 82

Concept books — Sounds
P: 53

Conduct of life — Fiction
P: 665

Conflict resolution — Fiction
P: 45

Conjunctions
PI: 2960

Conservation
See also Ecology and environment; Pollution; Wildlife conservation
I: 3222, 3226, 3240

Conservation — Fiction
P: 459   **I:** 1463   **IJ:** 1572

Constellations
PI: 3508

Constitution (U.S.)
P: 3135

Construction
See Building and construction

Construction equipment — Fiction
P: 1219

Consumerism
P: 3213

Contests — Fiction
I: 1609   **IJ:** 1429, 1483, 2159

Cookies — Fiction
P: 661

Cooking
See also Baking
PI: 3972   **I:** 3119, 3968, 3971, 3977, 3980   **IJ:** 3087, 3089, 3097, 3969, 3970, 3973, 3974, 3975

Cooking — Ethnic
IJ: 3976

Cooking — Fiction
P: 310, 681, 752, 1013

Coral reefs
P: 3712

Corwin, Jeff
IJ: 2844

Cougars
P: 3618   IJ: 3614

Counting books
P: 38, 83, 84, 86, 89, 90, 91, 92, 93,
94, 95, 99, 100, 101, 102, 103, 104,
107, 108, 109, 110, 111, 112, 161, 196,
613   I: 3689

Counting books — Fiction
P: 87, 88, 97, 98, 105, 106, 305, 1143

Courage
P: 3361   IJ: 4002

Courage — Fiction
P: 527

Cousins — Fiction
P: 773   IJ: 1561

Cowboys and cowgirls — Fiction
P: 1258

Cows
See Cattle

Coyotes
I: 3625

Crafts
See also specific crafts, e.g., Paper
crafts
P: 3937   PI: 3334, 3934   I: 3119,
3939   IJ: 3087, 3089, 3097, 3936,
3938, 3941, 3955, 3962

Crafts — Fiction
P: 796

Cranes (bird) — Fiction
P: 2227

Creative writing — Fiction
PI: 2390, 2430

Credit
IJ: 3207

Crickets
P: 3678

Crocodiles
P: 3538

Crop circles
I: 4008

Cross-dressing — Fiction
IJ: 2196

Crows — Fiction
P: 949

Cuba — Biography
IJ: 2706

Cuba — Fiction
P: 762   PI: 1492   IJ: 2260, 2327

Cuban Americans — Fiction
P: 1700

Cuban missile crisis — Fiction
IJ: 2350

Cupcakes — Fiction
P: 229, 1349

Curie, Marie
PI: 2845

Curie, Pierre
PI: 2845

Curiosities and wonders
IJ: 4016, 4026

Curiosity — Fiction
P: 673

Curses — Fiction
IJ: 1419

Cyberbullying
PI: 3369

Cyberterrorism
IJ: 3349

Cystic fibrosis — Fiction
IJ: 1742

D

da Vinci, Leonardo
IJ: 2686

Dadaism — Fiction
PI: 982

Dance
See also specific types of dance, e.g.,
Ballet
IJ: 3000, 3006

Dance — Fiction
P: 359, 426, 799   IJ: 2055

Dance — Folklore
PI: 2549

Dance — Poetry
PI: 2596

Daredevils
IJ: 4029

Darwin, Charles
IJ: 2846, 2847

Darwin, Charles — Fiction
P: 978

Dating (social) — Fiction
I: 1711   IJ: 2024, 2182, 2377

Davis, Jefferson
IJ: 2781

Day of the Dead
P: 3312

Deaf — Fiction
IJ: 2202

Death
I: 3305

Death — Fiction
P: 381, 444, 697, 1053, 1170,
1172   PI: 1451   I: 1455,
1532   IJ: 1476, 1486, 1707, 2137,
2138

**Declaration of Independence
(U.S.)**
PI: 17

Deer
P: 3627, 3629

Deforestation
PI: 3230

Demons
IJ: 4009

Demonstrations
IJ: 3116

Denmark
P: 3857   IJ: 3074

Dentistry
P: 3420, 3421

Depression (mental state)
IJ: 3411

**Depression (mental state) —
Fiction**
IJ: 2133

Depression, Great
PI: 3160, 3170   IJ: 3162, 3163

Depression, Great — Fiction
P: 960, 973, 1003, 1003   I: 2298,
2303, 2319   IJ: 2211, 2299, 2300,
2313, 2318

Deserts
P: 3806   I: 3805   IJ: 3807

Design
See also Fashion
I: 3870

Desks — Fiction
P: 2099

Desmond, Viola
PI: 2763

Detective stories
See Mystery stories

Dewey (cat)
IJ: 2954

Dewey Decimal System
PI: 2948

Diabetes
I: 3412

Diaries
See also Journals
P: 3697   I: 2969

Diaries — Fiction
P: 390, 2450   PI: 2043,
2198   IJ: 1446, 1493, 2044, 2230,

2270, 2284, 2310, 2332, 2378, 2379, 2409

Dickens, Charles
PI: 2742, 2743

Dickens, Charles — Fiction
IJ: 2248

Diemer, Walter
P: 2848

DiMaggio, Joe
PI: 4040

Dinosaurs
P: 3014, 3016, 3021, 3030 PI: 3017, 3024, 3027 I: 3012, 3015, 3019, 3025 IJ: 3023

Dinosaurs — Fiction
P: 231, 232, 252, 268, 554, 894, 899, 929, 1044, 1384

Dinosaurs — Poetry
P: 2613, 2643, 2650

Disabilities
See also Learning disabilities; Mental disabilities; Physical disabilities; Visual disabilities

Disabilities — Fiction
P: 710

Disasters
IJ: 3040, 3108, 3111

Discrimination
See Prejudice

Diseases and illness
See also Epidemics; Medicine; and specific diseases, e.g., Anorexia nervosa
IJ: 3408

Divorce — Fiction
P: 707, 1035 PI: 1423 IJ: 1491, 2155

Doby, Larry
P: 2870

Dodge Viper
I: 3909

Dog rescue
PI: 3762

Dog training
IJ: 3753

Dogs
See also Guide dogs; Sled dogs; Working dogs
P: 3745, 3757, 3759, 3766, 3779 PI: 3750, 3751, 3760, 3763, 3767 I: 3748, 3758 IJ: 3749, 3752, 3761, 3764

Dogs — Biography
IJ: 3756

Dogs — Fiction
P: 47, 180, 188, 191, 208, 467, 620, 830, 840, 853, 1041, 1046, 1047, 1050, 1052, 1053, 1057, 1060, 1061,

1063, 1067, 1071, 1072, 1078, 1080, 1081, 1082, 1085, 1086, 1090, 1091, 1098, 1103, 1105, 1108, 1121, 1124, 1134, 1135, 1137, 1138, 1139, 1144, 1160, 1161, 1163, 1170, 1172, 1174, 1179, 1338, 1369, 1370, 1392, 1530, 1531, 1678 PI: 917, 1452, 1665, 1675, 1680, 1682, 1687, 1715, 2035, 2154 I: 1455, 1472, 1668, 1670, 1671, 1679, 1683, 2152, 2302, 2330 IJ: 1499, 1673, 1686, 1695, 1732, 2082, 2128, 2231

Dogs — Poetry
P: 2637, 2642 PI: 2645

Dolls — Fiction
I: 2151, 2307 IJ: 1422

Dolphins
P: 3714 I: 3536, 3707 IJ: 3666

Dominican Americans — Fiction
IJ: 1709

Dominican Republic — Fiction
IJ: 1708

Donkeys
P: 3745 PI: 3778

Douglass, Frederick
PI: 2764 IJ: 2756, 2765

Douglass, Frederick — Fiction
PI: 954

Down syndrome — Fiction
IJ: 2167

Dr. Seuss
P: 2749

Dragons
PI: 4023 IJ: 2578

Dragons — Fiction
P: 196, 203, 248, 249, 251, 273, 303, 308, 385, 1344, 1350, 1816 PI: 1809 IJ: 1806, 1891, 1893, 1944

Drawing and painting
P: 3954 PI: 3946, 3948, 3950, 3951 I: 3944, 3947, 3952, 3953 IJ: 2929, 3943

Drawing and painting — Fiction
P: 193, 262, 953, 1179 IJ: 1722

Dreams — Fiction
P: 306, 1210 IJ: 1454, 1466

Dress
See Clothing and dress

Dressage
PI: 4060

Drought
IJ: 3234

Drugs and drug abuse
IJ: 3405

Drugs and drug abuse — Fiction
IJ: 1465, 1722

Drums — Fiction
P: 676, 889

Ducks — Fiction
PI: 1125

Ducks and geese
P: 3650

Ducks and geese — Fiction
P: 1097

Duct tape
PI: 3934

Dump trucks — Fiction
P: 1209

Dust Bowl
IJ: 3158, 3162, 3165

Dust Bowl — Fiction
IJ: 2101

Dylan, Bob
PI: 2711

Dyslexia — Fiction
IJ: 2260

E

Eagles
P: 3653, 3654

Earhart, Amelia
PI: 2677 IJ: 2678

Earhart, Amelia — Fiction
IJ: 2316

Earle, Sylvia
IJ: 2849

Earth
P: 3485 PI: 3483 I: 3482 IJ: 3477, 3484

Earth Day — Fiction
P: 368

Earth science
I: 3795 IJ: 3793, 3794

Earthquakes
PI: 3796, 3797, 3798 I: 3800 IJ: 3801

Earthworms — Fiction
P: 938, 1051

Easter
P: 107, 3327

Easter — Fiction
P: 1294, 1295, 1296, 1297

Easter Bunny — Fiction
P: 1298

Easter eggs — Fiction
P: 379, 1299

P = Primary; PI = Primary-Intermediate; I = Intermediate; IJ = Intermediate-Junior High

P = Primary; PI = Primary-Intermediate; I = Intermediate; IJ = Intermediate-Junior High

Eyeglasses — Fiction
P: 1337, 1355

F

Fables
P: 2563, 2566, 2570   PI: 2565, 2568

Fairies
IJ: 2578, 3098

Fairies — Fiction
P: 226, 278, 292   PI: 1820,
1967   I: 1993   IJ: 1767, 1774

Fairy tales
P: 2534, 2535, 2536, 2539, 2541, 2543,
2545, 2546   PI: 1803, 2537, 2538,
2540, 2542   I: 1835   IJ: 1420, 1949,
2020

Fairy tales — Poetry
PI: 2544

Faith — Fiction
P: 633

Family life
P: 3375   IJ: 3374

Family problems
See also specific problems, e.g.,
Divorce
P: 3282

Family problems — Fiction
PI: 1387   I: 2130, 2132   IJ: 1419,
2123, 2127, 2138, 2141

Family stories
See also specific family members, e.g.
Brothers and sisters; Grandfathers
P: 3371

Family stories — Fiction
P: 297, 642, 681, 683, 686, 688, 690,
692, 701, 704, 705, 708, 709, 711, 713,
717, 718, 720, 721, 724, 725, 726, 728,
730, 731, 732, 733, 736, 737, 738, 747,
754, 758, 759, 760, 761, 762, 764, 765,
769, 770, 774, 775, 776, 777, 779,
780, 782, 788, 818, 888, 890, 960,
1358, 1364, 1724   PI: 1424, 1435,
1447, 1452, 1475, 1694, 1699, 1701,
1713, 1715, 1718, 1719, 1726, 1727,
1738, 1743, 1745, 1756, 1757, 1882,
1909, 2177, 2181, 2192, 2369, 2374,
2416   I: 1690, 1704, 1706, 1711,
1714, 1717, 1720, 1729, 1741, 1748,
1750, 1752, 2073, 2126, 2142, 2197,
2255, 2329, 2330   IJ: 1399, 1406,
1416, 1425, 1429, 1436, 1441, 1453,
1457, 1461, 1467, 1469, 1476, 1488,
1616, 1698, 1708, 1709, 1710, 1712,
1728, 1732, 1734, 1736, 1737, 1739,
1742, 1744, 1747, 1753, 1755, 1807,
2124, 2125, 2128, 2129, 2136, 2137,
2140, 2143, 2144, 2145, 2179, 2203,
2293, 2318, 2324, 2326, 2342, 2500

Famines
IJ: 3234

Fantasy — Fiction
P: 194, 199, 200, 202, 205, 206, 207,
208, 211, 212, 213, 214, 216, 217, 222,
223, 228, 233, 238, 239, 242, 246, 247,
253, 254, 256, 258, 259, 260, 263, 265,
271, 272, 274, 275, 276, 279, 281, 283,
284, 286, 287, 288, 290, 294, 295, 297,
301, 305, 307, 312, 314, 315, 317, 583,
586, 588, 637, 872, 908, 1166, 1239,
1391, 1816, 1876   PI: 224, 311,
577, 1590, 1769, 1770, 1776, 1783,
1793, 1805, 1818, 1820, 1825, 1834,
1839, 1874, 1880, 1903, 1909, 1967,
1999, 2000, 2007, 2008   I: 1619,
1765, 1772, 1773, 1780, 1784, 1799,
1804, 1811, 1823, 1824, 1835, 1846,
1854, 1868, 1869, 1877, 1878, 1879,
1888, 1889, 1904, 1906, 1912, 1918,
1919, 1924, 1936, 1941, 1961, 1964,
1975, 1981, 1991, 1995, 2006,
2011   IJ: 1503, 1550, 1759, 1760,
1761, 1762, 1763, 1764, 1766, 1768,
1774, 1777, 1778, 1779, 1782, 1785,
1786, 1788, 1792, 1794, 1796, 1797,
1798, 1800, 1801, 1802, 1806, 1808,
1810, 1812, 1813, 1814, 1815, 1817,
1821, 1822, 1827, 1828, 1829, 1830,
1831, 1832, 1836, 1840, 1842, 1844,
1845, 1848, 1849, 1851, 1853, 1857,
1858, 1859, 1860, 1864, 1865, 1866,
1867, 1871, 1872, 1873, 1875, 1881,
1885, 1887, 1891, 1892, 1893, 1894,
1895, 1897, 1898, 1899, 1900, 1902,
1907, 1910, 1911, 1913, 1914, 1915,
1916, 1917, 1921, 1922, 1923, 1925,
1926, 1927, 1928, 1931, 1934, 1935,
1938, 1939, 1942, 1943, 1944, 1945,
1946, 1950, 1951, 1952, 1953, 1954,
1955, 1956, 1957, 1958, 1959, 1960,
1962, 1965, 1968, 1969, 1970, 1972,
1973, 1974, 1976, 1977, 1978, 1979,
1982, 1985, 1986, 1987, 1988, 1989,
1990, 1992, 1994, 1996, 1997, 1998,
2002, 2003, 2004, 2005, 2010, 2012,
2013, 2014, 2015, 2017, 2018, 2019,
2020, 2059, 2083, 2084, 2097, 2120,
2356, 2358, 2467

Farm animals
P: 55

Farm animals — Fiction
P: 859, 1083

Farm workers — Biography
IJ: 2777

Farmers' markets — Fiction
P: 639

Farms and farm life
P: 20, 3775, 3779   I: 3777   IJ: 3531

Farms and farm life — Fiction
P: 195, 310, 592, 594, 607, 655, 714,
807, 1101, 1111   I: 1748   IJ: 1418,
1430, 2164

Fashion
IJ: 3174

Fashion — Biography
IJ: 2863

Fashion — Fiction
IJ: 1400

Fathers — Fiction
P: 395, 693, 715, 716, 746,
785   IJ: 1707

Fathers and daughters — Fiction
P: 322, 745, 768   IJ: 2159

Fathers and sons — Fiction
P: 510, 953

Fear — Fiction
P: 220, 374, 477, 745, 786, 907, 1037

**Federal Bureau of Investigation
(U.S.)**
IJ: 3287, 3288, 3290, 3387

Feet
PI: 3440

Fenton, Margaret Lucy
IJ: 2795

Feral children — Fiction
I: 2257, 2258   IJ: 2259

Fernandez, Secundino — Fiction
PI: 1492

Ferrets
PI: 3739

Ferrets — Fiction
P: 1155

Festival — Fiction
P: 671

Fibonacci, Leonardo
PI: 2851

Fibonacci numbers — Fiction
PI: 96

Fighter pilots
IJ: 3822

Figures of speech
P: 2959, 2965   IJ: 2962

Fingerprints
IJ: 3284

Fire fighting
P: 3400   PI: 3399

Fire fighting — Fiction
P: 331, 533, 612

Fire prevention
P: 3455

Fire safety
P: 3455

Fireworks
PI: 3878

First Ladies (U.S.) — Biography
P: 2799, 2823   PI: 2824, 2825

Fish
See also different species of fish, e.g.,
Sharks
P: 3715   **PI:** 3768

Fishing
PI: 3106

Fitzgerald, Ella
PI: 2712

Fitzgerald, Larry
PI: 2889

Flags (U.S.)
P: 3128

Flamenco
IJ: 3000

Flamenco — Fiction
P: 782

Flatulence — Fiction
PI: 2359

Flight — Fiction
P: 237

Florida
I: 3202

Florida — Fiction
P: 1003   **IJ:** 1434

Flying machines — Poetry
IJ: 2612

Folk music — Fiction
P: 1008

Folklore
See also Mythology; and specific countries, e.g., Arabia — Folklore
P: 2547, 2558, 2559, 2564,
2567, 2569, 2573, 2574, 2575,
2577   **PI:** 2549   **IJ:** 2576

Folklore — China
P: 2551

Folklore — England
P: 2546, 2562   **IJ:** 2561

Folklore — Germany
P: 2556   **I:** 2557

Folklore — Greece
P: 2566, 2570

Folklore — India
P: 2552

Folklore — Ireland
P: 2560

Folklore — Italy
PI: 2571

Folklore — Japan
P: 2553, 2554

Folklore — Middle East
P: 99

Folklore — Muslim
PI: 2548

Folklore — Nigeria
PI: 2550

Folklore — Scandinavia
P: 2572

Folklore — Ukraine
P: 2555

Food
See also specific types of foods, e.g.,
Vegetables
P: 3780, 3781, 3783   **I:** 3776,
3777   **IJ:** 3448

Food allergies
P: 3416   **IJ:** 3413

Food chains
P: 3518   **IJ:** 3709, 3807, 3809

Football
P: 4055   **PI:** 4056, 4059   **IJ:** 4057,
4058

Football — Biography
PI: 2889, 2890, 2891, 2892, 2894,
2895, 2896, 2897   **I:** 2893

Football — Fiction
PI: 1665, 2506   **IJ:** 2502, 2503, 2519,
2521

Ford, Henry
IJ: 2852

Forensic sciences
I: 3279   **IJ:** 3281, 3283, 3284

**Forensic sciences —
Experiments and projects**
I: 3280

Forests
See also specific types of forests, e.g.,
Rain forests
IJ: 3245

Fort McHenry (Baltimore, MD)
I: 3184

Fortune telling — Fiction
IJ: 1416

Fossey, Dian
IJ: 2853

Foster care — Fiction
I: 2298   **IJ:** 1431, 1453, 1753

Foxes
P: 3622

Foxes — Fiction
P: 1097   **PI:** 1680

Fractions
P: 3819

France
IJ: 3097

France — Biography
PI: 2912

France — Fiction
P: 1013   **IJ:** 1600, 1837, 2237

Franklin, Benjamin
P: 2782

Franklin, Benjamin — Fiction
IJ: 1601

Frazee, Marla
PI: 2688

Friendship
IJ: 3572

Friendship — Fiction
P: 44, 229, 321, 328, 339, 340, 343,
357, 387, 412, 428, 431, 469, 475, 500,
521, 557, 559, 561, 790, 793, 794, 795,
796, 797, 798, 799, 800, 801, 802, 803,
804, 805, 806, 807, 808, 809, 810,
811, 812, 813, 814, 815, 816, 834,
843, 844, 1202, 1244, 1327, 1328,
1352, 1378, 2022, 2023, 2030, 2031,
2033   **PI:** 1404, 1423, 1432, 1435,
1682, 1726, 1805, 2021, 2026, 2029,
2032, 2035, 2036, 2043, 2048, 2374,
2418, 2422   **I:** 1402, 1415, 1438,
1439, 1440, 1487, 1679, 2025, 2027,
2038, 2040, 2042, 2045, 2046, 2047,
2049, 2157, 2382, 2392, 2433, 2435,
2446, 2457   **IJ:** 1405, 1408, 1413,
1416, 1445, 1461, 1482, 1484, 1488,
1491, 1632, 1886, 2024, 2028, 2034,
2039, 2041, 2050, 2051, 2141, 2168,
2236, 2301, 2342, 2352

Frogs and toads
P: 3542, 3544   **PI:** 3543, 3543,
3742   **I:** 3541   **IJ:** 3545

Frogs and toads — Fiction
P: 856, 1174   **I:** 1463

Frontier life (U.S.)
P: 3759   **PI:** 3142   **I:** 3148,
3149   **IJ:** 3145, 3146

Frontier life (U.S.) — Fiction
P: 964, 965, 984, 997, 2281,
2286   **PI:** 2283   **I:** 1729,
2285   **IJ:** 2284, 2311

Fruits
See specific types of fruits, e.g., Apples

Funerals
I: 3305

G

Games
See also Picture puzzles; Puzzles;
Sports; and specific games, e.g.,
Chess
I: 3119

Garages — Fiction
P: 632

Garbage
P: 3256   **IJ:** 3255

P = Primary; PI = Primary-Intermediate; I = Intermediate; IJ = Intermediate-Junior High

Great Depression
See Depression, Great

Great Plains
See Plains (U.S.)

Greece
PI: 3061   IJ: 3062

Greece — Ancient
See Greece — History

Greece — Biography
IJ: 2906

Greece — Fiction
IJ: 2207, 2238

Greece — Folklore
P: 2564, 2566, 2567, 2569, 2570

Greece — History
I: 3064   IJ: 3060

Greece — Mythology
P: 2563   PI: 2586, 2591   IJ: 2094,
2584, 2588, 2589

Greed — Fiction
P: 245

Green movement — Fiction
IJ: 1425

Greenberg, Hank
IJ: 2872

Grief — Fiction
I: 2298   IJ: 2134, 2139

Griffiths, Frances
IJ: 3098

Groundhog Day — Fiction
P: 406, 1250

Growing up — Fiction
See also Personal problems — Fiction
P: 324, 603, 640,
855   PI: 1490   IJ: 1459

Growth — Fiction
P: 82

Guardian angels — Fiction
I: 2188

Guernica
IJ: 2937

Guide dogs — Fiction
IJ: 2155

Guinea pigs — Fiction
PI: 1672

Gulf oil spill
I: 3259

Guyton, Tyree
PI: 2689

Gymnastics — Fiction
PI: 2512

Gypsies — Biography
I: 2732

H

Hair
PI: 3441   I: 4014

Hairstyles — Fiction
P: 863

Haiti
PI: 3796, 3797

Halifax (Nova Scotia)
IJ: 3108

Halley's comet — Fiction
IJ: 2317

Halloween
P: 89, 3328, 3954, 3992

Halloween — Fiction
P: 1300, 1301, 1302, 1303,
1304, 1305, 1306, 1307, 1308,
1309   PI: 1839   IJ: 1644, 2460

Halloween — Poetry
PI: 2649

Halvorsen, Gail S.
IJ: 2783

Hamsters
P: 3744

Hancock, John
IJ: 2784

Hands
P: 3438   PI: 3440

Hands — Fiction
P: 40

Hanukkah
PI: 3330

Hanukkah — Fiction
P: 1310

Happiness — Fiction
P: 611

Harlem (NY) — Fiction
IJ: 1465

Hawaii — Fiction
P: 439   PI: 1687, 1756, 2444

Hawaii Volcanoes National Park
IJ: 3197

Health and health care
I: 3419

**Health and health care —
Fiction**
P: 520

Hearing
See also Deaf
P: 3437

Heart
See also Circulatory system

Heart — Fiction
P: 620

Helicopters
PI: 2861, 3932   I: 3926

Hell — Fiction
IJ: 2357

Helpfulness — Fiction
P: 28

Hendrix, Jimi
PI: 2713

Henson, Jim
IJ: 2714

Hepburn, Audrey
P: 2715

Herons — Poetry
I: 2647

Hibernation
PI: 3568

Hibernation — Fiction
P: 404, 454, 486, 569, 942

Himalayas — Fiction
PI: 2222

Hindenburg (dirigible)
PI: 3880, 3884

Hinduism
IJ: 2579

Hip-hop (music)
I: 2976

Hip-hop (music) — Fiction
P: 1144

Hispanic Americans
See also specific groups, e.g., Cuban
Americans

**Hispanic Americans —
Biography**
P: 2829   PI: 2890, 2897   IJ: 2827,
2828

Hispanic Americans — Fiction
P: 739   IJ: 1708, 1710

History
See under Military history; World
history; and specific countries and
regions, e.g., Greece — History

HIV (virus)
See also AIDS
IJ: 3409, 3411

Hoaxes
IJ: 4025

Holidays
See specific holidays, e.g., Arbor Day

Hollywood — Fiction
IJ: 1496

Holmes, Benjamin C.
P: 2766

P = Primary; PI = Primary-Intermediate; I = Intermediate; IJ = Intermediate-Junior High

P = Primary; PI = Primary-Intermediate; I = Intermediate; IJ = Intermediate-Junior High

J

Itching — Fiction
P: 354

Jackhammers — Fiction
P: 1213

Jackson, Jesse
PI: 2767

Jackson, Michael
I: 2721　IJ: 2720, 2722

Jackson, Stonewall
IJ: 2785, 2786

Jaguars
I: 3620

James, LeBron
P: 2882

Japan
IJ: 3089

Japan — Fiction
P: 2227　IJ: 1576

Japan — Folklore
P: 2553, 2554

Japan — Mythology
IJ: 2580

Japanese Americans — Biography
I: 2694　IJ: 2699

Japanese Americans — Fiction
I: 2323, 2334　IJ: 2325

Jay-Z
IJ: 2723

Jazz — Biography
PI: 2707　I: 2732

Jazz — Fiction
P: 320, 481　PI: 2322

Jazz — Poetry
IJ: 2615

Jefferson, Thomas
P: 3138　PI: 3139　IJ: 2801

Jefferson, Thomas — Fiction
P: 1186

Jellyfish
PI: 3713

Jewish holy days
See specific holy days, e.g., Hanukkah

Jews — Biography
PI: 2875　IJ: 2753, 2872

Jews — Fiction
P: 623, 973, 1006, 1010,
2234　I: 2065　IJ: 2237, 2246

Jews — Folklore
P: 2575

Joan of Arc
PI: 2912

Jobs, Steve
PI: 2833

Johnson, Chris
PI: 2891

Johnson, Jack
P: 2887

Jokes and riddles
P: 3989, 3990, 3992　PI: 3988, 3991,
4024

Joseph, Chief
IJ: 2793

Journalism — Biography
IJ: 2779

Journalism — Fiction
PI: 819　IJ: 1551, 2456

Journals
See also Diaries
IJ: 3649

Judaism
See also Jews
I: 3102

Judaism — Fiction
P: 1012

Jumper, Betty Mae
PI: 2794

Jupiter (planet)
P: 3487　I: 3491　IJ: 3490

Justice — Fiction
IJ: 1393

K

Kahlo, Frida
P: 2690

Kamkwamba, William
P: 2913

Kangaroos — Fiction
P: 1162

Kansas — Fiction
IJ: 1428, 2295

Karate — Fiction
P: 371

Karting — Fiction
IJ: 1605

Kellogg, W. K.
PI: 2855

Kennedy, Edward M.
IJ: 2787

Kennedy family
PI: 2802

Kennedy, John Fitzgerald
PI: 2803

Kentucky — Fiction
IJ: 2324

Kenya
PI: 3083

Kenya — Biography
P: 2918　PI: 2917

Kenya — Fiction
P: 967　IJ: 1632

Key, Francis Scott
P: 2788

Kidnapping — Fiction
IJ: 1565

Killer whales
P: 3732

Kindness — Fiction
P: 1009

King, Martin Luther, Jr.
See also Martin Luther King Day
P: 2768　PI: 2769　IJ: 3172

King, Martin Luther, Jr. — Fiction
P: 971, 1002

Kings and queens
IJ: 3038

Kings and queens — Fiction
P: 777, 823　PI: 874

Kisses — Fiction
P: 49, 57

Kites — Fiction
P: 868

Knights — Fiction
PI: 1809, 2233, 2253　IJ: 1843, 2212

Knox, Henry
PI: 2789

Komodo dragons
PI: 3548　IJ: 3549

Korczak, Janusz
IJ: 2914

Korean Americans — Biography
PI: 2746

Korean Americans — Fiction
P: 1257　PI: 1701

Kouanchao, Malichansouk
P: 2915

Kublai Khan
PI: 2916

Kwanzaa
P: 3311, 3323

Kwanzaa — Fiction
P: 1256

L

Labor movements
PI: 3157

Lady Gaga
IJ: 2724

Ladybugs
P: 3694

Laffite, Jean
PI: 2790

Lamborghini
I: 3909

Language and languages — Fiction
P: 36

Laotian Americans — Biography
P: 2915

Lascaux (France)
P: 2931

Laurell, RoseAleta
P: 2953

Lawrence, Jennifer
IJ: 2725

Lazarus, Emma
P: 2818, 2819

Learning disabilities
See also Dyslexia

Learning disabilities — Fiction
IJ: 1723

Leaves
PI: 3512

Leaves — Fiction
P: 317, 951

Ledger, Heath
IJ: 2726

LEGO toys
PI: 3985

Lent
IJ: 3313

Leopards
I: 3616

Leopards — Fiction
P: 1079   IJ: 1977

Leprechauns — Fiction
P: 307, 1247   IJ: 1954

Leprosy — Fiction
IJ: 2218

Leshem, Yossi
IJ: 3648

Letters — Fiction
P: 524

Leukemia
IJ: 3417

Lewis, Ida
P: 2820

Lexicography — Biography
IJ: 2791

Libraries and librarians
P: 2953, 3388   PI: 2948   IJ: 2954

Libraries and librarians — Careers
P: 3385

Libraries and librarians — Fiction
P: 218, 598, 626, 979, 1115, 1193   PI: 992

Lice — Fiction
I: 2157

Lichtenstein, Roy
IJ: 2691

Light — Fiction
P: 128

Light bulbs
P: 3400

Lighthouses — Biography
P: 2820

Lighthouses — Fiction
P: 963

Lightning
IJ: 3847

Lincecum, Tim
PI: 2873

Lincoln, Abraham
P: 2804   PI: 2805   IJ: 2756

Lincoln, Abraham — Fiction
IJ: 2321

Lincoln Memorial (Washington, DC)
PI: 3277   I: 3185

Lions
IJ: 3617

Lions — Fiction
P: 1148

Literacy — Fiction
IJ: 1723, 2149

Lizards
See also Komodo dragons
PI: 3546   IJ: 3547

Loans
IJ: 3207

London (England)
P: 3099

London (England) — Fiction
IJ: 2248

Loneliness — Fiction
PI: 1743   I: 2151

Loons — Fiction
P: 1092

Lorenz, Konrad
P: 2856

Los Angeles (CA) — Fiction
IJ: 1444

Loss — Fiction
IJ: 2193

Lost — Fiction
P: 624

Lost articles — Fiction
P: 386, 423, 1039, 1384

Lost children — Fiction
P: 647

Louis, Joe
P: 2888

Louis, Joe — Fiction
IJ: 2313

Louisiana — Fiction
I: 2135   IJ: 1736

Love — Fiction
P: 432, 772   PI: 2241   IJ: 1464

Love — Poetry
IJ: 2610

Low, Juliette Gordon
PI: 2821   IJ: 2822

Luck — Fiction
IJ: 2501

Lullabies — Fiction
P: 144

M

Maathai, Wangari
P: 2918   PI: 2917

Machinery
See also Simple machines
P: 3900

Machinery — Fiction
P: 1214

Magic
I: 3984

Magic — Biography
PI: 2716   IJ: 2717, 2719

Magic — Fiction
P: 255, 376, 870, 1248   PI: 1850, 2410   I: 1811   IJ: 1393, 1408, 1592, 1621, 1759, 1806, 1864, 1913, 1933, 1942, 2020

Magic tricks
IJ: 3983

Maid Marian — Fiction
IJ: 2251

Maine — Fiction
IJ: 1453

P = Primary; PI = Primary-Intermediate; I = Intermediate; IJ = Intermediate-Junior High

Malawi — Biography
P: 2913

Mammals
See also specific mammals, e.g., Bears
I: 3586, 3588

Mammoths
P: 3022   IJ: 3013, 3026

Manatees
IJ: 3722

Manatees — Fiction
P: 1664

Mangrove trees
I: 3084

Manhattan Project (U.S.)
IJ: 3159

Manic depression — Fiction
I: 1735

Manley, Effa
P: 2874

Manners
See Etiquette

Manning, Peyton
PI: 2892   I: 2893

Marceau, Marcel
PI: 2728

March (month) — Fiction
P: 931

**March on Washington, 1965 —
Fiction**
P: 971

Marine animals
See also Birds; Fish; Reptiles; and
specific animals, e.g., Sharks

Marine animals — Poetry
P: 2635   IJ: 2633

Marine biology
IJ: 3711

Marine biology — Biography
IJ: 2849

Marine biology — Careers
I: 3402

Marine Corps (U.S.)
PI: 3930

Marine ecology
IJ: 3709

Marine life
PI: 3706   I: 3536, 3734   IJ: 3708,
3710

Marriage — Fiction
P: 990

Mars (planet)
IJ: 3499

Mars Inc.
PI: 3211

Marsupials
P: 3635

Martin Luther King Jr. Day
P: 3321   PI: 3317

Maserati
I: 3909

Masks
IJ: 3955

Mass media
IJ: 2940

Massachusetts
I: 3183

Mastodons
IJ: 3013

Materials
P: 3854

Mathematics
See also Counting books; branches of
mathematics, e.g., Algebra
PI: 3816, 3820, 3823, 3824   I: 3818,
3826   IJ: 3822, 3825

Mathematics — Biography
PI: 2851

Mathematics — Fiction
P: 294, 662

Mathematics — Puzzles
P: 3828, 3829

Matter (physics)
P: 3854   I: 3853

Matter (physics) — Fiction
PI: 1517

Mayan Indians
PI: 3050   IJ: 3047

Mayan Indians — Mythology
IJ: 2581

McCoy, Elijah
P: 2857

Meadowlands (NJ)
P: 3196

Measures and measurement
See Concept books — Measurement;
Weights and measures

Meat
IJ: 3451

Medicine
See also Diseases and illness
PI: 3124, 3410   I: 3419

Meerkats
P: 3590

Mennonites — Fiction
P: 774   IJ: 2189

Mental disabilities — Fiction
IJ: 1753

Mercury (planet)
P: 3493   IJ: 3492

Merian, Maria
P: 2858

**Mermaids and mermen —
Fiction**
IJ: 1395, 1895

Merry-go-rounds
P: 3872

Mesopotamia
IJ: 3056

Meteorology — Careers
IJ: 3401

Meteors
IJ: 3479, 3499

Mexican Americans
IJ: 3340

**Mexican Americans —
Biography**
PI: 2755, 2776   IJ: 2741, 2777

Mexican Americans — Fiction
P: 756   PI: 2440   I: 1696,
2323   IJ: 1478, 1698

Mexico
I: 3109, 3968

Mexico — Biography
P: 2698   PI: 2697

Mexico — Fiction
P: 773   I: 2509

M.I.A.
IJ: 2727

Mice — Fiction
P: 1129   PI: 1693   I: 1677,
2250   IJ: 1939

Michelangelo
I: 2925

Mid-autumn Festival — Fiction
P: 1252

Middle Ages
PI: 3071   IJ: 3070

Middle Ages — Fiction
P: 196   PI: 2233   IJ: 2004, 2212,
2247, 2251

Middle East — Folklore
P: 99

Middle East — Mythology
IJ: 2582

Middleton, Kate
IJ: 2923

Midwest (U.S.)
I: 3178

Migrant workers — Biography
P: 2778   PI: 2755

Migrant workers — Fiction
P: 774

Military history
IJ: 3043

P = Primary; PI = Primary-Intermediate; I = Intermediate; IJ = Intermediate-Junior High

Military vehicles
PI: 3932

Milk
P: 3784

Millionaires — Fiction
PI: 1396

Mills, Florence
P: 2729

Mines and mining
PI: 2982   IJ: 3111

Minnesota
I: 3176

Missing persons — Fiction
P: 514

Missions
I: 3122, 3198, 3202, 3203, 3205

Mississippi
IJ: 3273

Mites
IJ: 3684

Mixtures — Poetry
P: 2619

Model car racing — Fiction
PI: 1495

Monarch butterflies — Fiction
P: 941

Monet, Claude
P: 2933   PI: 2692

Money
P: 3210   PI: 3212

Money management — Fiction
P: 350

Money-making ideas — Fiction
P: 519   IJ: 2183, 2391

Mongolia
IJ: 3619

Mongols — Biography
PI: 2916   IJ: 2911

Monkeys — Fiction
P: 1079

Monsters
PI: 4001, 4023   I: 3953   IJ: 2578

Monsters — Fiction
P: 140, 168, 210, 215, 227,
244, 261, 262, 263, 299, 300,
1184   PI: 1825   I: 1781

Moon
I: 3486   IJ: 3477

Moon — Fiction
P: 147, 220

Moon — Poetry
PI: 2670

Moose — Fiction
P: 79

Moran, Thomas
P: 2693

Morgues
I: 4027

Morocco — Fiction
P: 178

Mortgage loans
IJ: 3207

Mosaics
IJ: 3936

Mother and child — Fiction
P: 383, 699, 950

Mother's Day — Fiction
P: 1253

Mothers — Fiction
P: 682, 706   PI: 837   IJ: 2351

**Mothers and daughters —
Fiction**
P: 727, 763   I: 2135   IJ: 1394

**Mothers and daughters —
Poetry**
IJ: 2631

Mothers and sons — Fiction
P: 786

Moths
See Butterflies and moths

Motion (physics)
P: 3854

**Motion (physics) — Experiments
and projects**
I: 3859

Motion pictures
IJ: 3899

Motion pictures — Fiction
I: 1668, 1702

Motocross .
I: 4063

Motorcycles
I: 4063

Mount Everest — Fiction
IJ: 1547

Mount Rushmore
I: 3177

Mount Rushmore (SD)
PI: 3179

Moving — Fiction
P: 582, 631, 1019, 1020, 1025,
1101, 1149, 1876   PI: 1442, 1682,
2198   I: 2131, 2330   IJ: 1403, 1418,
1496, 1500, 1563, 2155, 2158, 2171,
2186, 2213

Mozart, Maria Anna
P: 2730

Muir, John
P: 3164   PI: 3169

Mules — Fiction
P: 1002

Mummies
IJ: 3011, 3526

Muppets
IJ: 2714

Music
I: 2974, 2977   IJ: 2975, 3394

Music — Biography
P: 2705, 2730   IJ: 2710, 2722

Music — Fiction
P: 618, 644   IJ: 1410, 2124

Music — Poetry
PI: 2596

Musical instruments
See specific instruments, e.g., Clarinets
I: 2988

Muslims
See also Islam

Muslims — Fiction
P: 972

Myanmar (Burma)
I: 3092   IJ: 2907

Myanmar (Burma) — Fiction
IJ: 2223

Mystery stories — Fiction
P: 429, 1246, 1530, 1531, 1613, 1631,
1678   PI: 1245, 1525, 1526, 1529,
1546, 1554, 1555, 1556, 1571, 1581,
1602, 1614, 1651, 1652, 1653, 1654,
2087, 2088, 2089, 2104   I: 1506,
1507, 1513, 1514, 1515, 1516, 1523,
1524, 1532, 1537, 1538, 1549, 1557,
1567, 1578, 1583, 1595, 1597, 1609,
1618, 1625, 1639, 1641, 1643, 1657,
1658, 1720, 1904, 2060, 2091, 2110,
2255, 2319   IJ: 1497, 1502, 1504,
1508, 1510, 1518, 1519, 1520, 1534,
1535, 1539, 1540, 1542, 1544, 1550,
1551, 1552, 1553, 1559, 1561, 1563,
1564, 1566, 1569, 1570, 1572, 1577,
1579, 1582, 1584, 1586, 1591, 1598,
1601, 1607, 1608, 1621, 1624, 1626,
1632, 1633, 1635, 1642, 1644, 1645,
1655, 1659, 1661, 1883, 2105, 2162,
2248, 2280, 2414

Mythology
IJ: 2578, 2585, 2587, 2590, 2592

Mythology — Aztecs
IJ: 2581

Mythology — Egypt
PI: 2583

Mythology — Fiction
I: 1862

Mythology — Greece
See also specific gods, e.g., Athena
(Greek deity) — Fiction
P: 2563   PI: 2586, 2591   IJ: 2094,
2584, 2588, 2589

P = Primary; PI = Primary-Intermediate; I = Intermediate; IJ = Intermediate-Junior High

418

Mythology — Greece — Fiction
IJ: 1950

Mythology — India
IJ: 2579

Mythology — Japan
IJ: 2580

Mythology — Mayan Indians
IJ: 2581

Mythology — Middle East
IJ: 2582

N

Nails
PI: 3441

Names — Fiction
P: 529, 1227

NASCAR
IJ: 4039

National parks (U.S.)
See also specific national parks, e.g.,
Yosemite National Park
P: 3164   IJ: 3197

Native Americans
See also Inuit and specific Indian tribes,
e.g., Cherokee Indians
PI: 3118, 3120   I: 3119   IJ: 3121

Native Americans — Biography
See also Nez Perce Indians — Biography
PI: 2740, 2797, 2798   IJ: 2792, 2902,
2903

Native Americans — Fiction
IJ: 2266, 2297

Native Canadians
I: 3107

Naturalists — Biography
IJ: 2844

Nature
P: 3993   PI: 3519

Nature — Fiction
P: 939, 991

Nature — Poetry
P: 2662, 2668   PI: 2666,
2669   I: 2602

Navy (U.S.)
I: 3933

Neighborhoods — Fiction
P: 633

Neighbors — Fiction
P: 615

Neptune (planet)
IJ: 3490, 3498

Neruda, Pablo — Biography
P: 2745

Neruda, Pablo — Fiction
IJ: 2261

New Deal
IJ: 3156

New Mexico — Fiction
IJ: 1698

New Orleans (LA) — Fiction
I: 1523, 2273

New Year's Day — Fiction
P: 1254

New York (NY)
P: 3640

New York (NY) — Fiction
P: 624   I: 1523   IJ: 1608, 1626,
1635, 2292

New York (state)
IJ: 3195

New York (state) — Fiction
IJ: 2342

Newfoundland — Fiction
I: 2208

Newspapers — Fiction
P: 2030

Nez Perce Indians — Biography
IJ: 2793

Niagara Falls — Biography
PI: 2830

Nigeria
IJ: 3086

Nigeria — Folklore
PI: 2550

Night — Fiction
P: 128

Night — Poetry
I: 2667

1900s
IJ: 3039, 3161

1910s
IJ: 3039, 3161

1920s
IJ: 3039

1930s
IJ: 3039

1930s — Fiction
IJ: 1747, 2308, 2318

1940s — Fiction
IJ: 2309

1950s — Fiction
I: 2142, 2329   IJ: 2337, 2338, 2340

1960s
IJ: 3171

1960s — Fiction
IJ: 1500, 2321, 2326, 2327, 2328,
2335, 2336, 2343, 2348, 2350

1970s
IJ: 3174

1970s — Fiction
P: 994   IJ: 2331

19th century — Fiction
I: 1506   IJ: 2295

Ninja
PI: 3088

Ninja — Fiction
IJ: 1576

Nivola, Claire A.
PI: 2919

**Noah (Biblical character) —
Fiction**
P: 250

Noah's Ark — Fiction
P: 201

Noguchi, Isamu
I: 2694

Noise — Fiction
P: 131, 366, 889

Nonviolence
IJ: 3291

North America
I: 3104

Northeast (U.S.)
PI: 3190

Northup, Solomon
IJ: 2770

Nostradamus
I: 4004

Nova Scotia
PI: 3106

Nova Scotia — Fiction
P: 1126   PI: 2209

Nuclear energy
PI: 3863

Numbers
I: 3830

Nursery rhymes
P: 169, 170, 171, 172, 173, 175, 176,
177

Nursery rhymes — Fiction
P: 63, 174, 271, 277, 838

Nutrition
See also Eating habits
P: 3781   PI: 3446, 3447   IJ: 3444

Nylon
P: 3877

P = Primary; PI = Primary-Intermediate; I = Intermediate; IJ = Intermediate-Junior High

O

Obama, Barack
PI: 2808, 2809 I: 2810 IJ: 2806, 2807

Obama, Michelle
P: 2823 PI: 2824, 2825

Obesity
IJ: 3413

Occupations and work
P: 3391 IJ: 3076

Occupations and work — Fiction
P: 215, 449, 669 IJ: 1401

Oceanography
I: 3734

Oceans
P: 3705 PI: 3706 I: 3734 IJ: 3 710, 3711

Oceans — Fiction
P: 946

Odetta
PI: 2731

Oil pollution
PI: 3263 I: 3259

Oil spills
PI: 3258, 3263

Oil spills — Fiction
P: 1147

Olympic Games
PI: 10

Operation Moses — Fiction
P: 1006

Opossums
P: 3634

Optimism — Fiction
P: 27

Orangutans — Fiction
P: 1041

Orchestras
I: 2978

Oregon — Fiction
IJ: 1469

Oregon Trail — Fiction
P: 582 I: 2122

Orienteering
IJ: 3963

Origami
PI: 3959 I: 3958 IJ: 3957

Origami — Fiction
I: 2408

Orphans — Fiction
PI: 1396 I: 1409, 1714,

2302 IJ: 1473, 1943, 2218, 2247, 2310

Oryx
P: 3626

Otters — Fiction
P: 1058, 1113, 1141

Outdoor life
IJ: 4054

Outer space — Fiction
P: 266

Outer space — Poetry
PI: 2622

Owens, Jesse
IJ: 2901

Owls
PI: 3658 IJ: 3659

Owls — Fiction
P: 159, 1132

Ozone hole
PI: 3241

P

Paige, Satchel — Fiction
IJ: 2347

Painting
See Drawing and painting

Pakistan
I: 3093

Pakistani Americans — Fiction
P: 725

Paleontology
I: 3020 IJ: 3013, 3026

Palestinian Arabs — Fiction
IJ: 2262

Panama
P: 3110

Pandas
See Giant pandas

Paper crafts
IJ: 3956

Papier-mâché
IJ: 3957

Parades
P: 2733

Parasites
IJ: 3530

Park, Linda Sue
PI: 2746

Parks, Rosa
PI: 2771

Parks, Rosa — Fiction
P: 1004

Parrots
IJ: 3643

Parrots — Fiction
P: 1095

Parties
PI: 3333 I: 3964 IJ: 3360

Parties — Fiction
P: 791, 902 PI: 1417

Passover
P: 3331

Passover — Fiction
P: 1312

Passover — Folklore
P: 2574

Patagonia — Fiction
P: 957

Peace
P: 2995 IJ: 3300, 3301

Peace — Poetry
PI: 2601

Peacocks — Fiction
P: 1111

Peanut butter
P: 3782

Peanut butter — Fiction
P: 678

Peanuts
P: 3782

Peer pressure
IJ: 3381

Pelicans — Fiction
P: 1147

Pen pals — Fiction
P: 803 IJ: 2037

Penguins
P: 3660, 3661, 3662, 3664 I: 3663

Penguins — Fiction
P: 72, 237, 528, 1175

Perception
P: 70

Peregrine falcons
P: 3652

Personal finances
P: 3214 PI: 3215

Personal guidance
I: 3367, 3894 IJ: 3352, 3354, 3355, 3365, 3374, 3457

Personal guidance — Fiction
P: 360

Personal problems
See also topics such as Bullies and bullying; Death; Divorce; Moving

P = Primary; PI = Primary-Intermediate; I = Intermediate; IJ = Intermediate-Junior High

Personal problems — Fiction
P: 494, 1016 **PI:** 1468, 2154, 2178, 2194, 2198 **I:** 2150, 2152, 2161, 2165, 2170, 2173, 2174, 2176, 2180, 2438 **IJ:** 2139, 2148, 2156, 2158, 2162, 2163, 2169, 2179, 2185, 2187, 2191, 2195, 2336, 2340, 2411

Peter Pan (fictitious character) — Fiction
I: 1773

Peterson, Adrian
PI: 2894

Pets
See also specific species, e.g., Dogs
PI: 3741 **I:** 3740, 3977 **IJ:** 3566

Pets — Fiction
P: 1066, 1150, 1178 **PI:** 311

Philadelphia (PA)
I: 3191

Philosophy
IJ: 4016

Phobias
I: 3428 **IJ:** 4020

Phobias — Fiction
IJ: 2201, 2414

Photography
I: 2932 **IJ:** 3986

Physical disabilities — Fiction
P: 1033 **IJ:** 2203

Physical fitness
P: 3449

Physics
See also Energy (physics); Matter (physics); Motion (physics)

Physics — Experiments and projects
PI: 3856

Pianos — Fiction
P: 591

Picasso, Pablo
PI: 2695 **IJ:** 2937

Picture puzzles
P: 61, 3993, 3994, 3995, 3996, 3997, 3999, 4000

Picture puzzles — Fiction
PI: 581

Pies — Fiction
P: 555

Pigs — Fiction
P: 826, 1166

Pike, Lipman
PI: 2875

Pinkney, Jerry
PI: 2696

Pirates — Biography
PI: 2790

Pirates — Fiction
P: 204, 214, 304, 528, 579, 586 **PI:** 1612 **I:** 2396 **IJ:** 1548, 2271

Plains (U.S.) — Fiction
I: 2329

Planets
PI: 3488, 3495 **I:** 3491 **IJ:** 3496

Plants
P: 3790 **IJ:** 3469

Plastic bags — Fiction
P: 634

Play
PI: 3935

Play — Fiction
P: 22, 339, 596, 597, 619, 625, 629, 658, 765, 780, 1180

Play — Poetry
P: 2621

Pluto (dwarf planet)
IJ: 3494

Poe, Edgar Allan — Fiction
I: 1567

Poetry
See also as subdivision of other subjects, countries, or ethnic groups, e.g., African Americans — Poetry
P: 176, 2594, 2597, 2598, 2599, 2613, 2619, 2620, 2621, 2625, 2629, 2634, 2635, 2636, 2637, 2638, 2639, 2642, 2643, 2648, 2652, 2662, 2668 **PI:** 2544, 2596, 2601, 2603, 2604, 2605, 2606, 2609, 2616, 2622, 2623, 2624, 2628, 2640, 2644, 2645, 2660, 2661, 2664, 2665, 2666, 2670, 4024 **I:** 2600, 2602, 2608, 2632, 2647, 2663, 2667 **IJ:** 2593, 2607, 2610, 2611, 2612, 2614, 2615, 2618, 2626, 2630, 2631, 2633

Poetry — Biography
P: 2745, 2819

Poetry — Fiction
PI: 1743

Poisons
IJ: 3453

Pokiak-Fenton, Margaret
I: 2796

Polamalu, Troy
PI: 2895

Poland — Biography
IJ: 2921

Polar bears
P: 3575, 3605, 3606, 3610 **PI:** 3611 **IJ:** 3669

Polar bears — Fiction
P: 1131

Polar regions
See also Antarctic; Arctic
IJ: 3114

Police — Careers
P: 3398

Police — Fiction
P: 270

Politics
IJ: 3298

Politics — Fiction
I: 1522 **IJ:** 1407

Pollution
See also Air pollution; Oil pollution; Water pollution
P: 3236, 3264 **PI:** 3265 **IJ:** 3261, 3904

Pollution — Fiction
P: 614

Polo, Marco — Fiction
IJ: 1764

Ponds and pond life
P: 2999

Ponds and pond life — Fiction
P: 549

Ponies — Fiction
P: 1069, 1341, 1342

Pony Express
PI: 3144, 3147

Pony Express — Fiction
P: 985

Pop-up books
PI: 2542, 3330, 4023

Poppies — Fiction
P: 948

Popularity — Fiction
I: 1438, 1439, 2073, 2074 **IJ:** 1445, 1446, 1501, 1511, 2167, 2175, 2421

Population
IJ: 3267, 3268

Porcupines
P: 3636

Porcupines — Fiction
P: 1106

Possums — Fiction
IJ: 1666

Post, Emily — Fiction
P: 980

Post-traumatic stress disorder
PI: 3351

Postal Service (U.S.)
P: 3389

Poverty
IJ: 3234, 3266

Power resources
P: 3861

P = Primary; PI = Primary-Intermediate; I = Intermediate; IJ = Intermediate-Junior High

Religion
See also Bible; Prayers; and specific
religions, e.g., Islam
P: 3304   **IJ:** 3307

Renaissance — Fiction
IJ: 1508

Renewable energy
P: 3857   **IJ:** 3860

Report writing
I: 2947

Reptiles
See also specific reptiles, e.g., Alliga-
tors and crocodiles
IJ: 3537

Research
I: 2949, 2950, 2955, 2956,
2957   **IJ:** 2946

Responsibility — Fiction
P: 472

Restaurants — Fiction
I: 1750

Retail trade — Fiction
P: 862

Revere, Paul
P: 3135

Revolutionary period (U.S.)
I: 3137   **IJ:** 3133

Revolutionary War (U.S.)
PI: 3131, 3134   **IJ:** 3129, 3130, 3136

**Revolutionary War (U.S.) —
Biography**
PI: 2752, 2789   **IJ:** 2784

**Revolutionary War (U.S.) —
Fiction**
P: 974   **I:** 2272   **IJ:** 2267, 2268,
2269, 2270, 2271

Revolvers
PI: 2843

Rhinoceroses
IJ: 3667

Rhinoceroses — Fiction
P: 1040

Rice
I: 3094

Riddles
See Jokes and riddles

Ride, Sally
IJ: 2681

Rivera, Diego
P: 2698   **PI:** 2697

Roanoke Colony — Fiction
IJ: 2471

Robin Hood
P: 2562

Robin Hood — Fiction
IJ: 2251

Robinson, Jackie
P: 2876   **IJ:** 2877

Robinson, Jackie — Fiction
PI: 988

Robots
PI: 3985   **IJ:** 3895

Robots — Fiction
P: 266, 293, 588, 589, 1023,
1223   **I:** 1587

Rock music — Biography
PI: 2713   **I:** 2721   **IJ:** 2720

Rock music — Fiction
P: 920   **IJ:** 2067, 2399

Rocks and minerals
P: 3815   **IJ:** 3814, 3814

Rodia, Simon — Fiction
PI: 955

Roller skates — Fiction
P: 821

Rome
PI: 3067   **IJ:** 3066, 3100

Rome — Fiction
P: 1334   **PI:** 2244

Rome — History
I: 3069   **IJ:** 3065

Romo, Tony
PI: 2896

Roosevelt, Franklin D.
PI: 2812   **IJ:** 3156

Roosevelt, Theodore
P: 3164   **PI:** 3169

Rope jumping
IJ: 4028

Rose, Derrick
PI: 2883

Rothschild, Walter
P: 2859

Rowling, J. K.
IJ: 2747

Royalty — Fiction
IJ: 1813

Rubber stamps
I: 3940

Rulers
IJ: 3041

Rumors — Fiction
PI: 2181

Running away — Fiction
P: 1018   **IJ:** 1753, 2125, 2128, 2202,
2297

Rural life
PI: 3106

Russia — Fiction
PI: 2241   **IJ:** 2231

Ruth, Babe
IJ: 2878

S

Sabbath (Jewish)
P: 3329

Sacagawea — Fiction
P: 998

Safety
See also Fire safety
IJ: 3454

Sailors — Fiction
P: 241

Saints — Biography
PI: 2912

Salamanders — Fiction
P: 1112

San Francisco (CA) — Fiction
IJ: 2279, 2282

San Francisco earthquake
PI: 3008

Sanchez, Mark
PI: 2897

Sand castles — Fiction
P: 187

Santa Claus — Fiction
P: 1278

Santos-Dumont, Alberto
P: 2860

Sarg, Tony
P: 2733

Saturn (planet)
IJ: 3477

Say, Allen
IJ: 2699

Scandinavia — Folklore
P: 2572

School shootings — Fiction
IJ: 2200

School stories — Fiction
P: 185, 248, 277, 394, 512, 540,
571, 613, 654, 794, 805, 830, 836,
853, 880, 894, 984, 1032, 1098,
1180, 1181, 1182, 1183, 1184, 1185,
1186, 1187, 1188, 1189, 1191, 1192,
1194, 1195, 1197, 1198, 1199, 1200,
1201, 1202, 1203, 1204, 1205, 1206,
1338, 1356, 1543, 2033, 2415, 2423,
2450   **PI:** 1190, 1404, 1423, 1426,
1452, 1468, 1474, 1490, 1571, 1646,
1701, 1730, 1770, 1874, 2048, 2056,
2080, 2087, 2181, 2221, 2367, 2372,

2374, 2386, 2407, 2410, 2416, 2417,
2418, 2420, 2422, 2425, 2426, 2428,
2430, 2431, 2432, 2434, 2436, 2440,
2441, 2444, 2445, 2452, 2454, 2455,
2458, 2515   **I:** 1415, 1439, 1440,
1455, 1538, 1964, 2045, 2049, 2073,
2074, 2157, 2166, 2173, 2174, 2330,
2361, 2393, 2408, 2412, 2433,
2438, 2439, 2446, 2447, 2449,
2457   **IJ:** 1411, 1445, 1446, 1450,
1453, 1461, 1465, 1476, 1477, 1493,
1497, 1498, 1501, 1511, 1564, 1586,
1697, 1843, 1861, 2039, 2044, 2147,
2153, 2168, 2179, 2184, 2189, 2195,
2199, 2204, 2331, 2364, 2370, 2376,
2377, 2399, 2409, 2411, 2413, 2414,
2419, 2421, 2424, 2437, 2442, 2443,
2448, 2451, 2453, 2456, 2459, 2460

Schools
See also Boarding schools; Education;
Home schooling
P: 2951, 3359   **PI:** 3231   **I:** 2952

Schools — Integration
I: 2762

Schools — Integration — Fiction
P: 994

Schools — Poetry
P: 2594   **PI:** 2595

Schools — Segregation
IJ: 3275

Schulz, Charles
IJ: 2700

Schwartz, John
IJ: 3382

Scidmore, Eliza
P: 2826

Science
See also specific branches of science,
e.g., Physics
I: 3468, 4005   **IJ:** 3460, 3461, 3730,
3855, 4019

Science — Biography
P: 2856, 2858   **PI:** 2839, 2845,
2854   **IJ:** 2846, 2847, 2853

Science — Careers
IJ: 3403

**Science — Experiments and
projects**
See also under specific branches of
science, e.g., Physics — Experiments
and projects
I: 3279, 3465, 3473, 3853   **IJ:** 3464,
3467, 3469, 3470, 3471, 3472, 3793,
3851

**Science — Experiments and
projects — Fiction**
P: 886   **IJ:** 2429

Science — Poetry
I: 2602

Science fairs
IJ: 3469, 3471, 3690, 3793, 3851

Science fairs — Fiction
P: 1196   **PI:** 2077

Science fiction
See also Fantasy
P: 1242   **PI:** 2465, 2466   **I:** 2069,
2076, 2478, 2479   **IJ:** 1414, 1932,
2461, 2462, 2463, 2464, 2467, 2469,
2470, 2471, 2474, 2475, 2476, 2477,
2483, 2484, 2485, 2486, 2487, 2488,
2490, 2491

Scieszka, Jon
IJ: 2748

Scoliosis
IJ: 3413

Scorpions
P: 3701   **PI:** 3704   **IJ:** 3703

Scotland — Fiction
IJ: 2171

Scouts and scouting
PI: 2821   **IJ:** 2822

Scouts and scouting — Fiction
PI: 1495   **I:** 1471

Scrabble — Fiction
IJ: 1498

Scrapbooks
IJ: 3960

Sculpture — Fiction
P: 548

Sea horses
IJ: 3716

Sea lions
P: 3720

Sea stories — Fiction
IJ: 1548

Sea turtles
IJ: 3666

Sea turtles — Fiction
P: 1065   **PI:** 1721

Seagulls
PI: 3657

Seals
P: 3721   **I:** 3724

Seas — Poetry
PI: 2661

Seashores
See also Beaches
P: 3737

Seasons
See also specific seasons, e.g., Autumn
P: 3515   **PI:** 3512

Seasons — Fiction
P: 932, 935, 950, 1133

Seasons — Poetry
P: 2648   **PI:** 2665

Secret societies — Fiction
IJ: 2419

Seeds
P: 3789, 3790

Seesaws — Fiction
P: 550

Segregation (U.S.) — Fiction
P: 956   **PI:** 992, 996, 1001   **I:** 2323,
2339   **IJ:** 2320, 2333, 2335, 2338

Self-acceptance — Fiction
P: 81   **IJ:** 2203

Self-confidence
IJ: 3362

Self-confidence — Fiction
P: 319, 373   **IJ:** 1470, 2504

**Self-defense — Sports and
games**
IJ: 4064, 4065, 4066

Self-esteem
IJ: 3362

Self-esteem — Fiction
P: 50, 106, 1023

Selkies — Fiction
IJ: 1853

Selznick, Brian
PI: 2701

Seminole Indians — Biography
PI: 2794

Sendler, Irena
I: 2920   **IJ:** 2921

Senses
IJ: 3436

Separation anxiety — Fiction
P: 703

September 11, 2001
PI: 3347

Serengeti Plain
PI: 3811

Seuss, Dr.
See Dr. Seuss

17th century — Fiction
IJ: 1548

Sewing
I: 3961

Shadows — Fiction
P: 184, 411

Shakers (religion) — Fiction
IJ: 2310

Shakespeare, William — Fiction
IJ: 1411, 2256

Shakur, Tupac
IJ: 2734

P = Primary; PI = Primary-Intermediate; I = Intermediate; IJ = Intermediate-Junior High

P = Primary; PI = Primary-Intermediate; I = Intermediate; IJ = Intermediate-Junior High

Surfing — Fiction
P: 498

Survival
IJ: 3452, 4029

Survival skills
See also Wilderness survival
IJ: 3454

Survival stories — Fiction
PI: 3844, 3923 I: 1443,
1596 IJ: 1547, 1580, 1603, 1604,
1622, 2229, 2297

Swans — Fiction
P: 1117 IJ: 1406

Sweatshops — Fiction
IJ: 2228

Sweden — Fiction
IJ: 1458

Swift, Taylor
I: 2737

Swine flu
IJ: 3411

Swings — Fiction
P: 309

Swords
IJ: 3928

Symmetry
PI: 3827

T

T-ball — Fiction
P: 1346

Tai chi — Fiction
P: 1716

Tails
PI: 3522

Taiwanese Americans — Fiction
I: 1704

Talent shows — Fiction
P: 410 IJ: 1428

Tall tales — Fiction
P: 792, 861, 866, 910, 983

Tanks
PI: 3927

Tap dancing — Fiction
P: 691

Tarantulas
IJ: 3703

Tasmanian devils — Fiction
P: 1048

Tattoos
IJ: 3442

Taylor, Annie Edson
PI: 2830

Teachers — Fiction
IJ: 2427

Technology and engineering
P: 3993 I: 3876 IJ: 3154, 3281,
3461, 3875, 3897, 4037

Teddy bears — Fiction
P: 585, 587, 1010

Telepathy — Fiction
IJ: 1454

Television
I: 3898

Television — Fiction
P: 757

Television camera operators — Careers
P: 3385

Television personalities — Biography
P: 2738

Tennessee
I: 3200

Tennis — Biography
IJ: 2898, 2899

Terrorism
IJ: 3348, 3350

Terrorism – Fiction
IJ: 2344

Texas
I: 3203

Textiles
IJ: 2935

Texture
P: 26

Thailand
I: 3094

Thank-you notes — Fiction
P: 1199

Thanksgiving
P: 2733 IJ: 3332

Thanksgiving — Fiction
P: 1313

Theater
I: 3009

Theater — Fiction
P: 1338 PI: 1456, 2432

Thoreau, Henry David
IJ: 3188

Thoreau, Henry David — Fiction
IJ: 2280

Thorpe, Jim
IJ: 2902, 2903

Thumb sucking — Fiction
P: 896

Thunderstorms
PI: 3838

Tibetan Americans — Fiction
P: 760

Ticks
PI: 3685

Tidal pool animals — Poetry
P: 2646

Tigers
IJ: 3667

Time and clocks
IJ: 3459, 3833

Time and clocks — Fiction
P: 1331, 1331

Time capsules — Fiction
P: 185

Time travel — Fiction
PI: 2092, 2102 I: 1863, 2473,
2513 IJ: 1630, 1789, 1837, 1886,
1901, 2009, 2468, 2471, 2472, 2514

Time zones
P: 3832 PI: 3831

Time zones — Fiction
P: 650

Tingle, Tim
PI: 2797

***Titanic* (ship)**
PI: 3917, 3923,
3925 I: 3921 IJ: 1901, 3918, 3920,
3922

***Titanic* (ship) — Fiction**
IJ: 2305

Toads
See Frogs and toads

Toilet training
P: 3450

Toilet training — Fiction
P: 16, 651, 667

Toilets
I: 3037

Tornadoes
PI: 3845 I: 3841, 3842, 3843

Tornadoes — Fiction
P: 260 IJ: 1428

Toxins
PI: 3230

Toys
P: 3873

Toys — Fiction
P: 216, 228, 234, 238, 247, 296, 316,
492, 656, 664, 704, 712, 815, 1028,
1039, 1271

Track and field — Biography
PI: 2900   **IJ:** 2901, 2902, 2903

Tractors — Fiction
P: 260, 714

Trade
See International trade; Retail trade

Trains
See Railroads and trains

Transportation
See also Eisenhower Interstate System; also specific types of transportation, e.g., Automobiles
P: 3901   **PI:** 3257, 3902   **IJ:** 3908

Transportation — Fiction
P: 1207

Transportation (U.S.)
I: 3903

Traylor, Bill
PI: 2702

Trees
See also Deforestation; specific types, e.g., Cherry trees
PI: 3787

Trees — Fiction
P: 646, 933   **I:** 1398

Trees — Poetry
I: 2663

Tricks
I: 3984

Trivia
P: 4003   **IJ:** 4019

Trolls — Fiction
P: 1263

Troop transporters
I: 3926

Trucks and trucking
See also Dump trucks
P: 638

Truth, Sojourner
P: 2774   **IJ:** 2773

Tsunamis
I: 3736

Tubman, Harriet
IJ: 2775

Tuck, Justin — Fiction
P: 775

Tulips — Fiction
P: 814

Tunnels
IJ: 3889

Turkey — Fiction
P: 972

Turtles and tortoises — Fiction
P: 1059

Twain, Mark
PI: 2751

Twain, Mark — Fiction
PI: 1733

Twins — Fiction
P: 787, 1353   **I:** 1725, 1751, 1863, 2360   **IJ:** 1731, 2164, 2365, 2502

U

UFOs
IJ: 4007

Ukraine — Folklore
P: 2555

Uncles — Fiction
PI: 1850, 2353

Underground Railroad
IJ: 3036

Underground Railroad — Biography
IJ: 2775

Underground Railroad — Fiction
P: 970   **IJ:** 2278

Underground Railroad — Poetry
IJ: 2630

Underwater archaeology
IJ: 3919

Underwater exploration
IJ: 3738

Underwater exploration — Biography
IJ: 2849

Underwear
IJ: 4015

United Kingdom
See also England; Great Britain; Scotland

United Kingdom — Biography
IJ: 2923

United Nations
IJ: 2945, 3216, 3266, 3269, 3408, 3456

United States
IJ: 3115

United States — History
IJ: 3116

United States — History — Poetry
IJ: 2614

United States (1790–1850) — History
IJ: 3140

United States (1891–1913) — History
IJ: 3161

United States (1964–) — History
IJ: 3173

Upside-down books — Fiction
P: 240

Uranus (planet)
P: 3497   **IJ:** 3499

Urban planning
IJ: 3251

V

Vacations — Fiction
P: 358

Valentine's Day
PI: 3333, 3334

Valentine's Day — Fiction
P: 1314, 1315, 1316, 1317, 1318   **IJ:** 2034

Vampires — Fiction
P: 123   **I:** 1847   **IJ:** 1855, 1856

Van Lew, Elizabeth
IJ: 2831

Vegetables
P: 46, 3786

Vehicles — Fiction
P: 1215

Venice (Italy) — Fiction
P: 384   **IJ:** 1907

Venus (planet)
IJ: 3489

Vermont — Fiction
IJ: 1708, 1709, 1710

Veterinarians — Fiction
I: 1397

Video games
IJ: 3897, 4034

Video games — Careers
I: 3396

Vienna (Austria) — Fiction
PI: 989

Vietnam — Fiction
P: 1009   **IJ:** 2230

Vietnam War — Biography
IJ: 2922

Vietnamese Americans — Fiction
IJ: 1703

Vikings
IJ: 3036, 3054

P = Primary; PI = Primary-Intermediate; I = Intermediate; IJ = Intermediate-Junior High

Vikings — Fiction
I: 1628 **IJ:** 2254

Violins — Fiction
PI: 2242

Viruses
I: 3733

Vision — Fiction
P: 1032

Visual disabilities — Fiction
IJ: 1510

Vivaldi, Antonio — Fiction
P: 966

Volcanoes
PI: 3799 **IJ:** 3197, 3802

Volunteerism
IJ: 3292, 3297

Volunteerism — Fiction
PI: 1427

Vultures
PI: 3645

W

Wade, Dwyane
PI: 2884

Wagner, Honus
P: 2879

Wal-Mart
IJ: 2862

Walden Pond
IJ: 3188

Walruses
PI: 3723, 3725 **I:** 3724

Walton, Sam
IJ: 2862

Wang, Vera
IJ: 2863

War
I: 3049, 3059, 3064, 3069

Warhol, Andy
I: 2703

Warren, Mercy Otis
PI: 2752

Washington (DC)
P: 2826

Washington (state)
IJ: 3199

Washington (state) — Fiction
I: 1729

Washington, George
PI: 2813, 3134 **IJ:** 3130, 3136, 3941

Washington, George — Fiction
P: 1260

Watches
See Time and clocks

Water
P: 3850 **PI:** 3227 **I:** 3222 **IJ:** 3238, 3245

Water cycle
P: 3849

Water pollution
IJ: 3262

Waterskiing
IJ: 4031

Watts Towers — Fiction
PI: 955

Waves
PI: 3735

Weather
See also Storms; and specific types of weather, e.g., Hurricanes
IJ: 3851

Web sites
PI: 3896

Webster, Noah
IJ: 2791

Weddings — Fiction
P: 743, 789

Weight
IJ: 3444

Weight loss — Fiction
P: 1052

Weights and measures
PI: 3835 **IJ:** 3836

Weights and measures — Fiction
P: 999

Werewolves — Fiction
IJ: 1989

West (U.S.)
See also Frontier life (U.S.); and individual states, e.g., California
I: 3903 **IJ:** 3146

West (U.S.) — Biography
PI: 2761 **IJ:** 2757

West (U.S.) — Fiction
P: 255, 861

West Africa — Fiction
IJ: 2217

West African Americans
IJ: 3340

Wetland conservation
P: 3196

Whales
P: 3731 **I:** 3707 **IJ:** 3666, 3730

Whaling ships
IJ: 3166

Wheatley, Phillis
PI: 3134

Wheatley, Phillis — Fiction
IJ: 2275

White House (Washington, DC)
PI: 3187, 3979

White House (Washington, DC) — Fiction
P: 267 **PI:** 2417

Wild turkeys — Fiction
P: 1074

Wilderness survival
IJ: 3963

Wildfires
IJ: 3825

Wildlife conservation
PI: 3670

Wildlife rescue — Fiction
P: 1664

Wilheim, Lily Renee
IJ: 2753

William, Prince
IJ: 2923

Williams, Mary Lou — Fiction
PI: 981

Williams, Serena
IJ: 2899

Williams, Ted
P: 4041 **PI:** 2880, 4040

Williams, Venus
IJ: 2899

Williamsburg (VA)
IJ: 3201

Wind power
P: 3857

Windmills
P: 2913

Winds — Fiction
P: 947

Winfrey, Oprah
P: 2738

Winnie-the-Pooh (fictional character) — Fiction
PI: 2492

Winter — Fiction
P: 574 **PI:** 976

Wisconsin
IJ: 3180

Wishes — Fiction
P: 606, 968, 986, 1205 **IJ:** 1795, 1992, 2493

Witchcraft trials — Salem
I: 3127

Witches and wizards
IJ: 4013, 4013

Witches and wizards — Fiction
P: 197, 198, 210, 213, 919, 1267, 1306   PI: 1839   I: 1838, 1854   IJ: 1759, 1826, 1994

Wolves
P: 3623, 3624

Wolves — Fiction
P: 1164   IJ: 1899

Women
I: 3933

Women — Biography
P: 2680, 2690, 2708, 2715, 2730, 2738, 2774, 2778, 2818, 2819, 2820, 2823, 2826, 2829, 2858, 2874, 2904, 2918   PI: 2677, 2682, 2688, 2712, 2731, 2746, 2752, 2761, 2763, 2771, 2772, 2794, 2798, 2815, 2816, 2821, 2824, 2825, 2830, 2839, 2840, 2854, 2881, 2900, 2912, 2917   I: 2737, 2762, 2796, 2920   IJ: 2671, 2676, 2678, 2681, 2706, 2724, 2725, 2727, 2741, 2747, 2750, 2753, 2757, 2773, 2777, 2779, 2795, 2814, 2817, 2822, 2827, 2831, 2841, 2853, 2863, 2866, 2899, 2907, 2909, 2910, 2922

Women — Civil War
IJ: 3155

Women — Fiction
IJ: 2275, 2316, 2338

Women — Poetry
IJ: 2615

Women's rights
P: 3168

Women's suffrage — Fiction
I: 2312

Woods, Tiger
IJ: 2905

Wool — Fiction
P: 763

Wordplay
PI: 4024

Words
P: 47, 2966   PI: 2961   I: 2964

Words — Fiction
P: 685

Working dogs
P: 3745   PI: 3754, 3755, 3765

World history
P: 3993   IJ: 3010, 3039, 3051

World history — Fiction
P: 1007

World War I
I: 3073   IJ: 3072

World War II
I: 3075   IJ: 3074, 3079, 3080

World War II — Fiction
P: 1010   PI: 989   I: 2245, 2323, 2334, 2341   IJ: 2085, 2207, 2231, 2235, 2237, 2239, 2243, 2325, 2332, 2345

Wozniak, Steve
PI: 2833

Wrestling
PI: 4036

Wrestling — Fiction
I: 2509

Wright, Elsie
IJ: 3098

Writers
See Authors

Writing
See also Creative writing
PI: 2970   I: 3952   IJ: 2972, 3393

Writing — Fiction
P: 822, 1027, 1031

Y

Yaccarino, Dan
P: 2754

Yard sales — Fiction
P: 1364

Yellow fever
IJ: 3415

Yellowstone National Park
P: 2693

Yom Kippur
IJ: 3313

Yosemite National Park
PI: 3169

Young, Ed
PI: 2704

Z

Zambia — Biography
IJ: 3756

Zeus (Greek deity)
PI: 2586   IJ: 2589

Zimbabwe — Fiction
IJ: 1977

Zitkala-Sa
PI: 2798

Zodiac (astrology)
I: 4012, 4017

Zombies — Fiction
P: 845, 2384   I: 1908, 1983, 2361   IJ: 1819, 1861, 1890, 1920, 2355

Zoo animals
P: 3772, 3774

Zoo animals — Fiction
IJ: 2235

Zoology — Biography
P: 2859

Zoos
IJ: 3773

Zoos — Fiction
P: 88, 217   IJ: 1559, 1585

P = Primary; PI = Primary-Intermediate; I = Intermediate; IJ = Intermediate-Junior High

About the Author

CATHERINE BARR is the author of other volumes in the Best Books series (*Best Books for Middle School and Junior High Readers* and *Best Books for High School Readers*) and of *Popular Series Fiction for K–6 Readers*, *Popular Series Fiction for Middle School and Teen Readers*, and *High/ Low Handbook: Best Books and Web Sites for Reluctant Teen Readers*, 4th Edition.